D1310145

FOR REFERENCE

Do Not Take From This Room

THE WORLD BOOK
ATLAS

WORLD
BOOK

a Scott Fetzer company
Chicago
www.worldbookonline.com

THE WORLD BOOK ATLAS

Introductory Section

Index Map	iv-v
How to Use the Atlas	vi-vii
Time Zone Map	viii
Legend	1

Maps

World	**2-5**
World, Political	2-3
World, Physical	4-5

Europe	**6-29**
Europe, Political	6-7
Northern Europe and Scandinavia	8-9
Baltic Regions and Moscow	10-11
British Isles	12-13
Northern France, Belgium, and the Netherlands	14-15
Germany, Czech Republic, Slovakia, and Poland	16-17
Southern France and Switzerland	18-19
Spain and Portugal	20-21
Northern Italy, Austria, and the Balkans	22-23
Southern Italy	24-25
Hungary, Serbia, Romania, and Bulgaria	26-27
Greece and Western Turkey	28-29

Asia	**30-59**
Asia, Political	30-31
Northwestern Asia	32-33
Northeastern Asia	34-35
China, Korea, and Japan	36-37
Japan, Korea, and Northeastern China	38-39
Central and Southern Japan	40-41
Eastern China	42-43
Southeast Asia	44-45
Southern Asia	46-47
Myanmar, Thailand, and Singapore	48-49
Borneo, Java, and Sumatra	50-51
Philippines	52
Southern India	53
Northern India	54-55
Southwestern Asia	56-57
Israel, Lebanon, and Jordan	58-59

Africa	**60-71**
Africa, Political	60-61
Northeastern Africa	62-63
Northwestern Africa	64-65
Central Africa	66-67
Southern Africa	68-69
South Africa	70-71

The World Book Atlas
Published in 2008 by World Book, Inc.

World Book, Inc.
233 N. Michigan Avenue
Chicago, IL 60601

© 2008 by Rand McNally and Company

WORLD BOOK and the GLOBE DEVICE are registered trademarks or
trademarks of World Book, Inc.

ISBN: 978-0-7166-2656-5
LC: 2007937996

 4 5 6 7 8 12 11 10 09 08

For information about other World Book publications, visit our Web site
http://www.worldbookonline.com or call **1-800-WORLDBK (967-5325)**. For sales to
schools and libraries call **1-800-975-3250 (United States); 1-800-837-5365 (Canada)**.

This atlas is also published under the title **Classic World Atlas**
© 2008 Rand McNally and Company.

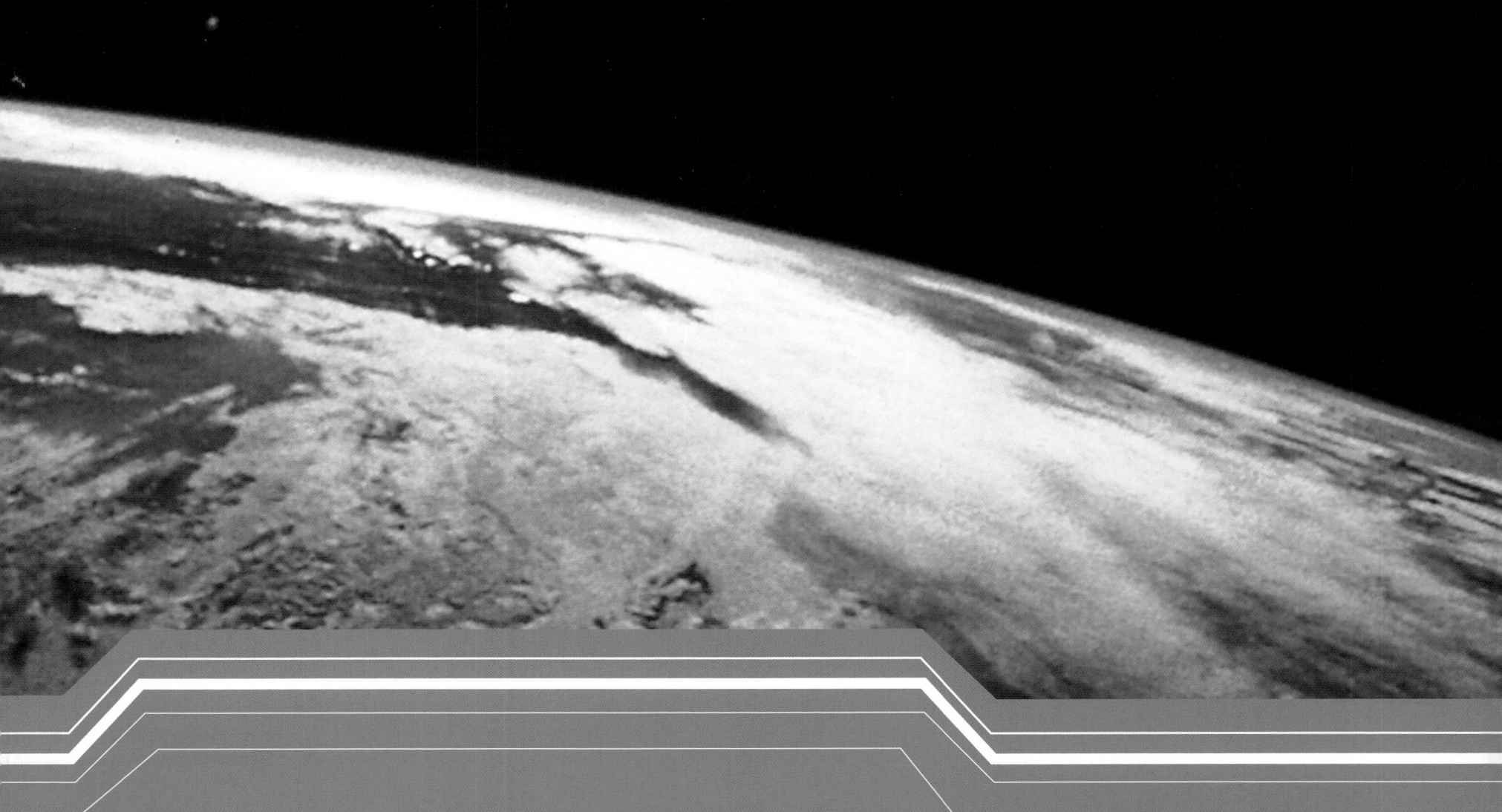

Australia and Oceania	**72-80**
Australia and Oceania, Political	72-73
Australia	74-75
Southeastern Australia	76-77
Islands of the Pacific	78-79
New Zealand	80
Antarctica	**81**
South America	**82-93**
South America, Political	82-83
Northern South America	84-85
Venezuela and Colombia	86-87
Eastern Brazil	88-89
Southern South America	90-91
Central Argentina and Chile	92-93
North America	**94-141**
North America, Political	94-95
Mexico, Central America, and the Caribbean	96-97
Northwestern Mexico and Southwestern United States	98-99
Central Mexico	100-101
Central America	102-103
Islands of the Caribbean	104-105
Canada	106-107

United States	108-109
Northeastern United States and Southeastern Canada	110-111
Great Lakes	112-113
Central Atlantic States	114-115
Southeastern United States	116-117
Northern Midwest	118-119
Midwest	120-121
Mississippi Delta	122-123
Northern Great Plains	124-125
Central Great Plains	126-127
Southern Great Plains	128-129
Southern Texas	130-131
Arizona and Utah	132-133
California, Nevada, and Hawaii	134-135
Northwestern United States	136-137
Southwestern Canada	138-139
Alaska and the Aleutians	140
Greenland	141
Oceans	**142-144**
Pacific and Indian Oceans	142-143
Atlantic Ocean	144

Index

Index to the Reference Maps	I•1-I•64

Cover photo credits:
Jacques Descloitres, MODIS Land Rapid Response Team/NASA/GSF; © Art Wolfe, Getty Images; NASA/GSFC and U.S. Japan ASTER Science Team

Cover design:
Norman Baugher

About the cover

The large photograph on the cover of **The World Book Atlas** features one of Earth's most identifiable shapes—the boot-shaped peninsula occupied by Italy. This peninsula extends into the Mediterranean Sea from southern Europe.

Italy also includes two large islands, Sicily and Sardinia. Sicily, which lies to the west of the boot's tip, is home to Mount Etna, one of the most famous volcanoes in the world. Etna rises on the eastern coast of the island. The volcano's eruptions, which have occurred periodically for thousands of years, are spectacular sights. As seen in the center inset photo, huge fiery clouds rise over the mountain, and glowing rivers of lava flow down its sides.

The inset photo on the bottom right is an ASTER (Advanced Spaceborne Thermal Emission and Reflection Radiometer) image of a sulfur dioxide plume that originated from Etna's summit. The plume, shown in reddish-purple in this view from space, drifts over the city of Catania and continues over the Ionian Sea.

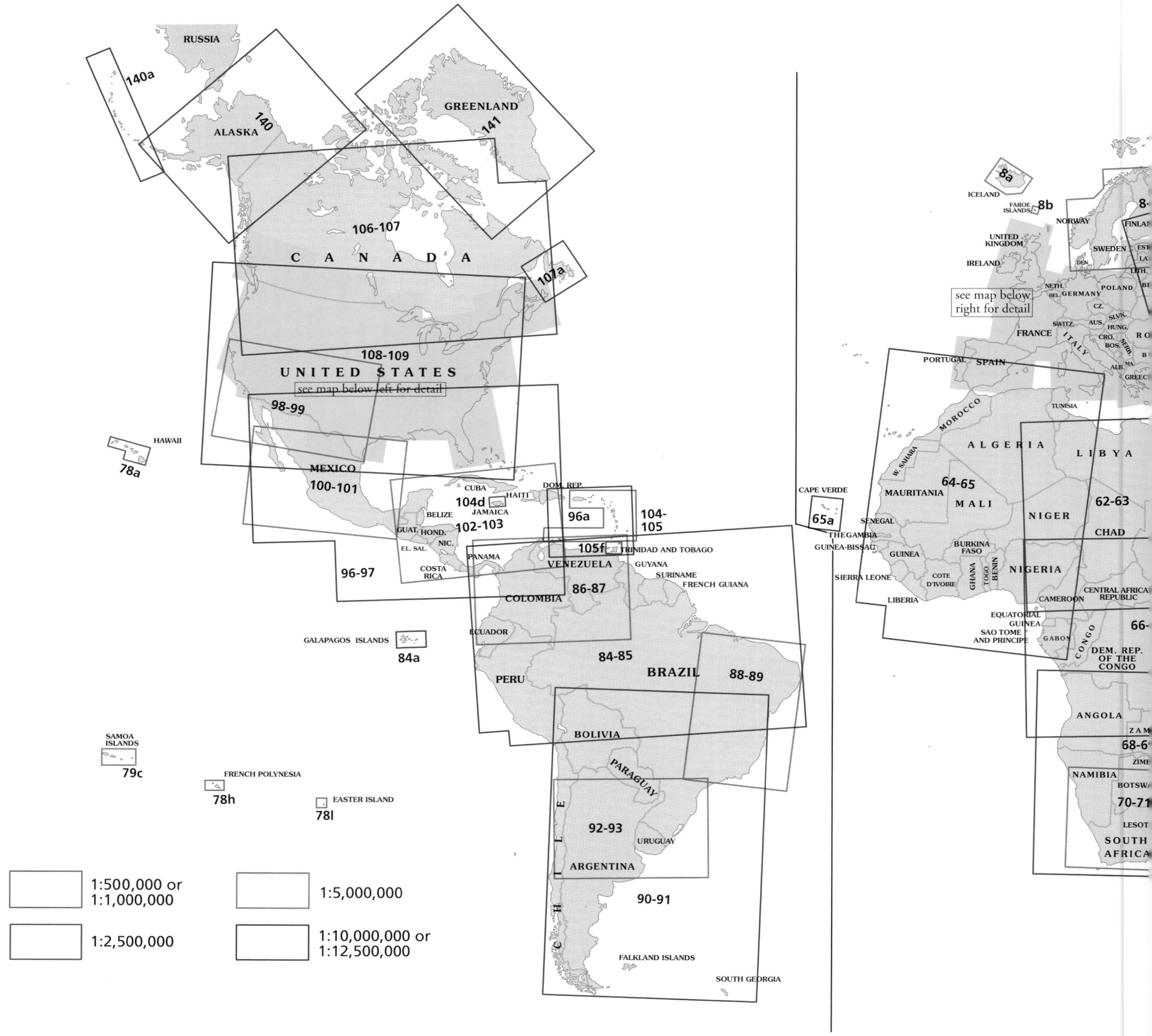

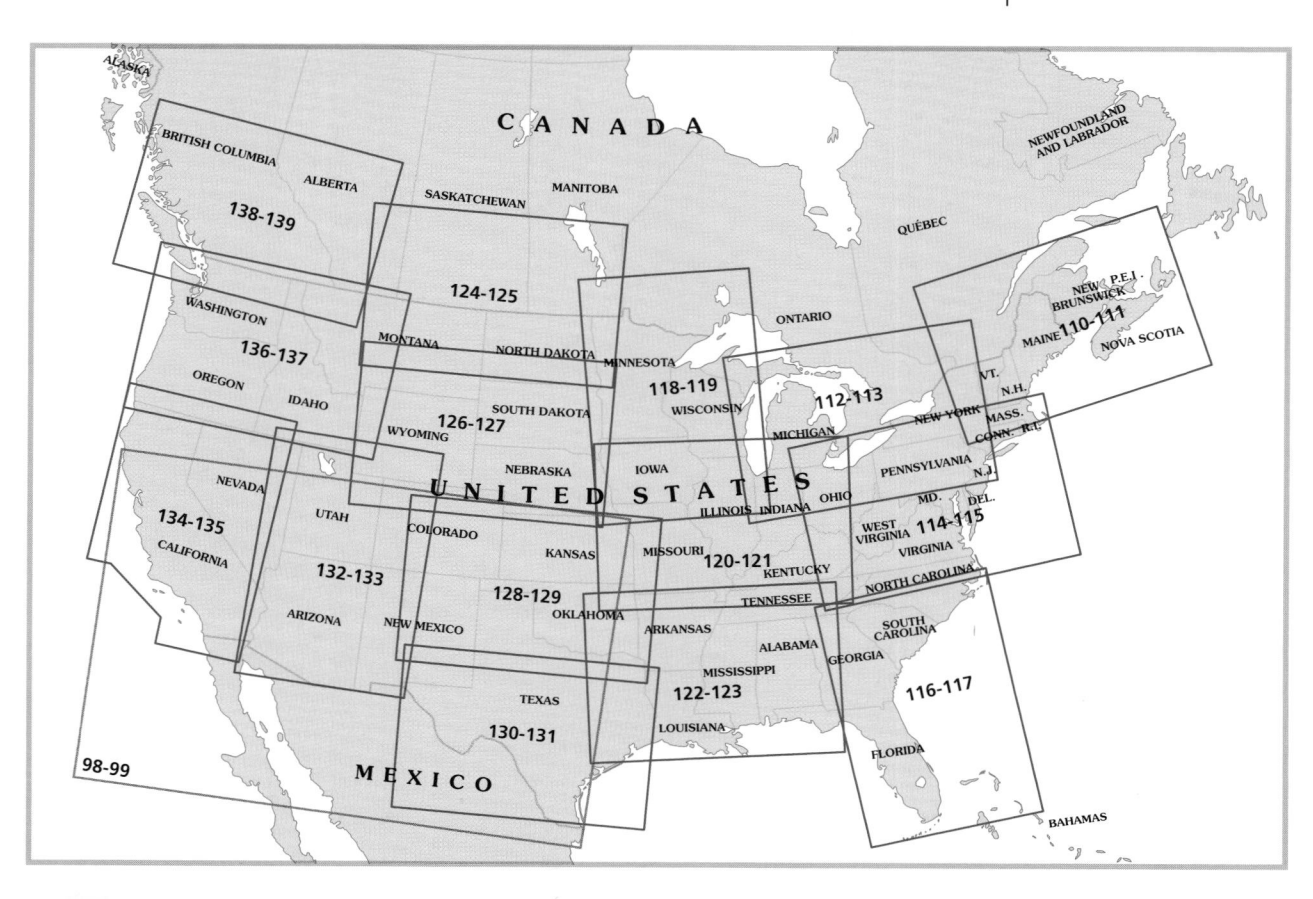

Index Map

R U S S I A

32-33

34-35

KAZAKHSTAN

MONGOLIA

38-39

JAPAN

NORTH KOREA

40-41

GEO.
ARM. AZER.
UZBEKISTAN
KYRG.
TURKMENISTAN
TAJIK.

C H I N A

SOUTH KOREA

42-43

35a

36-37

TURKEY
SYRIA
IRAQ
IRAN
JORDAN

AFGHANISTAN

54-55

NEPAL
BHU.

TAIWAN

59

KUWAIT
QATAR
U.A.E.

PAKISTAN

56-57

I N D I A

BNG.
MYANMAR

46-47

LAOS

SAUDI ARABIA

OMAN

53

THAILAND
CAMBODIA
VIETNAM

PHILIPPINES

52

PALAU

78b

DAN

YEMEN

ERITREA
DJIBOUTI

SRI LANKA

48-49

BRUNEI

ETHIOPIA

SOMALIA

MALDIVES

46a

MALAYSIA
SINGAPORE

44-45

KENYA

50-51

79a

UNDI
ANZANIA

SEYCHELLES

69b

I N D O N E S I A

PAPUA NEW GUINEA

79b

SOLOMON ISLANDS

COMOROS

EAST TIMOR

MADAGASCAR

VANUATU

79d

79e
FIJI

AMBIQUE

REUNION

MAURITIUS

69a

A U S T R A L I A

74-75

76-77

AZILAND

World	2-5
Europe	6-7
Asia	30-31
Africa	60-61
Australia and Oceania	72-73
Antarctica	81
South America	82-83
North America	94-95
Oceans	142-144

NEW ZEALAND

75a

77a
TASMANIA

80

© Rand McNally & Co.
M-101170-1-1-1-1

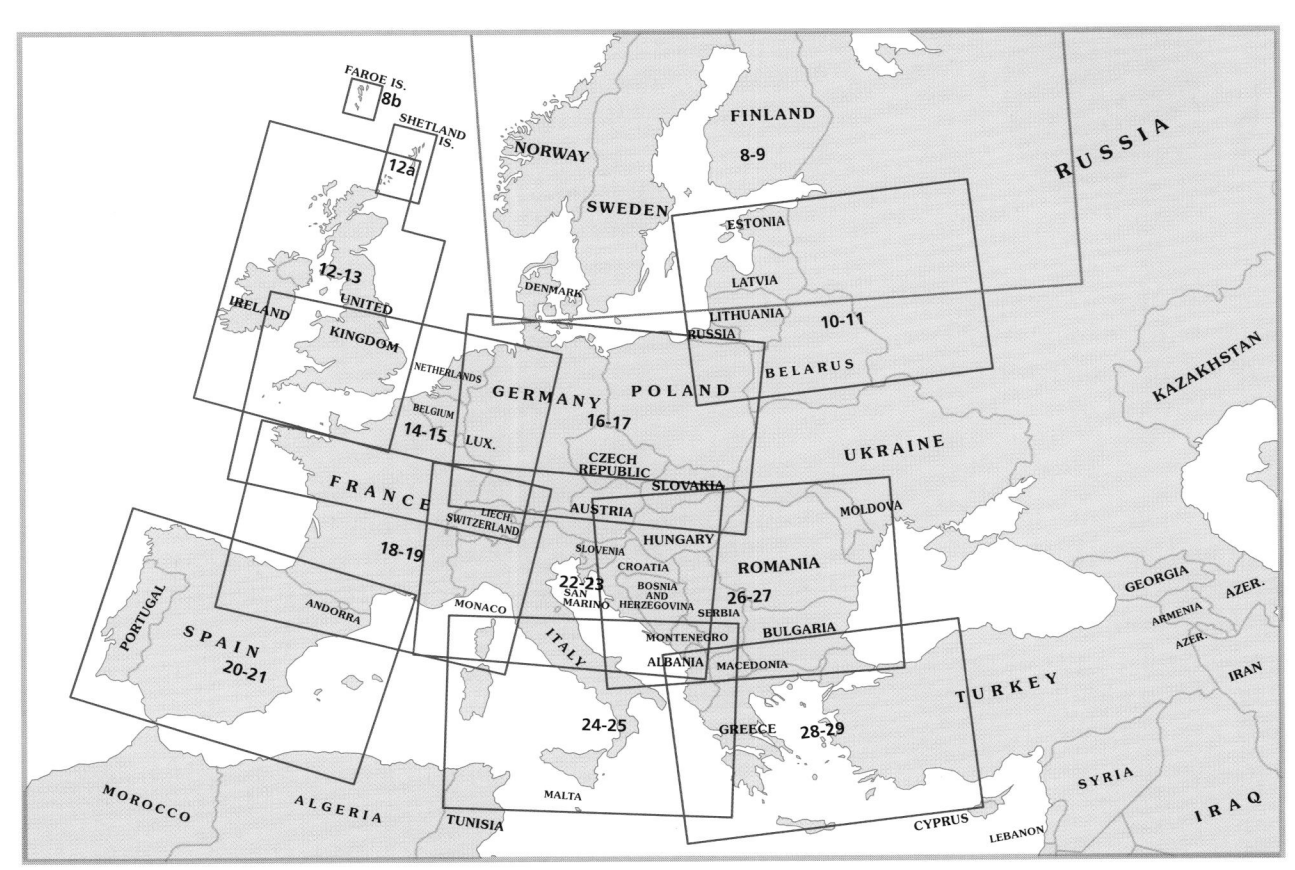

FAROE IS.
8b

SHETLAND IS.
12a

NORWAY

FINLAND

8-9

R U S S I A

SWEDEN

ESTONIA

12-13

IRELAND
UNITED KINGDOM

DENMARK

LATVIA

LITHUANIA

10-11

KAZAKHSTAN

RUSSIA

BELARUS

NETHERLANDS
BELGIUM
LUX.

G E R M A N Y

P O L A N D

16-17

14-15

CZECH REPUBLIC

UKRAINE

LIECH.
SWITZERLAND

F R A N C E

AUSTRIA

SLOVAKIA

MOLDOVA

18-19

SLOVENIA
CROATIA

HUNGARY

ROMANIA

26-27

GEORGIA

ARMENIA
AZER.

PORTUGAL

ANDORRA

MONACO

22-23
SAN MARINO

BOSNIA AND HERZEGOVINA
SERBIA

20-21

S P A I N

I T A L Y

MONTENEGRO

BULGARIA

ALBANIA
MACEDONIA

T U R K E Y

IRAN

MOROCCO

ALGERIA

TUNISIA

MALTA

24-25

GREECE

28-29

SYRIA

LEBANON

CYPRUS

I R A Q

How to use the atlas

What is an Atlas?

A set of maps bound together is called an atlas. Abraham Ortelius's *Theatrum orbis terrarum*, published in 1570, is considered to be the first modern "atlas," although it was not referred to as such for almost 20 years. In 1589, Gerardus Mercator coined the term when he named his collection of maps after Atlas, the mythological Titan who carried Earth on his shoulders as punishment for warring against Zeus. Since then, the definition of "atlas" has been expanded, and atlases often include additional geographic information in diagrams, tables, and text.

Latitude and Longitude

The terms "latitude" and "longitude" refer to the grid of horizontal and vertical lines found on most maps and globes. Any point on Earth can be located by its precise latitude and longitude coordinates.

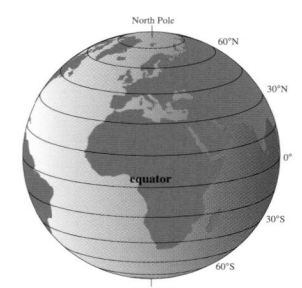

figure 1

The imaginary horizontal line that circles Earth halfway between the North and South poles is called the equator; it represents 0° latitude and lies 90° from either pole. The other lines of latitude, or parallels, measure distances north or south from the equator *(figure 1)*. The imaginary vertical line that measures 0° longitude runs through the Greenwich Observatory in the United Kingdom and is called the prime meridian. The other lines of longitude, or meridians, measure distances east or west from the prime meridian *(figure 2)*, up to a maximum of 180°. Lines of latitude and longitude cross each other, forming a grid *(figure 3)*.

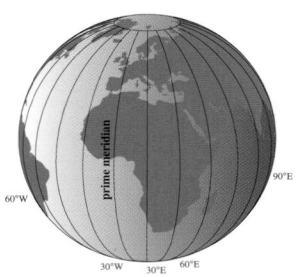

figure 2

figure 3

Map Projections

Every cartographer is faced with the problem of transforming the curved surface of Earth onto a flat plane with a minimum of distortion. The systematic transformation of locations on Earth (a spherical surface) to locations on a map (a flat surface) is called projection.

It is not possible to represent on a flat map the spatial relationships of angle, distance, direction, and area that only a globe can show faithfully. As a result, projections inevitably involve some distortion. On large-scale maps representing a few square miles, the distortion is generally negligible. But on maps depicting large countries, continents, or the entire world, the amount of distortion can be significant. On maps which use the Mercator projection *(figure 4)*, for example, distortion

increases with distance from the equator. Thus the island of Greenland appears larger than the entire continent of South America, although South America is in fact nine time larger. In contrast, the Robinson projection *(figure 5)* renders the world's major land areas in generally correct proportion to one another, although distortion is still apparent in areas such as Antarctica, which is actually smaller than all of the continents except Europe and Australia.

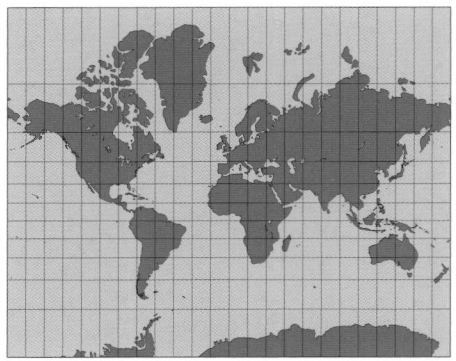

figure 4

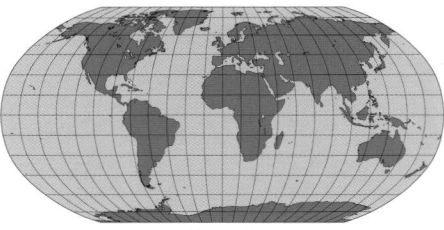

figure 5

There are an infinite number of possible map projections, all of which distort one or more of the characteristics of the globe in varying degrees. The projection that a cartographer chooses depends on the size and location of the area being projected and the purpose of the map. In this atlas, most of the maps are drawn on projections that give a consistent or only slightly distorted area scale, good land and ocean shape, parallels that are parallel, and as consistent a linear scale as possible throughout the projection.

Map Scale

The scale of a map is the relationship between distances or areas shown on the map and the corresponding distances or areas on Earth's surface. Large-scale maps show relatively small areas in greater detail than do small-scale maps, such as those of individual continents or of the world.

There are three different ways to express scale. Most often scale is given as a fraction, such as 1:10,000,000, which means that the ratio of distances on the map to actual distances on Earth is 1 to

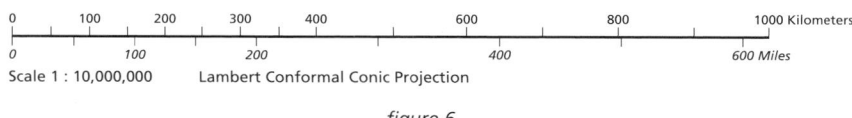

Scale 1 : 10,000,000   Lambert Conformal Conic Projection

figure 6

10,000,000. Scale can also be expressed as a phrase, such as "One inch represents approximately 10 million miles." Finally, scale can be illustrated via a bar scale on which various distances are labeled *(figure 6)*. Any of these three scale expressions can be used to calculate distances on a map.

Measuring Distances

Using a bar scale, it is possible to calculate the distance between any two points on a map. To find the approximate distance

between São Paulo and Rio de Janeiro, Brazil, for example, follow these steps:

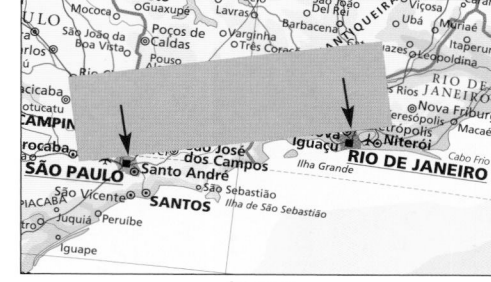

figure 7

1) Lay a piece of paper on the right-hand page of the "Eastern Brazil" map found on pages 88-89, lining up its edge with the city dots for São Paulo and Rio de Janeiro. Make a mark on the paper next to each dot (figure 7).

2) Place the paper along the scale bar found below the map, and position the first mark at 0. The second mark falls about a quarter of the way between the 200-mile tick and the 300-mile tick, indicating that the distance separating the two cities is approximately 225 miles (figure 8).

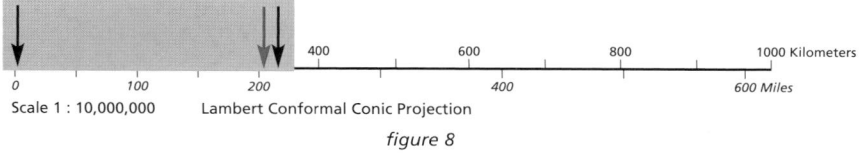

figure 8

3) To confirm this measurement, make a third pencil mark (shown in red in figure 8) at the 200-mile tick. Slide the paper to the left so that this mark lines up with 0. The Rio de Janeiro mark now falls about halfway between the 0 tick and the 50-mile tick. Thus, São Paulo and Rio de Janeiro are indeed approximately 225 (200 + 25) miles apart.

Using the Index to Find Places

One of the most important purposes of an atlas is to help the reader locate cities, towns, and geographic features such as rivers, lakes, and mountains. This atlas uses a "bingo key" indexing system. In the index, found on pages I•1 through I•64, every entry is assigned an alpha-numeric code that consists of a letter and a number. This code relates to the red letters and numbers that run along the perimeter of each map. To locate places or features, follow the steps outlined in this example for the city of Bratsk, Russia.

1) Look up Bratsk in the index. The entry (figure 9) contains the following information: the place name (Bratsk), the name of the country (Russia) in which Bratsk is located, the map reference key

Brassey, Banjaran, mts., Malay	A10	50
Brass Islands, is., V.I.U.S.	o7	104 b
Brasstown Bald, mtn., Ga., U.S.	B2	116
Bratca, Rom.	C9	26
Bratislava, Slov.	H13	16
Bratislava, state, Slov.	H13	16
Bratsk, Russia	C18	32
Bratskoe vodohranilisce, res., Russia	C18	32

figure 9

(C18) that corresponds to Bratsk's location on the map, and the page number (32) of the map on which Bratsk can be found.

2) Turn to the Northwestern Asia map on pages 32-33. Look along either the

left- or right-hand margin for the red letter "C"—the letter code given for Bratsk. The "C" denotes a band that arcs horizontally across the map, between the grid lines representing 55° and 60° North latitude. Then, look along either the top or bottom margin for the red number "18"—the numerical part of the code given for Bratsk. The "18" denotes a widening vertical band, between the grid lines representing 100° and 105° East longitude, which angles from the top center of the map to right-hand edge.

3) Using your finger, follow the horizontal "C" band and the vertical "18" band to the area where they overlap. Bratsk lies within this overlap area.

Physical Maps and Political Maps

Most of the maps in the atlas are physical maps (figure 10) emphasizing terrain, landforms, and elevation. Political maps, as in figure 11, emphasize countries and other political units over topography. The atlas includes political maps of the world and each of the continents except Antarctica.

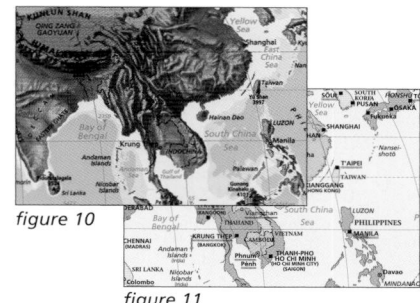

figure 10

figure 11

How Maps Show Topography

The physical maps in this atlas use two techniques to depict Earth's topography. Variations in elevation are shown through a series of colors called hypsometric tints. Areas below sea level appear as a dark green; as the elevation rises, the tints move successively through lighter green, yellow, and orange. Similarly, variations in ocean depth are represented by bathymetric tints. The shallowest areas appear as light blue; darker tints of blue indicate greater depths. The hypsometric/bathymetric scale that accompanies each map identifies, in feet and meters, all of the elevation and depth categories that appear on the map. Principal landforms, such as mountain ranges and valleys, are rendered

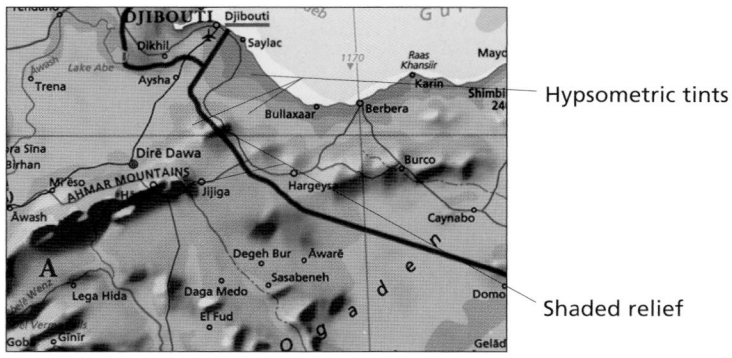

Hypsometric tints

Shaded relief

figure 12

in shades of gray, a technique known as shaded relief. The combination of hypsometric tints and shaded relief provides the map reader with a three-dimensional picture of Earth's surface (figure 12).

Time Zone Map

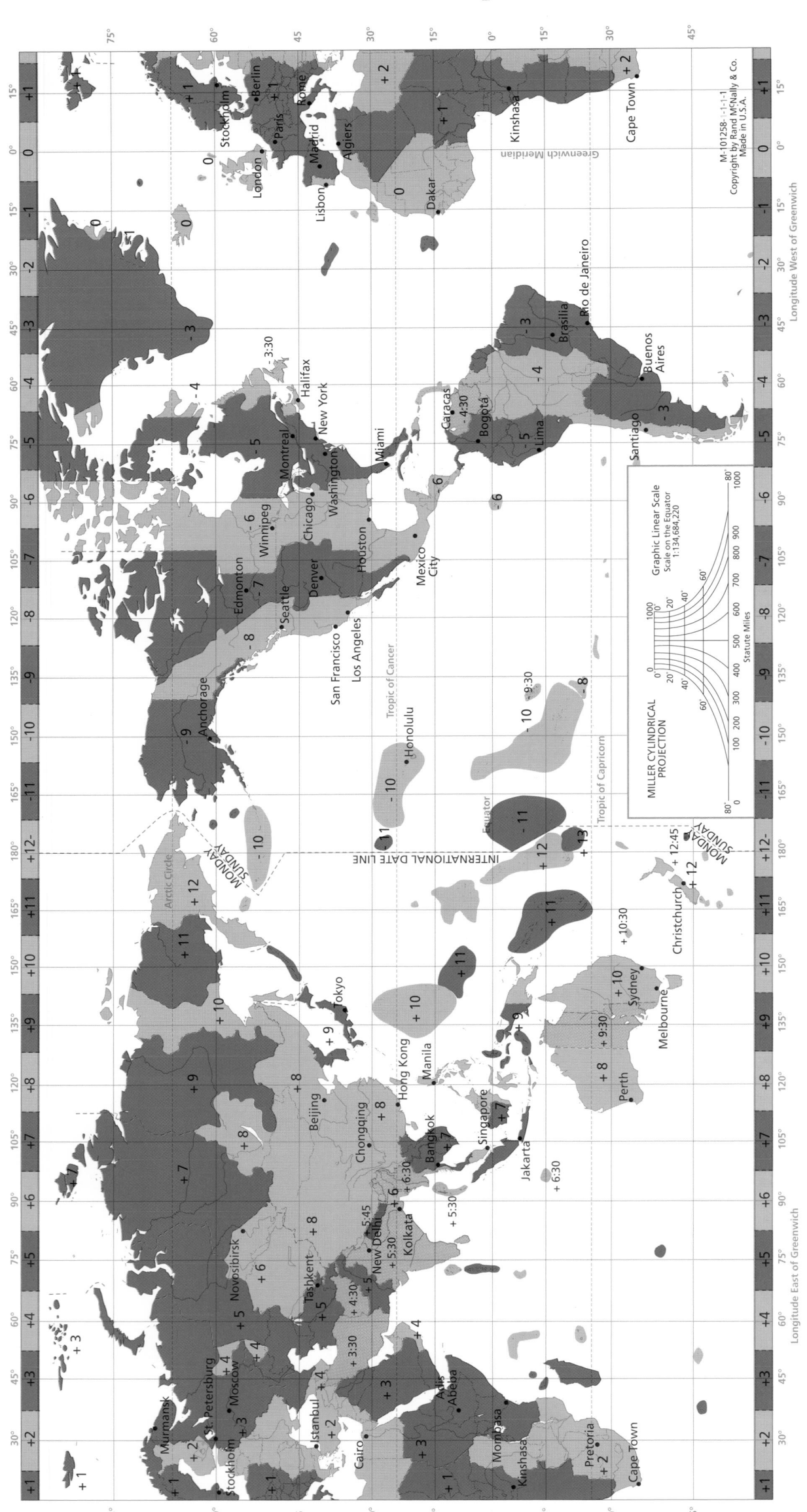

M-101258- -1-1-1
Copyright by Rand McNally & Co.
Made in U.S.A.

The surface of the earth is divided into 24 time zones. Each zone represents 15° of longitude or one hour of time. The time of the initial, or zero, zone is based on the Greenwich Meridian and extends eastward and westward for a distance of 7½° of longitude. Each of the zones is designated by a number representing the hours (+ or -) by which its standard time differs from Greenwich mean time. These standard time zones are indicated by bands of blue and yellow. Areas which have a fractional deviation from standard time are shown in special colors. The irregularities in the zones and the fractional deviations are due to political and economic factors.

Time Zones

Standard time zone of even-numbered hours from Greenwich time

Standard time zone of odd-numbered hours from Greenwich time

Time varies from standard time zone by half an hour

Time varies from standard time zone by other than half an hour

Legend

Hydrographic Features

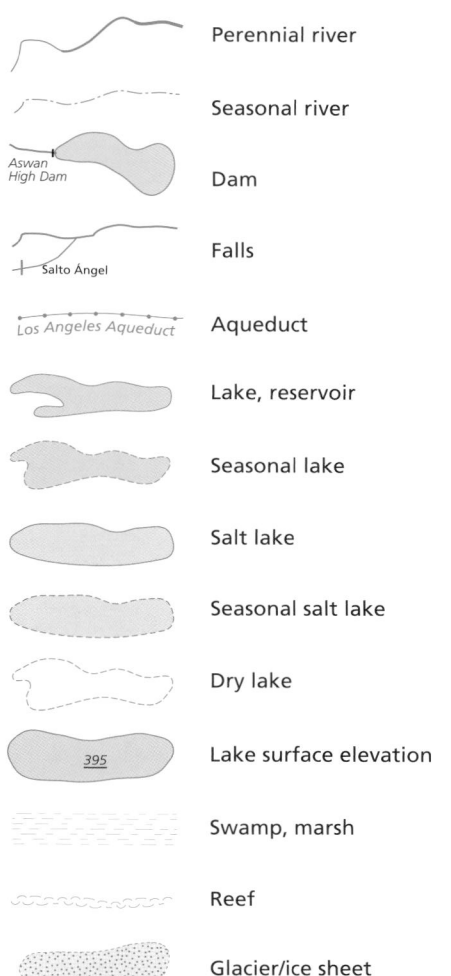

Perennial river

Seasonal river

Dam

Falls

Aqueduct

Lake, reservoir

Seasonal lake

Salt lake

Seasonal salt lake

Dry lake

Lake surface elevation

Swamp, marsh

Reef

Glacier/ice sheet

Topographic Features

764 ▽ Depth of water

2278 ▲ Elevation above sea level

1700 ▼ Elevation below sea level

⋈ Mountain pass

Huo Shan 1774 Mountain peak/elevation

The highest elevation on each continent is underlined.

The highest elevation in each country is shown in boldface.

Transportation Features

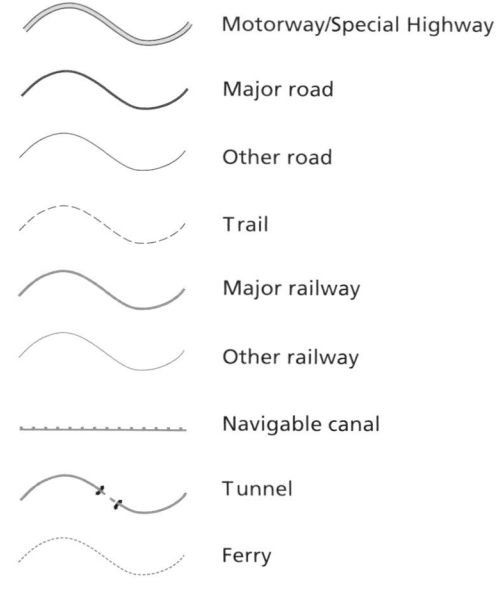

Motorway/Special Highway

Major road

Other road

Trail

Major railway

Other railway

Navigable canal

Tunnel

Ferry

✈ International airport

✈ Other airport

Political Features

International boundaries (First-order political unit)

 Demarcated

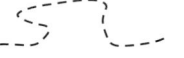 Disputed (de facto)

 Disputed (de jure)

 Indefinite/undefined

 Demarcation line

Internal boundaries

 State/province

Third-order (counties, oblasts, etc.)

NORMANDIE Cultural/historic region
(Denmark) Administering country

Cities and Towns

The size of symbol and type indicates the relative importance of the locality

■ **LONDON**

▣ **CHICAGO**

◉ **Milwaukee**

◎ Tacna

⊙ Iquitos

○ Old Crow

° Mettawa

⬬ Urban area

Capitals

MEXICO CITY
Bratislava Country, dependency

RIO DE JANEIRO
Perth State, province

MANCHESTER
Chester County

Cultural Features

⬚ or ■ National park, reservation

▪ Point of interest

⌐⌐⌐⌐⌐ Wall

∴ Ruins

⬚ Military installation

● Polar research station

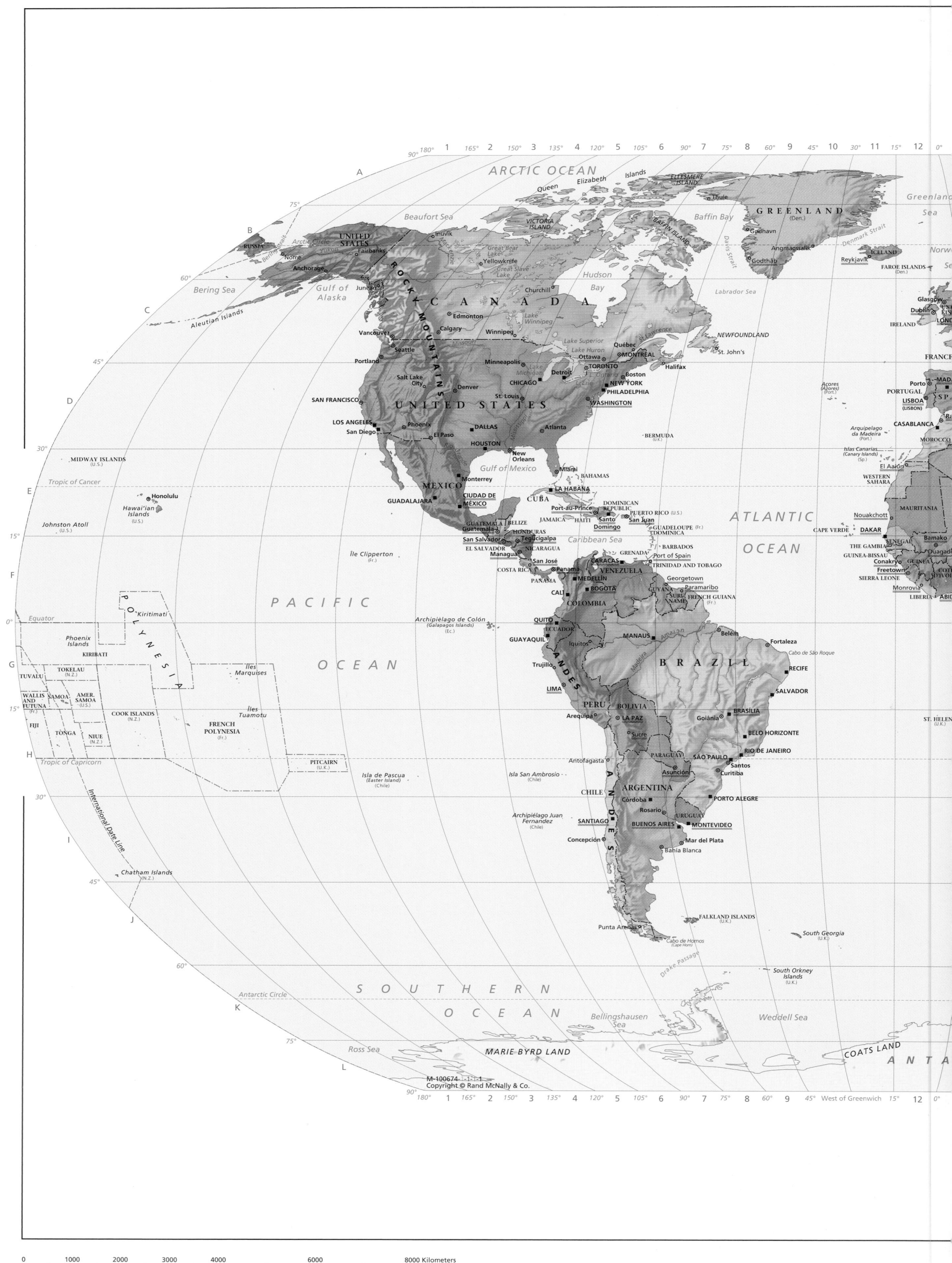

ARCTIC OCEAN

Queen Elizabeth Islands
ELLESMERE ISLAND
Thule
GREENLAND (Den.)
Greenland Sea

Beaufort Sea
VICTORIA ISLAND
Baffin Island
Baffin Bay
Godhavn
Angmagssalik
Denmark Strait

RUSSIA
Bering Strait
Nome
Inuvik
Great Bear Lake
Yellowknife
Great Slave Lake
Hudson Bay
Godthåb
Reykjavík
ICELAND
Norw
FAROE ISLANDS (Den.)

UNITED STATES
Fairbanks
Anchorage
Gulf of Alaska
Juneau
Churchill

CANADA

Glasgow
Dublin
LONG
IRELAND

Bering Sea
Aleutian Islands

Edmonton
Calgary
Lake Winnipeg
Winnipeg
Lake Superior
Lake Huron
Québec
MONTRÉAL
St. Lawrence
NEWFOUNDLAND
St. John's
Labrador Sea

Vancouver
Seattle
Portland
Minneapolis
Ottawa
TORONTO
Detroit
CHICAGO
Lake Michigan
Boston
Halifax
FRANCE

Salt Lake City
Denver
St. Louis
UNITED STATES
NEW YORK
PHILADELPHIA
WASHINGTON
Acores (Azores) (Port.)
Porto
PORTUGAL
MAD
SP

SAN FRANCISCO
Phoenix
DALLAS
Atlanta
BERMUDA (U.K.)
LISBOA (LISBON)
R

LOS ANGELES
San Diego
El Paso
HOUSTON
Arquipélago da Madeira (Port.)
CASABLANCA
MOROCCO

MIDWAY ISLANDS (U.S.)
New Orleans
Miami
BAHAMAS
Islas Canarias (Canary Islands) (Sp.)
El Aaiún
WESTERN SAHARA

Tropic of Cancer
Honolulu
Hawai'ian Islands (U.S.)
MEXICO
Monterrey
LA HABANA
CUBA
DOMINICAN REPUBLIC
PUERTO RICO (U.S.)
Nouakchott
MAURITANIA

Johnston Atoll (U.S.)
GUADALAJARA
CIUDAD DE MEXICO
Port-au-Prince
Santo Domingo
San Juan
ATLANTIC OCEAN
CAPE VERDE
DAKAR

GUATEMALA
BELIZE
HAITI
JAMAICA
GUADELOUPE (Fr.)
DOMINICA
SENEGAL
THE GAMBIA
Bamako

Île Clipperton (Fr.)
Guatemala
HONDURAS
Caribbean Sea
BARBADOS
GUINEA-BISSAU
Conakry
Ouagad

SAN SALVADOR
EL SALVADOR
Tegucigalpa
NICARAGUA
GRENADA
TRINIDAD AND TOBAGO
GUINEA
FREETOWN
GUINEA

Managua
San José
CARACAS
Port of Spain
SIERRA LEONE
COT
IVOIRE

COSTA RICA
PANAMA
Panama
MEDELLÍN
VENEZUELA
Georgetown
Paramaribo
LIBERIA
Monrovia
ABID

PACIFIC
COLOMBIA
CALI
BOGOTÁ
GUYANA
SURINAME
FRENCH GUIANA (Fr.)

Equator
QUITO
ECUADOR
Archipiélago de Colón (Galapagos Islands) (Ec.)

POLYNESIA
Kiritimati
GUAYAQUIL
Iquitos
MANAUS
Amazon
Belém
Fortaleza
Cabo de São Roque

OCEAN
Phoenix Islands
KIRIBATI
Trujillo
BRAZIL
RECIFE

TUVALU
TOKELAU (N.Z.)
Îles Marquises
LIMA
PERU
ANDES
SALVADOR

WALLIS AND FUTUNA (Fr.)
SAMOA
AMER. SAMOA (U.S.)
COOK ISLANDS (N.Z.)
Îles Tuamotu
BOLIVIA
La Paz
Sucre
Goiânia
BRASÍLIA
BELO HORIZONTE
ST. HELENA (U.K.)

FIJI
Arequipa
PARAGUAY
SÃO PAULO
RIO DE JANEIRO

TONGA
NIUE (N.Z.)
FRENCH POLYNESIA (Fr.)
Antofagasta
Asunción
Santos
Curitiba

Tropic of Capricorn
PITCAIRN (U.K.)
Isla de Pascua (Easter Island) (Chile)
Isla San Ambrosio (Chile)
ARGENTINA
PORTO ALEGRE

International Date Line
Archipiélago Juan Fernandez (Chile)
CHILE
Córdoba
Rosario
URUGUAY

Chatham Islands (N.Z.)
SANTIAGO
BUENOS AIRES
MONTEVIDEO
Mar del Plata

Concepción
Bahía Blanca

FALKLAND ISLANDS (U.K.)
Punta Arenas
Cabo de Hornos (Cape Horn)
South Georgia (U.K.)

SOUTHERN
South Orkney Islands (U.K.)

Antarctic Circle
OCEAN
Bellingshausen Sea
Drake Passage
Weddell Sea

Ross Sea
MARIE BYRD LAND
COATS LAND
ANTA

Scale 1 : 80,000,000   Robinson Projection

| 0 | 1000 | 2000 | 3000 | 4000 | 6000 | 8000 Kilometers |

| 0 | 500 | 1000 | 1500 | 2000 | 3000 | 4000 | 5000 Miles |

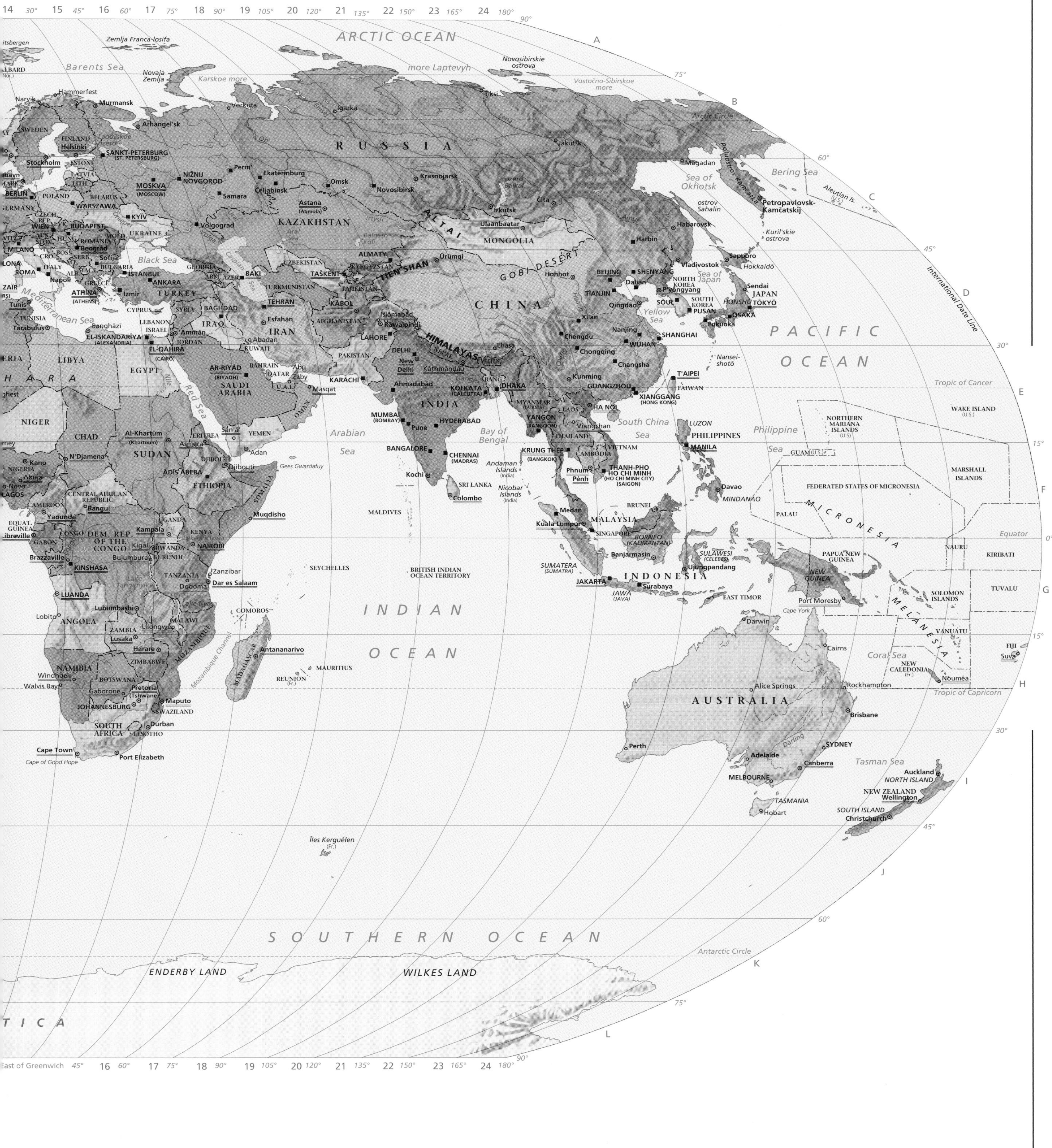

ARCTIC OCEAN

14 30° 15 45° 16 60° 17 75° 18 90° 19 105° 20 120° 21 135° 22 150° 23 165° 24 180°   90°

itsbergen
Zemlja Franca-Iosifa
Novosibirskie ostrova
A
LBARD
Nor.)
Barents Sea
Novaja Zemlja
Karskoe more
more Laptevyh
Vostočno-Sibirskoe more
75°
Narvik
Hammerfest
Murmansk
Vorkuta
Igarka
Tiksi
B
Arctic Circle
SWEDEN
FINLAND
Arhangel'sk
Magadan
Bering Sea
60°
Stockholm
Helsinki
ESTONIA
Jenisej
Ob'
RUSSIA
Jakutsk
Sea of Okhotsk
poluostrov Kamčatka
DARK
SANKT-PETERBURG (ST. PETERSBURG)
LATVIA
LITH.
NIŽNIJ NOVGOROD
Perm
Ekaterinburg
Omsk
Krasnojarsk
Cita
Irkutsk
Habarovsk
Petropavlovsk-Kamčatskij
C
45°
BERLIN
POLAND
WARSZAWA
BELARUS
MOSKVA (MOSCOW)
Samara
Celjabinsk
Novosibirsk
Amur
ostrov Sahalin
Kuril'skie ostrova
GERMANY
CZECH
WIEN
BUDAPEST
UKRAINE
Volgograd
KAZAKHSTAN
Astana (Aqmola)
Irtyš
Ulaanbaatar
Harbin
Vladivostok
Sapporo
Hokkaido
MILANO
AUS.
HUNG.
ROMANIA
Beograd
Sofiya
Aral Sea
Balqash köli
ALTAI
MONGOLIA
SHENYANG
NORTH KOREA
P'yongyang
Sea of Japan
Sendai
JAPAN
ROMA
ITALY
GREECE
Black Sea
GEORGIA
UZBEKISTAN
KYRGYZSTAN
TIEN SHAN
Ürümqi
GOBI DESERT
Hohhot
BEIJING
Dalian
Qingdao
SOUTH KOREA
SOUL
PUSAN
HONSHU
TOKYO
OSAKA
Fukuoka
LONA
Napoli
ISTANBUL
ANKARA
AZER.
BAKI
TURKMENISTAN
TAŠKENT
TAJIKISTAN
TIANJIN
CHINA
Xi'an
Nanjing
SHANGHAI
D
PACIFIC
30°
ATHINA (ATHENS)
Izmir
TURKEY
SYRIA
BAGHDAD
TEHRAN
KABOL
AFGHANISTAN
Islamabad
Rawalpindi
CHINA
Chengdu
Chongqing
Changsha
WUHAN
OCEAN
Nansei-shotō
Tunis
CYPRUS
LEBANON
ISRAEL
IRAQ
Esfahan
Abadan
IRAN
HIMALAYAS
Lhasa
Kunming
GUANGZHOU
XIANGGANG (HONG KONG)
T'AIPEI
TAIWAN
Tropic of Cancer
WAKE ISLAND (U.S.)
EL-ISKANDARIYA (ALEXANDRIA)
JORDAN
AMMAN
EL-QAHIRA (CAIRO)
KUWAIT
AR-RIYAD (RIYADH)
BAHRAIN
QATAR
Abu Zaby
U.A.E.
Masqat
PAKISTAN
LAHORE
DELHI
New Delhi
Kathmandu
NEPAL
Ganges
DHAKA
MYANMAR (BURMA)
HA NOI
LAOS
South China Sea
NORTHERN MARIANA ISLANDS (U.S.)
HARA
LIBYA
EGYPT
Red Sea
SAUDI ARABIA
OMAN
INDIA
KARACHI
Ahmadabad
KOLKATA (CALCUTTA)
E
15°
ERIA
NIGER
CHAD
Al-Khartum (Khartoum)
ERITREA
Ašmera
YEMEN
Adan
SAN'A'
MUMBAI (BOMBAY)
Pune
HYDERABAD
Arabian Sea
Bay of Bengal
YANGON (RANGOON)
THAILAND
KRUNG THEP (BANGKOK)
CAMBODIA
VIETNAM
PHILIPPINES
MANILA
LUZON
Philippine Sea
GUAM (U.S.)
MARSHALL ISLANDS
Kano
N'Djamena
SUDAN
DJIBOUTI
Djibouti
BANGALORE
CHENNAI (MADRAS)
Andaman Islands (India)
Phnum Penh
HANH-PHO HO CHI MINH (HO CHI MINH CITY) (SAIGON)
NIGERIA
Abuja
CENTRAL AFRICAN REPUBLIC
ADIS ABEBA
ETHIOPIA
Kochi
SRI LANKA
Nicobar Islands (India)
Davao
MINDANAO
FEDERATED STATES OF MICRONESIA
LAGOS
CAMEROON
Yaounde
Bangui
Gees Gwardafuy
Colombo
Medan
BRUNEI
MICRONESIA
PALAU
MALDIVES
Kuala Lumpur
MALAYSIA
SINGAPORE
BORNEO (KALIMANTAN)
Equator
0°
EQUAT. GUINEA
Libreville
GABON
CONGO DEM. REP. OF THE CONGO
UGANDA
Kampala
KENYA
NAIROBI
SUMATERA (SUMATRA)
Banjarmasin
SULAWESI (CELEBES)
PAPUA NEW GUINEA
NEW GUINEA
NAURU
KIRIBATI
Brazzaville
KINSHASA
Kigali
Bujumbura
BURUNDI
TANZANIA
Lake Victoria
Dodoma
SEYCHELLES
BRITISH INDIAN OCEAN TERRITORY
JAKARTA
Surabaya
Ujungpandang
EAST TIMOR
Port Moresby
SOLOMON ISLANDS
TUVALU
G
LUANDA
Lubumbashi
ZAMBIA
Lilongwe
Dar es Salaam
Zanzibar
Tanganyika
JAWA (JAVA)
Cape York
Darwin
MELANESIA
VANUATU
15°
Lobito
ANGOLA
Lusaka
MALAWI
INDIAN
FIJI
Suva
NAMIBIA
Windhoek
BOTSWANA
HARARE
ZIMBABWE
MOZAMBIQUE
Antananarivo
MADAGASCAR
MAURITIUS
OCEAN
Cairns
Coral Sea
NEW CALEDONIA (Fr.)
Nouméa
H
Tropic of Capricorn
Walvis Bay
Gaborone
Pretoria (Tshwane)
Maputo
SWAZILAND
JOHANNESBURG
REUNION (Fr.)
Alice Springs
Rockhampton
Darling
Brisbane
30°
SOUTH AFRICA
Durban
LESOTHO
AUSTRALIA
Cape Town
Cape of Good Hope
Port Elizabeth
Perth
Adelaide
SYDNEY
Canberra
Tasman Sea
Auckland
NORTH ISLAND
I
MELBOURNE
NEW ZEALAND
Wellington
TASMANIA
SOUTH ISLAND
Christchurch
45°
Hobart
Îles Kerguélen (Fr.)
J

S O U T H E R N   O C E A N
60°
Antarctic Circle
K
TICA
ENDERBY LAND
WILKES LAND
L
75°
East of Greenwich 45° 16 60° 17 75° 18 90° 19 105° 20 120° 21 135° 22 150° 23 165° 24 180°   90°

International Date Line

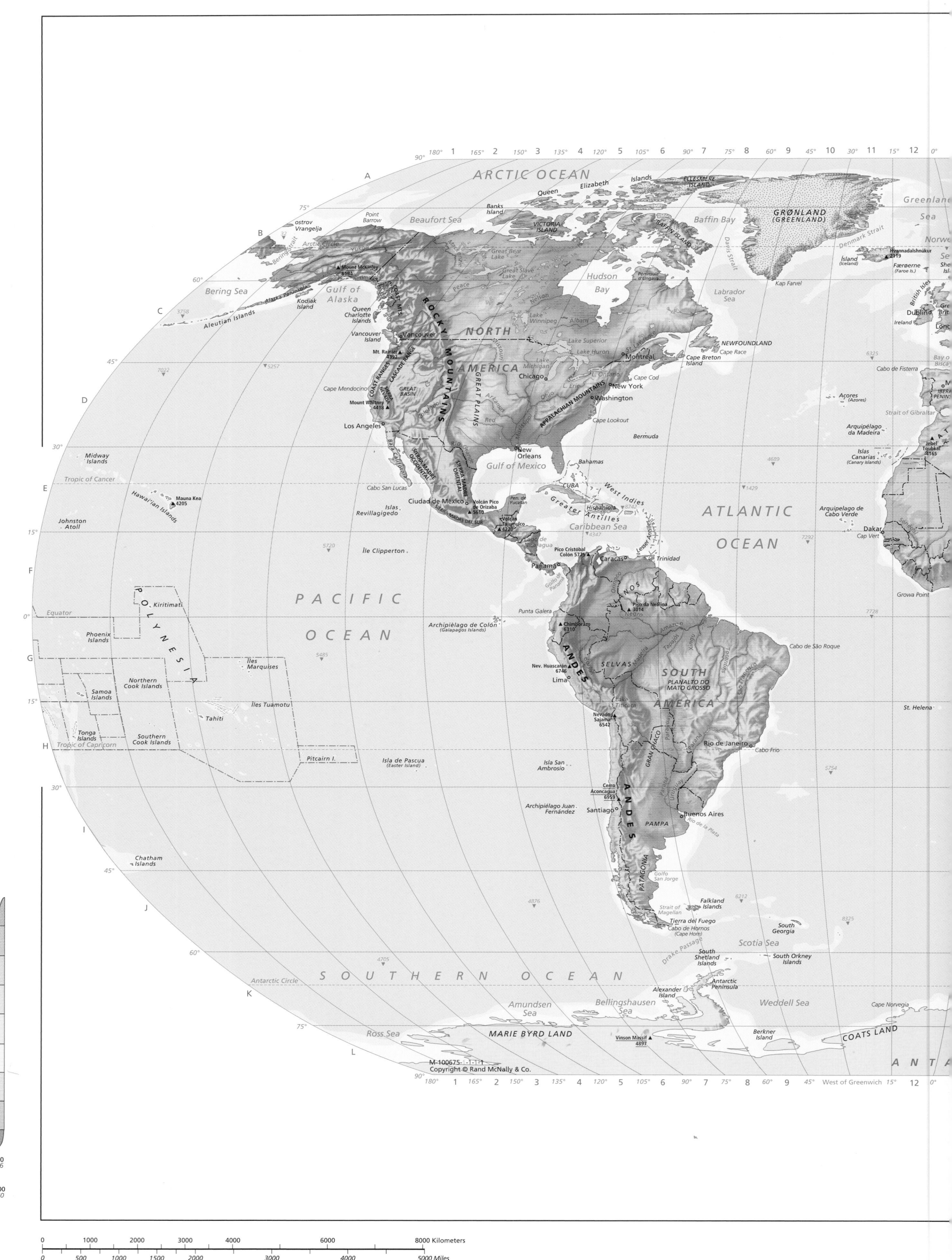

Meters / Feet
6000 / 19680
4000 / 13120
3000 / 9840
2000 / 6560
1000 / 3280
500 / 1640
200 / 656
Sea Level
200 / 656
2000 / 6560

0 1000 2000 3000 4000 6000 8000 Kilometers
0 500 1000 1500 2000 3000 4000 5000 Miles
Scale 1 : 80,000,000   Robinson Projection

M-100675- Copyright © Rand McNally & Co.

30° 15 45° 16 60° 17 75° 18 90° 19 105° 20 120° 21 135° 22 150° 23 165° 24 180° 90°

ARCTIC OCEAN

Zemlja Franca-Iosifa

Severnaja Zemlja

Barents Sea

Novosibirskie ostrova

more Laptevyh

Vostočno-Sibirskoe more

75°

A

Nordkapp

Karskoe more

Korsij poluostrov

Novaja Zemlja

ZAPADNO-SIBIRSKAJA

gora Kamen 1701

Arctic Circle

B

Koldhapigen

URAL'SKIE GORY

RAVNINA (WEST SIBERIAN PLAIN)

Nižnjaja Tunguska

SIBIR' (SIBERIA)

Omoloj gora Pobeda 3147

180°

Baltic

Ladožkoe ozero

Ekaterinburg

Ob

Lena

Kolyma

Bering Sea

C

Berlin

Moskva (Moscow)

Ishim

Irtyš

SIBIRSKOE

ostrov Sahalin

mys Lopatka

4027

ROPE

CARPATHIAN

Dnepr

Irkutsk

ozero Bajkal

ALTAI

Kuril'skie ostrova

45°

ALPS

Black Sea

gora El'brus 5642

Aral Sea

Balqash köli

Syr Darja

Pobedy 7439

A S I A

Sea of Okhotsk

D

APPENNINI

CAUCASUS

Caspian Sea

Amu Darja

TIEN SHAN

Ulaanbaatar

GOBI DESERT

Hokkaidō

Roma

BALKAN PENINSULA

Istanbul

pik Ismail Samani 7495

Beijing

HONSHŪ

Sea of Japan

Sicilia (Sicily)

Kriti

Cyprus

Tehrān

Qollehye Damāvand 5604

HINDU KUSH

(Qogir Feng) 8611

KUNLUN SHAN

Fuji-san 3776 Tōkyō

Shikoku

Kyūshū

297

30°

Mediterranean Sea

El-Qâhira (Cairo)

DASHT-E KAVIR

KÜHHA-YE ZAGROS

QING ZANG GAOYUAN

Gongga Shan 7590

Shanghai

East China Sea

9695

PACIFIC OCEAN

E

HARA

Red Sea

Persian Gulf

Gulf of Oman

HIMALAYAS

Delhi

Mount Everest 8848

Yellow Sea

Nansei-shotō

Tropic of Cancer

Wake Island

TIBESTI

Emi Koussi 3415

NUBIAN DESERT

ARABIAN PENINSULA

AR-RUB' AL-KHALI

Brahma

Ganges

Taiwan

Yü Shan 3997

Mariana Islands

15°

908

Mumbai (Bombay)

Godavari

2359

Hainan Dao

South China Sea

Philippine Sea

Guam 10915

Marshall Islands

F

AFRICA

Ras Dashen Terara 4620

Gulf of Aden

Suquṭrā

Arabian Sea

WESTERN GHATS

EASTERN GHATS

Bay of Bengal

Andaman Islands

Krung Thep

INDOCHINA

Manila

LUZON

Philippine

Chari

Adīs Abeba

Gees Gwardafuy

Cape Comorin

Pidurutalagala 2524

Sri Lanka

5423

Andaman Sea

Nicobar Islands

Gulf of Thailand

MINDANAO

Palau Islands

Caroline Islands

MICRONESIA

Congo

Margherita Peak 5109

Lake Rudolf

Maldive Islands

Malay Peninsula

Gunong Kinabalu 4101

Celebes Sea

Halmahera

Equator

0°

CONGO BASIN

Lake Victoria

Kirinyaga 5199

SUMATERA (SUMATRA)

BORNEO (KALIMANTAN)

SULAWESI (CELEBES)

Seram

Laut Banda

NEW GUINEA

New Britain

8940

Solomon Islands

RIFT VALLEY

Kilimanjaro 5895

5340

Greater Sunda Islands

Mount Wilhelm 4509

Lake Tanganyika

Zanzibar

Les Amirantes

Seychelles

Jakarta

Laut Jawa

JAWA (JAVA)

Timor

Arafura Sea

MELANESIA

Cape York

G

New Hebrides

15°

Cape Fria

Tanjona Bobaomby

Maromokotro 2876

5125

INDIAN

6090

1706

Timor Sea

Gulf of Carpentaria

CAPE YORK PENINSULA

Fiji Islands

Congo

OCEAN

Kimberley Plateau

Tanami Desert

Coral Sea

Nouvelle-Calédonie

Tropic of Capricorn

H

MADAGASCAR

Mauritius

North West Cape

Mount Meharry 1253

GREAT SANDY DESERT

AUSTRALIA

Mount Woodroffe 1435

GREAT DIVIDING RANGE

5303

KALAHARI DESERT

Réunion

Tanjona Vohimena

6420

GREAT VICTORIA DESERT

Sydney

North Cape

NAMIB DESERT

Orange

Thabana-Ntlenyana 3482

Cape Town

DRAKENSBERG

Île Amsterdam

Cape Leeuwin

Great Australian Bight

Darling

Murray

Melbourne

Mount Kosciuszko 2229

Tasman Sea

NORTH ISLAND

Mount Ruapehu 2797

30°

Cape of Good Hope

5536

2690

Mount Ossa 1617

TASMANIA

SOUTH ISLAND

Aoraki (Mount Cook) 3754

I

Prince Edward Islands

3079

Îles de Crozet

Îles Kerguélen

South East Cape

South West Cape

45°

Heard Island

6089

J

4425

60°

SOUTHERN OCEAN

5124

Cape Poinsett

Antarctic Circle

K

N MAUD LAND

ENDERBY LAND

WILKES LAND

Cape Adare

75°

VICTORIA LAND

Ross Sea

TICA

L

st of Greenwich 45° 16 60° 17 75° 18 90° 19 105° 20 120° 21 135° 22 150° 23 165° 24 180°

ATLANTIC OCEAN

GREENLAND SEA

NORWEGIAN SEA

ICELAND
Reykjavík
Akureyri
Hvannadalshnúkur 2119
Seydisfjördur
Hofn

Arctic Circle

Horn

FAROE ISLANDS (Den.) Tórshavn

SHETLAND ISLANDS (U.K.)

Rockall (U.K.)

NORTH SEA

NORWAY
Kristiansund
Ålesund Molde
Galdhøpiggen 2469
Dombås
Bergen
Haugesund
Stavanger
Oslo
Dramñen
Skien
Kristiansand
Lindesnes

SWEDEN
Trondheim
Namsos
Östersund
Sundsvall
Härnösand
Falun
Gävle
Uppsala
Västerås
Örebro
STOCKHOLM
Norrköping
Linköping

VESTERÅLEN
LOFOTEN
Narvik
Bodø
Mo i Rana
Tromsø

HEBRIDES
Thurso
Inverness
ORKNEY ISLANDS

UNITED KINGDOM
GLASGOW
EDINBURGH
Dundee
Aberdeen
Londonderry
Belfast
Carlisle
NEWCASTLE UPON TYNE
Middlesbrough

IRELAND
Sligo
Galway
DUBLIN
Limerick
Waterford
Cork
Mizen Head

IRISH SEA

LIVERPOOL
MANCHESTER
LEEDS
Sheffield
Nottingham
Leicester
BIRMINGHAM
Norwich
Ipswich
Swansea
Cardiff
Oxford
Bristol
LONDON
Southampton
Brighton
Dover
Plymouth
Penzance
Land's End
ISLES OF SCILLY

English Channel
Strait of Dover
GUERNSEY (U.K.)
JERSEY (U.K.)
Cherbourg
Le Havre
Rouen
Amiens
Pointe de Saint-Mathieu
Brest
Saint-Malo
Caen
Rennes
Le Mans

DENMARK
Holstebro
Esbjerg
Kolding
Odense
Flensburg
Kiel
Lübeck
Rostock
Stralsund
Rügen
KØBENHAVN (COPENHAGEN)
Malmö
Helsingborg
Århus
Aalborg
Frederikshavn
Göteborg
Jönköping
Halmstad
Växjö
Kalmar
Karlskrona
ÖLAND
GOTLAND
Bornholm (Den.)
Gdynia
Gdańsk
Szczecin
Bydgoszcz

Skagerrak
Kattegat
BALTIC SEA

NETHERLANDS
Groningen
's-Gravenhage (The Hague)
AMSTERDAM
ROTTERDAM
ANTWERPEN
BRUXELLES
LILLE
BELGIUM
Liège
Utrecht
Bremen
Bremerhaven
HAMBURG
Hannover
Münster
Dortmund
ESSEN
DÜSSELDORF
KÖLN
Bonn
Wiesbaden
FRANKFURT AM MAIN
LUXEMBOURG
Saarbrücken
MANNHEIM
Würzburg

GERMANY
Magdeburg
BERLIN
Leipzig
Dresden
Erfurt
Chemnitz

POLAND
Poznań
Wrocław
Częstochowa
Katowice
Walbrzych
Olomouc
PRAHA
CZECH REP
Ostrava
Brno
Plzeň

FRANCE
Nantes
Angers
Tours
Orléans
Bourges
Troyes
Reims
Metz
Nancy
Strasbourg
Mulhouse
Dijon
Besançon
La Rochelle
Poitiers
Limoges
A Coruña
Cabo de Fisterra
Gijón
Oviedo
Santander
Vigo
Ourense
León
Bilbao
Donostia San Sebastián
Pamplona
Burgos
Vitoria Gasteiz
Bordeaux
Bayonne
Toulouse
Montpellier
Nîmes
Avignon
LYON
Saint-Étienne
Grenoble
Mont Blanc 4807
Genève
Bern
Lausanne
Zürich
Basel
SWITZ
Vaduz
Innsbruck
Bolzano
STUTTGART
Augsburg
Regensburg
Nürnberg
MÜNCHEN (MUNICH)
Salzburg
Linz
WIEN (VIENNA)
Bratislava
Győr
BUDAPEST
AUSTRIA
Klagenfurt
Graz
SLOVENIA
Ljubljana
Zagreb
CROATIA
Rijeka
Trieste
Padova
Venezia (Venice)
Verona
Brescia
MILANO
Torino
GENOVA
La Spezia
Parma
Bologna
Pisa
Livorno
Firenze
Po
SLOVAKIA
HUNGARY
Pécs
Szeged
Osijek
BOSNIA AND HERZEGOVINA
Sarajevo
Split
MONTENEGRO
Podgorica
Dubrovnik

PYRENEES
ANDORRA
Andorra la Vella
MARSEILLE
Toulon
Nice
MONACO
LIGURIAN SEA
CORSE (CORSICA) (Fr.)
Ajaccio
Bastia
SAN MARINO
Perugia
Ancona
Pescara
L'Aquila
ROMA (ROME)
VATICAN CITY
APENNINES
ADRIATIC SEA
APPENNINO

PORTUGAL
PORTO
Braga
Coimbra
LISBOA (LISBON)
Setúbal
Évora
Badajoz
Faro
Cabo de São Vicente

SPAIN
Salamanca
Valladolid
Segovia
MADRID
Zaragoza
Lleida
Tarragona
BARCELONA
Toledo
VALÈNCIA
Albacete
Córdoba
Jaén
Sevilla
Granada
Murcia
Elx
Alacant
Cartagena
Huelva
Cádiz
Málaga
Mulhacén 3482
GIBRALTAR (U.K.)
Tánger
Ceuta (Sp.)
Tétouan
Al Hoceima
Melilla (Sp.)
Isla de Alborán (Sp.)

ILLES BALEARS (BALEARIC ISLANDS)
Menorca
Palma de Mallorca
MALLORCA
Eivissa

SARDEGNA (SARDINIA) (It.)
Sassari
Olbia
Nuoro
Oristano
Cagliari

TYRRHENIAN SEA

ITALY
NAPOLI (NAPLES)
Salerno
Foggia
Bari
Taranto
Brindisi
Lecce
Cosenza
Catanzaro
Reggio di Calabria
Messina
Palermo
Trapani
SICILIA (SICILY)
Catania
Siracusa
Agrigento
Monte Etna 3323
Cap Bon
Isola di Pantelleria (It.)
ISOLE PELAGIE (It.)
Isola delle Correnti
MALTA
Valletta

TIRANE
ALBANIA
IONIAN SEA

MEDITERRANEAN SEA

CASABLANCA
Rabat
Salé
Meknès
Fès
El-Jadida
Safi
Essaouira
Agadir
Jebel Toubkal 4165
Marrakech
Khouribga
Er-Rachidia

MOROCCO
Oujda
Taza
Sidi bel Abbès
Larache
Mestghanem
Wahran
EL DJAZAÏR (ALGIERS)
El Boulaïda
Tizi Ouzou
Béjaïa
Bouira
Ech Cheliff
Tihert
Laghouat
Beskra

ATLAS MOUNTAINS

ALGERIA
Annaba
Skikda
Qacentina
Sétif
Batna
Tbessa
Qsentina
Chott ech Chergui
Chott el Hodna
Chott Melrhir

TUNIS
TUNISIA
Bizerte
Nabeul
Sousse
Kairouan
Sfax
Béja
La Galite
Gafsa

M-100668
Copyright © Rand McNally & Co.

West of Greenwich 0° East of Greenwich

0   200   400   800   1200 Kilometers
0   100   200   400   600   800 Miles
Scale 1 : 12,500,000   Conic Equidistant Projection

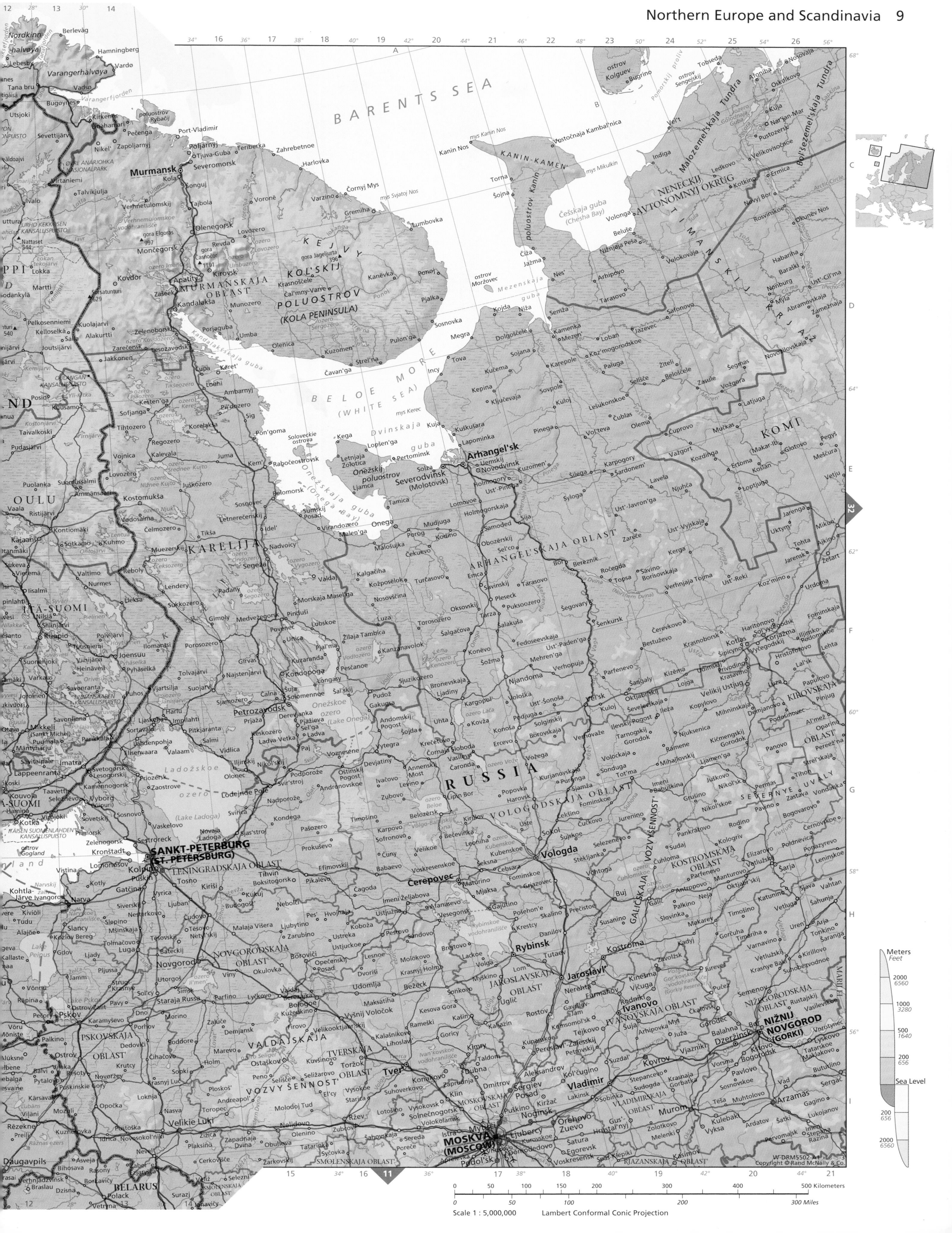

BARENTS SEA

KANIN-KAMEN

NENECKIJ AVTONOMNYJ OKRUG

KOLA PENINSULA
KOL'SKIJ POLUOSTROV
KEJVY

Murmansk

MURMANSKAJA OBLAST'

BELOE MORE
(WHITE SEA)

Čéšskaja guba (Chésha Bay)

Mezenskaja guba

Dvinskaja guba

Arhangel'sk
Severodvinsk (Molotovsk)

KOMI

KARELIJA

ARHANGEL'SKAJA OBLAST'

Onežskoe ozero (Lake Onega)

Petrozavodsk

Ladožskoe ozero (Lake Ladoga)

KIROVSKAJA OBLAST'

RUSSIA

VOLOGODSKAJA OBLAST'

SEVERNYE UVALY

SANKT-PETERBURG (ST. PETERSBURG)

LENINGRADSKAJA OBLAST'

Vologda

KOSTROMSKAJA OBLAST'

Čerepovec

Rybinsk

Jaroslavl'

JAROSLAVSKAJA OBLAST'

NOVGORODSKAJA OBLAST'

Novgorod

Ivanovo

IVANOVSKAJA OBLAST'

NIŽNIJ NOVGOROD (GORKI)

NIŽEGORODSKAJA OBLAST'

PSKOVSKAJA OBLAST'

Pskov

VALDAJSKAJA VOZVYŠENNOST'

TVERSKAJA OBLAST'

Tver'

Vladimir

VLADIMIRSKAJA OBLAST'

SMOLENSKAJA OBLAST'

MOSKVA (MOSCOW)

MOSKOVSKAJA OBLAST'

RJAZANSKAJA OBLAST'

Arzamas

BELARUS

OULU
ITÄ-SUOMI

Meters / Feet
2000 / 6560
1000 / 3280
500 / 1640
200 / 656
Sea Level
200 / 656
2000 / 6560

W-DRM5502-A1
Copyright © Rand McNally & Co.

0   50 100 150 200   300   400   500 Kilometers
0   50   100   200   300 Miles
Scale 1 : 5,000,000   Lambert Conformal Conic Projection

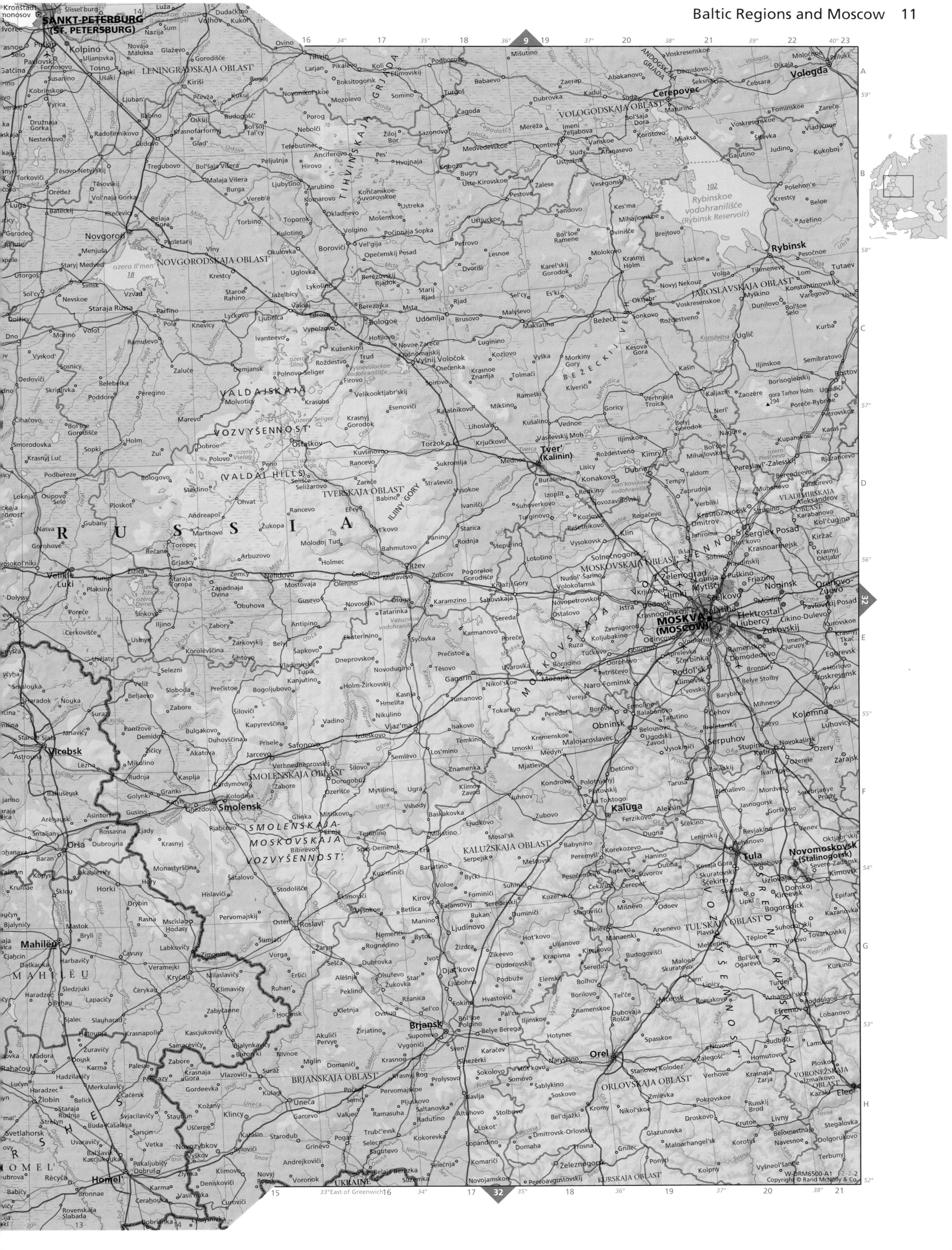

SANKT-PETERBURG
(ST. PETERSBURG)

LENINGRADSKAJA OBLAST'

NOVGORODSKAJA OBLAST'

VOLOGODSKAJA OBLAST'

Rybinskoe
vodohranilišče
(Rybinsk Reservoir)

Rybinsk

JAROSLAVSKAJA OBLAST'

VALDAJSKAJA

VOZVYŠENNOST'

(VALDAI HILLS)

R U S S I A

Tver'
(Kalinin)

TVERSKAJA OBLAST'

VLADIMIRSKAJA OBLAST'

MOSKOVSKAJA OBLAST'

MOSKVA
(MOSCOW)

Velikije
Luki

SMOLENSKAJA OBLAST'

SMOLENSKAJA-
MOSKOVSKAJA
VOZVYŠENNOST'

Smolensk

Vicebsk

KALUŽSKAJA OBLAST'

Kaluga

Tula

Novomoskovsk
(Stalinogorsk)

TUL'SKAJA OBLAST'

Mahilëu

MAHILËU

Brjansk

BRJANSKAJA OBLAST'

Orel

ORLOVSKAJA OBLAST'

Homel'

UKRAINE

VORONEŽSKAJA OBLAST'

KURSKAJA OBLAST'

Vologda

Čerepovec

Novgorod

Orša

12

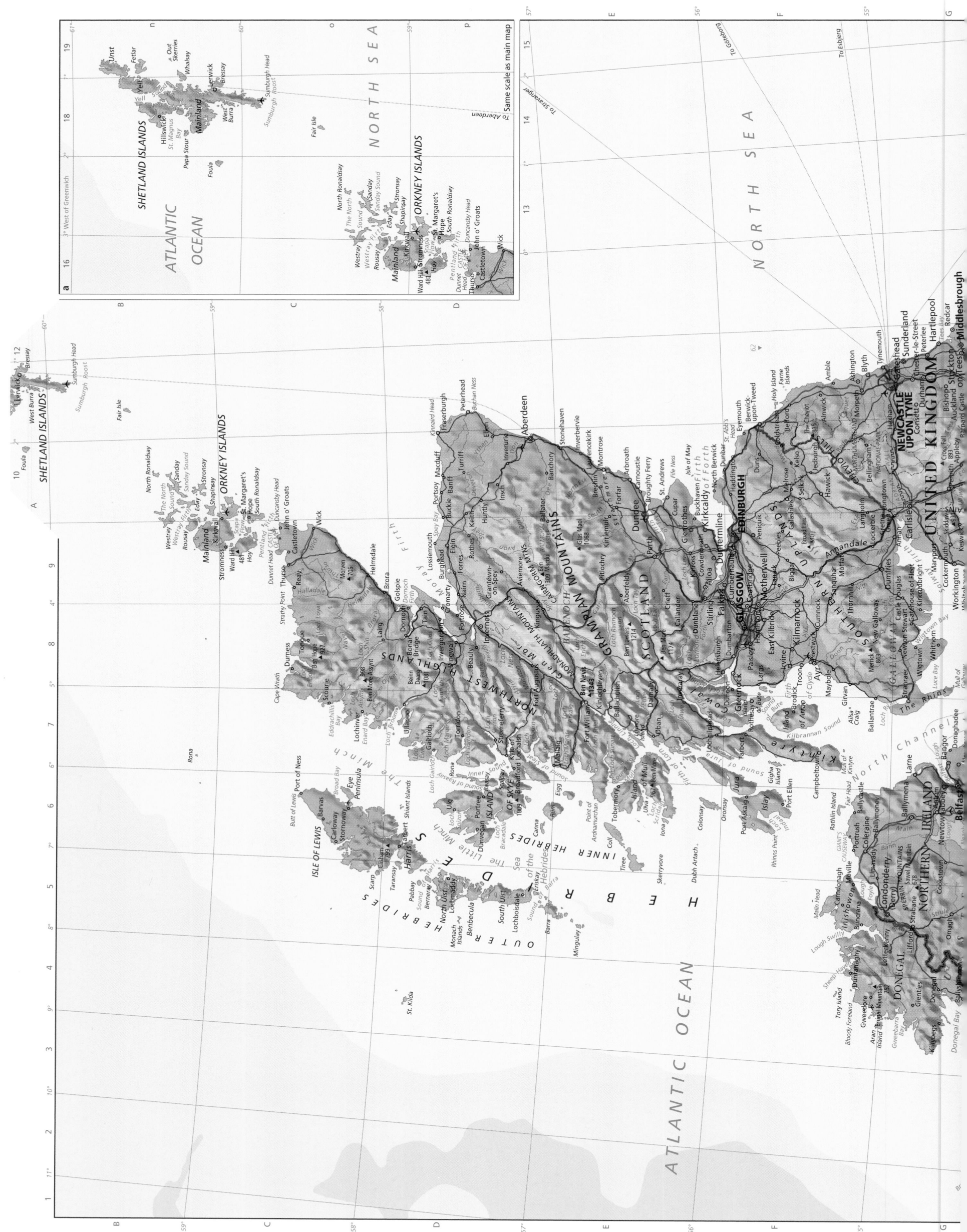

Same scale as main map

SHETLAND ISLANDS

Unst
Fetlar
Out Skerries
Whalsay
Lerwick
Bressay
Yell
Hillswick
St. Magnus Bay
Mainland
West Burra
Papa Stour
Sumburgh Head
Foula
Sumburgh Roost

ATLANTIC OCEAN

3° West of Greenwich

NORTH SEA

Fair Isle

ORKNEY ISLANDS

North Ronaldsay
The North Sound
Sanday
Sanday Sound
Stronsay
Eday
Shapinsay
St. Margaret's
Hope
South Ronaldsay
Duncansby Head
John o' Groats
Westray
Westray Firth
Rousay
Mainland
Kirkwall
Stromness
Ward Hill
48▲
Hoy
Scapa Flow
Pentland Firth
Dunnet Head
CASTLE
Thurso
Castletown
Wick

To Aberdeen
To Stranraer
To Gøteborg
To Esbjerg

NORTH SEA

SHETLAND ISLANDS

Lerwick 12
Bressay
West Burra
Sumburgh Head
Sumburgh Roost
Foula
Fair Isle

ORKNEY ISLANDS

North Ronaldsay
The North Sound
Sanday
Sanday Sound
Stronsay
Eday
Shapinsay
Westray
Westray Firth
Rousay
Mainland
Kirkwall
Stromness
Ward Hill
48▲
Hoy
Scapa Flow
St. Margaret's
Hope
South Ronaldsay
Pentland Firth
Dunnet Head CASTLE
Thurso
Castletown
Duncansby Head
John o' Groats
Wick

Rona

ATLANTIC OCEAN

St. Kilda

THE HEBRIDES

ISLE OF LEWIS
Butt of Lewis
Port of Ness
Barvas
Carloway
Stornoway
Eye Peninsula
Broad Bay
Shiant Islands
Scarp
Tarbert
Harris
Scalpay
Taransay
Pabbay
Berneray
North Uist
Monach Islands
Benbecula
Lochmaddy
Lochboisdale
South Uist
Barra
Mingulay
Eriskay
Sound of Barra

OUTER HEBRIDES

The Little Minch
The Minch

Raasay
ISLAND OF SKYE
Portree
Broadford
Dunvegan
Canna
Rum
Eigg
Muck
Point of Ardnamurchan
Coll
Tiree
Skerryvore
Dubh Artach

INNER HEBRIDES

Sea of the Hebrides
Iona
Mull
Colonsay
Oronsay
Port Askaig
Islay
Port Ellen
Gigha Island
Jura
Sound of Jura
Rhinns Point

NORTH WEST HIGHLANDS

Cape Wrath
Durness
Tongue
Loch Loyal
Strathy Point
Halladale
Reay
Thurso
Dunnet Head
Castletown
Wick
Helmsdale
Brora
Golspie
Dornoch
Dornoch Firth
Tain
Lairg
Bonar Bridge
Lochinver
Enard Bay
Ullapool
Gairloch
Loch Maree
Gruinard Bay
Poolewe
Torridon
Applecross
Stromeferry
Kyle of Lochalsh
Beinn Dearg 1084
Ben More Assynt 998
Eddrachillis
Loch Broom
Glen Mor
Beauly
Inverness
Dingwall
Cromarty
Nairn
Fortrose
Fort Augustus
Loch Ness
Loch Lochy
Loch Oich
Invergarry
Spean Bridge
Fort William
Ben Nevis 1343
Ballachulish
Glencoe
Kinlochleven
Loch Linnhe
Oban
Loch Etive
Loch Awe
Inveraray
Lochgilphead
Tarbert
Campbeltown
Mull of Kintyre
Fair Head

KINTYRE

Firth of Clyde
Isle of Arran
Bute
Brodick
Rothesay
Kilbrannan Sound
Ailsa Craig
Girvan
Ballantrae

CAIRNGORM MOUNTAINS

GRAMPIAN MOUNTAINS

MONADHLIATH MOUNTAINS

Ben Lawers 1214
Ben More 1174

SCOTLAND

Kinnaird Head
Fraserhead
Peterhead
Buchan Ness
Aberdeen
Stonehaven
Inverurie
Insch
Turriff
Banff
Buckie
Macduff
Portsoy
Portknockie
Spey Bay
Lossiemouth
Burghead
Elgin
Forres
Rothes
Keith
Huntly
Dufftown
Grantown-on-Spey
Aviemore
Kingussie
Blair Atholl
Pitlochry
Ballater
Braemar
Banchory
Loch Muick 1068
Brechin
Montrose
Forfar
Arbroath
Carnoustie
Broughty Ferry
Dundee
Cupar
St. Andrews
Perth
Auchterarder
Crieff
Callander
Dunblane
Stirling
Alloa
Kinross
Loch Leven
Cowdenbeath
Dunfermline
Falkirk
Kirkcaldy
Firth of Forth
Isle of May
North Berwick
Dunbar
Haddington
EDINBURGH
GLASGOW
Motherwell
Hamilton
Paisley
Greenock
Dumbarton
Loch Lomond
Helensburgh
Gourock
Largs
Ardrossan
Irvine
Troon
Prestwick
Ayr
Kilmarnock
East Kilbride
Cumnock
Maybole

PENTLAND HILLS
LAMMERMUIR HILLS

Berwick-upon-Tweed
Eyemouth
St. Abb's Head
Duns
Galashiels
Melrose
Peebles
Biggar
Lanark
Kelso
Jedburgh
Hawick
Selkirk

SOUTHERN UPLANDS

CHEVIOT HILLS

The Cheviot 816

Annandale
Moffat
Lockerbie
Langholm
Annan
Dumfries
Lochmaben
New Galloway
Castle Douglas
Kirkcudbright
Merrick 843
Newton Stewart
Wigtown
Wigtown Bay
Whithorn
Luce Bay
Stranraer
Portpatrick
Loch Ryan
The Rhins
Mull of Galloway

GALLOWAY

UNITED KINGDOM

Gateshead
Sunderland
Hartlepool
Tynemouth
NEWCASTLE UPON TYNE
Blyth
Ashington
Morpeth
Amble
Alnwick
Holy Island
Farne Islands
Bamburgh
Belford
Wooler
Rothbury
Bellingham
Consett
Chester-le-Street
Peterlee
Redcar
Middlesbrough
Stockton on Tees
Billingham
Bishop Auckland
Barnard Castle
Appleby
Penrith
Carlisle
Brampton
Longtown
Gretna
Workington
Cockermouth
Maryport
Keswick 978

NORTHERN IRELAND

Belfast
Larne
Carrickfergus
Newtownabbey
Bangor
Donaghadee
Ballymena
Ballymoney
Coleraine
Portrush
Portstewart
Ballycastle
Rathlin Island
Giant's Causeway

ANTRIM MOUNTAINS

Cookstown
Magherafelt
Londonderry (Derry)
Strabane
Omagh
Lifford
Letterkenny

SPERRIN MOUNTAINS

Sawel 683

DONEGAL

Malin Head
Buncrana
Moville
Lough Swilly
Lough Foyle
Inishowen
Carndonagh
Dungloe
Gweedore
Bloody Foreland
Tory Island
Gortahork
Donegal Bay
Glenties
Ardara
Killybegs
Aran Island
Gweebarra Bay
Slieve League
Donegal
Ballybofey
Stranorlar
Ballyshannon

ATLANTIC OCEAN

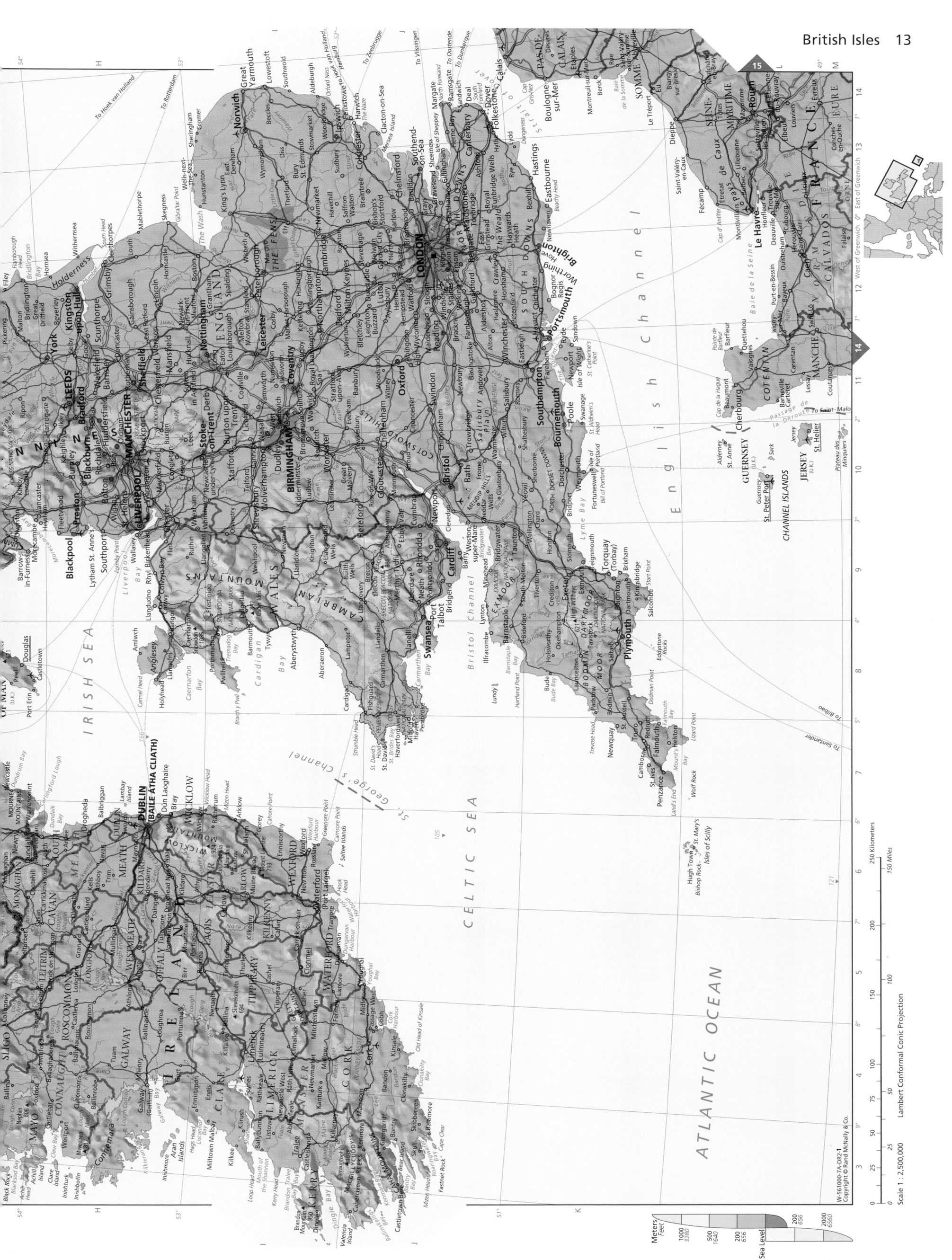

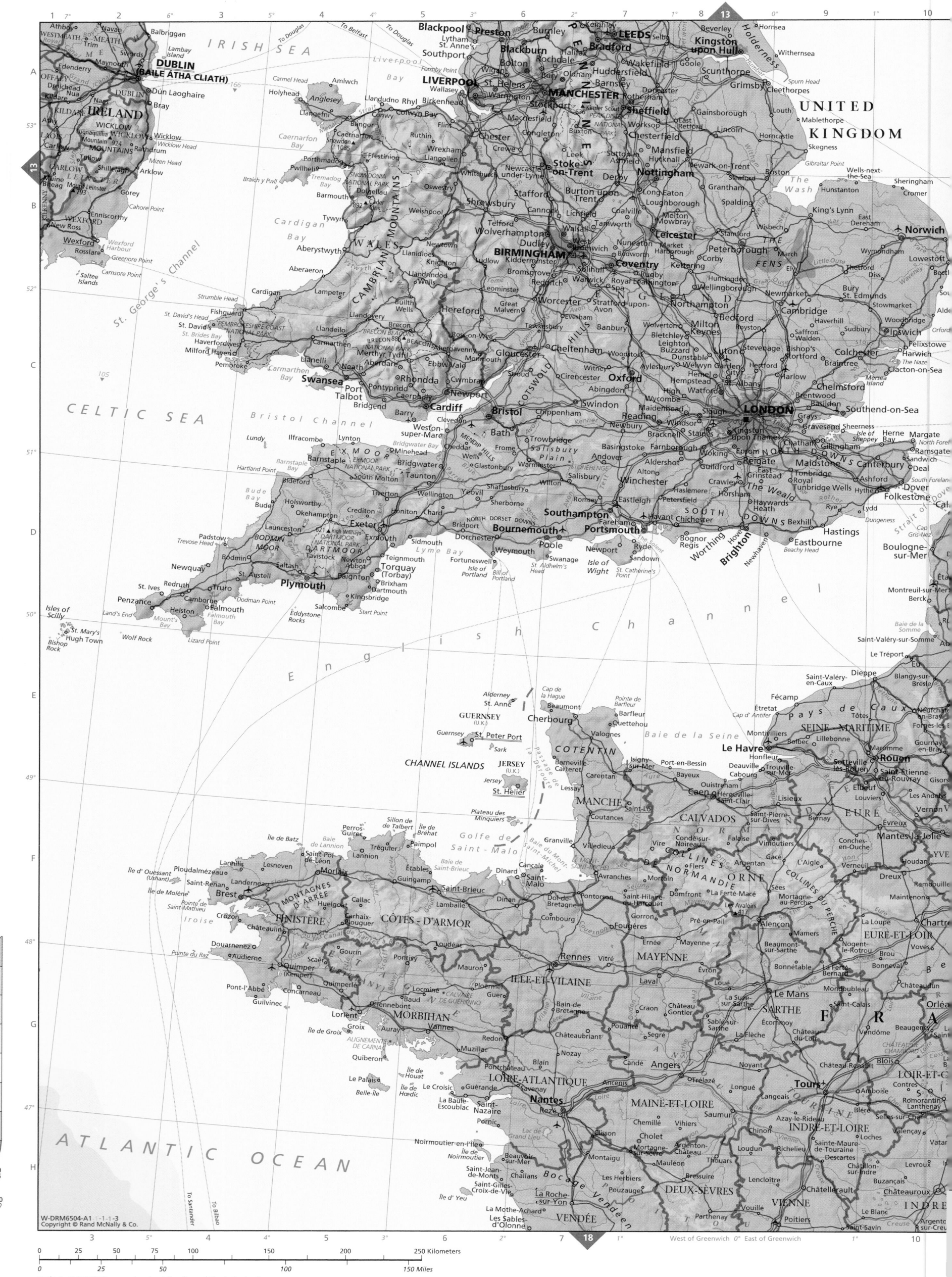

IRISH SEA

IRELAND

UNITED

KINGDOM

WALES

CELTIC SEA

Bristol Channel

CHANNEL ISLANDS

ATLANTIC OCEAN

English Channel

Meters
Feet

4000
13120

3000
9840

2000
6560

1000
3280

500
1640

200
656

Sea Level

200
656

2000
6560

W-DRM6504-A1   -1-1-3
Copyright © Rand McNally & Co.

0   25   50   75   150   200   250 Kilometers

0   25   50   100   150 Miles

Scale 1 : 2,500,000   Lambert Conformal Conic Projection

West of Greenwich 0° East of Greenwich

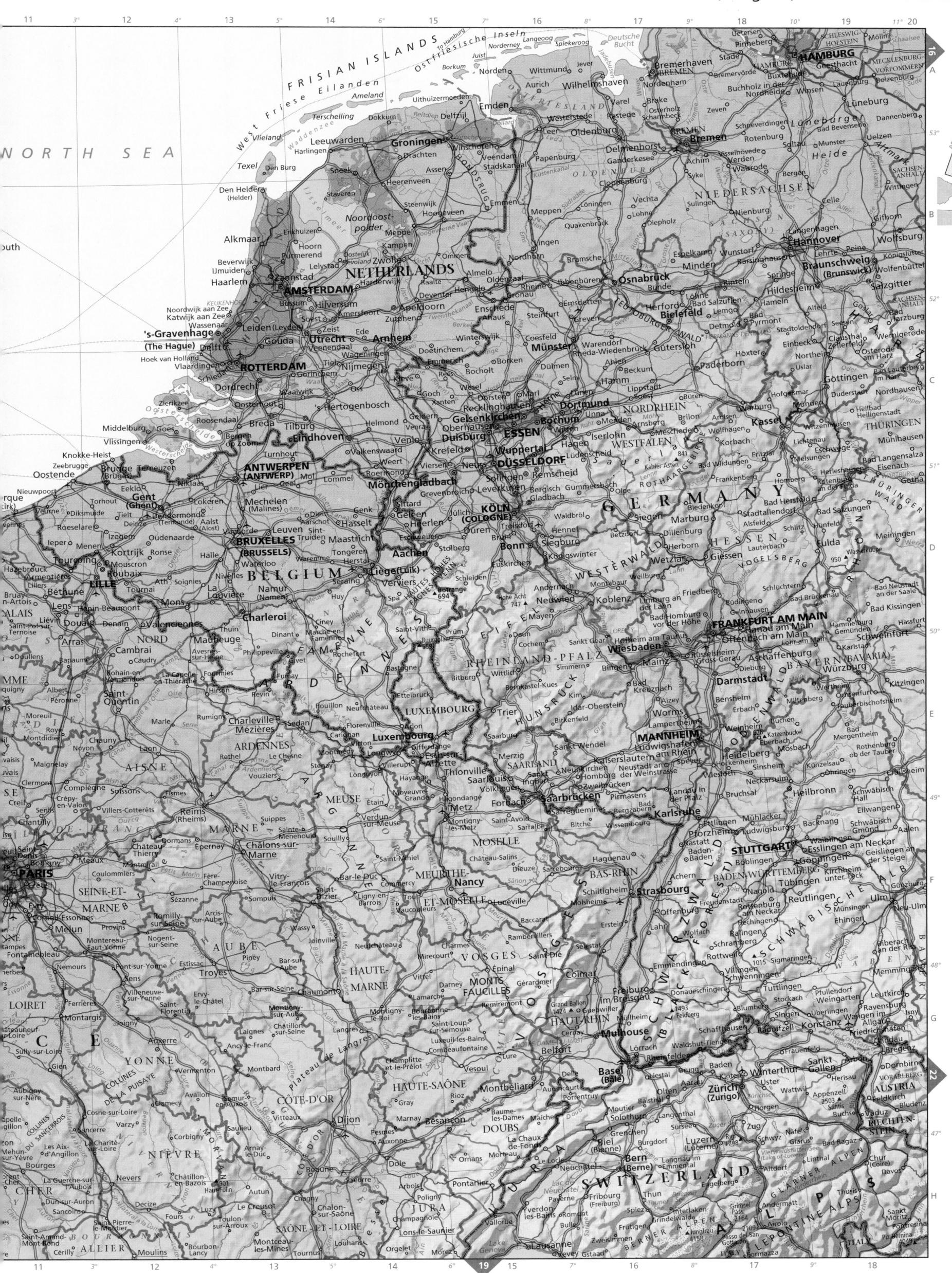

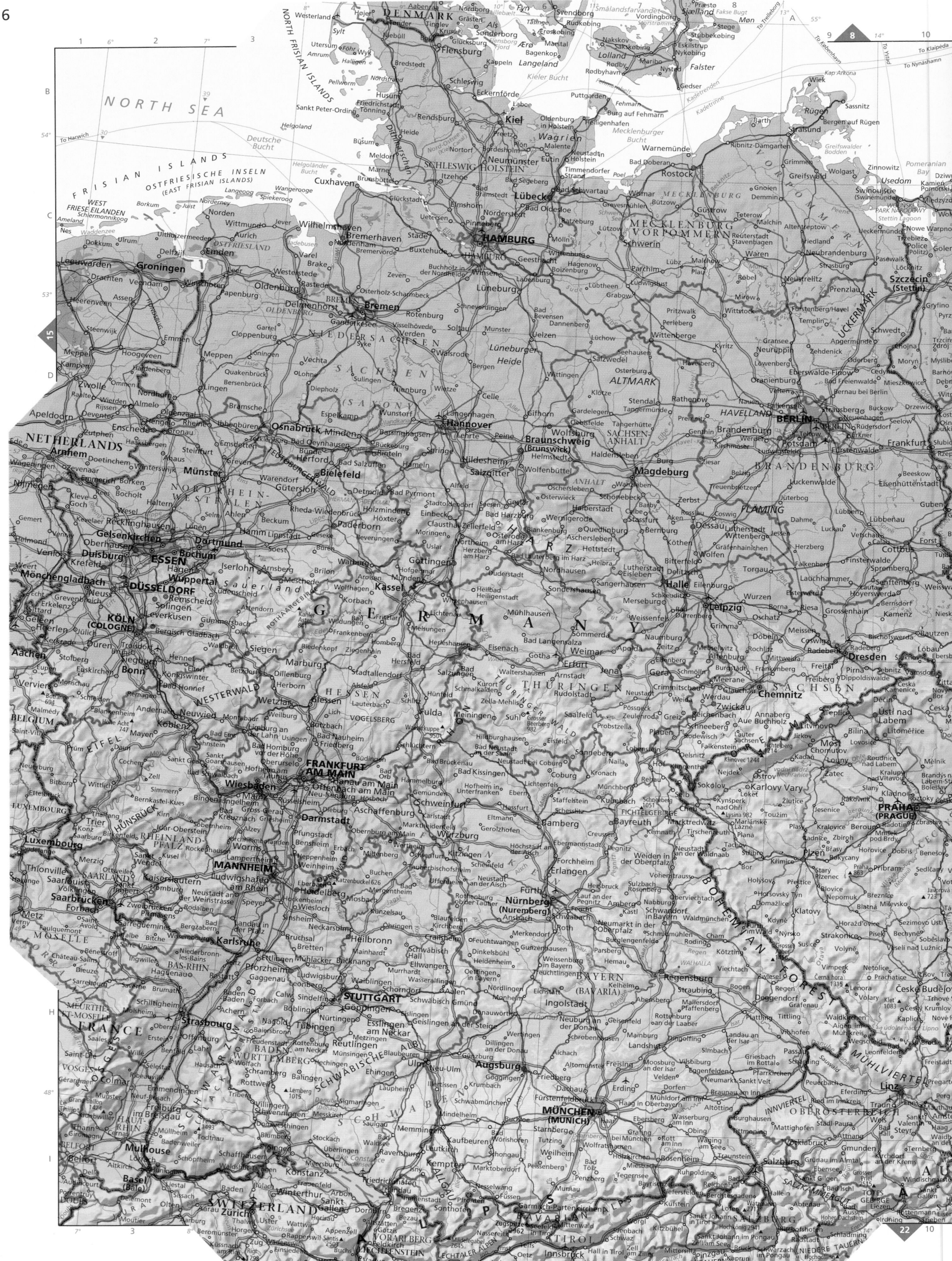

Scale 1 : 2,500,000   Lambert Conformal Conic Projection

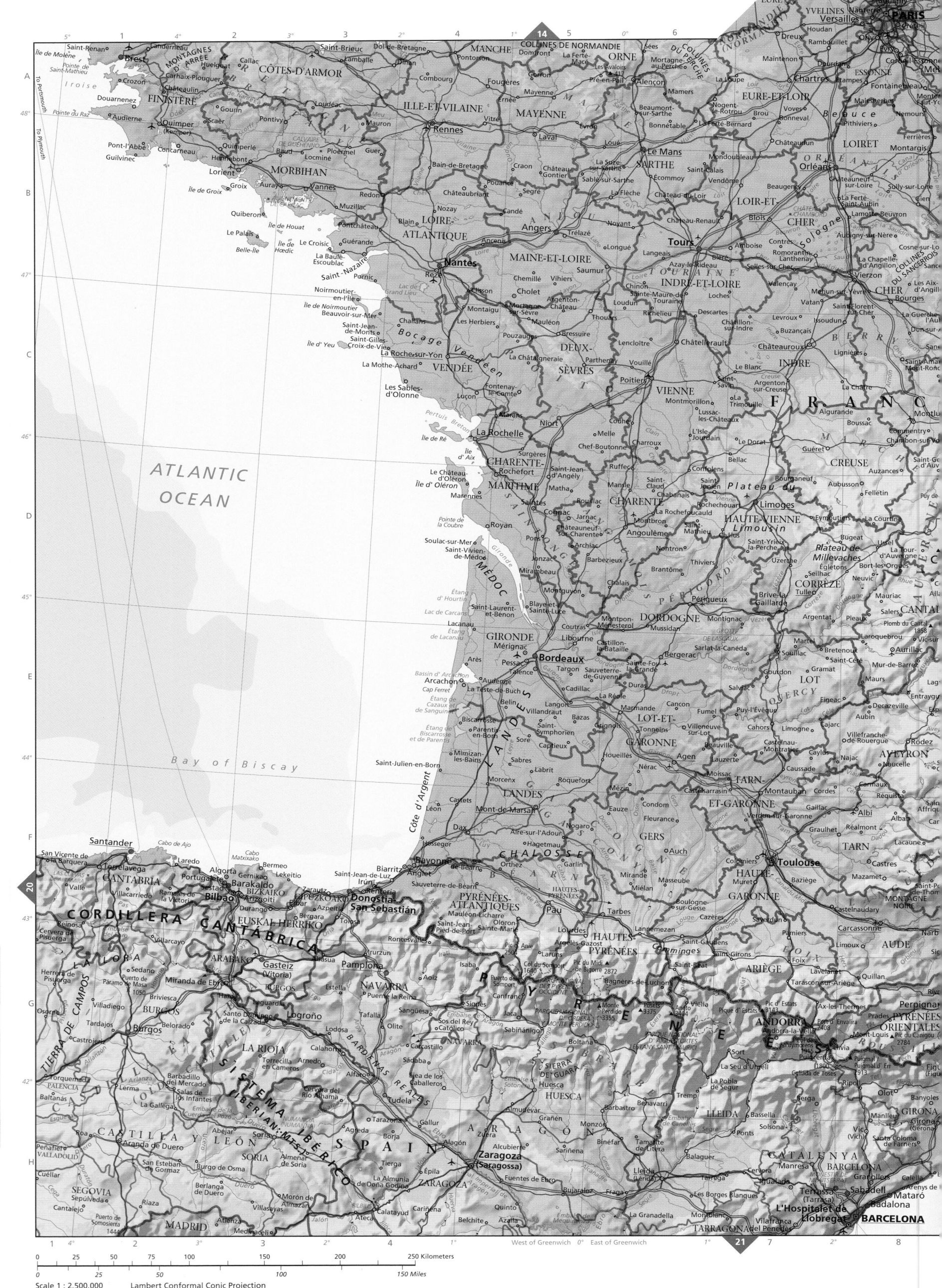

18

ATLANTIC OCEAN

Bay of Biscay

PARIS

BARCELONA

MADRID

SPAIN

FRANCE

Meters / Feet
4000 / 13120
3000 / 9840
2000 / 6560
1000 / 3280
500 / 1640
200 / 656
Sea Level
200 / 656
2000 / 6560

0   25   50   75   100   150   200   250 Kilometers
0   25   50   100   150 Miles

Scale 1 : 2 500 000   Lambert Conformal Conic Projection

West of Greenwich 0° East of Greenwich

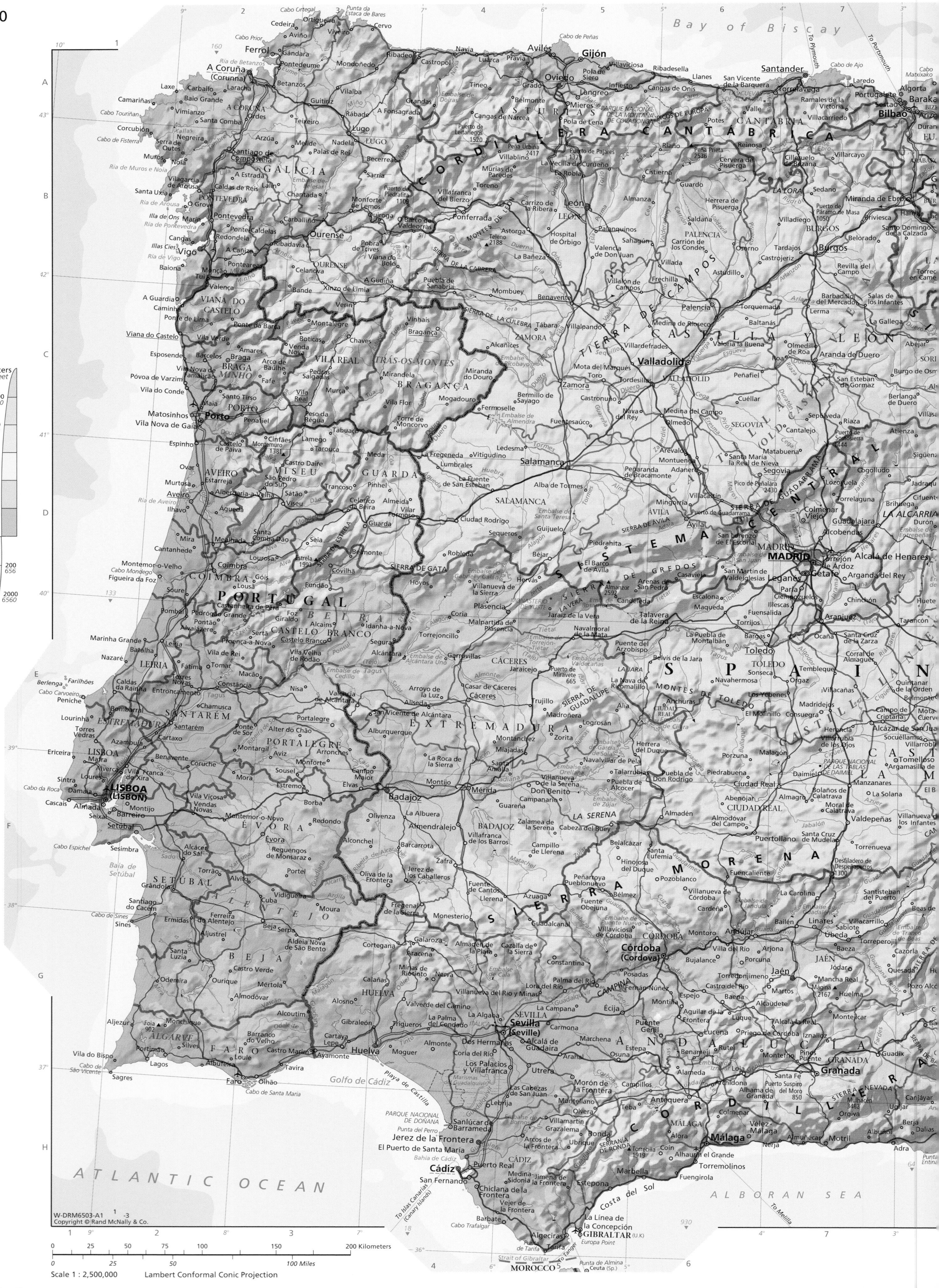

Bay of Biscay
ATLANTIC OCEAN
Golfo de Cádiz
ALBORAN SEA
PORTUGAL
SPAIN
MOROCCO
GIBRALTAR (U.K.)
CORDILLERA CANTABRICA
SISTEMA CENTRAL
SIERRA MORENA
CORDILLERA
MONTES DE TOLEDO
SIERRA DE GUADALUPE
SIERRA DE GREDOS
SIERRA DE GATA
TIERRA DE CAMPOS
CASTILLA Y LEÓN
ANDALUCIA
EXTREMADURA
GALICIA
ASTURIAS
CANTABRIA
BEIRA
TRÁS-OS-MONTES
MINHO
ESTREMADURA
ALENTEJO
ALGARVE
LA SERENA
LA ALCARRIA
Costa del Sol
Playa de Castilla
LISBOA (LISBON)
MADRID
Porto
A Coruña (Coruña)
Santiago de Compostela
Vigo
Ourense
Lugo
Ferrol
Oviedo
Gijón
Avilés
Santander
Bilbao
León
Burgos
Palencia
Valladolid
Salamanca
Zamora
Segovia
Ávila
Toledo
Cáceres
Badajoz
Mérida
Ciudad Real
Córdoba (Cordova)
Sevilla (Seville)
Huelva
Cádiz
Jerez de la Frontera
Málaga
Granada
Jaén
Coimbra
Aveiro
Braga
Viseu
Guarda
Bragança
Leiria
Santarém
Setúbal
Évora
Beja
Faro
Portalegre
Castelo Branco
Algeciras
Tarifa
Strait of Gibraltar
Cabo Trafalgar
Cabo de São Vicente
Cabo da Roca
Cabo Espichel
Cabo Finisterre
Cabo Ortegal
Meters
Feet
3000 9840
2000 6560
1000 3280
500 1640
200 656
Sea Level
200 656
2000 6560
W-DRM6503-A1
Copyright © Rand McNally & Co.
0 25 50 75 100 150 200 Kilometers
0 25 50 100 Miles
Scale 1 : 2,500,000
Lambert Conformal Conic Projection

FRANCE

PYRENEES

CATALUNYA

ARAGÓN

ZARAGOZA

BARCELONA
L'Hospitalet de Llobregat

VALÈNCIA

MEDITERRANEAN SEA

ILLES BALEARS (BALEARIC ISLANDS)

BALEARS

MALLORCA (Majorca)
Palma de Mallorca

MENORCA (Minorca)
Ciutadella de Menorca
Maó
Alaior

EIVISSA (IBIZA)
FORMENTERA

EL DJAZAÏR (ALGIERS)

ATLAS MOUNTAINS

KABYLIE

ALGERIA

NAVARRA

Donostia San Sebastián

Pamplona

Zaragoza (Saragossa)

Tudela

Huesca

Teruel

VALÈNCIA

Castelló de la Plana

Alacant (Alicante)

Murcia

Cartagena

Lorca

Tarragona

Reus

Tortosa

Girona

Figueres

Perpignan

Bayonne

Pau

Tarbes

Lourdes

Foix

Carcassonne

Narbonne

Béziers

ANDORRA
Andorra-la-Vella

La Seu d'Urgell

Berga

Manresa

Terrassa
Sabadell
Badalona
Mataró
Granollers

Vic

Olot

Ripoll

Banyoles

Vilafranca del Penedès

Igualada

Lleida

Balaguer

Cervera

Fraga

Monzón

Barbastro

Jaca

Sangüesa

Estella

Logroño

Calahorra

Tarazona

Soria

Calatayud

Daroca

Molina de Aragón

Cuenca

Albacete

Almansa

Yecla

Jumilla

Elx (Elche)

Orihuela

Benidorm

Dénia

Gandía

Cullera

Sagunt

Requena

Utiel

Alcoi

Xàtiva

Golfe du Lion

Golf de Roses

Costa Brava

Cap de Creus

Golf de Sant Jordi

Delta de l'Ebre

Cap de la Nau

Golf de València

Badia de Palma

Mar Menor

Cabo de Palos

Golfo de Mazarrón

Meters
Feet

4000
13120

3000
9840

2000
6560

1000
3280

500
1640

200
656

Sea Level

200
656

2000
6560

0   25   50   75   100   150 Kilometers

0   25   50   100 Miles

Scale 1 : 2,500,000   Lambert Conformal Conic Projection

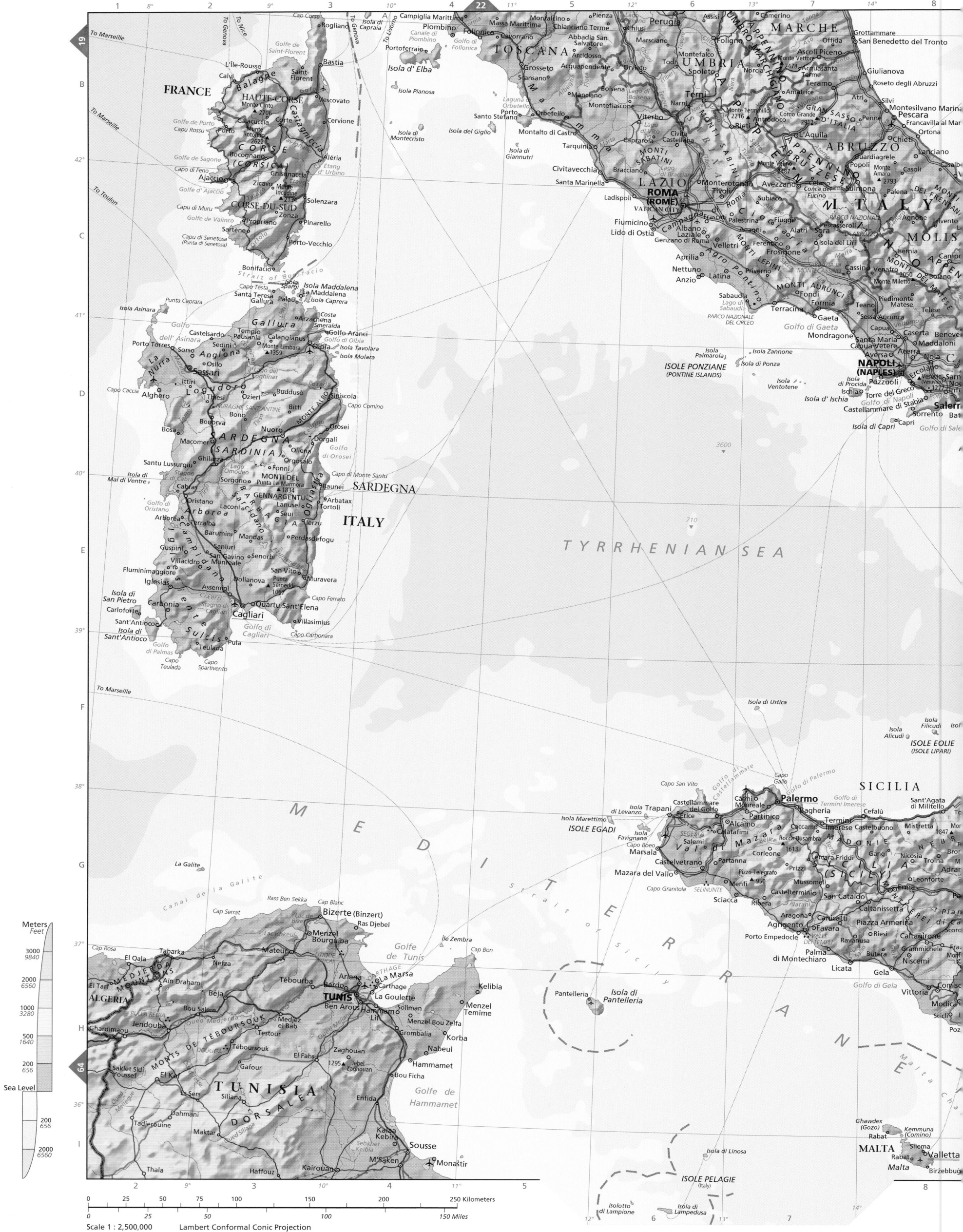

Scale 1 : 2,500,000   Lambert Conformal Conic Projection

ISOLE TREMITI
Isola Pianosa
Isola San Domino

A D R I A T I C   S E A

CROATIA
Otok Vis Vis
Svetac
Otok Biševo
Otok Šćedro Otok Hvar
Vela Luka Korčula
Otok Korčula
Otok Sušac
Otok Lastovo
Lastovski Kanal
MLJET NACIONALNI PARK
Mljetski Kanal
Otok Mljet
Poluotok Peljesac
Ston
Otok Šipan
Kardeljevo
Trpanj
Metković
BOSNIA AND HERZEGOVINA
Stolac
Ljubinje
Bileća
Trebinje
Dubrovnik
Cavtat
Herceg-Novi
Kotor
Cetinje

MONTENEGRO
Nikšić
Šavnik
DORMITOR NACIONALNI PARK
Bijelo Polje
Kolašin
Andrijevica
Ivangrad
Rožaj
VISOKA GORA
Plav
Podgorica
Virpazar
Bar
Ulcinj

SERBIA
Kosovska Mitrovica
Podujevo
Medveđa
Grdelica
Vladičin Han
Surdulica
Vranje
Trgovište
KOSOVO
Peć
METOHIJA
Đakovica
Prizren
Uroševac
Gnjilane
Preševo
Kriva Palanka
MANASTIR VISOKI DEČANI
MANASTIR GRAČANICA
Pristina
Kačanik
Kumanovo
Kratovo

ALBANIA
Shkodër
Lezhë
Rrëshen
Puke
Kukës
Burrel
Krujë
Debar
Zerqan
Gostivar
SAR PLANINA
Titov Veles
Tetovo
Skopje
Sveti Nikole
Štip
MACEDONIA
DYTIKI MAKEDONIA
KENTRIKI MAKEDONIA

Gjiri i Drinit
Kepi i Rodonit
Bishti i Pallës
Durrës
Tiranë
Kavajë
Librazhd
Struga
Ohrid
Resen
Bitola
GALIČICA NACIONALNI PARK
PELISTER NACIONALNI PARK
Flórina
Náousa
Véroia
Edessa
Ptolemaís
Kastoría
Grevena
Kozáni
Siátista
Sérvia
Deskáti

Rrogozhinë
Pegin
Cerrik
Elbasan
Prenjas
Pogradec
Korçë
Maliq
Lushnje
Kuçovë
Gramsh
Fier
Berat
Balish
Selenicë
Vlorë
Corovodë
Përmet
Tepelenë
Ersekë
Konitsa
Sazan
Kepi i Gjuhëzës
Himare
Gjirokaster
Delvinë
Sarande
Othonoí
Pogoniani
Kalpáki
Ioánnina
ÍPEIROS
Kérkyra (Corfu)
Liapádes
Kérkyra (Corfu)
Igoumenítsa
Paramythiá
Párga
Lefkímmi
Préveza
PINDOS
Métsovo
Kalampáka
Trikala
THESSALIA
DYTIKI ELLADA

G R E E C E
Arta
Amfilochía
Agrínio
Lefkáda
Lefkáda
Astakós
Mesolóngi
Aitolikó
Náfpaktos
Pátra
Káto Achaía
Kyllíni
Lecháiná
Gastoúni
Amaliáda
PELOPÓNNISOS (Peloponnesus)
Zákynthos
Pýrgos
Olympía
Kyparissía

Strait of Otranto

I O N I A N   S E A

IÓNIOI NÍSOI
Fiskárdo
Ithaki
Ithaki
Lixoúri
Kefalloniá
Argostóli
Zákynthos
Keri
Strofádes
Kyparissiakós Kólpos
Filiatrá
Gargaliánoi
Chora
Kyparissía
PELOPÓNNISOS
Pýlos
Schíza

PROMONTORIO DEL GARGANO
Lago di Lesina
Lago di Varano
Rodi Garganico
Vieste
Testa del Gargano
Peschici
Monte Calvo
1055
San Giovanni Rotondo
Monte Sant'Angelo
Manfredonia
Golfo di Manfredonia

Foggia
Troia
Orta Nova
Cerignola
Ascoli Satriano
Canosa di Puglia
Andria
Corato
Bitonto
Bari
Mola di Bari
Margherita di Savoia
Barletta
Trani
Bisceglie
Molfetta
PUGLIA
Grumo Appula
Conversano
Monopoli
Fasano
Ostuni
Brindisi
Carovigno
Francavilla Fontana
Mesagne
Lecce

BASILICATA
Melfi
Lavello
Venosa
Rionero in Vulture
Minervino Murge
Spinazzola
Gravina in Puglia
Altamura
Gioia del Colle
Castellana Grotte
Alberobello
Martina Franca
Ceglie Messápico
Manduria
Squinzano
Copertino
Galatina
Nardò
Gallipoli
Maglie
Óstuni
Taviano
Casarano
Santa Cesarea Terme
Tricase
Gagliano del Capo
Capo Santa Maria di Leuca

Acerenza
Tricarico
Irsina
Matera
Grottaglie
Taranto
Massafra
Ginosa
Ferrandina
Bernalda
Pisticci
METAPONTO
Isole Cheradi
Golfo di Taranto

Potenza
Avigliano
Muro Lucano
Stigliano
Sant'Arcangelo
Montalbano Ionico
Rotondella

APPENNINO LUCANO
Monte Volturino
1836
Monte Sirino
2005
Lagonegro
Lauria
Maratea

CALABRIA
CATENA COSTIERA
SILA GRANDE
Castrovillari
Cozzo Pellegrino
1987
Spezzano Albanese
Corigliano Calabro
Rossano
Cariati
Trebisacce
Cassano allo Ionio
Cirò Marina
Punta Alice
Acri
San Giovanni in Fiore
Monte Botte Donato
1928
Rende
Cosenza
Amantea
Paola
Monte Gariglione
1765
Strongoli
Petilia Policastro
Crotone
Capo Colonne
Cutro
Isola di Capo Rizzuto
Capo Rizzuto
Catanzaro
Filadelfia
Golfo di Sant'Eufemia
Pizzo
Golfo di Squillace
Squillace
Soverato
Vibo Valentia
Tropea
Nicotera
Monte Pecoraro
1423
Serra San Bruno
Gioia Tauro
Polistena
Cittanova
Palmi
Taurianova
Marina di Gioiosa Ionica
Siderno
Locri
Bovalino Marina
Messina
Villa San Giovanni
ASPROMONTE
1955
Reggio di Calabria
Melito di Porto Salvo
Capo Spartivento

Taormina
Giarre
Acireale
Catania
Augusta
Golfo di Augusta
Siracusa
Noto
Capo Passero

16° East of Greenwich
W-100632
Copyright © Rand McNally & Co.

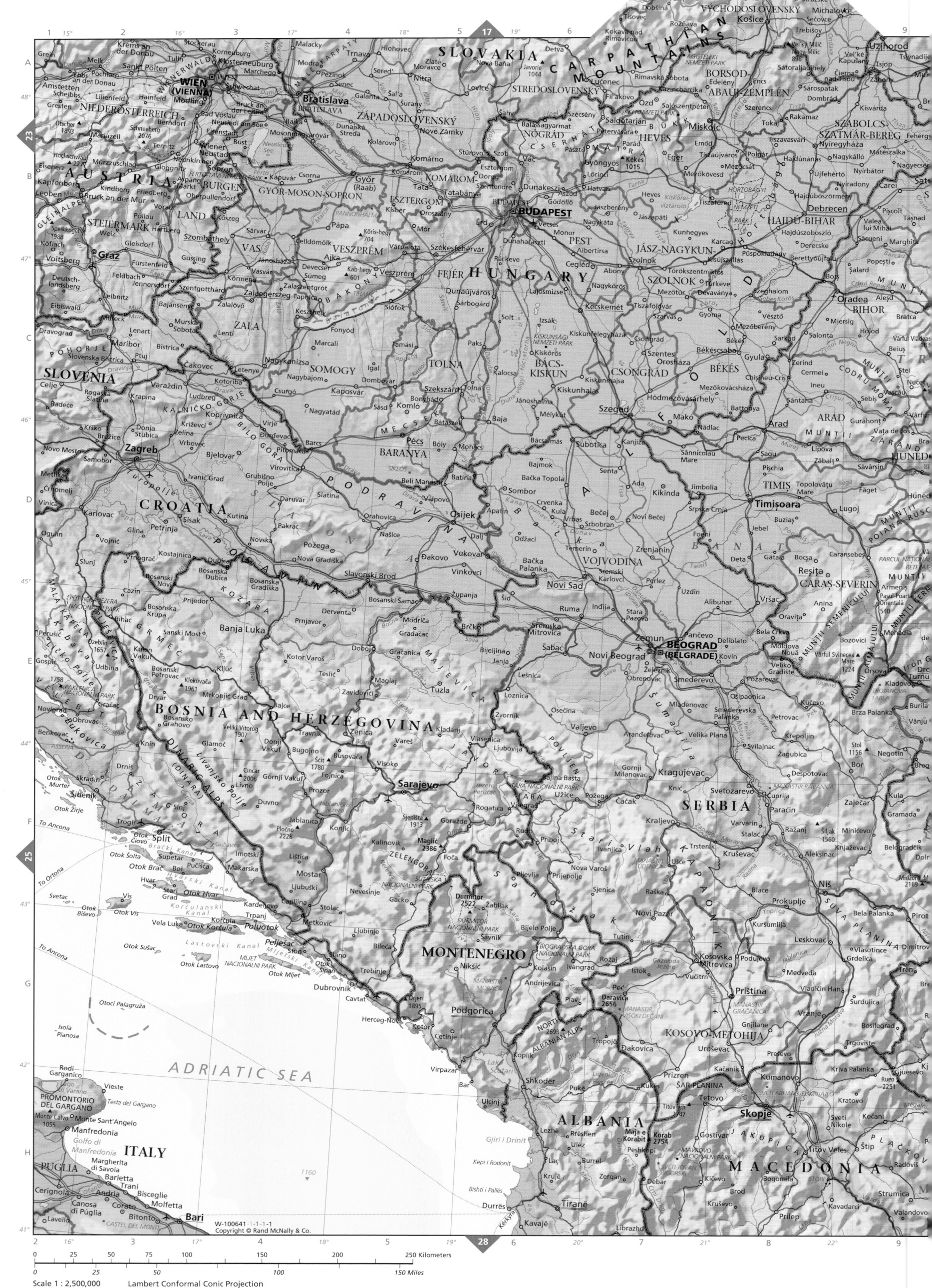

Scale 1 : 2,500,000   Lambert Conformal Conic Projection

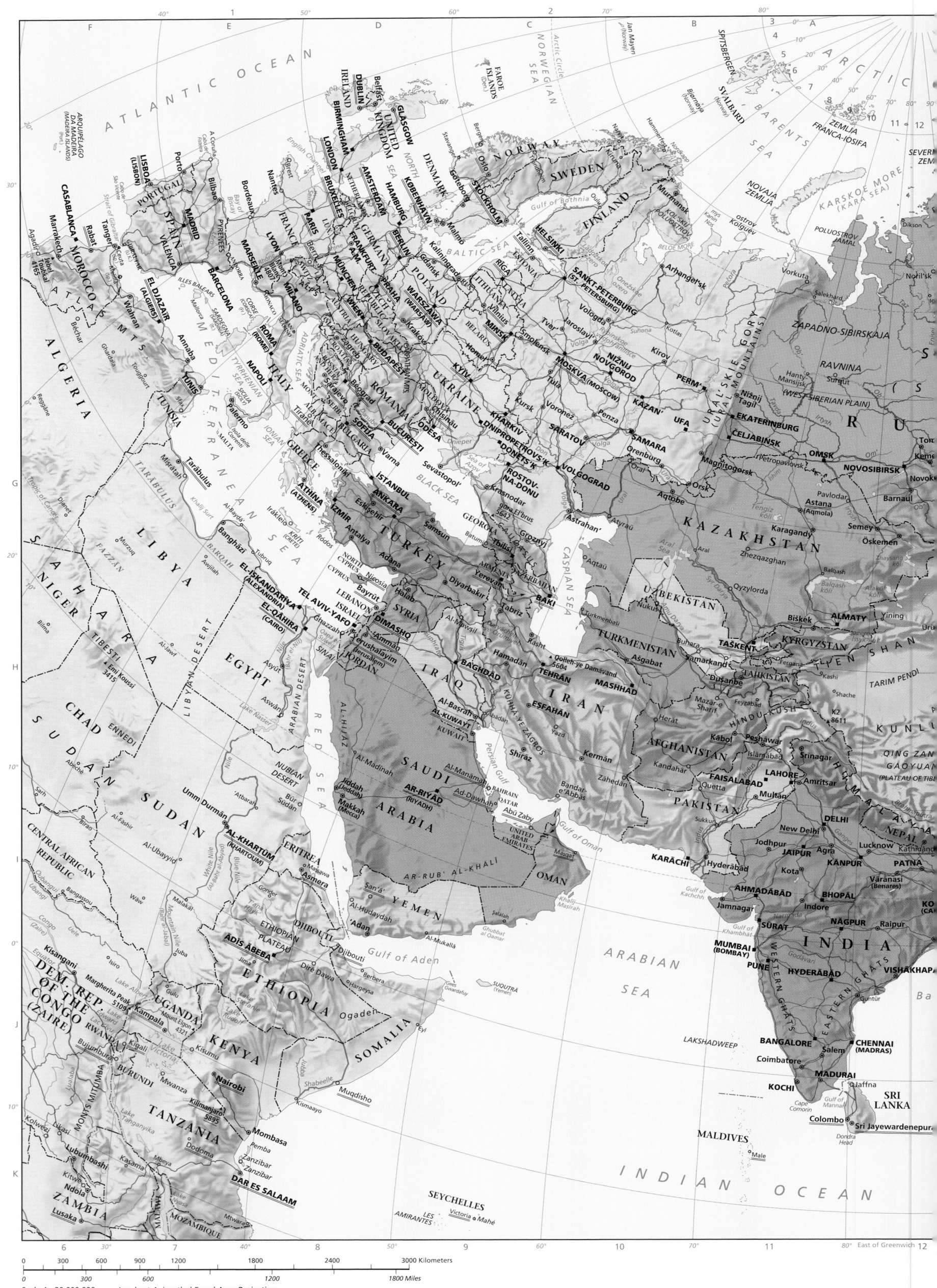

Scale 1 : 30,000,000   Lambert Azimuthal Equal Area Projection

A B C D E F

ostrov Vrangelja

St. Lawrence Island (U.S.)

Bering Strait

BERING SEA

ALEUTIAN ISLANDS (U.S.)

Attu Island

Cape Wrangell

KOMANDORSKIE OSTROVA

HAWAIIAN ISLANDS (U.S.)

MIDWAY ISLANDS (U.S.)

MORE LAPTEVYH (LAPTEV SEA)

NOVOSIBIRSKIE OSTROVA

VOSTOČNO-SIBIRSKOE MORE

HREBET ČERSKOGO

SREDINNYJ HREBET

Petropavlovsk-Kamčatskij

SEA OF OKHOTSK

POLUOSTROV KAMČATKA

TAJMYR

SEVERNOSIBIRSKOE

CENTRAL SIBERIAN PLATEAU

STANOVOJ HREBET

VERHOJANSKIJ HREBET

PLOSKOGOR'E

Hanga

Jakutsk

OSTROV SAHALIN

KURIL'SKIE OSTROVA (KURIL ISLANDS)

Tatarskij proliv

SIHOTE-ALIN'

PACIFIC OCEAN

Tropic of Cancer

Irkutsk

Angarsk

Bratsk

Ulan-Ude

Čita

Komsomol'sk-na-Amure

Blagoveščensk

Habarovsk

Vladivostok

HOKKAIDO

Sapporo

Hakodate

WAKE ISLAND (U.S.)

Aomori

Sendai

HARBIN

CHANGCHUN

SHENYANG FUSHUN

Jilin

NORTH KOREA

Ch'ŏngjin

SEA OF JAPAN

Niigata

HONSHŪ

TŌKYŌ

YOKOHAMA

Kanazawa NAGOYA JAPAN

MONGOLIA

Ulaanbaatar

GOBI DESERT

Hohhot

Zhangjiakou

BEIJING

P'yŏngyang

SŎUL (SEOUL)

SOUTH KOREA

KYŌTO OSAKA

HIROSHIMA

FUKUOKA

KYŪSHŪ

SHIKOKU

IZU-SHOTO (Japan)

OGASAWARA-GUNTO (Japan)

Minami-Tori-Shima (Japan)

HANGAYN NURUU

Baotou

TAIYUAN

TIANJIN

DALIAN

Bo Hai

Taegu PUSAN

Mokp'o

Cheju-do

KAZAN-RETTO (Japan)

NORTHERN MARIANA ISLANDS (U.S.)

MARSHALL ISLANDS

Enewetak

Ujelang

Shijiazhuang

JINAN

Qingdao

YELLOW SEA

Kagoshima

NANSEI-SHOTO (RYUKYU ISLANDS)

Amami-O-shima

Okinawa-jima

Naha

Farallon de Pajaros

Agrihan

Alamagan Pagan

Guguan

Anatahan MARIANA ISLANDS

Saipan

Tinian

Rota

Anxi

Yinchuan

Xining

Lanzhou

Qinghai Hu

Baoji

XI'AN

Zhengzhou

Xuzhou

SHANGHAI

Ningbo

EAST CHINA SEA

Lhasa

CHINA

CHENGDU

CHONGQING

WUHAN

Nanchang

NANJING

Hangzhou

Wenzhou

CHANGSHA

Hengyang

Zigong

Guiyang

Liuzhou

GUANGZHOU

Fuzhou

Xiamen

T'AIPEI

TAIWAN

T'ainan

KAOHSIUNG

GUAM (U.S.)

Hagåtña

MICRONESIA

HALL ISLANDS

Oroluk

MORTLOCK ISLANDS

Pohnpei Palikir

SENYAVIN ISLANDS

CHUUK

Kunming

Nanning

XIANGGANG (HONG KONG)

Zhanjiang

Luzon Strait

Taiwan Strait

PHILIPPINE SEA

YAP

Ulul

Gaferut

Lamotrek

Pulap

Sorol

Woleai

Eauripik

CAROLINE ISLANDS

FEDERATED STATES OF MICRONESIA

Kapingamarangi

Equator

BANGLADESH

DHAKA (DACCA)

CHITTAGONG

MYANMAR

Mandalay

(BURMA)

Sittwe

HA NOI (HANOI)

Haikou

HAINAN DAO

Gulf of Tonkin

LAOS

Hai Phong

Luangphrabang

VIETNAM

XISHA QUNDAO (PARACEL ISLANDS)

Chiang Mai

Udon Thani

Viangchan

Da Nang

LUZON

Baguio

Quezon City

MANILA

Mindoro

Samar

Masbate

Leyte

Cebu

Iloilo

Panay

PHILIPPINES

MINDANAO

Koror

PALAU ISLANDS

Ngulu

Ngulu

Sonsorol

SONSOROL ISLANDS

PALAU

ADMIRALTY ISLANDS

Manus Island

BISMARCK ARCHIPELAGO

NEW IRELAND

Kavieng

Rabaul

BISMARCK SEA

YANGON (RANGOON)

Gulf of Martaban

KRUNG THEP (BANGKOK)

THAILAND

CAMBODIA

Phnum Pénh

THANH PHO HO CHI MINH (HO CHI MINH CITY) (SAIGON)

Kâmpóng Saôm

SOUTH CHINA SEA

SPRATLY ISLANDS

Palawan

Balabac Island

SULU SEA

Zamboanga

Moro Gulf

Mount Apo 2954

Davao

Tinaca Point

Jolo Island

KEPULAUAN TALAUD

Morotai

HALMAHERA

Pulau Waigeo

Biak

Pulau Yapen

Jayapura

NEW GUINEA

PAPUA NEW GUINEA

Wewak

Madang

Mount Wilhelm 4509

Lae

Port Moresby

Gulf of Papua

NEW BRITAIN

SOLOMON SEA

COCO ISLANDS (India)

Dawei

Bangkok

Mui Ca Mau

MALAY PENINSULA

Phuket

Bandar Seri Begawan

BRUNEI

Gunong Kinabalu 4101

MALAYSIA

Kuching

BORNEO (KALIMANTAN)

Pontianak

Balikpapan

CELEBES SEA

Manado

KEPULAUAN SANGIHE

KEPULAUAN OBI

LAUT MALUKU

SERAM (CERAM)

LAUT SERAM

KEPULAUAN KAI

KEPULAUAN ARU

Pulau Yos Sudarso

Merauke

CAPE YORK PENINSULA

NICOBAR ISLANDS (India)

ANDAMAN ISLANDS (India)

ANDAMAN SEA

George Town (Penang)

MALAYSIA

KUALA LUMPUR

MEDAN

Banda Aceh

Pulau Nias

KEPULAUAN MENTAWAI

SUMATERA (SUMATRA)

Padang

Pulau Siberut

SINGAPORE

KEPULAUAN NATUNA BESAR

Strait of Malacca

Selat Karimata

SULAWESI (CELEBES)

Teluk Tomini

Selat Makasar

Kapuas

Banjarmasin

Pulau Laut

Ujungpandang

LAUT BANDA

Buru

Pulau Buton

KEPULAUAN SULA

KEPULAUAN TANIMBAR

ARAFURA SEA

Cape Wessel

Cape Arnhem

AUSTRALIA

Gulf of Carpentaria

Cape York

Melville Island

TIMOR SEA

CAPE YORK

Great Barrier Reef

CORAL SEA

Palembang

Bandar Lampung

Pulau Bangka

Belitung

INDONESIA

JAKARTA

BANDUNG

JAWA (JAVA)

SURABAYA

Madura

Bali

Lombok

Sumbawa

Sumba

FLORES

LAUT FLORES

LAUT SAWU

Kupang

EAST TIMOR

TIMOR

Pulau Wetar

M-100672-1-1-1-1

Copyright © Rand McNally & Co.

B

60°

C

55°

17

D

50°

E

45°

27

F

40°

G

Meters
Feet

6000
19680

4000
13120

3000
9840

2000
6560

1000
3280

500
1640

200
656

Sea Level

200
656

2000
6560

FINLAND

HELSINKI

ESTONIA

Tallinn

RIGA

LATVIA

LITHUANIA

MINSK

BELARUS

Chernihiv

KYÏV
(KIEV)

UKRAINE

Kirovohrad

Kryvyi
Rih

DNIPROPETROVS'K

Zaporizhzhia
DONETS'K

Mariupol'

Taganrog

ROSTOV-
NA-DONU

Krasnodar

Soči

BLACK SEA

Sankt-Peterburg
(ST. PETERSBURG)

Vicebsk

Mahilëŭ

Smolensk

Brjansk

Homel'

Kursk

Sumy

KHARKIV

Poltava

Cherkasy

Luhans'k

Kramators'k

MOSKVA
(MOSCOW)

Tula

Orel

Voronež

Belgorod

Lipeck

Tambov

Penza

SARATOV

VOLGOGRAD

Stavropol'

KALMYKIJA

CASPIAN DEPRESSION

Astrahan'

Rybinsk

Jaroslavl'

Ivanovo

Vladimir

Rjazan'

Novomoskovsk

NIŽNIJ
NOVGOROD
(GORKI)

Čeboksary

KAZAN'

MORDOVIJA

Saransk

Uljanovsk

ČUVAŠIJA

MARIJ EL

TATARIJA

Toljatti

SAMARA

Novokujbyševsk

Sterlitamak

UDMURTIJA

Iževsk

PERM'

EKATERINBURG

Nižnij
Tagil

UFA

BAŠKIRIJA

Magnitogorsk

ČELJABINSK

Orenburg

Orsk

Kirov

KOMI

ARHANGEL'SK

BELOE MORE
(WHITE SEA)

KARELIJA

KOL'SKIJ
POLUOSTROV
(KOLA PENINSULA)

Severodvinsk

Vologda

Čerepovec

Tver'

SEVERNYE UVALY

Syktyvkar

R U S S

Sea of Azov

CAUCASUS

GEORGIA

Tbilisi

ARMENIA

Yerevan

AZERBAIJAN

BAKI
(BAKU)

Grozny

Vladikavkaz

Mahačkala

DAGESTAN

TURKEY

Diyarbakir

SYRIA

IRAQ

IRAN

Tabriz

CASPIAN SEA

TURKMENISTAN

UST-URT
PLATEAU

Aral
Sea

UZBEKISTAN

Nukus

KAZAK

① ADYGEJA
② KARAČAEVO-ČERKESIJA
③ KABARDINO-BALKARIJA
④ SEVERNAJA OSETIJA
⑤ ČEČNJA
⑥ INGUŠETIJA

NL-DRM4711-A1-2-3-4-5
Copyright © Rand McNally & Co.

57

0   100   200   300   400   500   600 Kilometers
0   100   200   300   400 Miles

Scale 1 : 10,000,000   Lambert Conformal Conic Projection

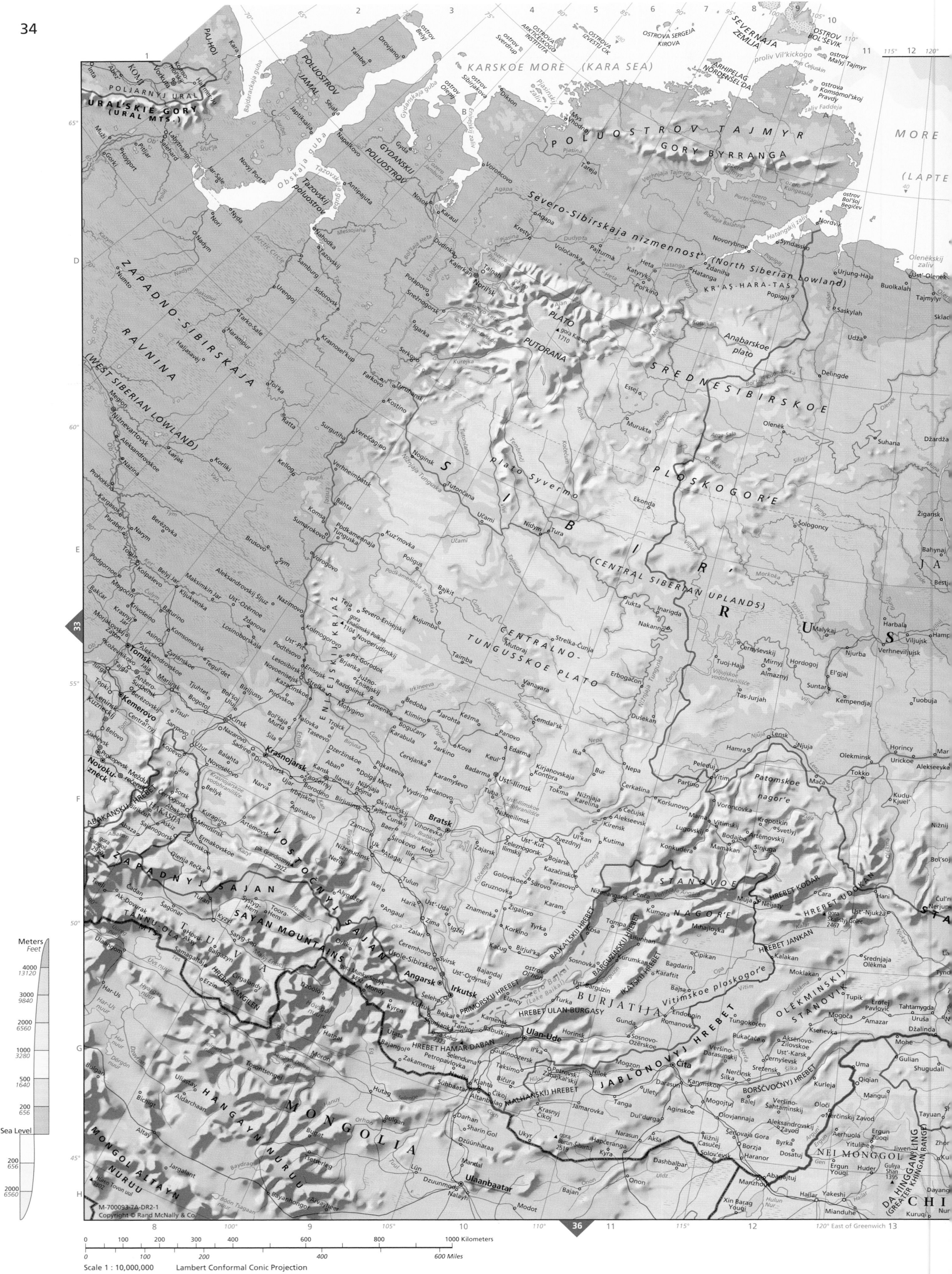

MORE

(LAPTE

KARSKOE MORE (KARA SEA)

POLUOSTROV TAJMYR
GORY BYRRANGA

Severo-Sibirskaja nizmennost' (North Siberian Lowland)

KOMJ-NAO
PALHOJ
POLJARNYJ URAL
URAL'SKIE GORY
(URAL MTS.)

POLUOSTROV JAMAL
GYDANSKIJ POLUOSTROV

ZAPADNO-SIBIRSKAJA RAVNINA
(WEST SIBERIAN LOWLAND)

PLATO PUTORANA
gora Kamen
1710

SREDNESIBIRSKOE

Anabarskoe plato

S I B I R '

plato Syverma

PLOSKOGOR'E

(CENTRAL SIBERIAN UPLANDS)

CENTRALNO-TUNGUSSKOE PLATO

R U S

JA

Tomsk
Kemerovo
Novokuzneck

Krasnojarsk

Bratsk

Irkutsk
Angarsk

Patomskoe nagor'e

STANOVOE NAGOR'E
HREBET KODAR
HREBET UDOKAN
STA

HREBET JANKAN

OLEKMINSKIJ STANOVIK

ZAPADNYJ SAJAN
VOSTOČNYJ SAJAN
SAYAN MOUNTAINS
TANNUOLA MTS.
T U V A

Ulan-Ude

BURJATIJA
Vitimskoe ploskogor'e

Čita

JABLONOVYJ HREBET

BORŠČOVOČNYJ HREBET

HANGAYN NURUU

MONGOL ALTAYN NURUU

M O N G O L I A

Ulaanbaatar

NEI MONGGOL

DA HINGGAN LING (GREATER KHINGAN RANGE)

CHI

Meters / Feet
4000 / 13120
3000 / 9840
2000 / 6560
1000 / 3280
500 / 1640
200 / 656
Sea Level
200 / 656
2000 / 6560

0 100 200 300 400 500 600 800 1000 Kilometers
0 100 200 300 400 600 Miles
Scale 1 : 10,000,000   Lambert Conformal Conic Projection

M-700093-7A-DR2-1
Copyright © Rand McNally & Co.

130° 15 135° 16 140° 17 145° 18 150° 19 155° 20 160° 21 165° 22 170° 23 175° 24
25 175° 26 70° 27 U.S.

NOVOSIBIRSKIE

OSTROVA

PTEVYH OSTROVA ANŽU

ostrov Genriety

OSTROVA DE-LONGA

ostrov Bennetta

ostrov Žannetty

ostrov Žohova

ostrov Vil'kickogo

OSTROV VRANGELJA (WRANGEL ISLAND)

proliv Longa

CHUKCHI SEA

Bering Strait

Cape Prince of Wales Tellk.

ALASKA

OSTROV KOTEL'NYJ

ostrov Bel'kovskij

proliv Sannikova

LJAHOVSKIJE OSTROV

LJAHOVSKIJE OSTROVA

OSTROV BOL'ŠOJ LJAHOVSKIJ

OSTROV FADDEEVSKIJ

OSTROV NOVAJA SIBIR'

ostrov Stolbovoj

proliv Dmitrija Lapteva

VOSTOČNO-SIBIRSKOE MORE (EAST SIBERIAN SEA)

MEDVEŽJI OSTROVA

ostrov Aën

Peljarnyj

Krasnoarmejsk

Enurmino

Vankarem

ČUKOTSKIJ POLUOSTROV (CHUKOTSK PEN.)

Uelkal

Anadyrskij zaliv (Gulf of Anadyr)

Campbell

Bykovskij

mys Buor-Haja

Janskij zaliv

Nižnejansk

Jano-Indigirskaja nizmennosť

Čokurdah

Logaškino

Pohodsk

Kolymskaja Anjuj

Čerskij

Ambarčik

Ust'-Čaun

ANADYRSKOE PLOSKOGOR'E

Egvekinot

HREBET PEKUL'NEJ

Uel'kal

Najba Hajyr

Ust'-Kujda

Tenkeli

Kolymskaja nizmennosť (Kolyma Plain)

Srednekolymsk

ANJUJSKIJ HREBET

Ostromoso Bilibino

Ust'-Belaja

Anadyr

Markovo

KORJAKSKOE NAGOR'E

Hatyrka

Deputatskij

Syagannah

Družina

Zyrjanka

Svatal

Nelemnje

JUKAGIRSKOE PLOSKOGOR'E

Omolon

Ščerbakovo

Omolon

Penžinskoe

Vaegi

HREBET KULAR

Namy Vlasovo

Tumat

VERHOJANSK MOUNTAINS

Batagaj Alyta

Verhojansk

Batagaj

Bala

Tomtor

HREBET (CHERSKIY MOUNTAINS

MOMSKIJ HREBET

gora Pobeda 3147

Balygyčan

OLOJSKIJ HREBET

Sčautnoe

Kamenskoe

Manily

PENŽINSKIJ HREBET

Paren

KORJAKSKOE NAGORE

Tylketyl

Hajlino

Slautnoe

Vetvej

Suordah

Junkur

Barylas

Ust'-Nera

Artyk

Omsukčan

Galimyj

Merenga

Evensk

Paren

Gižiga

Gižiginskaja guba

POLUOSTROV TAJGONOS

Oljutorskij zaliv

mys Oljutorskij

Karaginskij

ostrov Karaginskij

BERING SEA

Tompo

Borogoncy

HREBET SUNTAR-HAJATA

Ojmjakon

Mjaundža

Susuman

Taskan

Sejmčan

Orotukan

Talaja

gora Aborigen 2586

Tumany

zaliv Šelihova

Penžina

Ust'-Penžino

mys Govena

KAMČATSKIJ POLUOSTROV

KOMANDORSKIE OSTROVA

Karaga

Ossora

zaliv Ozernoj

zaliv Kronockij

ostrov Beringa

Nikol'sk

ostrov Beringa

Jakutsk

Bestjah

Majja

Pokrovsk

Ytyk-Kjuël'

Kangalassy

Dzebariki-Haja

Ohotskij Perevoz

HREBET SETTE-DABAN

gora Mus-Haja 2959

Atka

Omčak

Ust'-Omčug

Palatka

Stekol'nyj

Ola

SREDINNYJ HREBET

Palana

Vojampolka

Tigil'

Uka

zaliv Ozernoj

Ključi

vulkan Šiveluč 3283

Kamčatka

KAMČATSKIJ POLUOSTROV

Kamčatskij zaliv

Ulu

Hajsardah

Imeni Kirova

Amga

Bolugur

Ust'-Maja

El'dikan

Allah-Jun'

Jugorenok

Jun

Juodoma

Ynykčanskij

Taujsk

Armañ

Magadan

Siglan

mys Alevina

Tau-jskaja guba

Jamsk

mys Tolstoj

Morosečnoe

Sobolevo

Esso

Kozyrevsk

Atlasovo

VOSTOČNYJ HREBET

vulkan Ključevskaja Sopka 4750

vulkan Kronockaja Sopka 3456

Kronockij zaliv

'erhnjaja Amga

Ust'-Mil'

DANSKOE AGOR'E (AN PLATEAU)

Aim

Ust'-Judoma

HREBET DŽUGDŽUR

gora Topko 1906

Kemkara

Gonam

Nel'kan

Tomptokan

Aldoma

Ajan

Inja

Ohotsk

mys Duga-Zapadnaja

Ulja

ostrov Iony

SEA OF OKHOTSK

POLUOSTROV KAMČATKA

Kirovskij

Kihčik

Elizovo

Paratunka

Petropavlovsk-Kamčatskij

Malka

Apača

Koryakskaja Sopka

J HREBET

Zejskoe vodohranilišče

ŠANTARSKIE OSTROVA

Udskaja guba

Čumikan

Udskoe

Torom

Nyvrov

mys Elizavety

POLUOSTROV ŠMIDTA

Oha

Ust'-Bol'šereck

Oktjabr'skij

Bol'šereck

Pervyj Kuril'skij proliv

mys Lopatka

ostrov Atlasova

Severo-Kuril'sk

Paramušir

ostrov Šumšu

KURIL'SKIE OSTROVA (KURIL ISLANDS)

Zeja

Ovsjanka

Jasnyj

HREBET DŽAGDY

Baladek

Tugur

Sahalinskij zaliv Akademii

ozero Orel'

Mago

Nikolaevsk-na-Amure

Paromaj

Nogliki

Katangli

ostrov Onekotan

ostrov Šiaskotan

Oktjabr'skij

Norsk

Selemdžinsk

Sofijsk

HREBET JAM-ALIN'

Imeni Poliny Osipenko

Guga

Gurskoe

Bogorodskoe

Somineľnyj

Marijskoe

OSTROV SAHALIN (SAKHALIN)

Tymovskoe

Nyš

De-Kastri

ostrov Matua

ostrov Rasšua

ostrov Ketoj

Majskij

Ušman

Muhino

Ošimanovsk

Krasnojarovo

Seryševo

Svobodnyj

Belogorsk

Ivanovka

Aleksandrovsk-Sahalinskij

Sirokaja Pad'

Smirnyh

Pobedino

Kotikovo

ostrov Simušir

ostrov Urup

Ekaterinoslavka

Blagoveščensk

Zavitinsk

Rajčihinsk

Pojarkovo

HEI LONGJIANG

BUREINSKIJ HREBET

BADŽAL'SKIJ HREBET

Komsomol'sk-na-Amure

Amursk

El'ban

Pivan'

Mylki

Troickoe

Bošnjakovo

Lesogorsk

Uglegorsk

Makarov

Šahtërsk

Poronajsk

ZAPADNYJ HREBET

ostrov Broutona

Vysokogornyj

Vanino

Sovetskaja Gavan'

gora Tardoki-Jani 2077

Krasnogorsk

Iljinskij

Tomari

Vostočnyj

3300

Tyrma

Kul'dur

Obluč'e

Birakan

Birobidžan

Bira

Daotiandi

Habarovsk

Muhen

S HOTE ALIN'

Nel'ma

Adži

Čehov

Dolinsk

Južno-Sahalinsk

Bykov

Aldi

Tomari

gora Lopatina 1609

Pompejevka

Bidžan

Leninskoe

Fuyuan

Zhaoxing

Tongjiang

Antun

Vjazemskij

Nevel'sk

Anivа

zaliv Aniva

Korsakov

Novikovo

18 37 19 20

Meters | Feet
6000 / 19680
4000 / 13120
3000 / 9840
2000 / 6560
1000 / 3280
500 / 1640
200 / 656
Sea Level
200 / 656
2000 / 6560

0   100   200   300   400   600 Kilometers
0   100   200   300   400 Miles

Scale 1 : 10,000,000   Lambert Conformal Conic Projection

36

42

1   116°   2   118°   3   120°   4 **36** 122°   5   124°   6   126°   7   128°   8   130°

B

Ayulhai   Xi Ujimqin Qi   Sanshengchang   Dongwangfu   Horqin Youyi Zhongqi   Taonan   Shuanggang   Ping'an   Fuyu   Qian Gorlos   Xinglong   **HARBIN**   Acheng   Xiaoling   Lianhuapao   Husha

Xilinhot   Baiyinheshuo   Hanmiao   Jarud Qi   Ar Horqin Qi   Daodemiao   Gongyemiao   Kailu   Yuliangpu   Wulasitai   Maiqihamiao   Baixingt   Naiman   Dagongtai   Xiawa   Hure Qi   Houxinqiu   Kangping   Faku   Tieling

NEI MONGGOL

C   H   I   N   A

BEIJING (PEKING)   **TIANJIN (TIENTSIN)**   HEBEI

Bo Hai (Gulf of Chihli)

DALIAN (DAIREN)   Lüshun (Port Arthur)

Korea Bay

P'yŏngyang   Namp'o

NORTH KOREA

SHANDONG

Qingdao (Tsingtao)

YELLOW SEA

SŎUL (SEOUL)   **INCH'ŎN**

SOUTH KOREA

PUSAN (FUSAN)

Cheju   Halla-san 1950   **CHEJU-DO (QUELPART ISLAND)**

GOTŌ-RETTŌ

Nagasaki

EAST CHINA SEA

SHANGHAI

HANGZHOU   ZHEJIANG

ANHUI   **NANJING (NANKING)**   JIANGSU   **Nantong**   **Wuxi**   **Suzhou**

Meters / Feet
3000 / 9840
2000 / 6560
1000 / 3280
500 / 1640
200 / 656
Sea Level
200 / 656
2000 / 6560

0   50   100   150   200   300   400   500 Kilometers
0   50   100   200   300 Miles

Scale 1 : 5,000,000   Lambert Conformal Conic Projection

Japan, Korea, and Northeastern China

SEA OF OKHOTSK

Habomai, Shikotan, Kunashiri and
Etorofu, occupied since 1945, are
claimed by Japan pending a final peace treaty.

KURIL'SKIE OSTROVA
(KURIL ISLANDS)

RUSSIA

ostrov
Iturup
(Etorofu-
tô)

proliv Ekaterin

ostrov
Sikotan
(Shikotan-tô)

ostrov
Kunašir
(Kunashiri-tô)

Malaja
Kuril'skaja
Grjada
(Habomai-
shotô)

RUSSIA

SIHOTE ALIN'

Tamga
Lesozavodsk
Gornye Ključi
Ariadnoe
Tavaja
Ternej
Plastun
Pristan'
Velikaja Kema

Novokačalinsk
Kirovskij
Gornyj
gora Glucomanka
1598

Samarka
Krasnorečenskij
Dal'negorsk
Kamenka
Rudnaja Pristan'

Spassk-Dal'nij
Č12ernigovka
Arsenev
Kavalerovo

Monakino
Lazo
Olga
Gornovodnoe

Anučino
Sergeevka
Partizansk
Valentin

Vladivostok
Uglekamensk
Preobraženie

Nahodka
Zapovednyj

Rebun-tô
Rishiri-tô
Wakkanai
Sôya-misaki

Teshio
Hake-dake
1129

Mombetsu

Fukagawa
Nayoro
Shiretoko-
misaki

Asahikawa
Kitami
Bihoro
Shari-dake
1645

Takikawa
Akabira
Asahi dake
2290

Mikasa
Yûbari
Tokachi-dake
2077
AKAN-
KOKURITSU-
KÔEN

Abashiri

Akkeshi

Nemuro

HOKKAIDÔ

Kamui-misaki
Otaru
Ebetsu

Shakotan-
hantô

Sapporo
Chitose
Tomakomai
Obihiro
Kushiro

Oshamambe
Date
Yakumo
Noboribetsu
Shizunai

Uchiura-
wan

Muroran
783
Urakawa
Erimo-misaki

OSHIMA
HANTÔ

Okushiri-tô
Esashi

Hakodate
Tsugaru-kaikyô
Kamiishi
Mutsu

Aomori
Misawa

Hirosaki
Towada
Hachinohe

Iwaki-san
1625

Ôdate
Ninohe

Noshiro

Akita
Rida
Iwate-san
Miyako

Honjo
Ômagari
Morioka

Yuzawa
Hanamaki
Kamaishi

Sakata
Yokote
Mizusawa

Tsuruoka
Tendô
Kesennuma

Murakami
Yamagata
Ishinomaki

Niigata
Sendai

Nitsu
Yonezawa

Nagaoka
Aizu-wakamatsu
Fukushima

Sanjô
Kôriyama

Ojiya
Sukagawa
Iwaki

Joetsu
Tokamachi
Shirakawa

Itoigawa
Nikkô
Kitaibaraki

Nanao
Nagano
Numata
Yaita
Hitachi

Takaoka
Ueda
Utsunomiya

Kanazawa
Toyama
Takasaki
Ashikaga
Mito

Komatsu
Matsumoto
Okaya
Kumagaya
tsuchiura

Kaga
Takayama
Ômiya

Fukui
Ina
Nakatsugawa
Urawa
TÔKYÔ
Chôshi

Kofu
Hachiôji
Chiba

Gifu
Mino
Kasugai
Sagamihara
YOKOHAMA
KAWASAKI

Ôgaki
Toyota
Fuji-san
(Mount Fuji)
3776
Yokosuka

Matsue
Yonago
Toyooka
Miyazu
Tsuruga
Shizuoka
Fuji
Numazu
Katsuura

Izumo
Tottori
Fukuchiyama
Maizuru
Toyohashi
Itô
Ô-shima

KYÔTO
Ôtsu
Okazaki
Hamamatsu

Tsuyama
Biwa-ko
Tsu

Himeji
Nara
Toba
Enshû-nada

KÔBE
Higashiôsaka
Ise

Kurashiki
Okayama
ÔSAKA
Kishiwada
Wakayama

HIROSHIMA
Fukuyama
Awaji-
shima
Owase

Takamatsu
Tokushima
Kumano

Kure
Imabari
Anan
Gobô
Kumano-nada

Tokuyama
Niihama
Tanabe
Shingû

Matsuyama
Kôchi
Mugi
Shiono-misaki

SHIKOKU
Tosa
Muroto

Ôita
Uwajima
Sukumo
Tosa-wan

Beppu
Saiki
Bungo-suidô

KYÛSHÛ

Miyazaki

SEA OF JAPAN
(EAST SEA)

JAPAN

SADO

Noto-hantô

HIDA-
SAMMYAKU

CHÛGOKU-SANCHI

HONSHÛ

PACIFIC OCEAN

IZU-SHOTÔ
(IZU ISLANDS)

Nii-jima
Kôzu-shima
Miyake-jima
Hachijô-jima
Aoga-shima

Tok-to Take-shima
ed by S. Korea and Japan)

OKI-SHOTÔ
Dôgo

Vladivostok
zaliv Petra
Velikogo
(Peter the Great Bay)

Tok-to

1295
3685
244
2935
3735
1696

W-566400-7A-DR2-1
Copyright © Rand McNally & Co.

NANSEI-SHOTÔ (RYUKYU ISLANDS)

SATSUNAN-SHOTÔ

TOKARA-RETTO

AMAMI-SHOTÔ

EAST CHINA SEA

JAPAN

PACIFIC OCEAN

OKINAWA-SHOTÔ

Yaku-
shima
Tokara-kaikyô

Kuchino-shima
Nakano-shima

Suwanose-jima
Takara-jima

Yokoate-
jima

Amami-Ô-shima
Naze
Kikai-shima

Yewan-dake
694

Tokuno-
shima

Okino-Erabu-shima
Yoron-jima

Iheya-shima

Okinawa-jima
Nago
Okinawa

Kume-jima
Naha

Same scale as main map

NORTH KOREA

Kansŏng
Sohwa-ri
Sokch'o
Inje
Yangyang
T'ae-baek-san 1577
Hyŏn-ni
P'yŏngch'ang
Yŏyang-ni
Mukho
KANGWŎN-DO
Samch'ŏk
Chŏngsŏn
Imwŏn-ni
Checheŏn
Yŏngwŏl
Hambaeksan 1573
Ulchin
CHUNG-CH'ŎNG-BUKTO
Tanyang
Taebaek-san 1549
Ch'unyang
SOBAEK
Andong
Ilwŏl-san 1219
Yŏngju
Ulchin
SAMNAEK
Yech'ŏn
P'yŏnghae
Yŏngyang
Andong
Ŭisŏng
Yŏngdŏk
SOUTH KOREA
Sangju
Kusŏng
Ch'ŏngha
KYŎNGSANG-BUKTO
Kunwi
Sinnyŏng
Yŏngch'ŏn
P'ohang
Yŏngil-man Changgi-ap
Tabu-dong
Yŏngch'ŏn
Hayang
Ahwa-ri
Kuryŏngp'o
Waegwan
Taegu
Kyŏngsan
Kyŏngju
Sŏngju
Kyŏngsan
Kamp'o
Koryŏng
Ch'ŏngdo
Ch'ŏnan
Onyang
Ulsan
KYŎNGSANG-NAMDO
Miryang
Pangŏjin
Namji-ri
Sammangjin
Yangsan
Namch'ang
Haman
Changwŏn
Kimhae
Chindong
Masan
Kimhae
Chinhae
Ŭnghyŏn
PUSAN-JIKHALSI
Kosŏng
Paedun
Unch'ŏn
PUSAN (FUSAN)
Ch'ungmu
Changmong-ni
Chisep'o
KŎJE-DO
To Cheju-do
Western Channel

SEA OF JAPAN
(EAST SEA)

Ullŭng-do
(S. Korea)

Tok-to ° Take-shima
(Claimed by S. Korea and Japan)

Daimanji-san 608 Dōgo
OKI-SHOTŌ
Saigō
Dōzen

JAPA

Kamitsushima
Kamino-shima
TSUSHIMA
Shimono-Shima
Mishushima
Yatate-yama 649
Izuhara
Kō-zaki

Korea Strait
Tsushima-kaikyō
(Eastern Channel)

Mi-shima

Sakaiminato
Iwami
Kasumi
Hirata
Matsue
Yonago
Tōhaku
Aoya
Totton
Toyok
Taisha
Izumo
Yasugi
Kurayoshi
Misasa
Yōka
TOTTORI
Ōda
Sanbe-yama 1126
Daisen 1712
Chizu
Ikun
SHIMANE
Katsuyama
Tsuyama
CHUGOKU
SANCHI
Gōtsu
Shōbara
Tōjō
OKAYAMA
HYŌGO
Yama
Hamada
Miyoshi
Takahashi
Saeki
Bizen
Tatsuno
Shingū
Masuda
Kake
Fuchū
Kurashiki
Okayama
Akō
Takasac
Susa
HIROSHIMA
Higashihiroshima
Onomichi
Kasaoka
Tamano
Shodo-shima
Hagi
Tsuwano
HIROSHIMA
Mihara
Innoshima
Tobishi
AWAJI
SHIMA
Hōhoku
YAMAGUCHI
Nagato
Iwakuni
Ōtake
Kure
Ondo
INLAND SEA
Marugame
Sakaide
Zentsūji
Takamatsu
Toyoura
Mine
Sanyō
Hōfu
Tokuyama
Kudamatsu
SETO NAIKAI
Tadotsu
KAGAWA
Ōchi
Nandan
Shimonoseki
Onoda
Ube
Hikari
Yanai
Hiuchi-nada
Kanonji
Waki
Kamojima
Tokus
KITAKYŪSHŪ
Kanda
KŌKŪ-JIEITAI-CHIKUJŌ-KICHI
Suō-nada
Imabari
Niihama
Iyo-mimaki
TOKUSHIMA
Iki
Ashibe
Nakama
Yukuhashi
Buzen
Nakatsu
Kunisaki
Yashiro-jima
Hōjō
Tōyo
Saijō
An
Gōnoura
FUKUOKA
Iizuka
Tagawa
Takada
Kunisaki-hantō
Sada-misaki-hantō
Matsuyama
Ishizuchi-san 1981
SHIKOKU-SANCHI
Karatsu
FUKUOKA
Amagi
Kitsuki
Iyo
EHIME
Hirado
Maebaru
Chikugo
Hita
Kusu
Beppu
Sadamisaki
Nahama
Yawatahama
KŌCHI
Nankoku
Hirado-shima
SAGA
TSUKUSHI-SANCHI
Kurume
Yame
ŌITA
Ōita
Mikame
Uwa
Saketa
Emukae
Takeo
Okawa
Yanagawa
Kuju-san 1767
Usuki
Uwajima
Tosa
Sazu
Matsuura
Saga
Imari
Ōmuta
Yamaga
Kikuchi
Ichinomiya
Taketa
Mie
Saiki
Uwajima
Kōchi
Ōreshino
Ōshima
Isahaya
Arao
Tamana
Aso-san 1592
Tsukumi
Bungo-suidō
Iyan
Sukumo
Nakamura
NAGASAKI
Ōmura
KUMAMOTO
RIKUJŌ-JIEITAI
Takachiho
Kamae
Tosa-wan
Arikawa
Nakadōri-shima
Ōmura-wan
Unzen-dake 1360
Shimabara
KENGUN-CHUTONCHI
Kumamoto
Hinokage
Nobeoka
Ashizuri-misaki
Muroto
Nagasaki
Takashima
Obama
Uto
Takamori
SHIKOKU
Naru
Nomozaki
Misumi
Ogawa
Nōbeoka
Muroto-zaki
Fukue
Narao
Reihoku
Ōyano
Tsushiro
Itsuki
KYŪSHŪ-SANCHI
Kadogawa
Fukue-Jima
Amakusa-nada
Hondo
Tsuwa
MIYAZAKI
Hyūga
AMAKUSA-SHOTŌ
Ushibuka
Minamata
Hitoyoshi
Saito
Hyūga-nada
Amakuso-Shimo-shima
KYŪSHŪ
Ebino
Takanabe
Akune
Ōkuchi
Sadowara SHINDENBARU-KICHI
Kushima
Miyanojō
Kobayashi
Ōyodo
EAST CHINA SEA
Sendai
Kirishima-yama 1700
KIRISHIMA-YAKU-KOKURITSU-KŌEN
Miyazaki
Koshikijima-rettō
Kushikino
KAGOSHIMA
Kajiki
Kokubu
Miyakonojō
Nichinan
Higashiichiki
Kagoshima
On-take 1117
KIRISHIMA-YAKU-KOKURITSU-KŌEN
Tarumizu
Shibushi
Nangō
Danjo-guntō
Kaseda
Kanoya
Kushima
Satsuma-hantō
Makurazaki
Ibusuki
Ōsumi-hantō
Uchinoura
To Okinawa
Kaimon-dake 924
Yamagawa
Ei
KŌKŪ-DAIGAKU-UCHŪKŪKAN-KENKYŪSHO
Toi-misaki
Uji-guntō
Sata-misaki
KIRISHIMA-YAKU-KOKURITSU-KŌEN
134° East of Greenwich

Central and Southern Japan

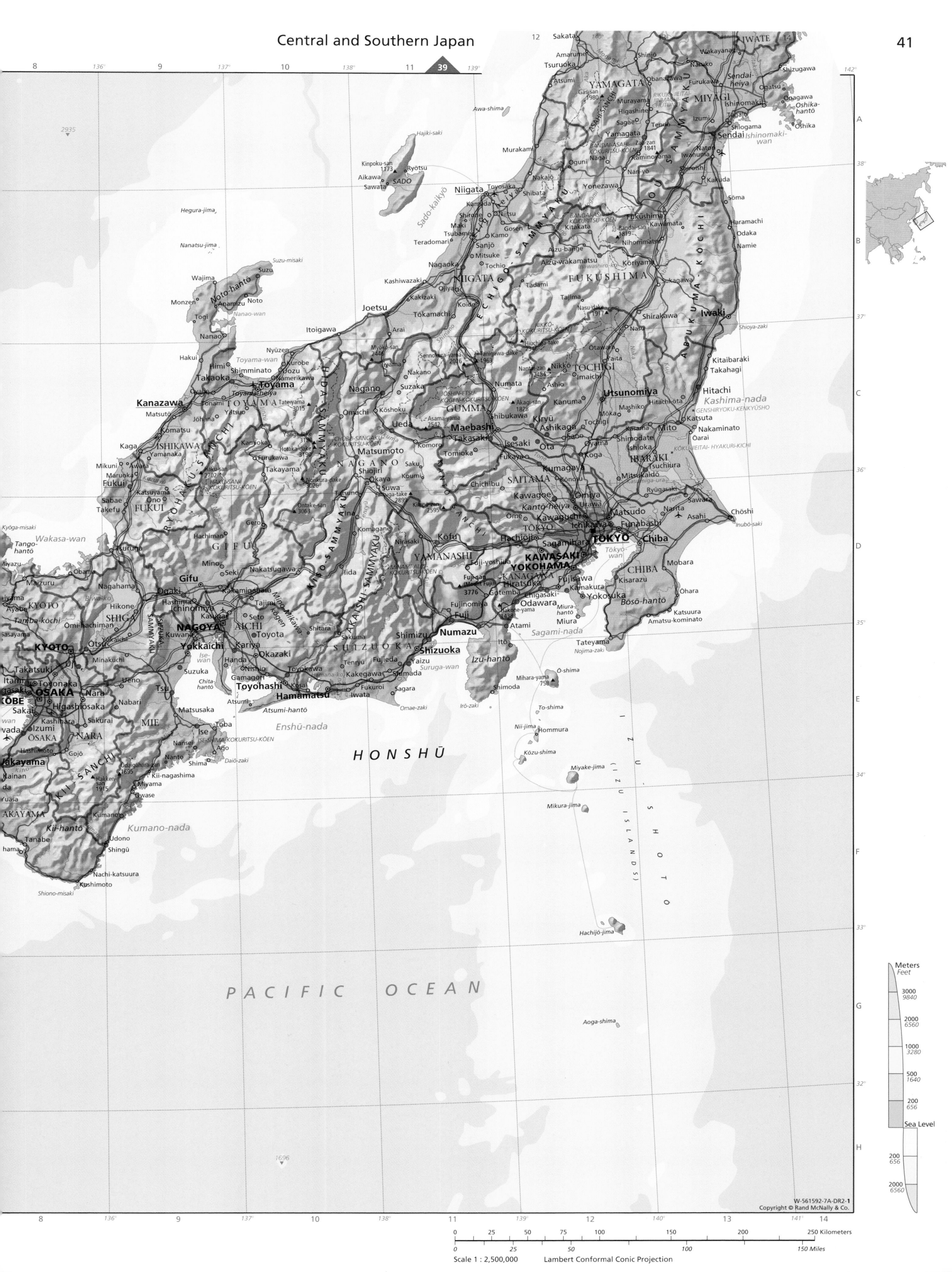

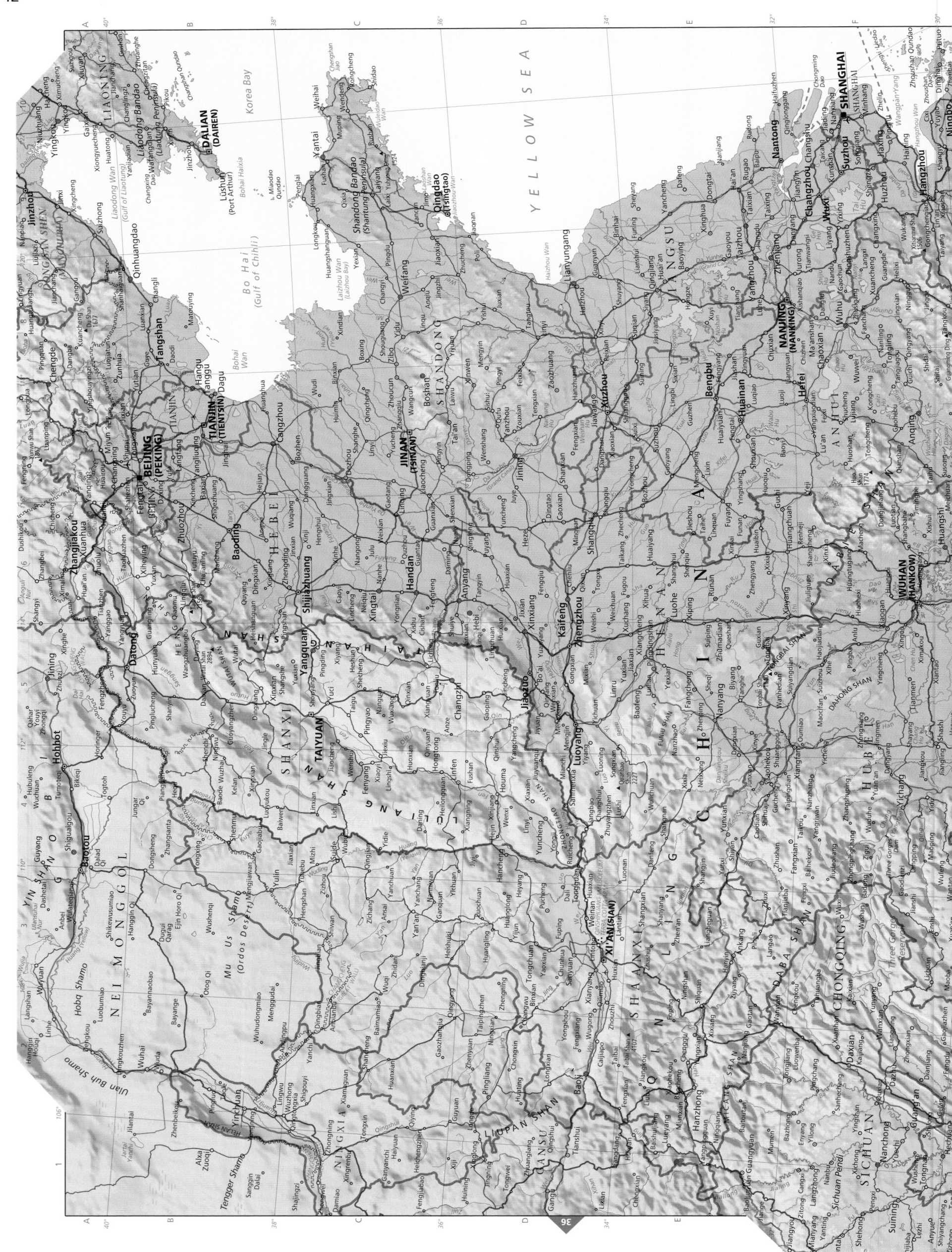

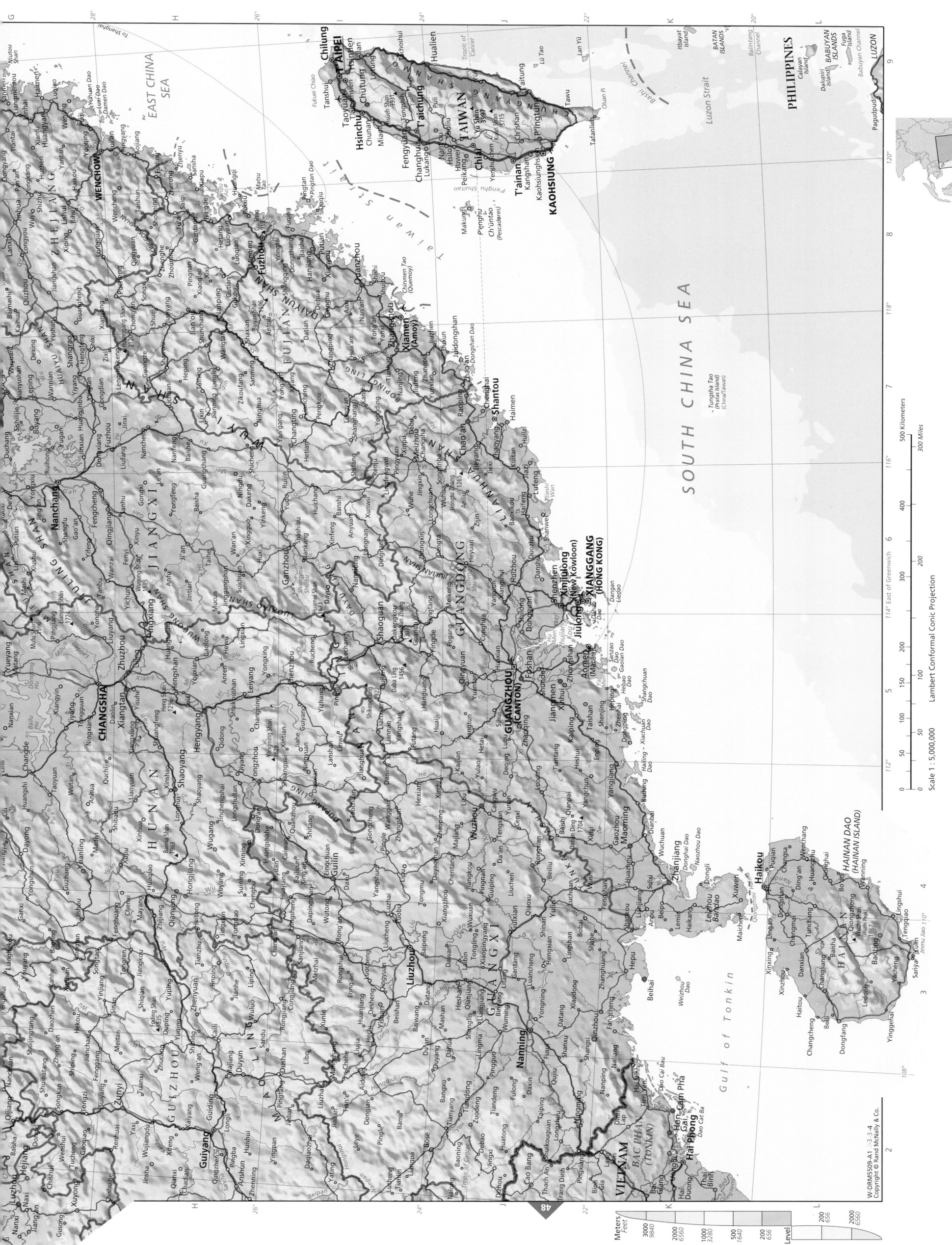

Scale 1 : 5,000,000   Lambert Conformal Conic Projection

44

47 | 2 | 4 | 5 | A | 36

HA NOI Hai Phong Gulf of Tonkin CHINA

Leizhou Bandao Xuwen Qiongzhou Haixia **Haikou**

Muang Ngoy Mong Hsan Ban Houayxay Viangphoukha Muang Nguey Xam Nua Thai Binh Nam Dinh Linga Qionghai

Hsipaw Chiang Rai Chiang Kham Muang Phiang Ban Ban Ninh Binh Changjiang Danxian Wenchang

Pyinmana Lei-kaw Phayao Muang Thadua Phou Bia 2819 Khe Bo Thanh Hoa Sam Son Dongfang Qionghai

Thayetmyo Nattalin 2620 Chiang Mai Doi Inthanon 2600 Viangchan (Vientiane) Muang Pakxan Vinh Wuzhi Shan 1840 Baoting

Prome Oktwin Lamphun Lampang Phrae Nam Pat Ban Nale Muang Ha Tinh Sanya Lingshui

Paungde Kyaukkyi Kyauktaw Mae Sariang Nam Pat Thoen Chiang Loei Udon Thani Nakhon Phanom Muang Khammuan Muang Phalan Lao Bao Dong Hoi HAINAN DAO (HAINAN ISLAND)

Sandoway Henzada Thonze Papun Uttaradit Sukhothai Sawankhalok Khon Kaen Sakon Nakhon Nong Han Muang Xepon Hue

YANGON (RANGOON) Thaton Pa-an Kamphaeng Phet Phitsanulok Lom Sak Kalasin Savannakhet Hoi An Da Nang

Kyeintali Gwa Pathein Myaungmya Syriam Thongwa Taphan Hin Phichit Chum Saeng Maha Sarakham Roi Et Muang Phin VIETNAM XISHA QUNDAO (PARACEL ISLANDS) (Claimed by China, Taiwan and Vietnam)

Bogale Pyapon Wakema Mawlamyine Chai Nat Nakhon Sawan THAILAND Buri Ram Si Sa Ket Ubon Ratchathani Champasak Tam Ky Quang Ngai

Myitta Dawei Lop Buri Takhli Nakhon Ratchasima Surin Muang Khong Saravan Muang Khongxedon Binh Son

Myinmoletkat Taung 2075 Palaw Suphan Buri Saraburi Phra Nakhon Si Ayutthaya PHANOM DONGRAK RANGE Choam Khsant Phumi Samraong Attapu Play Ku Dac Glei Kon Tum An Nhon Quy Nhon

MYANMAR (BURMA) Nakhon Pathom **KRUNG THEP (BANGKOK)** Samut Prakan ANGKOR WAT Phumi Kantuot Phumi Moung Phumi Srolau Stoeng Treng Virochey Dac To Song Cau Tuy Hoa

Kadan Kyun Dawna Kyun Songkhram Chon Buri Si Racha Cha-am Phetchaburi CAMBODIA Phumi Chhuk Kracheh Kampong Cham Lumphat Buon Ma Thuot Nha Trang

MERGUI Daung Kyun Tenasserim Hua Hin Rayong Chanthaburi Trat Ko Chang Battambang Phnum Aoral 1813 Kampong Thum Loc Ninh Da Lat Cam Ranh

Bentinck Island Letsok-aw Kyun Kanmaw Kyun Prachuap Khiri Khan Ko Kut **Phnum Penh (Phnom Penh)** Baeng Tonle Sab Kampong Chhnang Bao Lac Di Linh Phan Rang

ARCHIPELAGO Lanbi Kyun Phumi Kaoh Kong Krong Kaoh Kong Phumi Chhuk Svay Rieng Takev Bien Hoa Phan Thiet SOUTH CHINA SEA

Chumphon Isthmus of Kra Ko Tao Kaoh Rung Kampong Saom Dao Phu Quoc Long Xuyen Tan An My Tho **THANH PHO HO CHI MINH (HO CHI MINH CITY) (SAIGON)** Iles Catwick

Ranong Ao Ban Don Ko Phangan Ko Samui Rach Gia Can Tho Vinh Long Tra Vinh Nanshan Island

Andaman Sea Surat Thani Quan Dao Nam Du Soc Trang Bac Lieu SPRATLY ISLANDS (Claimed by Brunei, China, Malaysia, Philippines, Taiwan and Vietnam) Mount Mantaling

Phangnga Nakhon Si Thammarat Pak Phanang Ca Mau Mui Ca Mau Con Son Hon Khoai

Ko Phuket Phuket Thung Song Phatthalung Songkhla Balabac Island Pulau Balambangan Kudat

Trang Kantang Trale Luang Hat Yai Pattani Yala Narathiwat Kota Beludu Kota Kinabalu Gunong 4101

Satun Kangar Alor Setar Betong Sungai Kolok Pasir Mas Kota Bharu Pulau Labuan Labuan SABAH

Pulau We Banda Aceh Pulau Langkawi Sungai Petani Kuala Krai Kuala Terengganu BRUNEI Seria Bandar Seri Begawan

Lhokseumawe George Town (Penang) Butterworth Taiping Kuala Kangsar Gunong Mului 2377 Miri Niah Gunong Murud 2422

Meulaboh Gunung Abongabong 2985 Langsa Binjai Ipoh Kampar Teluk Intan Gunong Tahan 2187 Kuala Lipis MALAYSIA Pulau Laut KEPULAUAN NATUNA BESAR Bintulu Mukah MALAYSIA SARAWAK

Blangpidie Gunung Leuser 3381 Gunung Sinabung 2451 Raub Bentong Gunung Benum 2107 Kuantan Natuna Besar KEPULAUAN ANAMBAS Sibu Sarikei Kapit IRAN MTS.

Tapaktuan **MEDAN** Tebingtinggi Kuala Lumpur Shah Alam Klang SEMENANJUNG MALAYSIA Kuala Pilah Cukai Pulau Midai KEPULAUAN NATUNA SELATAN Kuching Betong Putussibau Gunong Kemul 2053

Pematangsiantar Kisaran Seremban Kajang Labis Mersing Pulau Tioman Pulau Serasan Sambas Serian UPPER KAPUAS MTS. Gunung Menyapa 2000

Pulau Simeulue Sinabang Tanjungbalai Segamat Keluang Pulau Jemaja Singkawang Semitau Longiram

Bagansiapiapi Rantauprapat Muar Batu Pahat Cape Datu KEPULAUAN TAMBELAN Selat Serasan Sambas Mempawah Sanggau Sintang BORNEO (KALIMANTAN)

Sibolga Pulau Rupat Dumai Melaka Johor Bahru **SINGAPORE** Singapore Pulau Batam Pontianak Putussibau

Padangsidempuan Pakanbaru Bengkalis Pulau Padang Pulau Bintan Tanjungpinang KEPULAUAN RIAU Pulau Subi Gunung Saran 1758 Bukit Raya 2278 Samarinda

Pulau Nias Gunungsitoli Bangkinang SUMATERA (SUMATRA) Pulau Kundur Pulau Lingga KEPULAUAN LINGGA Pulau Pejantan Nangatayap Balikpapan

Pulau Tuangku Pulau Mursala Equator Talu Pekanbaru Pulau Sebangka Ketapang Sukadana Buntok Bali

Pulau Babi Pulau Pini KEPULAUAN BATU Pulau Tanahmasa Bukittinggi Payakumbuh Taluk Tembilahan Pulau Basu Selat Berhala Pulau Singkep Sukaraja Kendawangan Palangkaraya Sampit Amuntai

Pulau Tanahbala Padangpanjang Pariaman Rengat Selat Gelasa Pangkalpinang Pulau Bangka Telukbatang Kumai Kualakapuas Kandangan

Pulau Siberut Padang Sungaidareh Jambi Muntok Pulau Karimata Teluk Kumai Banjarmasin Martapura Pulau Sebuku

Gunung Kerinci 3800 Muarabungo Bangko Selat Karimata (Karimata Strait) Tanjungpandan Belitung Teluk Sampit

KEPULAUAN MENTAWAI Pulau Sipura Mukomuko Surulangun Lubuklinggau **Palembang** Manggar Tanjung Puting Tanjung Selatan Kep. Balabalakang

Pulau Pagai Utara Pulau Pagai Selatan Lais Muaraenim GREATER SUNDA Pulau Sebuku

Bengkulu Lahat Gunung Dempo 3159 Kayuagung Perabumulih Baturaja LAUT JAWA (JAVA SEA) IND

Manna Martapura Menggala Pulau Masalembu Besar

Bintuhan Kotabumi Tulangbawang

Pulau Enggano Krui Kotaagung Bandar Lampung Pulau Bawean

Tanjung Cina Serang Karawang Indramayu Cirebon Pekalongan Kudus Bangkalan Pulau Kangean

JAKARTA Bogor Cianjur Purwakarta Sumedang Tegal Semarang Kudus Rembang Tuban Madura Sumenep Pulau Sapudi

Sukabumi **BANDUNG** Garut Purwokerto Purwakarta **SEMARANG** Surakarta **SURABAYA** Pamekasan Selat Madura

Ujunggenteng Sindangbarang Gunung Slamet 3428 Cilacap Yogyakarta Magelang Gunung Lawu 3265 Kediri **Malang** Probolinggo Banyuwangi

INDIAN OCEAN JAWA (JAVA) Tulungagung Blitar Jember Gunung Agung 3142 Bali Gunung Rinjani 3726 Mataram

Denpasar Nusa Penida Lombok Praya Taliwang

Meters / Feet
4000 / 13120
3000 / 9840
2000 / 6560
1000 / 3280
500 / 1640
200 / 656
Sea Level
200 / 656
2000 / 6560

M-DRM4708-A1-1-2-2-4
Copyright © Rand McNally & Co.

0 100 200 300 400 600 800 1000 Kilometers
0 200 400 600 Miles
Scale 1 : 10,000,000 Sinusoidal Projection

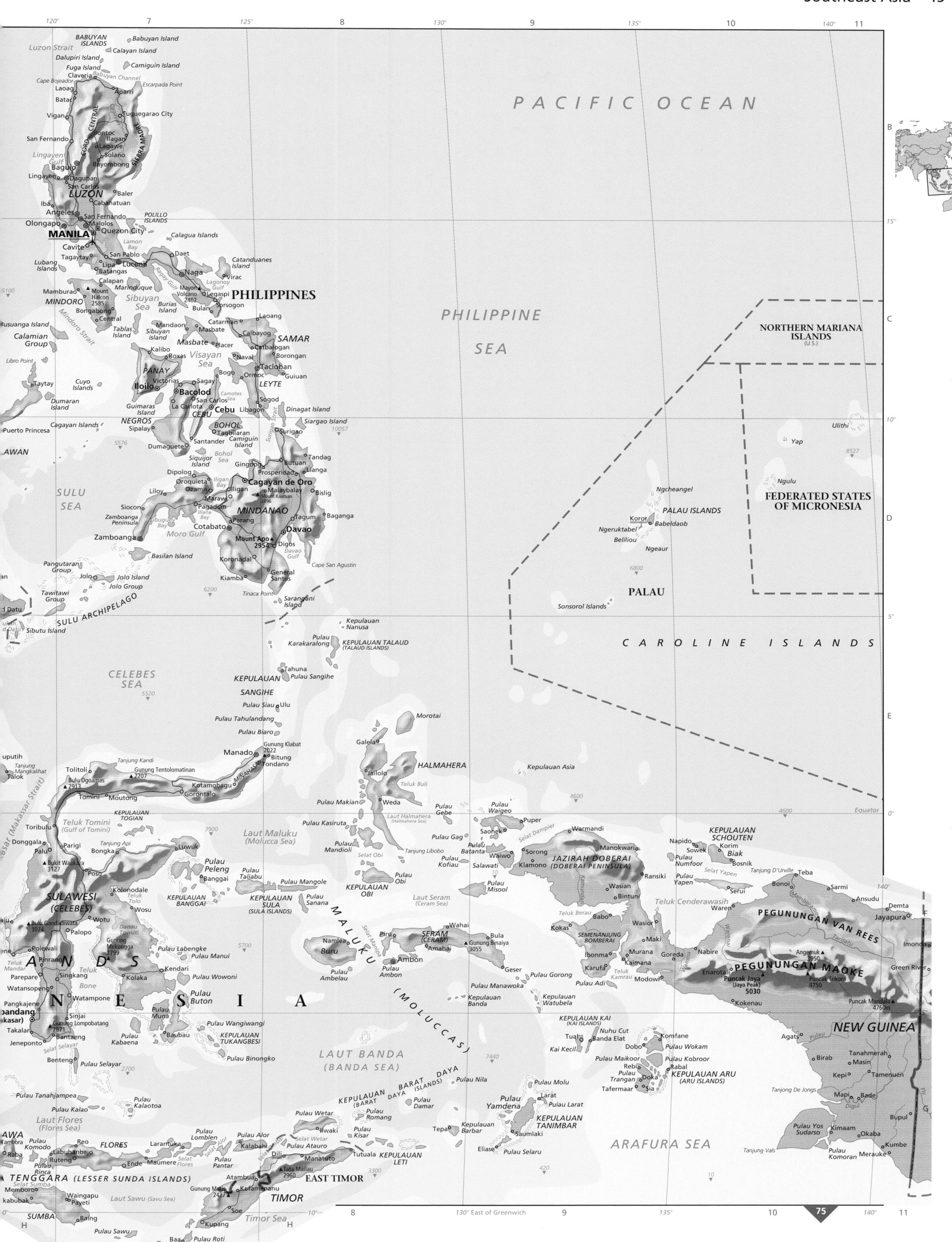

PACIFIC OCEAN

PHILIPPINE

SEA

NORTHERN MARIANA
ISLANDS
(U.S.)

BABUYAN
ISLANDS
Babuyan Island
Calayan Island
Dalupiri Island
Fuga Island
Camiguin Island
Luzon Strait
Claveria
Cape Bojeador
Aparri
Laoag
Tuguegarao City
Escarpada Point
Batac
Vigan
Ilagan
Bontoc
San Fernando
Baguio
Bayombong
Solano
San Carlos
Lingayen
Dagupan
Gulf
Iba
Cabanatuan
LUZON
Baler
Angeles
San Fernando
Olongapo
Malolos
Quezon City
MANILA
Cavite
Calagua Islands
Lamon
Bay
Tagaytay
San Pablo
Daet
Batangas
Lipa
Lucena
Naga
Catanduanes
Island
Calapan
Mamburao
Marinduque
Mount
Halcon
2585
Virac
Lubang
Islands
MINDORO
Bongabong
Central
Mayon
Volcano
2462
Legaspi
Orsogon
PHILIPPINES
Sibuyan
Sea
Burias
Island
Bulan
Tablas
Island
Masbate
Catarman
Laoang
Mandaon
Sibuyan
Island
Masbate
Calbayog
SAMAR
Busuanga Island
Calamian
Group
Kalibo
Roxas
Visayan
Sea
Placer
Borongan
Cuyo
Islands
PANAY
Victorias
Sagay
Bogo
Ormoc
Catbalogan
Naval
Tacloban
Guiuan
Libro Point
Iloilo
San Carlos
LEYTE
Taytay
Guimaras
Island
Bacolod
La Carlota
Cebu
Sogod
Dumaran
Island
NEGROS
CEBU
Libagon
Dinagat Island
Cagayan Islands
Sipalay
BOHOL
Tagbilaran
Siargao Island
Puerto Princesa
Dumaguete
Santander
Camiguin
Island
Surigao
Siquijor
Island
Bohol
Sea
Gingoog
Dipolog
Iligan
Tandag
Oroquieta
Bay
Liloy
Ozamis
Iligan
Butuan
Prosperidad
Cagayan de Oro
Llanga
SULU
SEA
Siocon
Pagadian
Malaybalay
Mount Kaatoan
2896
Bislig
Zamboanga
Peninsula
Parang
MINDANAO
Tagum
Baganga
Zamboanga
Cotabato
Moro Gulf
Mount Apo
2954
Davao
Digos
Basilan Island
Koronadal
Davao
Gulf
Pangutaran
Group
Kiamba
General
Santos
Cape San Agustin
Jolo
Jolo Island
Jolo Group
Tinaca Point
Sarangani
Island
Tawitawi
Group
SULU ARCHIPELAGO
Sibutu Island
Datu
Kepulauan
Nanusa
Pulau
Karakaralong
KEPULAUAN TALAUD
(TALAUD ISLANDS)
CELEBES
SEA
KEPULAUAN
SANGIHE
Tahuna
Pulau Sangihe
Pulau Siau
Ulu
Pulau Tahulandang
Pulau Biaro
Morotai
Manado
Gunung Klabat
2022
Bitung
Tondano
Galela
HALMAHERA
Kepulauan Asia
Tolitoli
Tanjung Kandi
Gunung Tentolomatinan
2207
Kotamobagu
MINAHASA
Jailolo
Bulu Ogoamas
2913
Gorontalo
Weda
Teluk Buli
Tomini
Moutong
Pulau Makian
Pulau Gebe
Teluk Tomini
(Gulf of Tomini)
KEPULAUAN
TOGIAN
Toribulu
Parigi
Tanjung Api
Bongka
Pulau Kasiruta
Pulau Gag
KEPULAUAN
SCHOUTEN
Donggala
Palu
Luwuk
Pulau
Waigeo
Puper
Warmandi
Napido
Sowek
Korim
Biak
Bosnik
Bukit Watuk Ira
3127
Poso
Pulau
Peleng
Banggai
Pulau
Mandioli
Saonek
Selat Dampier
Waiwo
Sorong
Manokwari
Pulau
Numfoor
Pulau
Batanta
Klamono
JAZIRAH DOBERAI
(DOBERAI PENINSULA)
Ransiki
SULAWESI
(CELEBES)
Pulau
Taljabu
Pulau Mangole
KEPULAUAN
OBI
Salawati
Pulau
Kofiau
Pulau
Misool
Wasian
Bintuni
Pulau
Yapen
Serui
Teba
Pulau
Labengke
Pulau Manui
KEPULAUAN
SULA
(SULA ISLANDS)
Pulau
Sanana
Pulau
Obi
Laut Seram
(Ceram Sea)
Wahai
Babo
Wasior
Teluk Cenderawasih
Waren
Bonoi
Sarmi
Ansudu
Bulu Gandang
3074
Palopo
Kolaka
Pulau Wowoni
MALUKU
Namlea
Buru
SERAM
(CERAM)
Gunung Binaiya
3055
Piru
Bula
Amahai
Kokas
SEMENANJUNG
BOMBERAI
Ibonma
Murana
Maki
Karufa
Kaimana
Goreda
Nabire
Demta
Jayapura
PEGUNUNGAN VAN REES
Angemuk
3950
Green River
Pinrang
Singkang
Teluk
Bone
Watampone
Kendari
Pulau
Ambelau
Pulau
Ambon
Ambon
Geser
Pulau Gorong
Pulau Adi
Modowi
Enarotali
Puncak Jaya
(Jaya Peak)
5030
Puncak Trikora
4750
PEGUNUNGAN MAOKE
Puncak Mandala
4760m
Pangkep
Sinjai
Gunung Lompobatang
2871
Baubau
Pulau
Buton
Kepulauan
Banda
Kepulauan
Watubela
Kokenau
NEW GUINEA
Takalar
Bantaeng
KEPULAUAN
TUKANGBESI
Pulau Wangiwangi
KEPULAUAN KAI
(KAI ISLANDS)
Nuhu Cut
Banda Elat
Komfane
Agats
Pulau
Birab
Jeneponto
Pulau
Muna
Kai Kecil
Tual
Dobo
Pulau Wokam
Pulau Kobroor
Rabal
Tanahmerah
Masin
Benteng
Pulau Selayar
Selat
Selayar
Pulau Binongko
LAUT BANDA
(BANDA SEA)
Pulau Maikoor
Rebi
Pulau
Trangan
KEPULAUAN ARU
(ARU ISLANDS)
Doka
Sia
Tafermaar
Kepi
Tamenun
Pulau Tanahjampea
Pulau Kalao
Pulau Nila
Larat
Pulau Larat
Mapi
Bade
LAUT FLORES
(Flores Sea)
Pulau Kalaotoa
Pulau Wetar
Pulau Molu
Pulau
Yamdena
Tanjong De Jongs
Digul
Bupul
Komodo
Labuhanbajo
FLORES
Larantuka
Pulau
Lomblen
Pulau Ataúro
Ilwaki
Pulau Kisar
Pulau
Romang
Tepa
Kepulauan
Barbar
KEPULAUAN
TANIMBAR
Pulau Yos
Sudarso
Kimaam
Okaba
Reo
Ruteng
Ende
Maumere
Dili
Manatúto
Tutuala
KEPULAUAN
LETI
Saumlaki
Eliase
ARAFURA SEA
Tanjung Vals
Pulau
Komoran
Merauke
Raba
Pulau
Pantar
Kalabahi
TENGGARA (LESSER SUNDA ISLANDS)
Atambua
Gunung Metis
2960
EAST TIMOR
TIMOR
Waingapu
Gunung Mutis
2427
Kefamenanu
Soe
Timor Sea
SUMBA
Payeti
Baing
Kupang
Pulau Sawu
Baa
Pulau Roti

Kepulauan Nanusa

Ngcheangel
Ngeruktabel
Koror
Babeldaob
Beliliou
PALAU ISLANDS
Ngeaur
FEDERATED STATES
OF MICRONESIA

Yap
Ngulu

Ulithi

PALAU

Sonsorol Islands

CAROLINE ISLANDS

Equator

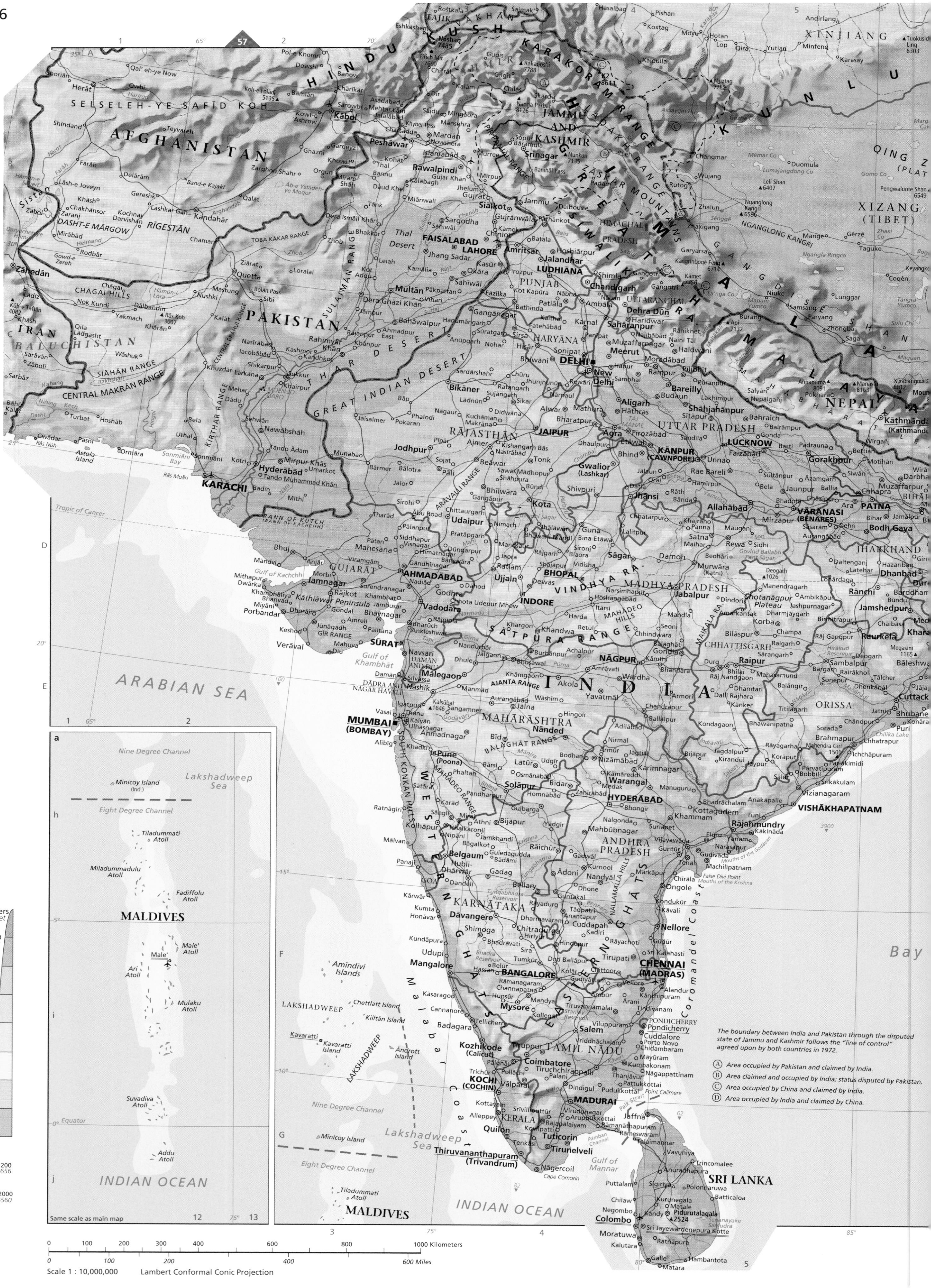

57

AFGHANISTAN

SELSELEH-YE SAFÎD KOH

HINDU KUSH

KARAKORAM RANGE

JAMMU AND KASHMIR

XINJIANG

KUN LUN

QING ZA (PLAT

XIZANG (TIBET)

NGANGLONG KANGRI

PAKISTAN

IRAN

BALUCHISTAN

CHAGAI HILLS

RÎGESTÂN

DASHT-E MÂRGOW

Sîstân

TOBA KÂKAR RANGE

SULAIMAN RANGE

CENTRAL BRÂHUI RANGE

KIRTHAR RANGE

SIÂHÂN RANGE

CENTRAL MAKRÂN RANGE

THAL DESERT

THAR DESERT

GREAT INDIAN DESERT

PUNJAB

LAHORE

FAISALABAD

LUDHIANA

Amritsar

Chandigarh

HIMACHAL PRADESH

UTTARANCHAL

HARYANA

DELHI

New Delhi

Meerut

UTTAR PRADESH

NEPAL

KÂTHMÂNDU (Kathmandu)

RÂJASTHÂN

JAIPUR

Jodhpur

Bikaner

Udaipur

Kota

LUCKNOW

KÂNPUR (CAWNPORE)

Gorakhpur

ALLAHÂBÂD

VÂRÂNASI (BENÂRES)

PATNA

BIHÂR

Bodh Gaya

GUJARÂT

AHMADÂBÂD

Vadodara

SÛRAT

RANN OF KUTCH (RANN OF KACHCHH)

Gulf of Kachchh

Tropic of Cancer

KARACHI

Hyderâbâd

Mirpur Khas

Gulf of Khambhât

DÂDRA AND NAGAR HAVELI

DAMÂN AND DIU

MAHÂRÂSHTRA

MUMBAI (BOMBAY)

Pune (Poona)

Solâpur

NÂGPUR

MADHYA PRADESH

BHOPÂL

INDORE

Ujjain

Jabalpur

VINDHYA RA.

SÂTPURA RANGE

MAHÂDEO HILLS

AJANTA RANGE

JHARKHAND

Ranchi

Jamshedpur

CHHATTISGARH

Raipur

ORISSA

Cuttack

Bhubane

Puri

ARABIAN SEA

INDIA

ANDHRA PRADESH

HYDERÂBÂD

Warangal

VISHÂKHAPATNAM

Râjahmundry

WEST

MAHÂDEO RANGE

SOUTH KONKAN HILLS

BALÂGHÂT RANGE

KARNATAKA

GOA

Panaji

Belgaum

Hubli-Dhârwâr

Mangalore

BANGALORE

Mysore

Coromandel Coast

GHÂTS

WESTERN GHÂTS

EASTERN GHÂTS

TAMIL NÂDU

CHENNAI (MADRAS)

PONDICHERRY

Salem

Coimbatore

Tiruchirâppalli

KERALA

KOCHI (COCHIN)

Kozhikode (Calicut)

MADURAI

Thiruvananthapuram (Trivandrum)

Tuticorin

Tirunelveli

Cape Comorin

Gulf of Mannar

SRI LANKA

Colombo

Sri Jayewardenepura Kotte

Kandy

Bay

Mouths of the Krishna

Mouths of the Godavari

Inset a — Lakshadweep

Nine Degree Channel

Minicoy Island (Ind.)

Lakshadweep Sea

Eight Degree Channel

Tiladummati Atoll

Miladummadulu Atoll

Fadiffolu Atoll

MALDIVES

Ari Atoll

Male' Atoll

Male'

Mulaku Atoll

Amîndivi Islands

LAKSHADWEEP

Chettlatt Island

Killtân Island

Kavaratti Island

Âncrott Island

Suvadiva Atoll

Equator

Minicoy Island

Addu Atoll

INDIAN OCEAN

MALDIVES

Malabar Coast

Same scale as main map

The boundary between India and Pakistan through the disputed state of Jammu and Kashmir follows the "line of control" agreed upon by both countries in 1972.

Ⓐ Area occupied by Pakistan and claimed by India.
Ⓑ Area claimed and occupied by India; status disputed by Pakistan.
Ⓒ Area occupied by China and claimed by India.
Ⓓ Area occupied by India and claimed by China.

Elevation scale

Meters / Feet

6000 / 19680
4000 / 13120
3000 / 9840
2000 / 6560
1000 / 3280
500 / 1640
200 / 656
Sea Level
200 / 656
2000 / 6560

0 100 200 300 400 600 800 1000 Kilometers
0 600 Miles

Scale 1 : 10,000,000   Lambert Conformal Conic Projection

M-DRM4707-A1-1-3-3-4
Copyright © Rand McNally & Co.

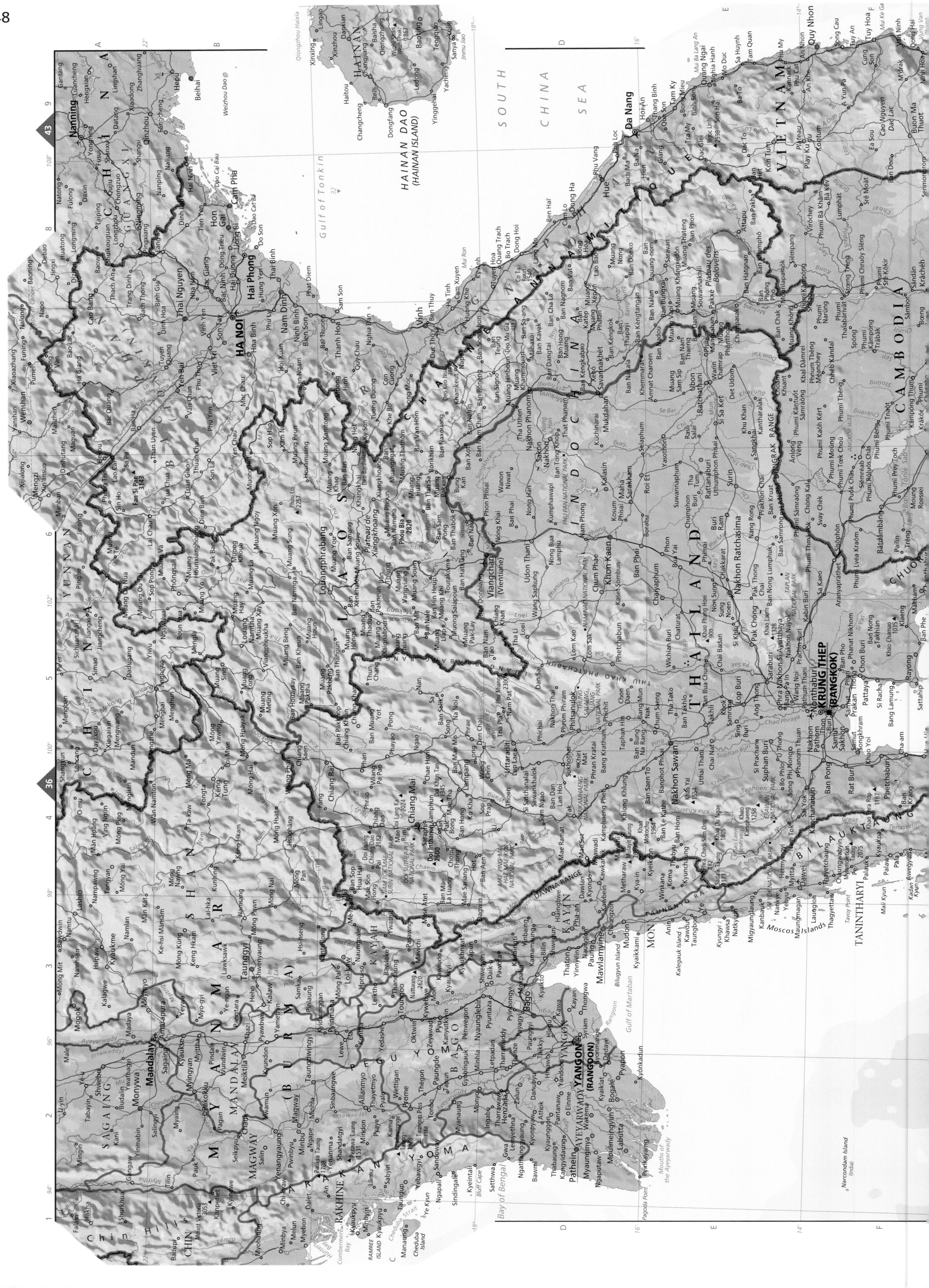

SOUTH CHINA SEA

HAINAN DAO (HAINAN ISLAND)

Gulf of Tonkin

CHINA

GUANGXI

YUNNAN

MYANMAR (BURMA)

LAOS

THAILAND

VIETNAM

CAMBODIA

Bay of Bengal

Gulf of Martaban

VIETNAM

Nanning

HA NOI

Hai Phong

Da Nang

Hue

Viangchan (Vientiane)

KRUNG THEP (BANGKOK)

YANGON (RANGOON)

Mandalay

Chiang Mai

Nakhon Ratchasima

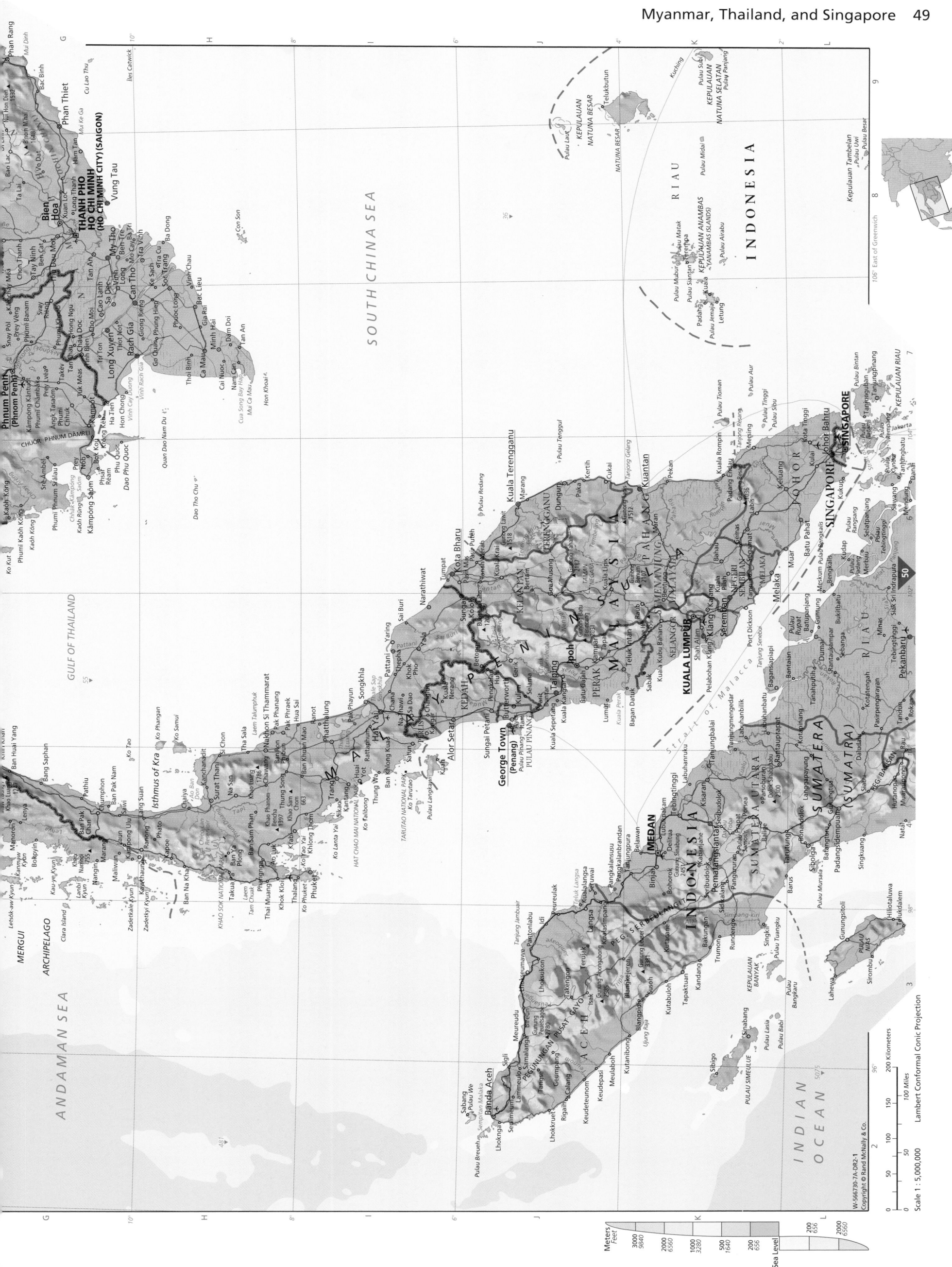

SOUTH CHINA SEA

INDONESIA

RIAU

KEPULAUAN
NATUNA BESAR

NATUNA BESAR

KEPULAUAN
NATUNA SELATAN

KEPULAUAN ANAMBAS
(ANAMBAS ISLANDS)

Kepulauan Tambelan

Phan Rang

Phan Thiet

Vung Tau

THANH PHO
HO CHI MINH
(HO CHI MINH CITY) (SAIGON)

Bien
Hoa

Phnum Penh
(Phnom Penh)

CHUOR PHNUM DAMREI

GULF OF THAILAND

ANDAMAN SEA

MERGUI

ARCHIPELAGO

Isthmus of Kra

KHAO SOK NATIONAL PARK

HAT CHAO MAI NATIONAL PARK

TARUTAO NATIONAL PARK

Kuala Terengganu

Kota Bharu

George Town
(Penang)
PULAU PINANG

Alor Setar

Ipoh

KUALA LUMPUR

MALAYSIA

PAHANG

TERENGGANU

KELANTAN

PERAK

KEDAH

Strait of Malacca

SINGAPORE

JOHOR

MELAKA

NEGERI
SEMBILAN

SELANGOR

MEDAN

SUMATERA UTARA

SUMATERA
(SUMATRA)

INDONESIA

RIAU

Pekanbaru

ACEH

Banda Aceh

PEGUNUNGAN

PUSAT
GAYO

KEPULAUAN
BANYAK

PULAU NIAS

PULAU SIMEULUE

INDIAN
OCEAN

Meters
feet

3000
9840

2000
6560

1000
3280

500
1640

200
656

Sea Level

200
656

2000
6560

Scale 1 : 5,000,000

Lambert Conformal Conic Projection

W-566730-7A-DR2-1
Copyright © Rand McNally & Co.

200 Kilometers

100 Miles

50

49

SOUTH CHINA SEA

KEPULAUAN NATUNA BESAR

Telukbutun

Natuna Besar

Pulau Laut

KELANTAN
Parit Buntar
Kuala Sepetang
Taiping
Kuala Kangsar
Gua Musang
TERENGGANU
Dungun
Paka
Kertih
Cukai
Ipoh
Gunong Batu Berembun 2031
Batu Gajah
Kampar
Tapah
Kuala Lipis
TAMAN NEGARA
Tembeling
Lumut
PERAK
Bagan Datuk
Teluk Intan
Gunong Benum 2107
PAHANG
Pint-Tree Hill 1450
Raub
Sabak
Kuala Kubu Baharo
Bentung
Maran
Pekan
Kuantan
Gunong Tapis
Tanjong Gelang
MALAY PENINSULA

MEDAN
Belawan
Labuhanruku
Delitua
Tebingtinggi
Pematangsiantar
Seribudolok
Serdudolok
Kisaran
Tanjungbalai
SELANGOR
KUALA LUMPUR
Klang
Kajang
NEGERI SEMBILAN
Bahau
Seremban
Port Dickson
Tampin
Kuala Pilah
Gemas
Gunong Besar 1036
Segamat
Labis
MELAKA
JOHOR
Melaka
Muar
Keluang
Batu Pahat
Kulai
Kota Tinggi
Kuala Rompin
Padang Endau
Tanjong Resang
Mersing
Pulau Tioman
Pulau Aur
Pulau Tinggi
Pulau Sibu

Pulau Mubor
Terempa
Pulau Siantan
Padang
Pulau Jemaja
Letung
Kuala
KEPULAUAN ANAMBAS (ANAMBAS ISLANDS)
Pulau Airabu
Pulau Midai
Pulau Panjang
KEPULAUAN NATUNA SELATAN
Pulau Subi
Pulau Serasan

R I A U

Selat Serasan

Pulau Samosir
Prapat
Pangururan
Baiige
SUMATERA UTARA
Parsoburan
Tarutung
Bonandolok
Sibolga
Batangtoru
Gunungtua
Padangsidempuan
Dolok Sibalabu 7300
Rantauprapat
Bagansiapiapi
Bantaian
Labuhanbilik
Pulau Rupat
Batupanjang
Dumai
Guntung
Pulau Bengkalis
Bengkalis
Kudap
Merbau
Selatpanjang
Pulau Tebingtinggi
Sawang
Pulau Kundur
Tanjungbatu
SINGAPORE
SINGAPORE
Kukup
Johor Bahru
Tanjunguban
Pulau Batam
Tanjungpinang
Pulau Bintan
Pulau Rempang
KEPULAUAN RIAU

KEPULAUAN TAMBELAN
Pulau Uwi
Pulau Tambelan
Pulau Tambelan Besar
Singkawang
Pulau Benua
Pulau Lemukutan
Pulau Temaju
Mempawah
Sungaipenyu

Pontian
Sungaikakap

Singkuang
Siabu
Kotatengah
Pasirpengarayan
Minas
Bukitbatu
Pekanbaru
Tandun
Taratakbuluh
Mendung
Danai
Siak Sri Indrapura
Pelalawan
Sungaiguntung
Teluklanjut
Pulau Bakung
Pulau Basu
Kerandin
Pulau Lingga
Kotadabok
Pulau Singkep
Penuba
Cukas
KEPULAUAN LINGGA (LINGGA ISLANDS)
Pulau Pejantan
Pulau Pengiki

Natal
Airbangis
Equator
Ujunggading
Rau
Cubadak
Bangkinang
Lubuksikaping
Tiku
Bonjol
Sulki
Lipatkain
Langgam
Lubukbertubung
Simpang
R I A U
Ukui
Pematang
Muaralembu
Airmolek
Cerenti
Kualacenako
Pulaukijang
Seberida
Keritang
Kampungbaru
Muarasabak
Tanjung Jabung
Tanjung Jabung

Pulau Pini
Bukittinggi
Payakumbuh
Padangpanjang
Batusangkar
Sawahlunto
Sijunjung
Lubukambacang
Muarapantai
Pelabuhandagang
Muarasabak

Sungailimau
Pariaman
Solok
Padang
SUMATERA BARAT
Gunung Talang 2585
Alahanpanjang
Kotabaru
Rantaupanjang
Peninjau
Muaratebo
Muaratebesi
JAMBI
Jambi
Betung
Tempino
Bayunglencir
Muarakumpe

Sigep
PULAU SIBERUT
Telukbayur
Painan
Muaralabuh
Iliki
Gunung Kerinci 3800
Sarolangun
Mandiangin
Bayat
Siulakderas

Kambang
Balaiselasa
Airhaji
Rantaupanjang
Airdikit
Sungaipenuh
Bangko
Pamenang
Pauh
Siulakderas
Belinyu
Sungailiat
Baturusa
PULAU BANGKA
Kelapa
Jebus
PULAU BANGKA
Pangkalpinang

Pulau Sipura
Pasirganting
Tapan
Silaut
Merangin
Pulaukida
Rawas
Surulangun
Sekeladi
Penuguan
Sungsang
Muntok
Bakem
Sungaiselan
Koba
Airgegas
Toboali
Pulau Liat
Tanjungpandan
Manggar
Belitung
Gantung

MENTAWAI
KEPULAUAN MENTAWAI (MENTAWAI ISLANDS)
Matobe
Pulau Pagai Utara
Mukomuko
Airdikit
SUMATERA (SUMATRA)
Gunung Masurai 2933
Gresik
Karangagung
Sekayu
Bedinggong
Kepo
Pulau Mendanau
Dendang
Membalong

Pulau Pagai Bake
Pulau Pagai Selatan
Pasirbantal
Ipuh
Lebongtandai
Muaraaman
Airtenang
BENGKULU
Ketaun
Muarabeliti
Lubuklinggau
Tebingbulan
Muaralakitan
Muararupit
Talangbetutu
PALEMBANG
Sungairotan
Pendopo
Gunungmegang
Tulungselapan
Pulau Lepar

Lais
Muarabeliti
Kapahiang
Curup
Tebingtinggi
Perabumulih
Tanjungraja
Kayuagung
Talangrimbo
Tanjung Kait

Padangbetuan
Bengkulu
Ujung Teluk Punggur
Kepahiang
Bungamas
Lahat
Beringin
Pagardewa
Tanjung Lumut

Tais
Gunung Dempo 3159
Pagaralam
Lubukbatang
Baturaja
Talangbatu

Manna
Martapura
Pasarseluma
Muaradua
Negeribatin
Menggala
Bintuhan
Kotabumi
Tulangbawang

Barhau
Pulau Enggano
Kayaapu
Liwa
Belambanganumpu
Gedongdalem
Sukadana
LAMPUNG
Krui
Talangpadang
Tegineneng
Pringsewu
Panjang
Bandar Lampung
Kotaagung
Rajabasa

GREATER S

I N D

LAUT

Balimbing
Tampang
Tanjung Tua
Kalianda
Ketapang
Tanjung Cina
Pulau Rakata (Krakatau)
Anyer
Mauk
Tanjung Karawang
Sungaibuntu
Cilamaya

Serang
Rangkasbitung
Tangerang
JAKARTA
Karawang
Pamanukan
Indramayu
Labuhan
Depok
Cikampek
Pagadenghaur
Gunungkencana
Bogor
Purwakarta
Subang
Cirebon

Pulau Panaitan
Cibaliung
Cibinong
Gunung Halimun
Cianjur
Sumedang
Klangenan
UJUNGKULON NATIONAL PARK
Tanjung Cangkuang
Malimping
Muarabinuangeun
Cisolok
Cicurug
JAWA BARAT
Gunung Gede 2958
Klangenan
Tegal
Pekalongan
Pemalang

INDIAN OCEAN

Pelabuhanratu
Sukabumi
BANDUNG
Léles
Ciawi
Kuningan
Rancah
Bantarkawung
Balapulang

Jampang-kulon
Sukanegara
Ibun
Garut
Ciamis
Gunung Slamet 3428
Bobotsar

Ujunggenteng
Sagaranten
Taraju
Sidareja
Tasikmalaya
Karangnunggal
Pangandaran
Purwokerto
Kroa

Sindangbarang
Bungbulang
Cipatujah
Cijulang
Cilacap

JAWA (JAVA)

Meters / Feet
3000 / 9840
2000 / 6560
1000 / 3280
500 / 1640
200 / 656
Sea Level
200 / 656
2000 / 6560

2939
6328
6650
28
48

0   50   100   150   200   300   400   500 Kilometers
0   50   100   200   300 Miles
Scale 1 : 5,000,000   Sinusoidal Projection

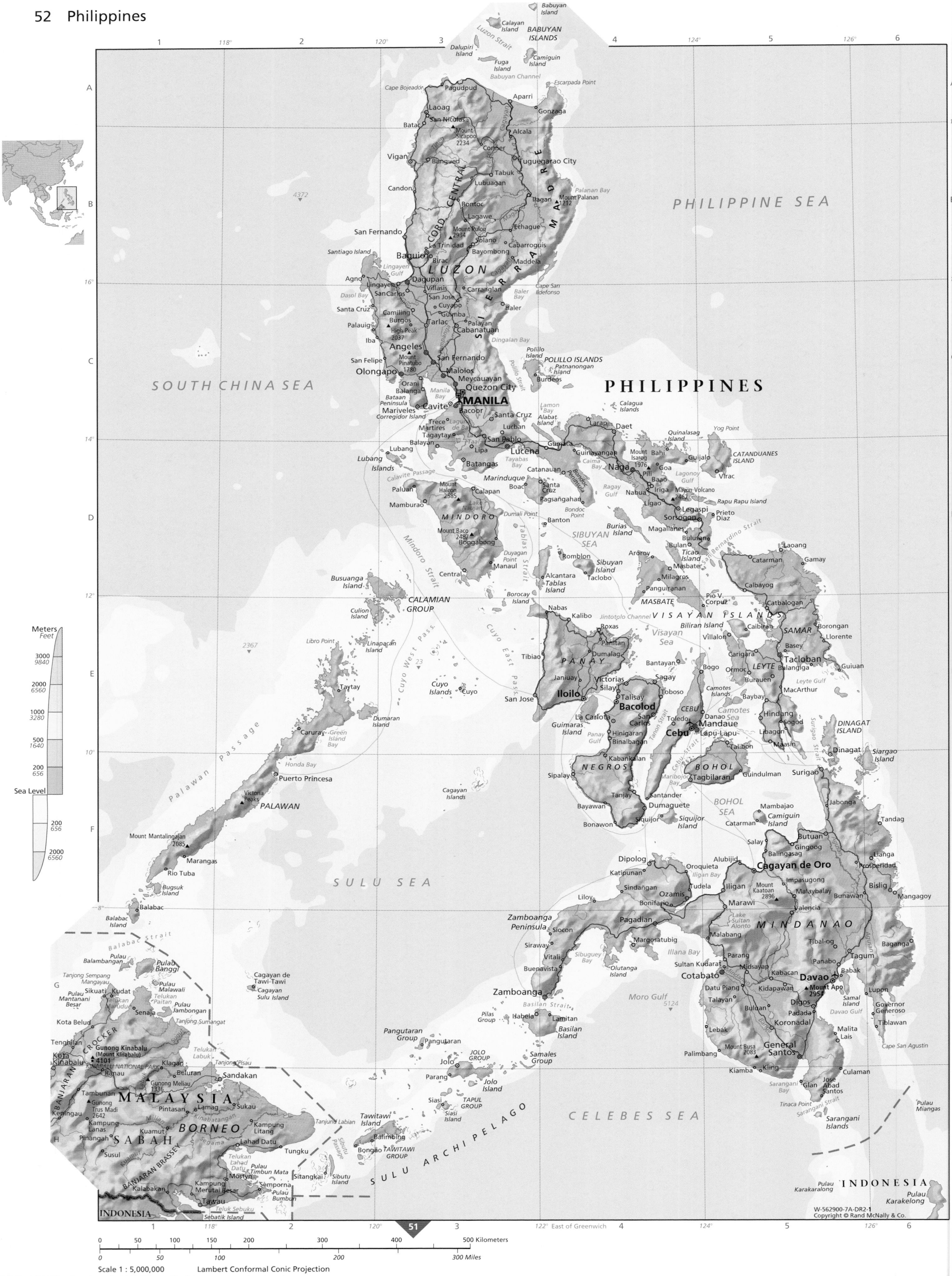

PHILIPPINES

PHILIPPINE SEA

SOUTH CHINA SEA

SULU SEA

CELEBES SEA

BABUYAN ISLANDS

LUZON

CORD. CENTRAL

SIERRA MADRE

MINDORO

CALAMIAN GROUP

PANAY

NEGROS

CEBU

BOHOL

LEYTE

SAMAR

MASBATE

VISAYAN ISLANDS

VISAYAN SEA

SIBUYAN SEA

CAMOTES SEA

BOHOL SEA

PALAWAN

MINDANAO

Zamboanga Peninsula

SULU ARCHIPELAGO

BORNEO

SABAH

MALAYSIA

INDONESIA

Moro Gulf

Davao Gulf

Babuyan Island
Calayan Island
Dalupiri Island
Fuga Island
Camiguin Island
Babuyan Channel
Luzon Strait
Escarpada Point
Cape Bojeador
Pagudpud
Laoag
Batac
San Nicolas
Aparri
Gonzaga
Alcala
Vigan
Bangued
Tuguegarao City
Candon
Tabuk
Cordon
Bontoc
Lagawe
Ilagan
Echague
Palanan Bay
Mount Palanan 1212
San Fernando
Mount Pulog 2934
La Trinidad
Solano
Bayombong
Cabarroguis
Maddela
Baguio
Birac
Santiago Island
Lingayen Gulf
Agno
Dagupan
Villasis
Carranglan
Baler Bay
Cape San Ildefonso
Lingayen
San Carlos
San Jose
Cuyapo
Baler
Santa Cruz
Dasol Bay
Camiling
Gumba
Palauig
Burgos High Peak 2037
Tarlac
Cabanatuan
Palayan
Dingalan Bay
Iba
Angeles
San Fernando
San Felipe
Mount Pinatubo 1780
Olongapo
Malolos
Meycauayan
Burdeos
POLILLO ISLANDS
Polillo
Patnanongan Island
Orani
Balanga
Quezon City
Bataan Peninsula
Mariveles
Cavite
MANILA
Bacoor
Santa Cruz
Lucban
Calagua Islands
Corregidor Island
Trece Martires
Tagaytay
Laguna de Bay
Lubang
Laguna
Larap
Daet
Lubang Islands
Lipa
San Pablo
Gumaca
Quinalasag Island
Yog Point
Batangas
Lucena
Guinayangan
Mount Isarog 1976
Bato
Naga
Goa
Guijalo
CATANDUANES ISLAND
Calavite Passage
Paluan
Marinduque
Catanauan
Pili
Iriga
Virac
Mount Halcon 2585
Calapan
Boac
Santa Cruz
Nahua
Mayon Volcano 2462
Rapu Rapu Island
Mamburao
Pagsañahan
Bondoc Point
Ligao
Legaspi
Prieto Diaz
Mount Baco 2488
Boggabong
Banton
Sorsogon
Bulusan
Central
Manaul
Romblon
Alcantara Tablas Island
Sibuyan Island
Taclobo
Magallanes
Ticao Island
Catarman
Laoang
Gamay
Duyagan Point
Tablas Strait
Borocay Island
Nabas
Panguiranan
Milagros
Pio V Corpuz
Calbayog
Catbalogan
Busuanga Island
Kalibo
Masbate
Aroroy
Catarman
Culion Island
Roxas
Bantayan
Borongan
Linapacan Island
Jintotolo Channel
Biliran Island
Caibiran
Libro Point
Tibiao
Pandan
Dumalag
Villalon
Carigara
Basey
Llorente
Cagayan Islands
Taytay
Janiuay
Victorias
Sagay
Bogo
Ormoc
Tacloban
Guiuan
Cuyo West Pass
Cuyo Islands
Cuyo
Silay
Toboso
Camotes Islands
Burauen
Belangiga
Cuyo East Pass
San Jose
Iloilo
Talisay
Danao
MacArthur
Dumaran Island
Green Island Bay
Caruray
La Carlota
San Carlos
Toledo
Mandaue
Hindang
Leyte Gulf
Guimaras Island
Panay Gulf
Hinigaran
Cebu
Lapu-Lapu
Inopacan
Honda Bay
Bacolod
Binalbagan
Lapu-Lapu
Maasin
Puerto Princesa
Kabankalan
Talibon
Dinagat
Siargao Island
DINAGAT ISLAND
Victoria Peaks
Sipalay
Tagbilaran
Guindulman
Surigao
Bayawan
Tanjay
Santander
Mambajao
Jabonga
Mount Mantalingajan 2085
Bonawon
Dumaguete
Squijor
Siquijor Island
Camiguin Island
Marangas
Catarman
Salay
Butuan
Tandag
Rio Tuba
Dipolog
Oroquieta
Gingoog
Bugsuk Island
Katipunan
Alubijid
Balingasag
Balabac
Iligan Bay
Cagayan de Oro
Ilianga
Balabac Island
Sindangan
Ozamis
Iligan
Impasugong
Prosperidad
Balabac Strait
Siocon
Tudela
Mount Kaatoan 2896
Bislig
Pulau Banggi
Balambangan
Zamboanga Peninsula
Malabang
Malaybalay
Bunawan
Pulau Malawali
Margosatubig
Marawi
Valencia
Mangagoy
Tanjong Sempang Mangayau
Siraway
Lake Sultan Alonto
Balambangan
Telukan Paitan
Vitali
Siocon
MINDANAO
Sikuati Kudat
Pulau Jambongan
Sibuguey Bay
Pagadian
Tibal-og
Baganga
Kudat
Tanjong Sumangat
Buenavista
Parang
Babak
Kota Belud
Cagayan de Tawi-Tawi
Olutanga Island
Sultan Kudarat
Midsayap
Panabo
Tagum
Pulau Banggi
Cagayan Sulu Island
Illana Bay
Kabacan
Tenghilan
Cotabato
Digos
Lupon
Gunong Kinabalu (Mount Kinabalu) 4101
Telukan Labuk
Tanjong Pisau
Talayan
Datu Piang
Kidapawan
Davao
Mount Apo 2954
Samal Island
Governor Generoso
Klagan
Zamboanga
Buluan
Ranau
Gunong Meliau 1336
Beluran
Lebak
Koronadal
Padada
Malita
Davao Gulf
Kota Kinabalu
Pilas Group
Isabela
Mount Busa 2083
Lais
Kampung Litang
Sandakan
JOLO GROUP
Samales Group
Palimbang
General Santos
Cape San Agustin
Tambunan
Pintasan
Lamag
Sukau
Siasi
Kiamba
Culaman
Kampung Nuluh
Glan
Jose Abad Santos
Gunong Trus Madi 2642
Parang
TAPUL GROUP
Jolo Island
Sarangani Bay
Kampung Kuamut
Kuamut
Jolo
Tinaca Point
Sarangani Islands
Kampung Gana
Lahad Datu
Siasi Island
Sarangani Strait
Kuala Penyu
Kuamut
TAWITAWI GROUP
Pinangah
Susul
Pulau Timbun Mata
Tawitawi Island
Pulau Miangas
Kalabakan
Tawau
Bongao
Sibutu Passage
CROCKER RANGE NATIONAL PARK
Mostyn
Balimbing
Kampung Merutai Besar
Sitangkai
Pulau Karakaralong
Sibutu Island
INDONESIA
Pulau Karakelong
Sebatik Island
Teluk Sebuku

Manila Bay
Lamon Bay
Alabat Island
Tayabas Bay
Ragay Gulf
Lagonoy Gulf
Bernardino Strait
Surigao Strait
Mindoro Strait
Palawan Passage
Bernardino Strait

Meters / Feet
3000 / 9840
2000 / 6560
1000 / 3280
500 / 1640
200 / 656
Sea Level
200 / 656
2000 / 6560

0 50 100 150 200 300 400 500 Kilometers
0 50 100 200 300 Miles
Scale 1 : 5,000,000
Lambert Conformal Conic Projection

W-562900-7A-DR2-1
Copyright © Rand McNally & Co.

118° 120° 122° East of Greenwich 124° 126°

Meters
Feet

6000
19680

4000
13120

3000
9840

2000
6560

1000
3280

500
1640

200
656

Sea Level

200
656

2000
6560

0   50   100   150   200   300   400   500 Kilometers

0   50   100   200   300 Miles

Scale 1 : 5,000,000   Lambert Conformal Conic Projection

Ⓐ Area occupied by Pakistan and claimed by India.
Ⓑ Area claimed and occupied by India; status disputed by Pakistan.
Ⓒ Area occupied by China and claimed by India.
Ⓓ Area occupied by India and claimed by China.

W-DRM5515-A1 ·2-2-4
Copyright © Rand McNally & Co.

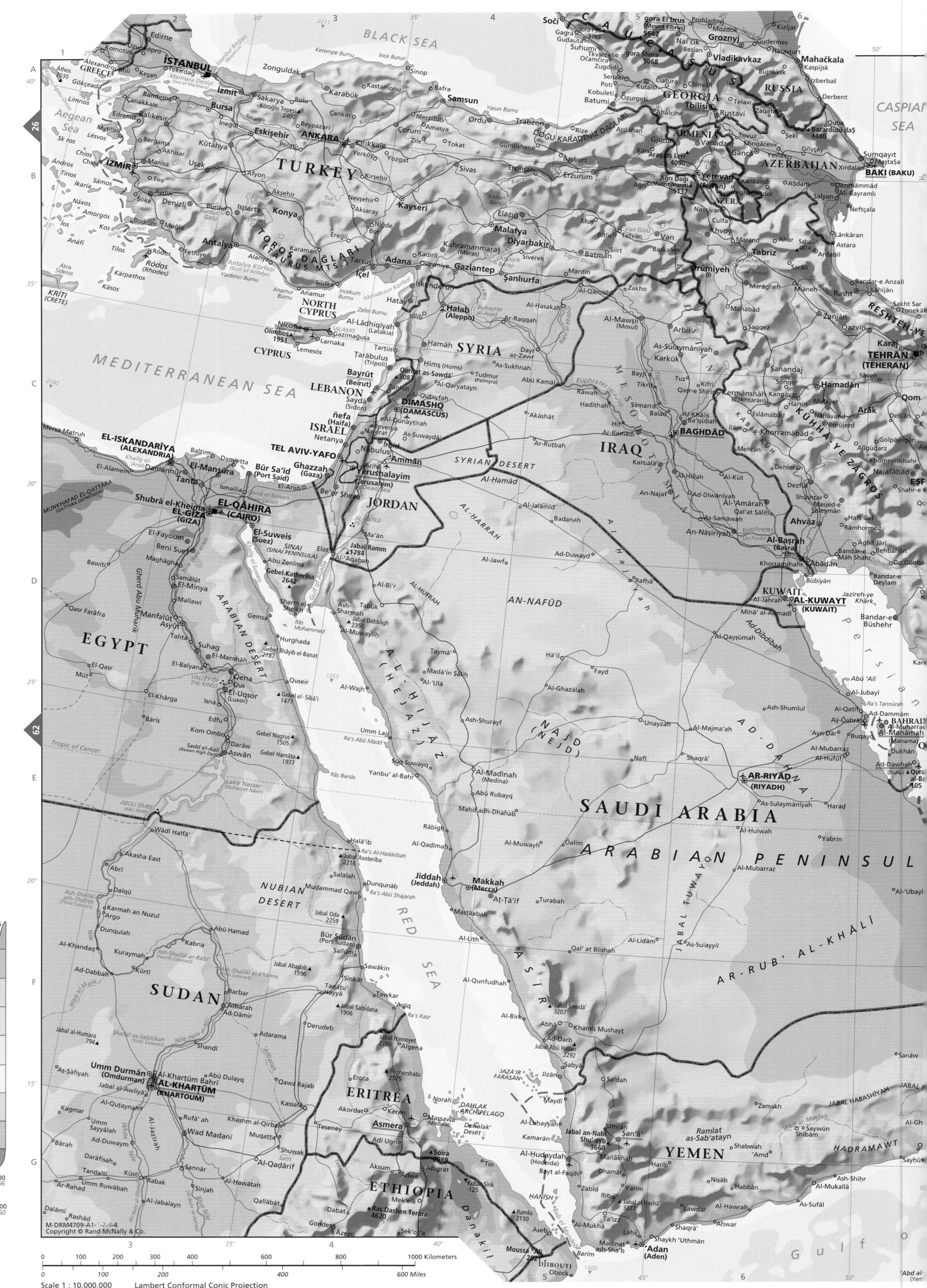

Meters
Feet

6000
19680

4000
13120

3000
9840

2000
6560

1000
3280

500
1640

200
656

Sea Level

200
656

2000
6560

M-DRM4709-A1-1-2-4-4
Copyright © Rand McNally & Co.

| 0 | 100 | 200 | 300 | 400 | 600 | 800 | 1000 Kilometers |

| 0 | 100 | 200 | 400 | 600 Miles |

Scale 1 : 10,000,000   Lambert Conformal Conic Projection

The boundary between India and Pakistan through the disputed
state of Jammu and Kashmir follows the "line of control"
agreed upon by both countries in 1972.

Ⓐ Area occupied by Pakistan and claimed by India.

Ⓑ Area claimed and occupied by India; status disputed by Pakistan.

Ⓒ Area occupied by China and claimed by India.

MEDITERRANEAN SEA

SYRIA

HIMS

HAMAH

HALAB

AR-RAQQAH

IRAQ

AL-ANBAR

SYRIAN DESERT
(BADIYAT ASH-SHAM)

DIMASHQ

LEBANON

NORTH CYPRUS

CYPRUS

TURKEY

KONYA

ADANA

ICEL

TOROS DAGLARI (TAURUS MOUNTAINS)

ANTALYA

ISPARTA

BURDUR

NIGDE

KARAMAN

GAZIANTEP

KAHRAMAN MARAS

SANLIURFA

ADIYAMAN

HATAY

SpanLiurfa (Urfa)

Gaziantep

Halab (Aleppo)

Hamah

Hims (Homs)

DIMASHQ (DAMASCUS)

Bayrūt (Beirut)

Tarābulus (Tripoli)

Al-Lādhiqīyah (Latakia)

Tartūs

Iskenderun (Alexandretta)

Adana

İçel (Mersin)

Antalya

Ⓐ Golan Heights. Occupied and unilaterally
annexed by Israel.

Ⓑ West Bank. Controlled by Israel, parts
administered by the Palestinian Authority.
Permanent status to be determined.

Ⓒ Gaza Strip. Administered by the Palestinian Authority
following unilateral withdrawal by Israel in 2005.
Permanent status to be determined.

In November 1983, Turkish Cypriots unilaterally
declared their independence as the Turkish
Republic of Northern Cyprus. A United Nations
buffer zone runs across the island.

SAUDI ARABIA

JORDAN

AMMĀN

AZ-ZARQĀ

MA'ĀN

EGYPT

SINAI
(SINAI PENINSULA)

ISRAEL

HA NEGEV
(NEGEV DESERT)

HA'ARAVA

GAZA STRIP

TEL AVIV-YAFO

Ghazzah (Gaza)

Rishon LeZiyyon
Yerushalayim (Jerusalem)
Reḥovot
Ashdod
Ashqelon

GEBEL EL TIH

GEBEL EL GILAL

AL-HIJAZ
(HEJAZ)

MIDYAN

RED SEA

Gulf of Aqaba

ARABIAN DESERT
(EASTERN DESERT)

Khalig el-Suweis
(Gulf of Suez)

EL-QAHIRA
(CAIRO)

EL-GĪZA (GIZA)

NILE DELTA

EL-SA'ĪD
(UPPER EGYPT)

Bûr Sa'îd
(Port Said)

El-Suweis
(Suez)

Ismailia

Gebel Katherîna
2642

Tabūk

Al-'Aqaba

Al-KARAK

AMMĀN
Ammān

Hurghada

Sharm el-Sheikh

Nakhl

El-Arîsh

El-Tûr

Beni Suef

El-Minya

Asyût

Scale 1 : 2,500,000

Lambert Conformal Conic Projection

Meters / Feet
3000 / 9840
2000 / 6560
1000 / 3280
500 / 1640
200 / 656
Sea Level

250 Kilometers
150 Miles

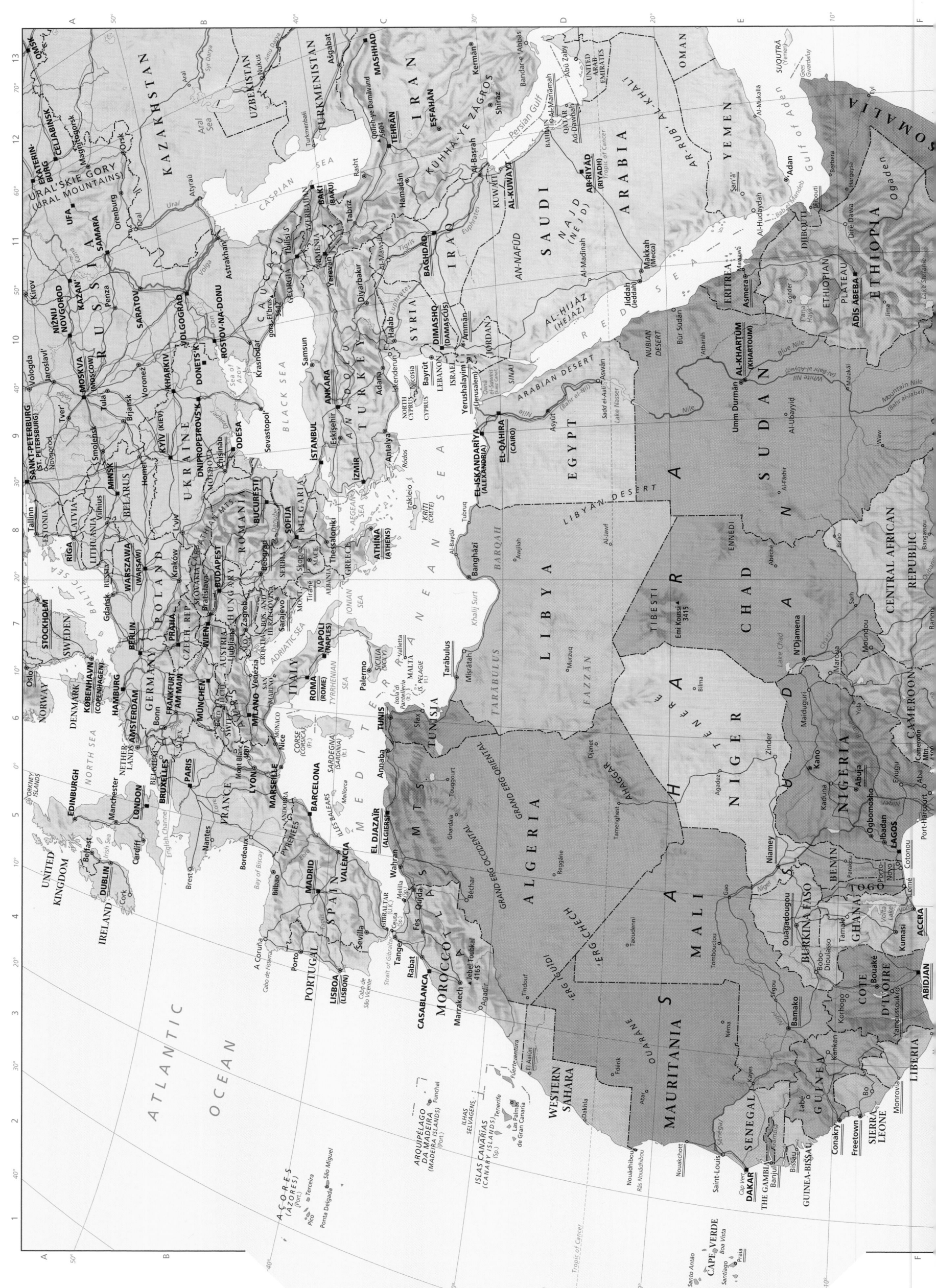

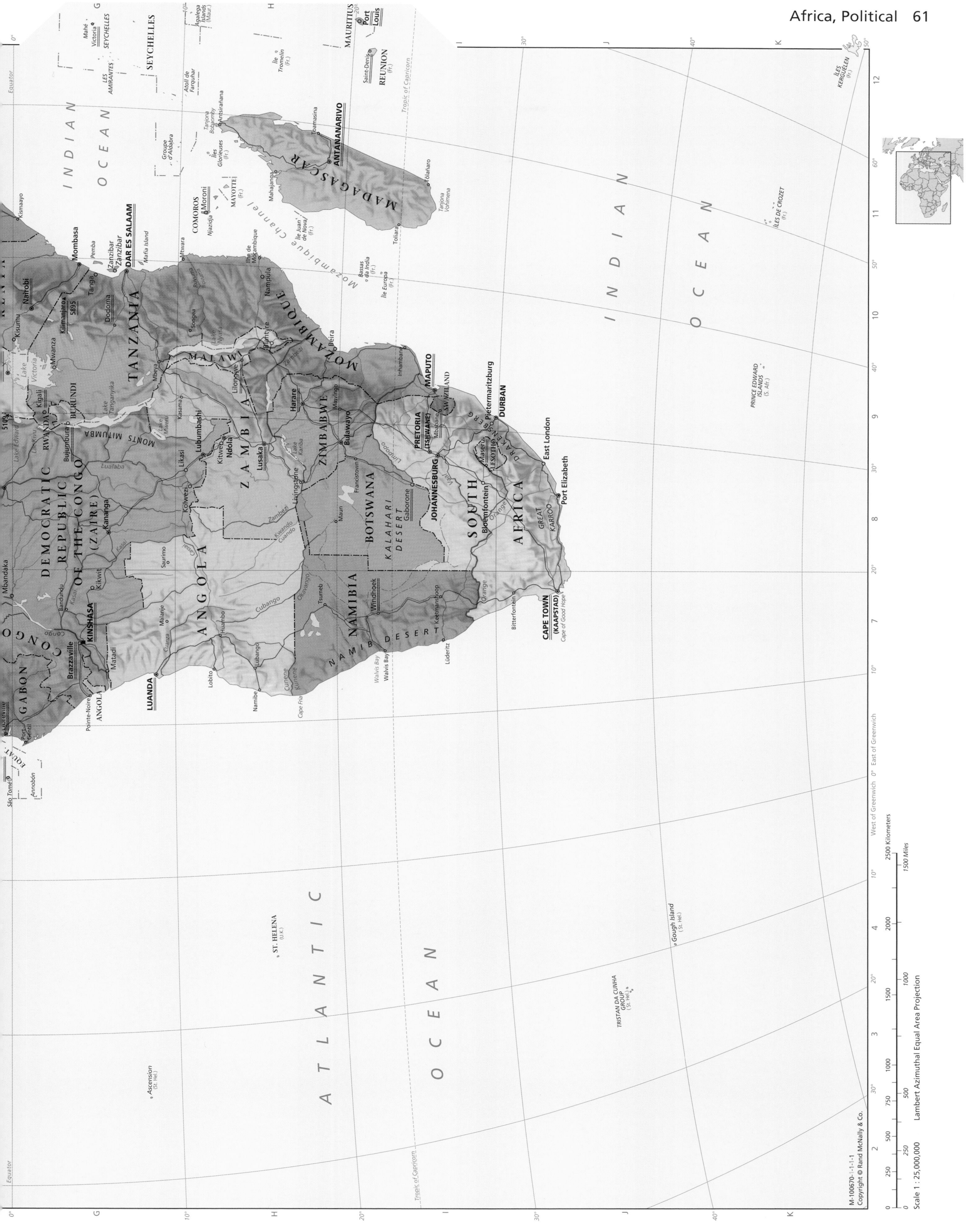

INDIAN OCEAN

Equator

SEYCHELLES

Mahé
Victoria
LES AMIRANTES

Agalega Islands (Maur.)

MAURITIUS
Port Louis

REUNION (Fr.)
Saint-Denis

Île Tromelin (Fr.)

Atoll de Farquhar

Tropic of Capricorn

ÎLES KERGUÉLEN (Fr.)

Groupe d'Aldabra

Îles Glorieuses (Fr.)

Antsiranana

Tanjona Bobaomby

MADAGASCAR

Toamasina

ANTANANARIVO

Mahajanga

COMOROS
Moroni
Njazidja

MAYOTTE (Fr.)

Île Juan de Nova (Fr.)

Bassas da India (Fr.)

Île Europa (Fr.)

Toliara

Tanjona Vohimena

ILES DE CROZET (Fr.)

Kismaayo

Mombasa

Pemba
Zanzibar
Zanzibar

DAR ES SALAAM

Mafia Island

KENYA

Nairobi
Kisumu
Mwanza

Kilimanjaro 5895

Lake Victoria

Dodoma

TANZANIA

Tanga

MOZAMBIQUE

PRINCE EDWARD ISLANDS (S. Afr.)

INDIAN OCEAN

Songea

Mtwara

Nampula

Mbeya

MALAWI

Lilongwe

Mozambique Channel

Ilha de Moçambique

Nacala

RWANDA
Kigali
BURUNDI
Bujumbura

Lake Kivu

5110

Lake Tanganyika

Lake Malawi

Lake Edward

MONTS MITUMBA

Kananga

Kikwit

Bandundu

DEMOCRATIC REPUBLIC OF THE CONGO (ZAIRE)

Lualaba

Lubumbashi
Likasi
Kolwezi
Kitwe
Ndola

ZAMBIA

Lusaka

Kasama

Lake Kariba

Harare

Beira

Inhambane

ZIMBABWE

Bulawayo

Francistown

MAPUTO

SWAZILAND
Mbabane

Pietermaritzburg

DURBAN

CONGO

KINSHASA

Brazzaville

Matadi

GABON

Libreville

Port-Gentil

Pointe-Noire

ANGOLA

Saurimo

Malanje

ANGOLA

LUANDA

Lobito

Namibe

Cape Frio

Huambo

Cubango

Cunene

Lubango

Menongue

Okavango

Cuando

Maun

BOTSWANA

KALAHARI DESERT

Gaborone

Livingstone

SOUTH

Johannesburg

PRETORIA (TSHWANE)

Maseru
LESOTHO

DRAKENSBERG

Bloemfontein

Orange

East London

Port Elizabeth

AFRICA

GREAT KARROO

CAPE TOWN (KAAPSTAD)
Cape of Good Hope

Bitterfontein

Keetmanshoop

Windhoek

NAMIBIA

NAMIB DESERT

Walvis Bay

Lüderitz

Tropic of Capricorn

ATLANTIC OCEAN

ST. HELENA (U.K.)

Ascension (St. Hel.)

Gough Island (St. Hel.)

TRISTAN DA CUNHA GROUP (St. Hel.)

São Tomé

Annobón

EQUAT.

Equator

West of Greenwich 0° East of Greenwich

2500 Kilometers
1500 Miles

2000

1500

1000

750

500

250

0

Scale 1 : 25,000,000

Lambert Azimuthal Equal Area Projection

M-100670--1-1-1
Copyright © Rand McNally & Co.

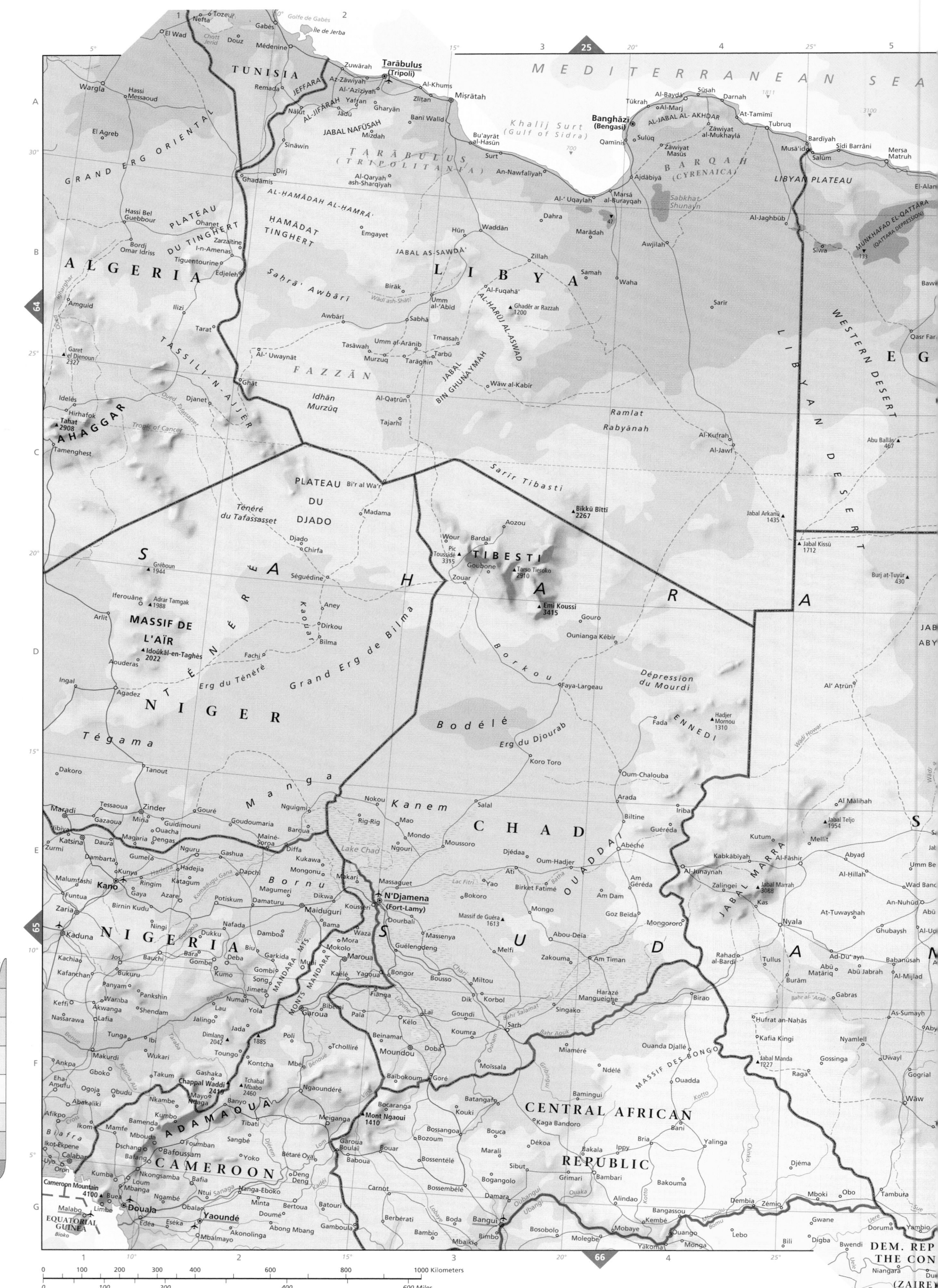

Meters
Feet

4000
13120

3000
9840

2000
6560

1000
3280

500
1640

200
656

Sea Level

200
656

2000
6560

0   100   200   300   400   500   600   700   800   900   1000 Kilometers

0   100   200   300   400   500   600 Miles

Scale 1 : 10,000,000   Lambert Conformal Conic Projection

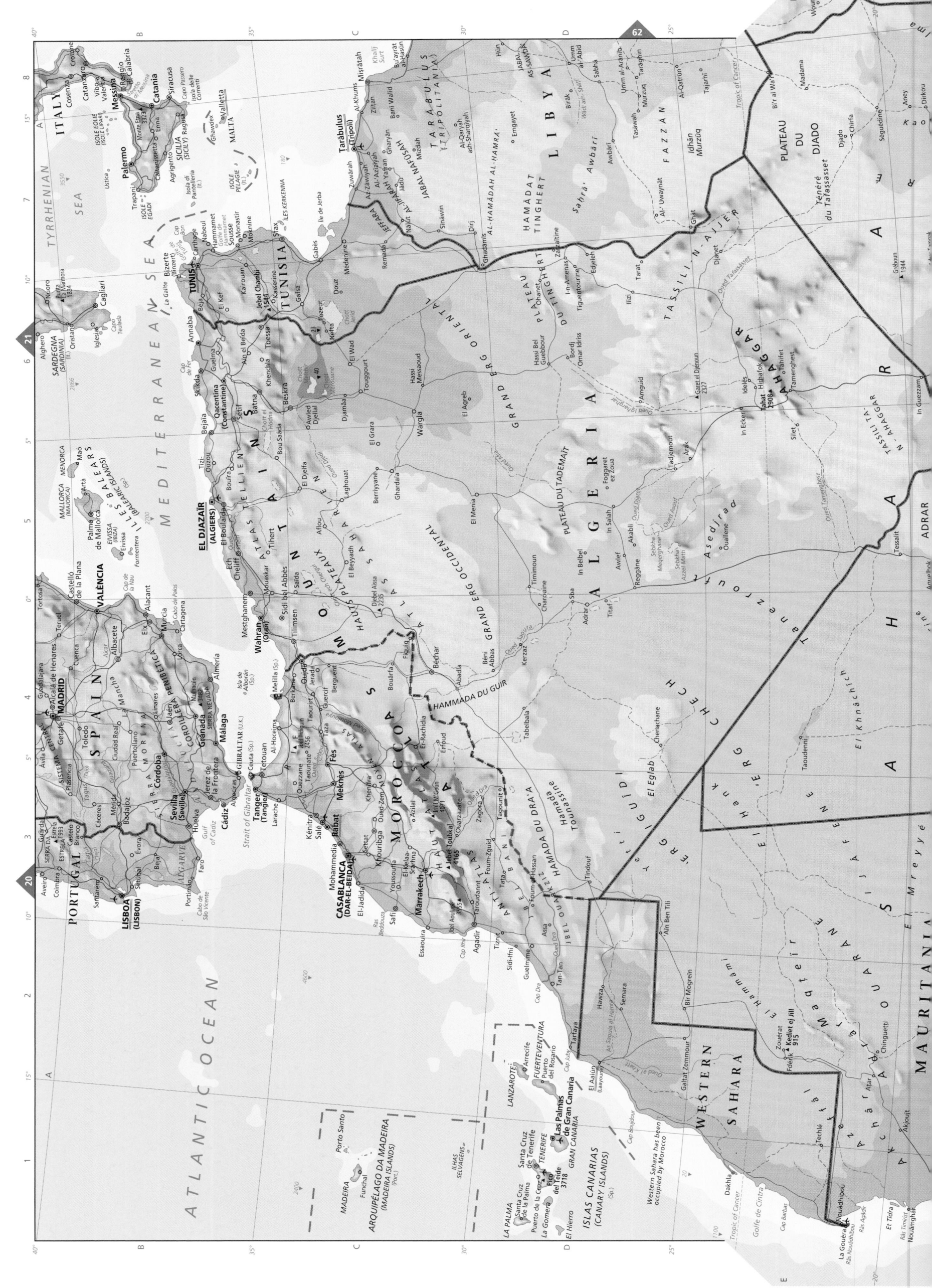

Countries

CHAD · NIGER · NIGERIA · MALI · BURKINA FASO · BENIN · TOGO · GHANA · COTE D'IVOIRE · LIBERIA · SIERRA LEONE · GUINEA · GUINEA-BISSAU · THE GAMBIA · SENEGAL · CAMEROON · ADAMAOUA · EQUATORIAL GUINEA · SAO TOME AND PRINCIPE · GABON · CONGO · CAPE VERDE

Capitals and Major Cities

N'Djamena · Niamey · Abuja · Lagos · Porto-Novo · Cotonou · Lomé · ACCRA · ABIDJAN · Yamoussoukro · Monrovia · Freetown · Conakry · Bissau · Banjul (Bathurst) · DAKAR · Bamako · Ouagadougou · Yaoundé · Douala · Malabo · Libreville · SÃO TOMÉ · PRAIA · SANTIAGO

Water Bodies and Physical Features

Lake Chad · Niger (river) · Lake Volta · White Volta · Black Volta · Benue · Gulf of Guinea · Bight of Benin · Bight of Biafra · Niger Delta · ATLANTIC OCEAN · Slave Coast · Gold Coast · Ivory Coast · Grain Coast · Cape Palmas · Cape Three Points · Cape Coast

Elevations

Hombori Tondo 1155 · Cameroon Mtn. 4100 · Pico de Santa Isabel 3008 · Pico de São Tomé 2024 · Chappal Waddi 2419 · Mount Nimba 1752 · Bintimani 1945 · Pico 2829 · Mont Pelé 872

Mountains / Regions

MONTS MANDARA · ADAMAOUA · BORNU · TÉGAMA · Erg du Ténéré · MONTS DE CRISTAL · FOUTA DJALON · EL 'AÇÂBA · HÔDH · MASSINA

Islands

BIOKO · Isla de Corisco · Annobón (Eq. Guinea) · Principe · São Tomé · SANTO ANTÃO · SÃO NICOLAU · SAL · Boa Vista · Maio · SANTIAGO · Fogo · Brava · ARQUIPÉLAGO DOS BIJAGÓS

Scale Information

Scale 1:10,000,000
Lambert Conformal Conic Projection

Meters / Feet:
4000 / 13120
3000 / 9840
2000 / 6560
1000 / 3280
500 / 1640
200 / 656
Sea Level
200 / 656
2000 / 6560

1000 Kilometers · 600 Miles

Meters
Feet

4000
13120

3000
9840

2000
6560

1000
3280

500
1640

200
656

Sea Level

200
656

2000
6560

M-DRM4712-A1-2-3-3-3
Copyright © Rand McNally & Co.

0   100   200   300   400   600   800   1000 Kilometers

0   100   200   400   600 Miles

Scale 1 : 10,000,000   Sinusoidal Projection

CONGO
Boko
Kasangulu
Kenge
Kandale
Kabinda

A
Pointe-Noire
Buco Zau
Tshela
Lukula
Luozi
Mbanza-Ngungu
Popokabaka
Feshi
Tshikapa
Dibaya
Mbuji-Mayi
(Bakwanga)
Gandajika
Ankoro
Sange

Lândana
Madimba
Kwango
Lóvua
Chitato
Cambulo
Luiza
Kaniama
Kabongo
Muyumba
Kiambi

Cabinda
Muanda
Boma
Matadi
M'banza
Congo
Maquela do Zombo
Cuango
Kasongo-Lunda
Kiamba
Camissombo
Luputa
Kabinda
Manono
Mulongo

ANGOLA
Nóqui
Songololo
Ngidinga
Kiama
Kahemba
Camaxilo
Caungula
Sombo
Kapanga
Kamina

Soyo
Nzeto
Quimaria
Damba
Kasongo-Lunda
Saurimo
Chiluage
Sandoa
Malonga
Kasaji
Mwenelunga

N'zeto
Nova Caipemba
Uige
Negage
Marimba
Luremo
Camaxilo
Muriege
Dilolo
Mutshatsha
Kolwezi
Likasi
(Jadotville)
Luishia
Sapwe
Kasenga
Kaw

Ambriz
Muxaluando
Quibaxe
Camabatela
Cuango
Cuango
Lubalo
Luau
Muconda
Cazombo
Kamwezi

DEMOCRATIC
REPUBLIC
OF THE CONGO
(ZAIRE)
Bukama
Luena
Lubudi
Samwe
Lac
Upemba

LUANDA
Ponta das Palmeirinhas
Barra do Cuanza
Catete
N'dalatando
Cacuaco
Malanje
Xá-Muteba
Mona Quimbundo
Chiluage
Solwezi
Chililabombwe
Mufulira
Lubumbashi
(Élisabethville)

Muxima
Dondo
Calulo
Cuanza
Cacuso
Cangandala
Cacolo
Cacolo
Mwinilunga
Kipushi
Chingola
Kitwe

Mussende
Capunda Cabilongo
Alto Chicapa
Cucumbi
Kabcompo
Kasempa
Kapiri Mposhi
Luanshya
Ndola

Porto Amboim
Gabela
Quibala
Waku Kungo
Andulo
Sautar
Muie
Cazombo
Zambezi
Chitokoloki
Kaoma
Kabwe
Old

Sumbe
Conda
Mungo
Camacupa
Cuemba
Munhango
Lutembo
Mussuma
Lukulu
ZAMBIA
Chisamba

Lobito
Balombo
Morro de Moco
2620
Kuito
Umpulo
Cangumbe
Luena
Lucusse
Lumbala
N'guimbo
Mongu
Mumbwa
Lusaka

Baía Farta
Benguela
Caála
Huambo
Chitembo
Luena
Lumbala
Kaquengue
Macondo
Senanga
Namwala
Mazabuka
Monze

Cubal
Ganda
Caconda
Cachingues
Longa
Cuito-Cuanavale
Chiume
Kalabo
Kataba
Pemba
Mulobezi
Kafue

Cabo de
Santa Maria
Chongoroi
Chicuma
Kuvango
Dongo
Menongue
Lupire
Mavinga
Neriquinha
Luiana
Zimba
Choma
Kalomo
Lake Kariba

Cabo de
Santa Marta
Lucira
Quilengues
Cacula
Matala
Capelongo
Cassinga
Caiundo
Senanga
Mulobezi
Livingstone
Victoria
Gwembe
Gwe

Bibala
Lubango
Chibia
Cahama
Humbe
Xangongo
Ondjiva
Cuangar
Caprivi
Strip
Singalamwe
Kasane
Victoria
Falls
Dete
Zi

Namibe
Chiange
Chibemba
Cunene
Dirico
Singalamwe
Hwange

Serra da Chela
Chitado
Oncócua
Ruacana Falls
Okavango
Rundu
Shakawe
Okavango
Delta
Gcoverega
Nyamandhlovu
Inyathi
Bulaw

Ponta Albina
Tombua
Iona
Cunene
Ondangwa
Tsumkwe
Nokaneng
Maun
Nata
Maitembge
Figtree
Plumtree
Kezi

Ponta de Marca
Foz do Cunene
OVAMBOLAND
Tsintsabis
Namutoni
Tsumeb
Tsumkwe
Nokaneng
Tsau
Lake
Ngami
Toteng
Makgadikgadi
Rakops
Gweta
Nata
Francistown
Old Tati
West Nichol

Cape Fria
KAOKO-VELD
Okaukuejo
Etosha Pan
Otavi
Grootfontein
KAUKAU
VELD
Maun
Botleti
Mmadinare
Shash

480
Sesfontein
Kamanjab
Outjo
Otjikondo
Otjiwarongo
Sukses
Otjinene
Epukiro
Rietfontein
Ghanzi
Tshootsha
Serowe
Selebi-
Phikwe
Bobonong

NAMIB
VELD
Brandberg
2579
Uis
Omaruru
Otjihavare
1289
Hochfeld
Epukiro
Okwa
Tswaane
Shoshong
Mahalapye
Palapye

Palgrave Point
Okombahe
Usakos
Omaruru
Karibib
Okahandja
Witvlei
Gobabis
Kule
BOTSWANA
Lephephe
Dinokwe
Baltimore

3700
Cape Cross
DAMARALAND
Windhoek
Gobabis
Ghanzi
Kang
KALAHARI
Mmathethe
Gaborone
Pietersburg
Potgietersrus

Swakopmund
Walvis Bay
Walvis Bay
Rehoboth
Olifants
Aminuis
Lehututu
Letlhakeng
Molepolole
Mochudi
Thabazimbi
Nylstroom

NAMIBIA
Kalkrand
Stampriet
Aranos
Tshane
Kokong
DESERT
Lobatse
Zeerust
Rustenburg
Warmbad
Ma

Conception Bay
Maltahöhe
Mariental
Gochas
Khakhea
Werda
Kanye
Mmabatho
Krugersdorp
PRETORIA
(TSHWANE)

Tropic of Capricorn
GREAT NAMAQUALAND
Gibeon
Tses
Koës
Tshabong
Molopo
Mafikeng
Lichtenburg
JOHANNESBURG
Benoni
Springs

365
Helmeringhausen
Bethanien
Keetmanshoop
Aroab
Askham
Kuruman
Vryburg
Klerksdorp
Vereenigi

Lüderitz
Aus
GROOT KARASBERG
Hotazel
Sishen
Olifantshoek
Wolmaransstad
Orkney
Parys
Heilbron

Hunsberg
1654
Karasburg
Upington
Postmasburg
Barkly West
Bloemhof
Welkom
Virginia
Senekal

Sendelingsdrif
Grünau
Warmbad
Augrabies
Falls
Kakamas
Kenhardt
Kuruman
Douglas
Kimberley
Koffiefontein
Bultfontein
Winburg
Ficksburg
Phofung
3299

Oranjemund
Alexander Bay
Orange
Onseepkans
Pofadder
Marydale
Prieska
Hopetown
Bloemfontein
Ladybrand
Maseru

LITTLE
NAMAQUALAND
Steinkopf
SOUTH AFRICA
Britstown
De Aar
Colesberg
Noupoort
Jagersfontein
Edenburg
LESOTHO
Mafeteng

Port Nolloth
Springbok
BUSHMAN
LAND
Kamieskroon
Brandvlei
Vanwyksvlei
Carnarvon
Hanover
Richmond
Middelburg
Steynsburg
Burgersdorp
Barkly
East
Maclear

ATLANTIC OCEAN
Gaties
Loeriesfontein
Nieuwoudtville
Williston
Loxton
Graaff-Reinet
Cradock
Tarkastad
Queenstown
Elliot
Dutywa

Hondeklipbaai
Bitterfontein
Calvinia
Fraserburg
Beaufort West
Aberdeen
Somerset East
Adelaide
Winterberg
2371
Bisho
East London
(Oos-Londen)
Butterwo

Vanrhynsdorp
Klawer
Clanwilliam
Sutherland
GREAT KARROO
Prince
Albert
Willowmore
Kirkwood
King
William's Town
Grahamstown
Port Alfred

Lambert's Bay
Citrusdal
Laingsburg
Oudtshoorn
Uniondale
Uitenhage
Algoabaai
Port Elizabeth

Sint Helenabaai
Cape Columbine
Piketberg
Tulbagh
LITTLE KARROO
George
Knysna
Humansdorp

Saldanha
Moorreesburg
Malmesbury
Paarl
Worcester
Swellendam
Riversdale
Mosselbaai
Cape
St. Francis

CAPE TOWN
(KAAPSTAD)
Stellenbosch
Strand
Bredasdorp
Kaap Agulhas

Simon's Town
Cape of Good Hope
Hermanus
False Bay

4080
150
4471

M-DRM4715-A1- - -2
Copyright © Rand McNally & Co.

0   100   200   300   400   600   800   1000 Kilometers
0   100   200   400   600 Miles

Scale 1 : 10,000,000   Lambert Conformal Conic Projection

INDIAN OCEAN

SEYCHELLES

Groupe d'Aldabra
Assomption
Atoll de Cosmoledo
Astove 4030
St. Pierre
Atoll de Providence
Atoll de Farquhar

COMOROS
Njazidja
Moroni ▲ Kartala 2361
Nzwani
Mwali
Fomboni
Mutsamudu
Dzaoudzi
MAYOTTE (Fr.)

ARCHIPEL DES COMORES

Îles Glorieuses (Fr.)

TANZANIA
Uruwira
Inyonga
Kitunda
Rungwa
Dodoma
Mpwapwa
Zanzibar
Kizimkazi
Zanzibar
arema
Kipili
Kilunda
Kipembawe
Kilosa
Morogoro
Bagamoyo
DAR ES SALAAM
ake Tanganyika
Namanyere
Rungwe
Njombe
Great Ruaha
Mikumi
anda
Sumbawanga
Usangu Flats
Iringa
Kidatu
Kisiju
Mafia Island
Kipili
Mpui
Makongolosi
Sao Hill
Ifakara
Utete
Kilindoni
Kasanga
Mkulwe
Chunya
Mbeya
Mahenge
Kilwa Kivinje
Mbala
Nakonde
Tukuyu
Mdandu
Njombe
Matandu
Kilwa Masoko
oso
Chitipa
Karonga
Zinga Mulike
Kipengere Range
Nyika Plateau 2606
Chilumba
Songea
Liwale
Kasama
Isoka
Livingstonia
Manda
Mbamba Bay
Njinjo
Lindi
Mpika
Chitambo
Rumphi
Olivenéa
Mtwara
Mikindani
Mbamba Bay 474
Tunduru
Mtama
Cabo Delgado
Palma
nga Mountains
Mzuzu
Lake Nyasa
Chamba
Newala
Masasi
Ruvuma
Diaca
Lundazi
Nkhata Bay
Mzimba
Cóbue
Mecula
Quiterajo
Chitambo
Metangula
Lichinga
Niassa
Maúa
Montepuez
Ancuabe
Pemba
Chipata
Mchinji
Salima
Catur
Belém
Marrupa
Balama
Katete
Lilongwe
Mandimba
Cuamba
Ribauè
Mecubúri
Monapo
MALAWI
Zomba
Mangochi
Malema
Nampula
Memba
ba
Vila Gamito
Ulóngue
Liwonde
Lake Chilwa
Serra Namúli 2419
Murrupula
Lúrio
Nacala-a-Velha
Nacala
Zámbué
Fingoè
Furancungo
Kazula
Blantyre
Sapitwa 3002
Milange
Namarrói
Alto Molócuè
Errego
Mogincual
Ilha de Moçambique
Lumbo
Albufeira Cahora Bassa
Moatize
Tete
Thyolo
Chiromo
Chiperone 2054
Lugela
Mulevala
Angoche
RMENT
Chioco
Changara
Chemba
Nsanje
Mocuba
Mocubela
Moma
Larde
VURADONHA MTS.
Shamva
Tambara
Doa
Morrumbala
Namacurta
Nama
Pebane
993
Bindura
Mazowe
Vila de Sena
Mopeia
Quelimane
Murewa
MOZAMBIQUE
Marromeu
e
Mutoko
Inyangani 2592
Serra da Gorongosa 1856
Vila Fontes
Inhaminga
Chinde
ngwiza
Marondera
Manica
Rusape
Macheke
Mutare
Chimoio
Dondo
Beira
WE
Chivhu
Monte Binga 2437
Chibabava
Sofala
Chipinge
Espungabera
vuma
Save
Nova Mambone
Ilha do Bazaruto
Mwenezi
Massangena
Mabote
Vilankulo
Ponta São Sebastião
nda
Malvernia
Mabalane
Mapinhane
Massinga
Chigubo
Funhalouro
Morrumbene
Ponta da Barra
Inhambane
Phalaborwa
Mabalane
Maxixe
Panda
Inharrime
Chibuto
Quissico
Chidenguele
burg
Xinavane
Macia
Xai-Xai
Komatipoort
Chókwè
fruit
Moamba
Baía de Maputo
MAPUTO
Barberton
Ilha da Inhaca
ZILAND
Manzini
Bela Vista
Zitundo
mba
Mbabane
Lavumisa
ryheid
Nongoma
Lake St. Lucia
Cape St. Lucia 1306
mpangeni
Mtubatuba
owns
Richard's Bay
ermaritzburg
Pinetown
DURBAN
mzinto
urg

INDIAN OCEAN

Mozambique Channel

5300

Île Juan de Nova (Fr.)

10

3000

Bassas da India (Fr.)

Ile Europa (Fr.)

4038

4300

MADAGASCAR
Antsiranana
Tanjona Bobaomby
Nosy Mitsio
Ambohitra 1475
Nosy Be
Ambilobe
Iharaña
Andoany
Ambanja
Maromandia
Maromokotro 2876
Alalalava
TSARATANANA
Sambava
Bealanana
Andapa
Antsohihy
Antalaha
Mahajanga
Soalala
Befandriana Avaratra
Mandritsara
Rantabe
Maroantsetra
Tanjona Masoala
Soalala
Marovoay
Tsaratanana
Mampikony
Mananara Avaratra
Besalampy
Madirovalo
Andilamena
Nosy Sainte Marie
Bekodoka
Maevatanana
Ambodifototra
Mahabe
Fenoarivo Atsinanana
Maintirano
Morafenobe
Kandreho
Andriamena
Farihy Alaotra
Ambodifototra
Nosy Barren
Antsalova
Ankazobe
Arivonimamo
ANTANANARIVO
Tsiroanomandidy
Ambatondrazaka
Toamasina
Tsiafajavona 2642
Moramanga
Ankavandra
Soavinandriana
Ampasimanolotra
Belo-Tsiribihina
Miandrivazo
Betafo
Ambatolampy
Vatomandry
5322
Tsiribihina
Morondava
Mahabo
Antsirabe
Manjakandriana
Mahanoro
Belo-sur-Mer
Malaimbandy
Ambatofinandrahana
Ambositra
Mandabe
Ambohimahasoa
Nosy-Varika
Andranopasy
Manja
Fianarantsoa
Ifanadiana
Mananjary
Morombe
Ambalavao
Befandriana Avaratra
Beroroha
Manakara
Mangoky
Ankazoabo
Ihosy
Vohipeno
Sakaraha
Ibity 2655
Farafangana
Manombo Atsimo
Ranohira
Ivohibe
Vondrozo
Vangaindrano
Toliara
Bezaha
Betroka
Midongy Atsimo
Ejeda
Bekily
Beraketa
Manantenina
Itampolo
Ampanihy
Androka
Amboasary
Tólañaro
Tsiombe
Ambovombe
Tanjona Vohimena

Tropic of Capricorn

INDIAN OCEAN

Tanjona Vilanandro

Tanjona Ankaboa

a Same scale as main map
INDIAN OCEAN
5300
2300
h
Port Louis
MAURITIUS
Piton de la Petite Rivière Noire ▲ 828
Curepipe
Mahébourg
Saint-Denis
Saint-Paul
Piton des Neiges ▲ 3070
Saint-Pierre
REUNION (Fr.)
5300
i
MASCARENE ISLANDS
4200
55° East of Greenwich
10

b Same scale as main map
INDIAN OCEAN
Groupe d'Aldabra
St. Pierre
Atoll de Providence
4406
Assomption
Atoll de Cosmoledo
Astove 4030
Atoll de Farquhar
SEYCHELLES
4495
Agalega Islands (Maur.)
50° East of Greenwich
11
12
13

Praslin
La Digue
Silhouette
Victoria
Mahé
SEYCHELLES
Poivre Atoll
Desroches
Île Plate
LES AMIRANTES
Alphonse
Coëtivy
j
k

67

5 35° 6 40° 67 7 45° 8 50° 9

5°
B
10°
C
15°
D
20°
E
25°
F

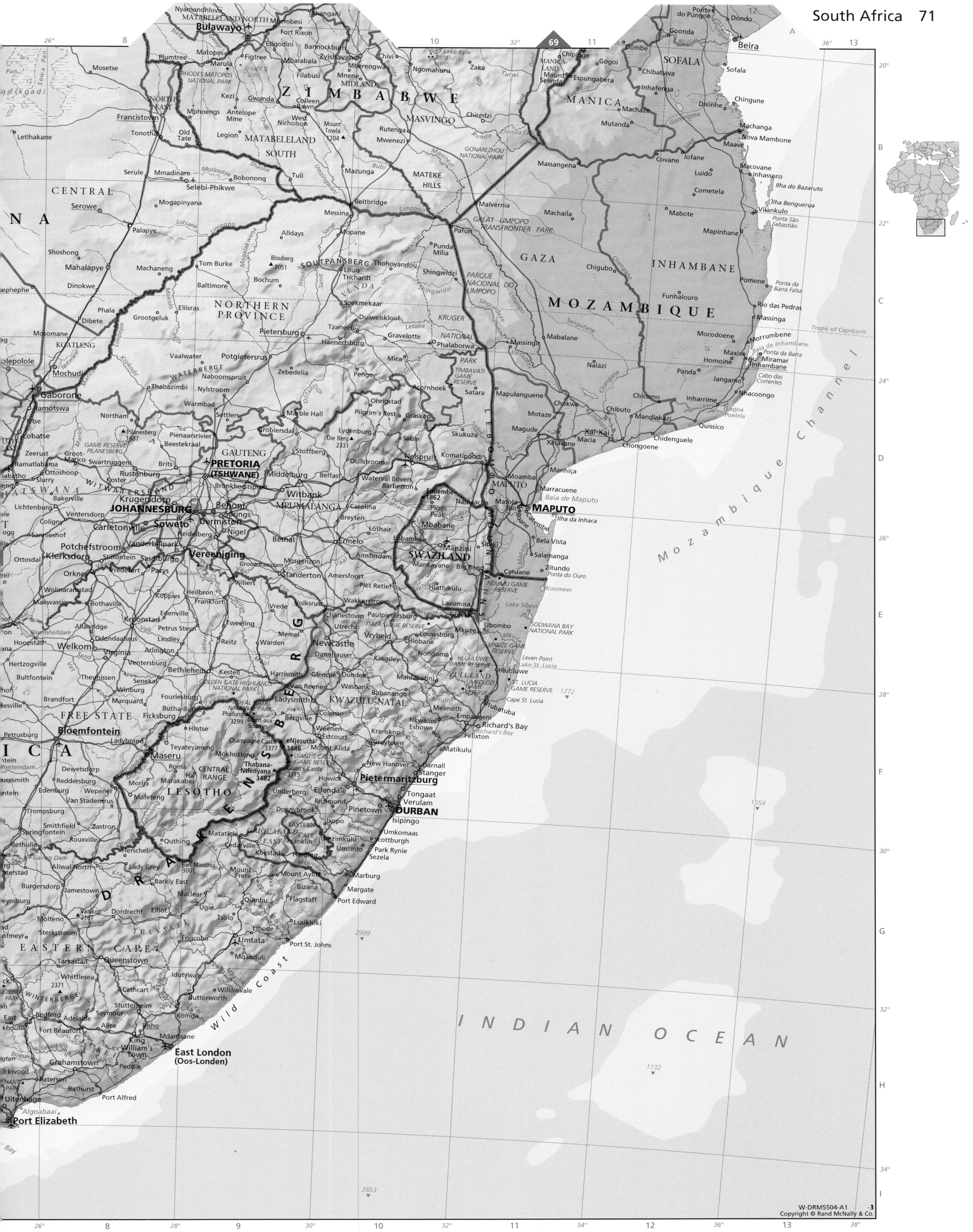

ZIMBABWE

Bulawayo

MATABELELAND NORTH

MATABELELAND SOUTH

MASVINGO

MIDLANDS

MANICA

SOFALA

Beira

MOZAMBIQUE

GAZA

INHAMBANE

NORTHERN PROVINCE

VENDA

KRUGER NATIONAL PARK

GAUTENG

PRETORIA (TSHWANE)

JOHANNESBURG

Soweto

MPUMALANGA

SWAZILAND

Mbabane

Manzini

MAPUTO

Vereeniging

FREE STATE

Bloemfontein

Maseru

LESOTHO

KWAZULU-NATAL

Pietermaritzburg

DURBAN

Richard's Bay

EASTERN CAPE

TRANSKEI

Umtata

East London (Oos-Londen)

Port Elizabeth

INDIAN OCEAN

Mozambique Channel

Tropic of Capricorn

Wild Coast

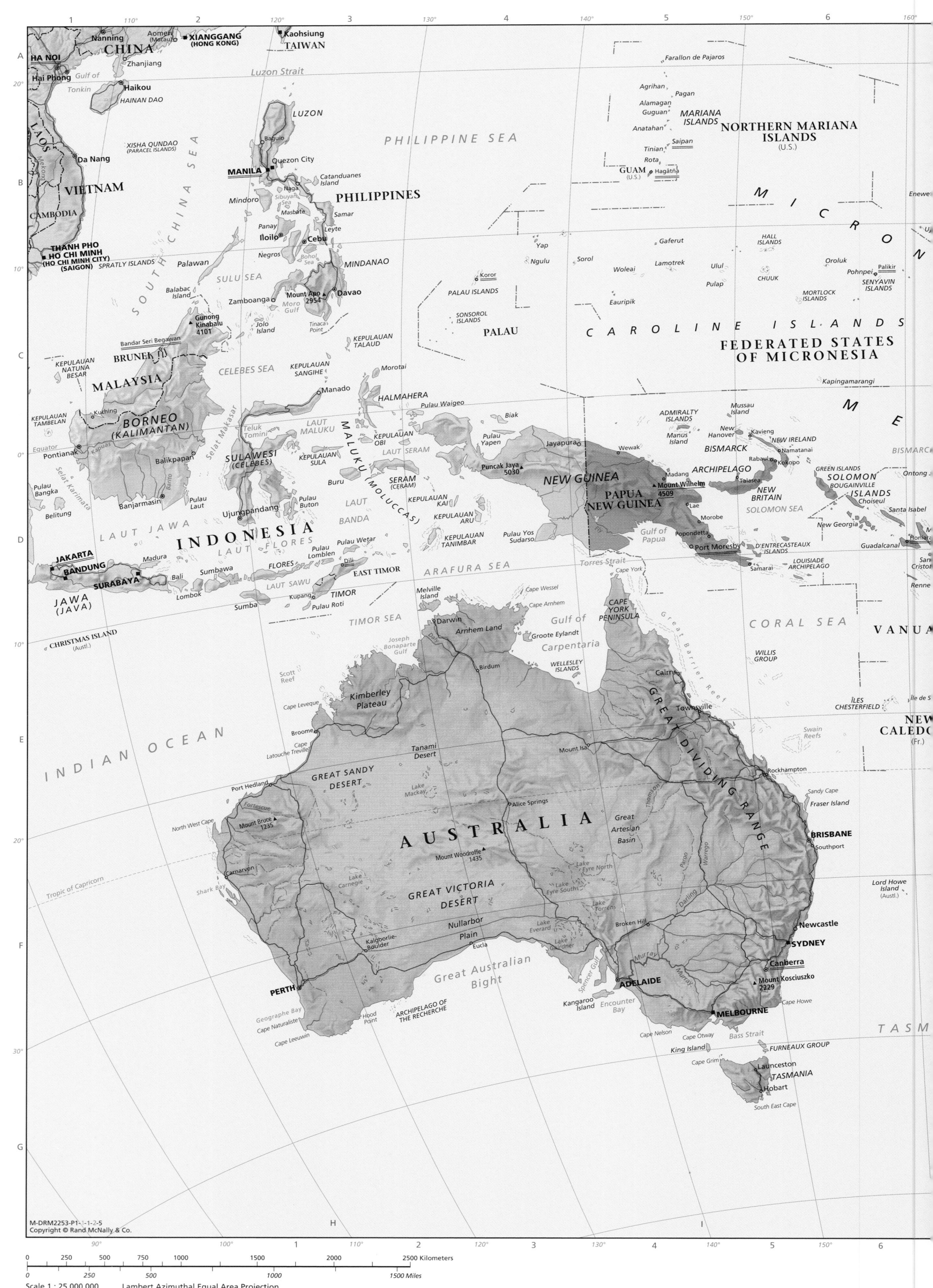

| 0 | 250 | 500 | 750 | 1000 | | 1500 | | 2000 | | 2500 Kilometers |

| 0 | 250 | | 500 | | 1000 | | 1500 Miles |

Scale 1 : 25,000,000   Lambert Azimuthal Equal Area Projection

AKE ISLAND
(U.S.)

Taongi

RSHALL ISLANDS

Rongelap   Bikar
Utrik
tho   RATAK
Kwajalein   CHAIN
        Maloelap
RALIK
CHAIN
Ailinglaplap   Majuro   Arno
Jaluit   Mili
    Ebon
            Butaritari

Tarawa Bairiki
Kuria Abemama
NAURU   Nonouti
        Banaba GILBERT ISLAND
            Nikunau
            Onotoa
            Arorae

N
E
S
I   Nanumea
A   Niutao
            Nui
SOLOMON
ISLANDS
        SANTA CRUZ
upua   ISLANDS
    Vanikolo   Rotuma
                Niulakita
    ÎLES BANKS
anua Lava   NEW
piritu   Pentecôte
Santo   Ambrym   ÎLES WALLIS
Malakula   WALLIS AND FUTUNA
    HEBRIDES   (Fr.)
Port Vila Éfaté   Île Futuna
        Erromango   FIJI   Île Alofi
OUVELLE-   Tanna   VANUA
LÉDONIE   Anatom   LEVU
    Lifou   VITI   LAU
    ÎLES LOYAUTÉ   LEVU Suva GROUP
uméa Maré   Tafahi   KORO SEA
    Île des   Kaduvu
    Pins   Vava'u
            TONGA
                Tongatapu Nuku' alofa
                    'Eua
                'Ata

PACIFIC   OCEAN

Johnston Atoll
(U.S.)

Kingman Reef
(U.S.)
Palmyra Atoll
(U.S.)
    Teraina
        Tabuaeran

Howland Island
(U.S.)
    Baker Island (U.S.)

KIRIBATI
        Kanton
        Rawaki
    Orona Manra
Nikumaroro   PHOENIX ISLANDS

P   O   L   Y

TUVALU   Funafuti   TOKELAU
                (N.Z.)
        SAMOA Swains AMERICAN
            Island SAMOA
                (U.S.)
            SAMOA ISLANDS
            Savai'i
            Upolu Apia
                Tutuila
                Pago Pago

        Nassau Island   Manihiki

        NORTHERN COOK
            ISLANDS
        Suwarrow

        COOK ISLANDS
            (N.Z.)

        Palmerston

        NIUE
        (N.Z.)   Aitutaki
SOUTHERN   Manuae
COOK   Takutea
ISLANDS   Atiu
    Rarotonga Avarua
        ÎLES MARIA
        Rimatara Rurutu
        ÎLES AUSTRALES
            Tubuai
        Ralvavae

HAWAI'IAN
ISLANDS
(U.S.)

Kaua'i   O'ahu
Ni'ihau   Moloka'i
    Honolulu   Maui
        Mauna Kea Hilo
        4205
        Kalae HAWAI'I

Kiritimati
(Christmas Island)

Jarvis
Island
(U.S.)
        Equator

            Malden

        Starbuck

N   E   S

Penrhyn

        Eiao
    Caroline   ÎLES
Vostok   MARQUISES
    Flint   Hiva Oa
                Fatu Hiva

Manuae   ÎLES DU
    Maupihaa Bora-Bora ROI GEORGES
        Mataiva   Raraka
        ARCHIPEL DE LA SOCIÉTÉ   Î L E S
        (SOCIETY ISLANDS)   Papeete
                Tahiti   Anaa
                    Marutea

LINE ISLANDS

I
A

S   I   A

D   U   T   U   A   M   O   T   U
        Pukaruha
            Reao

FRENCH POLYNESIA
    (Fr.)

Tureia
Tematangi Mururoa Marutea
            ÎLES
            GAMBIER
    Tropic of Capricorn

NORFOLK ISLAND
(Austl.)

Raoul
Island

KERMADEC ISLANDS
    (N.Z.)
    Curtis
    Island

THREE KINGS North
ISLANDS   Cape
    North
    Cape
    Great Barrier
    Island
Auckland   Bay of
        Plenty
NORTH ISLAND   East Cape

New Plymouth Mount Ruapehu
Cape Egmont   2797 Hawke Bay
    Napier
NEW
ZEALAND
SOUTH ISLAND   Cook Strait
        Wellington
Aoraki
(Mount Cook)   Christchurch
3754
    Canterbury
    Bight

    Dunedin
Island   Invercargill
th West-Cape

BOUNTY ISLANDS
    (N.Z.)

ANTIPODES ISLANDS
    (N.Z.)

AUCKLAND ISLANDS
(N.Z.)

Campbell Island
(N.Z.)

PACIFIC   OCEAN

Ahunui

    Rapa

        Ernest Legouvé
        Reef

    Maria Teresa
    Reef

PITCAIRN
(U.K.)
Adamstown

International Date Line

CHATHAM
ISLANDS
(N.Z.)

A
B
C
D
E
F
G

10°
0°
10°
20°
30°

170°   8   180°   9   170°   10   160°   11   150°   12   140°   13
8 East of Greenwich 180° West of Greenwich 9   170°   10   160°   11   150°   12   140°   13   14   130°   120°

INDONESIA

SUMBA

Baing

Kupang
Baa
Pulau Roti
Seba
Sedah
Pulau
Sawu
Nembala

TIMOR

Ashmore Islands

Cartier Islands

INDIAN OCEAN

Scott Reef

Browse
Island

TIMOR SEA

Cape Van Diemen
Croker Island
Cape Croker
Goulburn Is.
Coburg
Peninsula
Dundas Strait
Melville
Island
Bathurst
Island
Van Diemen
Gulf
Beagle
Gulf
Clarence Strait
Charles
Point
Darwin
Humpty Doo
Oenpelli
Jabiru

Rum Jungle
Batchelor
Adelaide River
Tipperary
Pine Creek
Arnhem Land
Katherine

Cape Londonderry
Joseph
Bonaparte
Gulf

Daly Waters

Adèle Island
Buccaneer
Archipelago
Collier
Bay
Cape Leveque
King
Sound
Kalumburu
Admiralty
Gulf
York Sound
Drysdale
Wyndham
Ord
Kununurra
Auvergne
Willeroo
Matarank
Larrimah
Birdum
Dunmarra
Newcastle
Top Springs

King Leopold Ranges
Kimberley
Plateau
Gibb River
Karunjie
Mount Wells
947
Mount Lush
781
Mount Napier
487
Ord River
Victoria River
Downs
Kildurk
Waterloo
Montejinni
Camfield
Wave Hill

Beagle Bay
Dampier Land
Derby
Yeeda
Kimberley
Downs
Liveringa
Fitzroy Crossing
Halls Creek
Turner
Inverway
Hooker Creek
Eva

Broome
Roebuck Bay
Cape Latouche Treville
Lagrange Bay
Thangoo
Noonkanbah
Christmas Creek
Gordon Downs
Banka Banka

LaGrange
Anna Plains
EDGAR RANGES
Billiluna
Sturt Creek
Mount Samuel
433

Eighty Mile Beach
Mandora
Wallal Downs
GREAT SANDY DESERT
Lake Gregory
Tanami
Tanami
Desert
The Granites
The Granites
436
NORTHERN TE
Wauchope

Port Hedland
Goldsworthy
Shay Gap
De Grey
Warrawagine
Lake
Waukarlycarly
Percival Lakes
Lake White
Lake Hazlett
Willowra

AUSTR
Dampier
Karratha
Wickham
Roebourne
Marble Bar
Nullagine
Lake Auld
Lake Dora
Lake Mackay
Mount Singleton
808
Mount Cockburn
846
Aileron

Barrow Island
Onslow
Millstream
Arraloola
Pannawonica
Mount Brockman
1132
Wittenoom
Mount Bruce
1235
Ethel
Creek
Lake George
Mount Liebig
1274
Narwietooma
Mount Zeil
1531
Ute

North West Cape
Glenroy
Minderoo
Boolaloo
HAMERSLEY RANGE
Tom Price
Mount Meharry
1253
Lake Disappointment
Mount Leisler
897
MACDONNELL RANGES
Alic

Exmouth
Learmonth
Paraburdoo
Newman
Gibson Desert
Lake Macdonald
Henbury

Ningaloo
Winning
BARLEE RANGE
WESTERN AUSTRALIA
Lake Neale
Petermann Ranges
Mount Olga
1066
Uluru
(Ayers Rock)
863
Curtin Springs
Erldunda

Chabjuwardoo
Bay
Cape Farquhar
Gnaraloo
Tropic of Capricorn
Gifford Creek
Mount Vernon
Mount Augustus
1105
Mount
Augustus
Mount Essendon
910
Mount Salvado
738
Mount Jenkins
Mount Cockburn
1134
Kulgera

Cape Cuvier
Minilya
Boologooro
Gascoyne
Junction
Peak
Hill
Granite Peak
Lake Burnside
Mount Squires
705
Timkinson
Ranges
Mount Woodroffe
1435

Bernier Island
Dorre Island
Dirk Hartog
Island
Cape Inscription
Shark
Bay
Carnarvon
Carey Downs
Mount Fraser
770
Carnegie
Baker Lake
Mount Aloysius
982
Sundown

Denham
Hamelin
Wooramel
Byro
Karalundi
Lake
Gregory
Lake
Nabberu
Lake
Carnegie
Lake
Gillen
Mount Sir Thomas
805
Wintinna

Tamala
Mount Murchison
520
Meekatharra
Wiluna
Lake Way
Lake Wells
Lake Throssel
GREAT VICTORIA DESERT
Lake
Meramangye
Mount Willoughby

Meeberrie
Cue
Lake
Darlot
Mount
Shenton
520
Serpentine
Lakes
Lake Dey-Dey

Kalbarri
Bluff Point
Northampton
Nannine
Tuckanarra
Wondinong
Agnew
Sandstone
Melrose
White Cliffs
Yeo Lake
Lake Maurice
SOU

Geraldton
Mingenew
Morawa
Yalgoo
Youanmi
Mount Magnet
Mount Redcliffe
562
Laverton
Leonora
Lake Carey
Rason
Lake
Plumridge
Lakes
Lake Gidgi
Coob

Houtman
Abrolhos
Dongara
Three Springs
Paynes Find
Mount Singleton
678
Lake Barlee
Gwalia
Malcolm
Kookynie
Lake
Ballard
Lake
Minigwal
Maralinga

Carnamah
Coorow
Dalwallinu
Menzies
Goongarrie
Lake Rebecca
Nullarbor
Deakin
Seemore Downs
Forrest
Cook
Ooldea
Malboom

Mount Lesueur
313
Watheroo
Pithara
Beacon
Mount Jackson
617
Kalgoorlie-
Boulder
Karonie
Zanthus
Rawlinna
Haig
Loongana
Plain
Hampton Tableland
Eucla
Head of
Bight
Colona
Penong

Lancelin
Gingin
Moora
New Norcia
Bencubbin
Mukinbudin
Bullfinch
Coolgardie
West
Lake Deborah
Lake
Seabrook
Mount Monger
Kambalda
Widgiemooltha
Madura
Mundrabilla
Fowlers Bay

Wanneroo
Stirling
PERTH
Fremantle
Rockingham
DARLING
Gosnells
Armadale
Trayning
Merredin
Kellerberrin
Bruce Rock
Southern Cross
Higginsville
Lake Lefroy
Lake Cowan
Fraser Range
Eyre
Streaky Bay
Anxiou

Pinjarra
Yarloop
RANGE
Topdyay
Northam
York
Corrigin
Hyden
Lake
Johnston
Norseman
Balladonia
Great Australian Bight

Bunbury
Collie
Darkan
Pingelly
Wickepin
Kondinin
Lake King
Salmon Gums
RUSSELL
RANGE
Point Dempster

Geographe Bay
Cape Naturaliste
Busselton
Donnybrook
Kojonup
Narrogin
Wagin
Lake
Grace
Nyabing
Newdegate
Ravensthorpe
Gibson
Esperance
Cape Arid

Margaret River
Augusta
Cape Leeuwin
Nannup
Bridgetown
Pemberton
Northcliffe
Katanning
Gnowangerup
Cranbrook
Mount
Barker
Denmark
Hopetoun
Hood Point
Bremer Bay
Cheyne
Bay
ARCHIPELAGO OF THE RECHERCHE

Flinders
Bay
Point D'Entrecasteaux
Walpole
West
Cape
Howe
Bald Head
Albany
King George Sound

Meters
Feet
2000
6560
1000
3280
500
1640
200
656
Sea Level
200
656
2000
6560

M-DRM4717-A1-·-1-2-2
Copyright © Rand McNally & Co.

0   100   200   300   400   600   800   1000 Kilometers
0   100   200   400   600 Miles
Scale 1 : 10,000,000   Lambert Conformal Conic Projection

A.C.T. = AUSTRALIAN CAPITAL TERRITORY

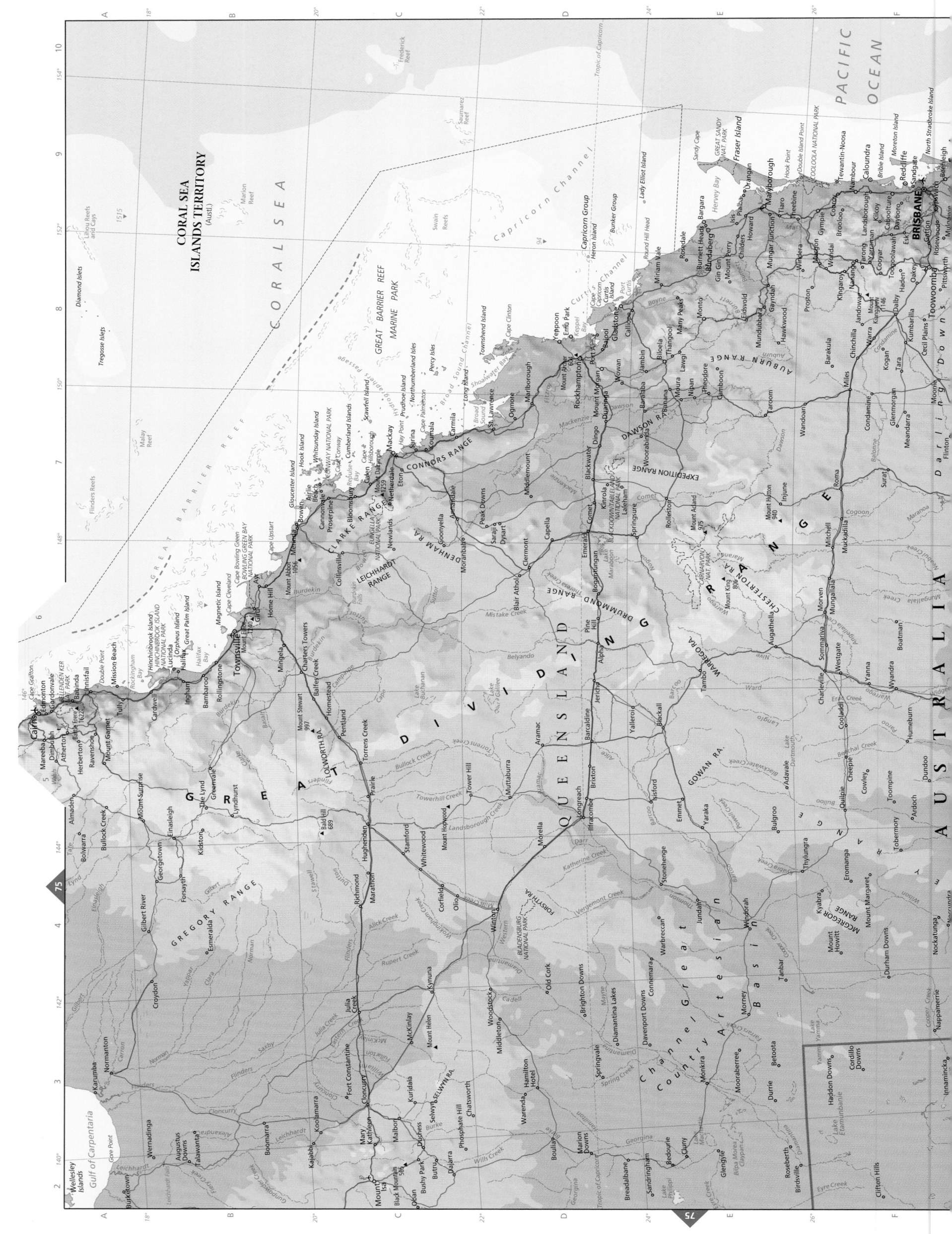

CORAL SEA
ISLANDS TERRITORY
(Aust.)

CORAL SEA

GREAT BARRIER REEF MARINE PARK

PACIFIC OCEAN

QUEENSLAND

AUSTRALIA

GREAT DIVIDING RANGE

Gulf of Carpentaria

BRISBANE

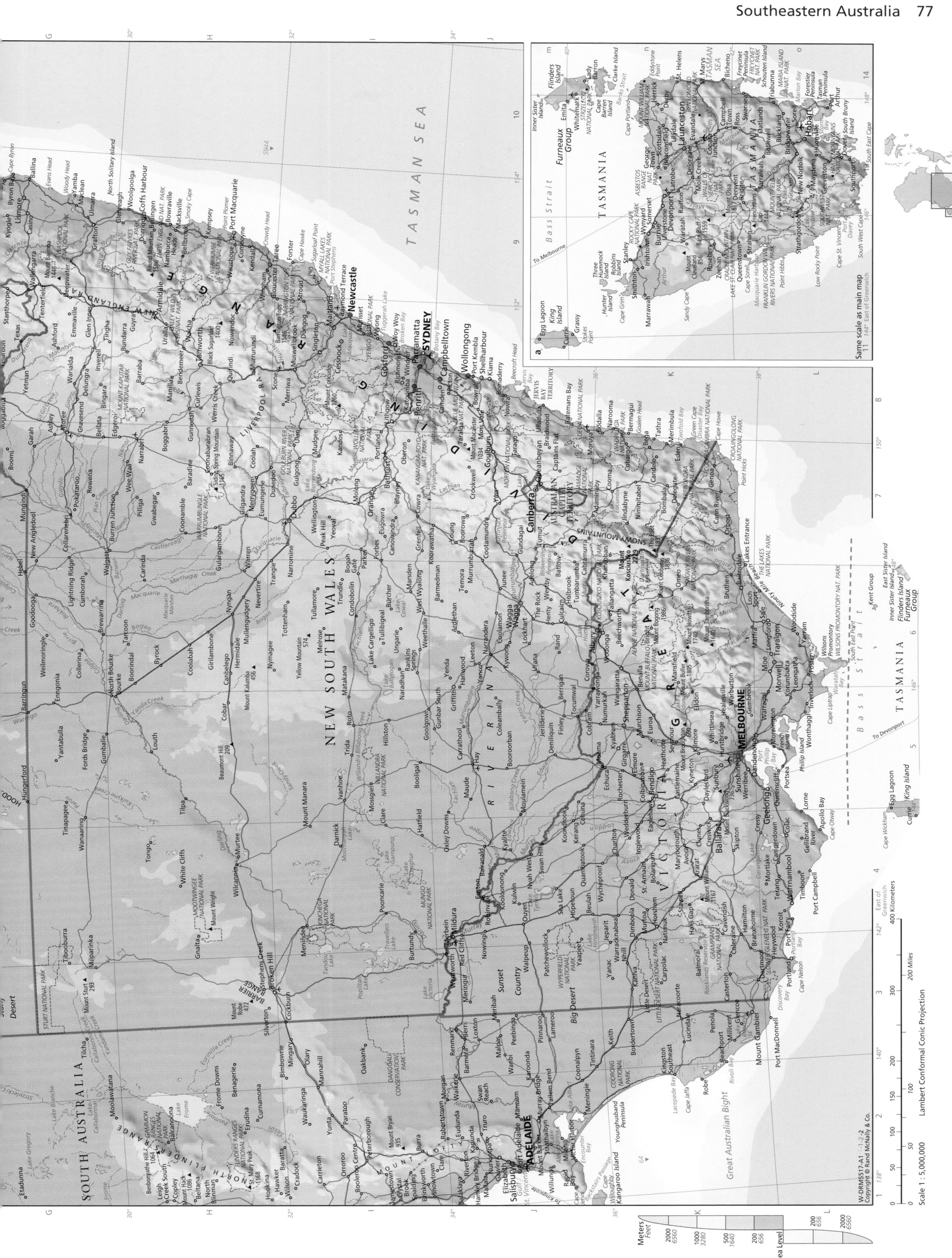

Lambert Conformal Conic Projection

W-DRM5517-A1 -1-2-2
Copyright © Rand McNally & Co.

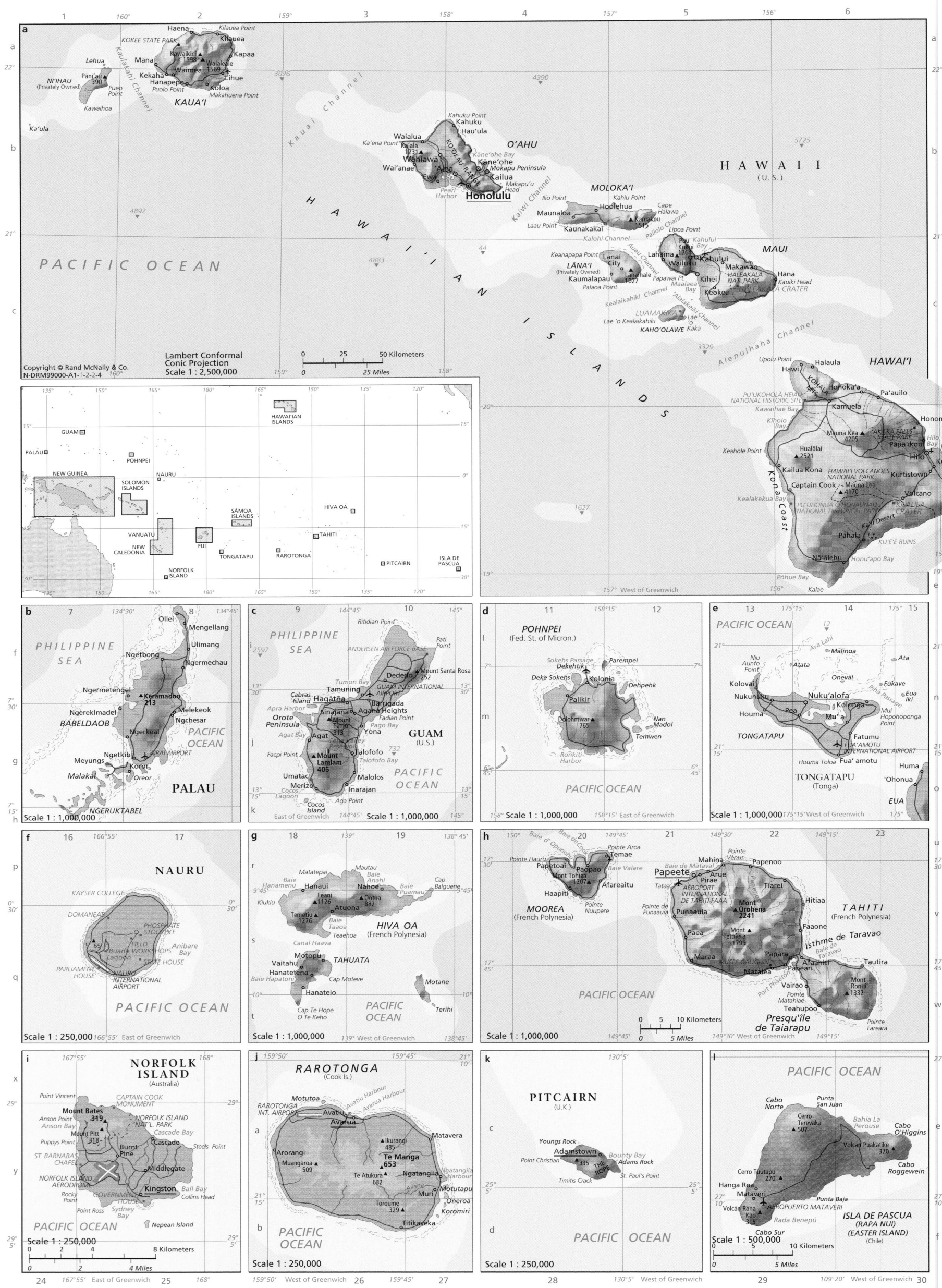

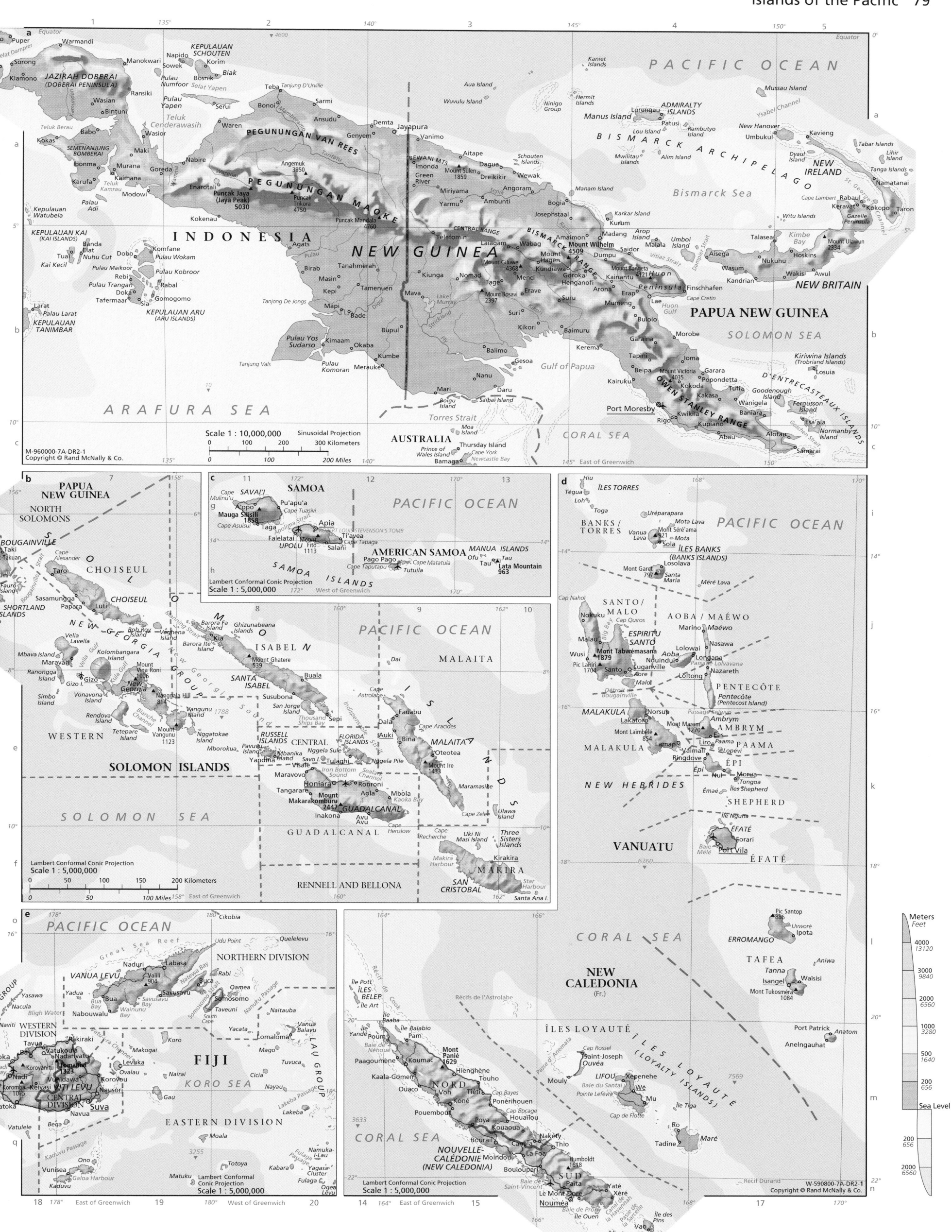

a (New Guinea map)

PACIFIC OCEAN
Equator

Warmandi
Puper
Klamono
Sorong
JAZIRAH DOBERAI
(DOBERAI PENINSULA)
Kokas
SEMENANJUNG
BOMBERAI
Babo
Ibonma
Murana
Karufa
Modowi
Kaimana
Teluk Berau
Teluk Kamrau
KEPULAUAN KAI
(KAI ISLANDS)
Kepulauan Watubela
Palau Adi
Banda
Elat
Dobo
Tual
Nuhu Cut
Kai Kecil
Pulau Maikoor
KEPULAUAN ARU
(ARU ISLANDS)
Pulau Kobroor
Rebi
Pulau Trangan
Doka
Sia
Tafermaar
Gomogomo
Larat
Palau Larat
KEPULAUAN TANIMBAR

Manokwari
Napido
KEPULAUAN SCHOUTEN
Sowek
Korim
Biak
Wasian
Ransiki
Bosnik
Nabire
Pulau Numfoor
Pulau Yapen
Serui
Teluk Cenderawasih
Waren
Bonoi
Demta
Jayapura
Vanimo
Sarmi
Ansudu
Genyem
Angemuk 3950
PEGUNUNGAN VAN REES
Enarotali
Puncak Jaya (Jaya Peak) 5030
PEGUNUNGAN MAOKE
Kokenau
Puncak Trikora 4750
Puncak Mandala 4760
INDONESIA
NEW GUINEA
Agats
Tanahmerah
Birab
Masin
Kepi
Mapi
Bade
Pulau Yos Sudarso
Kimaam
Okaba
Kumbe
Merauke
Pulau Komoran
Tanjung Vals
Tanjung De Jongs

ARAFURA SEA

Scale 1 : 10,000,000
0 100 200 300 Kilometers
0   100   200 Miles
Sinusoidal Projection
M-960000-7A-DR2-1
Copyright © Rand McNally & Co.

AUSTRALIA
Prince of Wales Island
Thursday Island
Cape York
Newcastle Bay
Bamaga

Torres Strait
Boigu Island
Saibai Island
Daru
Mari
Nanu
Gesoa
Gulf of Papua
Kairuku
Port Moresby
Rigo
Abau
Kupiano
OWEN STANLEY RANGE

CORAL SEA

PACIFIC OCEAN
Kaniet Islands
Mussau Island
Hermit Islands
Aua Island
Wuvulu Island
Ninigo Group
ADMIRALTY ISLANDS
Manus Island
Lorengau
Patusi
Rambutyo Island
Lou Island
Mwililu
Alim Island
BISMARCK ARCHIPELAGO
Ysabel Channel
New Hanover
Umbukul
Kavieng
Tabar Islands
Lihir Island
NEW IRELAND
Tanga Islands
Namatanai
St. George Channel
Rabaul
Kerevat
Kokopo
Taron
Gazelle Peninsula
Witu Islands
Cape Lambert
BISMARCK SEA
Madang
Bismarck Sea
Kimbe Bay
Talasea
Aisega
Wasum
Nukuhu
Awul
Hoskins
NEW BRITAIN
Mount Ulawun 2334
Kandrian

Kaniet Islands
Imonda
BEWANI MTS.
Aitape
Schouten Islands
Dagua
Wewak
TARITATU
Green River
Dreikikir
Angoram
Yarmu
Miriyama
Ambunti
CENTRAL RANGE
Wabag
Amaimon
Karkar Island
Arop
Bogia
Josephstaal
Manam Island
Lalagam
Mount Wilhelm 4509
Saidor
Madang
Dumpu
Umboi Island
Malala
BISMARCK RANGE
Mount Giluwe 4368
Mount Hagen
Kundiawa
Goroka
Henganofi
Bundi 4121
Kainantu
Mount Bangeta
Finschhafen
Cape Cretin
Arona
Erap
Huon Peninsula
Vitiaz Strait
Dampier Strait
Nomad
Tage
Mount Bosavi 2397
Erave
Suru
Suri
Mumeng
Lae
Bulolo
PAPUA NEW GUINEA
Kiunga
Mava
Lake Murray
Kikori
Baimuru
Morobe
SOLOMON SEA
Kerema
Tapini
Ioma
Garara
Bupul
Balimo
Kiriwina Islands (Trobriand Islands)
Losuia
D'ENTRECASTEAUX ISLANDS
Beipa
Mount Victoria 4035
Kokoda
Popondetta
Tufi
Goodenough Island
Fergusson Island
Wanigela
Baniara
Esa'ala
Normanby Island
Kwikila
Alotau
Samarai
Gochen Island

b (Solomon Islands map)

PAPUA NEW GUINEA
NORTH SOLOMONS
BOUGAINVILLE
Taki
Cape Alexander
Buka
Sasamungga
Papara
Luti
CHOISEUL
Taro
Fauro Island
SHORTLAND ISLANDS
Vella Lavella
Ranongga Island
Mbava Island
Maravari
Gizo
Vonavona Island
Simbo Island
Rendova Island
Tetepare Island
WESTERN
NEW GEORGIA GROUP
Rob Roy Island
Vaghena Island
Kia
Barora Fa Island
Barora Ite Island
Ghizunabeana Islands
ISABEL
Mount Ghatere 539
SANTA ISABEL
Buala
Susubona
San Jorge Island
Sepi
Mount Veu Roni 1006
Nggatokae Island
Mbarokua
Pavuvu Island
RUSSELL ISLANDS
Yandina
Mbanika Island
Savo Island
Maravovo
Tulaghi
Tangarare
Honiara
Mount Makarakomburu 2447
Inakona
Aola
SOLOMON SEA
GUADALCANAL
Cape Hunter
MALAITA
Dai
Faubu
Dala
Auki
Ngela Sule
Ngela Pile
Bina
MALAITA
Oteotea
Mount Ire 1433
Ronroni
Mbola
Kaoka Bay
Maramasike
Ulawa Island
Uki Ni Masi Island
Three Sisters Islands
Kirakira
Makira Harbour
MAKIRA
Star Harbour
SAN CRISTOBAL
Santa Ana I.
RENNELL AND BELLONA

Scale 1 : 5,000,000
Lambert Conformal Conic Projection
0 50 100 150 200 Kilometers
0   50   100 Miles

SOLOMON ISLANDS
WESTERN
New Georgia
Nggela Hill 314
CENTRAL
Thousand Ships Bay
Cape Astrolabe
Cape Aracides
Cape Recherche
Cape Zelee
GUADALCANAL

c (Samoa map)

SAMOA
SAVAI'I
Cape Mulinu'u
A'opo
Mauga Silisili 1858
Puapu'a
Cape Tuasivi
Taga
Cape Asuisui
Falelatai
Mount Fito 1113
UPOLU
Salani
Apia
ROBERT LOUIS STEVENSON'S TOMB
Ti'avea
Cape Tapaga
PACIFIC OCEAN
AMERICAN SAMOA
Pago Pago
Cape Taputapu
Tutuila
Cape Matatula
MANUA ISLANDS
Ofu
Tau
Lata Mountain 963
SAMOA ISLANDS

Lambert Conformal Conic Projection
Scale 1 : 5,000,000
West of Greenwich

d (Vanuatu map)

PACIFIC OCEAN
Hiu
ÎLES TORRES
Tégua
Loh
Toga
Uréparapara
Mota Lava
BANKS / TORRES
Vanua Lava
Mont Séré'ama
Sola
ÎLES BANKS (BANKS ISLANDS)
Losolava
Mont Garet 797
Santa Maria
Méré Lava
SANTO / MALO
Nokuku
Cap Nahoi
Malau
Cap Quiros
AOBA / MAÊWO
Marino
Maêwo
ESPIRITU SANTO
Wusi
Mont Tabwémasana 1879
Aoba
Nasawa
Pic Lahiri 1704
Luganville
Lolowai
Santo
Aore
Malol
Nduindui
Longana
Lolvana
Nazareth
Loltong
PENTECÔTE
Détroit de Bougainville
Pentecôte (Pentecost Island)
MALAKULA
Lakatoro
Norsup
Mont Marum 1270
AMBRYM
Mont Laimbélé 854
Lamap
Vaimali
PAAMA
MALAKULA
Liro
Ringdove
Lopévi
Épi
ÉPI
Ringdove
Nul
Morua
Tongoa
Émaé
Îles Shepherd
SHEPHERD
NEW HEBRIDES
Île Nguna
VANUATU
ÉFATÉ
Forari
Port Vila
Baie de Mélé
ÉFATÉ
Pic Santop 886
Uwworé
ERROMANGO
Ipota
TAFEA
Aniwa
Tanna
Isangel
Mont Tukosméra 1084
Waïsisi

e (Fiji map)

PACIFIC OCEAN
Cikobia
GROUP
Yasawa
Naviti
Nacula
Udu Point
Qelelevu
Great Sea Reef
Naduri
Labasa
VANUA LEVU
Valili 904
Yadua
Bua
Bua Bay
Nabouwalu
Buca Bay
Natewa Bay
Savusavu
Somosomo Bay
Savusavu Bay
Wainunu Bay
NORTHERN DIVISION
Qamea
Taveuni
Cape
South Cape
Yacata
Naitauba
Vanua Balavu
Mago
Cicia
Lomaloma
Tuvuca
WESTERN DIVISION
Tavua
Vatukoula
Nadarivatu
Makogai
Levuka
Ovalau
Nairai
Koro
Rakiraki
Tomanivi 1323
Nausori
Korovou
Gau
Nadi
Keiyasi
Korombasabasa
VITI LEVU 1075
CENTRAL DIVISION
Suva
Navua
Vatulele
Beqa
Nayau
Lakeba
LAU GROUP
KORO SEA
EASTERN DIVISION
FIJI
Moala
Totoya
Namuka-i-Lau
Kabara
Yagasa Cluster
Fulaga
Ogea
Matuku
Vunisea
Ono
Kaduvu
Galoa Harbour
Kaduvu Passage

Lambert Conformal Conic Projection
Scale 1 : 5,000,000
East of Greenwich

f (New Caledonia map)

CORAL SEA
Pic Santop
Récifs de l'Astrolabe
NEW CALEDONIA (Fr.)
Île Pott
ÎLES BELEP
Île Art
Île Baaba
Île Yandé
Île Balabio
Pam
Cap Rossel
Baie de Néhoué
Poum
Cap Saint-Joseph
ÎLES LOYAUTÉ (LOYALTY ISLANDS)
Ouvéa
Mont Panié 1629
Koumac
Hienghène
Touho
Kaala-Gomen
Voh
Koné
Saint-Joseph
Mouly
Paagoumene
Pouembout
Ponérihouen
Cap Bayes
Cap Bocage
Lifou
Xepenehe
Wé
Pouembout
Poya
Houailou
Mu
Ouaco
NORD
Ro
Kouaoua
Bourail
Nakéty
Thio
Kouaoua
Poya
La Foa
Moindou
Maré
Tadine
Humboldt 1618
Bouloupari
SUD
Paita
Le Mont-Dore
Yaté
Xéré
Cap Ndoua
Nouméa
NOUVELLE-CALÉDONIE (NEW CALEDONIA)
Baie de Saint-Vincent
Île Ouen
Île de Prony
Île des Pins
Baie de la Havannah
Île Kotomo
Récif Durand
Port Patrick
Anelngauhat
Port Patrick
Anatom
Aneityum
Pic 7569

Lambert Conformal Conic Projection
Scale 1 : 5,000,000
East of Greenwich
W-590800-7A-DR2-1
Copyright © Rand McNally & Co.

Meters / Feet
4000 / 13120
3000 / 9840
2000 / 6560
1000 / 3280
500 / 1640
200 / 656
Sea Level
200 / 656
2000 / 6560

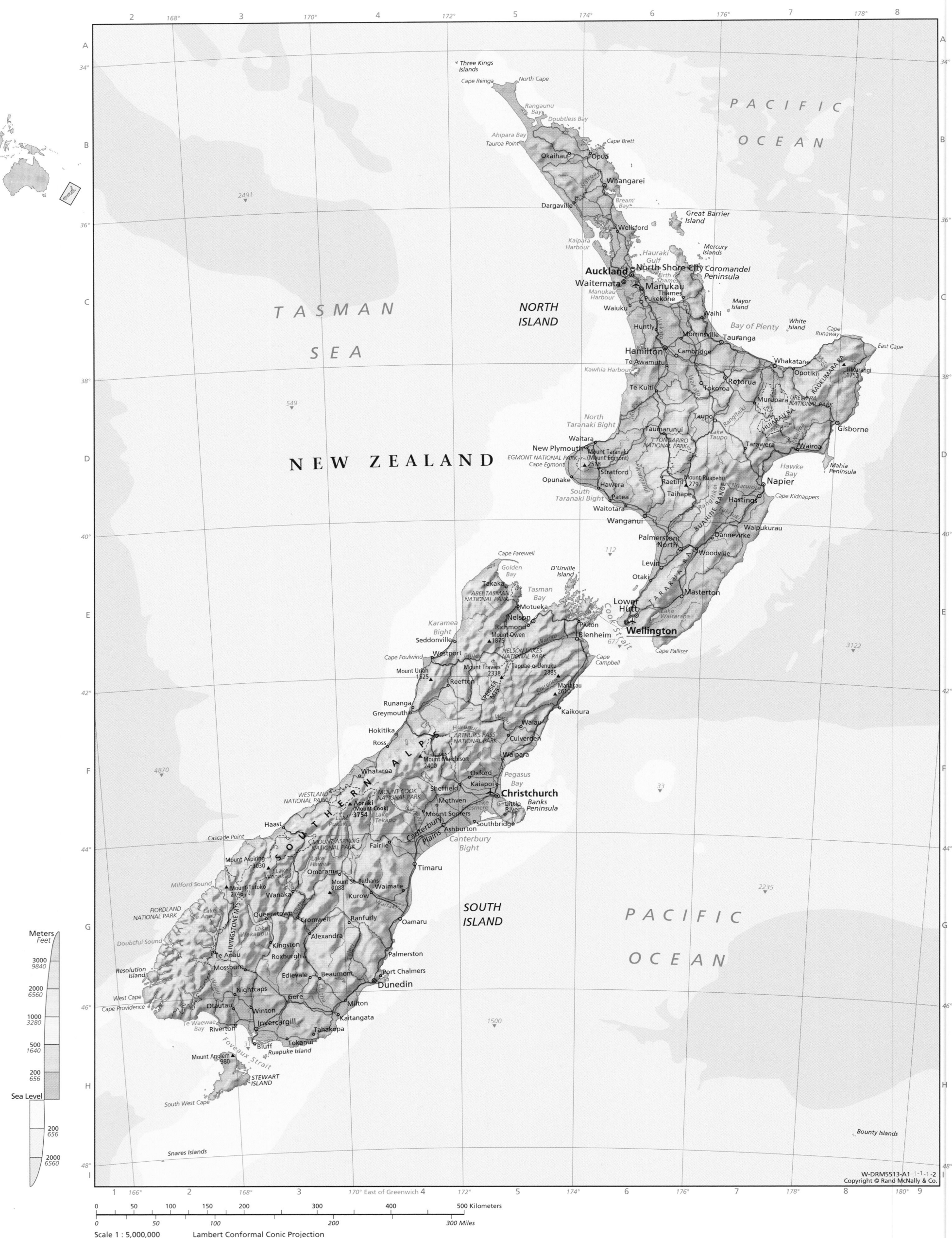

NEW ZEALAND

NORTH ISLAND

SOUTH ISLAND

TASMAN SEA

PACIFIC OCEAN

PACIFIC OCEAN

Three Kings Islands
Cape Reinga
North Cape
Rangaunu Bay
Doubtless Bay
Ahipara Bay
Tauroa Point
Cape Brett
Okaihau
Opua
Whangarei
Dargaville
Bream Bay
Wellsford
Great Barrier Island
Kaipara Harbour
Mercury Islands
Hauraki Gulf
North Shore City
Auckland
Coromandel Peninsula
Waitemata
Manukau
Firth of Thames
Thames
Manukau Harbour
Waiuku
Pukekohe
Waihi
Mayor Island
Bay of Plenty
White Island
Cape Runaway
Huntly
Morrinsville
Tauranga
Hamilton
Cambridge
Whakatane
Te Awamutu
Rotorua
Opotiki
East Cape
Kawhia Harbour
Te Kuiti
Tokoroa
Murupara
Hikurangi 1752
Taumarunui
Taupo
Lake Taupo
Tarawera
Gisborne
North Taranaki Bight
TONGARIRO NATIONAL PARK
Waitara
New Plymouth
Mount Taranaki (Mount Egmont)
EGMONT NATIONAL PARK
Cape Egmont 2518
Stratford
Wanganui
Raetihi
Mount Ruapehu 2797
Wairoa
Mahia Peninsula
Hawke Bay
Opunake
Hawera
Patea
Taihape
Napier
South Taranaki Bight
Waitotara
Hastings
Cape Kidnappers
Wanganui
Waipukurau
Palmerston North
Dannevirke
Cape Farewell
Golden Bay
D'Urville Island
Levin
Woodville
Takaka
ABEL TASMAN NATIONAL PARK
Tasman Bay
Otaki
Masterton
Karamea Bight
Motueka
Nelson
Richmond
Picton
Lower Hutt
Cook Strait
Seddonville
Mount Owen 1875
Blenheim
Wellington
NELSON LAKES NATIONAL PARK
Cape Palliser
Cape Foulwind
Westport
Mount Travers 2338
Tapuae-o-Uenuku 2885
Cape Campbell
Mount Una 1525
Reefton
SPENSER MTS
Manakau 2611
Runanga
Hurunui
Greymouth
Kaikoura
Hokitika
ARTHUR'S PASS NATIONAL PARK
Waiau
Ross
Culverden
Waipara
Whataroa
Mount Murchison 2400
Oxford
Pegasus Bay
Sheffield
Kaiapoi
SOUTHERN ALPS
MOUNT COOK NATIONAL PARK
Methven
Christchurch
WESTLAND NATIONAL PARK
Aoraki (Mount Cook) 3754
Mount Somers
Little River
Banks Peninsula
Haast
Lake Tekapo
Ashburton
Southbridge
Cascade Point
MOUNT ASPIRING NATIONAL PARK
Canterbury Plains
Canterbury Bight
Mount Aspiring 3030
Fairlie
Lake Hawea
Milford Sound
Mount Tutoko 2746
Lake Wanaka
Omarama
Timaru
Wanaka
Mount St Bathans 2088
Waimate
FIORDLAND NATIONAL PARK
LIVINGSTONE MTS
Queenstown
Kurow
Lake Wakatipu
Cromwell
Ranfurly
Oamaru
Doubtful Sound
Te Anau
Lake Te Anau
Alexandra
Resolution Island
Kingston
Palmerston
West Cape
Mossburn
Roxburgh
Port Chalmers
Cape Providence
Nightcaps
Edievale
Beaumont
Otautau
Gore
Dunedin
Te Waewae Bay
Winton
Milton
Riverton
Invercargill
Kaitangata
Tahakopa
Bluff
Tokanui
Mount Anglem 980
Ruapuke Island
Foveaux Strait
STEWART ISLAND
Snares Islands
South West Cape
Bounty Islands

Meters / Feet
3000 / 9840
2000 / 6560
1000 / 3280
500 / 1640
200 / 656
Sea Level
200 / 656
2000 / 6560

1 166° 2 3 168° 4 170° East of Greenwich 5 172° 6 7 174° 8 176° 9 178° 180°

0 50 100 150 200 300 400 500 Kilometers
0 100 200 300 Miles

Scale 1 : 5,000,000
Lambert Conformal Conic Projection

W-DRM5513-A1-1-1-1-2
Copyright © Rand McNally & Co.

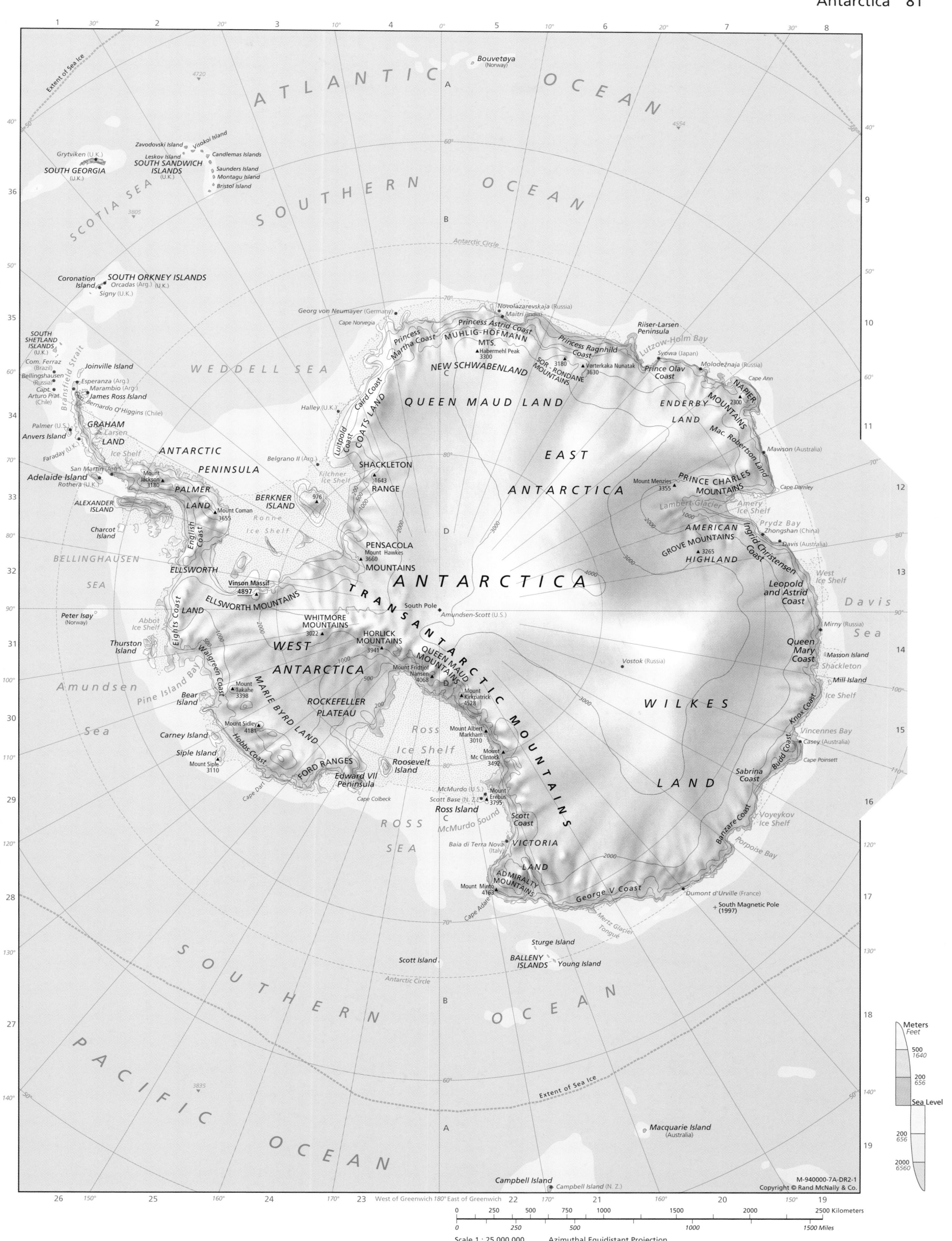

ATLANTIC OCEAN

Bouvetøya
(Norway)

SOUTHERN OCEAN

SCOTIA SEA

Grytviken (U.K.)
SOUTH GEORGIA
(U.K.)

Zavodovski Island
Leskov Island   Visokoi Island
SOUTH SANDWICH   Candlemas Islands
ISLANDS   Saunders Island
(U.K.)   Montagu Island
Bristol Island

Coronation   SOUTH ORKNEY ISLANDS
Island   Orcadas (Arg.) (U.K.)
Signy (U.K.)

Antarctic Circle

Georg von Neumayer (Germany)
Novolazarevskaja (Russia)
Maitri (India)

Princess Astrid Coast   Riiser-Larsen
Cape Norvegia   Princess   MÜHLIG-HOFMANN   Peninsula
SOUTH   Martha Coast   MTS.   Princess Ragnhild   Lützow-Holm Bay
SHETLAND   Coast   Syowa (Japan)
ISLANDS   Habermehl Peak   SOR-   3180   Molodežnaja (Russia)
(U.K.)   NEW SCHWABENLAND   3300   RONDANE   Vorterkaka Nunatak   Prince Olav
Com. Ferraz (Brazil)   MOUNTAINS   3630   Coast
Bellingshausen   QUEEN MAUD LAND   Cape Ann
(Russia)   Joinville Island   ENDERBY   NAPIER
Capt.   Esperanza (Arg.)   Halley (U.K.)   EAST   LAND   2300
Arturo Prat   Marambio (Arg.)   Caird Coast   Mac. Robertson Land   Mawson (Australia)
(Chile)   James Ross Island   Coats Land   ANTARCTICA
Bernardo O'Higgins (Chile)   SHACKLETON   PRINCE CHARLES
Palmer (U.S.)   GRAHAM   Belgrano II (Arg.)   RANGE   Mount Menzies   MOUNTAINS
Larsen   1643   3355   Cape Darnley
Anvers Island   LAND   Ice Shelf   Amery
Faraday (U.K.)   ANTARCTIC   Filchner   AMERICAN   Ice Shelf
Mount Jackson   PENINSULA   BERKNER   Ice Shelf   976   GROVE MOUNTAINS   3265   Prydz Bay
San Martin (Arg.)   3180   ISLAND   HIGHLAND   Zhongshan (China)
Adelaide Island   PALMER   Ronne   Davis (Australia)
Rothera (U.K.)   ALEXANDER   LAND   Mount Coman   Ice Shelf   PENSACOLA   Leopold   West
ISLAND   3655   Mount Hawkes   ANTARCTICA   and Astrid   Ice Shelf
BELLINGHAUSEN   Charcot   3660   MOUNTAINS   Coast   Davis
SEA   Island   ELLSWORTH   Vinson Massif   South Pole   Queen   Sea
Peter Isøy   4897   ELLSWORTH MOUNTAINS   Amundsen-Scott (U.S.)   Mary
(Norway)   Abbot   TRANSANTARCTIC   Coast   Mirny (Russia)
Ice Shelf   WHITMORE   Masson Island
Thurston   MOUNTAINS   HORLICK   MOUNTAINS   Vostok (Russia)   Shackleton
Island   3022   MOUNTAINS   QUEEN MAUD   WILKES   Mill Island
Amundsen   WEST   3941   MOUNTAINS   Ice Shelf
Mount   Mount Fridtjof   Vincennes Bay
Bear   Takahe   ANTARCTICA   Nansen   LAND   Knox Coast
Sea   Island   3398   4068   Casey (Australia)
Pine Island Bay   MARIE BYRD LAND   ROCKEFELLER   Mount   Mount Albert   Cape Poinsett
Mount Sidley   PLATEAU   Kirkpatrick   Markham   Sabrina
4181   4528   3010   Coast
Carney Island   Ross   Mount   Budd Coast
Siple Island   Ice Shelf   Mc Clintock
Mount Siple   FORD RANGES   Roosevelt   3492
3110   Edward VII   Island   McMurdo (U.S.)   Banzare Coast
Cape Dart   Peninsula   Mount   Voyeykov
Cape Colbeck   Scott Base (N.Z.)   Erebus   Ice Shelf
ROSS   Ross Island   3795   Porpoise Bay
SEA   McMurdo Sound   Scott
Baia di Terra Nova   Coast
(Italy)   VICTORIA
LAND
ADMIRALTY   George V Coast   Dumont d'Urville (France)
Mount Minto   MOUNTAINS
4163   South Magnetic Pole
Cape Adare   (1997)
Mertz Glacier
Tongue

Sturge Island
BALLENY   Young Island
Scott Island   ISLANDS

Antarctic Circle

SOUTHERN OCEAN

PACIFIC OCEAN

Macquarie Island
(Australia)

Campbell Island
Campbell Island (N.Z.)

West of Greenwich   East of Greenwich

WEDDELL SEA

English Coast

Eights Coast

Walgreen Coast

Hobbs Coast

Extent of Sea Ice

Meters   Feet
500   1640
200   656
Sea Level
200   656
2000   6560

M-940000-7A-DR2-1
Copyright © Rand McNally & Co.

0   250   500   750   1000   1500   2000   2500 Kilometers
0   250   500   1000   1500 Miles

Scale 1 : 25,000,000   Azimuthal Equidistant Projection

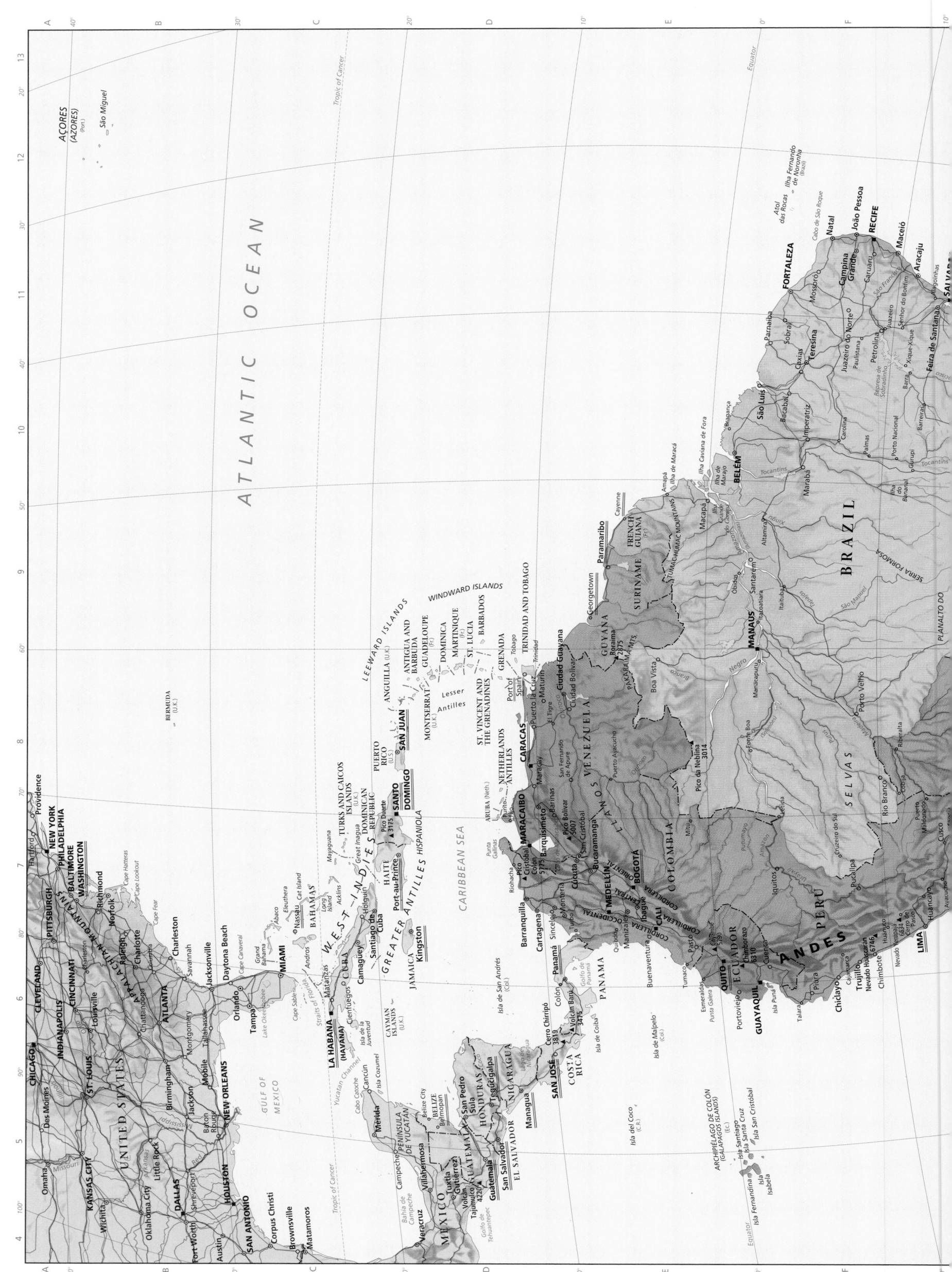

ATLANTIC OCEAN

AÇORES
(AZORES)
(Port.)

São Miguel

Tropic of Cancer

BERMUDA
(U.K.)

UNITED STATES

Omaha
Des Moines
KANSAS CITY
St. Louis
Wichita
Oklahoma City
Little Rock
Fort Worth
DALLAS
Austin
HOUSTON
SAN ANTONIO
Corpus Christi
Brownsville
Matamoros

CHICAGO
INDIANAPOLIS
CINCINNATI
Louisville
Nashville
Chattanooga
Birmingham
ATLANTA
Montgomery
Jackson
Mobile
Baton Rouge
NEW ORLEANS

CLEVELAND
PITTSBURGH
Charleston
Knoxville
Charlotte
Raleigh
Columbia
Savannah
Jacksonville
Daytona Beach
Orlando
Tampa
MIAMI

Providence
Hartford
NEW YORK
PHILADELPHIA
BALTIMORE
WASHINGTON
Richmond
Norfolk
Cape Hatteras
Cape Lookout
Cape Fear
Charleston

APPALACHIAN MTS

Mississippi
Missouri
Arkansas
Ohio

GULF OF
MEXICO

Tropic of Cancer

MEXICO
Veracruz
Tlajomulco
Volcán
Tajumulco 4220
GUATEMALA
Villahermosa
Tuxtla
Gutiérrez
PENINSULA
DE YUCATÁN
Campeche
Mérida
Cabo Catoche
Isla Cozumel
Yucatán Channel
Cabo Corrientes
Cabo San Antonio
BELIZE
Belmopan
Belize City
San Pedro
Sula
HONDURAS
Tegucigalpa
EL SALVADOR
San Salvador
NICARAGUA
Managua
León
Lago de
Nicaragua
COSTA
RICA
SAN JOSÉ
Cerro Chirripó
3819
Volcán Barú
3475
Panamá

Bahía de
Campeche
Golfo de
Tehuantepec
Equator

GULF OF
MEXICO

LA HABANA
(HAVANA)
Matanzas
Cienfuegos
CUBA
Camagüey
Santiago de
Cuba
Holguín
CAYMAN
ISLANDS
(U.K.)
Isla de la
Juventud

BAHAMAS
Grand
Bahama
Abaco
Nassau
Eleuthera
Cat Island
Andros
Long
Island
Acklins
Mayaguana
Great Inagua

TURKS AND CAICOS
ISLANDS
(U.K.)

W E S T - I N D I E S

G R E A T E R   A N T I L L E S

JAMAICA
Kingston

CARIBBEAN SEA

HAITI
Port-au-Prince
DOMINICAN
REPUBLIC
SANTO
DOMINGO
Pico Duarte
3175
HISPANIOLA

PUERTO
RICO
(U.S.)
SAN JUAN

Lesser
Antilles

ANGUILLA (U.K.)
ANTIGUA AND
BARBUDA
GUADELOUPE
(Fr.)
DOMINICA
MARTINIQUE
(Fr.)
ST. LUCIA
ST. VINCENT AND
THE GRENADINES
BARBADOS
GRENADA

LEEWARD ISLANDS

WINDWARD ISLANDS

MONTSERRAT
(U.K.)

Port of
Spain
TRINIDAD AND TOBAGO
Trinidad
Tobago

NETHERLANDS
ANTILLES
ARUBA (Neth.)

Punta
Gallinas
Riohacha
Barranquilla
Cartagena
Sincelejo
PANAMÁ
Colón
Golfo de
Panamá
Isla de San Andrés
(Col)

MARACAIBO
Cristóbal
Colón
5775
Maracay
Barquisimeto
VENEZUELA
CARACAS
Maturín
Ciudad Bolívar
Ciudad Guayana
Puerto la Cruz
Cumaná
El Tigre

Georgetown
GUYANA
Paramaribo
SURINAME
Cayenne
FRENCH
GUIANA
(Fr.)

Roraima
2875
SIERRA PACARAIMA MTS
TUMUCUMAQUE MOUNTAINS

Pico Bolívar
5007
San Cristóbal
Bucaramanga
Cúcuta
BOGOTÁ
MEDELLÍN
Ibagué
CALI
Pasto
COLOMBIA
Quibdó
Manizales
Buenaventura
CORDILLERA OCCIDENTAL
CORDILLERA CENTRAL
CORDILLERA ORIENTAL

San Fernando
de Apure
San Fernando
L O S   L L A N O S
Orinoco

Boa Vista
Branco
Negro
Pico da Neblina
3014
Manicouaque
Rio Branco

SERRA FORMOSA

BRAZIL

Amapá
Ilha de
Maracá
Macapá
Ilha do
Bailique
BELÉM
Ilha de
Marajó
Ilha
Caviana de Fora
Ilha de Fora
Óbidos
Santarém
Itaituba
Marabá
Carolina
Altamira
Tocantins
S E L V A S
MANAUS
Itaituba
Fonte Boa
Tabatinga
Tefé
Coari
Porto Velho
Cruzeiro do Sul

Atol
das Rocas
Ilha Fernando
de Noronha
(Brazil)

Cabo de São Roque
Natal
João Pessoa
RECIFE
Maceió
SALVADOR
Aracaju
FORTALEZA
Sobral
Parnaíba
Mossoró
Teresina
Juazeiro do Norte
Caxias
São Luís
Bacabal
Imperatriz
Campina
Grande
Caruaru
Petrolina
Juazeiro
Senhor do Bonfim
Feira de Santana
Barra
Xique-Xique
Paulistana
Bragança
São Manuel

São Francisco
DEPRESA DO
SOLIMÕES

Iquitos
PERU
Pucallpa
LIMA
Huancayo
Huánuco
Cerro de
Pasco
Nevado Huascarán
6768
Chimbote
Trujillo
Chiclayo
Cajamarca
Nevado
6634
Cusco
A N D E S

ECUADOR
QUITO
Cotopaxi
5897
Chimborazo
6310
GUAYAQUIL
Portoviejo
Esmeraldas
Tumaco
Punta Galera
Punta
Talara

ARCHIPIÉLAGO DE COLÓN
(GALÁPAGOS ISLANDS)
(Ec.)
Isla Santiago
Isla Santa Cruz
Isla San Cristóbal
Isla Fernandina
Isla
Isabela

Isla del Coco
(C.R.)
Isla de Malpelo
(Col)

Equator

PLANALTO DO

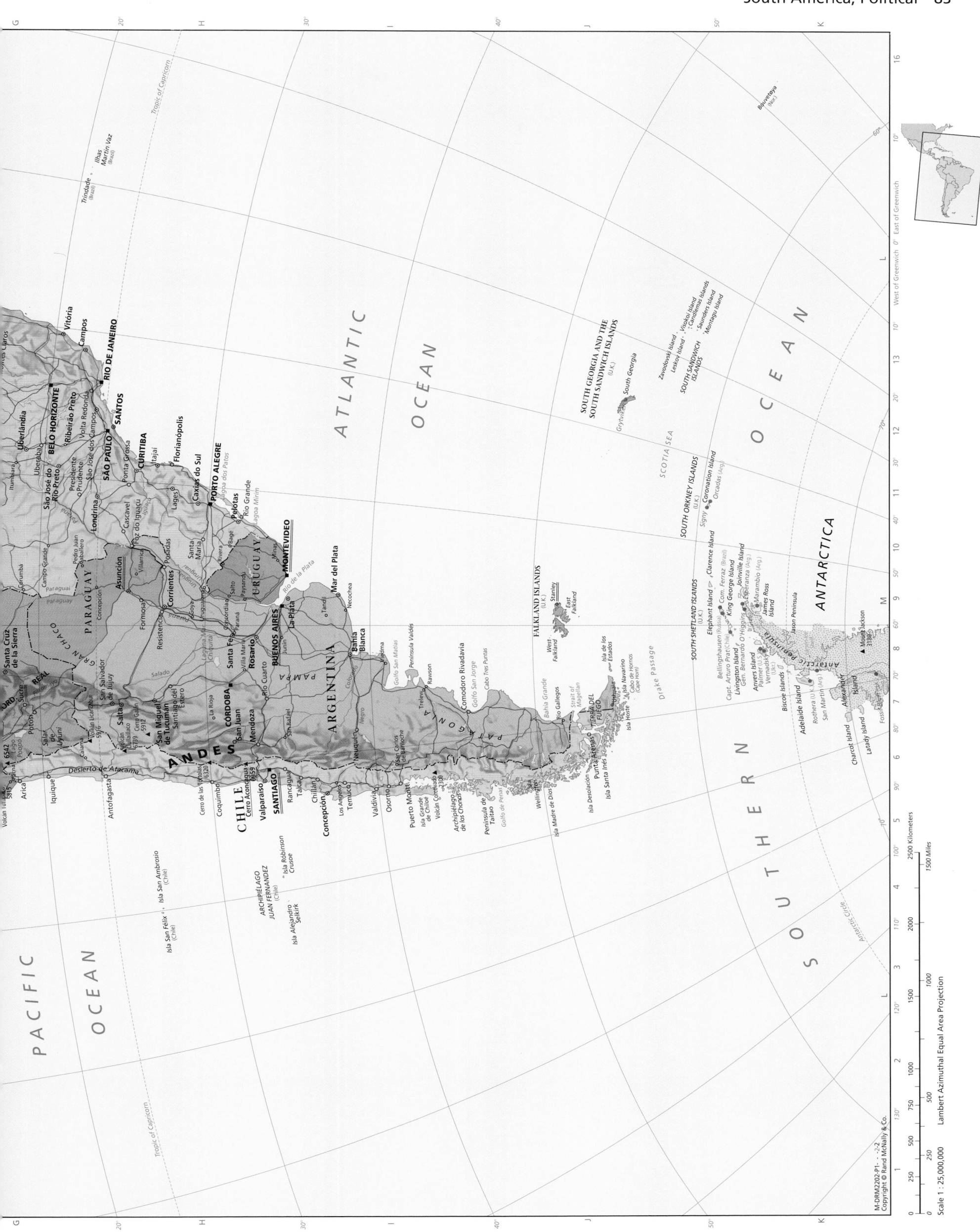

ATLANTIC

OCEAN

PACIFIC

OCEAN

SOUTHERN

OCEAN

ANTARCTICA

ARGENTINA

CHILE

PARAGUAY

URUGUAY

ANDES

PATAGONIA

PAMPA

GRAN CHACO

FALKLAND ISLANDS (U.K.)

SOUTH GEORGIA AND THE SOUTH SANDWICH ISLANDS (U.K.)

SOUTH ORKNEY ISLANDS

SOUTH SHETLAND ISLANDS (U.K.)

SCOTIA SEA

Drake Passage

Antarctic Peninsula

RIO DE JANEIRO
SÃO PAULO
BELO HORIZONTE
PORTO ALEGRE
MONTEVIDEO
BUENOS AIRES
La Plata
Rosario
CÓRDOBA
SANTIAGO
Valparaíso
Asunción
CURITIBA
SANTOS

Scale 1 : 25,000,000
Lambert Azimuthal Equal Area Projection
Copyright © Rand McNally & Co.

ATLANTIC

OCEAN

New Amsterdam
Nieuw
Nickerie
Totness   Paramaribo
Groningen   Onverwacht   Nieuw Amsterdam
Brokopondo   Albina   Moengo   Iracoubo
Kwakoegron   Saint-Laurent   Sinnamary
du Maroni   Kourou   Île du Diable
Brokopondo Stuwmeer   Saint-Élie   Tonate   Cayenne
                              Rémiré
SURINAME   FRENCH   Guisan Bourg   Rémiré
Juliana Top   GUIANA   Cabo Orange
▲1230   Ouanary   Saint-Georges
Saül   Clevelândia   Oiapoque   Cabo Caciporé
                    do Norte
TUMUC-HUMAC MOUNTAINS   Vila Velha
                              Cunani   Calçoene
                    Amapá
                        Ilha de Maracá
AMAPÁ   Cabo Norte
                    Sucuriju
Lago Novo
Serra do Navio   Aporema
            Ferreira   Ilha Bailique
            Gomes   Ilha do Curuá
Porto Grande   Ilha Janaucu
        Macapá   Ilha Caviana de Fora
    Porto Santana   Ilha Mexiana
    Mazagão   Equator

Cabo Maguari
Ilha Grande   Itatupá   Cabo de Marajó
de Gurupá   ILHA DE MARAJÓ   Soure   Salinópolis
Gurupá   Curumu   Anajás   Joanes   Curuçá   Bragança
        Ilha da   Breves   Mosqueiro   Maracanã
Carrazedo   Laguna   São Miguel   Muaná   Igarapé-   Açu
Alenquer   dos Macacos   BELÉM   Carutapera
Óbidos   Porto de   Abaetetuba   São Domingos do Capim   Turiaçu
Monte Alegre   Moz   Curralinho   Acará   Irituia   Curupu
    Portel   Cametá   Tomé-Açu   Camiranga   Guimarães
        Veiros   Juaba   Carapajó   Itamataré   Santa   Alcântara
Santarém   Baião   Pinheiro   Helena   Anil   Paulino
                        São Bento   São Luís   Neves
    Vitória   Pindaré-Mirim   Viana   Rosário   Barreirinhas   Parnaíba
    Altamira   Monção   Anajatuba   Urbano Santos   Tutóia   Cancoim
                        Itapecuru-Mirim   Luzilândia   Granja
Itaituba   Tucuruí   Cantanhede   Brejo   Piracuruca   Sobral   Maranguape
                        Bacabal   Coroatá   Chapadinha   Tianguá   Maracanaú   FORTALEZA
            Jacundá   Lago da Pedra   Codó   Miguel Alves   Ipu   Canindé   Itapipoca   Pacajus
PARÁ   Represa de   Caxias   Timon   Campo Maior   Pedro II   Baturité   Beberibe
        Tucuruí   Pedreiras   União   Barras   Pedro II   Acopiara   Itapiúna   Aracati
                                    Teresina   Pio IX   Taiá
            Itupiranga   Açailândia   MARANHÃO   Crateús   Senador Pompeu   Quixadá   Russas   São Bento
        São João   Amarante do   Presidente   Piquet Carneiro   Quixeramobim   do Norte
Marabá   Araguaí   Maranhão   Dutra   São Miguel do Tapuio   Iguatu   Tabuleiro   Mossoró   Macau   Touros
    Imperatriz   Montes Altos   Grajaú   Bacatuba   Água Branca   Jucás   do Norte   Assu   Macaíba   Cabo
Araguatins   Santa Isabel   Sítio   Colinas   Elesbão Veloso   Jaguaribe   RIO GRANDE   de
    do Araguaia   Nazaré   Novo   Amarante   Floriano   Vale do   Iguatu   DO NORTE   Natal   São Roque
Carajás   Xambioá   São Raimundo   Pastos Bons   Piauí   Oeiras   Campos Sales   Orós   Currais Novos
SERRA DOS CARAJÁS   das Mangabeiras   São João dos Patos   Picos   Crato   Juazeiro   Caicó
Cachoeira   Araguaína   Babaçulândia   Benedito Leite   PIAUÍ   do Norte   Cajazeiras   Patos   Campina
Cantagalo   Carolina   Riachão   Balsas   Simplício Mendes   CHAPADA DO ARARIPE   Itaporanga   Grande   João
Gradaús   Canto do Buriti   Paulistana   Salgueiro   Belém de   Flores   PARAÍBA   Pessoa
    Conceição do Araguaia   Cristino Castro   São Raimundo   Parnamirim   São Francisco   Sertânia   Timbaúba
BRAZIL   Pequizeiro   Itacajá   Nonato   Santa Maria da Boa Vista   Arcoverde   Jardim   Carpina   Olinda
SERRA DO CACHIMBO   Alto Parnaíba   Bom Jesus   Caracol   Casa Nova   Chorrochó   Garanhuns   RECIFE
    Araguacema   Pedro Afonso   Santa Filomena   Juazeiro   Petrolina   Palmeira   Palmares   Caruaru
Cachimbo   Dois Irmãos de Goiás   Miracema   Monte Alegre   Remanso   PERNAMBUCO   dos Índios   Ribeirão   Porto
        do Tocantins   do Piauí   Curimatá   Uauá   Paulo Afonso   União dos   de Pedras
    Porto dos Gaúchos   Tocantínia   Gilbués   Parnaguá   Jaguarari   Jeremoabo   ALAGOAS   Rio Largo
Cachoeira Aquili   Palmas   Curupá   Paulo Afonso   Maceió
    APIACÁS   Pium   Represa de   Jaguarari   Campo Formoso   Senhor do   Euclides da   Itabaiana   Propriá   Corunpe
                Cristalândia   Sono   Represa de   Bonfim   Cunha   SERGIPE   Junqueiro   Brejo Grande
    Ilha do   Porto Nacional   Sobradinho   Ribeira do Pombal   Lagarto
    Bananal   Brejinho de Nazaré   Barra   Xique-Xique   Jacobina   Tucano   Aracaju
    Duerê   Natividade   Dianópolis   Irecê   Serrinha   Olindina   Rio Real   Estância
MATO GROSSO   Gurupi   Peixe   Morro do Chapéu   Riachão do Jacuípe   Inhambupe   Esplanada
            TOCANTINS   Ponte Alta do   Barreiras   Ibotirama   BAHIA   Feira de Santana   Alagoinhas
PLANALTO DO   Bom Jesus   Taguatinga   Ruy Barbosa   Camaçari
MATO GROSSO   Araguaçu   Paranã   Santana   Ibitiara   Lençóis   Itaberaba   Iaçu   Santo Amaro   Candeias   SALVADOR
        São Miguel   Arraias   Correntina   Seabra   Santo Antônio   Maragogipe
        do Araguaia   Bandeirantes   São Domingos   Bom Jesus   Mucujê   Maracás   de Jesus   Valença
Diamantino   Porangatu   Cavalcante   Correntina   da Lapa   Paramirim   Jaguaquara   Ilha de Tinharé
Nobres   Minaçu   Nova Roma   Colinas   Posse   Pico das Almas   Jequié   Gandu   Camamu
Paraguai   GOIÁS   Colinas   Riacho de Santana   ▲1836   Maracás   Ubatá   Itacaré
rosário Oeste   Acorizal   Pilar de Goiás   Guanambi   Barra da Estiva   Gandu
    Cuiabá   São João   Formosa   Caculé   Poções   Coaraci
SERRA DE SÃO JERÔNIMO   da Aliança   Goianésia   Manga   Urandi   Vitória da   Ibicaraí   Ilhéus
Jaciara   General Carneiro   Barra do   Goiás   Brasília   Monte Azul   Conquista   Itambé   Itabuna
Poxoréu   Itapirapuã   Garças   Uruaçu   DISTRITO   São Francisco   Januária   Rio Pardo   Itapetinga   Una
Barão de Melgaço   Baliza   Aragarças   Iporá   Jussara   Goiás   FEDERAL   São Romão   Janaúba   de Minas   Pedra Azul   Canavieiras
Rondonópolis   Guiratinga   Piranhas   Jaraguá   Itaberaí   Anápolis   GOIÂNIA   Montes Claros   São João   Jordânia   Belmonte
Alto Garças   Aurilândia   Ceres   Silvânia   Luziânia   Unaí   do Paraíso   Jequitinhonha   Porto Seguro
Alto Araguaia   Caiapônia   Jandaia   Goiás   Cristalina   Mogol   Itaobim   Itamaraju
MATO GROSSO DO SUL   Minérios   Rio Verde   Cristianópolis   Pires do   MINAS GERAIS   Bocaiúva   Águas   Formosas   Prado
Pantanal de   Jatai   Santa Helena   Rio   Campo Alegre de Goiás   Caatinga   Piraporá   Minas Novas   Alcobaça
São Lourenço   Pedro Gomes   de Goiás   Bois   Morrinhos   João Pinheiro   Coronel   Carlos   Jequitinhonha   Caravelas
                        Pontalina   Ipameri   Capelinha   Murta   Chagas   Ponta da Baleia
                            Teófilo Otoni   Nanuque

M-DRM4705-A1- - - -2
Copyright © Rand McNally & Co.

CARIBBEAN SEA

PACIFIC

OCEAN

PANAMA

COLOMBIA

ECUADOR

PERU

Scale 1 : 5,000,000 Sinusoidal Projection

W-DRM5522-A1
Copyright © Rand McNally & Co.

72° West of Greenwich

ATLANTIC OCEAN

NETHERLANDS
ANTILLES

LESSER ANTILLES

TRINIDAD
AND TOBAGO

TRINIDAD

Gulf of Paria

CARACAS

V E N E Z U E L A

DISTRITO
FEDERAL

MIRANDA

ARAGUA

YARACUY

CARABOBO

COJEDES

GUÁRICO

PORTUGUESA

BARINAS

APURE

ANZOÁTEGUI

MONAGAS

SUCRE

Delta del Orinoco

DELTA
AMACURO

CUYUNI-MAZARUNI

BARIMA-WAINI

G U Y A N A

POTARO-
SIPARUNI

UPPER TAKUTU-
UPPER
ESSEQUIBO

B O L Í V A R

G U I A N A   H I G H L A N D S
(M A C I Z O   D E   G U A Y A N A)

LA GRAN SABANA

Parque Nacional Canaima

A M A Z O N A S

GUAINÍA

SIERRA PARIMA

Parque Nacional
Parima Tapirapecó

R O R A I M A

B R A Z I L

A M A Z O N A S

MANAUS

Pico da
Neblina
3014

Parque Nacional
Pico da Neblina

ILHA
PEDRO II

Parque Nacional
do Jaú

Equator

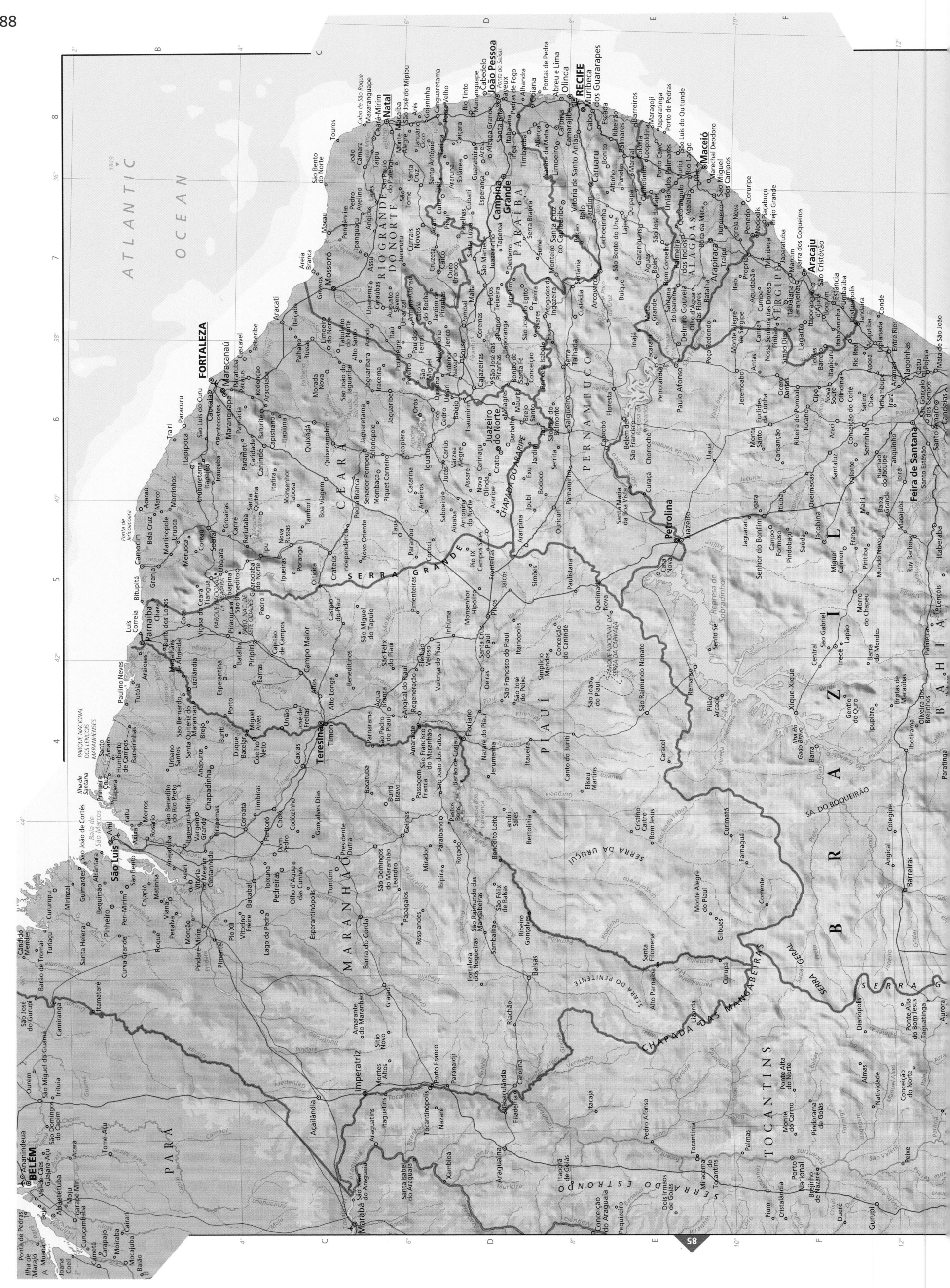

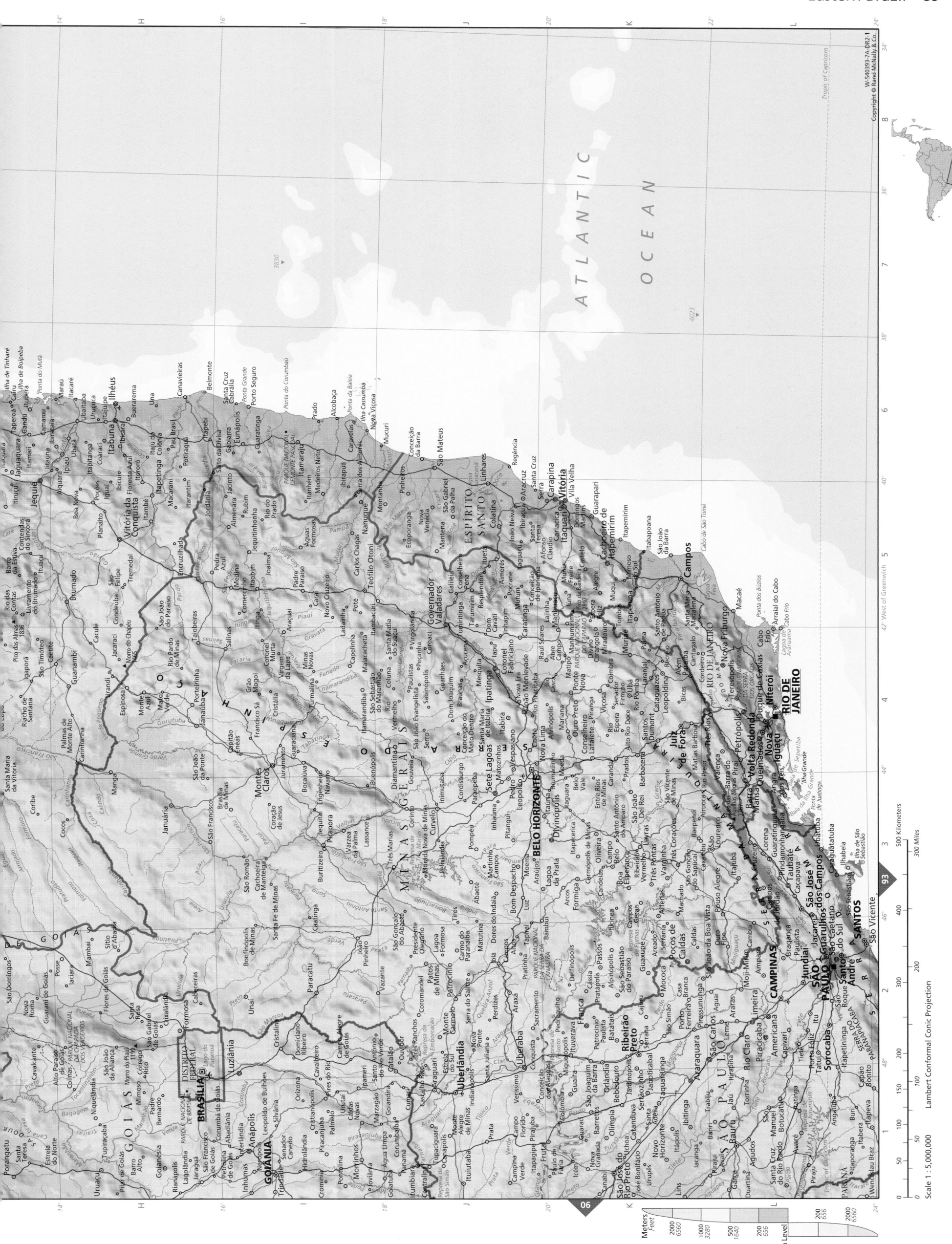

ATLANTIC

OCEAN

Tropic of Capricorn

GOIÁS

BRASÍLIA
DISTRITO FEDERAL

MINAS GERAIS

BELO HORIZONTE

ESPÍRITO SANTO

Vitória

Campos

RIO DE JANEIRO

RIO DE JANEIRO
Niterói

SÃO PAULO

SÃO PAULO

SANTOS

GOIÂNIA

Uberlândia

Montes Claros

Governador Valadares

Juiz de Fora

CAMPINAS

Ribeirão Preto

Sorocaba

Ilhéus

Vitória da Conquista

Meters / Feet
2000 / 6560
1000 / 3280
500 / 1640
200 / 656
Sea Level

200 / 656
2000 / 6560

Scale 1 : 5,000,000   Lambert Conformal Conic Projection

0   50   100   150   200   300   400   500 Kilometers
0   50   100   200   300 Miles

93

06

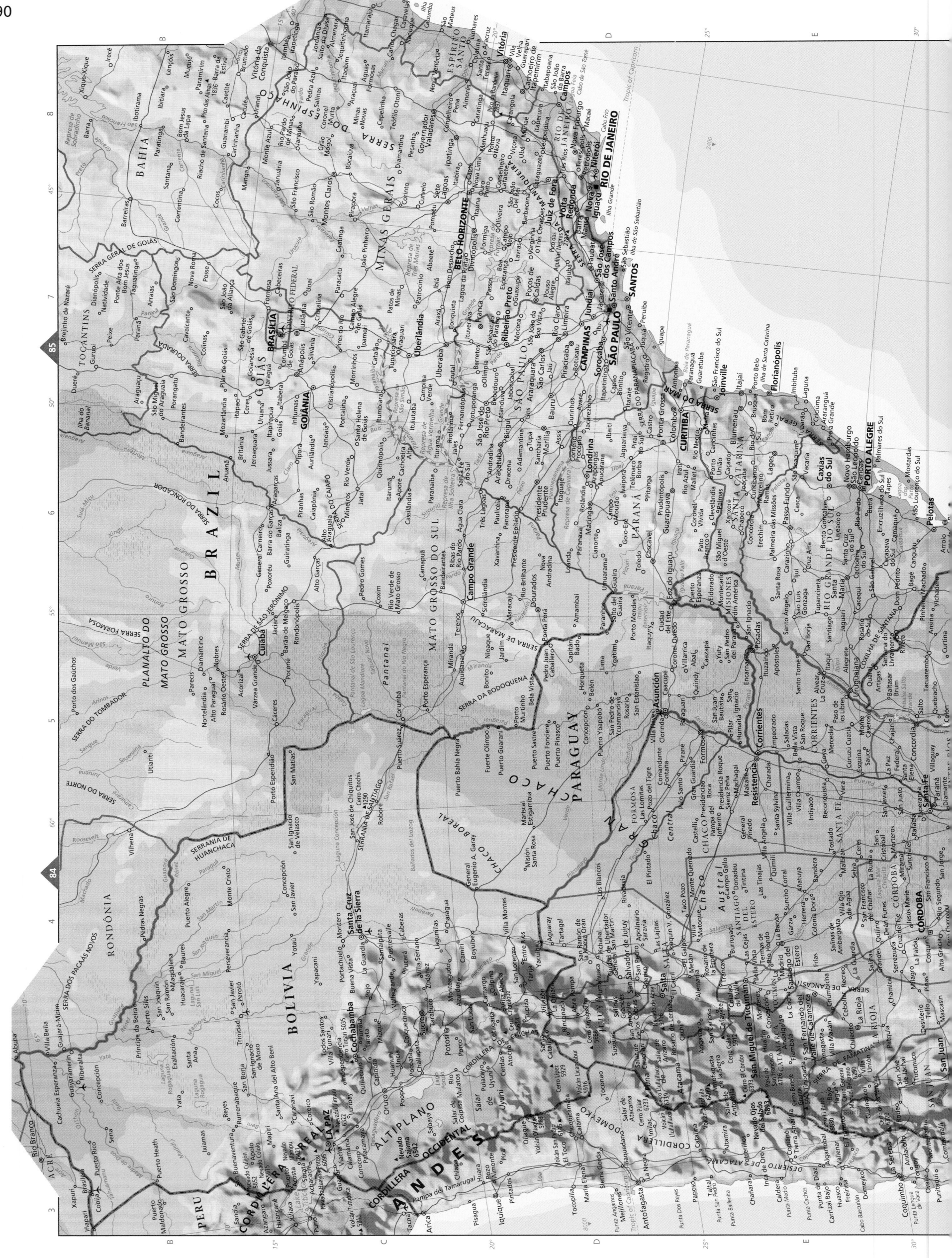

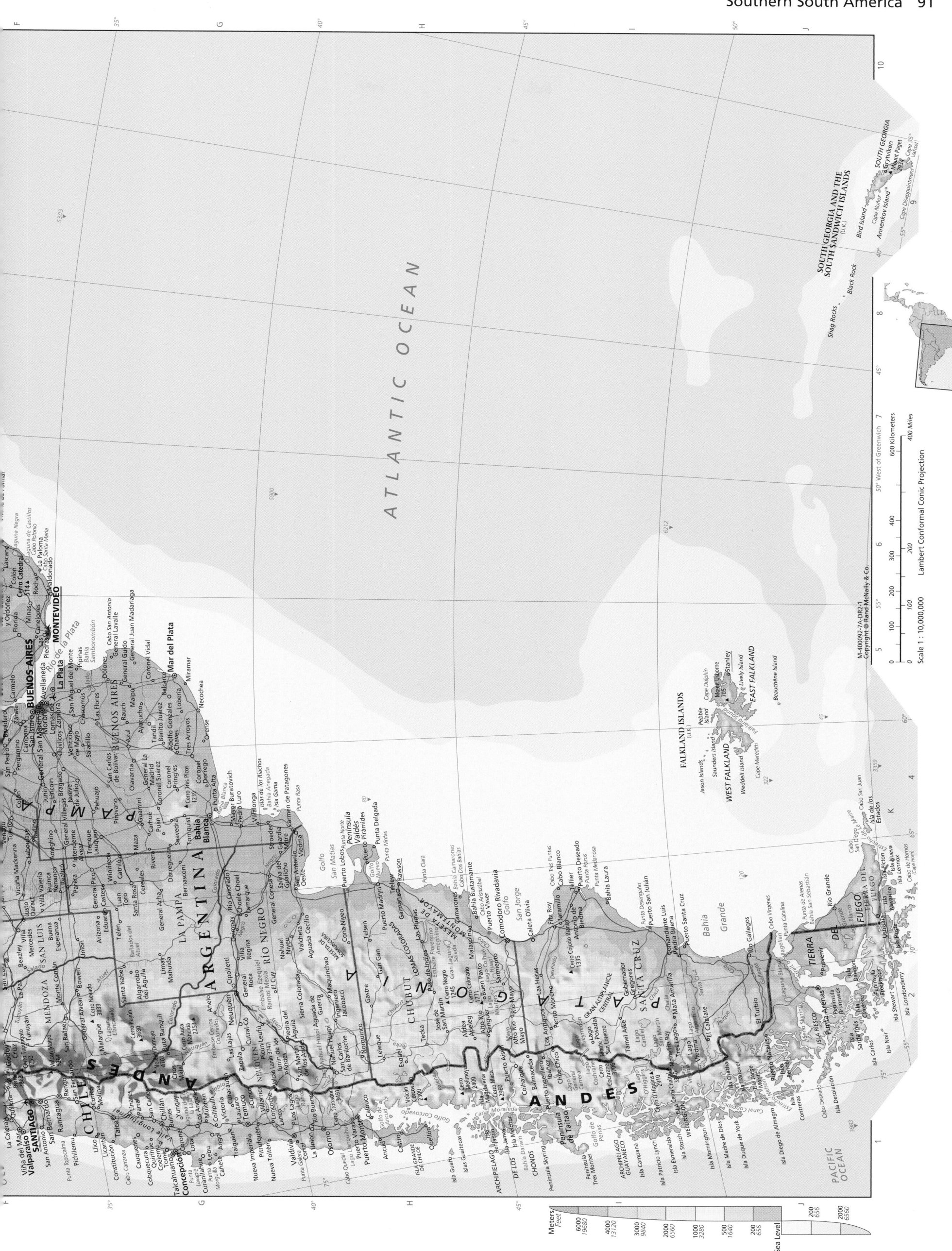

ATLANTIC OCEAN

SOUTH GEORGIA AND THE
SOUTH SANDWICH ISLANDS

SOUTH GEORGIA
Grytviken
Mount Paget
2934

Cape Nuñez
Annenkov Island
Cape Disappointment

Shag Rocks
Bird Island
Black Rock

FALKLAND ISLANDS
(U.K.)

Cape Dolphin
Mount Usborne
705
Stanley
Pebble Island
Saunders Island
WEST FALKLAND
Jason Islands
Weddell Island
Lively Island
EAST FALKLAND
Beauchene Island
Cape Meredith
322

50° West of Greenwich

Scale 1 : 10,000,000

Lambert Conformal Conic Projection

M-400092-7A-DR2.1
Copyright © Rand McNally & Co.

0   100   200   300   400   500   600 Kilometers
0   100   200   300   400 Miles

BUENOS AIRES
MONTEVIDEO
La Plata
Mar del Plata

URUGUAY
ARGENTINA
LA PAMPA
BUENOS AIRES
RIO NEGRO
NEUQUEN
CHUBUT
SANTA CRUZ
MENDOZA
SAN LUIS

PAMPA

ANDES

CHILE
SANTIAGO
Valparaíso
Concepción

P A T A G O N I A

TIERRA
DEL
FUEGO

ARCHIPIELAGO
DE LOS
CHONOS

ARCHIPIELAGO
GUAYANECO

Peninsula
de Taitao

PACIFIC
OCEAN

Meters Feet
6000 19680
4000 13120
3000 9840
2000 6560
1000 3280
500 1640
200 656
Sea Level
200 656
2000 6560

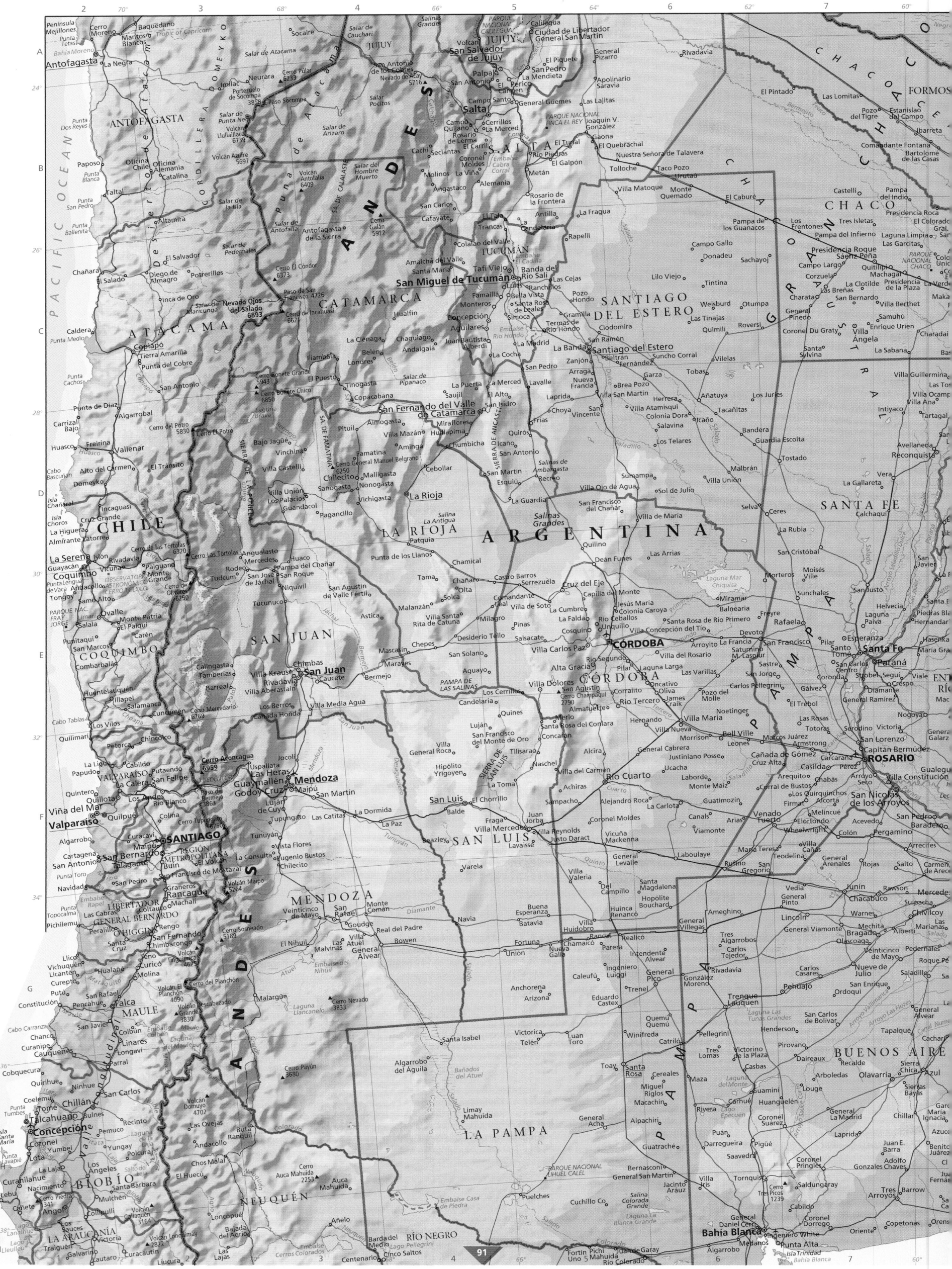

ATLANTIC OCEAN

BRAZIL

PARAGUAY

URUGUAY

CORRIENTES

RIO GRANDE DO SUL

SANTA CATARINA

PARANÁ

SÃO PAULO

BUENOS AIRES

MONTEVIDEO

CURITIBA

PORTO ALEGRE

Florianópolis

Asunción

Mar del Plata

La Plata

Joinville

Blumenau

Itajaí

Caxias do Sul

Novo Hamburgo

Pelotas

Rio Grande

Meters
Feet

6000
19680

4000
13120

3000
9840

2000
6560

1000
3280

500
1640

200
656

Sea Level

200
656

2000
6560

W-540195-7A-DR2-1
Copyright © Rand McNally & Co.

0   50   100   150   200   300   400   500 Kilometers
0   50   100   200   300 Miles

Scale 1 : 5,000,000   Lambert Conformal Conic Projection

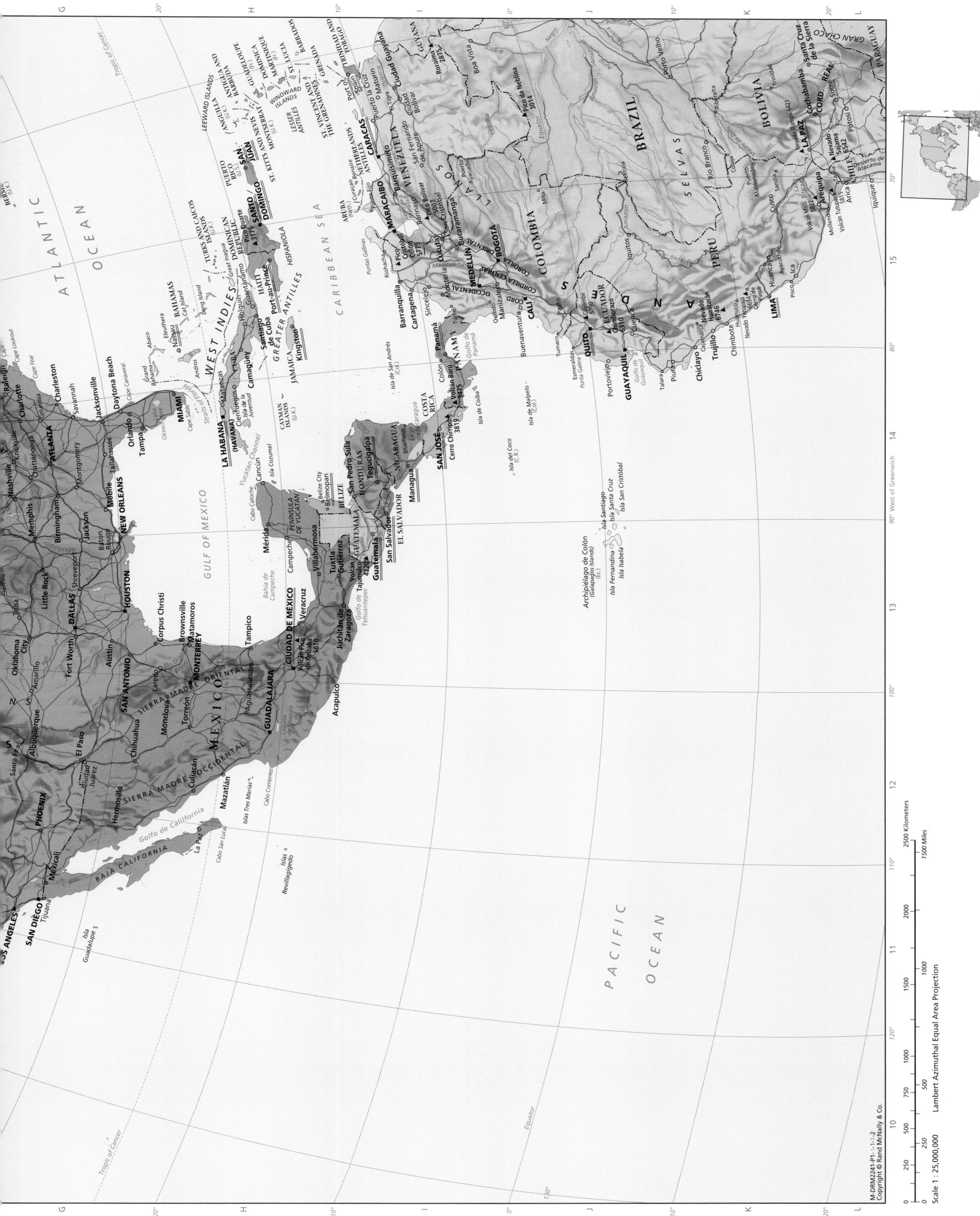

Scale 1 : 25,000,000   Lambert Azimuthal Equal Area Projection

Scale 1 : 10,000,000   Lambert Conformal Conic Projection

M-DRM4703-A1- -1- -2
Copyright © Rand McNally & Co.

ATLANTIC OCEAN

BERMUDA (U.K.)
Hamilton

MISSISSIPPI
ALABAMA
GEORGIA
SOUTH CAROLINA
N.C.
Wilmington
Cape Fear
Long Bay
Georgetown
Charleston
Beaufort
Savannah
Brunswick
Jacksonville
Jacksonville Beach
St. Augustine
Palatka
Daytona Beach
FLORIDA
Orlando
Titusville
Cape Canaveral
Cocoa
Melbourne
Tampa
St. Petersburg
Clearwater
Lakeland
Winter Haven
Vero Beach
Bradenton
Sarasota
Avon Park
Fort Pierce
Port Charlotte
Fort Myers
Cape Coral
West Palm Beach
Lake Worth
Boca Raton
Naples
Hialeah
Fort Lauderdale
Hollywood
Miami Beach
MIAMI
Homestead
Everglades City
Cape Sable
Key Largo
Florida Keys
Dry Tortugas
Key West

NEW ORLEANS
Houma
Chandeleur Islands
Mississippi Delta
Biloxi
Pascagoula
Pensacola
Panama City
Fort Walton Beach
Port St. Joe
Cape San Blas
Apalachee Bay
Perry
Gainesville
Ocala
De Land
Leesburg
Sanford

ATLANTA
Birmingham
Tuscaloosa
Montgomery
Columbus
Phenix City
Opelika
Auburn
Troy
Ozark
Dothan
Andalusia
Enterprise
Talladega
Anniston
Rome
Marietta
Covington
Augusta
Aiken
Orangeburg
Sumter
Columbia
Florence
Conway
Myrtle Beach
Camden
Anderson
Newberry
Greenwood
Athens
Gainesville
Huntsville
Decatur
Gadsden
Jasper
Bessemer

Oxford
Tupelo
Grenada
Columbus
Clarksdale
Cleveland
Greenville
Yazoo City
Canton
Jackson
Meridian
Demopolis
Selma
Laurel
Hattiesburg
McComb
Bogalusa
Gulfport
Mobile
Atmore

Huntsville
Cullman

BAHAMAS
Little Abaco
Marsh Harbour
Grand Bahama
Freeport
Abaco
Great Abaca
Berry Islands
Bimini Islands
Nicholl's Town
New Providence
Nassau
Andros
Kemps Bay
Eleuthera
Governor's Harbour
Arthur's Town
Cat Island
Mount Alvernia
63
San Salvador
Rum Cay
Long Island
Great Exuma
Exuma Cays
Exuma Sound

Tropic of Cancer

Clarence Town
Crooked Island
Acklins
Ragged Island Range
Mayaguana
Caicos Islands
TURKS AND CAICOS ISLANDS (U.K.)
Grand Turk
Turks Islands
Little Inagua
Great Inagua
Matthew Town

WEST   INDIES

CUBA
LA HABANA (HAVANA)
Matanzas
Cárdenas
Colón
Güines
Artemisa
Los Palacios
Pinar del Río
Guane
Cabo San Antonio
Nueva Gerona
Isla de la Juventud
Golfo de Batabanó
Santa Clara
Cienfuegos
Sagua la Grande
Caibarién
Placetas
Sancti Spíritus
Trinidad
Morón
Ciego de Ávila
Camagüey
Las Tunas
Santa Cruz del Sur
Golfo de Guacanayabo
Manzanillo
Bayamo
Holguín
Florida
Nuevitas
Gibara
Banes
Sagua de Tánamo
Baracoa
Palma Soriano
Santiago de Cuba
Guantánamo
Caimanera
SIERRA MAESTRA
Pico Turquino 1972
Cabo Cruz
Archipiélago de los Jardines de la Reina
Golfo de Ana María

GREATER   ANTILLES

CAYMAN ISLANDS (U.K.)
George Town
Little Cayman
Cayman Brac
Grand Cayman

JAMAICA
Montego Bay
Savanna-la-Mar
Spanish Town
Kingston
Blue Mountain Peak 2256
Mount Denham 986
St. Ann's Bay
Morant Cays

HAITI
HISPANIOLA
Cap-Haïtien
Gonaïves
Golfe de la Gonâve
Île de la Gonâve
Jérémie
Pic Macaya 2347
Les Cayes
Île à Vache
Port-au-Prince
Morne La Selle 2674
Jacmel

DOMINICAN REPUBLIC
Monte Cristi
Mao
Santiago de los Caballeros
La Vega
Pico Duarte 3175
San Juan de la Maguana
Azua
Barahona
Isla Beata
Cabo Beata
Cabo Engaño
SANTO DOMINGO
San Pedro de Macorís
La Romana
San Francisco de Macorís
Cabo Samaná
Isla de Mona
Cabo Rojo
Mayagüez
PUERTO RICO (U.S.)
Mona Passage

Windward Passage
Navassa Island (U.S.)

CARIBBEAN SEA

BELIZE
Belize City
Belmopan
Dangriga
Hill Bank
Orange Walk
Corozal
Chetumal
Victoria Peak 1120
Punta Gorda
La Libertad
San Luis

QUINTANA ROO
YUCATÁN PENINSULA
Mérida
Valladolid
Izamal
Tizimín
Río Lagartos
Cancún
Isla Cozumel
Tulum
Felipe Carrillo Puerto
Campeche
CAMPECHE
Escárcega
Hopelchén
Dzibalchén
Peto
Ticul
Maxcanú
Frogreso
Temax
Cabo Catoche
Puerto Juárez
Nueva Gerona
Corrientes
Arrecife Alacrán

GUATEMALA
GUATEMALA
Cobán
San Pedro Sula
HONDURAS
Tegucigalpa
Comayagua
Danlí
Juticalpa
Olanchito
El Progreso
Yoro
Santa Rosa de Copán
Cerro Las Minas 2849
Cerro El Pital 2730
Mogotón 2107
La Ceiba
Puerto Cortés
Tela
Trujillo
Balfate
Roatán
Isla de Roatán
Islas de la Bahía
Cabo Camarón
Laguna de Caratasca
Puerto Lempira
Cabo Gracias a Dios
Livingston
Puerto Barrios
Gulf of Honduras

EL SALVADOR
SAN SALVADOR
Nueva San Salvador
Santa Ana
Sonsonate
San Miguel
Unión
Golfo de Fonseca

NICARAGUA
Managua
Masaya
Jinotepe
Granada
León
Chinandega
Estelí
Jinotega
Matagalpa
Chichigalpa
Lago de Managua
Lago de Nicaragua
Bonanza
Siuna
Waspán
Puerto Cabezas
Prinzapolka
Bluefields
El Rama
Santo Tomás
Juigalpa
Laguna de Perlas
Islas del Maíz
Bahía de Punta Gorda
Punta Gorda
Cayos Miskitos
CORDILLERA ISABELIA
Ometepe
San Carlos
San Juan del Norte
Rivas
San Juan del Sur

COSTA RICA
SAN JOSÉ
Alajuela
Cartago
Volcán Irazú 3432
Cerro Chirripó 3819
Liberia
Santa Cruz
Nicoya
Puntarenas
Península de Nicoya
Golfo de Nicoya
San Isidro del General
Ciudad Cortés
Golfito
Puerto Limón
Volcán Barú 3475
David
Puerto Armuelles
Península de Osa
Golfo Dulce
Volcán Miravalles 2028
Cabo Santa Elena
Golfo de Papagayo

Quitasueño
Cayo de Serranilla (Col.)
Bayo Nuevo (Col.)
Cayo de Serrana
Cayos de Roncador
Isla de Providencia (Col.)
Isla de San Andrés (Col.)
Cayos de Albuquerque
San Andrés

PANAMA
PANAMÁ
Colón
Portobelo
Bocas del Toro
Almirante
Bajo Boquete
Boquete
Santiago
Chitré
Las Tablas
Penonomé
Aguadulce
La Chorrera
Canal de Panamá
SERRANÍA DEL DARIÉN
La Palma
Yaviza
Jaqué
Acandí
Golfo de Panamá
Isla del Rey
Sona
Chepo
Cabo Marzo
Las Perlas
Isla de Coiba
Isla de Cebaco
Punta Mala
Punta Mariato
Punta Burica
Golfo de Chiriquí
Golfo de los Mosquitos
Palmas Bellas
Santa Catalina

COLOMBIA
MEDELLÍN
BOGOTÁ
Barranquilla
Cartagena
Santa Marta
Ciénaga
Riohacha
Valledupar
Fundación
Plato
Magangué
Mompós
El Banco
Sincelejo
Corozal
Montería
San Marcos
Ayapel
Caucasia
Nechí
Segovia
Zaragoza
Puerto Berrío
Barrancabermeja
Aguachica
Ocaña
Cúcuta
Bucaramanga
San Gil
Socorro
Málaga
Chiquinquirá
Tunja
Ibagué
Armenia
Pereira
Manizales
Cartago
Quibdó
Istmina
Nuquí
Buenaventura
Cabo Corrientes
CORDILLERA OCCIDENTAL
CORDILLERA CENTRAL
Nevado del Tolima
Sabanalarga
El Carmen de Bolívar
Turbaco
Arjona
San Jacinto
San Onofre
Turbo
Chigorodó
Cristóbal Colón 5775
SERRANÍA DE PERIJÁ
Dabeiba
Frontino
Urrao
Pico Bolívar 5007
Trujillo
Valera
La Concepción
Cabimas
MARACAIBO
Lago de Maracaibo
Barinas
Guanare
Mérida
CORD. DE MÉRIDA
Barquisimeto
Carora
San Carlos del Zulia
VENEZUELA
Guasdualito
Arauca
Tame
Arauquita
Tibú
Pamplona
Puerto Santander
Cúcuta
Villavicencio
Chávita
LLANOS
Orocué
Cravo Norte
Yopal

ARUBA (Neth.)
NETH. ANT.
Curaçao
Oranjestad
Punta Gallinas
Cabo de la Vela
Península de la Guajira
Uribia
Maicao
Punto Fijo
Golfo de Venezuela
Punta Cardón
Coro
Paraguaná
Península de Paraguaná

PACIFIC OCEAN

NEVADA

CALIFORNIA

ARIZONA

UTAH

BAJA CALIFORNIA

BAJA CALIFORNIA SUR

Meters / Feet
4000 / 13120
3000 / 9840
2000 / 6560
1000 / 3280
500 / 1640
200 / 656
Sea Level
200 / 656
2000 / 6560

0 50 100 150 200 300 400 500 Kilometers
0 50 100 200 300 Miles
Scale 1 : 5,000,000   Lambert Conformal Conic Projection

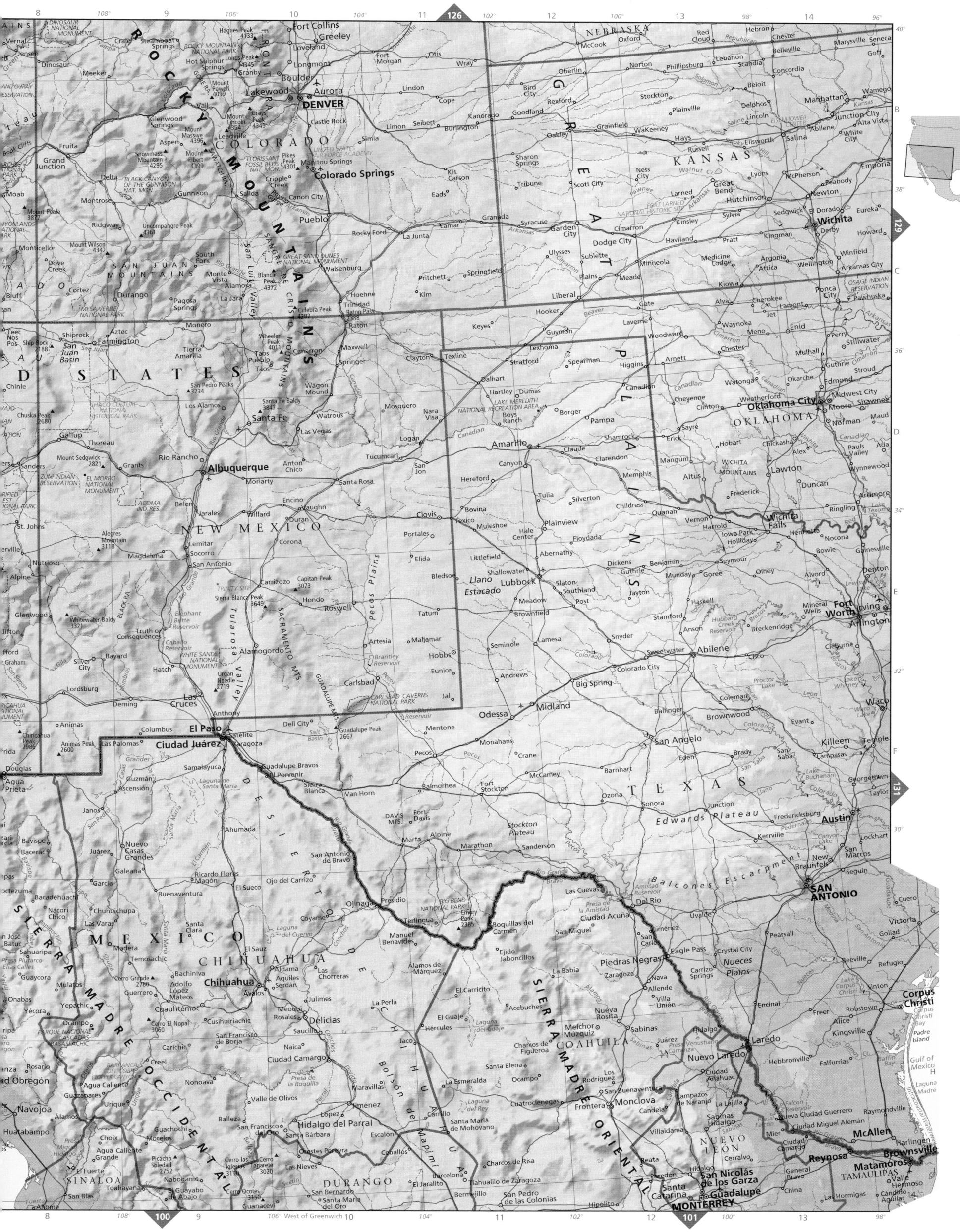

PACIFIC OCEAN

Scale 1 : 5,000,000   Lambert Conformal Conic Projection

W-532095-7A-DR2-1
Copyright © Rand McNally & Co.

Meters
Feet

4000
13120

3000
9840

2000
6560

1000
3280

500
1640

200
656

Sea Level

200
656

2000
6560

| 0 | 50 | 100 | 150 | 200 | 300 | 400 | 500 Kilometers |

| 0 | 50 | 100 | 200 | 300 Miles |

UNITED STATES

TEXAS

SAN ANTONIO

Corpus Christi

GULF OF MEXICO

Bahía de Campeche

MONTERREY
Saltillo

NUEVO LEÓN

TAMAULIPAS

COAHUILA

San Luis Potosí
Aguascalientes

León
GUANAJUATO
Querétaro
Irapuato

Morelia
MICHOACÁN

CIUDAD DE MÉXICO
(MEXICO CITY)
Toluca
PUEBLA
Cuernavaca

VERACRUZ
Xalapa
(Jalapa)
Veracruz

Acapulco

GUERRERO

OAXACA
Oaxaca de Juárez

ISTMO DE TEHUANTEPEC

TABASCO
Villahermosa

CAMPECHE
Ciudad del Carmen

CHIAPAS
Tuxtla Gutiérrez

Golfo de Tehuantepec

GUATEMALA
Tapachula
Puerto Madero

G u l f   o f   M e x i c o

Gulf of Honduras

Bahía de
Campeche

ISLAS DE LA BAHÍA

PENÍNSULA DE YUCATÁN

(YUCATAN PENINSULA)

Yucatan Channel

CAYMAN IS
(U.K.)

George Town   Grand
Cayman

LA HABANA
(HAVANA)   Matanzas

Cabo de San Antonio

Cabo Catoche

P A C I F I C

O C E A N

Scale 1 : 5,000,000   Lambert Conformal Conic Projection

W-536000-7A-DR2-1
Copyright © Rand McNally & Co.

CUBA

BAHAMAS

8   78°   9   76°   74°   72°   70°   13

Deadman
Cay
Long
Island   Clarence
Town
Cape Verde   Crooked
Island   Samana
Cay
Crooked Island Passage
Long Cay
Bight of
Acklins   Acklins   North East Point
Mayaguana   Mayaguana Passage
Salina Point

TURKS AND
CAICOS ISLANDS
(U.K.)

Providenciales
Middle
North Caicos   East
Caicos
CAICOS
ISLANDS   Grand Turk
TURKS
ISLANDS

ATLANTIC

OCEAN

22°

A

Ragged
Island
Ragged
Island Range   Cay Lobos
Cay Sal

West
Caicos

Little
Inagua   Palacca Point
North East Point
Lake
Rosa   Great
Inagua   Seal Cays

Matthew
Town

B

Turks Island Passage
Mouchoir Passage
Silver Bank Passage

Caibarién
Yaguajay
Placetas
Sancti
Spíritus
Ciego
de Ávila   Morón
Esmeralda   Cayo Romano
Cayo Sabinal
Cayo Guajaba
Nuevitas
Minas
Camagüey   Puerto
Manatí   Jesús
Menéndez   Rafael
Freyre   Gibara   Antilla   Banes
Bahía de Nipe
Puerto
Padre   Holguín
Las Tunas   Mayarí
Cueto   Sagua
de Tánamo   Tiguabos   Baracoa

Golfo de
Ana María

Manzanillo   Bayamo   Jiguaní
Palma
Soriano   San
Luis   Guantánamo
SIERRA MAESTRA   Santiago
de Cuba   Caimanera
GUANTÁNAMO BAY
NAVAL STATION (U.S.)   Imías

Niquero   Marea del
Portillo   Pico Turquino
1972   Cabo Cruz

HISPANIOLA

Île de la Tortue
Port-de-Paix   Cap-Haïtien   Manzanillo
Bay   Monte
Cristi   Cabo Isabela
Puerto Plata   Cabo Macoris
Cap du Môle   Cap à Foux   Limbé   Fort-Liberté   Dajabón   Mao   Pico Diego
de Ocampo
1749   Cabo Francés Viejo
Gonaïves   CITADELLE   Santiago de los
Caballeros   Moca   San Francisco
de Macorís   Nagua
Bahía
Escocesa   Cabo Samaná
Samaná
Bahía de Samaná
Saint-
Marc   HAITI   Morne Bonhomme
1788   Pico Duarte
3175   La Vega   Bonao   Hato Mayor del Rey   El Seibo
Higüey
Golfe de
la Gonâve   Île de la
Gonâve   Jérémie   Grande
Cayemite   Canal de Saint-Marc   Comendador   San Juan
de la Maguana   SANTO
DOMINGO   La Romana
San Pedro
de Macoris   Cabo
Engaño
Pic Macaya
2347   Anse-d'Hainault   Baie de Port
au-Prince   Port-au-Prince   Pétion-Ville   Neiba   San
Cristóbal   Azua
Canal du Sud   Léogâne   Petit-Goâve   Lago
Enriquillo   Bahía
de Ocoa   Punta
Palenque   Isla Saona
Bahía de Yuma
Coteaux   Aquin   Les Cayes   Jacmel   Morne
La Selle
2674   Barahona   DOMINICAN
REPUBLIC   Mona Passage
Pointe
Fanchon   Navassa
Island
(U.S.)   Pointe
Abacou   Île à Vache   Pedernales   Enriquillo   18°
Cabo Falso   Isla Beata   Cabo Beata

Cayman
Brac

JAMAICA   Montego Bay   Falmouth   Ocho
Rios   Saint Ann's
Bay   Port
Maria   Port
Antonio
Mount
Denham▲
986   Spanish
Town   Kingston   Blue Mountain Peak
2256   Morant
Bay
South Negril Point   Savanna-la-Mar   Mandeville   Portland
Bight   Morant Point
Portland Point

GREATER   ANTILLES   Windward Passage   Jamaica Channel

2184

Morant
Cays

Pedro
Cays

Cayo de Serranilla
(Col.)   Bajo Nuevo
(Col.)   16°

C

D

CARIBBEAN   SEA   14°   E

Roncador

5102

LESSER   ANTILLES

ARUBA
(Neth.)   Oranjestad   NETHERLANDS
ANTILLES
(Neth.) Bonaire   Willemstad   Curaçao   F

Bahía Honda   Punta Gallinas
Puerto Bolívar   Bahía
Portete   Cabo San Román   Pueblo
Nuevo   Península
de Paraguaná   12°
Cabo de La Vela   Punta Espada   Los Taques   Punta
Fijo   Puerto
Cardón   Cabo   La Vela
de Coro   Punta
Zamuro
Península
de La Guajira   Uribia   Golfo de
Venezuela   Coro   Cumarebo

Riohacha   Maicao   Ensenada
de Calabozo   Paraguaipoa   Capatárida   Pedregal   San Luis   Cabure
Santa Marta   Cabo de
La Aguja   Uribia   Sinamaica   San Rafael   Dabajuro   FALCÓN   Churuguara
Barranquilla   Ciénaga   Pico
Cristóbal
Colón
5775   Barrancas   Albania   Guasare   Altagracia   Cerro de Mauroa   Yumare   YARACUY
Soledad   LA GUAJIRA   Fonseca   MARACAIBO   Santa
Rita   Siquisique   PARQUE NACIONAL   YURUBÍ   San Felipe
ATLÁNTICO   Malambo   Fundación   Villanueva   Cabimas   Cabo   VENEZUELA   10°
Baranoa   Santa Marta   La Paz   Villa del
Rosario   Tía Juana   Ciudad Ojeda   Carora   LARA   Barquisimeto
Cartagena   Sabanalarga   Manatí   El Piñón   Valledupar   Agustín   Machiques   Lago de
Maracaibo   Bachaquero   Mene Grande   Quibor   MERIDA
Islas del
Rosario   Turbaco   Pivijay   Calamar   Codazzi   ZULIA   La Ceiba   Sabana de Mendoza   Carache   ARURI
Arjona   El Guamo   Pedraza   CESAR   Cerro Mu
2610   La Ceiba   Bobures   Valera   TRUJILLO   Acarigua   48
María La Baja   San
Juan   Mompós   Cerro   San Pedro
del Zulia   Trujillo   Ospino   PORTUGUESA
Islas de
San Bernardo   San
Onofre   El Carmen
de Bolívar   Magangué   Guamal   Chiriguaná   Casigua   El Vigía   Guárico   Santa
Cruz
Golfo de
Morrosquillo   San Antero   Ovejas   MAGDALENA   Tamalameque   San Pedro   Mucuchíes   Barinas   Barinitas
Sincelejo   San Pedro   Corozal   El Banco   BOLÍVAR   El Dividive   Tovar   Mérida   Guanare
Istmo de Panamá
(Isthmus of Panama)   Nombre
de Dios   El Porvenir   Tolú   Lorica   Planeta
Rica   Pueblo
Nuevo   SUCRE   Pinillos   Aguachica   Ocaña   Pico Bolívar
5007   Bocono   Barinas
SERRANÍA DE SAN BLAS   Montería   Cereté   Achí   El Carmen   Cúcuta   Santa
Panamá   Cabo
Tiburón   Punta
Caribana   Arboletes   San Pelayo   Caucasia   ANTIOQUIA   Gamarra   NORTE DE
SANTANDER   Barbara   LLANOS
Lago
Bayano   Turbo   Apartadó   Montelíbano   CÓRDOBA   San Marcos   Simití   Abrego   San Juan
de Colón   TÁCHIRA   APURE
ARCHIPIÉLAGO
DE LAS PERLAS   Golfo de
Urabá   Necoclí   Ayapel   Sardinata   San
Cristóbal   Palmarito   8°
Golfo de Panamá   PARQUE NACIONAL   DARIÉN   Yaviza   El Real de
Santa María   COLOMBIA   ANTIOQUIA   San Antonio del Táchira   Rubio

8   78° West of Greenwich   9   76°   86   74°   11   72°   12   70°   13

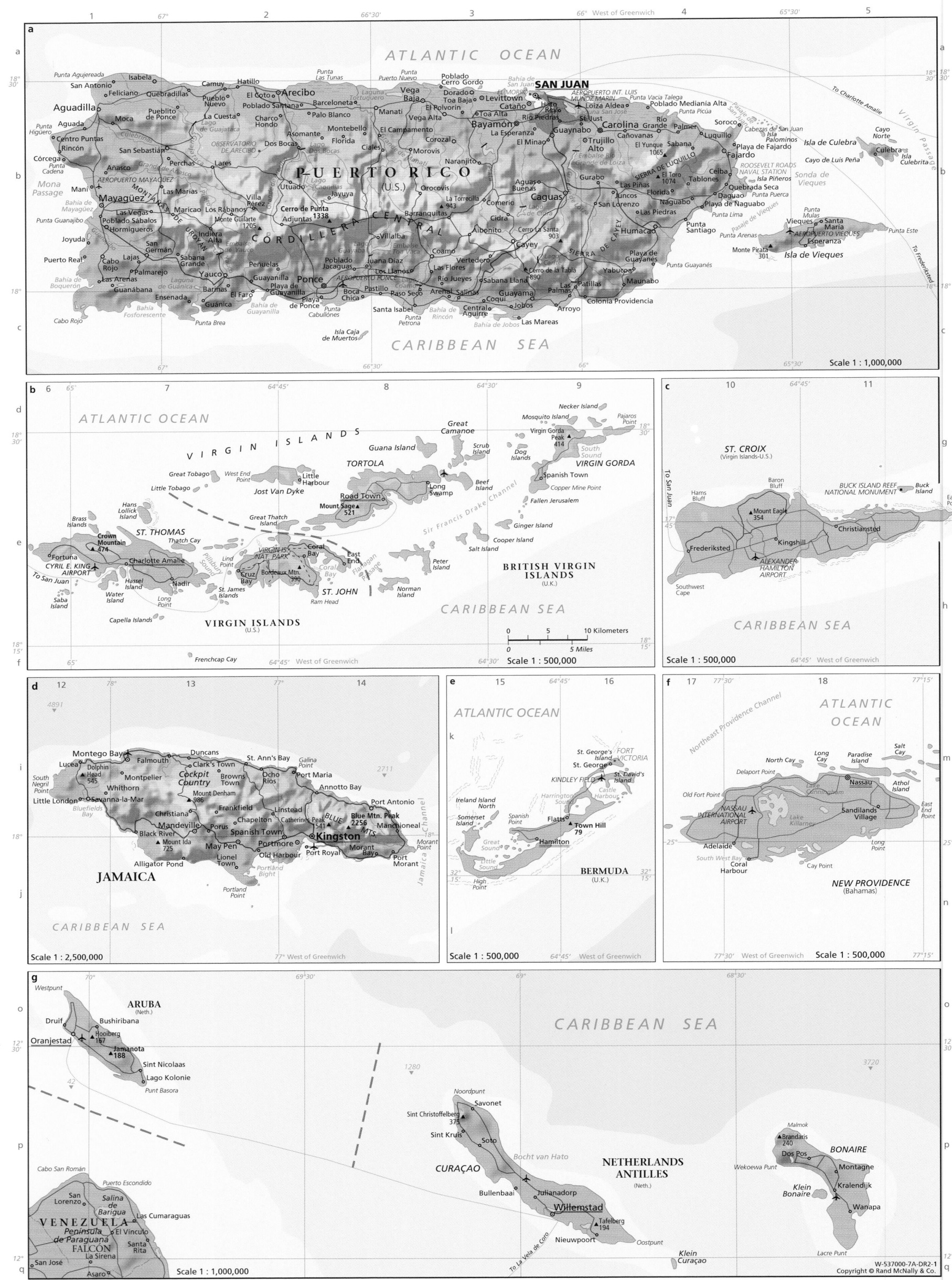

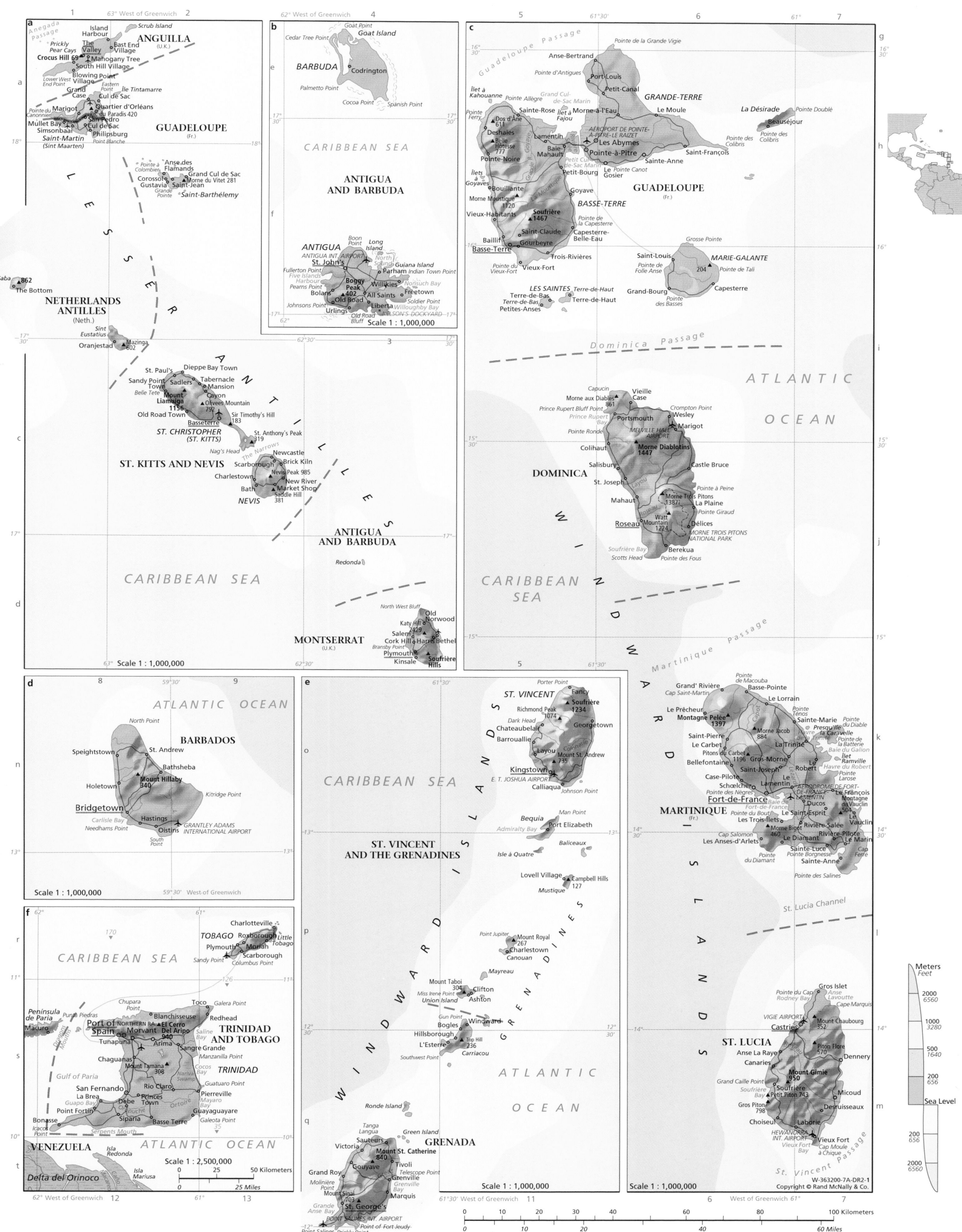

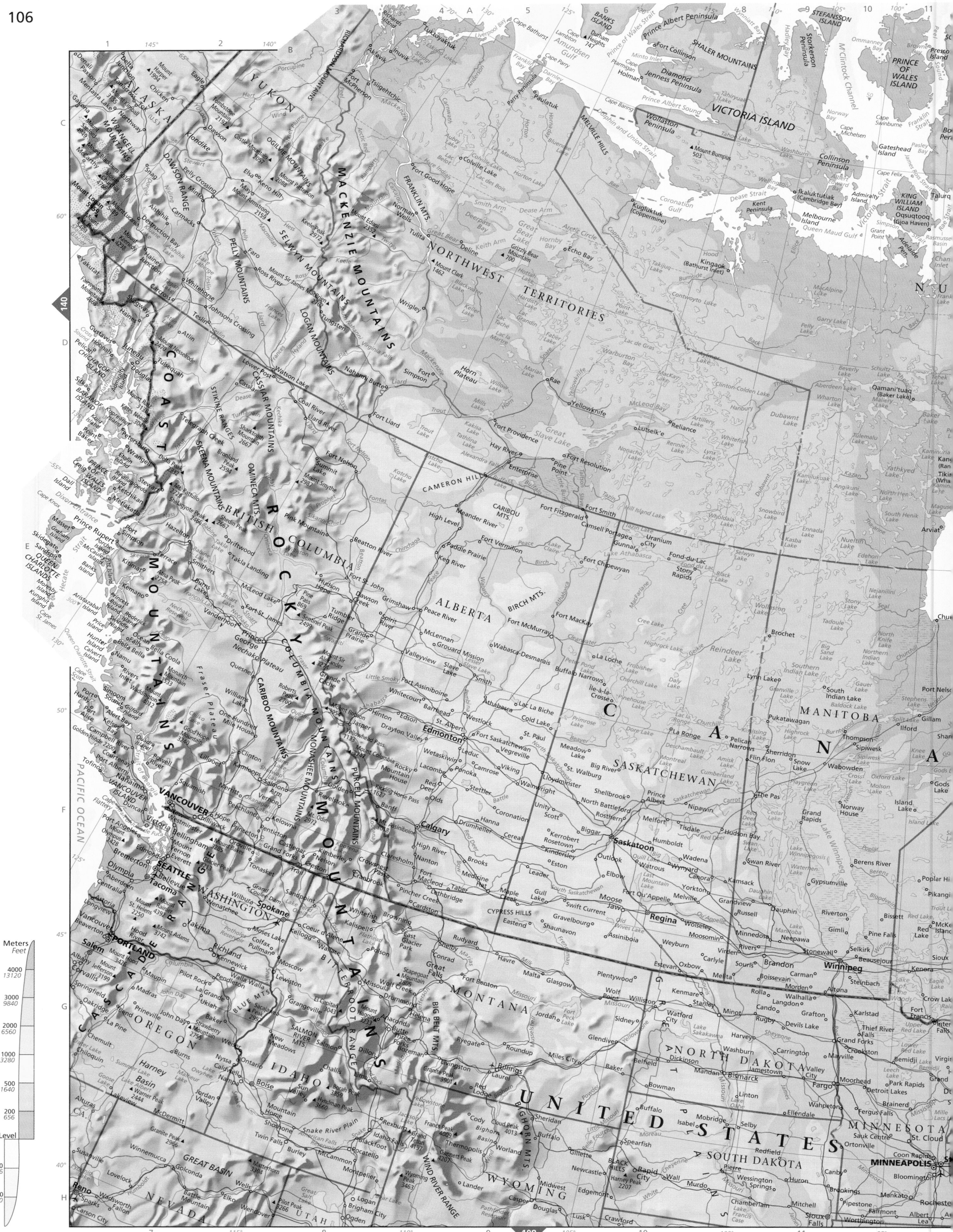

ALASKA (U.S.)
YUKON
NORTHWEST TERRITORIES
BRITISH COLUMBIA
ALBERTA
SASKATCHEWAN
MANITOBA
C A N A D A
WASHINGTON
OREGON
IDAHO
MONTANA
WYOMING
NEVADA
UTAH
NORTH DAKOTA
SOUTH DAKOTA
MINNESOTA
U N I T E D   S T A T E S

MACKENZIE MOUNTAINS
SELWYN MOUNTAINS
OGILVIE MOUNTAINS
PELLY MOUNTAINS
CASSIAR MOUNTAINS
LOGAN MOUNTAINS
OMINECA MOUNTAINS
SKEENA MOUNTAINS
COAST MOUNTAINS
ROCKY MOUNTAINS
CARIBOO MOUNTAINS
COLUMBIA MOUNTAINS
MONASHEE MOUNTAINS
PURCELL MOUNTAINS
CASCADE RANGE
BITTERROOT RANGE
WIND RIVER RANGE
GREAT BASIN

VANCOUVER
SEATTLE
TACOMA
PORTLAND
SALEM
SPOKANE
Calgary
Edmonton
Saskatoon
Regina
Winnipeg
MINNEAPOLIS
Reno

PACIFIC OCEAN
VICTORIA ISLAND
BANKS ISLAND
PRINCE OF WALES ISLAND
PRINCE OF WALES ISLAND (KING WILLIAM ISLAND)
QUEEN CHARLOTTE ISLANDS

Meters / Feet
4000 / 13120
3000 / 9840
2000 / 6560
1000 / 3280
500 / 1640
200 / 656
Sea Level
200 / 656
2000 / 6560

0 100 200 300 400 600 800 1000 Kilometers
0 100 200 400 600 Miles
Scale 1 : 10,000,000   Lambert Conformal Conic Projection

M-DRM4701-A1-1-2-2-3
Copyright © Rand McNally & Co.

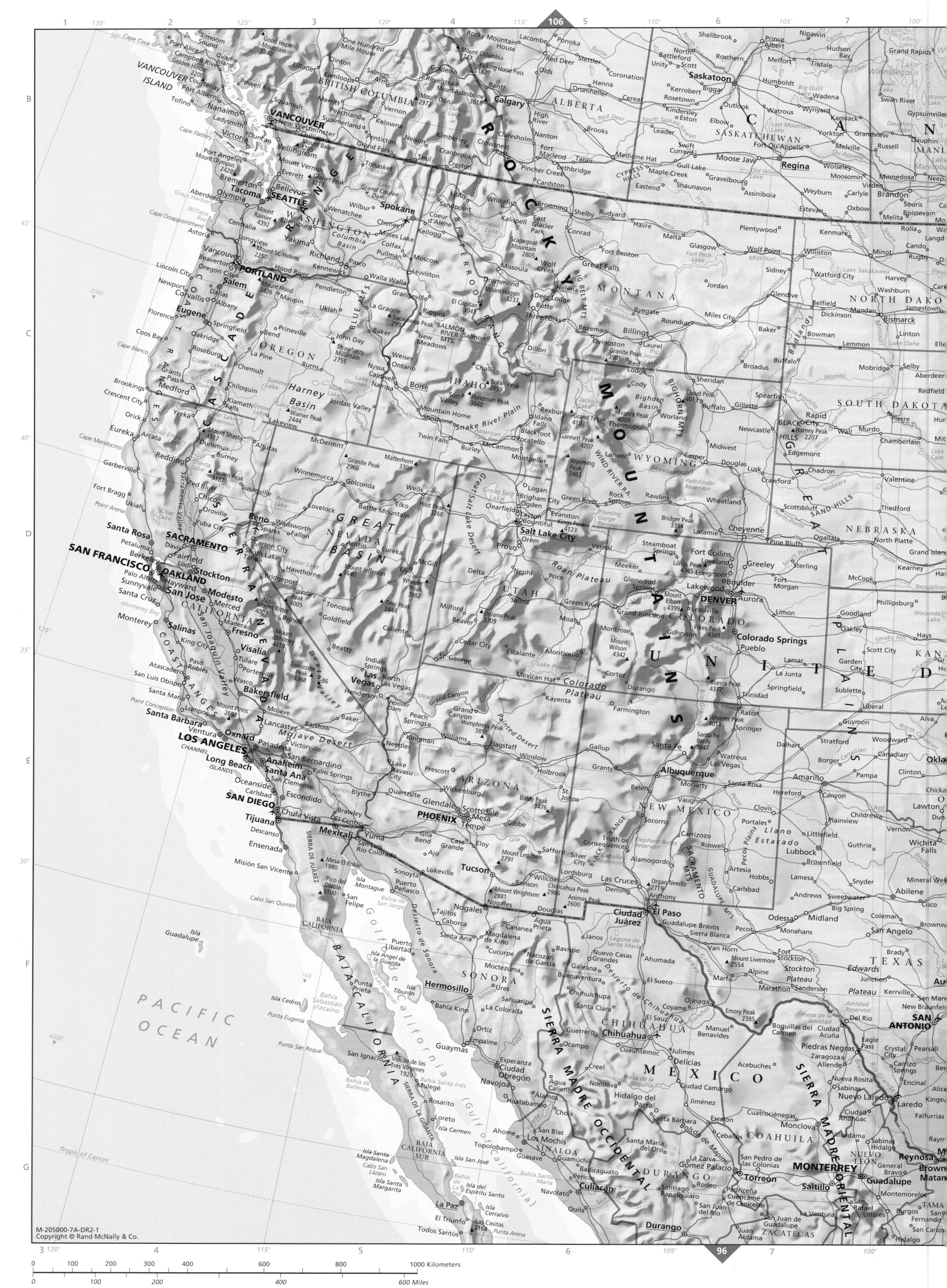

PACIFIC OCEAN

Meters / Feet
3000 / 9840
2000 / 6560
1000 / 3280
500 / 1640
200 / 656
Sea Level
200 / 656
2000 / 6560

0   100   200   300   400   600   800   1000 Kilometers
0   100   200   400   600 Miles
Scale 1 : 10,000,000   Lambert Conformal Conic Projection

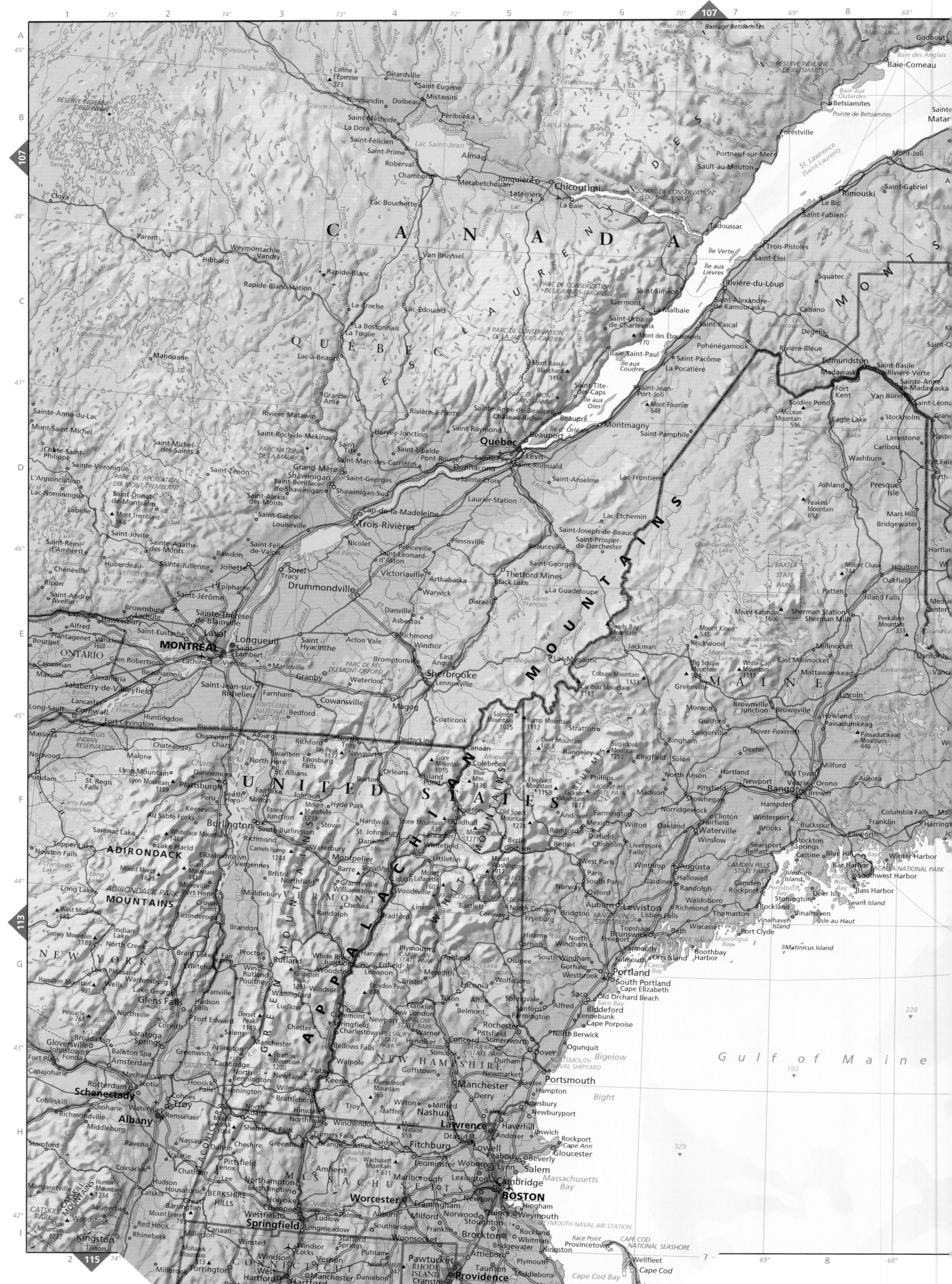

Gulf of St. Lawrence

NEWFOUNDLAND
AND LABRADOR

NEWFOUNDLAND

Cabot Strait

ÎLES DE LA
MADELEINE
(Que.)

NEW BRUNSWICK

PRINCE EDWARD ISLAND

CAPE BRETON
ISLAND

NOVA SCOTIA

Bay of Fundy

Halifax

ATLANTIC OCEAN

Sable Island
(N.S.)

Meters	
Feet	
1000	3280
500	1640
200	656
Sea Level	
200	656
2000	6560

0   25   50   75   100   150   200   250 Kilometers
0   25   50   100   150 Miles
Scale 1 : 2,500,000   Lambert Conformal Conic Projection

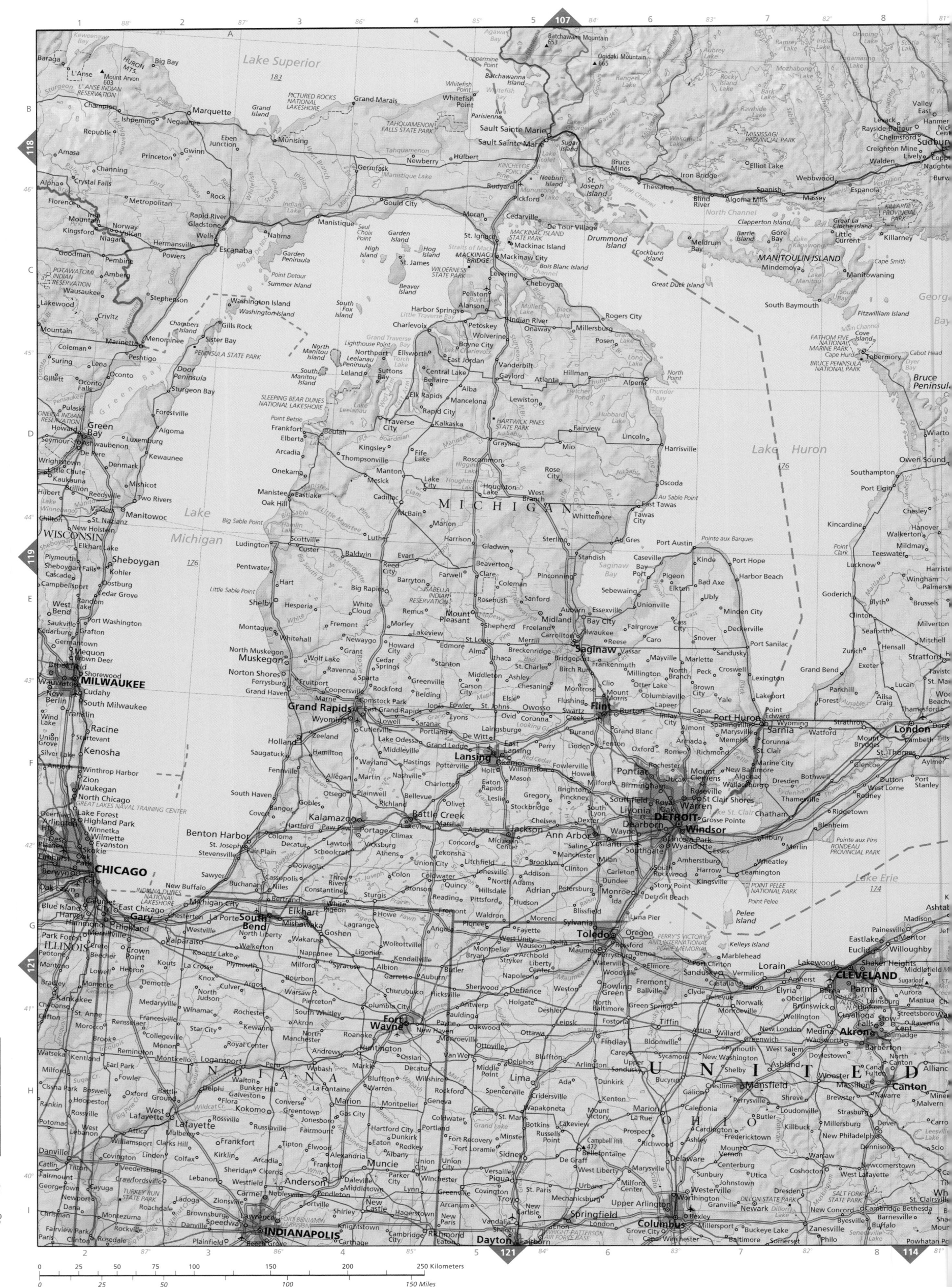

Meters
Feet

1000
3280

500
1640

200
656

Sea Level

200
656

2000
6560

0   25   50   75   100   150   200   250 Kilometers

0   25   50   100   150 Miles

Scale 1 : 2 500 000   Lambert Conformal Conic Projection

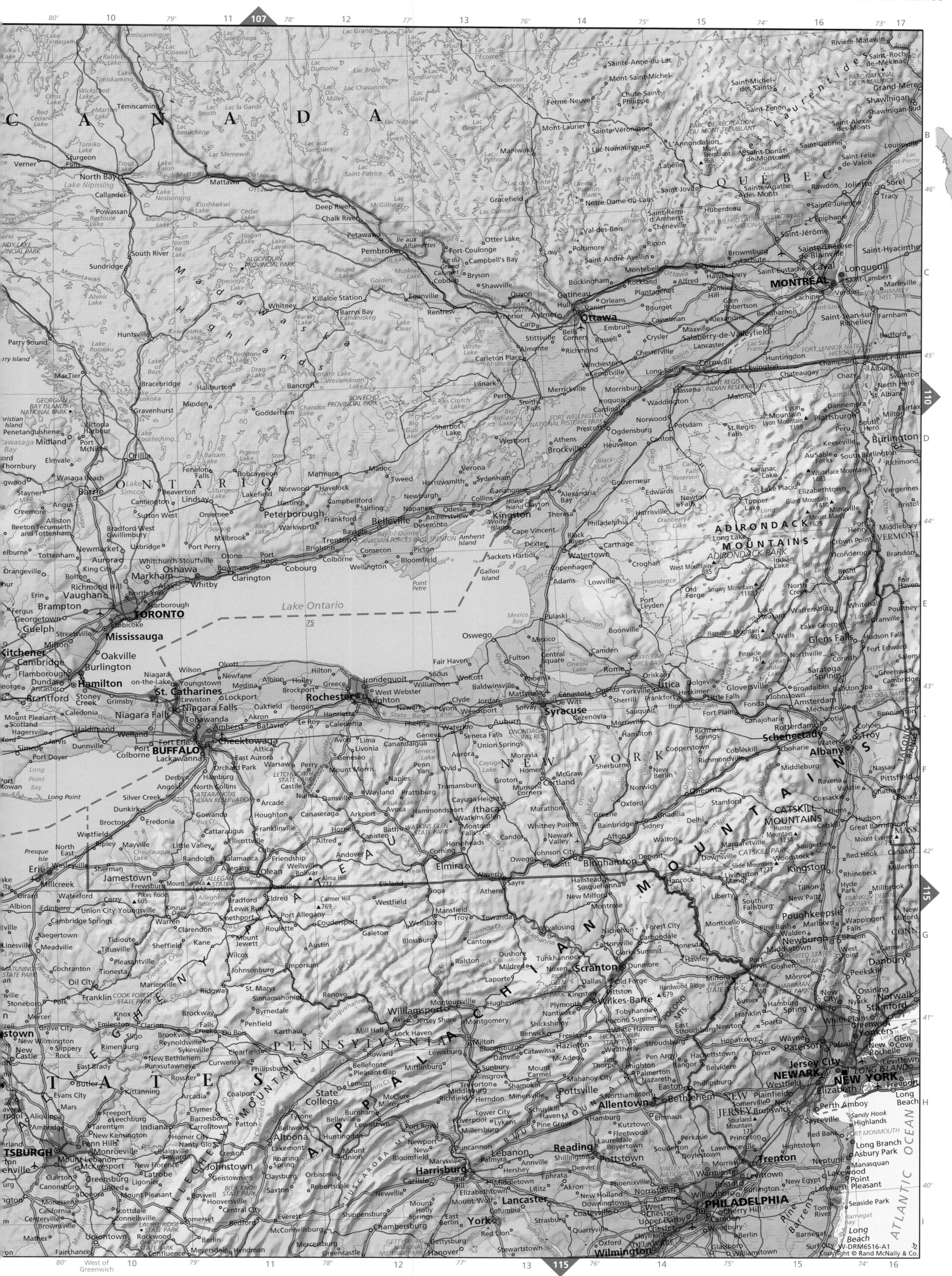

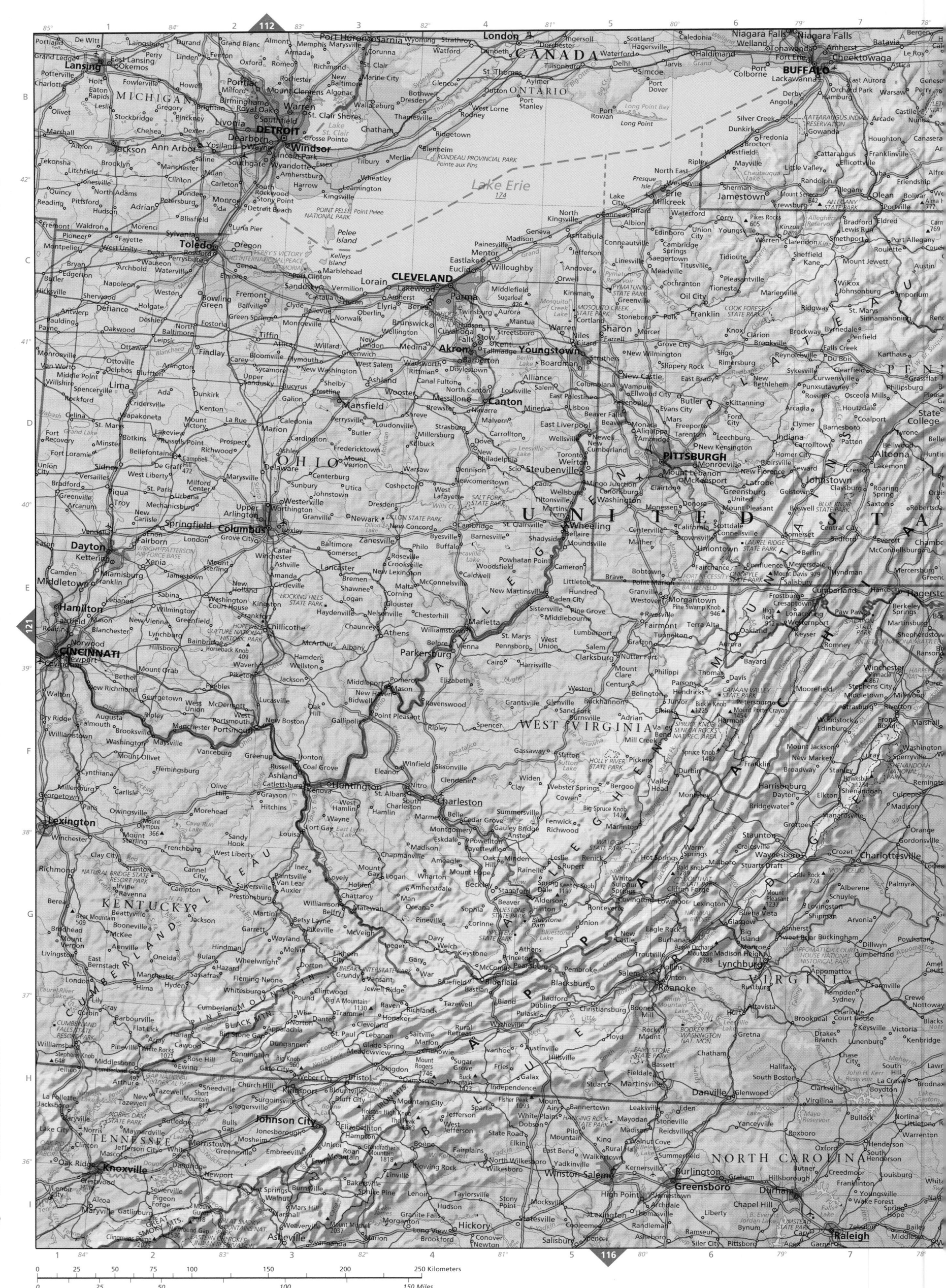

Scale 1 : 2,500,000   Lambert Conformal Conic Projection

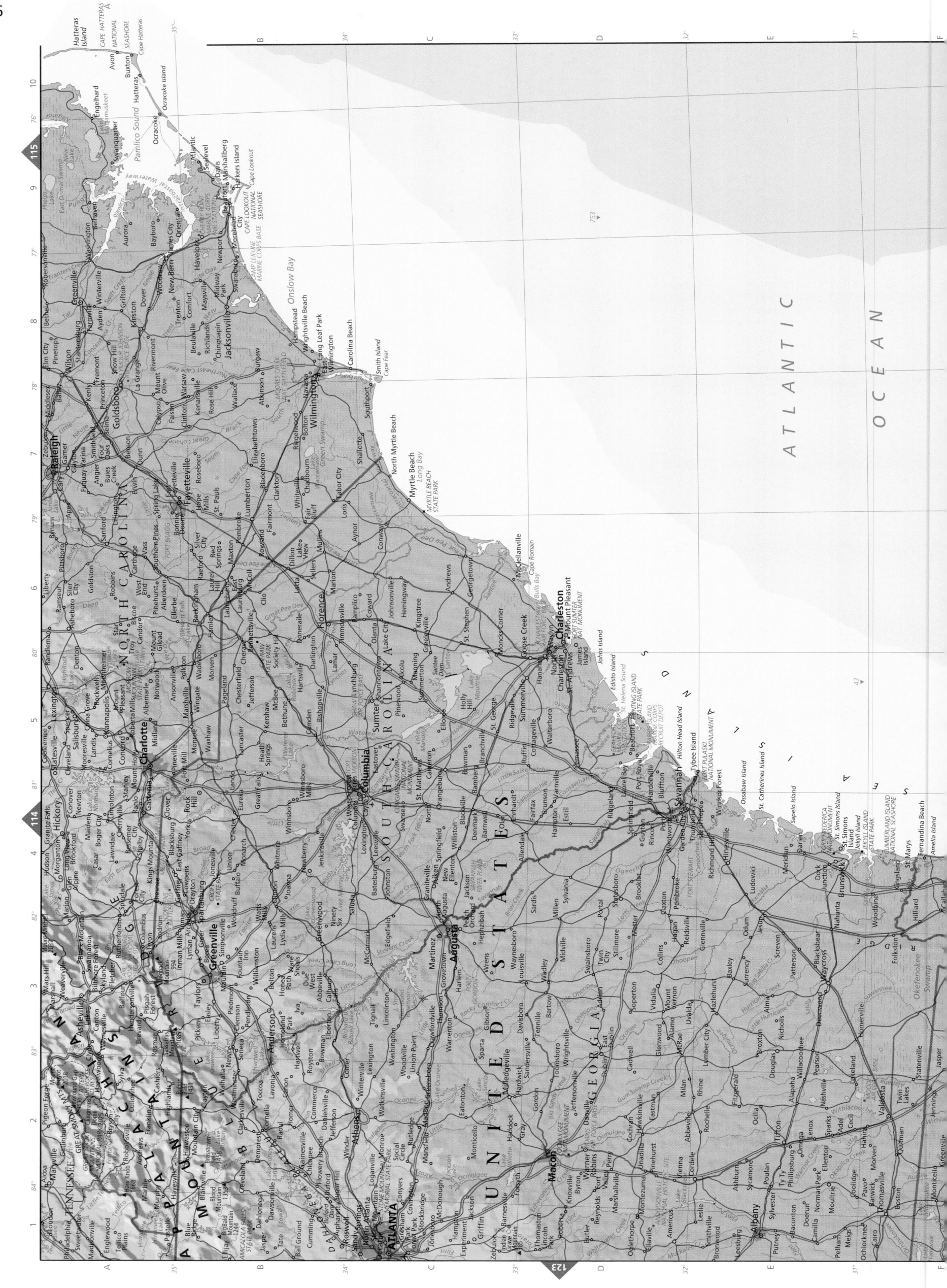

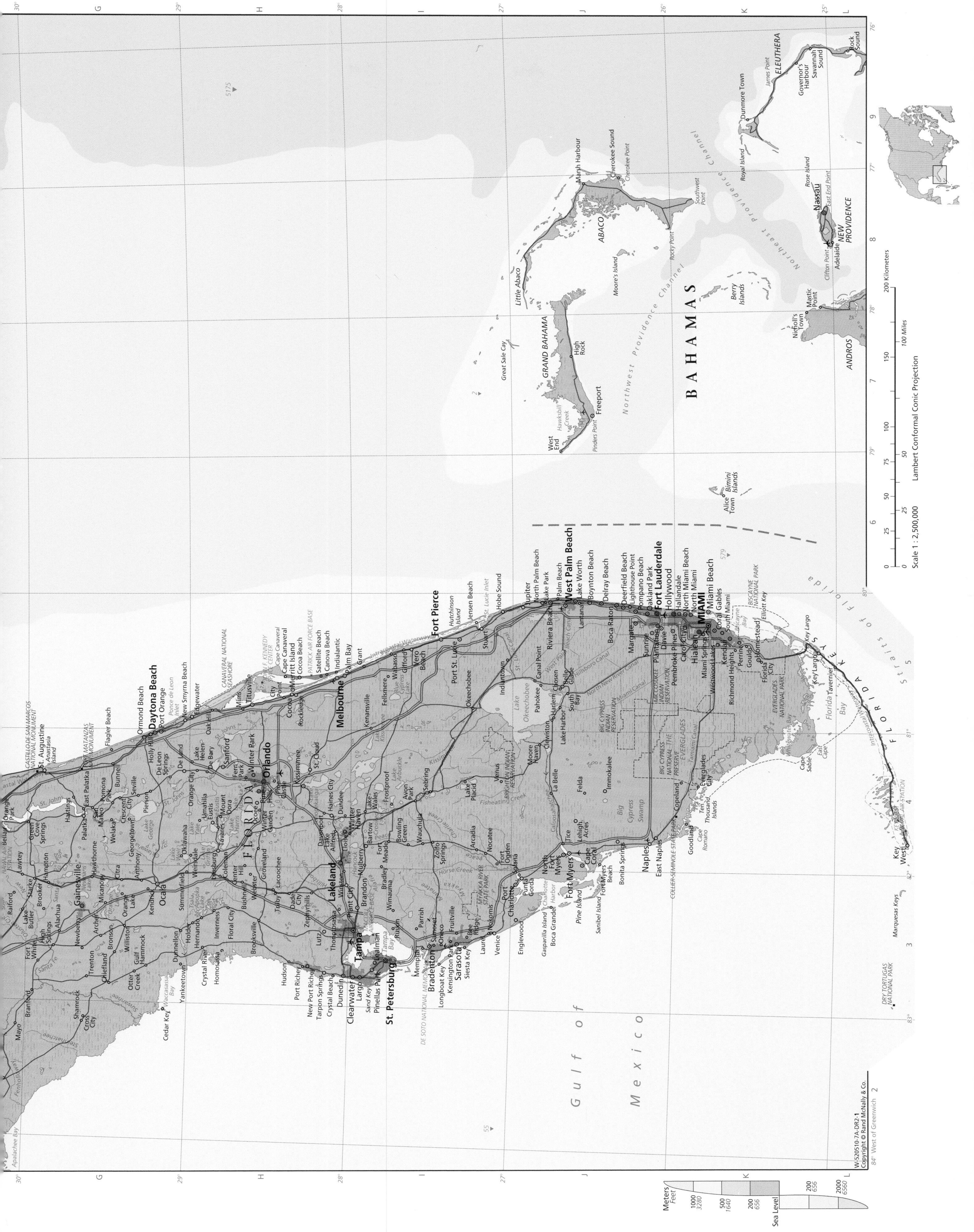

FLORIDA

BAHAMAS

ABACO
Little Abaco
Marsh Harbour
Cherokee Sound
Cherokee Point
Moore's Island
Southwest Point
Rocky Point
ELEUTHERA
James Point
Governor's Harbour
Savannah Sound
Rock Sound
Dunmore Town
Royal Island
Rose Island
East End Point
Nassau
NEW PROVIDENCE
Clifton Point
Adelaide
Berry Islands
Mastic Point
ANDROS
Nicholl's Town
Northwest Providence Channel
Northeast Providence Channel

GRAND BAHAMA
West End
Freeport
High Rock
Great Sale Cay
Hawksbill Creek
Pinders Point

Bimini Islands
Alice Town

Gulf of Mexico

Apalachee Bay
Mayo
Branford
Cross City
Cedar Key
Shamrock
Otter Creek
Yankeetown
Crystal River
Homosassa
Chiefland
Trenton
Newberry
High Springs
Alachua
Gainesville
Micanopy
Archer
Williston
Bronson
Brooksville
Inverness
Dunnellon
Floral City
Ocala
Anthony
Citra
Hawthorne
Starke
Keystone Heights
Palatka
Hastings
East Palatka
St. Augustine
CASTILLO DE SAN MARCOS NATIONAL MONUMENT
Anastasia Island
FORT MATANZAS NATIONAL MONUMENT
Flagler Beach
Bunnell
Crescent City
Seville
Pierson
De Leon Springs
Ormond Beach
Daytona Beach
Port Orange
New Smyrna Beach
Edgewater
DeLand
Orange City
Sanford
Lake Helen
Deltona
Titusville
CANAVERAL NATIONAL SEASHORE
J.F. KENNEDY SPACE CENTER
Cape Canaveral
Cocoa Beach
Merritt Island
Cocoa
Rockledge
PATRICK AIR FORCE BASE
Satellite Beach
Indialantic
Melbourne
Palm Bay
Palatka
Orlando
Winter Park
Kissimmee
St. Cloud
Grant
Sebastian
Vero Beach
Fellsmere
Fort Pierce
Hutchinson Island
Port St. Lucie
St. Lucie Inlet
Jensen Beach
Stuart
Hobe Sound
Jupiter
North Palm Beach
West Palm Beach
Lake Worth
Palm Beach
Lake Park
Riviera Beach
Belle Glade
South Bay
Pahokee
Canal Point
Lake Okeechobee
Clewiston
Moore Haven
La Belle
Immokalee
Okeechobee
Boynton Beach
Delray Beach
Boca Raton
Deerfield Beach
Lighthouse Point
Pompano Beach
Oakland Park
Fort Lauderdale
Hollywood
Hallandale
North Miami Beach
North Miami
Miami
Miami Beach
Coral Gables
South Miami
Hialeah
Miami Springs
Kendall
Perrine
Richmond Heights
Goulds
Homestead
Florida City
BISCAYNE NATIONAL PARK
Elliott Key
Key Largo
Tavernier
Florida Bay
EVERGLADES NATIONAL PARK
Cape Sable
East Cape
Flamingo
Whitewater Bay
Ten Thousand Islands
BIG CYPRESS NATIONAL PRESERVE
Everglades City
Chokoloskee
Marco Island
Goodland
Naples
East Naples
Bonita Springs
Fort Myers Beach
Fort Myers
North Fort Myers
Cape Coral
Sanibel Island
Pine Island
Captiva Island
Boca Grande
Gasparilla Island
Englewood
Venice
Nokomis
Laurel
Osprey
Siesta Key
Sarasota
Longboat Key
Bradenton
St. Petersburg
Pinellas Park
Largo
Clearwater
Dunedin
Tarpon Springs
Port Richey
New Port Richey
Hudson
Tampa
Plant City
Lakeland
Winter Haven
Bartow
Mulberry
Bowling Green
Wauchula
Arcadia
Zolfo Springs
Avon Park
Sebring
Lake Placid
Lehigh Acres
Marquesas Keys
DRY TORTUGAS NATIONAL PARK
Key West
FLORIDA KEYS
Straits of Florida

Scale 1 : 2,500,000
Lambert Conformal Conic Projection
0 25 50 75 100 150 200 Kilometers
0 25 50 75 100 Miles

W/520510-7A-DR2-1
Copyright © Rand McNally & Co.
84° West of Greenwich 2

Meters/Feet
2000/6560
1000/3280
500/1640
200/656
Sea Level

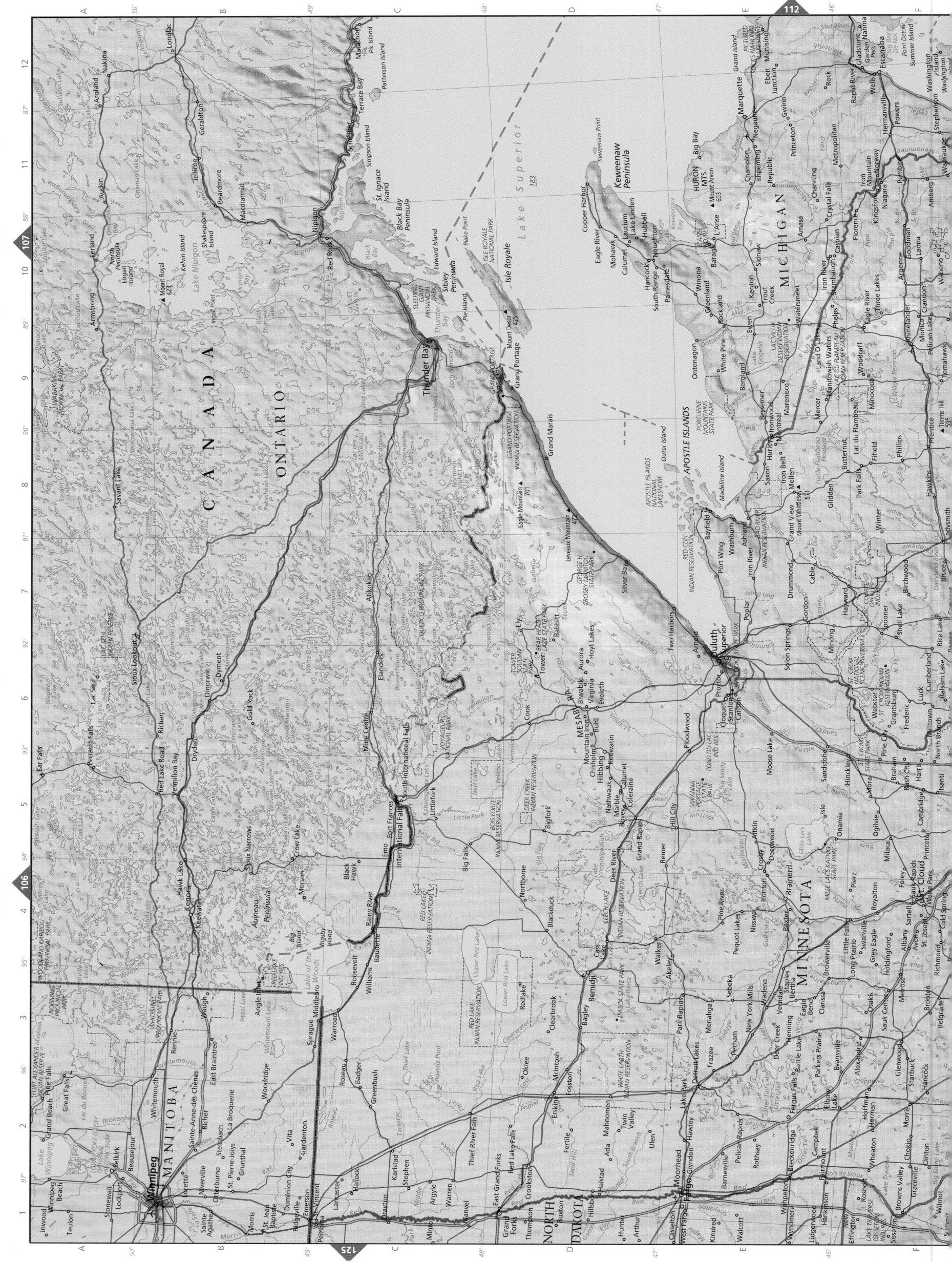

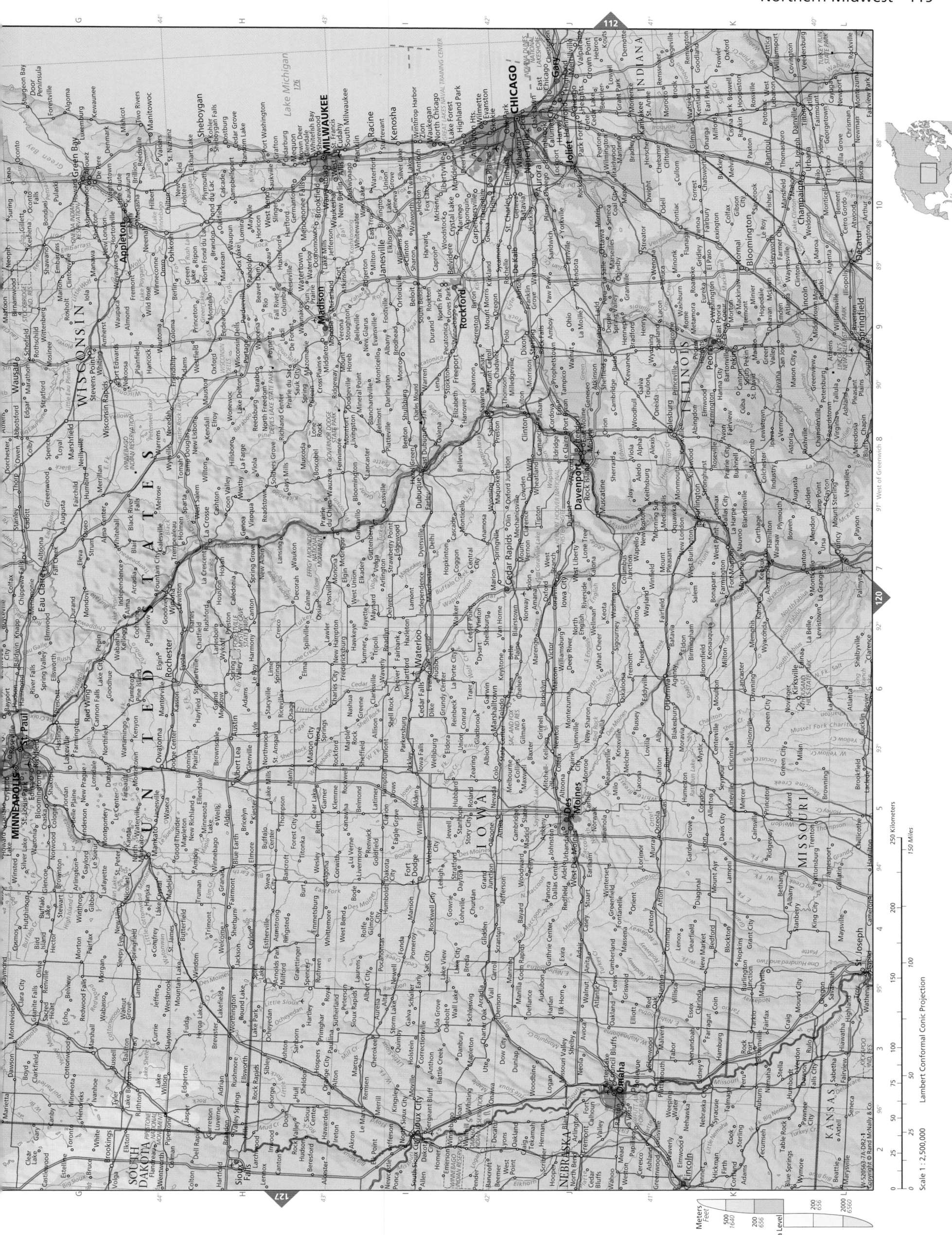

250 Kilometers   200   150   100   75   50   25   0
150 Miles   100   75   50   25   0
Scale 1 : 2,500,000
Lambert Conformal Conic Projection
Meters   Feet
2000 6560
500 1640
200 656
200 656
Sea Level
W:520563:7A:D92-1
Copyright © Rand McNally & Co.

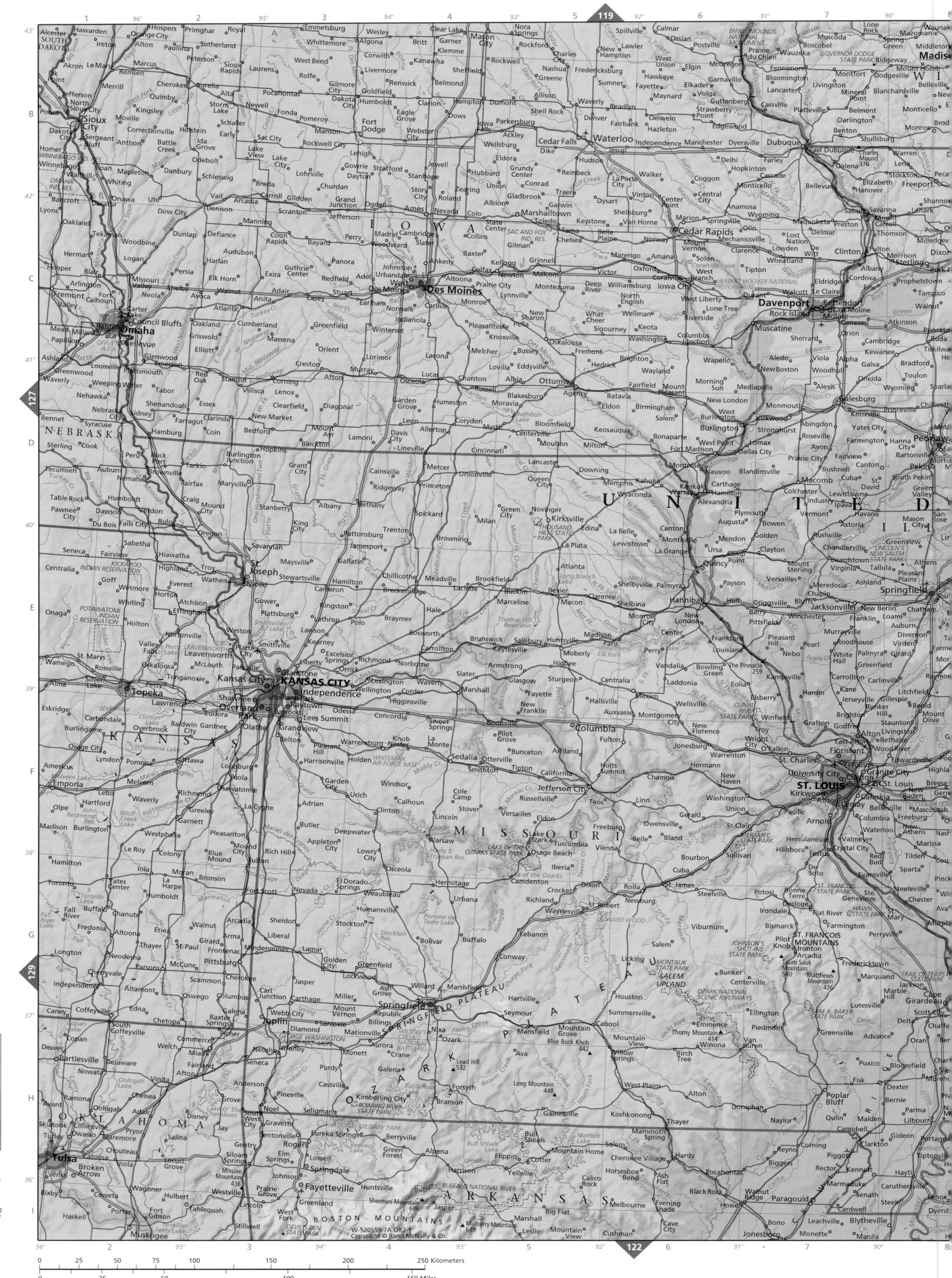

Meters
Feet

1000
3280

500
1640

200
656

Sea Level

200
656

2000
6560

0   25   50   75   100   150   200   250 Kilometers

0   25   50   75   100   150 Miles

Scale 1 : 2,500,000   Lambert Conformal Conic Projection

W-520559-7A-DR2-1
Copyright © Rand McNally & Co.

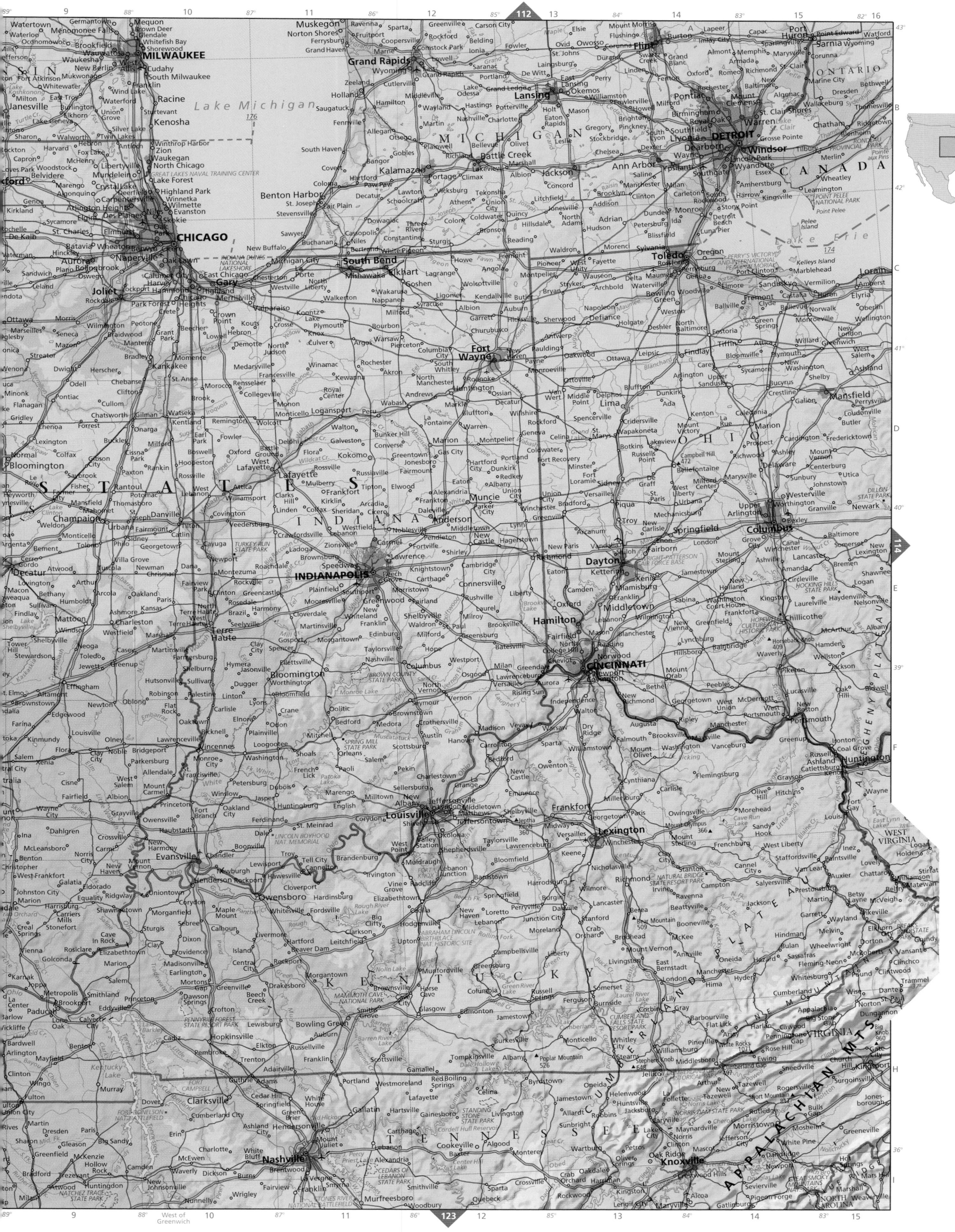

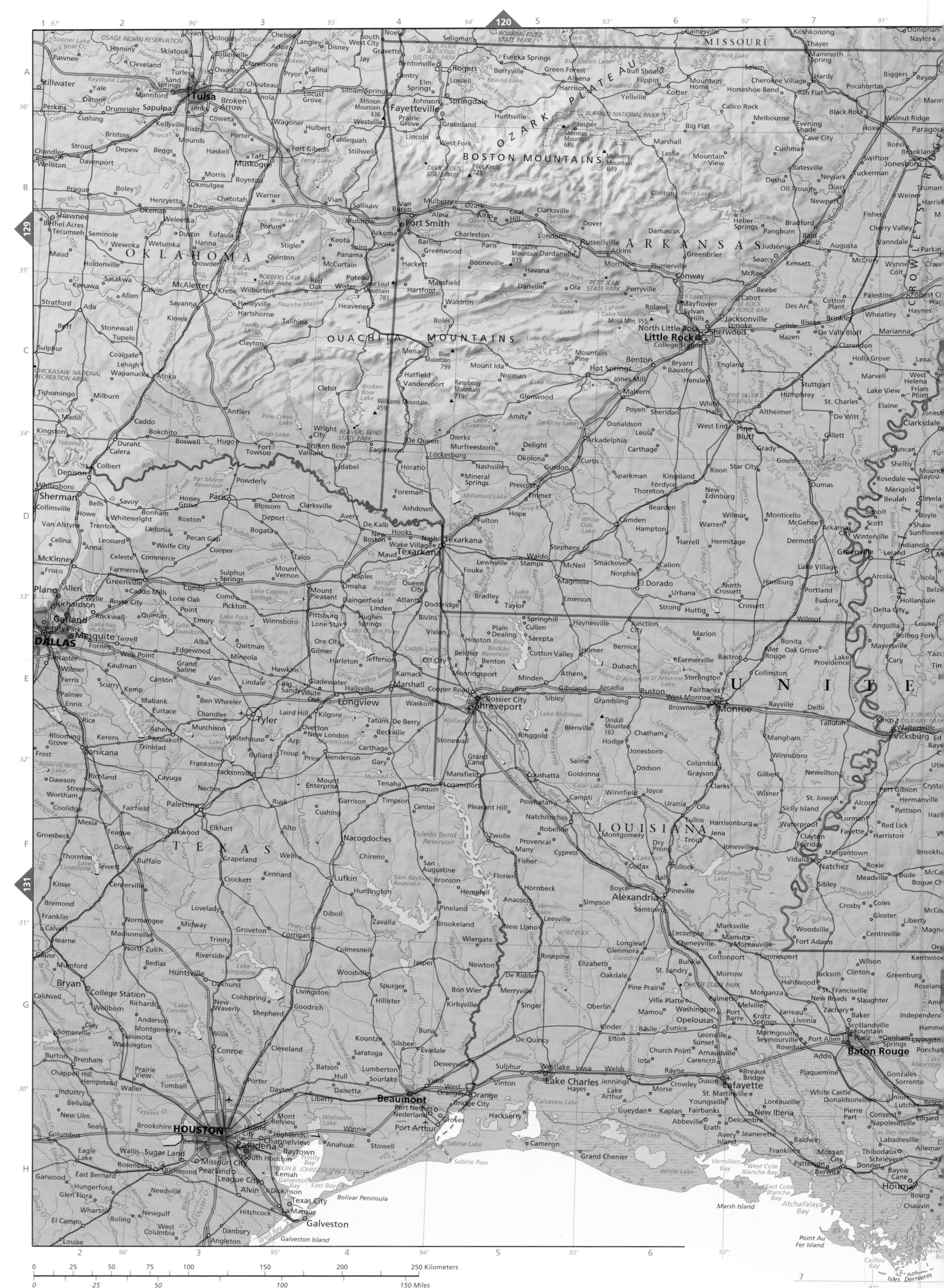

KENTUCKY

TENNESSEE

MISSISSIPPI

ALABAMA

GEORGIA

FLORIDA

NORTH CAROLINA

APPALACHIAN MOUNTAINS

CUMBERLAND PLATEAU

BLUE RIDGE

Memphis

Nashville

Knoxville

Chattanooga

Huntsville

Birmingham

Tuscaloosa

Montgomery

Atlanta

Columbus

Mobile

Pensacola

Fort Walton Beach

Panama City

Tallahassee

Dothan

Albany

Hattiesburg

Laurel

Meridian

NEW ORLEANS

Biloxi

Gulfport

Pascagoula

Mississippi Delta

Gulf of Mexico

Chandeleur Sound

Breton Sound

Gulf Islands National Seashore

Mobile Bay

Dauphin Island

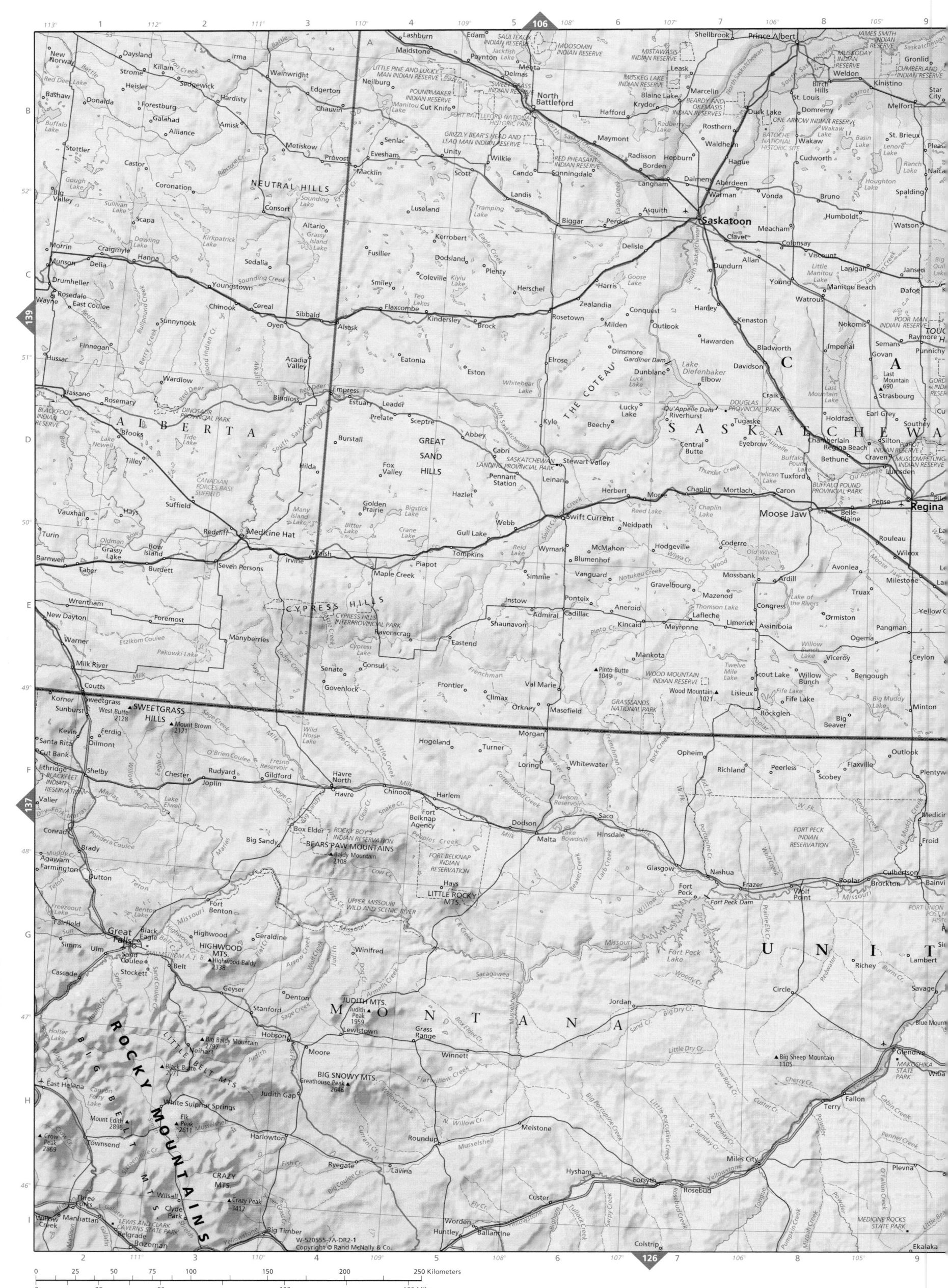

Meters
Feet

4000
13120

3000
9840

2000
6560

1000
3280

500
1640

200
656

Sea Level

200
656

2000
6560

0 25 50 75 100   150   200   250 Kilometers

0   25   50   100   150 Miles

Scale 1 : 2,500,000   Lambert Conformal Conic Projection

W-520555-7A-DR2-1
Copyright © Rand McNally & Co.

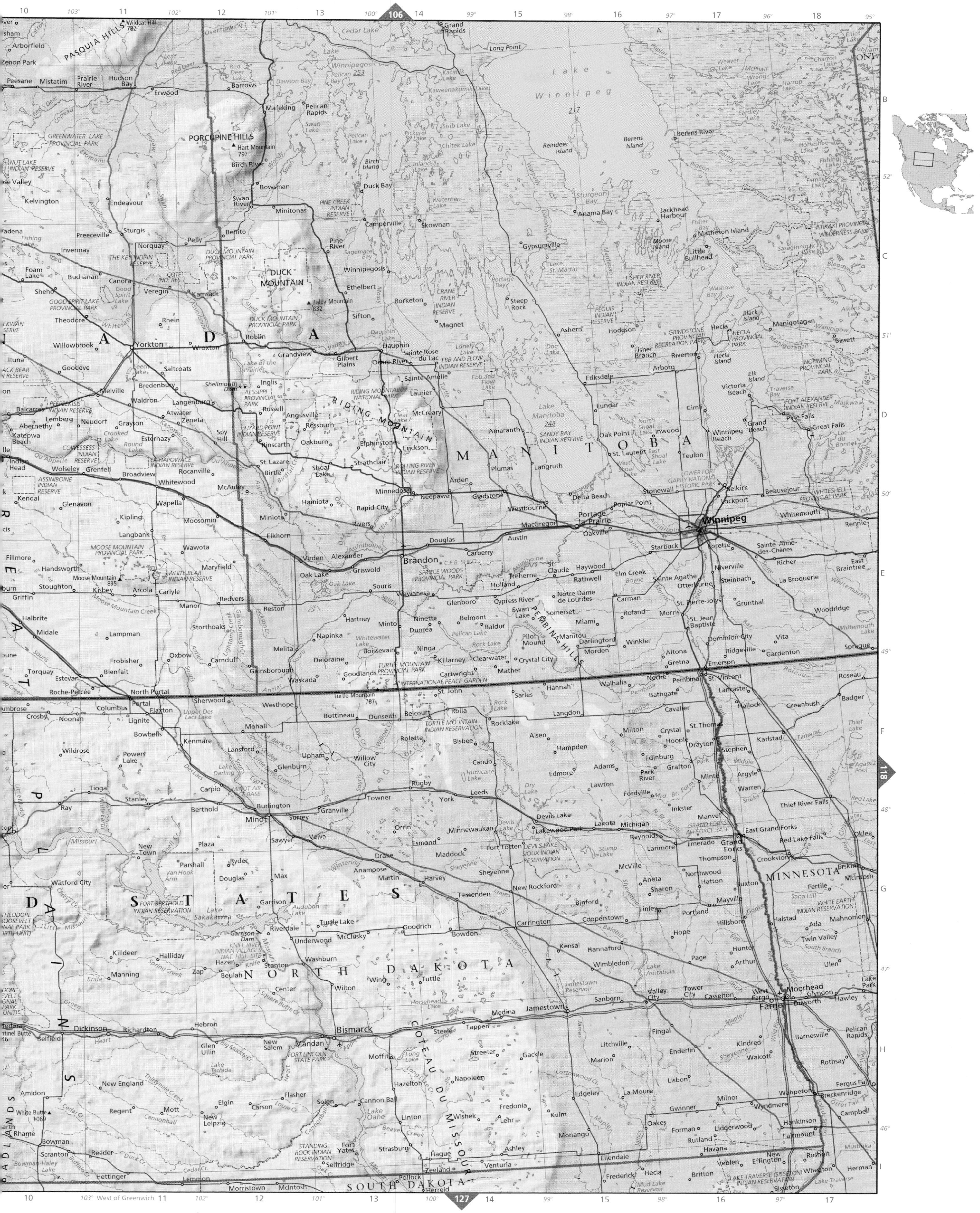

MANITOBA

NORTH DAKOTA

SOUTH DAKOTA

MINNESOTA

ONTARIO

UNITED STATES

CANADA

GREAT   PLAINS

PASQUA HILLS
PORCUPINE HILLS
Hart Mountain 797
GREENWATER LAKE PROVINCIAL PARK
DUCK MOUNTAIN
DUCK MOUNTAIN PROVINCIAL PARK
Baldy Mountain 832
RIDING MOUNTAIN NATIONAL PARK
RIDING MOUNTAIN
THE KEY INDIAN RESERVE
GOOD SPIRIT LAKE PROVINCIAL PARK
COTE IND. RES.
PINE CREEK INDIAN RESERVE
CRANE RIVER INDIAN RESERVE
PEGUIS INDIAN RESERVE
FISHER RIVER INDIAN RESERVE
GRINDSTONE PROVINCIAL RECREATION PARK
HECLA PROVINCIAL PARK
EBB AND FLOW INDIAN RESERVE
SANDY BAY INDIAN RESERVE
ROLLING RIVER INDIAN RESERVE
LIZARD POINT INDIAN RESERVE
WHITESHELL PROVINCIAL PARK
NOPIMING PROVINCIAL PARK
ATIKAKI PROVINCIAL WILDERNESS PARK
MOOSE MOUNTAIN PROVINCIAL PARK
Moose Mountain 835
WHITE BEAR INDIAN RESERVE
SPRUCE WOODS PROVINCIAL PARK
C.F.B. SHILO
PEMBINA HILLS
TURTLE MOUNTAIN PROVINCIAL PARK
Turtle Mountain 767
INTERNATIONAL PEACE GARDEN
TURTLE MOUNTAIN INDIAN RESERVATION
DEVILS LAKE SIOUX INDIAN RESERVATION
FORT TOTTEN
FORT BERTHOLD INDIAN RESERVATION
THEODORE ROOSEVELT NATIONAL PARK NORTH UNIT
GARRISON DAM
KNIFE RIVER INDIAN VILLAGES NAT HIST SITE
Lake Sakakawea
FORT LINCOLN STATE PARK
STANDING ROCK INDIAN RESERVATION
WHITE EARTH INDIAN RESERVATION
LAKE TRAVERSE (SISSETON) INDIAN RESERVATION
Lake Winnipeg
Lake Winnipegosis
Lake Manitoba
Cedar Lake
Cedar Lake

Winnipeg
Brandon
Yorkton
Dauphin
Minot
Bismarck
Mandan
Fargo
Moorhead
Grand Forks
East Grand Forks
West Fargo
Dilworth
Devils Lake
Jamestown
Dickinson
Valley City

Grand Rapids
Long Point
Berens River
Reindeer Island
Berens Island
Moose Island
Black Island
Hecla Island
Matheson Island
Manigotagan
Bissett
Pelican Rapids
Overflowing River
Wildcat Hill 782
Arborfield
Zenon Park
Peesane
Mistatim
Prairie River
Hudson Bay
Erwood
Mafeking
Pelican Rapids
Birch River
Bowsman
Swan River
Minitonas
Benito
Pelly
Kamsack
Veregin
Canora
Norquay
Invermay
Endeavour
Sturgis
Preeceville
Buchanan
Theodore
Rhein
Roblin
Grandview
Gilbert Plains
Ethelbert
Winnipegosis
Sifton
Camperville
Skownan
Gypsumville
Anama Bay
Jackhead Harbour
Hodgson
Fisher Branch
Ashern
Steep Rock
Eriksdale
Arborg
Riverton
Gimli
Victoria Beach
Winnipeg Beach
Pine Falls
Great Falls
Selkirk
Beausejour
Lockport
Stonewall
Portage la Prairie
Gladstone
Neepawa
Minnedosa
Rapid City
Rivers
MacGregor
Austin
Carberry
Virden
Alexander
Griswold
Oak Lake
Souris
Wawanesa
Glenboro
Cypress River
Holland
Treherne
St. Claude
Carman
Morris
Winkler
Morden
Altona
Gretna
Emerson
Roland
Steinbach
La Broquerie
Grunthal
Woodridge
Sprague
Vita
Gardenton
Dominion City
Ridgeville
Walhalla
Cavalier
Pembina
St. Vincent
Hallock
Greenbush
Badger
Grafton
Drayton
Crystal
Hoople
Edinburg
Park River
Grand Forks
Crookston
Red Lake Falls
Thief River Falls
Warren
Argyle
Karlstad
Stephen
Minto
Manvel
Emerado
Larimore
Northwood
Mayville
Hillsboro
Portland
Finley
Cooperstown
Carrington
Harvey
Fessenden
New Rockford
Rugby
Towner
York
Leeds
Minnewaukan
Esmond
Velva
Surrey
Burlington
Berthold
Stanley
Tioga
Ray
Williston
Watford City
New Town
Parshall
Ryder
Max
Garrison
Turtle Lake
Washburn
Underwood
McClusky
Goodrich
Bowdon
Kensal
Hannaford
Wimbledon
Valley City
Casselton
Sanborn
Jamestown
Medina
Steele
Tappen
Streeter
Gackle
Napoleon
Wishek
Ashley
Ellendale
Oakes
Forman
Lidgerwood
Hankinson
Wahpeton
Breckenridge
Fergus Falls
Barnesville
Hawley
Glyndon
Dilworth
Moorhead
Fergus Falls
Bismarck
Mandan
New Salem
Glen Ullin
Hebron
Richardton
Belfield
Dickinson
New England
Amidon
White Butte 1069
Regent
Mott
New Leipzig
Elgin
Flasher
Carson
Solen
Cannon Ball
Fort Yates
Selfridge
McIntosh
Morristown
Lemmon
Hettinger
Bowman
Scranton
Reeder
Haley
Rhame
Marmarth

103° West of Greenwich

Scale 1 : 2,500,000   Lambert Conformal Conic Projection

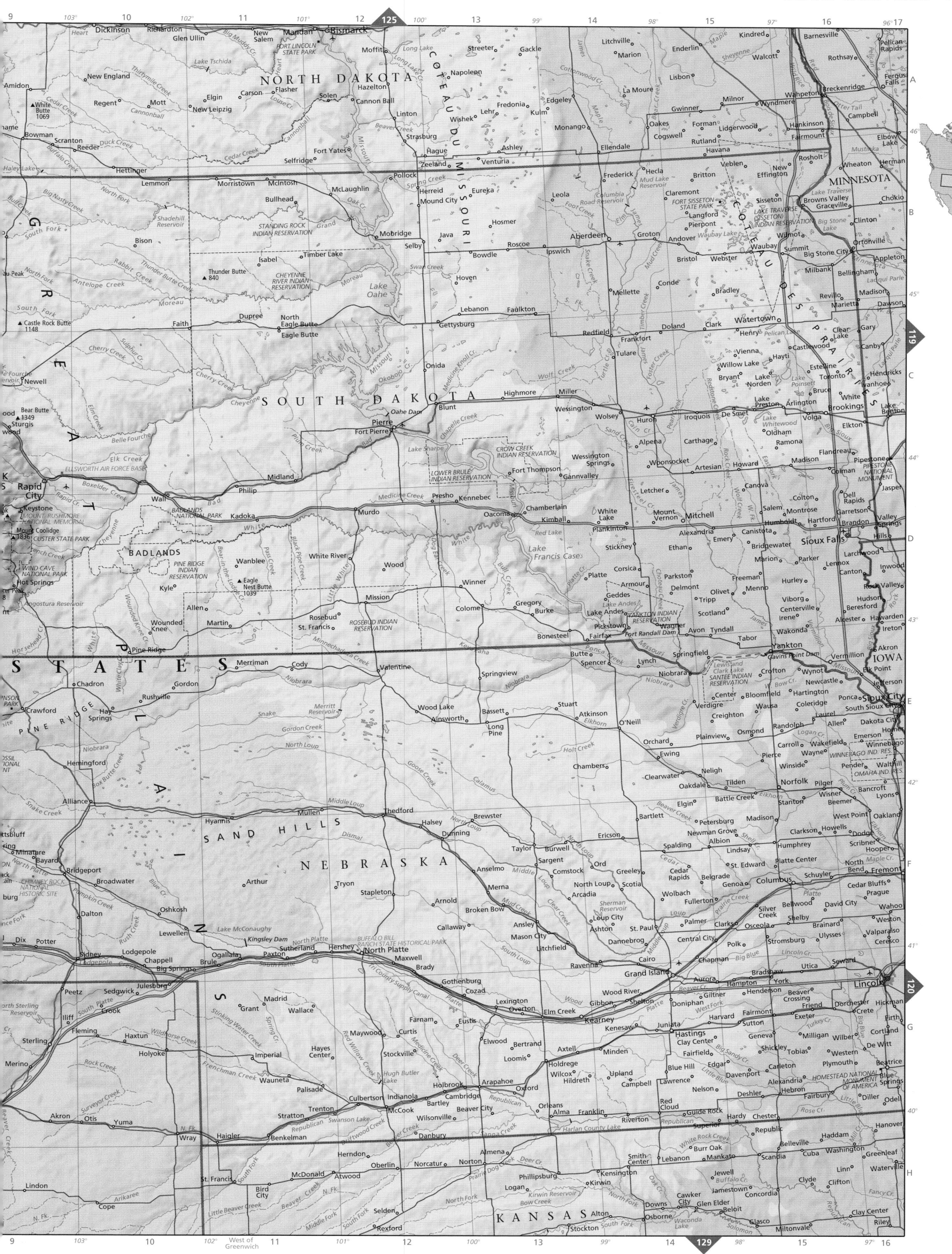

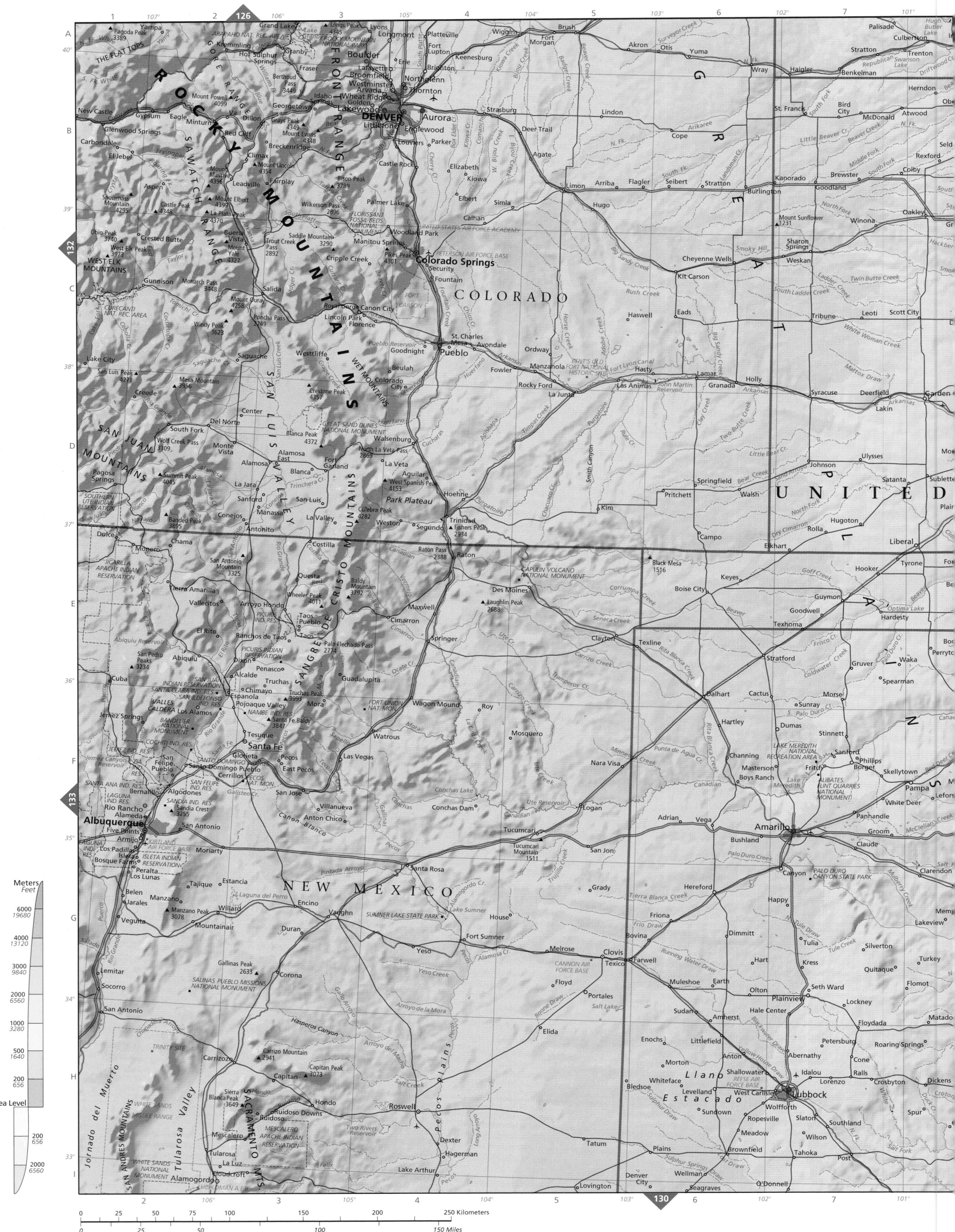

Meters
Feet

6000
19680

4000
13120

3000
9840

2000
6560

1000
3280

500
1640

200
656

Sea Level

200
656

2000
6560

0   25   50   75   100   150   200   250 Kilometers

0   25   50   100   150 Miles

Scale 1 : 2 500 000   Lambert Conformal Conic Projection

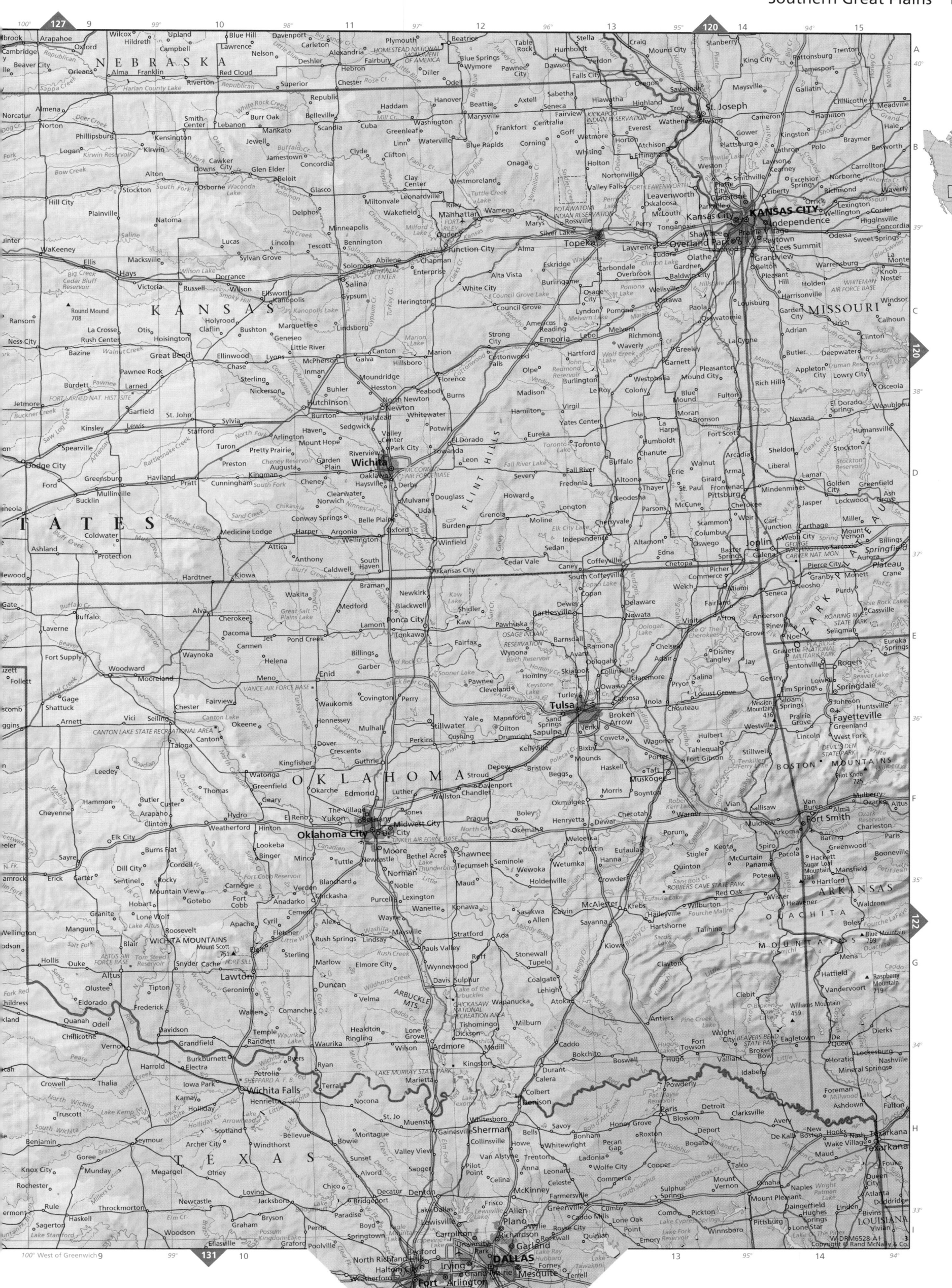

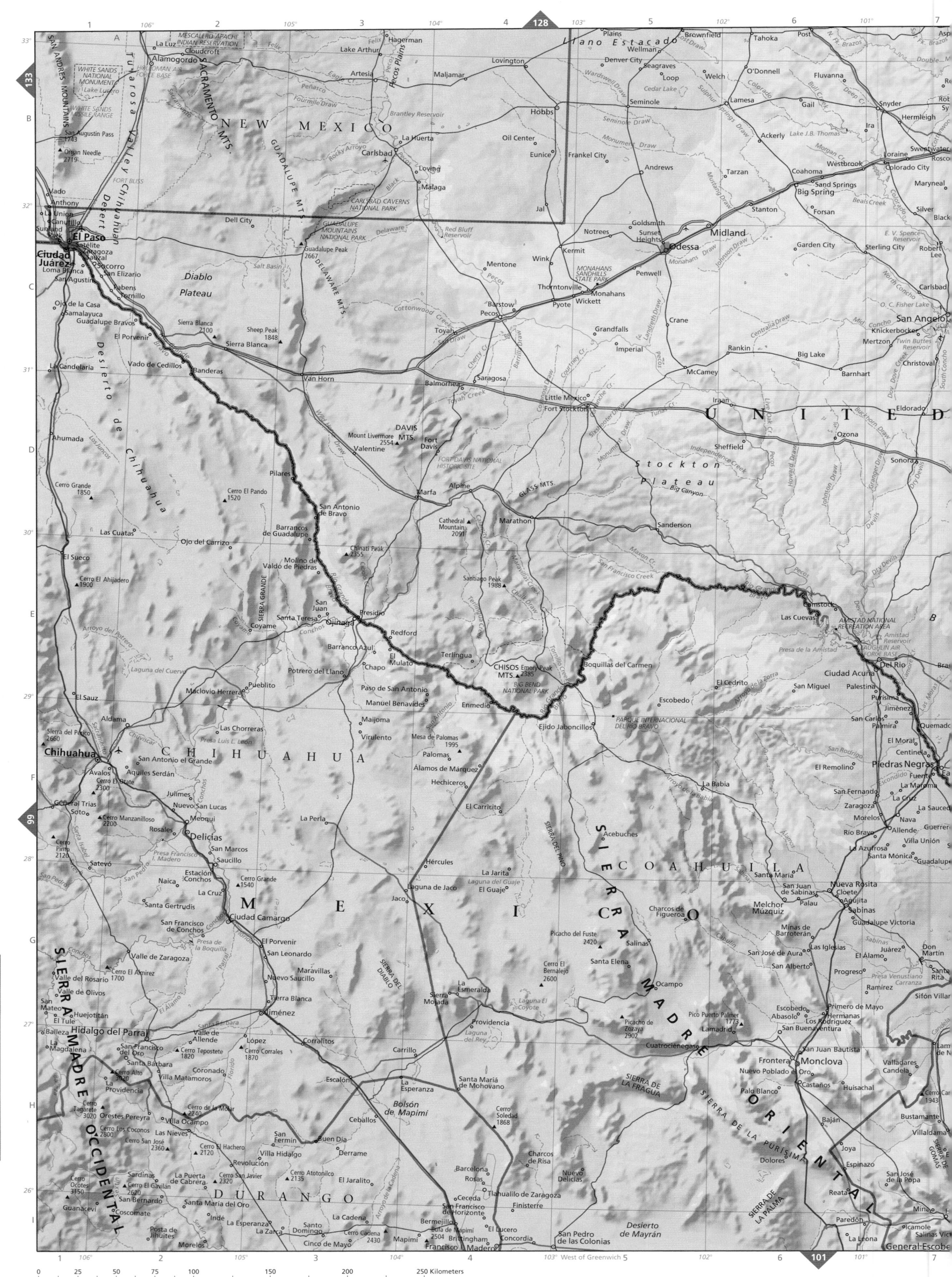

Meters
Feet

4000
13120

3000
9840

2000
6560

1000
3280

500
1640

200
656

Sea Level

200
656

2000
6560

0   25   50   75   100   150   200   250 Kilometers

0   25   50   100   150 Miles

Scale 1 : 2,500,000   Lambert Conformal Conic Projection

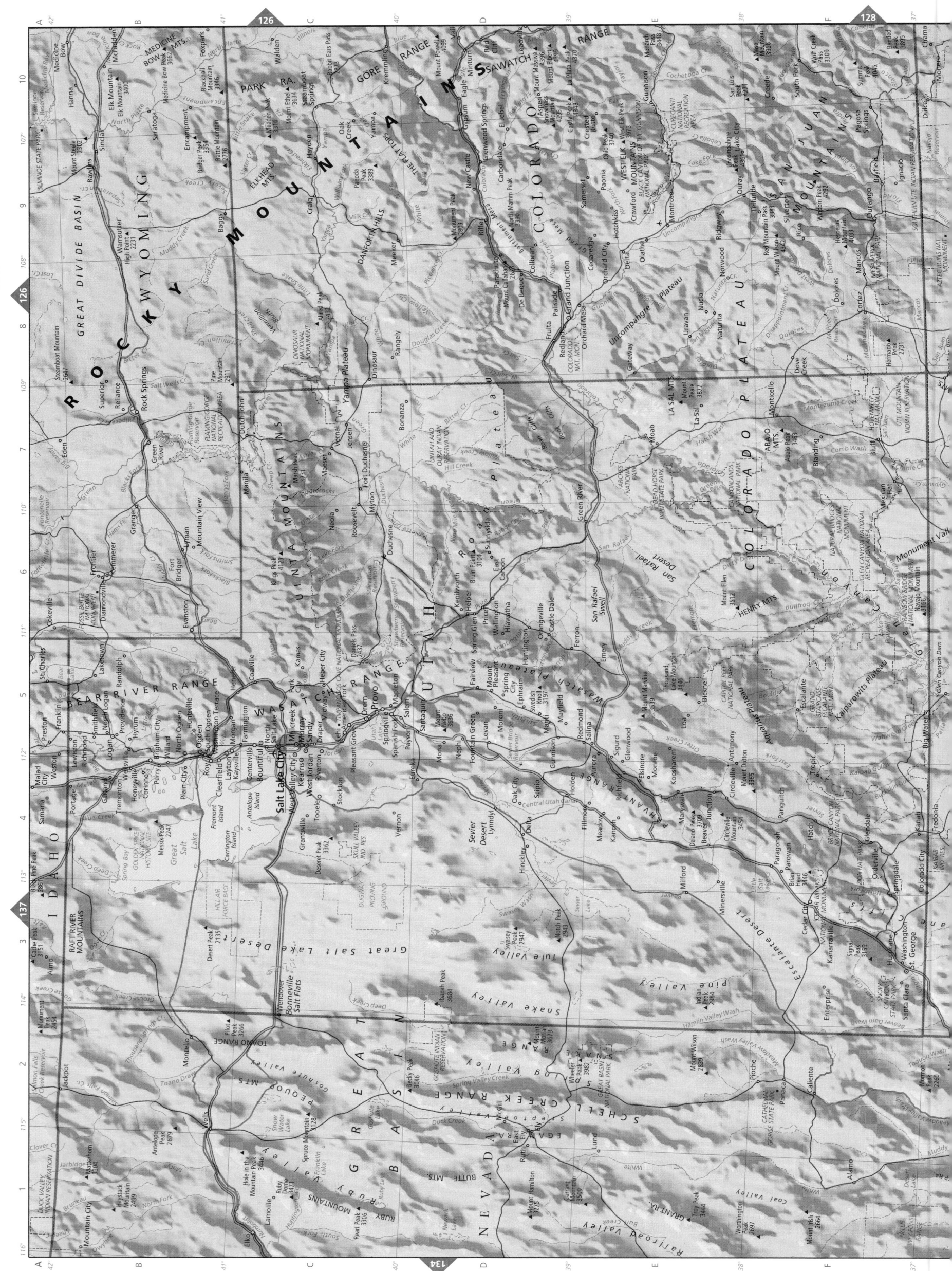

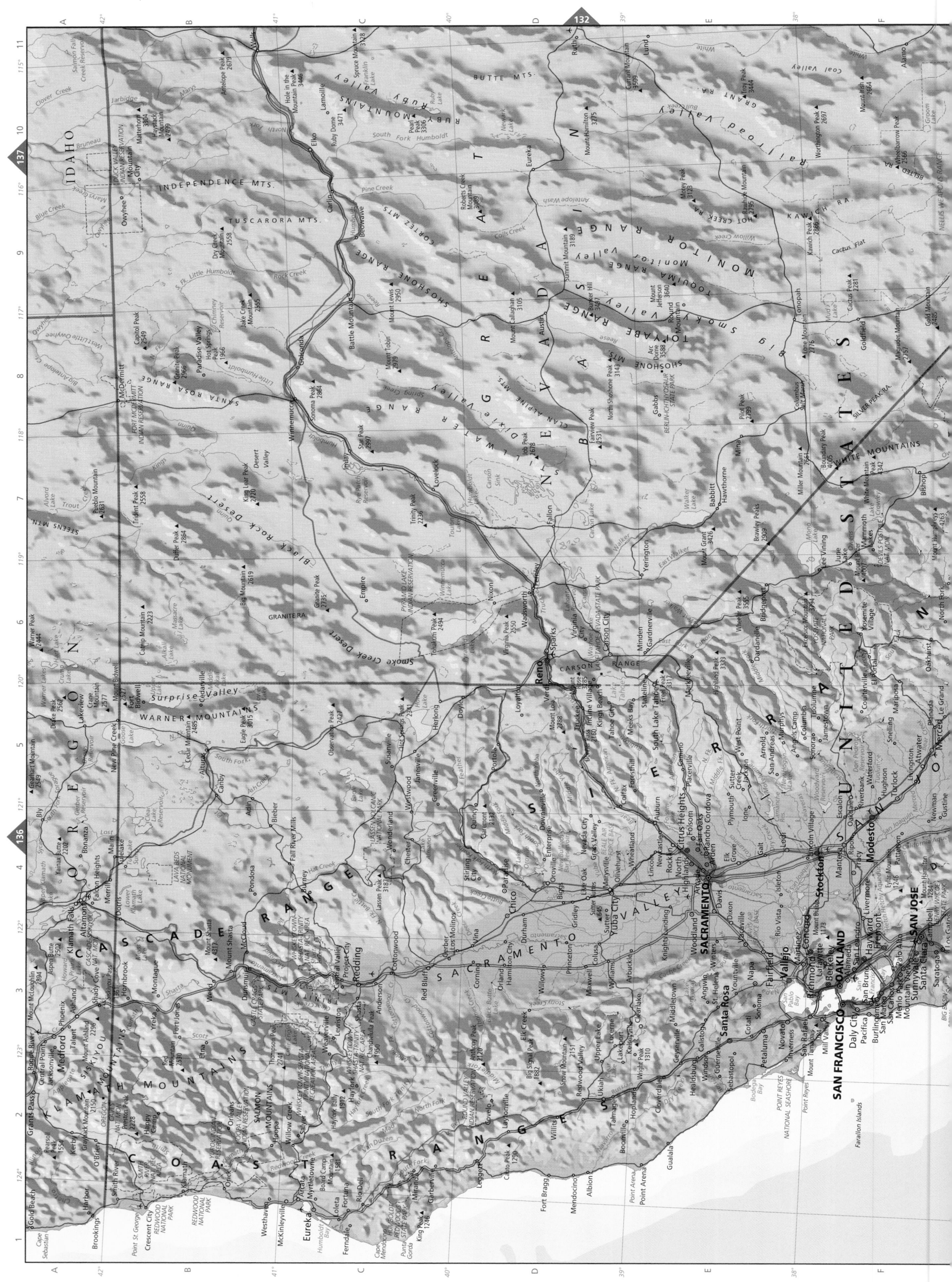

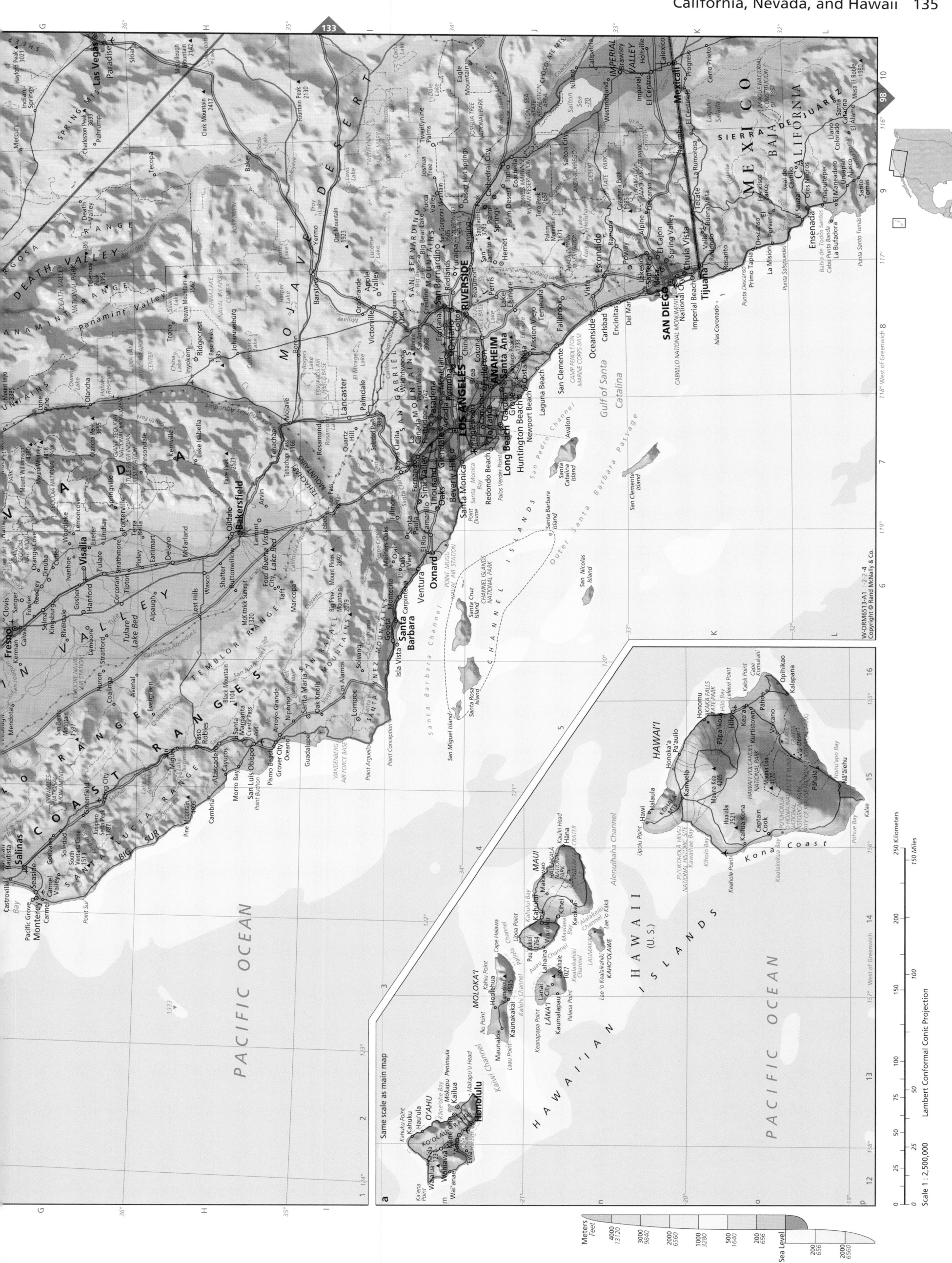

Scale 1 : 2,500,000

Lambert Conformal Conic Projection

W-DRM6513-A1 -2.2-.4
Copyright © Rand McNally & Co.

Same scale as main map

PACIFIC OCEAN

Meters / Feet
6000 / 19680
4000 / 13120
3000 / 9840
2000 / 6560
1000 / 3280
500 / 1640
200 / 656
Sea Level
200 / 656
2000 / 6560

Scale 1 : 2,500,000   Lambert Conformal Conic Projection

0 25 50 75 100   150   200   250 Kilometers
0   25   50   100   150 Miles

138

Scale 1 : 2,500,000   Lambert Conformal Conic Projection

Meters
Feet

4000
13120

3000
9840

2000
6560

1000
3280

500
1640

200
656

Sea Level

200
656

2000
6560

ARCTIC

OCEAN

BEAUFORT

SEA

CHUKCHI
SEA

RUSSIA

Bering Strait

Norton Sound

BERING

SEA

Bristol Bay

FOX ISLANDS

Gulf
of
Alaska

UNITED STATES

CANADA

BROOKS   RANGE

ALASKA   RANGE

CHUGACH MOUNTAINS

ST. ELIAS
MOUNTAINS

NORTHWEST
TERRITORIES

YUKON

BRITISH
COLUMBIA

ALEUTIAN   ISLANDS

BERING SEA

PACIFIC

OCEAN

NEAR ISLANDS

RAT ISLANDS

ANDREANOF ISLANDS

ISLANDS OF
FOUR MOUNTAINS

FOX ISLANDS

0   100   200   300   400   600   800   1000 Kilometers
0   100   200   300   400   600 Miles

Scale 1 : 10,000,000   Lambert Conformal Conic Projection

Scale 1 : 10,000,000   Lambert Conformal Conic Projection

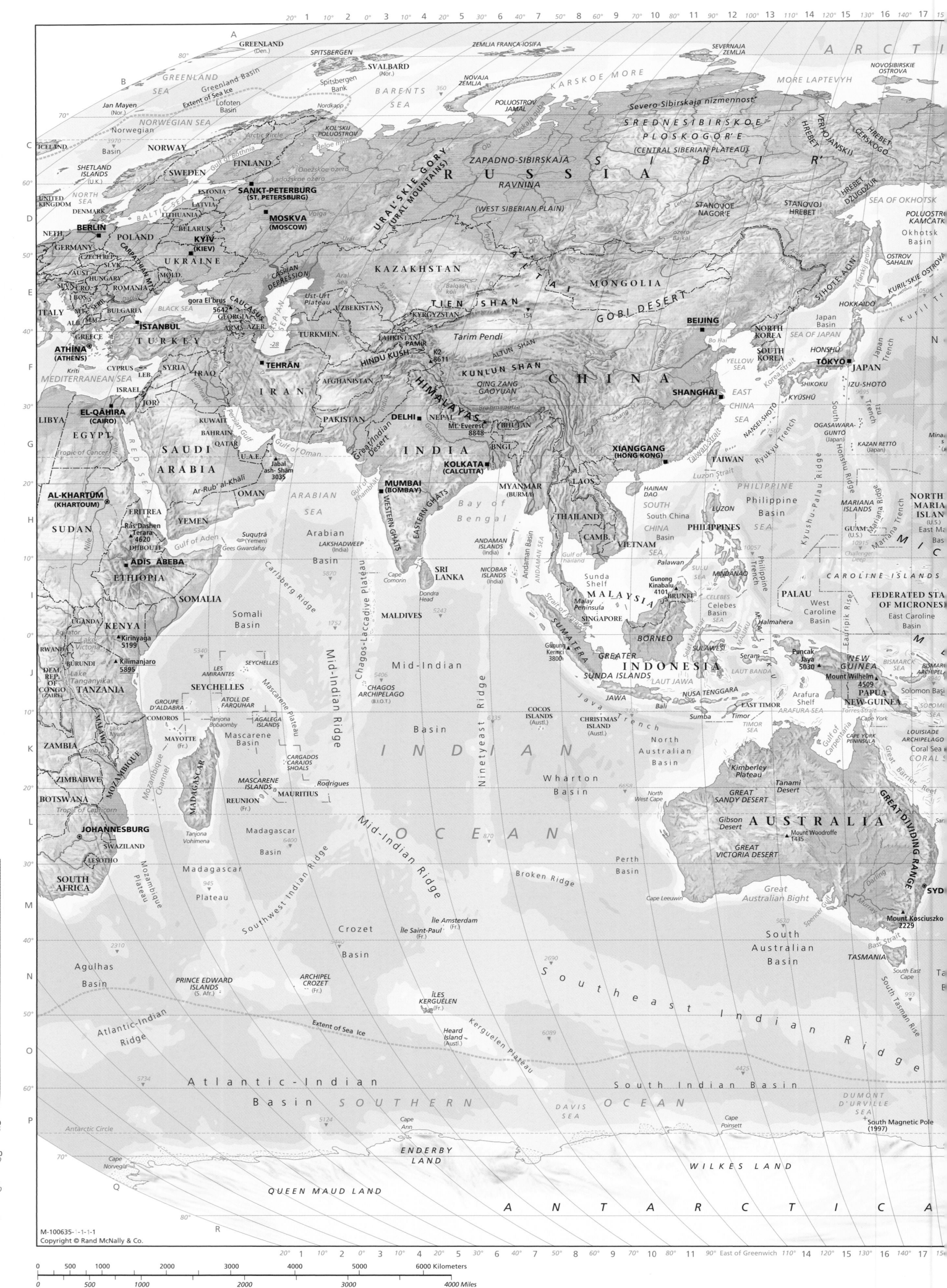

Scale 1 : 60,000,000   Robinson Projection

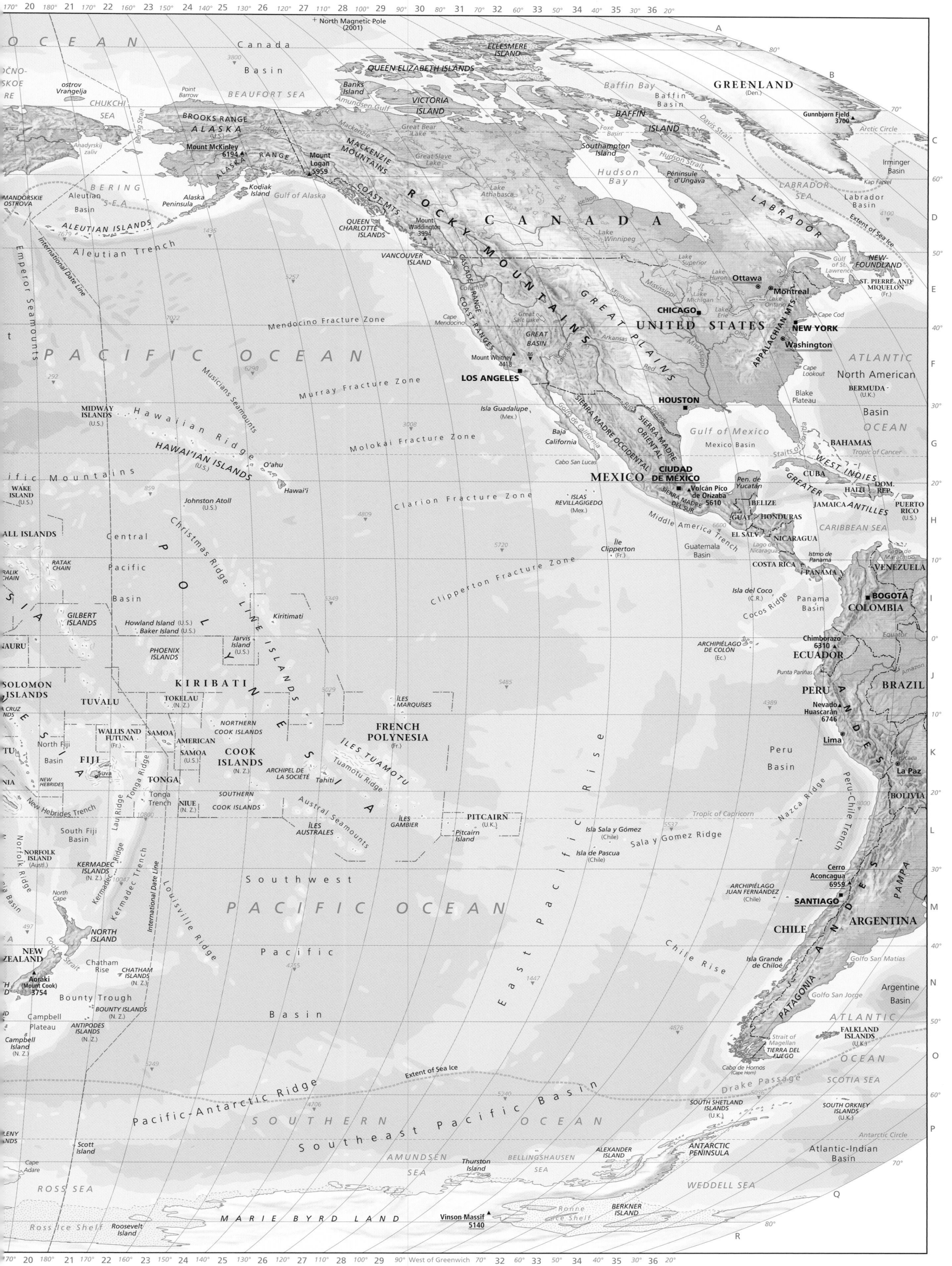

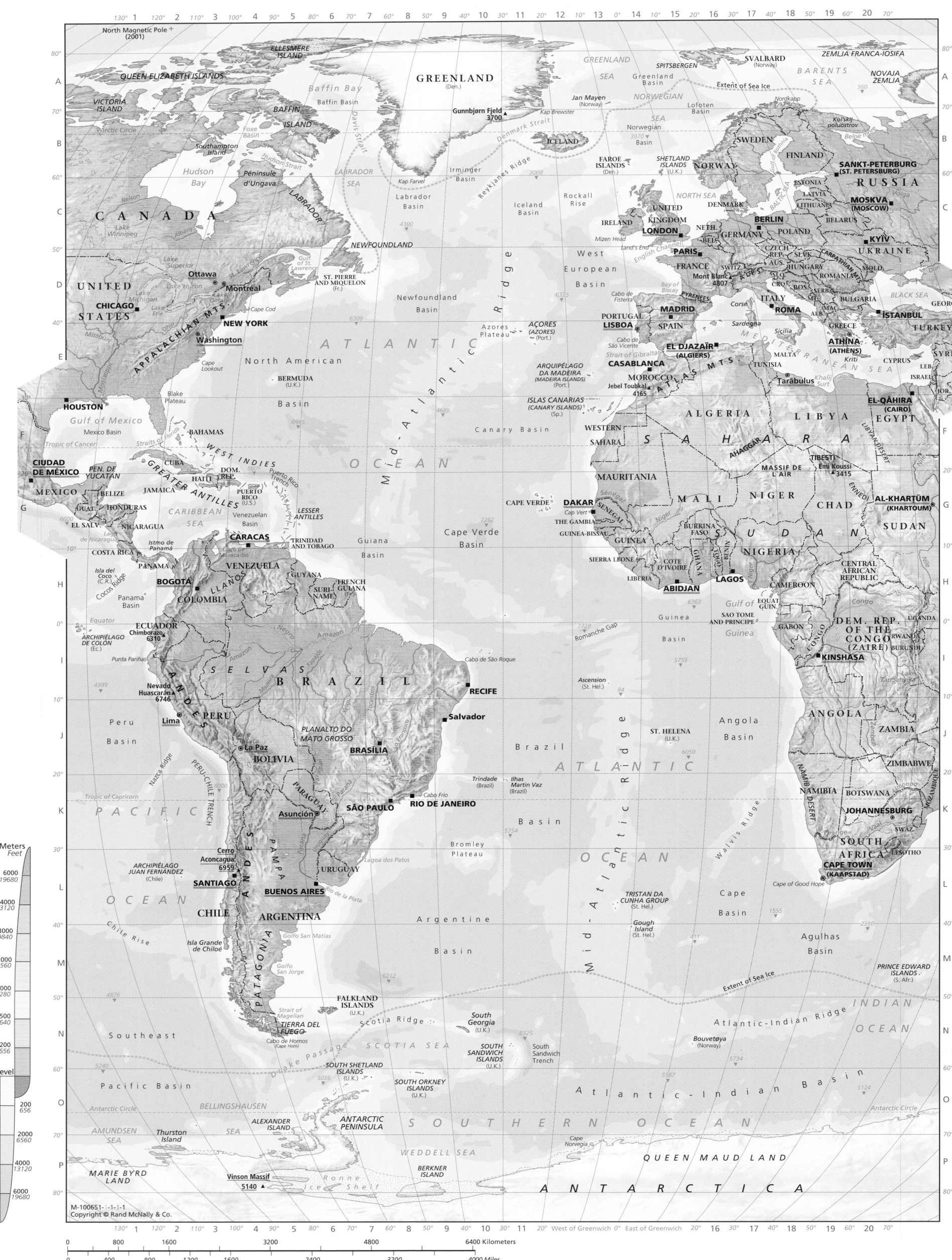

Meters / Feet

6000 / 19680
4000 / 13120
3000 / 9840
2000 / 6560
1000 / 3280
500 / 1640
200 / 656
Sea Level
200 / 656
2000 / 6560
4000 / 13120
6000 / 19680

M-100651- -1-1-1
Copyright © Rand McNally & Co.

0   800   1600   3200   4800   6400 Kilometers
0   400   800   1600   2400   3200   4000 Miles
Scale 1 : 60,000,000   Robinson Projection

Index to World Reference Maps

Introduction to the Index

This index includes in a single alphabetical list approximately 54,000 names of places and geographical features that appear on the reference maps. Each name is followed by the name of the country or continent in which it is located, an alpha-numeric map reference key and a page reference.

Names The names of cities and towns appear in the index in regular type. The names of all other features appear in *italics*, followed by descriptive terms (hill, mtn., state) to indicate their nature.

Abbreviations of names on the maps have been standardized as much as possible. Names that are abbreviated on the maps are generally spelled out in full in the index.

Country names and names of features that extend beyond the boundaries of one country are followed by the name of the continent in which each is located. Country designations follow the names of all other places in the index. The locations of places in the United States, Canada, and the United Kingdom are further defined by abbreviations that indicate the state, province, or other political division in which each is located.

All abbreviations used in the index are defined in the List of Abbreviations to the right.

Alphabetization Names are alphabetized in the order of the letters of the English alphabet. Spanish *ll* and *ch*, for example, are not treated as distinct letters. Furthermore, diacritical marks are disregarded in alphabetization — German or Scandinavian *ä* or *ö* are treated as *a* or *o*.

The names of physical features may appear inverted, since they are always alphabetized under the proper, not the generic, part of the name, thus: "Gibraltar, Strait of". Otherwise every entry, whether consisting of one word or more, is alphabetized as a single continuous entity. "Lakeland", for example, appears after "La Crosse" and before "La Salle". Names beginning with articles (Le Havre, Den Helder, Al-Manāmah) are not inverted. Names beginning "St.", "Ste." and "Sainte" are alphabetized as though spelled "Saint".

In the case of identical names, towns are listed first, then political divisions, then physical features. Entries that are completely identical are listed alphabetically by country name.

Map Reference Keys and Page References The map reference keys and page references are found in the last two columns of each entry.

Each map reference key consists of a letter and number. The letters correspond to letters along the sides of the maps. Lowercase letters refer to inset maps. The numbers correspond to numbers that appear across the tops and bottoms of the maps.

Map reference keys for point features, such as cities and mountain peaks, indicate the locations of the symbols for these features. For other features, such as countries, mountain ranges, or rivers, the map reference keys indicate the locations of the names.

The page number generally refers to the main map for the country in which the feature is located. Page references for two-page maps always refer to the left-hand page.

List of Abbreviations

Ab., Can.	Alberta, Can.
Afg.	Afghanistan
Afr.	Africa
Ak., U.S.	Alaska, U.S.
Al., U.S.	Alabama, U.S.
Alb.	Albania
Alg.	Algeria
Am. Sam.	American Samoa
anch.	anchorage
And.	Andorra
Ang.	Angola
Ant.	Antarctica
Antig.	Antigua and Barbuda
aq.	aqueduct
Ar., U.S.	Arkansas, U.S.
Arg.	Argentina
Arm.	Armenia
at.	atoll
Aus.	Austria
Austl.	Australia
Az., U.S.	Arizona, U.S.
Azer.	Azerbaijan
b.	bay, gulf, inlet, lagoon
B.C., Can.	British Columbia, Can.
Bah.	Bahamas
Bahr.	Bahrain
Barb.	Barbados
bas.	basin
Bdi.	Burundi
Bel.	Belgium
Bela.	Belarus
Ber.	Bermuda
Bhu.	Bhutan
B.I.O.T.	British Indian Ocean Territory
Blg.	Bulgaria
Bngl.	Bangladesh
Bol.	Bolivia
Bos.	Bosnia and Hercegovina
Bots.	Botswana
Braz.	Brazil
Bru.	Brunei
Br. Vir. Is.	British Virgin Islands
Burkina	Burkina Faso
c.	cape, point
Ca., U.S.	California, U.S.
Cam.	Cameroon
Camb.	Cambodia
Can.	Canada
can.	canal
C.A.R.	Central African Republic
Cay. Is.	Cayman Islands
Christ. I.	Christmas Island
C. Iv.	Cote d'Ivoire
clf.	cliff, escarpment
Co., U.S.	Colorado, U.S.
co.	county, district, etc.
Cocos Is.	Cocos (Keeling) Islands
Col.	Colombia
Com.	Comoros
cont.	continent
Cook Is.	Cook Islands
C.R.	Costa Rica
crat.	crater
Cro.	Croatia
cst.	coast, beach
Ct., U.S.	Connecticut, U.S.
ctry.	independent country
C.V.	Cape Verde
cv.	cave
Cyp.	Cyprus
Czech Rep.	Czech Republic
D.C., U.S.	District of Columbia, U.S.
De., U.S.	Delaware, U.S.
Den.	Denmark
dep.	dependency, colony
depr.	depression
des.	desert
Dji.	Djibouti
Dom.	Dominica
Dom. Rep.	Dominican Republic
D.R.C.	Democratic Republic of the Congo
Ec.	Ecuador
El Sal.	El Salvador
Eng., U.K.	England, U.K.
Eq. Gui.	Equatorial Guinea
Erit.	Eritrea
Est.	Estonia
est.	estuary
Eth.	Ethiopia
E. Timor	East Timor
Eur.	Europe
Falk. Is.	Falkland Islands
Far. Is.	Faroe Islands
Fin.	Finland
Fl., U.S.	Florida, U.S.
for.	forest, moor
Fr.	France
Fr. Gu.	French Guiana
Fr. Poly.	French Polynesia
Ga., U.S.	Georgia, U.S.
Gam.	The Gambia
Gaza	Gaza Strip
Geor.	Georgia
Ger.	Germany
Gib.	Gibraltar
Golan	Golan Heights
Grc.	Greece

Gren.	Grenada
Grnld.	Greenland
Guad.	Guadeloupe
Guat.	Guatemala
Guern.	Guernsey
Gui.	Guinea
Gui.-B.	Guinea-Bissau
Guy.	Guyana
gysr.	geyser
Hi., U.S.	Hawaii, U.S.
hist.	historic site, ruins
hist. reg.	historic region
Hond.	Honduras
Hung.	Hungary
i.	island
Ia., U.S.	Iowa, U.S.
Ice.	Iceland
ice	ice feature, glacier
Id., U.S.	Idaho, U.S.
Il., U.S.	Illinois, U.S.
In., U.S.	Indiana, U.S.
Indon.	Indonesia
I. of Man	Isle of Man
Ire.	Ireland
is.	islands
Isr.	Israel
isth.	isthmus
Jam.	Jamaica
Jer.	Jericho Area
Jord.	Jordan
Kaz.	Kazakhstan
Kir.	Kiribati
Kor., N.	Korea, North
Kor., S.	Korea, South
Ks., U.S.	Kansas, U.S.
Kuw.	Kuwait
Ky., U.S.	Kentucky, U.S.
Kyrg.	Kyrgyzstan
l.	lake, pond
La., U.S.	Louisiana, U.S.
Lat.	Latvia
lav.	lava flow
Leb.	Lebanon
Leso.	Lesotho
Lib.	Liberia
Liech.	Liechtenstein
Lith.	Lithuania
Lux.	Luxembourg
Ma., U.S.	Massachusetts, U.S.
Mac.	Macedonia
Madag.	Madagascar
Malay.	Malaysia
Mald.	Maldives
Marsh. Is.	Marshall Islands
Mart.	Martinique
Maur.	Mauritania
May.	Mayotte
Mb., Can.	Manitoba, Can.
Md., U.S.	Maryland, U.S.
Me., U.S.	Maine, U.S.
Mex.	Mexico
Mi., U.S.	Michigan, U.S.
Micron.	Micronesia, Federated States of
Mid. Is.	Midway Islands
misc. cult.	miscellaneous cultural
Mn., U.S.	Minnesota, U.S.
Mo., U.S.	Missouri, U.S.
Mol.	Moldova
Mon.	Monaco
Mong.	Mongolia
Mont.	Montenegro
Monts.	Montserrat
Mor.	Morocco
Moz.	Mozambique
Mrts.	Mauritius
Ms., U.S.	Mississippi, U.S.
Mt., U.S.	Montana, U.S.
mth.	river mouth or channel
mtn.	mountain
mts.	mountains
Mwi.	Malawi
Mya.	Myanmar
N.A.	North America
N.B., Can.	New Brunswick, Can.
N.C., U.S.	North Carolina, U.S.
N. Cal.	New Caledonia
N. Cyp.	North Cyprus
N.D., U.S.	North Dakota, U.S.
Ne., U.S.	Nebraska, U.S.
Neth.	Netherlands
Neth. Ant.	Netherlands Antilles
Nf., Can.	Newfoundland and Labrador, Can.
ngh.	neighborhood
N.H., U.S.	New Hampshire, U.S.
Nic.	Nicaragua
Nig.	Nigeria
N. Ire., U.K.	Northern Ireland, U.K.
N.J., U.S.	New Jersey, U.S.
N.M., U.S.	New Mexico, U.S.
N. Mar. Is.	Northern Mariana Islands
Nmb.	Namibia
Nor.	Norway
Norf. I.	Norfolk Island
N.S., Can.	Nova Scotia, Can.
N.T., Can.	Northwest Territories, Can.
Nu., Can.	Nunavut, Can.
Nv., U.S.	Nevada, U.S.
N.Y., U.S.	New York, U.S.
N.Z.	New Zealand

Oc.	Oceania
Oh., U.S.	Ohio, U.S.
Ok., U.S.	Oklahoma, U.S.
On., Can.	Ontario, Can.
Or., U.S.	Oregon, U.S.
p.	pass
Pa., U.S.	Pennsylvania, U.S.
Pak.	Pakistan
Pan.	Panama
Pap. N. Gui.	Papua New Guinea
Para.	Paraguay
P.E., Can.	Prince Edward Island, Can.
pen.	peninsula
Phil.	Philippines
Pit.	Pitcairn
pl.	plain, flat
plat.	plateau, highland
p.o.i.	point of interest
Pol.	Poland
Port.	Portugal
P.R.	Puerto Rico
Qc., Can.	Quebec, Can.
r.	rock, rocks
reg.	physical region
rel.	religious facility
res.	reservoir
Reu.	Reunion
rf.	reef, shoal
R.I., U.S.	Rhode Island, U.S.
Rom.	Romania
Rw.	Rwanda
s.	sea
S.A.	South America
S. Afr.	South Africa
sand	sand area
Sau. Ar.	Saudi Arabia
S.C., U.S.	South Carolina, U.S.
sci.	scientific station
Scot., U.K.	Scotland, U.K.
S.D., U.S.	South Dakota, U.S.
Sen.	Senegal
Serb.	Serbia
Sey.	Seychelles
S. Geor.	South Georgia
Sing.	Singapore
Sk., Can.	Saskatchewan, Can.
S.L.	Sierra Leone
Slov.	Slovakia
Slvn.	Slovenia
S. Mar.	San Marino
Sol. Is.	Solomon Islands
Som.	Somalia
Sp. N. Afr.	Spanish North Africa
Sri L.	Sri Lanka
state	state, province, etc.
St. Hel.	St. Helena
St. K./N.	St. Kitts and Nevis
St. Luc.	St. Lucia
stm.	stream (river, creek)
S. Tom./P.	Sao Tome and Principe
St. P./M.	St. Pierre and Miquelon
strt.	strait, channel, etc.
St. Vin.	St. Vincent and the Grenadines
Sur.	Suriname
sw.	swamp, marsh
Swaz.	Swaziland
Swe.	Sweden
Switz.	Switzerland
Tai.	Taiwan
Taj.	Tajikistan
Tan.	Tanzania
T./C. Is.	Turks and Caicos Islands
Thai.	Thailand
Tn., U.S.	Tennessee, U.S.
Tok.	Tokelau
Trin.	Trinidad and Tobago
Tun.	Tunisia
Tur.	Turkey
Turkmen.	Turkmenistan
Tx., U.S.	Texas, U.S.
U.A.E.	United Arab Emirates
Ug.	Uganda
U.K.	United Kingdom
Ukr.	Ukraine
unds.	undersea feature
Ur.	Uruguay
U.S.	United States
Ut., U.S.	Utah, U.S.
Uzb.	Uzbekistan
Va., U.S.	Virginia, U.S.
val.	valley, watercourse
Vat.	Vatican City
Ven.	Venezuela
Viet.	Vietnam
V.I.U.S.	Virgin Islands (U.S.)
vol.	volcano
Vt., U.S.	Vermont, U.S.
Wa., U.S.	Washington, U.S.
Wake I.	Wake Island
Wal./F.	Wallis and Futuna
W.B.	West Bank
well	well, spring, oasis
Wi., U.S.	Wisconsin, U.S.
W. Sah.	Western Sahara
wtfl.	waterfall, rapids
W.V., U.S.	West Virginia, U.S.
Wy., U.S.	Wyoming, U.S.
Yk., Can.	Yukon Territory, Can.
Zam.	Zambia
Zimb.	Zimbabwe

Index

A

Name	Map Ref.	Page
Å, Nor.	C5	8
Aabenraa, Den.	I3	8
Aachen, Ger.	F1	16
Aalborg, Den.	H4	8
Aalborg Bugt, b., Den.	H4	8
Aalen, Ger.	H6	16
Aali, Sadd el- (Aswan High Dam), dam, Egypt	C6	62
Aalst (Alost), Bel.	D13	14
Äänekoski, Fin.	E11	8
Aarau, Switz.	C4	22
Aare, stm., Switz.	C5	22
Aarlen see Arlon, Bel.	E14	14
Aarschot, Bel.	D14	14
Aasiaat see Egedesminde, Grnld.	D15	141
Aat see Ath, Bel.	D12	14
Aba, China	E5	36
Aba, D.R.C.	D6	66
Aba, Nig.	H6	64
Abā al-Bawl, Qurayn, hill, Qatar	E7	56
Abacaxis, stm., Braz.	E6	84
Abaco, i., Bah.	B9	96
Abacou, Pointe, c., Haiti	D10	102
Abadab, Jabal, mtn., Sudan	D7	62
Ābādān, Iran	C6	56
Ābādeh, Iran	C7	56
Abadla, Alg.	C4	64
Abaeté, Braz.	J3	88
Abaeté, stm., Braz.	J3	88
Abaetetuba, Braz.	A1	88
Abag Qi, China	C7	36
Abaí, Para.	C10	92
Abaj see Abay, Kaz.	E12	32
Abakaliki, Nig.	H6	64
Abakan, Russia	D16	32
Abakan, stm., Russia	D15	32
Abakanovo, Russia	A20	10
Abakanskij hrebet, mts., Russia	D15	32
Abala, Niger	G5	64
Abalak, Niger	F6	64
Aban, Russia	C17	32
Abancay, Peru	F3	84
Abashiri, Japan	B16	38
Abasolo, Mex.	C6	100
Abasolo, Mex.	I7	130
Abasolo, Mex.	G6	130
Abau, Pap. N. Gui.	c4	79a
Abay, Kaz.	E12	32
Ābay see Blue Nile, stm., Afr.	E6	62
Abaya, Lake see Ābaya Hāyk', l., Eth.	F7	62
Ābaya Hāyk', l., Eth.	F7	62
Abaza, Russia	D15	32
Abbadia San Salvatore, Italy	H8	22
Abbé, Lac see Abe, Lake, l., Afr.	E8	62
Abbeville, Fr.	D10	14
Abbeville, Ga., U.S.	D2	116
Abbeville, La., U.S.	H6	122
Abbeville, S.C., U.S.	B3	116
Abbey, Sk., Can.	D5	124
Abbeyfeale, Ire.	I3	12
Abbiategrasso, Italy	E5	22
Abbot, Mount, mtn., Austl.	B6	76
Abbot Ice Shelf, ice, Ant.	C31	81
Abbotsford, B.C., Can.	G8	138
Abbottābād, Pak.	A4	54
'Abd al-Kūrī, i., Yemen	G7	56
Ábdira, sci., Grc.	B7	28
Abdulino, Russia	D8	32
Abe, Lake, l., Afr.	E8	62
Abéché, Chad	E4	62
Abel Tasman National Park, p.o.i., N.Z.	E5	80
Abemama, at., Kir.	C8	72
Abengourou, C. Iv.	H4	64
Abenójar, Spain	F6	20
Abensberg, Ger.	H7	16
Abeokuta, Nig.	H5	64
Aberdare, Wales, U.K.	J9	12
Aberdeen, S. Afr.	H6	70
Aberdeen, Scot., U.K.	D10	12
Aberdeen, Id., U.S.	H14	136
Aberdeen, Md., U.S.	E9	114
Aberdeen, Ms., U.S.	D10	122
Aberdeen, N.C., U.S.	A6	116
Aberdeen, S.D., U.S.	B14	126
Aberdeen, Wa., U.S.	D3	136
Aberdeen Lake, l., Nu., Can.	C10	106
Aberdeen Lake, res., Ms., U.S.	D10	122
Aberfeldy, Scot., U.K.	E9	12
Abergavenny, Wales, U.K.	J9	12
Abernant, Al., U.S.	D11	122
Abernathy, Tx., U.S.	H7	128
Abernethy, Sk., Can.	D10	124
Abert, Lake, l., Or., U.S.	H6	136
Aberystwyth, Wales, U.K.	I8	12
Abez', Russia	A10	32
Abhā, Sau. Ar.	F5	56
Abidjan, C. Iv.	H4	64
Abilene, Tx., U.S.	B8	130
Abingdon, Eng., U.K.	J11	12
Abingdon, Il., U.S.	D7	120
Abingdon, Va., U.S.	H4	114
Abiquiu, N.M., U.S.	E2	128
Abiquiu Reservoir, res., N.M., U.S.	E2	128
Abisko, Swe.	B8	8
Abitibi, stm., On., Can.	E14	106
Abitibi, Lake, l., Can.	F15	106
Abja-Paluoja, Est.	B8	10
Abnûb, Egypt	K2	58
Åbo see Turku, Fin.	F9	8
Abohar, India	C5	54
Abomey, Benin	H5	64
Abongabong, Gunung, mtn., Indon.	J3	48
Abong Mbang, Cam.	D2	66
Abony, Hung.	B6	26
Aborigen, pik, mtn., Russia	D18	34
Abou-Deïa, Chad	E3	62
Abou Simbel (Abu Simbel), sci., Egypt	C6	62
Abraham Lake, res., Ab., Can.	D14	138
Abra Pampa, Arg.	D3	90
Abre Campo, Braz.	K4	88
Abreu e Lima, Braz.	D8	88
Abring, India	B6	54
Abrud, Rom.	C10	26
Abruzzo, state, Italy	H10	22
Abruzzo, Parco Nazionale d', p.o.i., Italy	C7	24
Absaroka Range, mts., U.S.	C3	126
Absarokee, Mt., U.S.	E17	136
Absecon, N.J., U.S.	E11	114
Abū 'Alī, i., Sau. Ar.	D6	56
Abu Ballâs, mtn., Egypt	C5	62
Abu Dhabi see Abū Ẓaby, U.A.E.	E7	56
Abū Dulayq, Sudan	D6	62
Abū el-Ḥul (Sphinx), hist., Egypt	I1	58
Abufari, Braz.	E5	84
Abū Ḥamad, Sudan	D6	62
Abu Ḥammâd, Egypt	H2	58
Abuja, Nig.	H6	64
Abū Jabrah, Sudan	E5	62
Abū Jubayhah, Sudan	E6	62
Abū Kamāl, Syria	C5	56
Abukuma, stm., Japan	B13	40
Abukuma-kōchi, plat., Japan	B13	40
Abū Madd, Ra's, c., Sau. Ar.	E4	56
Abu Mendi, Eth.	E7	62
Abunã, Braz.	E4	84
Abu Qîr, Khalîg, b., Egypt	G1	58
Abu Qurqâs, Egypt	K1	58
Ābu Road, India	F4	54
Abū Rubayq, Sau. Ar.	E4	56
Abū Shajarah Ra's, c., Sudan	C7	62
Abu Shâma, Gebel, mtn., Egypt	I2	58
Abu Simbel see Abou Simbel, sci., Egypt	C6	62
Abu Tîg, Egypt	K2	58
Abū Zabad, Sudan	E5	62
Abū Ẓaby (Abu Dhabi), U.A.E.	E7	56
Abwong, Sudan	F6	62
Abyei, Sudan	F5	62
Abyssinia see Ethiopia, ctry., Afr.	F7	62
Acacías, Col.	E5	86
Acadia National Park, p.o.i., Me., U.S.	F8	110
Acadia Valley, Ab., Can.	C3	124
Açailândia, Braz.	C2	88
Acajutiba, Braz.	F7	88
Acámbaro, Mex.	E8	100
Acandí, Col.	C3	86
Acaponeta, Mex.	D6	100
Acaponeta, stm., Mex.	D6	100
Acapulco de Juárez, Mex.	G8	100
Acará, Braz.	A1	88
Acará, stm., Braz.	A1	88
Acarai Mountains, mts., S.A.	C6	84
Acará-Mirim, stm., Braz.	B1	88
Acaraú, Braz.	B5	88
Acaraú, stm., Braz.	B5	88
Acaray, stm., Para.	B10	92
Acarí, Peru	G3	84
Acari, stm., Braz.	H3	88
Acarigua, Ven.	C7	86
Acatlán de Osorio, Mex.	F9	100
Acay, Nevado de, mtn., Arg.	B4	92
Acayucan, Mex.	F11	100
Acceglio, Italy	F3	22
Accomac, Va., U.S.	G10	114
Accra, Ghana	H5	64
Acebuches, Mex.	A7	100
Aceguá, Braz.	E10	92
Aceh, state, Indon.	J3	48
Acerra, Italy	D8	24
Achacachi, Bol.	C3	90
Achaguas, Ven.	D7	86
Achalpur, India	H6	54
Achar, Ur.	F9	92
Acharnés, Grc.	E6	28
Achelóos, stm., Grc.	E4	28
Acheng, China	B7	38
Achern, Ger.	H4	16
Achill Head, c., Ire.	G2	12
Achill Island, i., Ire.	H2	12
Achiras, Arg.	F5	92
Achit nuur, l., Mong.	E16	32
Achwa, stm., Afr.	D6	66
Acı Göl, l., Tur.	F12	28
Ačinsk, Russia	C16	32
Acıpayam, Tur.	F12	28
Acireale, Italy	G9	24
Ackerly, Tx., U.S.	B6	130
Ackley, Ia., U.S.	B4	120
Acklins, i., Bah.	C10	96
Acklins, Bight of, b., Bah.	A10	102
Acme, Ab., Can.	E17	138
Aconcagua, Cerro, mtn., Arg.	F3	92
Aconchi, Mex.	G7	98
Acopiara, Braz.	D6	88
Açores (Azores), is., Port.	C3	60
Acorizal, Braz.	G6	84
A Coruña (Corunna), Spain	A2	20
A Coruña, co., Spain	A2	20
Acquasanta Terme, Italy	H10	22
Acqui Terme, Italy	F5	22
Acre see 'Akko, Isr.	F6	58
Acre, state, Braz.	E4	84
Acre, stm., S.A.	F4	84
Acri, Italy	E10	24
Acton Vale, Qc., Can.	E4	110
Actopan, Mex.	E9	100
Açucena, Braz.	J4	88
Acuña, Arg.	D8	92
Ada, Mn., U.S.	D2	118
Ada, Oh., U.S.	D2	114
Ada, Ok., U.S.	C2	122
Ādaba, Eth.	F7	62
Adair, Ia., U.S.	C3	120
Adair, Bahía de, b., Mex.	F6	98
Adair, Cape, c., Nu., Can.	A16	106
Adairsville, Ga., U.S.	C14	122
Adairville, Ky., U.S.	H11	120
Adaja, stm., Spain	C6	20
Adak Island, i., Ak., U.S.	g23	140a
Adam, Oman	E8	56
Adamantina, Braz.	D6	90
Adamaoua, mts., Afr.	C2	66
Adamclisi, Rom.	E14	26
Adamello, mts., Italy	D7	22
Adaminaby, Austl.	K7	76
Adams, Mn., U.S.	H6	118
Adams, N.D., U.S.	F15	124
Adams, Ne., U.S.	K2	118
Adams, N.Y., U.S.	E13	112
Adams, stm., B.C., Can.	E11	138
Adams, Mount, vol., Wa., U.S.	D5	136
Adam's Bridge, rf., Asia	G4	53
Adams Lake, l., B.C., Can.	E11	138
Adams Peak, mtn., Sri L.	H5	53
Adams Rock, r., Pit.	c28	78k
Adamstown, Pit.	c28	78k
Adamsville, Tn., U.S.	B10	122
'Adan (Aden), Yemen	G6	56
Adana, Tur.	A6	58
Adana, state, Tur.	A6	58
Adanero, Spain	D6	20
Adarama, Sudan	D6	62
Adare, Cape, c., Ant.	C22	81
Adavale, Austl.	E5	76
Adda, stm., Italy	E6	22
Ad-Dabbah, Sudan	D6	62
Ad-Dahnā', des., Sau. Ar.	D6	56
Ad-Dāmir, Sudan	D6	62
Ad-Dammām, Sau. Ar.	D7	56
Ad-Dānā, Syria	B7	58
Ad-Dawḥah (Doha), Qatar	D7	56
Ad-Dibdibah, reg., Sau. Ar.	D6	56
Addis, La., U.S.	G7	122
Addis Ababa see Ādīs Ābeba, Eth.	F7	62
Addis Abeba see Ādīs Ābeba, Eth.	C7	66
Addison, Mi., U.S.	F5	112
Ad-Dīwānīyah, Iraq	C6	56
Addo Elephant National Park, p.o.i., S. Afr.	H7	70
Addu Atoll, at., Mald.	j12	46a
Ad-Du'ayn, Sudan	E5	62
Ad-Duwayd, Sau. Ar.	C5	56
Ad-Duwaym, Sudan	E6	62
Adel, Ga., U.S.	E2	116
Adelaide, Austl.	J2	76
Adelaide, Bah.	n18	104f
Adelaide Island, i., Ant.	B33	81
Adelaide Peninsula, pen., Nu., Can.	B11	106
Adelaide River, Austl.	B6	74
Adèle Island, i., Austl.	C4	74
Adélie, Terre, cst., Ant.	B18	81
Adelie Coast see Adélie, Terre, cst., Ant.	B18	81
Adelong, Austl.	J6	76
Aden see 'Adan, Yemen	G6	56
Aden, Gulf of, b.	E9	62
Adendorp, S. Afr.	H7	70
Adi, Pulau, i., Indon.	F9	44
Adiaké, C. Iv.	H4	64
Adige (Etsch), stm., Italy	E8	22
Ādīgrat, Eth.	E7	62
Adıgüzel Barajı, res., Tur.	E12	28
Ādilābād, India	B4	53
Adimi, Russia	G16	34
Adin, Ca., U.S.	B5	134
Adirondack Mountains, mts., N.Y., U.S.	E15	112
Ādīs Ābeba (Addis Ababa), Eth.	F7	62
Adi Ugri, Erit.	E7	62
Adıyaman, Tur.	A9	58
Adıyaman, state, Tur.	A9	58
Adjuntas, Presa de las see Vicente Guerrero, Presa, res., Mex.	D9	100
Admiral, Sk., Can.	E5	124
Admiralty Gulf, b., Austl.	B5	74
Admiralty Inlet, b., Nu., Can.	A13	106
Admiralty Island, i., Nu., Can.	B10	106
Admiralty Island, i., Ak., U.S.	E13	140
Admiralty Islands, is., Pap. N. Gui.	a4	79a
Admiralty Mountains, mts., Ant.	C21	81
Ado, Nig.	H5	64
Ado-Ekiti, Nig.	H6	64
Adolfo Gonzales Chaves, Arg.	H7	92
Adolfo López Mateos, Mex.	A5	100
Adolfo López Mateos, Presa, res., Mex.	C5	100
Adolfo Rodriguez Sáa see Santa Rosa del Conlara, Arg.	F5	92
Ādoni, India	D3	53
Adour, stm., Fr.	F4	18
Ādra, India	G11	54
Adra, Spain	H7	20
Adrano, Italy	G8	24
Adrar, Alg.	D4	64
Adrâr, reg., Maur.	E2	64
Adria, Italy	E9	22
Adrian, Mi., U.S.	C1	114
Adrian, Mo., U.S.	F3	120
Adrian, Or., U.S.	G9	136
Adrian, Tx., U.S.	F6	128
Adrian, W.V., U.S.	F5	114
Adriatic Sea, s., Eur.	G11	22
A Dun, stm., Viet.	F9	48
Adutiškis, Lith.	E9	10
Advance, Mo., U.S.	G7	120
Advocate Harbour, N.S., Can.	E11	110
Ādwa, Eth.	E7	62
Adyča, stm., Russia	C16	34
Adygea see Adygeja, state, Russia	F6	32
Adygeja, state, Russia	F6	32
Adygheya see Adygeja, state, Russia	F6	32
Adzopé, C. Iv.	H4	64
Aegean Sea, s.	E7	28
Aegina see Aígina, i., Grc.	F6	28
Aegviidu, Est.	A8	10
Aën, ostrov, i., Russia	B22	34
Aerku Hu, l., China	C9	54
Ærø, i., Den.	I4	8
Ærøskøbing, Den.	B6	16
A Estrada, Spain	B2	20
Aetna, Ab., Can.	G17	138
Afaahiti, Fr. Poly.	v22	78h
Afadjoto, mtn., Ghana	H5	64
Afareaitu, Fr. Poly.	v20	78h
Afars and Issas see Djibouti, ctry., Afr.	E8	62
Affton, Mo., U.S.	F7	120
Afghanistan, ctry., Asia	C9	56
Afgooye, Som.	D8	66
Afikpo, Nig.	H6	64
Aflou, Alg.	C5	64
Afmadow, Som.	D8	66
Afogados da Ingazeira, Braz.	D7	88
Afognak Island, i., Ak., U.S.	E9	140
Afoniha, Russia	B25	8
A Fonsagrada, Spain	A3	20
Africa, cont.	F14	4
'Afrīn, Syria	B7	58
Afton, N.Y., U.S.	B10	114
Afton, Ok., U.S.	H2	120
Afton, Wy., U.S.	H16	136
'Afula, Isr.	F6	58
Afyon, Tur.	E13	28
Afyon, state, Tur.	E13	28
Agadez, Niger	F6	64
Agadir, Mor.	C2	64
Agâdîr, Râs, c., Maur.	E1	64
Agadyr, Kaz.	E12	32
Agalak, Sudan	E6	62
Agalega Islands, is., Mrts.	K8	142
Agan, stm., Russia	B13	32
Agana see Hagåtña, Guam	j10	78c
Agana Heights, Guam	j10	78c
Agano, stm., Japan	B12	40
Agapa, Russia	B6	34
Aga Point, c., Guam	k10	78c
Agar, India	G5	54
Agartala, India	G13	54
Agassiz, B.C., Can.	G9	138
Agassiz Pool, res., Mn., U.S.	C3	118
Agate, Co., U.S.	B5	128
Agate Fossil Beds National Monument, p.o.i., Ne., U.S.	E9	126
Agattu Island, i., Ak., U.S.	g21	140a
Agawa Bay, b., On., Can.	A5	112
Agawam, Mt., U.S.	B14	136
Agboville, C. Iv.	H4	64
Ağdam, Azer.	B6	56
Ageevo, Russia	F19	10
Agen, Fr.	E6	18
Agency, Ia., U.S.	D5	120
Agency Lake, l., Or., U.S.	H5	136
Aggeneys, S. Afr.	F4	70
Aggteleki Nemzeti Park, p.o.i., Hung.	A7	26
Āghā Jārī, Iran	C6	56
Agía Marína, Grc.	F9	28
Agiásos, Grc.	D9	28
Aginskoe, Russia	F11	34
Ágio Óros, state, Grc.	C7	28
Ágio Óros, pen., Grc.	C7	28
Ágios Nikólaos, Grc.	H8	28
Agíou Órous, Kólpos (Singitic Gulf), b., Grc.	C6	28
Ağlasun, Tur.	F13	28
Agnes Lake, l., On., Can.	C7	118
Agnew, Austl.	E4	74
Agnibilékrou, C. Iv.	H4	64
Agno, Phil.	B2	52
Agno, stm., Phil.	C3	52
Ago, Japan	E9	40
Agogna, stm., Italy	E5	22
Agou, Mont, mtn., Togo	H5	64
Agout, stm., Fr.	F8	18
Āgra, India	E6	54
Agraciada, Ur.	F8	92
Agreda, Spain	C8	20
Ağrı, Tur.	B5	56
Agri, stm., Italy	D9	24
Ağrı Dağı (Ararat, Mount), mtn., Tur.	B5	56
Agrigento, Italy	G7	24
Agrihan, i., N. Mar. Is.	B5	72
Agrínio, Grc.	E4	28
Agrio, stm., Arg.	H2	92
Agrópoli, Italy	D9	24
Agro Pontino, reg., Italy	C6	24
Agto, Grnld.	D15	141
Água Branca, Braz.	C4	88
Agua Caliente, Mex.	B4	100
Agua Caliente Grande, Mex.	B4	100
Aguachica, Col.	C5	86
Água Clara, Braz.	D6	90
Aguada Cecilio, Arg.	H3	90
Aguada de Guerra, Arg.	H3	90
Aguada de Pasajeros, Cuba	A7	102
Aguadas, Col.	E4	86
Aguadilla, P.R.	B1	104a
Água Doce, Braz.	C12	92
Aguadulce, Pan.	H7	102
Agua Dulce, Tx., U.S.	G9	130
Agua Fria, stm., Az., U.S.	I4	132
Agua Fria National Monument, p.o.i., Az., U.S.	I5	132
Aguaí, Braz.	L2	88
Agualeguas, Mex.	H8	130
Aguán, stm., Hond.	E4	102
Aguanaval, stm., Mex.	C7	100
Aguapey, stm., Arg.	D9	92
Água Preta, Igarapé, stm., Braz.	H9	86
Agua Prieta, Mex.	F8	98
Aguaray Guazú, stm., Para.	A9	92
A Guardia, Spain	C1	20
Aguarico, stm., S.A.	H3	86
Aguaro-Guariquito, Parque Nacional, p.o.i., Ven.	C8	86
Aguaruto, Mex.	C5	100
Aguasabon, stm., On., Can.	C11	118
Águas Belas, Braz.	E7	88
Aguas Buenas, P.R.	B3	104a
Aguascalientes, Mex.	E7	100
Aguascalientes, state, Mex.	D7	100
Águas Formosas, Braz.	I5	88
Água Vermelha, Represa de, res., Braz.	C6	90
Aguayo, Arg.	E4	92
Agu Bay, b., Nu., Can.	A13	106
Agudos, Braz.	L1	88
Águeda, stm., Eur.	D4	20
Aguelhok, Mali	F5	64
Aguilar, Co., U.S.	D4	128
Aguilar de la Frontera, Spain	G6	20
Aguilares, Arg.	C5	92
Águilas, Spain	G9	20
Aguililla, Mex.	F7	100
Agujereada, Punta, c., P.R.	A1	104a
Agujita, Mex.	G6	130
Agulhas, Kaap, c., S. Afr.	I5	70
Agulhas Basin, unds.	M15	144
Agulhas Negras, Pico das, mtn., Braz.	L3	88
Agung, Gunung, vol., Indon.	G6	44
Agusan, stm., Phil.	F5	52
Agustín Codazzi, Col.	C5	86
Ağva, Tur.	B12	28
Ahaggar, mts., Alg.	E6	64
Ahaggar, Tassili ta-n-, plat., Alg.	E5	64
Ahalcihe, Geor.	F6	32
Ahar, Iran	B6	56
Ahaus, Ger.	D3	16
Ahipara Bay, b., N.Z.	B5	80
Ahlen, Ger.	E3	16
Ahmadābād, India	G4	54
Ahmadnagar, India	B2	53
Ahmadpur East, Pak.	D3	54
Ahmadpur Siāl, Pak.	C3	54
Ahmar Mountains, mts., Eth.	F8	62
Ahmetli, Tur.	E10	28
Ahmic Lake, l., On., Can.	C10	112
Ahoskie, N.C., U.S.	H9	114
Ahousat, B.C., Can.	G4	138
Ahraura, India	F9	54
Ahtuba, stm., Russia	E7	32
Ahtubinsk, Russia	E7	32
Ahuacatlán, Mex.	E6	100
Ahumada, Mex.	D1	130
Ahunui, at., Fr. Poly.	E12	72
Ahvāz, Iran	C6	56
Ahvenanmaa see Åland, state, Fin.	F9	8
Ahvenanmaa see Åland, is., Fin.	F8	8
Aḥwar, Yemen	G6	56
Ahwa-ri, Kor., S.	D2	40
Å i Åfjord, Nor.	D4	8
Aibonito, P.R.	B3	104a
Aichi, state, Japan	D10	40
Aidong, China	I2	42
'Aiea, Hi., U.S.	b3	78a
Aígina, Grc.	F6	28
Aígina, i., Grc.	F6	28
Aígio, Grc.	E5	28
Aigle, Switz.	D3	22
Aigle, stm., Qc., Can.	A1	110
Aiguá, Ur.	G10	92
Aigüestortes i Estany Sant Maurici, Parque Nacional d', p.o.i., Spain	B11	20
Aigüestortes i Llac de Sant Maurici, Parc Nacional d' see Aigüestortes i Esta, p.o.i., Spain	B11	20
Aikawa, Japan	A11	40
Aiken, S.C., U.S.	C4	116
Aikens Lake, l., Mb., Can.	C18	124
Ailao Shan, mts., China	G5	36
Aileron, Austl.	D6	74
Ailinglaplap, at., Marsh. Is.	C7	72
Ailsa Craig, On., Can.	E8	112
Ailsa Craig, i., Scot., U.K.	F7	12
Aim, Russia	E15	34
Aimorés, Braz.	J5	88
Ain, state, Fr.	D11	18
Ain, stm., Fr.	D11	18
Aïn Benian, Alg.	H13	20
Aïn Bessem, Alg.	H14	20
Aïn Defla, Alg.	H12	20
Aïn Draham, Tun.	H2	24
Aïn el Beïda, Alg.	B6	64
Ainslie Lake, l., N.S., Can.	D15	110
Aioi, Japan	E7	40
Aiora, Spain	E9	20
Aipe, Col.	F4	86
Aïr, Massif de l', mts., Niger	F6	64
Airai Airport, Palau	g8	78b
Airbangis, Indon.	C1	50
Airdrie, Ab., Can.	E16	138
Aire, stm., Fr.	F14	14
Aire, stm., Eng., U.K.	H11	12
Aire-sur-l'Adour, Fr.	F5	18
Air Force Island, i., Nu., Can.	B16	106
Airhaji, Indon.	D2	50
Airlie Beach, Austl.	C7	76
Airolo, Switz.	D5	22
Airuoca, Braz.	L3	88
Aishihik, Yk., Can.	C3	106
Aishihik Lake, l., Yk., Can.	C3	106
Aisne, state, Fr.	E12	14
Aisne, stm., Fr.	E12	14
Aïssa, Djebel, mtn., Alg.	C4	64
Aitape, Pap. N. Gui.	a3	79a
Aitkin, Mn., U.S.	E5	118
Aitolikó, Grc.	E4	28
Aitutaki, at., Cook Is.	E11	72
Aiuaba, Braz.	D5	88
Aiud, Rom.	C10	26
Aix, Île d', i., Fr.	C4	18
Aix, Mount, mtn., Wa., U.S.	D5	136
Aix-en-Provence, Fr.	F11	18
Aix-la-Chapelle see Aachen, Ger.	F1	16
Aix-les-Bains, Fr.	D11	18
Āīzawl, India	G14	54
Aizkraukle, Lat.	D8	10
Aizu-bange, Japan	B12	40
Aizu-wakamatsu, Japan	B12	40
Ajaccio, Fr.	H14	18
Ajaccio, Golfe d', b., Fr.	H14	18
Ajaguz see Ayaköz, Kaz.	E13	32
Ajajú, stm., Col.	G5	86
Ajan, Russia	E16	34
Ajan, stm., Russia	C7	34
Ajanta, India	H5	54
Ajanta Caves, hist., India	H5	54
Ajanta Range, mts., India	H5	54
Ajarani, stm., Braz.	F11	86
Ajax, On., Can.	E10	112
Ajdābiyā, Libya	A4	62
Ajdyrlinskij, Russia	D9	32
Ajjer, Tassili-n-, plat., Alg.	D6	64
Ajka, Hung.	B4	26
'Ajlūn, Jord.	F6	58
Ajmer, India	E5	54
Ajnāla, India	C5	54
Ajo, Az., U.S.	K4	132
Ajtos, Blg.	G14	26
Ajusco, Mex.	L9	134
Akabira, Japan	C15	38
Akabli, Alg.	D5	64
Akademii, zaliv, b., Russia	F16	34
Akagi-san, vol., Japan	C12	40
Akaishi-sammyaku, mts., Japan	D11	40
Āk'ak'ī Besek'a, Eth.	F7	62
Akalkot, India	C2	53
Akámas, Akrotírion, c., Cyp.	C3	58
Akan-kokuritsu-kōen, p.o.i., Japan	C16	38
'Akasha East, Sudan	C6	62
'Akāshāt, Iraq	C5	56
Akashi, Japan	E7	40
Akbarpur, India	E9	54
Akbulak, Russia	D9	32
Akçakale, Tur.	B9	58
Akçakoca, Tur.	B14	28
Akçakoyunlu, Tur.	B8	58
Akçaova, Tur.	F11	28
Akçay, Tur.	G12	28
Akçay, stm., Tur.	F11	28
Akchâr, reg., Maur.	E2	64
Akdoğan, N. Cyp.	C4	58
Ak-Dovurak, Russia	D15	32
Akeley, Mn., U.S.	D4	118
Aken, Ger.	E8	16
Akershus, state, Nor.	F4	8
Aketi, D.R.C.	D4	66
Akhaltsikhe see Ahalcihe, Geor.	F6	32
Akhḍar, Al-Jabal al-, mts., Libya	A4	62
Akhḍar, Al-Jabal al-, mts., Oman	E8	56
Akhḍar, Wādī al-, stm., Sau. Ar.	J7	58
Akhisar, Tur.	E10	28
Akhtarīn, Syria	B8	58
Akhtubinsk see Ahtubinsk, Russia	E7	32
Aki, Japan	F6	40
Akimiski Island, i., Nu., Can.	E14	106
Akıncı Burun, c., Tur.	B6	58
Akita, Japan	E13	38
Akjoujt, Maur.	F2	64
Akkeshi, Japan	C16	38
'Akko, Isr.	F6	58
Akköy, Tur.	F10	28
Aklavik, N.T., Can.	B4	106
'Aklé 'Aouâna, reg., Afr.	F3	64
Akmeņrags, c., Lat.	D3	10
Akmola see Astana, Kaz.	D12	32
Akō, Japan	E7	40
Ākobo (Akūbū), stm., Afr.	F6	62
Akola, India	H6	54
Akonolinga, Cam.	D2	66
Akordat, Erit.	D7	62
Akören, Tur.	F15	28
Akot, India	H6	54
Akpatok Island, i., Nu., Can.	C17	106
Akpınar, Tur.	A9	58
Akrítas, Ákra, c., Grc.	G4	28
Akrokórinthos, sci., Grc.	F5	28
Akron, Co., U.S.	A5	128
Akron, In., U.S.	G4	112
Akron, N.Y., U.S.	E11	112
Akron, Oh., U.S.	C4	114
Akron, Pa., U.S.	H13	112
Akrotíri, Cyp.	D3	58
Akša, Russia	F11	34
Aksaray, Tur.	B3	56
Aksay, Kaz.	D8	32
Aksayqin Hu, l., China	A7	54
Akşehir, Tur.	E14	28
Akşehir Gölü, l., Tur.	E14	28
Akseki, Tur.	F14	28
Aksu, China	F14	32
Aksu, stm., Tur.	A8	58
Aksu, stm., Tur.	F13	28
Āksum, Eth.	E7	62
Aktau see Aqtaū, Kaz.	F8	32
Aktjubinsk see Aqtöbe, Kaz.	D9	32
Akto, China	B12	56
Akūbū, Sudan	F6	62
Akūbū (Ākobo), stm., Afr.	F6	62
Akuliči Pervye, Russia	G16	10
Akune, Japan	G3	40
Akure, Nig.	H5	64
Akureyri, Ice.	k30	8a
Akutan Island, i., Ak., U.S.	F6	140
Akwanga, Nig.	H6	64
Akyazı, Tur.	C13	28
Ål, Nor.	F3	8
Alabama, state, U.S.	E12	122
Alabama, stm., Al., U.S.	F11	122
Alabaster, Al., U.S.	D12	122
Alacant (Alicante), Spain	F10	20
Alacant, co., Spain	F10	20
Alaçatı, Tur.	E9	28
Alachua, Fl., U.S.	G3	116
Alacrán, Arrecife, rf., Mex.	C7	96
Alacranes, Presa, res., Cuba	A7	102
Aladağ, mtn., Tur.	A6	58
Alagoa Grande, Braz.	D8	88
Alagoas, state, Braz.	E7	88
Alagoinhas, Braz.	G6	88
Alagón, Spain	C9	20
Alagón, stm., Spain	E4	20
Alahanpanjang, Indon.	D2	50
Alaior, Spain	E15	20
Alajku, Kyrg.	F12	32
Alajskij hrebet, mts., Asia	B11	56
Alajuela, C.R.	H5	102
Alajuela, Lago, res., Pan.	H8	102
Alakanuk, Ak., U.S.	D7	140
Alakol', ozero see Alaköl köli, l., Kaz.	E14	32
Alaköl köli, l., Kaz.	E14	32
Al-'Akrīshah, Egypt	G1	58
Alaktara, India	H9	54
Alakurtti, Russia	C13	8
'Alalakeiki Channel, strt., Hi., U.S.	c5	78a
Alalaú, stm., Braz.	H11	86
Alamagan, i., N. Mar. Is.	B5	72
Al-'Amārah, Iraq	C6	56
Alameda, Ca., U.S.	F3	134
Alameda, N.M., U.S.	H10	132
Alamo, Ga., U.S.	D3	116
Alamo, Tn., U.S.	B9	122
Alamo, stm., Ca., U.S.	K1	132
Alamogordo, N.M., U.S.	B2	130
Alamo Heights, Tx., U.S.	E9	130
Alamo Lake, res., Az., U.S.	I3	132
Álamos, Mex.	B4	100
Álamos, stm., Mex.	A8	100
Alamosa, Co., U.S.	D3	128
Alamosa East, Co., U.S.	D3	128
Álamos de Márquez, Mex.	A7	100
Aland, India	C3	53
Åland, state, Fin.	F9	8
Åland (Ahvenanmaa), is., Fin.	F8	8
Aland Islands see Åland, is., Fin.	F8	8
Aland Sea, s., Eur.	G8	8
Alandur, India	E5	53
Alanya, Tur.	G15	28
Alaotra, Farihy, l., Madag.	D8	68
Alapaevsk, Russia	C10	32
Alapaha, Ga., U.S.	E2	116
Alapaha, stm., U.S.	F2	116
Alaplı, Tur.	B14	28
Alappuzha see Alleppey, India	G3	53
Al-'Aqabah, Jord.	I6	58
Alarcón, Spain	E8	20
Alarcón, Embalse de, res., Spain	E9	20
Alas, stm., Indon.	K3	48
Alas, Selat, strt., Indon.	H10	50
Alaşehir, Tur.	E11	28
Alashanyouqi, China	C5	36
Alaska, state, U.S.	D9	140
Alaska, Gulf of, b., Ak., U.S.	E10	140
Alaska Peninsula, pen., Ak., U.S.	E7	140
Alaska Range, mts., Ak., U.S.	D9	140
Alassio, Italy	F5	22
Alatan'aola see Xin Barag Youqi, China	B8	36
Alatri, Italy	I10	22
Alatyr', Russia	D7	32
Alausí, Ec.	I2	86
Alava see Arabako, co., Spain	B8	20
Alava, Cape, c., Wa., U.S.	B2	136
Al-'Ayn, U.A.E.	E8	56
Alayor see Alaior, Spain	E15	20
Alazeja, stm., Russia	B19	34
Al-'Azīzīyah, Libya	A2	62
Alba, Italy	F5	22
Alba, Mi., U.S.	D5	112
Alba, Tx., U.S.	E3	122
Alba, state, Rom.	C10	26
Al-Bāb, Syria	B8	58
Albacete, Spain	E9	20
Albacete, co., Spain	F9	20
Al-Bad', Sau. Ar.	J6	58
Alba de Tormes, Spain	D5	20
Albaida, Spain	F10	20
Alba Iulia, Rom.	C10	26
Al-Balqā', state, Jord.	F6	58
Al-Bālū'ah, l., Syria	C7	58
Albanel, Lac, l., Qc., Can.	E16	106
Albania, Col.	B5	86
Albania, ctry., Eur.	C14	24
Albano Laziale, Italy	I9	22
Albany, Ga., U.S.	E1	116
Albany, In., U.S.	H4	112
Albany, Ky., U.S.	H12	120
Albany, Mn., U.S.	F4	118
Albany, Mo., U.S.	D3	120
Albany, N.Y., U.S.	B12	114
Albany, Oh., U.S.	E3	114
Albany, Or., U.S.	F3	136
Albany, Tx., U.S.	B8	130
Albany, stm., On., Can.	E14	106
Albarracín, Spain	D9	20
Al-Baṣrah (Basra), Iraq	C6	56
Al-Batrā' (Petra), sci., Jord.	H6	58
Albatross Bay, b., Austl.	B8	74
Al-Bayḍā', Libya	A4	62
Albemarle, N.C., U.S.	A5	116
Albemarle Island see Isabela, Isla, i., Ec.	i11	84a
Albemarle Sound, strt., N.C., U.S.	H9	114
Albenga, Italy	F5	22
Alberche, stm., Spain	D6	20
Alberdi, Para.	C8	92
Alberga Creek, stm., Austl.	E6	74
Alberni Inlet, b., B.C., Can.	G6	138
Alberobello, Italy	D11	24
Albert, Fr.	E11	14
Albert, Lake, l., Afr.	D6	66
Albert, Lake, l., Austl.	J2	76
Alberta, Al., U.S.	E11	122
Alberta, state, Can.	E8	106
Alberta, Mount, mtn., Ab., Can.	D13	138
Albert Canyon, B.C., Can.	E13	138
Albert City, Ia., U.S.	I3	118
Albert Edward Bay, b., Nu., Can.	B10	106
Alberti, Arg.	G7	92
Albertirsa, Hung.	B6	26
Albertkanaal, can., Bel.	D14	14
Albert Lea, Mn., U.S.	H5	118
Albert Markham, Mount, mtn., Ant.	D21	81
Albert Nile, stm., Afr.	D6	66
Alberton, P.E., Can.	D12	110
Albertville, Fr.	D12	18
Albertville, Al., U.S.	C12	122
Albi, Fr.	F8	18
Albia, Ia., U.S.	C5	120
Albin, Wy., U.S.	F8	126
Albina, Sur.	B7	84
Albina, Ponta, c., Ang.	D1	68
Albion, Ca., U.S.	D2	134
Albion, Id., U.S.	H13	136
Albion, Il., U.S.	F9	120
Albion, In., U.S.	G4	112
Albion, Mi., U.S.	B1	114
Albion, N.Y., U.S.	E11	112
Albion, Pa., U.S.	C5	114
Albion, Wa., U.S.	D9	136
Al-Biqā', state, Leb.	D7	58
Al-Biqā' (Bekaa Valley), val., Leb.	D7	58
Al-Bi'r, Sau. Ar.	J7	58
Albocàsser, Spain	D10	20
Alboran Sea, s.	B4	64
Alborz, Reshteh-ye Kūhhā-ye, mts., Iran	B7	56
Albuñol, Spain	H7	20
Albuquerque, N.M., U.S.	H10	132
Albuquerque, Cayos de, is., Col.	F6	102
Alburg, Vt., U.S.	E3	110
Alburquerque, Spain	E3	20
Albury, Austl.	J6	76
Alcains, Port.	E3	20
Alcalá de Guadaira, Spain	G5	20
Alcalá de Henares, Spain	D7	20
Alcalá la Real, Spain	G7	20
Alcalde, N.M., U.S.	E2	128

Name	Map Ref.	Page
Alcamo, Italy	G6	24
Alcanar, Spain	D11	20
Alcañices, Spain	C4	20
Alcañiz, Spain	C10	20
Alcântara, Braz.	B3	88
Alcántara, Spain	E3	20
Alcantarilla, Spain	G9	20
Alcaraz, Spain	F8	20
Alcaudete, Spain	G6	20
Alcázar de San Juan, Spain	E7	20
Alcester, S.D., U.S.	A1	120
Alcira, Arg.	F5	92
Alcira *see* Alzira, Spain	E10	20
Alcobaça, Braz.	I6	88
Alcobendas, Spain	D7	20
Alcoi, Spain	F10	20
Alcolea del Pinar, Spain	C8	20
Alcolu, S.C., U.S.	C5	116
Alcorn, Ms., U.S.	F7	122
Alcorta, Arg.	F7	92
Alcoutim, Port.	G3	20
Alcoy *see* Alcoi, Spain	F10	20
Alcúdia, Spain	E14	20
Alcúdia, Badia d', b., Spain	E14	20
Aldabra, Groupe d', is., Sey.	k11	69b
Aldama, Mex.	A5	100
Aldama, Mex.	D9	100
Aldan, Russia	E14	34
Aldan, stm., Russia	D15	34
Aldan Plateau see Aldanskoe nagor'e, plat., Russia	E14	34
Aldanskoe nagor'e (Aldan Plateau), plat., Russia	E14	34
Aldarchaan, Mong.	B4	36
Aldeia Nova de São Bento, Port.	G3	20
Alden, Mn., U.S.	H5	118
Alderney, i., Guern.	E6	14
Aldershot, Eng., U.K.	J12	12
Alderson, W.V., U.S.	G5	114
Aledo, Il., U.S.	C7	120
Aleg, Maur.	F2	64
Alegre, Braz.	K5	88
Alegrete, Braz.	D10	92
Alej, stm., Russia	D14	32
Alejandro Roca, Arg.	F5	92
Alejandro Selkirk, Isla, i., Chile	I6	82
Alejsk, Russia	D14	32
Aleksandrov, Russia	D21	10
Aleksandrovskij Zavod, Russia	F12	34
Aleksandrovskoe, Russia	B13	32
Aleksandrovsk-Sahalinskij, Russia	F17	34
Aleksandrów Kujawski, Pol.	D14	16
Alekseevka, Kaz.	D12	32
Alekseevka, Kaz.	E14	32
Alekseevka, Russia	D5	32
Alekseevsk, Russia	C19	32
Aleksejevka *see* Alekseevka, Kaz.	D12	32
Alekseyevka *see* Alekseevka, Kaz.	D12	32
Aleksin, Russia	F19	10
Aleksinac, Serb.	F8	26
Alemania, Arg.	B5	92
Além Paraíba, Braz.	K4	88
Alençon, Fr.	F9	14
Alenquer, Braz.	D7	84
Alentejo, hist. reg., Port.	F3	20
Alenuihaha Channel, strt., Hi., U.S.	c5	78a
Aleppo *see* Ḥalab, Syria	B8	58
Aléria, Fr.	G15	18
Alert, Nu., Can.	A13	141
Alert Bay, B.C., Can.	F4	138
Alert Point, c., Nu., Can.	A8	141
Alès, Fr.	E10	18
Alëšnja, Russia	G16	10
Alessándria, Italy	F5	22
Ålesund, Nor.	E1	8
Aleutian Basin, unds.	D20	142
Aleutian Islands, is., Ak., U.S.	g22	140a
Aleutian Range, mts., Ak., U.S.	E8	140
Aleutian Trench, unds.	E21	142
Aleutka, Russia	G19	34
Alevina, mys, c., Russia	E19	34
Alex, Ok., U.S.	G11	128
Alexander, Mb., Can.	E13	124
Alexander, N.D., U.S.	G10	124
Alexander, Kap, c., Grnld.	B11	141
Alexander Archipelago, is., Ak., U.S.	E12	140
Alexander Bay, S. Afr.	F3	70
Alexander City, Al., U.S.	E12	122
Alexander Island, i., Ant.	B33	81
Alexandra, N.Z.	G3	80
Alexandra, stm., Austl.	B3	76
Alexandra Falls, wtfl., N.T., Can.	C7	106
Alexandretta *see* İskenderun, Tur.	B6	58
Alexandretta, Gulf of see İskenderun Körfezi, b., Tur.	B6	58
Alexandria, Braz.	D6	88
Alexandria, B.C., Can.	D8	138
Alexandria, On., Can.	E2	110
Alexandria *see* El-Iskandarīya, Egypt	A6	62
Alexandria, Rom.	F12	26
Alexandria, La., U.S.	F6	122
Alexandria, Mn., U.S.	F3	118
Alexandria, Mo., U.S.	D6	120
Alexandria, S.D., U.S.	D15	126
Alexandria, Tn., U.S.	H11	120
Alexandria, Va., U.S.	F8	114
Alexandria Bay, N.Y., U.S.	D14	112
Alexandrina, Lake, l., Austl.	J2	76
Alexandroúpoli, Grc.	C8	28
Alexis, Il., U.S.	C7	120
Alfambra, Spain	D9	20
Alfaro, Spain	B9	20
Alfarràs, Spain	C11	20
Alfarrás *see* Alfarràs, Spain	C11	20
Al-Fāshir, Sudan	E5	62
Alfeiós, stm., Grc.	F4	28
Alfeld, Ger.	D5	16
Alfenas, Braz.	K3	88
Alföld, pl., Hung.	C7	26
Alfonsine, Italy	F9	22
Alfred, On., Can.	E2	110
Alfred, Me., U.S.	G6	110
Alfred, N.Y., U.S.	B8	114
Al-Fujayrah, U.A.E.	D8	56
Al-Fuqahā', Libya	B3	62
Al-Furāt see Euphrates, stm., Asia	C6	56
Ålgård, Nor.	G1	8
Algarrobal, Chile	D2	92
Algarrobo, Chile	F2	92
Algarrobo del Águila, Arg.	H4	92
Algarve, hist. reg., Port.	G2	20
Algeciras, Col.	F4	86
Algeciras, Spain	H5	20
Algemesí, Spain	E10	20
Algeria, ctry., Afr.	D5	64
Algha, Kaz.	E9	32
Al-Ghāb, sw., Syria	C7	58
Al-Ghayḍah, Yemen	F7	56
Al-Ghāzīyah, Leb.	E6	58
Alghero, Italy	D2	24
Algiers *see* El Djazaïr, Alg.	B5	64
Alginet, Spain	E10	20
Algoabaai, b., S. Afr.	H7	70
Algoa Bay see Algoabaai, b., S. Afr.	H7	70
Algodón, stm., Peru	I5	86
Algodones, N.M., U.S.	F2	128
Algoma Mills, On., Can.	B7	112
Algona, Ia., U.S.	A3	120
Algonac, Mi., U.S.	B3	114
Algonquin, Il., U.S.	B9	120
Algorta, Spain	A7	20
Algorta, Ur.	F9	92
Al-Ḥaffah, Syria	C7	58
Al-Ḥajarah, reg., Asia	C5	56
Al-Ḥamād, pl., Sau. Ar.	C4	56
Alhama de Murcia, Spain	G9	20
Alhandra, Braz.	D8	88
Al-Ḥarrah, lav., Sau. Ar.	C4	56
Al-Harūj al-Aswad, hills, Libya	B3	62
Al-Ḥasakah, Syria	B5	56
Alhaurín el Grande, Spain	H6	20
Al-Ḥawātah, Sudan	E7	62
Al-Ḥawrah, Yemen	G6	56
Al-Ḥijāz (Hejaz), reg., Sau. Ar.	D4	56
Al-Ḥillah, Iraq	C5	56
Al-Hirmil, Leb.	D7	58
Al-Hoceima, Mor.	B4	64
Al-Ḥudaydah (Hodeida), Yemen	G5	56
Al-Ḥufrah, reg., Sau. Ar.	J9	58
Al-Hufūf, Sau. Ar.	D6	56
Al Hūj, hills, Sau. Ar.	J9	58
Al-Ḥulwah, Sau. Ar.	E6	56
Alía, Spain	E5	20
Aliağa, Tur.	E9	28
Aliákmonas, stm., Grc.	C4	28
Aliança, Braz.	D8	88
Alībāg, India	B1	53
Alibates Flint Quarries National Monument, p.o.i., Tx., U.S.	F7	128
Äli Bayramlı, Azer.	B6	56
Alibei, ozero, l., Ukr.	D17	26
Alibey Adası, i., Tur.	D9	28
Alibunar, Serb.	D7	26
Alicante *see* Alacant, Spain	F10	20
Alicante see Alacant, co., Spain	F10	20
Alice, S. Afr.	H8	70
Alice, Tx., U.S.	G9	130
Alice, stm., Austl.	D5	76
Alice, Punta, c., Italy	E11	24
Alice Springs, Austl.	D6	74
Alice Town, Bah.	K6	116
Aliceville, Al., U.S.	D10	122
Alick Creek, stm., Austl.	C4	76
Alīgarh, India	E6	54
Alignements de Carnac, hist., Fr.	G5	14
Alīgūdarz, Iran	C6	56
'Alī Kheyl, Afg.	B2	54
Al-Ikhṣāṣ al-Qiblīyah, Egypt	I2	58
Alima, stm., Congo	E3	66
Alim Island, i., Pap. N. Gui.	a4	79a
Alindao, C.A.R.	C4	66
Alingsås, Swe.	G5	8
Alīpur, Pak.	D3	54
Ālīpur Duār, India	E12	54
Aliquippa, Pa., U.S.	D5	114
Alīrājpur, India	G5	54
Aliseda, Spain	E4	20
Alitak, Cape, c., Ak., U.S.	E9	140
Alivéri, Grc.	E7	28
Aliwal North, S. Afr.	G8	70
Alix, Ab., Can.	D17	138
Al-Jabalayn, Sudan	E6	62
Al-Jafr, Jord.	H7	58
Al-Jaghbūb, Libya	B4	62
Al-Jahrah, Kuw.	D6	56
Al-Jawārah, Oman	F8	56
Al-Jawf, Libya	C4	62
Al-Jawf, Sau. Ar.	D4	56
Al-Jazaïr *see* El Djazaïr, Alg.	B5	64
Al-Jazīrah, reg., Sudan	E6	62
Al-Jifārah (Jeffara), pl., Afr.	C7	64
Al-Jubayl, Sau. Ar.	D6	56
Al-Junaynah, Sudan	E4	62
Aljustrel, Port.	G2	20
Al-Kafr, Syria	F7	58
Al-Karak, Jord.	G6	58
Al-Karak, state, Jord.	G6	58
Al-Khalīl (Hebron), W.B.	G5	58
Al-Khāliṣ, Iraq	C5	56
Al-Khandaq, Sudan	D6	62
Al-Kharṭūm Baḥrī, Sudan	D6	62
Al-Kharṭūm (Khartoum), Sudan	D6	62
Al-Khaṣab, Oman	D8	56
Al-Khums, Libya	A2	62
Alkmaar, Neth.	B13	14
Al-Kufrah, Libya	C4	62
Al-Kūt, Iraq	C6	56
Al-Kuwayt (Kuwait), Kuw.	D6	56
Al-Labwah, Leb.	D7	58
Al-Lādhiqīyah (Latakia), Syria	C6	58
Al-Lādhiqīyah, state, Syria	C6	58
Allagash, stm., Me., U.S.	D7	110
Allahābād, India	F8	54
Allah-Jun', Russia	D16	34
Allakaket, Ak., U.S.	C9	140
Allan, Sk., Can.	C7	124
Allanmyo, Mya.	C2	48
Allanridge, S. Afr.	E8	70
Allatoona Lake, res., Ga., U.S.	C14	122
Alldays, S. Afr.	C9	70
Allegan, Mi., U.S.	F4	112
Allegany, N.Y., U.S.	B7	114
Allegheny, stm., U.S.	D6	114
Allegheny Mountains, mts., U.S.	E6	114
Allegheny Plateau, plat., U.S.	D5	114
Allegheny Reservoir, res., U.S.	C7	114
Allemands, Lac des, l., La., U.S.	H8	122
Allen, Ne., U.S.	I2	118
Allen, Ok., U.S.	C2	122
Allen, Tx., U.S.	D2	122
Allen, Lough, l., Ire.	G4	12
Allendale, Il., U.S.	F10	120
Allendale, S.C., U.S.	C4	116
Allende, Mex.	A8	100
Allenstein *see* Olsztyn, Pol.	C16	16
Allentown, Pa., U.S.	D10	114
Alleppey, India	G3	53
Aller, stm., Ger.	D5	16
Allevard, Fr.	D12	18
Allgäu *see* Kempten, Ger.	I6	16
Allgäu, reg., Ger.	I6	16
Alliance, Ab., Can.	D19	138
Alliance, Ne., U.S.	E10	126
Alliance, Oh., U.S.	D4	114
Al-Lidām, Sau. Ar.	E5	56
Allier, state, Fr.	C9	18
Allier, stm., Fr.	C9	18
Alligator Pond, Jam.	j13	104d
Allinagaram, India	F3	53
Allison, Ia., U.S.	B5	120
Al-Līth, Sau. Ar.	E5	56
Alloa, Scot., U.K.	E9	12
Allos, Fr.	E12	18
Allouez, Wi., U.S.	G11	118
Allred Peak, mtn., Co., U.S.	C8	132
All Saints, Antig.	f4	105b
Al-Luḥayyah, Yemen	F5	56
Allumette Lake, l., Can.	C12	112
Allumettes, Île aux, i., Qc., Can.	C12	112
Alma, N.B., Can.	E12	110
Alma, Qc., Can.	B5	110
Alma, Ar., U.S.	B4	122
Alma, Ga., U.S.	E3	116
Alma, Ks., U.S.	E1	120
Alma, Mi., U.S.	E5	112
Alma, Wi., U.S.	G7	118
Almada, Port.	F1	20
Almaden, Austl.	A5	76
Almadén, Spain	F6	20
Al-Madīnah (Medina), Sau. Ar.	E4	56
Al-Mafraq, Jord.	F7	58
Al-Mafraq, state, Jord.	F8	58
Almafuerte, Arg.	F5	92
Almagro, Spain	F7	20
Alma Hill, hill, N.Y., U.S.	B8	114
Al Māliḥah, Sudan	D5	62
Almalyk, Uzb.	F11	32
Al-Manāmah (Manama), Bahr.	D7	56
Almanor, Lake, res., Ca., U.S.	C4	134
Almansa, Spain	F9	20
Almanza, Spain	B5	20
Almanzor, mtn., Spain	D5	20
Al-Marj, Libya	A4	62
Almas, Braz.	F2	88
Almas, Pico das, mtn., Braz.	G4	88
Al-Mashrafah, Syria	D7	58
Almaty, Kaz.	F13	32
Al-Mawṣil (Mosul), Iraq	B5	56
Almeida, Port.	D3	20
Almejas, Bahía, b., Mex.	C3	100
Almelo, Neth.	B15	14
Almena, Ks., U.S.	B9	128
Almenara, Braz.	I5	88
Almendra, Embalse de, res., Spain	C4	20
Almendralejo, Spain	F4	20
Almería, Spain	H8	20
Almería, co., Spain	G8	20
Almería, Golfo de, b., Spain	H8	20
Al'metevsk, Russia	D8	32
Al-Mijlad, Sudan	E5	62
Al-Mīnā', Leb.	D6	58
Almira, Wa., U.S.	C7	136
Almirante, Pan.	H6	102
Almirante Latorre, Chile	D2	92
Almo, Id., U.S.	A3	132
Almodóvar del Campo, Spain	F6	20
Almont, Mi., U.S.	B2	114
Almonte, On., Can.	C13	112
Almonte, Spain	G4	20
Almonte, stm., Spain	E4	20
Almora, India	D7	54
Al-Mubarraz, Sau. Ar.	E6	56
Al-Mubarraz, Sau. Ar.	D6	56
Al-Mudawwarah, Jord.	I6	58
Almudévar, Spain	B10	20
Al-Muḥarraq, Bahr.	D7	56
Al-Mukallā, Yemen	G6	56
Al-Mukhā, Yemen	G5	56
Almuñécar, Spain	H7	20
Al-Muwayliḥ, Sau. Ar.	K6	58
Almyrós, Grc.	D5	28
Almyroú, Órmos, b., Grc.	H7	28
Alnwick, Eng., U.K.	F11	12
Alofi, Île, i., Wal./F.	E9	72
Alónnisos, Grc.	D6	28
Alónnisos, i., Grc.	D6	28
Alor, Pulau, i., Indon.	G7	44
Alor, Selat, strt., Indon.	G7	44
Alor Setar, Malay.	I5	48
Alosno, Spain	G3	20
Alost *see* Aalst, Bel.	D13	14
Alotau, Pap. N. Gui.	c5	79a
Aloysius, Mount, mtn., Austl.	E5	74
Alpachiri, Arg.	H5	92
Alpaugh, Ca., U.S.	H6	134
Alpena, Mi., U.S.	C6	112
Alpena, S.D., U.S.	C14	126
Alpercatas, stm., Braz.	D3	88
Alpes-de-Haute-Provence, state, Fr.	E12	18
Alpes-Maritimes, state, Fr.	F13	18
Alpha, Austl.	D6	76
Alpha, Il., U.S.	C7	120
Alpha, Mi., U.S.	B1	112
Alpharetta, Ga., U.S.	B1	116
Alphonse, i., Sey.	k12	69b
Alpine, Ca., U.S.	K9	134
Alpine, Tx., U.S.	D4	130
Alpine National Park, p.o.i., Austl.	K6	76
Alpinópolis, Braz.	K2	88
Alps, mts., Eur.	D6	22
Al-Qaḍārif, Sudan	E7	62
Al-Qaḍīmah, Sau. Ar.	E4	56
Al-Qāmishlī, Syria	B5	56
Al-Qaryah ash-Sharqīyah, Libya	A2	62
Al-Qaryatayn, Syria	D8	58
Al-Qaṭīf, Sau. Ar.	D6	56
Al-Qaṭrānah, Jord.	G7	58
Al-Qaṭrūn, Libya	C2	62
Al-Qayṣūmah, Sau. Ar.	D6	56
Al-Qunayṭirah, Syria	E6	58
Al-Qunayṭirah, state, Syria	E6	58
Al-Qunfudhah, Sau. Ar.	F5	56
Al-Quṭayfah, Syria	E7	58
Al-Quṭaynah, Sudan	E6	62
Als, i., Den.	I3	8
Alsace, hist. reg., Fr.	F16	14
Al'šany, Bela.	H10	10
Alsask, Sk., Can.	C4	124
Alsasua, Spain	B8	20
Alsea, Or., U.S.	F3	136
Alsek, stm., N.A.	D3	106
Alsen, N.D., U.S.	F15	124
Alsfeld, Ger.	F5	16
Alta, Nor.	B10	8
Altaelva, stm., Nor.	B10	8
Alta Gracia, Arg.	E5	92
Altagracia, Ven.	B6	86
Altagracia de Orituco, Ven.	C8	86
Altai, mts., Asia	E15	32
Altaj, state, Russia	D15	32
Altajskij, Russia	D14	32
Altamaha, stm., Ga., U.S.	E4	116
Altamira, Braz.	D7	84
Altamira, Chile	B3	92
Altamirano, Mex.	I10	130
Altamont, Ks., U.S.	G2	120
Altamont, Or., U.S.	A4	134
Altamont, Tn., U.S.	B13	122
Altamura, Italy	D10	24
Altamura, Isla, i., Mex.	C4	100
Altanbulag, Mong.	A6	36
Altar, Mex.	F7	98
Altar, stm., Mex.	F7	98
Altar, Desierto de, des., Mex.	F6	98
Altar de Los Sacrificios, sci., Guat.	D2	102
Altario, Ab., Can.	C3	124
Altata, Mex.	C4	100
Alta Vista, Ks., U.S.	C12	128
Altay, China	E15	32
Altay, Mong.	B4	36
Altay see Altaj, state, Russia	D15	32
Altay Mountains see Altai, mts., Asia	E15	32
Altdorf, Switz.	D5	22
Altenburg, Ger.	E8	16
Altentreptow, Ger.	C9	16
Alter do Chão, Port.	E3	20
Altevatnet, l., Nor.	B8	8
Altha, Fl., U.S.	G13	122
Altheimer, Ar., U.S.	C7	122
Altınekin, Tur.	E15	28
Altinho, Braz.	E7	88
Altınova, Tur.	D9	28
Altintaş, Tur.	D13	28
Altiplano, plat., S.A.	G4	84
Altmark, reg., Ger.	D7	16
Altmühl, stm., Ger.	G6	16
Alto, Tx., U.S.	F3	122
Alto Araguaia, Braz.	G7	84
Alto Chicapa, Ang.	C2	68
Alto Garças, Braz.	G7	84
Alto Longá, Braz.	C4	88
Altomünster, Ger.	H7	16
Alton, Eng., U.K.	J11	12
Alton, Ia., U.S.	B1	120
Alton, Il., U.S.	F7	120
Alton, Ks., U.S.	B9	128
Alton, N.H., U.S.	G5	110
Altona, Mb., Can.	E16	124
Altoona, Al., U.S.	C12	122
Altoona, Ia., U.S.	C4	120
Altoona, Pa., U.S.	D7	114
Altoona, Wi., U.S.	G7	118
Alto Paraguai, Braz.	F6	84
Alto Paraíso de Goiás, Braz.	G2	88
Alto Paraná, state, Para.	B10	92
Alto Parnaíba, Braz.	E2	88
Alto Río Mayo, Arg.	I2	90
Alto Río Senguer, Arg.	I2	90
Altos, Braz.	C4	88
Alto Santo, Braz.	C6	88
Altötting, Ger.	H8	16
Altun Shan, mts., China	D2	36
Alturas, Ca., U.S.	B5	134
Altus, Ar., U.S.	B5	122
Altus, Ok., U.S.	G9	128
Alu see Shortland Island, i., Sol. Is.	d6	79b
Al-'Ubaylah, Sau. Ar.	E7	56
Al-Ubayyiḍ, Sudan	E6	62
Alubijid, Phil.	F5	52
Al-Uḍayyah, Sudan	E5	62
Alūksne, Lat.	C9	10
Al-'Ulā, Sau. Ar.	D4	56
Al-'Uqaylah, Libya	A3	62
Al-'Uwaynāt, Libya	B2	62
Alva, Ok., U.S.	E10	128
Alvaiázere, Port.	E2	20
Alvarado, Mex.	F11	100
Alvarado, Tx., U.S.	B10	130
Álvaro Obregón, Presa, res., Mex.	B4	100
Alvear, Arg.	D9	92
Alverca, Port.	F1	20
Alvernia, Mount, hill, Bah.	C10	96
Alvesta, Swe.	H6	8
Alvin, Tx., U.S.	H3	122
Alvinópolis, Braz.	K4	88
Älvkarleby, Swe.	F7	8
Alvord, Tx., U.S.	H11	128
Alvord Desert, des., Or., U.S.	H8	136
Al-Wajh, Sau. Ar.	D4	56
Alwar, India	E6	54
Alwaye, India	F3	53
Alxa Zuoqi, China	B1	42
Alytus, Lith.	F6	10
Alzey, Ger.	G4	16
Alzira, Spain	E10	20
Amacuro (Amakura), stm., S.A.	C11	86
Amadeus, Lake, l., Austl.	D6	74
Amadjuak Lake, l., Nu., Can.	B16	106
Amagasaki, Japan	E8	40
Amagi, Japan	F3	40
Amahai, Indon.	F8	44
Amaichá del Valle, Arg.	C4	92
Amaimon, Pap. N. Gui.	b4	79a
Amajac, stm., Mex.	E9	100
Amakura (Amacuro), stm., S.A.	D11	86
Amakusa-nada, s., Japan	G2	40
Amakusa-shotō, is., Japan	G2	40
Åmål, Swe.	G5	8
Amalāpuram, India	C6	53
Amalfi, Col.	B2	84
Amaliáda, Grc.	F4	28
Amalner, India	H5	54
Amambaí, Braz.	D5	90
Amami Islands see Amami-Ō-shima, i., Japan	k19	39a
Amami-Ō-shima, i., Japan	k19	39a
Amami-shotō, is., Japan	I19	39a
Amana, Ia., U.S.	C6	120
Amana, stm., Ven.	C10	86
Amaná, Lago, l., Braz.	I9	86
Amanda, Oh., U.S.	E3	114
Amangeldi, Kaz.	D10	32
Amantea, Italy	E9	24
Amapá, Braz.	C7	84
Amapá, state, Braz.	C7	84
Amarante, Braz.	D4	88
Amaranth, Mb., Can.	D15	124
Amarapura, Mya.	B3	48
Amărăştii de Jos, Rom.	F11	26
Amarāvati, stm., India	F3	53
Amares, Port.	C2	20
Amargosa, Braz.	G6	88
Amargosa, stm., U.S.	H9	134
Amarillo, Tx., U.S.	F7	128
Amarkantak, India	G8	54
Amaro, Monte, mtn., Italy	H11	22
Amasra, Tur.	B15	28
Amasya, Tur.	A4	56
aMatikulu, S. Afr.	F10	70
Amatsu-kominato, Japan	D13	40
Amawbia Awka, Nig.	H6	64
Amazar, Russia	F13	34
Amazon (Amazonas) (Solimões), stm., S.A.	D7	84
Amazonas, state, Braz.	D4	84
Amazonas, state, Col.	H6	86
Amazonas, state, Ven.	F8	86
Ambājogāi, India	B3	53
Ambāla, India	C6	54
Ambalangoda, Sri L.	H4	53
Ambalavao, Madag.	E8	68
Ambam, Cam.	D2	66
Ambanja, Madag.	C8	68
Ambarčik, Russia	C21	34
Ambargasta, Salinas de, pl., Arg.	D5	92
Ambato, Ec.	H2	86
Ambatolampy, Madag.	D8	68
Ambatondrazaka, Madag.	D8	68
Ambelau, Pulau, i., Indon.	F8	44
Amberg, Ger.	G7	16
Amberg, Wi., U.S.	C2	112
Ambergris Cay, i., Belize	C4	102
Ambérieu-en-Bugey, Fr.	D11	18
Ambert, Fr.	D9	18
Ambidédi, Mali	G2	64
Ambikāpur, India	G9	54
Ambilobe, Madag.	C8	68
Ambla, Est.	A8	10
Amble, Eng., U.K.	F11	12
Ambo, Peru	F2	84
Ambodifototra, Madag.	D8	68
Ambohimahasoa, Madag.	E8	68
Amboise, Fr.	G10	14
Ambon, Indon.	F8	44
Ambon, Pulau, i., Indon.	F8	44
Amboseli, Lake, l., Afr.	E7	66
Amboseli National Park, p.o.i., Kenya	E7	66
Ambositra, Madag.	E8	68
Ambovombe, Madag.	F8	68
Amboy, Il., U.S.	C8	120
Amboy, Mn., U.S.	H4	118
Ambridge, Pa., U.S.	D5	114
Ambriz, Ang.	B1	68
Ambrosia Lake, N.M., U.S.	H9	132
Ambrym, state, Vanuatu	k17	79d
Ambrym, i., Vanuatu	k17	79d
Ambuntentimur, Indon.	G8	50
Ambunti, Pap. N. Gui.	a3	79a
Āmbūr, India	E4	53
Amchitka Island, i., Ak., U.S.	g22	140a
Amchitka Pass, strt., Ak., U.S.	g22	140a
Am Dam, Chad	E4	62
Amdo, China	B13	54
Ameagle, W.V., U.S.	G4	114
Ameca, Mex.	E6	100
Ameca, stm., Mex.	E6	100
Ameghino, Arg.	G6	92
Ameland, i., Neth.	A14	14
Amelia Court House, Va., U.S.	G8	114
Amelia Island, i., Fl., U.S.	F4	116
Āmer, India	E5	54
American, North Fork, stm., Ca., U.S.	D5	134
American, South Fork, stm., Ca., U.S.	E5	134
Americana, Braz.	L2	88
American Falls Reservoir, res., Id., U.S.	H13	136
American Fork, Ut., U.S.	C5	132
American Highland, plat., Ant.	C12	81
Americanos, Barra de los, i., Mex.	C10	100
American Samoa, dep., Oc.	h12	79c
Americus, Ga., U.S.	D1	116
Americus, Ks., U.S.	F1	120
Amersfoort, Neth.	B14	14
Amery, Wi., U.S.	F6	118
Amery Ice Shelf, ice, Ant.	B12	81
Ames, Ia., U.S.	B4	120
Amesbury, Ma., U.S.	B14	114
Amfilochía, Grc.	E4	28
Ámfissa, Grc.	E5	28
Amga, Russia	D15	34
Amga, stm., Russia	D15	34
Amguema, stm., Russia	C24	34
Amguid, Alg.	D6	64
Amgun', stm., Russia	F16	34
Amherst, N.S., Can.	E12	110
Amherst, Ma., U.S.	B13	114
Amherst, N.Y., U.S.	A7	114
Amherst, Oh., U.S.	C3	114
Amherst, Tx., U.S.	G6	128
Amherst, Wi., U.S.	G9	118
Amherstburg, On., Can.	F6	112
Amherstdale, W.V., U.S.	G4	114
Amherst Island, i., On., Can.	D13	112
Amherstview, On., Can.	D13	112
Amiens, Austl.	G8	76
Amiens, Fr.	E11	14
Amīndīvi Islands, is., India	F3	46
Amino, Japan	D8	40
Aminuis, Nmb.	C4	70
Amirantes, Les, is., Sey.	k12	69b
Amisk, Ab., Can.	B2	124
Amisk Lake, l., Sk., Can.	E10	106
Amistad, Parque Internacional de la, p.o.i., C.R.	H6	102
Amistad, Presa de la (Amistad Reservoir), res., N.A.	E6	130
Amistad National Recreation Area, p.o.i., Tx., U.S.	E6	130
Amistad Reservoir (Amistad, Presa de la), res., N.A.	E6	130
Amite, La., U.S.	G8	122
Amite, stm., La., U.S.	G8	122
Amity, Ar., U.S.	C5	122
Amla, India	H7	54
Åmli, Nor.	G3	8
'Ammān, Jord.	G6	58
'Ammān, state, Jord.	G7	58
Ämmänsaari, Fin.	D13	8
'Ammār, Tall, hill, Syria	F7	58
Ammasalik *see* Angmagssalik, Grnld.	D18	141
Ammon, Id., U.S.	G15	136
Amnat Charoen, Thai.	E7	48
Amnok-kang (Yalu), stm., Asia	D7	38
Amo (Torsa), stm., Asia	E12	54
Amo, stm., China	A5	48
Āmol, Iran	B7	56
Amorgós, i., Grc.	G8	28
Amory, Ms., U.S.	D10	122
Amos, Qc., Can.	F15	106
Åmot, Nor.	G2	8
Amoy *see* Xiamen, China	I7	42
Ampanihy, Madag.	E7	68
Amparo, Braz.	L2	88
Ampasimanolotra, Madag.	D8	68
Amposta, Spain	D11	20
Amqui, Qc., Can.	B9	110
Amrāvati, India	H6	54
Amreli, India	H3	54
Amritsar, India	C5	54
Amroha, India	D7	54
Amrum, i., Ger.	B4	16
Amsterdam, Neth.	B13	14
Amsterdam, S. Afr.	E10	70
Amsterdam, N.Y., U.S.	B11	114
Amsterdam, Île, i., Afr.	M10	142
Amstetten, Aus.	B11	22
Am Timan, Chad	E4	62
Amu Darya, stm., Asia	F10	32
Amugulang *see* Xin Barag Zuoqi, China	B8	36
Amund Ringnes Island, i., Nu., Can.	B6	141
Amundsen Gulf, b., Can.	B14	140
Amundsen-Scott, sci., Ant.	D19	81
Amundsen Sea, s., Ant.	P27	142
Amuntai, Indon.	E9	50
Amur (Heilong), stm., Asia	F16	34
Amursk, Russia	F16	34
Amuzhong, China	C10	54
Amvrakikós Kólpos, b., Grc.	E3	28
An, Mya.	C2	48
Ana, Parque Nacional dedo see Doñana, Parque Nacional de, p.o.i., Spain	H4	20
Anaa, at., Fr. Poly.	E12	72
Anabar, stm., Russia	B11	34
Anaco, Ven.	C9	86
Anaconda, Mt., U.S.	D14	136
Anaconda Range, mts., Mt., U.S.	E13	136
Anacortes, Wa., U.S.	B4	136
Anadarko, Ok., U.S.	F10	128
Anadolu (Anatolia), hist. reg., Tur.	H15	6
Anadyr', Russia	D24	34
Anadyr, stm., Russia	C23	34
Anadyr, Gulf of see Anadyrskij zaliv, b., Russia	C21	142
Anadyr Mountains see Anadyrskoe ploskogor'e, plat., Russia	C23	34
Anadyrskij liman, b., Russia	D24	34
Anadyrskij zaliv, b., Russia	C21	142
Anadyrskoe ploskogor'e, plat., Russia	C23	34
Anáfi, i., Grc.	G8	28
Anagni, Italy	C7	24
Anaheim, Ca., U.S.	J8	134
Anahim Lake, B.C., Can.	D5	138
Anáhuac, Mex.	I10	130
Ānai Mudi, mtn., India	F3	53
Anajás, Braz.	D8	84
Anakāpalle, India	C6	53
Anaktuvuk Pass, Ak., U.S.	C9	140
Analalava, Madag.	C8	68
Anamã, Braz.	D5	84
Anama Bay, Mb., Can.	C15	124
Ana María, Golfo de, b., Cuba	B8	102
Anambas, Kepulauan (Anambas Islands), is., Indon.	B5	50
Anambas Islands see Anambas, Kepulauan, is., Indon.	B5	50
Anamizu, Japan	B9	40
Anamoose, N.D., U.S.	G13	124
Anamur, Tur.	B3	58
Anamur Burnu, c., Tur.	B3	58
Anan, Japan	F7	40
Ānand, India	G4	54
Ānandapur, India	H11	54
Ananindeua, Braz.	A1	88
Anan'ïv, Ukr.	B16	26
Anantapur, India	D3	53
Anantnāg, India	B5	54
Anápolis, Braz.	I1	88
Anapurus, Braz.	B4	88
Añasco, P.R.	B1	104a
Anastasia Island, i., Fl., U.S.	G4	116
Anatahan, i., N. Mar. Is.	B5	72
Anatolia see Anadolu, hist. reg., Tur.	H15	6
Anatolikí Makedonía kai Thráki, state, Grc.	B8	28
Anatom, i., Vanuatu	m17	79d
Añatuya, Arg.	D6	92
Anauá, stm., Braz.	G11	86
Anavilhanas, Arquipélago das, is., Braz.	I11	86
Anbei, China	F17	32
Anbianbu, China	C2	42
Anbyŏn-ŭp, Kor., N.	E7	38
Ancaster, On., Can.	E9	112
Ancasti, Sierra de, mts., Arg.	D5	92
Anchiang *see* Qianyang, China	H3	42
Anch'ing *see* Anqing, China	F7	42
Anchorage, Ak., U.S.	D10	140
Anchuras, Spain	E6	20
Ancona, Italy	G10	22
Ancón de Sardinas, Bahía de, b., S.A.	G2	86
Ancuabe, Moz.	C6	68
Ancud, Chile	H2	90
Ancy-le-Franc, Fr.	G13	14
Anda, China	B10	36
Andacollo, Arg.	H2	92
Andahuaylas, Peru	F3	84
Andalgalá, Arg.	C4	92
Andalucía, state, Spain	G6	20
Andalusia *see* Jan Kempdorp, S. Afr.	E7	70
Andalusia, Al., U.S.	F12	122
Andalusia see Andalucía, state, Spain	G6	20
Andaman and Nicobar Islands, state, India	F7	46
Andaman Basin, unds.	H12	142
Andaman Islands, is., India	F7	46
Andaman Sea, s., Asia	G8	46
Andamook, Austl.	F7	74
Andapa, Madag.	C8	68
Andenes, Nor.	B6	8
Andéramboukane, Mali	F5	64
Andernach, Ger.	F3	16
Anderson, Ca., U.S.	C3	134
Anderson, In., U.S.	H4	112
Anderson, Mo., U.S.	H3	120
Anderson, S.C., U.S.	B3	116
Anderson, Tx., U.S.	G3	122
Anderson, stm., N.T., Can.	B5	106
Anderson, Mount, mtn., Wa., U.S.	C3	136
Anderson Dam, Id., U.S.	G11	136
Andes, Col.	E4	86
Andes, mts., S.A.	F7	82
Andfjorden, strt., Nor.	B7	8
Andhra Lake, res., India	B1	53
Andhra Pradesh, state, India	C4	53
Andilamena, Madag.	D8	68
Andingpu, China	B2	42
Andirlang, China	A5	46
Andižan, Uzb.	F12	32
Andkhvoy, Afg.	B10	56
Andoany, Madag.	C8	68
Andoga, stm., Russia	A19	10
Andong, Kor., S.	C1	40
Andong-chŏsuji, res., Kor., S.	C1	40
Andorra, ctry., Eur.	B12	20
Andorra, ctry., Eur.	B12	20
Andorra-la-Vella, And.	B12	20
Andover, Eng., U.K.	J11	12
Andover, Ma., U.S.	H5	110
Andover, Me., U.S.	F6	110
Andover, Oh., U.S.	C5	114
Andover, S.D., U.S.	B15	126
Andøya, i., Nor.	B6	8
Andradina, Braz.	D6	90
Andranopasy, Madag.	E7	68
Andreanof Islands, is., Ak., U.S.	g23	140a
Andreapol', Russia	D15	10
Andrews, In., U.S.	H4	112
Andrews, N.C., U.S.	A2	116
Andrews, S.C., U.S.	C6	116
Andrews, Tx., U.S.	B5	130
Andria, Italy	C10	24
Andriamena, Madag.	D8	68
Andriievo-Ivanivka, Ukr.	B17	26
Androka, Madag.	F7	68
Andronovskoe, Russia	F16	8
Andros, i., Bah.	C9	96
Ándros, i., Grc.	F7	28
Androscoggin, stm., Me., U.S.	F6	110
Āndrott Island, i., India	F1	53
Andrupene, Lat.	D10	10
Andudu, D.R.C.	D5	66
Andújar, Spain	F6	20
Andulo, Ang.	C2	68
Anduze, Fr.	E9	18
Anegada, Bahía, b., Arg.	H4	90
Anegada Passage, strt., N.A.	h15	96a
Aného, Togo	H5	64
Añelo, Arg.	I3	92
Anemata, Passe d', strt., N. Cal.	m16	79d
Anenii Noi, Mol.	C16	26
Aneroid, Sk., Can.	E6	124
Aneta, N.D., U.S.	G16	124
Anétis, Mali	F5	64
Aneto, mtn., Spain	B11	20
Anfu, China	H6	42
Angamos, Punta, c., Chile	D2	90
Ang'angxi, China	B9	36
Angara, stm., Russia	E8	34
Angarsk, Russia	D18	32
Angas Downs, Austl.	D6	74
Angastaco, Arg.	B4	92
Angaul, Russia	D18	32
Ånge, Swe.	E6	8
Ángel, Salto (Angel Falls), wtfl., Ven.	E10	86
Ángel de la Guarda, Isla, i., Mex.	G6	98
Angeles, Phil.	C3	52
Angel Falls see Ángel, Salto, wtfl., Ven.	E10	86
Ängelholm, Swe.	H5	8
Angelina, stm., Tx., U.S.	F4	122
Angellala Creek, stm., Austl.	F6	76
Angels Camp, Ca., U.S.	E5	134
Angemuk, mtn., Indon.	F10	44

Name	Map Ref.	Page

Name	Map Ref.	Page
Ångermanälven, stm., Swe.	E7	8
Angermünde, Ger.	C9	16
Angers, Fr.	G8	14
Angical, Braz.	F3	88
Angical do Piauí, Braz.	D4	88
Angicos, Braz.	C7	88
Angijak Island, i., Nu., Can.	D13	141
Angikuni Lake, l., Nu., Can.	C11	106
Angkor Wat, sci., Camb.	F6	48
Ångk Tasaŏm, Camb.	G7	48
Angle Inlet, Mn., U.S.	B3	118
Anglem, Mount, mtn., N.Z.	H2	80
Anglesey, i., Wales, U.K.	H8	12
Anglet, Fr.	F4	18
Angleton, Tx., U.S.	H3	122
Anglona, reg., Italy	D2	24
Angmagssalik (Ãmmasalik), Grnld.	D18	141
Angoche, Moz.	D6	68
Angol, Chile	H1	92
Angola, In., U.S.	G5	112
Angola, N.Y., U.S.	B6	114
Angola, ctry., Afr.	C2	68
Angola Basin, unds.	J14	144
Angora see Ankara, Tur.	D15	28
Angoram, Pap. N. Gui.	a3	79a
Angostura, Presa de la, res., Mex.	H12	100
Angoulême, Fr.	D6	18
Angoumois, hist. reg., Fr.	D5	18
Angra dos Reis, Braz.	L3	88
Angren, Uzb.	F12	32
Angu, D.R.C.	D4	66
Angualasto, Arg.	D3	92
Anguilla, Ms., U.S.	E8	122
Anguilla, dep., N.A.	h15	96a
Anguille, Cape c., Nf., Can.	C17	110
Anguli Nur, l., China	A6	42
Anguo, China	B6	42
Angus, On., Can.	D10	112
Angusville, Mb., Can.	D13	124
Anhalt, hist. reg., Ger.	D7	16
Anholt, i., Den.	H4	8
Anhua, China	G4	42
Anhui, state, China	F7	42
Anhwei see Anhui, state, China	F7	42
Aniak, Ak., U.S.	D8	140
Anibare Bay, b., Nauru	q17	78f
Anie, Pic d', mtn., Fr.	F5	18
Anil, Braz.	B3	88
Animas, N.M., U.S.	L8	132
Animas, stm., U.S.	G9	132
Animas Valley, val., N.A.	L8	132
Anina, Rom.	D8	26
Anita, Ia., U.S.	C3	120
Anitkaya, Tur.	E13	28
Aniva, mys, c., Russia	B13	36
Aniva, zaliv, b., Russia	G17	34
Aniwa, i., Vanuatu	l17	79d
Anjangaon, India	H6	54
Anjar, India	G2	54
'Anjar, Leb.	E6	58
Anjou, hist. reg., Fr.	G8	14
Anjouan see Nzwani, i., Com.	C7	68
Anjudin, Russia	B9	32
Anjujsk, Russia	C21	34
Anjujskij hrebet, mts., Russia	C21	34
Anju-ŭp, Kor., N.	G6	38
Anka, Nig.	G6	64
Ankaboa, Tanjona, c., Madag.	E7	68
Ankang, China	E3	42
Ankara, Tur.	D15	28
Ankara, state, Tur.	D15	28
Ankavandra, Madag.	D8	68
Ankazoabo, Madag.	E7	68
Ankazobe, Madag.	D8	68
Ankeny, Ia., U.S.	C4	120
Anking see Anqing, China.	F7	42
Ankleshwar, India.	H4	54
Ankoro, D.R.C.	F5	66
Anlong, China	F6	36
Ânlóng Vêng, Camb.	E6	48
Anlu, China	F5	42
An Muileann gCearr see Mullingar, Ire.	H5	12
Ånn, l., Swe.	E5	8
Ann, Cape, c., Ant.	B10	81
Ann, Cape, pen., Ma., U.S.	H6	110
Anna, Il., U.S.	G8	120
Anna, lake, res., Va., U.S.	F8	114
Annaba, Alg.	B6	64
An-Nabatiyah state, Leb.	E6	58
An-Nabatiyah at-Tahtã, Leb.	E6	58
Annaberg-Buchholz, Ger.	F9	16
An-Nabk, Syria	D7	58
An-Nafūd, des., Sau. Ar.	D5	56
An-Najaf, Iraq	C5	56
Annam see Trung Phan, hist. reg., Viet.	D8	48
Annamitique, Chaîne, mts., Asia	D8	48
Annan, Scot., U.K.	G9	12
Annandale, Austl.	C7	76
Annandale, Mn., U.S.	F4	118
Annandale, val., Scot., U.K.	F9	12
Anna Plains, Austl.	C4	74
Annapolis, Md., U.S.	F9	114
Annapolis Royal, N.S., Can.	F11	110
Annapūrna, mtn., Nepal	D9	54
Ann Arbor, Mi., U.S.	B2	114
An Nás see Naas, Ire.	H6	12
An-Nāsirīyah, Iraq	C6	56
An-Nāsirīyah, Syria	E7	58
An-Nawfalīyah, Libya	A3	62
Annecy, Fr.	D12	18
Annecy, Lac d', l., Fr.	D12	18
Annemasse, Fr.	C12	18
Annenkov Island, i., S. Geor.	J9	90
An Nhon, Viet.	F9	48
Anning, China	G5	36
Anniston, Al., U.S.	D13	122
Annobón, i., Eq. Gui.	J6	64
Annonay, Fr.	D10	18
An-Nuhūd, Sudan	E5	62
Annville, Ky., U.S.	G2	114
Annville, Pa., U.S.	D9	114
Anoka, Mn., U.S.	F5	118
Anori, China	D5	84
Anpu, China	K3	42
Anqing, China	F7	42
Anqiu, China	C8	42
Ansai, China	H5	42
Ansbach, Ger.	G6	16
Anse-d'Hainault, Haiti	C10	102
Anse La Raye, St. Luc.	m6	105c
Anselmo, Ne., U.S.	F13	120
Anserma, Col.	E4	86
Anshan, China	D5	38
Anshun, China	H1	42
Ansina, Ur.	F10	92
Ansley, Ne., U.S.	F13	120
Anson Bay, b., Austl.	B5	74
Anson Bay, b., Norf. I.	y24	78i
Ansongo, Mali	F5	64
Ansonville, N.C., U.S.	A5	116
Ansted, W.V., U.S.	F4	114
Antakya see Hatay, Tur.	B7	58
Antalaha, Madag.	C9	68
Antaliepté, Lith.	E7	10
Antalya, Tur.	G13	28
Antalya, state, Tur.	F14	28
Antalya, Gulf of see Antalya Körfezi, b., Tur.	G14	28
Antalya Körfezi (Antalya, Gulf of), b., Tur.	G14	28
An tAonach see Nenagh, Ire.	I4	12

Name	Map Ref.	Page
Antarctica, cont.	D11	81
Antarctic Peninsula, pen., Ant.	C35	81
Antas, Braz.	F6	88
Antas, stm., Braz.	D12	92
Antelope Island, i., Ut., U.S.	C4	132
Antelope Mine, Zimb.	B9	70
Antelope Peak, mtn., Nv., U.S.	B1	132
Antenor Navarro, Braz.	D6	88
Antequera, Para.	A9	92
Antequera, Spain.	H6	20
Anthon, Ia., U.S.	B2	120
Anthony, Ks., U.S.	D10	128
Anthony, N.M., U.S.	K10	132
Anthony, Tx., U.S.	E9	98
Anti-Atlas, mts., Mor.	D3	64
Antibes, Fr.	F13	18
Anticosti, Île d', i., Qc., Can.	F18	106
Antifer, Cap d', c., Fr.	E8	14
Antigonish, N.S., Can.	E14	110
Antigua, i., Antig.	f4	105b
Antigua and Barbuda, ctry., N.A.	h15	96a
Antigua International Airport, Antig.	f4	105b
Antiguo Morelos, Mex.	D9	100
Antikýthira, i., Grc.	H6	28
Anti-Lebanon (Sharqī, Al-Jabal ash-), mts., Asia	E7	58
Antilla, Cuba	B10	102
Antillen, Nederlandse see Netherlands Antilles, dep., N.A.	i14	96a
Antimony, Ut., U.S.	E5	132
Antioch see Hatay, Tur.	B7	58
Antioch, Il., U.S.	F11	112
Antioquia, Col.	D4	86
Antioquia, state, Col.	D4	86
Antipajuta, Russia	C4	34
Antipodes Islands, is., N.Z.	H9	72
Antisana, vol., Ec.	H2	86
Antler, stm., N.A.	E12	124
Antofagasta, Chile.	A2	92
Antofagasta, state, Chile	B3	92
Antofagasta de la Sierra, Arg.	C4	92
Antofalla, Salar de, pl., Arg.	C3	92
Antofalla, Volcán, vol., Arg.	B4	92
Antón, Pan.	H7	102
Anton, Tx., U.S.	H6	128
Anton Chico, N.M., U.S.	F3	128
Antongila, Helodrano, b., Madag.	D8	68
Antonina, Braz.	B13	92
Antonina do Norte, Braz.	D5	88
António Prado, Braz.	D12	92
Antonito, Co., U.S.	D2	128
Antón Lizardo, Punta, c., Mex.	F10	100
Antonovo, Kaz.	D8	32
Antopal', Bela.	H7	10
Antrim, N. Ire., U.K.	G6	12
Antropovo, Russia	G20	8
Antsalova, Madag.	D7	68
Antsirabe, Madag.	D8	68
Antsirañana, Madag.	C8	68
Antsohihy, Madag.	C8	68
Antulai, Gunong, mtn., Malay.	A10	50
Antuñ', Russia	G16	34
Antung see Dandong, China.	D5	38
Antwerp see Antwerpen, Bel.	C13	14
Antwerp, Oh., U.S.	C1	114
Antwerpen (Antwerp), Bel.	C13	14
An Uaimh see Navan, Ire.	H6	12
Anugul, India	H10	54
Anūpgarh, India	D4	54
Anuradhapura, Sri L.	G5	53
Anvers see Antwerpen, Bel.	C13	14
Anvers Island, i., Ant.	B34	81
Anvik, Ak., U.S.	D7	140
Anxi, China	I8	42
Anxi, China	C4	36
Anxiang, China	G5	42
Anxious Bay, b., Austl.	F6	74
Anyang, China	C6	42
Anyang, China	F7	38
A'nyêmaqên Shan, mts., China	D4	36
Anyer Kidul, Indon.	G4	50
Anykščiai, Lith.	E7	10
Anyuan, China	I6	42
Anyuanyi see Tianzhu, China	D5	36
Anyue, China	F1	42
Anze, China	C5	42
Anžero-Sudžensk, Russia	C15	32
Anzio, Italy	C6	24
Anzoátegui, state, Ven.	C9	86
Anžu, ostrova, is., Russia	A17	34
Aoba, i., Vanuatu	j16	79d
Aoba I Maéwo, state, Vanuatu	j17	79d
Aoga-shima, i., Japan	G12	40
Aohan Qi, China	C3	38
Aojiang, China	H9	42
Aoji-ri, Kor., N.	C9	38
Ao Luk, Thai.	H4	48
Aomar, Alg.	H14	20
Aomen (Macau), China.	J5	42
Aomori, Japan	D14	38
Aonla, India	D7	54
Aóós (Vjosës), stm., Eur.	D13	24
A'opo, Samoa	g11	79c
Aoraki (Cook, Mount), mtn., N.Z.	F4	80
Aôral, Phnum, mtn., Camb.	F7	48
Aore, i., Vanuatu	j16	79d
Aosta (Aoste), Italy	E4	22
Aoste see Aosta, Italy	E4	22
Aouderas, Niger	F6	64
Aouk, Bahr, stm., Afr.	F3	62
Aoukâr, reg., Maur.	F3	64
Aoya, Japan	D7	40
Aozou, Chad	D3	62
Apache Junction, Az., U.S.	J5	132
Apache Peak, mtn., Az., U.S.	L6	132
Apalachee, stm., Ga., U.S.	C2	116
Apalachicola, Fl., U.S.	H13	122
Apalachicola, stm., Fl., U.S.	H14	122
Apalachicola Bay, b., Fl., U.S.	H13	122
Apaporis, stm., S.A.	G6	86
Aparados da Serra, Parque Nacional de, p.o.i., Braz.	D12	92
Aparri, Phil.	A3	52
Apatzingán de la Constitución, Mex.	F7	100
Apaxtla de Castrejón, Mex.	F8	100
Apeldoorn, Neth.	B15	14
Apennines see Appennino, mts., Italy	G11	6
Apex, N.C., U.S.	I7	114
Api, mtn., Nepal	D8	54
Apia, Col.	E4	86
Apia, Samoa	g12	79c
Apiai, Braz.	B13	92
Apiaú, stm., Braz.	F11	86
Apishapa, stm., Co., U.S.	D4	128
Apizaco, Mex.	F9	100
Apo, Mount, mtn., Phil.	G5	52
Apodi, Braz.	C7	88

Name	Map Ref.	Page
Apodi, stm., Braz.	C7	88
Apolakkiá, Grc.	G10	28
Apolda, Ger.	E7	16
Apolinario Saravia, Arg.	B6	92
Apolo, Bol.	B3	90
Apón, stm., Ven.	B5	86
Aponguao, stm., Ven.	E11	86
Apopka, Lake, l., Fl., U.S.	H4	116
Aporá, Braz.	F6	88
Aporé, Braz.	C6	90
Apostle Islands, is., Wi., U.S.	E8	118
Apostle Islands National Lakeshore, p.o.i., Wi., U.S.	D8	118
Apóstoles, Arg.	C10	92
Apostolove, Ukr.	E4	32
Appalaches, Les see Appalachian Mountains, mts., N.A.	D12	108
Appalachia, Va., U.S.	H3	114
Appalachian Mountains, mts., N.A.	D12	108
Appennino (Apennines), mts., Italy	G11	6
Appennino Calabro, mts., Italy	E10	24
Appennino Abruzzese, mts., Italy	B7	24
Appennino Ligure, mts., Italy	F6	22
Appennino Lucano, mts., Italy	D9	24
Appennino Tosco-Emiliano, mts., Italy	F8	22
Appennino Umbro-Marchigiano, mts., Italy	G9	22
Appenzell, Switz.	C6	22
Apple Orchard Mountain, mtn., Va., U.S.	G6	114
Appleton, Mn., U.S.	F3	118
Appleton, Wi., U.S.	G10	118
Appleton City, Mo., U.S.	F3	120
Apple Valley, Ca., U.S.	I8	134
Appomattox, Va., U.S.	G7	114
Appomattox, stm., Va., U.S.	G7	114
Aprelevka, Russia	E20	10
Aprilia, Italy	C6	24
Apšeronsk, Russia	F5	32
Apt, Fr.	F11	18
Apucarana, Braz.	A12	92
Apulia see Puglia, state, Italy	C10	24
Apure, state, Ven.	D7	86
Apure, stm., Ven.	D8	86
Apurímac, stm., Peru	D3	84
Apurito, Ven.	D7	86
Aqaba, Gulf of, b.	J5	58
Áqchah, Afg.	B10	56
'Aqīq, Sudan	D7	62
Aqköl see Astana, Kaz.	D12	32
Aqköl, Kaz.	D13	32
Aqsū, Kaz.	D12	32
Aqsū, stm., Kaz.	E13	32
Aqsüat, Kaz.	E14	32
Aqsüat, Kaz.	E14	32
Aqtaü, Kaz.	D12	32
Aqtaü, Kaz.	F8	32
Aqtöbe, Kaz.	D9	32
Aquidabã, Braz.	F7	88
Aquidauana, Braz.	D5	90
Aquila, Mex.	F7	100
Aquiles Serdán, Mex.	A6	100
Aquiles Serdán, Mex.	C9	100
Aquin, Haiti	C11	102
Aquio, stm., Col.	F8	86
Ara, India	F10	54
Ara, stm., Japan	D12	40
Arab, Al., U.S.	C12	122
'Arab, Bahr al-, stm., Sudan	E5	62
'Araba, Wadi ('Arabah, Wādī), stm., Egypt	I3	58
'Arabah, Wādī al- (Ha'Arava), val., Asia	H6	58
Araban, Tur.	A8	58
Arabian Basin, unds.	H9	142
Arabian Desert (Eastern Desert), des., Egypt	B6	62
Arabian Gulf see Persian Gulf, b., Asia	D7	56
Arabian Peninsula, pen., Asia	E6	56
Arabian Sea, s.	F9	56
Araçá, stm., Braz.	G10	86
Aracaju, Braz.	F7	88
Aracataca, Col.	B4	86
Aracati, Braz.	C7	88
Araçatuba, Braz.	D6	90
Aracena, Spain	G4	20
Araci, Braz.	F6	88
Aracides, Cape, c., Sol. Is.	e9	79b
Aracoiaba, Braz.	C6	88
Aracruz, Braz.	J5	88
Araçuaí, Braz.	I4	88
Araçuaí, stm., Braz.	I4	88
Araçuao, Caño, stm., Ven.	C11	86
Araguaçu, Braz.	F1	88
Araguaia, stm., Braz.	J1	88
Araguaiana, Braz.	C6	90
Araguaína, Braz.	D1	88
Araguao, Caño, stm., Ven.	C11	86
Araguari, Braz.	J1	88
Araguari, stm., Braz.	C7	84
Araguatins, Braz.	C1	88
Araioses, Braz.	B4	88
Arak, Alg.	D5	64
Arāk, Iran	C6	56
Arakan see Rakhine, state, Mya.	C1	48
Arakan Yoma, mts., Mya.	C7	48
Arakkonam, India	E4	53
Araks see Araz, stm., Asia	B6	56
Aral, Kaz.	E10	32
Aralbay, Kaz.	E10	32
Aral Sea, l., Asia	E9	32
Aral'sk see Aral, Kaz.	E10	32
Aramac, Austl.	D5	76
Aramac, stm., Austl.	D5	76
Aramberri, Mex.	C8	100
Aran, India	C2	53
Arandānova, Russia	E7	10
Aranda de Duero, Spain	C7	20
Arandis, Nmb.	C2	70
Arang, India	H8	54
Aran Islands, is., Ire.	H3	12
Aranos, Nmb.	D3	70
Aransas, stm., Tx., U.S.	F10	130
Arantāngi, India	F4	53
Aranyaprathet, Thai.	F6	48
Arao, Japan	G3	40
Araouane, Mali	F4	64
Arapaho, Ok., U.S.	F9	128

Name	Map Ref.	Page
Arapahoe, Ne., U.S.	A9	128
Arapey Grande, stm., Ur.	E9	92
Arapiraca, Braz.	E7	88
Arapiraca, Braz.	D6	90
Arapongas, Braz.	D6	90
Arapoti, Braz.	B12	92
Araranguá, Braz.	D13	92
Araraquara, Braz.	K1	88
Araras, Braz.	L2	88
Araras, Açude, res., Braz.	C5	88
Ararat, Austl.	K4	76
Ararat, Mount see Ağrı Dağı, mtn., Tur.	B5	56
Arari, Braz.	B3	88
Arāria, India	E11	54
Araripe, Braz.	D5	88
Araripe, Chapada do, plat., Braz.	D6	88
Araripina, Braz.	D5	88
Ararirá, stm., Braz.	H10	86
Araruama, Lagoa de, b., Braz.	L4	88
Araruna, Braz.	D8	88
Aras (Araz), stm., Asia	B6	56
Aratuípe, Braz.	G6	88
Arauca, Col.	D6	86
Arauca, state, Col.	D6	86
Arauca, stm., S.A.	D8	86
Arauca, Braz.	B13	92
Arauquita, Col.	D6	86
Araure, Ven.	C7	86
Arāvalli Range, mts., India	F4	54
Arawa, Pap. N. Gui.	d6	79b
Araxá, Braz.	J2	88
Araya, Ven.	B9	86
Araya, Punta de, c., Ven.	B9	86
Araz (Aras), stm., Asia	B6	56
Arba Minch', Eth.	F7	62
Arbatax, Italy	E3	24
Arbil, Iraq	B5	56
Arboga, Swe.	G6	8
Arboledas, Arg.	H7	92
Arbon, Switz.	C6	22
Arborea, Italy	E2	24
Arborea, reg., Italy	E2	24
Arborfield, Sk., Can.	A10	124
Arbroath, Scot., U.K.	E10	12
Arbuckle, Ca., U.S.	D3	134
Arc, stm., Fr.	D12	18
Arcachon, Fr.	E4	18
Arcachon, Bassin d', b., Fr.	E4	18
Arcade, Ca., U.S.	E4	134
Arcade, N.Y., U.S.	B7	114
Arcadia, Ca., U.S.	I7	134
Arcadia, Fl., U.S.	I4	116
Arcadia, Ia., U.S.	B2	120
Arcadia, La., U.S.	E5	122
Arcadia, Mi., U.S.	D3	112
Arcadia, Mo., U.S.	G7	120
Arcadia, S.C., U.S.	B3	116
Arcadia, Wi., U.S.	G7	118
Arcanum, Oh., U.S.	D1	114
Arcas, Cayos, is., Mex.	E12	100
Arcata, Ca., U.S.	C1	134
Arc Dome, mtn., Nv., U.S.	E8	134
Arcelia, Mex.	F8	100
Arcevia, Italy	G9	22
Archangel see Arhangel'sk, Russia	D19	8
Archbold, Oh., U.S.	C1	114
Archer, Fl., U.S.	G3	116
Archer, stm., Austl.	B8	74
Archer, Mount, mtn., Austl.	D8	76
Archer City, Tx., U.S.	H10	128
Archer's Post, Kenya	D7	66
Arches National Park, p.o.i., Ut., U.S.	E7	132
Archiac, Fr.	D5	18
Archidona, Spain	G6	20
Arcis-sur-Aube, Fr.	F13	14
Arco, Id., U.S.	G13	136
Arcola, Il., U.S.	E9	120
Arcola, Ms., U.S.	D8	122
Arcos, Braz.	K3	88
Arcos de la Frontera, Spain	H5	20
Arcot, India	E4	53
Arcoverde, Braz.	E7	88
Arctic Bay see Tununirusiq, Nu., Can.	A14	106
Arctic Ocean	A21	4
Arctic Red, stm., N.T., Can.	B4	106
Arctic Village, Ak., U.S.	C10	140
Arda, stm., Eur.	H12	26
Ardabīl, Iran	A5	56
Ardahan, Tur.	A5	56
Ardakān, Iran	C7	56
Ardatov, Russia	I20	8
Ardèche, state, Fr.	E10	18
Arden, Ca., U.S.	E4	134
Ardennes, state, Fr.	E13	14
Ardennes, reg., Eur.	D14	14
Ardennes, Canal des, can., Fr.	E13	14
Ardestān, Iran	C7	56
Ardila, stm., Eur.	F3	20
Ardill, Sk., Can.	E8	124
Ardlethan, Austl.	J6	76
Ardmore, Al., U.S.	B12	122
Ardmore, Ok., U.S.	G11	128
Ardmore, Pa., U.S.	D10	114
Åre, Swe.	E5	8
Areado, Braz.	K2	88
Arecibo, P.R.	B2	104a
Arecibo, Observatorio de, sci., P.R.	B2	104a
Arecibo Observatory see Arecibo, Observatorio de, sci., P.R.	B2	104a
Arêhaušk, Bela.	F13	10
Areia, Braz.	D8	88
Areia, stm., Braz.	H3	88
Areia Branca, Braz.	C7	88
Arena, Point, c., Ca., U.S.	E2	134
Arena, Punta, c., Mex.	D4	100
Arena de la Ventana, Punta, c., Mex.	C4	100
Arenal, Braz.	J3	88
Arenas, Cayo, i., Mex.	D13	100
Arenas, Punta de, c., Arg.	J3	90
Arenas de San Pedro, Spain	D5	20
Arendal, Nor.	G3	8
Arenys de Mar, Spain	C13	20
Areópoli, Grc.	F5	28
Arequipa, Arg.	F7	92
Arequipa, Arg.	E2	84
Arévalo, Spain	C6	20
Arezzo, Italy	G8	22
Arga, stm., Spain	B9	20
Argadargada, Austl.	D7	74
Argamasilla de Alba, Spain	E7	20
Arganda del Rey, Spain	D7	20
Arga-Sala, stm., Russia	C10	34
Argelès-Gazost, Fr.	F5	18
Argens, stm., Fr.	F12	18
Argent, Côte d', cst., Fr.	E4	18
Argenta, Italy	F8	22
Argentan, Fr.	F8	14
Argenteuil, Fr.	F11	14
Argentina, ctry., S.A.	G3	90
Argentine Basin, unds.	L10	144
Argentino, Lago, l., Arg.	J2	90
Argenton-sur-Creuse, Fr.	H10	14
Argeș, state, Rom.	E11	26
Argeș, stm., Rom.	E13	26
Arghandāb, stm., Afg.	C10	56
Argolikós Kólpos (Argolis, Gulf of), b., Grc.	F6	28
Argolis, Gulf of see Argolikós Kólpos, b., Grc.	F6	28
Argonne, Wi., U.S.	F10	118

Name	Map Ref.	Page
Argonne, reg., Fr.	E14	14
Argos, Grc.	F5	28
Argos, In., U.S.	G3	112
Argostóli, Grc.	E3	28
Arguello, Point, c., Ca., U.S.	I5	134
Argun' (Ergun), stm., Asia	F12	34
Argungu, Nig.	G5	64
Argyle, Lake, l., Austl.	C5	74
Argyle, Lake, l., Austl.	C5	74
Ar-Rahad, Sudan	E6	62
Arraial do Cabo, Braz.	L5	88
Arraias, Braz.	G2	88
Ar-Ramādī, Iraq	C5	56
Ar-Ramthā, Jord.	F7	58
Arran, Island of, i., Scot., U.K.	F7	12
Ar-Rank, Sudan	E6	62
Ar-Raqqah, Syria	B9	58
Ar-Raqqah, state, Syria	B9	58
Arras, Fr.	D11	14
Ar-Rastan, Syria	D7	58
Arrecifes, Arg.	G7	92
Arrey, N.M., U.S.	K9	132
Arriaga, Mex.	G11	100
Arroio Grande, Braz.	F11	92
Arrojado, stm., Braz.	G3	88
Arronches, Port.	E3	20
Arros, stm., Fr.	F6	18
Arroux, stm., Fr.	B10	18
Arrowhead, Lake, res., Tx., U.S.	H10	128
Arrowwood, Ab., Can.	F17	138
Arroyito, Arg.	E6	92
Arroyo, P.R.	C3	104a
Arroyo de la Luz, Spain	E4	20
Arroyo Grande, Ca., U.S.	H5	134
Arroyo Hondo, N.M., U.S.	E3	128
Arroyo Seco, Arg.	F7	92
Arroyos y Esteros, Para.	B9	92
Ar-Rub' al-Khālī, des., Asia	E6	56
Ar-Ruqayyah, sci., Syria	F8	58
Ar-Rusāfah, sci., Syria	C9	58
Ar-Ruşayfah, Jord.	F7	58
Ar-Rusayris, Sudan	E6	62
Ar-Rutbah, Iraq	C5	56
Arsenev, Russia	B10	38
Arsenevka, stm., Russia	B10	38
Arsikere, India	E3	53
Årsos, Cyp.	D3	58
Arta, Ílle, i., N. Cal.	I14	79d
Árta, Grc.	D3	28
Art'em, Russia	D16	36
Artemisa, Cuba	A6	102
Artemisa, Chile	D16	32
Artëmovsk, Russia	C10	38
Artëmovskij, Russia	E12	34
Artesia, M.M., U.S.	B3	130
Arthabaska, ngh., Qc., Can.	D5	110
Arthal, India	B6	54
Arthur, On., Can.	E9	112
Arthur, Il., U.S.	E9	120
Arthur, N.D., U.S.	D1	118
Arthur, Tn., U.S.	H2	114
Arthur, stm., Austl.	n12	77a
Arthur's Pass National Park, p.o.i., N.Z.	F5	80
Arthur's Town, Bah.	C9	96
Artibonite, stm., Haiti	C11	102
Artigas, Ur.	E9	92
Artillery Lake, l., N.T., Can.	C9	106
Artois, hist. reg., Fr.	D11	14
Artsyz, Ukr.	D16	26
Artyk, Russia	D18	34
Aru, i., Kepulauan (Aru Islands), is., Indon.	G10	44
Aruã, Braz.	A9	92
Aruana, Braz.	F7	84
Aruba, dep., N.A.	F12	102
Aru Islands see Aru, Kepulauan, is., Indon.	G10	44
Arunachal Pradesh, state, India	C7	46
Arun Qi, China	B9	36
Aruppukkottai, India	G4	53
Arurandeua, stm., Braz.	C1	88
Arusha, Tan.	E7	66
Arut, stm., Indon.	E7	50
Aruvi, stm., Sri L.	G5	53
Aruwimi, stm., D.R.C.	D4	66
Arverde, Braz.	B3	128
Arvayheer, Mong.	B5	36
Arvi, India	H7	54
Arviat, Nu., Can.	C12	106
Arvidsjaur, Swe.	D8	8
Arvika, Swe.	G5	8
Arvin, Ca., U.S.	H7	134
Arvon, Mount, mtn., Mi., U.S.	B1	112
Arvorezinha, Braz.	D11	92
Arxan, China	B8	36
Arys, Kaz.	F11	32
Arys köli, l., Kaz.	E11	32
Arzachena, Italy	C3	24
Arzamas, Russia	I20	8
Arzignano, Italy	E8	22
Arz Lubnān, for., Leb.	D7	58
Aš, Czech Rep.	F8	16
Aša, stm., Russia	B9	32
Asaba, Nig.	H6	64
Asad, Buhayrat al- (Assad, Lake), res., Syria	B9	58
Asadābād, Afg.	C11	56
Asadābād, Iran	C6	56
Asagabostanci, N. Cyp.	C3	58
Asahan, stm., Indon.	B1	50
Asahi, Japan	D13	40
Asahi, stm., Japan	E6	40
Asahi-dake, vol., Japan	C15	38
Asahigawa see Asahikawa, Japan	C15	38
Asahikawa, Japan	C15	38
Asākā, Japan	C11	40
Asan-man, b., Kor., S.	F7	38
Āsānsol, India	G11	54
Åsarna, Swe.	E6	8
Asaro, Ven.	q20	104g
Asbestos, Qc., Can.	E4	110
Asbestos Range National Park, p.o.i., Austl.	n13	77a
Asbury Park, N.J., U.S.	D12	114
Ascensión, Braz.	E7	16
Ascension, i., St. Hel.	G4	60
Aschaffenburg, Ger.	F7	16
Aschersleben, Ger.	E7	16
Ascoli Piceno, Italy	H10	22
Ascoli Satriano, Italy	C9	24
Ascór (Ostër), stm., Eur.	H8	10
Aseb, Erit.	F8	62
Åsele, Swe.	D7	8
Asenovgrad, Blg.	G11	26
Aseri, Est.	A9	10
Aşgabat, Turkmen.	B8	56
Ashburton, N.Z.	F4	80
Ashburton, stm., Austl.	D3	74
Ashchysay, Kaz.	F11	32
Ashcroft, B.C., Can.	F9	138
Ashdod, Isr.	G5	58
Ashdod, Tel Aviv, Isr.	G5	58
Ashdown, Ar., U.S.	D4	122
Asheboro, N.C., U.S.	I6	114
Ashern, Mb., Can.	C15	124
Asheville, N.C., U.S.	I3	114
Ashford, Austl.	G8	76
Ashford, Eng., U.K.	J13	12
Ashford, Al., U.S.	F13	122
Ash Fork, Az., U.S.	H4	132
Ashgabat see Aşgabat, Turkmen.	B8	56
Ash Grove, Mo., U.S.	G4	120
Ashibe, Japan	F2	40

Name	Map Ref.	Page
Ashikaga, Japan	C12	40
Ashington, Eng., U.K.	F11	12
Ashio, Japan	C12	40
Ashizuri-misaki, c., Japan	G6	40
Ashland, Al., U.S.	D13	122
Ashland, Il., U.S.	E7	120
Ashland, Ks., U.S.	D9	128
Ashland, Ky., U.S.	F3	114
Ashland, Mo., U.S.	F5	120
Ashland, Mt., U.S.	B6	126
Ashland, Ne., U.S.	C1	120
Ashland, N.H., U.S.	G5	110
Ashland, Oh., U.S.	D3	114
Ashland, Or., U.S.	A3	134
Ashland, Va., U.S.	G8	114
Ashland, Wi., U.S.	E7	118
Ashland, Mount, mtn., Or., U.S.	A3	134
Ashley, Austl.	G7	76
Ashley, Il., U.S.	F8	120
Ashley, Mi., U.S.	E5	112
Ashley, Oh., U.S.	D3	114
Ashmore Islands, is., Austl.	B4	74
Ashoknagar, India	F6	54
Ashqelon, Isr.	G5	58
Ash-Shamāl, state, Leb.	D7	58
Ash-Shaqrā' see Shaqrā', Sau. Ar.	D6	56
Ash-Shāriqah, U.A.E.	D8	56
Ash-Shawbak, Jord.	H6	58
Ash-Shiḥr, Yemen	G6	56
Ash-Shurayf, Sau. Ar.	D4	56
Ashta, India	C2	53
Ashta, India	G6	54
Ashtabula, Oh., U.S.	C5	114
Ashtabula, Lake, res., N.D., U.S.	G16	124
Ashton, S. Afr.	H5	70
Ashton, St. Vin.	p11	105e
Ashton, Id., U.S.	F15	136
Ashton, Il., U.S.	C8	120
Ashton, Ne., U.S.	F14	126
Ashuanipi Lake, l., Nf., Can.	E17	106
Ashuapmushuan, stm., Qc., Can.	B3	110
Ashūm, Egypt	H1	58
Ashville, Al., U.S.	D12	122
Ashwaubenon, Wi., U.S.	D1	112
Asi see Orontes, stm., Asia	B7	58
Asia, cont.	C19	4
Asia, Kepulauan, is., Indon.	E9	44
Asia Minor, hist. reg., Tur.	E13	28
Āsīka, India	I10	54
Asinara, Golfo dell', b., Italy	D2	24
Asinara, Isola, i., Italy	C2	24
Asini, sci., Grc.	F5	28
Asino, Russia	C15	32
Asintorf, Bela.	F13	10
Asipovičy, Bela.	G11	10
'Asīr, reg., Sau. Ar.	E5	56
Askham, S. Afr.	E5	70
Askiz, Russia	D16	32
Askja, vol., Ice.	k31	8a
Aslanapa, Tur.	D12	28
Aslantaş Baraji, res., Tur.	A7	58
Asmara see Asmera, Erit.	D7	62
Asmera, Erit.	D7	62
Ašmjany, Bela.	F8	10
Asola, Italy	E7	22
Asomante, P.R.	B2	104a
Asosa, Eth.	E6	62
Asoteriba, Jabal, mtn., Sudan	C7	62
Asotin, Wa., U.S.	D9	136
Asouf, Oued, stm., Alg.	D5	64
Asp, Spain	F10	20
Aspe see Asp, Spain	F10	20
Aspen, Co., U.S.	D10	132
Aspendos, sci., Tur.	G14	28
Aspermont, Tx., U.S.	A7	130
Aspiring, Mount, mtn., N.Z.	G3	80
Assad, Lake see Asad, Buhayrat al-, res., Syria	B9	58
As-Safīrah, Syria	B8	58
Aṣ-Ṣāfiyah, Sudan	D6	62
As-Salt, Jord.	F6	58
Assam, state, India	C7	46
As-Samāwah, Iraq	C6	56
Aṣ-Ṣanamayn, Syria	E7	58
Aṣ-Ṣarafand, Leb.	E6	58
Assaré, Braz.	D6	88
Assateague Island, i., U.S.	F10	114
Assateague Island National Seashore, p.o.i., U.S.	G10	114
Assemini, Italy	E2	24
Assen, Neth.	A15	14
Asseria, sci., Cro.	F12	22
Assiniboia, Sk., Can.	E8	124
Assiniboine, stm., Can.	E16	124
Assiniboine, Mount, mtn., Can.	F15	138
Assis, Braz.	D6	90
Assis Chateaubriand, Braz.	B11	92
Assisi, Italy	G9	22
Assomption, i., Sey.	k11	69b
Assu, Braz.	C7	88
As-Sudd, reg., Sudan	F6	62
As-Sufāl, Yemen	G6	56
As-Sulaymānīyah, Iraq	B6	56
As-Sulaymānīyah, Sau. Ar.	E6	56
As-Sulayyil, Sau. Ar.	E6	56
Assumption, Il., U.S.	E8	120
As-Suwaydā', Syria	F7	58
As-Suwaydā', state, Syria	F7	58
Astakós, Grc.	E3	28
Astana (Aqmola), Kaz.	D12	32
Astara, Azer.	B6	56
Asti, Italy	F5	22
Astica, Arg.	E4	92
Astola Island, i., Pak.	D9	56
Astorga, Spain	B4	20
Astoria, Il., U.S.	D7	120
Astoria, Or., U.S.	D3	136
Astove, i., Sey.	I11	69b
Astrahan', Russia	E7	32
Astrahan' see Astrahan', Russia	E7	32
Astrašycki Haradok, Bela.	F10	10
Astrolabe, Cape, c., Sol. Is.	e9	79b
Astrolabe, Récifs de l', rf., N. Cal.	I15	79d
Astrolabe Reefs see Astrolabe, Récifs de l', rf., N. Cal.	I15	79d
Astrouna, Bela.	E12	10
Astudillo, Spain	B6	20
Asturias, state, Spain	A5	20
Astypálaia, i., Grc.	G9	28
Asunción, Para.	B9	92
Asunción, Bahía la, b., Mex.	B1	100
Asunción Nochixtlán, Mex.	G10	100
Āsunden, l., Swe.	H5	8
Asveja, Bela.	E11	10
Asvejskae, vozero, l., Bela.	D10	10
Aswān, Egypt	C6	62
Aswan High Dam see Aali, Sadd el-, dam, Egypt	C6	62
Asyūṭ, Egypt	K2	58
Asyūṭī, Wādī el- (Asyūṭī, Wādī al-), stm., Egypt	K2	58
'Ata, i., Tonga	F9	72
Atabapo, stm., S.A.	F8	86
Atacama, state, Chile	C3	92
Atacama, Desierto de, des., Chile	E2	90
Atacama, Puna de, plat., S.A.	B4	92
Atacama, Salar de, pl., Chile	D3	90
Atacama Desert see Atacama, Desierto de, des., Chile	B3	92
Ataco, Col.	F4	86
Atagaj, Russia	C17	32
Atakpamé, Togo	H5	64
Atalaia, Braz.	E7	88
Atambua, Indon.	G7	44
Atami, Japan	D12	40
Atangmik, Grnld.	E15	141
Aṭar, Maur.	E2	64
Atascadero, Ca., U.S.	H5	134
Atascosa, stm., Tx., U.S.	F9	130
Atasū, Kaz.	E12	32
Atata, i., Tonga	n14	78e
Atatürk Baraji, res., Tur.	A9	58
Atauro, Pulau, i., E. Timor	G8	44
Audenarde see Oudenaarde, Bel.	D12	14
'Aṭbarah, Sudan	D6	62
'Aṭbarah, stm., Afr.	D7	62
Atbasar, Kaz.	D11	32
Atchafalaya, stm., La., U.S.	G7	122
Atchafalaya Bay, b., La., U.S.	H7	122
Atchison, Ks., U.S.	E2	120
Ateca, Spain	C9	20
Aterno, stm., Italy	H10	22
Atfīh, Egypt	I2	58
Ath, Bel.	D12	14
Athabasca, Ab., Can.	B17	138
Athabasca, stm., Ab., Can.	D8	106
Athabasca, Lake, l., Can.	D9	106
Athalmer, B.C., Can.	F14	138
Athboy, Ire.	H6	12
Athens, On., U.S.	E8	136
Athens, On., Can.	D14	112
Athens see Athína, Grc.	E6	28
Athens, Al., U.S.	C11	122
Athens, Ga., U.S.	C2	116
Athens, Il., U.S.	E8	120
Athens, La., U.S.	E5	122
Athens, Mi., U.S.	F4	112
Athens, Oh., U.S.	E3	114
Athens, Pa., U.S.	C9	114
Athens, Tn., U.S.	B14	122
Athens, Tx., U.S.	E3	122
Athens, W.V., U.S.	G5	114
Atherton, Austl.	A5	76
Athi, stm., Kenya	E7	66
Athiainou, Cyp.	C4	58
Athlone, Ire.	H4	12
Athni, India	C2	53
Athok, Mya.	D2	48
Athol, Ma., U.S.	B13	114
Áthos, mtn., Grc.	C7	28
Athos, Mount see Áthos, mtn., Grc.	C7	28
Ati, Chad	E3	62
Atiak, Ug.	D6	66
Atico, Peru	G3	84
Atienza, Spain	C8	20
Atikokan, On., Can.	C7	118
Atirāmpattinam, India	F4	53
Atiu, i., Cook Is.	F11	72
Atka, Russia	D19	34
Atka Island, i., Ak., U.S.	g24	140a
Atkarsk, Russia	D6	32
Atkins, Ar., U.S.	B6	122
Atkinson, Il., U.S.	C8	120
Atkinson, N.C., U.S.	B7	116
Atlanta, Ga., U.S.	C1	116
Atlanta, Il., U.S.	D8	120
Atlanta, Mi., U.S.	C5	112
Atlanta, Mo., U.S.	E5	120
Atlantic, Ia., U.S.	C2	120
Atlantic, N.C., U.S.	B9	116
Atlantic Beach, Fl., U.S.	F4	116
Atlantic City, N.J., U.S.	E11	114
Atlantic-Indian Basin, unds.	O5	142
Atlantic-Indian Ridge, unds.	N15	144
Atlántico, state, Col.	B4	86
Atlantic Ocean	E9	144
Atlantic Peak, mtn., Wy., U.S.	E3	126
Atlas Mountains, mts., Afr.	C4	64
Atlasova, ostrov, i., Russia	F20	34
Atlas Saharien, mts., Alg.	C4	64
Atlin, B.C., Can.	D4	106
Atlin Lake, l., Can.	D4	106
'Atlit, Isr.	F5	58
Ātmakūr, India	D4	53
Atmore, Al., U.S.	F11	122
Atna Peak, mtn., B.C., Can.	D5	138
Atocha, Bol.	D3	90
Atoka, Ok., U.S.	C2	122
Atotonilco, Cerro, mtn., Mex.	H3	130
Atoyac, stm., Mex.	F9	100
Atoyac de Álvarez, Mex.	G8	100
Atrak (Atrek), stm., Asia	B7	56
Atran, stm., Swe.	H5	8
Atrato, stm., Col.	D3	86
Atrauli, India	D7	54
Atrek (Atrak), stm., Asia	B7	56
Atri, Italy	H10	22
Atsumi, Japan	E10	40
Atsumi-hantō, pen., Japan	E10	40
Aṭ-Ṭafīlah, Jord.	H6	58
Aṭ-Ṭafīlah, state, Jord.	H6	58
Aṭ-Ṭā'if, Sau. Ar.	E5	56
Aṭ-Ṭall, Syria	E7	58
Attalla, Al., U.S.	C12	122
Attapu, Laos	E8	48
Attawapiskat, On., Can.	E14	106
Attawapiskat, On., Can.	E13	106
Attawapiskat Lake, l., On., Can.	E13	106
Aṭ-Ṭawīl, mts., Sau. Ar.	D4	56
Aṭ-Ṭayyibah, Syria	C9	58
Attendorn, Ger.	E3	16
Attersee, l., Aus.	C10	22
Attica, In., U.S.	H2	112
Attica, Ks., U.S.	D10	128
Attica, N.Y., U.S.	B7	114
Attica see Attikí, hist. reg., Grc.	E6	28
Attikí, state, Grc.	F6	28
Attikí, hist. reg., Grc.	E6	28
Attleboro, Ma., U.S.	C14	114
'Avedat, Horvot, sci., Isr.	H5	58
Attock, Pak.	B4	54
Attu, Ak., U.S.	g21	140a
Attu Island, i., Ak., U.S.	g21	140a
Attūr, India	F4	53
Aṭ-Tuwayshah, Sudan	E5	62
Atuel, stm., Arg.	G3	92
Atuel, Bañados del, sw., Arg.	H4	92
Atuntaqui, Ec.	G2	86
Atuona, Fr. Poly.	s18	78g
Atwater, Ca., U.S.	F5	134
Atwater, Mn., U.S.	F4	118
Atwood, Il., U.S.	E9	120
Atwood, Ks., U.S.	B7	128
Atwood, i., Bah.	I9	120
Atyraū, Kaz.	E8	32
Aua Island, i., Pap. N. Gui.	a3	79a
Auari, stm., Braz.	G10	86
Auau Channel, strt., Hi., U.S.	c5	78a
Aubagne, Fr.	F11	18
Aube, state, Fr.	F13	14
Aube, stm., Fr.	F13	14
Aubigny-sur-Nère, Fr.	G11	14
Aubinadong, stm., On., Can.	A6	112
Aubrey Cliffs, clf., Az., U.S.	H3	132
Aubrey Lake, res., On., Can.	A6	112
Aubry Lake, l., N.T., Can.	B5	106
Auburn, Al., U.S.	E13	122
Auburn, Ca., U.S.	E4	134
Auburn, In., U.S.	G4	112
Auburn, Ky., U.S.	H11	120
Auburn, Ma., U.S.	B14	114
Auburn, Me., U.S.	F6	110
Auburn, Ne., U.S.	D1	120
Auburn, N.Y., U.S.	B9	114
Auburn, Wa., U.S.	C4	136
Aubusson, Fr.	D8	18
Auca Mahuida, Cerro, mtn., Arg.	H3	92
Auce, Lat.	D5	10
Auch, Fr.	F6	18
Auchi, Nig.	H6	64
Aucilla, stm., U.S.	F2	116
Auckland, N.Z.	C6	80
Auckland Islands, is., N.Z.	I7	72
Aude, state, Fr.	F8	18
Aude, stm., Fr.	F9	18
Auden, On., Can.	A11	118
Audierne, Fr.	F4	14
Audincourt, Fr.	G15	14
Audubon Lake, res., N.D., U.S.	G12	124
Aue, Ger.	F8	16
Augathella, Austl.	E6	76
Augrabies Falls National Park, p.o.i., S. Afr.	F4	70
Augrabiesvalle, wtfl., S. Afr.	F5	70
Augsburg, Ger.	H6	16
Augusta, Austl.	F2	74
Augusta, Italy	G9	24
Augusta, Ar., U.S.	B7	122
Augusta, Ga., U.S.	C3	116
Augusta, Il., U.S.	D6	120
Augusta, Ky., U.S.	F1	114
Augusta, Me., U.S.	F7	110
Augusta, Mt., U.S.	C14	136
Augusta, Wi., U.S.	G7	118
Augusto Severo, Braz.	C7	88
Augustów, Pol.	C18	16
Augustowski, Kanał, can., Eur.	C19	16
Augustus, Mount, mtn., Austl.	D3	74
Auki, Sol. Is.	e9	79b
Aukstaitijos nacionalnis parkas, p.o.i., Lith.	E8	10
Aulander, N.C., U.S.	H8	114
Auld, Lake, l., Austl.	D4	74
Aulla, Italy	F6	22
Aulne, stm., Fr.	F5	14
Aulneau Peninsula, pen., On., Can.	B4	118
Aumale, Fr.	E10	14
Auna, Nig.	G5	64
Auob, stm., Afr.	E5	70
Auraiya, India	E7	54
Aurangābād, India	B2	53
Aurangābād, India	F10	54
Aure, Nor.	E3	8
Aurelia, Ia., U.S.	B2	120
Aurich, Ger.	C3	16
Aurilândia, Braz.	G7	84
Aurillac, Fr.	E8	18
Aurine, Alpi (Zillertaler Alpen), mts., Eur.	C8	22
Aurora, On., Can.	D10	112
Aurora, Co., U.S.	B4	128
Aurora, Il., U.S.	C9	120
Aurora, In., U.S.	E13	120
Aurora, Me., U.S.	F8	110
Aurora, Mn., U.S.	D6	118
Aurora, N.C., U.S.	A9	116
Aurora, N.Y., U.S.	B9	114
Aurora, Oh., U.S.	C4	114
Aurora, Ut., U.S.	E5	132
Aurora, W.V., U.S.	E6	114
Aurora do Norte, Braz.	G2	88
Aursunden, l., Nor.	E4	8
Aurukun, Austl.	B8	74
Aus, Nmb.	E3	70
Ausable, stm., On., Can.	E8	112
Au Sable, stm., Mi., U.S.	D6	112
Au Sable Forks, N.Y., U.S.	F3	110
Au Sable Point, c., Mi., U.S.	D6	112
Auschwitz see Oświęcim, Pol.	F15	16
Aust-Agder, state, Nor.	G3	8
Austin, In., U.S.	F12	120
Austin, Mn., U.S.	H6	118
Austin, Nv., U.S.	D8	134
Austin, Pa., U.S.	C7	114
Austin, Tx., U.S.	D10	130
Austin, Lake, l., Austl.	E3	74
Australes, Îles, is., Fr. Poly.	F11	72
Australia, ctry., Oc.	D5	74
Australian Capital Territory, state, Austl.	J7	76
Austral Islands see Australes, Îles, is., Fr. Poly.	F11	72
Austral Plateau, unds.	E10	144
Austral Seamounts, unds.	L24	142
Austria, ctry., Eur.	C11	22
Austvågøy, i., Nor.	B6	8
Ausuittuq (Grise Fiord), Nu., Can.	B9	141
Autlán de Navarro, Mex.	F6	100
Autun, Fr.	H13	14
Auvergne, hist. reg., Fr.	D8	18
Auxerre, Fr.	G12	14
Auxier, Ky., U.S.	G3	114
Auxi-le-Château, Fr.	D11	14
Auxvasse, Mo., U.S.	E6	120
Auyán Tepuy, mtn., Ven.	E10	86
Auzances, Fr.	C8	18
Auzangate, Nevado, mtn., Peru	F3	84
Ava, Mo., U.S.	H5	120
Avaí, Braz.	L1	88
Avala, hist., Serb.	E7	26
Avallon, Fr.	G12	14
Avalon, Ca., U.S.	J7	134
Ávalos, Mex.	A5	100
Avanersuaq see Nordgrønland, state, Grnld.	B14	141
Avaré, Braz.	L1	88
Avarua, Cook Is.	a26	78j
Avarua Harbour, b., Cook Is.	a26	78j
Avatiu Harbour, b., Cook Is.	a26	78j
Aveiro, Port.	D2	20
Aveiro, state, Port.	D2	20
Aveiro, Ria de, mth., Port.	D1	20
Avellaneda, Arg.	G8	92
Avellaneda, Arg.	D8	92
Avellino, Italy	D8	24
Averøya, i., Nor.	E2	8
Aversa, Italy	D8	24
Avery, Id., U.S.	C11	136
Avery, Tx., U.S.	D4	122
Avery Island, La., U.S.	H6	122
Aves, Islas de, is., Ven.	B8	86
Avesnes-sur-Helpe, Fr.	D12	14
Avesta, Swe.	F6	8
Aveyron, state, Fr.	E8	18
Aveyron, stm., Fr.	E7	18
Avezzano, Italy	H10	22
Avigliano, Italy	D9	24
Avignon, Fr.	F10	18
Ávila, Spain	D6	20
Ávila, co., Spain	D6	20
Ávila, Sierra de, mts., Spain	D5	20
Avilés, Spain	A4	20
Avinurme, Est.	B9	10
Avispa, Cerro, mtn., Ven.	G9	86
Avoca, Austl.	K4	76
Avoca, Ia., U.S.	C2	120
Avoca, N.Y., U.S.	B8	114
Avoca, stm., Austl.	K4	76
Avola, B.C., Can.	D10	138
Avola, Italy	H9	24
Avon, Il., U.S.	D7	120
Avon, Mn., U.S.	F4	118
Avon, N.C., U.S.	A10	116
Avon, N.Y., U.S.	B8	114
Avon, stm., Austl.	F3	74
Avon, stm., Eng., U.K.	I11	12
Avon, stm., Eng., U.K.	K11	12
Avon, stm., Eng., U.K.	J10	12
Avondale, Az., U.S.	J4	132
Avondale, Co., U.S.	C4	128
Avon Downs, Austl.	D7	74
Avon Park, Fl., U.S.	I4	116
Avontuur, S. Afr.	H6	70
Avranches, Fr.	F7	14
Awaaso, Ghana	H4	64
Awaji, Japan	E8	40
Awaji-shima, i., Japan	E7	40
Awara, Japan	C9	40
Āwarē, Eth.	F8	62
Āwasa, Eth.	F7	62
Āwash, Eth.	F8	62
Awash, stm., Eth.	E8	62
Awa-shima, i., Japan	A12	40
Awbārī, Libya	B2	62
Awbārī, Şaḥrā', reg., Libya	B2	62
Awe, Loch, l., Scot., U.K.	E7	12
Awgyun, Mya.	F4	48
Awjilah, Libya	B4	62
Awled Djellal, Alg.	C6	64
Awo Omamma, Nig.	H6	64
Awul, Pap. N. Gui.	b5	79a
Axel Heiberg Island, i., Nu., Can.	A7	141
Axim, Ghana	I4	64
Axiós (Vardar), stm., Eur.	C5	28
Axis, Al., U.S.	G10	122
Axixá, Braz.	B3	88
Axtell, Ks., U.S.	L2	118
Axtell, Ne., U.S.	G13	126
Ayabe, Japan	D8	40
Ayacucho, Arg.	H8	92
Ayacucho, Peru	F3	84
Ayaguz, Kaz.	E13	32
Ayakōz, Kaz.	E13	32
Ayam, C. Iv.	H4	64
Ayamonte, Spain	G3	20
Ayapel, Col.	C4	86
Ayaş, Tur.	C15	28
Ayaviri, Peru	F3	84
Aydın, Tur.	F10	28
Aydın, state, Tur.	F11	28
Aydınkent, Tur.	F12	28
Ayer, Ma., U.S.	B14	114
Ayers Rock see Uluru, mtn., Austl.	E6	74
Ayeyarwady, state, Mya.	D2	48
Ayeyarwady (Irrawaddy), stm., Mya.	E8	46
Ayeyarwady, Mouths of the, mth., Mya.	E7	46
Aylesbury, Eng., U.K.	J12	12
Aylmer, On., Can.	F8	112
Aylmer, Qc., Can.	C14	112
Aylmer Lake, l., N.T., Can.	C9	106
Aylsham, Sk., Can.	A10	124
'Ayn Dār, Sau. Ar.	D6	56
Aynor, S.C., U.S.	B6	116
'Aynūnah, Sau. Ar.	J6	58
Ayon Island see Aën, ostrov, i., Russia	B22	34
Ayora see Aiora, Spain	E9	20
Ayorou, Niger	G5	64
'Ayoūn el 'Atroūs, Maur.	F3	64
Ayr, Austl.	B6	76
Ayr, Scot., U.K.	F8	12
Ayrancı, Tur.	A4	58
Ayre, Point of, c., I. of Man	G8	12
Aysha, Eth.	E8	62
Aytos see Ajtos, Blg.	G14	26
Ayutla, Mex.	D9	16
Ayutla de los Libres, Mex.	G9	100
Ayvacık, Tur.	D9	28
Ayvalık, Tur.	D9	28
Azaila, Spain	C10	20
Azamgarh, India	E9	54
Azángaro, Peru	F3	84
Azaouâd, reg., Mali	F4	64
Azare, Nig.	G6	64
Azaryčy, Bela.	H12	10
A'zāz, Syria	B8	58
Azdavay, Tur.	B16	28
Azeffâl, sand, Afr.	E2	64
Azerbaijan, ctry., Asia	A6	56
Āzezo, Eth.	E7	62
Azhikode, India	F2	53
Azilal, Mor.	C3	64
Azogues, Ec.	I2	86
Azores see Açores, is., Port.	C3	60
Azov, Russia	E5	32
Azov, Sea of, s., Eur.	E5	32
Azovskoje more see Azov, Sea of, s., Eur.	E5	32
Azraq, Al-Baḥr al- see Blue Nile, stm., Afr.	E6	62
Aztec, N.M., U.S.	G9	132
Aztec Peak, mtn., Az., U.S.	J5	132
Aztec Ruins National Monument, p.o.i., N.M., U.S.	G8	132
Azua, Dom. Rep.	C12	102
Azuaga, Spain	F5	20
Azuay, state, Ec.	I2	86
Azuer, stm., Spain	F7	20
Azuero, Península de, pen., Pan.	D1	86
Azufre, Volcán, vol., S.A.	B3	92
Azul, Arg.	H8	92
Azul, Cerro, mtn., Mex.	D12	26
Azur, Côte d', cst., Fr.	F13	18
Azurduy, Bol.	C4	90
Az-Zahrān, Sau. Ar.	D6	56
Az-Zarqā', Jord.	F7	58
Az-Zarqā', state, Jord.	G8	58
Az-Zāwiyah, Libya	A2	62
Azzel Matti, Sebkha, pl., Alg.	D5	64

B

Name	Map Ref.	Page
Ba, Fiji	p18	79e
Ba, stm., China	F2	42
Ba, stm., China	E5	42
Ba, stm., Viet.	F9	48
Baa, Indon.	H7	44
Baaba, Île, i., N. Cal.	l14	79d
Baao, Phil.	D4	52
Baardheere, Som.	D8	66
Baba Burnu, c., Tur.	D9	28
Babadag, Rom.	E15	26
Babaeski, Tur.	B10	28
Babahoyo, Ec.	H2	86
Babak, Phil.	G5	52
Babanango, S. Afr.	F10	70
Babanūsah, Sudan	E5	62
Babar, Kepulauan, is., Indon.	G8	44
Babbitt, Mn., U.S.	D7	118
Babbitt, Nv., U.S.	E7	134
B'abdā, Leb.	E6	58
Babeldaob, i., Palau	g7	78b
Bab el Mandeb see Mandeb, Bab el, strt.	E8	62
Babia, Arroyo de la, stm., Mex.	A5	100
Babian, stm., China	A5	48
Babícy, Bela.	H12	10
Babine, stm., B.C., Can.	A3	138
Babine Lake, l., B.C., Can.	B5	138
Babine Range, mts., B.C., Can.	B4	138
Babo, Indon.	F9	44
Bābol, Iran	B7	56
Baboquivari Peak, mtn., Az., U.S.	L5	132
Baborów, Pol.	F13	16
Babrujsk, Bela.	G12	10
Babruysk, Russia	F10	34
Babuyan Channel, strt., Phil.	A3	52
Babuyan Island, i., Phil.	A4	52
Babuyan Islands, is., Phil.	A3	52
Bacabal, Braz.	C3	88
Bacadéhuachi, Mex.	G8	98
Bacatuba, Braz.	C3	88
Bacău, Rom.	C13	26
Bacău, state, Rom.	C13	26
Bac Binh, Viet.	G9	48
Baccarat, Fr.	F15	14
Bačejkava, Bela.	F12	10
Bac Giang, Viet.	B8	48
Bachaquero, Ven.	B6	86
Bach Ma, Viet.	D8	48
Bach Thong, Viet.	A7	48
Bachu, China	B12	56
Back, stm., Nu., Can.	B11	106
Bačka, reg., Eur.	E16	22
Bačka Palanka, Serb.	D6	26
Bačka Topola, Serb.	D6	26
Back Creek, stm., Va., U.S.	F6	114
Backnang, Ger.	H5	16
Backstairs Passage, strt., Austl.	J1	76
Bacoachi, Mex.	F8	98
Bacolod, Phil.	E4	52
Bacontón, Ga., U.S.	E1	116
Bacoor, Phil.	C3	52
Bac Phan, hist. reg., Viet.	A7	48
Bács-Kiskun, state, Hung.	C6	26
Bâc, stm., Mol.	C15	26
Bacuri, Lago do, l., Braz.	B4	88
Bād, Iran	C7	56
Bad, stm., Mi., U.S.	E5	112
Bad, stm., S.D., U.S.	C12	126
Badagara, India	F2	53
Badajós, Lago, l., Braz.	D5	84
Badajoz, Spain	F4	20
Badajoz, co., Spain	F4	20
Badalona, Spain	C13	20
Bādāmi, India	D2	53
Badanah, Sau. Ar.	C5	56
Badarīnāth, India	C7	54
Badas, Kepulauan, is., Indon.	C5	50
Bad Axe, Mi., U.S.	E7	112
Bad Bergzabern, Ger.	G3	16
Bad Bevensen, Ger.	C6	16
Bad Bramstedt, Ger.	C5	16
Baddeck, N.S., Can.	D16	110
Bad Doberan, Ger.	B7	16
Bad Dürrenberg, Ger.	E8	16
Bad Ems, Ger.	F3	16
Baden, Switz.	C5	22
Baden-Baden, Ger.	H4	16
Badenoch, hist. reg., Scot., U.K.	E8	12
Badenweiler, Ger.	I3	16
Baden-Württemberg, state, Ger.	H4	16
Bad Freienwalde, Ger.	D9	16
Badgastein, Aus.	C10	22
Badger, Mn., U.S.	C3	118
Bad Hall, Aus.	B11	22
Bad Harzburg, Ger.	E6	16
Bad Hersfeld, Ger.	F5	16
Bad Homburg vor der Höhe, Ger.	F4	16
Bad Honnef, Ger.	F3	16
Badin Lake, res., N.C., U.S.	A5	116
Bad Ischl, Aus.	C10	22
Bad Kissingen, Ger.	F6	16
Bad Kreuznach, Ger.	G3	16
Bad Langensalza, Ger.	E6	16
Bad Lauterberg im Harz, Ger.	E6	16
Bad Mergentheim, Ger.	G5	16
Bad Muskau, Ger.	E10	16
Bad Nauheim, Ger.	F4	16
Bad Neustadt an der Saale, Ger.	F6	16
Bad Oeynhausen, Ger.	D4	16
Bad Oldesloe, Ger.	C6	16
Badong, China	F3	42
Bad Orb, Ger.	F5	16
Bad Pyrmont, Ger.	E5	16
Bad Reichenhall, Ger.	I8	16
Bad Salzuflen, Ger.	D4	16
Bad Salzungen, Ger.	F6	16
Bad Schwalbach, Ger.	F4	16
Bad Schwartau, Ger.	C6	16
Bad Segeberg, Ger.	C6	16
Bādshāhpur, India	F9	54
Bad Tölz, Ger.	I7	16
Badulla, Sri L.	H5	53
Badvel, India	D4	53
Bad Vöslau, Aus.	C13	22
Bad Wildungen, Ger.	E5	16
Bad Wörishofen, Ger.	I6	16
Badźarackaja guba, b., Russia	C2	34
Baena, Spain	G6	20
Baependi, Braz.	K3	88
Baer, Russia	C17	32
Baeza, Spain	G7	20
Baezaeko, stm., B.C., Can.	D7	138
Bafang, Cam.	C1	66
Bafatá, Gui.-B.	G2	64
Baffin Basin, unds.	A7	144
Baffin Bay, b., N.A.	C12	141
Baffin Bay, b., Tx., U.S.	G10	130
Baffin Island, i., Nu., Can.	B16	106
Bafia, Cam.	D2	66
Bafing, stm., Afr.	G2	64
Bafoulabé, Mali	G2	64
Bafoussam, Cam.	C1	66
Bafra, Tur.	A4	56
Bāft, Iran	D8	56
Bafwaboli, D.R.C.	D5	66
Bafwasende, D.R.C.	D5	66
Bagaces, C.R.	G5	102
Bagaha, India	E10	54
Bagalkot, India	C2	53
Bagamoyo, Tan.	F7	66
Baganga, Phil.	G6	52
Bagansiapiapi, Indon.	C2	50
Bagdad, Az., U.S.	I3	132
Bagdarin, Russia	F11	34
Bagé, Braz.	E11	92
Bagenkop, Den.	B6	16
Bāgeshwar, India	C7	54
Bāgevādi, India	C2	53
Baghdād, Iraq	C5	56
Bāghlān, Afg.	B10	56
Bagnères-de-Luchon, Fr.	G6	18
Bagni di Lucca, Italy	F7	22
Bagnols-sur-Cèze, Fr.	E10	18
Bago (Pegu), Mya.	D3	48
Bago, state, Mya.	C2	48
Bagoé, stm., Afr.	G3	64
Bağpınar, Tur.	A9	58
Baguio, Phil.	B3	52
Bāh, India	E7	54
Bahādurgarh, India	D6	54
Bahama, Canal Viejo de, strt., N.A.	A8	102
Bahamas, ctry., N.A.	C9	96
Baharampur, India	F11	54
Bahau, Malay.	K6	48
Bahau, stm., Indon.	B9	50
Bahāwalnagar, Pak.	C4	54
Bahāwalpur, Pak.	D3	54
Bahçe, Tur.	A7	58
Baheri, India	D7	54
Bahía see Salvador, Braz.	G6	88
Bahia, state, Braz.	G4	88
Bahía, Islas de la, is., Hond.	D4	102
Bahía Blanca, Arg.	I6	92
Bahía Bustamante, Arg.	I3	90
Bahía de Cáraquez, Ec.	H1	86
Bahía Kino, Mex.	A3	100
Bahir Dar, Eth.	E7	62
Bahraich, India	E8	54
Bahrain, ctry., Asia	D7	56
Bahtīm, Egypt	H2	58
Bahušèusk, Bela.	F13	10
Bai, stm., China	A7	42
Bai, stm., China	E5	42
Baia de Aramă, Rom.	E9	26
Baia di Terra Nova, sci., Ant.	C21	81
Baia Farta, Ang.	C1	68
Baia Mare, Rom.	B10	26
Baião, Braz.	B1	88
Baicheng, China	F14	32
Baicheng, China	B9	36
Baidoa see Baydhabo, Som.	D8	66
Baie-Comeau, Qc., Can.	A8	110
Baie-Saint-Paul, Qc., Can.	C6	110
Baie-Trinité, Qc., Can.	A9	110
Baie Verte, Nf., Can.	j22	107a
Baihe, China	B11	46
Baijnāth, India	D7	54
Baikal, Lake see Bajkal, ozero, l., Russia	F10	34
Baikal Mountains see Bajkal'skij hrebet, mts., Russia	F10	34
Baikonur see Bayqongyr, Kaz.	E11	32
Bailadores, Ven.	C6	86
Baile Átha Cliath see Dublin, Ire.	H6	12
Baile Átha Luain see Athlone, Ire.	H4	12
Baile Govora, Rom.	D11	26
Bailén, Spain	F7	20
Băileşti, Rom.	F10	26
Bailey, N.C., U.S.	I7	114
Bail Hongal, India	D2	53
Bailicun, China	I4	42
Bailique, Ilha, i., Braz.	C8	84
Baillie Islands, is., N.T., Can.	B14	140
Baillif, Guad.	h5	105c
Bailong, stm., China	E1	42
Bailu Hu, l., China	G5	42
Bailundo, Ang.	C2	68
Baimamiao, China	C2	42
Baima Shan, mtn., China	F5	36
Bainang, Pap. N. Gui.	b3	79a
Bainbridge, Ga., U.S.	G14	122
Bainbridge, N.Y., U.S.	B10	114
Bain-de-Bretagne, Fr.	G7	14
Baing, China	I12	50
Bainville, Mt., U.S.	F9	124
Baiona, Spain	B2	20
Baird, Tx., U.S.	B8	130
Baird Mountains, mts., Ak., U.S.	C7	140
Baird Peninsula, pen., Nu., Can.	B15	106
Bairiki, Kir.	C8	72
Bairin Zuoqi, China	C8	36
Bairnsdale, Austl.	K6	76
Baïse, stm., Fr.	F6	18
Baisha, China	L3	42
Baisha, China	I3	42
Baisha, China	H7	42
Baishuijiang, China	E1	42
Baisogala, Lith.	E6	10
Baixiang, China	B6	42
Baixingt, China	I3	42
Baixio, Braz.	D6	88
Baiyan Shan, mtn., China	H8	42
Baiyin, China	D5	36
Baja, Hung.	C5	26
Baja, Punta, c., Chile	e29	78l
Baja California, state, Mex.	F5	98
Baja California, pen., Mex.	B2	96
Baja California Sur, state, Mex.	C2	100
Bajada del Agrio, Arg.	I2	92
Baján, Mex.	H6	130
Bajan, Mong.	B7	36
Bajangol, Russia	F10	34
Bajanhongor, Mong.	C3	36
Bajawa, Indon.	H12	50
Bajestan, Iran	C8	56
Bajkal, Russia	F9	34
Bajkal, ozero (Baikal, Lake), l., Russia	F10	34
Bajkal'skij hrebet, mts., Russia	F10	34
Bajkit, Russia	B17	32
Bajkonur see Bayqongyr, Kaz.	E11	32
Bajmak, Russia	D9	32
Bajo Boquete, Pan.	H6	102
Bajool, Austl.	D8	76
Bajramaly, Turkmen.	B9	56
Bajsun, Uzb.	G11	32
Bakacak, Tur.	C10	28
Bakala, C.A.R.	C4	66
Bakel, Sen.	G2	64
Baker, Ca., U.S.	I9	134
Baker, La., U.S.	G7	122
Baker, Mt., U.S.	A8	126
Baker, Mount, vol., Wa., U.S.	B5	136
Baker Butte, mtn., Az., U.S.	I5	132
Baker City, Or., U.S.	F9	136
Baker Island, i., Oc.	C9	72
Baker Lake, l., Austl.	E5	74
Baker Lake, l., Nu., Can.	C11	106
Baker Lake, Nu., Can.	C11	106
Bakersfield, Ca., U.S.	H7	134
Bā Kêv, Camb.	F8	48
Bakhardok see Bakhardok, Turkmen.	B8	56
Bakhtīārī va Chahār Maḥall see Chahār Maḥall va Bakhtīārī, state, Iran	D7	56
Baki (Bākı), Azer.	A6	56
Baku see Bakı, Azer.	A6	56

Name	Map Ref.	Page
Bakumpai, Indon.	D8	50
Bakung, Pulau, i., Indon.	C4	50
Bakungan, Indon.	K3	48
Bakwanga see Mbuji-Mayi, D.R.C.	F4	66
Balâ, Tur.	D16	28
Balabac, Phil.	F1	52
Balabac Island, i., Phil.	G1	52
Balabac Strait, strt., Asia	G1	52
Ba'labakk, Leb.	D7	58
Balabalagan, Kepulauan, is., Indon.	E10	50
Balabanovo, Russia	E19	10
Balabio, Île, i., N. Cal.	m15	79d
Balad, Iraq	C5	56
Baladëk, Russia	F15	34
Bālāghāt, India	H8	54
Bālāghāt Range, mts., India	B3	53
Balagne, reg., Fr.	G14	18
Balaguer, Spain	C11	20
Balahna, Russia	H20	8
Balaikarangan, Indon.	C7	50
Balaisepuah, Indon.	C7	50
Balakirevo, Russia	D21	10
Balaklava, Austl.	J2	76
Balakovo, Russia	D7	32
Balama, Moz.	C6	68
Balambangan, Pulau, i., Malay.	G1	52
Bālā Morghāb, Afg.	B9	56
Balanga, Phil.	C3	52
Balāngīr, India	H9	54
Balapulang, Indon.	G6	50
Balarāmpur, India	G11	54
Balašiha, Russia	E20	10
Balašov, Russia	D6	32
Balassagyarmat, Hung.	A6	26
Balatina, Mol.	B14	26
Balaton, Mn., U.S.	G3	118
Balaton, l., Hung.	C4	26
Balayan, Phil.	D3	52
Balbieriškis, Lith.	F6	10
Balbina, Represa, res., Braz.	H12	86
Balcanoona, Austl.	H2	76
Balcarce, Arg.	H8	92
Balcarres, Sk., Can.	D10	124
Bălcești, Rom.	E10	26
Balcones Escarpment, clf., Tx., U.S.	D9	130
Balde, Arg.	F4	92
Bald Knob, Ar., U.S.	B7	122
Bald Knob, mtn., Va., U.S.	G6	114
Bald Mountain, mtn., Or., U.S.	G5	136
Bald Mountain, mtn., Or., U.S.	F3	136
Baldock Lake, l., Mb., Can.	D11	106
Baldone, Lat.	D7	10
Baldwin, La., U.S.	H7	122
Baldwin, Mi., U.S.	E4	112
Baldwin, Wi., U.S.	G6	118
Baldwinsville, N.Y., U.S.	E13	112
Baldwyn, Ms., U.S.	C10	122
Baldy Mountain, mtn., Mb., Can.	C13	124
Baldy Mountain, mtn., N.M., U.S.	E3	128
Baldy Peak, mtn., Az., U.S.	J7	132
Bâle see Basel, Switz.	C4	22
Baleares see Balears, state, Spain	E13	20
Baleares, Islas see Balears, Illes, is., Spain	E12	20
Balearic Islands see Balears, state, Spain	E13	20
Balearic Islands see Balears, Illes, is., Spain	E12	20
Balears, state, Spain	E13	20
Balears, Illes (Balearic Islands), is., Spain	E12	20
Balease, Gunung, mtn., Indon.	E12	50
Baleh, stm., Malay.	C8	50
Baleia, Ponta da, c., Braz.	I6	88
Baleine, stm., Qc., Can.	D17	106
Baleine, Grande rivière de la, stm., Qc., Can.	D15	106
Baleine, Petite rivière de la, stm., Qc., Can.	D15	106
Balej, Russia	F12	34
Baler, Phil.	C3	52
Baler Bay, b., Phil.	C3	52
Bāleshwar, India	H11	54
Balezino, Russia	C8	32
Balfate, Hond.	E4	102
Balfour, N.C., U.S.	A3	116
Balgazyn, Russia	D17	32
Balhaš, ozero see Balqash köli, l., Kaz.	E13	32
Bāli, India	F4	54
Bali, state, Indon.	G9	50
Bali, i., Indon.	G9	50
Bali, Laut (Bali Sea), s., Indon.	G9	50
Bali, Selat, strt., Indon.	H9	50
Bali Barat National Park, p.o.i., Indon.	H9	50
Baliceaux, i., St. Vin.	p11	105e
Balige, Indon.	B1	50
Balıkesir, Tur.	D10	28
Balıkesir, state, Tur.	D10	28
Balīkh, stm., Syria	B10	58
Balikpapan, Indon.	D10	50
Balimbing, Indon.	F4	50
Balimbing, Phil.	H2	52
Balimo, Pap. N. Gui.	b3	79a
Balingen, Ger.	H4	16
Balingian, Malay.	B8	50
Balintang Channel, strt., Phil.	K9	42
Bali Sea see Bali, Laut, s., Indon.	G9	50
Bali Strait see Bali, Selat, strt., Indon.	H9	50
Baliza, Braz.	G7	84
Balkan Mountains, mts., Eur.	G11	26
Balkan Peninsula, pen., Eur.	B6	28
Balkaria see Kabardino-Balkarija, state, Russia	F6	32
Balkh, Afg.	B10	56
Balkhash, Lake see Balqash köli, l., Kaz.	E13	32
Ballachulish, Scot., U.K.	E7	12
Balladonia, Austl.	F4	74
Ballālpur, India	B4	53
Ballangen, Nor.	B7	8
Ballantine, Mt., U.S.	B4	126
Ballarat, Austl.	K4	76
Ballard, Lake, l., Austl.	E4	74
Ballater, Scot., U.K.	D9	12
Ball Bay, b., Norf. I.	y25	78i
Ballenas, Bahía de, b., Mex.	B2	100
Ballenita, Punta, c., Chile	B2	92
Balleny Islands, is., Ant.	B21	81
Balleza, Mex.	B5	100
Balleza, stm., Mex.	B5	100
Ball Ground, Ga., U.S.	B1	116
Ballia, India	F10	54
Ballina, Austl.	G9	76
Ballina, Ire.	G3	12
Ballina, Ire.	I4	12
Ballinrobe, Ire.	H3	12
Ballston Spa, N.Y., U.S.	G2	110
Ballville, Oh., U.S.	C2	114
Ballybunnion, Ire.	I3	12
Ballyhaunis, Ire.	H4	12
Ballymena, N. Ire., U.K.	G6	12
Ballymoney, N. Ire., U.K.	F6	12
Ballyrogan, Lake, l., Austl.	I6	76
Balmaceda, Chile	I2	90
Balmoral, Austl.	K3	76
Balmorhea, Tx., U.S.	C4	130
Balnearia, Arg.	E6	92
Baloda Bāzār, India	H9	54
Balombo, Ang.	C1	68
Balong, Indon.	G7	50
Balonne, stm., Austl.	G7	76
Bālotra, India	F4	54
Balphakram National Park, p.o.i., India	F13	54
Balqash köli (Balkhash, Lake), l., Kaz.	E13	32
Balrāmpur, India	E8	54
Balranald, Austl.	J4	76
Balș, Rom.	E11	26
Balsam Lake, Wi., U.S.	F6	118
Balsam Lake, l., On., Can.	D11	112
Balsas, Braz.	D2	88
Balsas, stm., Braz.	F2	88
Balsas, stm., Braz.	D3	88
Balsas, stm., Mex.	F8	100
Balsas, stm., Pan.	C3	86
Balsthal, Switz.	C4	22
Balta, Ukr.	B16	26
Baltasar Brum, Ur.	E9	92
Bălți, Mol.	B14	26
Baltic Sea, s., Eur.	D12	6
Baltijsk, Russia	F2	10
Baltijskaja kosa, spit, Eur.	F2	10
Baltijskoje more see Baltic Sea, s., Eur.	D12	6
Baltim, Egypt	G2	58
Baltimore, Ire.	J3	12
Baltimore, Md., U.S.	E9	114
Baltimore, Oh., U.S.	E3	114
Ba Lu, stm., Viet.	E9	48
Baluchistān, state, Pak.	C2	54
Baluchistan, hist. reg., Asia	D9	56
Balui, stm., Malay.	B8	50
Bālurghāt, India	F12	54
Balvi, Lat.	C10	10
Balygyčan, Russia	D19	34
Balyqshy, Kaz.	E8	32
Balzac, Ab., Can.	E16	138
Balzar, Ec.	H2	86
Bam, Iran	D8	56
Bama, China	I2	42
Bama, Nig.	G7	64
Bamaga, Austl.	B8	74
Bamako, Mali	G3	64
Bamba, Mali	F4	64
Bambamarca, Peru	E2	84
Bambana, stm., Nic.	F6	102
Bambari, C.A.R.	C4	66
Bambaroo, Austl.	B6	76
Bamberg, Ger.	G6	16
Bamberg, S.C., U.S.	C4	116
Bambio, C.A.R.	D3	66
Bambuí, Braz.	K2	88
Bam Co, l., China	C13	54
Bamenda, Cam.	C1	66
Bami, Turkmen.	B8	56
Bāmīān, Afg.	C10	56
Bamingui, C.A.R.	C4	66
Bampūr, Iran	D9	56
Bāmra Hills, hills, India	H10	54
Bamumo, China	B14	54
Banaba, i., Kir.	D7	72
Banabuiú, stm., Braz.	C6	88
Banabuiú, Açude, l., Braz.	C6	88
Banalia, D.R.C.	D5	66
Banamba, Mali	G3	64
Banana Islands, is., S.L.	H2	64
Bananal, stm., Braz.	E1	88
Bananal, Ilha do, i., Braz.	F7	84
Banarlı, Tur.	B10	28
Banās, stm., India	E6	54
Banâs, Râs, c., Egypt	C7	62
Banat, hist. reg., Eur.	D7	26
Banaz, Tur.	E12	28
Ban Ban, Laos	C6	48
Ban Bouang-nom, Laos	E8	48
Banbridge, N. Ire., U.K.	G6	12
Ban Bung Na Rang, Thai.	D5	48
Banbury, Eng., U.K.	I11	12
Ban Cha La, Laos	D7	48
Bancroft, On., Can.	C12	112
Bancroft, Ia., U.S.	H4	118
Bancroft, Id., U.S.	H15	136
Bancroft, Ne., U.S.	C1	120
Bānda, India	F8	54
Banda, Kepulauan, is., Indon.	F9	44
Banda, Laut (Banda Sea), s., Indon.	G8	44
Banda Aceh, Indon.	J2	48
Bānda Dāūd Shāh, Pak.	B3	54
Banda del Río Salí, Arg.	C5	92
Bandai-Asahi-kokuritsu-kōen, p.o.i., Japan	B12	40
Bandai-san, vol., Japan	B13	40
Bandama, stm., C. Iv.	H3	64
Bandama Blanc, stm., C. Iv.	H3	64
Ban Dan, Thai.	E7	48
Ban Dangtai, Laos	D7	48
Bandar Beheshtī, Iran	D9	56
Bandarbeyla, Som.	C10	66
Bandar-e 'Abbās, Iran	D8	56
Bandar-e Anzalī, Iran	B6	56
Bandar-e Būshehr, Iran	D7	56
Bandar-e Deylam, Iran	D7	56
Bandar-e Lengeh, Iran	D7	56
Bandar-e Māh Shahr, Iran	C6	56
Bandar-e Moghūyeh, Iran	D7	56
Bandar-e Torkeman, Iran	B7	56
Bandar Lampung, Indon.	F4	50
Bandar Seri Begawan, Bru.	A9	50
Banda Sea see Banda, Laut, s., Indon.	G8	44
Bandeira, Pico da, mtn., Braz.	K5	88
Bandeirantes, Braz.	F7	84
Bandelier National Monument, p.o.i., N.M., U.S.	F2	128
Bandera, Arg.	D6	92
Bandera, Alto, mtn., Dom. Rep.	C12	102
Banderas, Mex.	C2	130
Banderas, Bahía de, b., Mex.	E6	100
Bandhavgarh National Park, p.o.i., India	G8	54
Bāndhi, Pak.	E2	54
Bandiagara, Mali	G4	64
Bandiantaolehai, China	C5	36
Bāndīkūi, India	E6	54
Bandipura, India	A5	54
Bandipur Tiger Reserve, India	F3	53
Bandırma, Tur.	C11	28
Bandon, Or., U.S.	G2	136
Ban Don, Ao, b., Thai.	H4	48
Ban Donhiang, Laos	C5	48
Bandundu, D.R.C.	E3	66
Bandung, Indon.	G5	50
Banes, Cuba	B10	102
Banff, Ab., Can.	E15	138
Banff, Scot., U.K.	D10	12
Banff National Park, p.o.i., Ab., Can.	E15	138
Banfora, Burkina	G4	64
Banga, D.R.C.	F4	66
Banga, India	C6	54
Banga, stm., Phil.	G5	52
Bangalore, India	E3	53
Bangaon, India	G12	54
Bangassou, C.A.R.	D4	66
Bangdag Co, l., China	A8	54
Banggai, Indon.	F7	44
Banggai, Kepulauan, is., Indon.	F7	44
Banggi, Pulau, i., Malay.	G1	52
Banggong Co, l., China	B7	54
Banghāzī (Bengasi), Libya	A3	62
Banghiang, stm., Laos	D7	48
Bangil, Indon.	G8	50
Bangka, Pulau, i., Indon.	E5	50
Bangka, Selat, strt., Indon.	E4	50
Bangkalan, Indon.	G8	50
Bangkaru, Pulau, i., Indon.	L3	48
Bangkinang, Indon.	C2	50
Bangkir, Indon.	C12	50
Bangko, Indon.	E3	50
Bangkog Co, l., China	C12	54
Bangkok see Krung Thep, Thai.	F5	48
Bangladesh, ctry., Asia	G13	54
Bang Lamung, Thai.	F5	48
Bang Mun Nak, Thai.	D5	48
Bangor, N. Ire., U.K.	G7	12
Bangor, Wales, U.K.	H8	12
Bangor, Me., U.S.	F8	110
Bangor, Pa., U.S.	D10	114
Bangriposi, India	G11	54
Bangs, Tx., U.S.	C8	130
Bangs, Mount, mtn., Az., U.S.	G3	132
Bang Saphan, Thai.	G4	48
Bangued, Phil.	B3	52
Bangui, C.A.R.	D3	66
Bangweulu, Lake, l., Zam.	C4	68
Bangweulu Swamps, sw., Zam.	C5	68
Bangxu, China	J2	42
Ban Hatgnao, Laos	E8	48
Ban Hèt, Laos	E8	48
Ban Hom, Thai.	E4	48
Ban Hong Muang, Laos	D7	48
Ban Houayxay, Laos	B5	48
Bani, C.A.R.	C4	66
Baní, Dom. Rep.	C12	102
Bani, Jbel, mts., Mor.	D3	64
Baniara, Pap. N. Gui.	b4	79a
Bani Bangou, Niger	F5	64
Banihāl Pass, p., India	B4	46
Banī Walīd, Libya	A2	62
Bāniyās, Golan	E6	58
Bāniyās, Syria	C6	58
Banja Luka, Bos.	E4	26
Banjarmasin, Indon.	E9	50
Banjul (Bathurst), Gam.	G1	64
Bānka, India	F11	54
Banka Banka, Austl.	C6	74
Ban Katèp, Laos	D7	48
Ban Kèngkabao, Laos	D7	48
Ban Kèngtangan, Laos	D7	48
Ban Kheun, Laos	B5	48
Ban Khuan Mao, Thai.	I4	48
Ban Kruat, Thai.	E6	48
Banks, Al., U.S.	F13	122
Banks, Îles (Banks Islands), is., Vanuatu	i16	79d
Banks Island, i., B.C., Can.	E4	106
Banks Island, i., N.T., Can.	B15	140
Banks Islands see Banks, Îles, is., Vanuatu	i16	79d
Banks Lake, res., Wa., U.S.	C7	136
Banks Peninsula, pen., N.Z.	F5	80
Banks Strait, strt., Austl.	n13	77a
Banks / Torres, state, Vanuatu	i16	79d
Bānkura, India	G11	54
Ban Mae La Luang, Thai.	C3	48
Ban Mit, Laos	C5	48
Ban Muangngat, Laos	C6	48
Bann, stm., N. Ire., U.K.	F6	12
Ban Nadou, Laos	E7	48
Ban Nahin, Laos	C7	48
Ban Nalan, Laos	E7	48
Ban Nam Chan, Thai.	C6	48
Ban Namnga, Laos	B6	48
Ban Nam Thaeng, Thai.	E7	48
Ban Naxouang, Laos	C7	48
Bannertown, N.C., U.S.	H5	114
Banning, Ca., U.S.	J9	134
Ban Nong Lumphuk, Thai.	E6	48
Bannu, Pak.	B3	54
Bañolas see Banyoles, Spain	B13	20
Baños, Ec.	H2	86
Banow, Afg.	B10	56
Ban Pak Bong, Thai.	C4	48
Ban Pakkhop, Laos	C5	48
Ban Pak Nam, Thai.	G4	48
Ban Phai, Thai.	D6	48
Ban Phai, Thai.	D6	48
Ban Pho, Thai.	F5	48
Ban Phông Pho, Laos	E7	48
Ban Pong, Thai.	F4	48
Ban Sa-ang, Laos	D7	48
Ban Salik, Thai.	C5	48
Ban Sam Pong, Laos	C6	48
Ban Samrong, Thai.	E6	48
Bānsda, India	H4	54
Banshadhāra, stm., India	B6	53
Banská Bystrica, Slov.	H15	16
Banská Štiavnica, Slov.	H14	16
Bansko, Blg.	H10	26
Ban Songkhon, Laos	C7	48
Bānswāra, India	G5	54
Bantaeng, Indon.	F11	50
Ban Takhlo, Thai.	E5	48
Bantarkawung, Indon.	G6	50
Bantayan, Phil.	E4	52
Ban Thabôk, Laos	C6	48
Ban Thapayi, Laos	D7	48
Ban Tian Sa, Laos	C6	48
Bantry, Ire.	J3	12
Bantry Bay, b., Ire.	J3	12
Ban Van Hom, Laos	C7	48
Ban Xènkhalôk, Laos	C5	48
Banya, Testa de la, c., Spain	D11	20
Banyak, Kepulauan, is., Indon.	K3	48
Ban Ya Plong, Thai.	H4	48
Banyo, Cam.	C2	66
Banyoles, Spain	B13	20
Banyuwangi, Indon.	H9	50
Banzare Coast, cst., Ant.	B17	81
Baode, China	B4	42
Baoding, China	B6	42
Baofeng, China	E5	42
Bao Ha, Viet.	A7	48
Baoji, China	D2	42
Baojing, China	G3	42
Bao Lac, Viet.	G8	48
Bao Lac, Viet.	A7	48
Baolunyuan, China	E1	42
Baoqing, China	B11	36
Baoshan, China	F4	36
Baoting, China	L3	42
Baotou, China	A4	42
Baoulé, stm., Mali	G3	64
Baowei, China	A8	48
Baoyi, China	E7	42
Baoying, China	E8	42
Bāpatla, India	D5	53
Bapaume, Fr.	D11	14
Baptiste Lake, res., On., Can.	C12	112
Bāqa el Gharbiyya, Isr.	F6	58
Baqanas, Kaz.	F13	32
Baqing, China	B14	54
Baqty, Kaz.	E14	32
Ba'qūbah, Iraq	C5	56
Baquedano, Chile	A3	92
Bar, Mont.	G6	26
Bara, Nig.	G7	64
Baraawe, Som.	D8	66
Barabinsk, Russia	C13	32
Barabinskaja step', pl., Russia	C13	32
Baraboo, Wi., U.S.	H9	118
Baraboo, stm., Wi., U.S.	H8	118
Baracaldo see Barakaldo, Spain	A8	20
Baracoa, Cuba	B10	102
Baradero, Arg.	F8	92
Baradine, Austl.	H7	76
Baraga, Mi., U.S.	B1	112
Bārah, Sudan	E6	62
Barahona, Dom. Rep.	C12	102
Barak, Tur.	B8	58
Barāk, stm., India	F14	54
Barakaldo, Spain	A8	20
Barakī Barak, Afg.	B2	54
Barakula, Austl.	F8	76
Baralaba, Austl.	E7	76
Baram, stm., Malay.	A9	50
Barama, stm., Guy.	D12	86
Bārāmati, India	B2	53
Bāramūla, India	A5	54
Baran', Bela.	F13	10
Bārān, India	F6	54
Baranagar, India	G12	54
Baranavičy, Bela.	G9	10
Barangbarang, Indon.	G12	50
Baranoa, Col.	B4	86
Baranof Island, i., Ak., U.S.	E12	140
Barany, Russia	C12	10
Baranya, state, Hung.	D5	26
Barão de Grajaú, Braz.	D4	88
Barão de Melgaço, Braz.	G6	84
Barão de Tromaí, Braz.	A3	88
Baraški, Russia	D24	8
Barataria, La., U.S.	H8	122
Barataria Bay, b., La., U.S.	H8	122
Barat Daya, Kepulauan (Barat Daya Islands), is., Indon.	G8	44
Barat Daya Islands see Barat Daya, Kepulauan, is., Indon.	G8	44
Barauana, stm., Braz.	G11	86
Barauni, India	F10	54
Baraut, India	D6	54
Baraya, Col.	F4	86
Barbacena, Braz.	K4	88
Barbacoas, Col.	G2	86
Barbadillo del Mercado, Spain	B7	20
Barbados, ctry., N.A.	h16	96a
Barbalha, Braz.	D6	88
Barbar, Sudan	D6	62
Barbaria, Cap de, c., Spain	F12	20
Barbas, Cap, c., W. Sah.	E1	64
Barbaši, Russia	C11	10
Barbastro, Spain	B10	20
Barbate, Spain	H4	20
Barbeau Peak, mtn., Nu., Can.	A10	141
Barberena, Guat.	E2	102
Barberton, S. Afr.	D10	70
Barberton, Oh., U.S.	C4	114
Barbil, India	G10	54
Barbosa, Col.	E5	86
Barbuda, i., Antig.	e4	105b
Barby, Ger.	E7	16
Bârca, Rom.	F10	26
Barcaldine, Austl.	D5	76
Barcău (Berettyó), stm., Eur.	B8	26
Barcellona Pozzo di Gotto, Italy	F9	24
Barcelona, Mex.	B7	100
Barcelona, Spain	C13	20
Barcelona, Ven.	B9	86
Barcelona, co., Spain	C13	20
Barceloneta, P.R.	B2	104a
Barcelos, Braz.	H10	86
Barcelos, Port.	C2	20
Barcin, Pol.	D13	16
Barcoo, stm., Austl.	E4	76
Barczewo, Pol.	C16	16
Barda del Medio, Arg.	I3	92
Bardaï, Chad	C3	62
Bardawîl, Sabkhet el-, b., Egypt	G4	58
Barddhamān, India	G11	54
Bardejov, Slov.	G17	16
Bardeskan, Iran	B8	56
Bardīyah, Libya	A5	62
Bardo, Tun.	H4	24
Bārdoli, India	H4	54
Bardstown, Ky., U.S.	G12	120
Bardwell Lake, res., Tx., U.S.	E2	122
Bareilly, India	D7	54
Barentsburg, Nor.	B29	141
Barentsøya, i., Nor.	B30	141
Barents Sea, s., Eur.	B7	30
Bareta, India	D5	54
Barfleur, Fr.	E7	14
Bargaal, Som.	B10	66
Bargara, Austl.	E9	76
Bargarh, India	D5	46
Barguzin, stm., Russia	F11	34
Barguzinskij hrebet, mts., Russia	F11	34
Bar Harbor, Me., U.S.	F8	110
Barharwa, India	F11	54
Barhi, India	F10	54
Bāri, India	E6	54
Bari, Italy	C10	24
Baria, stm., Ven.	G8	86
Barī Gāv, Afg.	B1	54
Barigua, Salina de, pl., Ven.	p20	104g
Barillas, Guat.	E2	102
Barīm, i., Yemen	G5	56
Barima, stm., S.A.	C12	86
Barima-Waini, state, Guy.	D12	86
Barinas, P.R.	B2	104a
Barinas, Ven.	C6	86
Barinas, state, Ven.	C7	86
Baring, Cape, c., N.T., Can.	A7	106
Baringo, Lake, l., Kenya	D7	66
Bāripada, India	H11	54
Bariri, Braz.	L1	88
Bârîs, Egypt	C6	62
Bari Sādri, India	F5	54
Barisāl, Bngl.	G13	54
Barisāl, state, Bngl.	G13	54
Barisan, Pegunungan, mts., Indon.	E2	50
Barito, stm., Indon.	E9	50
Barjols, Fr.	F11	18
Barkam, China	E5	36
Barkava, Lat.	D9	10
Barkerville, B.C., Can.	C9	138
Bark Lake, l., On., Can.	C12	112
Barkley, Lake, res., U.S.	H10	120
Barkley Sound, strt., B.C., Can.	H5	138
Barkly East, S. Afr.	G8	70
Barkly Tableland, plat., Austl.	C7	74
Barkly West, S. Afr.	F7	70
Barkol, China	C3	36
Bârlad, Rom.	C14	26
Bârlad, stm., Rom.	D14	26
Bar-le-Duc, Fr.	F14	14
Barlee, Lake, l., Austl.	E3	74
Barletta, Italy	C10	24
Barlinek, Pol.	D11	16
Barling, Ar., U.S.	B4	122
Barlow, Ky., U.S.	G8	120
Barmedman, Austl.	J6	76
Bārmer, India	F3	54
Barmera, Austl.	J3	76
Barnagar, India	G5	54
Barnard Castle, Eng., U.K.	G11	12
Barnaul, Russia	D14	32
Barn Bluff, mtn., Austl.	n12	77a
Barnegat, N.J., U.S.	E11	114
Barnegat Bay, b., N.J., U.S.	E11	114
Barnes Ice Cap, ice, Nu., Can.	A16	106
Barnesville, Ga., U.S.	C1	116
Barnesville, Mn., U.S.	E2	118
Barnesville, Oh., U.S.	E4	114
Barneville-Carteret, Fr.	E7	14
Barnsdall, Ok., U.S.	E12	128
Barnsley, Eng., U.K.	H11	12
Barnstable, Ma., U.S.	C15	114
Barnstaple, Eng., U.K.	J8	12
Barnstaple Bay, b., Eng., U.K.	J8	12
Barnwell, Ab., Can.	G18	138
Barnwell, S.C., U.S.	C4	116
Baro, stm., Afr.	F7	62
Baron Bluff, clf., V.I.U.S.	g10	104c
Baron'ki, Bela.	G15	10
Barora Fa Island, i., Sol. Is.	d8	79b
Barora Ite Island, i., Sol. Is.	d8	79b
Baroua, Niger	G7	64
Barpeta, India	E13	54
Barqah (Cyrenaica), hist. reg., Libya	A4	62
Barques, Pointe aux, c., Mi., U.S.	D7	112
Barquisimeto, Ven.	B7	86
Barra, Braz.	F4	88
Barra, i., Scot., U.K.	D5	12
Barra, Ponta da, c., Moz.	C12	70
Barraba, Austl.	H8	76
Barra da Estiva, Braz.	G5	88
Barra del Colorado, C.R.	G6	102
Barra de Rio Grande, Nic.	F6	102
Barra do Corda, Braz.	C3	88
Barra do Cuanza, Ang.	B1	68
Barra do Garças, Braz.	G7	84
Barra do Mendes, Braz.	F4	88
Barra do Piraí, Braz.	L3	88
Barra do Ribeiro, Braz.	E12	92
Barra Falsa, Ponta da, c., Moz.	C12	70
Barra Mansa, Braz.	L3	88
Barranca, Peru	F2	84
Barrancabermeja, Col.	D4	86
Barrancas, Ven.	C10	86
Barrancas, Ven.	C7	86
Barrancas, stm., Arg.	H2	92
Barranco Azul, Mex.	E3	130
Barranco do Velho, Port.	G3	20
Barranqueras, Arg.	C8	92
Barranquilla, Col.	B4	86
Barranquitas, P.R.	B3	104a
Barras, Braz.	C4	88
Barre, Vt., U.S.	F4	110
Barreal, Arg.	E3	92
Barreiras, Braz.	G3	88
Barreirinha, Braz.	D6	84
Barreiro, Port.	F1	20
Barreiros, Braz.	E8	88
Barren, stm., Ky., U.S.	H11	120
Barren, Nosy, is., Madag.	D7	68
Barren Islands, is., Ak., U.S.	E9	140
Barren River Lake, res., Ky., U.S.	H11	120
Barretos, Braz.	K1	88
Barrhead, Ab., Can.	B16	138
Barrie, On., Can.	D10	112
Barrie Island, i., On., Can.	C7	112
Barrière, B.C., Can.	E10	138
Barrier Range, mts., Austl.	H3	76
Barrigada, Guam	j10	78c
Barrington, N.S., Can.	G11	110
Barrington Tops National Park, p.o.i., Austl.	I8	76
Barringun, Austl.	G5	76
Barrouallie, St. Vin.	o11	105e
Barrow, Arg.	I7	92
Barrow, Ak., U.S.	B8	140
Barrow, stm., Ire.	I5	12
Barrow, Point, c., Ak., U.S.	B8	140
Barrow Creek, Austl.	D6	74
Barrow-in-Furness, Eng., U.K.	G9	12
Barrow Island, i., Austl.	D2	74
Barrows, Mb., Can.	B12	124
Barrow Strait, strt., Nu., Can.	C6	141
Barry, Wales, U.K.	J9	12
Barry, Il., U.S.	E6	120
Barryton, Mi., U.S.	E4	112
Barsalpur, India	D4	54
Bārsi, India	B2	53
Barsinghausen, Ger.	D5	16
Barstow, Ca., U.S.	I8	134
Barstow, Tx., U.S.	C4	130
Bar-sur-Seine, Fr.	F13	14
Bartang, Taj.	B11	56
Barth, Ger.	B8	16
Barthélemy, Deo, p., Viet.	C6	48
Bartholomew, Bayou, stm., U.S.	E7	122
Bartibougou, Burkina	G5	64
Bartica, Guy.	B6	84
Bartın, Tur.	B15	28
Bartın, state, Tur.	B15	28
Bartle Frere, mtn., Austl.	A5	76
Bartlesville, Ok., U.S.	H2	120
Bartlett, N.H., U.S.	F5	110
Bartlett, Tn., U.S.	B9	122
Bartlett, Tx., U.S.	D10	130
Bartley, Ne., U.S.	A8	128
Barton, Vt., U.S.	F4	110
Bartoszyce, Pol.	B16	16
Bartow, Fl., U.S.	I4	116
Bartow, Ga., U.S.	D3	116
Barú, Volcán, vol., Pan.	H6	102
Bārūk, Jabal al-, mtn., Leb.	E6	58
Barumini, Italy	E2	24
Barumun, stm., Indon.	C2	50
Barung, Nusa, i., Indon.	H8	50
Barus, Indon.	L4	48
Baruun-Urt, Mong.	B7	36
Barvas, Scot., U.K.	C6	12
Barview, Or., U.S.	G2	136
Barwāh, India	G5	54
Barwāni, India	H5	54
Barwick, Ga., U.S.	F2	116
Barwon, stm., Austl.	H6	76
Barybino, Russia	E20	10
Barycz, stm., Pol.	E13	16
Barysau, Bela.	F11	10
Basail, Arg.	C8	92
Basalt, stm., Austl.	B5	76
Basankusu, D.R.C.	D3	66
Basarabeasca, Mol.	C15	26
Basatongwula Shan, mtn., China	B13	54
Basavakalyān, India	C3	53
Basavilbaso, Arg.	F8	92
Bāsawul, Afg.	A3	54
Bascuñán, Cabo, c., Chile	D2	92
Basel (Bâle), Switz.	C4	22
Basella see Bassella, Spain	B12	20
Basey, Phil.	E5	52
Bashi Channel, strt., Asia	K9	42
Bashkortostan see Baškirija, state, Russia	D9	32
Basilan Island, i., Phil.	G4	52
Basilan Strait, strt., Phil.	G4	52
Basildon, Eng., U.K.	J13	12
Basile, La., U.S.	G6	122
Basilicata, state, Italy	D10	24
Basin, Mt., U.S.	D14	136
Basin, Wy., U.S.	C4	126
Basingstoke, Eng., U.K.	J11	12
Basin Lake, l., Sk., Can.	B8	124
Basīrhāt, India	G12	54
Baskahegan Lake, l., Me., U.S.	E8	110
Baskakovka, Russia	F17	10
Başkale, Tur.	B5	56
Baskatong, Réservoir, res., Qc., Can.	B13	112
Basket Lake, l., On., Can.	B6	118
Baškirija, state, Russia	D9	32
Baskomutan Milli Parkı, p.o.i., Tur.	E13	28
Basmat, India	B3	53
Bāsoda, India	G6	54
Basoko, D.R.C.	D4	66
Basora, Punt, c., Aruba	p20	104g
Basque Provinces see Euskal Herriko, state, Spain	A8	20
Basra see Al-Başrah, Iraq	C6	56
Bas-Rhin, state, Fr.	F16	14
Bassano, Ab., Can.	F18	138
Bassano del Grappa, Italy	E8	22
Bassari, Togo	H5	64
Bassas da India, rf., Reu.	E6	68
Bassein, stm., Mya.	D2	48
Bassella, Spain	B12	20
Basse Santa Su, Gam.	G2	64
Basse-Terre, Guad.	i5	105c
Basseterre, St. K./N.	C2	105a
Basse Terre, Trin.	s12	105f
Basse-Terre, i., Guad.	h5	105c
Bassett, Ne., U.S.	E13	126
Bassett, Va., U.S.	H6	114
Bassfield, Ms., U.S.	F9	122
Bassikounou, Maur.	F3	64
Bassila, Benin	H5	64
Bass River, N.S., Can.	E13	110
Bass Strait, strt., Austl.	L6	76
Basswood Lake, l., N.A.	C6	118
Båstad, Swe.	H5	8
Bastenaken see Bastogne, Bel.	D14	14
Bastersberge, hill, S. Afr.	G5	70
Basti, India	E9	54
Bastia, Fr.	G15	18
Bastogne, Bel.	D14	14
Bastrop, La., U.S.	E6	122
Bastrop, Tx., U.S.	D10	130
Basu, Pulau, i., Indon.	D3	50
Basutoland see Lesotho, ctry., Afr.	F9	70
Bata, Eq. Gui.	I6	64
Bataan Peninsula, pen., Phil.	C3	52
Batabanó, Golfo de, b., Cuba	A6	102
Batac, Phil.	A3	52
Batagaj, Russia	C15	34
Batagaj-Alyta, Russia	C15	34
Batak, Blg.	H11	26
Batala, India	C5	54
Batalha, Braz.	E7	88
Batalha, Port.	E2	20
Batam, Pulau, i., Indon.	C3	50
Batamaj, Russia	D14	34
Batang, China	E4	36
Batangafo, C.A.R.	C3	66
Batangas, Phil.	D3	52
Batangtoru, Indon.	C1	50
Batan Islands, is., Phil.	K9	42
Batanta, Pulau, i., Indon.	F9	44
Batatais, Braz.	K2	88
Batavia, Arg.	G5	92
Batavia see Jakarta, Indon.	G5	50
Batavia, Ia., U.S.	D5	120
Batavia, Il., U.S.	C9	120
Batavia, N.Y., U.S.	A7	114
Batchelor, Austl.	B6	74
Bătdâmbâng, Camb.	F6	48
Bateckij, Russia	B13	10
Batemans Bay, Austl.	J8	76
Bates, Mount, mtn., Norf. I.	y24	78i
Batesburg, S.C., U.S.	C4	116
Batesville, Ar., U.S.	B7	122
Batesville, Ms., U.S.	C9	122
Batesville, Tx., U.S.	F8	130
Bath, N.B., Can.	D9	110
Bath, Eng., U.K.	J10	12
Bath, Me., U.S.	G7	110
Bath, N.Y., U.S.	B8	114
Batha, stm., Chad	E3	62
Bathgate, N.D., U.S.	F16	124
Bathinda, India	C5	54
Bathsheba, Barb.	n8	105d
Bathurst, Austl.	I7	76
Bathurst, N.B., Can.	C11	110
Bathurst see Banjul, Gam.	G1	64
Bathurst, Cape, c., N.T., Can.	A5	106
Bathurst Inlet see Kingaok, Nu., Can.	B9	106
Bathurst Island, i., Austl.	B5	74
Bathurst Island, i., Nu., Can.	B5	141
Batlow, Austl.	J6	76
Batman, Tur.	B5	56
Batna, Alg.	B6	64
Ba To, Viet.	E9	48
Baton Rouge, La., U.S.	G7	122
Batouri, Cam.	D2	66
Batson, Tx., U.S.	G4	122
Batterie, Pointe de la, c., Mart.	k7	105c
Batticaloa, Sri L.	H5	53
Battipaglia, Italy	D8	24
Battle, stm., Can.	D19	138
Battle Creek, Mi., U.S.	F4	112
Battle Creek, Ne., U.S.	F15	126
Battle Creek, stm., N.A.	F4	124
Battle Ground, In., U.S.	H3	112
Battle Ground, Wa., U.S.	E4	136
Battle Harbour, Nf., Can.	i22	107a
Battle Mountain, Nv., U.S.	C8	134
Battle Mountain, mtn., Wy., U.S.	B9	132
Batu, mtn., Eth.	F7	62
Batu, Kepulauan, is., Indon.	F2	44
Batu-Batu, Indon.	F11	50
Batu Berincang, Gunong, mtn., Malay.	J5	48
Batubrok, Bukit, mtn., Indon.	C9	50
Batu Gajah, Malay.	J5	48
Batukelau, Indon.	C9	50
Batumi, Geor.	F6	32
Batu Pahat, Malay.	L6	48
Batupanjang, Indon.	C2	50
Baturaja, Indon.	F3	50
Baturino, Russia	C15	32
Baturité, Braz.	C6	88
Baturusa, Indon.	D5	50
Batusangkar, Indon.	D2	50
Batz, Île de, i., Fr.	F4	14
Bau, Malay.	C7	50
Baubau, Indon.	G7	44
Bauchi, Nig.	G6	64
Bauda, India	H10	54
Baudette, Mn., U.S.	C4	118
Baudó, stm., Col.	E3	86
Bauld, Cape, c., Nf., Can.	i22	107a
Bauman Fiord, b., Nu., Can.	B8	141
Baume-les-Dames, Fr.	G15	14
Baures, Bol.	B4	90
Bauru, Braz.	L1	88
Bauska, Lat.	D7	10
Bautzen, Ger.	E10	16
Bauxite, Ar., U.S.	C6	122
Bavaria see Bayern, state, Ger.	H7	16
Bavarian Alps, mts., Eur.	I7	16
Båven, l., Swe.	G7	8
Bavispe, Mex.	F8	98
Bavispe, stm., Mex.	F8	98
Bawang, Indon.	G6	50
Bawdwin, Mya.	A3	48
Bawean, Pulau, i., Indon.	F8	50
Bawiti, Egypt	B5	62
Bawmi, Mya.	D2	48
Baxaya, mtn., Som.	B9	66
Baxian, China	G2	42
Baxian, China	B7	42
Baxter, Ia., U.S.	C4	120
Baxter, Mn., U.S.	E4	118
Baxter, Tn., U.S.	H12	120
Baxterville, Ms., U.S.	F9	122
Bay, Ar., U.S.	B8	122
Bay, Laguna de, l., Phil.	C3	52
Bayamo, Cuba	B9	102
Bayamón, P.R.	B3	104a
Bayan, China	A7	38
Bayan, Indon.	H10	50
Bayāna, India	E6	54
Bayanaūyl, Kaz.	D13	32
Bayan Har Shan, mts., China	E4	36
Bayanhongor, Mong.	B5	36
Bayannaobao, China	B2	42
Bayano, Lago, res., Pan.	H8	102

Name	Map Ref.	Page
Bayan Obo, China	C7	36
Bayard, Ia., U.S.	C3	120
Bayard, N.M., U.S.	K8	132
Bayard, W.V., U.S.	E6	114
Bayawan, Phil.	F4	52
Baybay, Phil.	E5	52
Bayboro, N.C., U.S.	A9	116
Bayburt, Tur.	A5	56
Bay City, Mi., U.S.	E6	112
Bay City, Or., U.S.	E3	136
Bay City, Tx., U.S.	F12	130
Baydhabo (Baidoa), Som.	D8	66
Baydrag, stm., Mong.	B4	36
Bayern (Bavaria), state, Ger.	H7	16
Bayeux, Braz.	D8	88
Bayeux, Fr.	E8	14
Bayfield, Co., U.S.	F9	132
Bayfield, Wi., U.S.	E8	118
Bayındır, Tur.	E10	28
Bayjī, Iraq	C5	56
Baykonur see Bayqongyr, Kaz.	E11	32
Bay Minette, Al., U.S.	G11	122
Bayombong, Phil.	B3	52
Bayona see Baiona, Spain	B2	20
Bayonne, Fr.	F4	18
Bayou Bodcau Reservoir, res., La., U.S.	E5	122
Bayou Cane, La., U.S.	H8	122
Bayou D'Arbonne Lake, res., La., U.S.	E6	122
Bayovar, Peru	E1	84
Bay Port, Mi., U.S.	E6	112
Bayport, Mn., U.S.	F6	118
Bayqongyr, Kaz.	E11	32
Bayramiç, Tur.	D9	28
Bayreuth, Ger.	G7	16
Bayrūt (Beirut), Leb.	E6	58
Bays, Lake of, l., On., Can.	C10	112
Bay Saint Louis, Ms., U.S.	G9	122
Bay Shore, N.Y., U.S.	D12	114
Bayside, On., Can.	D12	112
Bay Springs Lake, res., Ms., U.S.	C10	122
Bayt ad-Dīn, Leb.	E6	58
Bayt al-Faqīh, Yemen	G5	56
Bayt Laḥm (Bethlehem), W.B.	G6	58
Baytown, Tx., U.S.	H4	122
Bayyā'īyah al-Kabīrah, Syria	C8	58
Baza, Spain	G8	20
Bazardüzü dağ, mtn., Azer.	A6	56
Bazaruto, Ilha do, i., Moz.	B12	70
Bazhong, China	F2	42
Bazièege, Fr.	F7	18
Bazine, Ks., U.S.	C9	128
Be, stm., Viet.	G8	48
Be, Nosy, i., Madag.	C8	68
Beach Haven, N.J., U.S.	E11	114
Beachport, Austl.	K3	76
Beachville, On., Can.	E9	112
Beachy Head, c., Eng., U.K.	K13	12
Beacon, Austl.	F3	74
Beacon, N.Y., U.S.	C12	114
Beacon Hill, Wa., U.S.	D3	136
Beaconsfield, Austl.	n13	77a
Beagle Gulf, b., Austl.	B5	74
Bealanana, Madag.	C8	68
Bealdoaivi see Peäldoajvi, mtn., Fin.	B12	8
Beale, Cape, c., B.C., Can.	H5	138
Beals Creek, stm., Tx., U.S.	B7	130
Bear, stm., Ca., U.S.	D4	134
Bear, stm., U.S.	I14	136
Bear Bay, b., Nu., Can.	B8	141
Bear Creek, stm., U.S.	C10	122
Bear Creek, stm., U.S.	D6	128
Bearden, Ar., U.S.	D6	122
Beardmore, On., Can.	B11	118
Bear Island, i., Ant.	C29	81
Bear Island, i., Ire.	J3	12
Bear Island see Bjørnøya, i., Nor.	B5	30
Bear Lake, l., Ab., Can.	A11	138
Bear Lake, l., U.S.	A5	132
Bear Mountain, mtn., Or., U.S.	G3	136
Béarn, hist. reg., Fr.	F5	18
Bear River, N.S., Can.	F11	110
Bear River Range, mts., U.S.	B5	132
Beartooth Pass, p., Wy., U.S.	C3	126
Bear Town, Ms., U.S.	F8	122
Beās, stm., India	C6	54
Beasain, Spain	A8	20
Beata, Cabo, c., Dom. Rep.	D12	102
Beata, Isla, i., Dom. Rep.	D12	102
Beaton, B.C., Can.	F13	138
Beatrice, Al., U.S.	F11	122
Beatrice, Ne., U.S.	A12	128
Beatrice, Cape, c., Austl.	B7	74
Beattie, Ks., U.S.	L2	118
Beatton, stm., B.C., Can.	D6	106
Beatty, Nv., U.S.	G9	134
Beattyville, Ky., U.S.	G2	114
Beaucaire, Fr.	F10	18
Beauce, reg., Fr.	F10	14
Beauceville, Qc., Can.	D6	110
Beauchêne, Lac, l., Qc., Can.	B11	112
Beauchêne Island, i., Falk. Is.	J5	90
Beaudesert, Austl.	F9	76
Beaufort, Malay.	A9	50
Beaufort, S.C., U.S.	D5	116
Beaufort Castle see Qal'at ash-Shaqīf, sci., Leb.	E6	58
Beaufort Sea, s., N.A.	B12	140
Beaufort West, S. Afr.	H6	70
Beaugency, Fr.	G10	14
Beauharnois, Qc., Can.	E2	110
Beaujolais, hist. reg., Fr.	C10	18
Beaumont, Fr.	E7	14
Beaumont, N.Z.	G3	80
Beaumont, Ca., U.S.	J8	134
Beaumont, Ms., U.S.	F9	122
Beaumont, Tx., U.S.	G4	122
Beaumont Hill, hill, Austl.	H5	76
Beaune, Fr.	G13	14
Beauport, Qc., Can.	D5	110
Beaupré, Qc., Can.	C6	110
Beaurepaire, Fr.	D11	18
Beausejour, Mb., Can.	D17	124
Beauséjour, Guad.	h6	105c
Beauvais, Fr.	E11	14
Beauvoir-sur-Mer, Fr.	H6	14
Beaver, Ak., U.S.	C10	140
Beaver, Ok., U.S.	E8	128
Beaver, Pa., U.S.	D5	114
Beaver, Ut., U.S.	E4	132
Beaver, stm., Can.	C6	106
Beaver, stm., Can.	D9	106
Beaver, stm., Ut., U.S.	E3	132
Beaver, stm., U.S.	E9	128
Beaver Creek, stm., Co., U.S.	G9	126
Beaver Creek, stm., Mt., U.S.	F6	124
Beaver Creek, stm., Ne., U.S.	G14	126
Beaver Creek, stm., Ne., U.S.	F14	126
Beaver Creek, stm., Ok., U.S.	G10	128
Beaver Creek, stm., Tx., U.S.	H9	128
Beaver Creek, stm., U.S.	A8	128
Beaver Creek, stm., U.S.	G9	124
Beaver Creek, stm., U.S.	D8	126
Beaver Crossing, Ne., U.S.	G15	126
Beaver Dam, Ky., U.S.	G11	120
Beaver Dam, Wi., U.S.	H9	118
Beaverdell, B.C., Can.	G11	138
Beaver Falls, Pa., U.S.	D5	114
Beaverhead, stm., Mt., U.S.	E14	136
Beaverhead Mountains, mts., U.S.	E13	136
Beaverhill Lake, l., Ab., Can.	C18	138
Beaverhouse Lake, l., On., Can.	C6	118
Beaver Island, i., Mi., U.S.	C4	112
Beaver Lake, l., Ab., Can.	B19	138
Beaver Lake, res., Ar., U.S.	H4	120
Beaverlodge, Ab., Can.	A11	138
Beaverton, On., Can.	D10	112
Beaverton, Mi., U.S.	E5	112
Beaverton, Or., U.S.	E4	136
Beāwar, India	E5	54
Beazley, Arg.	F4	92
Bebedouro, Braz.	K1	88
Becal, Mex.	B2	102
Bécancour, stm., Qc., Can.	D5	110
Beccles, Eng., U.K.	I14	12
Bečej, Serb.	D6	26
Beceni, Rom.	D13	26
Bečevinka, Russia	G17	8
Béchar, Alg.	C4	64
Becharof Lake, l., Ak., U.S.	E8	140
Bechevin Bay, b., Ak., U.S.	E7	140
Bechuanaland see Botswana, ctry., Afr.	E3	68
Bechuanaland, hist. reg., S. Afr.	E5	70
Bechyně, Czech Rep.	G10	16
Beckley, W.V., U.S.	G4	114
Beckum, Ger.	E4	16
Bédarieux, Fr.	F9	18
Bedelē, Eth.	F7	62
Bedford, Qc., Can.	E4	110
Bedford, S. Afr.	H8	70
Bedford, Eng., U.K.	I12	12
Bedford, Ia., U.S.	D3	120
Bedford, In., U.S.	F11	120
Bedford, Ky., U.S.	F12	120
Bedford, Pa., U.S.	D7	114
Bedford, Tx., U.S.	B10	130
Bedi, India	G3	54
Bedoba, Russia	C17	32
Bedourie, Austl.	E2	76
Bedworth, Eng., U.K.	I11	12
Beebe, Ar., U.S.	B7	122
Beechal Creek, stm., Austl.	F5	76
Beech Creek, Ky., U.S.	G10	120
Beech Fork, stm., Ky., U.S.	G12	120
Beech Grove, In., U.S.	I3	112
Beechworth, Austl.	K6	76
Beechy, Sk., Can.	D6	124
Beecroft Head, c., Austl.	J8	76
Beemer, Ne., U.S.	J2	118
Beenleigh, Austl.	F9	76
Bee Ridge, Fl., U.S.	I3	116
Beersheba see Be'ér Sheva', Isr.	G6	58
Beersheba Springs, Tn., U.S.	B13	122
Be'ér Sheva'(Beersheba), Isr.	G6	58
Beeskow, Ger.	D10	16
Beeville, Tx., U.S.	F10	130
Befale, D.R.C.	D4	66
Befandriana Avaratra, Madag.	E7	68
Bega, Austl.	K7	76
Bega, stm., Eur.	D9	26
Begamganj, India	G7	54
Begur, Cap de, c., Spain	C14	20
Begusarai, India	F11	54
Behbahān, Iran	C7	56
Behshahr, Iran	B7	56
Bei, stm., China	J5	42
Bei'an, China	B10	36
Beibei, China	G2	42
Beicheng, China	G5	36
Beigi, Eth.	F6	62
Beihai, China	K3	42
Beijing (Peking), China	B7	42
Beijing, state, China	B6	42
Beili, China	L3	42
Beiliu, China	J4	42
Beinamar, Chad	F3	62
Beipa, Pap. N. Gui.	b4	79a
Beipan, stm., China	I1	42
Beipiao, China	D4	38
Beira, Moz.	A12	70
Beira, hist. reg., Port.	E3	20
Beiru, stm., China	D5	42
Beirut see Bayrūt, Leb.	E6	58
Beiseker, Ab., Can.	E17	138
Beishan, China	I3	42
Bei Shan, mts., China	C4	36
Beitbridge, Zimb.	C10	70
Beizhen, China	D4	38
Beja, Port.	G3	20
Béja, Tun.	H3	24
Beja, state, Port.	G3	20
Bejaïa, Alg.	B6	64
Béjar, Spain	D5	20
Bejhi, stm., Pak.	D2	54
Bejuco, Pan.	H8	102
Bekaa Valley see Al-Biqā', val., Leb.	D7	58
Bekabad, Uzb.	F11	32
Bekdaš, Turkmen.	A7	56
Békés, Hung.	C8	26
Békés, state, Hung.	C7	26
Békéscsaba, Hung.	C7	26
Bekilli, Tur.	E12	28
Bekily, Madag.	E8	68
Bekodoka, Madag.	D7	68
Bekopaka, Madag.	D7	68
Bela, India	F9	54
Bela, Pak.	D10	56
Belaazërsk, Bela.	H8	10
Bela Crkva, Serb.	E8	26
Belaga, Malay.	B8	50
Bel Air, Md., U.S.	E9	114
Belaja, stm., Russia	C8	32
Belaja Gora, Russia	B14	10
Belambanganumpu, Indon.	F4	50
Belampalli, India	B4	53
Bela Palanka, Serb.	F9	26
Belarus, ctry., Eur.	E14	6
Belaruskaja hrada, mts., Bela.	F10	10
Belau see Palau, ctry., Oc.	g8	78b
Bela Vista, Braz.	D5	90
Bela Vista, Moz.	E11	70
Belawan, Indon.	B1	50
Belayan, stm., Indon.	C10	50
Bełchatów, Pol.	E15	16
Belcher, La., U.S.	E5	122
Belcherāgh, Afg.	B10	56
Belcher Channel, strt., Nu., Can.	B6	141
Belcher Islands, is., Nu., Can.	D14	106
Belding, Mi., U.S.	E4	112
Belebelka, Russia	C13	10
Beledweyne, Som.	D8	66
Belém, Braz.	A1	88
Belém, Moz.	C6	68
Belém de São Francisco, Braz.	E6	88
Belén, Arg.	C4	92
Belén, Nic.	G4	102
Belén, Para.	D5	90
Belen, Tur.	B7	58
Belén, Ur.	E9	92
Belen, N.M., U.S.	I10	132
Belén, stm., Arg.	C4	92
Belep, Îles, is., N. Cal.	I14	79d
Belesar, Embalse de, res., Spain	B3	20
Belëv, Russia	G19	10
Belfast, S. Afr.	D9	70
Belfast, N. Ire., U.K.	G6	12
Belfast, Me., U.S.	F7	110
Belfield, N.D., U.S.	H10	124
Belford, Eng., U.K.	F11	12
Belfort, Fr.	G15	14
Belfry, Mt., U.S.	B3	126
Belgaum, India	D2	53
Belgium, ctry., Eur.	D13	14
Belgorod, Russia	D5	32
Belgrade, Mt., U.S.	E15	136
Belgrade, Ne., U.S.	F14	126
Belgrade see Beograd, Serb.	E7	26
Belgrano II, sci., Ant.	C36	81
Belhaven, N.C., U.S.	A9	116
Belick, Bela.	H13	10
Beliliou, i., Palau	D9	44
Belin, Fr.	E5	18
Belin-Béliet see Belin, Fr.	E5	18
Belington, W.V., U.S.	E5	114
Belinyu, Indon.	D4	50
Belitung, i., Indon.	E5	50
Belize, ctry., N.A.	D3	102
Belize, stm., Belize	D3	102
Belize City, Belize	D3	102
Belkovski, ostrov see Bel'kovskij, ostrov, i., Russia	A16	34
Bel'kovskij, ostrov, i., Russia	A16	34
Bella Bella, B.C., Can.	D2	138
Bellac, Fr.	C7	18
Bella Coola, B.C., Can.	D4	138
Bella Coola, stm., B.C., Can.	D4	138
Bellair, Fl., U.S.	F4	116
Bellaire, Oh., U.S.	D5	114
Bellaire, Tx., U.S.	H3	122
Bellamy, Al., U.S.	E10	122
Bellaria, Italy	F9	22
Bellary, India	D3	53
Bellata, Austl.	G7	76
Bella Unión, Ur.	E9	92
Bella Vista, Arg.	D8	92
Bella Vista, Arg.	C5	92
Bellavista, Peru	E2	84
Bellbrook, Austl.	H9	76
Belle, W.V., U.S.	F4	114
Bellefontaine, Mart.	k6	105c
Bellefontaine, Oh., U.S.	D2	114
Bellefonte, Pa., U.S.	D8	114
Belle Fourche, S.D., U.S.	C9	126
Belle Fourche, stm., U.S.	C10	126
Bellegarde-sur-Valserine, Fr.	C11	18
Belle Glade, Fl., U.S.	J5	116
Belle Hôtesse, mtn., Guad.	h5	105c
Belle-Île, i., Fr.	G5	14
Belle Isle, i., Nf., Can.	i22	107a
Belle Isle, Strait of, strt., Nf., Can.	i22	107a
Bellenden Ker National Park, p.o.i., Austl.	A5	76
Belle Plaine, Ia., U.S.	C5	120
Belle Plaine, Ks., U.S.	D11	128
Belle Plaine, Mn., U.S.	G5	118
Belleview, Fl., U.S.	G11	122
Belleville, On., Can.	D12	112
Belleville, Il., U.S.	F8	120
Belleville, Ks., U.S.	B11	128
Belleville, Pa., U.S.	D8	114
Belleville-sur-Saône, Fr.	C10	18
Bellevue, Ab., Can.	G16	138
Bellevue, Ia., U.S.	B7	120
Bellevue, Id., U.S.	G12	136
Bellevue, Mi., U.S.	F4	112
Bellevue, Ne., U.S.	C2	120
Bellevue, Oh., U.S.	C3	114
Bellevue, Wa., U.S.	C4	136
Belley, Fr.	D11	18
Bellingham, Mn., U.S.	F2	118
Bellingham, Wa., U.S.	B4	136
Bellinghausen, sci., Ant.	B35	81
Bellingshausen Sea, s., Ant.	P29	142
Bellinzona, Switz.	D6	22
Bell Lake, l., On., Can.	B7	118
Bellmead, Tx., U.S.	C10	130
Bello, Col.	D4	86
Bellot Strait, strt., Nu., Can.	A12	106
Bell Peninsula, pen., Nu., Can.	C14	106
Bells, Tn., U.S.	B9	122
Bells, Tx., U.S.	D2	122
Bells Corners, On., Can.	C14	112
Belluno, Italy	D9	22
Bell Ville, Arg.	F6	92
Bellville, S. Afr.	H4	70
Bellwood, Ne., U.S.	F15	126
Bellwood, Pa., U.S.	D7	114
Belly, stm., N.A.	G17	138
Bellyk, Russia	D16	32
Belmond, Ia., U.S.	B4	120
Belmont, N.S., Can.	E13	110
Belmont, S. Afr.	F7	70
Belmont, N.H., U.S.	G5	110
Belmont, Wi., U.S.	B7	120
Belmonte, Braz.	H6	88
Belmonte, Port.	D3	20
Belmonte, Spain	A4	20
Belmopan, Belize	D3	102
Beloe, Russia	B22	10
Beloe, ozero, l., Russia	F17	8
Beloe more (White Sea), s., Russia	D18	8
Belogorsk, Russia	F14	34
Belo Horizonte, Braz.	J3	88
Beloit, Ks., U.S.	B10	128
Beloit, Wi., U.S.	B8	120
Belo Jardim, Braz.	E7	88
Belomestnaja, Russia	H20	10
Belomorsk, Russia	D16	8
Beloreck, Russia	D9	32
Belören, Tur.	F15	28
Belorussia see Belarus, ctry., Eur.	E14	6
Beloščele, Russia	D22	8
Belo sur Mer, Madag.	E7	68
Belot, Lac, l., N.T., Can.	B5	106
Belo Tsiribihina, Madag.	D7	68
Belousovo, Russia	E19	10
Belovo, Russia	D15	32
Belozërsk, Russia	F17	8
Belpre, Oh., U.S.	E4	114
Belt, Mt., U.S.	C16	136
Beltana, Austl.	H2	76
Belt Creek, stm., Mt., U.S.	C16	136
Belton, Mo., U.S.	F3	120
Belton, Tx., U.S.	C10	130
Belton Lake, res., Tx., U.S.	C10	130
Beltrán, Arg.	C5	92
Belukha, Mount, mtn., Asia	E15	32
Belūr, India	E2	53
Beluran, Malay.	H1	52
Belvedere Marittimo, Italy	E9	24
Belvidere, Il., U.S.	B9	120
Belvidere, N.J., U.S.	D10	114
Belview, Mn., U.S.	G3	118
Belvoir see Kokhav HaYarden, sci., Isr.	F6	58
Belyando, stm., Austl.	D6	76
Belye Berega, Russia	G17	10
Belye Stolby, Russia	E20	10
Belyj Gorodok, Russia	C20	10
Belyj Jar, Russia	C15	32
Bełżec, Pol.	F19	16
Belzig, Ger.	D8	16
Belzoni, Ms., U.S.	D8	122
Bement, Il., U.S.	E9	120
Bemidji, Mn., U.S.	D3	118
Benaco see Garda, Lago di, l., Italy	E7	22
Bena-Dibele, D.R.C.	E4	66
Benagerie, Austl.	H3	76
Benalla, Austl.	K6	76
Benares see Vārānasi, India	F9	54
Ben Arous, Tun.	H4	24
Benavarri, Spain	B11	20
Benavente, Spain	B5	20
Benbecula, i., Scot., U.K.	D5	12
Ben Bolt, Tx., U.S.	G9	130
Ben Cat, Viet.	G8	48
Bencha, Khao Phanom, mtn., Thai.	H4	48
Ben-Chicao, Col de, p., Alg.	H13	20
Bencubbin, Austl.	F3	74
Bend, Or., U.S.	F5	136
Bendemeer, Austl.	H8	76
Bender Cassim see Boosaaso, Som.	B9	66
Bendigo, Austl.	K5	76
Bēne, Lat.	D6	10
Benedito Leite, Braz.	D3	88
Benepú, Rada, anch., Chile	f29	78l
Benevento, Italy	C8	24
Bèng, stm., Laos	B5	48
Bengal, Bay of, b., Asia	F6	46
Bengara, Indon.	B10	50
Bengasi see Banghāzī, Libya	A3	62
Bengbu, China	E7	42
Benghazi see Banghāzī, Libya	A3	62
Bengkalis, Indon.	C3	50
Bengkalis, Pulau, i., Indon.	C3	50
Bengkayang, Indon.	C6	50
Bengkulu, Indon.	E3	50
Bengkulu, state, Indon.	E3	50
Bengough, Sk., Can.	E8	124
Benguela, Ang.	C1	68
Benguerua, Ilha, i., Moz.	B12	70
Benha, Egypt	H2	58
Beni, D.R.C.	D5	66
Beni, stm., Bol.	B3	90
Béni Abbas, Alg.	C4	64
Beni 'Adi el-Baharîya, Egypt	K1	58
Beni Ahmad, Egypt	J1	58
Benicarló, Spain	D11	20
Benidorm, Spain	F10	20
Beni Mazâr, Egypt	J1	58
Beni Muhammadîyat, Egypt	K2	58
Benin, ctry., Afr.	G5	64
Benin, Bight of, b., Afr.	I5	64
Benin City, Nig.	H6	64
Benisa see Benissa, Spain	F11	20
Benissa, Spain	F11	20
Beni Suef, Egypt	I2	58
Benito, Mb., Can.	C12	124
Benito Juárez, Arg.	H8	92
Benito Juárez, Presa, res., Mex.	G10	100
Benjamin, Tx., U.S.	H9	128
Benjamín, Isla, i., Chile	H2	90
Benjamin Constant, Braz.	D3	84
Benkelman, Ne., U.S.	A7	128
Benkovac, Cro.	F12	22
Benld, Il., U.S.	E8	120
Ben Lomond, Ca., U.S.	F3	134
Ben Lomond National Park, p.o.i., Austl.	n13	77a
Benndale, Ms., U.S.	G10	122
Bennetta, ostrov, i., Russia	A18	34
Bennett Island see Bennetta, ostrov, i., Russia	A18	34
Bennettsville, S.C., U.S.	B6	116
Bennington, Ks., U.S.	B11	128
Bennington, Vt., U.S.	B12	114
Benoit, Ms., U.S.	D7	122
Benoni, S. Afr.	E9	70
Ben Sekka, Rass, c., Tun.	G3	24
Bensheim, Ger.	G4	16
Benson, Az., U.S.	L6	132
Benson, Mn., U.S.	F3	118
Benson, N.C., U.S.	A7	116
Benteng, Indon.	G12	50
Ben Thuy, Viet.	C7	48
Bentinck Island, i., Austl.	C7	74
Bentinck Island, i., Mya.	G3	48
Bentiu, Sudan	F6	62
Bento Gonçalves, Braz.	D12	92
Benton, Ar., U.S.	C6	122
Benton, Il., U.S.	F9	120
Benton, Ky., U.S.	H9	120
Benton, La., U.S.	E5	122
Benton, Mo., U.S.	G8	120
Benton, Tn., U.S.	B14	122
Benton, Wi., U.S.	B7	120
Benton Harbor, Mi., U.S.	F3	112
Bentonia, Ms., U.S.	E8	122
Bentonville, Ar., U.S.	H3	120
Ben Tre, Viet.	G8	48
Bentung, Malay.	K5	48
Benua, Pulau, i., Indon.	C5	50
Benue, stm., Afr.	H6	64
Ben Wheeler, Tx., U.S.	E3	122
Benxi, China	D5	38
Beograd (Belgrade), Serb.	E7	26
Beohāri, India	F8	54
Béoumi, C. Iv.	H3	64
Beowawe, Nv., U.S.	C9	134
Beppu, Japan	F4	40
Bequia, i., St. Vin.	o11	105e
Bequimão, Braz.	B3	88
Berat, Alb.	D13	24
Berati see Berat, Alb.	D13	24
Berau, stm., Indon.	B10	50
Berau, Teluk, b., Indon.	F9	44
Berazino, Bela.	G11	10
Berazino, Bela.	F11	10
Berbera, Som.	B9	66
Berbérati, C.A.R.	D3	66
Berchtesgaden, Ger.	I8	16
Berck, Fr.	D10	14
Berclair, Tx., U.S.	F10	130
Berdians'k, Ukr.	E5	32
Berdigestjah, Russia	D14	34
Berdsk, Russia	D14	32
Berea, Oh., U.S.	C4	114
Berea, S.C., U.S.	B3	116
Berehomet, Ukr.	A12	26
Berehove, Ukr.	A9	26
Berekua, Dom.	j6	105c
Berekum, Ghana	H4	64
Berens, stm., Can.	B17	124
Berens Island, i., Mb., Can.	B16	124
Berens River, Mb., Can.	B16	124
Beresford, N.B., Can.	C11	110
Beresford, S.D., U.S.	H2	118
Bereşti, Rom.	C14	26
Berettyó (Barcău), stm., Eur.	B8	26
Berettyóújfalu, Hung.	B8	26
Berezivka, Ukr.	B17	26
Bereznik, Russia	E20	8
Berezniki, Russia	C9	32
Berëzovo, Russia	B10	32
Berëzovskij, Russia	C15	32
Berëzovskij Rjadok, Russia	B17	10
Berga, Spain	B12	20
Bergama, Tur.	D10	28
Bergamo, Italy	E6	22
Bergantín, Ven.	C9	86
Bergby, Swe.	F7	8
Bergen see Mons, Bel.	D12	14
Bergen, Ger.	D5	16
Bergen, Nor.	F1	8
Bergen, N.Y., U.S.	A7	114
Bergen auf Rügen, Ger.	B9	16
Bergen op Zoom, Neth.	C13	14
Bergerac, Fr.	E6	18
Bergisch Gladbach, Ger.	F3	16
Bergoo, W.V., U.S.	F5	114
Bergsjö, Swe.	E7	8
Berguent, Mor.	C4	64
Bergville, S. Afr.	F9	70
Berhala, Selat, strt., Indon.	D4	50
Beringa, ostrov, i., Russia	F22	34
Bering Glacier, ice, Ak., U.S.	D11	140
Beringovskij, Russia	D24	34
Bering Sea, s.	D21	142
Bering Strait, strt.	C6	140
Berja, Spain	H8	20
Berkåk, Nor.	E4	8
Berkakit, Russia	E14	34
Berkane, Mor.	C4	64
Berkeley, Ca., U.S.	F3	134
Berkeley Springs, W.V., U.S.	E7	114
Berkner Island, i., Ant.	C35	81
Berkshire Hills, hills, Ma., U.S.	B12	114
Berland, stm., Ab., Can.	B13	138
Berlevåg, Nor.	A13	8
Berlin, Ger.	D9	16
Berlin, N.H., U.S.	F5	110
Berlin, N.J., U.S.	E11	114
Berlin, Pa., U.S.	E7	114
Berlin, Wi., U.S.	H9	118
Berlin, state, Ger.	D9	16
Berlinguet Inlet, b., Nu., Can.	A14	106
Bermagui, Austl.	K8	76
Bermejillo, Mex.	C7	100
Bermejito, stm., Arg.	B7	92
Bermejo, stm., Arg.	E4	92
Bermejo, stm., S.A.	C8	92
Bermejo, Paso del, p., S.A.	F2	92
Bermen, Lac, l., Qc., Can.	E17	106
Bermeo, Spain	A8	20
Bermuda, dep., N.A.	k16	104e
Bern (Berne), Switz.	C4	22
Bernalda, Italy	D10	24
Bernasconi, Arg.	H5	92
Bernau bei Berlin, Ger.	D9	16
Bernay, Fr.	E9	14
Bernburg, Ger.	E7	16
Berndorf, Aus.	C12	22
Berne see Bern, Switz.	C4	22
Berner Alpen, mts., Switz.	D4	22
Berneray, i., Scot., U.K.	D5	12
Bernese Alps see Berner Alpen, mts., Switz.	D4	22
Bernice, La., U.S.	E6	122
Bernie, Mo., U.S.	H8	120
Bernier Bay, b., Nu., Can.	A12	106
Bernier Island, i., Austl.	D2	74
Bernina, Piz, mtn., Eur.	H18	14
Bernkastel-Kues, Ger.	G3	16
Bernsdorf, Ger.	E10	16
Berón de Astrada, Arg.	C9	92
Beroroha, Madag.	E8	68
Beroun, Czech Rep.	G9	16
Berounka, stm., Czech Rep.	F9	16
Berre, Étang de, l., Fr.	F11	18
Berri, Austl.	J3	76
Berriyyane, Alg.	C5	64
Berry, Al., U.S.	D11	122
Berry, hist. reg., Fr.	H11	14
Berry, Canal du, can., Fr.	G10	14
Berry Creek, stm., Ab., Can.	E19	138
Berryessa, Lake, res., Ca., U.S.	E3	134
Berry Islands, is., Bah.	B9	96
Berseba, Nmb.	D3	70
Bersenbrück, Ger.	D3	16
Bershad', Ukr.	A16	26
Bertha, Mn., U.S.	E3	118
Berthold, N.D., U.S.	F12	124
Berthoud, Co., U.S.	G7	126
Berthoud Pass, p., Co., U.S.	B3	128
Bertoua, Cam.	D2	66
Bertrand, Mi., U.S.	G3	112
Bertrand, Ne., U.S.	G13	126
Beruri, Braz.	D5	84
Berwick, La., U.S.	H7	122
Berwick, Pa., U.S.	C9	114
Berwick-upon-Tweed, Eng., U.K.	F11	12
Berwyn, Il., U.S.	G2	112
Besalampy, Madag.	D7	68
Besançon, Fr.	G14	14
Bešankovičy, Bela.	E12	10
Besar, Gunong, mtn., Malay.	K6	48
Besar, Gunung, vol., Indon.	E9	50
Besedz', stm., Eur.	H14	10
Beskid Mountains see Beskids, mts., Eur.	G15	16
Beskids, mts., Eur.	G15	16
Beskra, Alg.	C6	64
Beslan, Russia	F6	32
Besni, Tur.	A8	58
Bessarabia, hist. reg., Eur.	C15	26
Bessemer, Al., U.S.	D11	122
Bessemer, Mi., U.S.	E8	118
Bessemer City, N.C., U.S.	A4	116
Bestjah, Russia	D15	34
Bestöbe, Kaz.	D12	32
Bestuževo, Russia	F20	8
Betafo, Madag.	D8	68
Betanzos, Spain	A2	20
Bétaré Oya, Cam.	C2	66
Bétera, Spain	E10	20
Bethal, S. Afr.	E9	70
Bethalto, Il., U.S.	F7	120
Bethanien, Nmb.	E3	70
Bethany, Mo., U.S.	D3	120
Bethany, Ok., U.S.	F11	128
Bethel, Monts.	D3	105a
Bethel, Ak., U.S.	D7	140
Bethel, Me., U.S.	F6	110
Bethel, N.C., U.S.	I8	114
Bethel Acres, Ok., U.S.	B2	122
Bethel Springs, Tn., U.S.	B10	122
Bethlehem, S. Afr.	F9	70
Bethlehem, Pa., U.S.	D10	114
Bethlehem, W.V., U.S.	H9	112
Bethlehem see Bayt Laḥm, W.B.	G6	58
Bethune, Sk., Can.	D8	124
Béthune, Fr.	D11	14
Bethune, S.C., U.S.	B5	116
Betong, Malay.	C7	50
Betong, Thai.	J5	48
Betoota, Austl.	E3	76
Betpaqdala, des., Kaz.	E11	32
Betroka, Madag.	E8	68
Bet She'arim, Ḥorbat, sci., Isr.	F6	58
Betsiamites, stm., Qc., Can.	A8	110
Betsiamites, Barrage, dam, Qc., Can.	A7	110
Betsiamites, Pointe de, c., Qc., Can.	B8	110
Betsiboka, stm., Madag.	D8	68
Betsie, Point, c., Mi., U.S.	D3	112
Betsy Layne, Ky., U.S.	G3	114
Bettendorf, Ia., U.S.	C7	120
Bettiah, India	E10	54
Bettles Field, Ak., U.S.	C9	140
Bettola, Italy	F6	22
Betūl, India	H6	54
Betung, Indon.	E4	50
Betwa, stm., India	F7	54
Betzdorf, Ger.	F3	16
Beulah, Austl.	J4	76
Beulah, Co., U.S.	C4	128
Beulah, Mi., U.S.	D3	112
Beulah, Ms., U.S.	D8	122
Beulaville, N.C., U.S.	B8	116
Beuvron, stm., Fr.	G11	14
B. Everett Jordan Lake, res., N.C., U.S.	I6	114
Beverley, Eng., U.K.	H12	12
Beverly, Ma., U.S.	B15	114
Beverly Hills, Ca., U.S.	I7	134
Beverly Lake, l., Nu., Can.	C10	106
Beverungen, Ger.	E5	16
Beverwijk, Neth.	B13	14
Bewani Mountains, mts., Pap. N. Gui.	a3	79a
Bexhill, Eng., U.K.	K13	12
Bexley, Oh., U.S.	E3	114
Bey Dağları, mts., Tur.	G13	28
Beydagları Olimpos Milli Parkı, p.o.i., Tur.	G13	28
Beyla, Gui.	H3	64
Beyneū, Kaz.	E9	32
Beypazarı, Tur.	C14	28
Beypore, India	F2	53
Beyra, Som.	C9	66
Beyşehir, Tur.	F14	28
Beyşehir Gölü, l., Tur.	F14	28
Bežanickaja vozvyšennost', plat., Russia	D12	10
Bežanicy, Russia	D12	10
Bežeck, Russia	C19	10
Béziers, Fr.	F9	18
Bezmein, Turkmen.	B8	56
Bhadohi, India	F9	54
Bhādra, India	D5	54
Bhadrāchalam, India	C5	53
Bhadrak, India	H11	54
Bhadra Reservoir, res., India	E2	53
Bhadrāvati, India	E2	53
Bhāgalpur, India	F11	54
Bhainsa, India	B3	53
Bhāi Pheru, Pak.	C4	54
Bhairab Bāzār, Bngl.	F13	54
Bhaironghāti, India	C7	54
Bhakkar, Pak.	C3	54
Bhaktapur (Bhādgāon), Nepal	E10	54
Bhālki, India	C3	53
Bhalwāl, Pak.	B4	54
Bhamo, Mya.	D8	46
Bhandāra, India	H7	54
Bhanvad, India	H2	54
Bharatpur, India	E6	54
Bharatpur, Nepal	E10	54
Bharthana, India	E7	54
Bharūch, India	H4	54
Bhātāpāra, India	H8	54
Bhātghar Lake, res., India	B1	53
Bhatkal, India	E2	53
Bhātpāra, India	G12	54
Bhattiprolu, India	C5	53
Bhavāni, India	F3	53
Bhāvnagar, India	H4	54
Bhawani Mandi, India	F5	54
Bhawānipatna, India	I9	54
Bhera, Pak.	B4	54
Bhīkangaon, India	H5	54
Bhilai, India	H8	54
Bhīlwāra, India	F5	54
Bhīma, stm., India	C3	53
Bhīmavaram, India	C5	53
Bhind, India	E7	54
Bhīnmāl, India	F4	54
Bhiwandi, India	B1	53
Bhiwāni, India	D6	54
Bhojpur, Nepal	E11	54
Bhokardan, India	H5	54
Bhongīr, India	C4	53
Bhopāl, India	G6	54
Bhuban, India	H10	54
Bhubaneshwar, India	H10	54
Bhuj, India	G2	54
Bhusāwal, India	H5	54
Bhutan, ctry., Asia	E13	54
Bia, Phou, mtn., Laos	C6	48
Biafra, Bight of, b., Afr.	I6	64
Biak, i., Indon.	F10	44
Biała Piska, Pol.	C18	16
Biała Podlaska, Pol.	D19	16
Biała Podlaska, state, Pol.	E19	16
Białobrzegi, Pol.	E16	16
Białogard, Pol.	B12	16
Białowieski Park Narodowy, p.o.i., Pol.	D19	16
Białystok, Pol.	C19	16
Białystok, state, Pol.	C19	16
Bianco, Monte see Blanc, Mont, mtn., Eur.	D12	18
Biankouma, C. Iv.	H3	64
Biaora, India	F6	54
Biaro, Pulau, i., Indon.	E8	44
Biarritz, Fr.	F4	18
Biasca, Switz.	D5	22
Biba, Egypt	J2	58
Bibala, Ang.	C1	68
Bibb City, Ga., U.S.	E14	122
Bibbiena, Italy	G8	22
Bibémi, Cam.	C2	66
Bicas, Braz.	K4	88
Bicaz, Rom.	C13	26
Biche, Lac la, l., Ab., Can.	B18	138
Bichigt, Mong.	B4	36
Bicknell, In., U.S.	F10	120
Bicknell, Ut., U.S.	E5	132
Bicudo, stm., Braz.	J3	88
Bičura, Russia	F10	34
Bīd, India	B2	53
Bida, Nig.	H6	64
Bīdar, India	C3	53
Biddeford, Me., U.S.	G6	110
Bideford, Eng., U.K.	J8	12
Bieber, Ca., U.S.	B4	134
Biebrza, stm., Pol.	C18	16
Biebrzański Park Narodowy, p.o.i., Pol.	C18	16
Biecz, Pol.	G17	16
Biedenkopf, Ger.	F4	16
Biel (Bienne), Switz.	C4	22
Bielawa, Pol.	F12	16
Bielefeld, Ger.	D4	16
Bieler Lake, l., Nu., Can.	A15	106
Biella, Italy	E4	22
Bielsko-Biała, Pol.	G14	16
Bielsko-Biała, state, Pol.	G15	16
Bielsk Podlaski, Pol.	D19	16
Bienfait, Sk., Can.	E11	124
Bien Hoa, Viet.	G8	48
Bienne see Biel, Switz.	C4	22
Bien Son, Viet.	B7	48
Bienville, La., U.S.	E5	122
Bienville, Lac, l., Qc., Can.	D16	106
Bierutów, Pol.	E13	16
Bieszczadzki Park Narodowy, p.o.i., Pol.	G18	16
Bifoun, Gabon	E2	66
Big, stm., Mo., U.S.	F7	120
Biga, Tur.	C10	28
Bigadiç, Tur.	D11	28
Big A Mountain, mtn., Va., U.S.	G3	114
Big Bald Mountain, mtn., Ga., U.S.	B1	116
Big Baldy Mountain, mtn., Mt., U.S.	D16	136
Big Bay, Mi., U.S.	B2	112
Big Bay, b., Vanuatu	j16	79d
Big Bay De Noc, b., Mi., U.S.	C3	112
Big Bear Lake, Ca., U.S.	I9	134
Big Beaver, Sk., Can.	E8	124
Big Belt Mountains, mts., Mt., U.S.	D15	136
Big Bend, Swaz.	E10	70
Big Bend National Park, p.o.i., Tx., U.S.	E4	130
Big Bend Reservoir, res., Ab., Can.	D15	138
Big Black, stm., Ms., U.S.	E8	122
Big Blue, stm., U.S.	G16	126
Big Blue, West Fork, stm., Ne., U.S.	G15	126
Big Bonito Creek, stm., Az., U.S.	J7	132
Big Canyon, p., Tx., U.S.	D5	130
Big Chino Wash, stm., Az., U.S.	H4	132
Big Creek, B.C., Can.	E7	138
Big Creek, Ca., U.S.	F6	134
Big Creek, stm., B.C., Can.	E8	138
Big Creek, stm., Ar., U.S.	C8	122
Big Creek, stm., Ks., U.S.	C9	128
Big Cypress National Preserve, Fl., U.S.	J4	116
Big Cypress Swamp, sw., Fl., U.S.	J4	116
Big Delta, Ak., U.S.	D10	140
Big Desert, des., Austl.	J3	76
Big Diomede Island see Ratmanova, ostrov, i., Russia	C27	34
Big Dry Creek, stm., Mt., U.S.	G7	124
Bigelow Bight, b., U.S.	G6	110
Big Flat, Ar., U.S.	I5	120
Bigfork, Mn., U.S.	D5	118
Big Fork, stm., Mn., U.S.	C5	118
Big Frog Mountain, mtn., Tn., U.S.	C14	122
Biggar, Sk., Can.	B6	124
Biggers, Ar., U.S.	H7	120
Biggs, Ca., U.S.	D4	134
Big Gull Lake, l., On., Can.	D12	112

Name	Map Ref.	Page
Big Hole, stm., Mt., U.S.	E14	136
Bighorn, stm., U.S.	A5	126
Bighorn Basin, bas., U.S.	C4	126
Bighorn Canyon National Recreation Area, p.o.i., U.S.	B4	126
Bighorn Lake, res., U.S.	B4	126
Bighorn Mountains, mts., U.S.	C5	126
Bight, Head of b., Austl.	F6	74
Big Island, Va., U.S.	G6	114
Big Island, i., Nu., Can.	C17	106
Big Lake, I., Me., U.S.	E9	110
Big Lookout Mountain, mtn., Or., U.S.	F9	136
Big Lost, stm., Id., U.S.	G13	136
Big Muddy, stm., Il., U.S.	G8	120
Big Muddy Creek, stm., Mt., U.S.	F9	124
Big Nemaha, North Fork, stm., Ne., U.S.	K2	118
Bignona, Sen.	G1	64
Big Pine, Ca., U.S.	F7	134
Big Pine Mountain, mtn., Ca., U.S.	I6	134
Big Piney, Wy., U.S.	H16	136
Big Piney, stm., Mo., U.S.	G6	120
Bigpoint, Ms., U.S.	G10	122
Big Porcupine Creek, stm., Mt., U.S.	H6	124
Big Prairie Creek, stm., Al., U.S.	E11	122
Big Quill Lake, I., Sk., Can.	C9	124
Big Raccoon Creek, stm., In., U.S.	I2	112
Big Rapids, Mi., U.S.	E4	112
Big Rideau Lake, I., On., Can.	D13	112
Big River, Sk., Can.	E9	106
Big Sable Point, c., Mi., U.S.	D3	112
Big Sand Lake, I., Mb., Can.	D11	106
Big Sandy, Tn., U.S.	H9	120
Big Sandy, Tx., U.S.	E3	122
Big Sandy, stm., Wy., U.S.	F3	126
Big Sandy, stm., U.S.	F3	114
Big Sandy Creek, stm., Co., U.S.	C6	128
Bigsby Island, i., On., Can.	B4	118
Big Signal Peak, mtn., Ca., U.S.	D2	134
Big Sioux, stm., U.S.	E16	126
Big Sky, Mt., U.S.	E15	136
Big Smoky Valley, val., Nv., U.S.	E8	134
Big Spring, Tx., U.S.	B6	130
Big Spruce Knob, mtn., W.V., U.S.	F5	114
Big Stone City, S.D., U.S.	F2	118
Big Stone Gap, Va., U.S.	H3	114
Big Stone Lake, I., U.S.	F2	118
Big Sunflower, stm., Ms., U.S.	D8	122
Big Sur, reg., Ca., U.S.	H4	134
Big Timber, Mt., U.S.	E16	136
Big Trout Lake, I., On., Can.	E12	106
Biguaçu, Braz.	C13	92
Big Water, Ut., U.S.	F5	132
Big Wells, Tx., U.S.	F8	130
Big White Mountain, mtn., B.C., Can.	G12	138
Big Wood, stm., Id., U.S.	G12	136
Bihać, Bos.	E2	26
Bihar, India	F10	54
Bihar, state, India	E10	54
Biharamulo, Tan.	E6	66
Bihor, state, Rom.	C9	26
Bihor, Vârful, mtn., Rom.	C9	26
Bihoro, Japan	C16	38
Bihosawa, Bela.	E10	10
Bihu, China	G8	42
Bija, stm., Russia	D15	32
Bijagós, Arquipélago dos, is., Gui.-B.	G1	64
Bijainagar, India	F5	54
Bijapur, India	C2	53
Bijapur, India	B5	53
Bijeljina, Bos.	E6	26
Bijelo Polje, Mont.	F6	26
Bijie, China	F6	36
Bijnor, India	D7	54
Bikaner, India	D4	54
Bikar, at., Marsh. Is.	B8	72
Bikeqi, China	A4	42
Bikin, Russia	B11	36
Bikini, at., Marsh. Is.	B7	72
Bīkkū Bīttī, mtn., Libya	C3	62
Bikoro, D.R.C.	E3	66
Bilāra, India	E4	54
Bilāsipāra, India	D7	54
Bilāsipāra, India	E13	54
Bilāspur, India	C6	54
Bilāspur, India	G9	54
Bila Tserkva, Ukr.	F15	6
Bilauktaung Range, mts., Asia	F4	48
Bilbao, Spain	A7	20
Bilbeis, Egypt	H2	58
Bilbilis, sci., Spain	C9	20
Bileća, Bos.	G5	26
Bilecik, Tur.	C12	28
Bilecik, state, Tur.	C13	28
Biłgoraj, Pol.	F18	16
Bilgrām, India	E8	54
Bilhorod-Dnistrovs'kyi, Ukr.	C17	26
Bili, D.R.C.	D5	66
Biliaïvka, Ukr.	C17	26
Bilikol köli, I., Kaz.	F12	32
Bilīmora, India	H4	54
Bilin, Mya.	D3	48
Bilin, Mya.	D3	48
Bilina, Czech Rep.	F9	16
Biliran Island, i., Phil.	E5	52
Billabong Creek, stm., Austl.	J5	76
Billings, Mo., U.S.	G4	120
Billings, Mt., U.S.	B4	126
Billings Heights, Mt., U.S.	B4	126
Billiton see Belitung, i., Indon.	E5	50
Bill Williams, stm., Az., U.S.	I3	132
Bilma, Niger	F7	64
Biloela, Austl.	E8	76
Biloxi, Ms., U.S.	G10	122
Bilpa Morea Claypan, I., Austl.	E2	76
Bilqas Qism Awwal, Egypt	G2	58
Biltine, Chad	E4	62
Biltmore Forest, N.C., U.S.	A3	116
Bilugyun Island, i., Mya.	D3	48
Bimbo, C.A.R.	D3	66
Bimbowrie, Austl.	H3	76
Bimini Islands, is., Bah.	B9	96
Bina-Etāwa, India	F7	54
Binaija, Gunung, mtn., Indon.	F9	44
Binalbagan, Phil.	E4	52
Bin'an, China	B7	38
Bindki, India	E8	54
Bindloss, Ab., Can.	D3	124
Bindura, Zimb.	D5	68
Binéfar, Spain	C11	20
Binford, N.D., U.S.	G15	124
Binga, D.R.C.	D4	66
Binga, Monte, mtn., Afr.	D5	68
Bingara, Austl.	G8	76
Bingen, Ger.	G3	16
Binger, Ok., U.S.	F10	128
Binghamton, N.Y., U.S.	B10	114
Bin Ghunaymah, Jabal, mts., Libya	B3	62
Binhai, China	D8	42
Binh Gia, Viet.	B8	48
Binjai, Indon.	K4	48
Binnaway, Austl.	H7	76
Binongko, Pulau, i., Indon.	G7	44
Binscarth, Mb., Can.	D12	124
Bintan, Pulau, i., Indon.	C4	50
Bintimani, mtn., S.L.	H2	64
Bintuhan, Indon.	F3	50
Bintulu, Malay.	B8	50
Bintuni, Indon.	F9	44
Binxian, China	C7	42
Binxian, China	B7	38
Binyang, China	J3	42
Bin-Yauri, Nig.	G5	64
Biobío, state, Chile	H1	92
Biobío, stm., Chile	G2	90
Biogradska Gora Nacionalni Park, p.o.i., Mont.	G6	26
Bioko, i., Eq. Gui.	I6	64
Bira, Russia	G15	34
Birac, Phil.	B3	52
Birāk, Libya	B2	62
Birakan, Russia	G15	34
Bi'r al Wa'r, Libya	C2	62
Birao, C.A.R.	B4	66
Birch, stm., Ab., Can.	D8	106
Birch Creek, stm., Mt., U.S.	B14	136
Birch Hills, Sk., Can.	B8	124
Birch Island, B.C., Can.	E10	138
Birch Island, i., Mb., Can.	B13	124
Birch Mountains, hills, Ab., Can.	D8	106
Birch Run, Mi., U.S.	E6	112
Birch Tree, Mo., U.S.	H6	120
Birchwood, Wi., U.S.	F7	118
Bird Creek, stm., Ok., U.S.	E13	128
Bird Island, Mn., U.S.	G4	118
Bird Island, sci., S. Geor.	J9	90
Birdsville, Austl.	E2	76
Birdtail Creek, stm., Mb., Can.	D13	124
Birdum, Austl.	C6	74
Birecik, Tur.	A9	58
Bireun, Indon.	J3	48
Bir Ghbalou, Alg.	H14	20
Birigui, Braz.	D6	90
Biriljussy, Russia	C16	32
Birjand, Iran	C8	56
Birjul'ka, Russia	D19	32
Birjusa, stm., Russia	C17	32
Birjusinsk, Russia	C17	32
Birken, B.C., Can.	F8	138
Birkenfeld, Ger.	G3	16
Birkenhead, Eng., U.K.	H9	12
Birmingham, Eng., U.K.	I10	12
Birmingham, Al., U.S.	D11	122
Birmingham, Ia., U.S.	D6	120
Birmingham, Mi., U.S.	B2	114
Birmitrapur, India	G10	54
Bir Mogreïn, Maur.	D2	64
Birnin Gaouré, Niger	G5	64
Birnin-Kebbi, Nig.	G5	64
Birnin Konni, Niger	G5	64
Birnin Kudu, Nig.	G6	64
Birobidžan, Russia	G15	34
Birrie, stm., Austl.	G6	76
Birsk, Russia	C9	32
Birštonas, Lith.	F7	10
Birtle, Mb., Can.	D12	124
Birūr, India	E2	53
Biržai, Lith.	D7	10
Birżebbuġa, Malta	I8	24
Bisaccia, Italy	C9	24
Bisalpur, India	D7	54
Bisbee, Az., U.S.	L7	132
Bisbee, N.D., U.S.	F14	124
Biscarrosse et de Parentis, Étang de, l., Fr.	E4	18
Biscay, Bay of, b., Eur.	E2	18
Biscayne Bay, b., Fl., U.S.	K5	116
Biscayne National Park, p.o.i., Fl., U.S.	K5	116
Bisceglie, Italy	C10	24
Bischofshofen, Aus.	C10	22
Bischofswerda, Ger.	E10	16
Biscoe, N.C., U.S.	A6	116
Bishnupur, India	G11	54
Bisho, S. Afr.	H8	70
Bishop, Ca., U.S.	F7	134
Bishop, Tx., U.S.	G10	130
Bishop Auckland, Eng., U.K.	G11	12
Bishop Rock, r., Eng., U.K.	L6	12
Bishop's Falls, Nf., Can.	j22	107a
Bishop's Stortford, Eng., U.K.	J13	12
Bishopville, S.C., U.S.	B5	116
Bišķek, Kyrg.	F12	32
Biskupiec, Pol.	C16	16
Bislig, Phil.	F6	52
Bismarck, Mo., U.S.	G7	120
Bismarck, N.D., U.S.	A12	126
Bismarck Archipelago, is., Pap. N. Gui.	a4	79a
Bismarck Range, mts., Pap. N. Gui.	b3	79a
Bismarck Sea, s., Pap. N. Gui.	a4	79a
Bismark, Kap, c., Grnld.	B22	141
Bissau, Gui.-B.	G1	64
Bissett, Mb., Can.	C18	124
Bissikrima, Gui.	G2	64
Bistcho Lake, I., Ab., Can.	D7	106
Bistineau, Lake, res., La., U.S.	E5	122
Bistrica, Slvn.	D13	22
Bistrița, Rom.	B11	26
Bistrița, stm., Rom.	C13	26
Bistrița-Năsăud, state, Rom.	B11	26
Biswān, India	E8	54
Bitam, Gabon	D2	66
Bitburg, Ger.	G2	16
Bitche, Fr.	E16	14
Bitlis, Tur.	B5	56
Bitola, Mac.	B4	28
Bitola see Bitola, Mac.	B4	28
Bitonto, Italy	C10	24
Bitou, Burkina	G4	64
Bitter Creek, stm., Wy., U.S.	B8	132
Bitterfeld, Ger.	E8	16
Bitterfontein, S. Afr.	G4	70
Bitterroot, stm., Mt., U.S.	D13	136
Bitterroot, West Fork, stm., Mt., U.S.	E12	136
Bitterroot Range, mts., U.S.	C11	136
Bitung, Indon.	E8	44
Bitupitá, Braz.	B5	88
Biu, Nig.	G7	64
Biwabik, Mn., U.S.	D6	118
Biwa-ko, I., Japan	D8	40
Bixby, Ok., U.S.	I2	120
Biyala, Egypt	G2	58
Biyang, China	E5	42
Bizana, S. Afr.	G9	70
Bizen, Japan	E7	40
Bizerte (Binzert), Tun.	G3	24
Bizerte, Lac de, l., Tun.	A2	24
Bizkaiko, co., Spain	A8	20
Bjahoml', Bela.	F10	10
Bjala, Blg.	G14	26
Bjala Slatina, Blg.	F10	26
Bjalynicy, Bela.	F12	10
Bjarezina, stm., Bela.	H13	10
Bjaroza, Bela.	H8	10
Bjarozavka, Bela.	G9	10
Bjelovar, Cro.	E13	22
Bjørna, Swe.	E8	8
Björneborg see Pori, Fin.	F9	8
Bjorne Peninsula, pen., Nu., Can.	B8	141
Bjørnøya, i., Nor.	B5	30
Bla, Mali	G3	64
Blace, Serb.	F8	26
Black (Da, Song) (Lixian), stm., Asia	D9	46
Black, stm., Mb., Can.	D18	124
Black, stm., Ak., U.S.	C11	140
Black, stm., Az., U.S.	J6	132
Black, stm., La., U.S.	F7	122
Black, stm., Mi., U.S.	E7	112
Black, stm., N.Y., U.S.	E14	112
Black, stm., Wi., U.S.	G8	118
Black, stm., U.S.	I6	120
Blackall, Austl.	E5	76
Black Bay, b., On., Can.	C10	118
Black Bay Peninsula, pen., On., Can.	C10	118
Black Bear Creek, stm., Ok., U.S.	E11	128
Blackburn, Eng., U.K.	H10	12
Blackburn, Mount, mtn., Ak., U.S.	D11	140
Black Butte, mtn., Mt., U.S.	D15	136
Black Canyon of the Gunnison National Park, p.o.i., Co., U.S.	E9	132
Black Creek, stm., Ms., U.S.	G9	122
Black Creek, stm., S.C., U.S.	B6	116
Black Diamond, Ab., Can.	F16	138
Black Diamond, Wa., U.S.	C5	136
Blackdown Tableland National Park, p.o.i., Austl.	D7	76
Blackduck, Mn., U.S.	D4	118
Black Eagle, Mt., U.S.	C15	136
Blackfoot, Id., U.S.	G14	136
Blackfoot, Mt., U.S.	B14	136
Blackfoot, stm., Id., U.S.	G15	136
Blackfoot, stm., Mt., U.S.	D13	136
Blackfoot Reservoir, res., Id., U.S.	H15	136
Black Forest see Schwarzwald, mts., Ger.	H4	16
Black Hills, mts., U.S.	C9	126
Black Island, i., Mb., Can.	C17	124
Black Lake, Qc., Can.	D5	110
Black Lake, I., Mi., U.S.	C5	112
Black Lake, I., N.Y., U.S.	D14	112
Black Mesa, mtn., U.S.	E6	128
Blackmore, Mount, mtn., U.S.	E15	136
Black Mountain, N.C., U.S.	A3	116
Black Mountain, mtn., Az., U.S.	K5	132
Black Mountain, mtn., Ca., U.S.	H5	134
Black Mountain, mtn., Mt., U.S.	D14	136
Black Mountain, hill, Austl.	C2	76
Black Mountain, mtn., U.S.	H2	114
Black Nossob, stm., Nmb.	C4	70
Black Pine Peak, mtn., Id., U.S.	A3	132
Blackpool, Eng., U.K.	H9	12
Black Range, mts., N.M., U.S.	J9	132
Black River, N.Y., U.S.	D14	112
Black River Falls, Wi., U.S.	G8	118
Black Rock, Ar., U.S.	H6	120
Black Rock, r., Fr.	G2	12
Black Rock, r., S. Geor.	J8	90
Black Rock Desert, des., Nv., U.S.	B7	134
Blacksburg, S.C., U.S.	A4	116
Blacksburg, Va., U.S.	G5	114
Black Sea, s.	G15	6
Blacks Fork, stm., U.S.	B7	132
Blackshear, Lake, res., Ga., U.S.	D2	116
Blackstone, Va., U.S.	G8	114
Black Sturgeon Lake, I., On., Can.	B9	118
Blackville, S.C., U.S.	C4	116
Black Volta (Volta Noire) (Mouhoun), stm., Afr.	H4	64
Blackwater, Austl.	D7	76
Blackwater, Ire.	I4	12
Blackwater, stm., Mo., U.S.	F4	120
Blackwater Creek, stm., Austl.	E5	76
Blackwater Draw, stm., U.S.	H7	128
Blackwater Lake, I., N.T., Can.	C6	106
Blackwell, Tx., U.S.	B7	130
Bladenboro, N.C., U.S.	B7	116
Bladensburg National Park, p.o.i., Austl.	D4	76
Bladgrond-Noord, S. Afr.	F4	70
Bladworth, Sk., Can.	C7	124
Blāfell, mtn., Ice.	k30	8a
Blagoevgrad, Blg.	G10	26
Blaine, Mn., U.S.	F5	118
Blaine, Wa., U.S.	B4	136
Blair, Ne., U.S.	C1	120
Blair, Ok., U.S.	G9	128
Blair, Wi., U.S.	G7	118
Blair Athol, Austl.	D6	76
Blairsville, Ga., U.S.	B2	116
Blairsville, Pa., U.S.	D6	114
Blaj, Rom.	C10	26
Blakely, Ga., U.S.	F13	122
Blake Plateau, unds.	E6	144
Blakeslee, Oh., U.S.	C1	114
Blalock Island, i., Wa., U.S.	D7	136
Blanc, Mont, mtn., Eur.	D12	18
Blanca, Co., U.S.	D4	128
Blanca, Bahía, b., Arg.	G4	90
Blanca, Laguna, l., Chile	J2	90
Blanca, Punta, c., Chile	B2	92
Blanca, Sierra, mtn., Tx., U.S.	C2	130
Blanca Peak, mtn., Co., U.S.	D3	128
Blanchard, Ok., U.S.	F11	128
Blanchard, stm., Oh., U.S.	D2	114
Blanche, Lake, l., Austl.	G2	76
Blanche Channel, strt., Sol. Is.	e7	79b
Blanchester, Oh., U.S.	E1	114
Blanchisseuse, Trin.	s12	105f
Blanco, Tx., U.S.	D9	130
Blanco, stm., Arg.	D3	92
Blanco, stm., Ec.	H2	86
Blanco, Cabo, c., C.R.	H5	102
Blanco, Cañon, p., N.M., U.S.	H2	136
Blanco, Lago, l., Chile	J3	90
Blanco, Sablón, Qc., Can.	i22	107a
Bland, Va., U.S.	G4	114
Blanda, stm., Ice.	k30	8a
Blanding, Ut., U.S.	F7	132
Blanes, Spain	C13	20
Blangkejeren, Indon.	K3	48
Blangy-sur-Bresle, Fr.	E10	14
Blankenburg, Ger.	E6	16
Blanquilla, Isla, i., Ven.	B9	86
Blansko, Czech Rep.	G12	16
Blantyre, Mwi.	D6	68
Blarney Castle, sci., Ire.	J4	12
Blaszki, Pol.	E14	16
Blatná, Czech Rep.	G9	16
Blaubeuren, Ger.	H5	16
Blaufelden, Ger.	G5	16
Blazowa, Pol.	G18	16
Bledsoe, Tx., U.S.	H5	128
Blega, Indon.	G8	50
Bleik see Andenes, Nor.	B6	8
Blekinge, state, Swe.	H6	8
Blenheim, On., Can.	F8	112
Blenheim, N.Z.	E5	80
Blessing, Tx., U.S.	F11	130
Blethley, Eng., U.K.	J12	12
Bligh Water, strt., Fiji	p18	79e
Blind River, On., Can.	B6	112
Blissfield, Mi., U.S.	C2	114
Blitar, Indon.	H8	50
Block Island, i., R.I., U.S.	C14	114
Blockton, Ia., U.S.	D3	120
Bloedel, B.C., Can.	F5	138
Bloemfontein, S. Afr.	E7	70
Bloemhof, S. Afr.	E7	70
Bloemhofdam, res., S. Afr.	E7	70
Blois, Fr.	G10	14
Blönduós, Ice.	k29	8a
Bloodvein, stm., Can.	E11	106
Bloody Foreland, c., Ire.	F4	12
Bloomer, Wi., U.S.	F7	118
Bloomfield, On., Can.	E12	112
Bloomfield, Ky., U.S.	G12	120
Bloomfield, Mo., U.S.	H8	120
Bloomfield, Ne., U.S.	E15	126
Bloomfield, N.M., U.S.	G9	132
Blooming Grove, Tx., U.S.	E2	122
Blooming Prairie, Mn., U.S.	H5	118
Bloomington, Il., U.S.	D9	120
Bloomington, In., U.S.	E11	120
Bloomington, Mn., U.S.	G5	118
Bloomington, Tx., U.S.	F11	130
Bloomington, Wi., U.S.	B7	120
Bloomsburg, Pa., U.S.	C9	114
Bloomsbury, Austl.	C7	76
Bloomville, Oh., U.S.	C2	114
Blora, Indon.	G7	50
Blosseville Kyst, cst., Grnld.	D20	141
Blossom, Tx., U.S.	D3	122
Blountstown, Fl., U.S.	G13	122
Blountsville, Al., U.S.	C12	122
Blowering Reservoir, res., Austl.	J6	76
Blowing Point Village, Anguilla	A1	105a
Blowing Rock, N.C., U.S.	H4	114
Bludenz, Aus.	C6	22
Blue, stm., Az., U.S.	J7	132
Blue, stm., Ok., U.S.	C2	122
Blue Creek, Wa., U.S.	B8	136
Blue Cypress Lake, l., Fl., U.S.	I5	116
Blue Earth, Mn., U.S.	H4	118
Blue Earth, stm., U.S.	G8	16
Bluefield, Va., U.S.	G4	114
Bluefield, W.V., U.S.	G4	114
Bluefields, Nic.	F6	102
Blue Hill, Ne., U.S.	A10	128
Blue Hill Bay, b., Me., U.S.	F8	110
Blue Island, Il., U.S.	G2	112
Blue Mound, Ks., U.S.	F3	120
Blue Mountain, Ms., U.S.	C9	122
Blue Mountain, mtn., Ar., U.S.	C4	122
Blue Mountain, mtn., Mt., U.S.	G9	124
Blue Mountain, mts., Pa., U.S.	D8	114
Blue Mountain Peak, mtn., Jam.	i14	104d
Blue Mountains, mts., Jam.	i14	104d
Blue Mountains, mts., Me., U.S.	F6	110
Blue Mountains National Park, p.o.i., Austl.	B7	74
Blue Mud Bay, b., Austl.	B7	74
Blue Nile (Azraq, Al-Bahr al-) (Abay), stm., Afr.	E6	62
Bluenose Lake, l., Nu., Can.	B6	106
Blue Ridge, Ab., Can.	B15	138
Blue Ridge, Ga., U.S.	B1	116
Blue Ridge, Va., U.S.	H4	114
Blue River, B.C., Can.	D11	138
Bluestone Dam, dam, W.V., U.S.	G5	114
Bluestone Lake, res., W.V., U.S.	G5	114
Bluewater, N.M., U.S.	H9	132
Bluff, N.Z.	H3	80
Bluff, Ut., U.S.	F7	132
Bluff Cape, c., Mya.	D2	48
Bluff Creek, stm., U.S.	D11	128
Bluff Dale, Tx., U.S.	B9	130
Bluff Park, Al., U.S.	D12	122
Bluffs, Il., U.S.	E7	120
Bluffton, In., U.S.	H3	112
Bluffton, S.C., U.S.	D5	116
Blumberg, Ger.	I4	16
Blumenau, Braz.	C13	92
Blumenhof, Sk., Can.	D6	124
Bly, Or., U.S.	A4	134
Blyth, Eng., U.K.	F11	12
Blythe, Ca., U.S.	J2	132
Blytheville, Ar., U.S.	I7	120
Bø, Nor.	G3	8
Bo, S.L.	H2	64
Boac, Phil.	D3	52
Boaco, Nic.	F5	102
Boa Esperança, Braz.	K3	88
Boa Esperança, Represa, res., Braz.	D3	88
Bo'ai, China	D5	42
Boane, Moz.	E11	70
Board Camp Mountain, mtn., Ca., U.S.	C1	134
Boardman, Oh., U.S.	C5	114
Boatman, Austl.	F6	76
Boa Viagem, Braz.	C5	88
Boa Vista, Braz.	F11	86
Boa Vista, i., C.V.	k10	65a
Boawai, Indon.	H12	50
Boaz, Al., U.S.	C12	122
Bobai, China	J3	42
Bobaomby, Tanjona, c., Madag.	C8	68
Bobbili, India	B6	53
Bobcaygeon, On., Can.	D11	112
Bobigny, Fr.	F11	14
Böblingen, Ger.	H5	16
Bobo-Dioulasso, Burkina	G4	64
Bobolice, Pol.	C12	16
Bobonaza, stm., Ec.	H3	86
Bobonong, Bots.	B9	70
Bobr, Bela.	F12	10
Bóbr, stm., Pol.	E11	16
Bobtown, Pa., U.S.	E5	114
Bobures, Ven.	C6	86
Boby, mtn., Madag.	E8	68
Bôca da Mata, Braz.	E7	88
Boca do Acre, Braz.	E4	84
Boca do Jari, Braz.	D7	84
Bocage, Cap, c., N. Cal.	m15	79d
Bocaiúva, Braz.	I4	88
Bocanda, C.A.R.	C3	66
Bocaranga, C.A.R.	C3	66
Boca Raton, Fl., U.S.	J5	116
Bocas del Toro, Pan.	H6	102
Bocay, Nic.	E5	102
Bochnia, Pol.	G16	16
Bocholt, Ger.	E2	16
Bochum, Ger.	E3	16
Bocón, Caño, stm., Col.	F7	86
Bocsa, Rom.	D8	26
Boda, C.A.R.	D3	66
Bodajbo, Russia	E11	34
Bodalla, Austl.	K8	76
Bodaybo see Bodajbo, Russia	E11	34
Bode, stm., Ger.	E7	16
Bodélé, reg., Chad	D3	62
Boden, Swe.	D9	8
Bodensee see Constance, Lake, l., Eur.	I5	16
Bodhan, India	B3	53
Bodh Gaya, India	F10	54
Bodinäyakkanür, India	G3	53
Bodmin, Eng., U.K.	K8	12
Bodo, Nor.	C6	8
Bodoquena, Serra da, plat., Braz.	D5	90
Bodrum, Tur.	F10	28
Bodzentyn, Pol.	F16	16
Boende, D.R.C.	E4	66
Bœng Lvea, Camb.	F7	48
Boeo, Capo, c., Italy	G6	24
Boesmans, stm., S. Afr.	H7	70
Boeuf, stm., U.S.	E7	122
Boffa, Gui.	G2	64
Bogale, Mya.	D2	48
Bogalusa, La., U.S.	G9	122
Bogan, stm., Austl.	H6	76
Bogan Gate, Austl.	I6	76
Bogangolo, C.A.R.	C3	66
Bogata, Tx., U.S.	D3	122
Bogatić, Serb.	D6	26
Bogang, stm., China	C11	54
Bogda Shan, mts., China	C2	36
Bogen, Ger.	H8	16
Boger City, N.C., U.S.	A4	116
Boggabilla, Austl.	G8	76
Boggabri, Austl.	H7	76
Boggy Peak, mtn., Antig.	e11	105b
Bogles, Gren.	p11	105e
Bognor Regis, Eng., U.K.	K12	12
Bogo, Phil.	E5	52
Bogojubovo, Russia	E15	10
Bogong, Mount, mtn., Austl.	K6	76
Bogor, Indon.	G5	50
Bogorodick, Russia	G21	10
Bogorodsk, Russia	H20	8
Bogorodskoe, Russia	F17	34
Bogotá, Col.	E4	86
Bogotol, Russia	C15	32
Bogra, Bngl.	F12	54
Bogučany, Russia	C17	32
Bogué, Maur.	F2	64
Bogue Chitto, stm., U.S.	G8	122
Bogue Phalia, stm., Ms., U.S.	D8	122
Böğürtlen, Tur.	A8	58
Bo Hai (Chihli, Gulf of), b., China	B8	42
Bohai Haixia, strt., China	B9	42
Bohain-en-Vermandois, Fr.	D12	14
Bohai Wan, b., China	B8	42
Bohemian Forest, mts., Eur.	G8	16
Böhmer Wald see Bohemian Forest, mts., Eur.	G8	16
Bohol, i., Phil.	F4	52
Bohol Sea, s., Phil.	F5	52
Boiaçu, Braz.	H11	86
Boiano, Italy	C8	24
Boiestown, N.B., Can.	D10	110
Boipeba, Ilha de, i., Braz.	G6	88
Bois, stm., Braz.	C6	90
Bois, Lac des, l., N.T., Can.	B6	106
Bois Blanc Island, i., Mi., U.S.	C5	112
Bois de Sioux, stm., U.S.	F2	118
Boise, Id., U.S.	G10	136
Boise, stm., Id., U.S.	G10	136
Boise, Middle Fork, stm., Id., U.S.	G11	136
Boise, South Fork, stm., Id., U.S.	G11	136
Boise City, Ok., U.S.	E6	128
Boissevain, Mb., Can.	E13	124
Boissfort Peak, mtn., Wa., U.S.	D3	136
Boizenburg, Ger.	C6	16
Boja, Indon.	G7	50
Bojadła, Pol.	E11	16
Bojeador, Cape, c., Phil.	A3	52
Bojnūrd, Iran	B8	56
Bojonegoro, Indon.	G7	50
Bojuru, Braz.	E12	92
Bokāro Steel City, India	G10	54
Bokchito, Ok., U.S.	C2	122
Boké, Gui.	G2	64
Bokhara, stm., Austl.	G6	76
Bok Koŭ, Camb.	G6	48
Boknafjorden, strt., Nor.	G1	8
Boko, Congo	E2	66
Bokote, D.R.C.	E4	66
Boksitogorsk, Russia	A16	10
Bokungu, D.R.C.	E4	66
Bol, Cro.	G13	22
Bolama, Gui.-B.	G1	64
Bolaños, stm., Mex.	E7	100
Bolaños de Calatrava, Spain	F7	20
Bolán Pass, p., Pak.	D10	56
Bolayır, Tur.	C9	28
Bolbec, Fr.	E9	14
Bole, China	F14	32
Bole, Ghana	H4	64
Boles, Ar., U.S.	C4	122
Bolesławiec, Pol.	E11	16
Boley, Ok., U.S.	B2	122
Bolgatanga, Ghana	G4	64
Bolhrad, Ukr.	D15	26
Boli, China	B11	36
Bolibo, Indon.	E10	122
Bolingbrook, Il., U.S.	C9	120
Bolintin, China	D5	38
Bolívar, Col.	G3	86
Bolívar, Mo., U.S.	G4	120
Bolivar, Tn., U.S.	B9	122
Bolívar, state, Col.	C4	86
Bolívar, state, Ven.	D10	86
Bolívar, Cerro, mtn., Ven.	D10	86
Bolívar, Pico (La Columna), mtn., Ven.	C6	86
Bolivar Peninsula, pen., Tx., U.S.	H4	122
Bolivia, ctry., S.A.	C4	84
Bolivia, N.C., U.S.	B7	116
Bolkhov, Russia	H5	8
Bollène, Fr.	E10	18
Bollnäs, Swe.	F7	8
Bollon, Austl.	G6	76
Bolmen, l., Swe.	H5	8
Bolobo, D.R.C.	E3	66
Bologna, Italy	F8	22
Bologoe, Russia	C17	10
Bolognesi, Peru	E3	84
Bolohovo, Russia	F20	10
Bolomba, D.R.C.	D3	66
Bolon', ozero, l., Russia	F16	34
Bolotnoe, Russia	C14	32
Bolovens, Plateau des, plat., Laos	E8	48
Balahnja, stm., Russia	B9	34
Bol'saja Heta, stm., Russia	C5	34
Bol'saja Kuonamka, stm., Russia	C10	34
Bol'saja Murta, Russia	C16	32
Bol'saja Ussurka, stm., Russia	B11	36
Bol'saja Višera, Russia	B15	10
Bol'šakovo, Russia	F4	10
Bolsena, Italy	H8	22
Bolsena, Lago di, l., Italy	H8	22
Bol'šereck, Russia	F20	34
Bol'šereč'e, Russia	C12	32
Bol'ševik, ostrov, i., Russia	A10	34
Bolshevik see Bol'ševik, ostrov, i., Russia	A10	34
Bol'šie Uki, Russia	C12	32
Bol'šoe Mihajlovskoe, Russia	D20	8
Bol'soe Polpino, Russia	G17	10
Bol'šoe Selo, Russia	C21	10
Bol'šoj Anjuj, stm., Russia	C21	34
Bol'šoj Begičev, ostrov, i., Russia	B11	34
Bol'šoj Jugan, stm., Russia	B12	32
Bol'šoj Kamen', Russia	C10	38
Bol'šoj Ljahovskij, ostrov, i., Russia	B17	34
Bol'šoj Tal'cy, Russia	A15	10
Bolton, On., Can.	E10	112
Bolton, Eng., U.K.	H10	12
Bolton, Ms., U.S.	E8	122
Bolton, N.C., U.S.	B7	116
Bolu, Tur.	C14	28
Bolu, state, Tur.	C14	28
Bolva, stm., Russia	G17	10
Bolvadin, Tur.	E13	28
Bóly, Hung.	C5	26
Bolzano (Bozen), Italy	D8	22
Boma, D.R.C.	F2	66
Bomaderry, Austl.	J8	76
Bombala, Austl.	K7	76
Bombay see Mumbai, India	B1	53
Bomberai, Semenanjung, pen., Indon.	F9	44
Bomboma, D.R.C.	D3	66
Bom Conselho, Braz.	E7	88
Bom Despacho, Braz.	J3	88
Bomdila, India	E14	54
Bom Jardim, Braz.	E3	88
Bom Jesus, Braz.	E3	88
Bom Jesus da Lapa, Braz.	G4	88
Bommak, Russia	F14	34
Bomokandi, stm., D.R.C.	D5	66
Bomongo, D.R.C.	D3	66
Bom Retiro, Braz.	C13	92
Bomu, stm., Afr.	D4	66
Bon, Cap, c., Tun.	G5	24
Bon Air, Va., U.S.	G8	114
Bonaire, i., Neth. Ant.	p23	104g
Bonampak, sci., Mex.	D2	102
Bonandolok, Indon.	C1	50
Bonanza, Or., U.S.	A4	134
Bonanza, Ut., U.S.	C7	132
Bonanza Peak, mtn., Wa., U.S.	B5	136
Bonao, Dom. Rep.	C12	102
Bonaparte, La., U.S.	D6	120
Bonaparte, stm., B.C., Can.	F9	138
Bonaparte, Mount, mtn., Wa., U.S.	B7	136
Bonaparte Lake, l., B.C., Can.	E10	138
Bonar Bridge, Scot., U.K.	D8	12
Bonasse, Trin.	s12	105f
Bonaventure, Qc., Can.	B11	110
Bonaventure, stm., Qc., Can.	B11	110
Bonaventure, Île, i., Qc., Can.	B12	110
Bonavista, Nf., Can.	j23	107a
Bonavista Bay, b., Nf., Can.	j23	107a
Bondeno, Italy	F8	22
Bondo, D.R.C.	D4	66
Bondo, D.R.C.	E4	66
Bondoc Peninsula, pen., Phil.	D4	52
Bondoukou, Iv.	H4	64
Bondowoso, Indon.	G8	50
Bonduel, Wi., U.S.	G10	118
Bone, Teluk, b., Indon.	F7	44
Bonebone, Indon.	E12	50
Boneeogeh, Indon.	G12	50
Bonerate, Pulau, i., Indon.	G12	50
Bonesteel, S.D., U.S.	D13	126
Bonete Chico, Cerro, mtn., Arg.	D3	92
Bonete Grande, Cerro, mtn., Arg.	C3	92
Bongabong, Phil.	D3	52
Bongaigaon, India	E13	54
Bonganga, D.R.C.	D4	66
Bongka, Indon.	F7	44
Bongo, Gabon	E2	66
Bongo, Massif des, mts., C.A.R.	C4	66
Bongor, Chad	E3	62
Bonham, Tx., U.S.	D2	122
Bonhomme, Morne, mtn., Haiti	C11	102
Bonifacio, Fr.	H15	18
Bonifacio, Strait of, strt., Eur.	H15	18
Bonifati, Capo, c., Italy	E9	24
Bonin Islands see Ogasawara-guntō, is., Japan	G18	30
Bonita, La., U.S.	E7	122
Bonita Springs, Fl., U.S.	J4	116
Bonito, Braz.	D5	90
Bonito, Braz.	D6	88
Bonito de Santa Fé, Braz.	D6	88
Bonn, Ger.	F3	16
Bonners Ferry, Id., U.S.	B10	136
Bonnet, Lac du, res., Can.	D17	124
Bonne Terre, Mo., U.S.	F9	120
Bonnet Plume, stm., Yk., Can.	B3	106
Bonneville, Fr.	C12	18
Bonneville Peak, mtn.,	H14	136
Bonneville Salt Flats, pl., Ut., U.S.	C2	132
Bonney SE, Lake, l., Austl.	K3	76
Bonnie Rock, Austl.	F3	74
Bonny, Nig.	I6	64
Bonnyville, Ab., Can.	B20	138
Bono, Ar., U.S.	I7	120
Bonoi, Indon.	F10	44
Bonshaw, P.E., Can.	D13	110
Bontang, Indon.	C10	50
Bontebok National Park, p.o.i., S. Afr.	I5	70
Bonthe, S.L.	H2	64
Bontoc, Phil.	B3	52
Bon Wier, Tx., U.S.	G5	122
Booker, Tx., U.S.	E8	128
Booker T. Washington National Monument, p.o.i., Va., U.S.	H6	114
Boola, Gui.	H3	64
Boolaloo, Austl.	D3	74
Booleroo Centre, Austl.	D2	76
Boologooro, Austl.	D2	76
Boomi, Austl.	G7	76
Boone, Ia., U.S.	I5	118
Boone, N.C., U.S.	H4	114
Boone, stm., Ia., U.S.	B4	120
Booneville, Ar., U.S.	B5	122
Booneville, Ky., U.S.	G2	114
Booneville, Ms., U.S.	C10	122
Boon Tsagaan nuur, l., Mong.	B4	36
Boorabbin, Austl.	F3	74
Booral, Austl.	D2	134
Boorindal, Austl.	H6	76
Booroorban, Austl.	J5	76
Boosaaso, Som.	B9	66
Booth, Al., U.S.	E12	122
Boothbay Harbor, Me., U.S.	G7	110
Boothia, Gulf of, b., Nu., Can.	A12	106
Boothia Peninsula, pen., Nu., Can.	A12	106
Boothville, La., U.S.	H9	122
Booué, Gabon	E2	66
Bophuthatswana, hist. reg., S. Afr.	E7	70
Boping Ling, mts., China	I7	42
Bopolu, Gui.	H2	64
Boquein, Tur.	F10	28
Boqueirão, Serra do, hills, Braz.	F4	88

Name	Map Ref.	Page
Boquilla, Presa de la, res., Mex.	B6	100
Boquim, Braz.	F7	88
Bor, Russia	H20	8
Bor, Russia	E20	8
Bor, Sudan	F6	62
Bor, Tur.	B3	56
Bor, Serb.	E9	26
Bor, Lak, stm., Kenya	D7	66
Bora-Bora, i., Fr. Poly.	E11	72
Borabu, Thai.	E6	48
Borah Peak, mtn., Id., U.S.	F13	136
Borås, Swe.	H5	8
Borba, Braz.	D6	84
Bordeaux, Fr.	E5	18
Bordeaux Mountain, hill, V.I.U.S.	e8	104b
Borden, Sk., Can.	B6	124
Borden Peninsula, pen., Nu., Can.	A14	106
Bordertown, Austl.	K3	76
Bordesholm, Ger.	B6	16
Bordighera, Italy	G4	22
Bordj Menaïel, Alg.	H14	20
Bordj Omar Idriss, Alg.	D6	64
Borđoy, i., Far. Is.	m34	8b
Borgå see Porvoo, Fin.	F11	8
Borgarnes, Ice.	k28	8a
Børgefjell Nasjonalpark, p.o.i., Nor.	D5	8
Borger, Tx., U.S.	F7	128
Borgholm, Swe.	H7	8
Borgne, Lake, b., La., U.S.	G9	122
Borgnesse, Pointe, c., Mart.	I7	105c
Borgomanero, Italy	E5	22
Borgo San Dalmazzo, Italy	F4	22
Borgosesia, Italy	E5	22
Borgo Val di Taro, Italy	F6	22
Borgworm see Waremme, Bel.	D14	14
Borikhan, Laos	C6	48
Borisoglebsk, Russia	D6	32
Borisoglebskij, Russia	C21	10
Borjas Blancas see Les Borges Blanques, Spain	C11	20
Borkavičy, Bela.	E11	10
Borken, Ger.	E2	16
Borkou, reg., Chad	D3	62
Borkum, i., Ger.	C2	16
Borlänge, Swe.	F6	8
Bormes, Fr.	F12	18
Borna, Ger.	E9	16
Borneo (Kalimantan), i., Asia	E5	44
Bornholm, state, Den.	I6	8
Bornholm, i., Den.	I6	8
Borocay Island, i., Phil.	E3	52
Borodino, Russia	C17	32
Borogoncy, Russia	D15	34
Borohoro Shan, mts., China	F14	32
Boromo, Burkina	G4	64
Boron, Ca., U.S.	H8	134
Boronga Islands, is., Mya.	I14	54
Borongan, Phil.	E5	52
Borovan, Blg.	F10	26
Boroviči, Russia	B16	10
Borovljanka, Russia	D14	32
Borovsk, Russia	E19	10
Borovskij, Russia	C11	32
Borovskoy, Kaz.	D10	32
Borrachudo, stm., Braz.	J3	88
Borrazópolis, Braz.	A12	92
Borriana, Spain	E10	20
Borroloola, Austl.	C7	74
Borş, Rom.	B8	26
Borşa, Rom.	B11	26
Borsad, India	G4	54
Borščovočnyj hrebet, mts., Russia	F12	34
Borsod-Abaúj-Zemplén, state, Hung.	A8	26
Bort-les-Orgues, Fr.	D8	18
Borūjerd, Iran	C6	56
Borzja, Russia	F12	34
Bosa, Italy	D2	24
Bosanska Dubica, Bos.	D3	26
Bosanska Gradiška, Bos.	D4	26
Bosanska Krupa, Bos.	E3	26
Bosanski Novi, Bos.	D3	26
Bosanski Šamac, Bos.	D5	26
Bosavi, Mount, mtn., Pap. N. Gui.	b3	79a
Boscobel, Wi., U.S.	A7	120
Bose, China	J2	42
Boshan, China	C7	42
Boshof, S. Afr.	F7	70
Bosilegrad, Serb.	G9	26
Bosna, stm., Bos.	E5	26
Bosnia and Herzegovina, ctry., Eur.	E3	26
Bosnik, Indon.	F10	44
Bošnjakovo, Russia	G17	34
Bosobolo, D.R.C.	D3	66
Bōsō-hantō, pen., Japan	D13	40
Bosporus see İstanbul Boğazı, strt., Tur.	B12	28
Bossangoa, C.A.R.	C3	66
Bossembélé, C.A.R.	C3	66
Bossey Bangou, Niger	G5	64
Bossier City, La., U.S.	E5	122
Bosten Hu, l., China	C2	36
Boston, Eng., U.K.	H12	12
Boston, Ga., U.S.	F2	116
Boston, Ma., U.S.	B14	114
Boston Bar, B.C., Can.	G9	138
Boston Mountains, mts., Ar., U.S.	B5	122
Boswell, In., U.S.	H2	112
Boswell, Ok., U.S.	C3	122
Bosworth, Mo., U.S.	E4	120
Botād, India	G3	54
Botany Bay, b., Austl.	J8	76
Boteti, stm., Bots.	E3	68
Bothaville, S. Afr.	E8	70
Bothnia, Gulf of, b., Eur.	E9	8
Bothwell, On., Can.	F8	112
Boticas, Port.	C3	20
Botna, stm., Mol.	C15	26
Botoşani, Rom.	B13	26
Botoşani, state, Rom.	B13	26
Bo Trach, Viet.	D8	48
Botrange, mtn., Bel.	D15	14
Botswana, ctry., Afr.	E3	68
Botte Donato, Monte, mtn., Italy	E10	24
Bottineau, N.D., U.S.	F13	124
Botucatu, Braz.	L1	88
Botwood, Nf., Can.	j22	107a
Bouaflé, C. Iv.	H3	64
Bouaké, C. Iv.	H3	64
Bouar, C.A.R.	C3	66
Bouârfa, Mor.	C4	64
Bouca, C.A.R.	C3	66
Boucher, stm., Qc., Can.	A7	110
Bouches-du-Rhône, state, Fr.	F11	18
Bouctouche, N.B., Can.	D12	110
Boufarik, Alg.	H13	20
Bou Ficha, Tun.	H4	24
Bougainville, i., Pap. N. Gui.	d7	79b
Bougainville, Détroit de, strt., Vanuatu	j16	79d
Bougainville Strait, strt., Oc.	d7	79b
Bougouni, Mali	G3	64
Bouillante, Guad.	h5	105c
Bouillon, Bel.	E14	14
Bouïra, Alg.	B5	64
Boujdour, Cap, c., W. Sah.	D2	64
Boularderie Island, i., N.S., Can.	D16	110
Boulder, Co., U.S.	A3	128
Boulder, Mt., U.S.	D14	136
Boulder, stm., Mt., U.S.	D15	136
Boulder City, Nv., U.S.	H2	132
Boulia, Austl.	D2	76
Boulogne-sur-Mer, Fr.	D10	14
Bouloupari, N. Cal.	m15	79d
Boulsa, Burkina	G4	64
Bou Medfaa, Alg.	H13	20
Bouna, C. Iv.	H4	64
Boundary Peak, mtn., Nv., U.S.	F7	134
Boundiali, C. Iv.	H3	64
Boun Nua, Laos	B5	48
Bountiful, Ut., U.S.	C4	132
Bounty Bay, b., Pit.	c28	78k
Bounty Islands, is., N.Z.	H8	80
Bounty Trough, unds.	N20	142
Bourail, N. Cal.	m15	79d
Bourbeuse, stm., Mo., U.S.	F6	120
Bourbon, In., U.S.	G3	112
Bourbonnais, hist. reg., Fr.	C9	18
Bourbonne-les-Bains, Fr.	G14	14
Bourem, Mali	F4	64
Bourg, La., U.S.	H8	122
Bourg-en-Bresse, Fr.	C11	18
Bourges, Fr.	G11	14
Bourget, On., Can.	E1	110
Bourget, Lac du, l., Fr.	D11	18
Bourgogne (Burgundy), hist. reg., Fr.	B10	18
Bourgogne, Canal de, can., Fr.	G13	14
Bourgoin-Jallieu, Fr.	D11	18
Bourke, Austl.	H5	76
Bournemouth, Eng., U.K.	K11	12
Bou Saâda, Alg.	B5	64
Bou Salem, Tun.	H2	24
Bouse Wash, stm., Az., U.S.	J3	132
Bou Smail, Alg.	H13	20
Boussac, Fr.	C8	18
Bousso, Chad	E3	62
Boutilimit, Maur.	F2	64
Bouvetøya, i., Ant.	A5	81
Bouza, Niger	G6	64
Bøvågen, Nor.	F1	8
Bovec, Slvn.	D10	22
Bovey, Mn., U.S.	D5	118
Bovill, Id., U.S.	D10	136
Bovina, Tx., U.S.	G6	128
Bow, stm., Ab., Can.	G19	138
Bo-Wadrif, S. Afr.	H4	70
Bowbells, N.D., U.S.	F11	124
Bow Creek, stm., Ks., U.S.	B9	128
Bowden, Ab., Can.	E16	138
Bowdle, S.D., U.S.	B13	126
Bowdon, N.D., U.S.	G14	124
Bowen, Arg.	G4	92
Bowen, Austl.	C7	76
Bowen, Il., U.S.	D7	120
Bowen, stm., Austl.	C6	76
Bowie, Az., U.S.	K7	132
Bowie, Md., U.S.	F9	114
Bowling Green, Fl., U.S.	I4	116
Bowling Green, Ky., U.S.	H11	120
Bowling Green, Mo., U.S.	E6	120
Bowling Green, Oh., U.S.	C2	114
Bowling Green, Va., U.S.	F8	114
Bowling Green, Cape, c., Austl.	B6	76
Bowling Green Bay National Park, p.o.i., Austl.	B6	76
Bowman, N.D., U.S.	A9	126
Bowman, S.C., U.S.	C5	116
Bowman, Mount, mtn., B.C., Can.	E9	138
Bowmanville, On., Can.	E11	112
Bowral, Austl.	J8	76
Bowraville, Austl.	H9	76
Bowron, stm., B.C., Can.	C9	138
Bowsman, Mb., Can.	B12	124
Box Elder Creek, stm., Mt., U.S.	G5	124
Boxelder Creek, stm., S.D., U.S.	C10	126
Boxelder Creek, stm., U.S.	B8	126
Boxing, China	C8	42
Boyacá, state, Col.	E5	86
Boyang, China	G7	42
Boyce, La., U.S.	F6	122
Boyceville, Wi., U.S.	F6	118
Boyd, Tx., U.S.	A10	130
Boyd, stm., Austl.	G9	76
Boydton, Va., U.S.	H7	114
Boyer, stm., Ia., U.S.	C2	120
Boyertown, Pa., U.S.	D10	114
Boykins, Va., U.S.	H8	114
Boyle, Ms., U.S.	D8	122
Boylston, Al., U.S.	E12	122
Boyne, stm., Austl.	E8	76
Boyne, stm., Mb., Can.	E16	124
Boyne, stm., Ire.	H5	12
Boyne City, Mi., U.S.	C5	112
Boynton Beach, Fl., U.S.	J5	116
Boysen Reservoir, res., Wy., U.S.	D4	126
Boys Ranch, Tx., U.S.	F6	128
Bozburun, Tur.	G11	28
Bozburun Yarımadası, pen., Tur.	G11	28
Boz Dağ, mtn., Tur.	E11	28
Boz Dağlar, mts., Tur.	E10	28
Bozdoğan, Tur.	F11	28
Bozeman, Mt., U.S.	E15	136
Bozen see Bolzano, Italy	D8	22
Bozhen, China	B7	42
Bozhou, China	E6	42
Bozkurt, Tur.	F12	28
Bozoum, C.A.R.	C3	66
Bozova, Tur.	A9	58
Bozovici, Rom.	E9	26
Bozshakö̈l, Kaz.	D12	32
Bozüyük, Tur.	D13	28
Bra, Italy	F4	22
Brač, Otok, i., Cro.	G13	22
Bracciano, Italy	H9	22
Bracciano, Lago di, l., Italy	H9	22
Bracebridge, On., Can.	C10	112
Brackendale, B.C., Can.	G7	138
Brackettville, Tx., U.S.	E7	130
Bracknell, Eng., U.K.	J12	12
Braço do Norte, Braz.	D13	92
Brad, Rom.	C9	26
Bradano, stm., Italy	D10	24
Bradenton, Fl., U.S.	I3	116
Bradford, Eng., U.K.	H11	12
Bradford, Ar., U.S.	B7	122
Bradford, Pa., U.S.	C7	114
Bradford, Tn., U.S.	H9	120
Bradford, Vt., U.S.	G4	110
Bradford West Gwillimbury, On., Can.	D10	112
Bradley, Ar., U.S.	D5	122
Bradley, Fl., U.S.	I3	116
Bradley, Il., U.S.	G2	112
Bradley, S.D., U.S.	B15	126
Brady, Mt., U.S.	B15	136
Brady, Ne., U.S.	F12	126
Brady, Tx., U.S.	C8	130
Brady Creek, stm., Tx., U.S.	C8	130
Braga, Port.	C2	20
Braga, state, Port.	C2	20
Bragado, Arg.	G7	92
Bragança, Braz.	D8	84
Bragança, Port.	C4	20
Bragança, state, Port.	C4	20
Bragança Paulista, Braz.	L2	88
Brāhmanbāria, Bngl.	F13	54
Brāhmani, stm., India	H10	54
Brahmapur, India	B7	53
Brahmaputra (Yarlung), stm., Asia	C7	46
Braich y Pwll, c., Wales, U.K.	I8	12
Braidwood, Austl.	J7	76
Braidwood, Il., U.S.	C9	120
Brăila, Rom.	D14	26
Brăila, state, Rom.	D14	26
Brainard, Ne., U.S.	F15	126
Brainerd, Mn., U.S.	E4	118
Braintree, Eng., U.K.	J13	12
Brak, stm., S. Afr.	G6	70
Brake, Ger.	C4	16
Bralorne, B.C., Can.	F8	138
Brampton, On., Can.	E10	112
Bramsche, Ger.	D3	16
Branchville, S.C., U.S.	C5	116
Branco, stm., Braz.	H11	86
Branco, stm., Braz.	F3	88
Brandaris, hill, Neth. Ant.	p23	104g
Brandberg, mtn., Nmb.	B2	70
Brandbu, Nor.	F4	8
Brandenburg, Ger.	D8	16
Brandenburg, Ky., U.S.	G11	120
Brandenburg, state, Ger.	D9	16
Brandfort, S. Afr.	F8	70
Brandon, Mb., Can.	E14	124
Brandon, Fl., U.S.	I3	116
Brandon, Ms., U.S.	E9	122
Brandon, S.D., U.S.	H2	118
Brandon, Vt., U.S.	G3	110
Brandsen, Arg.	G8	92
Brandvlei, S. Afr.	G5	70
Brandy Peak, mtn., Or., U.S.	H3	136
Brandýs nad Labem-Stará Boleslav, Czech Rep.	F10	16
Branford, Fl., U.S.	G2	116
Braniewo, Pol.	B15	16
Bransby, Austl.	G4	76
Bransby Point, c., Monts.	D3	105a
Bransfield Strait, strt., Ant.	B35	81
Branson, Mo., U.S.	H4	120
Brantford, On., Can.	E9	112
Brantley, Al., U.S.	F12	122
Brantley Tank, res., N.M., U.S.	B3	130
Brantôme, Fr.	D6	18
Brantville, N.B., Can.	C12	110
Bras d'Or Lake, l., N.S., Can.	E16	110
Brasiléia, Braz.	F4	84
Brasília, Braz.	H1	88
Brasília, Parque Nacional de, p.o.i., Braz.	H1	88
Brasília de Minas, Braz.	I3	88
Braslau, Bela.	E9	10
Braşov, Rom.	D12	26
Braşov, state, Rom.	D12	26
Brassey, Banjaran, mts., Malay.	A10	50
Brass Islands, is., V.I.U.S.	e7	104b
Brasstown Bald, mtn., Ga., U.S.	B2	116
Bratca, Rom.	C9	26
Bratislava, Slov.	H13	16
Bratislava, state, Slov.	H13	16
Bratsk, Russia	C18	32
Bratskoe vodohranilišče, res., Russia	C18	32
Bratsk Reservoir see Bratskoe vodohranilišče, res., Russia	C18	32
Brattleboro, Vt., U.S.	B13	114
Braulio Carrillo, Parque Nacional, p.o.i., C.R.	G5	102
Braúnas, Braz.	J4	88
Braunau am Inn, Aus.	B10	22
Braunschweig (Brunswick), Ger.	D6	16
Brava, i., C.V.	I10	65a
Brava, Costa, cst., Spain	C14	20
Brava, Laguna, l., Arg.	D3	92
Brava, Punta, c., Ur.	G9	92
Brave, Pa., U.S.	E5	114
Bravo (Rio Grande), stm., N.A.	H13	98
Bravo, Cerro, mtn., Peru	E2	84
Bravo del Norte see Bravo, stm., N.A.	H13	98
Brawley, Ca., U.S.	K10	134
Bray, Ire.	H6	12
Bray Island, i., Nu., Can.	B15	106
Brazeau, stm., Ab., Can.	D15	138
Brazeau, Mount, mtn., Ab., Can.	D13	138
Brazeau Dam, dam, Ab., Can.	C15	138
Brazil, In., U.S.	E10	120
Brazil, ctry., S.A.	F9	82
Brazil Basin, unds.	J11	144
Brazoria, Tx., U.S.	E12	130
Brazos, stm., Tx., U.S.	E8	108
Brazos, Clear Fork, stm., Tx., U.S.	B8	130
Brazos, Double Mountain Fork, stm., Tx., U.S.	H8	128
Brazos, North Fork, stm., Tx., U.S.	H3	122
Brazzaville, Congo	E2	66
Brčko, Bos.	E5	26
Brda, stm., Pol.	C13	16
Bré see Bray, Ire.	H6	12
Brea, Ca., U.S.	J8	134
Bream Bay, b., N.Z.	B6	80
Brea Pozo, Arg.	D6	92
Breaux Bridge, La., U.S.	G7	122
Brebes, Indon.	G6	50
Brechin, Scot., U.K.	E10	12
Breckenridge, Mi., U.S.	E5	112
Breckenridge, Mn., U.S.	E2	118
Breckenridge, Mo., U.S.	E4	120
Brecknock, Península, pen., Chile	J2	90
Břeclav, Czech Rep.	H12	16
Brecon, Wales, U.K.	J9	12
Brecon Beacons, hills, Wales, U.K.	J9	12
Brecon Beacons National Park, p.o.i., Wales, U.K.	J9	12
Breda, Neth.	C13	14
Breda, Ia., U.S.	B3	120
Bredasdorp, S. Afr.	I5	70
Bredenbury, Sk., Can.	D11	124
Bredy, Russia	D9	32
Breë, stm., S. Afr.	I5	70
Breese, Il., U.S.	F8	120
Bregalnica, stm., Mac.	A5	28
Bregenz, Aus.	C6	22
Bregovo, Blg.	E9	26
Bréhat, Île de, i., Fr.	F6	14
Breiðafjörður, b., Ice.	k28	8a
Brejinho de Nazaré, Braz.	F1	88
Brejo, Braz.	B4	88
Brejo Grande, Braz.	F7	88
Brejo Santo, Braz.	D6	88
Brekstad, Nor.	E3	8
Bremen, Ger.	C4	16
Bremen, Ga., U.S.	D13	122
Bremen, Oh., U.S.	E3	114
Bremen, state, Ger.	C4	16
Bremer Bay, Austl.	F3	74
Bremer Bay, b., Austl.	F3	74
Bremerhaven, Ger.	C4	16
Bremerton, Wa., U.S.	C4	136
Bremervörde, Ger.	C4	16
Bremond, Tx., U.S.	F2	122
Brenham, Tx., U.S.	G2	122
Brenner Pass, p., Eur.	C8	22
Brent, Fl., U.S.	G11	122
Brenta, stm., Italy	D8	22
Brentwood, Eng., U.K.	J13	12
Brentwood, N.Y., U.S.	D12	114
Brentwood, Tn., U.S.	H11	120
Breo, Italy	F4	22
Brescia, Italy	E7	22
Breslau see Wrocław, Pol.	E13	16
Bressanone, Italy	D8	22
Bressay, i., Scot., U.K.	n18	12a
Bresse, reg., Fr.	C11	18
Bressuire, Fr.	H8	14
Brèst, Bela.	H6	10
Brest, Fr.	F4	14
Brèst, state, Bela.	H8	10
Bretagne (Brittany), hist. reg., Fr.	F5	14
Bretenoux, Fr.	E7	18
Breton, Ab., Can.	C16	138
Breton Islands, is., La., U.S.	H9	122
Breton Sound, strt., La., U.S.	H9	122
Brett, Cape, c., N.Z.	B6	80
Bretten, Ger.	G4	16
Breueh, Pulau, i., Indon.	J2	48
Breuil-Cervinia, Italy	E4	22
Brevard, N.C., U.S.	A3	116
Breves, Braz.	D7	84
Brevoort Island, i., Nu., Can.	E13	141
Brewarrina, Austl.	G6	76
Brewer, Me., U.S.	F8	110
Brewster, Mn., U.S.	H3	118
Brewster, Ne., U.S.	F13	126
Brewster, Wa., U.S.	B7	136
Brewster, Kap, c., Grnld.	C21	141
Brewton, Al., U.S.	F11	122
Breyten, S. Afr.	E10	70
Březnice, Czech Rep.	G9	16
Brezno, Slov.	H15	16
Bria, C.A.R.	C4	66
Brian Boru Peak, mtn., B.C., Can.	A3	138
Briançon, Fr.	E12	18
Brian Head, mtn., Ut., U.S.	F4	132
Briare, Canal de, can., Fr.	G11	14
Bribie Island, i., Austl.	F9	76
Bricelyn, Mn., U.S.	H5	118
Briceni, Mol.	A14	26
Briceville, Tn., U.S.	A14	122
Bri Chuallan see Bray, Ire.	H6	12
Bridge, stm., B.C., Can.	F7	138
Bridge City, Tx., U.S.	G5	122
Bridge Lake, B.C., Can.	E10	138
Bridgend, Wales, U.K.	J9	12
Bridgeport, Ca., U.S.	E6	134
Bridgeport, Ct., U.S.	C12	114
Bridgeport, Mi., U.S.	E6	112
Bridgeport, Ne., U.S.	F9	126
Bridgeport, Tx., U.S.	H11	128
Bridgeport, Wa., U.S.	C7	136
Bridgeport, Lake, res., Tx., U.S.	H10	128
Bridger, Mt., U.S.	B4	126
Bridger Peak, mtn., Wy., U.S.	B9	132
Bridgeton, N.J., U.S.	E10	114
Bridgetown, Austl.	F3	74
Bridgetown, Barb.	n8	105d
Bridgetown, N.S., Can.	F11	110
Bridgeville, De., U.S.	F10	114
Bridgewater, N.S., Can.	F12	110
Bridgewater, Ma., U.S.	B15	114
Bridgewater, S.D., U.S.	D15	126
Bridgewater, Va., U.S.	F6	114
Bridgwater, Eng., U.K.	J9	12
Bridgwater Bay, b., Eng., U.K.	J9	12
Bridlington, Eng., U.K.	G12	12
Bridport, Eng., U.K.	K10	12
Brie, reg., Fr.	F12	14
Brier Creek, stm., Ga., U.S.	C4	116
Brig, Switz.	D5	22
Briggs, Tx., U.S.	D10	130
Brigham City, Ut., U.S.	B4	132
Bright, Austl.	K6	76
Brighton, On., Can.	D12	112
Brighton, Eng., U.K.	K12	12
Brighton, Co., U.S.	A4	128
Brighton, Ia., U.S.	C6	120
Brighton, Mi., U.S.	B2	114
Brighton, N.Y., U.S.	E12	112
Brighton Downs, Austl.	D3	76
Brignoles, Fr.	F11	18
Brijuni, i., Cro.	F10	22
Brilliant, B.C., Can.	G13	138
Brilliant, Al., U.S.	C11	122
Brillion, Wi., U.S.	D1	112
Brilon, Ger.	E4	16
Brindisi, Italy	D11	24
Brinkworth, Austl.	I2	76
Brion, Île, i., Qc., Can.	C15	110
Brioude, Fr.	D9	18
Brisbane, Austl.	F9	76
Brisighella, Italy	F8	22
Bristol, Eng., U.K.	J10	12
Bristol, Ct., U.S.	C12	114
Bristol, Fl., U.S.	G14	122
Bristol, N.H., U.S.	G5	110
Bristol, Pa., U.S.	D11	114
Bristol, R.I., U.S.	C14	114
Bristol, Tn., U.S.	H3	114
Bristol, Vt., U.S.	F3	110
Bristol Bay, b., Ak., U.S.	E7	140
Bristol Channel, strt., U.K.	J8	12
Bristol Island, i., S. Geor.	A2	81
Bristol Lake, l., Ca., U.S.	I10	134
Bristow, Ok., U.S.	B2	122
Britannia Beach, B.C., Can.	G7	138
British Columbia, state, Can.	E5	106
British Guiana see Guyana, ctry., S.A.	C6	84
British Honduras see Belize, ctry., N.A.	D3	102
British Indian Ocean Territory, dep., Afr.	G17	2
British Isles, is., Eur.	C12	4
British Mountains, mts., N.A.	C11	140
British Solomon Islands see Solomon Islands, ctry., Oc.	D7	72
British Virgin Islands, dep., N.A.	h15	96a
Brits, S. Afr.	D8	70
Britstown, S. Afr.	G6	70
Britt, Ia., U.S.	A4	120
Brittany see Bretagne, hist. reg., Fr.	F5	14
Britton, S.D., U.S.	B15	126
Brive-la-Gaillarde, Fr.	D7	18
Brixen see Bressanone, Italy	D8	22
Brixham, Eng., U.K.	K9	12
Brixton, Austl.	D5	76
Brjanka, Russia	C16	32
Brjansk, Russia	G17	10
Brjanskaja oblast', co., Russia	H16	10
Brno, Czech Rep.	G12	16
Broa, Ensenada de la, b., Cuba	A6	102
Broad, stm., Ga., U.S.	B2	116
Broad, stm., U.S.	B4	116
Broadalbin, N.Y., U.S.	G2	110
Broad Sound, b., Austl.	D7	76
Broad Sound Channel, strt., Austl.	C8	76
Broadus, Mt., U.S.	B7	126
Broadwater, Ne., U.S.	F10	126
Broadway, Va., U.S.	F7	114
Brocēni, Lat.	D5	10
Brochet, Mb., Can.	D10	106
Brock, Sk., Can.	C5	124
Brockman, Mount, mtn., Austl.	D3	74
Brockton, Ma., U.S.	B14	114
Brockton, Mt., U.S.	F9	124
Brockville, On., Can.	D14	112
Brockway, Pa., U.S.	C7	114
Brocton, N.Y., U.S.	B6	114
Brodeur Peninsula, pen., Nu., Can.	A13	106
Brodhead, Wi., U.S.	B8	120
Brodick, Scot., U.K.	F7	12
Brodnax, Va., U.S.	H7	114
Brodnica, Pol.	C15	16
Brogan, Or., U.S.	F9	136
Brok, Pol.	D17	16
Broken Arrow, Ok., U.S.	H2	120
Broken Bay, b., Austl.	I8	76
Broken Bow, Ok., U.S.	C4	122
Broken Bow Lake, res., Ok., U.S.	C4	122
Broken Hill, Austl.	H3	76
Broken Hill see Kabwe, Zam.	C4	68
Broken Ridge, unds.	M12	142
Brokopondo, Sur.	B6	84
Brokopondo Stuwmeer, res., Sur.	C6	84
Bromley Plateau, unds.	K10	144
Bromptonville, Qc., Can.	E4	110
Bromsgrove, Eng., U.K.	I10	12
Bronkhorstspruit, S. Afr.	D9	70
Bronlund Peak, mtn., B.C., Can.	D5	106
Bronnae, Bela.	H13	10
Bronnicy, Russia	E21	10
Bronson, Fl., U.S.	G3	116
Bronson, Ks., U.S.	G2	120
Bronson, Mi., U.S.	G4	112
Bronte, Italy	G8	24
Bronte, Tx., U.S.	C7	130
Brook, In., U.S.	H2	112
Brookeland, Tx., U.S.	F5	122
Brooker, Fl., U.S.	G3	116
Brookfield, N.S., Can.	E13	110
Brookfield, Wi., U.S.	E1	112
Brookford, N.C., U.S.	I4	114
Brookhaven, Ms., U.S.	F8	122
Brookings, Or., U.S.	A1	134
Brookings, S.D., U.S.	G2	118
Brookland, Ar., U.S.	B8	122
Brooklyn, N.S., Can.	F12	110
Brooklyn, Ia., U.S.	J6	118
Brooklyn, Mi., U.S.	B1	114
Brooklyn Center, Mn., U.S.	F5	118
Brookmere, B.C., Can.	G10	138
Brookneal, Va., U.S.	G7	114
Brookport, Il., U.S.	G9	120
Brooks, Ab., Can.	F19	138
Brooks Bay, b., B.C., Can.	F2	138
Brookshire, Tx., U.S.	H3	122
Brooks Range, mts., Ak., U.S.	C8	140
Brooksville, Fl., U.S.	H3	116
Brooksville, Ms., U.S.	D10	122
Brookville, In., U.S.	E12	120
Brookville, Pa., U.S.	C6	114
Brookville Lake, res., In., U.S.	E13	120
Broome, Austl.	C4	74
Broomfield, Co., U.S.	B3	128
Brooten, Mn., U.S.	F3	118
Brora, Scot., U.K.	C9	12
Brosna, stm., Ire.	H5	12
Brotas de Macaúbas, Braz.	G4	88
Brou, Fr.	F10	14
Broughton, Mount, mtn., Austl.	K5	76
Broughty Ferry, Scot., U.K.	E10	12
Browerville, Mn., U.S.	E4	118
Brown, Mount, mtn., Mt., U.S.	B15	136
Brown, Point, c., Wa., U.S.	D2	136
Brown Deer, Wi., U.S.	E2	112
Browne Bay, b., Nu., Can.	A11	106
Brownfield, Tx., U.S.	A5	130
Browning, Mo., U.S.	D4	120
Browning, Mt., U.S.	B13	136
Brownlee Reservoir, res., U.S.	F9	136
Brownsburg, Qc., Can.	E2	110
Brownsburg, In., U.S.	I3	112
Brownsdale, Mn., U.S.	H5	118
Browns Town, Jam.	i13	104d
Brownstown, In., U.S.	F11	120
Brownsville, Ky., U.S.	G11	120
Brownsville, La., U.S.	E6	122
Brownsville, Or., U.S.	F4	136
Brownsville, Tn., U.S.	B9	122
Brownsville, Tx., U.S.	I10	130
Brownton, Mn., U.S.	G4	118
Brownville, Me., U.S.	E7	110
Brownville, Ne., U.S.	D2	120
Brownville Junction, Me., U.S.	E7	110
Brownwood, Tx., U.S.	C8	130
Brownwood, Lake, res., Tx., U.S.	C9	130
Browse Island, i., Austl.	B4	74
Broxton, Ga., U.S.	E3	116
Broža, Bela.	H12	10
Bruay-en-Artois, Fr.	D11	14
Bruce, S.D., U.S.	G2	118
Bruce, Wi., U.S.	F7	118
Bruce, Mount, mtn., Austl.	D3	74
Bruce Mines, On., Can.	B6	112
Bruce Peninsula, pen., On., Can.	C8	112
Bruce Peninsula National Park, p.o.i., On., Can.	C8	112
Bruce Rock, Austl.	F3	74
Bruchsal, Ger.	G4	16
Bruck an der Leitha, Aus.	B13	22
Bruck an der Mur, Aus.	C12	22
Bruges see Brugge, Bel.	C12	14
Brugg, Switz.	C5	22
Brugge (Bruges), Bel.	C12	14
Brühl, Ger.	F2	16
Bruit, Pulau, i., Malay.	B7	50
Brule, Ne., U.S.	F11	126
Brumado, Braz.	H5	88
Brundidge, Al., U.S.	F13	122
Bruneau, Id., U.S.	H11	136
Bruneau, stm., U.S.	H11	136
Bruneck see Brunico, Italy	D8	22
Brunei, ctry., Asia	A9	50
Brunico, Italy	D8	22
Brunsbüttel, Ger.	C4	16
Brunson, S.C., U.S.	D4	116
Brunswick see Braunschweig, Ger.	D6	16
Brunswick, Ga., U.S.	E4	116
Brunswick, Md., U.S.	E8	114
Brunswick, Me., U.S.	G6	110
Brunswick, Mo., U.S.	E4	120
Brunswick, Oh., U.S.	C4	114
Brunswick, Península, pen., Chile	J2	90
Bruntál, Czech Rep.	F13	16
Brus, Laguna de, b., Hond.	E5	102
Brush, Co., U.S.	A5	128
Brusovo, Russia	C18	10
Brusque, Braz.	C13	92
Brussel see Bruxelles, Bel.	D13	14
Brussels see Bruxelles, Bel.	D13	14
Brussels, On., Can.	E8	112
Bruthen, Austl.	K6	76
Bruxelles (Brussels), Bel.	D13	14
Bruzual, Ven.	D7	86
Bryan, Oh., U.S.	C1	114
Bryan, Tx., U.S.	G2	122
Bryan, Mount, mtn., Austl.	I2	76
Bryant, Ar., U.S.	C6	122
Bryce Canyon National Park, p.o.i., Ut., U.S.	F4	132
Bryli, Bela.	G13	10
Bryson, Qc., Can.	C13	112
Bryson, Tx., U.S.	A9	130
Brzeg, Pol.	F13	16
Brześć Kujawski, Pol.	D14	16
Brzesko, Pol.	F16	16
Brzeziny, Pol.	E15	16
Bsharrī, Leb.	D6	58
Bua, Fiji	p19	79e
Bua Bay, b., Fiji	p19	79e
Buada Lagoon, b., Nauru	q17	78f
Buala, Sol. Is.	e8	79b
Bua Yai, Thai.	E6	48
Bubanza, Bdi.	E5	66
Bubaque, Gui.-B.	G1	64
Bubi, stm., Zimb.	B10	70
Būbiyān, i., Kuw.	D6	56
Bubuduo, China	C10	54
Bucak, Tur.	F13	28
Bucaramanga, Col.	D5	86
Buccaneer Archipelago, is., Austl.	C4	74
Buchanan, Sk., Can.	C11	124
Buchanan, Lib.	H2	64
Buchanan, Ga., U.S.	D13	122
Buchanan, Mi., U.S.	G3	112
Buchanan, Lake, l., Austl.	C5	76
Buchanan, Lake, l., Tx., U.S.	D9	130
Buchan Ness, c., Scot., U.K.	D11	12
Buchans, Nf., Can.	j22	107a
Bucharest see București, Rom.	E13	26
Buchen, Ger.	G5	16
Buchholz in der Nordheide, Ger.	C5	16
Buchloe, Ger.	H6	16
Buchon, Point, c., Ca., U.S.	H4	134
Buchs, Switz.	C6	22
Buckatunna, Ms., U.S.	F10	122
Buckatunna Creek, stm., Ms., U.S.	F10	122
Bückeburg, Ger.	D5	16
Buckeye, Az., U.S.	J4	132
Buckeye Lake, Oh., U.S.	I7	112
Buckhaven, Scot., U.K.	E9	12
Buckholts, Tx., U.S.	D10	130
Buckhorn Draw, stm., Tx., U.S.	D7	130
Buckie, Scot., U.K.	D10	12
Buckingham, Qc., Can.	C14	112
Buckingham, Va., U.S.	G7	114
Buckingham Bay, b., Austl.	B7	74
Buck Island, i., V.I.U.S.	g11	104c
Buck Island Reef National Monument, p.o.i., V.I.U.S.	g11	104c
Buck Lake, l., Ab., Can.	D16	138
Buckland, Ak., U.S.	C7	140
Buckley, Wa., U.S.	C4	136
Bucklin, Ks., U.S.	D9	128
Bucklin, Mo., U.S.	E5	120
Buck Mountain, mtn., Wa., U.S.	B7	136
Bucovăţ, Mol.	B15	26
Buco Zau, Ang.	A1	68
București (Bucharest), Rom.	E13	26
București, state, Rom.	E13	26
Bucyrus, Oh., U.S.	D3	114
Buda, Il., U.S.	C8	120
Buda, Tx., U.S.	D10	130
Budalin, Mya.	A2	48
Budapest, Hung.	B6	26
Budapest, state, Hung.	B6	26
Budaun, India	D7	54
Budd Coast, cst., Ant.	B16	81
Buddh Gaya see Bodh Gaya, India	F10	54
Buddusò, Italy	D3	24
Bude, Ms., U.S.	F8	122
Bude Bay, b., Eng., U.K.	K8	12
Budënnovsk, Russia	F6	32
Budeşti, Rom.	E13	26
Büdingen, Ger.	F5	16
Budišov nad Budišovkou, Czech Rep.	G13	16
Budjala, D.R.C.	D3	66
Budogovišči, Russia	G19	10
Budrio, Italy	F8	22
Budweis see České Budějovice, Czech Rep.	H10	16
Buea, Cam.	D1	66
Buena Esperanza, Arg.	G5	92
Buenaventura, Col.	F3	86
Buenaventura, Mex.	G9	98
Buena Vista, Bol.	C4	90
Buena Vista, Mex.	K9	134
Buenavista, Phil.	G4	52
Buena Vista, Co., U.S.	C2	128
Buena Vista, Ga., U.S.	E14	122
Buena Vista, Va., U.S.	G6	114
Buena Vista Lake Bed, reg., Ca., U.S.	H6	134
Buendía, Embalse de, res., Spain	D8	20
Buenópolis, Braz.	I3	88
Buenos Aires, Arg.	G8	92
Buenos Aires, Col.	F3	86
Buenos Aires, C.R.	H6	102
Buenos Aires, state, Arg.	G5	90
Buenos Aires, Lago see General Carrera, Lago, l., S.A.	I2	90
Buen Pasto, Arg.	I3	90
Buerarema, Braz.	H6	88
Buffalo, Ks., U.S.	G2	120
Buffalo, Mn., U.S.	F5	118
Buffalo, Mo., U.S.	G4	120
Buffalo, N.Y., U.S.	B7	114
Buffalo, Oh., U.S.	E4	114
Buffalo, S.C., U.S.	B4	116
Buffalo, S.D., U.S.	B9	126
Buffalo, Tx., U.S.	F2	122
Buffalo, stm., Can.	C8	106
Buffalo, stm., Ar., U.S.	H4	120
Buffalo, stm., Tn., U.S.	B11	122
Buffalo Creek, stm., Mn., U.S.	G4	118
Buffalo Lake, Mn., U.S.	G4	118
Buffalo Lake, l., Ab., Can.	D18	138
Buffalo Lake, l., N.T., Can.	C7	106
Buffalo Narrows, Sk., Can.	D8	106
Buffalo Pound Lake, l., Sk., Can.	D8	124
Buffels, stm., S. Afr.	F3	70
Buffels, stm., S. Afr.	F10	70
Buford, Ga., U.S.	B2	116
Buford Dam, dam, Ga., U.S.	B1	116
Buftea, Rom.	E12	26
Bug (Buh) (Zakhidnyy Buh), stm., Eur.	D17	16
Buga, Col.	F3	86
Bugala Island, i., Ug.	E6	66
Bugeat, Fr.	D7	18
Bugojno, Bos.	E4	26
Bugrino, Russia	B23	8
Bugsuk Island, i., Phil.	F1	52
Bugt, China	C4	38
Bugul'ma, Russia	D8	32
Buguruslan, Russia	D8	32
Buh, stm., China	D4	36
Buh (Bug) (Zakhidnyy Buh), stm., Eur.	D19	16
Buhara, Uzb.	G10	32
Buhl, Mn., U.S.	D6	118
Buhler, Ks., U.S.	C11	128
Buhuşi, Rom.	C13	26
Buies Creek, N.C., U.S.	A7	116
Builth Wells, Wales, U.K.	I9	12
Buin, Chile	F2	92
Buin, Pap. N. Gui.	d6	79b
Buíque, Braz.	E7	88
Buitsivango (Rietfontein), stm., Afr.	B4	70
Buj, Russia	G19	8
Bujalance, Spain	G6	20
Buje, Cro.	E10	22
Bujnaksk, Russia	F7	32
Bujumbura, Bdi.	E5	66
Bukačača, Russia	F12	34
Bukama, D.R.C.	F5	66
Bukan', Russia	G17	10
Bukavu, D.R.C.	E5	66
Bukeya, D.R.C.	G5	66
Bukhara see Buhara, Uzb.	G10	32
Bukittinggi, Indon.	D2	50
Bükki Nemzeti Park, p.o.i., Hung.	A7	26
Bukoba, Tan.	E6	66
Bukovica, reg., Cro.	F12	22
Bukovina, hist. reg., Eur.	B12	26
Bukuru, Nig.	H6	64
Bula, Indon.	F9	44
Būlaevo, Kaz.	C12	32
Bulajevo see Būlaevo, Kaz.	C12	32
Bulan, Phil.	D4	52

Name	Map Ref.	Page
Bulandshahr, India	D6	54
Bulawayo, Zimb.	B9	70
Bulbul, Syria	B7	58
Buldan, Tur.	E11	28
Buldāna, India	H6	54
Buldir Island, i., Ak., U.S.	g22	140a
Bulgan, Mong.	B5	36
Bulgan, Mong.	B3	36
Bulgaria, ctry., Eur.	G12	26
Bulkley, stm., B.C., Can.	B3	138
Bullard, Tx., U.S.	E3	122
Bulla Regia, sci., Tun.	H2	24
Bullas, Spain	F9	20
Bullaxaar, Som.	B8	66
Bulle, Switz.	D4	22
Buller, stm., N.Z.	E5	80
Buller, Mount, mtn., Austl.	K6	76
Bullfinch, Austl.	F3	74
Bull Harbour, B.C., Can.	F2	138
Bullhead, S.D., U.S.	B11	126
Bullhead City, Az., U.S.	H2	132
Bullock, N.C., U.S.	H7	114
Bullock Creek, Austl.	A5	76
Bullock Creek, stm., Austl.	C5	76
Bulloo, stm., Austl.	G4	76
Bullpound Creek, stm., Ab., Can.	E19	138
Bulls Gap, Tn., U.S.	H2	114
Bull Shoals, Ar., U.S.	H5	120
Bull Shoals Lake, res., U.S.	H5	120
Bulnes, Chile	H1	92
Bulolo, Pap. N. Gui.	b4	79a
Bulsār, India	H4	54
Buluan, Phil.	G5	52
Bulukumba, Indon.	F12	50
Bululawang, Indon.	H8	50
Bumba, D.R.C.	D4	66
Bumpus, Mount, hill, Nu., Can.	B8	106
Bumu Hu, l., China	C13	54
Buna, Kenya	D7	66
Bunawan, Phil.	F5	52
Bunbury, Austl.	F3	74
Bunceton, Mo., U.S.	F5	120
Bundaberg, Austl.	E9	76
Bundarra, Austl.	H8	76
Bünde, Ger.	D4	16
Būndi, India	F5	54
Bundoran, Ire.	G4	12
Būndu, India	G10	54
Bungamas, Indon.	E3	50
Bungo-suidō, strt., Japan	G5	40
Bungo-takada, Japan	F4	40
Bungtlang, India	G14	54
Bunia, D.R.C.	D6	66
Bunker, Mo., U.S.	G6	120
Bunker Group, is., Austl.	D9	76
Bunker Hill, In., U.S.	H3	112
Bunker Hill, Or., U.S.	G2	136
Bunker Hill, mtn., Nv., U.S.	D8	134
Bunkie, La., U.S.	G6	122
Bunnell, Fl., U.S.	G4	116
Buñol see Bunyolo, Spain	E10	20
Buntok, Indon.	D9	50
Bunyolo, Spain	E10	20
Bunyu, Pulau, i., Indon.	B10	50
Buolkalah, Russia	B12	34
Buolkalakh see Buolkalah, Russia	B12	34
Buon Ma Thuot, Viet.	F9	48
Buor-Haja, guba, b., Russia	B15	34
Buor-Haja, mys, c., Russia	B15	34
Bupul, Indon.	G11	44
Buqayq, Sau. Ar.	D6	56
Bura, Kenya	E7	66
Burām, Sudan	E5	62
Burang, China	C8	54
Buranhém, stm., Braz.	I6	88
Burāq, Syria	E7	58
Burauen, Phil.	E5	52
Burbank, Wa., U.S.	D8	136
Burç, Tur.	A8	58
Burcher, Austl.	I6	76
Burco, Som.	C9	66
Burdekin, stm., Austl.	C6	76
Burdekin Falls, wtfl., Austl.	C6	76
Burden, Ks., U.S.	D12	128
Burdett, Ks., U.S.	C9	128
Burdur, Tur.	F13	28
Burdur, state, Tur.	F13	28
Burdur Gölü, l., Tur.	F12	28
Bureinskij hrebet, mts., Russia	G15	34
Bureja, Russia	G15	34
Bureja, stm., Russia	F15	34
Büren, Ger.	E4	16
Bürenhayrhan, Mong.	B3	36
Burford, On., Can.	E9	112
Burg, Ger.	D7	16
Burg, Den see Den Burg, Neth.	A13	14
Burgas, Blg.	G14	26
Burgas, state, Blg.	G13	26
Burgas, Gulf of see Burgaski Zaliv, b., Blg.	G14	26
Burgaski Zaliv, b., Blg.	G14	26
Burg auf Fehmarn, Ger.	B7	16
Burgaw, N.C., U.S.	B8	116
Burgdorf, Switz.	C4	22
Burgenland, state, Aus.	C13	22
Burgeo, Nf., Can.	j22	107a
Burgersdorp, S. Afr.	G8	70
Burghausen, Ger.	H8	16
Burghead, Scot., U.K.	D9	12
Burgin, Ky., U.S.	G13	120
Burgo de Osma, Spain	C7	20
Burgos, Mex.	C9	100
Burgos, Phil.	C3	52
Burgos, Spain	B7	20
Burgos, co., Spain	B7	20
Burgstädt, Ger.	F8	16
Burgundy see Bourgogne, hist. reg., Fr.	B10	18
Burhan Budai Shan, mts., China	D4	36
Burhaniye, Tur.	D9	28
Burhānpur, India	H5	54
Burias Island, i., Phil.	D4	52
Burica, Punta, c., N.A.	I6	102
Burien, Wa., U.S.	C4	136
Burila Mare, Rom.	E9	26
Buri Ram, Thai.	E6	48
Buriti, Braz.	B4	88
Buriti Bravo, Braz.	C4	88
Buriticupu, stm., Braz.	C2	88
Buriti dos Lopes, Braz.	B5	88
Buritizeiro, Braz.	I3	88
Burjasot see Burjassot, Spain	E10	20
Burjassot, Spain	E10	20
Burjatija, state, Russia	F11	34
Burkburnett, Tx., U.S.	G10	128
Burke, S.D., U.S.	D13	126
Burke, stm., Austl.	D2	76
Burketown, Austl.	A2	76
Burkina Faso, ctry., Afr.	G4	64
Burleson, Tx., U.S.	B10	130
Burley, Id., U.S.	H13	136
Burlingame, Ca., U.S.	F3	134
Burlingame, Ks., U.S.	F2	120
Burlington, On., Can.	E10	112
Burlington, Co., U.S.	B6	128
Burlington, Ia., U.S.	D6	120
Burlington, Ks., U.S.	F2	120
Burlington, N.C., U.S.	H6	114
Burlington, Vt., U.S.	F3	110
Burlington, Wa., U.S.	B4	136
Burlington, Wi., U.S.	B9	120
Burlington, Wy., U.S.	C4	126
Burlington Junction, Mo., U.S.	D2	120
Burma see Myanmar, ctry., Asia	D8	46
Burnaby, B.C., Can.	G7	138
Burnet, Tx., U.S.	D9	130
Burnett, stm., Austl.	E8	76
Burnett Bay, b., N.T., Can.	B14	140
Burney, Ca., U.S.	C4	134
Burnie, Austl.	n12	77a
Burnley, Eng., U.K.	H10	12
Burns, Ks., U.S.	C12	128
Burns, Or., U.S.	G7	136
Burns, Tn., U.S.	H10	120
Burns, Wy., U.S.	F8	126
Burnside, Ky., U.S.	G13	120
Burnside, stm., Nu., Can.	B8	106
Burnside, Lake, l., Austl.	E4	74
Burns Lake, B.C., Can.	B5	138
Burnsville, Ms., U.S.	C10	122
Burnsville, N.C., U.S.	I3	114
Burnsville, W.V., U.S.	F5	114
Burnt, stm., Or., U.S.	F9	136
Burnt Pine, Norf. I.	y25	78i
Burntwood, stm., Mb., Can.	D11	106
Burqin, China	B2	36
Burra, Austl.	I2	76
Burragorang, Lake, res., Austl.	J7	76
Burrel, Alb.	C13	24
Burreli see Burrel, Alb.	C13	24
Burrendong, Lake, res., Austl.	I7	76
Burren Junction, Austl.	H7	76
Burriana see Borriana, Spain	E10	20
Burrinjuck Reservoir, res., Austl.	J7	76
Burr Oak, Ks., U.S.	B10	128
Burrton, Ks., U.S.	C11	128
Burruyacú, Arg.	E4	90
Bursa, Tur.	C11	28
Bursa, state, Tur.	C11	28
Būr Sa'īd (Port Said), Egypt	G3	58
Burstall, Sk., Can.	D4	124
Būr Sūdān (Port Sudan), Sudan	D7	62
Burt, Ia., U.S.	H4	118
Burt Lake, l., Mi., U.S.	C5	112
Burtnieks ezers, l., Lat.	C8	10
Burton, Mi., U.S.	E6	112
Burton, Tx., U.S.	G2	122
Burton upon Trent, Eng., U.K.	I11	12
Buru, i., Indon.	F8	44
Burullus, Buheirat el-, l., Egypt	G1	58
Burundi, ctry., Afr.	E6	66
Burun-Šibertuj, gora, mtn., Russia	G10	34
Bururi, Bdi.	E5	66
Burwash, On., Can.	B9	112
Burwell, Ne., U.S.	F13	126
Bury, Eng., U.K.	H10	12
Buryatia see Burjatija, state, Russia	F11	34
Bury Saint Edmunds, Eng., U.K.	I13	12
Burzil, Pak.	A5	54
Busa, Mount, mtn., Phil.	G5	52
Busan see Pusan-jikhalsi, state, Kor., S.	D2	40
Busanga, D.R.C.	E4	66
Busby, Mt., U.S.	B5	126
Bûsh, Egypt	I2	58
Bushire see Bandar-e Būshehr, Iran	D7	56
Bushland, Tx., U.S.	F6	128
Bushman Land, reg., S. Afr.	F4	70
Bushnell, Fl., U.S.	H3	116
Bushnell, Il., U.S.	D7	120
Bushtyna, Ukr.	A10	26
Busia, Ug.	D6	66
Businga, D.R.C.	D4	66
Busira, stm., D.R.C.	E3	66
Buskerud, state, Nor.	F3	8
Busko-Zdrój, Pol.	F16	16
Buṣrá ash-Shām, Syria	F7	58
Busselton, Austl.	F3	74
Bussey, Ia., U.S.	C5	120
Bussum, Neth.	B14	14
Bustamante, Mex.	B8	100
Busto Arsizio, Italy	E5	22
Busuanga Island, i., Phil.	D2	52
Busu-Djanoa, D.R.C.	D4	66
Büsum, Ger.	B4	16
Buta, D.R.C.	D4	66
Buta Ranquil, Arg.	H2	92
Butare, Rw.	E5	66
Butaritari, at., Kir.	C8	72
Bute, Island of, i., Scot., U.K.	F7	12
Bute Inlet, b., B.C., Can.	F5	138
Butembo, D.R.C.	D5	66
Butera, Italy	G8	24
Butere, Kenya	D6	66
Butha-Buthe, Leso.	F9	70
Buthidaung, Mya.	D7	46
Butiá, Braz.	E11	92
Butler, Ga., U.S.	D1	116
Butler, In., U.S.	C1	114
Butler, Mo., U.S.	F3	120
Butler, Oh., U.S.	D3	114
Butler, Pa., U.S.	D6	114
Butner, N.C., U.S.	H7	114
Buto, hist., Egypt	G1	58
Buton, Pulau, i., Indon.	F7	44
Butrint, sci., Alb.	E14	24
Butru, Austl.	C2	76
Butte, Mt., U.S.	D14	136
Butte, Ne., U.S.	E14	126
Butte Creek, stm., Ca., U.S.	D4	134
Butte Falls, Or., U.S.	H4	136
Butternut, Wi., U.S.	E8	118
Butterworth, Malay.	J5	48
Butterworth, S. Afr.	H9	70
Buttle Lake, l., B.C., Can.	G5	138
Button Islands, is., Nu., Can.	C17	106
Buttonwillow, Ca., U.S.	H6	134
Butuan, Phil.	F5	52
Buturlino, Russia	I21	8
Buṭwal, Nepal	E9	54
Butzbach, Ger.	F4	16
Bützow, Ger.	C7	16
Buulobarde, Som.	D9	66
Buur Gaabo, Som.	E8	66
Buurgplaatz, mtn., Lux.	D15	14
Buxtehude, Ger.	C5	16
Buxton, S. Afr.	E7	70
Buxton, Eng., U.K.	H11	12
Buxton, N.C., U.S.	A10	116
Buxton, Mount, mtn., B.C., Can.	E2	138
Buyant-Uhaa, Mong.	C7	36
Buyr nuur, l., Asia	B8	36
Büyükada, Tur.	C12	28
Büyükçekmece, Tur.	B11	28
Büyükkarıştıran, Tur.	B10	28
Büyükkemikli Burnu, c., Tur.	C9	28
Büyükmenderes, stm., Tur.	F10	28
Buzău, Rom.	D13	26
Buzău, state, Rom.	D13	26
Buzău, stm., Rom.	D13	26
Buzen, Japan	F4	40
Búzi, stm., Moz.	A12	70
Buziaș, Rom.	D8	26
Buzuluk, Russia	D8	32
Byādgi, India	D2	53
Byam Channel, strt., Nu., Can.	A19	140
Byam Martin Island, i., Nu., Can.	B19	140
Bycen', Bela.	H8	10
Byčki, Russia	F17	10
Byczyna, Pol.	E14	16
Bydgoszcz, Pol.	C13	16
Bydgoszcz, state, Pol.	C13	16
Byelorussia see Belarus, ctry., Eur.	E14	6
Byers, Tx., U.S.	G10	128
Byesville, Oh., U.S.	E4	114
Bygdin, l., Nor.	F3	8
Byhalia, Ms., U.S.	C9	122
Byhau, Bela.	G13	10
Bykle, Nor.	G2	8
Bylnice, Czech Rep.	G14	16
Bylot Island, i., Nu., Can.	A15	106
Byng Inlet, On., Can.	C9	112
Bynum, Mt., U.S.	C14	136
Bynum, N.C., U.S.	I6	114
Byrd, Lac, l., Qc., Can.	A13	112
Byrnedale, Pa., U.S.	C7	114
Byro, Austl.	E3	74
Byron, Ga., U.S.	D2	116
Byron, Il., U.S.	B8	120
Byron, Cape, c., Austl.	G9	76
Byron Bay, Austl.	G9	76
Byrranga, gory, mts., Russia	B8	34
Bystřice pod Hostýnem, Czech Rep.	G13	16
Bytantaj, stm., Russia	C15	34
Bytča, Slov.	G14	16
Bytom, Pol.	F14	16
Bytoš', Russia	G17	10
Bytów, Pol.	B13	16

C

Name	Map Ref.	Page
Ca, stm., Asia	C7	48
Caacupé, Para.	B9	92
Caaguazú, Para.	B9	92
Caaguazú, state, Para.	B10	92
Caála, Ang.	C2	68
Caapiranga, Braz.	I11	86
Caatinga, Braz.	I3	88
Caazapá, Para.	C9	92
Caazapá, state, Para.	C9	92
Cabaiguán, Cuba	A8	102
Cabaliana, Lago, l., Braz.	I11	86
Caballococha, Peru	D3	84
Caballo Reservoir, res., N.M., U.S.	K9	132
Cabanatuan, Phil.	C3	52
Cabano, Qc., Can.	C8	110
Cabarroguis, Phil.	B3	52
Cabedelo, Braz.	D8	88
Cabeza del Buey, Spain	F5	20
Cabezas, Bol.	C4	90
Cabildo, Arg.	I7	92
Cabimas, Ven.	B6	86
Cabinda, Ang.	B1	68
Cabinda, state, Ang.	B1	68
Cabinet Mountains, mts., U.S.	B10	136
Cable, Wi., U.S.	E7	118
Cabo, Braz.	E8	88
Cabo Blanco, Arg.	I3	90
Cabo Frio, Braz.	L4	88
Cabonga, Réservoir, res., Qc., Can.	F15	106
Cabool, Mo., U.S.	G5	120
Caboolture, Austl.	F9	76
Caborca, Mex.	F6	98
Cabo Rojo, P.R.	B1	104a
Cabot, Ar., U.S.	C7	122
Cabot Head, c., On., Can.	C8	112
Cabot Strait, strt., Can.	j21	107a
Cabourg, Fr.	E8	14
Cabra Corral, Embalse, res., Arg.	B5	92
Cabramurra, Austl.	J7	76
Cabrera, stm., Col.	F4	86
Cabrera, Illa de, i., Spain	E13	20
Cabri, Sk., Can.	D5	124
Cabriel, stm., Spain	E9	20
Cabrillo National Monument, p.o.i., Ca., U.S.	K8	134
Cabrobó, Braz.	E6	88
Cabruta, Ven.	D8	86
Cabullónes, Punta, c., P.R.	C2	104a
Čabusy, Bela.	H11	10
Cabuyaro, Col.	E5	86
Caçador, Braz.	C12	92
Čačak, Serb.	F7	26
Caçapava, Braz.	L3	88
Caçapava do Sul, Braz.	E11	92
Cacapon, stm., W.V., U.S.	E7	114
Cacequi, Braz.	D10	92
Cáceres, Braz.	G6	84
Cáceres, Col.	D4	86
Cáceres, Spain	E4	20
Cáceres, co., Spain	E4	20
Čačèrsk, Bela.	H13	10
Cache, stm., Ar., U.S.	B7	122
Cache, stm., Il., U.S.	G8	120
Cache Creek, B.C., Can.	F9	138
Cache Creek, stm., Ca., U.S.	E3	134
Cache la Poudre, stm., Co., U.S.	G7	126
Cache Peak, mtn., Id., U.S.	A3	132
Cachi, Arg.	B4	92
Cachimbo, Braz.	E7	84
Cachimbo, Serra do, mts., Braz.	E6	84
Cachoeira Alta, Braz.	C6	90
Cachoeira de Manteiga, Braz.	I3	88
Cachoeira do Sul, Braz.	E11	92
Cachoeiro de Itapemirim, Braz.	K5	88
Cachos, Punta, c., Chile	C2	92
Cachuela Esperanza, Bol.	B3	90
Căciulați, Rom.	E13	26
Cacolo, Ang.	C2	68
Caconda, Ang.	C2	68
Cactus, Tx., U.S.	E6	128
Cactus Flat, pl., Nv., U.S.	F9	134
Cacuaco, Ang.	B1	68
Caculé, Braz.	H4	88
Cacuri, Ven.	E9	86
Čadan, Russia	D16	32
Čadca, Slov.	G14	16
Caddo, Ok., U.S.	C2	122
Caddo, stm., Ar., U.S.	C5	122
Caddo Lake, res., U.S.	E4	122
Caddo Mills, Tx., U.S.	D2	122
Cadell, stm., Austl.	D3	76
Cadena, Cerro, mtn., Mex.	I3	130
Cadena, Punta, c., P.R.	B1	104a
Cadillac, Sk., Can.	E6	124
Cadillac, Fr.	E5	18
Cadillac, Mi., U.S.	D4	112
Cádiz, Spain	H4	20
Cadiz, Ky., U.S.	H10	120
Cádiz, co., Spain	H5	20
Cádiz, Bahía de, b., Spain	H4	20
Cadiz Lake, l., Ca., U.S.	I1	132
Čadobec, stm., Russia	C17	32
Cadomin, Ab., Can.	C13	138
Cadore, reg., Italy	D9	22
Cadott, Wi., U.S.	G7	118
Cadwell, Ga., U.S.	D2	116
Čaek, Kyrg.	F12	32
Caen, Fr.	E8	14
Caengo (Kwenge), stm., Afr.	B2	68
Caernarfon, Wales, U.K.	H8	12
Caernarfon Bay, b., Wales, U.K.	H8	12
Caerphilly, Wales, U.K.	J9	12
Caesarea see Qesari, Horbat, sci., Isr.	F5	58
Caeté, Braz.	J4	88
Caetité, Braz.	H4	88
Cafayate, Arg.	C4	92
Cagayan, stm., Phil.	A3	52
Cagayan de Oro, Phil.	F5	52
Cagayan Islands, is., Phil.	F3	52
Cagayan Sulu Island, i., Phil.	G2	52
Čagda, Russia	E15	34
Çağış, Tur.	D10	28
Cagliari, Italy	E3	24
Cagliari, Golfo di, b., Italy	E3	24
Cagliari, Stagno di, l., Italy	E2	24
Cagnes-sur-Mer, Fr.	F13	18
Čagoda, stm., Russia	A17	10
Čagodošča, stm., Russia	A18	10
Caguán, stm., Col.	G4	86
Caguas, P.R.	B3	104a
Cahaba, stm., Al., U.S.	E11	122
Cahama, Ang.	D1	68
Caher, Ire.	I4	12
Cahokia, Il., U.S.	F7	120
Cahora Bassa, Albufeira, res., Moz.	D5	68
Cahors, Fr.	E7	18
Cahto Peak, mtn., Ca., U.S.	D2	134
Cahuinari, stm., Col.	H6	86
Cahul, Mol.	D15	26
Caí, stm., Braz.	D12	92
Caianda, Ang.	C3	68
Caiapó, Serra do, mts., Braz.	G7	84
Caibarién, Cuba	A8	102
Cai Bau, Dao, i., Viet.	B8	48
Caiçara, Braz.	D8	88
Caicara, Caño, stm., Ven.	D7	86
Caicara de Maturín, Ven.	C10	86
Caicara de Orinoco, Ven.	D8	86
Caicedonia, Col.	E4	86
Caicó, Braz.	D7	88
Caicos Islands, is., T./C. Is.	B11	102
Caicos Passage, strt., N.A.	B11	102
Caijiapo, China	D2	42
Caima Bay, b., Phil.	D4	52
Caimanera, Cuba	C10	102
Caimanero, Laguna del, l., Mex.	D5	100
Cain Creek, stm., S.D., U.S.	C14	126
Cai Nuoc, Viet.	H7	48
Cairari, Braz.	B1	88
Caird Coast, cst., Ant.	C3	81
Cairns, Austl.	A5	76
Cairo see El-Qâhira, Egypt	H2	58
Cairo, Ga., U.S.	F1	116
Cairo, Il., U.S.	G8	120
Cairo, Ne., U.S.	F14	126
Cairo, W.V., U.S.	E4	114
Cairo Montenotte, Italy	F5	22
Cairu, Braz.	G6	88
Caisleán an Bharraigh see Castlebar, Ire.	H3	12
Caiundo, Ang.	D2	68
Caiwan, China	I4	42
Caizi Hu, l., China	F7	42
Caja de Muertos, Isla, i., P.R.	C2	104a
Cajamarca, Peru	E2	84
Cajapió, Braz.	B3	88
Cajazeiras, Braz.	D6	88
Cajon Summit, p., Ca., U.S.	I8	134
Cajuru, Braz.	K2	88
Caka, China	D4	36
Çakmak, Tur.	A5	58
Čakovec, Cro.	D13	22
Calabar, Nig.	H6	64
Calabozo, Ven.	C8	86
Calabozo, Ensenada de, b., Ven.	B6	86
Calabria, state, Italy	F10	24
Calafat, Rom.	F9	26
Calagua Islands, is., Phil.	C4	52
Calahorra, Spain	B8	20
Calais, Fr.	C10	14
Calalaste, Sierra de, mts., Arg.	B4	92
Calama, Chile	D3	90
Calamar, Col.	B4	86
Calamar, Col.	F5	86
Calamian Group, is., Phil.	E3	52
Calamus, stm., Ne., U.S.	E13	126
Calañas, Spain	G4	20
Calang, Indon.	J2	48
Calapan, Phil.	D3	52
Călărași, Mol.	B15	26
Călărași, Rom.	E14	26
Călărași, state, Rom.	E14	26
Calarcá, Col.	E4	86
Calatafimi, Italy	G6	24
Calatayud, Spain	C9	20
Calau, Ger.	E9	16
Calavite Passage, strt., Phil.	D3	52
Calayan Island, i., Phil.	A3	52
Calbayog, Phil.	D5	52
Calbe, Ger.	E7	16
Calbuco, Chile	H2	90
Calcasieu, stm., La., U.S.	G5	122
Calcasieu Lake, l., La., U.S.	G5	122
Calceta, Ec.	H1	86
Calchaquí, Arg.	D7	92
Calchaquí, stm., Arg.	B4	92
Calçoene, Braz.	C7	84
Calcutta see Kolkata, India	G12	54
Caldaro, Italy	D8	22
Caldas, Col.	D4	86
Caldas, state, Col.	E4	86
Caldas da Rainha, Port.	E1	20
Caldas de Reis, Spain	B2	20
Caldas de Reyes see Caldas de Reis, Spain	B2	20
Caldas Novas, Braz.	I1	88
Caldera, Chile	C2	92
Caldwell, Id., U.S.	G10	136
Caldwell, Ks., U.S.	D11	128
Caldwell, Oh., U.S.	E4	114
Caldwell, Tx., U.S.	G2	122
Caledon, S. Afr.	I4	70
Caledon (Mohokare), stm., Afr.	F8	70
Caledonia, Belize	C3	102
Caledonia, N.S., Can.	F11	110
Caledonia, Ms., U.S.	D10	122
Caledonia, N.Y., U.S.	A8	114
Caledonia, Oh., U.S.	D3	114
Calella, Spain	C13	20
Calen, Austl.	C7	76
Calera, Al., U.S.	D12	122
Caleta Olivia, Arg.	I3	90
Caleufú, Arg.	G5	92
Calexico, Ca., U.S.	K10	134
Calgary, Ab., Can.	E16	138
Calhan, Co., U.S.	B4	128
Calhoun, Al., U.S.	E12	122
Calhoun, Ga., U.S.	C14	122
Calhoun, Mo., U.S.	F4	120
Calhoun, Tn., U.S.	B14	122
Calhoun City, Ms., U.S.	D9	122
Cali, Col.	F3	86
Calico Rock, Ar., U.S.	H5	120
Calicut see Kozhikode, India	F2	53
Caliente, Nv., U.S.	F2	132
California, Mo., U.S.	F5	120
California, state, U.S.	D3	108
California, Golfo de (California, Gulf of), b., Mex.	B2	96
California, Gulf of see California, Golfo de, b., Mex.	B2	96
California Aqueduct, aq., Ca., U.S.	I8	134
Calilegua, Parque Nacional, p.o.i., Arg.	A5	92
Calimere, Point, c., India	F4	53
Calingasta, Arg.	E3	92
Calion, Ar., U.S.	D6	122
Calipatria, Ca., U.S.	J10	134
Calispell Peak, mtn., Wa., U.S.	B9	136
Calistoga, Ca., U.S.	E3	134
Calitri, Italy	D9	24
Calitzdorp, S. Afr.	H5	70
Callabonna, Lake, l., Austl.	G2	76
Callabonna Creek, stm., Austl.	G3	76
Callahan, Mount, mtn., Co., U.S.	D8	132
Callan, Ire.	I5	12
Callander, On., Can.	B10	112
Callao, Peru	F2	84
Callaquén, Volcán, vol., Chile	H2	92
Callaway, Ne., U.S.	F12	126
Calliaqua, St. Vin.	o11	105e
Calling Lake, Ab., Can.	A17	138
Calling Lake, l., Ab., Can.	A17	138
Callosa de Segura, Spain	F9	20
Calmar, Ab., Can.	C17	138
Calmar, Ia., U.S.	A6	120
Calm Lake, l., On., Can.	C6	118
Čal'mny-Varre, Russia	C17	8
Čalna, Russia	F15	8
Caloundra, Austl.	F9	76
Calp, Spain	F11	20
Calpe see Calp, Spain	F11	20
Caltagirone, Italy	G8	24
Caltanissetta, Italy	G8	24
Călugăreni, Rom.	E12	26
Calulo, Ang.	B2	68
Calumet, Mn., U.S.	D5	118
Calumet City, Il., U.S.	G2	112
Calunda, Ang.	C3	68
Caluula, Som.	B10	66
Calvados, state, Fr.	E8	14
Calvert, Al., U.S.	F10	122
Calvert, Tx., U.S.	G2	122
Calvert Island, i., B.C., Can.	E2	138
Calvillo, Mex.	E7	100
Calvin, Ok., U.S.	C2	122
Calvinia, S. Afr.	G4	70
Calw, Ger.	H4	16
Calwa, Ca., U.S.	G6	134
Calypso, N.C., U.S.	A7	116
Camabatela, Ang.	B2	68
Camaçari, Braz.	G6	88
Camacupa, Ang.	C2	68
Camaguán, Ven.	C8	86
Camagüey, Cuba	B9	102
Camaiore, Italy	G7	22
Camajuaní, Cuba	A8	102
Camaná, Peru	G3	84
Camaná, stm., Peru	G3	84
Camanaú, stm., Braz.	H11	86
Camanche Reservoir, res., Ca., U.S.	E4	134
Camapuã, Braz.	C6	90
Camaquã, Braz.	E12	92
Camaquã, stm., Braz.	E11	92
Camará, Braz.	D5	84
Camarajibe, Braz.	D8	88
Camararé, stm., Braz.	F6	84
Camarat, Cap, c., Fr.	F12	18
Camarès, Fr.	F8	18
Camargo, Bol.	D3	90
Camargue, reg., Fr.	F10	18
Camarillo, Ca., U.S.	I6	134
Camarón, Arroyo, stm., Mex.	G7	130
Camarón, Cabo, c., Hond.	D5	102
Camarones, Arg.	H3	90
Camarones, Bahía, b., Arg.	H3	90
Camas Creek, stm., Id., U.S.	F14	136
Camatagua, Embalse de, l., Ven.	C8	86
Ca Mau, Viet.	H7	48
Ca Mau, Mui, c., Viet.	H7	48
Camba, Indon.	F11	50
Cambodia, ctry., Asia	C3	48
Camboon, Austl.	E8	76
Camboriú, Braz.	C13	92
Camborne, Eng., U.K.	K7	12
Cambrai, Fr.	D12	14
Cambria, Ca., U.S.	H4	134
Cambrian Mountains, mts., Wales, U.K.	I9	12
Cambridge, On., Can.	E9	112
Cambridge, N.Z.	C6	80
Cambridge, Eng., U.K.	I12	12
Cambridge, Ia., U.S.	C4	120
Cambridge, Il., U.S.	C7	120
Cambridge, Ma., U.S.	B14	114
Cambridge, Md., U.S.	F9	114
Cambridge, Mn., U.S.	F5	118
Cambridge, Ne., U.S.	A8	128
Cambridge, N.Y., U.S.	G3	110
Cambridge, Oh., U.S.	D4	114
Cambridge Bay see Ikaluktutiak, Nu., Can.	B10	106
Cambridge Fiord, b., Nu., Can.	A15	106
Cambridge Springs, Pa., U.S.	C5	114
Cambrils, Spain	C11	20
Cambuí, Braz.	L2	88
Cambulo, Ang.	B3	68
Cambundi-Catembo, Ang.	C2	68
Camden, Austl.	J8	76
Camden, Al., U.S.	F11	122
Camden, Ar., U.S.	D6	122
Camden, Me., U.S.	F7	110
Camden, N.C., U.S.	H9	114
Camden, N.J., U.S.	E10	114
Camden, N.Y., U.S.	E14	112
Camden, Oh., U.S.	E1	114
Camden, S.C., U.S.	B5	116
Camden, Tn., U.S.	H9	120
Camden Bay, b., Ak., U.S.	B11	140
Camdenton, Mo., U.S.	G5	120
Camels Hump, mtn., Vt., U.S.	F3	110
Camenca, Mol.	A15	26
Camerino, Italy	G10	22
Cameron, Mo., U.S.	E3	120
Cameron, Tx., U.S.	D10	130
Cameron, Wi., U.S.	F7	118
Cameron, W.V., U.S.	E5	114
Cameron Hills, hills, Can.	D7	106
Cameroon, ctry., Afr.	C2	66
Cameroon Mountain, vol., Cam.	D1	66
Camerota, Italy	D9	24
Cametá, Braz.	B1	88
Çamiçi Gölü, l., Tur.	F10	28
Camiguin Island, i., Phil.	F5	52
Camiguin Island, i., Phil.	A3	52
Camiling, Phil.	C3	52
Camilla, Ga., U.S.	E1	116
Camino, Ca., U.S.	E5	134
Camiranga, Braz.	A2	88
Camiri, Bol.	D4	90
Camissombo, Ang.	B3	68
Çamlıdere, Tur.	C15	28
Çamlıdere, Tur.	A10	58
Cam Lo, Viet.	D8	48
Camocim, Braz.	B5	88
Camooweal, Austl.	C7	74
Camorta Island, i., India	G7	46
Camotes Islands, is., Phil.	E5	52
Camotes Sea, s., Phil.	E5	52
Campagna di Roma, reg., Italy	C6	24
Campaign, Tn., U.S.	B13	122
Campana, Arg.	G8	92
Campana, Isla, i., Chile	I1	90
Campanario, Spain	F5	20
Campania, state, Italy	D8	24
Campano, Appennino, mts., Italy	C8	24
Campaspe, stm., Austl.	C6	76
Campbell, S. Afr.	F6	70
Campbell, Ca., U.S.	F4	134
Campbell, Mo., U.S.	H7	120
Campbell, Ne., U.S.	A10	128
Campbell, Cape, c., N.Z.	E6	80
Campbellford, On., Can.	D12	112
Campbell Hill, hill, Oh., U.S.	D2	114
Campbell Hills, hill, St. Vin.	p11	105e
Campbell Island, B.C., Can.	D2	138
Campbell Island, i., N.Z.	I7	72
Campbell Lake, l., B.C., Can.	G5	138
Campbell Plateau, unds.	O20	142
Campbellpore, Pak.	B4	54
Campbell River, B.C., Can.	F5	138
Campbell's Bay, Qc., Can.	C13	112
Campbellsport, Wi., U.S.	E1	112
Campbellton, N.B., Can.	C10	110
Campbellton, P.E., Can.	D12	110
Campbellton, Fl., U.S.	G13	122
Campbelltown, Austl.	J8	76
Campbell Town, Austl.	n13	77a
Campbeltown, Scot., U.K.	F7	12
Campeche, Mex.	C2	102
Campeche, state, Mex.	C2	102
Campeche, Bahía de, b., Mex.	D6	96
Campeche, Gulf of see Campeche, Bahía de, b., Mex.	E13	100
Campechuela, Cuba	B9	102
Câmpeni, Rom.	C10	26
Camperdown, Austl.	L4	76
Camperville, Mb., Can.	C13	124
Cam Pha, Viet.	B8	48
Camp Hill, Al., U.S.	E13	122
Camp Hill, Pa., U.S.	H12	112
Câmpia Turzii, Rom.	C10	26
Campidano, val., Italy	E2	24
Campiglia Marittima, Italy	G7	22
Campillos, Spain	G6	20
Câmpina, Rom.	D12	26
Campina, reg., Spain	G5	20
Campina Grande, Braz.	D7	88
Campinas, Braz.	L2	88
Campina Verde, Braz.	J1	88
Campoalegre, Col.	F4	86
Campo Alegre de Goiás, Braz.	I2	88
Campobasso, Italy	C8	24
Campo Belo, Braz.	K3	88
Campo de Criptana, Spain	E7	20
Campo Erê, Braz.	C11	92
Campo Florido, Braz.	J1	88
Campo Formoso, Braz.	F5	88
Campo Gallo, Arg.	C6	92
Campo Grande, Braz.	D6	90
Campo Largo, Arg.	C7	92
Campo Largo, Braz.	B13	92
Campo Maior, Braz.	C4	88
Campo Maior, Port.	F3	20
Campo Mourão, Braz.	A11	92
Campo Novo, Braz.	C11	92
Campos, Braz.	K5	88
Campos Altos, Braz.	J2	88
Campo Santo, Arg.	B5	92
Campos Belos, Braz.	G2	88
Campos do Jordão, Braz.	L3	88
Campos Gerais, Braz.	K2	88
Campos Novos, Braz.	C12	92
Campos Sales, Braz.	D5	88
Camp Point, Il., U.S.	D6	120
Campti, La., U.S.	F5	122
Campton, Ky., U.S.	G2	114
Câmpulung, Rom.	D11	26
Câmpulung Moldovenesc, Rom.	B12	26
Campuya, stm., Peru	H4	86
Camp Verde, Az., U.S.	I4	132
Cam Ranh, Viet.	G9	48
Cam Ranh, Vinh, b., Viet.	G9	48
Cam Ranh Bay see Cam Ranh, Vinh, b., Viet.	G9	48
Camrose, Ab., Can.	C18	138
Camsell, stm., N.T., Can.	B7	106
Camuy, P.R.	B2	104a
Çan, Tur.	C10	28
Canaan, Vt., U.S.	E5	110
Cana-brava, stm., Braz.	G1	88
Cana-brava, stm., Braz.	G1	88
Canada, ctry., N.A.	D9	106
Canada Basin, unds.	A25	142
Cañada de Gómez, Arg.	F7	92
Cañada Honda, Arg.	F3	92
Canadian, Tx., U.S.	F8	128
Canadian, stm., U.S.	F13	128
Canadian, Deep Fork, stm., Ok., U.S.	F13	128
Canaguá, stm., Ven.	D7	86
Canaima, Parque Nacional, p.o.i., Ven.	E10	86
Canajoharie, N.Y., U.S.	B11	114
Çanakkale, Tur.	C9	28
Çanakkale, state, Tur.	D9	28
Çanakkale Boğazı (Dardanelles), strt., Tur.	C9	28
Canala, N. Cal.	m15	79d
Canal Fulton, Oh., U.S.	D4	114
Canal Point, Fl., U.S.	J5	116
Canals, Arg.	F6	92
Canal Winchester, Oh., U.S.	E3	114
Canandaigua, N.Y., U.S.	B8	114
Cananea, Mex.	F7	98
Canápolis, Braz.	J1	88
Cañar, Ec.	I2	86
Cañar, state, Ec.	I2	86
Canarias, Islas (Canary Islands), is., Spain	D1	64
Canarreos, Archipiélago de los, is., Cuba	B6	102
Canary Basin, unds.	F11	144
Canary Islands see Canarias, Islas, is., Spain	D1	64
Cañas, C.R.	G5	102
Canaseraga, N.Y., U.S.	B8	114
Canastota, N.Y., U.S.	E14	112
Canatlán, Mex.	C6	100
Canaveral, Cape, c., Fl., U.S.	H5	116
Canaveral National Seashore, p.o.i., Fl., U.S.	H5	116
Cañaveras, Spain	D8	20
Canavese, hist. reg., Italy	E4	22
Canavieiras, Braz.	H6	88
Canbelego, Austl.	H6	76
Canberra, Austl.	J7	76
Canby, Ca., U.S.	B5	134
Canby, Mn., U.S.	G2	118
Canby, Or., U.S.	E4	136
Cancon, Fr.	E6	18
Cancún, Mex.	B4	102
Cancún, Punta, c., Mex.	B4	102
Çandarlı Körfezi, b., Tur.	E9	28
Candé, Fr.	G7	14
Candeias, Braz.	G6	88
Candeias, Braz.	K3	88
Candela, stm., Mex.	B8	100
Candelaria, Arg.	C10	92
Candelária, Braz.	D11	92
Candelaria, stm., Mex.	C2	102
Candelo, Austl.	K7	76
Cándido Aguilar, Mex.	C9	100
Cândido Mendes, Braz.	A3	88
Candlemas Islands, is., S. Geor.	K12	82
Candlestick, Ms., U.S.	E8	122
Cando, N.D., U.S.	F14	124
Candon, Phil.	B3	52
Candor, N.C., U.S.	A6	116
Candor, N.Y., U.S.	B9	114
Canea see Chaniá, Grc.	H7	28
Canela, Braz.	D12	92
Canelas, Mex.	C5	100
Canelli, Italy	F5	22
Canelones, Ur.	G9	92
Cañete, Chile	H1	92
Caney, stm., U.S.	E13	128
Caney Creek, stm., Tx., U.S.	F12	130
Canfranc, Spain	B10	20
Cangas de Narcea, Spain	A4	20
Cangas de Onís, Spain	A5	20
Cangkuang, Tanjung, c., Indon.	G4	50
Cangombe, Ang.	C2	68
Canguaretama, Braz.	D8	88
Canguçu, Braz.	E11	92
Cangumbe, Ang.	C2	68
Cangxi, China	F1	42
Cangzhou, China	B7	42
Caniapiscau, stm., Qc., Can.	D17	106
Caniapiscau, Lac, res., Qc., Can.	E17	106
Canicattì, Italy	G7	24

Name | Map Ref. | Page

Canim Lake, B.C., Can. — E10 138
Canim Lake, l., B.C., Can. — E9 138
Canindé, Braz. — C8 88
Canindé, stm., Braz. — D4 88
Canindeyú, state, Para. — B10 92
Canisteo, N.Y., U.S. — B8 114
Canistota, S.D., U.S. — D15 126
Cañitas de Felipe Pescador, Mex. — D7 100
Canjáyar, Spain — G8 20
Çankiri, Tur. — A3 56
Çankiri, state, Tur. — C15 28
Canmore, Ab., Can. — E15 138
Cannanore, India — F2 53
Cannelton, In., U.S. — G11 120
Cannes, Fr. — F13 18
Canning, N.S., Can. — E12 110
Cannington, On., Can. — D10 112
Cannock, Eng., U.K. — I10 12
Cannon, stm., Mn., U.S. — G5 118
Cannonball, stm., N.D., U.S. — A11 126
Cannon Beach, Or., U.S. — E2 136
Cannon Falls, Mn., U.S. — G6 118
Cannonvale, Austl. — C7 76
Cann River, Austl. — K7 76
Canoas, Braz. — D12 92
Canoas, stm., Braz. — C12 92
Canoe, B.C., Can. — F11 138
Canoe, stm., B.C., Can. — D12 138
Canoinhas, Braz. — C12 92
Canon City, Co., U.S. — C3 128
Cañon de Río Blanco, Parque Nacional, p.o.i., Mex. — F10 100
Canonsburg, Pa., U.S. — D5 114
Canoochee, stm., Ga., U.S. — C4 116
Canora, Sk., Can. — C11 124
Canosa di Puglia, Italy — C10 24
Canossa, sci., Italy — F7 22
Canouan, i., St. Vin. — p11 105e
Canova, S.D., U.S. — D15 126
Canova Beach, Fl., U.S. — H5 116
Cañovanas, P.R. — B4 104a
Canowindra, Austl. — I7 76
Canso, N.S., Can. — E16 110
Cantabria, state, Spain — A6 20
Cantabrian Mountains see Cantábrica, Cordillera, mts., Spain — A5 20
Cantábrica, Cordillera, mts., Spain — A5 20
Cantagalo, Braz. — K4 88
Cantal, state, Fr. — D8 18
Cantanhede, Braz. — B3 88
Cantaura, Ven. — C9 86
Canterbury, Eng., U.K. — J14 12
Canterbury Bight, b., N.Z. — G4 80
Canterbury Plains, pl., N.Z. — G4 80
Can Tho, Viet. — G7 48
Canton see Guangzhou, China — J5 42
Canton, Il., U.S. — D7 120
Canton, Ks., U.S. — C11 128
Canton, Mn., U.S. — H7 118
Canton, Mo., U.S. — D6 120
Canton, Ms., U.S. — E8 122
Canton, N.Y., U.S. — D14 112
Canton, Oh., U.S. — D4 114
Canton, Ok., U.S. — E10 128
Canton, S.D., U.S. — C9 114
Canton, S.D., U.S. — H2 118
Canton, Tx., U.S. — E3 122
Canton see Kanton, i., Kir. — D9 72
Canton Lake, res., Ok., U.S. — E10 128
Cantonment, Fl., U.S. — G11 122
Cantù, Italy — E6 22
Cantu, stm., Braz. — B11 92
Cantwell, Ak., U.S. — D10 140
Cañuelas, Arg. — G8 92
Canumã, Braz. — D6 84
Canutama, Braz. — E5 84
Çany, Russia — C13 32
Çany, ozero, l., Russia — D13 32
Canyon, Tx., U.S. — G7 128
Canyon City, Or., U.S. — F8 136
Canyon Creek, Ab., Can. — A15 138
Canyon de Chelly National Monument, p.o.i., Az., U.S. — G7 132
Canyon Ferry Lake, res., Mt., U.S. — D15 136
Canyon Lake, res., Tx., U.S. — E9 130
Canyonlands National Park, p.o.i., Ut., U.S. — E6 132
Canyonville, Or., U.S. — H3 136
Cao Bang, Viet. — A7 48
Cao Lanh, Viet. — G7 48
Caombo, Ang. — B2 68
Caorle, Italy — E9 22
Caoxian, China — D6 42
Cap, Pointe du, c., St. Luc. — l7 105c
Capac, Mi., U.S. — E7 112
Capanaparo, stm., S.A. — D8 86
Capanema, Braz. — D8 84
Capão Bonito, Braz. — L1 88
Capão Doce, Morro do, mtn., Braz. — C12 92
Caparaó, Parque Nacional do, p.o.i., Braz. — K4 88
Caparo Viejo, stm., Ven. — D6 86
Capatárida, Ven. — B6 86
Cap aux Meules, Île du, i., Qc., Can. — C14 110
Cap-Chat, Qc., Can. — A10 110
Cap-de-la-Madeleine, Qc., Can. — D4 110
Cape, stm., Austl. — C5 76
Cape Barren Island, i., Austl. — n13 77a
Cape Basin, unds. — L14 144
Cape Breton Highlands National Park, p.o.i., N.S., Can. — D16 110
Cape Breton Island, i., N.S., Can. — D16 110
Cape Charles, Va., U.S. — G9 114
Cape Coast, Ghana — H4 64
Cape Cod Bay, b., Ma., U.S. — C15 114
Cape Cod National Seashore, p.o.i., Ma., U.S. — B16 114
Cape Coral, Fl., U.S. — J4 116
Cape Dorset see Kinngait, Nu., Can. — C15 106
Cape Elizabeth, Me., U.S. — G6 110
Cape Fear, stm., N.C., U.S. — B8 116
Cape Girardeau, Mo., U.S. — G8 120
Cape Hatteras National Seashore, p.o.i., N.C., U.S. — A10 116
Capelinha, Braz. — I4 88
Cape Lisburne, Ak., U.S. — C6 140
Capel'ka, Russia — B11 10
Capella, Austl. — D7 76
Capelongo, Ang. — C2 68
Cape Lookout National Seashore, p.o.i., N.C., U.S. — B9 116
Cape May, N.J., U.S. — F10 114
Cape May Court House, N.J., U.S. — E11 114
Cape Porpoise, Me., U.S. — G6 110
Capernaum see Kefar Naḥum, sci., Isr. — F6 58
Cape Sable Island, i., N.S., Can. — G11 110
Capesterre, Guad. — i6 105c
Capesterre, Pointe de la, c., Guad. — h5 105c
Capesterre-Belle-Eau, Guad. — i6 105c
Cape Tormentine, N.B., Can. — D12 110
Cape Town (Kaapstad), S. Afr. — H4 70
Cape Verde, ctry., Afr. — k9 65a
Cape Verde Basin, unds. — G10 144
Cape Vincent, N.Y., U.S. — D13 112
Cape York Peninsula, pen., Austl. — B8 74
Cap-Haïtien, Haiti — C11 102

Capilla del Monte, Arg. — E5 92
Capim, stm., Braz. — A2 88
Capinota, Bol. — C3 90
Capira, Pan. — H8 102
Capitan, N.M., U.S. — H3 128
Capitán Arturo Prat, sci., Ant. — B34 81
Capitán Bado, Para. — D5 90
Capitán Bermúdez, Arg. — F7 92
Capitán Meza, Para. — C10 92
Capitán Enéas, Braz. — I4 88
Capitola, Ca., U.S. — G4 134
Capitol Peak, mtn., Nv., U.S. — B8 134
Capitol Reef National Park, p.o.i., Ut., U.S. — E5 132
Capivara, Represa de, res., Braz. — D6 90
Capivari, Braz. — L2 88
Capivari, stm., Braz. — G6 88
Capoeiras, Braz. — D12 110
Capraia, Italy — G6 22
Capraia, Isola di, i., Italy — G6 22
Caprara, Punta, c., Italy — C2 24
Caprarola, Italy — B6 24
Capreol, On., Can. — B9 112
Capri, Italy — D8 24
Capri, Isola di, i., Italy — D8 24
Capricorn Channel, strt., Austl. — D9 76
Capricorn Group, is., Austl. — D9 76
Caprivi Strip, hist. reg., Nmb. — D3 68
Capron, Il., U.S. — B9 120
Captain Cook Monument, hist., Norf. I. — x25 78i
Captains Flat, Austl. — J7 76
Capua, Italy — C8 24
Capucapu, stm., Braz. — H12 86
Capucin, c., Dom. — i5 105c
Capulin Volcano National Monument, p.o.i., N.M., U.S. — E5 128
Caquetá, state, Col. — G4 86
Caquetá (Japurá), stm., S.A. — H7 86
Cara, Russia — E12 34
Cara, stm., Russia — E12 34
Carabinani, stm., Braz. — I10 86
Carabobo, state, Ven. — B7 86
Caracal, Rom. — E11 26
Caracaraí, Braz. — G11 86
Caracas, Ven. — B8 86
Caracol, Braz. — E4 88
Caraguatatuba, Braz. — L3 88
Caraguatay, Para. — B9 92
Carajás, Braz. — E7 84
Carajás, Serra dos, hills, Braz. — E7 84
Carakol, is., Belize. — D3 102
Caranavi, Bol. — C3 90
Carandaí, Braz. — K4 88
Carangola, Braz. — K4 88
Caransebeş, Rom. — D9 26
Carapá, stm., Para. — B10 92
Carapajó, Braz. — A1 88
Cara-Paraná, stm., Col. — H5 86
Carapina, Braz. — K5 88
Caraquet, N.B., Can. — C11 110
Caras-Severin, state, Rom. — D8 26
Carataska, Laguna de, b., Hond. — E5 102
Caratinga, Braz. — J4 88
Carauari, Braz. — D4 84
Caraúbas, Braz. — C7 88
Caravaca de la Cruz, Spain — F8 20
Caravelas, Braz. — I6 88
Caravelí, Peru — G3 84
Caravelle, Presqu'île la, pen., Mart. — k7 105c
Caraway, Ar., U.S. — B8 122
Carayaó, Para. — B9 92
Carazinho, Braz. — D11 92
Carballiño, Spain — B2 20
Carballo, Spain — A2 20
Carbon, Ab., Can. — E17 138
Carbon, Tx., U.S. — B9 130
Carbonara, Capo, c., Italy — E3 24
Carbondale, Co., U.S. — D9 132
Carbondale, Il., U.S. — G8 120
Carbondale, Pa., U.S. — C10 114
Carbonear, Nf., Can. — j23 107a
Carboneras de Guadazaón, Spain — E9 20
Carbon Hill, Al., U.S. — D11 122
Carbonia, Italy — E2 24
Carcagente see Carcaixent, Spain — E10 20
Carcaixent, Spain — E10 20
Carcajou, stm., N.T., Can. — B5 106
Carcans, Lac de, b., Fr. — D4 18
Carcaraña, Arg. — F7 92
Carcarañá, stm., Arg. — F7 92
Carcassonne, Fr. — F8 18
Carchi, state, Ec. — G3 86
Carcross, Yk., Can. — C3 106
Çardak, Tur. — F12 28
Cárdenas, Cuba — A7 102
Cárdenas, Mex. — F12 100
Cárdenas, Mex. — E13 100
Cárdenas, Bahía de, b., Cuba — A7 102
Cardiel, Lago, l., Arg. — I2 90
Cardiff, Wales, U.K. — J9 12
Cardigan, P.E., Can. — D14 110
Cardigan, Wales, U.K. — I8 12
Cardigan Bay, b., Wales, U.K. — I8 12
Cardinal, On., Can. — D14 112
Cardona, Ur. — F9 92
Cardonal, Punta, c., Mex. — A3 100
Cardoso, Ur. — F9 92
Cardston, Ab., Can. — G17 138
Cardwell, Austl. — B5 76
Cardwell, Mo., U.S. — H7 120
Cardwell Mountain, mtn., Tn., U.S. — B13 122
Çardžev, Turkmen. — B9 56
Carei, Rom. — B9 26
Careiro, Braz. — I12 86
Careiro, Ilha do, i., Braz. — I12 86
Cárema, Austl. — F14 14
Carinda, Austl. — H6 76
Carinhanha, Braz. — H3 88
Carinhanha, stm., Braz. — H3 88
Carini, Italy — F7 24
Carinhanha see Kärnten, state, Aus. — D10 22
Caripito, Braz. — B10 86
Caririê, Braz. — C5 88
Carirés, Braz. — D6 88
Carleton, Mi., U.S. — B2 114

Carleton, Mount, mtn., N.B., Can. — C10 110
Carleton Place, On., Can. — C13 112
Carletonville, S. Afr. — E8 70
Cârlibaba, Rom. — B12 26
Carlin, Nv., U.S. — C9 134
Carlingford Lough, b., Eur. — H7 12
Carlinville, Il., U.S. — E8 120
Carlisle, Eng., U.K. — G9 12
Carlisle, In., U.S. — C4 120
Carlisle, In., U.S. — F10 120
Carlisle, Ky., U.S. — F1 114
Carlisle, Pa., U.S. — D8 114
Carl Junction, Mo., U.S. — G3 120
Carlos, Isla i., Chile — J2 90
Carlos Casares, Arg. — G7 92
Carlos Chagas, Braz. — I5 88
Carlos Pellegrini, Arg. — E6 92
Carlow, Ire. — I5 12
Carlow, state, Ire. — I6 12
Carloway, Scot., U.K. — C6 12
Carlsbad see Karlovy Vary, Czech Rep. — F8 16
Carlsbad, Ca., U.S. — J8 134
Carlsbad, N.M., U.S. — B3 130
Carlsbad, Tx., U.S. — C7 130
Carlsbad Caverns National Park, p.o.i., N.M., U.S. — B3 130
Carlsberg Ridge, unds. — I9 142
Carlton, Or., U.S. — E3 136
Carlton, Tx., U.S. — C9 130
Carlyle, Sk., Can. — E11 124
Carlyle Lake, res., Il., U.S. — F8 120
Carmacks, Yk., Can. — C3 106
Carmagnola, Italy — F4 22
Carman, Mb., Can. — E16 124
Carmanthen, Wales, U.K. — J8 12
Carmarthen, Wales, U.K. — F17 138
Carmarthen Bay, b., Wales, U.K. — J8 12
Carmel, Ca., U.S. — G3 134
Carmel, In., U.S. — I3 112
Carmel, N.Y., U.S. — G16 112
Carmel Head, c., Wales, U.K. — H8 12
Carmelo, Ur. — F8 92
Carmel Valley, Ca., U.S. — G4 134
Carmen see Ciudad del Carmen, stm., Chile — D2 92
Carmen, Isla, i., Mex. — C3 100
Carmen, Isla del, i., Mex. — F13 100
Carmen de Areco, Arg. — G8 92
Carmen de Patagones, Arg. — H4 90
Carmi, Il., U.S. — F9 120
Carmila, Austl. — C7 76
Carmine, Tx., U.S. — D11 130
Carmo do Paranaíba, Braz. — J2 88
Carmona, Spain — G5 20
Carmona, Braz. — C6 88
Carmópolis de Minas, Braz. — K3 88
Carnarvon, Austl. — D2 74
Carnarvon, S. Afr. — G5 70
Carnarvon National Park, p.o.i., Austl. — E6 76
Carnaúby, Bela. — H6 10
Carndonald, Ire. — I5 12
Carnegie, Austl. — E4 74
Carnegie, Pa., U.S. — D5 114
Carnegie, Lake, l., Austl. — E4 74
Carney Island, i., Ant. — C29 81
Carnic Alps, mts., Eur. — D9 22
Carniça, reg., Italy — C5 22
Car Nicobar Island, i., India — G7 46
Carnot, C.A.R. — D3 66
Carnoustie, Scot., U.K. — E10 12
Carnsore Point, c., Ire. — I6 12
Carnwath, stm., N.T., Can. — B5 106
Carnwath, Scot., U.K. — F9 12
Carol City, Fl., U.S. — K5 116
Carolina, Braz. — D2 88
Carolina, P.R. — B4 104a
Carolina, S. Afr. — E10 70
Carolina Beach, N.C., U.S. — B8 116
Caroline, at., Kir. — D12 72
Caroline Islands, is., Oc. — C5 72
Caron, Sk., Can. — D8 124
Caroni, stm., Ven. — C10 86
Carora, Ven. — B6 86
Carpathian Mountains, mts., Eur. — B13 26
Carpentaria, Gulf of, b., Austl. — B7 74
Carpenter, Wy., U.S. — F8 126
Carpenter Lake, res., B.C., Can. — F8 138
Carpentersville, Il., U.S. — B9 120
Carpentras, Fr. — E11 18
Carpi, Italy — F7 22
Carpina, Braz. — D8 88
Cărpineni, Mol. — C15 26
Carpinteria, Ca., U.S. — I6 134
Carp Lake, l., B.C., Can. — B7 138
Carpolac, Austl. — K3 76
Carrabelle, Fl., U.S. — H14 122
Carranza, Cabo, c., Chile — G1 92
Carrara, Italy — F7 22
Carrathool, Austl. — J5 76
Carretera, Punta, c., Peru — F1 84
Carriacou, i., Gren. — q11 105e
Carrick on Shannon, Ire. — H4 12
Carrick-on-suir, Ire. — I5 12
Carrie, Mount, mtn., Wa., U.S. — C3 136
Carriers Mills, Il., U.S. — G9 120
Carrieton, Austl. — I2 76
Carrington, N.D., U.S. — G14 124
Carrión, stm., Spain — B6 20
Carrión de los Condes, Spain — B6 20
Carrizal Bajo, Chile — D2 92
Carrizo Creek, stm., U.S. — E5 128
Carrizo Mountain, mtn., N.M., U.S. — H3 128
Carrizo Springs, Tx., U.S. — F7 130
Carrizozo, N.M., U.S. — H3 128
Carroll, Ia., U.S. — B3 120
Carroll, Ne., U.S. — E15 126
Carrollton, Al., U.S. — D10 122
Carrollton, Ga., U.S. — D13 122
Carrollton, Il., U.S. — E7 120
Carrollton, Ky., U.S. — F12 120
Carrollton, Mi., U.S. — E5 112
Carrollton, Mo., U.S. — E4 120
Carrollton, Ms., U.S. — D8 122
Carrollton, Oh., U.S. — D4 114
Carrollton, Tx., U.S. — A10 130
Carrolltown, Pa., U.S. — D7 114
Carron, stm., Austl. — A3 76
Carrot, stm., Can. — E10 106
Carrot, stm., Can. — A10 124
Carry Falls Reservoir, res., N.Y., U.S. — E15 136
Carseland, Ab., Can. — F17 138
Carson, Wa., U.S. — E5 136
Carson, East Fork, stm., U.S. — E6 134
Carson City, Mi., U.S. — D6 134
Carson City, Nv., U.S. — D6 134
Carson Lake, res., Nv., U.S. — D7 134
Carson Range, mts., U.S. — D6 134
Carson Sink, l., Nv., U.S. — D7 134
Cartagena, Chile — F2 92
Cartagena, Col. — B4 86
Cartagena, Spain — G10 20
Cartago, Col. — E3 86
Cartago, C.R. — H6 102
Cartaxo, Port. — E2 20
Cartaya, Spain — G3 20
Carter, Ok., U.S. — F9 128
Carter Lake, Ia., U.S. — C2 120
Cartersville, Ga., U.S. — C14 122
Carthage, Ar., U.S. — C6 122
Carthage, Mo., U.S. — G3 120
Carthage, Ms., U.S. — E9 122

Carthage, N.C., U.S. — A6 116
Carthage, S.D., U.S. — C15 126
Carthage, Tn., U.S. — H11 120
Carthage, Tx., U.S. — E4 122
Castle Rock, Co., U.S. — B3 128
Castle Rock, Wa., U.S. — D3 136
Castle Rock, mtn., Or., U.S. — F8 136
Castle Rock Butte, mtn., S.D., U.S. — B9 126
Cartier Islands, is., Austl. — B4 74
Cartwright, Mb., Can. — E14 124
Caruaru, Braz. — D8 84
Carúpano, Ven. — B10 86
Carutapera, Braz. — D8 84
Caruthersville, Mo., U.S. — H8 120
Carutu, stm., Ven. — E10 86
Carvoeiro, Braz. — H10 86
Carvoeiro, Cabo, c., Port. — E1 20
Cary, Ms., U.S. — E8 122
Cary, N.C., U.S. — I7 114
Câryšskoe, Russia — D14 32
Caryville, Fl., U.S. — G13 122
Casablanca (Dar-el-Beida), Mor. — C3 64
Casa Branca, Braz. — K2 88
Casa de Piedra, Embalse, res., Arg. — I4 92
Casa Grande, Az., U.S. — K5 132
Casa Grande Ruins National Monument, p.o.i., Az., U.S. — K5 132
Casale Monferrato, Italy — E5 22
Casanare, state, Col. — E6 86
Casanare, stm., Col. — D6 86
Casa Nova, Braz. — E5 88
Casar, N.C., U.S. — A4 116
Casarano, Italy — D12 24
Casar de Cáceres, Spain — E4 20
Casas Adobes, Az., U.S. — K6 132
Casas Grandes, stm., Mex. — F9 98
Casavieja, Spain — D6 20
Casca, Braz. — D12 92
Cascade, Id., U.S. — F12 100
Cascade, stm., Chile — D2 92
Cascade, Norf. I. — y25 78i
Cascade, Ia., U.S. — B6 120
Cascade, Mt., U.S. — C15 136
Cascade, Wi., U.S. — E1 112
Cascade Bay, b., Norf. I. — y25 78i
Cascade Mountains see Cascade Range, mts., N.A. — C3 108
Cascade Range, mts., N.A. — C3 108
Cascade Reservoir, res., Id., U.S. — F10 136
Cascade-Siskiyou National Monument, p.o.i., Or., U.S. — H4 136
Cascais, Port. — F1 20
Cascapédia, stm., Qc., Can. — B10 110
Cascavel, Braz. — B11 92
Cascavel, Braz. — C6 88
Cascina, Italy — G7 22
Case-Pilote, Mart. — k6 105c
Caserta, Italy — C8 24
Casey, Il., U.S. — E9 120
Casey, sci., Ant. — B16 81
Casey, Mount, mtn., Id., U.S. — B10 136
Cashel, Ire. — I5 12
Cashiers, N.C., U.S. — A2 116
Cashmere, Wa., U.S. — C6 136
Cashton, Wi., U.S. — H8 118
Casigua, Ven. — C5 86
Casigua, Ven. — C5 86
Casino, Austl. — G9 76
Casiquiare, stm., Ven. — F8 86
Časlav, Czech Rep. — G11 16
Casma, Peru — E2 84
Čašniki, Bela. — F12 10
Casoli, Italy — H11 22
Caspe, Spain — C10 20
Casper, Wy., U.S. — E6 126
Caspian Depression (Prikaspijskaja nizmennost′), pl. — E7 32
Caspian Sea, s. — F7 32
Cass, stm., Mi., U.S. — E6 112
Cassano allo Ionio, Italy — E10 24
Cass City, Mi., U.S. — E6 112
Casselman, On., Can. — C14 112
Cássia, Braz. — K2 88
Cassiar, B.C., Can. — D5 106
Cassiar Mountains, mts., Can. — D5 106
Cassilândia, Braz. — C6 90
Cassinga, Ang. — D2 68
Cassino, Italy — C7 24
Cass Lake, Mn., U.S. — D4 118
Cassongue, Ang. — C1 68
Cassopolis, Mi., U.S. — G3 112
Cassumba, Ilha, i., Braz. — I6 88
Cassville, Mo., U.S. — H4 120
Cassville, Wi., U.S. — B7 120
Castagniccia, reg., Fr. — G15 18
Castanea, Pa., U.S. — H6 130
Castanhal, Braz. — A1 88
Castanheiro, Braz. — H8 86
Castanho, Braz. — G8 86
Castanheira de Pêra, Port. — D2 20
Castaños, Mex. — H8 130
Casteggio, Italy — F6 22
Castelbuono, Italy — G8 24
Castelfranco Veneto, Italy — E8 22
Castellammare, Golfo di, b., Italy — F6 24
Castellammare del Golfo, Italy — F6 24
Castellammare di Stabia, Italy — D8 24
Castellana Grotte, Italy — D11 24
Castellane, Fr. — F12 18
Castellaneta, Italy — D10 24
Castelli, Arg. — H9 92
Castelli, Arg. — D8 22
Castelló, co., Spain — D10 20
Castelló de la Plana see Castelló de la Plana, Spain — E11 20
Castellón de la Plana see Castelló, co., Spain — D10 20
Castellón see Castelló, co., Spain — D10 20
Castelnau-Montratier, Fr. — E7 18
Castelo, Braz. — K5 88
Castelo Branco, Port. — E3 20
Castelo Branco, state, Port. — E3 20
Castelo de Paiva, Port. — C2 20
Castel San Giovanni, Italy — E6 22
Castelsarrasin, Fr. — E6 18
Castelo Sul, Braz. — e8 79b
Casterton, Austl. — K3 76
Castets, Fr. — F4 18
Castiglione del Lago, Italy — G8 22
Castilla, Peru — E1 84
Castilla, Playa de, cst., Spain — A10 124
Castilla-La Mancha, state, Spain — E9 20
Castilla la Nueva, hist. reg., Spain — E7 20
Castilla la Vieja (Old Castile), hist. reg., Spain — C7 20
Castillon-la-Bataille, Fr. — E5 18
Castillos, Ur. — G11 92
Castine, Me., U.S. — F8 110
Castle Bruce, Dom. — j6 105c
Castle Dome Peak, mtn., Az., U.S. — J2 132
Castle Hills, Tx., U.S. — E9 130
Castleisland, Ire. — I3 12
Castlemaine, Austl. — K5 76
Castle Mountain, mtn., Yk., Can. — C3 106

Castle Peak, mtn., Co., U.S. — D9 132
Castlerea, Ire. — H4 12
Castlereagh, stm., Austl. — H7 76
Castle Rock, Co., U.S. — B3 128
Castle Rock, Wa., U.S. — D3 136
Castle Rock, mtn., Or., U.S. — F8 136
Castle Rock Butte, mtn., S.D., U.S. — B9 126
Castletown, I. of Man — G8 12
Castlewood, S.D., U.S. — C15 126
Castor, Ab., Can. — D19 138
Castor, stm., Mo., U.S. — G7 120
Castres, Fr. — F8 18
Castries, St. Luc. — l6 105c
Castro, Braz. — B13 92
Castro, Chile — H2 90
Castro Barros, Arg. — E5 92
Castro Daire, Port. — D3 20
Castro del Río, Spain — G6 20
Castronuño, Spain — C5 20
Castro Verde, Port. — G2 20
Castrovillari, Italy — E10 24
Castroville, Ca., U.S. — G4 134
Catacamas, Hond. — E5 102
Catacaos, Peru — E1 84
Catacocha, Ec. — D2 84
Cataguases, Braz. — K4 88
Catahoula Lake, l., La., U.S. — F6 122
Catalan, Tur. — A6 58
Catalão, Braz. — J2 88
Çatalca, Tur. — B11 28
Catalina, Chile — B3 92
Catalina see Santa Catalina Island, i., Ca., U.S. — J7 134
Catalina, Punta, c., Chile — J3 90
Catalonia see Catalunya, state, Spain — C12 20
Catalunya, state, Spain — C12 20
Catamarca, state, Arg. — C4 92
Catamayo, Ec. — D2 84
Catanauan, Phil. — D4 52
Catanduanes Island, i., Phil. — D5 52
Catanduva, Braz. — K1 88
Catania, Italy — G9 24
Catania, Golfo di, b., Italy — G9 24
Cataño, P.R. — B3 104a
Catanzaro, Italy — F10 24
Cataract Canyon, p., Az., U.S. — H4 132
Catarino Rodríguez, Mex. — C8 100
Catarman, Phil. — F5 52
Catarman, Phil. — D5 52
Catarroja, Spain — E10 20
Catatumbo, stm., Ven. — C5 86
Catawba, stm., U.S. — B5 116
Catawissa, Pa., U.S. — D9 114
Cat Ba, Dao, i., Viet. — B8 48
Catbalogan, Phil. — E5 52
Catedral, Cerro, hill, Ur. — G10 92
Catete, Ang. — B1 68
Cathcart, S. Afr. — H8 70
Cathedral City, Ca., U.S. — J9 134
Catherine, Mount see Katherina, Gebel, mtn., Egypt — J4 58
Catherines Peak, mtn., Jam. — i14 104d
Cat Island, i., Bah. — C9 96
Cat Lake, l., On., Can. — E12 106
Catlettsburg, Ky., U.S. — F3 114
Catlin, Il., U.S. — H2 112
Catoche, Cabo, c., Mex. — B4 102
Catoosa, Ok., U.S. — H2 120
Catrió, Arg. — D12 14
Catrimani, stm., Braz. — G11 86
Catskill, N.Y., U.S. — B12 114
Catskill Mountains, mts., N.Y., U.S. — B11 114
Catt, Mount, mtn., B.C., Can. — B2 138
Cattaraugus, N.Y., U.S. — B7 114
Cattolica, Italy — G9 22
Catuane, Moz. — E11 70
Catur, Moz. — C6 68
Catyrtaš, Kyrg. — F13 32
Cau, stm., Viet. — A7 48
Cauabeuri, stm., Braz. — G8 86
Caubvick, Mount, mtn., Can.. — F13 141
Cauca, state, Col. — F3 86
Cauca, stm., Col. — D4 86
Caucaia, Braz. — B6 88
Caucasia, Col. — D4 86
Caucasus, mts. — F6 32
Caucete, Arg. — E3 92
Cauchari, Salar de, pl., Arg. — D3 90
Caudry, Fr. — D12 14
Caungula, Ang. — B2 68
Čaunskaja guba, b., Russia — C22 34
Cauquenes, Chile — G1 92
Caura, stm., Ven. — D9 86
Caurés, stm., Braz. — H10 86
Căuşani, Mol. — C16 26
Caussapscal, Qc., Can. — B9 110
Caussade, Fr. — E7 18
Cauto, stm., Cuba — B9 102
Caux, Pays de, reg., Fr. — E9 14
Cávado, stm., Port. — C2 20
Cavaillon, Fr. — F11 18
Cavalcante, Braz. — G2 88
Cavalese, Italy — D8 22
Cavalier, N.D., U.S. — F16 124
Cavalla (Cavally), stm., Afr. — H3 64
Cavally (Cavalla), stm., Afr. — H3 64
Cavan, Ire. — G5 12
Cavan, state, Ire. — H5 12
Cavarzere, Italy — E9 22
Çavdir, Tur. — F12 28
Cave City, Ky., U.S. — G11 120
Cave in Rock, Il., U.S. — G9 120
Cavendish, Austl. — K4 76
Cave Run Lake, res., Ky., U.S. — F2 114
Cave Spring, Ga., U.S. — C13 122
Caviana de Fora, Ilha, i., Braz. — C8 84
Cavite, Phil. — C3 52
Cavour, Canale, can., Italy — E5 22
Çavuş, Tur. — G14 28
Cawood, Ky., U.S. — H2 114
Cawston, B.C., Can. — G11 138
Caxias, Braz. — C4 88
Caxias do Sul, Braz. — D12 92
Caxito, Braz. — B1 88
Çay, Tur. — E13 28
Cayambe, Ec. — G3 86
Caylus, Fr. — E7 18
Çaycuma, Tur. — B15 28
Cay Sal Bank, Bah. — K7 116
Cayce, S.C., U.S. — B3 116
Cayenne, Fr. Gu. — C7 84
Cayey, P.R. — B3 104a
Caylus see above — —
Cayman Brac, i., Cay. Is. — C8 102
Cayman Islands, dep., N.A. — C7 102
Caynaba, Som. — C9 66
Cayon, St. K./N. — C2 105a
Cayuga, In., U.S. — I2 112
Cayuga, Tx., U.S. — F3 122
Cayuga Heights, N.Y., U.S. — B9 114
Cayuga Lake, res., N.Y., U.S. — B9 114
Cazalla de la Sierra, Spain — G5 20
Cazaux et de Sanguinet, Étang de, b., Fr. — E4 18
Cazères, Fr. — F6 18
Cazombo, Ang. — C3 68

Cazorla, Spain — G7 20
Cea, stm., Spain — B5 20
Ceanannas see Kells, Ire. — H6 12
Ceará, state, Braz. — C6 88
Ceará-Mirim, Braz. — C8 88
Ceará-Mirim, stm., Braz. — C8 88
Ceatharlach see Carlow, Ire. — I5 12
Cebaco, Isla de, i., Pan. — I7 102
Ceballos, Mex. — B6 100
Čeboksary, Russia — C7 32
Cebollar, Arg. — D4 92
Cebollas, Mex. — D6 100
Cebollati, Ur. — F11 92
Cebollatí, stm., Ur. — F10 92
Čebsara, Russia — A21 10
Cebu, Phil. — E4 52
Cebu, i., Phil. — E4 52
Cebu Strait, strt., Phil. — F4 52
Ceceda, Mex. — H4 130
Čechtice, Czech Rep. — G11 16
Čechy, hist. reg., Czech Rep. — G10 16
Cecilia, Ky., U.S. — G12 120
Cecil Plains, Austl. — F8 76
Cecina, Italy — G7 22
Čečnja, state, Russia — F7 32
Cedar, stm., Ne., U.S. — F14 126
Cedar, stm., U.S. — J7 118
Cedar Bluffs, Ne., U.S. — J2 118
Cedar Breaks National Monument, p.o.i., Ut., U.S. — F3 132
Cedarburg, Wi., U.S. — E1 112
Cedar City, Ut., U.S. — F3 132
Cedar Creek, stm., Id., U.S. — C5 120
Cedar Creek, stm., N.D., U.S. — A11 126
Cedar Falls, Ia., U.S. — B5 120
Cedar Grove, Wi., U.S. — E1 112
Cedar Hill, Tx., U.S. — H10 120
Cedar Key, Fl., U.S. — G2 116
Cedar Lake, In., U.S. — J11 118
Cedar Lake, l., On., Can. — B11 112
Cedar Lake, res., Mb., Can. — E10 106
Cedar Mountain, mtn., Ca., U.S. — B5 134
Cedar Rapids, Ia., U.S. — C6 120
Cedars of Lebanon see Arz Lubnān, for., Leb. — D7 58
Cedar Springs, Mi., U.S. — E4 112
Cedartown, Ga., U.S. — C13 122
Cedar Tree Point, c., Antig. — e4 105b
Cedarvale, B.C., Can. — A2 138
Cedar Vale, Ks., U.S. — D12 128
Cedarville, Ca., U.S. — B5 134
Cedarville, Mi., U.S. — B5 112
Cedeira, Spain — A2 20
Cedillo, Embalse de, res., Eur. — E3 20
Cedro, Braz. — D6 88
Cedros, Mex. — C8 100
Cedros, Isla, i., Mex. — A1 100
Ceduna, Austl. — F6 74
Ceelbuur, Som. — D9 66
Ceepeecee, B.C., Can. — G4 138
Ceerigaabo, Som. — B9 66
Cefalonia see Kefalloniá, i., Grc. — E3 28
Cefalù, Italy — F8 24
Cega, stm., Spain — C6 20
Cegdomyn, Russia — F15 34
Ceglédi, Hung. — B6 26
Ceglie Messapico, Italy — D11 24
Cehegín, Spain — F9 20
Čehov, Russia — E20 10
Čehov, Russia — G17 34
Čekalin, Russia — F19 10
Čekuevo, Russia — E18 8
Čeľabinsk, Russia — C10 32
Čelákovice, Czech Rep. — F10 16
Celano, Italy — H10 22
Celaya, Mex. — E8 100
Celebes see Sulawesi, i., Indon. — F7 44
Celebes Basin, unds. — I15 142
Celebes Sea, s., Asia — E7 44
Čeleken, Turkmen. — B7 56
Celeste, Tx., U.S. — D2 122
Celestún, Mex. — B2 102
Celina, Tn., U.S. — H12 120
Celina, Tx., U.S. — D2 122
Čeljabinsk, Russia — C10 32
Celje, Slvn. — D12 22
Čeljuskin, mys, c., Russia — A9 34
Celle, Ger. — D6 16
Čelmozero, Russia — D14 8
Celtic Sea, s., Eur. — J6 12
Çeltikçi, Tur. — A1 58
Čemal, Russia — D15 32
Cenajo, Embalse del, res., Spain — F9 20
Cenderawasih, Teluk, b., Indon. — F10 44
Cenovo, Blg. — F12 26
Centenario, Arg. — I3 92
Center, Co., U.S. — D2 128
Center, Mo., U.S. — E6 120
Center, N.D., U.S. — G12 124
Center, Tx., U.S. — F4 122
Centerburg, Oh., U.S. — D3 114
Center Hill, Fl., U.S. — H3 116
Center Hill Lake, res., Tn., U.S. — H12 120
Center Moriches, N.Y., U.S. — D13 114
Center Point, Al., U.S. — D12 122
Center Point, Ia., U.S. — B6 120
Centerville, Ia., U.S. — D5 120
Centerville, Mo., U.S. — G7 120
Centerville, Tn., U.S. — B11 122
Centerville, Tx., U.S. — F2 122
Centerville, Ut., U.S. — C4 132
Central, Braz. — G4 88
Central, Phil. — D3 52
Central, Az., U.S. — K7 132
Central, N.M., U.S. — K8 132
Central, state, Bots. — B9 70
Central, state, Para. — B9 92
Central, state, Sol. Is. — e8 79b
Central, Cordillera, mts., Col. — E2 84
Central, Cordillera, mts., Peru — E2 84
Central, Cordillera, mts., Phil. — B3 52
Central, Massif, mts., Fr. — D8 18
Central, Sistema, mts., Spain — D6 20
Central African Republic, ctry., Afr. — C4 66
Central Aguirre, P.R. — C3 104a
Central Arizona Project Aqueduct, ca., U.S. — J3 132
Central Bohemia see Středočeský, state, Czech Rep. — G10 16
Central Borneo see Kalimantan Tengah, state, Indon. — D8 50
Central Brãhui Range, mts., Pak. — D10 56
Central Celebes see Sulawesi Tengah, state, Indon. — D12 50
Central City, Ia., U.S. — B6 120
Central City, Il., U.S. — F8 120
Central City, Ky., U.S. — G10 120
Central Division, state, Fiji — q19 79e
Centralia, Il., U.S. — F8 120
Centralia, Mo., U.S. — E5 120
Centralia, Wa., U.S. — D4 136
Centralina, Braz. — J1 88

Name	Map Ref.	Page
Central Java see Jawa Tengah, state, Indon.	G7	50
Central Kalahari Game Reserve, Bots.	C6	70
Central Lake, Mi., U.S.	C4	112
Central Makrān Range, mts., Pak.	D9	56
Central'nyj, Russia	C15	32
Central Pacific Basin, unds.	I21	142
Central Point, Or., U.S.	A2	134
Central Range, mts., Pap. N. Gui.	a3	79a
Central Russian Upland see Srednerusskaja vozvyšennost', plat., Russia	H20	10
Central Siberian Plateau see Srednesibirskoe ploskogor'e, plat., Russia	C10	34
Central Siberian Uplands see Srednesibirskoe ploskogor'e, plat., Russia	C10	34
Central Slovakia see Stredoslovenský Kraj, state, Slov.	H15	16
Central Utah Canal, can., Ut., U.S.	D4	132
Central Valley, Ca., U.S.	C3	134
Central Valley see Longitudinal, Valle, val., Chile	H1	92
Centre, Canal du, can., Fr.	C10	18
Centreville, Al., U.S.	E11	122
Centreville, Md., U.S.	E9	114
Centreville, Ms., U.S.	F7	122
Centro Puntas, P.R.	B1	104a
Century, Fl., U.S.	G11	122
Ceos see Kéa, i., Grc.	F7	28
Čepelare, Blg.	H11	26
Cephalonia see Kefalloniá, i., Grc.	E3	28
Cepu, Indon.	G7	50
Ceram see Seram, i., Indon.	F8	44
Ceram Sea see Seram, Laut, s., Indon.	F8	44
Čerčany, Czech Rep.	G10	16
Cerdas, Bol.	D3	90
Cereal, Ab., Can.	C3	124
Čereha, stm., Russia	C11	10
Čeremhovo, Russia	D18	32
Čeremšany, Russia	B11	38
Čerepanovo, Russia	D14	32
Čerepet', Russia	F19	10
Čerepovec, Russia	A20	10
Ceres, Arg.	D7	92
Ceres, Braz.	G8	84
Ceres, S. Afr.	H4	70
Ceresco, Ne., U.S.	J2	118
Ceresio see Lugano, Lago di, l., Eur.	D14	18
Cereté, Col.	C4	86
Čerevkovo, Russia	F21	8
Cerignola, Italy	C9	24
Cérilly, Fr.	H11	14
Çerkeş, Tur.	C15	28
Čerkessk, Russia	F6	32
Çerkezköy, Tur.	B10	28
Čerlak, Russia	D12	32
Cermei, Rom.	C8	26
Čermoz, Russia	C9	32
Cerna, Rom.	D15	26
Černá hora, mtn., Czech Rep.	G9	16
Cernavodă, Rom.	E15	26
Cernay, Fr.	G16	14
Černigovka, Russia	B10	38
Černjahovsk, Russia	F4	10
Černogorsk, Russia	D16	32
Černuška, Russia	C9	32
Černyševsk, Russia	F12	34
Černyševskij, Russia	D11	34
Cerralvo, Isla, i., Mex.	C4	100
Cërrik, Alb.	C14	24
Cërriku see Cërrik, Alb.	C14	24
Cerrillos, Arg.	B5	92
Cerrillos, N.M., U.S.	F2	128
Cerritos, Mex.	D8	100
Cerro Azul, Arg.	C10	92
Cerro Azul, Mex.	E9	100
Cerro Azul, Peru	F2	84
Cerro Chato, Ur.	F10	92
Cerro de las Mesas, sci., Mex.	F10	100
Cerro de Pasco, Peru	F2	84
Cerro Gordo, Il., U.S.	E9	120
Cerro Largo, Braz.	D10	92
Cerro Moreno, Chile	A2	92
Cerrón, Cerro, mtn., Ven.	B6	86
Cerrón Grande, Embalse, res., El Sal.	E3	102
Cerro Prieto, Mex.	K10	134
Cerros Colorados, Embalse, res., Arg.	I3	92
Cerro Tololo, Observatorio Astronómico, sci., Chile	E2	92
Čerskij, Russia	C21	34
Čerskogo, hrebet (Cherskiy Mountains), mts., Russia	C17	34
Čertolino, Russia	D16	10
Červen', Bela.	G11	10
Červen Brjag, Blg.	F11	26
Cervera, Spain	C12	20
Cervera de Pisuerga, Spain	B6	20
Cervia, Italy	F9	22
Cervialto, Monte, mtn., Italy	D9	24
Cervino see Matterhorn, mtn., Eur.	D13	18
Cervione, Fr.	G15	18
Cervo, Spain	A3	20
Cesar, state, Col.	C5	86
Cesar, stm., Col.	B5	86
Cesena, Italy	F9	22
Cesenatico, Italy	F9	22
Cēsis, Lat.	C8	10
Česká Kamenice, Czech Rep.	F10	16
Česká Lípa, Czech Rep.	F10	16
Česká Třebová, Czech Rep.	G12	16
České Budějovice, Czech Rep.	H10	16
Český Brod, Czech Rep.	F10	16
Çeşme, Tur.	E9	28
Češskaja guba (Chesha Bay), b., Russia	C21	8
Cessnock, Austl.	I8	76
Cesvaine, Lat.	D9	10
Cetina, stm., Cro.	G13	22
Cetinje, Mont.	G5	26
Ceuta, Sp. N. Afr.	B3	64
Cévennes, reg., Fr.	E9	18
Cévennes, Parc National des, p.o.i., Fr.	E9	18
Cevizli, Tur.	F14	28
Ceyhan, Tur.	A6	58
Ceyhan, stm., Tur.	B6	58
Ceylon, Mn., U.S.	H4	118
Ceylon see Sri Lanka, ctry., Asia	G5	53
Cèze, stm., Fr.	E10	18
Cha-am, Thai.	F5	48
Chabanais, Fr.	D6	18
Chabás, Arg.	F7	92
Chabjuwardoo Bay, b., Austl.	D2	74
Chablais, reg., Fr.	C12	18
Chacabuco, Arg.	G7	92
Chachani, Nevado, vol., Peru	G3	84
Chachapoyas, Peru	E2	84
Chāchora, India	F6	54
Chāchro, Pak.	F3	54
Chaco, state, Arg.	C7	92
Chaco, stm., N.M., U.S.	G8	132
Chaco, Parque Nacional, p.o.i., Arg.	C8	92
Chaco Austral, reg., Arg.	C7	92
Chaco Boreal, reg., Para.	D4	90
Chaco Central, reg., Arg.	D4	90
Chaco Mesa, mtn., N.M., U.S.	H9	132
Chad, ctry., Afr.	E3	62
Chad, Lake, l., Afr.	G7	64
Chadbourn, N.C., U.S.	B7	116
Chadian, China	H1	42
Chadron, Ne., U.S.	E10	126
Chadwick, Il., U.S.	I9	118
Chaem, stm., Thai.	C4	48
Chāgai, Pak.	D9	56
Chāgai Hills, hills, Asia	D9	56
Chagos Archipelago, is., B.I.O.T.	J10	142
Chagos-Lacadive Plateau, unds.	J10	142
Chaguanas, Trin.	s12	105f
Chaguaramas, Ven.	C8	86
Chahal, Guat.	E3	102
Chahanwusu see Dulan, China	D4	36
Chahe, China	E4	36
Chāībāsa, India	G10	54
Chaihe, China	B8	38
Chai Nat, Thai.	E4	48
Chaiya, Thai.	H4	48
Chaiyaphum, Thai.	E6	48
Chajarí, Arg.	E8	92
Chakaria, Bngl.	H14	54
Chākdaha, India	G12	54
Chake Chake, Tan.	F7	66
Chākia, India	E10	54
Chakkarat, Thai.	E6	48
Chakradharpur, India	G10	54
Chāksu, India	E5	54
Chakwāl, Pak.	B4	54
Chala, Peru	G3	84
Chalais, Fr.	D6	18
Chalatenango, El Sal.	F3	102
Chalaxung, China	E4	36
Chalbi Desert, des., Kenya	D7	66
Chalcidice see Chalkidikí, hist. reg., Grc.	C6	28
Chalcis see Chalkída, Grc.	E6	28
Chaleur Bay, b., Can.	C11	110
Chalía, stm., Arg.	I2	90
Chālisgaon, India	H5	54
Chalke see Chálki, i., Grc.	G10	28
Chálki, i., Grc.	G10	28
Chalkída, Grc.	E6	28
Chalkidikí, hist. reg., Grc.	C6	28
Chalk River, On., Can.	B12	112
Challakere, India	D3	53
Challapata, Bol.	C3	90
Challenger Deep, unds.	H17	142
Chalmette, La., U.S.	H9	122
Châlons-sur-Marne, Fr.	F13	14
Chalon-sur-Saône, Fr.	H13	14
Chalosse, reg., Fr.	F5	18
Chaltel, Cerro (Fitz Roy, Monte), mtn., S.A.	I2	90
Chaluhe, China	C6	38
Cham, Ger.	G8	16
Chama, N.M., U.S.	G10	132
Chama, stm., U.S.	E2	128
Chama, stm., Ven.	C6	86
Chamaicó, Arg.	G5	92
Chaman, Pak.	C10	56
Chamba, India	B6	54
Chambal, stm., India	E6	54
Chamberlain, Sk., Can.	D8	124
Chamberlain, S.D., U.S.	D13	126
Chamberlain, stm., Austl.	C5	74
Chamberlain Lake, l., Me., U.S.	D7	110
Chambers, Ne., U.S.	E14	126
Chambersburg, Pa., U.S.	E8	114
Chambers Island, i., Wi., U.S.	C2	112
Chambéry, Fr.	D11	18
Chambi, Jebel, mtn., Tun.	B6	64
Chamblee, Ga., U.S.	D14	122
Chambord, Qc., Can.	B4	110
Chamdo see Qamdo, China	E4	36
Chamical, Arg.	E4	92
Chamo, Lake see Ch'amo Hāyk', l., Eth.	F7	62
Ch'amo Hāyk', l., Eth.	F7	62
Chamois, Mo., U.S.	F6	120
Chamoli, India	C7	54
Chamonix-Mont-Blanc, Fr.	D12	18
Chāmpa, India	G9	54
Champagne, hist. reg., Fr.	F13	14
Champagne Castle, mtn., S. Afr.	F9	70
Champagnole, Fr.	H14	14
Champaign, Il., U.S.	D9	120
Champaquí, Cerro, mtn., Arg.	F5	92
Champasak, Laos	E7	48
Champdoré, Lac, l., Qc., Can.	D17	106
Champion, Ab., Can.	F17	138
Champion, Mi., U.S.	B1	112
Champion, Oh., U.S.	G9	112
Champlain, Lake, l., N.A.	D16	112
Champlitte-et-le-Prélot, Fr.	G14	14
Champotón, Mex.	C2	102
Chāmrājnagar Rāmasamudram, India	F3	53
Chana, Thai.	I5	48
Chañar, Arg.	E4	92
Chañaral, Chile	C2	92
Chañaral, Isla, i., Chile	D2	92
Chancay, Peru	F2	84
Chanchiang see Zhanjiang, China	K4	42
Chanco, Chile	G1	92
Chandalar, Ak., U.S.	C10	140
Chandalar, stm., Ak., U.S.	C10	140
Chandannagar, India	G11	54
Chandausi, India	D7	54
Chāndbāli, India	H11	54
Chandeleur Islands, is., La., U.S.	H10	122
Chandeleur Sound, strt., La., U.S.	H9	122
Chandīgarh, India	C6	54
Chandler, Qc., Can.	B12	110
Chandler, Az., U.S.	J5	132
Chandler, In., U.S.	F10	120
Chandler, Tx., U.S.	E3	122
Chandlerville, Il., U.S.	D7	120
Chāndpur, Bngl.	G13	54
Chāndpur, Bngl.	G14	54
Chāndpur, India	D7	54
Chandrapur, India	B4	53
Chāndvad, India	H5	54
Chang (Yangtze), stm., China	F8	36
Chang, stm., China	G1	42
Chang, Ko, i., Thai.	F6	48
Changan see Xi'an, China	D3	42
Changanācheri, India	G3	53
Changane, stm., Moz.	D11	70
Changcheng, China	L3	42
Chang Cheng (Great Wall), misc. cult., China	D6	36
Chang Chenmo, stm., Asia	A7	54
Changchiak'ou see Zhangjiakou, China	A6	42
Ch'angchih see Changzhi, China	C5	42
Changchou see Changzhou, China	F8	42
Changchou see Zhangzhou, China	I7	42
Changchow see Changzhou, China	F8	42
Changchow see Zhangzhou, China	I7	42
Changchun, China	C6	38
Changde, China	G4	42
Chang Hu, l., China	F5	42
Changhua, Tai.	I9	42
Changhŭng, Kor., S.	G7	38
Changji, China	C2	36
Changjiang, China	L3	42
Changkiakow see Zhangjiakou, China	A6	42
Changli, China	B8	42
Changling, China	B5	38
Changlun, Malay.	I5	48
Changmar, China	A7	54
Changning, China	G4	36
Changning, China	H5	42
Ch'angnyŏng, Kor., S.	D1	40
Changping, China	A7	42
Changsa, China	L4	42
Changsan-got, c., Kor., N.	E6	38
Changsha, China	G5	42
Changshan Qundao, is., China	B10	42
Changshou, China	G2	42
Changshu, China	F9	42
Ch'angte see Changde, China	G4	42
Changteh see Anyang, China	C6	42
Changtien see Zibo, China	C8	42
Changting, China	I7	42
Changting, China	B8	38
Changwŏn, Kor., S.	D1	40
Changwu, China	D2	42
Changxing, China	F8	42
Changxing Dao, i., China	B9	42
Changyi, China	C8	42
Changyŏn-ŭp, Kor., N.	E6	38
Changzhi, China	C5	42
Changzhou, China	F8	42
Chaniá, Grc.	H7	28
Chanión, Kólpos, b., Grc.	H6	28
Chankiang see Zhanjiang, China	K4	42
Channagiri, India	D2	53
Channapatna, India	E3	53
Channel Country, reg., Austl.	E3	76
Channel Islands, is., Eur.	L10	12
Channel Islands, is., Ca., U.S.	J6	134
Channel Islands National Park, p.o.i., Ca., U.S.	J6	134
Channel-Port aux Basques, Nf., Can.	j22	107a
Channelview, Tx., U.S.	H3	122
Channing, Mi., U.S.	B1	112
Channing, Tx., U.S.	F6	128
Chan-si see Shanxi, state, China	B5	42
Chantada, Spain	B3	20
Chanthaburi, Thai.	F6	48
Chantilly, Fr.	E11	14
Chan-tong see Shandong, state, China	C7	42
Chantrey Inlet, b., Nu., Can.	B11	106
Chanute, Ks., U.S.	G2	120
Chao, stm., China	A7	42
Chao'an, China	J7	42
Ch'aochou see Chao'an, China	J7	42
Chaochow see Chao'an, China	J7	42
Chao Hu, l., China	F7	42
Chao Phraya, stm., Thai.	E5	48
Chaor, stm., China	B9	36
Chaoxian, China	F7	42
Chaoyang, China	J7	42
Chaoyang, China	B7	38
Chaoyang, China	D4	38
Chaoyangshan, China	C6	38
Chapada dos Veadeiros, Parque Nacional da, p.o.i., Braz.	H2	88
Chapadinha, Braz.	B4	88
Chapaevo, Kaz.	D8	32
Chapala, Mex.	E7	100
Chapala, Laguna de, l., Mex.	E7	100
Chāparmukh, India	E14	54
Chaparral, Col.	F4	86
Chapecó, Braz.	C11	92
Chapel Hill, N.C., U.S.	I6	114
Chapelton, Jam.	i13	104d
Chapéu, Morro do, mtn., Braz.	H4	88
Chapicuy, Ur.	E9	92
Chapin, Il., U.S.	E7	120
Chapleau, On., Can.	F14	106
Chaplin, Sk., Can.	D7	124
Chaplin Lake, l., Sk., Can.	D7	124
Chapman, Ne., U.S.	F14	126
Chapman, Cape, c., Nu., Can.	B13	106
Chapmanville, W.V., U.S.	G3	114
Chapo, Mex.	E3	130
Chappal, Waddi, mtn., Afr.	H7	64
Chappell Hill, Tx., U.S.	G2	122
Chapultepec, Mex.	L9	134
Chaquiago, Arg.	C4	92
Charadai, Arg.	C8	92
Charalá, Col.	D5	86
Charata, Arg.	C7	92
Chār Borjak, Afg.	C9	56
Charcas, Mex.	D8	100
Charco Hondo, P.R.	B2	104a
Charcos de Risa, Mex.	B7	100
Charcot Island, i., Ant.	B33	81
Chard, Eng., U.K.	K10	12
Charente, state, Fr.	D6	18
Charente, stm., Fr.	C6	18
Charente-Maritime, state, Fr.	C5	18
Chari, stm., Afr.	E3	62
Chārīkār, Afg.	B10	56
Chariton, Ia., U.S.	C4	120
Chariton, stm., U.S.	E5	120
Chariton, Mussel Fork, stm., Mo., U.S.	E5	120
Charity, Guy.	B6	84
Charkhāri, India	F7	54
Charkhlik see Ruoqiang, China	D2	36
Charleroi, Bel.	D13	14
Charles, Cape, c., Va., U.S.	G10	114
Charles, Peak, mtn., Austl.	F4	74
Charles City, Ia., U.S.	A5	120
Charles City, Va., U.S.	G8	114
Charles Island, i., Nu., Can.	C16	106
Charles Mound, hill, Il., U.S.	B7	120
Charles Point, c., Austl.	B6	74
Charleston, Ar., U.S.	B4	122
Charleston, Il., U.S.	E9	120
Charleston, Mo., U.S.	H8	120
Charleston, Ms., U.S.	C8	122
Charleston, S.C., U.S.	D6	116
Charleston, W.V., U.S.	F4	114
Charleston Peak, mtn., Nv., U.S.	G10	134
Charlestown, S. Afr.	E9	70
Charlestown, St. K./N.	C2	105a
Charlestown, St. Vin.	p11	105e
Charlestown, In., U.S.	F12	120
Charleville, Austl.	F5	76
Charleville-Mézières, Fr.	E13	14
Charlevoix, Lake, l., Mi., U.S.	C5	112
Charlieu, Fr.	C10	18
Charlotte, Mi., U.S.	B1	114
Charlotte, N.C., U.S.	A5	116
Charlotte, Tn., U.S.	H10	120
Charlotte, Tx., U.S.	F9	130
Charlotte Amalie, V.I.U.S.	e7	104b
Charlotte Harbor, b., Fl., U.S.	J3	116
Charlotte Lake, l., B.C., Can.	D5	138
Charlottesville, Va., U.S.	F7	114
Charlottetown, P.E., Can.	D13	110
Charlotteville, Trin.	r13	105f
Charlton Island, i., Nu., Can.	E14	106
Charouine, Alg.	D4	64
Charron Lake, l., Mb., Can.	B18	124
Charroux, Fr.	C6	18
Chārsadda, Pak.	A3	54
Charter Oak, Ia., U.S.	I3	118
Charters Towers, Austl.	C6	76
Chartres, Fr.	F10	14
Chascomús, Arg.	G8	92
Chase, B.C., Can.	F11	138
Chase, Mount, mtn., Me., U.S.	D8	110
Chase City, Va., U.S.	H7	114
Chaska, Mn., U.S.	G5	118
Chateaubelair, St. Vin.	o11	105e
Châteaubriant, Fr.	G7	14
Château-du-Loir, Fr.	G9	14
Châteaudun, Fr.	F10	14
Chateaugay (Châteauguay), stm., N.A.	D15	112
Châteaulin, Fr.	F4	14
Châteauneuf-sur-Charente, Fr.	D5	18
Château-Renault, Fr.	G9	14
Château-Richer, Qc., Can.	C5	110
Châteauroux, Fr.	H10	14
Château-Thierry, Fr.	E12	14
Châtellerault, Fr.	H9	14
Chatfield, Mn., U.S.	H6	118
Chatham, N.B., Can.	C11	110
Chatham, On., Can.	F7	112
Chatham, Eng., U.K.	J13	12
Chatham, Il., U.S.	E8	120
Chatham, La., U.S.	E6	122
Chatham, Ma., U.S.	C15	114
Chatham, N.Y., U.S.	B12	114
Chatham, Isla, i., Chile	J2	90
Chatham Islands, is., N.Z.	H9	72
Chatham Rise, unds.	N20	142
Chatham Strait, strt., Ak., U.S.	E13	140
Châtillon-en-Bazois, Fr.	G12	14
Châtillon-sur-Seine, Fr.	G13	14
Chatkal Range, mts., Asia	F12	32
Chatom, Al., U.S.	F10	122
Chatra, India	F10	54
Chatsworth, Austl.	C3	76
Chatsworth, Ga., U.S.	C14	122
Chatsworth, Il., U.S.	D9	120
Chattahoochee, stm., U.S.	G14	122
Chattanooga, Tn., U.S.	B13	122
Chattaroy, W.V., U.S.	G3	114
Chaturat, Thai.	E5	48
Chaubourg, Mount, hill, St. Luc.	I7	105c
Chaudière, stm., Qc., Can.	D5	110
Chau Doc, Viet.	G7	48
Chauk, Mya.	B2	48
Chaumont, Fr.	F13	14
Chauncey, Oh., U.S.	E3	114
Chaungwabyin, Mya.	F4	48
Chauny, Fr.	E12	14
Chaupāran, India	F10	54
Chautauqua Lake, l., N.Y., U.S.	B6	114
Chauvin, La., U.S.	H8	122
Chavakkad, India	F2	53
Chavarría, Arg.	D8	92
Chaves, Port.	C3	20
Cháviva, Col.	E5	86
Chawa'nanake, China	C12	54
Chay, stm., Viet.	A7	48
Chayuan, China	G9	42
Chazy, N.Y., U.S.	F3	110
Chbar, stm., Camb.	F8	48
Cheaha Mountain, mtn., Al., U.S.	D13	122
Cheat, stm., U.S.	E6	114
Cheat, Shavers Fork, stm., W.V., U.S.	E6	114
Cheb, Czech Rep.	F8	16
Chebanse, Il., U.S.	G2	112
Cheboygan, Mi., U.S.	C5	112
Chech, 'Erg, des., Afr.	E4	64
Chechnya see Čečnja, state, Russia	F7	32
Chech'on, Kor., S.	B1	40
Chęciny, Pol.	F16	16
Checleset Bay, b., B.C., Can.	F3	138
Checotah, Ok., U.S.	B3	122
Chedabucto Bay, b., N.S., Can.	E15	110
Cheduba Island, i., Mya.	C1	48
Cheduba Strait, strt., Mya.	C1	48
Cheektowaga, N.Y., U.S.	B7	114
Cheepie, Austl.	F5	76
Chef-Boutonne, Fr.	C5	18
Chefoo see Yantai, China	C9	42
Chehalis, Wa., U.S.	D4	136
Chehalis, stm., Wa., U.S.	D3	136
Cheju, Kor., S.	H7	38
Cheju-do (Quelpart Island), i., Kor., S.	H7	38
Chekiang see Zhejiang, state, China	G8	42
Chela, Serra da, mts., Ang.	D1	68
Chelan, Lake, res., Wa., U.S.	B6	136
Chelif, Oued, stm., Alg.	B5	64
Chełm, Pol.	E19	16
Chełm, state, Pol.	E19	16
Chełmno, Pol.	C14	16
Chelmsford, On., Can.	B8	112
Chelmsford, Eng., U.K.	J13	12
Chełmża, Pol.	C14	16
Chelsea, Ia., U.S.	C5	120
Chelsea, Mi., U.S.	B1	114
Chelsea, Vt., U.S.	F4	110
Cheltenham, Eng., U.K.	J10	12
Chelva see Xelva, Spain	E9	20
Chelyuskin, Cape see Čeljuskin, mys, c., Russia	A9	34
Chemainus, B.C., Can.	H7	138
Chemba, Moz.	D5	68
Chemnitz, Ger.	F8	16
Chemult, Or., U.S.	G5	136
Chenāb, stm., Asia	D3	54
Chenango, stm., N.Y., U.S.	B10	114
Chenchiang see Zhenjiang, China	E8	42
Chenderoh, Tasik, l., Malay.	J5	48
Chénéville, Qc., Can.	E1	110
Cheney, Wa., U.S.	C9	136
Cheney Reservoir, res., Ks., U.S.	D10	128
Cheneyville, La., U.S.	F6	122
Chengbu, China	H4	42
Chengchou see Zhengzhou, China	D5	42
Chengchow see Zhengzhou, China	D5	42
Chengde, China	A7	42
Chengdu, China	E5	36
Chenggu, China	E2	42
Chenghai, China	J7	42
Chengmai, China	L3	42
Chengshan Jiao, c., China	C10	42
Chengteh see Chengde, China	A7	42
Chengtu see Chengdu, China	E5	36
Chengxian, China	E1	42
Chengyang, China	G8	42
Chengzitan, China	B10	42
Ch'enhsien see Chenzhou, China	I5	42
Chen Hu, l., China	F5	42
Chenliu, China	D6	42
Chennai (Madras), India	E5	53
Chenoa, Il., U.S.	D9	120
Chen-si see Shaanxi, state, China	E3	42
Chentang, China	J4	42
Chenxi, China	H3	42
Chenxiangtun, China	D5	38
Chenyang see Shenyang, China	D5	38
Chenzhou, China	I5	42
Cheonan see Ch'ŏnan, Kor., S.	F7	38
Cheongju see Ch'ŏngju, Kor., S.	F7	38
Chepén, Peru	E2	84
Chepes, Arg.	E4	92
Chepkotet, mtn., Kenya	D7	66
Chepo, Pan.	H8	102
Cher, state, Fr.	B8	18
Cher, stm., Fr.	B7	18
Cheradi, Isole, i., Italy	D11	24
Cherbourg, Fr.	E7	14
Cherchell, Alg.	H13	20
Chergui, Chott ech, l., Alg.	C5	64
Cheriton, Va., U.S.	G10	114
Cheriyam Island, i., India	F1	53
Cherkassy see Cherkasy, Ukr.	E4	32
Cherkasy, Ukr.	E4	32
Cherkessia see Karačaevo-Čerkesija, state, Russia	F6	32
Chernihiv, Ukr.	D4	32
Chernivtsi, Ukr.	A12	26
Chernivtsi, co., Ukr.	A13	26
Chernobyl see Chornobyl', Ukr.	D4	32
Cherokee, Ia., U.S.	B2	120
Cherokee, Ks., U.S.	G3	120
Cherokee, Ok., U.S.	E10	128
Cherokee, Tx., U.S.	C9	130
Cherokee Lake, res., Tn., U.S.	H2	114
Cherokee Point, c., Bah.	J8	116
Cherokees, Lake O' The, res., Ok., U.S.	H2	120
Cherokee Sound, Bah.	J8	116
Cherrapunji, India	F13	54
Cherry Creek, stm., S.D., U.S.	C11	126
Cherry Hill, N.J., U.S.	E10	114
Cherryvale, Ks., U.S.	G2	120
Cherry Valley, Ar., U.S.	B8	122
Cherryville, N.C., U.S.	A4	116
Cherskiy Mountains see Čerskogo, hrebet, mts., Russia	C17	34
Chesapeake, Va., U.S.	H9	114
Chesapeake Bay, b., U.S.	F9	114
Chesapeake Bay Bridge-Tunnel, Va., U.S.	G9	114
Chesapeake Beach, Md., U.S.	F9	114
Chesaw, Wa., U.S.	B7	136
Chesha Bay see Češskaja guba, b., Russia	C21	8
Cheshire, Ma., U.S.	B12	114
Cheslatta Lake, l., B.C., Can.	C5	138
Chesnee, S.C., U.S.	A4	116
Chest Creek, stm., Pa., U.S.	D7	114
Chester, Eng., U.K.	H10	12
Chester, Ca., U.S.	C4	134
Chester, Il., U.S.	G8	120
Chester, Mt., U.S.	B15	136
Chester, Ne., U.S.	A11	128
Chester, Ok., U.S.	E10	128
Chester, Pa., U.S.	E10	114
Chester, Va., U.S.	G8	114
Chester Basin, N.S., Can.	F12	110
Chesterfield, Eng., U.K.	H11	12
Chesterfield, S.C., U.S.	B5	116
Chesterfield, Îles, is., N. Cal.	E6	72
Chesterfield Inlet see Igluligaarjuk, Nu., Can.	C12	106
Chesterfield Inlet, b., Nu., Can.	C12	106
Chesterfield Islands see Chesterfield, Îles, is., N. Cal.	E6	72
Chesterhill, Oh., U.S.	E4	114
Chester-le-Street, Eng., U.K.	G11	12
Chestertown, Md., U.S.	E9	114
Chesterville, On., Can.	C14	112
Chesuncook Lake, l., Me., U.S.	E7	110
Chetek, Wi., U.S.	F7	118
Chéticamp, N.S., Can.	D16	110
Chetumal, Mex.	C3	102
Chetumal, Bahía, b., N.A.	C3	102
Chevelon Creek, stm., Az., U.S.	I6	132
Cheviot, Oh., U.S.	E13	120
Cheviot Hills, hills, U.K.	F10	12
Ch'ew Bahir see Stefanie, Lake, l., Afr.	G7	62
Chewelah, Wa., U.S.	B9	136
Cheyenne, Ok., U.S.	F9	128
Cheyenne, Wy., U.S.	F8	126
Cheyenne, stm., U.S.	C11	126
Cheyenne Wells, Co., U.S.	C6	128
Cheyne Bay, b., Austl.	F3	74
Chhabra, India	F6	54
Chhapra, India	F10	54
Chhātak, Bngl.	F13	54
Chhatarpur, India	F7	54
Chhatrapur, India	E6	46
Chhattisgarh, state, India	D5	46
Chhay Arêng, stm., Camb.	G6	48
Chhêb Kândal, Camb.	F7	48
Chhindwāra, India	H7	54
Chhlong, stm., Camb.	F8	48
Chhota-Chhindwāra, India	G7	54
Chhota Udepur Mhow, India	D3	46
Chi, stm., China	E7	42
Chi, stm., Thai.	E7	48
Chía, Col.	E4	86
Chiahsing see Jiaxing, China	F9	42
Chiai, Tai.	J9	42
Chiamussu see Jiamusi, China	B11	36
Chian see Ji'an, China	H6	42
Chiang Dao, Thai.	C4	48
Chiange, Ang.	D1	68
Chiang Kham, Thai.	C5	48
Chiang Khan, Thai.	D5	48
Chiang Mai, Thai.	C4	48
Chiangmen see Jiangmen, China	J5	42
Chiang Rai, Thai.	C4	48
Chiang Saen, Thai.	B4	48
Chiangtu see Yangzhou, China	E8	42
Chiangyin see Jiangyin, China	F9	42
Chiaohsien see Jiaoxian, China	C8	42
Chiaotso see Jiaozuo, China	D5	42
Chiapas, state, Mex.	D6	96
Chiavari, Italy	F6	22
Chiavenna, Italy	D6	22
Chiba, Japan	D13	40
Chiba, state, Japan	D13	40
Chibabava, Moz.	B11	70
Chibemba, Ang.	D1	68
Chibougamau, Qc., Can.	F15	106
Chibuto, Moz.	D11	70
Chibuzhangchu Hu, l., China	B13	54
Chicago, Il., U.S.	G2	112
Chicago Heights, Il., U.S.	C10	120
Chicapa, stm., Afr.	B3	68
Chichagof Island, i., Ak., U.S.	E12	140
Chīchāwatni, Pak.	C4	54
Chicheng, China	A6	42
Chichén Itzá, sci., Mex.	B3	102
Chichester, Eng., U.K.	K12	12
Chichibu, Japan	C11	40
Ch'ich'ihaerh see Qiqihar, China	B9	36
Chichiriviche, Ven.	B7	86
Chickamauga, Ga., U.S.	C13	122
Chickamauga Lake, res., Tn., U.S.	B14	122
Chickasaw, Al., U.S.	G10	122
Chickasawhay, stm., Ms., U.S.	F10	122
Chickasaw National Recreation Area, p.o.i., Ok., U.S.	G12	128
Chickasha, Ok., U.S.	F11	128
Chicken, Ak., U.S.	D11	140
Chiclana de la Frontera, Spain	H4	20
Chiclayo, Peru	E2	84
Chico, Ca., U.S.	D4	134
Chico, Tx., U.S.	H11	128
Chico, stm., Arg.	I2	90
Chico, stm., Arg.	I3	90
Chico, stm., Phil.	B3	52
Chicomba, Ang.	C2	68
Chicopee, Ga., U.S.	B2	116
Chicopee, Ma., U.S.	B13	114
Chicoutimi, Qc., Can.	B5	110
Chicoutimi, stm., Qc., Can.	B5	110
Chicuma, Ang.	C1	68
Chidambaram, India	F4	53
Chidenguele, Moz.	D12	70
Chiefland, Fl., U.S.	G3	116
Chiehyang see Jieyang, China	J7	42
Chiemsee, l., Ger.	I8	16
Chieo Lan Reservoir, res., Thai.	H4	48
Chieri, Italy	F4	22
Chiese, stm., Italy	E7	22
Chieti, Italy	H11	22
Chifeng, China	C3	38
Chigasaki, Japan	D12	40
Chignahuapan, Mex.	F9	100
Chignecto, Cape, c., N.S., Can.	E11	110
Chignecto Bay, b., Can.	E12	110
Chignik, Ak., U.S.	E8	140
Chigoubiche, Lac, l., Qc., Can.	A3	110
Chigubo, Moz.	C11	70
Chigu Co, l., China	D13	54
Ch'ihfeng see Chifeng, China	C3	38
Chihli, Gulf of see Bo Hai, b., China	B8	42
Chihsi see Jixi, China	B9	38
Chihuahua, Mex.	A5	100
Chihuahua, state, Mex.	B3	96
Chihuahua, Desierto de, des., N.A.	F6	108
Chihuahuan Desert see Chihuahua, Desierto de, des., N.A.	F6	108
Chii-san, mtn., Kor., S.	G7	38
Chikaskia, stm., U.S.	E11	128
Chik Ballāpur, India	E3	53
Chikhli, India	H6	54
Chikmagalūr, India	E2	53
Chiknāyakanhalli, India	E3	53
Chikodi, India	C2	53
Chikrêng, stm., Camb.	F7	48
Chikuma, stm., Japan	C11	40
Chi-kyaw, Mya.	B1	48
Chilakalūrupet, India	C4	53
Chilako, stm., B.C., Can.	C7	138
Chilanko Forks, B.C., Can.	D6	138
Chilapa de Álvarez, Mex.	G9	100
Chilās, Pak.	B11	56
Chilcotin, stm., B.C., Can.	E8	138
Childers, Austl.	E9	76
Childersburg, Al., U.S.	D12	122
Childress, Tx., U.S.	G8	128
Chile, ctry., S.A.	F2	90
Chile Chico, Chile	I2	90
Chilecito, Arg.	D4	92
Chilecito, Arg.	F3	92
Chile Rise, unds.	M5	144
Chilhowie, Va., U.S.	H4	114
Chilia, Bratul, stm., Eur.	D16	26
Chilika Lake, l., India	I10	54
Chililabombwe, Zam.	C4	68
Chilin see Jilin, China	C7	38
Chilko, stm., B.C., Can.	D7	138
Chilko Lake, l., B.C., Can.	E6	138
Chillagoe, Austl.	C8	74
Chillán, Chile	H1	92
Chillicothe, Mo., U.S.	E4	120
Chillicothe, Oh., U.S.	E3	114
Chillicothe, Tx., U.S.	G9	128
Chilliwack, B.C., Can.	G9	138
Chiloé, Isla Grande de, i., Chile	H2	90
Chilón, Mex.	G12	100
Chiloquin, Or., U.S.	H5	136
Chilpancingo de los Bravo, Mex.	G9	100
Chiluage, Ang.	B3	68
Chilumba, Mwi.	C5	68
Chilung, Tai.	I9	42
Chilwa, Lake, l., Afr.	D6	68
Chimaltenango, Guat.	E2	102
Chimán, Pan.	H8	102
Chimayo, N.M., U.S.	E3	128
Chimbarongo, Chile	G2	92
Chimbas, Arg.	E3	92
Chimborazo, state, Ec.	H2	86
Chimborazo, vol., Ec.	H2	86
Chimbote, Peru	E2	84
Chimoio, Moz.	D5	68
Chimpay, Arg.	G3	90
Chin, state, Mya.	B1	48
China, Mex.	C9	100
China, ctry., Asia	B8	46
Chinan see Jinan, China	C7	42
Chinandega, Nic.	F4	102
Chinati Peak, mtn., Tx., U.S.	E3	130
Chincha Alta, Peru	F2	84
Chinchaga, stm., Can.	D7	106
Chinchilla, Austl.	F8	76
Chinchilla de Monte-Aragón, Spain	F9	20
Chinchiná, Col.	E4	86
Chinchou see Jinzhou, China	A9	42
Chinchow see Jinzhou, China	A9	42
Chincolco, Chile	F2	92
Chincoteague, Va., U.S.	G10	114
Chinde, Moz.	D6	68
Chindo, Kor., S.	G7	38
Chin-do, i., Kor., S.	G7	38
Chindong, Kor., S.	D1	40
Chindwinn, stm., Mya.	D7	46
Ch'ingchiang see Qingjiang, China	E8	42
Chingleput, India	E4	53
Chingola, Zam.	C4	68
Chingshih see Jinshi, China	G4	42
Ch'ingtao see Qingdao, China	C9	42
Chingtechen see Jingdezhen, China	G7	42
Chinguețți, Maur.	E2	64
Chinhae, Kor., S.	D1	40
Chin Hills, hills, Mya.	D7	46
Chinhoyi, Zimb.	D5	68
Chinhsien see Jinzhou, China	B9	42
Chinhua see Jinhua, China	G8	42
Ch'inhuangtao see Qinhuangdao, China	B8	42
Chining see Jining, China	D7	42
Chining see Jining, China	A5	42
Chiniot, Pak.	C4	54
Chinĭt, stm., Camb.	F7	48

Name | Map Ref. | Page

Chinjan, Pak. C1 54
Chinju, Kor., S. G7 38
Chinkiang see Zhenjiang, China E8 42
Chinko, stm., C.A.R. C4 66
Chinle, Az., U.S. G7 132
Chinle Wash, stm., Az., U.S. G7 132
Chinmen Tao (Quemoy), i., Tai. I8 42
Chino, Ca., U.S. J8 134
Chinon, Fr. G9 14
Chinook, Ab., Can. C2 124
Chinook Cove, B.C., Can. E10 138
Chino Valley, Az., U.S. I4 132
Chinquapin, N.C., U.S. B8 116
Chinsali, Zam. C5 68
Chintāmani, India E4 53
Chinú, Col. C4 86
Chinwangtao see Qinhuangdao, China B8 42
Chioco, Moz. D5 68
Chioggia, Italy E9 22
Chíos, Grc. E9 28
Chíos, i., Grc. E8 28
Chios see Chíos, i., Grc. E8 28
Chipata, Zam. C5 68
Chip Lake, l., Ab., Can. C15 138
Chiplūn, India C1 53
Chipman, N.B., Can. D11 110
Chipola, stm., Fl., U.S. G13 122
Chippenham, Eng., U.K. J10 12
Chippewa, stm., Mn., U.S. F3 118
Chippewa, stm., Wi., U.S. G6 118
Chippewa, East Fork, stm., Wi., U.S. F8 118
Chippewa Falls, Wi., U.S. G7 118
Chiquimula, Guat. E3 102
Chiquinquirá, Col. E4 86
Chīrāla, India D5 53
Chirāwa, India D5 54
Chiredzi, Zimb. B10 70
Chireno, Tx., U.S. F4 122
Chirfa, Niger E7 64
Chirgaon, India F7 54
Chiribiquete, Parque Nacional, p.o.i., Col. G5 86
Chiricahua Mountains, mts., Az., U.S. L7 132
Chiricahua National Monument, p.o.i., Az., U.S. L7 132
Chiricahua Peak, mtn., Az., U.S. L7 132
Chiriguaná, Col. C5 86
Chirikof Island, i., Ak., U.S. E8 140
Chiriquí, Golfo de, b., Pan. H6 102
Chiriquí, Laguna de, b., Pan. H6 102
Chiromo, Mwi. D5 68
Chirpan see Čirpan, Blg. G12 26
Chirripó, Cerro, mtn., C.R. H6 102
Chirripó, Parque Nacional, p.o.i., C.R. H6 102
Chisago City, Mn., U.S. F5 118
Chisamba, Zam. C4 68
Chisasibi, Qc., Can. E15 106
Chisep'o, Kor., S. E1 40
Ch'ishan, Tai. J9 42
Chisholm, Ab., Can. B16 138
Chisholm, Me., U.S. F6 110
Chisholm, Mn., U.S. D5 118
Chishtiān Mandi, Pak. D4 54
Chishui, China G1 42
Chishui, stm., China F6 36
Chisimayu see Kismaayo, Som. E8 66
Chişinău, Mol. B15 26
Chişineu-Criş, Rom. C8 26
Chita, Col. D5 86
Chitado, Ang. D1 68
Chitagá, Col. D5 86
Chita-hantō, pen., Japan E9 40
Chitato, Ang. B3 68
Chitek Lake, l., Mb., Can. B14 124
Chitembo, Ang. C2 68
Chitina, Ak., U.S. D11 140
Chitina, stm., Ak., U.S. D11 140
Chitipa, Mwi. B5 68
Chitokoloki, Zam. C3 68
Chitose, Japan C14 38
Chitradurga, India D3 53
Chitrakūt Dham, India F8 54
Chitrāl, Pak. B11 56
Chitrāvati, stm., India D3 53
Chitré, Pan. H7 102
Chittagong, Bngl. G13 54
Chittagong, state, Bngl. G13 54
Chittāpur, India C3 53
Chittaurgarh, India F5 54
Chittoor, India E4 53
Chittūr, India F3 53
Chitungwiza, Zimb. D5 68
Chiuchiang see Jiujiang, China G6 42
Chiumbe (Tshumbe), stm., Afr. B3 68
Chiume, Ang. D3 68
Chiusi, Italy G8 22
Chiva see Xiva, Spain E10 20
Chivacoa, Ven. B7 86
Chivasso, Italy E4 22
Chivi, Zimb. B10 70
Chivilcoy, Arg. G7 92
Chivirira Falls, wtfl., Zimb. B11 70
Chizu, Japan D7 40
Chloride, Az., U.S. H2 132
Chmielnik, Pol. F16 16
Chŏâm Khsant, Camb. E7 48
Choapa, stm., Chile E2 92
Choceň, Czech Rep. F12 16
Chochís, Cerro, mtn., Bol. C5 90
Choch'iwŏn, Kor., S. F7 38
Chociwel, Pol. C11 16
Chocó, state, Col. E3 86
Chocolate Mountains, mts., U.S. J1 132
Choconta, Col. E5 86
Chocope, Peru E2 84
Choctawhatchee, West Fork, stm., Al., U.S. G13 122
Choctawhatchee Bay, b., Fl., U.S. G12 122
Chodzież, Pol. D12 16
Choele Choel, Arg. G3 90
Choiseul, St. Luc. m6 105c
Choiseul, state, Sol. Is. d7 79b
Choiseul, i., Sol. Is. d7 79b
Chojna, Pol. D10 16
Chojnice, Pol. C13 16
Chojnów, Pol. E11 16
Ch'ok'ē, mts., Eth. E7 62
Choke Canyon Reservoir, res., Tx., U.S. F9 130
Chokio, Mn., U.S. F2 118
Chókwe, Moz. D11 70
Cholet, Fr. G8 14
Choluteca, Hond. F4 102
Choluteca, stm., Hond. F4 102
Choma, Zam. D4 68
Chomo Lhāri, mtn., Asia E12 54
Chomūn, India E5 54
Chomutov, Czech Rep. F9 16
Ch'ŏnan, Kor., S. F7 38
Chon Buri, Thai. F5 48
Chon Daen, Thai. D5 48
Chone, Ec. H1 86
Chong'an, China H8 42
Ch'ŏngdo, Kor., S. D1 40
Ch'ŏngjin, Kor., N. D8 38
Ch'ŏngju, Kor., S. F7 38
Chŏng Kal, Camb. E6 48
Chongming, China I4 38
Chongming Dao, i., China F9 42
Chongoroi, Ang. C1 68
Chongqing (Chungking), China G2 42
Chongqing, state, China F6 36
Chŏngsŏn, Kor., S. B1 40
Chŏngŭp, Kor., S. G7 38
Chongxin, China D2 42
Chongzuo, China A8 48
Chŏnju, Kor., S. G7 38
Chonos, Archipiélago de los, is., Chile I1 90
Ch'ŏnsu-ri, Kor., N. D8 38
Chontaleña, Cordillera, mts., Nic. G5 102
Cho Oyu see Chopu, mtn., Asia D11 54
Cho Oyu see Qowowuyag, mtn., Asia D11 54
Chop, Ukr. A9 26
Chopda, India H5 54
Chopim, stm., Braz. C11 92
Chopinzinho, Braz. B11 92
Chopu (Qowowuyag), mtn., Asia D11 54
Chorna, Ukr. B16 26
Chornobyl', Ukr. D4 32
Choros, Isla, i., Chile D2 92
Ch'ŏrwŏn, Kor., S. E7 38
Chorzele, Pol. C16 16
Chosen, Fl., U.S. J5 116
Chōshi, Japan D13 40
Chosica, Peru F2 84
Chos Malal, Arg. H2 92
Choszczno, Pol. C11 16
Choteau, Mt., U.S. C14 136
Chotila, India G3 54
Chouchiak'ou see Shangshui, China E6 42
Chouk'ou see Shangshui, China E6 42
Choushan Islands see Zhoushan Qundao, is., China F10 42
Chowchilla, Ca., U.S. F5 134
Chown, Mount, mtn., Ab., Can. C11 138
Choya, Arg. D5 92
Choybalsan, Mong. B7 36
Choyr, Mong. B6 36
Chrisman, Il., U.S. I2 112
Christanshåb (Qasigiannguit), Grnld. D15 141
Christchurch, N.Z. F5 80
Christian, Cape, c., Nu., Can. A17 106
Christian, Point, c., Pit. c28 78k
Christiana, Jam. i13 104d
Christiana, S. Afr. E7 70
Christian Island, i., On., Can. D9 112
Christiansburg, Va., U.S. G5 114
Christian Sound, strt., Ak., U.S. E12 140
Christianstad, V.I.U.S. h11 104c
Christmas Island, dep., Oc. K13 142
Christmas Island, i., Christ. I. E1 72
Christmas Island see Kiritimati, at., Kir. C11 72
Christmas Ridge, unds. I22 142
Christoval, Tx., U.S. C7 130
Chrudim, Czech Rep. G11 16
Chrzanów, Pol. F15 16
Chu (Xam), stm., Asia B7 48
Chuādanga, Bngl. G12 54
Chuanchou see Quanzhou, China I8 42
Chubbuck, Id., U.S. H14 136
Chūbu-Sangaku-kokuritsu-kōen, p.o.i., Japan C10 40
Chubut, state, Arg. H3 90
Chubut, stm., Arg. H3 90
Ch'üchiang see Shaoguan, China I5 42
Chuchi Lake, l., B.C., Can. A6 138
Chuchou see Zhuzhou, China H5 42
Chuchow see Zhuzhou, China H5 42
Chu Chua, B.C., Can. E10 138
Chucunaque, stm., Pan. H9 102
Chugach Mountains, mts., Ak., U.S. D10 140
Chuginadak Island, i., Ak., U.S. g25 140a
Chūgoku-sanchi, mts., Japan D6 40
Chugwater Creek, stm., Wy., U.S. F8 126
Chuhuichupa, Mex. G8 98
Chuí, Braz. F11 92
Chukchi Sea, s. C7 94
Chuke Hu, l., China C11 54
Chukotsk Peninsula see Čukotskij poluostrov, pen., Russia C26 34
Chula Vista, Ca., U.S. K8 134
Chulucanas, Peru E1 84
Chumbicha, Arg. D4 92
Chum Phae, Thai. D6 48
Chumphon, Thai. G4 48
Chumphon Buri, Thai. E6 48
Chum Saeng, Thai. E5 48
Chumunjin, Kor., S. B1 40
Chun'an, China G8 42
Chunan, Tai. I9 42
Chuncheon see Ch'unch'ŏn, Kor., S. F7 38
Chunchi, Ec. I2 86
Ch'unch'ŏn, Kor., S. F7 38
Chunchula, Al., U.S. G10 122
Ch'ungch'ŏng-bukto, state, Kor., S. B1 40
Ch'ungju, Kor., S. F7 38
Chungking see Chongqing, China G2 42
Ch'ungmu, Kor., S. E1 40
Chungshan see Zhongshan, China J5 42
Chungyang Shanmo, mts., Tai. J9 42
Chunhua, China D3 42
Chunhuhux, Mex. C3 102
Chuquibamba, Peru G3 84
Chuquicamata, Chile D3 90
Chur (Coire), Switz. D6 22
Church Hill, Tn., U.S. H3 114
Churchill, Mb., Can. D12 106
Churchill, stm., Nf., Can. E18 106
Churchill, stm., Can. D11 106
Churchill, Mount, mtn., B.C., Can. G7 138
Churchill, Mount, vol., Ak., U.S. D11 140
Churchill Falls, wtfl., Nf., Can. E17 106
Churchill Lake, l., Sk., Can. D9 106
Church Point, La., U.S. G6 122
Church Rock, N.M., U.S. H8 132
Chūru, India D5 54
Churubusco, In., U.S. G4 112
Churuguara, Ven. B7 86
Chushul, India B7 54
Chute-Saint-Philippe, Qc., Can. D1 110
Chutung, Tai. I9 42
Chuuk, is., Micron. C6 72
Chuvashia see Čuvašija, state, Russia C7 32
Chuxian, China E8 42
Chuxiong, China F5 36
Ci, stm., China B6 42
Ci, stm., China B6 42
Ciadâr Lunga, Mol. C15 26
Ciales, P.R. B3 104a
Ciamis, Indon. G6 50
Cianjur, Indon. G5 50
Cianorte, Braz. A11 92
Ciatura, Geor. F6 32
Ciawi, Indon. G5 50
Cibaliung, Indon. G4 50
Cibatu, Indon. G6 50
Cibinong, Indon. G5 50
Cibolo Creek, stm., Tx., U.S. E3 130
Cibolo Creek, stm., Tx., U.S. E10 130
Cicero, Il., U.S. G2 112
Cicero, In., U.S. H3 112
Cicero Dantas, Braz. F6 88
Cicurug, Indon. G5 50
Cidra, P.R. B3 104a
Ciechanów, Pol. D16 16
Ciechanów, state, Pol. C16 16
Ciechanowiec, Pol. D18 16
Ciego de Ávila, Cuba B8 102
Ciempozuelos, Spain D7 20
Ciénaga, Col. B4 86
Ciénega de Flores, Mex. H7 130
Cienfuegos, Cuba A7 102
Cíes, Illas, is., Spain B1 20
Cies, Islas see Cíes, Illas, is., Spain B1 20
Cieszanów, Pol. F19 16
Cieszyn, Pol. G14 16
Cieza, Spain F9 20
Çifteler, Tur. D13 28
Cifuentes, Spain D8 20
Cigüela, stm., Spain E7 20
Cihanbeyli, Tur. E15 28
Cijara, Embalse de, res., Spain E6 20
Cijulang, Indon. G6 50
Cikampek, Indon. G5 50
Čikobia, i., Fiji o20 79e
Čikoj, Russia F10 34
Cilacap, Indon. G6 50
Cilamaya, Indon. E6 50
Cilento, reg., Italy D9 24
Cili, China G4 42
Cilician Gates see Gülek Boğazı, p., Tur. A5 58
Čilik see Shelek, Kaz. F13 32
Cill Chainnigh see Kilkenny, Ire. I5 12
Cilleruelo de Bezana, Spain B7 20
Cil'ma, stm., Russia D24 8
Cimarron, N.M., U.S. E4 128
Cimarron, stm., U.S. F12 128
Cimarron, North Fork, stm., U.S. D7 128
Čimbaj, Uzb. F9 32
Cimişlia, Mol. C15 26
Cimljanskoe vodohranilišče, res., Russia E6 32
Cimone, Monte, mtn., Italy F7 22
Cimpu, Indon. E12 50
Cina, Tanjung, c., Indon. G4 50
Cinaruco, stm., Ven. D7 86
Cinaruco-Capanaparo Santos Luzardo, Parque Nacional, p.o.i., Ven. D8 86
Cinca, stm., Spain C11 20
Cincinnati, Ia., U.S. D4 120
Cincinnati, Oh., U.S. E1 114
Cinco, Canal Numero, can., Arg. H9 92
Cinco de Mayo, Mex. I3 130
Cinco Saltos, Arg. I3 92
Çine, Tur. F10 28
Ciney, Bel. D14 14
Cinfães, Port. C2 20
Cinişeuți, Mol. B15 26
Cintalapa, Mex. G12 100
Cinto, Monte, mtn., Fr. G14 18
Cintra, Golfe de, b., W. Sah. E1 64
Ciociaria, reg., Italy I10 22
Cipa, stm., Russia F11 34
Cipatujah, Indon. G5 50
Cipó, Braz. F6 88
Cipó, stm., Braz. J4 88
Cipolletti, Arg. G3 90
Circeo, Parco Nazionale del, p.o.i., Italy C6 24
Čirčik, Uzb. F11 32
Circle, Ak., U.S. C11 140
Circle, Mt., U.S. G8 124
Circleville, Oh., U.S. E3 114
Circleville, Ut., U.S. E4 132
Circleville Mountain, mtn., Ut., U.S. E4 132
Cirebon, Indon. G6 50
Ciremay, Gunung, vol., Indon. G6 50
Cirencester, Eng., U.K. J11 12
Čirgalandy, Russia D17 32
Ciriè, Italy E4 22
Cirò Marina, Italy E11 24
Čirpan, Blg. G12 26
Ciskei, hist. reg., S. Afr. H8 70
Cisnădie, Rom. D11 26
Cisne, Il., U.S. F9 120
Cisne, Islas del see Santanilla, Islas, is., Hond. D6 102
Cisneros, Col. D4 86
Cisolok, Indon. G5 50
Cissna Park, Il., U.S. H2 112
Čistoozërnoe, Russia D13 32
Čistopol', Russia C8 32
Čita, Russia F11 34
Citlaltépetl, Volcán see Pico de Orizaba, Volcán, vol., Mex. F10 100
Citra, Fl., U.S. G3 116
Citrus Heights, Ca., U.S. E4 134
Città di Castello, Italy G9 22
Cittanova, Italy F10 24
City of Sunrise see Sunrise, Fl., U.S. J5 116
City Point, Fl., U.S. H5 116
Ciudad Acuña, Mex. A8 100
Ciudad Altamirano, Mex. F8 100
Ciudad Anáhuac, Mex. B8 100
Ciudad Bolívar, Ven. C10 86
Ciudad Bolivia, Ven. C6 86
Ciudad Camargo, Mex. B6 100
Ciudad Camargo, Mex. B9 100
Ciudad Constitución, Mex. C3 100
Ciudad Cortés, C.R. H6 102
Ciudad Darío, Nic. F4 102
Ciudad del Carmen, Mex. F12 100
Ciudad del Este, Para. B10 92
Ciudad de Libertador General San Martín, Arg. A5 92
Ciudad de México (Mexico City), Mex. F9 100
Ciudad de Nutrias, Ven. C7 86
Ciudadela see Ciutadella de Menorca, Spain D14 20
Ciudad Guayana, Ven. C10 86
Ciudad Hidalgo, Mex. F8 100
Ciudad Jiménez see Jiménez, Mex. B6 100
Ciudad Juárez, Mex. C1 130
Ciudad Lerdo see Lerdo, Mex. C7 100
Ciudad Madero, Mex. D10 100
Ciudad Mante, Mex. D9 100
Ciudad Miguel Alemán, Mex. B9 100
Ciudad Morelos, Mex. E5 98
Ciudad Netzahualcóyotl, Mex. F9 100
Ciudad Obregón, Mex. B4 100
Ciudad Ojeda, Ven. B6 86
Ciudad Piar, Ven. D10 86
Ciudad Real, Spain F6 20
Ciudad Real, co., Spain F6 20
Ciudad Rodrigo, Spain D4 20
Ciudad Valles, Mex. E9 100
Ciudad Victoria, Mex. D9 100
Ciutadella de Menorca, Spain D14 20
Civita Castellana, Italy H9 22
Civitanova Marche, Italy G10 22
Civitavecchia, Italy H8 22
Çivril, Tur. E12 28
Çixi, China F9 42
Čiža, Russia C21 8
Čjaluša, Bela. G12 10
Čkalovsk, Russia H20 8
Clackamas, stm., Or., U.S. E4 136
Clacton-on-Sea, Eng., U.K. J14 12
Claflin, Ks., U.S. C10 128
Claiborne, Al., U.S. F11 122
Clain, stm., Fr. C6 18
Claire, Lake, l., Ab., Can. D8 106
Clair Engle Lake, res., Ca., U.S. C3 134
Clairton, Pa., U.S. D6 114
Clallam Bay, Wa., U.S. B2 136
Clanton, Al., U.S. E12 122
Clanwilliam, S. Afr. H4 70
Clapperton Island, i., On., Can. B7 112
Clara, Ire. H5 12
Clara, Ms., U.S. F10 122
Clara, stm., Austl. B4 76
Clara, Punta, c., Arg. H4 90
Clare, Austl. I4 76
Clare, Mi., U.S. E5 112
Clare, state, Ire. I3 12
Clare Island, i., Ire. H2 12
Claremont, N.H., U.S. G4 110
Claremont, S.D., U.S. B15 126
Claremont, mtn., Ca., U.S. D4 134
Claremore, Ok., U.S. H2 120
Clarence, Mo., U.S. E5 120
Clarence, stm., Austl. G9 76
Clarence, stm., N.Z. F5 80
Clarence, Cape, c., Nu., Can. A13 106
Clarence, Isla, i., Chile J2 90
Clarence Strait, strt., Austl. B6 74
Clarence Strait, strt., Ak., U.S. E13 140
Clarence Town, Bah. C9 96
Clarendon, Ar., U.S. C7 122
Clarendon, Tx., U.S. G8 128
Clarenville, Nf., Can. j23 107a
Claresholm, Ab., Can. F17 138
Clarinda, Ia., U.S. D2 120
Clarines, Ven. C9 86
Clarington, On., Can. E11 112
Clarion, Ia., U.S. B4 120
Clarion, Pa., U.S. C6 114
Clarion, stm., Pa., U.S. C6 114
Clarion Fracture Zone, unds. H25 142
Clarissa, Mn., U.S. E3 118
Clark, Mount, mtn., N.T., Can. C6 106
Clarke, stm., Austl. B5 76
Clarke Island, i., Austl. n14 77a
Clarkesville, Ga., U.S. B2 116
Clarkfield, Mn., U.S. G3 118
Clark Fork, Id., U.S. B10 136
Clark Fork, stm., U.S. C11 136
Clarks, La., U.S. E6 122
Clarksburg, W.V., U.S. E5 114
Clarksdale, Ms., U.S. C8 122
Clark's Harbour, N.S., Can. G11 110
Clarks Hill, In., U.S. H3 112
Clarkson, Ky., U.S. G11 120
Clarks Summit, Pa., U.S. C10 114
Clarkston, Wa., U.S. D9 136
Clark's Town, Jam. i13 104d
Clarksville, Ar., U.S. B5 122
Clarksville, Ia., U.S. I6 118
Clarksville, Tn., U.S. H10 120
Clarksville, Va., U.S. H7 114
Clarkton, Mo., U.S. H7 120
Clarkton, N.C., U.S. B7 116
Claro, stm., Braz. G7 84
Claude, Tx., U.S. F7 128
Clausthal-Zellerfeld, Ger. E5 16
Claveria, Phil. B7 44
Clavering Ø, i., Grnld. C22 141
Clavet, Sk., Can. B7 124
Claxton, Ga., U.S. D4 116
Clay, Ky., U.S. G10 120
Clay, Tx., U.S. G2 122
Clay Center, Ne., U.S. G14 126
Clay City, Il., U.S. F9 120
Clay City, In., U.S. E10 120
Clay City, Ky., U.S. G1 114
Claymont, De., U.S. E10 114
Claypool, Az., U.S. J6 132
Claysburg, Pa., U.S. D7 114
Clayton, Al., U.S. F13 122
Clayton, Ga., U.S. B2 116
Clayton, Il., U.S. D7 120
Clayton, La., U.S. F7 122
Clayton, Mo., U.S. F7 120
Clayton, N.M., U.S. E5 128
Clayton, N.Y., U.S. D13 112
Clayton, Ok., U.S. C4 122
Clayton, Wa., U.S. B9 136
Clear, Cape, c., Ire. J3 12
Clear Boggy Creek, stm., Ok., U.S. C2 122
Clearbrook, Mn., U.S. D3 118
Clear Creek, stm., Wy., U.S. C7 114
Clearfield, Pa., U.S. C7 114
Clearfield, Ut., U.S. B4 132
Clearlake, Ca., U.S. E3 134
Clear Lake, Ia., U.S. A4 120
Clear Lake, S.D., U.S. G2 118
Clear Lake, Wi., U.S. F6 118
Clear Lake, l., Mb., Can. D14 124
Clear Lake, l., Ca., U.S. D3 134
Clear Lake, res., La., U.S. F5 122
Clear Lake Reservoir, res., Ca., U.S. B4 134
Clearmont, Wy., U.S. C6 126
Clearwater, B.C., Can. E10 138
Clearwater, Mb., Can. E14 124
Clearwater, Fl., U.S. I3 116
Clearwater, Ne., U.S. E14 126
Clearwater, stm., Ab., Can. D15 138
Clearwater, stm., B.C., Can. D10 138
Clearwater, stm., Can. D8 106
Clearwater, stm., Id., U.S. D10 136
Clearwater, stm., Mn., U.S. D3 118
Clearwater, stm., Mt., U.S. C13 136
Clearwater, Middle Fork, stm., Id., U.S. D11 136
Clearwater, North Fork, stm., Id., U.S. D11 136
Clearwater Lake, l., B.C., Can. D10 138
Clearwater Mountains, mts., Id., U.S. D11 136
Clebit, Ok., U.S. C4 122
Cleburne, Tx., U.S. B10 130
Cle Elum, stm., Wa., U.S. C5 136
Cle Elum Lake, res., Wa., U.S. C6 136
Cleethorpes, Eng., U.K. H12 12
Clementsport, N.S., Can. F11 110
Clemson, S.C., U.S. B3 116
Clermont, Austl. D6 76
Clermont, Qc., Can. C6 110
Clermont, Fr. E11 14
Clermont-Ferrand, Fr. D9 18
Clevedon, Eng., U.K. J10 12
Cleveland, Al., U.S. D12 122
Cleveland, Ms., U.S. D8 122
Cleveland, N.C., U.S. A5 116
Cleveland, Oh., U.S. C4 114
Cleveland, Ok., U.S. A2 122
Cleveland, Tn., U.S. B14 122
Cleveland, Tx., U.S. G3 122
Cleveland, Va., U.S. H3 114
Cleveland, Cape, c., Austl. B6 76
Cleveland, Mount, mtn., Mt., U.S. B13 136
Clevelândia, Braz. C11 92
Cleves see Kleve, Ger. E2 16
Clew Bay, b., Ire. H3 12
Clewiston, Fl., U.S. J4 116
Clifton, St. Vin. p11 105e
Clifton, Az., U.S. J7 132
Clifton, Tn., U.S. B11 122
Clifton, Tx., U.S. C10 130
Clifton Forge, Va., U.S. G6 114
Clifton Hills, Austl. F2 76
Climax, Sk., Can. E5 124
Climax, Co., U.S. B2 128
Clinch, stm., U.S. I13 120
Clinchco, Va., U.S. G15 120
Clingmans Dome, mtn., U.S. I2 114
Clinton, B.C., Can. E9 138
Clinton, On., Can. E8 112
Clinton, Al., U.S. E11 122
Clinton, Ar., U.S. B6 122
Clinton, Ia., U.S. C7 120
Clinton, In., U.S. I2 112
Clinton, Ky., U.S. H9 120
Clinton, La., U.S. G7 122
Clinton, Mi., U.S. B2 114
Clinton, Mn., U.S. F2 118
Clinton, Ms., U.S. E8 122
Clinton, N.C., U.S. A7 116
Clinton, Ok., U.S. F9 128
Clinton, S.C., U.S. B4 116
Clinton, Wi., U.S. B9 120
Clinton, Cape, c., Austl. D8 76
Clinton Lake, res., Il., U.S. D9 120
Clinton-Colden Lake, l., N.T., Can. C9 106
Clinton Lake, res., Ks., U.S. F2 120
Clintonville, Wi., U.S. G10 118
Clintwood, Va., U.S. G3 114
Clio, Mi., U.S. E6 112
Clio, S.C., U.S. B6 116
Clipperton, Île, at., Oc. H28 142
Clipperton Fracture Zone, unds. I25 142
Clipperton Island see Clipperton, Île, at., Oc. H28 142
Clisson, Fr. G7 14
Clodomira, Arg. C5 92
Cloete, Mex. G6 130
Cloncurry, Austl. C3 76
Cloncurry, stm., Austl. B3 76
Clonmel, Ire. I5 12
Clo-oose, B.C., Can. H6 138
Cloppenburg, Ger. D3 16
Cloquet, Mn., U.S. E6 118
Clorinda, Arg. B9 92
Cloud Peak, mtn., Wy., U.S. C5 126
Clova, Qc., Can. B1 110
Clover, S.C., U.S. A4 116
Cloverdale, Ca., U.S. E2 134
Cloverdale, In., U.S. E11 120
Cloverport, Ky., U.S. G11 120
Clovis, Ca., U.S. G6 134
Clovis, N.M., U.S. G5 128
Cluain Meala see Clonmel, Ire. I5 12
Cluj, state, Rom. C10 26
Cluj-Napoca, Rom. C10 26
Clunes, Austl. K4 76
Cluny, Austl. E2 76
Cluny, Fr. C10 18
Clusone, Italy E7 22
Clute, Tx., U.S. E12 130
Clutha, stm., N.Z. H3 80
Clyde, Ks., U.S. B11 128
Clyde, N.C., U.S. A3 116
Clyde, Oh., U.S. C3 114
Clyde, Tx., U.S. B8 130
Clyde, stm., Scot., U.K. F9 12
Clyde, Firth of, b., Scot., U.K. F7 12
Clyde Inlet, b., Nu., Can. A17 106
Clyde Park, Mt., U.S. E16 136
Clyde River see Kangiqtugaapik, Nu., Can. A16 106
Clymer, Pa., U.S. D6 114
Ćmielów, Pol. F17 16
Cna, stm., Russia C17 10
Cna, stm., Russia D6 32
Cnossus see Knosós, sci., Grc. H8 28
Côa, stm., Port. D3 20
Coachella, Ca., U.S. J9 134
Coachella Canal, can., Ca., U.S. K1 132
Coahoma, Tx., U.S. B6 130
Coahuila, state, Mex. B7 100
Coal City, Il., U.S. J10 118
Coalcomán de Matamoros, Mex. F7 100
Coal Creek, stm., Wa., U.S. C8 136
Coaldale, Ab., Can. G18 138
Coalgate, Ok., U.S. C2 122
Coal Grove, Oh., U.S. F3 114
Coal Hill, Ar., U.S. B5 122
Coalinga, Ca., U.S. G5 134
Coalmont, B.C., Can. G10 138
Coalport, Pa., U.S. D7 114
Coal River, B.C., Can. D5 106
Coal Valley, val., Nv., U.S. F1 132
Coalville, Eng., U.K. I11 12
Coalville, Ut., U.S. C5 132
Coamo, P.R. B3 104a
Coaraci, Braz. H6 88
Coari, Braz. D5 84
Coari, stm., Braz. E5 84
Coast Mountains, mts., N.A. D4 106
Coast Ranges, mts., U.S. C2 134
Coatbridge, Scot., U.K. F9 12
Coatesville, Pa., U.S. E10 114
Coaticook, Qc., Can. E5 110
Coats Island, i., Nu., Can. C14 106
Coats Land, reg., Ant. C2 81
Coatzacoalcos, Mex. F11 100
Cobá, sci., Mex. B4 102
Cobalt, On., Can. F14 106
Cobán, Guat. E2 102
Cobar, Austl. H5 76
Cobberas, Mount, mtn., Austl. K6 76
Cobden, On., Can. C12 112
Cobequid Bay, b., N.S., Can. E13 110
Cobh, Ire. J4 12
Cobham, stm., Can. B18 124
Cobija, Bol. B3 90
Coblence see Koblenz, Ger. F3 16
Coblenz see Koblenz, Ger. F3 16
Cobleskill, N.Y., U.S. B11 114
Cobourg, On., Can. E11 112
Cobquecura, Chile H1 92
Cobram, Austl. J5 76
Cobre, Barranca del (Copper Canyon), misc. cult., Mex. B5 100
Cóbuè, Moz. C5 68
Coburg, Ger. F6 16
Coburg Island, i., Nu., Can. B10 141
Coburg Peninsula, pen., Austl. B6 74
Coca, stm., Ec. H3 86
Cocal, Braz. B5 88
Cocentaina, Spain F10 20
Cōch, stm., Asia B6 36
Cochabamba, Bol. C3 90
Coche, Isla, i., Ven. B10 86
Cochem, Ger. F3 16
Cochin see Kochi, India F3 53
Cochin China see Nam Phan, hist. reg., Viet. G8 48
Cochinos, Bahía de (Pigs, Bay of), b., Cuba B7 102
Cochise Head, mtn., Az., U.S. K7 132
Cochrane, Ab., Can. E16 138
Cochrane, On., Can. F14 106
Cochrane, Wi., U.S. G7 118
Cochrane, Lago (Pueyrredón, Lago), l., S.A. I2 90
Cochranton, Pa., U.S. C5 114
Cockburn, Austl. I3 76
Cockburn, Mount, mtn., Austl. E5 74
Cockburn, Mount, mtn., Austl. D5 74
Cockburn Island, i., On., Can. C6 112
Cockermouth, Eng., U.K. G9 12
Cockpit Country, reg., Jam. i13 104d
Côco, stm., Braz. F1 88
Coco, stm., N.A. E6 102
Coco, Cayo, i., Cuba A8 102
Coco, Isla del, i., C.R. F7 96
Cocoa, Fl., U.S. H5 116
Cocoa Beach, Fl., U.S. H5 116
Coco Channel, strt., Asia F7 46
Cocodrie Lake, res., La., U.S. G6 122
Coco Islands, is., Mya. F7 46
Coconino Plateau, plat., Az., U.S. H4 132
Cocos, Braz. H3 88
Cocos Islands, dep., Oc. K12 142
Cocos Lagoon, b., Guam k9 78c
Cocos Ridge, unds. H5 144
Cocula, Mex. E7 100
Cod, Cape, pen., Ma., U.S. C15 114
Codajás, Braz. D5 84
Codera, Cabo, c., Ven. B8 86
Coderre, Sk., Can. D7 124
Codigoro, Italy F9 22
Cod Island, i., Nf., Can. F13 141
Codlea, Rom. D12 26
Codó, Braz. C3 88
Codogno, Italy E6 22
Codòzinho, Braz. C3 88
Codroy, Nf., Can. C17 110
Cody, Ne., U.S. E11 126
Cody, Wy., U.S. C3 126
Coelho Neto, Braz. C4 88
Coen, Austl. B8 74
Coëtivy, i., Sey. k13 69b
Coeur d'Alene, Id., U.S. C10 136
Coeur d'Alene, stm., Id., U.S. C10 136
Coeur d'Alene Lake, res., Id., U.S. C10 136
Coffeeville, Ms., U.S. D9 122
Coffeyville, Ks., U.S. G2 120
Coffs Harbour, Austl. H9 76
Cofre de Perote, Cerro, mtn., Mex. F10 100
Cofre de Perote, Parque Nacional, p.o.i., Mex. F10 100
Cofrentes see Cofrents, Spain E9 20
Cofrents, Spain E9 20
Cogâlnic (Kohyl'nyk), stm., Eur. C15 26
Coggon, Ia., U.S. B6 120
Cognac, Fr. D5 18
Cogolludo, Spain D7 20
Cogoon, stm., Austl. F7 76
Cogswell, N.D., U.S. A15 126
Cohocton, stm., N.Y., U.S. F12 112
Cohoes, N.Y., U.S. B12 114
Cohuna, Austl. J5 76
Coiba, Isla de, i., Pan. I6 102
Coig, stm., Arg. J3 90
Coihaique, Chile I2 90
Coimbatore (Koyambattur), India F3 53
Coimbra, Braz. K4 88
Coimbra, Port. D2 20
Coimbra, state, Port. D2 20
Coín, Spain H6 20
Coipasa, Lago, l., Bol. C3 90
Coipasa, Salar de, pl., S.A. C3 90
Coire see Chur, Switz. D6 22
Cojedes, state, Ven. C7 86
Cojudo Blanco, Cerro, mtn., Arg. I3 90
Cojutepeque, El Sal. F3 102
Cokato, Mn., U.S. F4 118
Cokeville, Wy., U.S. A6 132
Čokurdah, Russia B18 34
Colac, Austl. L4 76
Colatina, Braz. J5 88
Colbeck, Cape, c., Ant. C25 81
Colbert, Ok., U.S. D2 122
Colbinabbin, Austl. K5 76
Colbún, Chile G2 92
Colbún, Embalse, res., Chile G2 92
Colby, Ks., U.S. B7 128
Colby, Wi., U.S. G8 118
Colchester, Eng., U.K. J13 12
Colchester, Il., U.S. D7 120
Cold Bay, Ak., U.S. E7 140
Cold Lake, Ab., Can. E8 106
Cold Spring, Mn., U.S. F4 118
Coldstream, Scot., U.K. F10 12
Coldwater, Ks., U.S. D9 128
Coldwater, Mi., U.S. G4 112
Coldwater, Oh., U.S. H5 112
Coldwater, stm., Ms., U.S. C8 122
Coldwater Creek, stm., U.S. E7 128
Coleambally, Austl. J5 76
Colebrook, N.H., U.S. F5 110
Cole Camp, Mo., U.S. F4 120
Coleman, Ab., Can. G16 138
Coleman, Fl., U.S. H3 116
Coleman, Mi., U.S. E5 112
Coleman, Wi., U.S. C1 112
Coleman, stm., Austl. B8 74
Colenso, S. Afr. F9 70
Coleraine, Austl. K3 76
Coleraine, N. Ire., U.K. F6 12
Coleridge, Ne., U.S. E15 126
Coles, Ms., U.S. F7 122
Colesberg, S. Afr. G7 70
Coleville, Sk., Can. C4 124
Colfax, Ia., U.S. C4 120
Colfax, In., U.S. H3 112
Colfax, La., U.S. F6 122
Colfax, Wa., U.S. D9 136
Colfax, Wi., U.S. F7 118
Colgong, India F11 54
Colhué Huapi, Lago, l., Arg. I3 90
Colibris, Pointe des, c., Guad. h6 105c
Colico, Italy D6 22
Coligny, S. Afr. E8 70
Colihaut, Dom. j5 105c
Colima, Mex. F7 100
Colima, state, Mex. F7 100
Colima, Nevado de, vol., Mex. F7 100
Colinas, Braz. D3 88
Colinas, Braz. H1 88
Colinton, Ab., Can. B17 138
Coll, i., Scot., U.K. E6 12
Collarenebri, Austl. G7 76
College, Ak., U.S. D10 140
Collegedale, Tn., U.S. B13 122
College Park, Ga., U.S. D14 122
College Place, Wa., U.S. D8 136
College Station, Ar., U.S. C6 122
College Station, Tx., U.S. G2 122
Collerina, Austl. G6 76
Colleymount, B.C., Can. B4 138
Collie, Austl. F3 74
Collier Bay, b., Austl. C4 74
Collierville, Tn., U.S. B9 122
Collingwood, On., Can. D9 112
Collins, Ga., U.S. D3 116
Collins, Ms., U.S. F9 122
Collins Bay, On., Can. D13 112
Collins Head, c., Norf. I. y25 78i
Collinston, La., U.S. E7 122
Collinsville, Austl. C6 76
Collinsville, Al., U.S. C13 122
Collinsville, Ok., U.S. H2 120
Collinsville, Tx., U.S. D2 122
Collinwood, Tn., U.S. B11 122
Collipulli, Chile H1 92
Colman, S.D., U.S. H2 118
Colmar, Fr. F16 14
Colmenar, Spain H6 20
Colmenar Viejo, Spain D7 20
Colmeneros, Mex. F8 100
Colmesneil, Tx., U.S. G4 122
Colnett, Punta, c., Mex. F4 98

Name	Map Ref.	Page
Cologne see Köln, Ger.	F2	16
Cologne, Mn., U.S.	G5	118
Coloma, Mi., U.S.	F3	112
Coloma, Wi., U.S.	G9	118
Colomb-Béchar see Béchar, Alg.	C4	64
Colombia, Col.	F4	86
Colombia, ctry., S.A.	C3	84
Colombie-Britannique see British Columbia, state, Can.	E5	106
Colombo, Braz.	B13	92
Colombo, Sri L.	H4	53
Colome, S.D., U.S.	D13	126
Colomiers, Fr.	F7	18
Colón, Arg.	F8	92
Colón, Arg.	F7	92
Colón, Cuba	A7	102
Colón, Pan.	H7	102
Colón, Ur.	F10	92
Colon, Mi., U.S.	G4	112
Colón, Archipiélago de (Galapagos Islands), is., Ec.	h12	84a
Colona, Austl.	F6	74
Colonelganj, India	E8	54
Colônia, stm., Braz.	H6	88
Colonia Alvear Norte see General Alvear, Arg.	G3	92
Colonia del Sacramento, Ur.	G9	92
Colonia Dora, Arg.	D6	92
Colonia Elisa, Arg.	C8	92
Colonia Lavalleja, Ur.	E9	92
Colonial Heights, Va., U.S.	G8	114
Colonia Providencia, P.R.	C4	104a
Colonia Suiza, Ur.	G9	92
Colonias Unidas, Arg.	C8	92
Colonne, Capo, c., Italy	E11	24
Colonsay, Sk., Can.	B8	124
Colonsay, i., Scot., U.K.	E6	12
Colony, Ks., U.S.	F2	120
Colorada Grande, Salina, pl., Arg.	I5	92
Coloradas, Lomas, hills, Arg.	H3	90
Colorado, Hond.	E4	102
Colorado, state, U.S.	D6	108
Colorado, stm., Arg.	G4	90
Colorado, stm., N.A.	E5	98
Colorado, stm., Tx., U.S.	F11	130
Colorado, Cerro, mtn., Arg.	H3	90
Colorado City, Co., U.S.	C4	128
Colorado City, Tx., U.S.	B7	130
Colorado Kolonie see Lago Kolonie, Aruba	p20	104g
Colorado National Monument, p.o.i., Co., U.S.	D8	132
Colorado Plateau, plat., U.S.	E7	132
Colorado River Aqueduct, aq., Ca., U.S.	E5	98
Colorado Springs, Co., U.S.	C4	128
Colotlán, Mex.	D7	100
Colquechaca, Bol.	C3	90
Colstrip, Mt., U.S.	B6	126
Colt, Ar., U.S.	B8	122
Coltauco, Chile	G2	92
Colton, Ca., U.S.	I8	134
Colton, S.D., U.S.	H2	118
Columbia, Ca., U.S.	E5	134
Columbia, Il., U.S.	F7	120
Columbia, Ky., U.S.	G12	120
Columbia, La., U.S.	E6	122
Columbia, Md., U.S.	E9	114
Columbia, Mo., U.S.	F5	120
Columbia, N.C., U.S.	I9	114
Columbia, Pa., U.S.	D9	114
Columbia, S.C., U.S.	C4	116
Columbia, Tn., U.S.	B11	122
Columbia, stm., N.A.	D3	136
Columbia, Cape, c., Nu., Can.	A11	141
Columbia, Mount, mtn., Ab., Can.	D13	138
Columbia Basin, bas., Wa., U.S.	C8	136
Columbia City, In., U.S.	G4	112
Columbia Falls, Me., U.S.	F9	110
Columbia Icefield, ice, Can.	D13	138
Columbia Mountains, mts., N.A.	G13	138
Columbiana, Al., U.S.	D12	122
Columbiana, Oh., U.S.	D5	114
Columbine, Cape, c., S. Afr.	H3	70
Columbrets, Illes, is., Spain	E11	20
Columbus, Ga., U.S.	E14	122
Columbus, In., U.S.	E12	120
Columbus, Ks., U.S.	G3	120
Columbus, Ms., U.S.	D10	122
Columbus, N.C., U.S.	A3	116
Columbus, N.D., U.S.	F11	124
Columbus, Ne., U.S.	F15	126
Columbus, N.M., U.S.	L9	132
Columbus, Oh., U.S.	E2	114
Columbus, Tx., U.S.	H2	122
Columbus, Wi., U.S.	H9	118
Columbus Point, c., Trin.	r13	105f
Columbus Salt Marsh, pl., Nv., U.S.	E8	134
Colusa, Ca., U.S.	D3	134
Colville, Wa., U.S.	B9	136
Colville, stm., Ak., U.S.	C9	140
Colville Lake, l., N.T., Can.	B5	106
Colwyn Bay, Wales, U.K.	H9	12
Comacchio, Italy	F9	22
Comacchio, Valli di, l., Italy	F9	22
Comala, Mex.	F7	100
Comalcalco, Mex.	F12	100
Comales, Mex.	H9	130
Coman, Mount, mtn., Ant.	C34	81
Comana, Rom.	F15	26
Comanche, Ok., U.S.	G10	128
Comandante Ferraz, sci., Ant.	B35	81
Comandante Fontana, Arg.	B7	92
Comandante Leal, Arg.	E5	92
Comandante Luis Piedra Buena, Arg.	I3	90
Comănești, Rom.	C13	26
Comayagua, Hond.	E4	102
Combarbalá, Chile	E2	92
Combermere Bay, b., Mya.	C1	48
Combourg, Fr.	F7	14
Comboyne, Austl.	H9	76
Comendador, Dom. Rep.	C12	102
Comer, Ga., U.S.	B2	116
Comercinho, Braz.	I5	88
Comet, stm., Austl.	E7	76
Cometela, Moz.	B12	70
Comfort, N.C., U.S.	B8	116
Comfort, Tx., U.S.	E8	130
Comfort, Cape, c., Nu., Can.	B14	106
Comfrey, Mn., U.S.	G4	118
Comilla, Bngl.	G13	54
Comino see Kemmuna, i., Malta	H8	24
Comiso, Italy	H8	24
Comitán de Domínguez, Mex.	G12	100
Commerce, Ga., U.S.	B2	116
Commerce, Ok., U.S.	H3	120
Commercy, Fr.	F14	14
Comminges, reg., Fr.	F6	18
Committee Bay, b., Nu., Can.	B13	106
Communism Peak see Ismail Samani, pik, mtn., Taj.	B11	56
Como, Italy	E6	22
Como, Tx., U.S.	D3	122
Como, Lago di, l., Italy	D6	22
Comodoro Rivadavia, Arg.	I3	90
Comores, Archipel des, is., Afr.	C7	68
Comorin, Cape, c., India	G3	53
Comoros, ctry., Afr.	C7	68
Comox, B.C., Can.	G6	138
Compiègne, Fr.	E11	14
Compostela, Mex.	E6	100
Compton, Ca., U.S.	J7	134
Comrat, Mol.	C15	26
Comstock, Ne., U.S.	F13	126
Comstock, Tx., U.S.	E6	130
Comstock Park, Mi., U.S.	E4	112
Con, stm., Viet.	C7	48
Čona, stm., Russia	B19	32
Co Nag, l., China	B13	54
Conakry, Gui.	H2	64
Conambo, stm., Ec.	H3	86
Cona Niyeo, Arg.	H3	90
Conasauga, stm., U.S.	C14	122
Concarán, Arg.	F5	92
Concarneau, Fr.	G5	14
Conceição, Braz.	D6	88
Conceição da Barra, Braz.	J6	88
Conceição das Alagoas, Braz.	J1	88
Conceição do Araguaia, Braz.	E1	88
Conceição do Canindé, Braz.	D5	88
Conceição do Coité, Braz.	F6	88
Conceição do Mato Dentro, Braz.	J4	88
Conceição do Norte, Braz.	G2	88
Concepción, Arg.	C5	92
Concepción, Arg.	D9	92
Concepción, Bol.	C4	90
Concepción, Chile	H1	92
Concepción, Col.	D5	86
Concepción, Para.	D5	90
Concepción, Bahía, b., Mex.	B2	100
Concepción, Canal, strt., Chile	J2	90
Concepción, Laguna, l., Bol.	C4	90
Concepción, Volcán, vol., Nic.	G5	102
Concepción de la Sierra, Arg.	D10	92
Concepción del Oro, Mex.	C8	100
Concepción del Uruguay, Arg.	F8	92
Conception, Point, c., Ca., U.S.	I5	134
Conception Bay, b., Nf., Can.	j23	107a
Conception Bay, b., Nmb.	C2	70
Conchas, stm., Arg.	B5	92
Conchas Dam, N.M., U.S.	F4	128
Conchas Lake, res., N.M., U.S.	F4	128
Concho, Az., U.S.	I7	132
Concho, stm., Tx., U.S.	C8	130
Conchos, stm., Mex.	A6	100
Conchos, stm., Mex.	C10	100
Conconully, Wa., U.S.	B7	136
Concord, Ca., U.S.	E4	134
Concord, Ga., U.S.	D14	122
Concord, N.C., U.S.	A5	116
Concord, N.H., U.S.	G5	110
Concordia, Arg.	E8	92
Concórdia, Braz.	C11	92
Concordia, Mex.	D5	100
Concordia, Mex.	I4	130
Concordia, Mo., U.S.	F4	120
Concrete, Wa., U.S.	B5	136
Con Cuong, Viet.	C7	48
Conda, Ang.	C1	68
Condamine, Austl.	F7	76
Condamine, stm., Austl.	F8	76
Condat, Fr.	D8	18
Conde, S.D., U.S.	B14	126
Condeúba, Braz.	H5	88
Condobolin, Austl.	I6	76
Condom, Fr.	F6	18
Condon, Or., U.S.	E6	136
Condoto, Col.	E3	86
Condroz, hist. reg., Bel.	D14	14
Cone, Tx., U.S.	H7	128
Conecuh, stm., U.S.	F12	122
Conegliano, Italy	E9	22
Conejos, Co., U.S.	D2	128
Conejos, stm., Co., U.S.	D3	128
Confuso, stm., Para.	B8	92
Congaree Swamp National Monument, p.o.i., S.C., U.S.	C5	116
Congaz, Mol.	C15	26
Conghua, China	J5	42
Congjiang, China	I3	42
Congleton, Eng., U.K.	H10	12
Congo, ctry., Afr.	E3	66
Congo (Zaïre), stm., Afr.	F2	66
Congo, Democratic Republic of the (Zaire), ctry., Afr.	E4	66
Congo Basin, bas., Afr.	E4	66
Congonhinhas, Braz.	A12	92
Congress, Sk., Can.	E8	124
Conitaca, Mex.	C5	100
Conn, Lough, l., Ire.	G3	12
Connacht see Connaught, hist. reg., Ire.	H3	12
Connaught, hist. reg., Ire.	H3	12
Conneaut, Oh., U.S.	C5	114
Conneautville, Pa., U.S.	C5	114
Connecticut, state, U.S.	C13	114
Connecticut, stm., U.S.	H4	110
Connellsville, Pa., U.S.	D6	114
Connemara, reg., Ire.	H3	12
Connersville, In., U.S.	E12	120
Conn Lake, l., Nu., Can.	A15	106
Connors Range, mts., Austl.	C7	76
Cononaco, stm., Ec.	H3	86
Conorochite, stm., Ven.	F8	86
Conover, N.C., U.S.	I4	114
Conquest, Sk., Can.	C6	124
Conquista, Braz.	J2	88
Conrad, Ia., U.S.	B5	120
Conroe, Tx., U.S.	G3	122
Conroe, Lake, res., Tx., U.S.	G3	122
Consecon, On., Can.	D12	112
Conselheiro Lafaiete, Braz.	K4	88
Conselheiro Pena, Braz.	J5	88
Conselice, Italy	F8	22
Consett, Eng., U.K.	G10	12
Consolación del Sur, Cuba	A6	102
Con Son, is., Viet.	H8	48
Consort, Ab., Can.	B3	124
Constance see Konstanz, Ger.	I4	16
Constance, Lake (Bodensee), l., Eur.	I5	16
Constância, Port.	E2	20
Constanța, Rom.	E15	26
Constanța, state, Rom.	E15	26
Constantina, Spain	G5	20
Constantine see Qacentina, Alg.	B6	64
Constantine, Mi., U.S.	G4	112
Constantine, Cape, c., Ak., U.S.	E8	140
Constantinople see İstanbul, Tur.	B12	28
Constitución, Chile	G1	92
Constitución, Ur.	E9	92
Constitución de 1857, Parque Nacional, p.o.i., Mex.	K10	134
Consuegra, Spain	E7	20
Contai, India	H11	54
Contas, stm., Braz.	H6	88
Contentnea Creek, stm., N.C., U.S.	A8	116
Continental Peak, mtn., Wy., U.S.	E4	126
Contratación, Col.	D5	86
Contreras, Embalse de, res., Spain	E9	20
Contreras, Isla, i., Chile	J1	90
Contursi, Italy	D9	24
Contwoyto Lake, l., Can.	B8	106
Convent, La., U.S.	G8	122
Conversano, Italy	D10	24
Converse, In., U.S.	H4	112
Conway, Ar., U.S.	B6	122
Conway, Mo., U.S.	G5	120
Conway, N.C., U.S.	H8	114
Conway, N.H., U.S.	F5	110
Conway, S.C., U.S.	C6	116
Conway, Lake, res., Ar., U.S.	C6	122
Conway National Park, p.o.i., Austl.	C7	76
Conway Springs, Ks., U.S.	D11	128
Conwy, Wales, U.K.	H9	12
Coober Pedy, Austl.	E6	74
Cook, Austl.	F6	74
Cook, Mn., U.S.	D6	118
Cook, Ne., U.S.	D1	120
Cook, Cape, c., B.C., Can.	F2	138
Cook, Mount see Aoraki, mtn., N.Z.	F4	80
Cook, Récif de, rf., N. Cal.	I14	79d
Cookeville, Tn., U.S.	H12	120
Cooking Lake, l., Ab., Can.	C17	138
Cook Inlet, b., Ak., U.S.	D9	140
Cook Islands, dep., Oc.	E10	72
Cook Strait, strt., N.Z.	E6	80
Cooktown, Austl.	C9	74
Coolabah, Austl.	H6	76
Cooladdi, Austl.	F5	76
Coolamon, Austl.	J6	76
Coolangatta, Austl.	G9	76
Cooleemee, N.C., U.S.	I5	114
Coolgardie, Austl.	F4	74
Coolidge, Ga., U.S.	E2	116
Coolidge, Tx., U.S.	F2	122
Coolidge, Mount, mtn., S.D., U.S.	D9	126
Coolidge Dam, dam, Az., U.S.	J6	132
Coolin, Id., U.S.	B10	136
Cooloola National Park, p.o.i., Austl.	F9	76
Cooma, Austl.	K7	76
Coonabarabran, Austl.	H7	76
Coonalpyn, Austl.	J2	76
Coonamble, Austl.	H7	76
Coonoor, India	F3	53
Coon Rapids, Mn., U.S.	F5	118
Coon Valley, Wi., U.S.	H8	118
Cooper, Tx., U.S.	D3	122
Cooper Creek, stm., Austl.	G2	76
Cooper Road, La., U.S.	E5	122
Coopers, Al., U.S.	E12	122
Cooperstown, N.Y., U.S.	B11	114
Coopersville, Mi., U.S.	E4	112
Coopracambra National Park, p.o.i., Austl.	K7	76
Coorong National Park, p.o.i., Austl.	K2	76
Coorow, Austl.	E3	74
Cooroy, Austl.	F9	76
Coosa, stm., U.S.	E12	122
Coos Bay, Or., U.S.	G2	136
Cootamundra, Austl.	J7	76
Cootehill, Ire.	G5	12
Copacabana, Arg.	D4	92
Copacabana, Col.	D4	86
Copainalá, Mex.	G12	100
Copan, Ok., U.S.	H2	120
Copán, sci., Hond.	E3	102
Copatana, Braz.	I8	86
Copeland, Fl., U.S.	K4	116
Copenhagen see København, Den.	I4	8
Copenhagen, N.Y., U.S.	E14	112
Copertino, Italy	D11	24
Copiapó, Chile	C2	92
Copiapó, stm., Chile	C2	92
Copley, Austl.	H2	76
Copparo, Italy	F8	22
Copper, stm., Ak., U.S.	D11	140
Copperas Cove, Tx., U.S.	C9	130
Copper Butte, mtn., Wa., U.S.	B8	136
Copper Canyon see Cobre, Barranca del, misc. cult., Mex.	B5	100
Copper Center, Ak., U.S.	D10	140
Copper Harbor, Mi., U.S.	D10	118
Coppermine see Kugluktuk, Nu., Can.	B8	106
Coppermine, stm., Can.	B7	106
Copper Mine Point, c., Br. Vir. Is.	e9	104b
Copper Mountain, B.C., Can.	G10	138
Coquí, P.R.	C3	104a
Coquilhatville see Mbandaka, D.R.C.	D3	66
Coquimbo, Chile	E2	92
Coquimbo, state, Chile	E2	92
Corabia, Rom.	F11	26
Coração de Jesus, Braz.	I3	88
Coradi, Isole see Cheradi, Isole, i., Italy	D11	24
Coral Gables, Fl., U.S.	K5	116
Coral Harbour, Bah.	n18	104f
Coral Harbour see Salliq, Nu., Can.	C14	106
Coral Sea, s., Oc.	E6	72
Coral Sea Basin, unds.	K18	142
Coral Sea Islands Territory, dep., Oc.	B9	76
Coralville, Ia., U.S.	C6	120
Coram, Mt., U.S.	B12	136
Corangamite, Lake, l., Austl.	K4	76
Corato, Italy	C10	24
Corbeil-Essonnes, Fr.	F11	14
Corbett National Park, p.o.i., India	D7	54
Corbigny, Fr.	G12	14
Corbin, Ky., U.S.	H1	114
Corbones, stm., Spain	G5	20
Corby, Eng., U.K.	I12	12
Corcaigh see Cork, Ire.	J4	12
Córcega, P.R.	B1	104a
Corcoran, Ca., U.S.	G6	134
Corcovado, Golfo, b., Chile	H2	90
Corcovado, Parque Nacional, p.o.i., C.R.	H6	102
Corcovado, Volcán, vol., Chile	H2	90
Corcubión, Spain	B1	20
Cordeiro, Braz.	L4	88
Cordele, Ga., U.S.	E2	116
Cordell Hull Reservoir, res., Tn., U.S.	H12	120
Corder, Mo., U.S.	E4	120
Cordillera, state, Para.	B9	92
Cordillo Downs, Austl.	F3	76
Córdoba, Arg.	E5	92
Córdoba, Mex.	F10	100
Córdoba (Cordova), Spain	G6	20
Córdoba, state, Arg.	E5	92
Córdoba, state, Col.	C4	86
Córdoba, co., Spain	F6	20
Córdova, Peru	F2	84
Cordova see Córdoba, Spain	G6	20
Cordova, Ak., U.S.	D10	140
Cordova, Al., U.S.	D11	122
Cordova, Il., U.S.	C7	120
Cordova Peak, mtn., Ak., U.S.	D10	140
Coreaú, Braz.	B5	88
Coreaú, stm., Braz.	B5	88
Corentyne, stm., S.A.	C6	84
Corfield, Austl.	C4	76
Corfu see Kérkyra, Grc.	D2	28
Corfu see Kérkyra, i., Grc.	D2	28
Coria, Spain	D4	20
Coria del Río, Spain	G4	20
Coribe, Braz.	G3	88
Coricudgy, Mount, mtn., Austl.	I8	76
Corigliano Calabro, Italy	E10	24
Corinne, Ut., U.S.	B4	132
Corinne, W.V., U.S.	G4	114
Corinth see Kórinthos, Grc.	F5	28
Corinth, Ms., U.S.	C10	122
Corinth, N.Y., U.S.	G3	110
Corinth, Gulf of see Korinthiakós Kólpos, b., Grc.	E5	28
Corinto, Braz.	J3	88
Corisco, Isla de, i., Eq. Gui.	I6	64
Corjeuți, Mol.	A14	26
Cork, Ire.	J4	12
Cork, state, Ire.	I4	12
Corleone, Italy	G7	24
Çorlu, Tur.	B10	28
Cornelia, Ga., U.S.	B2	116
Cornélio Procópio, Braz.	D6	90
Cornelius, N.C., U.S.	A5	116
Cornelius Grinnell Bay, b., Nu., Can.	E13	141
Cornell, Wi., U.S.	F7	118
Corner Brook, Nf., Can.	j22	107a
Cornești, Mol.	B14	26
Corneta, Punta, c., Mex.	H10	100
Corning, Ar., U.S.	H7	120
Corning, Ca., U.S.	D3	134
Corning, Ia., U.S.	D3	120
Corning, Ks., U.S.	B12	128
Corning, N.Y., U.S.	B8	114
Cornish, Me., U.S.	G6	110
Čornoe more see Black Sea, s.	G15	6
Corno Grande, mtn., Italy	H10	22
Cornwall, On., Can.	E2	110
Cornwallis Island, i., Nu., Can.	B7	141
Cornwall Island, i., Nu., Can.	B6	141
Coro, Ven.	B7	86
Coro, Golfete de, b., Ven.	B6	86
Coroaci, Braz.	J4	88
Coroatá, Braz.	C3	88
Corocoro, Bol.	C3	90
Corocoro, Isla, i., S.A.	C11	86
Coroico, Bol.	C3	90
Coromandel, Braz.	J2	88
Coromandel Coast, cst., India	E5	53
Coromandel Peninsula, pen., N.Z.	C6	80
Corona, Ca., U.S.	J8	134
Corona, N.M., U.S.	G3	128
Coronado, Mex.	D8	100
Coronado, Bahía de, b., C.R.	H6	102
Coronado, Islas, is., Mex.	K8	134
Coronation, Ab., Can.	D19	138
Coronation Gulf, b., Nu., Can.	B8	106
Coronation Island, i., Ant.	B36	81
Coronda, Arg.	E7	92
Coronel, Chile	H1	92
Coronel Bogado, Para.	C9	92
Coronel Dorrego, Arg.	I7	92
Coronel Fabriciano, Braz.	J4	88
Coronel Moldes, Arg.	B5	92
Coronel Moldes, Arg.	F5	92
Coronel Oviedo, Para.	B9	92
Coronel Pringles, Arg.	H7	92
Coronel Suárez, Arg.	H6	92
Coronel Vidal, Arg.	H9	92
Coronel Vivida, Braz.	C11	92
Corongo, Peru	E2	84
Coropuna, Nevado, vol., Peru	G3	84
Corossol, Guad.	B2	105a
Çorovodë, Alb.	D14	24
Corowa, Austl.	J6	76
Corozal, Belize	C3	102
Corozal, Col.	C4	86
Corozal, P.R.	B3	104a
Corpus Christi, Tx., U.S.	G10	130
Corpus Christi, Lake, res., Tx., U.S.	F9	130
Corpus Christi Bay, b., Tx., U.S.	G10	130
Corral, Chile	H2	90
Corral de Almaguer, Spain	E7	20
Corral de Bustos, Arg.	F6	92
Corrales, Cerro, mtn., Mex.	H2	130
Corralito, Arg.	F5	92
Correctionville, Ia., U.S.	B2	120
Corregidor Island, i., Phil.	C3	52
Corrente, Braz.	F3	88
Corrente, stm., Braz.	G4	88
Correntes, Cabo das, c., Moz.	D12	70
Correntina, Braz.	G3	88
Corrèze, state, Fr.	D7	18
Corrib, Lough, l., Ire.	H3	12
Corrientes, Arg.	C8	92
Corrientes, state, Arg.	D9	92
Corrientes, stm., Arg.	D8	92
Corrientes, stm., S.A.	D2	84
Corrientes, Bahía de, b., Cuba	B5	102
Corrientes, Cabo, c., Arg.	I9	92
Corrientes, Cabo, c., Col.	E3	86
Corrientes, Cabo, c., Mex.	E6	100
Corrigan, Tx., U.S.	F4	122
Corrigin, Austl.	F3	74
Corriverton, Guy.	B6	84
Corrumpa Creek, stm., U.S.	E5	128
Corry, Pa., U.S.	C6	114
Corse (Corsica), i., Fr.	G15	18
Corse, Cap, c., Fr.	F15	18
Corse-du-Sud, state, Fr.	H15	18
Corsica see Corse, i., Fr.	G15	18
Corsicana, Tx., U.S.	E2	122
Cort Adelaer, Kap, c., Grnld.	E17	141
Cortazar, Mex.	E8	100
Corte, Fr.	G15	18
Cortés, Mar de see California, Golfo de, b., Mex.	B2	96
Cortez, Co., U.S.	F8	132
Cortez, Sea of see California, Golfo de, b., Mex.	B2	96
Cortina d'Ampezzo, Italy	D8	22
Cortland, Ne., U.S.	K2	118
Cortland, N.Y., U.S.	B9	114
Cortland, Oh., U.S.	C5	114
Cortona, Italy	G8	22
Corubal, stm., Afr.	G2	64
Coruche, Port.	F2	20
Çorum, Tur.	A4	56
Corumbá, Braz.	C5	90
Corumbá, stm., Braz.	I1	88
Corumbaíba, Braz.	J1	88
Corumbataí, stm., Braz.	B11	92
Corumo, stm., Ven.	D11	86
Corunna see A Coruña, Spain	A2	20
Corunna, Mi., U.S.	F5	112
Coruripe, Braz.	F7	88
Corvallis, Mt., U.S.	D12	136
Corvallis, Or., U.S.	F3	136
Corwith, Ia., U.S.	B3	120
Corydon, In., U.S.	F11	120
Corydon, Ky., U.S.	G10	120
Corzu, Rom.	E10	26
Corzuela, Arg.	C7	92
Cos see Kos, i., Grc.	G10	28
Cosamaloapan de Carpio, Mex.	F10	100
Coscomate, Mex.	I2	130
Cosenza, Italy	E10	24
Coshocton, Oh., U.S.	D4	114
Cosigüina, Punta, c., Nic.	F4	102
Cosigüina, Volcán, vol., Nic.	F4	102
Cosmoledo, Atoll de, i., Sey.	k11	69b
Cosmos, Mn., U.S.	G4	118
Cosne-sur-Loire, Fr.	G11	14
Cosquín, Arg.	E5	92
Cossato, Italy	E5	22
Cossatot, stm., Ar., U.S.	C4	122
Costa Mesa, Ca., U.S.	J8	134
Costa Rica, Mex.	C5	100
Costa Rica, ctry., N.A.	H5	102
Coswig, Ger.	E9	16
Coswig, Ger.	E8	16
Cotabato, Phil.	G4	52
Cotahuasi, Peru	G3	84
Cotati, Ca., U.S.	E3	134
Coteaux, Haiti	C10	102
Cote d'Ivoire, ctry., Afr.	H3	64
Côte-d'Or, state, Fr.	G13	14
Cotegipe, Braz.	F3	88
Cotentin, pen., Fr.	E7	14
Côtes-d'Armor, state, Fr.	F6	14
Cotingo, stm., Braz.	E11	86
Cotiujeni, Mol.	B15	26
Cotonou, Benin	H5	64
Cotopaxi, state, Ec.	H2	86
Cotopaxi, vol., Ec.	H2	86
Cotopaxi, Parque Nacional, p.o.i., Ec.	H2	86
Cotswold Hills, hills, Eng., U.K.	J10	12
Cottage Grove, Or., U.S.	G3	136
Cottbus, Ger.	E10	16
Cotter, Ar., U.S.	H5	120
Cottian Alps, mts., Eur.	E12	18
Cottondale, Fl., U.S.	G13	122
Cotton Plant, Ar., U.S.	C7	122
Cottonport, La., U.S.	G6	122
Cotton Valley, La., U.S.	E5	122
Cottonwood, Az., U.S.	I5	132
Cottonwood, Ca., U.S.	C3	134
Cottonwood, Mn., U.S.	G3	118
Cottonwood, stm., Ks., U.S.	C12	128
Cottonwood, stm., Mn., U.S.	G3	118
Cottonwood Creek, stm., Mt., U.S.	F5	124
Cottonwood Falls, Ks., U.S.	C12	128
Coubre, Pointe de la, c., Fr.	D4	18
Couchiching, Lake, l., On., Can.	D10	112
Coudersport, Pa., U.S.	C8	114
Coudres, Île aux, i., Qc., Can.	C6	110
Coulee City, Wa., U.S.	C7	136
Coulee Dam, Wa., U.S.	B8	136
Coulommiers, Fr.	F12	14
Coulonge, stm., Qc., Can.	C13	112
Coulterville, Il., U.S.	F8	120
Counce, Tn., U.S.	B10	122
Council, Id., U.S.	F10	136
Council Bluffs, Ia., U.S.	C2	120
Council Grove, Ks., U.S.	C12	128
Coupeville, Wa., U.S.	B4	136
Courantyne see Corentyne, stm., S.A.	C6	84
Courland (Kurzeme), hist. reg., Lat.	C5	10
Courland Lagoon, b., Eur.	E3	10
Courmayeur, Italy	E3	22
Courtenay, B.C., Can.	G5	138
Courtland, Al., U.S.	C11	122
Courtland, Va., U.S.	H8	114
Courtrai see Kortrijk, Bel.	D12	14
Coutras, Fr.	D5	18
Coutts, Ab., Can.	G19	138
Couture, Lac, l., Qc., Can.	C16	106
Covasna, state, Rom.	C12	26
Cove, Or., U.S.	E9	136
Cove Island, i., On., Can.	C8	112
Covelo, Ca., U.S.	D2	134
Coventry, Eng., U.K.	I11	12
Covert, Mi., U.S.	F3	112
Covilhã, Port.	D3	20
Covington, Ga., U.S.	C2	116
Covington, In., U.S.	H2	112
Covington, Ky., U.S.	E1	114
Covington, La., U.S.	G8	122
Covington, Oh., U.S.	H5	112
Covington, Ok., U.S.	E11	128
Covington, Tn., U.S.	B9	122
Covington, Va., U.S.	G5	114
Cowal, pen., Scot., U.K.	E7	12
Cowal, Lake, l., Austl.	I6	76
Cowan, Tn., U.S.	B13	122
Cowan, Lake, l., Austl.	F4	74
Cowansville, Qc., Can.	E4	110
Cowarie, Austl.	E7	74
Cow Creek, stm., Ks., U.S.	C10	128
Cow Creek, stm., Or., U.S.	H3	136
Cowdenbeath, Scot., U.K.	E9	12
Cowell, Austl.	F7	74
Cowen, W.V., U.S.	F5	114
Coweta, Ok., U.S.	I2	120
Cowhouse Creek, stm., Tx., U.S.	C10	130
Cowichan Bay, B.C., Can.	H7	138
Cowichan Lake, l., B.C., Can.	H6	138
Cowley, Austl.	F5	76
Cowley, Wy., U.S.	C4	126
Cowlic, Az., U.S.	L4	132
Cowlitz, stm., Wa., U.S.	D4	136
Cowpasture, stm., Va., U.S.	F6	114
Cowpens, S.C., U.S.	A4	116
Cowra, Austl.	I7	76
Coxá, stm., Braz.	H3	88
Coxim, Braz.	C6	90
Cox's Bāzār, Bngl.	H13	54
Coyaguaima, Cerro, mtn., Arg.	D3	90
Coyame, Mex.	A6	100
Coyle see Coig, stm., Arg.	J3	90
Coyote, stm., Mex.	F6	98
Coyote Wash, stm., N.M., U.S.	G8	132
Coyuca de Benítez, Mex.	G8	100
Coyuca de Catalán, Mex.	F8	100
Cozad, Ne., U.S.	G13	126
Cozumel, Mex.	B4	102
Cozumel, Isla, i., Mex.	B4	102
Crab Orchard, Tn., U.S.	I13	120
Crab Orchard Lake, res., Il., U.S.	G9	120
Cradle Mountain-Lake Saint Clair National Park, p.o.i., Austl.	n12	77a
Cradock, S. Afr.	H7	70
Craig, Co., U.S.	C9	132
Craig, Mo., U.S.	D2	120
Craig, Ne., U.S.	J2	118
Craigellachie, B.C., Can.	E12	138
Craigmont, Id., U.S.	D10	136
Craigsville, Va., U.S.	F6	114
Craik, Sk., Can.	C8	124
Crailsheim, Ger.	G6	16
Craiova, Rom.	E10	26
Cranberry Lake, l., N.Y., U.S.	F1	110
Cranbrook, Austl.	F3	74
Cranbrook, B.C., Can.	G15	138
Crandon, Wi., U.S.	F9	118
Crane, Az., U.S.	K2	132
Crane, In., U.S.	F11	120
Crane, Tx., U.S.	C5	130
Crane Lake, l., Sk., Can.	D4	124
Crane Mountain, mtn., Or., U.S.	A5	134
Crângeni, Rom.	E11	26
Cranston, R.I., U.S.	C14	114
Crasna, Rom.	D13	26
Crasna, stm., Eur.	I18	16
Crasnoe, Mol.	C16	26
Crater Lake, l., Or., U.S.	H4	136
Crater Lake National Park, p.o.i., Or., U.S.	H5	136
Craters of the Moon National Monument, p.o.i., Id., U.S.	G13	136
Crateús, Braz.	C5	88
Crato, Braz.	D6	88
Crauford, Cape, c., Nu., Can.	A14	106
Cravo Norte, Col.	D6	86
Cravo Norte, stm., Col.	D6	86
Cravo Sur, stm., Col.	E6	86
Crawford, Co., U.S.	E9	132
Crawford, Ms., U.S.	D10	122
Crawford, Tx., U.S.	C10	130
Crawford Bay, B.C., Can.	G14	138
Crawfordsville, Ar., U.S.	B8	122
Crawfordsville, In., U.S.	H2	112
Crawfordville, Ga., U.S.	C3	116
Crawley, Eng., U.K.	J12	12
Crazy Woman Creek, stm., Wy., U.S.	C6	126
Creal Springs, Il., U.S.	G9	120
Cree, stm., Sk., Can.	D9	106
Creede, Co., U.S.	F10	132
Creedmoor, N.C., U.S.	H7	114
Cree Lake, l., Sk., Can.	D9	106
Creemore, On., Can.	D9	112
Creighton, Ne., U.S.	E15	126
Creighton Mine, On., Can.	B8	112
Creil, Fr.	E11	14
Crema, Italy	E6	22
Cremona, Italy	E7	22
Crenshaw, Ms., U.S.	C8	122
Crepori, stm., Braz.	E6	84
Crépy-en-Valois, Fr.	E11	14
Cres, Cro.	E11	22
Cres, Otok, i., Cro.	F11	22
Cresaptown, Md., U.S.	E7	114
Crescent, Or., U.S.	G5	136
Crescent City, Ca., U.S.	B1	134
Crescent City, Fl., U.S.	G4	116
Crescent Spur, B.C., Can.	C10	138
Cresco, Ia., U.S.	H6	118
Crespo, Arg.	F7	92
Cresson, Tx., U.S.	B10	130
Cressy, Austl.	K4	76
Crested Butte, Co., U.S.	E9	132
Crestline, Ca., U.S.	I8	134
Creston, B.C., Can.	G14	138
Creston, Ia., U.S.	C3	120
Crestone Peak, mtn., Co., U.S.	D3	128
Crestview, Fl., U.S.	G12	122
Crestwood Hills, Tn., U.S.	I1	114
Creswell, Or., U.S.	G3	136
Creswell Bay, b., Nu., Can.	A12	106
Crete, Il., U.S.	G2	112
Crete, Ne., U.S.	G16	126
Crete see Kríti, i., Grc.	H7	28
Crete, Sea of see Kritikón Pélagos, s., Grc.	H8	28
Créteil, Fr.	F11	14
Cretin, Cape, c., Pap. N. Gui.	b4	79a
Creus, Cap de, c., Spain	B14	20
Creuse, state, Fr.	C8	18
Creuse, stm., Fr.	C6	18
Creussen, Ger.	G7	16
Creve Coeur, Il., U.S.	K9	118
Crevillent, Spain	F10	20
Crevillente see Crevillent, Spain	F10	20
Crewe, Eng., U.K.	H10	12
Crewe, Va., U.S.	G7	114
Cricaré, stm., Braz.	J5	88
Criciúma, Braz.	D13	92
Crikvenica, Cro.	E11	22
Crimea see Kryms'kyi pivostriv, pen., Ukr.	E4	32
Crimean Peninsula see Kryms'kyi pivostriv, pen., Ukr.	E4	32
Crimmitschau, Ger.	F8	16
Cripple Creek, Co., U.S.	C3	128
Crisfield, Md., U.S.	F10	114
Criss Creek, B.C., Can.	E10	138
Crissiumal, Braz.	C10	92
Cristal, Monts de, mts., Afr.	I7	64
Cristalândia, Braz.	F1	88
Cristália, Braz.	I4	88
Cristalina, Braz.	I2	88
Cristinápolis, Braz.	F7	88
Cristino Castro, Braz.	E3	88
Cristóbal Colón, Pico, mtn., Col.	B5	86
Crișul Alb, stm., Eur.	C8	26
Crișul Negru, stm., Eur.	C8	26
Crișul Repede (Sebes Körös), stm., Eur.	B8	26
Crivitz, Wi., U.S.	C1	112
Crna, stm., Mac.	B4	28
Crni Drim (Drinit të Zi), stm., Eur.	C14	24
Črnomelj, Slvn.	E12	22
Croajingolong National Park, p.o.i., Austl.	K7	76
Croatia, ctry., Eur.	E13	22
Croche, stm., Qc., Can.	C4	110
Crocker, Mo., U.S.	G5	120
Crocker, Banjaran, mts., Malay.	H1	52
Crockett, Tx., U.S.	F3	122
Crocodilopolis, hist., Egypt	I1	58
Crocus Hill, hill, Anguilla	A1	105a
Crofton, Ky., U.S.	G10	120
Croghan, N.Y., U.S.	E14	112
Croix, Lac la, l., N.A.	C6	118
Croker, Cape, c., Austl.	B6	74
Croker, Cape, c., On., Can.	D9	112
Croker Island, i., Austl.	B6	74
Cromer, Eng., U.K.	I14	12
Cromínia, Braz.	I1	88
Crompton Point, c., Dom.	i6	105c
Cromwell, N.Z.	G3	80
Cromwell, Al., U.S.	E10	122
Crooked, stm., Or., U.S.	F5	136
Crooked Creek, Ak., U.S.	D8	140
Crooked Creek, stm., U.S.	D8	128
Crooked Island, i., Bah.	A10	102
Crooked Island Passage, strt., Bah.	A10	102
Crooked River, Sk., Can.	B10	124
Crookston, Mn., U.S.	D2	118
Crooksville, Oh., U.S.	E3	114
Crosby, Mn., U.S.	E5	118
Crosby, N.D., U.S.	F10	124
Crosby, Mount, mtn., Wy., U.S.	D3	126
Crosbyton, Tx., U.S.	H7	128
Cross, stm., Afr.	H6	64
Crossett, Ar., U.S.	D7	122
Cross Lake, res., Mb., Can.	E11	106
Crossman Peak, mtn., Az., U.S.	I2	132
Cross Plains, Tx., U.S.	B8	130
Cross Plains, Wi., U.S.	H9	118
Cross Sound, strt., Ak., U.S.	E12	140
Crossville, Il., U.S.	F9	120
Crossville, Tn., U.S.	I12	120
Croswell, Mi., U.S.	E7	112
Crotone, Italy	E11	24
Crow, North Fork, stm., Mn., U.S.	F5	118
Crow, South Fork, stm., Mn., U.S.	G4	118
Crow Agency, Mt., U.S.	B5	126
Crow Creek, stm., U.S.	G8	126
Crowder, Ms., U.S.	C8	122
Crowduck Lake, l., Mb., Can.	A3	118
Crowdy Head, c., Austl.	H9	76

Name	Map Ref.	Page
Crowell, Tx., U.S.	H9	128
Crow Lake, On., Can.	B5	118
Crowley, La., U.S.	G6	122
Crowleys Ridge, mts., U.S.	B8	122
Crown Mountain, mtn., V.I.U.S.	e7	104b
Crown Point, In., U.S.	G2	112
Crownpoint, N.M., U.S.	H8	132
Crown Point, N.Y., U.S.	G3	110
Crown Prince Frederik Island, i., Nu., Can.	A13	106
Crowsnest Pass, Ab., Can.	G16	138
Crowsnest Pass, p., Can.	G16	138
Crows Nest Peak, mtn., S.D., U.S.	C8	126
Crow Wing, stm., Mn., U.S.	E4	118
Croydon, Austl.	B4	76
Croydon Station, B.C., Can.	C11	138
Crozet, Va., U.S.	F7	114
Crozet, Îles, is., Afr.	J16	4
Crozet Basin, unds.	M9	142
Crucea, Rom.	E15	26
Cruces, Cabo, c., Cuba	C9	102
Cruz Alta, Arg.	F6	92
Cruz Alta, Braz.	D11	92
Cruz Bay, V.I.U.S.	e7	104b
Cruz del Eje, Arg.	E5	92
Cruzeiro, Braz.	L3	88
Cruzeiro do Oeste, Braz.	A11	92
Cruzeiro do Sul, Braz.	E3	84
Cruzeta, Braz.	D7	88
Cruz Grande, Chile	D2	92
Crysler, On., Can.	C14	112
Crystal, Mn., U.S.	F15	118
Crystal, N.D., U.S.	F16	124
Crystal Brook, Austl.	I2	76
Crystal City, Mb., Can.	E15	124
Crystal City, Mo., U.S.	F7	120
Crystal City, Tx., U.S.	F8	130
Crystal Falls, Mi., U.S.	B1	112
Crystal Lake, Il., U.S.	B9	120
Crystal Lake, l., Mi., U.S.	D3	112
Crystal Springs, Ms., U.S.	E8	122
Csongrád, Hung.	C7	26
Csongrád, state, Hung.	C7	26
Csorna, Hung.	B4	26
Cu see Shù, stm., Asia	F12	32
Cúa, Ven.	B8	86
Cuajinicuilapa, Mex.	G9	100
Cuamba, Moz.	C6	68
Cuando (Kwando), stm., Afr.	D3	68
Cuangar, Ang.	D2	68
Cuango, Ang.	B2	68
Cuango see Kwango, stm., Afr.	F3	66
Cuanza, stm., Ang.	C2	68
Cuao, stm., Ven.	E8	86
Cuareim (Quaraí), stm., S.A.	E9	92
Cuaró, Ur.	E9	92
Cuarto, stm., Arg.	F5	92
Cuatrociénegas, Mex.	B7	100
Cuauhtémoc, Mex.	A5	100
Cuautitlán, Mex.	F6	100
Cuba, Port.	F3	20
Cuba, Al., U.S.	E10	122
Cuba, Il., U.S.	D7	120
Cuba, Mo., U.S.	F6	120
Cuba, N.M., U.S.	G10	132
Cuba, ctry., N.A.	C9	96
Cubagua, Isla, i., Ven.	B9	86
Cubal, Ang.	C1	68
Cubango (Okavango), stm., Afr.	D2	68
Cubati, Braz.	D7	88
Cublas, Russia	D21	8
Cubuk, Tur.	C15	28
Cuchi, stm., Ang.	C2	68
Cuchillo Co, Arg.	I5	92
Cuchivero, stm., Ven.	D9	86
Cucui, Braz.	G8	86
Cucurpe, Mex.	F7	98
Cúcuta, Col.	D5	86
Cucuy, Piedra de, hill, Ven.	G8	86
Cudahy, Wi., U.S.	F2	112
Cuddalore, India	F4	53
Cuddapah, India	D4	53
Čudovo, Russia	A14	10
Cudworth, Sk., Can.	B8	124
Cudzin, Bela.	H9	10
Cue, Austl.	E3	74
Cuemba, Ang.	C2	68
Cuenca, Ec.	I2	86
Cuenca, Spain	D8	20
Cuenca, co., Spain	E9	20
Cuencamé de Ceniceros, Mex.	C7	100
Cuernavaca, Mex.	F9	100
Cuero, Tx., U.S.	E10	130
Cuers, Fr.	F12	18
Cuervo, Laguna del, l., Mex.	A6	100
Cuesta Pass, p., Ca., U.S.	H5	134
Cueto, Cuba	B9	102
Cugir, Rom.	D10	26
Čuguevka, Russia	B10	38
Čuhlomskoe, ozero, l., Russia	G19	8
Cuiabá, Braz.	G6	84
Cuiabá, stm., Braz.	G6	84
Cuiari, Braz.	G7	86
Cuicatlán, Mex.	G10	100
Cuilapa, Guat.	E2	102
Cuilco see Grijalva, stm., N.A.	G12	100
Cuíto (Kwilu), stm., Afr.	F3	66
Cuité, Braz.	D7	88
Cuíto, Braz.	D2	68
Cuito Cuanavale, Ang.	D2	68
Cuitzeo, Lago de, l., Mex.	F8	100
Cuiuni, stm., Braz.	H10	86
Cukai, Malay.	J6	48
Čukas, Indon.	D4	50
Čukotskij, mys, c., Russia.	D26	34
Čukotskij, mys, c., Russia (Chukotsk Peninsula), pen., Russia	C26	34
Culbertson, Mt., U.S.	F9	124
Cul de Sac, Guad.	A1	105a
Cul de Sac, Neth. Ant.	A1	105a
Culebra, P.R.	B5	104a
Culebra, Isla de, i., P.R.	B5	104a
Culebra Peak, mtn., Co., U.S.	D3	128
Culfa, Azer.	B6	56
Culgoa, stm., Austl.	G6	76
Culiacán, Mex.	C5	100
Culiacán, Mex.	C5	100
Culion Island, i., Phil.	D2	52
Cúllar, Spain	G8	20
Cullen, La., U.S.	D5	122
Culleoka, Tn., U.S.	B12	122
Cullera, Spain	E10	20
Cullman, Al., U.S.	C12	122
Cullom, Il., U.S.	D9	120
Čul'man, Russia	E13	34
Culpeper, Va., U.S.	F7	114
Culpina, Bol.	D4	90
Culuene, stm., Braz.	F7	84
Culver, Or., U.S.	F5	136
Culverden, N.Z.	F5	80
Čulym, Russia	C14	32
Čulym, stm., Russia.	C14	32
Čum, Russia	A9	32
Cumaná, Ven.	B9	86
Cumare, Cerro, hill, Col.	H5	86
Cumari, Braz.	J1	88
Cumbal, Nevado de, vol., Col.	G3	86
Cumberland, Braz.	F7	88
Cumberland, B.C., Can.	G5	138
Cumberland, Ky., U.S.	G2	114
Cumberland, Md., U.S.	E7	114
Cumberland, Va., U.S.	G7	114
Cumberland, Wi., U.S.	F6	118
Cumberland, stm., U.S.	H2	114
Cumberland, Lake, res., Ky., U.S.	H13	120
Cumberland, South Fork, stm., U.S.	H13	120
Cumberland Gap, p., U.S.	H2	114
Cumberland Island National Seashore, p.o.i., Ga., U.S.	F4	116
Cumberland Islands, is., Austl.	C7	76
Cumberland Lake, l., Sk., Can.	E10	106
Cumberland Peninsula, pen., Nu., Can.	B17	106
Cumberland Plateau, plat., U.S.	G14	120
Cumberland Sound, strt., Nu., Can.	B17	106
Cumbernauld, Scot., U.K.	F9	12
Cumbrian Mountains, mts., Eng., U.K.	G9	12
Cumby, Tx., U.S.	D3	122
Čumikan, Russia	F16	34
Cumming, Ga., U.S.	B1	116
Cummins, Austl.	F7	74
Cummock, Scot., U.K.	F8	12
Cumpas, Mex.	F8	98
Çumra, Tur.	F15	28
Čumyš, stm., Russia	D15	32
Čuna, stm., Russia	C17	32
Cunani, Braz.	C7	84
Cunaviche, Ven.	D8	86
Cunco, Chile	G2	90
Cundinamarca, state, Col.	E4	86
Cunene (Kunene), stm., Afr.	D1	68
Cuneo (Coni), Italy	F4	22
Cunha Porã, Braz.	C11	92
Čunja, stm., Russia	B17	32
Cunnamulla, Austl.	G5	76
Cunningham, Ks., U.S.	D10	128
Čunskij, Russia	C17	32
Cununurra, stm., Ven.	F9	86
Čuny, Russia.	G17	8
Cuorgnè, Italy	E4	22
Cupar, Sk., Can.	D9	124
Cupar, Scot., U.K.	E9	12
Cupica, Golfo de, b., Col.	D3	86
Čuprovo, Russia	D22	8
Cuquenán, stm., Ven.	E11	86
Curaçá, Braz.	E6	88
Curaçao, i., Neth. Ant.	p21	104g
Curacautín, Chile	I2	92
Curanilahue, Chile	H1	92
Curanipe, Chile	G1	92
Curapça, Russia	D15	34
Curaray, stm., S.A.	H4	86
Curepipe, Mrts.	i10	69a
Curepto, Chile	G1	92
Curicó, Chile	G2	92
Curicuriari, stm., Braz.	H8	86
Curimatá, Braz.	E3	88
Curitiba, Braz.	B13	92
Curitibanos, Braz.	C12	92
Curiuaú, stm., Braz.	H11	86
Curiúva, Braz.	B12	92
Curlew, Wa., U.S.	B8	136
Curnamona, Austl.	H2	76
Čurovići, Russia	H15	10
Currais Novos, Braz.	D7	88
Curralinho, Braz.	D8	84
Currant Mountain, mtn., Nv., U.S.	E1	132
Current, stm., U.S.	H7	120
Currie, Austl.	m12	77a
Currituck, N.C., U.S.	H9	114
Currituck Sound, strt., N.C., U.S.	H10	114
Curtea de Argeş, Rom.	D11	26
Curtina, Ur.	F9	92
Curtis, Ar., U.S.	D5	122
Curtis, Ne., U.S.	G12	126
Curtis Bank, Port. s., Austl.	D8	74
Curtis Channel, strt., Austl.	D8	76
Curtis Island, i., Austl.	D8	76
Curtis Island, i., N.Z.	G9	72
Curu, stm., Braz.	B6	88
Curuá, stm., Braz.	D7	84
Curuá, stm., Braz.	E7	84
Curuá, Ilha do, i., Braz.	C7	84
Curuá-Una, stm., Braz.	D7	84
Curuçá, Braz.	D8	84
Curumu, Braz.	D7	84
Curup, Indon.	E3	50
Curupá, Braz.	E2	88
Cururupu, Braz.	A3	88
Curuzú Cuatiá, Arg.	D8	92
Curvelo, Braz.	J3	88
Cusco, Peru	F3	84
Cushing, Ok., U.S.	B2	122
Cushing, Tx., U.S.	F4	122
Cushman, Ar., U.S.	I6	120
Cusiana, stm., Col.	E5	86
Cusihuiriachic, Mex.	A5	100
Čusovaja, stm., Russia	C9	32
Čusovoj, Russia	C9	32
Cusset, Fr.	C9	18
Cusseta, Ga., U.S.	E14	122
Čust, Uzb.	F12	32
Custer, Mi., U.S.	E3	112
Custer, Mt., U.S.	A5	126
Custer, S.D., U.S.	D9	126
Custódia, Braz.	E7	88
Cut, Nuhu, i., Indon.	G9	44
Cut Bank, Mt., U.S.	B14	136
Cutbank, stm., Ab., Can.	B12	138
Cut Bank Creek, stm., Mt., U.S.	F12	124
Cut Bank Creek, stm., U.S.	F12	124
Cutervo, Peru	E2	84
Cuthbert, Ga., U.S.	F14	122
Cutler, Ca., U.S.	G6	134
Cutler, Me., U.S.	F9	110
Cutlerville, Mi., U.S.	F4	112
Cutral-Có, Arg.	G3	90
Cutro, Italy	E10	24
Cuttack, India	H10	54
Cutzamalá, stm., Mex.	F8	100
Čuvašija, state, Russia	C7	32
Cuvier, Cape, c., Austl.	D2	74
Cuxhaven, Ger.	C4	16
Cuyahoga Falls, Oh., U.S.	C4	114
Cuyamaca Peak, mtn., Ca., U.S.	J9	134
Cuyari, stm., S.A.	G7	86
Cuyo, Phil.	E3	52
Cuyo East Pass, strt., Phil.	E3	52
Cuyo Islands, is., Phil.	E3	52
Cuyo West Pass, strt., Phil.	E3	52
Cuyuni, stm., S.A.	D11	86
Cuyuni-Mazaruni, state, Guy.	D11	86
Cwmbran, Wales, U.K.	J10	12
Cyclades see Kikládes, is., Grc.	F7	28
Cypress, La., U.S.	F5	122
Cypress Hills, hills, Can.	E5	124
Cypress River, Mb., Can.	E14	124
Cypress Springs, Lake, res., Tx., U.S.	D3	122
Cyprus, ctry., Asia	C4	58
Cyprus, North, ctry., Asia	D15	4
Cyprus see Kýpros, i., Asia	C4	58
Cyrenaica see Barqah, hist. reg., Libya	A4	62
Cyril, Ok., U.S.	G10	128
Cyril E. King Airport, V.I.U.S.	e7	104b
Cyrus Field Bay, b., Nu., Can.	E13	141
Çyrvonae, vozero, l., Bela.	H10	10
Cythera see Kýthira, i., Grc.	G5	28
Czaplinek, Pol.	C12	16
Czarna Woda, Pol.	C14	16
Czarnków, Pol.	D12	16
Czechoslovakia see Czech Republic, ctry., Eur.	G11	16
Czech Republic, ctry., Eur.	G11	16
Czechowice-Dziedzice, Pol.	G15	16
Czerniejewo, Pol.	D13	16
Czersk, Pol.	D11	16
Częstochowa, Pol.	F15	16
Częstochowa, state, Pol.	F15	16
Człuchów, Pol.	C13	16

D

Name	Map Ref.	Page
Da, stm., China	G8	42
Da, Song see Black, stm., Asia	D9	46
Da'an, China	J4	42
Dabajuro, Ven.	B6	86
Daba Ling, mtn., China	I5	42
Daba Shan, mts., China	E3	42
Dabat, Eth.	E7	62
Dabeiba, Col.	D3	86
Dabhoi, India	G4	54
Dabie, Pol.	D14	16
Dabie Shan, mts., China.	F6	42
Dabnou, Niger.	G5	64
Dabola, Gui.	G2	64
Dabou, C. Iv.	H4	64
Daboya, Ghana	H4	64
Dabra, India	F7	54
Dabrowa Białostocka, Pol.	C19	16
Dabu, China	I7	42
Dacca see Dhaka, Bngl.	G13	54
Dac Glei, Viet.	E8	48
Dachau, Ger.	H7	16
Dačice, Czech Rep.	G11	16
Dacoma, Ok., U.S.	E10	128
Dadanawa, Guy.	F12	86
Dade City, Fl., U.S.	H3	116
Dādeldhurā, Nepal.	D8	54
Dadeville, Al., U.S.	E13	122
Dādra and Nagar Haveli, state, India.	I4	54
Dādu, India.	D10	56
Daegu see Taegu, Kor., S.	D1	40
Daejeon see Taejŏn, Kor., S.	F7	38
Daerhanwangfu, China.	B5	38
Daet, Phil.	C4	52
Dafang, China	F6	36
Dafeng, China	E9	42
Dáfni, Grc.	F5	28
Dafoe, sk., Can.	C9	124
Dafu, China	F5	42
Dagâ, stm., Mya.	D2	48
Dagana, Sen.	F1	64
Daga Post, Sudan	F6	62
Dağardı, Tur.	D12	28
Dagda, Lat.	D10	10
Dagestan, state, Russia	F7	32
Daglung, China	D13	54
Dagu, China	B7	42
Dagua, Pap. N. Gui.	a3	79a
Daguan, China	F5	36
Daguan Hu, l., China	F7	42
Daguao, P.R.	B4	104a
Dagujia, China	C6	38
Dagupan, Phil.	B3	52
Dagzê Co, l., China	B11	54
Dahab, Egypt	J5	58
Dahei, India.	H4	54
Daheiding Shan, mtn., China	B10	36
Da Hinggan Ling (Greater Khingan Range), mts., China	B9	36
Dahlak Archipelago, is., Erit.	D8	62
Dahlonega, Ga., U.S.	B1	116
Dahlonega Plateau, plat., U.S.	C14	122
Dahmani, Tun.	I2	24
Dahme, Ger.	E9	16
Dāhod, India	G5	54
Dahomey see Benin, ctry., Afr.	G5	64
Dahra, Libya	B3	62
Dahra, mts., Alg.	H11	20
Dahshur, Pyramides de (Dashur, Pyramides of), hist., Egypt	I1	58
Dai, i., Sol. Is.	d9	79b
Daia, Rom.	E12	26
Dai Hai, l., China	A5	42
Dai-uk-u, Mya.	D3	48
Da'il, Syria	F7	58
Daimiel, Spain	E7	20
Daingean, Ire.	H5	12
Daingerfield, Tx., U.S.	D4	122
Dainkog, China	E4	36
Daireaux, Arg.	H7	92
Dairen see Dalian, China.	B9	42
Dairût, Egypt	K1	58
Dai-sen, vol., Japan.	D6	40
Daisetta, Tx., U.S.	G4	122
Daixian, China	B5	42
Daiyun Shan, mts., China	I8	42
Dajarra, Austl.	C2	76
Dajian Shan, mtn., China.	F5	36
Dakar, Sen.	G1	64
Dakeng, China	H6	42
Dakhin Shāhbāzpur Island, i., Bngl.	G13	54
Dakhla, W. Sah.	E1	64
Dākoānk, India	G7	46
Dakoro, Niger	G6	64
Dakota City, Ia., U.S.	B3	120
Dakota City, Ne., U.S.	B1	120
Dakovo, Serb.	F11	6
Dakovo, Cro.	E15	22
Dala, Sol. Is.	e9	79b
Dalaba, Gui.	G2	64
Dalad Qi, China	A4	42
Dalälven, stm., Swe.	F7	8
Dalaman, stm., Tur.	G11	28
Dalālmī, Sudan	E6	62
Dalandzadgad, Mong.	C5	36
Da Lat, Viet.	G9	48
Dālbandin, Pak.	D9	56
Dalbosjön, b., Swe.	G5	8
Dalby, Austl.	F8	76
Dale, Nor.	F1	8
Dale, In., U.S.	F10	120
Dale Hollow Lake, res., U.S.	H12	120
Dalga, Egypt	K1	58
Dalhart, Tx., U.S.	E6	128
Dalhousie, N.B., Can.	B10	110
Dalhousie, India	B5	54
Dalhousie, Cape, c., N.T., Can.	B14	140
Dali, China	G5	36
Dali, China	D3	42
Daliang Shan, mts., China.	F5	36
Dalin, China	C4	38
Dalj, Cro.	E15	22
Dālkola, India	F11	54
Dallas, Ga., U.S.	D14	122
Dallas, Or., U.S.	F3	136
Dallas, Pa., U.S.	C10	114
Dallas, Tx., U.S.	B11	130
Dallas, Wi., U.S.	F7	118
Dallas Center, Ia., U.S.	J4	118
Dallas City, Il., U.S.	D6	120
Dalli Rājhara, India	H8	54
Dall Island, i., Ak., U.S.	F13	140
Dall Lake, l., Ak., U.S.	D7	140
Dalmacija see Dalmatia, hist. reg., Eur.	G12	22
Dalmatia, hist. reg., Eur.	G12	22
Dalmau, India.	E8	54
Dal'negorsk, Russia.	B11	38
Dal'nerečensk, Russia.	B11	36
Dal'nyk, Ukr.	C17	26
Daloa, C. Iv.	H3	64
Dalqū, Sudan	C6	62
Dalroy, Ab., Can.	E17	138
Dalrymple, Mount, mtn., Austl.	C7	76
Dar-el-Beida see Casablanca, Mor.	C3	64
Dar es Salaam, Tan.	F7	66
Darfo, Italy	E7	22
Dargai, Pak.	A3	54
Dargan-Ata, Turkmen.	A9	56
Dargaville, N.Z.	B5	80
Dargol, Niger	G5	64
Darhan, Mong.	B6	36
Darıca, Tur.	C12	28
Darién, Col.	F3	86
Darien, Ga., U.S.	E4	116
Darién, Parque Nacional, p.o.i., Pan.	D2	86
Darién, Serranía del, mts.	C3	86
Dārjiling, India	E12	54
Dark Head, c., St. Vin.	o11	105e
Darlag, China	E4	36
Darling, S. Afr.	H4	70
Darling, Ms., U.S.	C8	122
Darling, stm., Austl.	I4	76
Darling Downs, reg., Austl.	F8	76
Darlingford, Mb., Can.	E15	124
Darling Range, mts., Austl.	F3	74
Darlington, Eng., U.K.	G11	12
Darlington, Wi., U.S.	B7	120
Darlington Dam, res., S. Afr.	H7	70
Darlot, Lake, l., Austl.	E4	74
Darłowo, Pol.	B12	16
Darmstadt, Ger.	G4	16
Darnah, Libya	A4	62
Darnall, S. Afr.	F10	70
Darney, Fr.	F15	14
Darnley, Cape, c., Ant.	B11	81
Darnley Bay, b., N.T., Can.	B6	106
Daroca, Spain	C9	20
Darovskoe, Russia	C7	32
Darregueira, Arg.	H6	92
Darreh Gaz, Iran	B8	56
Darrington, Wa., U.S.	B5	136
Darrouzett, Tx., U.S.	E8	128
Dartmoor, Austl.	K3	76
Dartmoor National Park, p.o.i., Eng., U.K.	K9	12
Dartmouth, N.S., Can.	F13	110
Dartmouth, Eng., U.K.	K9	12
Dartmouth, Lake, l., Austl.	E5	76
Dartmouth Reservoir, res., Austl.	K6	76
Daru, Pap. N. Gui.	b3	79a
Daruvar, Cro.	E14	22
Darvaza, Turkmen.	A8	56
Darwha, India	H6	54
Darwin, Austl.	B6	74
Darwin, Bahía, b., Chile	I2	90
Darya Khān, Pak.	C3	54
Dashbalbar, Mong.	B7	36
Dashitou, China	C3	50
Dašhovuz, Turkmen.	A8	56
Dasht, stm., Pak.	D9	56
Dashur, Pyramids of see Dahshur, Pyramides de, hist., Egypt	I1	58
Dashutang, China	A6	48
Dasol Bay, b., Phil.	C2	52
Dastgardān, Iran	C8	56
Datang, China	I3	42
Datça, Tur.	G10	28
Datia, India	F7	54
Datian, China	I7	42
Datian Ding, mtn., China	J4	42
Datong, China	D5	36
Datong, China	B5	42
Datong, China	B9	36
Datong, stm., China	D5	36
Datu, Cape, c., Asia	B10	50
Datumakuta, Indon.	B10	50
Datu Piang, Phil.	G5	52
Daua (Dawa), stm., Afr.	G8	62
Daudnagar, India	F10	54
Daugai, Lith.	F7	10
Daugavpils, Lat.	D9	10
Daŭhinava, Bela.	F10	10
Daule, Ec.	H1	86
Daule, stm., Ec.	H1	86
Daund, India	B2	53
Dauphin, Mb., Can.	C13	124
Dauphin, stm., Mb., Can.	C15	124
Dauphin Island, i., Al., U.S.	G10	122
Dauphin Island, i., Al., U.S.	G10	122
Dauphiné, hist. reg., Fr.	D11	18
Dauphin Lake, l., Mb., Can.	C13	124
Dauphin, Nig.	G6	64
Davangere, India	D2	53
Davant, La., U.S.	H9	122
Davao, Phil.	G5	52
Davao Gulf, b., Phil.	G5	52
Dāvarzan, Iran	B8	56
Davenport, Ia., U.S.	C7	120
Davenport, Ok., U.S.	B2	122
Davenport, Wa., U.S.	C8	136
Davenport Downs, Austl.	E3	76
Davenport Range, mts., Austl.	D6	74
David, Pan.	H6	102
David City, Ne., U.S.	F15	126
Davidson, Sk., Can.	C7	124
Davidson Mountains, mts., Ak., U.S.	C11	140
Davie, Fl., U.S.	J5	116
Davis, Ca., U.S.	E4	134
Davis, N.C., U.S.	A9	116
Davis, Ok., U.S.	C2	122
Davis, W.V., U.S.	E6	114
Davis, sci., Ant.	B11	81
Davis, Mount, mtn., Pa., U.S.	E6	114
Davis Dam, dam, U.S.	H2	132
Davis Inlet, Nf., Can.	D18	106
Davis Mountains, mts., Tx., U.S.	D3	130
Davis Sea, s., Ant.	P11	142
Davis Strait, strt., N.A.	D14	141
Davlekanovo, Russia	D8	32
Davos, Switz.	D6	22
Davyd-Haradok, Bela.	H9	10
Dawa (Daua), stm., Afr.	G8	62
Dawaki, Nig.	G6	64
Dawei, Mya.	H4	48
Dawen, stm., China	D7	42
Dawna Range, mts., Mya.	D4	48
Dawson, Ga., U.S.	F14	122
Dawson, Mn., U.S.	G2	118
Dawson, N.D., U.S.	A12	126
Dawson, stm., Austl.	D7	76
Dawson, Isla, i., Chile	J2	90
Dawson Bay, b., Mb., Can.	B13	124
Dawson Creek, B.C., Can.	D7	138
Dawson Inlet, b., Nu., Can.	C12	106
Dax, Fr.	F4	18
Daxian, China	F2	42
Daxing, China	B7	42
Daxu, China	I4	42
Daxue Shan, mts., China	F5	36
Dayang, stm., China	D5	38
Dayangshu, China	B9	36
Dayao, China	F5	36
Daye, China	F6	42
Daying, China	B5	42
Daylesford, Austl.	K5	76
Daymán, stm., Ur.	E9	92
Dayong, China	G4	42
Dayr az-Zawr, Syria	B4	56
Daysland, Ab., Can.	D18	138
Dayton, Oh., U.S.	E1	114
Dayton, Tn., U.S.	B13	122
Dayton, Tx., U.S.	G4	122
Dayton, Wa., U.S.	D9	136
Dayton, Wy., U.S.	C5	126
Daytona Beach, Fl., U.S.	G5	116
Dayu, China	I6	42
Dayu Ling, mts., China	I6	42
Da Yunhe (Grand Canal), can., China	E8	42
Dayville, Or., U.S.	F7	136
Dazhou, China	F2	42
Dazkırı, Tur.	F12	28
Deadhorse, Ak., U.S.	B10	140
Deadman's Cay, Bah.	A10	102
Dead Sea, l., Asia	G6	58
Deadwood, S.D., U.S.	C9	126
Deakin, Austl.	F5	74
Deal, Eng., U.K.	J14	12
Dealesville, S. Afr.	F7	70
Deal Island, Md., U.S.	F10	114
De'an, China	G6	42
Dean, stm., B.C., Can.	D4	138
Deán Funes, Arg.	E5	92
Deans Dundas Bay, b., N.T., Can.	B16	140
Dearborn, Mi., U.S.	B2	114
Dearg, Beinn, mtn., Scot., U.K.	D8	12
Dease, stm., B.C., Can.	D5	106
Dease Arm, b., N.T., Can.	B6	106
Dease Strait, strt., Nu., Can.	B9	106
Death Valley, Ca., U.S.	G9	134
Death Valley, val., Ca., U.S.	G9	134
Death Valley National Park, p.o.i., Ca., U.S.	G8	134
Deatsville, Al., U.S.	E12	122
Deauville, Fr.	E8	14
Deba, Nig.	G7	64
Debao, China	J2	42
Debar, Mac.	B3	28
De Bary, Fl., U.S.	H4	116
Debre Birhan, Eth.	F7	62
Debrecen, Hung.	B8	26
Debre Mark'os, Eth.	E7	62
Debre Tabor, Eth.	E7	62
Debre Zeyt, Eth.	F7	62
Debrzno, Pol.	C13	16
Decatur, Al., U.S.	C11	122
Decatur, Ga., U.S.	C1	116
Decatur, Il., U.S.	E9	120
Decatur, In., U.S.	H4	112
Decatur, Mi., U.S.	F3	112
Decatur, Ms., U.S.	E9	122
Decatur, Tn., U.S.	B14	122
Decatur, Tx., U.S.	H11	128
Decaturville, Tn., U.S.	B10	122
Decazeville, Fr.	E8	18
Deccan, plat., India	B4	53
Decelles, Réservoir, res., Qc., Can.	F15	106
Deception, stm., Bots.	B6	70
Deception, Mount, mtn., Wa., U.S.	C3	136
Decherd, Tn., U.S.	B12	122
Dechhu, India	E4	54
Děčín, Czech Rep.	F10	16
Decize, Fr.	H12	14
Decker Lake, B.C., Can.	B5	138
Decorah, Ia., U.S.	H7	118
Dédougou, Burkina	G4	64
Dedoviči, Russia	C12	10
Dee, stm., Scot., U.K.	D11	12
Dee, stm., U.K.	H10	12
Deenwood, Ga., U.S.	A6	116
Deep, stm., N.C., U.S.	A6	116
Deep Creek, stm., U.S.	H14	136
Deep River, On., Can.	B12	112
Deepwater, Mo., U.S.	F4	120
Deep Well, Austl.	D6	74
Deer Creek, stm., Ms., U.S.	E8	122
Deerfield, Il., U.S.	F2	112
Deerfield Beach, Fl., U.S.	J5	116
Deering, Ak., U.S.	C7	140
Deer Island, i., N.B., Can.	F10	110
Deer Isle, Me., U.S.	F8	110
Deer Lake, Nf., Can.	j22	107a
Deer Lodge, Mt., U.S.	D14	136
Deer Park, Al., U.S.	F10	122
Deer Park, Wa., U.S.	C9	136
Deerpass Bay, b., N.T., Can.	B6	106
Deer Trail, Co., U.S.	B4	128
Defiance, Ia., U.S.	C2	120
Defiance, Oh., U.S.	C1	114
Defiance, Mount, mtn., Or., U.S.	E5	136
De Forest, Wi., U.S.	H9	118
De Funiak Springs, Fl., U.S.	G12	122
Dêgê, China	E4	36
Degeh Bur, Eth.	F8	62
Dégelis, Qc., Can.	C8	110
Degerfors, Swe.	G6	8
Deggendorf, Ger.	H8	16
De Gray Lake, res., Ar., U.S.	C5	122
De Grey, stm., Austl.	D3	74
Dehalwiwa-Mount Lavinia, Sri L.	H4	53
Dehra Dün, India	C7	54
Dehri, India	F10	54
Dehua, China	I8	42
Dehui, China	B6	38
Deinze, Bel.	D12	14
Deir Mawās, Egypt	K1	58
Dej, Rom.	B11	26
Dejnau, Turkmen.	B9	56
De Kalb, Ms., U.S.	E10	122
De Kalb, Tx., U.S.	D4	122
Dekese, D.R.C.	E4	66
Deke Sokehs, i., Micron.	m11	78d
De Land, Fl., U.S.	H4	116
Delano, Ca., U.S.	H6	134
Delano, Mn., U.S.	F5	118

Name	Map Ref.	Page

Delaport Point, c., Bah. m18 104f
Delapu, China C13 54
Delarof Islands, is., Ak., U.S. .. g23 140a
Delaware, Oh., U.S. D2 114
Delaware, Ok., U.S. H2 120
Delaware, state, U.S. F10 114
Delaware, stm., Ks., U.S. E2 120
Delaware, stm., U.S. D10 114
Delaware, East Branch,
  stm., N.Y., U.S. B10 114
Delaware, West Branch,
  stm., U.S. B11 114
Delaware Bay, b., U.S. E10 114
Delaware City, De., U.S. E10 114
Delburne, Ab., Can. D17 138
Del Campillo, Arg. G5 92
Del City, Ok., U.S. F11 128
Delegate, Austl. K7 76
Delémont, Switz. C4 22
De Leon, Tx., U.S. B9 130
Delfinópolis, Braz. K2 88
Délfoi, sci., Grc. E5 28
Delft, Neth. B13 14
Delft Island, i., Sri L. G4 53
Delfzijl, Neth. A15 14
Delgado, Cabo, c., Moz. C7 68
Delger, stm., Mong. G8 34
Delgerhet, Mong. B7 36
Delhi, On., Can. F9 112
Delhi, India D6 54
Delhi, Ia., U.S. B6 120
Delhi, La., U.S. E7 122
Delhi, N.Y., U.S. B11 114
Delhi, state, India D6 54
Delia, Ab., Can. E18 138
Deliblato, Serb. E8 26
Delicias, Mex. A6 100
Delight, Ar., U.S. C5 122
Delijān, Iran C7 56
Deline, N.T., Can. B6 106
Delingde, Russia B11 34
Delingha, China D4 36
Delínkalns, hill, Lat. C9 10
Delisle, Sk., Can. C6 124
Delitzsch, Ger. E8 16
Dell City, Tx., U.S. C2 130
Delle, Fr. G16 14
Dellys, Alg. H14 20
Del Mar, Ca., U.S. K8 134
Delmar, Ia., U.S. C7 120
Delmar, Md., U.S. F10 114
Delmarva Peninsula,
  pen., U.S. F10 114
Delmas, Sk., Can. B5 124
Delmenhorst, Ger. C4 16
Delmiro Gouveia, Braz. E7 88
Delnice, Cro. E11 22
Del Norte, Co., U.S. D2 128
De-Longa, ostrova, is.,
  Russia A19 34
De Long Mountains, mts.,
  Ak., U.S. C7 140
Deloraine, Mb., Can. E13 124
Delorme, Lac, l., Qc., Can. .. E16 106
Delphi, In., U.S. H3 112
Delphi see Délfoi, sci., Grc. .. E5 28
Delphos, Ks., U.S. B11 128
Delportshoop, S. Afr. F7 70
Delray Beach, Fl., U.S. J5 116
Del Río, Tx., U.S. E7 130
Delta, Co., U.S. E8 132
Delta, Ut., U.S. D4 132
Delta Amacuro, state, Ven. .. C11 86
Delta Beach, Mb., Can. D15 124
Delta City, Ms., U.S. D8 122
Delta Downs, Austl. C8 74
Delta Junction, Ak., U.S. D10 140
Delta Peak, mtn., B.C., Can. .. D4 106
Del Valle, Tx., U.S. D10 130
Del Verme Falls, wtfl., Eth. .. F8 62
Delvinë, Alb. E14 24
Demak, Indon. G7 50
Demarcation Point, c.,
  Ak., U.S. C11 140
Demavend, Mount see
  Damāvand, Qolleh-ye,
  vol., Iran B7 56
Demba, D.R.C. F4 66
Dembi, Eth. F7 62
Dembia, C.A.R. C4 66
Dembi Dolo, Eth. F6 62
Demidov, Russia E14 10
Deming, N.M., U.S. K9 132
Demini, stm., Braz. H10 86
Demirci, Tur. D11 28
Demirköy, Tur. B10 28
Demjanka, stm., Russia C12 32
Demjanovo, Russia F22 8
Demjanskoe, Russia C11 32
Demmin, Ger. C8 16
Demmitt, Ab., Can. A11 138
Demopolis, Al., U.S. E11 122
Demorest, Ga., U.S. B2 116
Dempo, Gunung, vol.,
  Indon. F3 50
Demta, Indon. F11 44
Denain, Fr. D12 14
Denali, Ak., U.S. D10 140
Denali National Park,
  Ak., U.S. D10 140
Denan, Eth. F8 62
Denau, Uzb. G11 32
Den Burg, Neth. A13 14
Dendang, Indon. E5 50
Dendermonde (Termonde),
  Bel. C12 14
Dengkou, China C2 66
Dengkou, China A2 42
Dênggên, China E4 36
Dengxian, China E4 42
Denham, Austl. E2 74
Denham, Mount, mtn., Jam. .. i13 104d
Denham Range, mts., Austl. .. C6 76
Denham Springs, La., U.S. .. G8 122
Den Helder (Helder), Neth. .. B13 14
Dénia, Spain F11 20
Deniliquin, Austl. J5 76
Deniskovići, Russia H14 10
Denison, Tx., U.S. D2 122
Denison, Mount, vol.,
  Ak., U.S. E9 140
Denizli, Tur. F12 28
Denizli, state, Tur. F12 28
Denkanikota, India E3 53
Denmark, Austl. F3 74
Denmark, S.C., U.S. C4 116
Denmark, Wi., U.S. D2 112
Denmark, ctry., Eur. D10 6
Denmark Strait, strt. C20 94
Dennery, St. Luc. m7 105c
Denpasar, Indon. H9 50
Denton, Md., U.S. F10 114
Denton, Mt., U.S. C17 136
Denton, Tx., U.S. A5 116
Denton Creek, stm., Tx., U.S. H11 128
D'Entrecasteaux,
  Point, c., Austl. F3 74
D'Entrecasteaux
  Islands, is., Pap. N. Gui. .. D6 72
Denver, Co., U.S. B3 128
Denver, Pa., U.S. D9 114
Denver City, Tx., U.S. A5 130
Deoband, India D6 54
Deogarh, India F4 54
Deoghar, India F11 54
Deogarh, mtn., India G9 54
Deogarh Hills hills, India ... F9 54
Deoghar, India F11 54
Deoli, India G7 54
Deoria, India E9 54

De Pere, Wi., U.S. D1 112
Depew, Ok., U.S. B2 122
Depoe Bay, Or., U.S. F2 136
Depok, Indon. G5 50
Deposit, N.Y., U.S. B10 114
Depue, Il., U.S. C8 120
Dêqên, China F4 36
Deqing, China J4 42
De Queen, Ar., U.S. C4 122
De Quincy, La., U.S. G5 122
Dera, Lach, stm., Afr. D8 66
Dera Bugti, Pak. D2 54
Dera Ghāzi Khān, Pak. C3 54
Dera Ismāīl Khān, Pak. C3 54
Derāwar Fort, Pak. D3 54
Derbent, Russia F7 32
Derby, Eng., U.K. C4 74
Derby, Austl. n13 77a
Derby, Eng., U.K. I11 12
Derby, Ks., U.S. D11 128
Derby, N.Y., U.S. B6 114
Derecske, Hung. B10 28
Dereköy, Tur. B10 28
Derg, Lough, l., Ire. I4 12
Dergači, Russia D7 32
De Ridder, La., U.S. G5 122
Dermott, Ar., U.S. D7 122
Dernieres, Isles, is., La., U.S. H8 122
Dêrong, China F4 36
Derrame, Mex. H3 130
Derry see Londonderry,
  N. Ire., U.K. F6 12
Derry, N.H., U.S. B14 114
Derudeb, Sudan D7 62
Derwent, Ab., Can. E4 26
Derwent, stm., Austl. C19 138
Derwent, stm., Austl. o13 77a
Derwent, stm., Eng., U.K. ... G12 12
Derwent Water, l., Eng.,
  U.K. G9 12
Derzhavinsk, Kaz. D11 32
Desaguadero, stm., Arg. F4 92
Desaguadero, stm., S.A. G4 84
Désappointement,
  Îles du, is., Fr. Poly. E12 72
Des Arc, Ar., U.S. C7 122
Descabezado Grande,
  Volcán, vol., Chile G2 92
Descanso, Braz. C11 92
Descanso, Ca., U.S. K9 134
Descanso, Punta, c., Mex. ... K8 134
Descartes, Fr. G9 14
Deschambault Lake, l.,
  Sk., Can. E10 106
Deschutes, stm., Or., U.S. ... E6 136
Desdunes, Haiti C11 102
Desē, Eth. E7 62
Deseado, stm., Arg. I3 90
Desengaño, Punta, c., Arg. .. I3 90
Desenzano del Garda, Italy .. E7 22
Deseret Peak, mtn., Ut., U.S. C4 132
Deseronto, On., Can. D12 112
Désert, stm., Qc., Can. B13 112
Désert, Lac, l., Qc., Can. B13 112
Desert Hot Springs, Ca., U.S. J9 90
Desert Lake, l., Nv., U.S. F1 132
Desert Peak, mtn., Ut., U.S. . B3 132
Desert Valley, val., Nv., U.S. . B7 132
Desha, Ar., U.S. B7 122
Deshaies, Guad. h5 105c
Deshler, Oh., U.S. C1 114
Deshnok, India E4 54
Desiderio Tello, Arg. E4 92
Deskáti, Grc. D4 28
Desloge, Mo., U.S. G7 120
Des Moines, Ia., U.S. C4 120
Des Moines, N.M., U.S. E5 128
Des Moines, stm., U.S. D3 122
Des Moines, East Fork,
  stm., U.S. H4 118
Desna, stm., Eur. D4 32
Desolación, Isla, i., Chile J2 90
De Soto, Il., U.S. G8 120
De Soto, Mo., U.S. F7 120
Despatch, S. Afr. H7 70
Despeñaperros,
  Desfiladero de, p., Spain ... F7 20
Des Plaines, Il., U.S. F11 112
Des Plaines, stm., U.S. C9 120
Desroches, i., Sey. k12 69b
Desruisseaux, St. Luc. m7 105c
Dessau, Ger. E8 16
Destruction Bay, Yk., Can. .. C3 106
Desvres, Fr. D10 14
Detčino, Russia F19 10
Dete, Zimb. D4 68
Detmold, Ger. E4 16
Detour, Point, c., Mi., U.S. .. C3 112
De Tour Village, Mi., U.S. ... C5 112
Detrital Wash, stm., Az., U.S. H2 132
Detroit, Mi., U.S. B2 114
Detroit, Tx., U.S. D3 122
Detroit Beach, Mi., U.S. C2 114
Dettifoss, wtfl., Ice. k31 8a
Det Udom, Thai. E7 48
Detva, Slov. H15 16
Deua National Park, p.o.i.,
  Austl. J7 76
Deúlgaon Rāja, India H5 54
Deutsche Bucht, b., Ger. C4 16
Deutschlandsberg, Aus. D12 22
Deux-Sèvres, state, Fr. C5 18
Deva, Rom. D9 26
Devakottai, India G4 53
Dévaványa, Hung. B7 26
Deventer, Neth. B15 14
Devgadh Bāriya, India G4 54
De View, Bayou, stm., Ar.,
  U.S. B8 122
Devikot, India E3 54
Devils, stm., Tx., U.S. E6 130
Devils Island see
  Diable, Île du, i., Fr. Gu. ... B7 84
Devils Lake, N.D., U.S. F15 124
Devils Lake, l., N.D., U.S. ... F14 124
Devils Postpile National
  Monument, p.o.i., Ca.,
  U.S. F6 134
Devils Tower National
  Monument, p.o.i., Wy.,
  U.S. C8 126
Devine, B.C., Can. F8 138
Devine, Tx., U.S. E9 130
Devjatiny, Russia F17 8
Devli, India F5 54
Devoll, stm., Alb. D14 24
Devon, Ab., Can. C17 138
Devon Island, i., Nu., Can. .. n13 77a
Devoto, Arg. E6 92
Devrek, Tur. B14 28
Dewakang-lompo, Pulau,
  i., Indon. F11 50
Dewar, Ok., U.S. B3 122
Dewās, India H6 54
Dewey, Ok., U.S. H1 120
Deweyville, Tx., U.S. C7 122
De Witt, Ar., U.S. C7 122
De Witt, Ia., U.S. G16 126
De Witt, N.Y., U.S. A9 114
Dexing, China G7 42
Dexter, Me., U.S. E7 110
Dexter, Mi., U.S. B2 114
Dexter, Mo., U.S. H4 128
Dexter, N.Y., U.S. D13 112
Dexterity Fiord, b., Nu., Can. A16 106
Dey-Dey, Lake, l., Austl. E5 36
Dezfūl, Iran C6 56
Dezhou, China C7 42
Dežneva, mys, c., Russia C27 34
Dezong, China B13 54

Dhahran see Az-Zahrān,
  Sau. Ar. D6 56
Dhaka (Dacca), Bngl. G13 54
Dhaka, state, Bngl. F13 54
Dhamār, Yemen G5 56
Dhāmpur, India D7 54
Dhamtari, India H8 54
Dhanbād, India G11 54
Dhandhuka, India G3 54
Dhangadhi, Nepal D8 54
Dhankuta, Nepal E11 54
D'Hanis, Tx., U.S. E8 130
Dharān, Nepal E11 54
Dhār, India G5 54
Dharāpuram, India F3 53
Dharmābād, India B3 53
Dharmapuri, India E4 53
Dharmavaram, India D3 53
Dharmjaygarh, India G9 54
Dharmshāla, India B6 54
Dhaulpur, India E6 54
Dhawalāgiri, mtn., Nepal ... D9 54
Dhenkānāl, India H10 54
Dherínia, Cyp. C4 58
Dhofar see Zufar, reg.,
  Oman F7 56
Dholka, India G4 54
Dhone, India D3 53
Dhoomadheere, Som. D8 66
Dhorāji, India H3 54
Dhrāngadhra, India G3 54
Dhrol, India G3 54
Dhuburi, India E13 54
Dhule, India H5 54
Dhuliān, India F12 54
Dhupgāri, India E12 54
Dhuusamarreeb, Som. C9 66
Diable, Île du (Devils Island),
  i., Fr. Gu. B7 84
Diable, Pointe du, c., Mart. .. k7 105c
Diables, Morne aux,
  vol., Dom. i5 105c
Diablo, Canyon, p., Az., U.S. H5 132
Diablo, Mount, mtn.,
  Ca., U.S. F4 134
Diablo, Pico del, mtn., Mex. . F4 98
Diablo Range, mts., Ca., U.S. G4 134
Diablotins, Morne, vol.,
  Dom. j6 105c
Diaca, Moz. C6 68
Dialakoto, Sen. G2 64
Diamante, Arg. F7 92
Diamante, stm., Arg. G4 92
Diamantina, Braz. J4 88
Diamantina, stm., Austl. E2 76
Diamantina Lakes, Austl. ... D3 76
Diamantino, Braz. F6 84
Diamond, Mo., U.S. G3 120
Diamond Harbour, India G12 54
Diamond Islets, is., Austl. ... A8 76
Diamond Peak, mtn., Id.,
  U.S. F13 136
Diamond Peak, mtn., Wa.,
  U.S. D9 136
Diamondville, Wy., U.S. B6 132
Diana Bay, b., Can. C16 106
Dianbai, China K4 42
Dian Chi, l., China G5 36
Dianjiang, China F2 42
Dianópolis, Braz. F2 88
Diapaga, Burkina G5 64
Diaz, Ar., U.S. B7 122
Díaz Point, c., Nmb. E2 70
Dibai, India D7 54
Dibaya, D.R.C. F4 66
Dibeng, S. Afr. E6 70
D'Iberville, Ms., U.S. G9 122
Dibete, Bots. C8 70
Dibrugarh, India C7 46
Dickens, Tx., U.S. H8 128
Dickinson, N.D., U.S. A10 126
Dickinson, Tx., U.S. H3 122
Dickson, Tn., U.S. H10 120
Didao, China B9 38
Didsbury, Ab., Can. E16 138
Didwana, India E5 54
Didymóteicho, Grc. B9 28
Dieburg, Ger. G4 16
Dieciocho de Julio, Ur. F11 92
Diefenbaker, Lake, res.,
  Sk., Can. C7 124
Diego de Almagro, Chile C2 92
Diego de Almagro, Isla,
  i., Chile J1 90
Diego de Ocampo, Pico,
  mtn., Dom. Rep. C12 102
Diégo-Suarez see
  Antsiranana, Madag. C8 68
Diemuchuoke, China B7 54
Dien Bien, Viet. B6 48
Dien Bien Phu see Dien
  Bien, Viet. B6 48
Diepholz, Ger. D4 16
Dieppe, N.B., Can. D12 110
Dieppe, Fr. E9 14
Dieppe Bay Town, St. K./N. .. C2 105a
Dierks, Ar., U.S. C4 122
Di'er Songhua, stm., China .. B6 38
Diest, Bel. D14 14
Dieulefit, Fr. E10 18
Dieveniškės, Lith. F8 10
Diez de Octubre, Mex. C6 100
Dif, Kenya D8 66
Diffa, Niger G7 64
Differdange, Lux. E14 14
Dig, India E6 54
Digba, D.R.C. D5 66
Digboi, India C8 46
Digby, N.S., Can. F11 110
Digby Neck, pen., N.S., Can. F10 110
Digges Islands, is., Nu., Can. C15 106
Dighton, Ks., U.S. C8 128
Diglūr, India B3 53
Digne-les-Bains, Fr. E12 18
Digos, Phil. G5 52
Digras, India H6 54
Digul, stm., Indon. G10 44
Diinsoor, Som. D8 66
Dijon, Fr. G14 14
Dikaja, Russia A22 10
Dike, Ia., U.S. B5 120
Dikhil, Dji. E8 62
Dikili, Tur. D9 28
Dikirnis, Egypt H2 58
Dikodougou, C. Iv. H3 64
Dikson, Russia B5 34
Dikwa, Nig. G7 64
Dīla, Eth. F7 62
Dilek Yarımdası Milli
  Parkı, p.o.i., Tur. F10 28
Dili, E. Timor G8 44
Dillenburg, Ger. F4 16
Diller, Ne., U.S. A12 128
Dilley, Tx., U.S. E9 130
Dilling, Sudan E5 62
Dillingen an der Donau, Ger. H6 16
Dillingham, Ak., U.S. E8 140
Dillon, S.C., U.S. B6 116
Dillon, Mount, mtn., N.M.,
  U.S. J8 132
Dillwyn, Va., U.S. G7 114
Dilolo, D.R.C. G4 66
Dilos, sci., Grc. F8 28
Dilworth, Mn., U.S. H17 124
Dimāpur, India C7 46
Dimashq (Damascus), Syria . E7 58
Dimbelenge, D.R.C. F4 66
Dimbokro, C. Iv. H4 64
Dimbulah, Austl. A5 76
Dimitrovgrad, Blg. F14 26

Dimitrovgrad, Russia D8 32
Dimitsána, Grc. F4 28
Dimlang, mtn., Nig. H7 64
Dimmitt, Tx., U.S. G6 128
Dimona, Isr. G6 58
Dinagat, Phil. E5 52
Dinagat Island, i., Phil. E5 52
Dinājpur, Bngl. F12 54
Dinan, Fr. F6 14
Dinant, Bel. D13 14
Dinar, Tur. E13 28
Dinard, Fr. F6 14
Dinaric Alps (Dinara), mts.,
  Eur. G13 22
Dindi, stm., India C4 53
Dindigul, India F4 53
Dindori, India G8 54
Ding'an, China L4 42
Dingbian, China C2 42
Dingbiānji, China D11 54
Dinggyê, China D11 54
Dinghai, China F9 42
Dingle, Ire. I2 12
Dingle Bay, b., Ire. I2 12
Dingnan, China I6 42
Dingo, Austl. D7 76
Dingolfing, Ger. H8 16
Dingshuzhen, China F8 42
Dingtao, China D6 42
Dinguiraye, Gui. G2 64
Dingwall, N.S., Can. D16 110
Dingxian, China B6 42
Dingxiang, China B5 42
Dinh, India E7 60
Dinhäta, India E12 54
Dinh Hoa, Viet. B7 48
Dinh Lap, Viet. B8 48
Dinkelsbühl, Ger. G6 16
Dinnebito Wash, stm., Az.,
  U.S. H5 132
Dinorwic, On., Can. B6 118
Dinorwic Lake, l., On., Can. . B6 118
Dinosaur National
  Monument, p.o.i., U.S. ... C8 132
Dinsmore, Sk., Can. C6 124
Dinuba, Ca., U.S. G6 134
Dioka, Mali G3 64
Diolouloukou, Sen. G1 64
Diourbel, Sen. G1 64
Dīpālpur, Pak. C4 54
Diplo, Pak. F2 54
Dipolog, Phil. F4 52
Dippoldiswalde, Ger. F9 16
Dir, Pak. B11 56
Dirê, Mali F4 64
Dirê Dawa, Eth. F8 62
Diriamba, Nic. G4 102
Dirico, Ang. D3 68
Dīrj, Libya A2 62
Dirk Hartog Island, i., Austl. E2 74
Dirkou, Niger F7 64
Dirranbandi, Austl. G7 76
Dīsa, India F4 54
Disappointment, Cape, c.,
  S. Geor. J9 90
Disappointment, Cape, c.,
  Wa., U.S. D2 136
Disappointment, Lake,
  l., Austl. D4 74
Disaster Bay, b., Austl. K8 76
Discovery Bay, b., Austl. L3 76
Dishman, Wa., U.S. C9 136
Disko, i., Grnld. D15 141
Disko Bugt, b., Grnld. D15 141
Dismal, stm., Ne., U.S. F12 126
Dispur, India E13 54
Disraëli, Qc., Can. E5 110
Distrito Capital, state, Col. .. E4 86
Distrito Federal, state, Braz. . H2 88
Distrito Federal, state, Mex. . F9 100
Distrito Federal, state, Ven. .. B8 86
Ditā, Uq, Egypt G1 58
Dithmarschen, reg., Ger. ... B5 16
Diu, India H3 54
Dive, can., Fr. B9 18
Divenskaja, Russia A12 10
Divernon, Il., U.S. E8 120
Divinhe, Moz. B12 70
Divinópolis, Braz. K3 88
Divi Point, c., India D5 53
Divisor, Serra do, plat., S.A. . E3 84
Divnoe, Russia E6 32
Divnogorsk, Russia C16 32
Divo, C. Iv. H3 64
Dīwāl Qol, Afg. A1 54
Dix, Ne., U.S. F9 126
Dixon, Ca., U.S. E4 134
Dixon, Il., U.S. C8 120
Dixon, Ky., U.S. G10 120
Dixon, Mo., U.S. G5 120
Dixon, N.M., U.S. E3 128
Dixon Entrance, strt., N.A. .. E4 106
Diyarbakır, Tur. B4 56
Dizhou, China J2 42
Djado, Niger E7 64
Djado, Plateau du, plat.,
  Niger E7 64
Djambala, Congo E2 66
Djanet, Alg. E6 64
Djat'kovo, Russia G17 10
Djéma, C.A.R. C5 66
Djenné, Mali G4 64
Djenoun, Garet el, mtn.,
  Alg. D6 64
Djérem, stm., Cam. C2 66
Djibo, Burkina G4 64
Djibouti, Dji. E8 62
Djibouti, ctry., Afr. E8 62
Djoku-Punda, D.R.C. F4 66
Djolu, D.R.C. D4 66
Djougou, Benin H5 64
Djourab, Erg du, sand, Chad . D3 62
Djugu, D.R.C. D6 66
Djúrás, Swe. F6 8
Djurtjuli, Russia C8 32
Dmitrija Lapteva,
  proliv, strt., Russia B16 34
Dmitrov, Russia D20 10
Dmitrovsk, Russia E16 10
Dnieper, stm., Eur. E15 6
Dniester (Dnister), stm., Eur. G19 16
Dnipro, stm., Ukr. E4 32
Dniprodzerzhyns'k, Ukr. E4 32
Dnipropetrovs'k, Ukr. E4 32
Dnistrovs'kyi
  lyman, l., Ukr. C17 26
Dnjaprouska Buhski,
  kanal, can., Bela. H7 10
Dno, Russia C12 10
Do, Lac, l., Mali F4 64
Dôa, Moz. D5 68
Doaktown, N.B., Can. D10 110
Doany, Madag. C8 68
Doba, Chad F3 62
Dobczyce, Pol. G15 16
Dobele, Lat. D6 10
Döbeln, Ger. E8 16
Doberai, Jazirah (Doberai
  Peninsula), pen., Indon. ... F9 44
Doberai Peninsula see
  Doberai, Jazirah,
  pen., Indon. F9 44
Dobiegniew, Pol. D11 16
Doboj, Bos. E5 26
Dobra, Pol. B10 16
Dobre Miasto, Pol. C16 16
Dobric, Blg. F14 26

Dobříš, Czech Rep. G10 16
Dobrjanka, Russia C9 32
Dobroe, Russia C15 10
Dobroteasa, Rom. E11 26
Dobruja, hist. reg., Eur. E15 26
Dobruš, Bela. H14 10
Dobrušnad Wisła, Pol. D15 16
Doce, stm., Braz. J6 88
Dock Junction, Ga., U.S. ... E4 116
Doctor Cecilio Báez, Para. .. B9 92
Doctor Coss, Mex. I8 130
Doctor González, Mex. I8 130
Dod Ballāpur, India E3 53
Doddridge, Ar., U.S. D4 122
Dodecanese see
  Dodekánisoy, is., Grc. G10 28
Dodekanisoy
  (Dodecanese), is., Grc. ... G10 28
Dodge Center, Mn., U.S. ... G5 118
Dodge City, Ks., U.S. D9 128
Dodgeville, Wi., U.S. B7 120
Dodoma, Tan. F7 66
Dodoni, sci., Grc. D3 28
Dodsland, Sk., Can. C5 124
Dodson, Mt., U.S. F5 124
Dodson, Tx., U.S. G8 128
Doerun, Ga., U.S. E1 116
Doetinchem, Neth. C15 14
Dogai Coring, l., China A12 54
Doğanhisar, Tur. E14 28
Dog Island, i., Fl., U.S. H14 122
Dog Lake, l., Mb., Can. C15 124
Dog Lake, l., On., Can. C9 118
Dogliani, Italy F4 22
Dôgo, i., Japan C6 40
Do Gonbadan, Iran C7 56
Dogondoutchi, Niger G5 64
Doğu Karadeniz
  Dağları, mts., Tur. A5 56
Doha see Ad-Dawhah,
  Qatar D7 56
Dohrighāt, India E9 54
Doiran, Lake, l., Eur. B5 28
Dois Irmãos de Goiás, Braz. . E1 88
Dois Suthep-Pui National
  Park, p.o.i., Thai. C4 48
Doka, Indon. G9 44
Dokkum, Neth. A14 14
Doksy, Czech Rep. F10 16
Doland, S.D., U.S. C14 126
Dolbeau, Qc., Can. B4 110
Dol-de-Bretagne, Fr. F7 14
Dolbeau, Qc., Can. B4 110
Dole, Fr. F11 18
Dolega, Pan. H6 102
Dolgellau, Wales, U.K. I9 12
Dolgij Most, Russia C17 32
Dolgoščele, Russia C11 8
Dolinsk, Russia G17 34
Dolj, state, Rom. E10 26
Dolni Dăbnik, Blg. F11 26
Dolny Kubin, Slov. G15 16
Dolomites see Dolomiti,
  mts., Italy D8 22
Dolomiti, mts., Italy D8 22
Dolores, Arg. H9 92
Dolores, Col. F4 86
Dolores, Guat. D3 102
Dolores, Mex. H6 130
Dolores, Ur. F8 92
Dolores, stm., U.S. E7 132
Dolores Hidalgo, Mex. E8 100
Dolphin, Cape, c., Falk. Is. .. J5 90
Dolphin and Union
  Strait, strt., Nu., Can. B7 106
Dolphin Head, mtn., Jam. .. i12 104d
Dolsk, Pol. D13 16
Dolžicy, Russia C12 10
Domaniči, Russia G16 10
Domažlice, Czech Rep. G8 16
Dombås, Nor. E3 8
Dombóvár, Hung. C4 26
Dom Cavati, Braz. J4 88
Dôme, Puy de, mtn., Fr. D8 18
Dome Creek, B.C., Can. C9 138
Domeyko, Chile C2 92
Domeyko, Cordillera, mts.,
  Chile D3 90
Domfront, Fr. F8 14
Domiciano Ribeiro, Braz. ... I2 88
Domingo M. Irala, Para. B10 92
Dominica, ctry., N.A. j5 105c
Dominica Channel see
  Martinique Passage,
  strt., N.A. k6 105c
Dominicana, República
  see Dominican Republic,
  ctry., N.A. D10 96
Dominican Republic,
  ctry., N.A. D10 96
Dominion City, Mb., Can. ... E16 124
Dominion, Cape, c., Nu., Can. B15 106
Domo, Eth. F9 62
Domodedovo, Russia E20 10
Domodossola, Italy D4 22
Dom Pedrito, Braz. E10 92
Dom Pedro, Braz. C3 88
Dompu, Indon. H11 50
Domžale, Slvn. D11 22
Don, stm., Russia E6 32
Don, stm., Scot., U.K. D10 12
Don, stm., India B3 53
Don, stm., Laos E7 48
Don, stm., Scot., U.K. D10 12
Dona Ana, Moz. D5 68
Donald, Ar., U.S. K7 120
Donaldson, Ar., U.S. C5 122
Donaldsonville, La., U.S. ... G7 122
Donalsonville, Ga., U.S. F13 122
Doña Inés, Cerro, mtn.,
  Chile C2 92
Doñana, Parque Nacional
  de, p.o.i., Spain H4 20
Donau see Danube,
  stm., Eur. F11 6
Donauwörth, Ger. H6 16
Don Benito, Spain F5 20
Doncaster, Eng., U.K. H11 12
Dondaicha, India H5 54
Dondo, Ang. B1 68
Dondo, Moz. A12 70
Dondo, Teluk, b., Indon. E12 50
Dondra Head, c., Sri L. I5 53
Doneşti, Mol. B14 26
Donegal, Ire. G4 12
Donegal Bay, b., Ire. G3 12
Donets, stm., Eur. E5 32
Donets'k, Ukr. E5 32
Doneţi, Blg. C12 10
Dong, stm., China J6 42
Dong'an, China B11 38
Dongara, Austl. E2 74
Dongfang, China L3 42
Dongfang, China B7 42
Donggala, Indon. D11 50
Dongge, Indon. H10 50
Dongguan, China J5 42
Donggou, China K4 42
Dong Hai see East China
  Sea, China F9 36
Dong Hoi, Viet. D8 48
Dong Hu, l., China B10 54
Dong Trieu, Viet. B8 48

Dongjingcheng, China B8 38
Donglan, China I2 42
Dongliao, stm., China C5 38
Dong Nai, stm., Viet. G8 48
Dongning, China B9 38
Dongo, D.R.C. D3 66
Dongou, Congo D3 66
Dongping, China D7 42
Dongping, China K5 42
Dong San Shen (Manchuria),
  hist. reg., China B5 38
Dongshan, China L4 42
Dongsheng, China B4 42
Dongtai, China E9 42
Dongting Hu, l., China G5 42
Dongwe, stm., Zam. C3 68
Dongxi, China G2 42
Dongxiang, China G7 42
Dongyang, China G9 42
Dongzhi, China F7 42
Doniphan, Ne., U.S. G14 126
Donja Stubica, Cro. E12 22
Donjek, stm., Yk., Can. C3 106
Don Martín, Mex. G7 130
Donna, Tx., U.S. H9 130
Donnacona, Qc., Can. D5 110
Donnelly, Id., U.S. F10 136
Donner, La., U.S. H7 122
Donner Pass, p., Ca., U.S. .. D5 134
Donner und Blitzen,
  stm., Or., U.S. G8 136
Donnybrook, Austl. F3 74
Donora, Pa., U.S. D6 114
Donostia see Donostia-San
  Sebastián, Spain A9 20
Donostia-San Sebastián,
  Spain A9 20
Don Pedro Reservoir, res.,
  Ca., U.S. F5 134
Don Peninsula, pen., B.C.,
  Can. D2 138
Donskoj, Russia G21 10
Doolow, som. D8 66
Doornik see Tournai, Bel. ... D12 14
Door Peninsula, pen., Wi.,
  U.S. D2 112
Dor, Isr. F5 58
Dora, Al., U.S. D11 122
Dora, Lake, l., Austl. D4 74
Dora Baltea, stm., Italy E4 22
Dorado, P.R. B3 104a
Doraville, Ga., U.S. D14 122
Dorcheat, Bayou, stm., U.S. . D5 122
Dorchester, N.B., Can. E12 110
Dorchester, On., Can. F7 112
Dorchester, Eng., U.K. K10 12
Dorchester, Ne., U.S. G15 126
Dorchester, Cape, c.,
  Nu., Can. B15 106
Dordabis, Nmb. C3 70
Dordogne, state, Fr. D6 18
Dordogne, stm., Fr. D6 18
Dordrecht, Neth. C13 14
Dordrecht, S. Afr. H8 70
Dore Lake, l., Sk., Can. E9 106
Dorena, Or., U.S. G4 136
Dores do Indaiá, Braz. J3 88
Dorfen, Ger. H8 16
Dorgali, Italy D3 24
Dörgön nuur, l., Mong. B3 36
Dori, Burkina G4 64
Doring, stm., S. Afr. G4 70
Dornbirn, Aus. C6 22
Dornoch, Scot., U.K. D8 12
Dorog, Hung. B5 26
Dorogobuž, Russia F16 10
Dorohoi, Rom. A13 26
Dorokempo, Indon. H11 50
Dorre Island, i., Austl. E2 74
Dorrigo, Austl. H8 76
Dorris, Ca., U.S. B4 134
Dorsale, mts., Tun. I3 24
Dort see Dordrecht, Neth. .. C13 14
Dortmund, Ger. E3 16
Dorton, Ky., U.S. G3 114
Dörtyol, Tur. B7 58
Doruma, D.R.C. D5 66
Dos, Canal Numero, can.,
  Arg. H9 92
Dosatuj, Russia A8 36
Döşemealtı, Tur. F13 28
Dos Bocas, P.R. B2 104a
Dos Hermanas, Spain G4 20
Dos Palos, Ca., U.S. G5 134
Dos Pos, Neth. Ant. p23 104g
Dos Quebradas, Col. E4 86
Dossor, Kaz. E8 32
Dossor, Niger G6 64
Dostyq, Kaz. E14 32
Dothan, Al., U.S. F13 122
Dotnuva, Lith. E6 10
Douai, Fr. D11 14
Douala, Cam. D1 66
Douarnenez, Fr. F4 14
Doublé, Pointe, c., Guad. ... h7 105c
Double Island Point, c.,
  Austl. E9 76
Double Springs, Al., U.S. ... C11 122
Doubletop Peak, mtn.,
  Wy., U.S. G16 136
Doubs, state, Fr. G15 14
Doubs, stm., Eur. H14 14
Doubtful Sound, strt., N.Z. .. G2 80
Doubtless Bay, b., N.Z. B5 80
Douentza, Mali F4 64
Dougga, sci., Tun. H3 24
Douglas, Mb., Can. E12 124
Douglas, Isle of Man G8 12
Douglas, S. Afr. F7 70
Douglas, Az., U.S. L7 132
Douglas, Ga., U.S. E3 116
Douglas, Wy., U.S. E7 126
Douglas, Cape, c.,
  Ak., U.S. E9 140
Douglas Channel, strt.,
  B.C., Can. C1 138
Douglas Lake, B.C., Can. ... F10 138
Douglas Lake, l., Mi., U.S. .. C5 112
Douglasville, Ga., U.S. D14 122
Doullens, Fr. D11 14
Dourada, Serra, plat., Braz. . G1 88
Dourados, Braz. D6 90
Dourados, Serra dos,
  mts., Braz. B11 92
Douro (Duero), stm., Eur. ... C2 20
Douz, Tun. C6 64
Dove Creek, Co., U.S. F7 132
Dover, Austl. o13 77a
Dover, Eng., U.K. J14 12
Dover, De., U.S. E10 114
Dover, N.H., U.S. C15 114
Dover, N.J., U.S. D11 114
Dover, Oh., U.S. D4 114
Dover, Tn., U.S. H10 120
Dover, Strait of, strt., Eur. .. K14 12
Dover-Foxcroft, Me., U.S. ... E7 110
Dovrefjell Nasjonalpark,
  p.o.i., Nor. E3 8
Dow City, Ia., U.S. C2 120
Dowagiac, Mi., U.S. G3 112
Dowlatābād, Iran D8 56
Downey, Id., U.S. H14 136
Downieville, Ca., U.S. D5 134
Downing, Mo., U.S. D5 120
Downingtown, Pa., U.S. D10 114

Name	Map Ref.	Page
Downpatrick, N. Ire., U.K.	G7	12
Downs, Ks., U.S.	B10	128
Downton, Mount, mtn., B.C., Can.	D6	138
Dows, Ia., U.S.	B4	120
Dowshī, Afg.	B10	56
Doyle, Ca., U.S.	C5	134
Doyles, Nf., Can.	C17	110
Doylestown, Pa., U.S.	D10	114
Doyline, La., U.S.	E5	122
Dōzen, is., Japan	C5	40
Dozier, Al., U.S.	F12	122
Dra, Cap, c., Mor.	D2	64
Dra'a, Hamada du, des., Alg.	D3	64
Drâa, Oued, stm., Afr.	D2	64
Drac, stm., Fr.	E2	22
Dracena, Braz.	D6	90
Drachten, Neth.	A15	14
Dracut, Ma., U.S.	B14	114
Dragalina, Rom.	E14	26
Drăgăneşti-Vlaşca, Rom.	E12	26
Drăgăşani, Rom.	E11	26
Dragonera, Sa, i., Spain	E13	20
Dragons Mouths, strt.	s12	105f
Dragoon, Az., U.S.	K6	132
Draguignan, Fr.	F12	18
Drahičyn, Bela.	H8	10
Drake, N.D., U.S.	G13	124
Drakensberg, mts., Afr.	F9	70
Drake Passage, strt.	K8	82
Drakesboro, Ky., U.S.	G10	120
Drakes Branch, Va., U.S.	H7	114
Dráma, Grc.	B7	28
Drammen, Nor.	G3	8
Drang, stm., Asia	F8	48
Drangajökull, ice, Ice.	j28	8a
Dranov, Ostrovul, i., Rom.	E16	26
Drau (Dráva), stm., Eur.	D11	22
Dráva (Drau), stm., Eur.	D14	22
Dravograd, Slvn.	D12	22
Drawsko Pomorskie, Pol.	C11	16
Drayton, N.D., U.S.	C1	118
Drayton, S.C., U.S.	B4	116
Drayton Valley, Ab., Can.	C15	138
Dresden, On., Can.	F7	112
Dresden, Ger.	E9	16
Dresden, Oh., U.S.	D3	114
Drètun', Bela.	E12	10
Dreux, Fr.	F10	14
Drew, Ms., U.S.	D8	122
Drienov, Slov.	H17	16
Driftwood, B.C., Can.	D5	106
Driftwood, stm., In., U.S.	E12	120
Driggs, Id., U.S.	G15	136
Drin, stm., Alb.	C13	24
Drina, stm., Eur.	F16	22
Drinit, Gjiri i, b., Alb.	C13	24
Drinit të Zi (Crni Drim), stm., Eur.	C14	24
Driskill Mountain, hill, La., U.S.	E6	122
Drissa (Drysa), stm., Eur.	E11	10
Drniš, Cro.	G13	22
Drobeta-Turnu Severin, Rom.	E9	26
Drochia, Mol.	A14	26
Drogheda, Ire.	H6	12
Droichead Átha *see* Drogheda, Ire.	H6	12
Droichead Nua, Ire.	H6	12
Drôme, state, Fr.	E11	18
Dronero, Italy	F4	22
Dronne, stm., Fr.	D6	18
Dronning Louise Land, reg., Grnld.	B20	141
Druc', stm., Bela.	G12	10
Druif, Aruba	o19	104g
Druja, Bela.	E10	10
Drūkšiai, l., Eur.	E9	10
Drumheller, Ab., Can.	E18	138
Drummond, Mt., U.S.	D13	136
Drummond, Wi., U.S.	E7	118
Drummond Island, i., Mi., U.S.	C6	112
Drummondville, Qc., Can.	E4	110
Druskininkai, Lith.	F7	10
Družba *see* Dostyq, Kaz.	E14	32
Druzhba *see* Dostyq, Kaz.	E14	32
Družina, Russia	C18	34
Drvar, Bos.	E3	26
Dry Arm, b., Mt., U.S.	G7	124
Dry Bay, b., Ak., U.S.	E12	140
Dryberry Lake, l., On., Can.	B4	118
Dry Cimarron, stm., U.S.	B2	122
Dry Creek Mountain, mtn., Nv., U.S.	B9	134
Dryden, On., Can.	B6	118
Dry Devils, stm., Tx., U.S.	D7	130
Dry Prong, La., U.S.	F6	122
Dry Ridge, Ky., U.S.	F1	114
Drysdale, stm., Austl.	C5	74
Dry Tortugas, is., Fl., U.S.	G11	108
Dry Tortugas National Park, p.o.i., Fl., U.S.	L3	116
Drzewica, Pol.	E16	16
Dschang, Cam.	C1	66
Du, stm., China	E4	42
Du'an, China	I3	42
Duaringa, Austl.	D7	76
Duarte, Pico, mtn., Dom. Rep.	C12	102
Duartina, Braz.	L1	88
Ḍubā, Sau. Ar.	K6	58
Dubach, La., U.S.	E6	122
Dubai *see* Dubayy, U.A.E.	D8	56
Dubăsari, Mol.	B16	26
Dubăsari, Lacul, res., Mol.	B15	26
Dubawnt, stm., Can.	C10	106
Dubawnt Lake, l., Can.	C10	106
Dubayy (Dubai), U.A.E.	D8	56
Dubbo, Austl.	I7	76
Dubh Artach, r., Scot., U.K.	E6	12
Dublin (Baile Átha Cliath), Ire.	H6	12
Dublin, Ga., U.S.	D3	116
Dublin, Tx., U.S.	B9	130
Dublin, Va., U.S.	G5	114
Dublin, state, Ire.	H6	12
Dubna, Russia	D20	10
Dubna, Russia	F19	10
Dubna, stm., Russia	D21	10
Dubnica nad Váhom, Slov.	H14	16
Dubois, In., U.S.	F11	120
Du Bois, Ne., U.S.	D1	120
Du Bois, Pa., U.S.	C7	114
Dubois, Wy., U.S.	D3	126
Dubossary Reservoir see Dubăsari, Lacul, res., Mol.	B15	26
Dubovka, Russia	E6	32
Dubrājpur, India	G11	54
Dubréka, Gui.	H2	64
Dubrouna, Bela.	F13	10
Dubrovka, Russia	G16	10
Dubrovnik, Cro.	H15	22
Dubrovnoe, Russia	C11	32
Dubuque, Ia., U.S.	B7	120
Dubysa, stm., Lith.	E6	10
Duchang, China	G7	42
Duchesne, Ut., U.S.	C6	132
Duchesne, stm., Ut., U.S.	C7	132
Duchess, Austl.	C2	76
Duck, stm., Tn., U.S.	B11	122
Duck Creek, stm., Nv., U.S.	D2	132
Duck Hill, Ms., U.S.	D9	122
Duck Lake, Sk., Can.	B7	124
Ducktown, Tn., U.S.	B14	122
Duda, stm., Col.	F4	86
Dudačkino, Russia	A15	10
Duderstadt, Ger.	E6	16
Dudinka, Russia	C6	34
Dudley, Eng., U.K.	I10	12
Dudleyville, Az., U.S.	K6	132
Dudna, stm., India	B2	53
Dudorovskij, Russia	G18	10
Dudwa National Park, p.o.i., India	D8	54
Dueré, stm., Braz.	F1	88
Duero (Douro), stm., Eur.	C2	20
Due West, S.C., U.S.	B3	116
Dufourspitze, mtn., Eur.	D13	18
Dufur, Or., U.S.	E5	136
Duga-Zapadnaja, mys, c., Russia	E18	34
Dugdemona, stm., La., U.S.	F6	122
Dugi Otok, i., Cro.	F11	22
Dugna, Russia	F19	10
Du Gué, stm., Qc., Can.	D16	106
Duhovščina, Russia	E15	10
Duida, Cerro, mtn., Ven.	F9	86
Duisburg, Ger.	E2	16
Duitama, Col.	E5	86
Duiwelskloof, S. Afr.	C10	70
Dujuuma, Som.	D8	66
Duke, Ok., U.S.	G9	128
Duke of York Bay, b., Nu., Can.	B13	106
Duk Fadiat, Sudan	F6	62
Dukhān, Qatar	D7	56
Duki, Pak.	C2	54
Dukla Pass, p., Eur.	G17	16
Dukou, China	F5	36
Dūkštas, Lith.	E9	10
Dulan, China	D4	36
Dulce, N.M., U.S.	G9	132
Dulce, stm., Arg.	D6	92
Dulce, Golfo, b., C.R.	H6	102
Dul'durga, Russia	F11	34
Dulgalah, stm., Russia	C15	34
Dullstroom, S. Afr.	D10	70
Dulovka, Russia	C11	10
Dulq Maghār, Syria	B9	58
Duluth, Ga., U.S.	C14	122
Duluth, Mn., U.S.	E6	118
Dūmā, Syria	E7	58
Dumaguete, Phil.	F4	52
Dumai, Indon.	C2	50
Dumalag, Phil.	E4	52
Dumali Point, c., Phil.	D3	52
Dumaran Island, i., Phil.	E2	52
Dumaresq, stm., Austl.	G8	76
Dumaring, Indon.	C11	50
Dumas, Tx., U.S.	F7	128
Dumbarton, Scot., U.K.	F8	12
Dumbrăveni, Rom.	C11	26
Dume, Point, c., Ca., U.S.	J7	134
Dumfries, Scot., U.K.	F9	12
Dumka, India	F11	54
Dumlupınar, Tur.	E12	28
Dummar, Syria	E7	58
Dumoine, Lac, l., Qc., Can.	B12	112
Dumont, Ia., U.S.	B4	120
Dumont d'Urville, sci., Ant.	B18	81
Dumpu, Pap. N. Gui.	b4	79a
Dumraon, India	F10	54
Dumyât, Masabb (Damietta Mouth), mth., Egypt	G3	58
Duna see Danube, stm., Eur.	F11	6
Dunaharaszti, Hung.	B6	26
Dunaj see Danube, stm., Eur.	F11	6
Dunajec, stm., Eur.	F16	16
Dunajská Streda, Slov.	H13	16
Dunakeszi, Hung.	B6	26
Dunărea Veche, Braţul, stm., Rom.	E15	26
Dunaújváros, Hung.	C5	26
Dunavăţu de Sus, Rom.	E16	26
Duna-völgyi-főcsatorna, can., Hung.	C6	26
Dunav-Tisa-Dunav, Kanal, can., Serb.	D6	26
Dunbar, Scot., U.K.	E10	12
Dunblane, Sk., Can.	C6	124
Duncan, B.C., Can.	H7	138
Duncan, Az., U.S.	K7	132
Duncan, Ok., U.S.	G11	128
Duncan, stm., B.C., Can.	F13	138
Duncan Lake, res., B.C., Can.	F14	138
Duncannon, Pa., U.S.	D8	114
Duncan Passage, strt., India	F7	46
Duncans, Jam.	i13	104d
Duncansby Head, c., Scot., U.K.	C9	12
Dundaga, Lat.	C5	10
Dundalk, On., Can.	D9	112
Dundalk (Dún Dealgan), Ire.	G6	12
Dundalk, Md., U.S.	E9	114
Dundalk Bay, b., Ire.	H6	12
Dundas, On., Can.	E9	112
Dundas, Lake, l., Austl.	F4	74
Dundas Peninsula, pen., Can.	B17	140
Dundas Strait, strt., Austl.	B6	74
Dún Dealgan *see* Dundalk, Ire.	G6	12
Dundee, S. Afr.	F10	70
Dundee, Scot., U.K.	E10	12
Dundee, Fl., U.S.	H4	116
Dundee, Mi., U.S.	C2	114
Dundurn, Sk., Can.	C7	124
Dund-Us, Mong.	B3	36
Dunedin, N.Z.	G4	80
Dunedin, Fl., U.S.	H3	116
Dunedoo, Austl.	I7	76
Dunfermline, Scot., U.K.	E9	12
Dungannon, N. Ire., U.K.	G6	12
Dūngarpur, India	G4	54
Dungarvan, Ire.	I5	12
Dungeness, c., Eng., U.K.	K13	12
Dungog, Austl.	I8	76
Dungu, D.R.C.	D5	66
Dungun, Malay.	J6	48
Dunhua, China	C8	38
Dunhuang, China	C3	36
Dunilovo, Russia	C21	10
Dunkerque (Dunkirk), Fr.	C11	14
Dunkirk *see* Dunkerque, Fr.	C11	14
Dunkirk, In., U.S.	H4	112
Dunkirk, N.Y., U.S.	B6	114
Dunkirk, Oh., U.S.	D2	114
Dunkwa, Ghana	H4	64
Dún Laoghaire, Ire.	H6	12
Dunlap, Tn., U.S.	B13	122
Dunmore, Pa., U.S.	C10	114
Dunmore Town, Bah.	K9	116
Dunn, N.C., U.S.	A7	116
Dunnellon, Fl., U.S.	G3	116
Dunnet Head, c., Scot., U.K.	C9	12
Dunning, Ne., U.S.	F12	126
Dunnville, On., Can.	F10	112
Dunoon, Scot., U.K.	F8	12
Dunqulah, Sudan	D5	62
Dunqunāb, Sudan	C7	62
Duns, Scot., U.K.	F10	12
Dunseith, N.D., U.S.	F13	124
Dunsmuir, Ca., U.S.	B3	134
Dunstable, Eng., U.K.	J12	12
Dunster, B.C., Can.	C11	138
Dunyāpur, Pak.	D3	54
Duolun, China	C2	38
Duolundabohuer, China	B14	54
Duomula, China	A9	54
Duozhu, China	J6	42
Dupang Ling, mts., China	I4	42
Dupnica, Blg.	G10	26
Dupnitsa *see* Dupnica, Blg.	G10	26
Dupuyer, Mt., U.S.	B14	136
Duque Bacelar, Braz.	C4	88
Duque de Caxias, Braz.	L4	88
Duque de York, Isla, i., Chile	J1	90
Duran, N.M., U.S.	G3	128
Durance, stm., Fr.	F11	18
Durand, Il., U.S.	B8	120
Durand, Wi., U.S.	G7	118
Durand, Récif, rf., N. Cal.	n17	79d
Durand Reef see Durand, Récif, rf., N. Cal.	n17	79d
Durango, Mex.	C6	100
Durango, Spain	A8	20
Durango, Co., U.S.	F9	132
Durango, state, Mex.	C6	100
Durant, Ia., U.S.	C6	120
Durant, Ms., U.S.	D9	122
Durant, Ok., U.S.	D2	122
Duras, Fr.	E6	18
Durazno, Ur.	F9	92
Durban, S. Afr.	F10	70
Đurđevac, Cro.	D14	22
Düren, Ger.	F2	16
Durg, India	H8	54
Durgāpur, India	G11	54
Durham, On., Can.	D9	112
Durham, Eng., U.K.	G11	12
Durham, Ca., U.S.	D4	134
Durham, N.C., U.S.	H6	114
Durham, N.H., U.S.	G5	110
Durham Downs, Austl.	F3	76
Durham Heights, mtn., N.T., Can.	A6	106
Durlas éile *see* Thurles, Ire.	I5	12
Durleşti, Mol.	B15	26
Durmitor, mtn., Mont.	F5	26
Durmitor Nacionalni Park, p.o.i., Mont.	F6	26
Dürnkrut, Aus.	B13	22
Durrës, Alb.	C13	24
Durrësi *see* Durrës, Alb.	C13	24
Durrie, Austl.	E3	76
Dursunbey, Tur.	D11	28
Duru Gölü, l., Tur.	B11	28
Durūz, Jabal ad-, mtn., Syria	F7	58
D'Urville, Tanjung, c., Indon.	F10	44
D'Urville Island, i., N.Z.	E5	80
Dušak, Turkmen.	B9	56
Dusa Marreb *see* Dhuusamarreeb, Som.	C9	66
Dušanbe, Taj.	B10	56
Dušekan, Russia	B19	32
Dusetos, Lith.	E8	10
Dushan, China	I2	42
Du Shan, mtn., China	A8	42
Dushanzi, China	C1	36
Duson, La., U.S.	G6	122
Düsseldorf, Ger.	E2	16
Dustin, Ok., U.S.	B2	122
Dutch John, Ut., U.S.	C7	132
Dutton, Mt., U.S.	C15	136
Dutton, stm., Austl.	C4	76
Duvno, Bos.	F4	26
Duxun, China	J7	42
Duyfken Point, c., Austl.	B8	74
Duyun, China	H2	42
Düzce, Tur.	C14	28
Dve Mogili, Blg.	F12	26
Dvine, ozero, l., Russia	D14	10
Dvinskaja guba, b., Russia	D17	8
Dvuh Cirkov, gora, mtn., Russia	C22	34
Dvůr Králové nad Labem, Czech Rep.	F11	16
Dwārka, India	G2	54
Dwight, Il., U.S.	C9	120
Dworshak Reservoir, res., Id., U.S.	D11	136
Dwyka, stm., S. Afr.	H5	70
Dyer, Tn., U.S.	H8	120
Dyer, Cape, c., Nu., Can.	D13	141
Dyer Bay, b., On., Can.	C8	112
Dyersburg, Tn., U.S.	H8	120
Dyje (Thaya), stm., Eur.	H12	16
Dyment, On., Can.	B6	118
Dynów, Pol.	G18	16
Dysart, Sk., Can.	D9	124
Dysart, Ia., U.S.	B5	120
Dysna (Dzisna), stm., Eur.	E9	10
Dytikí Elláda, state, Grc.	E4	28
Dytikí Makedonía, state, Grc.	C4	28
Džagdy, hrebet, mts., Russia	F15	34
Džalal-Abad, Kyrg.	F12	32
Džalinda, Russia	F13	34
Dzaoudzi, May.	C8	68
Džardžan, Russia	C13	34
Dzavhan, stm., Mong.	B3	36
Dzeržinsk, Russia	H20	8
Dzeržinskoe, Russia	C16	32
Džetygara *see* Zhetiqara, Kaz.	D10	32
Dzhankoi, Ukr.	E4	32
Dzhugdzhur Mountains see Džugdžur, hrebet, mts., Russia	E16	34
Dzhungarian Alatau Mountains, mts., Asia	E14	32
Działoszyce, Pol.	F16	16
Dzibilchaltún, sci., Mex.	B3	102
Dzierżoniów, Pol.	F12	16
Dzilam González, Mex.	B3	102
Dzisna, Bela.	E11	10
Dzisna (Dysna), stm., Eur.	E9	10
Dzitbalché, Mex.	B2	102
Dziwnów, Pol.	B10	16
Džizak, Uzb.	F11	32
Dzjarèčyn, Bela.	G7	10
Dzjaršynskaja, hara, hill, Bela.	G9	10
Dzjaržynsk, Bela.	G9	10
Dzjatlavičy, Bela.	H9	10
Dzöölön, Mong.	F8	34
Džugdžur, hrebet, mts., Russia	E16	34
Dzūkijos nacionalinis parkas, p.o.i., Lith.	F7	10
Dzungarian Basin see Junggar Pendi, bas., China	B2	36
Dzungarian Gate, p., Asia	E14	32
Dzüünharaa, Mong.	B6	36
Dzuunmod, Mong.	B6	36
Dzyhivka, Ukr.	A15	26

E

Name	Map Ref.	Page
Eads, Co., U.S.	C6	128
Eagle, Ak., U.S.	D11	140
Eagle, Co., U.S.	D10	132
Eagle, stm., Co., U.S.	B2	128
Eagle Bay, B.C., Can.	F11	138
Eagle Butte, S.D., U.S.	C11	126
Eagle Creek, stm., Sk., Can.	B6	124
Eagle Grove, Ia., U.S.	B4	120
Eaglehawk, Austl.	K4	76
Eagle Lake, Tx., U.S.	H2	122
Eagle Lake, l., On., Can.	B5	118
Eagle Lake, l., Ca., U.S.	C5	134
Eagle Lake, l., Me., U.S.	D7	110
Eagle Mountain, Ca., U.S.	J1	132
Eagle Mountain, mtn., Id., U.S.	D11	136
Eagle Mountain, mtn., Mn., U.S.	D8	118
Eagle Mountain Lake, res., Tx., U.S.	A10	130
Eagle Pass, Tx., U.S.	F7	130
Eagle Peak, mtn., Ca., U.S.	B5	134
Eagle River, Mi., U.S.	D10	118
Eagle River, Wi., U.S.	F9	118
Eagletown, Ok., U.S.	C4	122
Ear Falls, On., Can.	A5	118
Earle, Ar., U.S.	B8	122
Earl Grey, Sk., Can.	D9	124
Earlham, Ia., U.S.	C3	120
Earlimart, Ca., U.S.	H6	134
Earlville, Il., U.S.	C8	120
Early, Ia., U.S.	B2	120
Early, Tx., U.S.	C9	130
Eas, Vanuatu	k17	79d
Easley, S.C., U.S.	B3	116
East Alton, Il., U.S.	F7	120
East Angus, Qc., Can.	E5	110
East Antarctica, reg., Ant.	C8	81
East Aurora, N.Y., U.S.	B7	114
East Bay, b., Tx., U.S.	H4	122
East Bend, N.C., U.S.	H5	114
East Bernard, Tx., U.S.	H2	122
East Bernstadt, Ky., U.S.	G1	114
East Borneo see Kalimantan Timur, state, Indon.	C10	50
Eastbourne, Eng., U.K.	K13	12
East Brady, Pa., U.S.	D6	114
East Brewton, Al., U.S.	F11	122
East Cache Creek, stm., Ok., U.S.	G10	128
East Caicos, i., T./C. Is.	B12	102
East Cape, c., N.Z.	C8	80
East Cape, c., Fl., U.S.	K4	116
East Carbon, Ut., U.S.	D6	132
East Caroline Basin, unds.	I17	142
East Chicago, In., U.S.	G2	112
East China Sea, s., Asia	F9	36
East Cote Blanche Bay, b., La., U.S.	H7	122
East Coulee, Ab., Can.	E18	138
East Dereham, Eng., U.K.	I13	12
East Dismal Swamp, sw., N.C., U.S.	A9	116
East Dubuque, Il., U.S.	B7	120
East Ely, Nv., U.S.	D2	132
East End, V.I.U.S.	e8	104b
Easter Island see Pascua, Isla de, i., Chile	f30	78l
Eastern Cape, state, S. Afr.	G8	70
Eastern Channel see Tsushima-kaikyō, strt., Japan	F2	40
Eastern Creek, stm., Austl.	C3	76
Eastern Desert see Arabian Desert, des., Egypt	B6	62
Eastern Division, state, Fiji	q20	79e
Eastern Ghāts, mts., India	E4	53
Eastern Point, c., Guad.	A1	105a
Eastern Sayans see Vostočnyj Sajan, mts., Russia	D17	32
East Falkland, i., Falk. Is.	J5	90
East Fayetteville, N.C., U.S.	A7	116
East Frisian Islands see Ostfriesische Inseln, is., Ger.	C3	16
East Gaffney, S.C., U.S.	A4	116
East Germany see Germany, ctry., Eur.	E6	16
East Glacier Park, Mt., U.S.	B13	136
East Grand Forks, Mn., U.S.	D2	118
East Grand Rapids, Mi., U.S.	F4	112
East Grinstead, Eng., U.K.	J12	12
Easthampton, Ma., U.S.	B13	114
East Java see Jawa Timur, state, Indon.	G8	50
East Jordan, Mi., U.S.	C4	112
East Kelowna, B.C., Can.	G11	138
East Kilbride, Scot., U.K.	F8	12
Eastlake, Mi., U.S.	D3	112
Eastlake, Oh., U.S.	C4	114
Eastland, Tx., U.S.	B9	130
East Lansing, Mi., U.S.	B1	114
East Laurinburg, N.C., U.S.	B6	116
Eastleigh, Eng., U.K.	K11	12
East Liverpool, Oh., U.S.	D5	114
East London (Oos-Londen), S. Afr.	H9	70
Eastmain, Qc., Can.	E15	106
Eastmain, stm., Qc., Can.	E15	106
Eastmain-Opinaca, Réservoir, res., Qc., Can.	E15	106
Eastman, Ga., U.S.	D2	116
East Mariana Basin, unds.	H18	142
East Matagorda Bay, b., Tx., U.S.	F11	130
East Missoula, Mt., U.S.	D13	136
East Moline, Il., U.S.	C7	120
East Naples, Fl., U.S.	J4	116
East Nishnabotna, stm., Ia., U.S.	C2	120
East Nusa Tenggara see Nusa Tenggara Timur, state, Indon.	H12	50
East Olympia, Wa., U.S.	D3	136
Easton, Md., U.S.	F9	114
Easton, Pa., U.S.	D10	114
East Pacific Rise, unds.	N27	142
East Palatka, Fl., U.S.	G4	116
East Pecos, N.M., U.S.	F3	128
East Peoria, Il., U.S.	D8	120
Eastpoint, Fl., U.S.	H14	122
East Point, Ga., U.S.	D14	122
East Point, c., P.E., Can.	D15	110
East Point, c., V.I.U.S.	g11	104c
Eastport, Id., U.S.	B10	136
Eastport, Me., U.S.	F9	110
East Prairie, Mo., U.S.	H8	120
East Prairie, stm., Ab., Can.	A14	138
East Pryor Mountain, mtn., Mt., U.S.	B4	126
East Retford, Eng., U.K.	H12	12
East Saint Louis, Il., U.S.	F7	120
East Sea (Japan, Sea of), s., Asia	D11	38
East Shoal Lake, l., Mb., Can.	D16	124
East Siberian Sea see Vostočno-Sibirskoe more, s., Russia	B20	34
East Sister Island, i., Austl.	L6	76
East Slovakia see Východoslovenský Kraj, state, Slov.	H17	16
East Stroudsburg, Pa., U.S.	D11	114
East Timor, ctry., Asia	G8	44
East Troy, Wi., U.S.	B9	120
Eastville, Va., U.S.	G10	114
East Wenatchee, Wa., U.S.	C6	136
East Wilmington, N.C., U.S.	B8	116
Eaton, In., U.S.	H4	112
Eaton, Oh., U.S.	E1	114
Eaton Rapids, Mi., U.S.	B1	114
Eatonton, Ga., U.S.	C2	116
Eatonville, Wa., U.S.	D4	136
Eau Claire, Wi., U.S.	G7	118
Eau Claire, Lac à l', l., Qc., Can.	D16	106
Eauripik, at., Micron.	C5	72
Eauripik Rise, unds.	I17	142
Eauze, Fr.	F6	18
Ebano, Mex.	D9	100
Ebb and Flow Lake, l., Mb., Can.	D14	124
Ebbw Vale, Wales, U.K.	J9	12
Ebebiyín, Eq. Gui.	I7	64
Eben Junction, Mi., U.S.	B2	112
Ebensee, Aus.	C10	22
Eberbach, Ger.	G4	16
Eber Gölü, l., Tur.	E14	28
Ebern, Ger.	F6	16
Ebersbach, Ger.	E10	16
Eberswalde-Finow, Ger.	D9	16
Ebetsu, Japan	C14	38
Ebino, Japan	G3	40
Ebinur Hu, l., China	F14	32
Eboli, Italy	D9	24
Ebolowa, Cam.	D2	66
Ebon, at., Marsh. Is.	C7	72
Ebre see Ebro, stm., Spain	C11	20
Ebre, Delta de l', Spain	D11	20
Ebro (Ebre), stm., Spain	C11	20
Ebro, Delta del see Ebre, Delta de l', Spain	D11	20
Ebro, Embalse del, res., Spain	B7	20
Eceabat, Tur.	C9	28
Ech Cheliff, Alg.	B5	64
Echeng, China	E7	36
Echínos, Grc.	B7	28
Echt, Neth.	E1	16
Echuca, Austl.	K5	76
Écija, Spain	G5	20
Eckernförde, Ger.	B5	16
Eckerö, i., Fin.	F8	8
Eckville, Ab., Can.	D16	138
Eclectic, Al., U.S.	E12	122
Eclipse Sound, strt., Nu., Can.	A14	106
Ecoporanga, Braz.	J5	88
Écorce, Lac de l', res., Qc., Can.	B13	112
Écrins, Barre des, mtn., Fr.	E12	18
Écrins, Massif des, plat., Fr.	E12	18
Ecru, Ms., U.S.	C9	122
Ecuador, ctry., S.A.	D2	84
Ed, Swe.	G4	8
Edam, Sk., Can.	A5	124
Eddrachillis Bay, b., Scot., U.K.	C7	12
Eddystone Rocks, r., Eng., U.K.	K8	12
Eddyville, Ia., U.S.	C5	120
Eddyville, Ky., U.S.	G9	120
Ede, Neth.	B14	14
Ede, Nig.	H5	64
Edéa, Cam.	D2	66
Edehon Lake, l., Nu., Can.	C11	106
Edelény, Hung.	A7	26
Eden, Austl.	K7	76
Eden, Ms., U.S.	D8	122
Eden, N.C., U.S.	H6	114
Eden, Wy., U.S.	A7	132
Eden, stm., Eng., U.K.	G10	12
Edendale, S. Afr.	F10	70
Eden Valley, Mn., U.S.	F4	118
Edenville, S. Afr.	E8	70
Eder, stm., Ger.	E4	16
Édessa, Grc.	C4	28
Edfu, Egypt	C6	62
Edgar, Ne., U.S.	G14	126
Edgar, Wi., U.S.	G8	118
Edgard, La., U.S.	H8	122
Edgartown, Ma., U.S.	C15	114
Edgeley, N.D., U.S.	A14	126
Edgell Island, i., Grnld.	E13	141
Edgemont, S.D., U.S.	D9	126
Edgeøya, i., Nor.	B30	141
Edgeroi, Austl.	H7	76
Edgerton, Ab., Can.	B3	124
Edgerton, Mn., U.S.	H2	118
Edgerton, Oh., U.S.	C1	114
Edgerton, Wi., U.S.	B8	120
Edgewater, Fl., U.S.	H5	116
Edgewood, Ia., U.S.	B6	120
Edgewood, Il., U.S.	F9	120
Edgewood, Md., U.S.	E9	114
Edgewood, Tx., U.S.	E3	122
Edina, Mn., U.S.	G5	118
Edina, Mo., U.S.	D5	120
Edinburg, Il., U.S.	E8	120
Edinburg, In., U.S.	E11	120
Edinburg, Ms., U.S.	E9	122
Edinburg, Tx., U.S.	H9	130
Edinburg, Va., U.S.	F7	114
Edinburgh, Scot., U.K.	F9	12
Edincik, Tur.	C10	28
Edineţ, Mol.	A14	26
Edirne, Tur.	B9	28
Edirne, state, Tur.	B9	28
Edison, Ga., U.S.	F14	122
Edisto, stm., S.C., U.S.	D5	116
Edisto, North Fork, stm., S.C., U.S.	C4	116
Edisto Island, i., S.C., U.S.	D5	116
Edith, Mount, mtn., Mt., U.S.	D15	136
Edith Cavell, Mount, mtn., Ab., Can.	D12	138
Edjeleh, Alg.	D6	64
Edmond, Ok., U.S.	F11	128
Edmonds, Wa., U.S.	C4	136
Edmonton, Austl.	A5	76
Edmonton, Ab., Can.	C17	138
Edmonton, Ky., U.S.	G12	120
Edmore, N.D., U.S.	F15	124
Edmundston, N.B., Can.	C8	110
Edna, Ks., U.S.	G2	120
Edna, Tx., U.S.	E11	130
Edremit, Tur.	D10	28
Edremit Körfezi, b., Tur.	D9	28
Edrovo, Russia	C16	10
Edson, Ab., Can.	C14	138
Eduardo Castex, Arg.	G5	92
Eduni, Mount, mtn., N.T., Can.	C5	106
Edward, stm., Austl.	J5	76
Edward, Lake, l., Afr.	E5	66
Edward Island, i., On., Can.	C10	118
Edwards, Ms., U.S.	E8	122
Edwards Air Force Base, Ca., U.S.	I8	134
Edwards Plateau, plat., Tx., U.S.	D7	130
Edwardsville, Il., U.S.	F8	120
Edward VII Peninsula, pen., Ant.	C25	81
Eek, Ak., U.S.	D7	140
Eeklo, Bel.	C12	14
Eel, stm., Ca., U.S.	D2	134
Eel, stm., In., U.S.	E10	120
Eel, stm., In., U.S.	G4	112
Eems (Ems), stm., Eur.	A16	14
Éfaté, state, Vanuatu	k17	79d
Éfaté, i., Vanuatu	k17	79d
Eferding, Aus.	B10	22
Efes (Ephesus), sci., Tur.	F10	28
Effigy Mounds National Monument, p.o.i., Ia., U.S.	A6	120
Effingham, Il., U.S.	E9	120
Effingham, Ks., U.S.	E2	120
Eflâni, Tur.	B15	28
Eforie Nord, Rom.	E15	26
Eforie Sud, Rom.	F15	26
Efremov, Russia	G20	10
Eg, stm., Mong.	F9	34
Egadi, Isole, is., Italy	G5	24
Egaña, Arg.	H8	92
Egan Range, mts., Nv., U.S.	D2	132
Egedesminde (Aasiaat), Grnld.	D15	141
Egegik, Ak., U.S.	E8	140
Eger, Hung.	B7	26
Egersund, Nor.	G1	8
Eggenfelden, Ger.	H8	16
Egg Harbor City, N.J., U.S.	E11	114
Égletons, Fr.	D7	18
Egmont, Cape, c., N.Z.	D5	80
Egmont, Mount see Taranaki, Mount, vol., N.Z.	D6	80
Egmont Bay, b., P.E., Can.	D12	110
Egmont National Park, p.o.i., N.Z.	D5	80
Egorevsk, Russia	E22	10
Egremont, Ab., Can.	B17	138
Eğridir, Tur.	F13	28
Eğridir Gölü, l., Tur.	E13	28
Éguas, stm., Braz.	G3	88
Egvekinot, Russia	C25	34
Egypt, ctry., Afr.	B5	62
Eha-Amufu, Nig.	H6	64
Ehime, state, Japan	F5	40
Ehingen, Ger.	H5	16
Ehrhardt, S.C., U.S.	C4	116
Eibar, Spain	A8	20
Eibiswald, Aus.	D12	22
Eichstätt, Ger.	H7	16
Eidsvold, Austl.	E8	76
Eifel, mts., Ger.	F2	16
Eigg, i., Scot., U.K.	E6	12
Eight Degree Channel, strt., Asia	h12	46a
Eights Coast, cst., Ant.	C31	81
Eighty Mile Beach, cst., Austl.	C4	74
Eildon, Austl.	K5	76
Eildon, Lake, res., Austl.	K5	76
Eilenburg, Ger.	E8	16
Eiler Rasmussen, Kap, c., Grnld.	A21	141
Einasleigh, Austl.	B5	76
Einasleigh, stm., Austl.	A4	76
Einbeck, Ger.	E5	16
Eindhoven, Neth.	C14	14
Einme, Mya.	D2	48
Eirunepé, Braz.	E4	84
Eiseb, stm., Afr.	B4	70
Eisenach, Ger.	E6	16
Eisenberg, Ger.	F7	16
Eisenerz, Aus.	C11	22
Eisenhüttenstadt, Ger.	D10	16
Eisenstadt, Aus.	C13	22
Eisfeld, Ger.	F6	16
Eišiškės, Lith.	F7	10
Eislingen, Ger.	H5	16
Eitorf, Ger.	F3	16
Eivissa (Iviza), Spain	F12	20
Eivissa (Ibiza), i., Spain	F12	20
Ejea de los Caballeros, Spain	B9	20
Ejeda, Madag.	E7	68
Ejido Jaboncillos, Mex.	A7	100
Ejin Horo Qi, China	B3	42
Ejin Qi, China	C5	36
Ejsk, Russia	E5	32
Ejura, Ghana	H4	64
Ejutla de Crespo, Mex.	G10	100
Ekaterinburg, Russia	C10	32
Ekaterinino, Russia	E16	10
Ekateriny, proliv, strt., Russia	B17	38
Ekenäs *see* Tammisaari, Fin.	G10	8
Ekibastuz, Kaz.	D13	32
Ekimčan, Russia	F15	34
Ekonda, Russia	C10	34
Ekwan, stm., On., Can.	E14	106
Ela, Mya.	C3	48
El Aaiún (Laayoune), W. Sah.	D2	64
El 'Açâba, plat., Maur.	F2	64
El Affroun, Alg.	H13	20
El Agreb, Alg.	C6	64
El Ahijadero, Cerro, mtn., Mex.	E1	130
Elaine, Ar., U.S.	C8	122
El-'Aiyât, Egypt	I2	58
El-Alamein, Egypt	A5	62
El Álamo, Mex.	G7	130
El Álamo, Mex.	L9	134
El Álamo, Mex.	H8	130
El Alto, Arg.	D5	92
Elan', Russia	D6	32
Elancy, Russia	F10	34
El Ángel, Ec.	G2	86
El-Arish, Egypt	G4	58
Elat, Isr.	I5	58
Elat, Gulf of see Aqaba, Gulf of, b.	J5	58
El Ávila, Parque Nacional, p.o.i., Ven.	B8	86
Elazığ, Tur.	B4	56
Elba, Isola d', i., Italy	H7	22
El-Badâri, Egypt	K2	58
El-Bahnasa, Egypt	J1	58
El-Balyana, Egypt	B6	62
El'ban, Russia	F16	34
El Banco, Col.	C4	86
El Barco de Ávila, Spain	D5	20
Elbasan, Alb.	C13	24
Elbasani *see* Elbasan, Alb.	C13	24
El Baúl, Ven.	C7	86
El Baúl, Cerro, mtn., Mex.	G11	100
Elbe (Labe), stm., Eur.	C5	16
Elbe-Havel-Kanal, can., Ger.	D8	16
Elbert, Co., U.S.	B4	128
Elbert, Mount, mtn., Co., U.S.	D10	132
Elberta, Mi., U.S.	D3	112
Elberton, Ga., U.S.	B3	116
Elbeuf, Fr.	E10	14
Elbeyli, Tur.	B8	58
El Beyyadh, Alg.	C5	64
Elbląg, Pol.	B15	16
Elbląg, state, Pol.	B15	16
El Bluff, Nic.	G6	102
El Bonillo, Spain	F8	20
El Boulaïda, Alg.	B5	64
Elbow, stm., Ab., Can.	E16	138
Elbow Lake, Mn., U.S.	E3	118
El'brus, gora, mtn., Russia	F6	32
Elbrus, Mount see El'brus, gora, mtn., Russia	F6	32
El-Burg, Egypt	G1	58
El-Burgâya, Egypt	J1	58
Elburs see Alborz, Reshteh-ye Kūhhā-ye, mts., Iran	B7	56
Elburz Mountains see Alborz, Reshteh-ye Kūhhā-ye, mts., Iran	B7	56
El Cadilla, Embalse, res., Arg.	C5	92
El Cajon, Ca., U.S.	K9	134
El Calafate, Arg.	J2	90
El Callao, Ven.	D11	86
El Calvario, Ven.	C8	86
El Campamento, P.R.	B3	104a
El Campo, Tx., U.S.	H2	122
El Capitan, mtn., Mt., U.S.	D12	136
El Carmen, Arg.	B5	92
El Carmen, Col.	C5	86
El Carmen, stm., Mex.	F9	98
El Carmen de Bolívar, Col.	C4	86
El Carricito, Mex.	A7	100
El Carril, Arg.	B5	92
El Centinela, Mex.	K10	134
El Centro, Ca., U.S.	K10	134
El Cerrito, Col.	F3	86
El Cerro Del Aripo, mtn., Trin.	s12	105f
Elche *see* Elx, Spain	F10	20
El Chile, Montaña, mtn., Nic.	E4	102
Elcho, Wi., U.S.	F9	118
Elcho Island, i., Austl.	B7	74
El Cocuy, Col.	D5	86
El Colorado, Arg.	C8	92
El Cóndor, Cerro, vol., Arg.	C3	92
El Corazón, Ec.	H2	86
El Corpus, Hond.	F4	102
El Coto, P.R.	B2	104a
El'cy, Russia	D16	10
Elda, Spain	F10	20
El Desemboque, Mex.	G6	98
El Desemboque, Mex.	F6	98
El'dikan, Russia	D16	34
El-Dilingât, Egypt	H1	58
El Diviso, Col.	G2	86
El Djazaïr (Algiers), Alg.	B5	64
El Djelfa, Alg.	C5	64
Eldon, Ia., U.S.	D5	120
Eldora, Ia., U.S.	B4	120
Eldorado, Arg.	C10	92
Eldorado, Braz.	B13	92
El Dorado, Ar., U.S.	D6	122
Eldorado, Il., U.S.	G9	120
El Dorado, Ks., U.S.	D12	128
Eldorado, Ok., U.S.	G9	128
El Dorado, Ven.	D11	86
El Dorado Springs, Mo., U.S.	G3	120
Eldoret, Kenya	D7	66
Eldred, Pa., U.S.	C7	114
Eldridge, Ia., U.S.	C7	120
Eleanor, W.V., U.S.	F3	114
Elec, Russia	H21	10
Electric City, Wa., U.S.	C7	136
Elefantes (Olifants), stm., Afr.	D10	70
Elefsína, Grc.	E6	28
Eleftheroúpoli, Grc.	C7	28
Elektrostal', Russia	E21	10

Name	Map Ref.	Page
Elena, Blg.	G12	26
El Encanto, Col.	H5	86
Elephant Butte Reservoir, res., N.M., U.S.	J9	132
Elephant Mountain, mtn., Me., U.S.	F6	110
Elesbão Veloso, Braz.	D4	88
El Estor, Guat.	E3	102
Eleuthera, i., Bah.	B9	96
Eleva, Wi., U.S.	G7	118
Eleven Point, stm., U.S.	H6	120
El Fahs, Tun.	H3	24
El Faro, P.R.	C2	104a
El-Fashn, Egypt	J1	58
El-Fayoum, Egypt	I1	58
El Ferrol del Caudillo *see* Ferrol, Spain	A2	20
El-Fiqriya, Egypt	K1	58
Elfrida, Az., U.S.	L7	132
El Fuerte, Mex.	B4	100
El Galpón, Arg.	B5	92
Elgin, Scot., U.K.	D9	12
Elgin, Ia., U.S.	B6	120
Elgin, Il., U.S.	B9	120
Elgin, Mn., U.S.	G6	118
Elgin, N.D., U.S.	A11	126
Elgin, Ne., U.S.	F14	126
Elgin, Ok., U.S.	G10	128
Elgin, Or., U.S.	E8	136
El-Gindîya, Egypt	J1	58
El-Gîza (Giza), Egypt	H1	58
Elgon, Mount, mtn., Afr.	D6	66
El Grara, Alg.	C5	64
El Grove *see* O Grove, Spain	B2	20
El Guaje, Mex.	A7	100
El Guamo, Col.	B4	86
El Guapo, Ven.	B9	86
El Hachero, Cerro, mtn., Mex.	H2	130
El Ḥammâmi, reg., Maur.	E2	64
El-Ḥamûl, Egypt	G2	58
El Ḥank, clf., Afr.	E3	64
El-Hawâmdîya, Egypt	I2	58
Elhovo, Blg.	G13	26
El Huisache, Mex.	D8	100
Eliase, Indon.	G9	44
Elida, N.M., U.S.	H5	128
Elila, stm., D.R.C.	E5	66
Elim, Ak., U.S.	D7	140
Elisenvaara, Russia	F13	8
Eliseu Martins, Braz.	E4	88
El-Iskandarîya (Alexandria), Egypt	A6	62
Elista, Russia	E6	32
Elizabeth, Austl.	J2	76
Elizabeth, Co., U.S.	B4	128
Elizabeth, Il., U.S.	B7	120
Elizabeth, N.J., U.S.	D11	114
Elizabeth, W.V., U.S.	E4	114
Elizabeth City, N.C., U.S.	H9	114
Elizabethton, Tn., U.S.	H3	114
Elizabethtown, Il., U.S.	G9	120
Elizabethtown, Ky., U.S.	G11	120
Elizabethtown, N.Y., U.S.	F3	110
Elizabethtown, Pa., U.S.	D9	114
Elizavety, mys, c., Russia	F17	34
Elizovo, Russia	F20	34
El-Jadida, Mor.	C3	64
El Jaralito, Mex.	B6	100
El Jebel, Co., U.S.	D9	132
Ełk, Pol.	C18	16
Elk, stm., B.C., Can.	F16	138
Elk, stm., Ks., U.S.	D12	128
Elk, stm., W.V., U.S.	F4	114
Elk, stm., U.S.	C12	122
Elkader, Ia., U.S.	B6	120
Elk City, Ok., U.S.	F9	128
Elk Creek, Ca., U.S.	D3	134
Elk Creek, stm., S.D., U.S.	C10	126
El Kef, Tun.	H2	24
El-Kelaa-Srarhna, Mor.	C3	64
Ēl Kerē, Eth.	F8	62
Elk Grove, Ca., U.S.	E4	134
El-Khânka, Egypt	H2	58
El-Khārga, Egypt	B6	62
Elkhart, In., U.S.	G4	112
Elkhart, Ks., U.S.	D7	128
Elkhart, Tx., U.S.	F3	122
El Khnâchîch, clf., Mali	E4	64
Elkhorn, Mb., Can.	D12	124
Elk Horn, Ia., U.S.	C2	120
Elkhorn, Wi., U.S.	B9	120
Elkhorn, stm., Ne., U.S.	F16	126
Elkhorn City, Ky., U.S.	G3	114
Elkhorn Mountain, mtn., B.C., Can.	G4	138
Elkhovo *see* Elhovo, Blg.	G13	26
Elkins, W.V., U.S.	F6	114
Elk Island, i., Mb., Can.	D17	124
Elk Island National Park, p.o.i., Ab., Can.	C18	138
Elkland, Pa., U.S.	C8	114
Elk Mountain, mtn., Wy., U.S.	B10	132
Elko, B.C., Can.	G15	138
Elko, Nv., U.S.	C1	132
Elk Point, Ab., Can.	C19	138
Elk Point, S.D., U.S.	B1	120
Elk Rapids, Mi., U.S.	D4	112
Elk River, Mn., U.S.	F5	118
Elkton, Md., U.S.	E10	114
Elkton, Mi., U.S.	E6	112
Elkton, S.D., U.S.	G2	118
Elkton, Va., U.S.	F7	114
Ellaville, Ga., U.S.	D1	116
Ellef Ringnes Island, i., Nu., Can.	B5	141
Ellen, Mount, mtn., Ut., U.S.	E6	132
Ellendale, Mn., U.S.	H5	118
Ellendale, N.D., U.S.	A14	126
Ellensburg, Wa., U.S.	C6	136
Ellenton, Ga., U.S.	E2	116
Ellesmere, Lake, l., N.Z.	F5	80
Ellesmere Island, i., Nu., Can.	B9	141
Ellettsville, In., U.S.	E11	120
Ellice, stm., Nu., Can.	B10	106
Ellice Islands see Tuvalu, ctry., Oc.	D8	72
Ellicottville, N.Y., U.S.	B7	114
Ellijay, Ga., U.S.	B1	116
Ellinwood, Ks., U.S.	C10	128
Elliot, S. Afr.	G8	70
Elliot, Mount, mtn., Austl.	B6	76
Elliot Lake, On., Can.	B7	112
Elliot Lake, l., Mb., Can.	B18	124
Elliott, Ia., U.S.	C2	120
Elliott, Ms., U.S.	D9	122
Ellisras, S. Afr.	C8	70
Elliston, Austl.	F6	74
Elliston, Mt., U.S.	D14	136
Ellisville, Ms., U.S.	F9	122
Ellon, Scot., U.K.	D10	12
Ellora, India	H5	54
Ellora Caves, hist., India	A2	53
Elloree, S.C., U.S.	C5	116
Ellsworth, Ks., U.S.	C10	128
Ellsworth, Me., U.S.	F8	110
Ellsworth, Mi., U.S.	C4	112
Ellsworth, Mn., U.S.	H3	118
Ellsworth, Wi., U.S.	G6	118
Ellsworth Land, reg., Ant.	C32	81
Ellsworth Mountains, mts., Ant.	C32	81
El Lucero, Mex.	I4	130
Ellwangen, Ger.	H5	16
Ellwood City, Pa., U.S.	D5	114
Elm, stm., U.S.	B14	126
Elma, Wa., U.S.	D3	136
El-Mahalla el-Kubra, Egypt	H2	58
El-Maimûn, Egypt	I2	58
Elmalı, Tur.	G12	28
El Maneadero, Mex.	L9	134
El-Mansûra, Egypt	G2	58
El Manteco, Ven.	D10	86
El-Manzala, Egypt	G2	58
El-Matariya, Egypt	G3	58
Elm Creek, Mb., Can.	E16	124
Elm Creek, Ne., U.S.	G13	126
El Médano, Mex.	C3	100
El Menia, Alg.	C5	64
Elmer, N.J., U.S.	E10	114
Elmhurst, Il., U.S.	G2	112
El-Minya (Minya), Egypt	J1	58
Elmira, On., Can.	E9	112
Elmira, P.E., Can.	D14	110
Elmira, N.Y., U.S.	B9	114
El Moral, Mex.	F7	130
Elmore, Austl.	K5	76
Elmore, Mn., U.S.	H4	118
Elmore, Oh., U.S.	C2	114
Elmore City, Ok., U.S.	G11	128
El Morro, hist., P.R.	B3	104a
El Morro National Monument, p.o.i., N.M., U.S.	H8	132
El Mreyyé, reg., Maur.	F3	64
Elmshorn, Ger.	C5	16
Elm Springs, Ar., U.S.	H3	120
El Mulato, Mex.	E3	130
El-Mutî'a, Egypt	K2	58
Elmvale, On., Can.	D10	112
Elmwood, Il., U.S.	K8	118
Elmwood, Ne., U.S.	K2	118
El Negrito, Hond.	E4	102
Elnora, Ab., Can.	D17	138
Elnora, In., U.S.	F10	120
Eloguj, stm., Russia	B15	32
Eloise, Fl., U.S.	H4	116
Elora, On., Can.	E9	112
Elorza, Ven.	D7	86
El Otate, Cerro, mtn., Mex.	F1	130
Ëloten, Turkmen.	B9	56
Eloy, Az., U.S.	K5	132
Eloy Alfaro, Ec.	I2	86
El Palmar, Ven.	D10	86
El Palmar de los Sepúlveda, Mex.	C5	100
El Palmito, Mex.	I8	130
El Palqui, Chile	E2	92
El Pao, Ven.	C7	86
El Paso, Il., U.S.	D8	120
El Paso, Tx., U.S.	L10	132
El Paso de Robles *see* Paso Robles, Ca., U.S.	H5	134
El Paso Peaks, mtn., Ca., U.S.	H8	134
El Perú, Ven.	D11	86
Elphinstone, Mb., Can.	D13	124
El Piñón, Col.	B4	86
El Pintado, Arg.	B7	92
El Pital, Cerro, mtn., N.A.	E3	102
El Planchón, Volcán (Planchón, Cerro del), vol., S.A.	G2	92
El Polvorín, P.R.	B3	104a
El Portal, Ca., U.S.	F6	134
El Porvenir, Mex.	G3	130
El Porvenir, Mex.	K9	134
El Porvenir, Pan.	H8	102
El Potrero, Mex.	H7	130
El Potro, Cerro (Potro, Cerro del), mtn., S.A.	D3	92
El Prat de Llobregat, Spain	C12	20
El Progreso, Hond.	E4	102
El Puerto de Santa María, Spain	H4	20
El Puesto, Arg.	C4	92
El-Qâhira (Cairo), Egypt	H2	58
El-Qantara el-Sharqîya, Egypt	H3	58
El-Qasr, Egypt	B5	62
El Quebrachal, Arg.	B5	92
El Quelite, Mex.	D5	100
Elqui, stm., Chile	D2	92
El-Qûsîya, Egypt	K1	58
El Real de Santa María, Pan.	H9	102
El Remolino, Mex.	F6	130
El Reno, Ok., U.S.	F10	128
El Rio, Ca., U.S.	I6	134
El Roble, Mesa, mtn., Mex.	L10	134
Elroy, Wi., U.S.	H8	118
Elsa, Yk., Can.	C3	106
Elsa, Tx., U.S.	H9	130
El-Saff, Egypt	I2	58
El-Sa'îd (Upper Egypt), hist. reg., Egypt	J2	58
El Salado, Chile	C2	92
El Salado, Parque Nacional, p.o.i., Ec.	I1	86
El Salto, Mex.	D6	100
El Salvador, Chile	C3	92
El Salvador, ctry., N.A.	F3	102
El Samán de Apure, Ven.	D7	86
El Sauz, Mex.	A5	100
El Sauzal, Mex.	L9	134
Elsberry, Mo., U.S.	E7	120
El Seibo, Dom. Rep.	C13	102
Elsen Nur, l., China	D3	36
El-Simbillawein, Egypt	H2	58
Elsinore *see* Helsingør, Den.	H5	8
Elsinore, Ut., U.S.	E4	132
El Sombrero, Ven.	C8	86
Elsterwerda, Ger.	E9	16
El Sueco, Mex.	E1	130
El-Suweis (Suez), Egypt	I3	58
El Tajín, sci., Mex.	E10	100
El Tala, Arg.	C5	92
El Tanque, Mex.	H8	130
El Tecuán, Mex.	C5	100
El-Thamad, Egypt	I5	58
El Tigre, Ven.	C9	86
Eltmann, Ger.	G6	16
El Toco, Chile	D3	90
El Tocuyo, Ven.	C7	86
Elton, La., U.S.	G6	122
El Tránsito, Chile	D2	92
El Trébol, Arg.	F7	92
El Tule, Mex.	G1	130
El Tuparro, Parque Nacional, p.o.i., Col.	E7	86
El-Tûr, Egypt	J4	58
El Turbio, Arg.	J2	90
El-Uqsor (Luxor), Egypt	B6	62
Elūru, India	C5	53
El Valle, Pan.	H7	102
Elvas, Port.	F3	20
El Vendrell, Spain	C12	20
Elverum, Nor.	F4	8
El Viejo, Nic.	F4	102
El Vigía, Ven.	C6	86
El Vínculo, Ven.	p20	104g
Elvira, Arg.	G8	92
El Volcán, Chile	F2	92
El Wad, Alg.	C6	64
El-Wâsta, Egypt	I2	58
Elwell, Lake, res., Mt., U.S.	B15	136
Elwood, In., U.S.	H4	112
Elwood, Ne., U.S.	G13	126
Elx, Spain	F10	20
Ely, Eng., U.K.	I13	12
Ely, Mn., U.S.	D7	118
Ely, Nv., U.S.	D2	132
El Yagual, Ven.	D7	86
Elyria, Oh., U.S.	C3	114
El Yunque, mtn., P.R.	B4	104a
El-Zarqa, Egypt	G2	58
Émaé, i., Vanuatu	k17	79d
Emajõgi, stm., Est.	B9	10
Emāmshahr, Iran	B8	56
Emba see Embi, stm., Kaz.	E9	32
Embarras, stm., Il., U.S.	F10	120
Embarrass, Wi., U.S.	G10	118
Embi, Kaz.	E9	32
Embi, stm., Kaz.	E9	32
Emborcação, Represa da, res., Braz.	J2	88
Embreeville, Tn., U.S.	H3	114
Embrun, Fr.	E12	18
Embu, Kenya	E7	66
Emca, stm., Russia	E19	8
Emden, Ger.	C3	16
Emden, Il., U.S.	K9	118
Emelle, Al., U.S.	E10	122
Emerado, N.D., U.S.	G16	124
Emerald, Austl.	D6	76
Emerson, Mb., Can.	E16	124
Emerson, Ar., U.S.	D5	122
Emerson, Ia., U.S.	C2	120
Emery, S.D., U.S.	D15	126
Emery, Ut., U.S.	E5	132
Emet, Tur.	D12	28
Emiliano Zapata, Mex.	G13	100
Emilia-Romagna, state, Italy	F8	22
Emin, China	B1	36
Emine, nos, c., Blg.	G14	26
Eminence, Mo., U.S.	G6	120
Emirdağ, Tur.	D14	28
Emır Dağları, mts., Tur.	E14	28
Emita, Austl.	m13	77a
Emlembe, mtn., Afr.	D10	70
Emlenton, Pa., U.S.	G10	112
Emmaste, Est.	B5	10
Emmaus, Pa., U.S.	D10	114
Emmaville, Austl.	G8	76
Emmen, Neth.	B15	14
Emmendingen, Ger.	H3	16
Emmerich, Ger.	E2	16
Emmet, Ar., U.S.	D5	122
Emmetsburg, Ia., U.S.	A3	120
Emmiganūru, India	D3	53
Emmitsburg, Md., U.S.	E8	114
Emmonak, Ak., U.S.	D7	140
Emo, On., Can.	C5	118
Emory Peak, mtn., Tx., U.S.	E4	130
Empalme, Mex.	A3	100
Empangeni, S. Afr.	F10	70
Empedrado, Arg.	C8	92
Emperor Seamounts, unds.	E19	142
Empire, La., U.S.	H9	122
Empire, Nv., U.S.	C6	134
Empoli, Italy	G7	22
Emporia, Ks., U.S.	F1	120
Emporia, Va., U.S.	H8	114
Emporium, Pa., U.S.	C7	114
Empty Quarter see Ar-Rub' al-Khālī, des., Asia	E6	56
Ems, stm., Eur.	C3	16
Emsdetten, Ger.	D3	16
Emu, China	C8	38
Emu Park, Austl.	D8	76
Enarotali, Indon.	F10	44
Enašimskij Polkan, gora, mtn., Russia	C16	32
Encampment, Wy., U.S.	B10	132
Encantado, Braz.	D11	92
Encarnación, Para.	C9	92
Enchi, Ghana	H4	64
Enchilayas, Mex.	F6	98
Encinal, Tx., U.S.	F8	130
Encinitas, Ca., U.S.	J8	134
Encino, N.M., U.S.	G3	128
Encontrados, Ven.	C5	86
Encounter Bay, b., Austl.	J2	76
Encruzilhada, Braz.	H5	88
Encruzilhada do Sul, Braz.	E11	92
Encs, Hung.	A8	26
Endako, B.C., Can.	B5	138
Ende, Indon.	G7	44
Endeavor, Wi., U.S.	H9	118
Endeavour Strait, strt., Austl.	B8	74
Enderby, B.C., Can.	F11	138
Enderby Land, reg., Ant.	B10	81
Enderlin, N.D., U.S.	A15	126
Endicott, N.Y., U.S.	B9	114
Endicott, Wa., U.S.	D9	136
Endicott Mountains, mts., Ak., U.S.	C9	140
Ene, stm., Peru	F3	84
Enewetak, at., Marsh. Is.	B7	72
Enez, Tur.	C9	28
Enfield, N.C., U.S.	H8	114
Engaño, Cabo, c., Dom. Rep.	C13	102
Engcobo, S. Afr.	G9	70
Engelhard, N.C., U.S.	A10	116
Engel's, Russia	D7	32
Engen, B.C., Can.	B6	138
Engenheiro Navarro, Braz.	I3	88
Enggano, Pulau, i., Indon.	F2	50
England, state, U.K.	I12	12
Englefield, Cape, c., Nu., Can.	B13	106
Englehart, On., Can.	F15	106
Englewood, B.C., Can.	F3	138
Englewood, Co., U.S.	B4	128
Englewood, Fl., U.S.	J3	116
Englewood, Ks., U.S.	D8	128
Englewood, Tn., U.S.	A1	116
English, stm., On., Can.	A4	118
English Channel, strt., Eur.	D7	14
English Coast, cst., Ant.	C33	81
Engure, Lat.	C6	10
Engures ezers, l., Lat.	C6	10
Enid, Ok., U.S.	E11	128
Enid Lake, res., Ms., U.S.	C9	122
Enisej, stm., Russia	C6	34
Enisejsk, Russia	C16	32
Enisejskij krjaž, mts., Russia	C16	32
Enisejskij zaliv, b., Russia	B5	34
Eniwetok see Enewetak, at., Marsh. Is.	B7	72
eNjesuthi, mtn., Afr.	F9	70
Enka, N.C., U.S.	A3	116
Enkhuizen, Neth.	B14	14
Enköping, Swe.	G7	8
Enmedio, Mex.	E4	130
Enmedio, Cerro de, mtn., Mex.	F8	100
Enna, Italy	G8	24
Ennadai Lake, l., Nu., Can.	C10	106
Ennedi, plat., Chad	D4	62
Ennis, Ire.	I3	12
Ennis, Mt., U.S.	E15	136
Ennis, Tx., U.S.	E2	122
Enniscorthy, Ire.	I6	12
Enniskillen, N. Ire., U.K.	G5	12
Enns, Aus.	B11	22
Enns, stm., Aus.	B11	22
Enon, Oh., U.S.	E2	114
Enontekiö, Fin.	B10	8
Enoree, stm., S.C., U.S.	B3	116
Enosburg Falls, Vt., U.S.	F4	110
Enping, China	J5	42
Enrekang, Indon.	E11	50
Enrique Urien, Arg.	C7	92
Enriquillo, Dom. Rep.	D12	102
Enriquillo, Lago, l., Dom. Rep.	C12	102
Enschede, Neth.	B15	14
Ensenada, Arg.	G9	92
Ensenada, Mex.	L9	134
Enshi, China	F3	42
Enshū-nada, s., Japan	E10	40
Entebbe, Ug.	D6	66
Enterprise, N.T., Can.	C7	106
Enterprise, Al., U.S.	F13	122
Enterprise, Ca., U.S.	D4	134
Enterprise, Ms., U.S.	E10	122
Enterprise, Or., U.S.	E9	136
Enterprise, Ut., U.S.	F3	132
Entrepeñas, Embalse de, res., Spain	D8	20
Entre Ríos, Bol.	D4	90
Entre Rios, Braz.	G7	88
Entre Ríos, state, Arg.	F8	92
Entrevaux, Fr.	F12	18
Entroncamento, Port.	E2	20
Entwistle, Ab., Can.	C16	138
Enugu, Nig.	H6	64
Enurmino, Russia	C26	34
Envalira, Port d', p., And.	B12	20
Envigado, Col.	D4	86
Envira, stm., Braz.	E3	84
Enyamba, D.R.C.	E5	66
Enyellé, Congo	D3	66
Eolia, Mo., U.S.	E6	120
Eolie, Isole (Lipari, Isole), is., Italy	F8	24
Epanomí, Grc.	C5	28
Epecuén, Lago, l., Arg.	H6	92
Épernay, Fr.	E12	14
Epes, Al., U.S.	E10	122
Ephesus see Efes, sci., Tur.	F10	28
Ephraim, Ut., U.S.	D5	132
Ephrata, Pa., U.S.	D9	114
Ephrata, Wa., U.S.	C7	136
Épi, state, Vanuatu	k17	79d
Épi, i., Vanuatu	k17	79d
Epídavros, sci., Grc.	F6	28
Épila, Spain	C9	20
Épinal, Fr.	F15	14
Epirus see Ípeiros, hist. reg., Grc.	D3	28
Epsom, Eng., U.K.	J12	12
Epukiro, Nmb.	B4	70
Epukiro, stm., Nmb.	B4	70
Eqlīd, Iran	C7	56
Equatorial Guinea, ctry., Afr.	I6	64
Erap, Pap. N. Gui.	b4	79a
Erath, La., U.S.	H6	122
Erave, Pap. N. Gui.	b3	79a
Erawan National Park, p.o.i., Thai.	E4	48
Erbach, Ger.	G5	16
Erbogačon, Russia	B19	32
Ercevo, Russia	F18	8
Ercolano, Italy	D8	24
Érd, Hung.	B5	26
Erdao, stm., China	C8	38
Erdaohezi, China	B8	38
Erdek, Tur.	C10	28
Erdemli, Tur.	B5	58
Erding, Ger.	H7	16
Erebato, stm., Ven.	E9	86
Erebus, Mount, mtn., Ant.	C21	81
Erechim, Braz.	C11	92
Ereğli, Tur.	A4	58
Ereğli, Tur.	B14	28
Erenhot, China	C7	36
Erepecuru, Lago do, l., Braz.	D6	84
Ereymentaū, Kaz.	D12	32
Erfoud, Mor.	C4	64
Erft, stm., Ger.	E2	16
Erfurt, Ger.	F7	16
Ergene, stm., Tur.	B10	28
Ergeni, hills, Russia	E6	32
Ērgļi, Lat.	D8	10
Ergun Youqi, China	A9	36
Ergun Zuoqi, China	F13	34
Er Hai, l., China	F5	36
Erice, Italy	F6	24
Ericeira, Port.	F1	20
Erichsen Lake, l., Nu., Can.	A14	106
Erick, Ok., U.S.	F9	128
Erickson, Mb., Can.	D14	124
Ericson, Ne., U.S.	F14	126
Erie, Co., U.S.	A3	128
Erie, Il., U.S.	C7	120
Erie, Pa., U.S.	B5	114
Erie, Lake, l., N.A.	B4	114
Erie Canal see New York State Barge Canal, can., N.Y., U.S.	E12	112
Eriksdale, Mb., Can.	D15	124
Erimo-misaki, c., Japan	D15	38
Erin, On., Can.	E9	112
Erin, Tn., U.S.	H10	120
Eriskay, i., Scot., U.K.	D5	12
Eritrea, ctry., Afr.	D7	62
Erivan *see* Yerevan, Arm.	A5	56
Erkelenz, Ger.	E2	16
Erkner, Ger.	D9	16
Erlangen, Ger.	G7	16
Ermelo, S. Afr.	E10	70
Ermenek, Tur.	B3	58
Ermenek, stm., Tur.	B3	58
Ermica, Russia	C25	8
Ermolaevo, Russia	D9	32
Ermolino, Russia	E19	10
Ermoúpoli, Grc.	F7	28
Erne, Lower Lough, l., N. Ire., U.K.	G4	12
Erne, Upper Lough, l., Eur.	G5	12
Ernée, Fr.	F8	14
Erode, India	F3	53
Erofej Pavlovič, Russia	F13	34
Eromanga, Austl.	F4	76
Erongo, state, Nmb.	C2	70
Erongo, mtn., Nmb.	B2	70
Eropol, Russia	C22	34
Erota, Erit.	D7	62
Er-Rachidia, Mor.	C4	64
Errego, Moz.	D6	68
Errigal Mountain, mtn., Ire.	F4	12
Errinundra National Park, p.o.i., Austl.	K7	76
Erris Head, c., Ire.	G2	12
Errol Heights, Or., U.S.	E4	136
Erromango, i., Vanuatu	l17	79d
Erši, Russia	F17	10
Eršov, Russia	D7	32
Erstein, Fr.	F16	14
Ertai, China	B3	36
Ertis, Kaz.	D12	32
Ertis see Irtysh, stm., Asia	D13	32
Ertix see Irtysh, stm., Asia	E15	32
Ertoma, Russia	E22	8
Erval, Braz.	F11	92
Ervy-le-Châtel, Fr.	F12	14
Erwin, N.C., U.S.	A7	116
Erwin, Tn., U.S.	H3	114
Erwood, Sk., Can.	B11	124
Erýmanthos, mtn., Grc.	F4	28
Eryuan, China	F4	36
Erzhan, China	B8	38
Erzin, Russia	D17	32
Erzincan, Tur.	B4	56
Erzurum, Tur.	B5	56
Esa'ala, Pap. N. Gui.	b5	79a
Esashi, Japan	D13	38
Esbjerg, Den.	I3	8
Esbo *see* Espoo, Fin.	F11	8
Escada, Braz.	E8	88
Escalante, stm., Ut., U.S.	F6	132
Escalante, stm., Ven.	C5	86
Escalón, Mex.	B6	100
Escalon, Ca., U.S.	F5	134
Escambia, stm., Fl., U.S.	G11	122
Escanaba, Mi., U.S.	C2	112
Escanaba, stm., Mi., U.S.	B2	112
Escandón, Puerto, p., Spain	D10	20
Escárcega, Mex.	C2	102
Escarpada Point, c., Phil.	A4	52
Escatawpa, stm., U.S.	G10	122
Esch-sur-Alzette, Lux.	E15	14
Escobedo, Mex.	G6	130
Escocesa, Bahía, b., Dom. Rep.	C13	102
Escondido, Ca., U.S.	J8	134
Escondido, stm., Mex.	F7	130
Escondido, stm., Nic.	F6	102
Escuinapa de Hidalgo, Mex.	D5	100
Escuintla, Guat.	E2	102
Escuintla, Mex.	H12	100
Eséka, Cam.	D2	66
Eşen, Tur.	G12	28
Eşfahān, Iran	C7	56
Esgueva, stm., Spain	C6	20
Eshkāshem, Afg.	B11	56
Eshowe, S. Afr.	F10	70
Esil, Kaz.	D11	32
Esil see Ishim, stm., Asia	D11	32
Esk, Austl.	F9	76
Ëškar-Ola, Russia	C7	32
Eskdale, W.V., U.S.	F4	114
Es'ki, Russia	C19	10
Eskilstrup, Den.	B7	16
Eskilstuna, Swe.	G7	8
Eskimo Lakes, l., N.T., Can.	B4	106
Eskimo Point *see* Arviat, Nu., Can.	C12	106
Eskişehir, Tur.	D13	28
Eskişehir, state, Tur.	D13	28
Eskridge, Ks., U.S.	F1	120
Esla, stm., Spain	C5	20
Eslāmābād, Iran	C6	56
Eşme, Tur.	E11	28
Esmeralda, Austl.	B4	76
Esmeralda, Cuba	B8	102
Esmeralda, Isla, i., Chile	I1	90
Esmeraldas, Ec.	G2	86
Esmeraldas, state, Ec.	G2	86
Esmeraldas, stm., Ec.	G2	86
Esnagami Lake, l., On., Can.	A11	118
Espada, Punta, c., Col.	A6	86
Espalion, Fr.	E8	18
Espanola, On., Can.	B8	112
Espanola, N.M., U.S.	F2	128
Espejo, Spain	G6	20
Espelkamp, Ger.	D4	16
Espera Feliz, Braz.	K5	88
Esperança, Braz.	D7	88
Esperança, Braz.	D4	84
Esperance, Austl.	F4	74
Esperantina, Braz.	B4	88
Esperanza, Arg.	E7	92
Esperanza, Mex.	B4	100
Esperanza, P.R.	B5	104a
Esperanza, sci., Ant.	B35	81
Espichel, Cabo, c., Port.	F1	20
Espinal, Col.	E4	86
Espinazo, Mex.	H6	130
Espinhaço, Serra do, mts., Braz.	I4	88
Espinho, Port.	D2	20
Espinillo, Arg.	B8	92
Espino, Ven.	C9	86
Espinosa, Braz.	H4	88
Espírito Santo, state, Braz.	J5	88
Espiritu Santo, i., Vanuatu	j16	79d
Espíritu Santo, Isla del, i., Mex.	C3	100
Espita, Mex.	B3	102
Esplanada, Braz.	F7	88
Espoo, Fin.	F11	8
Espungabera, Moz.	B11	70
Esquel, Arg.	H2	90
Esquimalt, B.C., Can.	H7	138
Esquina, Arg.	D8	92
Esquiú, Arg.	D5	92
Essaouira, Mor.	C3	64
Essej, Russia	C9	34
Essen, Ger.	E3	16
Essendon, Mount, mtn., Austl.	D3	74
Essequibo, stm., Guy.	C6	84
Es Sers, Tun.	H2	24
Essex, On., Can.	F7	112
Essex, Md., U.S.	E9	114
Essex, Mt., U.S.	B13	136
Essex Junction, Vt., U.S.	F3	110
Essexville, Mi., U.S.	E6	112
Esslingen am Neckar, Ger.	H5	16
Essonne, state, Fr.	F11	14
Est, Pointe de l', c., Qc., Can.	A15	110
Estacada, Or., U.S.	E4	136
Estaca de Bares, Punta da, c., Spain	A3	20
Estaca de Bares, Punta de la see Estaca de Bares, Punta da, c., Spain	A3	20
Estacado, Llano, pl., U.S.	H6	128
Estación Adolfo Rodriguez Sáa *see* Santa Rosa del Conlara, Arg.	F5	92
Estación Colonia Alvear Norte *see* General Alvear, Arg.	G3	92
Estación Foguista J. F. Juárez *see* El Galpón, Arg.	B5	92
Estación Gobernador Vera *see* Vera, Arg.	D7	92
Estación J. J. Castelli *see* Castelli, Arg.	B7	92
Estación Justino Solari *see* Mariano I. Loza, Arg.	D8	92
Estación Manuel F. Mantilla *see* Pedro R. Fernández, Arg.	D8	92
Estación Vela *see* María Ignacia, Arg.	H8	92
Estados, Isla de los, i., Arg.	J4	90
Eşţahbān, Iran	D7	56
Estância, Braz.	F7	88
Estancia, N.M., U.S.	G2	128
Estanislao del Campo, Arg.	B7	92
Estarreja, Port.	D2	20
Estats, Pic d' (Estats, Pique d'), mtn., Eur.	G7	18
Estats, Pico de see Estats, Pic d', mtn., Eur.	G7	18
Estats, Pique d' (Estats, Pic d'), mtn., Eur.	G7	18
Estcourt, S. Afr.	F9	70
Este, Italy	E8	22
Esteio, Braz.	D12	92
Estelí, Nic.	F4	102
Estella, Spain	B8	20
Estelline, S.D., U.S.	G2	118
Estelline, Tx., U.S.	G8	128
Estepa, Spain	G6	20
Estepona, Spain	H5	20
Estes Park, Co., U.S.	G7	126
Este Sudeste, Cayos del, is., Col.	F7	102
Estevan, Sk., Can.	E10	124
Estevan Point, B.C., Can.	G4	138
Estherville, Ia., U.S.	H4	118
Estill, S.C., U.S.	D4	116
Estiva, stm., Braz.	G3	88
Eston, Sk., Can.	C5	124
Estonia, ctry., Eur.	G11	8
Estrela, Braz.	D11	92
Estrela, mtn., Port.	D3	20
Estrela do Sul, Braz.	J2	88
Estremadura, hist. reg., Port.	E1	20
Estremoz, Port.	F3	20
Estrondo, Serra do, plat., Braz.	E1	88
Esztergom, Hung.	B5	26
Etadunna, Austl.	G2	76
Etah, Grnld.	B11	141
Etah, India	E7	54
Étain, Fr.	E14	14
Étampes, Fr.	F11	14
Etamunbanie, Lake, l., Austl.	F2	76
Étaples, Fr.	D10	14
Etāwah, India	E7	54
Etchojoa, Mex.	B4	100
Etelä-Suomi, state, Fin.	F12	8
Ethan, S.D., U.S.	D14	126
Ethel, Ms., U.S.	D9	122
Ethel, Mount, mtn., Co., U.S.	C10	132
Ethiopia, ctry., Afr.	F7	62
Ethiopian Plateau, plat., Eth.	E7	62
Ethridge, Mt., U.S.	B14	136
Ethridge, Tn., U.S.	B11	122
Etigo-heiya, pl., Japan	B12	40
Etive, Loch, l., Scot., U.K.	E7	12
E. T. Joshua Airport, St. Vin.	o11	105e
Etna, Ca., U.S.	B3	134
Etna, Monte, vol., Italy	G8	24
Etobicoke, ngh., On., Can.	E10	112
Etolin Island, i., Ak., U.S.	E13	140
Etolin Strait, strt., Ak., U.S.	D6	140
Etomami, stm., Sk., Can.	B11	124
Eton, Austl.	C7	76
Etorofu-tō (Iturup, ostrov), i., Russia	B17	38
Etosha Pan, pl., Nmb.	D2	68
Etoumbi, Congo	D2	66
Etowah, Tn., U.S.	B14	122
Etowah, stm., Ga., U.S.	C14	122
Étretat, Fr.	E9	14
Etsch see Adige, stm., Italy	E8	22
Et Tîdra, i., Maur.	F1	64
Ettlingen, Ger.	H4	16
Etzikom Coulee, stm., Ab., Can.	E2	124
Etzná, sci., Mex.	C2	102
Eu, Fr.	D10	14
Eua, i., Tonga	F9	72
Eua Iki, i., Tonga	n15	78e
Euboea see Évvoia, i., Grc.	E6	28
Euboea, Gulf of see Vóreios Evvoïkós, b., Grc.	E5	28
Eucla, Austl.	F5	74
Euclid, Oh., U.S.	C4	114
Euclides da Cunha, Braz.	F6	88
Eucumbene, Lake, res., Austl.	K7	76
Eudora, Ar., U.S.	D7	122
Eudora, Ks., U.S.	F2	120
Eufaula, Al., U.S.	F13	122
Eufaula Lake, res., Ok., U.S.	B3	122
Eugene, Or., U.S.	F3	136
Eugenia, Punta, c., Mex.	B1	100
Eugenio Bustos, Arg.	F3	92
Eugowra, Austl.	I7	76
Eumungerie, Austl.	H7	76
Eunápolis, Braz.	I6	88
Eungella National Park, p.o.i., Austl.	C7	76
Eunice, La., U.S.	G6	122
Eunice, N.M., U.S.	B4	130
Euphrates (Al-Furāt), stm., Asia	C6	56
Eupora, Ms., U.S.	D9	122
Eure, state, Fr.	E9	14
Eure, stm., Fr.	E10	14
Eure-et-Loir, state, Fr.	F10	14
Eureka, Can.	A8	141
Eureka, Ca., U.S.	C1	134
Eureka, Il., U.S.	K9	118
Eureka, Ks., U.S.	D12	128
Eureka, Mt., U.S.	B11	136
Eureka, Nv., U.S.	D10	134
Eureka, S.C., U.S.	B4	116
Eureka Springs, Ar., U.S.	H4	120
Eurinilla Creek, stm., Austl.	H3	76
Euroa, Austl.	K5	76
Europa, Île, i., Reu.	E7	68
Europa, Picos de, mts., Spain	A6	20
Europa Island see Europa, Île, i., Reu.	E7	68
Europa Point, c., Gib.	H5	20
Europe, cont.	C13	4
Euskal Herriko, state, Spain	A8	20
Euskirchen, Ger.	F2	16
Eustace, Tx., U.S.	E2	122
Eustis, Fl., U.S.	H4	116
Eustis, Lake, l., Fl., U.S.	H4	116
Euston, Austl.	J4	76
Eutaw, Al., U.S.	E11	122
Eutin, Ger.	B6	16
Eutsuk Lake, l., B.C., Can.	C4	138
Eva, Al., U.S.	C12	122
Evadale, Tx., U.S.	G4	122
Evandale, Austl.	n13	77a
Evans, Lac, l., Qc., Can.	E15	106
Evans, Mount, mtn., Co., U.S.	B3	128
Evansburg, Ab., Can.	C15	138
Evans City, Pa., U.S.	D5	114
Evansdale, Ia., U.S.	I6	118
Evans Strait, strt., Nu., Can.	C14	106
Evanston, Il., U.S.	F2	112
Evanston, Wy., U.S.	B6	132
Evansville, In., U.S.	F10	120
Evansville, Mn., U.S.	E3	118
Evansville, Wi., U.S.	B8	120
Evansville, Wy., U.S.	E6	126
Evart, Mi., U.S.	E4	112
Eveleth, Mn., U.S.	D6	118
Evening Shade, Ar., U.S.	H6	120
Evensk, Russia	D20	34
Everard, Lake, l., Austl.	F6	74
Everest, Mount (Qomolangma Feng), mtn., Asia	D11	54
Everett, Pa., U.S.	E7	114
Everett, Wa., U.S.	C4	136
Everett, Mount, mtn., Ma., U.S.	B12	114
Everglades, The, sw., Fl., U.S.	K4	116
Everglades City, Fl., U.S.	K4	116
Everglades National Park, p.o.i., Fl., U.S.	K5	116
Evergreen, Al., U.S.	F12	122
Evergreen, Mt., U.S.	B12	136
Evermann, Cerro, vol., Mex.	F3	100
Evesham, Sk., Can.	B4	124
Evesham, Eng., U.K.	I11	12
Évian-les-Bains, Fr.	C12	18
Evje, Nor.	G2	8
Évora, Port.	F3	20
Évora, state, Port.	F3	20
Evoron, ozero, l., Russia	F16	34
Évreux, Fr.	E10	14
Évry, Fr.	F11	14
E. V. Spence Reservoir, res., Tx., U.S.	C7	130
Évvoia, i., Grc.	E6	28
'Ewa, Hi., U.S.	b3	78a
Ewing, Ne., U.S.	E14	126
Ewing, Va., U.S.	H2	114
Ewo, Congo	E2	66
Exaltación, Bol.	B3	90
Excelsior Mountain, mtn., Ca., U.S.	E6	134
Excelsior Springs, Mo., U.S.	E3	120
Exeter, On., Can.	E8	112
Exeter, Eng., U.K.	K9	12
Exeter, Ca., U.S.	G6	134
Exeter, N.H., U.S.	G6	110
Exeter Sound, strt., Nu., Can.	D13	141
Exira, Ia., U.S.	C3	120
Exmoor, plat., Eng., U.K.	J9	12
Exmoor National Park, p.o.i., Eng., U.K.	J9	12
Exmore, Va., U.S.	G10	114
Exmouth, Austl.	D2	74
Exmouth, Eng., U.K.	K9	12
Exmouth Gulf, b., Austl.	D2	74
Exshaw, Ab., Can.	E15	138
Extremadura, state, Spain	E4	20
Exuma Cays, is., Bah.	C9	96
Exuma Sound, strt., Bah.	C9	96
Eyasi, Lake, l., Tan.	E6	66
Eyebrow, Sk., Can.	D7	124
Eyemouth, Scot., U.K.	F10	12
Eye Peninsula, pen., Scot., U.K.	C6	12
Eyjafjördur, b., Ice.	j30	8a
Eyl, Som.	C9	66
Eyl, val., Som.	C9	66
Eylar Mountain, mtn., Ca., U.S.	F4	134
Eyota, Mn., U.S.	H6	118
Eyrarbakki, Ice.	I29	8a
Eyre, Austl.	F5	74

Name	Map Ref.	Page
Eyre Creek, stm., Austl.	F2	76
Eyre North, Lake, l., Austl.	E7	74
Eyre Peninsula, pen., Austl.	F7	74
Eyre South, Lake, l., Austl.	E7	74
Ezequiel Ramos Mexía, Embalse, res., Arg.	G3	90
Ežerėlis, Lith.	F6	10
Ezine, Tur.	D9	28

F

Name	Map Ref.	Page
Faaone, Fr. Poly.	v22	78h
Faber Lake, l., N.T., Can.	C7	106
Fabriano, Italy	G9	22
Facatativá, Col.	E4	86
Fachi, Niger	F7	64
Facpi Point, c., Guam	j9	78c
Factoryville, Pa., U.S.	C10	114
Fada, Chad	D4	62
Fada-Ngourma, Burkina	G5	64
Faddeevskij, ostrov, i., Russia	A18	34
Faddeja, zaliv, b., Russia	A10	34
Fadiffolu Atoll, at., Mald.	h12	46a
Faenza, Italy	F8	22
Fafe, Port.	C2	20
Fagaras, Rom.	D11	26
Fagernes, Nor.	F3	8
Fagersta, Swe.	F6	8
Faguibine, Lac, l., Mali	F4	64
Fagurhólsmýri, Ice.	l31	8a
Fairbank, Ia., U.S.	B5	120
Fairbanks, Ak., U.S.	D10	140
Fairbanks, La., U.S.	E6	122
Fair Bluff, N.C., U.S.	B6	116
Fairborn, Oh., U.S.	E1	114
Fairbury, Il., U.S.	K10	118
Fairbury, Ne., U.S.	A11	128
Fairchance, Pa., U.S.	E6	114
Fairchild, Wi., U.S.	G8	118
Fairfax, Mn., U.S.	G4	118
Fairfax, Mo., U.S.	D2	120
Fairfax, S.C., U.S.	D4	116
Fairfax, S.D., U.S.	D14	126
Fairfax, Va., U.S.	F8	114
Fairfax, Vt., U.S.	F3	110
Fairfield, Al., U.S.	D11	122
Fairfield, Ca., U.S.	E3	134
Fairfield, Id., U.S.	G12	136
Fairfield, Il., U.S.	F9	120
Fairfield, Me., U.S.	F7	110
Fairfield, Ne., U.S.	G14	126
Fairfield, Oh., U.S.	E6	114
Fairfield, Tx., U.S.	F2	122
Fairgrove, Mi., U.S.	E6	112
Fairhaven, Ma., U.S.	C15	114
Fair Haven, N.Y., U.S.	E13	112
Fair Head, c., N. Ire., U.K.	F6	12
Fairhope, Al., U.S.	G11	122
Fair Isle, i., Scot., U.K.	B11	12
Fairland, In., U.S.	E12	120
Fairlie, N.Z.	G4	80
Fairmont, Mn., U.S.	H4	118
Fairmont, N.C., U.S.	B6	116
Fairmont, Ne., U.S.	G15	126
Fairmont, W.V., U.S.	E5	114
Fairmont Hot Springs, B.C., Can.	F14	138
Fairmount, Il., U.S.	H4	112
Fairmount, In., U.S.	H4	112
Fairmount, N.D., U.S.	E2	118
Fair Ness, c., Nu., Can.	C16	106
Fair Oaks, Ca., U.S.	E4	134
Fair Plain, Mi., U.S.	F3	112
Fairplay, Co., U.S.	B3	128
Fairview, Ga., U.S.	C13	122
Fairview, Il., U.S.	D7	120
Fairview, Mi., U.S.	D5	112
Fairview, Mt., U.S.	G9	124
Fairview, Tn., U.S.	I10	122
Fairview, Ut., U.S.	D5	132
Fairview Park, In., U.S.	I2	112
Fairview Peak, mtn., Nv., U.S.	D7	134
Fairweather Mountain, mtn., N.A.	D3	106
Faisalabad (Lyallpur), Pak.	C4	54
Faison, N.C., U.S.	A7	116
Faistós, sci., Grc.	H7	28
Faith, S.D., U.S.	B10	126
Faizābād, India	E9	54
Fajardo, P.R.	B4	104a
Fajou, Îlet à, i., Guad.	h5	105c
Fajr, Bi'r, well, Sau. Ar.	J8	58
Fajr, Wādī, stm., Sau. Ar.	H9	58
Fajr, Wādī, stm., Sau. Ar.	J8	58
Fakse Bugt, b., Den.	A8	10
Faku, China	C5	38
Falaba, S.L.	H2	64
Falaise, Fr.	F8	14
Falakáta, India	E12	54
Falam, Mya.	A1	48
Falcón, state, Ven.	B7	86
Falcón, Presa (Falcon Reservoir), res., N.A.	H8	130
Falcón Reservoir (Falcón, Presa), res., N.A.	H8	130
Falconara Marittima, Italy	G10	22
Faleleitai, Samoa	g11	79c
Falémé, stm., Afr.	G2	64
Fălești, Mol.	B14	26
Falfurrias, Tx., U.S.	G9	130
Falkenberg, Ger.	E9	16
Falkenberg, Swe.	H5	8
Falkensee, Ger.	D9	16
Falkenstein, Ger.	E8	16
Falkirk, Scot., U.K.	E9	12
Falkland, B.C., Can.	F11	138
Falkland Islands, dep., S.A.	J4	90
Falkland Sound, strt., Falk. Is.	J5	90
Falköping, Swe.	G5	8
Falkville, Al., U.S.	C11	122
Fall, stm., Ks., U.S.	D13	128
Fallbrook, Ca., U.S.	J8	134
Fallon, Nv., U.S.	D7	134
Fall River, Ks., U.S.	G1	120
Fall River, Ma., U.S.	C14	114
Fall River, Wi., U.S.	H9	118
Fall River Mills, Ca., U.S.	B4	134
Falls City, Ne., U.S.	D2	120
Falls City, Or., U.S.	F3	136
Falls Creek, Pa., U.S.	C10	102
Falls Lake, res., N.C., U.S.	I7	114
Falmouth, Jam.	i13	104d
Falmouth, Eng., U.K.	K7	12
Falmouth, Ma., U.S.	C15	114
Falmouth, Me., U.S.	G6	110
False Bay, S. Afr.	I4	70
False Divi Point, c., India	D5	53
False Pass, Ak., U.S.	F7	140
Falset, Spain	C11	20
Falso, Cabo, c., Dom. Rep.	D12	102
Falster, i., Den.	I4	8
Fălticeni, Rom.	B13	26
Falun, Swe.	F6	8
Famagusta see Gazimağusa, N. Cyp.	C4	58
Famaillá, Arg.	C5	92
Famatina, Sierra de, mts., Arg.	D4	92
Famenne, reg., Bel.	D14	14
Family Lake, l., Mb., Can.	B18	124
Fanchang, China.	F8	42
Fanch'eng see Xiangfan, China	F4	42
Fanchon, Pointe, c., Haiti	C10	102
Fancy, Thai.	o11	105e
Fandjiang, Sudan	F6	62
Fangcheng, China	E5	42
Fangxian, China	E4	42
Fangzheng, China	B10	36
Fanipal', Bela.	G10	10
Fanjiatun, China	C6	38
Fanny Bay, B.C., Can.	G6	138
Fano, Italy	G10	22
Fan Si Pan, mtn., Viet.	A6	48
Faraday, sci., Ant.	B34	81
Faradje, D.R.C.	D5	66
Farafangana, Madag.	E8	68
Farāh, Afg.	C9	56
Farāh, stm., Afg.	C9	56
Farallon de Pajaros, i., N. Mar. Is.	A5	72
Farallon Islands, is., Ca., U.S.	F2	134
Faranah, Gui.	G2	64
Farasān, Jazā'ir, is., Sau. Ar.	F5	56
Fareham, Eng., U.K.	K11	12
Farewell, Ak., U.S.	D9	140
Farewell, Cape, c., N.Z.	E5	80
Fargo, N.D., U.S.	E2	118
Faribault, Mn., U.S.	G5	118
Faribault, Lac, l., Qc., Can.	D16	106
Farīdābād, India	D6	54
Faridkot, India	C5	54
Farīdpur, Bngl.	G12	54
Farīdpur, India	D7	54
Farilhões, is., Port.	E1	20
Farim, Gui.-B.	G2	64
Farīmān, Iran	F9	120
Farinha, stm., Braz.	D2	88
Fārīskur, Egypt	G2	58
Farit, Amba, mtn., Eth.	E7	62
Farjestaden, Swe.	H7	8
Farley, Ia., U.S.	B7	120
Farmer City, Il., U.S.	D9	120
Farmersville, Il., U.S.	E8	120
Farmersville, Tx., U.S.	D2	122
Farmerville, La., U.S.	E6	122
Farmington, Il., U.S.	D7	120
Farmington, Me., U.S.	F6	110
Farmington, Mn., U.S.	G5	118
Farmington, Mo., U.S.	G7	120
Farmington, Mt., U.S.	C14	136
Farmington, N.H., U.S.	G5	110
Farmington, N.M., U.S.	G8	132
Farmington, Ut., U.S.	C5	132
Far Mountain, mtn., B.C., Can.	D5	138
Farmville, N.C., U.S.	A8	116
Farmville, Va., U.S.	G7	114
Farnborough, Eng., U.K.	J12	12
Farne Islands, is., Eng., U.K.	F11	12
Farnham, Qc., Can.	E3	110
Faro, Braz.	D6	84
Faro, Yk., Can.	C4	106
Faro, Port.	H3	20
Faro, state, Port.	G3	20
Faroe Islands, dep., Eur.	n34	8b
Fârôn, i., Swe.	H8	8
Farquhar, Atoll de, i., Sey.	I12	69b
Farquhar, Cape, c., Austl.	D2	74
Farragut, Ia., U.S.	D2	120
Farrars Creek, stm., Austl.	E3	76
Farrell, Pa., U.S.	C5	114
Farrukhābād, India	E7	54
Fārsala, Grc.	D5	28
Fársala, Grc.	D5	28
Fartak, Ra's, c., Yemen.	F7	56
Farvel, Kap, c., Grnld.	F17	141
Farwell, Mi., U.S.	E5	112
Fasà, Iran	D7	56
Fasano, Italy	D11	24
Fastnet Rock, r., Ire.	J3	12
Fatehābād, India	D5	54
Fatehjang, Pak.	B4	54
Fatehpur, India	F8	54
Fatehpur, India	E8	54
Fatehpur Sikri, India	E6	54
Fathom Five National Marine Park, p.o.i., On., Can.	C8	112
Fatick, Sen.	G1	64
Fátima, Port.	E2	20
Fatshan see Foshan, China	F5	42
Fatu Hiva, i., Fr. Poly.	E13	72
Fatumu, Tonga	n14	78e
Fatwā, India	F10	54
Fauabu, Sol. Is.	e9	79b
Faucilles, Monts de, mts., Fr.	F15	14
Faulkton, S.D., U.S.	B13	126
Fauquier, B.C., Can.	G12	138
Fâurei, Rom.	D14	26
Fauresmith, S. Afr.	F7	70
Faura Island, i., Sol. Is.	d6	79b
Fauske, Nor.	C6	8
Faust, Ab., Can.	A15	138
Fauva, Italy	G7	24
Fawcett Lake, l., Ab., Can.	A17	138
Fawn, stm., On., Can.	E13	106
Fawnie Nose, mtn., B.C., Can.	C5	138
Faxafló, b., Ice.	k28	8a
Faxinal do Soturno, Braz.	D11	92
Faya-Largeau, Chad	D3	62
Fayette, Al., U.S.	D11	122
Fayette, Ia., U.S.	B6	120
Fayette, lakes, res., Tx., U.S.	E3	122
Fayette, Ms., U.S.	F7	122
Fayetteville, Ar., U.S.	H3	120
Fayetteville, Ga., U.S.	D14	122
Fayetteville, N.C., U.S.	A7	116
Fayetteville, W.V., U.S.	F4	114
Fâyid, Egypt	H3	58
Fāzilka, India	C5	54
Fāzilpur, Pak.	D3	54
Fazzān, hist. reg., Libya	B2	62
Fderîk, Maur.	E2	64
Fear, Cape, c., N.C., U.S.	C8	116
Feather, stm., Ca., U.S.	D4	134
Feather, Middle Fork, stm., Ca., U.S.	D5	134
Feather, North Fork, East Branch, stm., Ca., U.S.	C5	134
Fécamp, Fr.	E9	14
Federación, Arg.	E8	92
Federal, Arg.	E8	92
Federally Administered Tribal Areas, state, Pak.	B2	54
Federal Republic of Germany see Germany, ctry., Eur.	E6	16
Federalsburg, Md., U.S.	F10	114
Federated States of Micronesia see Micronesia, Federated States of, ctry., Oc.	C6	72
Fehérgyarmat, Hung.	A9	26
Fehmarn, i., Ger.	B7	16
Feia, Lagoa, b., Braz.	L5	88
Fei Huang, stm., China	D8	42
Feijó, Braz.	E3	84
Feira de Santana, Braz.	G6	88
Feixi, China	F7	42
Feixian, China	D7	42
Fejér, state, Hung.	B5	26
Felanitx, Spain	E14	20
Felda, Fl., U.S.	J4	116
Feldbach, Aus.	D12	22
Feldberg, mtn., Ger.	I4	16
Feldkirch, Aus.	C6	22
Feldkirchen, Ger.	C6	22
Felício, P.R.	B1	104a
Feliciano, Arroyo, stm., Arg.	E8	92
Felipe Carrillo Puerto, Mex.	C4	102
Felix, Cape, c., Nu., Can.	B11	106
Felixlândia, Braz.	J3	88
Felixstowe, Eng., U.K.	I14	12
Felletin, Fr.	D8	18
Fellsmere, Fl., U.S.	I5	116
Feltre, Italy	D8	22
Femunden, l., Nor.	E4	8
Femundsmarka Nasjonalpark, p.o.i., Nor.	E4	8
Fen, stm., China.	D4	42
Fenelon Falls, On., Can.	D11	112
Fengcheng, China.	G6	42
Fengcheng, China.	B11	8
Fengcheng, China.	D6	38
Fengdu, China.	G2	42
Fengfeng, China.	C6	42
Fenggang, China.	G2	42
Fenghuang, China.	H3	42
Fengjiabao, China.	C1	42
Fengning, China.	A7	42
Fengqing, China.	G4	36
Fengqiu, China.	D6	42
Fengtai, China.	B7	42
Fengtai, China.	E7	42
Fengtien see Shenyang, China	D5	38
Fengxi, China	F3	42
Fengxian, China	D7	42
Fengxiang, China	D2	42
Fengyang, China	E7	42
Fengyüan, Tai.	I9	42
Fengzhen, China	A5	42
Feni, Bngl.	G13	54
Feodosiia, Ukr.	F5	32
Fer, Cap de, c., Alg.	B6	64
Ferdinand, In., U.S.	F10	120
Ferdows, Iran	C8	56
Ferentino, Italy	I10	22
Fergana, Uzb.	F12	32
Fergana Mountains see Ferganskij hrebet, mts., Kyrg.	F12	32
Ferganskij hrebet, mts., Kyrg.	F12	32
Fergus, On., Can.	E9	112
Fergus Falls, Mn., U.S.	E10	130
Ferguson, B.C., Can.	F13	138
Ferguson, Ky., U.S.	G13	120
Ferguson, Mo., U.S.	F7	120
Fergusson Island, i., Pap. N. Gui.	b5	79a
Ferkéssédougou, C. Iv.	H4	64
Ferlo, reg., Sen.	F2	64
Ferme-Neuve, Qc., Can.	B14	112
Fermo, Italy	G10	22
Fermont, Qc., Can.	E17	106
Fermoselle, Spain	C4	20
Fernández, Arg.	C6	92
Fernandina, Isla, i., Ec.	i11	84a
Fernandina Beach, Fl., U.S.	F4	116
Fernando de la Mora, Para.	B9	92
Fernando de Noronha, Ilha, i., Braz.	F11	82
Fernandópolis, Braz.	D6	90
Fernando Póo see Bioko, i., Eq. Gui.	I6	64
Fernán-Núñez, Spain	G6	20
Ferndale, Ca., U.S.	C1	134
Ferne, B.C., Can.	G15	138
Fernley, Nv., U.S.	D6	134
Fern Park, Fl., U.S.	H4	116
Fern Ridge Lake, res., Or., U.S.	F3	136
Fernwood, Id., U.S.	C10	136
Ferokh, India	F2	53
Ferrandina, Italy	D10	24
Ferrara, Italy	F8	22
Ferrato, Capo, c., Italy	E3	24
Ferreira Gomes, Braz.	C7	84
Ferrenafe, Peru	C6	118
Ferret, Cap, c., Fr.	E4	18
Ferrières, Fr.	F11	14
Ferris, Tx., U.S.	E2	122
Ferrol, Spain	A2	20
Ferrysburg, Mi., U.S.	E3	112
Ferto-tavi Nemzeti Park, p.o.i., Hung.	B3	26
Fès, Mor.	C3	64
Feshi, D.R.C.	F3	66
Fessenden, N.D., U.S.	G14	124
Fethiye, Tur.	F12	120
Fetisovo, Kaz.	F8	32
Fetlar, i., Scot., U.K.	n19	12a
Feucht, Ger.	G7	16
Feuchtwangen, Ger.	G6	16
Feuilles, stm., Qc., Can.	D16	106
Feuilles, Baie aux, b., Qc., Can.	D16	106
Feurs, Fr.	D10	18
Fevzipaşa, Tur.	B8	58
Fez see Fès, Mor.	C3	64
Fezzan see Fazzān, hist. reg., Libya	B2	62
Ffestiniog, Wales, U.K.	I9	12
Fianarantsoa, Madag.	E8	68
Fianga, Chad	F3	62
Fichê, Eth.	F7	62
Fichtelgebirge, mts., Eur.	F7	16
Ficksburg, S. Afr.	F8	70
Fidalgo, Wn., Braz.	E5	88
Fidenza, Italy	F7	22
Field, B.C., Can.	E14	138
Fier, Alb.	D13	24
Fieri see Fier, Alb.	D13	24
Fiery Creek, stm., Austl.	B2	76
Fierzës, Liqeni i, res., Alb.	B14	24
Fife Lake, Sk., Can.	E8	124
Fife Lake, Mi., U.S.	D4	112
Fife Lake, i., Sk., Can.	E8	124
Fife Ness, c., Scot., U.K.	E10	12
Fifield, Wi., U.S.	F8	118
Fifth Cataract see Khāmis, Ash-Shallāl al-, wtfl., Sudan.	D6	62
Figeac, Fr.	E8	18
Figtree, Zimb.	B9	70
Figueira da Foz, Port.	D1	20
Figueiras see Figueres, Spain	B13	20
Figueres, Spain	B13	20
Figuig, Mor.	C4	64
Fiji, ctry., Oc.	E8	72
Filabusi, Zimb.	B9	70
Filadelfia, Italy	F9	24
Filchner Ice Shelf, ice, Ant.	C1	81
Filey, Eng., U.K.	G12	12
Filiaşi, Rom.	E10	26
Filiátes, Grc.	D3	28
Filingué, Niger	G5	64
Filippoi, sci., Grc.	B7	28
Fillmore, Sk., Can.	E10	124
Fillmore, Ca., U.S.	I7	134
Fillmore, Ut., U.S.	E4	132
Filtu, Eth.	F8	62
Fimi, stm., D.R.C.	E3	66
Finale Emilia, Italy	F8	22
Finale Ligure, Italy	F5	22
Finca El Rey, Parque Nacional, p.o.i., Arg.	B5	92
Findlay, Oh., U.S.	C2	114
Findlay, Mount, mtn., B.C., Can.	F14	138
Fingôa, Moz.	D5	68
Finistère, state, Fr.	F5	14
Finisterre, Cabo de see Fisterra, Cabo de, c., Spain	A1	20
Finke, Austl.	E6	74
Finland, ctry., Eur.	C12	8
Finland, Gulf of, b., Eur.	G11	8
Finlay, stm., B.C., Can.	D5	106
Finley, Austl.	J5	76
Finley, N.D., U.S.	G16	124
Finmoore, B.C., Can.	C7	138
Finnegan, Ab., Can.	E18	138
Finnis, Cape, c., Austl.	F6	74
Finniss, state, Nor.	B11	8
Finnmark, state, Nor.	B11	8
Finnsnes, Nor.	B8	8
Finschhafen, Pap. N. Gui.	b4	79a
Finse, Nor.	F2	8
Finspång, Swe.	G6	8
Finsterwalde, Ger.	E9	16
Fiordland National Park, p.o.i., N.Z.	G2	80
Fiorenzuola d'Arda, Italy.	F6	22
Firat (Euphrates), stm., Asia	B4	56
Firebaugh, Ca., U.S.	G5	134
Firenze (Florence), Italy	G8	22
Firmat, Arg.	F7	92
Firminy, Fr.	D10	18
Firovo, Russia	C16	10
Firozābād, India	E7	54
Fīrozpūr, India	C5	54
Firozpur Jhirka, India	E6	54
First Cataract, wtfl., Egypt.	C6	62
Firth, Ne., U.S.	K2	118
Firth, stm., N.A.	C11	140
Fīrūzābād, Iran	D7	56
Fisher, Ar., U.S.	B7	122
Fisher, Il., U.S.	D9	120
Fisher Bay, b., Mb., Can.	C17	124
Fisher Branch, Mb., Can.	C16	124
Fisher Peak, mtn., Va., U.S.	H5	114
Fishers Island, i., N.Y., U.S.	C14	114
Fisher Strait, strt., Nu., Can.	C14	106
Fishing Creek, Md., U.S.	F9	114
Fishing Creek, stm., N.C., U.S.	H8	114
Fishing Lake, l., Mb., Can.	B18	124
Fisk, Mo., U.S.	H7	120
Fiskárdo, Grc.	E3	28
Fisterra, Cabo de, c., Spain	B1	20
Fitchburg, Ma., U.S.	B14	114
Fito, Mount, vol., Samoa	g12	79c
Fitri, Lac, l., Chad	E3	62
Fitz Roy, Arg.	I3	90
Fitzroy, stm., Austl.	D8	76
Fitzroy, stm., Austl.	C4	74
Fitz Roy, Monte (Chaltel, Cerro), mtn., S.A.	I2	90
Fitzroy Crossing, Austl.	C5	74
Fitzwilliam Island, i., On., Can.	C8	112
Fiuggi, Italy	I10	22
Fiume see Rijeka, Cro.	E11	22
Fiumicino, Italy	I9	22
Five Islands, N.S., Can.	E12	110
Five Islands Harbour, b., Antig.	f4	105b
Fivemile Creek, stm., Wy., U.S.	D4	126
Five Points, N.M., U.S.	H10	132
Fivizzano, Italy	F7	22
Fizi, D.R.C.	E5	66
Fjällåsen, Swe.	C8	8
Fjällsjö, i., Swe.	B5	128
Flagstaff, Az., U.S.	H5	132
Flagstaff Lake, res., Me., U.S.	E6	110
Flamands, Anse des, Guad.	B2	105a
Flambeau, stm., Wi., U.S.	F8	118
Flamborough, On., Can.	E9	112
Flamborough Head, c., Eng., U.K.	G12	12
Flåming, reg., Ger.	E8	16
Flaming Gorge National Recreation Area, p.o.i., U.S.	B7	132
Flaming Gorge Reservoir, res., U.S.	B7	132
Flanagan, Il., U.S.	D9	120
Flanders, On., Can.	C6	118
Flasher, N.D., U.S.	A11	126
Flåsjön, l., Swe.	D6	8
Flat, Ak., U.S.	D8	140
Flat, Tx., U.S.	C10	130
Flat, stm., N.T., Can.	C5	106
Flat, stm., Mi., U.S.	E4	112
Flatey, Ice.	k28	8a
Flathead (Flathead, North Fork), stm., N.A.	H16	138
Flathead, stm., N.A.	C12	136
Flathead, Middle Fork, stm., Mt., U.S.	B13	136
Flathead, North Fork (Flathead), stm., N.A.	H16	138
Flathead, South Fork, stm., Mt., U.S.	B13	136
Flathead Lake, l., Mt., U.S.	C12	136
Flat Lake, l., Ab., Can.	B17	138
Flatonia, Tx., U.S.	E10	130
Flat River, P.E., Can.	D13	110
Flat River, Mo., U.S.	G7	120
Flat Rock, Il., U.S.	C13	122
Flattery, Cape, c., Wa., U.S.	B2	136
Flatts, Ber.	k15	104e
Flattwillow Creek, stm., Mt., U.S.	H5	124
Flatwood, U.S.	E11	122
Flaxton, N.D., U.S.	F11	124
Flaxville, Mt., U.S.	F8	124
Fleetwood, Eng., U.K.	H10	12
Fleetwood, Pa., U.S.	D10	114
Flekkefjord, Nor.	G2	8
Fleming-Neon, Ky., U.S.	G3	114
Flemingsburg, Ky., U.S.	F2	114
Flen, Swe.	G7	8
Flensburg, Ger.	B5	16
Fletcher, N.C., U.S.	A3	116
Fletcher Pond, l., Mi., U.S.	D5	112
Fleurance, Fr.	F6	18
Flinders, stm., Austl.	A3	76
Flinders Bay, b., Austl.	G2	74
Flinders Island, i., Austl.	m14	77a
Flinders Ranges National Park, p.o.i., Austl.	H2	76
Flinders Reefs, rf., Austl.	A7	76
Flin Flon, Mb., Can.	E10	106
Flint, Wales, U.K.	H9	12
Flint, Mi., U.S.	E6	112
Flint, i., Kir.	E12	72
Flint, stm., U.S.	C12	122
Flint, stm., U.S.	C1	112
Flint Lake, l., Nu., Can.	B16	106
Flinton, Austl.	F7	76
Flintville, Tn., U.S.	B12	122
Flix, Pantà de, res., Spain	C11	20
Flomaton, Al., U.S.	F11	122
Floodwood, Mn., U.S.	E6	118
Flora, Il., U.S.	F9	120
Flora, In., U.S.	H3	112
Florac, Fr.	E9	18
Floral Park, N.Y., U.S.	H15	116
Flora Vista, N.M., U.S.	I7	134
Flore, Piton, mtn., St. Luc.	m7	105c
Florence see Firenze, Italy	G8	22
Florence, Al., U.S.	C11	122
Florence, Az., U.S.	J5	132
Florence, Co., U.S.	C3	128
Florence, Ks., U.S.	C12	128
Florence, S.C., U.S.	B6	116
Florence, Wi., U.S.	C1	112
Florencia, Col.	G4	86
Florentino Ameghino, Arg.	H3	90
Flores, Braz.	D7	88
Flores, Guat.	D2	102
Flores, i., C.V.	k10	65a
Flores, state, Arg.	C8	92
Flores, Laut (Flores Sea), s., Indon.	G11	50
Flores, Selat, strt., Indon.	G7	44
Flores de Goiás, Braz.	H2	88
Flores Island, i., B.C., Can.	G4	138
Flores Sea see Flores, Laut, s., Indon.	G11	50
Floresta, Braz.	E6	88
Florești, Mol.	B15	26
Floresville, Tx., U.S.	E9	130
Floriano, Braz.	D4	88
Floriano Peixoto, Braz.	E4	84
Florianópolis, Braz.	C13	92
Florida, Col.	F3	86
Florida, Cuba	B8	102
Florida, P.R.	B4	104a
Florida, Ur.	G9	92
Florida, state, U.S.	F11	108
Florida, Straits of, strt., N.A.	G11	108
Florida Bay, b., Fl., U.S.	K5	116
Floridablanca, Col.	D5	86
Florida City, Fl., U.S.	K5	116
Florida Islands, is., Sol. Is.	e9	79b
Florida Keys, is., Fl., U.S.	L4	116
Floridia, Italy	G9	24
Florido, stm., Mex.	B6	100
Florien, La., U.S.	F5	122
Flórina, Grc.	C4	28
Florissant, Mo., U.S.	F7	120
Florissant Fossil Beds National Monument, p.o.i., Co., U.S.	B3	128
Florø, Nor.	F1	8
Flotte, Cap de, c., N. Cal.	m16	79d
Floyd, N.M., U.S.	G5	128
Floyd, Va., U.S.	H5	114
Floyd, stm., Ia., U.S.	I2	118
Floydada, Tx., U.S.	G7	128
Flumendosa, stm., Italy.	E3	24
Fluminimaggiore, Italy.	E2	24
Flushing see Vlissingen, Neth.	C12	14
Fluvanna, Tx., U.S.	B6	130
Fly, stm.	b3	79a
Foam Lake, Sk., Can.	C10	124
Foça, Tur.	E9	28
Foça, Tur.	E9	28
Focşani, Rom.	D14	26
Fogang, China	J5	42
Foggaret ez Zoua, Alg.	D5	64
Foggia, Italy	C9	24
Fogo, i., C.V.	k10	65a
Fogo Island, i., Nf., Can.	j23	107a
Foguista J. F. Juárez see El Galpón, Arg.	B5	92
Föhr, i., Ger.	B4	16
Fóia, mtn., Port.	G2	20
Foix, Fr.	G7	18
Foix, hist. reg., Fr.	F7	18
Fojnica, Bos.	F4	26
Fokino, Russia	G17	10
Foládí, Koh-e, mtn., Afg.	C10	56
Folda, b., Nor.	C6	8
Foley, Al., U.S.	G11	122
Foleyet, On., Can.	F14	106
Foley Island, i., Nu., Can.	B15	106
Folgefonni, ice, Nor.	G2	8
Foligno, Italy	H9	22
Folkestone, Eng., U.K.	J14	12
Folkston, Ga., U.S.	F3	116
Folkston, Ga., U.S.	E9	118
Föllinge, Swe.	E6	8
Follonica, Italy	H7	22
Follonica, Golfo di, b., Italy.	H7	22
Folsom, Ca., U.S.	E4	134
Folsom Lake, res., Ca., U.S.	E4	134
Fomboni, Com.	C7	68
Fominiči, Russia	F17	10
Fominskoe, Russia	A22	10
Fond-du-Lac, Sk., Can.	D9	106
Fond du Lac, Wi., U.S.	H10	118
Fond du Lac, stm., Sk., Can.	D9	106
Fondi, Italy	C7	24
Fonni, Italy	D3	24
Fonseca, Col.	B5	86
Fonseca, Golfo de, b., N.A.	F4	102
Fontainebleau, Fr.	F11	14
Fontana, Arg.	C8	92
Fontana, Ca., U.S.	I8	134
Fontana Lake, res., N.C., U.S.	A2	116
Fontanelle, Ia., U.S.	J4	118
Fontas, stm., Can.	D6	106
Fonte Boa, Braz.	I8	86
Fontenay-le-Comte, Fr.	C5	18
Fontenelle, Qc., Can.	B12	110
Fontenelle Reservoir, res., Wy., U.S.	B3	132
Fontur, c., Ice.	j32	8a
Fonyód, Hung.	C4	26
Foochow see Fuzhou, China.	H8	42
Foothills, Ab., Can.	C14	138
Foram, Vanuatu	k17	79d
Forbach, Ger.	H4	16
Forbach, Fr.	E15	14
Forbes, Austl.	I7	76
Forbes, Mount, mtn., Ab., Can.	E14	138
Forbesganj, India	E11	54
Forchheim, Ger.	G7	16
Ford, Ks., U.S.	D9	128
Ford, stm., Mi., U.S.	B2	112
Ford City, Ca., U.S.	H6	134
Ford City, Pa., U.S.	D6	114
Førde, Nor.	F1	8
Ford Ranges, mts., Ant.	C26	81
Fords Bridge, Austl.	G5	76
Fordville, N.D., U.S.	F16	124
Fordyce, Ar., U.S.	D6	122
Forécariah, Gui.	H2	64
Forel, Mont, mtn., Grnld.	D18	141
Foreman, Ar., U.S.	D4	122
Forest, On., Can.	E8	112
Forest, Ms., U.S.	E9	122
Forest Acres, S.C., U.S.	B4	116
Forestburg, Ab., Can.	D18	138
Forest City, N.C., U.S.	A4	116
Forest City, Pa., U.S.	C10	114
Forest Grove, B.C., Can.	E9	138
Foresthill, Ca., U.S.	D5	134
Forestier Peninsula, pen., Austl.	o14	77a
Forest Lake, Mn., U.S.	F5	118
Forest Park, Ga., U.S.	D14	122
Forestville, Qc., Can.	B8	110
Forez, Monts du, mts., Fr.	D9	18
Forfar, Scot., U.K.	E10	12
Forges-les-Eaux, Fr.	E10	14
Forillon, Parc national de, p.o.i., Qc., Can.	B12	110
Forked Deer, stm., Tn., U.S.	I8	120
Forks, Wa., U.S.	C2	136
Forli, Italy	F9	22
Formby Point, c., Eng., U.K.	H9	12
Formentera, i., Spain	F12	20
Formentor, Cap de, c., Spain	E14	20
Formia, Italy	C7	24
Formiga, Braz.	K3	88
Formosa, Arg.	B8	92
Formosa, Braz.	H2	88
Formosa see Taiwan, ctry., Asia	I9	42
Formosa, stm., Arg.	D4	90
Formosa, Serra, plat., Braz.	F6	84
Formosa Strait see Taiwan Strait, strt., Asia	I8	42
Formoso, stm., Braz.	G3	88
Forncelle, Italy	E2	122
Forney, Tx., U.S.	E2	122
Foros, stm., Arg.	A13	10
Forrest, Austl.	F5	74
Forrest, Il., U.S.	D9	120
Forrest City, Ar., U.S.	B8	122
Forrester Island, i., Ak., U.S.	E13	140
Forsayth, Austl.	A4	76
Forst, Ger.	E10	16
Förster, Aust.	I7	76
Forsyth, Ga., U.S.	D2	116
Forsyth, Mo., U.S.	H4	120
Forsyth, Mt., U.S.	A6	126
Fort Abbās, Pak.	D4	54
Fort Albany, On., Can.	E14	106
Fortaleza, Braz.	B6	88
Fortaleza do Ituxi, Braz.	E4	84
Fort Assiniboine, Ab., Can.	B15	138
Fort Atkinson, Wi., U.S.	B9	120
Fort Bayard see Zhanjiang, China	K4	42
Fort Beaufort, S. Afr.	H8	70
Fort Belknap Agency, Mt., U.S.	F5	124
Fort Benton, Mt., U.S.	C16	136
Fort Bragg, Ca., U.S.	D2	134
Fort Branch, In., U.S.	F10	120
Fort Bridger, Wy., U.S.	B6	132
Fort Calhoun, Ne., U.S.	C1	120
Fort Chipewyan, Ab., Can.	D8	106
Fort Collins, Co., U.S.	G7	126
Fort-Coulonge, Qc., Can.	C13	112
Fort Covington, N.Y., U.S.	E2	110
Fort Davis, Al., U.S.	E13	122
Fort Davis, Tx., U.S.	D4	130
Fort-de-France, Mart.	k6	105c
Fort-de-France-Lamentin, Aérodrome de, Mart.	k7	105c
Fort Deposit, Al., U.S.	F12	122
Fort Dodge, Ia., U.S.	B3	120
Fort Duchesne, Ut., U.S.	C7	132
Forte dei Marmi, Italy	G7	22
Fort Edward, N.Y., U.S.	G3	110
Fort Erie, On., Can.	F10	112
Fortescue, stm., Austl.	D3	74
Fortezza, Italy	D8	22
Fort Frances, On., Can.	C5	118
Fort Fraser, B.C., Can.	B6	138
Fort Frederica National Monument, p.o.i., Ga., U.S.	E4	116
Fort Gaines, Ga., U.S.	F13	122
Fort Garland, Co., U.S.	D3	128
Fort Gibson, Ok., U.S.	I2	120
Fort Good Hope, N.T., Can.	B5	106
Forth, Firth of, b., Scot., U.K.	E10	12
Fort Hall, Id., U.S.	G14	136
Fortine, Mt., U.S.	B12	136
Fortín Jones, Arg.	I5	92
Fort Jones, Ca., U.S.	B3	134
Fort Klamath, Or., U.S.	H4	136
Fort Knox, Ky., U.S.	G12	120
Fort-Lamy see N'Djamena, Chad	E3	62
Fort Laramie, Wy., U.S.	E8	126
Fort Lauderdale, Fl., U.S.	J5	116
Fort Liard, N.T., Can.	C6	106
Fort Loramie, Oh., U.S.	D1	114
Fort Loudoun Lake, res., Tn., U.S.	B15	122
Fort Lyon Canal, can., Co., U.S.	C5	128
Fort MacKay, Ab., Can.	D8	106
Fort Macleod, Ab., Can.	G17	138
Fort Madison, Ia., U.S.	D6	120
Fort Matanzas National Monument, p.o.i., Fl., U.S.	G4	116
Fort McMurray, Ab., Can.	D8	106
Fort McPherson, N.T., Can.	B4	106
Fort Meade, Fl., U.S.	I4	116
Fort Mill, S.C., U.S.	A5	116
Fort Morgan, Co., U.S.	G8	126
Fort Myers, Fl., U.S.	J3	116
Fort Myers Beach, Fl., U.S.	J3	116
Fort Nelson, B.C., Can.	D6	106
Fort Nelson, stm., B.C., Can.	D6	106
Fort Ogden, Fl., U.S.	I4	116
Fort Payne, Al., U.S.	C13	122
Fort Peck, Mt., U.S.	F7	124
Fort Peck Dam, dam, Mt., U.S.	G7	124
Fort Peck Lake, res., Mt., U.S.	G7	124
Fort Pierce, Fl., U.S.	I5	116
Fort Plain, N.Y., U.S.	B11	114
Fort Portal, Ug.	D6	66
Fort Providence, N.T., Can.	C7	106
Fort Pulaski National Monument, p.o.i., Ga., U.S.	E5	116
Fort Qu'Appelle, Sk., Can.	D10	124
Fort Randall Dam, dam, S.D., U.S.	D14	126
Fort Recovery, Oh., U.S.	D1	114
Fort Resolution, N.T., Can.	C8	106
Fort Rixon, Zimb.	B9	70
Fort Saint James, B.C., Can.	B6	138
Fort Saint John, B.C., Can.	D6	106
Fort Saskatchewan, Ab., Can.	C17	138
Fort Scott, Ks., U.S.	G3	120
Fort Severn, On., Can.	D13	106
Fort-Shevchenko, Kaz.	F7	32
Fort Simpson, N.T., Can.	C6	106
Fort Smith, N.T., Can.	C8	106
Fort Smith, Ar., U.S.	B4	122
Fort Stockton, Tx., U.S.	D4	130
Fort Sumner, N.M., U.S.	G4	128
Fort Sumter National Monument, p.o.i., S.C., U.S.	D6	116
Fort Supply, Ok., U.S.	E9	128
Fort Thomas, Az., U.S.	J7	132
Fort Totten, N.D., U.S.	G14	124
Fort Towson, Ok., U.S.	C3	122
Fortuna, Arg.	G5	92
Fortuna, C.R.	G5	102
Fortuna, Ca., U.S.	C1	134
Fortuna, V.I.U.S.	e6	104b
Fortune Bay, b., Nf., Can.	j22	107a
Fortuneswell, Eng., U.K.	K10	12
Fort Union National Monument, p.o.i., N.M., U.S.	F3	128
Fort Valley, Ga., U.S.	D2	116
Fort Vermilion, Ab., Can.	D7	106
Fort Victoria, sci., Ber.	k16	104e
Fort Walton Beach, Fl., U.S.	G12	122
Fort Wayne, In., U.S.	G4	112
Fort White, Fl., U.S.	G3	116
Fort William, Scot., U.K.	E7	12
Fort Worth, Tx., U.S.	B10	130
Fort Yates, N.D., U.S.	A12	126
Fort Yukon, Ak., U.S.	C10	140
Foshan, China	J5	42
Fosheim Peninsula, pen., Nu., Can.	B9	141
Foso, Ghana	H4	64
Fossil, Or., U.S.	E6	136
Fossil Butte National Monument, p.o.i., Wy., U.S.	B6	132
Fossil Lake, l., Or., U.S.	G6	136
Fossombrone, Italy	G9	22
Fosston, Mn., U.S.	D3	118
Foster, Austl.	L6	76
Foster Bugt, strt., Grnld.	C21	141
Fosters, Al., U.S.	D11	122
Fostoria, Oh., U.S.	C2	114
Fougamou, Gabon	E2	66
Fougères, Fr.	F7	14
Fou-hsien see Fujian, state, China	I8	42
Foula, i., Scot., U.K.	n17	12a
Foulay see Fuling, China, stm.	F8	42
Foulwind, Cape, c., N.Z.	E4	80
Foumban, Cam.	D2	66
Foumban, Cam.	D2	66
Foum-el-Hassan, Mor.	D3	64
Foum-Zguid, Mor.	C3	64
Foundiougne, Sen.	G1	64
Fountain, Co., U.S.	C4	128
Fountain, Fl., U.S.	G13	122
Fountain City, Wi., U.S.	G7	118
Fountain Green, Ut., U.S.	D5	132
Fountain Peak, mtn., Ca., U.S.	I1	132

Name	Map Ref.	Page
Fountain Place, La., U.S.	G7	122
Fourche LaFave, stm., Ar., U.S.	C6	122
Fourchu, N.S., Can.	E16	110
Four Corners, Or., U.S.	F4	136
Fourmies, Fr.	D13	14
Four Mountains, Islands of, is., Ak., U.S.	g24	140a
Four Oaks, N.C., U.S.	A7	116
Fourth Cataract see Rābi', Ash-Shallāl ar-, wtfl., Sudan	D6	62
Fous, Pointe des, c., Dom.	j6	105c
Fouta Djalon, reg., Gui.	G2	64
Foux, Cap à, c., Haiti	C11	102
Fouyang see Fuyang, China	E6	42
Foveaux Strait, strt., N.Z.	H3	80
Fowler, Co., U.S.	C4	128
Fowler, In., U.S.	H2	112
Fowler, Mi., U.S.	E5	112
Fowlers Bay, Austl.	F6	74
Fowlerville, Mi., U.S.	B1	114
Fox, stm., Wi., U.S.	H10	118
Fox, stm., U.S.	D5	120
Fox, stm., U.S.	C9	120
Fox Creek, Ab., Can.	B14	138
Foxe Basin, b., Nu., Can.	B15	106
Foxe Channel, strt., Nu., Can.	C15	106
Foxe Peninsula, pen., Nu., Can.	C15	106
Foxford, Ire.	H3	12
Fox Islands, is., Ak., U.S.	g25	140a
Fox Lake, Il., U.S.	B9	120
Foxpark, Wy., U.S.	B10	132
Fox Valley, Sk., Can.	D4	124
Foxworth, Ms., U.S.	F9	122
Foyle, Lough, b., Eur.	F5	12
Foz do Areia, Represa de, res., Braz.	B12	92
Foz do Cunene, Ang.	D1	68
Foz do Iguaçu, Braz.	B10	92
Foz do Jordão, Braz.	E3	84
Foz Giraldo, Port.	E3	20
Fraga, Spain	C11	20
Fraile Muerto, Ur.	F10	92
Framingham, Ma., U.S.	B14	114
Franca, Braz.	K2	88
França, Braz.	F5	88
Franca-Iosifa, Zemlja, is., Russia	B9	30
Francavilla al Mare, Italy	H11	22
Francavilla Fontana, Italy	D11	24
France, ctry., Eur.	C8	18
Frances, stm., Yk., Can.	C5	106
Frances Lake, l., Yk., Can.	C4	106
Francés Viejo, Cabo, c., Dom. Rep.	C13	102
Franceville, Gabon	E2	66
Franche-Comté, hist. reg., Fr.	B12	18
Francis, Sk., Can.	D10	124
Francis Case, Lake, res., S.D., U.S.	D13	126
Francisco Beltrão, Braz.	B11	92
Francisco I. Madero, Mex.	I4	130
Francisco I. Madero, Mex.	C6	100
Francisco Murguía, Mex.	C7	100
Francisco Sá, Braz.	I4	88
Francistown, Bots.	B8	70
Francofonte, Italy	G8	24
François Lake, B.C., Can.	B5	138
Francois Lake, l., B.C., Can.	C5	138
Francs Peak, mtn., Wy., U.S.	C3	126
Frankel City, Tx., U.S.	B5	130
Franken, hist. reg., Ger.	G6	16
Frankenberg, Ger.	F9	16
Frankenberg, Ger.	E4	16
Frankenmuth, Mi., U.S.	E6	112
Frankford, On., Can.	D12	112
Frankford, Mo., U.S.	E6	120
Frankfort, S. Afr.	E9	70
Frankfort, In., U.S.	H3	112
Frankfort, Ks., U.S.	B12	128
Frankfort, Ky., U.S.	F13	120
Frankfort, N.Y., U.S.	A10	114
Frankfort, Oh., U.S.	E2	114
Frankfort, S.D., U.S.	C14	126
Frankfurt, Ger.	D10	16
Frankfurt am Main, Ger.	F4	16
Franklin, Az., U.S.	K7	132
Franklin, Ga., U.S.	D13	122
Franklin, Id., U.S.	A5	132
Franklin, Il., U.S.	E7	120
Franklin, In., U.S.	E11	120
Franklin, Ma., U.S.	B14	114
Franklin, N.C., U.S.	A2	116
Franklin, Ne., U.S.	A9	128
Franklin, N.H., U.S.	G5	110
Franklin, N.J., U.S.	C11	114
Franklin, Oh., U.S.	E1	114
Franklin, Pa., U.S.	C6	114
Franklin, Tn., U.S.	I11	120
Franklin, Tx., U.S.	F2	122
Franklin, Va., U.S.	H9	114
Franklin, Wi., U.S.	F2	112
Franklin Bay, b., N.T., Can.	B5	106
Franklin D. Roosevelt Lake, res., Wa., U.S.	B4	108
Franklin Gordon Wild Rivers National Park, p.o.i., Austl.	o12	77a
Franklin Grove, Il., U.S.	C8	120
Franklin Lake, l., Nu., Can.	B12	106
Franklin Mountains, mts., N.T., Can.	B5	106
Franklin Strait, strt., Nu., Can.	A11	106
Franklinton, La., U.S.	G8	122
Franklinville, N.Y., U.S.	B7	114
Frankston, Tx., U.S.	E3	122
Frankton, In., U.S.	H4	112
Fransfontein, Nmb.	B2	70
Franzensfeste see Fortezza, Italy	D8	22
Franz Josef Land see Franca-Iosifa, Zemlja, is., Russia	B9	30
Frascati, Italy	I9	22
Fraser, B.C., Can.	G13	138
Fraser, Co., U.S.	B3	128
Fraser, stm., B.C., Can.	G9	138
Fraser, Mount, mtn., Austl.	E3	74
Fraserburgh, Scot., U.K.	D11	12
Fraser Island, i., Austl.	E9	76
Fraser Lake, B.C., Can.	B6	138
Fraser Lake, l., B.C., Can.	B6	138
Fraser Plateau, plat., B.C., Can.	E8	138
Fraser Range, Austl.	F4	74
Frauenfeld, Switz.	C5	22
Fray Bentos, Ur.	F8	92
Fray Jorge, Parque Nacional, p.o.i., Chile	E2	92
Fray Marcos, Ur.	G10	92
Frazer, Mt., U.S.	F7	124
Frederic, Wi., U.S.	F6	118
Frederica, De., U.S.	E10	114
Fredericia, Den.	I3	8
Frederick, Md., U.S.	E8	114
Frederick, S.D., U.S.	B14	126
Frederick Hills, hills, Austl.	B7	74
Frederick Reef, rf., Austl.	C10	76
Fredericksburg, Ia., U.S.	B5	120
Fredericksburg, Tx., U.S.	D9	130
Fredericksburg, Va., U.S.	F8	114
Fredericktown, Oh., U.S.	D3	114
Frederico Westphalen, Braz.	C11	92
Fredericton, N.B., Can.	E10	110
Fredericton Junction, N.B., Can.	E10	110
Frederiksborg, state, Den.	H5	8
Frederiksdal, Grnld.	E17	141
Frederikshåb (Paamiut), Grnld.	E15	141
Frederikshavn, Den.	H4	8
Frederiksted, V.I.U.S.	h10	104c
Fredonia, Ks., U.S.	G2	120
Fredonia, N.D., U.S.	A13	126
Fredonia, N.Y., U.S.	B6	114
Fredrika, Swe.	D8	8
Fredrikstad, Nor.	G4	8
Freeburg, Il., U.S.	F8	120
Freeland, Mi., U.S.	E5	112
Freeland, Pa., U.S.	C9	114
Freel Peak, mtn., Ca., U.S.	E5	134
Freels, Cape, c., Nf., Can.	j23	107a
Freeman, S.D., U.S.	D15	126
Freeport, Bah.	B9	96
Freeport, N.S., Can.	F10	110
Freeport, Fl., U.S.	G12	122
Freeport, Il., U.S.	B8	120
Freeport, N.Y., U.S.	H16	112
Freeport, Pa., U.S.	D6	114
Freeport, Tx., U.S.	F12	130
Free State, state, S. Afr.	F8	70
Freetown, Antig.	f4	105b
Freetown, S.L.	H2	64
Fregenal de la Sierra, Spain	F4	20
Freiberg, Ger.	F9	16
Freiburg see Fribourg, Switz.	D4	22
Freiburg im Breisgau, Ger.	I3	16
Freirina, Chile	D2	92
Freising, Ger.	H7	16
Freistadt, Aus.	B11	22
Freital, Ger.	F9	16
Fréjus, Fr.	F12	18
Fremantle, Austl.	F3	74
Fremont, Ca., U.S.	F4	134
Fremont, Ia., U.S.	C5	120
Fremont, In., U.S.	C1	114
Fremont, Mi., U.S.	E4	112
Fremont, Ne., U.S.	C1	120
Fremont, Oh., U.S.	C2	114
Fremont, Wi., U.S.	G10	118
Fremont, stm., Ut., U.S.	E6	132
French, stm., On., Can.	B9	112
French Broad, stm., U.S.	I3	114
Frenchcap Cay, i., V.I.U.S.	f7	104b
French Guiana, dep., S.A.	C7	84
French Island, i., Austl.	L5	76
French Lick, In., U.S.	F11	120
Frenchman (Frenchman Creek), stm., N.A.	E5	124
Frenchman Creek (Frenchman), stm., N.A.	E5	124
Frenchman Creek, stm., U.S.	G11	126
Frenchmans Cap, mtn., Austl.	o12	77a
French Polynesia, dep., Oc.	K24	142
French Somaliland see Djibouti, ctry., Afr.	E8	62
Fresco, C. Iv.	H3	64
Fresco, stm., Braz.	E7	84
Fresnillo, Mex.	D7	100
Fresno, Ca., U.S.	G6	134
Fresno, stm., Ca., U.S.	F6	134
Fresno Reservoir, res., Mt., U.S.	B16	136
Freu, Cap des, c., Spain	E14	20
Freudenstadt, Ger.	H4	16
Frewena, Austl.	C7	74
Frewsburg, N.Y., U.S.	B6	114
Freycinet National Park, p.o.i., Austl.	o14	77a
Freycinet Peninsula, pen., Austl.	o14	77a
Freyre, Arg.	E6	92
Fria, Gui.	G2	64
Fria, Cape, c., Nmb.	D1	68
Friant, Ca., U.S.	G6	134
Friars Point, Ms., U.S.	C8	122
Frías, Arg.	D5	92
Fribourg (Freiburg), Switz.	D4	22
Fridley, Mn., U.S.	F5	118
Fridtjof Nansen, Mount, mtn., Ant.	D25	81
Friedberg, Aus.	C12	22
Friedberg, Ger.	H7	16
Friedberg, Ger.	F4	16
Friedland, Ger.	C9	16
Friedrichshafen, Ger.	I5	16
Friend, Ne., U.S.	G15	126
Friendship, N.Y., U.S.	B7	114
Friendship, Tn., U.S.	I8	120
Fries, Va., U.S.	H4	114
Friesach, Aus.	D11	22
Frio, stm., Tx., U.S.	F9	130
Frio, Cabo, c., Braz.	L5	88
Frio Draw, stm., U.S.	G6	128
Friona, Tx., U.S.	G6	128
Frisco, Tx., U.S.	D2	122
Frisian Islands, is., Eur.	A14	14
Fritch, Tx., U.S.	F7	128
Fritzlar, Ger.	E5	16
Friuli, hist. reg., Italy	E9	22
Friuli-Venezia Giulia, state, Italy	D9	22
Frjazino, Russia	E21	10
Frobisher, Sk., Can.	E11	124
Frobisher Bay, b., Nu., Can.	C17	106
Frobisher Lake, l., Sk., Can.	D9	106
Froid, Mt., U.S.	F9	124
Frolovo, Russia	E6	32
Frome, Eng., U.K.	J10	12
Frome, stm., Austl.	G2	76
Frome, Lake, l., Austl.	H2	76
Fronteiras, Braz.	D5	88
Frontenac, Ks., U.S.	G3	120
Frontera, Mex.	F12	100
Frontera, Mex.	B8	100
Frontier, Sk., Can.	E5	124
Frontier, Wy., U.S.	B6	132
Frontino, Col.	B2	84
Frontino, Páramo, mtn., Col.	D3	86
Front Range, mts., Co., U.S.	H7	126
Front Royal, Va., U.S.	F7	114
Frosinone, Italy	C7	24
Frostburg, Md., U.S.	E6	114
Frostproof, Fl., U.S.	I4	116
Frøya, i., Nor.	E3	8
Fruges, Fr.	D11	14
Fruita, Co., U.S.	D8	132
Fruitdale, Or., U.S.	H3	136
Fruithurst, Al., U.S.	D13	122
Fruitland, Id., U.S.	F10	136
Fruitport, Mi., U.S.	E3	112
Fruitvale, B.C., Can.	G13	138
Fruitvale, Wa., U.S.	D6	136
Frunzivka, Ukr.	B16	26
Frutal, Braz.	J1	88
Frutigen, Switz.	D4	22
Frýdek-Místek, Czech Rep.	G14	16
Fryeburg, Me., U.S.	G6	110
Fu, stm., China	G7	42
Fu, stm., China	F2	42
Fu, stm., China	G6	42
Fua'amotu International Airport, Tonga	n14	78e
Fu'an, China	H8	42
Fuchou see Fuzhou, China	H8	42
Fuchow see Fuzhou, China	G7	42
Fuchū, Japan	E6	40
Fuchun, stm., China	G8	42
Fuding, China	H9	42
Fuego, Volcán de, vol., Guat.	E2	102
Fuencaliente, Spain	F6	20
Fuengirola, Spain	H6	20
Fuensalida, Spain	D6	20
Fuente, Mex.	F7	130
Fuente de Cantos, Spain	F4	20
Fuente de Oro, Col.	F5	86
Fuentes de Ebro, Spain	C10	20
Fuerte, stm., Mex.	B4	100
Fuerte Olimpo, Para.	D5	90
Fuga Island, i., Phil.	A3	52
Fugou, China	D6	42
Fuhai, China	B2	36
Fuhsien see Wafangdian, China	B9	42
Fuji, Japan	D11	40
Fuji, Mount see Fuji-san, vol., Japan	D11	40
Fujian, state, China	I7	42
Fujieda, Japan	E11	40
Fujin, China	B11	36
Fujinomiya, Japan	D11	40
Fuji-san (Fuji, Mount), vol., Japan	D11	40
Fujisawa, Japan	D12	40
Fujiyama see Fuji-san, vol., Japan	D11	40
Fuji-yoshida, Japan	D11	40
Fukagawa, Japan	C14	38
Fukang, China	C2	36
Fukave, i., Tonga	n14	78e
Fukaya, Japan	C12	40
Fukien see Fujian, state, China	I7	42
Fukuchiyama, Japan	D8	40
Fukue, Japan	G1	40
Fukue-jima, i., Japan	G1	40
Fukui, Japan	C9	40
Fukui, state, Japan	D9	40
Fukuoka, Japan	F3	40
Fukuoka, state, Japan	F3	40
Fukuroi, Japan	E10	40
Fukushima, Japan	B13	40
Fukushima, state, Japan	B12	40
Fukuyama, Japan	E6	40
Fulaga Passage, strt., Fiji	q20	79e
Fulda, Ger.	F5	16
Fulda, Mn., U.S.	H3	118
Fulda, stm., Ger.	E5	16
Fuling, China	G2	42
Fullarton, stm., Austl.	C3	76
Fullerton, Ca., U.S.	J8	134
Fullerton Point, c., Antig.	f4	105b
Fulong, China	J2	42
Fulton, Al., U.S.	F11	122
Fulton, Ar., U.S.	D5	122
Fulton, Il., U.S.	C7	120
Fulton, Ks., U.S.	F3	120
Fulton, Ky., U.S.	H9	120
Fulton, Mo., U.S.	F5	120
Fulton, N.Y., U.S.	E13	112
Fulton, Tx., U.S.	F10	130
Fumay, Fr.	D13	14
Funabashi, Japan	D12	40
Funafuti, i., Tuvalu	D8	72
Funan, China	E6	42
Funchal, Port.	C1	64
Fundación, Col.	B4	86
Fundão, Port.	D3	20
Fundy, Bay of, b., Can.	F10	110
Fundy National Park, p.o.i., N.B., Can.	E11	110
Funhalouro, Moz.	C12	70
Funing, China	E8	42
Funiu Shan, mts., China	E5	42
Funsi, Ghana	G4	64
Funtua, Nig.	G6	64
Fuping, China	D3	42
Fuqing, China	I8	42
Fuquay-Varina, N.C., U.S.	A7	116
Furculești, Rom.	F12	26
Furmanov, Russia	H19	8
Furnas, Represa de, res., Braz.	K2	88
Furneaux Group, is., Austl.	m13	77a
Furnes see Veurne, Bel.	C11	14
Fürstenberg / Havel, Ger.	C9	16
Fürstenfeld, Aus.	C12	22
Fürstenfeldbruck, Ger.	H7	16
Fürstenwalde, Ger.	D9	16
Fürth, Ger.	G6	16
Furth im Wald, Ger.	G8	16
Furukawa, Japan	C10	40
Furukawa, Japan	A13	40
Fury and Hecla Strait, strt., Nu., Can.	B14	106
Fusagasugá, Col.	E4	86
Fusan see Pusan, Kor., S.	D2	40
Fushan, China	C9	42
Fushan, China	D4	42
Fushih see Yan'an, China	C3	42
Fushun, China	G1	42
Fushun, China	D5	38
Fusilier, Sk., Can.	C4	124
Fusong, China	C7	38
Füssen, Ger.	I6	16
Fuste, Picacho del, mtn., Mex.	G5	130
Fusui, China	J2	42
Futun, stm., China	H7	42
Futuna, Île, i., Wal./F.	E9	72
Futuyu, China	B6	42
Fuwa, Egypt	G1	58
Fuxian Hu, l., China	G5	36
Fuxin, China	C4	38
Fuyang, China	E6	42
Fuyang, stm., China	C6	42
Fuyu, China	B6	38
Fuyu, China	B9	36
Fuyuan, China	F5	36
Fuyuan see Tongjiang, China	B11	36
Fuyuan, China	B11	36
Fuzhou, China	G7	42
Fuzhou, China	H8	42
Fylí, sci., Grc.	E6	28
Fyn, state, Den.	I4	8
Fyn, i., Den.	I4	8
Fyne, Loch, b., Scot., U.K.	E7	12
Fyresvatnet, l., Nor.	G2	8

G

Name	Map Ref.	Page
Gaalkacyo, Som.	C9	66
Gabare, Blg.	F10	26
Gabarus, N.S., Can.	E16	110
Gabela, Ang.	C1	68
Gaberones see Gaborone, Bots.	D7	70
Gabès, Tun.	C7	64
Gabiarra, Braz.	I6	88
Gabon, ctry., Afr.	E2	66
Gaborone, Bots.	D7	70
Gabras, Sudan	E5	62
Gabriel Strait, strt., Nu., Can.	C17	106
Gabriel y Galán, Embalse de, res., Spain	D4	20
Gabrovo, Blg.	G12	26
Gacé, Fr.	F9	14
Gackle, N.D., U.S.	A13	126
Gadag, India	D2	53
Gādarwāra, India	G7	54
Gäddede, Swe.	D6	8
Gado Bravo, Ilha do, i., Braz.	F4	88
Gádor, Spain	H8	20
Gadsden, Al., U.S.	C12	122
Gadsden, Az., U.S.	K2	132
Gadwāl, India	C3	53
Gael Hamke Bugt, b., Grnld.	C22	141
Găești, Rom.	E12	26
Gaeta, Italy	C7	24
Gaeta, Golfo di, b., Italy	C7	24
Gaferut, i., Micron.	C5	72
Gaffney, S.C., U.S.	A4	116
Gafour, Tun.	H3	24
Gafsa, Tun.	C6	64
Gag, Pulau, i., Indon.	F8	44
Gagarin, Russia	E17	10
Gage, Ok., U.S.	E9	128
Gaggenau, Ger.	H4	16
Gagliano del Capo, Italy	E12	24
Gagnoa, C. Iv.	H3	64
Gagra, Geor.	F5	32
Gaibandha, Bngl.	F12	54
Gail, Tx., U.S.	B6	130
Gaillac, Fr.	F7	18
Gaillimh see Galway, Ire.	H3	12
Gaimán, Arg.	H3	90
Gainesboro, Tn., U.S.	H12	120
Gainesville, Fl., U.S.	G3	116
Gainesville, Ga., U.S.	B2	116
Gainesville, Mo., U.S.	H5	120
Gainesville, Tx., U.S.	H11	128
Gainsborough, Eng., U.K.	H12	12
Gainsborough Creek, stm., Can.	E12	124
Gairdner, Lake, l., Austl.	F7	74
Gaithersburg, Md., U.S.	E8	114
Gaixian, China	A10	42
Gaizina Kalns, hill, Lat.	D8	10
Gajendragarh, India	D2	53
Gajny, Russia	B8	32
Gajuapara, stm., Braz.	C2	88
Gajutino, Russia	B21	10
Gakarosa, mtn., S. Afr.	E6	70
Gakona, Ak., U.S.	D10	140
Galahad, Ab., Can.	D19	138
Galâla el Baharîya, Gebel el-, mts., Egypt	I3	58
Galâla el-Qiblîya, Gebel el-, mts., Egypt	J3	58
Galán, Cerro, mtn., Arg.	C4	92
Galana, stm., Kenya	E7	66
Galanta, Slov.	H13	16
Galapagos Islands see Colón, Archipiélago de, is., Ec.	h12	84a
Galashiels, Scot., U.K.	F9	12
Galați, Rom.	D14	26
Galați, state, Rom.	D14	26
Galatia, Il., U.S.	G9	120
Galatina, Italy	D12	24
Galaxídi, Grc.	E5	28
Galdhøpiggen, mtn., Nor.	F2	8
Galeana, Mex.	C8	100
Galeana, Mex.	F9	98
Galela, Indon.	E8	44
Galena, Ak., U.S.	D8	140
Galena, Il., U.S.	B7	120
Galena, Mo., U.S.	H4	120
Galena Park, Tx., U.S.	E12	130
Galeota Point, c., Trin.	s13	105f
Galera, Punta, c., Chile	G2	90
Galera, Punta, c., Ec.	G1	86
Galera Point, c., Trin.	s13	105f
Galeras, Volcán, vol., Col.	G3	86
Galesburg, Il., U.S.	D7	120
Galesville, Wi., U.S.	G7	118
Galeton, Pa., U.S.	C8	114
Galiano Island, i., B.C., Can.	H7	138
Galič, Russia	G20	8
Galicia, state, Spain	B3	20
Galicia, hist. reg., Eur.	G18	16
Galičica Nacionalni Park, p.o.i., Mac.	C3	28
Galičskaja vozvyšennost', hills, Russia	G20	8
Galičskoe, ozero, l., Russia	G20	8
Galilee, Lake, l., Austl.	D5	76
Galilee, Sea of see Kinneret, Yam, l., Isr.	F6	58
Galiléia, Braz.	J5	88
Galina Point, c., Jam.	i14	104d
Galion, Oh., U.S.	D3	114
Galite, Canal de la, strt., Tun.	G3	24
Gallarate, Italy	E5	22
Gallatin, Tn., U.S.	H11	120
Gallatin, stm., U.S.	E15	136
Galle, Sri L.	H5	53
Gállego, stm., Spain	B10	20
Gallegos, stm., Arg.	J3	90
Galliano, La., U.S.	H8	122
Gallinas, stm., N.M., U.S.	F4	128
Gallinas, Punta, c., Col.	A6	86
Gallipoli, Italy	D11	24
Gallipoli see Gelibolu, Tur.	C9	28
Gallipoli Peninsula see Gelibolu Yarımadası, pen., Tur.	C9	28
Gallipolis, Oh., U.S.	F3	114
Gällivare, Swe.	C9	8
Gallo, Capo, c., Italy	F7	24
Gallo Arroyo, stm., N.M., U.S.	G3	128
Galloo Island, i., N.Y., U.S.	E13	112
Galloway, hist. reg., Scot., U.K.	G8	12
Galloway, Mull of, c., Scot., U.K.	G8	12
Gallup, N.M., U.S.	H8	132
Gallura, reg., Italy	C3	24
Galoa Harbour, b., Fiji	q19	79e
Galt, Ca., U.S.	E4	134
Galtat Zemmour, W. Sah.	D2	64
Galty Mountains, mts., Ire.	I4	12
Galva, Il., U.S.	C7	120
Galva, Ks., U.S.	C11	128
Galveston, In., U.S.	H3	112
Galveston, Tx., U.S.	H4	122
Galveston Bay, b., Tx., U.S.	H4	122
Galveston Island, i., Tx., U.S.	E13	130
Gálvez, Arg.	F7	92
Galway (Gaillimh), Ire.	H3	12
Galway, state, Ire.	H4	12
Galway Bay, b., Ire.	H3	12
Gam (Jin), stm., Asia	A7	48
Gama, Isla, i., Arg.	H4	90
Gamagōri, Japan	E10	40
Gamarra, Col.	C5	86
Gamay, Phil.	D5	52
Gamba, China	D12	54
Gambaga, Ghana	G4	64
Gambēla, Eth.	F6	62
Gambell, Ak., U.S.	D5	140
Gambia (Gambie), stm., Afr.	G1	64
Gambia, The, ctry., Afr.	G1	64
Gambie (Gambia), stm., Afr.	G2	64
Gambier, Îles, is., Fr. Poly.	F13	72
Gamboa, Pan.	C2	86
Gamboma, Congo	E3	66
Gamboula, C.A.R.	D2	66
Gamka, stm., S. Afr.	H5	70
Gamlakarleby see Kokkola, Fin.	E10	8
Gamleby, Swe.	H7	8
Gammon Ranges National Park, p.o.i., Austl.	H2	76
Ga-Mogara, stm., S. Afr.	E6	70
Gan, stm., China	B10	36
Gan, stm., China	G6	42
Ganado, Az., U.S.	H7	132
Ganado, Tx., U.S.	E11	130
Gananoque, On., Can.	D13	112
Gäncä, Azer.	A6	56
Gand see Gent, Bel.	C12	14
Ganda, Ang.	C1	68
Gandadiwata, Bulu, mtn., Indon.	E11	50
Gandajika, D.R.C.	F4	66
Gandak (Nārāyaṇi), stm., Asia	E10	54
Gándara, Spain	A2	20
Gander, Nf., Can.	j23	107a
Ganderkesee, Ger.	C4	16
Gandesa, Spain	C11	20
Gandevi, India	H4	54
Gāndhinagar, India	G4	54
Gandhi Reservoir see Gāndhi Sāgar, res., India	F5	54
Gāndhi Sāgar, res., India	F5	54
Gandia, Spain	F10	20
Gandu, Braz.	G6	88
Ganga see Ganges, stm., Asia	F11	54
Gan Gan, Arg.	H3	90
Gangānagar, India	D4	54
Gangāpur, India	B2	53
Gangāpur, India	E6	54
Gangāpur, India	F5	54
Gāngārāmpur, India	F12	54
Gangaw, Mya.	A2	48
Gangāwati, India	D3	53
Gangdhār, India	G5	54
Gangdisê Shan, mts., China	C9	54
Ganges, B.C., Can.	H7	138
Ganges (Ganga) (Padma), stm., Asia	G13	54
Ganges, Mouths of the, mth., Asia	H12	54
Ganghu, China	B11	54
Gangmar Co, l., China	B10	54
Gangneung see Kangnŭng, Kor., S.	B1	40
Gangoa, China	D5	36
Gangotri, India	C7	54
Gangotri, India	C7	54
Gangoumen, China	D2	38
Gangtok, India	E12	54
Gangu, China	D1	42
Gangweon see Kangwŏn-do, state, Kor., S.	B1	40
Gannan, China	B9	36
Gannett Peak, mtn., Wy., U.S.	D3	126
Gannvalley, S.D., U.S.	C14	126
Ganquan, China	C3	42
Gansbaai, S. Afr.	I4	70
Gansu, state, China	D5	36
Gantang, China	H8	42
Gantt, Al., U.S.	F12	122
Gantung, Indon.	E6	50
Ganyanchi, China	C1	42
Ganyesa, S. Afr.	E7	70
Ganzê, China	E4	36
Ganzhou, China	I6	42
Gao, Mali	F4	64
Gao'an, China	G6	42
Gaochun, China	F8	42
Gaohebu, China	F7	42
Gaojian, China	F9	36
Gaolan, China	D5	36
Gaolong, China	H5	42
Gaona, Arg.	B5	92
Gaoping, China	D5	42
Gaotan, China	E3	42
Gaotang, China	C7	42
Gaoua, Burkina	G4	64
Gaoual, Gui.	G2	64
Gaoxian, China	F5	36
Gaoyi, China	C6	42
Gaoyou, China	E8	42
Gaoyou Hu, l., China	E8	42
Gaozhou, China	K4	42
Gap, Fr.	E12	18
Gar, China	B8	54
Gar, stm., China	C8	54
Gara, Lough, l., Ire.	H4	12
Garagumskij kanal (Kara-Kum Canal), can., Turkmen.	B9	56
Garagumy (Kara-Kum), des., Turkmen.	A8	56
Garaina, Pap. N. Gui.	b4	79a
Garanhuns, Braz.	E7	88
Garapan, N. Mar. Is.	B5	72
Garara, Pap. N. Gui.	b4	79a
Garber, Ok., U.S.	E11	128
Garberville, Ca., U.S.	C2	134
Gârbovu, Rom.	E10	26
Garça, Braz.	L1	88
García, Mex.	G8	98
García de Sola, Embalse de, res., Spain	E5	20
Gard, state, Fr.	F10	18
Garda, Italy	E7	22
Garda, Lago di, l., Italy	E7	22
Gardelegen, Ger.	D7	16
Garden City, Ks., U.S.	C8	128
Garden City, Mo., U.S.	F3	120
Garden City, Tx., U.S.	C6	130
Gardendale, Al., U.S.	D12	122
Garden Grove, Ca., U.S.	J7	134
Garden Grove, Ia., U.S.	D4	120
Garden Island, i., Mi., U.S.	C4	112
Garden Peninsula, pen., Mi., U.S.	C3	112
Garden Reach, India	G11	54
Gardenton, Mb., Can.	E17	124
Gardey, Arg.	H8	92
Gardeyz, Afg.	C10	56
Gardiner, Mt., U.S.	E16	136
Gardiner, Or., U.S.	G2	136
Gardiner Dam, dam, Sk., Can.	C6	124
Gardner, Ks., U.S.	F2	120
Gardner, Ma., U.S.	B13	114
Gardner Canal, b., B.C., Can.	C2	138
Gardnerville, Nv., U.S.	E6	134
Garessio, Italy	F5	22
Garet, Mont, vol., Vanuatu	j16	79d
Garfield, Ks., U.S.	C9	128
Garfield, N.M., U.S.	K9	132
Garfield Mountain, mtn., Mt., U.S.	F14	136
Gargano, Promontorio del, mts., Italy	I12	22
Gargano, Testa del, c., Italy	I13	22
Gargždai, Lith.	E4	10
Garhākota, India	G7	54
Garibaldi, Braz.	D12	92
Garibaldi, B.C., Can.	G7	138
Garibaldi, Or., U.S.	E2	136
Garibaldi, Mount, vol., B.C., Can.	G8	138
Gariep Dam, res., S. Afr.	G7	70
Garies, S. Afr.	G4	70
Garigliano, stm., Italy	C7	24
Gariglione, Monte, mtn., Italy	E10	24
Garissa, Kenya	E7	66
Garland, Tx., U.S.	E2	122
Garland, Ut., U.S.	B4	132
Garlasco, Italy	E5	22
Garlin, Fr.	F5	18
Garm, Taj.	B11	56
Garmisch-Partenkirchen, Ger.	I7	16
Garnavillo, Ia., U.S.	B6	120
Garner, Ia., U.S.	A4	120
Garner, N.C., U.S.	I7	114
Garnpung Lake, l., Austl.	I4	76
Garona (Garonne), stm., Eur.	E5	18
Garonne (Garona), stm., Eur.	E5	18
Garoowe, Som.	C9	66
Garoua, Cam.	C2	66
Garoua Boulaï, Cam.	C2	66
Garqu Yan, China	B14	54
Garqu Yan, China	A14	54
Garrel, Ger.	D3	16
Garretson, S.D., U.S.	H2	118
Garrett, In., U.S.	G4	112
Garrett, Ky., U.S.	G3	114
Garrison, N.D., U.S.	G12	124
Garrison, Tx., U.S.	F4	122
Garrison Dam, dam, N.D., U.S.	G12	124
Garry Bay, b., Nu., Can.	B13	106
Garry Lake, l., Nu., Can.	B10	106
Garsen, Kenya	E7	66
Garson, On., Can.	B9	112
Garut, Indon.	G5	50
Garwolin, Pol.	E17	16
Garwood, Tx., U.S.	H2	122
Gary, In., U.S.	G2	112
Gary, Tx., U.S.	E4	122
Gary, W.V., U.S.	G4	114
Garyarsa, China	C8	54
Garza, Arg.	D6	92
Garza Ayala, Mex.	H7	130
Garzón, Col.	F4	86
Garzón, Ur.	G10	92
Gasan-Kuli, Turkmen.	B7	56
Gas City, In., U.S.	H4	112
Gascogne (Gascony), hist. reg., Fr.	F6	18
Gasconade, stm., Mo., U.S.	F6	120
Gasconade, Osage Fork, stm., Mo., U.S.	G5	120
Gascony see Gascogne, hist. reg., Fr.	F6	18
Gascoyne, stm., Austl.	D2	74
Gashaka, Nig.	H7	64
Gashua, Nig.	G7	64
Gaspar, Braz.	C13	92
Gasparilla Island, i., Fl., U.S.	J3	116
Gaspé, Qc., Can.	B12	110
Gaspé, Baie de, b., Qc., Can.	B12	110
Gaspé, Cap, c., Qc., Can.	B12	110
Gaspe Peninsula see Gaspésie, Péninsule de la, pen., Qc., Can.	B11	110
Gaspésie, Péninsule de la (Gaspe Peninsula), pen., Qc., Can.	B11	110
Gassaway, W.V., U.S.	F5	114
Gasteiz (Vitoria), Spain	B8	20
Gaston, Lake, res., U.S.	H7	114
Gastonia, N.C., U.S.	A4	116
Gastre, Arg.	H3	90
Gata, Cabo de, c., Spain	H8	20
Gata, Sierra de, mts., Spain	D4	20
Gătaia, Rom.	D8	26
Gátas, Akrotírion, c., Cyp.	D4	58
Gatčina, Russia	A12	10
Gate City, Va., U.S.	H3	114
Gateshead, Eng., U.K.	G11	12
Gateshead Island, i., Nu., Can.	A11	106
Gatesville, N.C., U.S.	H9	114
Gatesville, Tx., U.S.	C10	130
Gateway, Co., U.S.	E8	132
Gatineau, Qc., Can.	C14	112
Gatineau, stm., Qc., Can.	C14	112
Gatineau, Parc de la, p.o.i., Qc., Can.	C13	112
Gatlinburg, Tn., U.S.	I2	114
Gattinara, Italy	E5	22
Gatton, Austl.	F9	76
Gatún, Lago, res., Pan.	H7	102
Gatun Lake see Gatún, Lago, res., Pan.	H7	102
Gauer Lake, l., Mb., Can.	D11	106
Gauja (Koiva), stm., Eur.	C7	10
Gaujiena, Lat.	C9	10
Gauley, stm., W.V., U.S.	F4	114
Gauley Bridge, W.V., U.S.	F4	114
Gaurela, India	G8	54
Gauribidanūr, India	E3	53
Gause, Tx., U.S.	G2	122
Gaustatoppen, mtn., Nor.	G3	8
Gauteng, state, S. Afr.	D9	70
Gavà, Spain	C12	20
Gávdos, i., Grc.	I7	28
Gavião, stm., Braz.	H5	88
Gavins Point Dam, dam, U.S.	E15	126
Gävle, Swe.	F7	8
Gävleborg, state, Swe.	F7	8
Gavorrano, Italy	H7	22
Gavrilov-Jam, Russia	H18	8
Gawachab, Nmb.	E3	70
Gāwān, India	F10	54
Gawler, Austl.	J2	76
Gawler Ranges, mts., Austl.	F7	74
Gaya, India	F10	54
Gaya, Nig.	G6	64
Gaya, Niger	G5	64
Gaylord, Mn., U.S.	G4	118
Gayndah, Austl.	E8	76
Gays Mills, Wi., U.S.	H8	118
Gaza see Ghazzah, Gaza	G5	58
Gaza, state, Moz.	C11	70
Gazandzhyk see Gazandzyk, Turkmen.	B8	56
Gazandzyk, Turkmen.	B8	56
Gazaoua, Niger	G6	64
Gaza Strip, dep., Asia	G5	58
Gazelle Peninsula, pen., Pap. N. Gui.	a5	79a
Gaziantep, Tur.	A8	58
Gaziantep, state, Tur.	B8	58
Gazimağusa (Famagusta), N. Cyp.	C4	58
Gazimağusa Körfezi, b., N. Cyp.	C4	58
Gazipaşa, Tur.	G15	28
Gazivoda Jezero, res., Serb.	G7	26
Gbanga, Lib.	H3	64
Gboko, Nig.	H6	64
Gdańsk (Danzig), Pol.	B14	16
Gdańsk, state, Pol.	B14	16
Gdansk, Gulf of, b., Eur.	B15	16
Gdov, Russia	B10	10
Gdynia, Pol.	B14	16
Gearhart Mountain, mtn., Or., U.S.	A5	134
Geary, N.B., Can.	E10	110
Geary, Ok., U.S.	F10	128
Gebe, Pulau, i., Indon.	E8	44
Gebze, Tur.	C12	28
Geçitkale, N. Cyp.	C4	58
Gediz, Tur.	D12	28
Gediz (Hermus), stm., Tur.	E10	28
Gedser, Den.	B7	16
Geel, Bel.	C13	14
Geelong, Austl.	L5	76
Geelvink Channel, strt., Austl.	E2	74
Geesthacht, Ger.	C6	16
Geeveston, Austl.	o13	77a
Ge Hu, l., China	F8	42
Geiger, Al., U.S.	E10	122
Geikie, stm., Sk., Can.	D9	106
Geisenfeld, Ger.	H7	16
Geislingen an der Steige, Ger.	H5	16
Geistown, Pa., U.S.	D7	114
Geita, Tan.	E6	66
Gejiu, China	G5	36
Gela, Italy	G8	24
Gela, Golfo di, b., Italy	H7	24
Gelādī, Eth.	F9	62
Gelang, Tanjong, c., Malay.	K6	48
Gelasa, Selat, strt., Indon.	E5	50
Geleen, Neth.	D14	14
Gelembe, Tur.	D10	28
Gelendžik, Russia	F5	32
Gelgaudiškis, Lith.	E6	10
Gelibolu, Tur.	C9	28
Gelibolu Yarımadası (Gallipoli Peninsula), pen., Tur.	C9	28
Gellibrand River, Austl.	L4	76
Gelsenkirchen, Ger.	E2	16
Gemas, Malay.	K6	48
Gemena, D.R.C.	D3	66
Gemert, Neth.	E1	16
Gemlik, Tur.	C12	28
Gemlik Körfezi, b., Tur.	C11	28
Gemona del Friuli, Italy	D10	22
Gemsa, Egypt	K4	58
Gemsbok National Park, p.o.i., Bots.	D5	70

Name — Map Ref. — Page

Gemünden, Ger. — F5 16
Gen, stm., China — A9 36
Genalē (Jubba), stm., Afr. — C8 66
Gending, Indon. — G8 50
General Acha, Arg. — H5 92
General Alvear, Arg. — G3 92
General Alvear, Arg. — H8 92
General Belgrano, Arg. — G8 92
General Bernardo
  O'Higgins, sci., Ant. — B35 81
General Bravo, Mex. — C9 100
General Cabrera, Arg. — F6 92
General Campos, Arg. — E8 92
General Carrera, Lago, l.,
  S.A. — I2 90
General Conesa, Arg. — H4 90
General Conesa, Arg. — H9 92
General Daniel Cerri, Arg. — I6 92
General Elizardo Aquino,
  Para. — C9 92
General Enrique
  Martínez, Ur. — F10 92
General Escobedo, Mex. — I7 130
General Eugenio A.
  Garay, Para. — D4 90
General Galarza, Arg. — F8 92
General Güemes, Arg. — B5 92
General Guido, Arg. — H8 92
General José de San
  Martín, Arg. — C8 92
General Juan José Ríos,
  Mex. — C4 100
General Juan Madariaga,
  Arg. — H9 92
General La Madrid, Arg. — H7 92
General Lavalle, Arg. — H9 92
General Levalle, Arg. — G5 92
General Manuel Belgrano,
  Cerro, mtn., Arg. — D4 92
General Pico, Arg. — G6 92
General Pinedo, Arg. — C7 92
General Pizarro, Arg. — B6 92
General Ramírez, Arg. — F7 92
General Roca, Arg. — G3 90
General San Martín, Arg. — G8 92
General Santos, Phil. — G5 52
General Terán, Mex. — C9 100
General Toševo, Blg. — F14 26
General Toshevo see
  General Toševo, Blg. — F14 26
General Treviño, Mex. — H8 130
General Trias, Mex. — F1 130
General Viamonte, Arg. — G7 92
General Villegas, Arg. — G6 92
Genesee, Id., U.S. — D9 136
Genesee, stm., U.S. — F12 112
Geneseo, Il., U.S. — C7 120
Geneseo, Ks., U.S. — C10 128
Geneseo, N.Y., U.S. — B8 114
Geneva see Genève, Switz. — D3 22
Geneva, Il., U.S. — J10 118
Geneva, In., U.S. — H5 112
Geneva, Ne., U.S. — G15 126
Geneva, N.Y., U.S. — B8 114
Geneva, Oh., U.S. — C4 114
Geneva, Lake, l., Eur. — C12 18
Genève (Geneva), Switz. — D3 22
Genève, Lac de see
  Geneva, Lake, l., Eur. — C12 18
Genf see Genève, Switz. — D3 22
Gengma, China — G4 36
Genil, stm., Spain — G5 20
Genk, Bel. — C14 14
Genkai-nada, s., Japan — F2 40
Genoa, Austl. — K7 76
Genoa see Genova, Italy — F5 22
Genoa, Ne., U.S. — F15 126
Genoa, Oh., U.S. — C2 114
Genoa, Wi., U.S. — H7 118
Genova (Genoa), Italy — F5 22
Genova, Golfo di, b., Italy — G5 22
Genrietty, ostrov, i., Russia — A20 34
Gens de Terre, stm.,
  Qc., Can. — B13 112
Genshiryoku-kenkyūsho,
  sci., Japan — C13 40
Gent (Ghent), Bel. — C12 14
Genteng, Gili, i., Indon. — G8 50
Genthin, Ger. — D8 16
Gentio do Ouro, Braz. — F4 88
Genzano di Roma, Italy — I9 22
Geographe Bay, b., Austl. — F3 74
Geographical Society
  Ø, i., Grnld. — C21 141
Geok-Tepe, Turkmen. — B8 56
Geokčaj see
George, Ia., U.S. — H2 118
George, stm., Qc., Can. — D17 106
George, Lake, l., Austl. — J7 76
George, Lake, l., Austl. — D4 74
George, Lake, l., Ug. — E6 66
George, Lake, l., Fl., U.S. — G4 116
George, Lake, res., N.Y., U.S. — G3 110
George Town, Austl. — n13 77a
Georgetown, Austl. — B4 76
Georgetown, On., Can. — E9 112
Georgetown, P.E.I., Can. — D14 110
George Town, Cay. Is. — C7 102
Georgetown, Gam. — G2 64
Georgetown, Guy. — B6 84
George Town (Penang),
  Malay. — J4 48
Georgetown, St. Vin. — o11 105e
Georgetown, Co., U.S. — B3 128
Georgetown, De., U.S. — F10 114
Georgetown, Fl., U.S. — G4 116
Georgetown, Id., U.S. — H15 136
Georgetown, Ky., U.S. — F1 114
Georgetown, Ms., U.S. — F8 122
Georgetown, Oh., U.S. — F2 114
Georgetown, S.C., U.S. — C6 116
Georgetown, Tx., U.S. — D10 130
George V Coast, cst., Ant. — B19 81
George Washington
  Birthplace National
  Monument, p.o.i.,
  Va., U.S. — F9 114
George Washington Carver
  National Monument,
  p.o.i., Mo., U.S. — H3 120
George West, Tx., U.S. — F9 130
Georgia, ctry., Asia — F6 32
Georgia, state, U.S. — E11 108
Georgia, Strait of, strt., N.A. — G7 138
Georgian Bay, b., On., Can. — C8 112
Georgian Bay Islands
  National Park, p.o.i.,
  On., Can. — D9 112
Georgievka, Kaz. — E14 32
Georgina, stm., Austl. — D2 76
Georg von Neumayer,
  sci., Ant. — B3 81
Gera, Ger. — F7 16
Geral, Serra, mts., Braz. — C12 92
Geral, Serra, clff, Braz. — F2 88
Gerald, Mo., U.S. — F6 120
Geral de Goiás,
  Serra, clff, Braz. — G2 88
Geraldine, N.Z. — F5 80
Geraldton, Austl. — E2 74
Geraldton, On., Can. — B11 118
Gérardmer, Fr. — F15 14
Gerber, Ca., U.S. — C3 134
Gerdine, Mount, mtn.,
  Ak., U.S. — D9 140
Gerede, Tur. — C15 28
Gereshk, Afg. — C9 56
Gérgal, Spain — G8 20
Gerik, Malay. — J5 48
Gerlachovský
  štít, mtn., Slov. — G16 16
German Democratic
  Republic see Germany,
  ctry., Eur. — E6 16
Germania Land, reg., Grnld. — B21 141

Germantown, Il., U.S. — F8 120
Germantown, Tn., U.S. — B9 122
Germantown, Wi., U.S. — E1 112
Germany, ctry., Eur. — E6 16
Germany, Federal Republic
  of see Germany, ctry., Eur. — E6 16
Germencik, Tur. — F10 28
Germfask, Mi., U.S. — B4 112
Gernika, Spain — A8 20
Gero, Japan — D10 40
Geroliménas, Grc. — G5 28
Gerona see Girona, Spain — B13 20
Geronimo, Ok., U.S. — G10 128
Gers, state, Fr. — F6 18
Gers, stm., Fr. — F6 18
Gérzē, China — B10 54
Geseke, Ger. — E4 16
Geser, Indon. — F9 44
Getafe, Spain — D7 20
Gettysburg, Pa., U.S. — E8 114
Getúlio Vargas, Braz. — C11 92
Geumpang, Indon. — J2 48
Gevgelija, Mac. — B5 28
Geyikli, Tur. — D9 28
Geyser, Mt., U.S. — C16 136
Geyserville, Ca., U.S. — E3 134
Geyve, Tur. — C13 28
Ghaapplato, plat., S. Afr. — E7 70
Ghadāmis, Libya — B1 62
Ghaghar, stm., India — D5 54
Ghāghara (Kauriālā), stm.,
  Asia — E9 54
Ghāghra see
  Ghāghara, stm., Asia — E9 54
Ghakhar, Pak. — B4 54
Ghana, ctry., Afr. — H4 64
Ghanzi, Bots. — B5 70
Ghanzi, state, Bots. — C6 70
Gharandal, sci., Jord. — H6 58
Gharaunda, India — D6 54
Ghardaïa, Alg. — C5 64
Ghardimaou, Tun. — H2 24
Gharyān, Libya — A2 62
Ghāt, Libya — C2 62
Ghātere, Mount, mtn.,
  Sol. Is. — d8 79b
Ghātprabha, stm., India — C2 53
Ghātsīla, India — G11 54
Ghawdex (Gozo), i., Malta — H8 24
Ghazāl, Bahr al-, stm.,
  Sudan — F6 62
Ghāziābād, India — D6 54
Ghazipur, India — F9 54
Ghazlūna, Pak. — C1 54
Ghazni, Afg. — C10 56
Ghazni, state, Afg. — B1 54
Ghazni, stm., Afg. — B2 54
Ghazzah (Gaza), Gaza — G5 58
Ghazzah, Leb. — E6 58
Ghent see Gent, Bel. — C12 14
Gheorgheni, Rom. — C12 26
Gherla, Rom. — C10 26
Gheroo, Geziret, i., Egypt — G1 58
Ghinah, Wādī al-, stm.,
  Sau. Ar. — H9 58
Ghisonaccia, Fr. — H15 18
Ghizo see Gizo Island,
  i., Sol. Is. — e7 79b
Ghizunabeana Islands,
  is., Sol. Is. — d8 79b
Ghorīān, Afg. — C9 56
Ghotki, Pak. — E2 54
Ghubaysh, Sudan — E5 62
Gianh, stm., Viet. — C7 48
Giannitsá, Grc. — C5 28
Giant Mountain, mtn.,
  N.Y., U.S. — F3 110
Giant's Castle, mtn., S. Afr. — F9 70
Giant's Castle Game
  Reserve, S. Afr. — F9 70
Giant Sequoia National
  Monument, p.o.i.,
  Ca., U.S. — G7 134
Gia Rai, Viet. — H7 48
Giarre, Italy — G9 24
Gibara, Cuba — B9 102
Gibbon, Mn., U.S. — G4 118
Gibbons, Ab., Can. — C17 138
Gibbonsville, Id., U.S. — E13 136
Gibb River, Austl. — C5 74
Gibeon, Nmb. — D3 70
Gibraléon, Spain — G3 20
Gibraltar, Gib. — H5 20
Gibraltar, dep., Eur. — H5 20
Gibraltar, Strait of, strt. — B3 64
Gibraltar Point, c.,
  Eng., U.K. — H13 12
Gibsland, La., U.S. — E5 122
Gibson City, Il., U.S. — D9 120
Gibson Desert, des., Austl. — D4 74
Gibsons, B.C., Can. — G7 138
Giddalūr, India — D4 53
Giddings, Tx., U.S. — D11 130
Gīdgī, Lake, l., Austl. — E5 74
Giedraičiai, Lith. — E8 10
Gien, Fr. — G11 14
Giessen, Ger. — F4 16
Gifatīn, Gezira, is., Egypt — K4 58
Gifford, Fl., U.S. — I5 116
Gifford, stm., Nu., Can. — A14 106
Gifford Creek, Austl. — D3 74
Gifgāfa, Bîr, well, Egypt — H4 58
Gifhorn, Ger. — D6 16
Gifu, Japan — D9 40
Gifu, state, Japan — D10 40
Giganta, Sierra de la,
  mts., Mex. — C3 100
Gigena see Alcira, Arg. — F5 92
Gigha Island, i., Scot., U.K. — F7 12
Giglio, Isola del, i., Italy — H7 22
Gihu see Gifu, Japan — D9 40
Gijón, Spain — A5 20
Gila, stm., U.S. — K2 132
Gila Bend, Az., U.S. — K4 132
Gila Cliff Dwellings
  National Monument,
  p.o.i., N.M., U.S. — J8 132
Gilbert, La., U.S. — E7 122
Gilbert, stm., Austl. — C8 74
Gilbert Islands see
  Kiribati, ctry., Oc. — D9 72
Gilbert Islands, is., Kir. — D9 72
Gilbert Peak, mtn., Wa., U.S. — D5 136
Gilbert Plains, Mb., Can. — C13 124
Gilbuès, Braz. — E3 88
Gilchrist, Or., U.S. — G5 136
Gilford Island, i., B.C., Can. — F4 138
Gilgandra, Austl. — H7 76
Gilgil, Kenya — E7 66
Gil Gil Creek, stm., Austl. — G8 76
Gilgit, Pak. — B11 56
Gilgit, stm., Pak. — B11 56
Giljuj, stm., Russia — F14 34
Gillam, Mb., Can. — D12 106
Gillen, Lake, l., Austl. — E5 74
Gillespie, Il., U.S. — E8 120
Gillett, Ar., U.S. — C7 122
Gillette, Wy., U.S. — C7 126
Gillian, Lake, l., Nu., Can. — B16 106
Gillingham, Eng., U.K. — J13 12
Gills Rock, Wi., U.S. — C3 112
Gilman, Il., U.S. — D10 120
Gilman, Wi., U.S. — F8 118
Gilmer, Tx., U.S. — E4 122
Gilmore City, Ia., U.S. — B3 120
Gilroy, Ca., U.S. — F4 134
Giltner, Ne., U.S. — G14 126
Giluwe, Mount, mtn.,
  Pap. N. Gui. — b3 79a
Gimbi, Eth. — F7 62
Gimie, Mount, vol., St. Luc. — m6 105c

Gimli, Mb., Can. — D16 124
Gimpu, Indon. — D12 50
Gineina, Râs el-,
  mtn., Egypt — I4 58
Gin Gin, Austl. — E8 76
Gingoog, Phil. — F5 52
Giniṛ, Eth. — F8 62
Ginosa, Italy — D10 24
Gioia, Golfo di b., Italy — F9 24
Gioia del Colle, Italy — D10 24
Gioia Tauro, Italy — F9 24
Giong Rieng, Viet. — H7 48
Gipuzkoako, co., Spain — A8 20
Girafi, Wadi (Paran, Naḥal),
  stm. — I5 58
Giralia, Austl. — D2 74
Girard, Il., U.S. — E8 120
Girard, Ks., U.S. — G3 120
Girard, Oh., U.S. — C5 114
Girard, Pa., U.S. — C5 114
Girardot, Col. — E4 86
Giraud, Pointe, c., Dom. — j6 105c
Girgarre, Austl. — K5 76
Girīdīh, India — F11 54
Girna, stm., India — H5 54
Gir National Park,
  p.o.i., India — H3 54
Girne (Kyrenia), N. Cyp. — C4 58
Girón, Ec. — D2 84
Girona, co., Spain — B13 20
Gironde, state, Fr. — E5 18
Gironde, est., Fr. — D5 18
Gir Range, mts., India — H3 54
Giru, Austl. — B6 76
Giruá, Braz. — D10 92
Girvan, Scot., U.K. — F8 12
Gisborne, N.Z. — D8 80
Giscome, B.C., Can. — B8 138
Gislaved, Swe. — H5 8
Gisors, Fr. — E10 14
Gitarama, Rw. — E5 66
Gitega, Bdi. — E5 66
Giulianova, Italy — H10 22
Giurgiu, Rom. — F12 26
Giurgiu, state, Rom. — E13 26
Giuvala, Pasul, p., Rom. — D12 26
Givet, Fr. — D13 14
Givors, Fr. — D10 18
Giyon, Eth. — F7 62
Giza see El-Gîza, Egypt — H1 58
Gizduvan, Uzb. — F10 32
Gižiga, Russia — D21 34
Gižiginskaja guba,
  b., Russia — D20 34
Gizo, Sol. Is. — e7 79b
Gizo Island, i., Sol. Is. — e7 79b
Gižycko, Pol. — B17 16
Gjirokastër, Alb. — D14 24
Gjirokastra see
  Gjirokastër, Alb. — D14 24
Gjoa Haven see
  Oqsuqtooq, Nu., Can. — B11 106
Gjøvik, Nor. — F4 8
Gjuhëzës, Kepi i, c., Alb. — D13 24
Gjumri, Arm. — A5 56
Glace Bay, N.S., Can. — D17 110
Glacier, B.C., Can. — E13 138
Glacier Bay, b., Ak., U.S. — E12 140
Glacier National Park,
  p.o.i., B.C., Can. — E13 138
Glacier National Park,
  p.o.i., Mt., U.S. — B12 136
Glacier Peak, vol., Wa., U.S. — B5 136
Glacier Strait, strt.,
  Nu., Can. — B10 141
Glad', Russia — A15 10
Gladbrook, Ia., U.S. — B5 120
Gladewater, Tx., U.S. — E4 122
Gladstone, Austl. — D8 76
Gladstone, Mb., Can. — D14 124
Gladstone, Mi., U.S. — C2 112
Gladstone, Mo., U.S. — E3 120
Glâma, stm., Nor. — F4 8
Glan, Phil. — H5 52
Glaris see Glarus, Switz. — C5 22
Glarner Alpen, mts., Switz. — D6 22
Glarus, Switz. — C5 22
Glarus Alps see Glarner
  Alpen, mts., Switz. — D6 22
Glasco, Ks., U.S. — B11 128
Glasgow, Scot., U.K. — F8 12
Glasgow, Ky., U.S. — G12 120
Glasgow, Mo., U.S. — E5 120
Glasgow, Mt., U.S. — F7 124
Glasgow, Va., U.S. — G6 114
Glassboro, N.J., U.S. — E10 114
Glastonbury, Eng., U.K. — J10 12
Glauchau, Ger. — F8 16
Glazov, Russia — C8 32
Glazunovka, Russia — H19 10
Gleichen, Ab., Can. — F17 138
Glen Alpine, N.C., U.S. — A4 116
Glenavon, Sk., Can. — D10 124
Glenboro, Mb., Can. — E14 124
Glenburn, N.D., U.S. — F12 124
Glen Burnie, Md., U.S. — E9 114
Glen Canyon, p., U.S. — F6 132
Glen Canyon Dam, dam,
  Az., U.S. — G5 132
Glen Canyon National
  Recreation Area,
  p.o.i., U.S. — G5 132
Glencoe, On., Can. — F8 112
Glencoe, S. Afr. — F9 70
Glencoe, Mn., U.S. — G4 118
Glen Cove, N.Y., U.S. — D12 114
Glendale, Az., U.S. — J4 132
Glendale, Ca., U.S. — I7 134
Glendale, Ms., U.S. — F9 122
Glendale, Ut., U.S. — F4 132
Glendale, Wi., U.S. — A10 120
Glendive, Mt., U.S. — G9 124
Glendo, Wy., U.S. — E7 126
Glendon, Ab., Can. — B19 138
Glendo Reservoir, res.,
  Wy., U.S. — E8 126
Glen Elder, Ks., U.S. — B10 128
Glengarriff, Ire. — J3 12
Glengyle, Austl. — E2 76
Glen Innes, Austl. — G8 76
Glenmora, La., U.S. — G6 122
Glennallen, Ak., U.S. — D10 140
Glennie, Mi., U.S. — D6 112
Glenns Ferry, Id., U.S. — H11 136
Glenoma, Wa., U.S. — D4 136
Glenormiston, Austl. — D7 74
Glennreagh, Austl. — H9 76
Glen Robertson, On., Can. — E2 110
Glenrock, Wy., U.S. — E7 126
Glenrose, Tx., U.S. — B10 130
Glenrothes, Scot., U.K. — E9 12
Glens Falls, N.Y., U.S. — G3 110
Glenville, Mn., U.S. — H5 118
Glenwood, Ab., Can. — G18 138
Glenwood, Al., U.S. — F12 122
Glenwood, Ar., U.S. — C5 122
Glenwood, Ia., U.S. — C2 120
Glenwood, Mn., U.S. — F3 118
Glenwood, N.M., U.S. — J7 132
Glenwood, Va., U.S. — H6 114
Glenwood Springs, Co., U.S. — D9 132
Glidden, Wi., U.S. — E8 118
Glide, Or., U.S. — G3 136
Glina, Cro. — E13 22
Glittertind see
  Glittertinden, mtn., Nor. — F3 8
Glittertinden, mtn., Nor. — F3 8
Gliwice, Pol. — F14 16
Gljadjanskoje, Russia — D10 32
Globe, Az., U.S. — J6 132
Głodeni, Mol. — B14 26
Głogów, Pol. — E11 16

Głogów Małopolski, Pol. — F17 16
Glomma see Glâma,
  stm., Nor. — F4 8
Glommersträsk, Swe. — D8 8
Glorieta, N.M., U.S. — F3 128
Glorieuses, Îles, is., Reu. — C8 68
Glorioso Islands see
  Glorieuses, Îles, is., Reu. — C8 68
Gloucester, Austl. — H9 76
Gloucester, Eng., U.K. — J10 12
Gloucester, Ma., U.S. — B15 114
Gloucester, Va., U.S. — G9 114
Gloucester Island, i., Austl. — B7 76
Glouster, Oh., U.S. — E3 114
Gloversville, N.Y., U.S. — A11 114
Głowno, Pol. — E15 16
Głubczyce, Pol. — F13 16
Glūbokoe, Kaz. — D14 32
Glubokoje see
  Glūbokoe, Kaz. — D14 32
Głuchołazy, Pol. — F13 16
Glücksburg, Ger. — B5 16
Glückstadt, Ger. — C5 16
Glucomanka, gora, mtn.,
  Russia — B11 38
Glyndon, Mn., U.S. — E2 118
Gmünd, Aus. — B12 22
Gmünd, Aus. — D10 22
Gmunden, Aus. — C10 22
Gnalta, Austl. — H4 76
Gnezdovo, Russia — E15 10
Gniew, Pol. — C14 16
Gniezno, Pol. — D13 16
Gnilec, Russia — H19 10
Gnjilane, Serb. — G8 26
Gnowangerup, Austl. — F3 74
Gŏ, stm., Japan — E5 40
Goa, state, India — D2 53
Goālpāra, India — E13 54
Goaso, Ghana — H4 64
Goat Island, i., Antig. — e4 105b
Goat Point, c., Antig. — e4 105b
Goba, Eth. — F8 62
Gobabis, Nmb. — C4 70
Göbel, Tur. — D11 28
Gobernador Gregores, Arg. — I2 90
Gobernador Ingeniero
  Valentín Virasoro, Arg. — D9 92
Gobernador Juan E.
  Martínez, Arg. — D8 92
Gobernador Vera see
  Vera, Arg. — D7 92
Gobi Desert, des., Asia — C5 36
Gobô, Japan — F8 40
Goce Delčev, Blg. — H10 26
Goch, Ger. — E2 16
Godafoss, wtfl., Ice. — k31 8a
Godāvari, stm., India — C5 53
Godāvari, Mouths of
  the, mth., India — C5 53
Godbout, Qc., Can. — A9 110
Goderich, On., Can. — E8 112
Godfrey, Il., U.S. — F7 120
Godhavn (Qeqertarsuaq),
  Grnld. — D15 141
Godhra, India — G4 54
Gödöllő, Hung. — B6 26
Godoy Cruz, Arg. — F3 92
Gods, stm., Mb., Can. — D12 106
Gods Lake, Mb., Can. — E12 106
Gods Lake, l., Mb., Can. — E12 106
Gods Mercy, Bay of, b.,
  Nu., Can. — C13 106
Godthåb (Nuuk), Grnld. — E15 141
Godwin Austen see K2,
  mtn., Asia — B12 56
Goeie Hoop, Kaap die see
  Good Hope, Cape of,
  c., S. Afr. — I4 70
Goeland, Lac au, l.,
  Qc., Can. — E15 106
Goes, Neth. — C12 14
Goffstown, N.H., U.S. — G5 110
Gogebic, Lake, l.,
  Mi., U.S. — E9 118
Gogoi, Moz. — B11 70
Gogrial, Sudan — F5 62
Gohad, India — E7 54
Gohpur, India — E14 54
Goiana, Braz. — D8 88
Goianésia, Braz. — H1 88
Goiânia, Braz. — I1 88
Goianinha, Braz. — D8 88
Goiás, Braz. — G7 84
Goiás, state, Braz. — C7 90
Goiatuba, Braz. — J1 88
Goio-Erê, Braz. — B11 92
Gôio-Erê, stm., Braz. — B11 92
Góis, Port. — D2 20
Gojō, Japan — E8 40
Gojra, Pak. — C4 54
Gokāk, India — C2 53
Gökçeada, i., Tur. — D9 28
Gökova Körfezi
  (Kerme, Gulf of), b., Tur. — G10 28
Göksu, stm., Tur. — B4 58
Göksu, stm., Tur. — A6 58
Göktepe, Tur. — F11 28
Gokwe, Zimb. — D4 68
Golāghāt, India — C7 46
Gola Gokarannāth, India — D8 54
Gölbaşı, Tur. — D13 16
Gölbaşı, Tur. — A8 58
Golcanda, sci., India — C4 53
Golconda, Il., U.S. — G9 120
Golconda, Nv., U.S. — C8 134
Gölcük, Tur. — C12 28
Gołdap, Pol. — B18 16
Gold Bridge, B.C., Can. — F8 138
Golden, B.C., Can. — E13 138
Golden, Co., U.S. — B3 128
Golden, Il., U.S. — D7 120
Golden Bay, b., N.Z. — E5 80
Golden City, Mo., U.S. — G3 120
Goldendale, Wa., U.S. — E6 136
Golden Gate Highlands
  National Park, p.o.i.,
  S. Afr. — F9 70
Golden Hinde, mtn.,
  B.C., Can. — G5 138
Golden Lake, l., On., Can. — C12 112
Goldfield, Nv., U.S. — F8 134
Gold Meadow, Ca., U.S. — H8 122
Goldonna, La., U.S. — E5 122
Gold River, B.C., Can. — G5 138
Gold Rock, On., Can. — B6 118
Goldsboro, N.C., U.S. — A6 116
Goldsworthy, Austl. — D3 74
Goldthwaite, Tx., U.S. — C9 130
Goleta, Ca., U.S. — I6 134
Golfito, C.R. — H6 102
Golfo Aranci, Italy — D3 24
Gölhisar, Tur. — F12 28
Goliad, Tx., U.S. — F10 130
Golicyno, Russia — E19 10
Golina, Pol. — D13 16
Golin Baixing, China — B4 38
Golmud, China — D8 36
Gölmarmara, Tur. — E10 28
Golmud, China — A7 46
Golo, stm., Fr. — F7 18
Golovnin, La., U.S. — E5 122 — see
Golpāyegān, Iran — C7 56
Golspie, Scot., U.K. — D9 12
Golub-Dobrzyń, Pol. — C14 16

Golva, N.D., U.S. — A8 126
Golyšmanovo, Russia — C11 32
Goma, D.R.C. — E5 66
Gomang Co, l., China — C12 54
Gomati, stm., India — E8 54
Gombe, Nig. — G7 64
Gombi, Nig. — G7 64
Gómez Farias, Mex. — A5 100
Gómez Palacio, Mex. — C7 100
Gómez Plata, Col. — D4 86
Gomo Co, l., China — B10 54
Gomogomo, Indon. — b1 79a
Gomoh, India — G10 54
Gonābād, Iran — C8 56
Gonaïves, Haiti — C11 102
Gonam, Russia — E15 34
Gonam, stm., Russia — E14 34
Gonarezhou National
  Park, p.o.i., Zimb. — B10 70
Gonâve, Golfe de la,
  b., Haiti — C11 102
Gonâve, Île de la, i., Haiti — C11 102
Gonbad-e Qābūs, Iran — B8 56
Gonda, India — E8 54
Gondal, India — G3 54
Gondar see Gonder, Eth. — E7 62
Gondarbal, India — A5 54
Gonder, Eth. — E7 62
Gondia, India — H8 54
Gönen, Tur. — C10 28
Gong'an, China — I6 42
Gongcheng, China — I4 42
Gongchengqiao, China — F8 42
Gongga Shan, mtn., China — F5 36
Gonggar, China — D13 54
Gonghe, China — D5 36
Gongliu, China — F14 32
Gongola, stm., Nig. — G7 64
Gongshiya, China — C10 54
Gongxi, China — H6 42
Gongxian, China — D5 42
Gongzhuling, China — C6 38
Goñi, Ur. — F9 92
Goniądz, Pol. — C18 16
Gonoura, Japan — F2 40
Gonzales, Ca., U.S. — G4 134
Gonzales, La., U.S. — G8 122
Gonzales, Tx., U.S. — E10 130
González Moreno, Arg. — G6 92
Goochland, Va., U.S. — G8 114
Goodenough Island, i.,
  Pap. N. Gui. — b5 79a
Gooderham, On., Can. — D11 112
Goodeve, Sk., Can. — C10 124
Good Hope, Cape of
  (Goeie Hoop, Kaap die),
  c., S. Afr. — I4 70
Good Hope Mountain,
  mtn., B.C., Can. — E6 138
Goodhue, Mn., U.S. — G6 118
Gooding, Id., U.S. — H12 136
Goodland, Fl., U.S. — K4 116
Goodland, In., U.S. — K11 118
Goodland, Ks., U.S. — B7 128
Goodlands, Mb., Can. — E13 124
Goodman, Wi., U.S. — C1 112
Goodnews Bay, Ak., U.S. — E7 140
Goodnight, Co., U.S. — C4 128
Goodooga, Austl. — G6 76
Goodrich, N.D., U.S. — G13 124
Good Spirit Lake, l.,
  Sk., Can. — C11 124
Goodview, Mn., U.S. — G7 118
Goodwater, Al., U.S. — D12 122
Goodyear, Az., U.S. — J4 132
Goole, Eng., U.K. — H12 12
Goolgowi, Austl. — I5 76
Goomalling, Austl. — F3 74
Goondiwindi, Austl. — G8 76
Goongarrie, Austl. — F4 74
Goose, stm., N.D., U.S. — G17 124
Goose Creek, S.C., U.S. — C6 116
Goose Island, i., B.C., Can. — D2 138
Goose Lake, l., Sk., Can. — C6 124
Goose Lake, l., U.S. — B5 134
Gooty, India — D3 53
Gopālganj, Bngl. — G12 54
Gopālganj, India — E10 54
Gopichettipālaiyam, India — F3 53
Göppingen, Ger. — H5 16
Goqën, China — F4 36
Go Quao, Viet. — H7 48
Góra Kalwaria, Pol. — E17 16
Gorakhpur, India — E9 54
Goražde, Bos. — F5 26
Gordeevka, Russia — H14 10
Gorda, Punta, c., Cuba — A6 102
Gorda, Punta, c., Nic. — E6 102
Gordon, Ga., U.S. — D2 116
Gordon, Al., U.S. — D11 122
Gordon, Ne., U.S. — E7 118
Gordon, Lake, res., Austl. — o13 77a
Gordon Creek, stm., Ne.,
  U.S. — E11 126
Gordon Downs, Austl. — C5 74
Gordon Horne Peak, mtn.,
  B.C., Can. — E12 138
Gordonsville, Va., U.S. — F7 114
Gordonvale, Austl. — A5 76
Gore, N.S., Can. — E13 110
Gore, Chad — F3 62
Gore, Eth. — F7 62
Gore, N.Z. — H3 80
Gore, Indon. — E7 44
Gorée, Tx., U.S. — H9 128
Gore Range, mts., Co., U.S. — H6 126
Goreville, Il., U.S. — G8 120
Gorgān, Iran — B7 56
Gorgona, Isla, i., Col. — F2 86
Gorgota, Rom. — E13 26
Gorham, Me., U.S. — G6 110
Gori, Geor. — F6 32
Gorica see Gorizia, Italy — E10 22
Goricy, Russia — C19 10
Gorinchem, Neth. — C14 14
Gorizia (Gorica), Italy — E10 22
Gorj, state, Rom. — D10 26
Gorkhā, Nepal — E10 54
Gorki Reservoir see
  Gor'kovskoe
  vodohranilišče,
  res., Russia — H20 8
Gor'kovskoe vodohranilišče
  (Gorky Reservoir),
  res., Russia — H20 8
Gorlice, Pol. — G17 16
Görlitz, Ger. — E10 16
Gorman, Tx., U.S. — B9 130
Gorna Orjahovica, Blg. — F12 26
Gornjak, Russia — D14 32
Gornji Vakuf, Bos. — F4 26
Gorno-Altajsk, Russia — D15 32
Gorno-Altaysk see
  Gorno-Altajsk, Russia — D15 32
Gornozavodsk, Russia — B13 36
Gornye Ključi, Russia — B10 38
Gornyj, Russia — F20 10
Gorodec, Russia — B12 10
Gorodišče, Russia — D7 32
Gorodnja, Russia — H13 10
Gorodok, Russia — B12 10
Goroka, Pap. N. Gui. — b4 79a
Gorong, Pulau, i., Indon. — F9 44
Gorongosa, stm., Moz. — B12 70
Gorontalo, Indon. — E7 44
Górowo Iławeckie, Pol. — B16 16
Goršečnoe, Russia — F20 10
Gorūkleh, Tur. — ? ? — see
Gorutuba, stm., Braz. — H4 88
Gorzów, state, Pol. — D11 16
Gorzów Wielkopolski
  (Landsberg), Pol. — D11 16

Goschen Strait, strt.,
  Pap. N. Gui. — c5 79a
Gosford, Austl. — I8 76
Goshen, N.S., Can. — E15 110
Goshen, Ca., U.S. — G6 134
Goshen, In., U.S. — G4 112
Goshen, N.Y., U.S. — C11 114
Goshute Lake, l., Nv., U.S. — C2 132
Goshute Valley, val., Nv., U.S. — C2 132
Goslar, Ger. — E6 16
Gosnells, Austl. — F3 74
Gossinga, Sudan — F5 62
Gostivar, Mac. — B3 28
Gostyn, Ok., U.S. — F10 128
Gostynin, Pol. — D15 16
Göteborg (Gothenburg),
  Swe. — H4 8
Gotemba, Japan — D11 40
Goteşti, Mol. — C15 26
Gotha, Ger. — F6 16
Gothenburg see
  Göteborg, Swe. — H4 8
Gothenburg, Ne., U.S. — G12 126
Gothèye, Niger — G5 64
Gotland, state, Swe. — G8 8
Gotland, i., Swe. — G8 8
Gotō-rettō, is., Japan — F1 40
Gotska Sandön, i., Swe. — G8 8
Gōtsu, Japan — D5 40
Göttingen, Ger. — E5 16
Goubangzi, China — D4 38
Gouda, Neth. — B13 14
Goudge, Arg. — G3 92
Goudiri, Sen. — G2 64
Gough Island, i., St. Hel. — K5 60
Gough Lake, l., Ab., Can. — D18 138
Gouin, Réservoir, res.,
  Qc., Can. — B1 110
Goulais, stm., On., Can. — B6 112
Goulburn, Austl. — J7 76
Goulburn Islands, is., Austl. — B6 74
Goulburn River National
  Park, p.o.i., Austl. — I7 76
Gould, Ar., U.S. — D7 122
Goulds, Fl., U.S. — K5 116
Goumbou, Mali — G3 64
Goundam, Mali — F4 64
Goundi, Chad — F3 62
Gouré, Niger — G7 64
Gourma-Rharous, Mali — F4 64
Gournay-en-Bray, Fr. — E10 14
Gouro, Chad — D3 62
Gouverneur, N.Y., U.S. — D14 112
Govan, Sk., Can. — C9 124
Gove, Ks., U.S. — C8 128
Govena, mys, c., Russia — E22 34
Govenlock, Sk., Can. — E4 124
Governador Valadares,
  Braz. — J5 88
Govind Ballabh Pant
  Reservoir see Govind
  Ballabh Pant Sāgar,
  res., India — F9 54
Govind Ballabh Pant
  Sāgar, res., India — F9 54
Govind Reservoir see
  Govind Sāgar, res., India — C6 54
Govind Sāgar, res., India — C6 54
Gowanda, N.Y., U.S. — B7 114
Gowd-e Zereh, l., Afg. — D9 56
Gowmal (Gumal), stm., Asia — B2 54
Gowrie, Ia., U.S. — B3 120
Goya, Arg. — D8 92
Goyaves, Îlets à, is., Guad. — h5 105c
Göyçay, Azer. — A6 56
Goz Beïda, Chad — E4 62
Gozdnica, Pol. — E11 16
Gozha Co, l., China — A5 46
Gozo see Ghawdex,
  i., Malta — H8 24
Graaff-Reinet, S. Afr. — H7 70
Grabo, C. Iv. — I3 64
Grabow, Ger. — C7 16
Grabów nad Prosną, Pol. — E13 16
Gračanica, Bos. — E5 26
Grace, Id., U.S. — H15 136
Gracefield, Qc., Can. — B13 112
Graceville, Fl., U.S. — G13 122
Gracias a Dios, Cabo, c., N.A. — E6 102
Gradaús, Braz. — E7 84
Grado, Italy — E10 22
Grado, Spain — A4 20
Grady, Ar., U.S. — C7 122
Grady, N.M., U.S. — G5 128
Graettinger, Ia., U.S. — H4 118
Grafenau, Ger. — H9 16
Gräfenhainichen, Ger. — E8 16
Grafing bei München, Ger. — H7 16
Grafton, Austl. — G9 76
Grafton, Il., U.S. — F7 120
Grafton, N.D., U.S. — F16 124
Grafton, Oh., U.S. — C3 114
Grafton, Wi., U.S. — E2 112
Grafton, W.V., U.S. — E5 114
Grafton, Cape, c., Austl. — A5 76
Graham, N.C., U.S. — H6 114
Graham, Tx., U.S. — H10 128
Graham, Mount, mtn.,
  Az., U.S. — K7 132
Graham Island, i., B.C., Can. — E4 106
Graham Island, i., Nu., Can. — B7 141
Graham Lake, res., Me., U.S. — F8 110
Graham Land, reg., Ant. — B34 81
Graham Moore, Cape, c.,
  Nu., Can. — A15 106
Grahamstad see
  Grahamstown, S. Afr. — H8 70
Grahamstown, S. Afr. — H8 70
Graian Alps, mts., Fr. — E12 18
Grain Coast, cst., Lib. — I3 64
Grainfield, Ks., U.S. — B8 128
Grajaú, Braz. — C2 88
Grajaú, stm., Braz. — B3 88
Grajewo, Pol. — C18 16
Gramada, Blg. — F9 26
Grambling, La., U.S. — E6 122
Gramilla, Arg. — C5 92
Grammichele, Italy — G8 24
Grampian Mountains,
  mts., Scot., U.K. — E8 12
Grampians National Park,
  p.o.i., Austl. — K3 76
Gramsh, Alb. — D14 24
Granada, Nic. — G5 102
Granada, Spain — G7 20
Granada, co., Spain — G7 20
Granada, Co., U.S. — D6 128
Granadella, Spain — C11 20
Granby, Qc., Can. — E4 110
Granby, Co., U.S. — A3 128
Granby, Mo., U.S. — H3 120
Granby, Lake, res., Co., U.S. — A3 128
Gran Chaco, reg., S.A. — D5 90
Grand, stm., On., Can. — E9 112
Grand, stm., Mi., U.S. — F4 112
Grand, stm., Mo., U.S. — E4 120
Grand, stm., S.D., U.S. — B11 126
Grand, East Fork, stm., U.S. — A3 120
Grand, Lac, l., Qc., Can. — A12 112
Grand, North Fork, stm.,
  S.D., U.S. — B10 126
Grand, South Fork, stm.,
  S.D., U.S. — B9 126

Name — Map Ref. — Page

Grandas, Spain A4 20
Grand Bahama, i., Bah. B9 96
Grand Ballon, mtn., Fr. G16 14
Grand Bank, Nf., Can. j22 107a
Grand-Bassam, C. Iv. H4 64
Grand Bay, Al., U.S. G10 122
Grand Beach, Mb., Can. D17 124
Grand Bend, On., Can. E8 112
Grand-Bourg, Guad. i6 105c
Grand Caille Point, c., St. Luc. m6 105c
Grand Calumet, Île du, i., Qc., Can. C13 112
Grand Canal see Da Yunhe, can., China E8 42
Grand Canal, can., Ire. H6 12
Grand Cane, La., U.S. E5 122
Grand Canyon, Az., U.S. G4 132
Grand Canyon, p., Az., U.S. G4 132
Grand Canyon National Park, p.o.i., Az., U.S. G4 132
Grand Canyon-Parashant National Monument, p.o.i., Az., U.S. G3 132
Grand Case, Guad. A1 105a
Grand Cayman, i., Cay. Is. C7 102
Grand Cess, Lib. I3 64
Grand Chenier, La., U.S. H6 122
Grand Coulee Dam, dam, Wa., U.S. C8 136
Grand Cul de Sac, Guad. B2 105a
Grande, stm., Arg. A5 92
Grande, stm., Arg. H3 92
Grande, stm., Bol. C4 90
Grande, stm., Braz. F4 88
Grande, stm., Braz. C7 90
Grande, stm., S.A. J3 90
Grande, stm., Ven. C11 86
Grande, Arroyo, stm., Ur. F9 92
Grande, Bahía, b., Arg. J3 90
Grande, Boca, mth., Ven. C11 86
Grande, Cerro, mtn., Mex. G2 130
Grande, Cerro, mtn., Mex. E7 100
Grande, Ilha, i., Braz. L3 88
Grande, Ilha, i., Braz. A11 92
Grande, Ponta, c., Braz. I6 88
Grande, Rio see Rio Grande, stm., N.A. H13 98
Grande, Serra, mts., Braz. D5 88
Grande-Anse, Qc., Can. C4 110
Grande Cache, Ab., Can. C11 138
Grande Cayemite, i., Haiti C11 102
Grande de Manacapuru, Lago, l., Braz. I11 86
Grande de Matagalpa, stm., Nic. F6 102
Grande de Santiago, stm., Mex. E6 100
Grande do Gurupá, Ilha, i., Braz. D7 84
Grande-Entrée, Qc., Can. C15 110
Grande Prairie, Ab., Can. A12 138
Grand Erg de Bilma, des., Niger F7 64
Grand Erg Occidental, des., Alg. C5 64
Grand Erg Oriental, des., Alg. C6 64
Grande-Rivière, Qc., Can. B12 110
Grande Rivière, La, stm., Qc., Can. E15 106
Grande Ronde, stm., U.S. E9 136
Grandes, Salinas, pl., Arg. A4 92
Grandes, Salinas, pl., Arg. D5 92
Grand-Étang, N.S., Can. D15 110
Grande-Terre, i., Guad. h6 105c
Grande Vigie, Pointe de la, c., Guad. g6 105c
Grand Falls, N.B., Can. C9 110
Grandfather Mountain, mtn., N.C., U.S. H4 114
Grandfield, Ok., U.S. G10 128
Grand Forks, B.C., Can. G12 138
Grand Forks, N.D., U.S. D1 118
Grand Haven, Mi., U.S. E3 112
Grandin, Lac, l., N.T., Can. C7 106
Grand Island, Ne., U.S. G14 126
Grand Island, i., Mi., U.S. B3 112
Grand Isle, La., U.S. H9 122
Grand Junction, Co., U.S. D8 132
Grand Junction, Ia., U.S. B3 120
Grand Lake, Co., U.S. A3 128
Grand Lake, l., N.B., Can. D11 110
Grand Lake, l., N.A. E9 110
Grand Lake, l., La., U.S. H6 122
Grand Lake, l., Mi., U.S. C6 112
Grand Lake, res., Oh., U.S. D1 114
Grand Ledge, Mi., U.S. B1 114
Grand Manan, N.B., Can. F10 110
Grand Manan Island, i., N.B., Can. F10 110
Grand Marais, Mi., U.S. B4 112
Grand Meadow, Mn., U.S. H6 118
Grand-Mère, Qc., Can. D4 110
Grand Morin, stm., Fr. F12 14
Grand Portage, Mn., U.S. D9 118
Grand Portage National Monument, p.o.i., Mn., U.S. C9 118
Grand Prairie, Tx., U.S. B11 130
Grand Rapids, Mb., Can. A14 124
Grand Rapids, Mi., U.S. F4 112
Grand Rapids, Mn., U.S. D5 118
Grand Rhône, stm., Fr. F10 18
Grand Saline, Tx., U.S. E3 122
Grand Staircase – Escalante National Monument, p.o.i., Ut., U.S. F5 132
Grand Teton, mtn., Wy., U.S. G16 136
Grand Teton National Park, p.o.i., Wy., U.S. F16 136
Grand Tower, Il., U.S. G8 120
Grand Traverse Bay, b., Mi., U.S. C4 112
Grand Turk, T./C. Is. B12 102
Grandview, Mb., Can. C13 124
Grandview, Mo., U.S. F3 120
Grandview, Tx., U.S. B10 130
Grandview, Wa., U.S. D6 136
Grand View, Wi., U.S. E7 118
Grand Wash Cliffs, clf., Az., U.S. H3 132
Grañén, Spain C10 20
Graneros, Chile G2 92
Granger, Wa., U.S. D6 136
Granger, Wy., U.S. B6 132
Granger Draw, stm., Tx., U.S. D7 130
Granger Lake, res., Tx., U.S. D10 130
Granges see Grenchen, Switz. C4 22
Grangeville, Id., U.S. E10 136
Granite City, Il., U.S. F7 120
Granite Falls, Mn., U.S. G3 118
Granite Falls, N.C., U.S. I4 114
Granite Falls, Wa., U.S. B5 136
Granite Pass, p., Wy., U.S. C5 126
Granite Peak, Austl. E4 74
Granite Peak, mtn., Mt., U.S. E17 136
Granite Peak, mtn., Mt., U.S. E14 136
Granite Peak, mtn., Nv., U.S. C6 134
Graniteville, S.C., U.S. C4 116
Granitola, Capo, c., Italy G6 24
Granja, Braz. B5 88
Gran Laguna Salada, l., Arg. H3 90
Gränna, Swe. G6 8
Granollers, Spain C13 20
Gran Paradiso, mtn., Italy E4 22
Gran Paradiso, Parco Nazionale del, p.o.i., Italy E4 22
Gran Rio, stm., Sur. C6 84
Gran Sasso d'Italia, mts., Italy H10 22
Gransee, Ger. C9 16
Grant, Fl., U.S. I5 116
Grant, Mi., U.S. E4 112
Grant City, Mo., U.S. D3 120
Grantham, Eng., U.K. I12 12
Grantley Adams International Airport, Barb. n9 105d
Grant Park, Il., U.S. C10 120
Grant Point, c., Nu., Can. B11 106
Grants, N.M., U.S. H9 132
Grantsburg, Wi., U.S. F6 118
Grants Pass, Or., U.S. A2 134
Grant-Suttie Bay, b., Nu., Can. B15 106
Grantsville, W.V., U.S. F4 114
Grantville, Ga., U.S. D14 122
Granum, Ab., Can. G17 138
Granville, Fr. F7 14
Granville, Il., U.S. J9 118
Granville, N.D., U.S. F13 124
Granville, W.V., U.S. E5 114
Granville Lake, l., Mb., Can. D10 106
Granvin, Nor. F2 8
Grão Mogol, Braz. I4 88
Grapeland, Tx., U.S. F3 122
Grapevine Lake, res., Tx., U.S. B10 130
Grapevine Peak, mtn., Nv., U.S. G8 134
Gras, Lac de, l., N.T., Can. C8 106
Gräsö, i., Swe. F8 8
Grasonville, Md., U.S. F9 114
Grass, stm., N.Y., U.S. D15 112
Grass Creek, Wy., U.S. D4 126
Grasse, Fr. F12 18
Grassflat, Pa., U.S. D7 114
Grasslands National Park, p.o.i., Sk., Can. E6 124
Grass Valley, Ca., U.S. D4 134
Grass Valley, Or., U.S. E6 136
Grassy, Austl. n12 77a
Grassy Plains, B.C., Can. C4 138
Graulhet, Fr. F7 18
Gravelbourg, Sk., Can. E7 124
Gravelines, Fr. D11 14
Gravelotte, S. Afr. C10 70
Gravenhage, 's- see 's-Gravenhage, Neth. B12 14
Gravenhurst, On., Can. D10 112
Gravesend, Eng., U.K. J13 12
Gravette, Ar., U.S. H3 120
Gravina in Puglia, Italy D10 24
Gray, Fr. G14 14
Gray, Ga., U.S. D2 116
Grayback Mountain, mtn., Or., U.S. A2 134
Grayling, Mi., U.S. D5 112
Grays, Eng., U.K. J13 12
Grays Harbor, b., Wa., U.S. D2 136
Grays Lake, sw., Id., U.S. G15 136
Grayson, Sk., Can. D11 124
Grayson, Al., U.S. C11 122
Grayson, La., U.S. E6 122
Grays Peak, mtn., Co., U.S. B3 128
Graysville, Tn., U.S. B13 122
Grayville, Il., U.S. F9 120
Graz, Aus. C12 22
Grdelica, Serb. G9 26
Great Artesian Basin, bas., Austl. E3 76
Great Australian Bight, b., Austl. F5 74
Great Barrier Island, i., N.Z. C6 80
Great Barrier Reef, rf., Austl. C9 74
Great Basin, bas., U.S. C4 108
Great Basin National Park, p.o.i., Nv., U.S. E2 132
Great Bear, stm., N.T., Can. B6 106
Great Bear Lake, l., N.T., Can. B6 106
Great Beaver Lake, l., B.C., Can. B7 138
Great Belt see Storebælt, strt., Den. I4 8
Great Bend, Ks., U.S. C10 128
Great Bitter Lake see Murrat el-Kubra, Buheirat, l., Egypt H3 58
Great Britain see United Kingdom, ctry., Eur. D8 6
Great Camanoe, i., Br. Vir. Is. e8 104b
Great Central, B.C., Can. G6 138
Great Channel, strt., Asia G7 46
Great Dismal Swamp, sw., U.S. H9 114
Great Divide Basin, bas., Wy., U.S. F4 126
Great Dividing Range, mts., Austl. C8 74
Great Driffield, Eng., U.K. G12 12
Greater Antilles, is., N.A. H15 94
Greater Khingan Range see Da Hinggan Ling, mts., China B9 36
Greater Sunda Islands, is., Asia F4 44
Great Exuma, i., Bah. C9 96
Great Falls, Mb., Can. D18 124
Great Falls, Mt., U.S. C15 136
Great Falls, S.C., U.S. B4 116
Great Himalayan National Park, p.o.i., India C6 54
Great Inagua, i., Bah. B11 102
Great Indian Desert (Thar Desert), des., Asia D3 54
Great Karroo (Groot Karroo), plat., S. Afr. H6 70
Great La Cloche Island, i., On., Can. B8 112
Great Lake, res., Austl. n13 77a
Great Limpopo Transfrontier Park, p.o.i., Afr. C10 70
Great Malvern, Eng., U.K. I10 12
Great Miami, stm., U.S. E13 120
Great Namaqualand (Groot Namaland), hist. reg., Nmb. D3 70
Great Nicobar, i., India G7 46
Great Ouse, stm., Eng., U.K. I13 12
Great Palm Island, i., Austl. B6 76
Great Pee Dee, stm., S.C., U.S. C6 116
Great Plain of the Koukdjuak, pl., Nu., Can. B16 106
Great Plains, pl., N.A. C4 108
Great Point, c., Ma., U.S. C15 114
Great Ruaha, stm., Tan. F7 66
Great Sacandaga Lake, res., N.Y., U.S. G2 110
Great Sale Cay, i., Bah. I7 116
Great Salt Lake, l., Ut., U.S. B4 132
Great Salt Lake Desert, des., Ut., U.S. C3 132
Great Salt Plains Lake, res., Ok., U.S. E10 128
Great Sand Dunes National Monument, p.o.i., Co., U.S. D3 128
Great Sand Hills, hills, Sk., Can. D4 124
Great Sandy Desert, des., Austl. D4 74
Great Sandy National Park, p.o.i., Austl. E9 76
Great Scarcies, stm., Afr. H2 64
Great Sea Reef, rf., Fiji p19 79e
Great Slave Lake, l., N.T., Can. C8 106
Great Smoky Mountains, mts., U.S. A2 116
Great Smoky Mountains National Park, p.o.i., U.S. A2 116
Great Tenasserim, stm., Mya. F4 48
Great Thatch Island, i., Br. Vir. Is. e7 104b
Great Tobago, i., Br. Vir. Is. e7 104b
Great Victoria Desert, des., Austl. E5 74
Great Wall see Chang Cheng, misc. cult., China D6 36
Great Yarmouth, Eng., U.K. I14 12
Gréboun, mtn., Niger F6 64
Grecco, Ur. F9 92
Gredos, Sierra de, mts., Spain D5 20
Greece, N.Y., U.S. E12 112
Greece, ctry., Eur. H13 6
Greeley, Co., U.S. G8 126
Greeley, Ks., U.S. F2 120
Greeleyville, S.C., U.S. C6 116
Greely Fiord, b., Nu., Can. A9 141
Green, stm., Il., U.S. C8 120
Green, stm., Ky., U.S. G10 120
Green, stm., N.D., U.S. G17 136
Green, stm., Wa., U.S. C5 136
Green, stm., U.S. E7 132
Green Bay, Wi., U.S. D1 112
Green Bay, b., U.S. D2 112
Greenbrier, Ar., U.S. B6 122
Green Brier, Tn., U.S. H11 120
Greenbrier, stm., W.V., U.S. F5 114
Greenburg, La., U.S. G8 122
Greenbush, Mn., U.S. C2 118
Greencastle, In., U.S. E10 120
Greencastle, Pa., U.S. E8 114
Green Cove Springs, Fl., U.S. G4 116
Greendale, In., U.S. E13 120
Greene, Ia., U.S. B5 120
Greeneville, Tn., U.S. H3 114
Greenfield, Ca., U.S. B13 114
Greenfield, Ia., U.S. C3 120
Greenfield, Il., U.S. E7 120
Greenfield, Ma., U.S. H4 110
Greenfield, Mo., U.S. G4 120
Greenfield, Oh., U.S. E2 114
Greenfield, Ok., U.S. F10 128
Green Forest, Ar., U.S. H4 120
Green Island Bay, b., Phil. E2 52
Green Islands, is., Pap. N. Gui. D6 72
Green Lake, Wi., U.S. H10 118
Green Lake, l., B.C., Can. E9 138
Green Lake, l., Wi., U.S. H9 118
Greenland, Ar., U.S. I3 120
Greenland, dep., N.A. B19 94
Greenland Basin, unds. A14 144
Greenland Sea, s. B21 94
Greenleaf, Ks., U.S. B11 128
Green Lookout Mountain, mtn., Wa., U.S. E4 136
Green Mountains, mts., N.A. G4 110
Greenock, Scot., U.K. F8 12
Greenore Point, c., Ire. I6 12
Greenough, stm., Austl. E3 74
Greenport, N.Y., U.S. C13 114
Green River, Pap. N. Gui. a3 79a
Green River, Ut., U.S. D7 132
Green River, Wy., U.S. B7 132
Green River Lake, res., Ky., U.S. G12 120
Greensboro, Fl., U.S. G14 122
Greensboro, Ga., U.S. C2 116
Greensboro, N.C., U.S. H6 114
Greensburg, In., U.S. E12 120
Greensburg, Ks., U.S. D9 128
Greensburg, Pa., U.S. D6 114
Green Springs, Oh., U.S. C2 114
Green Swamp, sw., N.C., U.S. B7 116
Greentown, In., U.S. H4 112
Greenup, Il., U.S. E9 120
Greenup, Ky., U.S. F3 114
Greenvale, Austl. B5 76
Green Valley, Az., U.S. L6 132
Greenville, Lib. H3 64
Greenville, Al., U.S. F12 122
Greenville, Ga., U.S. D14 122
Greenville, Il., U.S. F8 120
Greenville, Ky., U.S. G10 120
Greenville, Me., U.S. E7 110
Greenville, Mi., U.S. E4 112
Greenville, Mo., U.S. G7 120
Greenville, Ms., U.S. D7 122
Greenville, N.C., U.S. A8 116
Greenville, Oh., U.S. D1 114
Greenville, Pa., U.S. C5 114
Greenville, S.C., U.S. B3 116
Greenville, Tx., U.S. D2 122
Greenwater Lake, l., On., Can. C8 118
Greenwich, Ct., U.S. C12 114
Greenwich, Oh., U.S. C3 114
Greenwood, B.C., Can. G12 138
Greenwood, Ar., U.S. B4 122
Greenwood, In., U.S. E11 120
Greenwood, Ms., U.S. D8 122
Greenwood, S.C., U.S. B3 116
Greenwood, Wi., U.S. G8 118
Greenwood, Lake, res., S.C., U.S. B4 116
Greer, S.C., U.S. B3 116
Greers Ferry Lake, res., Ar., U.S. B6 122
Greeson, Lake, res., Ar., U.S. C5 122
Gregório, stm., Braz. E3 84
Gregory, Mi., U.S. B1 114
Gregory, S.D., U.S. D13 126
Gregory, Tx., U.S. G10 130
Gregory, stm., Austl. C7 74
Gregory, Lake, l., Austl. E3 74
Gregory, Lake, l., Austl. G2 76
Gregory, Lake, l., Austl. D5 74
Gregory Range, mts., Austl. B4 76
Greifswald, Ger. B9 16
Greifswalder Bodden, b., Ger. B9 16
Greiz, Ger. F8 16
Gremiha, Russia B18 8
Grenaa, Den. H4 8
Grenada, Ms., U.S. D9 122
Grenada, ctry., N.A. q11 105e
Grenada Lake, res., Ms., U.S. D9 122
Grenadines, is., N.A. p11 105e
Grenchen, Switz. C4 22
Grenen, c., Den. H4 8
Grenfell, Austl. I7 76
Grenoble, Fr. D11 18
Grenola, Ks., U.S. D12 128
Grenora, N.D., U.S. F10 124
Grenville, Gren. q10 105e
Gresham, Or., U.S. E4 136
Gresik, Indon. G8 50
Gresik, Indon. E3 50
Gressåmoen Nasjonalpark, p.o.i., Nor. D5 8
Gretna, Mb., Can. E16 124
Gretna, La., U.S. H8 122
Gretna, Va., U.S. H6 114
Gretna Green, Scot., U.K. F9 12
Greven, Ger. D3 16
Grevená, Grc. C4 28
Grevenbroich, Ger. E2 16
Grevesmühlen, Ger. C7 16
Greybull, stm., Wy., U.S. C4 126
Grey Eagle, Mn., U.S. F4 118
Grey Islands, is., Nf., Can. i22 107a
Greylock, Mount, mtn., Ma., U.S. B12 114
Greymouth, N.Z. F4 80
Grey Range, mts., Austl. F4 76
Greytown, S. Afr. F10 70
Gribbel Island, i., B.C., Can. C1 138
Gribingui, stm., C.A.R. C3 66
Gridley, Ca., U.S. D4 134
Gridley, Il., U.S. D9 120
Griesheim, Ger. G4 16
Griffin, Sk., Can. E10 124
Griffin, Ga., U.S. C1 116
Griffin, Lake, l., Fl., U.S. H4 116
Griffith, Austl. J5 76
Griggsville, Il., U.S. E7 120
Grignols, Fr. E5 18
Grigoriopol, Mol. B16 26
Grijalva (Cuilco), stm., N.A. G12 100
Grim, Cape, c., Austl. n12 77a
Grimari, C.A.R. C3 66
Grimma, Ger. E8 16
Grimmen, Ger. B9 16
Grimsby, On., Can. E10 112
Grimsby, Eng., U.K. H12 12
Grimsel Pass, p., Switz. D5 22
Grímsey, i., Ice. j30 8a
Grimshaw, Ab., Can. D7 106
Grimstad, Nor. G3 8
Grímsvötn, vol., Ice. k31 8a
Grindelwald, Switz. D5 22
Grinnell, Ia., U.S. C5 120
Grinnell Peninsula, pen., Nu., Can. B7 141
Grintavec, mtn., Slvn. D11 22
Griqualand East, hist. reg., S. Afr. G9 70
Griqualand West, hist. reg., S. Afr. F6 70
Grise Fiord see Ausuittuq, Nu., Can. B9 141
Gris-Nez, Cap, c., Fr. D10 14
Griswold, Mb., Can. E13 124
Griswold, Ia., U.S. C2 120
Grizzly Bear Mountain, mtn., N.T., Can. B6 106
Grizzly Mountain, mtn., Id., U.S. C10 136
Grjadcy, Russia D14 10
Grjazovec, Russia G18 8
Groaíras, Braz. B5 88
Groblersdal, S. Afr. D9 70
Grodków, Pol. F13 16
Grodzisk Mazowiecki, Pol. D16 16
Groen, stm., S. Afr. G6 70
Groesbeck, Tx., U.S. F2 122
Grofa, hora, mtn., Ukr. A10 26
Groix, Fr. G5 14
Groix, Île de, i., Fr. G5 14
Grójec, Pol. E16 16
Grombalia, Tun. H4 24
Gronau, Ger. D3 16
Grong, Nor. D5 8
Groningen, Neth. A15 14
Groningen, Sur. B6 84
Groom, Tx., U.S. F7 128
Groot, stm., S. Afr. H7 70
Groot-Berg, stm., S. Afr. H4 70
Groot-Brakrivier, S. Afr. I6 70
Grootdraaidam, res., S. Afr. E9 70
Groote Eylandt, i., Austl. B7 74
Grootfontein, Nmb. D2 68
Grootgeluk, S. Afr. C8 70
Groot Karasberge, mts., Nmb. E4 70
Groot Karroo see Great Karroo, plat., S. Afr. H6 70
Groot-Kei, stm., S. Afr. H9 70
Groot Laagte, stm., Afr. B5 70
Groot Namaland see Great Namaqualand, hist. reg., Nmb. D3 70
Groot-Swartberge, mts., S. Afr. H6 70
Groot-Vis, stm., S. Afr. H8 70
Grootvloer, pl., S. Afr. F5 70
Gros Islet, St. Luc. I7 105c
Gros-Morne, Mart. k6 105c
Gros Morne, mtn., Nf., Can. j22 107a
Gros Piton, vol., St. Luc. m6 105c
Grossenhain, Ger. E9 16
Grosse Pointe, Mi., U.S. B3 114
Grosse Pointe, c., Guad. h6 105c
Grosser Beerberg, mtn., Ger. F6 16
Grosseto, Italy H7 22
Gross-Gerau, Ger. G4 16
Grossglockner, mtn., Aus. C9 22
Grossos, Braz. C7 88
Grossvenediger, mtn., Aus. C9 22
Groton, N.Y., U.S. F13 112
Groton, S.D., U.S. B14 126
Grottaglie, Italy D11 24
Grottammare, Italy G11 22
Grottoes, Va., U.S. F7 114
Grouard Mission, Ab., Can. D7 106
Groundhog, stm., On., Can. F14 106
Grove City, Mn., U.S. F4 118
Grove City, Oh., U.S. E2 114
Grove City, Pa., U.S. C5 114
Grove Hill, Al., U.S. F11 122
Grove Mountains, mts., Ant. C12 81
Grover City, Ca., U.S. H5 134
Groves, Tx., U.S. H5 122
Groveton, N.H., U.S. F5 110
Groveton, Tx., U.S. F3 122
Grovetown, Ga., U.S. C3 116
Growa Point, c., Lib. I3 64
Growler Peak, mtn., Az., U.S. K3 132
Groznyj, Russia F7 32
Grubišno Polje, Cro. E14 22
Grudziądz, Pol. C14 16
Grulla, Tx., U.S. H9 130
Grumo Appula, Italy D10 24
Grundy, Va., U.S. G3 114
Grundy Center, Ia., U.S. B5 120
Grušino, Russia G21 8
Gruver, Tx., U.S. E7 128
Gruznovka, Russia E10 34
Gryfice, Pol. C11 16
Gryfino, Pol. C10 16
Grytviken, S. Geor. J9 90
Guacanayabo, Golfo de, b., Cuba B9 102
Guacara, Ven. B7 86
Guacarí, Col. F3 86
Gu Achi, Az., U.S. K4 132
Guachiría, stm., Col. E6 86
Guachochi, Mex. B5 100
Guadajoz, stm., Spain G6 20
Guadalajara, Mex. E7 100
Guadalajara, Spain D7 20
Guadalajara, co., Spain D8 20
Guadalcanal, state, Sol. Is. f8 79b
Guadalcanal, i., Sol. Is. e9 79b
Guadalete, stm., Spain H4 20
Guadalhorce, stm., Spain G6 20
Guadalimar, stm., Spain F7 20
Guadalmena, stm., Spain F8 20
Guadalope, stm., Spain D10 20
Guadalquivir, stm., Spain H4 20
Guadalquivir, Marismas del, sw., Spain G4 20
Guadalupe, Mex. D7 100
Guadalupe, Mex. C8 100
Guadalupe, Ca., U.S. I5 134
Guadalupe, stm., Tx., U.S. F11 130
Guadalupe, Isla, i., Mex. G3 98
Guadalupe Bravos, Mex. C1 130
Guadalupe Mountains, mts., U.S. B3 130
Guadalupe Mountains National Park, p.o.i., Tx., U.S. C3 130
Guadalupe Peak, mtn., Tx., U.S. C3 130
Guadalupe Victoria, Mex. C6 100
Guadalupe Victoria, Mex. G6 130
Guadarrama, Puerto de, p., Spain D6 20
Guadarrama, Sierra de, mts., Spain D6 20
Guadeloupe, dep., N.A. h15 96a
Guadeloupe Passage, strt., N.A. g5 105c
Guadiana, stm., Eur. G3 20
Guadiana Menor, stm., Spain G7 20
Guadiato, stm., Spain F5 20
Guadiela, stm., Spain D8 20
Guadix, Spain G7 20
Guafo, Isla, i., Chile H1 90
Guaíba, Braz. E12 92
Guaíba, est., Braz. E12 92
Guaimaca, Hond. E4 102
Guainía, state, Col. F7 86
Guainía, stm., S.A. F8 86
Guaiquinima, Cerro, mtn., Ven. E10 86
Guaíra, Braz. B10 92
Guaíra, Braz. K1 88
Guairá, state, Para. B9 92
Guairá, Salto del (Sete Quedas, Salto das), wtfl., S.A. B10 92
Guáitara, stm., Col. G3 86
Guaitecas, Islas, is., Chile H2 90
Guajaba, Cayo, i., Cuba B9 102
Guajará-Açu, Braz. A1 88
Guajará-Mirim, Braz. F4 84
Guaje, Laguna del, l., Mex. B7 100
Gualaca, Pan. H6 102
Gualaceo, Ec. I2 86
Gualala, Ca., U.S. E2 134
Gualdo Tadino, Italy G9 22
Gualeguay, Arg. F8 92
Gualeguay, stm., Arg. F8 92
Gualeguaychú, Arg. F8 92
Gualicho, Salina del, pl., Arg. H4 90
Guam, dep., Oc. j10 78c
Guamá, stm., Braz. A1 88
Guamal, Col. F5 86
Guamal, Col. C4 86
Guaminí, Arg. H6 92
Guam International Airport, Guam i10 78c
Guamote, Ec. H2 86
Guamúchil, Mex. C4 100
Guamués, stm., Col. G3 86
Gua Musang, Malay. J5 48
Guanacaste, Cordillera de, mts., C.R. G5 102
Guanaceví, Mex. C6 100
Guanahacabibes, Golfo de, b., Cuba A5 102
Guana Island, i., Br. Vir. Is. e8 104b
Guanaja, Hond. D5 102
Guanaja, Isla de, i., Hond. D5 102
Guanajuato, Mex. E8 100
Guanajuato, state, Mex. E8 100
Guanambi, Braz. H4 88
Guanaparo, Caño, stm., Ven. C7 86
Guañape, Islas, is., Peru E2 84
Guanare, Ven. C7 86
Guanare, stm., Ven. C7 86
Guanarito, Ven. C7 86
Guandacol, Arg. D3 92
Guandu, China I5 42
Guane, Cuba A5 102
Guang'an, China F2 42
Guangchang, China H7 42
Guangde, China F8 42
Guangdong, state, China J6 42
Guangfeng, China G8 42
Guangji, China G6 42
Guangling, China B6 42
Guangming Ding, mtn., China F7 42
Guangnan, China G5 36
Guangxi, state, China G6 36
Guangxi Zhuangzu Zizhiqu see Guangxi, state, China G6 36
Guangyuan, China E1 42
Guangze, China H7 42
Guangzhou (Canton), China J5 42
Guanhães, Braz. J4 88
Guánica, P.R. C2 104a
Guanipa, stm., Ven. C10 86
Guanta, Ven. B9 86
Guantánamo, Cuba B10 102
Guantao, China C6 42
Guanting Shuiku, res., China A6 42
Guanxian, China E5 36
Guanxian, China C6 42
Guanyun, China D8 42
Guapí, Col. F3 86
Guapiara, Braz. B13 92
Guápiles, C.R. G6 102
Guaporé, Braz. D11 92
Guaporé (Iténez), stm., S.A. F5 84
Guaqui, Bol. C3 90
Guará, stm., Braz. G3 88
Guarabira, Braz. D8 88
Guaraciaba do Norte, Braz. C5 88
Guaraciana, Braz. I4 88
Guaranda, Ec. H2 86
Guaraniaçu, Braz. B11 92
Guarapari, Braz. K5 88
Guarapuava, Braz. B12 92
Guaraqueçaba, Braz. B13 92
Guaratinguetá, Braz. L3 88
Guaratuba, Braz. B13 92
Guarda, Port. D3 20
Guarda, state, Port. D3 20
Guardafui, Cape see Gwardafuy, Gees, c., Som. B10 66
Guardia Escolta, Arg. D6 92
Guardiagrele, Italy H11 22
Guardia Mitre, Arg. H4 90
Guardo, Spain B6 20
Guareña, Spain F4 20
Guarenas, Ven. B8 86
Guárico, state, Ven. C8 86
Guárico, stm., Ven. C8 86
Guárico, Embalse del, l., Ven. C8 86
Guariquito, stm., Ven. C8 86
Guarulhos, Braz. L2 88
Guasare, stm., Ven. B5 86
Guasave, Mex. C4 100
Guasdualito, Ven. D6 86
Guasipati, Ven. D11 86
Guastalla, Italy F7 22
Guatemala, Guat. E2 102
Guatemala, ctry., N.A. E2 102
Guatemala Basin, unds. H29 142
Guateque, Col. E5 86
Guatimozín, Arg. F6 92
Guatopo, Parque Nacional, p.o.i., Ven. B8 86
Guatuaro Point, c., Trin. s13 105f
Guaviare, state, Col. G5 86
Guaviare, stm., Col. E8 86
Guaxupé, Braz. K2 88
Guayabal, Cuba B9 102
Guayabal, Ven. D8 86
Guayabero, stm., Col. F5 86
Guayacán, Chile D2 92
Guayaguayare, Trin. s12 105f
Guayama, P.R. C3 104a
Guayana see Guyana, ctry., S.A. C6 84
Guayana, Macizo de (Guiana Highlands), mts., S.A. E10 86
Guayaneco, Archipiélago, is., Chile I1 90
Guayanilla, P.R. B2 104a
Guayape, stm., Hond. E4 102
Guayapo, stm., Ven. E8 86
Guayaquil, Ec. I1 86
Guayaquil, Golfo de, b., S.A. D1 84
Guayaramerín, Bol. B3 90
Guayas, state, Ec. H1 86
Guayas, stm., Ec. I2 86
Guaymallén, Arg. F3 92
Guaymas, Mex. B3 100
Guaynabo, P.R. B3 104a
Guayquiraró, stm., Arg. E8 92
Guazapares, Mex. B4 100
Guazárachi, Mex. B5 100
Guba, D.R.C. G5 66
Gubaha, Russia C9 32
Gûbâl, Madîq (Jubal, Strait of), strt., Egypt K4 58
Gubavica, wtfl., Cro. G13 22
Gubbi, India E3 53
Gubbio, Italy G9 22
Guben, Ger. E10 16
Gubin, Pol. E10 16
Gucheng, China E4 42
Gūdalūr, India G3 53
Gúdar, Sierra de, mts., Spain D10 20
Gudauta, Geor. F6 32
Gudermes, Russia F7 32
Gudivāda, India C5 53
Gudiyāttam, India E4 53
Güdül, Tur. C15 28
Gūdūr, India D4 53
Guebwiller, Fr. G16 14
Güejar, stm., Col. F5 86
Guékédou, Gui. H2 64
Guélengdeng, Chad E3 62
Guelma, Alg. B6 64
Guelmime, Mor. D2 64
Guelph, On., Can. E9 112
Guérande, Fr. G6 14
Guercif, Mor. C4 64
Guerdjoumane, Djebel, mtn., Alg. H13 20
Güere, stm., Ven. C9 86
Guéréda, Chad E4 62
Guéret, Fr. C7 18
Guerla Mandata Shan, mtn., China C8 54
Guernesey see Guernsey, dep., Eur. L10 12
Guerneville, Ca., U.S. E3 134
Guernica see Gernika, Spain A8 20
Guernica y Luno see Gernika, Spain A8 20
Guernsey, dep., Eur. E6 14
Guernsey, i., Guern. E6 14
Guerrero, Mex. A5 100
Guerrero, Mex. F7 130
Guerrero, state, Mex. G8 100
Guerrero Negro, Mex. B1 100
Gueydan, La., U.S. G6 122
Guga, Russia F16 34
Gugē, mtn., Eth. F7 62
Guguan, i., N. Mar. Is. B5 72
Gui, stm., China I4 42
Guiana Basin, unds. G9 144
Guiana Highlands (Guayana, Macizo de), mts., S.A. E10 86
Güicán, Col. D5 86
Guichi, China F7 42
Guide, China D5 36
Guidimouni, Niger G6 64
Guiding, China H2 42
Guier, Lac de, l., Sen. F1 64
Guijuelo, Spain D5 20
Guilarte, Monte, mtn., P.R. B2 104a
Guildford, Eng., U.K. J12 12
Guildhall, Vt., U.S. F5 110
Guilford, Me., U.S. E7 110
Guilin, China I4 42
Guillaume-Delisle, Lac, l., Qc., Can. D15 106
Guillestre, Fr. E12 18
Guimarães, Braz. B3 88
Guimaras Island, i., Phil. E4 52
Guimba, Phil. C3 52
Guin, Al., U.S. D11 122
Guinan, China D5 36
Guindulman, Phil. F5 52
Guinea, ctry., Afr. G2 64
Guinea, Gulf of, b., Afr. I6 64
Guinea Basin, unds. H13 144
Guinea-Bissau, ctry., Afr. G1 64
Güines, Cuba A7 102
Guingamp, Fr. F5 14
Güinope, Hond. F4 102
Guiping, China J4 42
Guipúzcoa see Gipuzkoako, co., Spain A8 20
Guiratinga, Braz. G7 84
Güiria, Ven. B10 86
Guitry, C. Iv. H3 64
Guiuan, Phil. E5 52
Guixian, China J3 42
Guiyang, China I5 42
Guiyang, China H2 42
Güiza, stm., Col. G2 86
Guizhou, state, China F6 36
Gujarāt, state, India G3 54
Gūjar Khān, Pak. B4 54
Gujrānwāla, Pak. B4 54
Gujrāt, Pak. B4 54
Gukou, China H8 42
Gulargambone, Austl. H7 76
Gulbarga, India C3 53
Gulbene, Lat. C9 10
Güldüzü, Tur. B8 58
Guledagudda, India C2 53
Gülek Boğazı, p., Tur. A5 58
Gulf Islands National Seashore, p.o.i., U.S. G10 122
Gulfport, Ms., U.S. G9 122
Gulf Shores, Al., U.S. G11 122
Gulgong, Austl. I7 76
Gulian, China F13 34
Gulistan, Uzb. F11 32
Gulkana, Ak., U.S. D10 140
Gull, stm., On., Can. B9 118
Gullfoss, wtfl., Ice. k29 8a
Gull Lake, Sk., Can. D5 124
Gull Lake, l., Ab., Can. D17 138
Gull Lake, l., Mn., U.S. E4 118
Güllük, Tur. F10 28
Güllük Körfezi, b., Tur. F10 28
Gülpınar, Tur. D9 28
Gulu, Ug. D6 66
Guluogongba, China A10 54
Gumaca, Phil. D4 52
Gumal (Gowmal), stm., Asia B2 54
Gumbalie, Austl. G5 76
Gumdag, Turkmen. B7 56
Gumel, Nig. G6 64
Gumla, India G10 54
Gumma, state, Japan C11 40
Gummersbach, Ger. E3 16
Gümüşhane, Tur. A4 56
Gümüşsu, Tur. E12 28
Guna, India F6 54
Gundagai, Austl. J7 76
Gundji, D.R.C. D4 66
Gundlupet, India F3 53
Gündoğdu, Tur. C9 28
Güney, Tur. E12 28
Gungu, D.R.C. F3 66
Gunmi, Nig. G6 64
Gunnar, Sk., Can. D9 106
Gunnarn, Swe. D7 8
Gunnbjørn Fjeld, mtn., Grnld. D19 141
Gunnedah, Austl. H7 76
Gunnison, Ut., U.S. D5 132
Gunnison, stm., Co., U.S. E8 132

Name | Map Ref. | Page

Gunong Mulu National Park, p.o.i., Malay. A9 50
Gun Point, c., Gren. p11 105e
Gunpowder Creek, stm., Austl. B2 76
Gunsan see Kunsan, Kor., S. F7 38
Guntakal, India D3 53
Guntersville, Al., U.S. C12 122
Guntersville Dam, dam, Al., U.S. C12 122
Guntersville Lake, res., Al., U.S. C12 122
Guntūr, India C5 53
Gunungkencana, Indon. G4 50
Gunungsahilan, Indon. C2 50
Gunungsitoli, Indon. L3 48
Gunupur, India B6 53
Günzburg, Ger. H6 16
Gunzenhausen, Ger. G6 16
Guo, stm., China E7 42
Guoyang, China E7 42
Guoyangzhen, China B5 42
Gupis, Pak. B11 56
Gurabo, P.R. B4 104a
Gura Humorului, Rom. B12 26
Gurais, India A5 54
Gurdāspur, India B5 54
Gurdon, Ar., U.S. D5 122
Güre, Tur. E12 28
Gurevsk, Russia D15 32
Gurgueia, stm., Braz. D4 88
Gurha, India F3 54
Guri, Embalse de, res., Ven. D10 86
Gurskoe, Russia F16 34
Gurskøya, i., Nor. E1 8
Gürsu, Tur. C12 28
Gurupá, Braz. D7 84
Gurupi, Braz. F1 88
Gurupi, stm., Braz. D8 84
Guru Sikhar, mtn., India F4 54
Gurvan Sayhan uul, mts., Mong. C5 36
Gusau, Nig. G6 64
Gusev, Russia F5 10
Gušgy, Turkmen. B9 56
Gushan, China B10 42
Gushi, China E6 42
Gus'-Hrustal'nyj, Russia I19 8
Gusino, Russia F14 10
Gusinoozersk, Russia F10 34
Gus'-Khrustal'nyy see Gus'-Hrustal'nyj, Russia I19 8
Guspini, Italy E2 24
Güssing, Aus. C13 22
Gustav Holm, Kap, c., Grnld. D19 141
Gustavus, Ak., U.S. E12 140
Gustine, Ca., U.S. F5 134
Gustine, Tx., U.S. C9 130
Güstrow, Ger. C8 16
Gütersloh, Ger. E4 16
Guthrie, Ok., U.S. F11 128
Guthrie, Tx., U.S. H8 128
Guthrie Center, Ia., U.S. C3 120
Gutian, China H8 42
Gutiérrez Zamora, Mex. E10 100
Guttenberg, Ia., U.S. B6 120
Guwāhāti, India E13 54
Guxian, China E5 42
Guyana, ctry., S.A. C6 84
Guyang, China A4 42
Guye, China B8 42
Guy Fawkes River National Park, p.o.i., Austl. H9 76
Guymon, Ok., U.S. E7 128
Guyot, Mount, mtn., U.S. I2 114
Guyra, Austl. H8 76
Guyton, Ga., U.S. D4 116
Guyuan, China D2 42
Guzar, Uzb. G11 32
Güzelyurt, N. Cyp. C3 58
Güzelyurt Körfezi, b., N. Cyp. C3 58
Guzhen, China E7 42
Guzmán, Mex. F7 100
Guzmán, Mex. F9 98
Gvardejsk, Russia F4 10
Gwa, Mya. D2 48
Gwaai, Zimb. D4 68
Gwādar, Pak. D9 56
Gwalia, Austl. E4 74
Gwalior (Lashkar), India E7 54
Gwanda, Zimb. B9 70
Gwane, D.R.C. D5 66
Gwangju see Kwangju, Kor., S. G7 38
Gwardafuy, Gees, c., Som. B10 66
Gwātar Bay, b., Asia E9 56
Gwayi, stm., Zimb. D4 68
Gwda, stm., Pol. C12 16
Gweedore, Ire. F4 12
Gweru, Zimb. D4 68
Gwinn, Mi., U.S. B2 112
Gwydir, stm., Austl. G7 76
Gyangtse see Gyangzê, China D12 54
Gyangzê, China D12 54
Gyaring Co, l., China C12 54
Gyaring Hu, l., China E4 36
Gyda, Russia B4 34
Gydanskaja guba, b., Russia B4 34
Gydanskij poluostrov, pen., Russia B4 34
Gyeongju see Kyŏngju, Kor., S. D2 40
Gyirong, China D10 54
Gyldenløves Fjord, b., Grnld. E17 141
Gym Peak, mtn., N.M., U.S. K9 132
Gympie, Austl. F9 76
Gyobingauk, Mya. C2 48
Gyoma, Hung. C7 26
Gyöngyös, Hung. B6 26
Győr (Raab), Hung. B4 26
Győr-Moson-Sopron, state, Hung. B4 26
Gypsum, Co., U.S. D10 132
Gypsum, Ks., U.S. C11 128
Gypsumville, Mb., Can. C15 124
Gyula, Hung. C8 26
Gyulafehérvár see Alba Iulia, Rom. C10 26
Gyzylarbat, Turkmen. B8 56

H

Haag in Oberbayern, Ger. H8 16
Haaksbergen, Neth. D2 16
Haapiti, Fr. Poly. v20 78h
Haapsalu, Est. G10 8
Haar, Ger. H7 16
Ha'Arava ('Arabah, Wādī al-), val., Asia H6 58
Ha'Arava (Jayb, Wādī al-), stm., Asia H6 58
Haarlem, Neth. B13 14
Habaqila, China C6 36
Habarovsk, Russia G16 34
Habary, Russia D13 32
Habashiyah, Jabal, mts., Yemen F7 56
Habbān, Yemen G6 56
Habermehl Peak, mtn., Ant. C6 81
Habiganj, Bngl. F13 54
Habomai Islands see Malaja Kuril'skaja Grjada, is., Russia C17 38
Hachijō-jima, i., Japan F12 40
Hachiman, Japan D9 40
Hachinohe, Japan D14 38
Hachiōji, Japan D12 40
Hackberry, La., U.S. H5 122
Hackberry Creek, stm., Ks., U.S. C8 128
Hackett, Ar., U.S. B4 122
Hackettstown, N.J., U.S. D11 114
Hadāli, Pak. B4 54
HaDarom, state, Isr. H5 58
Hadd, Ra's al-, c., Oman E8 56
Haddam, Ks., U.S. B11 128
Haddington, Scot., U.K. F10 12
Haddock, Ga., U.S. C2 116
Haddon Downs, Austl. F3 76
Hadejia, Nig. G7 64
Hadejia, stm., Nig. G6 64
Haden, Austl. F8 76
Hadera, Isr. F5 58
Haderslev, Den. I3 8
Hadībū, Yemen G7 56
Hadīthah, Iraq C5 56
Hadley Bay, b., Nu., Can. A9 106
Hadlock, Wa., U.S. B4 136
Ha Dong, Viet. B7 48
Hadramawt, reg., Yemen F6 56
Hadrian's Wall, misc. cult., Eng., U.K. G10 12
Hadzilavičy, Bela. G13 10
Haeju, Kor., N. E6 38
Haenam, Kor., S. G7 38
Haerhpin see Harbin, China B7 38
Haffner Bjerg, mtn., Grnld. B13 141
Hafford, Sk., Can. B6 124
Haffouz, Tun. I3 24
Hāfizābād, Pak. B4 54
Hāflong, India F14 54
Hafnarfjörður, Ice. k28 8a
Haft Gel, Iran C6 56
Hagan, Ga., U.S. D3 116
Hagari, stm., India D3 53
Hagåtña (Agana), Guam j10 78c
Hagemeister Island, i., Ak., U.S. E7 140
Hagen, Ger. E3 16
Hagenow, Ger. C7 16
Hagensborg, B.C., Can. D4 138
Hagerman, N.M., U.S. A3 130
Hagerstown, In., U.S. I4 112
Hagerstown, Md., U.S. E8 114
Hagersville, On., Can. F9 112
Hagfors, Swe. F5 8
Haggin, Mount, mtn., Mt., U.S. D13 136
Hagi, Japan E4 40
Ha Giang, Viet. A7 48
Hagondange, Fr. E15 14
Hags Head, c., Ire. I3 12
Hague, Sk., Can. B7 124
Hague, Cap de la, c., Fr. E7 14
Haguenau, Fr. F16 14
Hagues Peak, mtn., Co., U.S. G7 126
Hahira, Ga., U.S. F2 116
Hai'an, China E9 42
Haibei, China B10 36
Haicheng, China A10 42
Haichow Bay see Haizhou Wan, b., China D8 42
Haidargarh, India E8 54
Hai Duong, Viet. B8 48
Haifa see Hefa, Isr. F5 58
Haifa see Hefa, state, Isr. F5 58
Haifeng, China J6 42
Haig, Austl. F5 74
Haigler, Ne., U.S. A7 128
Haikang, China K3 42
Haikou, China K4 42
Haikou, China G9 42
Hā'il, Sau. Ar. D5 56
Hailākāndi, India F14 54
Hailar, China B8 36
Hailar, stm., China B8 36
Haileyville, Ok., U.S. C3 122
Hailin, China B8 38
Hailun, China B10 36
Hailuoto, i., Fin. D11 8
Haimen, China J7 42
Haimen, China G9 42
Hainan, state, China L3 42
Hainan Dao (Hainan Island), i., China L4 42
Hainan Island see Hainan Dao, i., China L4 42
Hainan Strait see Qiongzhou Haixia, strt., China K4 42
Haines, Ak., U.S. E12 140
Haines, Or., U.S. F8 136
Haines City, Fl., U.S. H4 116
Haines Junction, Yk., Can. C3 106
Haining, China F9 42
Hai Ninh, Viet. B8 48
Hai Phong, Viet. B8 48
Haiphong see Hai Phong, Viet. B8 48
Haiti, ctry., N.A. C11 102
Haitun, China D4 36
Haivoron, Ukr. A16 26
Haiyuan, China C1 42
Haizhou, China D8 42
Haizhou Wan, b., China D8 42
Hajdú-Bihar, state, Hung. B8 26
Hajdúböszörmény, Hung. B8 26
Hajdúnánás, Hung. B8 26
Hajdúszoboszló, Hung. B8 26
Hājīpur, India F10 54
Hajnówka, Pol. D19 16
Hakasija, state, Russia D16 32
Hakha, Mya. A1 48
Hakken-san, mtn., Japan E8 40
Hakodate, Japan D14 38
Hakone-yama, vol., Japan D12 40
Hakui, Japan C9 40
Haku-san, vol., Japan C9 40
Haku-san-kokuritsu-kōen, p.o.i., Japan C9 40
Hal see Halle, Bel. D13 14
Halab (Aleppo), Syria B8 58
Halab, state, Syria B8 58
Halachó, Mex. B2 102
Halahai, China B6 38
Halā'ib, Sudan C7 62
Halawa, Cape, c., Hi., U.S. b5 78a
Halberstadt, Ger. E7 16
Halbrite, Sk., Can. E10 124
Halcon, Mount, mtn., Phil. D3 52
Halden, Nor. G4 8
Haldensleben, Ger. D7 16
Haldimand, On., Can. F10 112
Haldwāni, India D7 54
Hale, Mo., U.S. E4 120
Haleakalā Crater, crat., Hi., U.S. c5 78a
Haleakalā National Park, p.o.i., Hi., U.S. c5 78a
Hale Center, Tx., U.S. G7 128
Halenkov, Czech Rep. G14 16
Halfmoon Bay, B.C., Can. G6 138
Halfway, Md., U.S. E8 114
Halfway, Or., U.S. F9 136
Halicarnassus, sci., Tur. F10 28
Halifax, Austl. B6 76
Halifax, N.S., Can. F13 110
Halifax, Eng., U.K. H11 12
Halifax, N.C., U.S. H8 114
Halifax, Va., U.S. H6 114
Halifax Bay, b., Austl. B6 76
Haliyāl, India D2 53
Haljala, Est. A9 10
Halkapınar, Tur. A5 58
Halland, state, Swe. H5 8
Hallandale, Fl., U.S. K5 116
Hallāniyah, Juzur al- (Kuria Muria Islands), is., Oman F8 56
Halla-san, mtn., Kor., S. H7 38
Hall Basin, b., N.A. A13 141
Halle, Bel. D13 14
Halle, Ger. E7 16
Hällefors, Swe. G6 8
Hallein, Aus. C10 22
Hallettsville, Tx., U.S. E11 130
Halley, sci., Ant. C2 81
Halligen, is., Ger. B4 16
Hall in Tirol, Aus. C8 22
Hall Islands, is., Micron. C6 72
Hall Lake, l., Nu., Can. B14 106
Hall Land, reg., Grnld. A14 141
Hall Mountain, mtn., Wa., U.S. B9 136
Hallock, Mn., U.S. C2 118
Hallowell, Me., U.S. F7 110
Hall Peninsula, pen., Nu., Can. C17 106
Halls, Tn., U.S. I8 120
Hallsberg, Swe. G6 8
Halls Creek, Austl. C5 74
Hallstahammar, Swe. G7 8
Hallstavik, Swe. F8 8
Hallstead, Pa., U.S. C10 114
Hallsville, Mo., U.S. E5 120
Halmahera, i., Indon. E8 44
Halmahera, Laut (Halmahera Sea), s., Indon. F8 44
Halmahera Sea see Halmahera, Laut, s., Indon. F8 44
Hal'mer-Ju, Russia A10 32
Halmstad, Swe. H5 8
Haloučyn, Bela. F12 10
Hal'šany, Bela. F8 10
Halsey, Ne., U.S. F12 126
Halsey, Or., U.S. F3 136
Halstead, Ks., U.S. D11 128
Haltern, Ger. E3 16
Haltiatunturi, mtn., Eur. B9 8
Haltom City, Tx., U.S. B10 130
Halton Hills see Georgetown, On., Can. E9 112
Halvorson, Mount, mtn., B.C., Can. C10 138
Ham, stm., Nmb. F4 70
Hamada, Japan E4 40
Hamadān, Iran C6 56
Hamāh, Syria C7 58
Hamāh, state, Syria C8 58
Hamamatsu, Japan E10 40
Haman, Kor., S. D1 40
Hamana-ko, l., Japan E10 40
Hamar, Nor. F4 8
Ha Marakabei, Leso. F9 70
Hamar-Daban, hrebet, mts., Russia F9 34
Hamâta, Gebel, mtn., Egypt C6 62
Hamburg, Ger. C6 16
Hamburg, Ar., U.S. D7 122
Hamburg, Ia., U.S. D2 120
Hamburg, N.J., U.S. C11 114
Hamburg, N.Y., U.S. B7 114
Hamburg, state, Ger. C6 16
Hamden, Ct., U.S. C13 114
Hamden, Oh., U.S. E3 114
Hämeenlinna (Tavastehus), Fin. F10 8
Hamelin, Austl. E2 74
Hameln, Ger. D5 16
HaMerkaz, state, Isr. F5 58
Hamersley Range, mts., Austl. D3 74
Hamgyŏng-sanjulgi, mts., Kor., N. D8 38
Hamhŭng, Kor., N. E7 38
Hami, China C3 36
Hamilton, Austl. K4 76
Hamilton, Ber. k15 104e
Hamilton, On., Can. E10 112
Hamilton, N.Z. C6 80
Hamilton, Scot., U.K. F8 12
Hamilton, Al., U.S. C11 122
Hamilton, Ga., U.S. E14 122
Hamilton, Il., U.S. D6 120
Hamilton, Mi., U.S. F4 112
Hamilton, Mo., U.S. E3 120
Hamilton, Mt., U.S. D12 136
Hamilton, N.Y., U.S. B10 114
Hamilton, Oh., U.S. E1 114
Hamilton, stm., Austl. D3 74
Hamilton, Lake, res., Ar., U.S. C5 122
Hamilton, Mount, mtn., Ca., U.S. F4 134
Hamilton City, Ca., U.S. D3 134
Hamilton Dome, Wy., U.S. D4 126
Hamilton Hotel, Austl. D3 76
Hamilton Mountain, mtn., N.Y., U.S. G2 110
Hamina, Fin. F12 8
Hamiota, Mb., Can. D13 124
Hamīrpur, India F7 54
Hamlin, Tx., U.S. B7 130
Hamlin, W.V., U.S. F3 114
Hamlin Valley Wash, stm., U.S. E3 132
Hamm, Ger. E3 16
Hammamet, Tun. H4 24
Hammamet, Golfe de, b., Tun. H4 24
Hammam Lif, Tun. H4 24
Hammelburg, Ger. F5 16
Hammerdal, Swe. E6 8
Hammerfest, Nor. A10 8
Hammon, Ok., U.S. F9 128
Hammond, In., U.S. G2 112
Hammond, La., U.S. G8 122
Hammondsport, N.Y., U.S. F12 112
Hampden, Me., U.S. F8 110
Hampden, N.D., U.S. F15 124
Hampi, India D3 53
Hampshire, Il., U.S. I10 118
Hampstead, N.C., U.S. B8 116
Hampton, N.B., Can. E11 110
Hampton, Ar., U.S. D6 122
Hampton, Fl., U.S. G3 116
Hampton, Ga., U.S. C1 116
Hampton, Ne., U.S. G15 126
Hampton, N.H., U.S. H6 110
Hampton, Tn., U.S. H3 114
Hampton, Va., U.S. G9 114
Hampton Butte, mtn., Or., U.S. G6 136
Hampton Tableland, plat., Austl. F5 74
Hamra, Swe. F6 8
Hamrā', Al-Ḥamādah al-, des., Libya B2 62
Hamra, As Saquia al, stm., W. Sah. D2 64
Hamsara, stm., Russia D16 32
Hams Fork, stm., Wy., U.S. F2 126
Ham Tan, Viet. G8 48
Hāmūn, Daryācheh-ye, l., Iran C9 56
Han, stm., China F6 42
Han, stm., China I7 42
Han, Nong, l., Thai. D7 48
Hāna, Hi., U.S. c6 78a
Hanahan, S.C., U.S. D5 116
Hanamaki, Japan E14 38
Hanamui see Anglem, Mount, mtn., N.Z. H2 80
Hanapepe, Hi., U.S. b2 78a
Hanateio, Fr. Poly. s18 78g
Hanatetena, Fr. Poly. s18 78g
Hanau, Ger. F4 16
Hanbury, stm., N.T., Can. C9 106
Hancavičy, Bela. H9 10
Hâncești, Mol. C15 26
Hanceville, Al., U.S. C12 122
Hancheng, China D7 36
Hancheng, China D4 42
Hanchung see Hanzhong, China E2 42
Hancock, Md., U.S. E7 114
Hancock, Mi., U.S. D10 118
Hancock, Mn., U.S. F3 118
Hancock, N.Y., U.S. C10 114
Handa, Japan E9 40
Handan, China C6 42
Handlová, Slov. H14 16
Handsworth, Sk., Can. E10 124
Handyga, Russia D16 34
HaNegev (Negev Desert), reg., Isr. H5 58
Hanford, Ca., U.S. G6 134
Hanga Roa, Chile e29 78l
Hangayn nuruu, mts., Mong. B4 36
Hangchou see Hangzhou, China F9 42
Hangchow see Hangzhou, China F9 42
Hangchow Bay see Hangzhou Wan, b., China F9 42
Hanggin Houqi, China A2 42
Hanggin Qi, China B3 42
Hangman Creek, stm., U.S. C9 136
Hangö see Hanko, Fin. G10 8
Hangokurt, Russia B10 32
Hangu, China B7 42
Hangu, Pak. B3 54
Hanguang, China I5 42
Hangzhou, China F9 42
Hangzhou Wan, b., China F9 42
Hanino, Russia F19 10
Hanish, is., Yemen G5 56
Hanish Islands see Hanish, is., Yemen G5 56
Hanjiang, China I8 42
Hankinson, N.D., U.S. E2 118
Hanko, Fin. G10 8
Hankow see Wuhan, China F6 42
Hanku see Hangu, China B7 42
Hānle, India B7 54
Hanley, Sk., Can. C7 124
Hanna, Ab., Can. E19 138
Hanna, Ok., U.S. B3 122
Hanna, Wy., U.S. B10 132
Hanna City, Il., U.S. D8 120
Hannah, N.D., U.S. F15 124
Hannah Bay, b., On., Can. E14 106
Hannibal, Mo., U.S. E6 120
Hannover, Ger. D5 16
Ha Noi (Hanoi), Viet. B7 48
Hanoi see Ha Noi, Viet. B7 48
Hanover, On., Can. D8 112
Hanover see Hannover, Ger. D5 16
Hanover, S. Afr. G7 70
Hanover, Il., U.S. B7 120
Hanover, In., U.S. F12 120
Hanover, N.H., U.S. G4 110
Hanover, N.M., U.S. K8 132
Hanover, Pa., U.S. E9 114
Hanover, Va., U.S. G8 114
Hanover, Isla, i., Chile J2 90
Hansdiha, India F11 54
Hānsi, India D5 54
Hanska, Mn., U.S. G4 118
Hantajskoe, ozero, l., Russia C6 34
Hantan see Handan, China C6 42
Hantsport, N.S., Can. E12 110
Hanty-Mansijsk, Russia B11 32
Hantzsch, stm., Nu., Can. B16 106
Hanumāngarh, India C3 46
Hanumangarh, India D4 54
Hanuy, stm., Mong. B5 36
Hanyin, China E3 42
Hanzhong, China E2 42
Hanzhuang, China D7 42
Haojiadian, China F5 42
Haoli see Hegang, China B11 36
Hāora, India G12 54
Haparanda, Swe. D10 8
Hapčeranga, Russia G11 34
Happy, Tx., U.S. G7 128
Happy Jack, Az., U.S. I5 132
Happy Valley-Goose Bay, Nf., Can. E18 106
Hāpur, India D6 54
Ḩaql, Sau. Ar. I5 58
Harad, Sau. Ar. E6 56
Haradok, Bela. E13 10
Haradzec, Bela. H7 10
Haradzeja, Bela. G10 10
Haradzišča, Bela. G8 10
Haramachi, Japan B13 40
Haranor, Russia A8 36
Harar see Hārer, Eth. F8 62
Harare, Zimb. D5 68
Harazé Mangueigne, Chad E4 62
Harbala, Russia D13 34
Harbavičy, Bela. G13 10
Harbin, China B7 38
Harbiye, Tur. B7 58
Harbor, Or., U.S. A1 134
Harbor Beach, Mi., U.S. E7 112
Harbour Breton, Nf., Can. j22 107a
Harbourville, N.S., Can. E12 110
Harda, India G6 54
Hardangerfjorden, b., Nor. F2 8
Hardangerjøkulen, ice, Nor. F2 8
Hardangervidda Nasjonalpark, p.o.i., Nor. F2 8
Hardap, state, Nmb. D3 70
Hardeeville, S.C., U.S. D4 116
Harderwijk, Neth. B14 14
Hardin, Il., U.S. E7 120
Hardin, Mt., U.S. B5 126
Harding, S. Afr. G9 70
Harding, Lake, res., U.S. E13 122
Hardinsburg, Ky., U.S. G11 120
Hardisty Lake, l., N.T., Can. C7 106
Hardoi, India E7 54
Hardtner, Ks., U.S. D10 128
Hardwick, Ga., U.S. C2 116
Hardwick, Vt., U.S. F4 110
Hardy, Ar., U.S. H6 120
Hardy, Ne., U.S. G15 126
Hardy Bay, b., N.T., Can. B16 140
Hare Bay, b., Nf., Can. i22 107a
Hare Indian, stm., N.T., Can. B5 106
Hareøen, i., Grnld. C14 141
Hārer, Eth. F8 62
Hargeysa, Som. C8 66
Harghita, state, Rom. C12 26
Har Hu, l., China D4 36
Hari, stm., Indon. D3 50
Harīb, Yemen G6 56
Haridwār, India D7 54
Harihar, India D2 53
Hārim, Syria B7 58
Harīpur, Pak. B4 54
Harīrūd (Tedžen), stm., Asia C9 56
Harischandra Range, mts., India B1 53
Haritonovo, Russia F22 8
Harkers Island, N.C., U.S. B9 116
Harlan, Ky., U.S. H2 114
Harlan County Lake, res., Ne., U.S. A9 128
Harlem, Fl., U.S. J5 116
Harlem, Ga., U.S. C3 116
Harleton, Tx., U.S. E4 122
Harlingen, Neth. A14 14
Harlingen, Tx., U.S. H10 130
Harlovka, Russia B17 8
Harlow, Eng., U.K. J13 12
Harlowton, Mt., U.S. D17 136
Harman, W.V., U.S. F6 114
Harmancık, Tur. D12 28
Harmanli, Blg. H12 26
Harmony, In., U.S. E10 120
Harnai, India C1 53
Harney Basin, bas., Or., U.S. G8 136
Harney Lake, l., Or., U.S. G7 136
Harney Peak, mtn., S.D., U.S. D9 126
Härnösand, Swe. E8 8
Har nuur, l., Mong. B3 36
Haro, Spain B8 20
Haro, Cabo, c., Mex. B3 100
Hārot, stm., Afg. C9 56
Harovsk, Russia F18 8
Harpanahalli, India D3 53
Harper, Lib. I3 64
Harper, Ks., U.S. D10 128
Harper, Tx., U.S. D8 130
Harper, Mount, mtn., Ak., U.S. D11 140
Harqin Qi, China D3 38
Harrai, India G7 54
Harricana, stm., Can. E15 106
Harriman, Tn., U.S. I13 120
Harrington, De., U.S. F10 114
Harrington, Me., U.S. F9 110
Harris, Sk., Can. C6 124
Harris, Monts. D3 105a
Harris, Mn., U.S. F5 118
Harris, reg., Scot., U.K. D6 12
Harris, Lake, l., Fl., U.S. H4 116
Harrisburg, Ar., U.S. B8 122
Harrisburg, Ne., U.S. F9 126
Harrisburg, Or., U.S. F3 136
Harrisburg, Pa., U.S. D8 114
Harrismith, S. Afr. F9 70
Harrison, Ar., U.S. H4 120
Harrison, Mi., U.S. D5 112
Harrison, Ne., U.S. E9 126
Harrison Bay, b., Ak., U.S. B9 140
Harrisonburg, La., U.S. F7 122
Harrisonburg, Va., U.S. F6 114
Harrison Islands, is., Nu., Can. B13 106
Harrison Lake, l., B.C., Can. G9 138
Harriston, On., Can. E9 112
Harriston, Ms., U.S. F7 122
Harrisville, N.Y., U.S. D14 112
Harrisville, W.V., U.S. E4 114
Harrodsburg, Ky., U.S. G13 120
Harrogate, Eng., U.K. H11 12
Harrold, Tx., U.S. G9 128
Harrowsmith, On., Can. D13 112
Harry S. Truman Reservoir, res., Mo., U.S. F4 120
Har Sai Shan, mtn., China D4 36
Harsīn, Iran C6 56
Hârşova, Rom. E14 26
Harstad, Nor. B7 8
Harsūd, India G6 54
Hart, Mi., U.S. E3 112
Hart, Tx., U.S. G6 128
Hart, stm., Yk., Can. B3 106
Hartbees, stm., S. Afr. F5 70
Hartberg, Aus. C12 22
Hartford, Ar., U.S. C4 122
Hartford, Ct., U.S. C13 114
Hartford, Ks., U.S. F2 120
Hartford, Mi., U.S. F3 112
Hartford, S.D., U.S. H2 118
Hartford, Wi., U.S. H10 118
Hartford City, In., U.S. H4 112
Hartland, N.B., Can. D9 110
Hartland, Me., U.S. F7 110
Hartlepool, Eng., U.K. G11 12
Hartley, Ia., U.S. H3 118
Hartley Bay, B.C., Can. C1 138
Hart Mountain, mtn., Mb., Can. B12 124
Hartney, Mb., Can. E13 124
Harts, stm., S. Afr. E7 70
Hartselle, Al., U.S. C12 122
Hartshorne, Ok., U.S. C3 122
Hartsville, S.C., U.S. B5 116
Hartville, Mo., U.S. G5 120
Hartwell, Ga., U.S. B3 116
Hartwell Lake, res., U.S. B2 116
Hartz Mountains National Park, p.o.i., Austl. o13 77a
Hārūnābād, Pak. D4 54
Haruniye, Tur. A7 58
Harūr, India E4 53
Har-Us nuur, l., Mong. B3 36
Harvard, Ne., U.S. G14 126
Harvey, N.B., Can. E12 110
Harvey, Il., U.S. G2 112
Harvey, N.D., U.S. G14 124
Harwich, Eng., U.K. J14 12
Haryāna, state, India D6 54
Haryn', stm., Eur. H10 10
Harz, mts., Ger. E6 16
Hasavjurt, Russia F7 32
Hasdo, stm., India G9 54
Hase, stm., Ger. D3 16
Hasenkamp, Arg. E8 92
Hashima, Japan D9 40
Hashimoto, Japan E8 40
Hāsilpur, Pak. D4 54
Haskell, Ok., U.S. I2 120
Haskell, Tx., U.S. A8 130
Haskovo, Blg. H12 26
Haskovo, state, Blg. G12 26
Haslemere, Eng., U.K. J12 12
Hasperos Canyon, p., N.M., U.S. H3 128
Ḥaṣṣ, Jabal al-, hill, Syria C8 58
Hassa, Tur. B7 58
Hassan, India E3 53
Hassayampa, stm., Az., U.S. J4 132
Hassel Sound, strt., Nu., Can. B6 141
Hasselt, Bel. D14 14
Hassfurt, Ger. F6 16
Hassi Messaoud, Alg. C6 64
Hässleholm, Swe. H5 8
Hastings, Barb. n8 105d
Hastings, On., Can. D11 112
Hastings, N.Z. D7 80
Hastings, Eng., U.K. K13 12
Hastings, Mi., U.S. F4 112
Hastings, Mn., U.S. G6 118
Hastings, Ne., U.S. G14 126
Haswell, Co., U.S. C5 128
Hatanga, Russia B9 34
Hatanga, stm., Russia B9 34
Hatangskij zaliv, b., Russia B10 34
Hatay (Antioch), Tur. B7 58
Hatay, state, Tur. B7 58
Hatch, N.M., U.S. K9 132
Hatch, Ut., U.S. F4 132
Hat Chao Mai National Park, p.o.i., Thai. I4 48
Hatchie, stm., U.S. B9 122
Hatfield, Austl. I4 76
Hatfield, Ar., U.S. C4 122
Hatfield, Ma., U.S. B13 114
Hatgal, Mong. F9 34
Hāthras, India E7 54
Ha Tien, Viet. G7 48
Hatillo, P.R. A2 104a
Ha Tinh, Viet. C7 48
Hatip, Tur. F15 28
Hato, Bocht van, b., Neth. Ant. p21 104g
Hato Mayor del Rey, Dom. Rep. C13 102
Hāt Pīplia, India G6 54
Hatta, India F7 54
Hatteras, N.C., U.S. A10 116
Hatteras, Cape, c., N.C., U.S. A10 116
Hatteras Island, i., N.C., U.S. A10 116
Hattiesburg, Ms., U.S. F9 122
Hatton, Al., U.S. C11 122
Hatton, N.D., U.S. G16 124
Hatunsaray, Tur. A3 58
Hatvan, Hung. B6 26
Hat Yai, Thai. I5 48
Hatyrka, Russia D24 34
Haugesund, Nor. G1 8
Haukeligrend, Nor. G2 8
Haukivesi, l., Fin. E12 8
Hauraki Gulf, b., N.Z. C6 80
Hausach, Ger. H4 16
Haut, Isle au, i., Me., U.S. F8 110
Haut Atlas, mts., Mor. C3 64
Haute-Corse, state, Fr. G15 18
Haute-Garonne, state, Fr. F7 18
Haute-Loire, state, Fr. D9 18
Haute-Marne, state, Fr. F14 14
Hautes-Alpes, state, Fr. E12 18
Haute-Saône, state, Fr. G14 14
Haute-Savoie, state, Fr. C12 18
Hautes-Pyrénées, state, Fr. F6 18
Haute-Vienne, state, Fr. D7 18
Haut-Rhin, state, Fr. G16 14
Haut Sheila, N.B., Can. C11 110
Hauts Plateaux, reg., Afr. C5 64
Hau'ula, Hi., U.S. b4 78a
Hauwâret el-Maqta', Egypt I1 58
Havana see La Habana, Cuba A6 102
Havana, Fl., U.S. G14 122
Havana, Il., U.S. D7 120
Havana, N.D., U.S. B15 126
Havannah, Canal de la, strt., N. Cal. n16 79d
Havant, Eng., U.K. K12 12
Havast, Uzb. F11 32
Havasu, Lake, res., U.S. I2 132
Havasu Creek, stm., Az., U.S. H4 132
Havel, stm., Ger. D8 16
Havelberg, Ger. D8 16
Haveli, Pak. C4 54
Havelland, reg., Ger. D8 16
Havelock, On., Can. D12 112
Havelock, N.C., U.S. B8 116
Haverfordwest, Wales, U.K. J7 12
Haverhill, Eng., U.K. I13 12
Haverhill, Ma., U.S. B14 114
Hāveri, India D2 53
Haviland, Ks., U.S. D9 128
Havířov, Czech Rep. G14 16
Havlíčkův Brod, Czech Rep. G11 16
Havre see Le Havre, Fr. E8 14
Havre, Mt., U.S. B17 136
Havre-Aubert, Qc., Can. C15 110
Havre Aubert, Île du, i., Qc., Can. C14 110
Havre de Grace, Md., U.S. E9 114
Havre North, Mt., U.S. B17 136
Havsa, Tur. B9 28
Haw, stm., N.C., U.S. A7 116
Hawaii, state, U.S. b5 78a
Hawai'i, i., Hi., U.S. c6 78a
Hawai'ian Islands, is., Hi., U.S. c4 78a
Hawaiian Ridge, unds. G21 142
Hawai'i Volcanoes National Park, p.o.i., Hi., U.S. d6 78a
Hawarden, Sk., Can. C7 124
Hawea, Lake, l., N.Z. G3 80
Hawera, N.Z. D6 80
Hawesville, Ky., U.S. G11 120
Hawi, Hi., U.S. c6 78a
Hawick, Scot., U.K. F10 12
Hawke, Cape, c., Austl. I9 76
Hawke Bay, b., N.Z. D7 80
Hawker, Austl. H2 76
Hawkes, Mount, mtn., Ant. D36 81
Hawkesbury, On., Can. E2 110
Hawkesbury Island, i., B.C., Can. C1 138
Hawkeye, Ia., U.S. B6 120
Hawkins, Tx., U.S. E3 122
Hawkins, Wi., U.S. F8 118
Haw Knob, mtn., U.S. A1 116
Hawksbill Creek, b., Bah. J7 116
Hawkwood, Austl. E8 76
Hawley, Mn., U.S. E2 118
Hawley, Pa., U.S. C10 114
Hawthorne, Fl., U.S. G3 116
Hawthorne, Nv., U.S. E7 134
Hawwāret 'Adlan, Egypt I1 58
Hay, Austl. J5 76
Hay, stm., Austl. D7 74
Hay, stm., Can. D7 106
Hay, Cape, c., N.T., Can. B17 140
Hayang, Kor., S. D1 40
Hayange, Fr. E14 14
Haybān, Jabal, mtn., Sudan E6 62
Haydarlı, Tur. E13 28
Hayden, Co., U.S. C9 132
Haydenville, Oh., U.S. E3 114
Hayes, La., U.S. G6 122
Hayes, stm., Mb., Can. D12 106
Hayes, stm., Nu., Can. B11 106
Hayes, Mount, mtn., Ak., U.S. D10 140
Hayes Center, Ne., U.S. G11 126
Hayesville, Or., U.S. F4 136
Hayfield, Mn., U.S. H6 118
Hayford Peak, mtn., Nv., U.S. G1 132
Hayfork, Ca., U.S. C2 134
Hay Lakes, Ab., Can. C17 138
Haynes, Ar., U.S. C8 122
Hayneville, Al., U.S. E12 122
Hayrabolu, Tur. B10 28
Hay River, N.T., Can. C7 106
Hays, Ab., Can. F19 138
Hays, Ks., U.S. C9 128
Hays, Mt., U.S. F5 124
Hay Springs, Ne., U.S. E10 126
Haystack Mountain, mtn., Nv., U.S. B1 132
Hayti, Mo., U.S. H8 120
Hayti, S.D., U.S. C15 126
Hayward, Ca., U.S. F3 134
Hayward, Wi., U.S. E7 118
Haywards Heath, Eng., U.K. J13 12
HaZafon, state, Isr. F6 58
Hazard, Ky., U.S. G2 114
Hazārībāg, India G10 54
Ḥaẓawẓā, Sabkhat, l., Sau. Ar. H9 58
Hazebrouck, Fr. D11 14
Hazel Green, Wi., U.S. I8 118
Hazelton, B.C., Can. A3 138
Hazelton, N.D., U.S. A12 126
Hazelton Mountains, mts., B.C., Can. B3 138
Hazelwood, N.C., U.S. A2 116
Hazen, Ar., U.S. C7 122
Hazen, N.D., U.S. G12 124
Hazen, Lake, l., Nu., Can. A11 141
Hazlehurst, Ms., U.S. F8 122
Hazlet, Sk., Can. D5 124
Hazleton, Ia., U.S. B6 120
Hazleton, Pa., U.S. D9 114
Hazlett, Lake, l., Austl. D5 74
Hazor HaGelilit, Isr. E6 58
He, stm., China H6 42
He, stm., China I4 42
Healdsburg, Ca., U.S. E2 134
Healdton, Ok., U.S. G11 128
Healesville, Austl. K5 76
Healy, Ks., U.S. C8 128
Heard Island, i., Austl. O10 142
Hearst, On., Can. F14 106
Heart, stm., N.D., U.S. H12 124
Heart Lake, l., Ab., Can. A19 138
Heath, Pointe, c., Qc., Can. A15 110
Heathcote, Austl. K5 76
Heath Springs, S.C., U.S. B5 116
Heathsville, Va., U.S. G9 114
Heavener, Ok., U.S. C4 122
Hebei, state, China D8 36
Hebel, Austl. G6 76
Heber, Az., U.S. I6 132
Heber City, Ut., U.S. C5 132
Heber Springs, Ar., U.S. B6 122

Name	Map Ref.	Page
Hebgen Lake, res., Mt., U.S.	F15	136
Hebi, China	D6	42
Hebrides, is., Scot., U.K.	D5	12
Hebrides, Sea of the, s., Scot., U.K.	D6	12
Hebron, Nf., Can.	F13	141
Hebron, Il., U.S.	B9	120
Hebron, N.D., U.S.	H11	124
Hebron, Ne., U.S.	A11	128
Hebron *see* Al-Khalīl, W.B.	G5	58
Hecate Strait, strt., B.C., Can.	E4	106
Hecelchakán, Mex.	B2	102
Hechi, China	I3	42
Hechiceros, Mex.	F4	130
Hechingen, Ger.	H4	16
Hechuan, China	G2	42
Hecla, Mb., Can.	C17	124
Hecla, Cape, c., Nu., Can.	A13	141
Hecla Island, i., Mb., Can.	D17	124
Hectanooga, N.S., Can.	F10	110
Hector, Mn., U.S.	G4	118
Hede, Swe.	E5	8
Hedemora, Swe.	F6	8
He Devil, mtn., Id., U.S.	E10	136
Hedley, Tx., U.S.	G8	128
Hedmark, state, Nor.	F4	8
Hedrick, Ia., U.S.	C5	120
Heerenveen, Neth.	B14	14
Heerlen, Neth.	D15	14
H̱efa (Haifa), Isr.	F5	58
H̱efa, state, Isr.	F5	58
Hefei, China	F7	42
Heflin, Al., U.S.	D13	122
Hegang, China	B11	36
Heho, Mya.	B3	48
Hei, stm., China	A7	42
Heide, Ger.	B5	16
Heidelberg, Ger.	G4	16
Heidelberg, S. Afr.	E9	70
Heidelberg, Ms., U.S.	F10	122
Heidenheim, Ger.	G6	16
Heihe, China	A10	36
Heilbad Heiligenstadt, Ger.	E6	16
Heilbron, S. Afr.	E8	70
Heilbronn, Ger.	G5	16
Heiligenhafen, Ger.	B6	16
Heilong (Amur), stm., Asia	F14	34
Heilongguan, China	C4	42
Heilongjiang, state, China	B10	36
Heilungkiang see Heilongjiang, state, China	B8	38
Heimaey, i., Ice.	I29	8a
Heinola, Fin.	F12	8
Heishan, China	D4	38
Heishuisi, China	C3	42
Hejaz see Al-Ḥijāz, reg., Sau. Ar.	D4	56
Hejian, China	B7	42
Hejiang, China	G1	42
Hejing, China	C2	36
Hekla, vol., Ice.	k30	8a
Hekou, China	A6	48
Hekou, China	G4	42
Helagsfjället, mtn., Swe.	E5	8
Helan Mountains see Helan Shan, mts., China	B1	42
Helan Shan, mts., China	B1	42
Helbra, Ger.	E7	16
Helder *see* Den Helder, Neth.	B13	14
Helder, Den *see* Den Helder, Neth.	B13	14
Helen, Mount, hill, Austl.	C3	76
Helena, Ar., U.S.	C8	122
Helena, Mt., U.S.	D14	136
Helena, Ok., U.S.	E10	128
Helensburgh, Scot., U.K.	E8	12
Helenwood, Tn., U.S.	H13	120
Helgoland, i., Ger.	B3	16
Helgoländer Bucht, b., Ger.	C4	16
Heli, China	B11	36
Heliopolis, sci., Egypt	H2	58
Helixi, China	F8	42
Hellesylt, Nor.	E2	8
Hellín, Spain	F9	20
Hells Canyon, p., U.S.	E10	136
Hells Canyon National Recreation Area, p.o.i., Or., U.S.	E10	136
Hells Gate, p., B.C., Can.	G9	138
Helmand, stm., Asia	C9	56
Helmcken Falls, wtfl., B.C., Can.	E10	138
Helmond, Neth.	C14	14
Helmstedt, Ger.	D6	16
Helong, China	C8	38
Helper, Ut., U.S.	D6	132
Helsingborg, Swe.	H5	8
Helsingfors *see* Helsinki, Fin.	F11	8
Helsingør, Den.	H5	8
Helsinki (Helsingfors), Fin.	F11	8
Helska, Mierzeja, pen., Pol.	B14	16
Helston, Eng., U.K.	K7	12
Helvecia, Arg.	E7	92
Helwan, Egypt	I2	58
Helwan Observatory, sci., Egypt	I2	58
Hemau, Ger.	G7	16
Hemāvati, stm., India	E2	53
Hemel Hempstead, Eng., U.K.	J12	12
Hemet, Ca., U.S.	J9	134
Hemingford, Ne., U.S.	E9	126
Hemingway, S.C., U.S.	C6	116
Hemphill, Tx., U.S.	F5	122
Hemsön, i., Swe.	E8	8
Henan, state, China	E5	42
Henares, stm., Spain	D7	20
Henbury, Austl.	D6	74
Hendek, Tur.	C13	28
Henderson, Ky., U.S.	G10	120
Henderson, Mn., U.S.	G5	118
Henderson, N.C., U.S.	H7	114
Henderson, Ne., U.S.	G15	126
Henderson, Nv., U.S.	G1	132
Henderson, Tn., U.S.	B10	122
Henderson, Tx., U.S.	E4	122
Hendersonville, Tn., U.S.	H11	120
Hendricks, Mn., U.S.	G2	118
Hendricks, W.V., U.S.	E6	114
Henefer, Ut., U.S.	B5	132
Henganofi, Pap. N. Gui.	b4	79a
Hengchow *see* Hengyang, China	H5	42
Hengdaozi, China	C7	38
Hengelo, Neth.	B15	14
Hengfeng, China	G7	42
Henglu, China	D7	38
Hengshan, China	C3	42
Hengshan, China	H5	42
Heng Shan, mts., China	B5	42
Hengshui, China	C6	42
Hengxian, China	J3	42
Hengyang, China	H5	42
Hénin-Beaumont, Fr.	D11	14
Henlopen, Cape, c., De., U.S.	F10	114
Hennebont, Fr.	G5	14
Hennef, Ger.	F3	16
Hennessey, Ok., U.S.	E11	128
Henniker, N.H., U.S.	G5	110
Henning, Mn., U.S.	E3	118
Henrietta, N.Y., U.S.	A8	114
Henrietta, Tx., U.S.	H10	128
Henrietta Island see Genrietty, ostrov, i., Russia	A20	34
Henrietta Maria, Cape, c., On., Can.	D14	106
Henri Pittier, Parque Nacional, p.o.i., Ven.	B8	86
Henry, Il., U.S.	C8	120
Henry, Cape, c., Va., U.S.	H10	114
Henry, Mount, mtn., Mt., U.S.	B11	136
Henryetta, Ok., U.S.	B2	122
Henry Kater, Cape, c., Nu., Can.	B17	106
Henrys Fork, stm., Id., U.S.	F15	136
Hensall, On., Can.	E8	112
Hensley, Ar., U.S.	C6	122
Henslow, Cape, c., Sol. Is.	e9	79b
Hentiesbaai, Nmb.	C2	70
Hentiyn nuruu, mts., Mong.	G10	34
Henzada, Mya.	D2	48
Hephzibah, Ga., U.S.	C3	116
Heping, China	H7	42
Heppenheim, Ger.	G4	16
Heppner, Or., U.S.	E7	136
Hepu, China	K3	42
Hequ, China	B4	42
Héraðsflói, b., Ice.	k32	8a
Herāt, Afg.	C9	56
Hérault, state, Fr.	F9	18
Hérault, stm., Fr.	F9	18
Herbert, Sk., Can.	D6	124
Herberton, Austl.	A5	76
Herbertsdale, S. Afr.	H5	70
Herborn, Ger.	F4	16
Herceg-Novi, Mont.	G5	26
Hércules, Mex.	A7	100
Herðubreið, vol., Ice.	k31	8a
Heredia, C.R.	G5	102
Hereford, Eng., U.K.	I10	12
Hereford, Az., U.S.	L6	132
Hereford, Tx., U.S.	G6	128
Hereke, Tur.	C12	28
Herencia, Spain	E7	20
Herford, Ger.	D4	16
Herington, Ks., U.S.	C11	128
Herisau, Switz.	C6	22
Herkimer, N.Y., U.S.	E15	112
Hermagor, Aus.	D10	22
Herman, Mn., U.S.	F2	118
Herman, Ne., U.S.	C1	120
Hermanas, Mex.	G6	130
Hermanns-Denkmal, hist., Ger.	E4	16
Hermansverk, Nor.	F2	8
Hermansville, Mi., U.S.	C2	112
Hermanus, S. Afr.	I4	70
Hermanville, Ms., U.S.	F8	122
Hermiston, Or., U.S.	E7	136
Hermitage, Ar., U.S.	D6	122
Hermit Islands, is., Pap. N. Gui.	a4	79a
Hermleigh, Tx., U.S.	B7	130
Hermon, Mount (Shaykh, Jabal ash-), mtn., Asia	E6	58
Hermosillo, Mex.	A3	100
Hermyingyi, Mya.	E4	48
Hernád (Hornad), stm., Eur.	H17	16
Hernandarias, Arg.	E8	92
Hernandarias, Para.	B10	92
Hernando, Arg.	F6	92
Hernando, Fl., U.S.	H3	116
Hernando, Ms., U.S.	C9	122
Herndon, Pa., U.S.	D9	114
Herne Bay, Eng., U.K.	J14	12
Herning, Den.	H3	8
Heroica Zitácuaro, Mex.	F8	100
Heron Island, i., Austl.	D8	76
Heron Lake, Mn., U.S.	H3	118
Hérouville-Saint-Clair, Fr.	E8	14
Herradura, Arg.	C8	92
Herreid, S.D., U.S.	B12	126
Herrera de Pisuerga, Spain	B6	20
Herrick, Austl.	n13	77a
Herrin, Il., U.S.	G8	120
Hersbruck, Ger.	G7	16
Herschel, Sk., Can.	C5	124
Herschel, S. Afr.	G8	70
Herschel Island, i., Yk., Can.	C12	140
Herscher, Il., U.S.	C9	120
Hershey, Ne., U.S.	F11	126
Hershey, Pa., U.S.	D9	114
Herstal, Bel.	D14	14
Hertford, Eng., U.K.	J12	12
Hertogenbosch, 's- *see* 's-Hertogenbosch, Neth.	C14	14
Herval d'Oeste, Braz.	C12	92
Hervás, Spain	D5	20
Hervey Bay, b., Austl.	E9	76
Hervey-Jonction, Qc., Can.	D4	110
Herzberg, Ger.	E9	16
Herzberg am Harz, Ger.	E6	16
Heshan, China	J3	42
Heshui, China	J4	42
Heshun, China	C5	42
Hesperia, Mi., U.S.	E3	112
Hesperus Mountain, mtn., Co., U.S.	F8	132
Hess, stm., Yk., Can.	C4	106
Hessen, state, Ger.	F5	16
Hesston, Ks., U.S.	C11	128
Het, stm., Laos	B6	48
Heta, stm., Russia	B8	34
Hetang, China	H8	42
Heṭauṇḍā, Nepal	E10	54
Hetch Hetchy Aqueduct, aq., Ca., U.S.	F4	134
Hetögeln, l., Swe.	D6	8
Hettstedt, Ger.	E7	16
Heuvelton, N.Y., U.S.	D14	112
Heves, Hung.	B7	26
Heves, state, Hung.	A7	26
Hewanorra International Airport, St. Luc.	m6	105c
Hewu, China	H5	42
Hexham, Eng., U.K.	F11	12
Hexian, China	I4	42
Heyang, China	D3	42
Heyburn, Id., U.S.	H13	136
Heysham, Eng., U.K.	G10	12
Heyuan, China	J6	42
Heywood, Austl.	L3	76
Heyworth, Il., U.S.	D9	120
Heze, China	D6	42
Hezheng, China	D5	36
Hialeah, Fl., U.S.	K5	116
Hiawatha, Ks., U.S.	E2	120
Hiawatha, Ut., U.S.	D6	132
Hibbard, Qc., Can.	C2	110
Hibbing, Mn., U.S.	D5	118
Hickman, Ky., U.S.	H8	120
Hickory, Ms., U.S.	E9	122
Hickory, N.C., U.S.	I4	114
Hickory Flat, Ms., U.S.	C9	122
Hicks, Point, c., Austl.	K7	76
Hico, Tx., U.S.	C9	130
Hida *see* Hita, Japan	F3	40
Hidalgo, Mex.	C9	100
Hidalgo, Mex.	B8	100
Hidalgo, Mex.	B9	100
Hidalgo, state, Mex.	E9	100
Hidalgo del Parral, Mex.	B6	100
Hida-sammyaku, mts., Japan	C10	40
Hidrolândia, Braz.	I1	88
Hieflau, Aus.	C11	22
Hienghène, N. Cal.	m15	79d
Hierapolis see Pamukkale, sci., Tur.	F12	28
Higashihiroshima, Japan	E5	40
Higashiichiki, Japan	H3	40
Higashine, Japan	A13	40
Higashiōsaka, Japan	E8	40
Higgins, Tx., U.S.	E8	128
Higgins Lake, l., Mi., U.S.	D5	112
Higginsville, Mo., U.S.	E4	120
Highbury, Austl.	C8	74
Highland, Il., U.S.	F8	120
Highland, In., U.S.	G2	112
Highland, Ks., U.S.	E2	120
Highland Park, Il., U.S.	F2	112
Highlands, N.C., U.S.	A2	116
Highlands, N.J., U.S.	D12	114
Highlands, Tx., U.S.	H3	122
High Level, Ab., Can.	D7	106
High Point, N.C., U.S.	I5	114
High Point, mtn., N.J., U.S.	C11	114
High Point, mtn., Wy., U.S.	B9	132
High Point, c., Ber.	I15	104e
High River, Ab., Can.	F17	138
Highrock Lake, l., Mb., Can.	D10	106
Highrock Lake, l., Sk., Can.	D9	106
High Rock Lake, res., N.C., U.S.	A5	116
High Springs, Fl., U.S.	G3	116
Hightstown, N.J., U.S.	D11	114
High Willhays, mtn., Eng., U.K.	K9	12
Highwood, Mt., U.S.	C16	136
Highwood, stm., Ab., Can.	F17	138
Highwood Baldy, mtn., Mt., U.S.	C16	136
High Wycombe, Eng., U.K.	J11	12
Higuera de Abuya, Mex.	C5	100
Higueras, Mex.	I8	130
Higüero, Punta, c., P.R.	B1	104a
Higüey, Dom. Rep.	C13	102
Hiiumaa, i., Est.	G10	8
Hikari, Japan	F4	40
Hikone, Japan	D9	40
Hilbert, Wi., U.S.	D1	112
Hilda, Ab., Can.	D3	124
Hildburghausen, Ger.	F6	16
Hildesheim, Ger.	D5	16
Hiliotaluwa, Indon.	L3	48
Hillaby, Mount, mtn., Barb.	n8	105d
Hill Bank, Belize	D3	102
Hill City, Ks., U.S.	B9	128
Hill City, S.D., U.S.	D9	126
Hillcrest Mines, Ab., Can.	G16	138
Hillerød, Den.	I4	8
Hilliard, Fl., U.S.	F4	116
Hill Island Lake, l., N.T., Can.	C9	106
Hillister, Tx., U.S.	G4	122
Hills, Mn., U.S.	H2	118
Hillsboro, Il., U.S.	E8	120
Hillsboro, Ks., U.S.	C11	128
Hillsboro, Mo., U.S.	F7	120
Hillsboro, N.D., U.S.	D1	118
Hillsboro, Oh., U.S.	E2	114
Hillsboro, Or., U.S.	E3	136
Hillsboro, Wi., U.S.	H8	118
Hillsboro Canal, can., Fl., U.S.	J5	116
Hillsborough, Gren.	q10	105e
Hillsborough, N.C., U.S.	H6	114
Hillsborough, stm., Fl., U.S.	H3	116
Hillsborough, Cape, c., Austl.	C7	76
Hillsborough Bay, b., P.E., Can.	D13	110
Hillsdale, Mi., U.S.	G5	112
Hillston, Austl.	I5	76
Hillsville, Va., U.S.	H5	114
Hillswick, Scot., U.K.	n18	12a
Hilo, Hi., U.S.	d6	78a
Hilok, Russia	F11	34
Hilok, stm., Russia	F10	34
Hilton, N.Y., U.S.	E12	112
Hilton Head Island, i., S.C., U.S.	D5	116
Hilvan, Tur.	A9	58
Hilversum, Neth.	B14	14
Himāchal Pradesh, state, India	B6	54
Himalayas, mts., Asia	F10	142
Himarë, Alb.	D13	24
Himatnagar, India	G4	54
Himeji, Japan	E7	40
Himi, Japan	C9	40
Himki, Russia	E20	10
Ḥimṣ (Homs), Syria	D7	58
Ḥimṣ, state, Syria	D8	58
Hinchinbrook Island, i., Austl.	B6	76
Hinchinbrook Island, i., Ak., U.S.	D10	140
Hinchinbrook Island National Park, p.o.i., Austl.	B6	76
Hinckley, Il., U.S.	C9	120
Hinckley, Mn., U.S.	E5	118
Hinckley, Ut., U.S.	D4	132
Hindang, Phil.	E5	52
Hindaun, India	E6	54
Hindmarsh, Lake, l., Austl.	J3	76
Hindu Kush, mts., Asia	B10	56
Hindupur, India	E3	53
Hines, Or., U.S.	G7	136
Hinesville, Ga., U.S.	E4	116
Hinganghāt, India	H7	54
Hingham, Ma., U.S.	B15	114
Hingol, stm., Pak.	D10	56
Hingoli, India	B3	53
Hinigaran, Phil.	E4	52
Hinnøya, i., Nor.	B6	8
Hinojosa del Duque, Spain	F5	20
Hinokage, Japan	G4	40
Hinsdale, Mt., U.S.	F6	124
Hinterrhein, stm., Switz.	D6	22
Hinton, Ab., Can.	C13	138
Hinton, Ok., U.S.	F10	128
Hinton, W.V., U.S.	G5	114
Hipólito, Mex.	C8	100
Hipólito Yrigoyen, Arg.	F4	92
Hirado, Japan	F2	40
Hirado-shima, i., Japan	F2	40
Hīrākud, India	H9	54
Hīrākud Reservoir, res., India	H10	54
Hirara, Japan	G10	36
Hirata, Japan	D5	40
Hiratsuka, Japan	D12	40
Hiriyūr, India	E3	53
Hirosaki, Japan	D14	38
Hiroshima, Japan	E5	40
Hiroshima, state, Japan	E5	40
Hirosima *see* Hiroshima, Japan	E5	40
Hirovo, Russia	B16	10
Hirson, Fr.	E13	14
Hisār, India	D5	54
Hisarönü, Tur.	B14	28
Hispaniola, i., N.A.	D10	96
Hisua, India	F10	54
Ḥisyah, Syria	D7	58
Hita, Japan	F3	40
Hitachi, Japan	C13	40
Hitachi-ōta, Japan	C13	40
Hitchcock, Tx., U.S.	H3	122
Hitchins, Ky., U.S.	F3	114
Hitiaa, Fr. Poly.	v22	78h
Hitoyoshi, Japan	G3	40
Hitra, i., Nor.	E3	8
Hiuchiga-take, vol., Japan	C12	40
Hiuchi-nada, s., Japan	E6	40
Hiva, Uzb.	F10	32
Hiva Oa, i., Fr. Poly.	s19	78g
Hiwannee, Ms., U.S.	F10	122
Hiwasa, Japan	F7	40
Hiwassee, stm., U.S.	B14	122
Hiwassee Lake, res., N.C., U.S.	A1	116
Hixson, Tn., U.S.	B13	122
Hjälmaren, l., Swe.	G6	8
Hjo, Swe.	G6	8
Hjørring, Den.	H3	8
Hkakabo Razi, mtn., Mya.	C8	46
Hkok (Kok), stm., Asia	B4	48
Hlaingbwe, Mya.	D3	48
Hlathikulu, Swaz.	E10	70
Hlinsko, Czech Rep.	G11	16
Hlohovec, Slov.	H13	16
Hlotse, Leso.	F9	70
Hluhluwe, S. Afr.	F11	70
Hluhluwe Game Reserve, S. Afr.	F10	70
Hluša, Bela.	G11	10
Hlyboka, Ukr.	A12	26
Hlybokae, Bela.	E10	10
Hmelita, Russia	E16	10
H. Neely Henry Lake, res., Al., U.S.	D12	122
Ho, Ghana	H5	64
Hoa Binh, Viet.	B7	48
Hoare Bay, b., Nu., Can.	D13	141
Hobart, Austl.	o13	77a
Hobart, Ok., U.S.	F9	128
Hobbs, N.M., U.S.	B4	130
Hobbs Coast, cst., Ant.	C28	81
Hobe Sound, Fl., U.S.	I5	116
Hobgood, N.C., U.S.	H8	114
Hobq Shamo, des., China	A2	42
Hobson Lake, l., B.C., Can.	D10	138
Hobyo, Som.	C9	66
Hochalmspitze, mtn., Aus.	C10	22
Hochfeld, Nmb.	B3	70
Ho Chi Minh City *see* Thanh Pho Ho Chi Minh, Viet.	G8	48
Hochkönig, mtn., Aus.	C10	22
Höchstadt an der Aisch, Ger.	G6	16
Hochstetter Forland, pen.	B21	141
Hoch'uan *see* Hechuan, China	G2	42
H̱ocimsk, Bela.	G15	10
Hockenheim, Ger.	G4	16
Hocking, stm., Oh., U.S.	E15	120
Ḥôḍ, reg., Maur.	F3	64
Hodal, India	E6	54
Hodeida *see* Al-Ḥudaydah, Yemen	G5	56
Hodge, La., U.S.	E6	122
Hodgenville, Ky., U.S.	G12	120
Hodgeville, Sk., Can.	D7	124
Hódmezővásárhely, Hung.	C7	26
Hodna, Chott el, l., Alg.	B6	64
Hodonín, Czech Rep.	H12	16
Hodžanur'jah, gora, mtn., Uzb.	G11	32
Hodžejli, Uzb.	F9	32
Hœdic, Île de, i., Fr.	G6	14
Hoehne, Co., U.S.	D4	128
Hoei *see* Huy, Bel.	D14	14
Hoek van Holland, Neth.	C12	14
Hoeryŏng-ŭp, Kor., N.	C8	38
Hoeyang-ŭp, Kor., N.	E7	38
Hof, Ger.	F7	16
Hof, Ice.	k32	8a
Hofei *see* Hefei, China	F7	42
Hoffman, Mn., U.S.	F3	118
Hofgeismar, Ger.	E5	16
Hofheim am Taunus, Ger.	F4	16
Hofheim in Unterfranken, Ger.	F6	16
Hofors, Swe.	F7	8
Hofsjökull, ice, Ice.	k30	8a
Hōfu, Japan	E4	40
Hofuf *see* Al-Hufūf, Sau. Ar.	D6	56
Hogansville, Ga., U.S.	D14	122
Hogback Mountain, mtn., Ne., U.S.	F9	126
Hogback Mountain, mtn., S.C., U.S.	A3	116
Högsby, Swe.	H6	8
Hohenwald, Tn., U.S.	B11	122
Hoher Dachstein, mtn., Aus.	C10	22
Hohe Tauern, mts., Aus.	C9	22
Hohhot, China	A4	42
Hohoe, Ghana	H5	64
Hōhoku, Japan	E3	40
Hoh Xil Hu, l., China	D3	36
Hoh Xil Shan, mts., China	D2	36
Hoi An, Viet.	E9	48
Hoihong *see* Haikang, China	K3	42
Hoihow *see* Haikou, China	K4	42
Hoima, Ug.	D6	66
Hoisington, Ks., U.S.	C10	128
Hojāi, India	E14	54
Højer, Den.	B4	16
Hōjō, Japan	F5	40
Hokah, Mn., U.S.	H7	118
Hokang *see* Hegang, China	B11	36
Hokitika, N.Z.	F4	80
Hokkaidō, i., Japan	C15	38
Holalkere, India	D3	53
Holberg, B.C., Can.	F2	138
Holbrook, Austl.	J6	76
Holbrook, Az., U.S.	I6	132
Holbrook, Ne., U.S.	A8	128
Holden, Ab., Can.	C18	138
Holden, Mo., U.S.	F4	120
Holden, W.V., U.S.	G3	114
Holden Village, Wa., U.S.	B6	136
Holder, Fl., U.S.	H3	116
Holderness, pen., Eng., U.K.	H12	12
Holdfast, Sk., Can.	D8	124
Holdingford, Mn., U.S.	F4	118
Hold With Hope, reg., Grnld.	C22	141
Hole in the Mountain Peak, mtn., Nv., U.S.	C1	132
Hole Narsipur, India	E2	53
Holetown, Barb.	n8	105d
Holgate, Oh., U.S.	C1	114
Holguín, Cuba	B9	102
Holíč, Slov.	H13	16
Hollabrunn, Aus.	B13	22
Holland, Mi., U.S.	F3	112
Holland, Tx., U.S.	D10	130
Holland see Netherlands, ctry., Eur.	B15	14
Holland, hist. reg., Neth.	B13	14
Hollandale, Ms., U.S.	D8	122
Hollandia *see* Jayapura, Indon.	F11	44
Hollandsbird Island, i., Nmb.	D2	70
Holley, N.Y., U.S.	E11	112
Holliday, Tx., U.S.	H10	128
Hollins, Va., U.S.	G6	114
Hollister, Ca., U.S.	G4	134
Hollow Rock, Tn., U.S.	H9	120
Holly, Co., U.S.	C6	128
Holly Grove, Ar., U.S.	C7	122
Holly Hill, Fl., U.S.	G4	116
Holly Springs, Ms., U.S.	C9	122
Hollywood, Fl., U.S.	J5	116
Holm, Russia	C14	10
Holman, N.T., Can.	A7	106
Hólmavík, Ice.	k28	8a
Holmen, Wi., U.S.	H7	118
Holmes, Mount, mtn., Wy., U.S.	F16	136
Holm Land, pen., Grnld.	A22	141
Holm Ø, i., Grnld.	C14	141
Holmogorskaja, Russia	E19	8
Holmsk, Russia	G17	34
Holmsund, Swe.	E9	8
H̱olon, Isr.	F5	58
Holoog, Nmb.	E4	70
Holovanivs'k, Ukr.	A17	26
Holstebro, Den.	H3	8
Holstein, Ia., U.S.	B2	120
Holsteinsborg (Sisimiut), Grnld.	D15	141
Holston, stm., Tn., U.S.	H2	114
Holston, North Fork, stm., U.S.	H3	114
Holsworthy, Eng., U.K.	K8	12
Holt, Fl., U.S.	G12	122
Holt, Mi., U.S.	B1	114
Holton, Ks., U.S.	E2	120
Holts Summit, Mo., U.S.	F5	120
Holy Cross, Ak., U.S.	D8	140
Holy Cross Mountain, mtn., B.C., Can.	C10	138
Holyhead, Wales, U.K.	H8	12
Holy Island, i., Eng., U.K.	F11	12
Holyoke, Co., U.S.	G10	126
Holyoke, Ma., U.S.	B13	114
Holyrood, Ks., U.S.	C10	128
Holzkirchen, Ger.	I7	16
Holzminden, Ger.	E5	16
Hom, stm., Nmb.	F4	70
Homa Bay, Kenya	E6	66
Homalin, Mya.	D7	46
Homathko, stm., B.C., Can.	E6	138
Homathko Icefield, ice, B.C., Can.	E6	138
Homberg, Ger.	E5	16
Hombori Tondo, mtn., Mali	F4	64
Hombre Muerto, Salar del, pl., Arg.	B4	92
Homburg, Ger.	G3	16
Home Bay, b., Nu., Can.	B17	106
Home Hill, Austl.	B6	76
Homel', Bela.	H13	10
Homel', state, Bela.	H12	10
Homeland Park, S.C., U.S.	B3	116
Homer, Ak., U.S.	E9	140
Homer, Ga., U.S.	B2	116
Homer, La., U.S.	E5	122
Homer, Ne., U.S.	B1	120
Homer City, Pa., U.S.	D6	114
Homerville, Ga., U.S.	E3	116
Homestead, Fl., U.S.	K5	116
Homestead National Monument of America, p.o.i., Ne., U.S.	A11	128
Homewood, Al., U.S.	D12	122
Hommura, Japan	E12	40
Homnābād, India	C3	53
Homochitto, stm., Ms., U.S.	F7	122
Homoíne, Moz.	C12	70
Homosassa, Fl., U.S.	H3	116
Homs *see* Al-Khums, Libya	A2	62
Homs *see* Ḥimṣ, Syria	D7	58
Honaker, Va., U.S.	H4	114
Honan *see* Luoyang, China	D5	42
Honan see Henan, state, China	E5	42
Honāvar, India	D2	53
Hon Chong, Viet.	G7	48
Honda, Col.	E4	86
Honda, Bahía, b., Col.	A5	86
Honda Bay, b., Phil.	F2	52
Hondeklipbaai, S. Afr.	G3	70
Hon Dien, Nui, mtn., Viet.	G9	48
Hondo, Ab., Can.	A16	138
Hondo, Japan	G3	40
Hondo, N.M., U.S.	H3	128
Hondo, stm., N.A.	C3	102
Hondo Creek, stm., Tx., U.S.	E8	130
Honduras, ctry., N.A.	E4	102
Honduras, Cabo de, c., Hond.	D5	102
Honduras, Gulf of, b., N.A.	D4	102
Honea Path, S.C., U.S.	B3	116
Hønefoss, Nor.	F4	8
Honesdale, Pa., U.S.	C10	114
Honey Grove, Tx., U.S.	D3	122
Honey Lake, l., Ca., U.S.	C5	134
Honeyville, Ut., U.S.	B4	132
Honfleur, Fr.	E9	14
Hong, stm., China	E6	42
Hong, Song see Red, stm., Asia	D9	46
Hon Gai, Viet.	B8	48
Hong Hu, l., China	F5	42
Hongjiang, China	H4	42
Hong Kong *see* Xianggang, China	J6	42
Hongliuyuan, China	F17	32
Hong Ngu, Viet.	G7	48
Hongqi, China	B7	38
Hongshi, China	C7	38
Hongshui, stm., China	J3	42
Hongtong, China	C4	42
Honguedo, Détroit d', strt., Qc., Can.	A12	110
Hongze, China	E8	42
Hongze Hu, l., China	E8	42
Honiara, Sol. Is.	e8	79b
Honjō, Japan	E13	38
Honningsvåg, Nor.	A11	8
Honoka'a, Hi., U.S.	c6	78a
Honolulu, Hi., U.S.	b4	78a
Honomu, Hi., U.S.	d6	78a
Hon Quan, Viet.	G8	48
Honshū, i., Japan	G12	38
Honuu, Russia	C17	34
Hood, stm., Nu., Can.	B9	106
Hood, Mount, vol., Or., U.S.	E5	136
Hood Canal, b., Wa., U.S.	C4	136
Hoodoo Peak, mtn., Wa., U.S.	B6	136
Hood Point, c., Austl.	F3	74
Hoodsport, Wa., U.S.	C3	136
Hoogeveen, Neth.	B15	14
Hoogeveense Vaart, can., Neth.	B15	14
Hooker, Ok., U.S.	E7	128
Hook Head, c., Ire.	I6	12
Hookina, Austl.	H2	76
Hook Island, i., Austl.	C7	76
Hook Point, c., Austl.	E9	76
Hooks, Tx., U.S.	D4	122
Hoonah, Ak., U.S.	E12	140
Hoopa, Ca., U.S.	B2	134
Hooper, Ne., U.S.	C1	120
Hooper Bay, Ak., U.S.	D6	140
Hoople, N.D., U.S.	F16	124
Hoopstad, S. Afr.	E7	70
Hoorn, Neth.	B14	14
Hoosick Falls, N.Y., U.S.	H3	110
Hoover Dam, dam, U.S.	G2	132
Hooversville, Pa., U.S.	H11	112
Hopatcong, N.J., U.S.	D11	114
Hope, B.C., Can.	G9	138
Hope, Ar., U.S.	D5	122
Hope, In., U.S.	E12	120
Hope, Ben, mtn., Scot., U.K.	C8	12
Hope, Point, c., Ak., U.S.	C6	140
Hopedale, La., U.S.	H9	122
Hopeh see Hebei, state, China	D8	36
Ho-pei see Hebei, state, China	D8	36
Hopelchén, Mex.	C3	102
Hope Mills, N.C., U.S.	B7	116
Hopër, stm., Russia	E17	6
Hopes Advance, Cap, c., Qc., Can.	C17	106
Hopetoun, Austl.	F4	74
Hopetoun, Austl.	J4	76
Hopetown, S. Afr.	F6	70
Hope Valley, R.I., U.S.	C14	114
Hopewell, Va., U.S.	G8	114
Hopewell Culture National Historic Park, p.o.i., Oh., U.S.	E2	114
Hopewell Islands, is., Nu., Can.	D14	106
Hopi *see* Hebi, China	D6	42
Hopkins, Mo., U.S.	D3	120
Hopkins, stm., Austl.	K4	76
Hopkinsville, Ky., U.S.	H10	120
Hopkinton, Ia., U.S.	B6	120
Hopólite Bouchard, Arg.	G6	92
Hoppo *see* Hepu, China	K3	42
Hopwood, Mount, hill, Austl.	C5	76
Hoquiam, Wa., U.S.	C2	136
Hor, Russia	G16	34
Hor, stm., Russia	B12	36
Hor, stm., Russia	G16	34
Horatio, Ar., U.S.	D4	122
Hordaland, state, Nor.	F2	8
Horezu, Rom.	D10	26
Horicon, Wi., U.S.	H10	118
Horinger, China	A4	42
Horinsk, Russia	F10	34
Horizontina, Braz.	C10	92
Horlick Mountains, mts., Ant.	D29	81
Horlivka, Ukr.	E5	32
Horlovo, Russia	E21	10
Hormigueros, P.R.	B1	104a
Hormuz, Strait of, strt., Asia	D8	56
Horn, Aus.	B12	22
Horn, c., Ice.	j28	8a
Horn, stm., N.T., Can.	C7	106
Horn, Cape see Hornos, Cabo de, c., Chile	K3	90
Hornad (Hernád), stm., Eur.	H17	16
Hornaday, stm., Can.	B6	106
Hornafjörður, b., Ice.	k32	8a
Hornavan, l., Swe.	C7	8
Hornbeck, La., U.S.	F5	122
Hornbrook, Ca., U.S.	B3	134
Hornby Bay, b., N.T., Can.	B7	106
Hornell, N.Y., U.S.	B8	114
Hornepayne, On., Can.	F13	106
Horn Island, i., Ms., U.S.	G10	122
Horn Lake, Ms., U.S.	C8	122
Hornos, Cabo de (Horn, Cape), c., Chile	K3	90
Horn Plateau, plat., N.T., Can.	C6	106
Hornsea, Eng., U.K.	H12	12
Horodkivka, Ukr.	A15	26
Horodok, Ukr.	G19	16
Horog, Taj.	B11	56
Horol', Russia	B10	38
Horqin Youyi Zhongqi, China	B4	38
Horqin Zuoyi Houqi, China	C4	38
Horqin Zuoyi Zhongqi, China	B5	38
Horqueta, Para.	D5	90
Horse Cave, Ky., U.S.	G12	120
Horse Creek, stm., Co., U.S.	C5	128
Horse Creek, stm., U.S.	F8	126
Horsefly, B.C., Can.	D9	138
Horsefly Lake, l., B.C., Can.	D10	138
Horseheads, N.Y., U.S.	B9	114
Horse Islands, is., Nf., Can.	i22	107a
Horsens, Den.	I3	8
Horseshoe Bend, Id., U.S.	G10	136
Horsham, Austl.	K4	76
Horsham, Eng., U.K.	J12	12
Horšovský Týn, Czech Rep.	G8	16
Horten, Nor.	G4	8
Hortobágy, reg., Hung.	B8	26
Hortobágyi Nemzeti Park, p.o.i., Hung.	B8	26
Horton, Ks., U.S.	E2	120
Horton, stm., N.T., Can.	B6	106
Horton Lake, l., N.T., Can.	B6	106
Hortonville, Wi., U.S.	G10	118
Hory, Bela.	F14	10
Hosa'ina, Eth.	F7	62
Hösbach, Ger.	F5	16
Hosedahard, Russia	A9	32
Hosford, Fl., U.S.	G14	122
Hoshāb, Pak.	D9	56
Hoshangābād, India	G6	54
Hoshiārpur, India	C5	54
Hosh Isa, Egypt	H1	58
Hosmer, B.C., Can.	G15	138
Hospers, Ia., U.S.	A2	120
Hospet, India	D3	53
Hospitalet *see* L'Hospitalet de Llobregat, Spain	C13	20
Hossegor, Fr.	F4	18
Hosston, La., U.S.	E5	122
Hosta Butte, mtn., N.M., U.S.	H8	132
Hoste, Isla, i., Chile	K3	90
Hosūr, India	E3	53
Hotagen, l., Swe.	E5	8
Hotaka-dake, mtn., Japan	C10	40
Hotamış, Tur.	A4	58
Hotan, China	A5	46
Hotazel, S. Afr.	E6	70
Hotevilla, Az., U.S.	H6	132
Hotilovo, Russia	C17	10
Hot'kovo, Russia	D21	10
Hot'kovo, Russia	G18	10
Hot Springs, Ar., U.S.	C5	122
Hot Springs, N.C., U.S.	I3	114
Hot Springs, S.D., U.S.	D9	126
Hot Springs, Va., U.S.	F6	114
Hot Springs National Park *see* Hot Springs, Ar., U.S.	C5	122
Hot Springs Peak, mtn., Nv., U.S.	B8	134
Hot Sulphur Springs, Co., U.S.	A2	128
Hottah Lake, l., N.T., Can.	B7	106
Hottentotsbaai, b., Nmb.	E2	70
Hotynec, Russia	G18	10
Houaïlou, N. Cal.	m15	79d
Houat, Île de, i., Fr.	G6	14
Houdan, Fr.	F10	14
Houghton, Mi., U.S.	D10	118
Houghton, N.Y., U.S.	B7	114
Houghton Lake, l., Mi., U.S.	D4	112
Houlka, Ms., U.S.	C10	122
Houlton, Me., U.S.	D9	110
Houma, China	D4	42
Houma, Tonga	n13	78e
Houma, La., U.S.	H8	122
Hou-pei see Hubei, state, China	F5	42
Hourtin, Étang d', l., Fr.	D4	18
Housatonic, Ma., U.S.	B12	114
House, N.M., U.S.	G5	128
Houston, B.C., Can.	B4	138
Houston, Mn., U.S.	H7	118
Houston, Mo., U.S.	G6	120
Houston, Tx., U.S.	H3	122
Houston, Lake, res., Tx., U.S.	H3	122
Hout, stm., S. Afr.	C9	70
Houtman Abrolhos, is., Austl.	E2	74
Houxinqiu, China	C5	38
Hovd, Mong.	C5	36
Hovd, stm., Mong.	E16	32
Hove, Eng., U.K.	K12	12
Hoven, S.D., U.S.	B13	126
Hovenweep National Monument, p.o.i., U.S.	F7	132
Hoverla, hora, mtn., Ukr.	A11	26
Hovgaard Ø, i., Grnld.	A22	141
Hövsgöl nuur, l., Mong.	F9	34
Hovu-Aksy, Russia	D16	32
Howar, Wādī, val., Afr.	D5	62
Howard, Austl.	E9	76
Howard, Ks., U.S.	D12	128
Howard, Pa., U.S.	D8	114
Howard, S.D., U.S.	C15	126
Howard City, Mi., U.S.	E4	112
Howard Draw, stm., Tx., U.S.	D6	130
Howard Lake, Mn., U.S.	F4	118
Howe, In., U.S.	G4	112
Howe, Cape, c., Austl.	K7	76
Howe Island, i., On., Can.	D13	112
Howell, Mi., U.S.	B2	114
Howells, Ne., U.S.	F15	126
Howick, S. Afr.	F10	70
Howitt, Mount, mtn., Austl.	K6	76
Howland Island, i., Oc.	C9	72
Howser, B.C., Can.	F13	138
Howson Peak, mtn., B.C., Can.	B3	138
Hoxie, Ar., U.S.	H6	120
Hoxie, Ks., U.S.	B8	128

Name	Map Ref.	Page
Höxter, Ger.	E5	16
Hoxtolgay, China	B2	36
Hoy, i., Scot., U.K.	C9	12
Hoyerswerda, Ger.	E10	16
Hoyos, Spain	D4	20
Höytiäinen, l., Fin.	E13	8
Hoyt Lakes, Mn., U.S.	D6	118
Hradec Králové, Czech Rep.	F11	16
Hradzjanka, Bela.	G11	10
Hranice, Czech Rep.	G13	16
Hrèsk, Bela.	G10	10
Hristoforovo, Russia	F22	8
Hrodna, Bela.	G6	10
Hrodna, state, Bela.	G7	10
Hroma, stm., Russia	B17	34
Hron, stm., Slov.	H14	16
Hronov, Czech Rep.	F12	16
Hrubieszów, Pol.	F19	16
Hrustal'nyj, Russia	B11	38
Hsiakuan *see* Dali, China	F5	36
Hsiamen *see* Xiamen, China	I7	42
Hsian *see* Xi'an, China	D3	42
Hsiangt'an *see* Xiangtan, China	H5	42
Hsiangyang *see* Xiangfan, China	F4	42
Hsienyang *see* Xianyang, China	D3	42
Hsi-hseng, Mya.	B3	48
Hsilo, Tai.	J9	42
Hsim, stm., Mya.	B4	48
Hsinchu, Tai.	I9	42
Hsinghua *see* Xinghua, China	E8	42
Hsingt'ai *see* Xingtai, China	C6	42
Hsinhailien *see* Lianyungang, China	D8	42
Hsinhsiang *see* Xinxiang, China	D5	42
Hsining *see* Xining, China	D5	36
Hsinking *see* Changchun, China	C6	38
Hsinp'u *see* Lianyungang, China	D8	42
Hsintien, Tai.	I9	42
Hsinyang *see* Xinyang, China	E6	42
Hsipaw, Mya.	A3	48
Hsüanhua *see* Xuanhua, China	A6	42
Hsüch'ang *see* Xuchang, China	D5	42
Hsüchou *see* Xuzhou, China	D7	42
Hua'an, China	I7	42
Huab, stm., Nmb.	B2	70
Huacaraje, Bol.	B4	90
Huacho, Peru	F2	84
Huachuca City, Az., U.S.	L6	132
Huadian, China	C7	38
Huading Shan, mtn., China	G9	42
Hua Hin, Thai.	F4	48
Huai, stm., China	E8	42
Huai, stm., China	C6	42
Huai'an, China	E8	42
Huai'an, China	A6	42
Huaibin, China	E6	42
Huaicheng *see* Huai'an, China	E8	42
Huaidezhen, China	C6	38
Huaiji, China	I5	42
Huailai, China	A6	42
Huainan, China	E7	42
Huairou, China	A7	42
Huaite *see* Gongzhuling, China	C6	38
Huaiyang, China	E6	42
Huai Yot, Thai.	I4	48
Huaiyuan, China	E7	42
Huajuapan de León, Mex.	G10	100
Hualahuises, Mex.	C9	100
Hualālai, vol., Hi., U.S.	d6	78a
Hualañé, Chile	G2	92
Hualfín, Arg.	C4	92
Hualien, Tai.	J9	42
Huallaga, stm., Peru	E2	84
Huallanca, Peru	E2	84
Hualong, China	D5	36
Huambo, Ang.	C2	68
Huamei Shan, mtn., China	I5	42
Huan, stm., China	F6	42
Huanan, China	B11	36
Huancabamba, Peru	E2	84
Huancané, Peru	G4	84
Huancavelica, Peru	F2	84
Huancayo, Peru	F2	84
Huang (Yellow), stm., China	D8	36
Huangchuan, China	E6	42
Huanggai Hu, l., China	G5	42
Huanggang, China	F6	42
Huanggangliang, mtn., China	C2	38
Huanghua, China	B7	42
Huangjinbu, China	G7	42
Huangling, China	D3	42
Huanglong, China	D3	42
Huangnihe, China	C7	38
Huangpi, China	F6	42
Huangqi, China	H8	42
Huangshahe, China	H4	42
Huangshan, China	G8	42
Huangshan see Guangming Ding, mtn., China	F7	42
Huangshi, China	G4	42
Huangshi, China	F6	42
Huangtang Hu, l., China	G6	42
Huangtuliangzi, China	A8	42
Huanguelén, Arg.	H6	92
Huangxian, China	C9	42
Huangyan, China	G9	42
Huangyuan, China	D5	36
Huangzhong, China	D5	36
Huangzhu, China	L4	42
Huanjiang, China	I3	42
Huanren, China	D6	38
Huánuco, Peru	E2	84
Huanuni, Bol.	C3	90
Huanxian, China	C2	42
Huara, Chile	C3	90
Huaral, Peru	F2	84
Huaraz, Peru	E2	84
Huariaca, Peru	F2	84
Huarmey, Peru	F2	84
Huarong, China	G5	42
Huasaga, stm., S.A.	I3	86
Hua Sai, Thai.	H5	48
Huascarán, Nevado, mtn., Peru	E2	84
Huasco, Chile	D2	92
Huasco, stm., Chile	D2	92
Huatabampo, Mex.	B4	100
Huating, China	D2	42
Huatong, China	A9	42
Huauchinango, Mex.	E9	100
Huaxian, China	J5	42
Huaxian, China	D6	42
Huaxian, China	D3	42
Huaynamota, stm., Mex.	D6	100
Huazamota, Mex.	D6	100
Huazhou, China	K4	42
Hubbard, Ia., U.S.	B4	120
Hubbard Creek Reservoir, l., Tx., U.S.	B8	130
Hubbard Lake, l., Mi., U.S.	D6	112
Hubbards, N.S., Can.	F12	110
Hubbell, Mi., U.S.	D10	118
Hubei, state, China	F5	42
Huberdeau, Qc., Can.	E2	110
Hubli-Dhārwār, India	D2	53
Hubuleng, China	A4	42
Huchow *see* Huzhou, China	F9	42
Huckleberry Mountain, mtn., Or., U.S.	G4	136
Hucknall, Eng., U.K.	H11	12
Huddersfield, Eng., U.K.	H11	12
Huddinge, Swe.	G8	8
Huder, China	A9	36
Hudiksvall, Swe.	F7	8
Hudson, Fl., U.S.	H3	116
Hudson, Ia., U.S.	B5	120
Hudson, N.C., U.S.	I4	114
Hudson, N.Y., U.S.	H3	110
Hudson, Oh., U.S.	C4	114
Hudson, S.D., U.S.	H2	118
Hudson, Wy., U.S.	E4	126
Hudson, stm., U.S.	G16	112
Hudson, Baie d' see Hudson Bay, b., Can.	C13	106
Hudson Bay, Sk., Can.	B11	124
Hudson Bay, b., Can.	C13	106
Hudson Falls, N.Y., U.S.	G3	110
Hudson's Hope, B.C., Can.	D6	106
Hudson Strait, strt., Can.	C16	106
Hudžand, Taj.	A10	56
Hue, Viet.	D8	48
Huebra, stm., Spain	D4	20
Huehuetenango, Guat.	E2	102
Huejutla de Reyes, Mex.	E9	100
Huelgoat, Fr.	F5	14
Huelva, Spain	G3	20
Huelva, co., Spain	G4	20
Huentelauquén, Chile	E2	92
Huércal-Overa, Spain	G8	20
Huerfano, stm., Co., U.S.	C4	128
Huerlumada, China	B13	54
Huerva, stm., Spain	C9	20
Huesca, Spain	B10	20
Huesca, co., Spain	B10	20
Huéscar, Spain	G8	20
Huetamo de Núñez, Mex.	F8	100
Hueytown, Al., U.S.	D11	122
Ḥufrat an-Naḥās, Sudan	F4	62
Hughenden, Austl.	C4	76
Hughes, Ak., U.S.	C9	140
Hughes, Ar., U.S.	C8	122
Hughes Springs, Tx., U.S.	E4	122
Hugh Keenleyside Dam, dam, B.C., Can.	G12	138
Hughson, Ca., U.S.	F5	134
Hugh Town, Eng., U.K.	L6	12
Hugli, stm., India	G12	54
Hugo, Co., U.S.	B5	128
Hugo, Ok., U.S.	C3	122
Hugoton, Ks., U.S.	D7	128
Huhar, stm., China	B4	38
Huhehaote *see* Hohhot, China	A4	42
Huhehot *see* Hohhot, China	A4	42
Huichang, China	I6	42
Huicheng *see* Huilai, China	J7	42
Hŭich'ŏn, Kor., N.	D7	38
Huichou *see* Huizhou, China	J6	42
Huila, state, Col.	F4	86
Huila, Nevado del, vol., Col.	F3	86
Huilai, China	J7	42
Huili, China	F5	36
Huillapima, Arg.	D4	92
Huimin, China	C7	42
Huinan, China	C7	38
Huisachal, Mex.	H6	130
Huishui, China	H2	42
Huisne, stm., Fr.	F9	14
Huitong, China	H3	42
Huitzo, Mex.	G10	100
Huitzuco de los Figueroa, Mex.	F9	100
Huixian, China	E2	42
Huixian, China	D5	42
Huixtla, Mex.	H12	100
Huize, China	F5	36
Huizhou, China	J6	42
Hŭksan-chedo, is., Kor., S.	G6	38
Hukuntsi, Bots.	D5	70
Hulan, China	B7	38
Hulan Ergi, China	B9	36
Hulbert, Mi., U.S.	B4	112
Hulett, Wy., U.S.	C8	126
Hulga, stm., Russia	B10	32
Hulin, China	B11	36
Hulin, stm., China	B4	38
Huliu, stm., China	A6	42
Hull, Ia., U.S.	H2	118
Hull, Il., U.S.	E6	120
Hull, ngh., Qc., Can.	C14	112
Hullo, Est.	A6	10
Hulun *see* Hailar, China	B8	36
Hulun Nur, l., China	B8	36
Huma, China	F14	34
Huma, Tonga	o15	78e
Humacao, P.R.	B4	104a
Humahuaca, Arg.	D3	90
Humaitá, Braz.	E5	84
Humaitá, Para.	C8	92
Humansdorp, S. Afr.	I7	70
Humansville, Mo., U.S.	G4	120
Humara, Jabal al-, hill, Sudan	D6	62
Humbe, Ang.	D1	68
Humber, stm., Eng., U.K.	H12	12
Humbird, Wi., U.S.	G8	118
Humboldt, Sk., Can.	B8	124
Humboldt, Az., U.S.	I4	132
Humboldt, Ia., U.S.	B3	120
Humboldt, Il., U.S.	E9	120
Humboldt, Ne., U.S.	D2	120
Humboldt, S.D., U.S.	D15	126
Humboldt, stm., Nv., U.S.	C7	134
Humboldt, North Fork, stm., Nv., U.S.	B1	132
Humboldt, South Fork, stm., Nv., U.S.	C1	132
Humboldt Gletscher, ice, Grnld.	B13	141
Humboldt Lake, l., Nv., U.S.	D7	134
Hume, Ca., U.S.	G7	134
Hume, Lake, res., Austl.	J6	76
Humeburn, Austl.	F5	76
Humenné, Slov.	H17	16
Humeston, Ia., U.S.	D4	120
Hummi, ozero, l., Russia	F16	34
Humphrey, Ne., U.S.	F15	126
Humphreys, Mount, mtn., Ca., U.S.	F7	134
Humphreys Peak, mtn., Az., U.S.	H5	132
Humpolec, Czech Rep.	G11	16
Humpty Doo, Austl.	B6	74
Hūn, Libya	B3	62
Hun, stm., China	D5	38
Hun, stm., China	D6	38
Húnaflói, b., Ice.	j29	8a
Hunan, state, China	H4	42
Hunchun, China	C9	38
Hundred, W.V., U.S.	E5	114
Hunedoara, Rom.	D9	26
Hunedoara, state, Rom.	C9	26
Hünfeld, Ger.	F5	16
Hungary, ctry., Eur.	B6	26
Hungchiang *see* Hongjiang, China	H4	42
Hŭngdŏki-dong, Kor., N.	E7	38
Hungerford, Austl.	G5	76
Hungerford, Tx., U.S.	H2	122
Hungry Horse Dam, dam, Mt., U.S.	B13	136
Hungry Horse Reservoir, res., Mt., U.S.	B12	136
Hung Yen, Viet.	B8	48
Hunjiang, China	C7	38
Hunlen Falls, wtfl., B.C., Can.	D5	138
Hunsberge, mts., Nmb.	E3	70
Hunsrück, mts., Ger.	G3	16
Hunsūr, India	E3	53
Hunte, stm., Ger.	D4	16
Hunter, N.D., U.S.	D1	118
Hunter, stm., Austl.	I8	76
Hunter Island, i., Austl.	n12	77a
Hunter Island, i., B.C., Can.	E2	138
Hunter Mountain, mtn., N.Y., U.S.	B11	114
Hunter River, P.E., Can.	D13	110
Hunters, Wa., U.S.	B8	136
Hunters Bay, b., Mya.	C1	48
Huntingdon, Qc., Can.	E2	110
Huntingdon, Eng., U.K.	I12	12
Huntingdon, Pa., U.S.	D7	114
Huntingdon, Tn., U.S.	I9	120
Huntington, In., U.S.	H4	112
Huntington, Tx., U.S.	F4	122
Huntington, Ut., U.S.	D5	132
Huntington, W.V., U.S.	F3	114
Huntington Beach, Ca., U.S.	J7	134
Huntland, Tn., U.S.	B12	122
Huntley, Mt., U.S.	B4	126
Huntly, N.Z.	C6	80
Huntly, Scot., U.K.	D10	12
Huntsville, On., Can.	C10	112
Huntsville, Al., U.S.	C12	122
Huntsville, Mo., U.S.	E5	120
Huntsville, Tn., U.S.	H13	120
Huntsville, Tx., U.S.	G3	122
Huntsville, Ut., U.S.	B5	132
Hunyuan, China	B5	42
Huong Hoa, Viet.	D8	48
Huon Gulf, b., Pap. N. Gui.	b4	79a
Huon Peninsula, pen., Pap. N. Gui.	b4	79a
Huonville, Austl.	o13	77a
Huoqiu, China	E7	42
Huoshan, China	F7	42
Huoxian, China	C4	42
Hurd, Cape, c., On., Can.	C8	112
Hüren Tovon uul, mtn., Mong.	C4	36
Hure Qi, China	C4	38
Hurghada, Egypt	K4	58
Hurley, N.M., U.S.	K8	132
Hurley, S.D., U.S.	D15	126
Hurley, Wi., U.S.	E8	118
Huron, Ca., U.S.	G5	134
Huron, Oh., U.S.	C3	114
Huron, S.D., U.S.	C14	126
Huron, stm., Mi., U.S.	B2	114
Huron, Lake, l., N.A.	D7	112
Huron Mountains, hills, Mi., U.S.	B2	112
Hurricane, Ut., U.S.	F3	132
Hurstbridge, Austl.	K5	76
Hurtado, stm., Chile	E2	92
Hurtsboro, Al., U.S.	E13	122
Hurunui, stm., N.Z.	F5	80
Husainīwāla, India	C5	54
Húsavik, Far. Is.	n34	8b
Húsavík, Ice.	j31	8a
Hushitai, China	C5	38
Huși, Rom.	C15	26
Huslia, Ak., U.S.	C8	140
Hussar, Ab., Can.	E18	138
Husum, Ger.	B4	16
Hutag, Mong.	B5	36
Hutanopan, Indon.	C1	50
Hutchinson, S. Afr.	G6	70
Hutchinson, Ks., U.S.	C11	128
Hutchinson, Mn., U.S.	G4	118
Hutch Mountain, mtn., Az., U.S.	I5	132
Hutsonville, Il., U.S.	E10	120
Huttig, Ar., U.S.	D6	122
Hutto, Tx., U.S.	D10	130
Hutuo, stm., China	B5	42
Huwei, Tai.	J9	42
Huxi, China	H6	42
Huxian, China	D3	42
Huxley, Ab., Can.	E17	138
Huy, Bel.	D14	14
Huzhen, China	G9	42
Huzhou, China	F9	42
Hvannadalshnúkur, mtn., Ice.	k31	8a
Hvar, Cro.	G13	22
Hvar, Otok, i., Cro.	G13	22
Hveragerđi, Ice.	k29	8a
Hvolsvöllur, Ice.	I29	8a
Hwainan *see* Huainan, China	E7	42
Hwange, Zimb.	D4	68
Hwang Ho see Huang, stm., China	D8	36
Hwangju-ŭp, Kor., N.	E6	38
Hwangshih *see* Huangshi, China	F6	42
Hyannis, Ma., U.S.	C15	114
Hyannis, Ne., U.S.	F11	126
Hyargas nuur, l., Mong.	B3	36
Hyattville, Wy., U.S.	C5	126
Hyden, Austl.	F3	74
Hyden, Ky., U.S.	G2	114
Hyde Park, Guy.	B6	84
Hyde Park, N.Y., U.S.	C12	114
Hyde Park, Vt., U.S.	F4	110
Hyderābād, India	C4	53
Hyderābād, Pak.	F2	54
Hydra see Ýdra, i., Grc.	F6	28
Hydraulic, B.C., Can.	D9	138
Hydro, Ok., U.S.	F10	128
Hydrographers Passage, strt., Austl.	C8	76
Hyères, Fr.	F12	18
Hyères, Îles d', is., Fr.	G12	18
Hyesan, Kor., N.	D8	38
Hyland, stm., Can.	C5	106
Hyndman, Pa., U.S.	E7	114
Hyndman Peak, mtn., Id., U.S.	G12	136
Hyōgo, state, Japan	D7	40
Hyrum, Ut., U.S.	B5	132
Hysham, Mt., U.S.	A5	126
Hythe, Eng., U.K.	J13	12
Hyūga, Japan	G4	40
Hyūga-nada, s., Japan	G4	40
Hyvinge *see* Hyvinkää, Fin.	F11	8
Hyvinkää, Fin.	F11	8
I		
Iaciara, Braz.	H2	88
Iaco (Yaco), stm., S.A.	F4	84
Iaçu, Braz.	G5	88
Iaeger, W.V., U.S.	G4	114
Ialomița, state, Rom.	E14	26
Ialomița, stm., Rom.	E13	26
Ialomiței, Balta, sw., Rom.	E14	26
Iamonia, Lake, l., Fl., U.S.	F1	116
Iapu, Braz.	J4	88
Iargara, Mol.	C15	26
Iași, Rom.	B14	26
Iași, state, Rom.	B14	26
Iatt, Lake, res., La., U.S.	F6	122
Ib, stm., India	G10	54
Iba, Phil.	C2	52
Ibadan, Nig.	H5	64
Ibagué, Col.	E4	86
Ibaiti, Braz.	A12	92
Ibănești, Rom.	A13	26
Ibapah Peak, mtn., Ut., U.S.	D3	132
Ibar, stm., Eur.	F7	26
Ibaraki, state, Japan	C13	40
Ibarra, Ec.	G2	86
Ibarreta, Arg.	B8	92
Ibb, Yemen	G5	56
Ibbenbüren, Ger.	D3	16
Ibembo, D.R.C.	D4	66
Iberá, Esteros del, sw., Arg.	D8	92
Iberia, Mo., U.S.	F5	120
Iberian Mountains see Ibérico, Sistema, mts., Spain	D8	20
Iberian Peninsula, pen., Eur.	D12	4
Ibérico, Sistema (Iberian Mountains), mts., Spain	D8	20
Ibiá, Braz.	J2	88
Ibiapina, Braz.	B5	88
Ibicaraí, Braz.	H6	88
Ibicuí, Braz.	H5	88
Ibicuí, stm., Braz.	D9	92
Ibiquera, Braz.	G5	88
Ibiraçu, Braz.	J5	88
Ibirapuã, Braz.	I5	88
Ibirapuitã, stm., Braz.	D10	92
Ibirataia, Braz.	H6	88
Ibirubá, Braz.	D11	92
Ibitiara, Braz.	G4	88
Ibitinga, Braz.	K1	88
Ibiza *see* Eivissa, Spain	F12	20
Ibiza see Eivissa, i., Spain	F12	20
Ibotirama, Braz.	G4	88
İbriktepe, Tur.	B9	28
Ibshawâi, Egypt	I1	58
Ibusuki, Japan	H3	40
Ica, Peru	F2	84
Içá (Putumayo), stm., S.A.	D4	84
Icabarú, stm., Ven.	E10	86
Icacos Point, c., Trin.	s11	105f
Icamaquã, stm., Braz.	D10	92
Icamole, Mex.	I7	130
Içana, Braz.	G8	86
Içana (Isana), stm., S.A.	G7	86
Icaño, Arg.	D5	92
Icatu, Braz.	B3	88
Iceberg Pass, p., Co., U.S.	G7	126
İçel (Mersin), Tur.	B5	58
İçel, state, Tur.	B4	58
Iceland, ctry., Eur.	k30	8a
Iceland Basin, unds.	C11	144
Ice Mountain, mtn., B.C., Can.	B9	138
Ichaikaronji, India	C2	53
Ichchāpuram, India	B7	53
Ichikawa, Japan	D12	40
Ichinomiya, Japan	D9	40
Ichkeul, Lac, l., Tun.	G3	24
Ichnia, Ukr.	D4	32
Ich'un *see* Yichun, China	B10	36
Ičinskaja Sopka, vulkan, vol., Russia	E20	34
Icó, Braz.	D6	88
Icy Cape, c., Ak., U.S.	B7	140
Ida, Mount see Ídi Óros, mtn., Grc.	H7	28
Idabel, Ok., U.S.	D4	122
Ida Grove, Ia., U.S.	B2	120
Idah, Nig.	H6	64
Idaho, state, U.S.	G12	136
Idaho City, Id., U.S.	G11	136
Idaho Falls, Id., U.S.	G14	136
Idaho National Engineering Laboratory, sci., Id., U.S.	G14	136
Idalou, Tx., U.S.	H7	128
Idanha-a-Nova, Port.	E3	20
Idāppādi, India	F3	53
Idar, India	G4	54
Idar-Oberstein, Ger.	G3	16
Idelès, Alg.	E6	64
Idi, Indon.	J3	48
Idiofa, D.R.C.	F3	66
Ídi Óros, mtn., Grc.	H7	28
Idku, Bahra el-, l., Egypt	G1	58
Idlib, Syria	C7	58
Idlib, state, Syria	C7	58
Ídolo, Isla del, i., Mex.	E10	100
Idoûkâl-en-Taghès, mtn., Niger	F6	64
Idre, Swe.	F5	8
Idrija, Slvn.	D11	22
Idutywa, S. Afr.	H9	70
Iecava, stm., Lat.	D7	10
Ieper, Bel.	D11	14
Ierápetra, Grc.	H8	28
Ierzu, Italy	E3	24
Iesolo, Italy	E9	22
Ifakara, Tan.	F7	66
Ife, Nig.	H5	64
Iferouâne, Niger	F6	64
Iferten *see* Yverdon-les-Bains, Switz.	D3	22
Ifôghas, Adrar des, mts., Afr.	F5	64
Igan, Malay.	B7	50
Igan, stm., Malay.	B7	50
Iganga, Ug.	D6	66
Igaporã, Braz.	G4	88
Igara, Braz.	F5	88
Igara Paraná, stm., Col.	H5	86
Igarapé-Açu, Braz.	D8	84
Igarapé-Miri, Braz.	B1	88
Igarka, Russia	A15	32
Igatpuri, India	B1	53
Igboho, Nig.	H5	64
Igharghar, Oued, stm., Alg.	D6	64
Igiugig, Ak., U.S.	E8	140
Iglesias, Italy	E2	24
Iglesias, Cerro las, mtn., Mex.	B5	100
Iglesiente, reg., Italy	E2	24
Igluligaarjuk (Chesterfield Inlet), Nu., Can.	C12	106
Iglulik, Nu., Can.	B14	106
'Igma, Gebel el-, mts., Egypt	I4	58
Ignacio, Co., U.S.	F9	132
Ignalina, Lith.	E9	10
Ignaței, Mol.	B15	26
Igoumenítsa, Grc.	D3	28
Igra, Russia	C8	32
Iguaçu (Iguazú), stm., S.A.	B10	92
Iguaçu, Parque Nacional do, p.o.i., Braz.	B11	92
Iguaí, Braz.	H5	88
Iguala, Mex.	F9	100
Igualada, Spain	C12	20
Iguana, stm., Ven.	D9	86
Iguape, Braz.	B14	92
Iguape, stm., Braz.	B13	92
Iguassu Falls, wtfl., S.A.	B10	92
Iguatemi, stm., Braz.	A10	92
Iguatu, Braz.	D6	88
Iguazú (Iguaçu), stm., S.A.	B10	92
Iguazú, Parque Nacional, p.o.i., S.A.	B10	92
Iguéla, Gabon	E1	66
Iguéla, Lagune, b., Gabon	E1	66
Iguîdi, 'Erg, sand, Afr.	D3	64
Igžej, Russia	D18	32
Iharaña, Madag.	C9	68
Iheya-shima, i., Japan	I18	39a
Ihnâsiya el-Madina, Egypt	I1	58
Ihosy, Madag.	E8	68
Ihtiman, Blg.	G10	26
Iida, Japan	D10	40
Iisalmi, Fin.	E12	8
Iiyama, Japan	C11	40
Iizuka, Japan	F3	40
Ijâfene, des., Maur.	E3	64
Ijebu-Ode, Nig.	H5	64
IJmuiden, Neth.	B13	14
IJssel, stm., Neth.	B15	14
IJsselmeer, l., Neth.	B14	14
Ijuí, Braz.	D11	92
Ijuí, stm., Braz.	D10	92
Ika, Russia	C19	32
Ikali, D.R.C.	E4	66
Ikaluktutiak (Cambridge Bay), Nu., Can.	B10	106
Ikaría, i., Grc.	F9	28
Ikatskij hrebet, mts., Russia	F11	34
Ikeda, Japan	E6	40
Ikej, Russia	D17	32
Ikeja, Nig.	H5	64
Ikela, D.R.C.	E4	66
Ikerre, Nig.	H6	64
İkizce, Tur.	D15	28
Ikom, Nig.	H6	64
Ikot-Ekpene, Nig.	H6	64
Ikuno, Japan	D7	40
Ikurangi, hill, Cook Is.	a26	78j
Ila, Nig.	H6	64
Ilagan, Phil.	B3	52
Ilaiyānkudi, India	G4	53
Īlām, Iran	C6	56
Ilām, Nepal	E11	54
Ilan, Tai.	I9	42
Ilanskij, Russia	C17	32
Ilaro, Nig.	H5	64
Iława, Pol.	C15	16
Ilbenge, Russia	D13	34
Île-à-la-Crosse, Sk., Can.	D9	106
Ilebo, D.R.C.	E4	66
Île-de-France, hist. reg., Fr.	E11	14
Île de France, i., Grnld.	B22	141
Île-du-Prince-Édouard see Prince Edward Island, state, Can.	D13	110
Ilek, stm., Asia	D8	32
Ilesha, Nig.	H5	64
Îles Loyauté, state, N. Cal.	m16	79d
Île Tintamarre, i., Anguilla	A2	105a
Ilevskij Pogost, Russia	F20	8
Ileza, Russia	F20	8
Ilfracombe, Austl.	D5	76
Ilfracombe, Eng., U.K.	J8	12
Ilhabela, Braz.	L3	88
Ilha Grande, Baía da, b., Braz.	L3	88
Ilha Solteira, Represa de, res., Braz.	D6	90
Ilhea Point, c., Nmb.	C2	70
Ilhéus, Braz.	H6	88
Ilia, Rom.	D9	26
Iliamna, Ak., U.S.	E8	140
Iliamna Lake, l., Ak., U.S.	D9	140
Ilicinea, Braz.	K3	88
Iliff, Co., U.S.	G9	126
Iligan, Phil.	F5	52
Iligan Bay, b., Phil.	F4	52
Iliniza, vol., Ec.	H2	86
Ilion, N.Y., U.S.	A10	114
Ilir, Russia	C18	32
Ilizi, Alg.	D6	64
Il'ja, Bela.	F10	10
Iljino, Russia	E14	10
Iljinskij, Russia	G17	34
Iljinskoe, Russia	D19	10
Iljinsko-Podomskoe, Russia	F23	8
Iljiny gory, hills, Russia	D17	10
Ilkal, India	D2	53
Ilkley, Eng., U.K.	H11	12
Illampu, Nevado, mtn., Bol.	C3	90
Illana Bay, b., Phil.	G4	52
Illapel, Chile	E2	92
Ille-et-Vilaine, state, Fr.	F7	14
Illéla, Niger	G6	64
Iller, stm., Ger.	I6	16
Illertissen, Ger.	H6	16
Illescas, Mex.	D7	100
Illichivs'k, Ukr.	C17	26
Illimani, Nevado, mtn., Bol.	C3	90
Illinois, state, U.S.	D8	120
Illinois, stm., Il., U.S.	E7	120
Illinois, stm., Or., U.S.	H3	136
Illinois, stm., U.S.	B3	122
Il'men', ozero, l., Russia	B14	10
Ilo, Peru	G3	84
Iloilo, Phil.	E4	52
Ilomantsi, Fin.	E14	8
Ilorin, Nig.	H5	64
Il'pyrskij, Russia	D21	34
Ilūkste, Lat.	E9	10
Ilulissat *see* Jakobshavn, Grnld.	D15	141
Ilwaki, Indon.	G8	44
Ilwŏl-san, mtn., Kor., S.	C1	40
Īlyīch, Kaz.	F11	32
Imabari, Japan	E5	40
Imaichi, Japan	C12	40
Imandra, ozero, l., Russia	C14	8
Imari, Japan	F2	40
Imaruí, Braz.	D13	92
Imaruí, Lagoa do, l., Braz.	D13	92
Imatra, Fin.	F13	8
Imavere, Est.	B8	10
Imbabura, state, Ec.	G2	86
Imbituba, Braz.	D13	92
Imeni Cjurupy, Russia	E21	10
Imeni Kirova, Russia	E14	34
Imeni Poliny Osipenko, Russia	F16	34
Imeni Stepana Razina, Russia	I21	8
Imeni Željabova, Russia	A19	10
Īmī, Eth.	F8	62
Imías, Cuba	B10	102
Imilac, Chile	B3	92
Imlay, Nv., U.S.	C7	134
Imlay City, Mi., U.S.	E6	112
Immenstadt, Ger.	I6	16
Immokalee, Fl., U.S.	J4	116
Imnaha, stm., Or., U.S.	E10	136
Imola, Italy	F8	22
Imonda, Pap. N. Gui.	a3	79a
Impasugong, Phil.	F5	52
Imperatriz, Braz.	C2	88
Imperia, Italy	G5	22
Imperial, Sk., Can.	C8	124
Imperial, Ca., U.S.	K10	134
Imperial, Tx., U.S.	C5	130
Imperial Beach, Ca., U.S.	K8	134
Imperial Dam, dam, U.S.	K2	132
Imperial de Aragón, Canal, can., Spain	C9	20
Imperial Valley, val., Ca., U.S.	E5	98
Impfondo, Congo	D3	66
Imphāl, India	D7	46
Imroz, Tur.	C8	28
Imst, Aus.	C7	22
Imuris, Mex.	F7	98
Ina, Japan	D10	40
Ina, Il., U.S.	F9	120
Inajá, Braz.	E7	88
I-n-Amenas, Alg.	D6	64
Iñapari, Peru	F4	84
Inarajan, Guam	j10	78c
Inari, Fin.	B12	8
Inarigda, Russia	B19	32
Inarijärvi, l., Fin.	B12	8
Inawashiro-ko, l., Japan	B12	40
Inca, Spain	E13	20
Inca de Oro, Chile	C3	92
Incahuasi, Cerro de, mtn., S.A.	C3	92
İnce Burun, c., Tur.	C10	28
İncekum Burnu, c., Tur.	B4	58
Inchelium, Wa., U.S.	B8	136
Inch'ŏn, Kor., S.	F7	38
İncirliova, Tur.	F10	28
Incomati (Komati), stm., Afr.	E10	70
Incudine, Monte, mtn., Fr.	H15	18
Incy, Russia	D19	8
Indaiá, stm., Braz.	J3	88
Indalsälven, stm., Swe.	E6	8
Indé, Mex.	I2	130
Independence, Ca., U.S.	G7	134
Independence, Ia., U.S.	B6	120
Independence, Ks., U.S.	G2	120
Independence, Ky., U.S.	F13	120
Independence, La., U.S.	G8	122
Independence, Mo., U.S.	E3	120
Independence, Va., U.S.	H4	114
Independence, Wi., U.S.	G7	118
Independence Fjord, b., Grnld.	A20	141
Independencia, Bol.	C3	90
Independência, Braz.	C5	88
Inderbor, Kaz.	E8	32
Indi, India	C2	53
India, ctry., Asia	D4	46
Indialantic, Fl., U.S.	H5	116
Indiana, Pa., U.S.	D6	114
Indiana, state, U.S.	D11	120
Indiana Dunes National Lakeshore, p.o.i., In., U.S.	G2	112
Indianapolis, In., U.S.	I3	112
Indian Bayou, stm., Ar., U.S.	C7	122
Indian Church, Belize	D3	102
Indian Head, Sk., Can.	D10	124
Indian Lake, N.Y., U.S.	G2	110
Indian Lake, l., On., Can.	A7	112
Indian Lake, l., Mi., U.S.	B3	112
Indian Ocean	K11	142
Indianola, Ia., U.S.	C4	120
Indianola, Ms., U.S.	D8	122
Indianola, Ne., U.S.	A8	128
Indian Peak, mtn., Ut., U.S.	E3	132
Indian River, Mi., U.S.	C5	112
Indian Rock, mtn., Wa., U.S.	E6	136
Indiantown, Fl., U.S.	I5	116
Indiera Alta, P.R.	B2	104a
Indiga, Russia	C23	8
Indigirka, stm., Russia	C18	34
Indin, Mya.	H14	54
Indio, Ca., U.S.	J9	134
Indira Gandhi Canal, can., India	E4	54
Indispensable Strait, strt., Sol. Is.	e9	79b
Indochina, reg., Asia	D7	48
Indonesia, ctry., Asia	J16	30
Indore, India	G5	54
Indragiri, stm., Indon.	D2	50
Indramayu, Indon.	G6	50
Indrāvati, stm., India	B5	53
Indravati Tiger Reserve, p.o.i., India	B5	53
Indre, state, Fr.	C7	18
Indre, stm., Fr.	G10	14
Indre-et-Loire, state, Fr.	G9	14
Indus, stm., Asia	D2	46
Industry, Tx., U.S.	H2	122
İnece, Tur.	B10	28
In Ecker, Alg.	E6	64
İnegöl, Tur.	C12	28
Ineu, Rom.	C8	26
Inez, Ky., U.S.	G3	114
Inez, Tx., U.S.	F11	130
Inferior, Laguna, b., Mex.	G11	100
Infiernillo, Canal del, strt., Mex.	G6	98
Infiernillo, Presa del, res., Mex.	F7	100
Ing, stm., Thai.	C5	48
Ingá, Braz.	D8	88
Ingabu, Mya.	D2	48
Ingal, Niger	F6	64
Ingall Point, c., On., Can.	B10	118
Ingelheim, Ger.	G4	16
Ingende, D.R.C.	E3	66
Ingeniero Jacobacci, Arg.	H3	90
Ingeniero Luiggi, Arg.	G5	92
Ingham, Austl.	B6	76
Inglefield Land, reg., Grnld.	B12	141
Ingleside, Tx., U.S.	G10	130
Inglewood, Austl.	G8	76
Inglewood, Austl.	K4	76
Inglewood, Ca., U.S.	J7	134
Inglis, Mb., Can.	D12	124
Ingolf Fjord, b., Grnld.	A22	141
Ingolstadt, Ger.	H7	16
Ingonish, N.S., Can.	D16	110
Ingrāj Bāzār, India	F12	54
Ingrid Christensen Coast, cst., Ant.	B12	81
In Guezzam, Alg.	F6	64
Ingušetija, state, Russia	F6	32
Ingushetia see Ingušetija, state, Russia	F6	32
Inhaca, Ilha da, i., Moz.	E11	70
Inhambane, Moz.	C12	70
Inhambane, state, Moz.	C12	70
Inhambane, Baía de, b., Moz.	C12	70
Inhambupe, Braz.	F6	88
Inhaminga, Moz.	D5	68
Inhapim, Braz.	J4	88
Inharrime, Moz.	D12	70
Inhassoro, Moz.	B12	70
Inhuma, Braz.	D5	88
Inhumas, Braz.	I1	88
Inimutaba, Braz.	J3	88
Ining *see* Yining, China	F14	32
Inírida, stm., Col.	F7	86
Inis *see* Ennis, Ire.	I3	12
Inis Córthaidh *see* Enniscorthy, Ire.	I6	12
Inishbofin, i., Ire.	H2	12
Inishmore, i., Ire.	H3	12
Inishowen, pen., Ire.	F5	12
Inishturk, i., Ire.	H2	12
Inja, Russia	E17	34
Inja, stm., Russia	D18	34
Injune, Austl.	E7	76
Inkom, Id., U.S.	H14	136
Inkster, N.D., U.S.	F16	124
Inland Lake, l., Mb., Can.	B14	124
Inland Sea see Seto-naikai, s., Japan	E5	40
Inle Lake, l., Mya.	B3	48
Inman, Ks., U.S.	C11	128
Inman Mills, S.C., U.S.	A3	116
Inn, stm., Eur.	B10	22
Innamincka, Austl.	F3	76
Inner Channel, strt., Belize	D3	102
Inner Hebrides, is., Scot., U.K.	E6	12
Inner Mongolia see Nei Monggol, state, China	C7	36
Inner Sister Island, i., Austl.	m13	77a
Innisfail, Austl.	A6	76
Innisfail, Ab., Can.	D17	138
Innisfree, Ab., Can.	C19	138
Innokentevka, Russia	G16	34
Innoko, stm., Ak., U.S.	D8	140
Innoshima, Japan	E6	40
Innsbruck, Aus.	C8	22
Innviertel, reg., Aus.	B10	22
Inola, Ok., U.S.	H2	120
Inongo, D.R.C.	E3	66
İnönü, Tur.	D13	28
Inowrocław, Pol.	D14	16
In Salah, Alg.	D5	64
Instow, Sk., Can.	E5	124
Inta, Russia	A10	32
Intendente Alvear, Arg.	G6	92
İntepe, Tur.	D9	28
Interlaken, Switz.	D4	22
Interlândia, Braz.	I1	88
International Falls, Mn., U.S.	C5	118
Inthanon, Doi, mtn., Thai.	C4	48
Intiyaco, Arg.	D7	92
Intracoastal Waterway, strt., U.S.	H10	130
Intracoastal Waterway, strt., U.S.	L5	116
Intu, Indon.	D9	50
Inubō-saki, c., Japan	D13	40
Inukjuak, Qc., Can.	D15	106
Inuvik, N.T., Can.	B4	106
Inverbervie, Scot., U.K.	E10	12
Invercargill, N.Z.	H3	80
Inverell, Austl.	G8	76
Inverloch, Austl.	L5	76
Invermay, Sk., Can.	C10	124
Invermere, B.C., Can.	F14	138
Inverness, N.S., Can.	D15	110
Inverness, Scot., U.K.	D8	12
Inverness, Ca., U.S.	E3	134
Inverness, Fl., U.S.	H3	116

Name | Map Ref. | Page

Inverurie, Scot., U.K. D10 12
Inverway, Austl. C5 74
Investigator Strait, strt., Austl. G7 74
Inwood, Mb., Can. D16 124
Inyangani, mtn., Zimb. D5 68
Inyathi, Zimb. D4 68
Inyo, Mount, mtn., Ca., U.S. G8 134
Inyokern, Ca., U.S. H8 134
Inyo Mountains, mts., Ca., U.S. G7 134
Inzana Lake, l., B.C., Can. B6 138
Ioánnina, Grc. D3 28
Iokanga, stm., Russia C18 8
Iola, Ks., U.S. G2 120
Ioma, Pap. N. Gui. b4 79a
Iona, Ang. D1 68
Iona, N.S., Can. D16 110
Iona, Id., U.S. G15 136
Iona, i., Scot., U.K. E6 12
Ione, Ca., U.S. E5 134
Ione, Wa., U.S. B9 136
Ionia, Mi., U.S. E4 112
Ionian Islands see Iónioi Nísoi, is., Grc. E3 28
Ionian Sea, s., Eur. F11 24
Iónioi Nísoi, state, Grc. E3 28
Iónioi Nísoi (Ionian Islands), is., Grc. E3 28
Iony, ostrov, i., Russia E17 34
Íos, i., Grc. G8 28
Iosegun Lake see Fox Creek, Ab., Can. B14 138
Iowa, La., U.S. G5 122
Iowa, state, U.S. I5 118
Iowa, stm., Ia., U.S. C6 120
Iowa City, Ia., U.S. C6 120
Iowa Falls, Ia., U.S. B4 120
Iowa Park, Tx., U.S. H10 128
Ipameri, Braz. I1 88
Ipanema, stm., Braz. E7 88
Ipanguaçu, Braz. C7 88
Ipatinga, Braz. J4 88
Ipatovo, Russia E6 32
Ipaumirim, Braz. D6 88
Ípeiros, state, Grc. D3 28
Ípeiros, hist. reg., Grc. D3 28
Ipel' (Ipoly), stm., Eur. I14 16
Ipiales, Col. G3 86
Ipiaú, Braz. H6 88
Ipin see Yibin, China F5 36
Ipirá, Braz. G6 88
Ipixuna, Braz. C3 88
Ipoh, Malay. J5 48
Ipojuca, stm., Braz. E7 88
Ipoly (Ipel'), stm., Eur. I14 16
Iporã, Braz. G7 84
Iporã, Braz. A11 92
Ipota, Vanuatu I17 79d
İpsala, Tur. C9 28
Ipswich, Austl. F9 76
Ipswich, Eng., U.K. I14 12
Ipswich, Ma., U.S. B15 114
Ipswich, S.D., U.S. B13 126
Ipu, Braz. C5 88
Ipubi, Braz. D5 88
Ipuc' (Iput'), stm., Eur. H14 10
Ipueiras, Braz. C5 88
Iput' (Ipuc'), stm., Eur. H14 10
Iqaluit, Nu., Can. C17 106
Iqfahs, Egypt J1 58
Iquique, Chile D2 90
Iquitos, Peru D3 84
Ira, Tx., U.S. B7 130
Iracema, Braz. C6 88
Irákleia, i., Grc. G8 28
Irákleio, Grc. H8 28
Iran, ctry., Asia C7 56
Iran Mountains, mts., Asia C9 50
Īrānshahr, Iran D9 56
Irapa, Ven. B10 86
Irapuato, Mex. E8 100
Iraq, ctry., Asia C5 56
Irará, Braz. F6 88
Irati, Braz. B12 92
Irazú, Volcán, vol., C.R. G6 102
Irbejskoe, Russia C17 32
Irbid, Jord. F6 58
Irbid, state, Jord. F6 58
Irbit, Russia C10 32
Irdning, Aus. C11 22
Irebu, D.R.C. E3 66
Irecê, Braz. F5 88
Ireland, ctry., Eur. H4 12
Ireland Island North, i., Ber. k15 104e
Irene, S.D., U.S. D15 126
Ireng (Maú), stm., S.A. F12 86
Ireton, Ia., U.S. B1 120
Iri, Kor., S. G7 38
Iriba, Chad E4 62
Iriga, Phil. D4 52
Irîgui, reg., Afr. F3 64
Iringa, Tan. F7 66
Irinjālakuda, India F3 53
Iriomote-jima, i., Japan G9 36
Iriri, stm., Braz. D7 84
Irish, Mount, mtn., Nv., U.S. F1 132
Irish Sea, s., Eur. H7 12
Irituia, Braz. A2 88
Irkutsk, Russia D18 32
Irma, Ab., Can. D19 138
Irminger Basin, unds. B10 144
Irnijärvi, l., Fin. D13 8
Iroise, b., Fr. F4 14
Iron Bottom Sound, strt., Sol. Is. e8 79b
Iron Bridge, On., Can. B6 112
Iron City, Tn., U.S. B11 122
Irondale, Al., U.S. D12 122
Irondale, Mo., U.S. G7 120
Irondequoit, N.Y., U.S. E12 112
Iron Gate, p., Eur. E9 26
Iron Knob, Austl. F7 74
Iron Mountain, Mi., U.S. C1 112
Iron Range, Austl. B8 74
Iron River, Mi., U.S. E10 118
Ironton, Mn., U.S. E4 118
Ironton, Mo., U.S. G7 120
Ironton, Oh., U.S. F3 114
Ironwood, Mi., U.S. E8 118
Ironwood Forest National Monument, p.o.i., Az., U.S. K5 132
Iroquois, On., Can. D14 112
Iroquois, stm., U.S. H2 112
Iroquois Falls, On., Can. F14 106
Irō-zaki, c., Japan E11 40
Irrawaddy see Ayeyarwady, stm., Mya. E8 46
Irricana, Ab., Can. E17 138
Irrigon, Or., U.S. E7 136
Irshava, Ukr. A10 26
Irsina, Italy D10 24
Irtyš see Irtysh, stm., Asia C11 32
Irtysh (Irtyš) (Ertis) (Ertix), stm., Asia C11 32
Irún, Spain A9 20
Iruña see Pamplona, Spain B9 20
Irurzun, Spain B9 20
Irú Tepuy, mtn., Ven. E11 86
Irvine, Ab., Can. E3 124
Irvine, Scot., U.K. F8 12
Irvines Landing, B.C., Can. G6 138
Irving, Tx., U.S. B10 130
Irvington, Ky., U.S. G11 120
Isa, Nig. G6 64
Isaac, stm., Austl. D7 76
Isaac Lake, l., B.C., Can. C10 138
Isabel, state, Sol. Is. d8 79b
Isabela, Phil. G3 52
Isabela, P.R. A1 104a
Isabela, Cabo, c., Dom. Rep. C12 102
Isabela, Isla, i., Ec. i11 84a
Isabelia, Cordillera, mts., Nic. F5 102
Isaccea, Rom. D15 26
Isachsen, Cape, c., Nu., Can. B4 141
Ísafjarđardjúp, b., Ice. j28 8a
Ísafjörður, Ice. j28 8a
Isahaya, Japan G3 40
Isak, Indon. J3 48
Isaka, Tan. E6 66
Īsa Khel, Pak. B3 54
Işalniţa, Rom. E10 26
Isana (Içana), stm., S.A. G7 86
Isangel, Vanuatu I17 79d
Isanti, Mn., U.S. F5 118
Isar, stm., Eur. H8 16
Isarog, Mount, vol., Phil. D4 52
İscehisar, Tur. E13 28
Ischia, Italy D7 24
Ischia, Isola d', i., Italy D7 24
Ise, Japan E9 40
Iseo, Lago d', l., Italy E6 22
Isère, state, Fr. D11 18
Isère, stm., Fr. D11 18
Iserlohn, Ger. E3 16
Isernia, Italy C8 24
Isesaki, Japan C12 40
Ise-shima-kokuritsu-kōen, p.o.i., Japan E9 40
Ise-wan, b., Japan E9 40
Iseyin, Nig. H5 64
Isezaki see Isesaki, Japan C12 40
Isfahan see Eşfahān, Iran C7 56
Isfara, Taj. A11 56
Isherton, Guy. F12 86
Ishigaki, Japan G9 36
Ishikari, stm., Japan C14 38
Ishikari-wan, b., Japan C14 38
Ishikawa, state, Japan C9 40
Ishim (Esil) (Išim), stm., Asia C12 32
Ishinomaki, Japan A14 40
Ishioka, Japan C13 40
Ishizuchi-san, mtn., Japan F5 40
Ishpeming, Mi., U.S. B2 112
Ishurdi, Bngl. F12 54
Isigny-sur-Mer, Fr. E7 14
Işıklı, Tur. E12 28
Isil'kul', Russia C12 32
Išim, Russia C11 32
Išimskaja ravnina, pl., Asia C11 32
Isiolo, Kenya D7 66
Isipingo, ngh., S. Afr. G10 70
Isiro, D.R.C. D5 66
Isis, Austl. E9 76
Iskăr, stm., Blg. F11 26
Iskăr, Jazovir, res., Blg. G10 26
İskenderun (Alexandretta), Tur. B6 58
İskenderun Körfezi, b., Tur. B6 58
Iskitim, Russia D14 32
Iskut, stm., B.C., Can. D4 106
Isla, Mex. G11 100
Isla, Salar de la, pl., Chile B3 92
İslâhiye, Tur. A7 58
Islāmābād, Pak. B4 54
Islāmkot, Pak. F3 54
Islāmpur, India F10 54
Islāmpur, India E12 54
Islāmpur, India C2 53
Island, Ky., U.S. G10 120
Island Falls, Me., U.S. E8 110
Island Harbour, Anguilla A1 105a
Island Lake, l., Mb., Can. E12 106
Island Park, Id., U.S. F15 136
Island Pond, Vt., U.S. F5 110
Islands, Bay of, b., Nf., Can. j22 107a
Isla Patrulla, Ur. F10 92
Isla Vista, Ca., U.S. I5 134
Islay, i., Scot., U.K. F6 12
Isle, Mn., U.S. E5 118
Isle, stm., Fr. E5 18
Isle of Man, dep., Eur. G8 12
Isle of Wight, Va., U.S. H9 114
Isle Royale National Park, p.o.i., Mi., U.S. C10 118
Islesboro Island, i., Me., U.S. F8 110
Isleta, N.M., U.S. I10 132
Isleton, Ca., U.S. E4 134
Islón, Chile D2 92
Ismailia (Al-Ismā'īlīyah), Egypt H3 58
Ismail Samani, pik, mtn., Taj. B11 56
Isna, Egypt B6 62
Isny, Ger. I5 16
Isoka, Zam. C5 68
Isola del Liri, Italy I10 22
Isola di Capo Rizzuto, Italy F11 24
Isonzo, stm., Eur. E10 22
Isparta, Tur. F13 28
Isparta, state, Tur. F13 28
Ispica, Italy H8 24
Israel, ctry., Asia G5 58
Isrā'īl see Israel, ctry., Asia G5 58
Issa, stm., Russia D11 10
Isser, Oued, stm., Alg. H14 20
Issia, C. Iv. H3 64
Issoire, Fr. D9 18
Issoudun, Fr. H10 14
Issuna, Tan. F6 66
Issyk-Kul', Kyrg. F13 32
Issyk-Kul, Lake see Issyk-Kul', ozero, l., Kyrg. F13 32
Issyk-Kul', ozero, l., Kyrg. F13 32
İstanbul, Tur. B12 28
İstanbul, state, Tur. B11 28
İstanbul Boğazı (Bosporus), strt., Tur. B12 28
Istiaía, Grc. E6 28
Istmina, Col. E3 86
Isto, Mount, mtn., Ak., U.S. C11 140
Istra, Russia E19 10
Istria, pen., Eur. E10 22
Itá, Para. B9 92
Itabaiana, Braz. D8 88
Itabaiana, Braz. F7 88
Itabaianinha, Braz. F7 88
Itabapoana, Braz. K5 88
Itaberaba, Braz. G5 88
Itaberaí, Braz. G8 84
Itabi, Braz. F7 88
Itabira, Braz. J4 88
Itabuna, Braz. H6 88
Itacajá, Braz. E2 88
Itacambiruçu, stm., Braz. I4 88
Itacoatiara, Braz. D6 84
Itacurubí del Rosario, Para. B9 92
Itaeté, Braz. G5 88
Itaguajé, Braz. D6 90
Itaguara, Braz. K3 88
Itaguari, stm., Braz. H3 88
Itagüí, Col. D4 86
Itaí, Braz. A13 92
Itaiçaba, Braz. C7 88
Itaim, stm., Braz. D5 88
Itainópolis, Braz. D5 88
Itaipu Reservoir, res., S.A. B10 92
Itäisen Suomenlahden kansallispuisto, p.o.i., Fin. F12 8
Itaituba, Braz. D6 84
Itajaí, Braz. C13 92
Itajubá, Braz. L3 88
Itaju do Colônia, Braz. H6 88
Itajuípe, Braz. H6 88
Itala Game Reserve, S. Afr. E10 70
Itálica, sci., Spain G4 20
Italy, Tx., U.S. B11 130
Italy, ctry., Eur. G11 6
Itamaraju, Braz. I6 88
Itamarandiba, Braz. I4 88
Itamarandiba, stm., Braz. I4 88
Itamari, Braz. G6 88
Itambacuri, Braz. I5 88
Itambé, Braz. H5 88
Itami, Japan E8 40
Itampolo, Madag. E7 68
Itānagar, India E14 54
Itanhaém, Braz. B14 92
Itanhém, Braz. I5 88
Itaobim, Braz. I5 88
Itapagipe, Braz. J1 88
Itapajé, Braz. B6 88
Itaparica, Ilha de, i., Braz. G6 88
Itaparica, Represa de, res., Braz. E6 88
Itapebi, Braz. H6 88
Itapecerica, Braz. K3 88
Itapecuru-Mirim, Braz. B3 88
Itapemirim, Braz. K5 88
Itaperuna, Braz. K5 88
Itapetim, Braz. D7 88
Itapetinga, Braz. H5 88
Itapetininga, Braz. L1 88
Itapetininga, stm., Braz. A14 92
Itapeva, Braz. L1 88
Itapicuru, Braz. F6 88
Itapicuru, stm., Braz. F6 88
Itapicuru, stm., Braz. B3 88
Itapipoca, Braz. B6 88
Itapiranga, Braz. D6 84
Itapirapuã, Braz. G7 84
Itapiúna, Braz. C6 88
Itápolis, Braz. K1 88
Itaporã de Goiás, Braz. D1 88
Itaporanga, Braz. D6 88
Itaporanga d'Ajuda, Braz. F7 88
Itapúa, state, Para. C10 92
Itaquara, Braz. G6 88
Itaquari, Braz. K5 88
Itaqui, Braz. D9 92
Itarantim, Braz. H5 88
Itararé, Braz. B13 92
Itararé, stm., Braz. A13 92
Itārsi, India G6 54
Itarumã, Braz. C6 90
Itasca, Tx., U.S. B10 130
Itasca, Lake, l., Mn., U.S. D3 118
Itä-Suomi, state, Fin. E12 8
Itata, stm., Chile H1 92
Itatinga, Braz. L1 88
Itatira, Braz. C6 88
Itatupã, Braz. D7 84
Itaueira, Braz. D4 88
Itaueira, stm., Braz. D4 88
Itaúna, Braz. K3 88
Itbayat Island, i., Phil. K9 42
Itéa, Grc. E5 28
Iténez (Guaporé), stm., S.A. F5 84
Ithaca, Mi., U.S. E5 112
Ithaca, N.Y., U.S. B9 114
Ithaca see Itháki, i., Grc. E3 28
Itháki, i., Grc. E3 28
Itimbiri, stm., D.R.C. D4 66
Itinga, Braz. I5 88
Itiquira, stm., Braz. G6 84
Itiruçu, Braz. G5 88
Itiúba, Braz. F5 88
Itla el-Bâsha, hill, Egypt K3 58
Itō, Japan E12 40
Itoigawa, Japan B10 40
Iton, stm., Fr. F9 14
Itororó, Braz. H5 88
Itsuki, Japan G3 40
Ittiri, Italy D2 24
Ittoqqortoormiit see Scoresbysund, Grnld. C21 141
Itu, Braz. L2 88
Itu, stm., Braz. D10 92
Ituaçu, Braz. G5 88
Ituango, Col. D4 86
Ituberá, Braz. G6 88
Itueta, Braz. J5 88
Ituí, stm., Braz. E3 84
Ituiutaba, Braz. J1 88
Itumbiara, Braz. J1 88
Ituna, Sk., Can. C10 124
Itupiranga, Braz. E8 84
Ituporanga, Braz. C13 92
Iturama, Braz. C6 90
Iturbide, Mex. C3 102
Iturup, ostrov (Etorofu-tō), i., Russia B17 38
Ituverava, Braz. K2 88
Ituxi, stm., Braz. E4 84
Ituzaingó, Arg. C9 92
Itzehoe, Ger. C5 16
Iuka, Ms., U.S. C10 122
Iul'tin, Russia C25 34
Iúna, Braz. K5 88
Ivacèvičy, Bela. H8 10
Ivačovo, Russia F17 8
Ivaí, stm., Braz. D6 90
Ivaiporã, Braz. B12 92
Ivalo, Fin. B12 8
Ivalojoki, stm., Fin. B12 8
Ivanava, Bela. H8 10
Ivančice, Czech Rep. G12 16
Ivangorod, Russia A11 10
Ivangrad, Mont. G6 26
Ivanhoe, Austl. I5 76
Ivanhoe, Ca., U.S. G6 134
Ivanhoe, Mn., U.S. G2 118
Ivanhoe, Va., U.S. H4 114
Ivanišči, Russia D18 10
Ivanjica, Serb. F7 26
Ivan'kovo, Russia F20 10
Ivan'kovskoe vodohranilišče, res., Russia D19 10
Ivano-Frankivs'k, Ukr. F13 6
Ivano-Frankivs'k, co., Ukr. A11 26
Ivanovka, Russia F14 34
Ivanovo, Russia H19 8
Ivanovskaja oblast', co., Russia H19 8
Ivanovskoe, Russia A11 10
Ivanpah Lake, l., Ca., U.S. H1 132
Ivdel', Russia B9 32
Ivigtut, Grnld. E16 141
Ivindo, stm., Gabon D2 66
Ivinheíma, stm., Braz. D6 90
Iviza see Eivissa, Spain F12 20
Ivjanec, Bela. G9 10
Ivohibe, Madag. E8 68
Ivory Coast see Cote d'Ivoire, ctry., Afr. H3 64
Ivory Coast, cst., C. Iv. I3 64
Ivrea, Italy E4 22
İvrindi, Tur. D10 28
Ivujivik, Qc., Can. C15 106
Iwaki, Japan B13 40
Iwaki-san, vol., Japan D14 38
Iwakuni, Japan E5 40
Iwami, Japan D7 40
Iwanuma, Japan A13 40
Iwata, Japan E10 40
Iwate, state, Japan A14 40
Iwate-san, vol., Japan E14 38
'Iweibid, Gebel, mtn., Egypt H3 58
Iwo, Nig. H5 64
Ixmiquilpan, Mex. E9 100
Ixopo, S. Afr. G10 70
Ixtapa, Mex. G8 100
Ixtepec, Mex. G11 100
Ixtlán del Río, Mex. E6 100
Iyang see Yiyang, China G5 42
Iyo, Japan F5 40
Iyo-mishima, Japan F6 40
Iyo-nada, s., Japan F5 40
Izabal, Lago de, l., Guat. E3 102
Izamal, Mex. B3 102
Izapa, sci., Mex. H12 100
Izberbaš, Russia F7 32
Izbica, Pol. F19 16
Izegem, Bel. D12 14
Iževsk, Russia C8 32
Izium, Ukr. E5 32
Ižma, stm., Russia B8 32
Izmaïl, Ukr. D15 26
Izmalkovo, Russia H21 10
Izmayil see Izmaïl, Ukr. D15 26
İzmir (Smyrna), Tur. E10 28
İzmir, state, Tur. E10 28
İzmir Körfezi, b., Tur. E9 28
İzmit (Kocaeli), Tur. C12 28
İzmit Körfezi, b., Tur. C12 28
İznik, Tur. C12 28
İznik Gölü, l., Tur. C12 28
Iznoski, Russia E18 10
Izozog, Bañados del, sw., Bol. C4 90
Izra', Syria F7 58
Izsák, Hung. C6 26
Iztaccíhuatl, Volcán, vol., Mex. F9 100
Iztaccíhuatl y Popocatéptl, Parques Nacionales, p.o.i., Mex. F9 100
Izucar de Matamoros, Mex. F9 100
Izu-hantō, pen., Japan E11 40
Izuhara, Japan E2 40
Izu Islands see Izu-shotō, is., Japan E12 40
Izumi, Japan G3 40
Izumi, Japan A13 40
Izumi, Japan E8 40
Izumo, Japan D5 40
Izu-shotō (Izu Islands), is., Japan E12 40
Izu Trench, unds. G17 142
Izvestij CIK, ostrova, is., Russia A5 34
Izvorul Muntelui, Lacul, l., Rom. C12 26

J

Jabal, Baḩr al- see Mountain Nile, stm., Afr. F6 62
Jabal al-Awliyā', Sudan D6 62
Jabal Lubnān, state, Leb. D6 58
Jabalón, stm., Spain F7 20
Jabalpur, India G7 54
Jabālyah, Gaza G5 58
Jabbūl, Sabkhat al-, l., Syria C8 58
Jabiru, Austl. B6 74
Jablah, Syria C6 58
Jablanica, Bos. F4 26
Jablaničko jezero, res., Bos. F4 26
Jablonec nad Nisou, Czech Rep. F11 16
Jabłonka, Pol. G15 16
Jablonovyj hrebet, mts., Russia F11 34
Jablunkov, Czech Rep. G14 16
Jaboticabal, Braz. K1 88
Jaca, Spain B10 20
Jacala, Mex. E9 100
Jacaré, stm., Braz. F5 88
Jacareí, Braz. L2 88
Jacarezinho, Braz. D7 90
Jáchal, stm., Arg. E4 92
Jaciara, Braz. G6 84
Jacinto, Braz. I5 88
Jacinto Aráuz, Arg. I6 92
Jacinto City, Tx., U.S. H3 122
Jackfish Lake, l., Sk., Can. A5 124
Jackhead Harbour, Mb., Can. C16 124
Jack Mountain, mtn., Mt., U.S. D14 136
Jackpot, Nv., U.S. B2 132
Jacksboro, Tn., U.S. H1 114
Jacksboro, Tx., U.S. H10 128
Jackson, Ca., U.S. E5 134
Jackson, Ky., U.S. G2 114
Jackson, La., U.S. G7 122
Jackson, Mi., U.S. B1 114
Jackson, Mn., U.S. H4 118
Jackson, Ms., U.S. E8 122
Jackson, N.C., U.S. H8 114
Jackson, Oh., U.S. E3 114
Jackson, S.C., U.S. C4 116
Jackson, Tn., U.S. B10 122
Jackson, Wy., U.S. G16 136
Jackson, stm., Va., U.S. G6 114
Jackson, Mount, mtn., Ant. C34 81
Jackson, Mount, mtn., Austl. F3 74
Jackson Creek, stm., Can. E12 124
Jackson Lake, l., Wy., U.S. G16 136
Jacksonville, Al., U.S. D13 122
Jacksonville, Ar., U.S. C6 122
Jacksonville, Fl., U.S. F4 116
Jacksonville, Il., U.S. E7 120
Jacksonville, N.C., U.S. B8 116
Jacksonville, Or., U.S. A2 134
Jacksonville, Tx., U.S. F3 122
Jacksonville Beach, Fl., U.S. F4 116
Jacmel, Haiti C11 102
Jaco, Mex. B6 100
Jacobābād, Pak. D2 54
Jacobina, Braz. F5 88
Jacobsdal, S. Afr. F7 70
Jacques-Cartier, Mont, mtn., Qc., Can. A11 110
Jacu, stm., Braz. D8 88
Jacuí, stm., Braz. D11 92
Jacuípe, stm., Braz. F5 88
Jacumba, Ca., U.S. K9 134
Jacundá, Braz. D8 84
Jacupiranga, Braz. B13 92
Jacuriaí, stm., Braz. F6 88
Jadebusen, b., Ger. C4 16
J.A.D. Jensens Nunatakker, mtn., Grnld. E16 141
Jadraque, Spain D8 20
Jādū, Libya A2 62
Jaén, Peru E2 84
Jaén, Spain G7 20
Jaén, co., Spain G7 20
Jāfarābād, India H3 54
Jaffa, Cape, c., Austl. K2 76
Jaffna, Sri L. G4 53
Jaffna Lagoon, b., Sri L. G4 53
Jaffrey, N.H., U.S. B13 114
Jafr, Qā' al-, depr., Jord. H7 58
Jagalūr, India D3 53
Jagannāthganj Ghāt, Bngl. F12 54
Jagatsingpur, India H11 54
Jagdalpur, India B6 53
Jageljurta, gora, hill, Russia C17 8
Jagersfontein, S. Afr. F7 70
Jaggayyapeta, India C5 53
Jagodnoe, Russia D18 34
Jagraon, India C5 54
Jagtiāl, India B4 53
Jaguaquara, Braz. G6 88
Jaguarão, Braz. F11 92
Jaguarão (Yaguarón), stm., S.A. F11 92
Jaguarari, Braz. F5 88
Jaguari, Braz. D10 92
Jaguariaíva, Braz. B13 92
Jaguaribara, Braz. C6 88
Jaguaribe, Braz. C6 88
Jaguaribe, stm., Braz. C7 88
Jaguaruna, Braz. D13 92
Jagüey Grande, Cuba A7 102
Jahānābād, India F10 54
Jahrom, Iran D7 56
Jahroma, Russia D20 10
Jaicós, Braz. D5 88
Jailolo, Indon. E8 44
Jaintiāpur, Bngl. F14 54
Jaipur, India E5 54
Jaipur Hāt, Bngl. F12 54
Jais, India E8 54
Jaisalmer, India E3 54
Jaito, India C5 54
Jaja, Russia C15 32
Jājapur, India H11 54
Jajce, Bos. E4 26
Jakarta, Indon. G5 50
Jakarta, Teluk, b., Indon. F5 50
Jakaŭlevičy, Bela. F13 10
Jakhāu, India G2 54
Jakobshavn (Ilulissat), Grnld. D15 141
Jakobstad see Pietarsaari, Fin. E10 8
Jakovlevka, Russia B10 38
Jakša, Russia B9 32
Jakutija, state, Russia C14 34
Jakutsk, Russia D14 34
Jal, N.M., U.S. B4 130
Jalaid Qi, China B9 36
Jalālābād, Afg. C11 56
Jalālpur, India E9 54
Jalandhar, India C5 54
Jalapa, Guat. E3 102
Jalapa see Xalapa, Mex. F10 100
Jālaun, India E7 54
Jales, Braz. D6 90
Jalesar, India E7 54
Jaleshwar, India H11 54
Jālgaon, India H5 54
Jālgaon, India H6 54
Jalingo, Nig. H7 64
Jalisco, state, Mex. E6 100
Jālna, India B2 53
Jalón, stm., Spain C9 20
Jālor, India F4 54
Jalostotitlán, Mex. E7 100
Jalpa, Mex. E7 100
Jalpāiguri, India E12 54
Jaluit, at., Marsh. Is. C7 72
Jalutorovsk, Russia C11 32
Jamaame, Som. E8 66
Jamaica, ctry., N.A. D8 102
Jamaica Channel, strt., N.A. D9 102
Jamal, poluostrov, pen., Russia B2 34
Jam-Alin', hrebet, mts., Russia F15 34
Jamālpur, Bngl. F12 54
Jamālpur, India F11 54
Jamanota, hill, Aruba o20 104g
Jamantau, gora, mtn., Russia D9 32
Jamanxim, stm., Braz. E6 84
Jamari, stm., Braz. E5 84
Jamarovka, Russia F11 34
Jambelí, Canal de, strt., Ec. I2 86
Jambi, Indon. D3 50
Jambi, state, Indon. D3 50
Jamboaye, stm., Indon. J3 48
Jambol, Blg. G13 26
Jambongan, Pulau, i., Malay. G1 52
Jambuair, Tanjung, c., Indon. J3 48
Jambusar, India G4 54
James, stm., Mo., U.S. H4 120
James, stm., Va., U.S. G8 114
James, stm., U.S. C8 108
James, Isla, i., Chile H2 90
James Bay, b., Can. E14 106
James City, N.C., U.S. A8 116
James Craik, Arg. F6 92
James Island, S.C., U.S. D5 116
James Point, c., Bah. K9 116
Jamesport, Mo., U.S. E4 120
James Ross, Cape, c., N.T., Can. B17 140
James Ross Island, i., Ant. B35 81
James Ross Strait, strt., Nu., Can. A11 106
Jamestown, Austl. I2 76
Jamestown, S. Afr. G8 70
Jamestown, Ca., U.S. F5 134
Jamestown, Ky., U.S. H12 120
Jamestown, N.C., U.S. I6 114
Jamestown, N.D., U.S. H15 124
Jamestown, N.Y., U.S. B6 114
Jamestown, Tn., U.S. H13 120
Jamestown, misc. cult., Va., U.S. G9 114
Jām Jodhpur, India H3 54
Jamkhandi, India C2 53
Jamm, Russia B10 10
Jammerbugten, b., Den. H3 8
Jammu, India B5 54
Jammu and Kashmir see Kashmir, hist. reg., Asia B4 46
Jamnagar (Navanagar), India G3 54
Jampang-kulon, Indon. G5 50
Jāmpur, Pak. D3 54
Jämsä, Fin. F11 8
Jamshedpur, India G10 54
Jamsk, Russia E19 34
Jämtland, state, Swe. E6 8
Jamūi, India F11 54
Jamuna, stm., Bngl. F12 54
Jana, stm., Russia C16 34
Janaúba, Braz. H4 88
Janaucu, Ilha, i., Braz. C7 84
Jand, Pak. B4 54
Jandaia, Braz. G7 84
Jandiāla, India C5 54
Jandowae, Austl. F8 76
Jándula, stm., Spain F7 20
Janeiro, stm., Braz. F3 88
Janesville, Ca., U.S. C5 134
Janesville, Mn., U.S. G5 118
Janesville, Wi., U.S. B9 120
Jangamo, Moz. D12 70
Jangeru, Indon. E10 50
Jangijul', Uzb. F11 32
Jangīpur, India F11 54
Jangoon, India C4 53
Janīn, W.B. F6 58
Janisjarvi, ozero, l., Russia E14 8
Janiuay, Phil. E4 52
Jankan, hrebet, mts., Russia E12 34
Jan Kempdorp, S. Afr. E7 70
Janlohong, Indon. B10 50
Jan Mayen, i., Nor. B22 94
Janos, Mex. F8 98
Jánosháza, Hung. B4 26
Janowiec Wielkopolski, Pol. D13 16
Janskij, Russia C15 34
Janskij zaliv, b., Russia B16 34
Jantra, stm., Blg. F12 26
Januária, Braz. H3 88
Januário Cicco, Braz. D8 88
Jaora, India G5 54
Japan, ctry., Asia E12 38
Japan, Sea of (East Sea), s., Asia D11 38
Japan Basin, unds. E16 142
Japan Trench, unds. F17 142
Japaratinga, Braz. E8 88
Japi, Braz. D7 88
Japonskoje more see East Sea, s., Asia D11 38
Japonskoje more see Japan, Sea of, s., Asia D11 38
Japtiksalja, Russia C3 34
Japurá, Braz. H8 86
Japurá (Caquetá), stm., S.A. D5 84
Jaqué, Pan. D2 86
Jarābulus, Syria B9 58
Jaraguá, Braz. H1 88
Jaraguá do Sul, Braz. C13 92
Jaraíz de la Vera, Spain D5 20
Jarales, N.M., U.S. I10 132
Jarama, stm., Spain D7 20
Jaramānah, Syria E7 58
Jaransk, Russia C7 32
Jarānwāla, Pak. C4 54
Jarash, Jord. F6 58
Jarash, sci., Jord. F6 58
Jarcevo, Russia E15 10
Jardim, Braz. D6 88
Jardim, Braz. D5 90
Jardim de Piranhas, Braz. D7 88
Jardín América, Arg. C10 92
Jardines de la Reina, Archipiélago de los, is., Cuba B8 102
Jardinópolis, Braz. K1 88
Jarej-Uliga-Delap, Marsh. Is. C8 72
Jarenga, Russia E23 8
Jarensk, Russia E23 8
Jargalant, Mong. B4 36
Jari, stm., Braz. C7 84
Jaridih, India G11 54
Jarkand see Shache, China B12 56
Jarkino, Russia C17 32
Jarocin, Pol. D13 16
Jarohta, Russia C17 32
Jaroměř, Czech Rep. F11 16
Jaroslavl', Russia H19 8
Jaroslavskaja oblast', co., Russia H18 8
Jarosław, Pol. F18 16
Jarratt, Va., U.S. H8 114
Jar-Sale, Russia A12 32
Jartai Yanchi, l., China B1 42
Jarud Qi, China B4 38
Järvakandi, Est. G11 8
Järvenpää, Fin. F11 8
Jarvie, Ab., Can. B17 138
Jarvis, On., Can. F9 112
Jarvisburg, N.C., U.S. H10 114
Jarvis Island, i., Oc. D10 72
Jasdan, India G3 54
Jasel'da, stm., Bela. H8 10
Jashpurnagar, India D5 46
Jasień, Pol. E11 16
Jāsk, Iran D8 56
Jaškul', Russia E7 32
Jasło, Pol. G17 16
Jasnogorsk, Russia F20 10
Jasnyj, Russia F14 34
Jason Islands, is., Falk. Is. J4 90
Jasper, Ab., Can. D12 138
Jasper, Al., U.S. D11 122
Jasper, Ar., U.S. I4 120
Jasper, Fl., U.S. F3 116
Jasper, Ga., U.S. B1 116
Jasper, In., U.S. F10 120
Jasper, Mn., U.S. H2 118
Jasper, Mo., U.S. G3 120
Jasper, Tn., U.S. B13 122
Jasper Lake, l., Ab., Can. C13 138
Jasper National Park, p.o.i., Ab., Can. D13 138
Jastarnia, Pol. B14 16
Jászapáti, Hung. B7 26
Jászberény, Hung. B6 26
Jász-Nagykun-Szolnok, state, Hung. B7 26
Jataí, Braz. G7 84
Jatapu, stm., Braz. D6 84
Jataté, stm., Mex. G13 100
Jati, Braz. D6 88
Jāti, Pak. F2 54
Játiva see Xàtiva, Spain F10 20
Jatni, India H10 54
Jaú, Braz. L1 88
Jaú, stm., Braz. H11 86
Jaú, Parque Nacional do, p.o.i., Braz. I10 86
Jauaperi, stm., Braz. H11 86
Jauá Sarisariñama, Parque Nacional, p.o.i., Ven. E9 86
Jauja, Peru F2 84
Jaunjelgava, Lat. D7 10
Jaunpiebalga, Lat. C9 10
Jaunpur, India F9 54
Java see Jawa, i., Indon. H6 50
Javalambre, mtn., Spain D9 20
Java Sea see Jawa, Laut, s., Indon. F6 50
Java Trench, unds. J13 142
Jávea see Xàbia, Spain F11 20
Javorník, Czech Rep. F13 16
Javorová skála, mtn., Czech Rep. G10 16
Jawa (Java), i., Indon. H6 50
Jawa, Laut (Java Sea), s., Indon. F6 50
Jawa Barat, state, Indon. G5 50
Jawa Tengah, state, Indon. G7 50
Jawa Timur, state, Indon. G8 50
Jawhar, Som. D9 66
Jawi, Indon. D6 50
Jawor, Pol. E12 16
Jaworzno, Pol. F15 16
Jay, Fl., U.S. G11 122
Jay, Ok., U.S. H3 120
Jaya, Puncak (Jaya Peak), mtn., Indon. F10 44
Jaya Peak see Jaya, Puncak, mtn., Indon. F10 44
Jayapura, Indon. F11 44
Jayb, Wādī al- (Ha'Arava), stm., Asia H6 58
Jaynes, Az., U.S. K5 132
Jaypur, India B6 53
Jayuya, P.R. B2 104a
Jažełbicy, Russia B15 10
Jažma, Russia C21 8
Jeanerette, La., U.S. H7 122
Jeannette Island see Žannetty, ostrov, i., Russia A20 34
Jebba, Nig. H5 64
Jebel, Rom. D8 26
Jedburgh, Scot., U.K. F10 12
Jeddah see Jiddah, Sau. Ar. E4 56
Jędrzejów, Pol. F16 16
Jeffara (Al-Jifārah), pl., Afr. C7 64
Jeffers, Mn., U.S. G3 118
Jefferson, Ga., U.S. B2 116
Jefferson, Oh., U.S. C5 114
Jefferson, Or., U.S. F3 136
Jefferson, S.C., U.S. B5 116
Jefferson, S.D., U.S. B1 120
Jefferson, Wi., U.S. A9 120
Jefferson, Mount, mtn., Nv., U.S. E8 134
Jefferson, Mount, mtn., U.S. F15 136
Jefferson, Mount, vol., Or., U.S. F5 136
Jefferson City, Mo., U.S. F5 120
Jefferson City, Tn., U.S. H2 114
Jeffersontown, Ky., U.S. F12 120
Jeffersonville, Ga., U.S. D2 116
Jeffersonville, In., U.S. F12 120
Jeffrey City, Wy., U.S. E5 126
Jega, Nig. G5 64
Jehol see Chengde, China A7 42
Jejsk see Ejsk, Russia E5 32
Jeju see Cheju, Kor., S. H7 38
Jēkabpils, Lat. D8 10
Jekyll Island, i., Ga., U.S. E4 116
Jelai, stm., Indon. E7 50
Jelenia Góra, Pol. F11 16
Jelenia Góra, state, Pol. E11 16
Jelgava, Lat. D6 10
Jelgavkrasti, Lat. C7 10
Jellicoe, On., Can. B11 118

Name	Map Ref.	Page
Jelm Mountain, mtn., Wy., U.S.	F7	126
Jemaja, Pulau, i., Indon.	B4	50
Jember, Indon.	H8	50
Jemez Canyon Reservoir, res., N.M., U.S.	H9	132
Jemez Springs, N.M., U.S.	H10	132
Jemnice, Czech Rep.	H11	16
Jempang, Kenohan, l., Indon.	D9	50
Jena, Ger.	F7	16
Jena, La., U.S.	F6	122
Jendouba, Tun.	H2	24
Jeneponto, Indon.	F11	50
Jenks, Ok., U.S.	H2	120
Jennings, Fl., U.S.	F2	116
Jennings, La., U.S.	G6	122
Jensen, Ut., U.S.	C7	132
Jens Munk Island, i., Nu., Can.	B14	106
Jens Munks Ø, i., Grnld.	E17	141
Jenu, Indon.	D6	50
Jeonju see Chŏnju, Kor., S.	G7	38
Jepara, Indon.	G7	50
Jeparit, Austl.	K4	76
Jeptha Knob, hill, Ky., U.S.	F12	120
Jequié, Braz.	G5	88
Jequitinhonha, Braz.	I5	88
Jequitinhonha, stm., Braz.	H5	88
Jerada, Mor.	C4	64
Jerba, Île de, i., Tun.	C7	64
Jerécuaro, Mex.	E8	100
Jérémie, Haiti	C10	102
Jeremoabo, Braz.	F6	88
Jerevan see Yerevan, Arm.	A5	56
Jerez de García Salinas, Mex.	D7	100
Jerez de la Frontera, Spain	H4	20
Jerez de los Caballeros, Spain	F4	20
Jericho, Austl.	D5	76
Jericho see Arīḥā, Gaza	G6	58
Jericó, Braz.	D7	88
Jerid, Chott, l., Tun.	C6	64
Jerimoth Hill, hill, R.I., U.S.	C14	114
Jeroaquara, Braz.	G7	84
Jerome, Az., U.S.	I4	132
Jerome, Id., U.S.	H12	136
Jersey, dep., Eur.	E6	14
Jersey, i., Jersey	E6	14
Jersey City, N.J., U.S.	D11	114
Jerseyville, Il., U.S.	E7	120
Jerumenha, Braz.	D4	88
Jerusalem see Yerushalayim, Isr.	G6	58
Jervis, Cape, c., Austl.	J1	76
Jervis Bay, b., Austl.	J8	76
Jervis Bay Territory, co., Austl.	J8	76
Jervis Inlet, b., B.C., Can.	F7	138
Jesenice, Czech Rep.	F9	16
Jeseník, Czech Rep.	F13	16
Jesi (Iesi), Italy	G10	22
Jessen, Ger.	E9	16
Jessore, Bngl.	G12	54
Jesup, Ga., U.S.	E4	116
Jesup, Ia., U.S.	B5	120
Jesús Carranza, Mex.	G11	100
Jesús María, Arg.	E5	92
Jesús Menéndez, Cuba	B9	102
Jet, Ok., U.S.	E10	128
Jetmore, Ks., U.S.	C9	128
Jetpur, India	H3	54
Jeune Landing, B.C., Can.	F3	138
Jever, Ger.	C3	16
Jewel Cave National Monument, p.o.i., S.D., U.S.	D8	126
Jewell, Ks., U.S.	B10	128
Jewell Ridge, Va., U.S.	G4	114
Jewett, Il., U.S.	E9	120
Jewett City, Ct., U.S.	C13	114
Jezercës, maja e, mtn., Alb.	B13	24
Jeziorany, Pol.	B16	16
Jhābua, India	G5	54
Jha Jha, India	F11	54
Jhālakāti, Bngl.	G13	54
Jhālāwār, India	F6	54
Jhang Sadar, Pak.	C4	54
Jhānsi, India	F7	54
Jhārgrām, India	G11	54
Jharia, India	G11	54
Jharkhand, state, India	G10	54
Jhārsuguda, India	H10	54
Jhelum, Pak.	B4	54
Jhelum, stm., Asia	C4	54
Jhinkpāni, India	G10	54
Jhok Rind, Pak.	C3	54
Jhunjhunūn, India	D5	54
Jiaban, China	I2	42
Jiading, China	F9	42
Jiāganj, India	F12	54
Jiahe, China	I5	42
Jiali, China	C14	54
Jialing, stm., China	G2	42
Jialu, stm., China	E5	42
Jiamusi, China	B11	36
Ji'an, China	D7	38
Ji'an, China	H6	42
Jian, stm., China	H8	42
Jianchang, China	A8	42
Jianchang, China	B10	42
Jianchuan, China	F4	36
Jiande, China	G8	42
Jiang'an, China	G1	42
Jiangcheng, China	A5	48
Jiangdu, China	E8	42
Jiange, China	E1	42
Jianghua, China	I4	42
Jiangjin, China	G2	42
Jiangkou, China	J4	42
Jiangkou, China	H3	42
Jiangkou, China	F4	42
Jiangle, China	H7	42
Jiangling, China	F4	42
Jiangmen, China	J5	42
Jiangmifeng, China	B7	38
Jiangshan, China	G8	42
Jiangsu, state, China	E8	42
Jiangtun, China	J5	42
Jiangxi, state, China	H6	42
Jiangya, China	G4	42
Jiangyin, China	F9	42
Jiangyou, China	F1	42
Jiangzhong, China	D14	54
Jianli, China	G5	42
Jianning, China	H7	42
Jian'ou, China	H8	42
Jianping, China	D3	38
Jianshi, China	F3	42
Jianshui, China	G5	36
Jianyang, China	E5	36
Jianyang, China	H8	42
Jiaocheng, China	C4	42
Jiaohe, China	C7	38
Jiaolai, stm., China	C4	38
Jiaonan, China	D8	42
Jiaoxian, China	C8	42
Jiaozhou Wan, b., China	C9	42
Jiaozuo, China	D5	42
Jiashan, China	E7	42
Jiashi, China	B12	56
Jiashun Hu, l., China	A10	54
Jiawang, China	D7	42
Jiaxian, China	D5	42
Jiaxian, China	B4	42
Jiaxing, China	F9	42
Jiazi, China	J6	42
Jibuti see Djibouti, Dji.	E8	62
Jicarón, Isla, i., Pan.	I7	102
Jičín, Czech Rep.	F11	16
Jiddah (Jeddah), Sau. Ar.	E4	56
Jidingxilin, China	B14	54
Jieshi Wan, b., China	J6	42
Jieshou, China	E6	42
Jiexi, China	J6	42
Jiexiu, China	C4	42
Jieyang, China	J7	42
Jieznas, Lith.	F7	10
Jiguaní, Cuba	B9	102
Jigüey, Bahía de, strt., Cuba	A8	102
Jigzhi, China	E5	36
Jihlava, Czech Rep.	G11	16
Jihlava, stm., Czech Rep.	G12	16
Jihočeský kraj, state, Czech Rep.	G10	16
Jihomoravský kraj, state, Czech Rep.	G12	16
Jijia, stm., Rom.	B14	26
Jijiga, Eth.	F8	62
Jilantai, China	B1	42
Jilib, Som.	D8	66
Jili Hu, l., China	B2	36
Jilin, China	C7	38
Jilin, state, China	C10	36
Jill, Kediet ej, mtn., Maur.	E2	64
Jiloca, stm., Spain	C9	20
Jīma, Eth.	F7	62
Jimbolia, Rom.	D7	26
Jimena de la Frontera, Spain	H5	20
Jiménez, Mex.	B6	100
Jiménez, Mex.	A8	100
Jiménez del Téul, Mex.	D7	100
Jimeta, Nig.	H7	64
Jim Ned Creek, stm., Tx., U.S.	C8	130
Jimo, China	C9	42
Jimsar, China	C2	36
Jim Thorpe, Pa., U.S.	D10	114
Jin (Gam), stm., Asia	A7	48
Jin, stm., China	H7	42
Jinan (Tsinan), China	C7	42
Jincang, China	C9	38
Jincheng, China	D5	42
Jīnd, India	D6	54
Jindabyne, Austl.	K7	76
Jindřichův Hradec, Czech Rep.	G11	16
Jing, stm., China	D3	42
Jing'an, China	G6	42
Jingbian, China	C3	42
Jingbohu, res., China	C8	38
Jingde, China	F8	42
Jingdezhen, China	G7	42
Jinggangshan, China	H6	42
Jinghai, China	B7	42
Jinghe, China	F14	32
Jinghong, China	B5	48
Jingle, China	B4	42
Jingmen, China	F5	42
Jingning, China	D1	42
Jingxi, China	J2	42
Jingxian, China	F8	42
Jingxian, China	C7	42
Jingxian, China	H3	42
Jingxin, China	I6	42
Jingyu, China	C7	38
Jingzhi, China	C8	42
Jinhae see Chinhae, Kor., S.	D1	40
Jinhua, China	G8	42
Jining, China	D7	42
Jining, China	A5	42
Jinja, Ug.	D6	66
Jinjiazhen, China	C5	38
Jinju see Chinju, Kor., S.	G7	38
Jinmu Jiao, c., China	L3	42
Jinning, China	G5	36
Jinotega, Nic.	F5	102
Jinotepe, Nic.	G4	102
Jinping, China	H3	42
Jinqian, stm., China	E3	42
Jinsha, China	H1	42
Jinsha (Yangtze), stm., China	F5	36
Jinshi, China	G4	42
Jintian, China	H6	42
Jintotolo Channel, strt., Phil.	E4	52
Jinxi, China	A9	42
Jinxi, China	H7	42
Jinxian, China	G7	42
Jinxian, China	B6	42
Jinzhou, China	B9	42
Jinzhou, China	A9	42
Ji-Paraná, Braz.	F5	84
Jipijapa, Ec.	H1	86
Jiquiriçá, stm., Braz.	G6	88
Jiri, stm., India	F14	54
Jirkov, Czech Rep.	F9	16
Jishou, China	G3	42
Jisr ash-Shughūr, Syria	C7	58
Jitaúna, Braz.	G6	88
Jiu, stm., Rom.	F10	26
Jiudaoliang, China	F4	42
Jiufeng, China	I7	42
Jiujiang, China	G6	42
Jiulian Shan, mts., China	I6	42
Jiuliguan, China	F6	42
Jiuling Shan, mts., China	G6	42
Jiulong, China	J5	42
Jiulong, stm., China	I7	42
Jiuquan, China	D4	36
Jiutai, China	B6	38
Jiuyuanqu, China	D4	42
Jiuzhan, China	C7	38
Jiuzhen, China	I7	42
Jiwen, China	A9	36
Jixi, China	B9	38
Jixi, China	F8	42
Jixian, China	A7	42
Jixian, China	D6	42
Jiyi, China	D4	42
Jiyuan, China	D5	42
Jiyun, stm., China	B7	42
Jīzān, Sau. Ar.	F5	56
Jizl, Wādī al-, stm., Sau. Ar.	K8	58
J. J. Castelli see Castelli, Arg.	B7	92
J.M. Lencinas see Las Catitas, Arg.	F3	92
Joaçaba, Braz.	C12	92
Joana Coeli, Braz.	A1	88
Joanes, Braz.	D8	84
João Câmara, Braz.	C8	88
João Monlevade, Braz.	J4	88
João Pessoa, Braz.	D8	88
João Pinheiro, Braz.	I2	88
Joaquim Távora, Braz.	A12	92
Joaquin, Tx., U.S.	F4	122
Joaquín V. González, Arg.	B5	92
Jobos, P.R.	C3	104a
Job Peak, mtn., Nv., U.S.	D7	134
Jocolí, Arg.	F3	92
Jódar, Spain	G7	20
Jodhpur, India	E4	54
Jodiya, India	G3	54
Joensuu, Fin.	E13	8
Joetsu, Japan	B11	40
Jõgeva, Est.	G12	8
Jog Falls, wtfl., India	D2	53
Joggins, N.S., Can.	E12	110
Jogjakarta see Yogyakarta, Indon.	G7	50
Jōhana, Japan	C9	40
Johannesburg, S. Afr.	E8	70
John Day, Or., U.S.	F8	136
John Day, stm., Or., U.S.	E6	136
John Day, Middle Fork, stm., Or., U.S.	F8	136
John Day, North Fork, stm., Or., U.S.	F8	136
John Day Fossil Beds National Monument, p.o.i., Or., U.S.	F7	136
John F. Kennedy Space Center, sci., Fl., U.S.	H5	116
John H. Kerr Reservoir, res., U.S.	H7	114
John Martin Reservoir, res., Co., U.S.	C6	128
John o' Groats, Scot., U.K.	C9	12
John Redmond Reservoir, res., Ks., U.S.	F1	120
Johns Island, i., S.C., U.S.	D5	116
Johnson, Ar., U.S.	H3	120
Johnson, Ks., U.S.	D7	128
Johnsonburg, Pa., U.S.	C7	114
Johnson City, N.Y., U.S.	B10	114
Johnson City, Tn., U.S.	H3	114
Johnson City, Tx., U.S.	D9	130
Johnsondale, Ca., U.S.	H7	134
Johnson Draw, stm., Tx., U.S.	D6	130
Johnson Point, c., St. Vin.	o11	105e
Johnsonville, S.C., U.S.	C6	116
Johnston, Ia., U.S.	C4	120
Johnston, S.C., U.S.	C4	116
Johnston, Lake, l., Austl.	F4	74
Johnston Atoll, at., Oc.	B10	72
Johnstown, Co., U.S.	G8	126
Johnstown, N.Y., U.S.	G2	110
Johnstown, Oh., U.S.	D3	114
Johnstown, Pa., U.S.	D7	114
Johor, state, Malay.	L6	48
Johor Bahru, Malay.	L6	48
Joigny, Fr.	G12	14
Joiner, Ar., U.S.	B8	122
Joinville, Braz.	C13	92
Joinville Island, i., Ant.	B35	81
Jojogan, Indon.	G7	50
Jokkmokk, Swe.	C8	8
Jökulsá á Brú, stm., Ice.	k32	8a
Jökulsårgljúfur Nasjonalpark, p.o.i., Ice.	k32	8a
Joliet, Il., U.S.	C9	120
Joliette, Qc., Can.	D3	110
Jolo, Phil.	G3	52
Jolo Group, is., Phil.	G3	52
Jolo Island, i., Phil.	H3	52
Jombang, Indon.	G8	50
Jomda, China	E4	36
Jonava, Lith.	E7	10
Jones, Ok., U.S.	F11	128
Jonesboro, Ar., U.S.	I7	120
Jonesboro, Ga., U.S.	C1	116
Jonesboro, Il., U.S.	G8	120
Jonesboro, La., U.S.	E6	122
Jonesborough, Tn., U.S.	H3	114
Jones Mill, Ar., U.S.	C6	122
Jonesport, Me., U.S.	F9	110
Jones Sound, strt., Nu., Can.	B8	141
Jonestown, Ms., U.S.	C8	122
Jonesville, La., U.S.	F7	122
Jonesville, Mi., U.S.	B1	114
Jonglei Canal, can., Sudan	F6	62
Joniškėlis, Lith.	D6	10
Joniškis, Lith.	D6	10
Jönköping, Swe.	H6	8
Jönköping, state, Swe.	H6	8
Jonquière, Qc., Can.	B5	110
Jonuta, Mex.	F12	100
Jonzac, Fr.	D5	18
Joplin, Mo., U.S.	G3	120
Joplin, Mt., U.S.	B16	136
Joppa, Il., U.S.	G9	120
Jora, India	E6	54
Jordan, Mn., U.S.	G5	118
Jordan, Mt., U.S.	G6	124
Jordan, ctry., Asia	H7	58
Jordan (Al-Urdunn) (HaYarden), stm., Asia	F6	58
Jordan, stm., Ut., U.S.	C5	132
Jordan Creek, stm., U.S.	H10	136
Jordânia, Braz.	H5	88
Jordan Valley, Or., U.S.	G10	136
Jordão, stm., Braz.	B12	92
Jorge Montt, Isla, i., Chile	J2	90
Jorhāt, India	C7	46
Jornado del Muerto, des., N.M., U.S.	J10	132
Joroinen, Fin.	E12	8
Jos, Nig.	G6	64
Jose Abad Santos, Phil.	H5	52
José Batlle y Ordóñez, Ur.	F10	92
José Bonifácio, Braz.	K1	88
José de Freitas, Braz.	C4	88
José de San Martín, Arg.	H2	90
José Pedro Varela, Ur.	F10	92
Joseph, Or., U.S.	E9	136
Joseph, Lac, l., Nf., Can.	E17	106
Joseph Bonaparte Gulf, b., Austl.	B5	74
Joshīmath, India	C7	54
Jōshin-Etsu-kōgen-kokuritsu-kōen, p.o.i., Japan	C11	40
Joshua, Tx., U.S.	B10	130
Joshua Tree, Ca., U.S.	I9	134
Joshua Tree National Park, p.o.i., Ca., U.S.	J10	134
Jostedalsbreen, ice, Nor.	F2	8
Jostedalsbreen Nasjonalpark, p.o.i., Nor.	F2	8
Jotunheimen Nasjonalpark, p.o.i., Nor.	F2	8
Joubertina, S. Afr.	H6	70
Jourdanton, Tx., U.S.	F9	130
Joutsijärvi, Fin.	C13	8
Joviânia, Braz.	I1	88
Jowai, India	F14	54
Joya, Mex.	H6	130
Joyce, La., U.S.	F6	122
Joyuda, P.R.	B1	104a
J. Percy Priest Lake, res., Tn., U.S.	H11	120
J. Strom Thurmond Reservoir, res., U.S.	C3	116
Juami, stm., Braz.	I7	86
Juana Díaz, P.R.	B2	104a
Juan Aldama, Mex.	C7	100
Juan Bautista Alberdi, Arg.	C5	92
Juan de Fuca, Strait of, strt., N.A.	B2	136
Juan de Garay, Arg.	I5	92
Juan de Nova, Île, i., Reu.	D7	68
Juan E. Barra, Arg.	H7	92
Juan Fernández, Archipiélago, is., Chile	I6	82
Juanjuí, Peru	E2	84
Juan N. Fernández, Arg.	I8	92
Juan Viñas, C.R.	H6	102
Juárez see Benito Juárez, Arg.	H8	92
Juárez, Mex.	B8	100
Juárez, Mex.	F8	98
Juatinga, Ponta de, c., Braz.	L3	88
Juazeirinho, Braz.	D7	88
Juazeiro, Braz.	E5	88
Juazeiro do Norte, Braz.	D6	88
Juba, Sudan	G6	62
Juba see Jubba, stm., Afr.	D8	66
Juba see Genalē, stm., Afr.	C8	66
Jubal, Strait of see Gûbâl, Madîq, strt., Egypt	K4	58
Jubayl, Leb.	D6	58
Jubba (Genalē), stm., Afr.	D8	66
Juby, Cap, c., Mor.	D2	64
Júcar (Xúquer), stm., Spain	E10	20
Juchipila, Mex.	E7	100
Juchitán de Zaragoza, Mex.	G11	100
Jucurucu, stm., Braz.	I5	88
Jucurutu, Braz.	C7	88
Judenburg, Aus.	C11	22
Judino, Russia	B22	10
Judique, N.S., Can.	E15	110
Judith, stm., Mt., U.S.	C17	136
Judith Gap, Mt., U.S.	D17	136
Judith Peak, mtn., Mt., U.S.	C17	136
Judoma, stm., Russia	E16	34
Jufari, stm., Braz.	H10	86
Jug, stm., Russia	G21	8
Jugorskij poluostrov, pen., Russia	A10	32
Juhnov, Russia	F18	10
Juidongshan, China	J7	42
Juigalpa, Nic.	F5	102
Juist, i., Ger.	C2	16
Juiz de Fora, Braz.	K4	88
Jujuy, state, Arg.	D3	90
Jukagirskoe ploskogor'e, plat., Russia	C19	34
Jukta, Russia	B19	32
Jula, stm., Russia	E21	8
Julesburg, Co., U.S.	G10	126
Juliaca, Peru	G3	84
Julia Creek, Austl.	C3	76
Julia Creek, stm., Austl.	C3	76
Julianadorp, Neth. Ant.	p22	104g
Julian Alps, mts., Eur.	D10	22
Juliana Top, mtn., Sur.	C6	84
Julianehåb (Qaqortoq), Grnld.	E16	141
Jülich, Ger.	F2	16
Juliette, Lake, res., Ga., U.S.	D2	116
Julimes, Mex.	A6	100
Júlio de Castilhos, Braz.	D11	92
Juma, Russia	D15	8
Juma, stm., China	B6	42
Jumba, Som.	E8	66
Jumilla, Spain	F9	20
Jumlā, Nepal	D9	54
Jūnāgadh, India	H3	54
Juncos, P.R.	B4	104a
Junction, Tx., U.S.	D8	130
Junction City, Ar., U.S.	E6	122
Junction City, Ks., U.S.	B12	128
Junction City, Ky., U.S.	G13	120
Jundah, Austl.	E4	76
Jundiaí, Braz.	L2	88
Juneau, Ak., U.S.	E13	140
Juneau, Wi., U.S.	H10	118
Junee, Austl.	J6	76
June Lake, Ca., U.S.	F6	134
Jungar Qi, China	B4	42
Jungfrau, mtn., Switz.	D4	22
Junggar Pendi, bas., China	B2	36
Juniata, Ne., U.S.	G14	126
Juniata, stm., Pa., U.S.	D8	114
Junín, Arg.	G7	92
Junín, Ec.	H1	86
Junín de los Andes, Arg.	G2	90
Juniper, N.B., Can.	D9	110
Junipero Serra Peak, mtn., Ca., U.S.	G4	134
Jūniyah, Leb.	E6	58
Junlian, China	F5	36
Junnar, India	B1	53
Junqueiro, Braz.	E7	88
Junxian, China	E4	42
Juodkrantė, Lith.	E3	10
Juozapinės kalnas, hill, Lith.	F8	10
Juparanã, Lagoa, l., Braz.	J5	88
Jupiter, Fl., U.S.	J5	116
Juquiá, Braz.	B14	92
Juquiá, Ponta do, c., Braz.	B14	92
Jur, Russia	E16	34
Jur, stm., Sudan	F5	62
Jura, Mol.	B16	26
Jura, state, Fr.	C11	18
Jura, mts., Eur.	B12	18
Jura, i., Scot., U.K.	F7	12
Jūra, stm., Lith.	E5	10
Jurbarkas, Lith.	E5	10
Jurenino, Russia	G20	8
Jurevec, Russia	H20	8
Jurga, Russia	C15	32
Juriti, Braz.	D6	84
Jūrmala, Lat.	C6	10
Jurong, China	F8	42
Juruá, stm., S.A.	D4	84
Juruena, stm., Braz.	E6	84
Jurumirim, Represa de, res., Braz.	L1	88
Jusepín, Ven.	C10	86
Juškovo, Russia	G21	8
Justiniano Posse, Arg.	F6	92
Justino Solari see Mariano I. Loza, Arg.	D8	92
Justo Daract, Arg.	F5	92
Jutaí, stm., Braz.	D4	84
Jüterbog, Ger.	D9	16
Jutiapa, Guat.	E3	102
Juticalpa, Hond.	E4	102
Jutland see Jylland, reg., Den.	H3	8
Jutrosin, Pol.	E13	16
Juventud, Isla de la (Pines, Isle of), i., Cuba	B6	102
Juxian, China	D8	42
Juye, China	D6	42
Juža, Russia	H20	8
Južna Morava, stm., Serb.	F8	26
Južno-Enisejskij, Russia	C17	32
Južno-Sahalinsk, Russia	G17	34
Južno-Ural'sk, Russia	D10	32
Južnyj, mys, c., Russia	E20	34
Južnyj Ural, mts., Russia	D9	32
Jwayyā, Leb.	E6	58
Jyekundo see Yushu, China	E4	36
Jylland (Jutland), reg., Den.	H3	8
Jyväskylä, Fin.	E11	8

K

Name	Map Ref.	Page
K2, mtn., Asia	B12	56
Kaabong, Ug.	D6	66
Kaahka, Turkmen.	B8	56
Ka'ala, mtn., Hi., U.S.	b3	78a
Kaala-Gomen, N. Cal.	m15	79d
Kaapstad see Cape Town, S. Afr.	H4	70
Kaarli, Est.	A9	10
Kaatoan, Mount, mtn., Phil.	F5	52
Kabacan, Phil.	G5	52
Kabaena, Pulau, i., Indon.	G7	44
Kabah, sci., Mex.	B3	102
Kabala, S.L.	H2	64
Kabale, Ug.	E5	66
Kabalega Falls, wtfl., Ug.	D6	66
Kabalo, D.R.C.	F5	66
Kabambare, D.R.C.	E5	66
Kabanjahe, Indon.	K4	48
Kabankalan, Phil.	F4	52
Kabardin-Balkaria see Kabardino-Balkarija, state, Russia	F6	32
Kabardino-Balkarija, state, Russia	F6	32
Kabba, Nig.	H6	64
Kabbani, stm., India	F3	53
Kåbdalis, Swe.	C8	8
Kabetogama Lake, l., Mn., U.S.	C5	118
Kab-hegy, mtn., Hung.	B4	26
Kabinda, D.R.C.	F4	66
Kabinu, Indon.	A9	50
Kabīr Kūh, mts., Iran	C6	56
Kabna, Sudan	D6	62
Kābol, Afg.	C10	56
Kābol, state, Afg.	A2	54
Kabompo, Zam.	C3	68
Kabompo, stm., Zam.	C3	68
Kabongo, D.R.C.	F5	66
Kābul see Kābol, Afg.	C10	56
Kabul (Kābol), stm., Asia	A4	54
Kabwe, Zam.	C4	68
Kabylie, reg., Alg.	H14	20
Kačanik, Serb.	G8	26
Kačerginė, Lith.	F6	10
Kachchh, Gulf of, b., India	G2	54
Kachīry, Kaz.	D13	32
Kačkanar, Russia	C10	32
Kačug, Russia	D19	32
Kadaiyanallūr, India	G3	53
Kadaň, Czech Rep.	F9	16
Kadan Kyun, i., Mya.	F4	48
Kadapongan, Pulau, i., Indon.	F9	50
Kaddam, res., India	B4	53
Kade, Ghana	H4	64
Kadéï, stm., Afr.	G2	62
Kadi, India	G4	54
Kadina, Austl.	F7	74
Kading, stm., Laos	C7	48
Kadınhanı, Tur.	E15	28
Kadiolo, Mali	G3	64
Kādīpur, India	E9	54
Kadiri, India	D4	53
Kadirli, Tur.	A7	58
Kadoka, S.D., U.S.	D11	126
Kadoma, Zimb.	D4	68
Kaduj, Russia	A20	10
Kaduna, Nig.	G6	64
Kaduna, stm., Nig.	G6	64
Kāduqlī, Sudan	E5	62
Kadūr, India	E3	53
Kaduvu, i., Fiji	q19	79e
Kaduvu Passage, strt., Fiji	q18	79e
Kadyj, Russia	H20	8
Kadžerom, Russia	B9	32
Kaédi, Maur.	F2	64
Kaélé, Cam.	B2	66
Ka'ena Point, c., Hi., U.S.	b3	78a
Kaesŏng, Kor., N.	F7	38
Kafanchan, Nig.	H6	64
Kaffrine, Sen.	G1	64
Kafia Kingi, Sudan	F4	62
Kafr el-Dauwar, Egypt	G1	58
Kafr el-Sheikh, Egypt	G1	58
Kafr el-Zaiyât, Egypt	H1	58
Kafr Sa'd, Egypt	G2	58
Kafue, Zam.	D4	68
Kafue, stm., Zam.	D4	68
Kaga, Japan	C9	40
Kaga Bandoro, C.A.R.	C3	66
Kāgān, Pak.	A4	54
Kagan, Uzb.	G10	32
Kagawa, state, Japan	E6	40
Kagawong, Lake, l., On., Can.	C7	112
Kagaznagar, India	B4	53
Kagera, stm., Afr.	E6	66
Kagmar, Sudan	E6	62
Kagoshima, Japan	H3	40
Kagoshima, state, Japan	H3	40
Kagoshima-wan, b., Japan	H3	40
Kahama, Tan.	E6	66
Kahayan, stm., Indon.	D8	50
Ka-Hem see Malyj Enisej, stm., Russia	F8	34
Kahemba, D.R.C.	F3	66
Kahiu Point, c., Hi., U.S.	b5	78a
Kahoka, Mo., U.S.	D6	120
Kaho'olawe, i., Hi., U.S.	c5	78a
Kahouanne, Îlet à, i., Guad.	h5	105c
Kahramanmaraş (Maraş), Tur.	A7	58
Kahraman Maraş, state, Tur.	A7	58
Kahuku Point, c., Hi., U.S.	b4	78a
Kahului, Hi., U.S.	c5	78a
Kai, Kepulauan (Kai Islands), is., Indon.	G9	44
Kaiapoi, N.Z.	F5	80
Kaibab Plateau, plat., Az., U.S.	G4	132
Kaidu, stm., China	F15	32
Kaieteur Fall, wtfl., Guy.	E12	86
Kaieteur National Park, p.o.i., Guy.	E12	86
Kaifeng, China	D6	42
Kaihua, China	G8	42
Kai Islands see Kai, Kepulauan, is., Indon.	G9	44
Kaijian, China	J4	42
Kaijiang, China	F2	42
Kai Kecil, i., Indon.	G9	44
Kaikoura, N.Z.	F5	80
Kailahun, S.L.	H2	64
Kailas see Kangrinboqê Feng, mtn., China	C8	54
Kailāshahar, India	F14	54
Kailas Range see Gangdisê Shan, mts., China	C9	54
Kaili, China	H2	42
Kailu, China	C4	38
Kailua, Hi., U.S.	b4	78a
Kailua Kona, Hi., U.S.	d6	78a
Kaïmaktsalán (Kajmakčalan), mtn., Eur.	C15	24
Kaimana, Indon.	F9	44
Kaimon-dake, vol., Japan	H3	40
Kainabrivier, stm., Nmb.	E4	70
Kainan, Japan	E8	40
Kainantu, Pap. N. Gui.	b4	79a
Kainji Reservoir, res., Nig.	G5	64
Kaipara Harbour, b., N.Z.	C5	80
Kaiparowits Plateau, plat., Ut., U.S.	F5	132
Kaiping, China	J5	42
Kairouan, Tun.	I3	24
Kairuku, Pap. N. Gui.	b4	79a
Kaiserslautern, Ger.	G3	16
Kaišiadorys, Lith.	F7	10
Kait, Tanjung, c., Indon.	E5	50
Kaitangata, N.Z.	H3	80
Kaithal, India	D6	54
Kaituma, stm., Guy.	D12	86
Kaiwi Channel, strt., Hi., U.S.	b4	78a
Kaixian, China	F3	42
Kaiyang, China	H2	42
Kaiyuan, China	G5	36
Kaiyuan, China	C6	38
Kaiyuancheng, China	C6	38
Kaiyuh Mountains, mts., Ak., U.S.	D8	140
Kajaani, Fin.	D12	8
Kajabbi, Austl.	B2	76
Kajakī, Band-e, res., Afg.	C10	56
Kajang, Malay.	K5	48
Kajmysovy, Russia	C13	32
Kajo Kaji, Sudan	G6	62
Kaka, Sudan	E6	62
Kakabeka Falls, wtfl., On., Can.	C9	118
Kakagi Lake, l., On., Can.	B5	118
Kakamas, S. Afr.	F5	70
Kakamega, Kenya	D6	66
Kakamigahara, Japan	D9	40
Kakata, Lib.	H2	64
Kākdwīp, India	H12	54
Kakegawa, Japan	E10	40
Kakhonak, Ak., U.S.	E9	140
Kakhovka Reservoir see Kakhovs'ke vodoskhovyshche, res., Ukr.	E4	32
Kakhovs'ke vodoskhovyshche, res., Ukr.	E4	32
Kākināda (Cocanada), India	C6	53
Kakisa Lake, l., N.T., Can.	C7	106
Kakizaki, Japan	B11	40
Kakogawa, Japan	E7	40
Kakšaal-Too, hrebet, mts., Asia	F13	32
Kaktovik, Ak., U.S.	B11	140
Kakuda, Japan	B13	40
Kakus, stm., Malay.	B8	50
Kakwa, stm., Ab., Can.	B12	138
Kala, stm., Sri L.	G4	53
Kalaa Kebira, Tun.	I4	24
Kalabahi, Indon.	G7	44
Kalabakan, Malay.	A10	50
Kalabo, Zam.	D3	68
Kalač, Russia	D6	32
Kalačinsk, Russia	D12	32
Kalač-na-Donu, Russia	E6	32
Kaladan, stm., Asia	G14	54
Kalae, c., Hi., U.S.	e6	78a
Kalahari Desert, des., Afr.	C5	70
Kalahari Gemsbok National Park, p.o.i., S. Afr.	D5	70
Kalajoki, Fin.	D10	8
Kalakan, Russia	E12	34
Kalām, Pak.	B11	56
Kalama, Wa., U.S.	D4	136
Kalamalka Lake, l., B.C., Can.	F11	138
Kalamáta, Grc.	F5	28
Kalamazoo, Mi., U.S.	F4	112
Kalamazoo, stm., Mi., U.S.	F4	112
Kalamb, India	B1	53
Kalampising, Indon.	B10	50
Kalao, Pulau, i., Indon.	G12	50
Kalaotoa, Pulau, i., Indon.	G7	44
Kalar, stm., Russia	E12	34
Kalasin, Thai.	D6	48
Kalašnikovo, Russia	C18	10
Kalāt, Pak.	D10	56
Kalávryta, Grc.	E5	28
Kalaw, Mya.	B3	48
Kalbarri, Austl.	E2	74
Kale, Tur.	G12	28
Kale, Tur.	F11	28
Kaleden, B.C., Can.	G11	138
Kalegauk Island, i., Mya.	E3	48
Kalehe, D.R.C.	E5	66
Kalemie, D.R.C.	F5	66
Kalemyo, Mya.	D7	46
Kaletwa, Mya.	H14	54
Kalevala, Russia	D14	8
Kalewa, Mya.	D7	46
Kálfafell, Ice.	k31	8a
Kalgan see Zhangjiakou, China	A6	42
Kalgoorlie-Boulder, Austl.	F4	74
Kaliakra, nos, c., Blg.	F15	26
Kalianda, Indon.	F4	50
Kalibo, Phil.	E4	52
Kalima, D.R.C.	E5	66
Kalimantan (Borneo), i., Asia	F5	44
Kalimantan Barat, state, Indon.	D7	50
Kalimantan Selatan, state, Indon.	E9	50
Kalimantan Tengah, state, Indon.	D8	50
Kalimantan Timur, state, Indon.	C10	50
Kālimpang, India	E12	54
Kālīnadi, stm., India	D2	53
Kalinin see Tver', Russia	D18	10
Kaliningrad (Königsberg), Russia	F3	10
Kaliningradskaja oblast', co., Russia	F4	10
Kalinkavičy, Bela.	H12	10
Kaliro, Ug.	D6	66
Kalisat, Indon.	H8	50
Kāli Sindh, stm., India	F6	54
Kalispell, Mt., U.S.	B12	136
Kalisz, Pol.	E14	16
Kalisz, state, Pol.	E13	16
Kalisz Pomorski, Pol.	C11	16
Kaliua, Tan.	E6	66
Kaliveli Tank, l., India	E4	53
Kalixälven, stm., Swe.	C9	8
Kaljazin, Russia	C20	10
Kālka, India	C6	54
Kalkaska, Mi., U.S.	D4	112
Kalkfonteindam, res., S. Afr.	F7	70
Kalkım, Tur.	D10	28
Kalkrand, Nmb.	D3	70
Kallar Kahār, Pak.	B4	54
Kallavesi, l., Fin.	E12	8
Kallsjön, l., Swe.	E5	8
Kalmar, Swe.	H6	8
Kalmar, state, Swe.	H7	8
Kalmarsund, strt., Swe.	H7	8
Kalmykia see Kalmykija, state, Russia	E7	32
Kalmykija, state, Russia	E7	32
Kālna, India	G12	54
Kalocsa, Hung.	C5	26
Kalofer, Blg.	G12	26
Kalohi Channel, strt., Hi., U.S.	b4	78a
Kalol, India	G4	54
Kālol, India	G4	54
Kalomo, Zam.	D4	68
Kalona, Ia., U.S.	J7	118
Kalone Peak, mtn., B.C., Can.	D4	138
Kalpeni Island, i., India	F1	53
Kālpi, India	E7	54
Kalpin, China	A12	56
Kalsūbai, mtn., India	B1	53
Kaltag, Ak., U.S.	D8	140
Kaluga, Russia	F19	10
Kalukalukuang, Pulau, i., Indon.	F10	50
Kalumburu, Austl.	B5	74
Kałuszyn, Pol.	D17	16
Kalutara, Sri L.	H4	53
Kalužskaja oblast', co., Russia	F18	10
Kalyān, India	B1	53
Kalyāndurg, India	D3	53
Kálymnos, Grc.	G9	28
Kálymnos, i., Grc.	F9	28
Kama, stm., Russia	C8	32
Kamae, Japan	G4	40
Kamaishi, Japan	E14	38
Kamakou, mtn., Hi., U.S.	b5	78a
Kamakura, Japan	D12	40
Kamālia, Pak.	C4	54
Kamamaung, Mya.	D3	48
Kaman, stm., Laos	E8	48
Kamanjab, Nmb.	D1	68
Kamarān, i., Yemen	F5	56
Kāmāreddi, India	B4	53
Kama Reservoir see Kamskoe vodohranilišče, res., Russia	C9	32
Kamas, Ut., U.S.	C5	132
Kamay, Tx., U.S.	H10	128
Kambalda, Austl.	F4	74
Kambam, India	G3	53
Kambarka, Russia	C8	32
Kambja, Est.	B9	10
Kambove, D.R.C.	G5	66
Kamčatka, stm., Russia	E21	34
Kamčatka, poluostrov, pen., Russia	E19	34
Kamčatskij poluostrov, pen., Russia	E21	34
Kamčatskij zaliv, b., Russia	E21	34
Kamchatka Peninsula see Kamčatka, poluostrov, pen., Russia	E20	34
Kameda, Japan	B12	40
Kámeiros, sci., Grc.	G10	28
Kamen', gora, mtn., Russia	C8	34
Kameng, stm., India	E14	54
Kamenjak, Rt, c., Cro.	F10	22
Kamenka, Kaz.	D11	32
Kamenka, Russia	D6	32
Kamenka, Russia	D21	8
Kamen'-na-Obi, Russia	D14	32
Kameno, Blg.	G14	26
Kamen-Rybolov, Russia	B9	38
Kamenskoe, Russia	D22	34
Kamensk-Ural'skij, Russia	C10	32
Kamenz, Ger.	E10	16
Kāmet, mtn., Asia	C7	54
Kam'ians'ke, Ukr.	D16	26
Kamień Krajeński, Pol.	C13	16
Kamienna Góra, Pol.	F12	16
Kamieńsk, Pol.	E15	16

Name	Map Ref.	Page
Kamieskroon, S. Afr.	G3	70
Kamiiso, Japan	D14	38
Kamilukuak Lake, l., Can.	C10	106
Kamina, D.R.C.	F4	66
Kaminak Lake, l., Nu., Can.	C12	106
Kaminoyama, Japan	A13	40
Kaminuriak Lake, l., Nu., Can.	C12	106
Kamioka, Japan	C10	40
Kamjanec, Bela.	H6	10
Kamkhat Muḩaywir, hill, Jord.	G7	58
Kamloops, B.C., Can.	F10	138
Kamnik, Slvn.	D11	22
Kamo, Japan	B12	40
Kamoa Mountains, mts., Guy.	C6	84
Kamojima, Japan	E7	40
Kāmoke, Pak.	B5	54
Kampala, Ug.	D6	66
Kampar, Malay.	J5	48
Kampar, stm., Indon.	C3	50
Kamparkalns, hill, Lat.	C5	10
Kampar Kanan, stm., Indon.	C2	50
Kampen, Neth.	B14	14
Kamphaeng Phet, Thai.	D4	48
Kampinoski Park Narodowy, p.o.i., Pol.	D16	16
Kâmpóng Cham, Camb.	F7	48
Kâmpóng Chhnăng, Camb.	F7	48
Kâmpóng Kântuŏt, Camb.	G7	48
Kâmpóng Saôm, Camb.	G6	48
Kâmpóng Saôm, Chhâk, b., Camb.	G6	48
Kâmpóng Thum, Camb.	F7	48
Kampong Ulu, Mya.	G4	48
Kâmpôt, Camb.	G7	48
Kampsville, Il., U.S.	E7	120
Kampti, Burkina	G4	64
Kampuchea see Cambodia, ctry., Asia	C3	48
Kampungbaru, Indon.	D3	50
Kampung Litang, Malay.	A11	50
Kamrau, Teluk, b., Indon.	F9	44
Kamsack, Sk., Can.	C12	124
Kamskoe vodohranilišče, res., Russia	C9	32
Kāmthi, India	H7	54
Kamuela, Hi., U.S.	d6	78a
Kámuk, Cerro, mtn., C.R.	H6	102
Kamundan, stm., Indon.	F9	44
Kamyšin, Russia	D7	32
Kamyšlov, Russia	C10	32
Kan, stm., Russia	C17	32
Kanaaupscow, stm., Qc., Can.	E15	106
Kanab, Ut., U.S.	F4	132
Kanab Creek, stm., U.S.	G4	132
Kanaga Island, i., Ak., U.S.	g23	140a
Kanagawa, state, Japan	D12	40
Kanakapura, India	E3	53
Kananga (Luluabourg), D.R.C.	F4	66
Kananggar, Indon.	I12	50
Kanangra-Boyd National Park, p.o.i., Austl.	I7	76
Kanaš, Russia	C7	32
Kanawha, Ia., U.S.	B4	120
Kanawha, stm., W.V., U.S.	F4	114
Kanazawa, Japan	C9	40
Kanbauk, Mya.	E3	48
Kanchanaburi, Thai.	F4	48
Kanchanjanggā (Kānchenjunga), mtn., Asia	E11	54
Kānchenjunga (Kanchanjanggā), mtn., Asia	E11	54
Kānchipuram, India	E4	53
Kanchow *see* Ganzhou, China	I6	42
Kańczuga, Pol.	F18	16
Kanda, Japan	F3	40
Kandahār, Afg.	C10	56
Kandahar, Sk., Can.	C9	124
Kandalakša, Russia	C15	8
Kandalakšskaja guba, b., Russia	C15	8
Kandale, D.R.C.	F3	66
Kandang, Indon.	K3	48
Kandangan, Indon.	E9	50
Kandanghaur, Indon.	G6	50
Kandé, Togo	H5	64
Kandhkot, Pak.	D2	54
Kandi, India	G12	54
Kandi, Tanjung, c., Indon.	E7	44
Kandıra, Tur.	B13	28
Kandla, India	G3	54
Kandos, Austl.	I7	76
Kandreho, Madag.	D8	68
Kandy, Sri L.	H5	53
Kane, Pa., U.S.	C7	114
Kane Basin, b., N.A.	B12	141
Kanem, state, Chad	E3	62
Kāne'ohe, Hi., U.S.	b4	78a
Kanëvka, Russia	C18	8
Kang, Bots.	C6	70
Kangaba, Mali	G3	64
Kangalassy, Russia	D15	34
Kangâmiut, Grnld.	D15	141
Kangān, Iran	D7	56
Kangar, Malay.	I5	48
Kangaroo Island, i., Austl.	G7	74
Kangāvar, Iran	C6	56
Kangbao, China	C7	36
Kangding, China	C9	46
Kangean, Kepulauan (Kangean Islands), is., Indon.	G9	50
Kangean, Pulau, i., Indon.	G9	50
Kangean Islands see Kangean, Kepulauan, is., Indon.	G9	50
Kangeeak Point, c., Nu., Can.	B18	106
Kangerlussuaq, b., Grnld.	D19	141
Kangersuatsiaq *see* Prøven, Grnld.	C14	141
Kanger Valley National Park, p.o.i., India	B6	53
Kanggye, Kor., N.	D7	38
Kanghwa-do, i., Kor., S.	F7	38
Kangiqsliniq (Rankin Inlet), Nu., Can.	C12	106
Kangiqsualujjuaq, Qc., Can.	D17	106
Kangiqsujuaq, Qc., Can.	C16	106
Kangiqtugaapik (Clyde River), Nu., Can.	A16	106
Kangirsuk, Qc., Can.	C17	106
Kangmar, China	D12	54
Kangnŭng, Kor., S.	B1	40
Kango, Gabon	D2	66
Kangping, China	C5	38
Kangpu, China	F4	36
Kangrinboqê Feng, mtn., China	C8	54
Kangshan, Tai.	J9	42
Kangsŏ, Kor., N.	E6	38
Kangto, mtn., Asia	D14	54
Kangwŏn-do, state, Kor., S.	B1	40
Kanha National Park, p.o.i., India	G8	54
Kanhar, stm., India	F9	54
Kanhsien *see* Ganzhou, China	I6	42
Kani, Mya.	A2	48
Kaniama, D.R.C.	F4	66
Kanibadam, Taj.	A11	56
Kaniet Islands, is., Pap. N. Gui.	a4	79a
Kanigiri, India	D4	53
Kanin, poluostrov, pen., Russia	C21	8
Kanin-Kamen', mts., Russia	B21	8
Kanin Nos, Russia	B20	8
Kanin Nos, mys, c., Russia	B20	8
Kaniva, Austl.	K3	76
Kanjiža, Serb.	C7	26
Kankaanpää, Fin.	F10	8
Kankakee, Il., U.S.	G2	112
Kankan, Gui.	G3	64
Kānker, India	H8	54
Kankunskij, Russia	E14	34
Kanmaw Kyun, i., Mya.	G4	48
Kannack, Viet.	E9	48
Kannad, India	H5	54
Kannapolis, N.C., U.S.	A5	116
Kannauj, India	E7	54
Kanniyākumari, India	G3	53
Kannod, India	G6	54
Kannur *see* Cannanore, India	F2	53
Kannus, Fin.	E10	8
Kano, Nig.	G6	64
Kanonji, Japan	E6	40
Kanopolis, Ks., U.S.	C10	128
Kanorado, Ks., U.S.	B6	128
Kanosh, Ut., U.S.	E4	132
Kanoya, Japan	H3	40
Kanpetlet, Mya.	B1	48
Kānpur (Cawnpore), India	E7	54
Kansas, state, U.S.	C10	128
Kansas, stm., Ks., U.S.	B13	128
Kansas City, Ks., U.S.	E3	120
Kansas City, Mo., U.S.	E3	120
Kansk, Russia	C17	32
Kansŏng, Kor., S.	A1	40
Kan-sou see Gansu, state, China	D5	36
Kansu see Gansu, state, China	D5	36
Kantang, Thai.	I4	48
Kantchari, Burkina	G5	64
Kānth, India	D7	54
Kantishna, stm., Ak., U.S.	D9	140
Kantō-heiya, pl., Japan	D12	40
Kanton, i., Kir.	D9	72
Kantō-sanchi, mts., Japan	D11	40
Kantu-long, Mya.	C3	48
Kantunilkin, Mex.	B4	102
Kanuku Mountains, mts., Guy.	F12	86
Kanuma, Japan	C12	40
Kanye, Bots.	D7	70
Kanyutkwin, Mya.	C3	48
Kaohiung *see* Kaohsiung, Tai.	J8	42
Kaohsiung, Tai.	J8	42
Kaohsiunghsien, Tai.	J9	42
Kaoka Bay, b., Sol. Is.	e9	79b
Kaoko Veld, plat., Nmb.	D1	68
Kaolack, Sen.	G1	64
Kaolinovo, Blg.	F14	26
Kaoma, Zam.	C3	68
Kaouar, reg., Niger	F7	64
Kapaa, Hi., U.S.	a2	78a
Kapadvanj, India	G4	54
Kapanga, D.R.C.	F4	66
Kapaonik, mts., Serb.	G8	26
Kapatkevičy, Bela.	H11	10
Kapčagajskoe vodohranilišče see Kapshaghay bögeni, res., Kaz.	F13	32
Kapchagay Reservoir see Kapshaghay bögeni, res., Kaz.	F13	32
Kapfenberg, Aus.	C12	22
Kapıdağ Yarımadası, pen., Tur.	C10	28
Kapikotongwa, stm., On., Can.	A11	118
Kapingamarangi, at., Micron.	C6	72
Kapiri Mposhi, Zam.	C4	68
Kapisigdlit, Grnld.	E16	141
Kapiskau, stm., On., Can.	E14	106
Kapit, Malay.	C8	50
Kaplan, La., U.S.	G6	122
Kaplice, Czech Rep.	H10	16
Kapoeta, Sudan	G6	62
Kapona, D.R.C.	F5	66
Kapos, stm., Hung.	C5	26
Kaposvár, Hung.	C4	26
Kaposvar Creek, stm., Sk., Can.	D11	124
Kappeln, Ger.	B5	16
Kapshaghay bögeni, res., Kaz.	F13	32
Kaptai, Bngl.	G14	54
Kaptai Lake see Karnaphuli Reservoir, res., Bngl.	G14	54
Kapuas, stm., Indon.	D6	50
Kapuas, stm., Indon.	E9	50
Kapunda, Austl.	J2	76
Kapūrthala, India	C5	54
Kapuskasing, On., Can.	F14	106
Kapuvár, Hung.	B4	26
Kapyl', Bela.	G9	10
Kara, Russia	C1	34
Kara-Balta, Kyrg.	F12	32
Karabanovo, Russia	D21	10
Karabaš, Russia	C9	32
Kara-Bogaz-Gol, zaliv, b., Turkmen.	A7	56
Kara-Bogaz-Gol Gulf see Kara-Bogaz-Gol, zaliv, b., Turkmen.	A7	56
Karabük, Tur.	B15	28
Karabula, Russia	C17	32
Karaburun, Tur.	E9	28
Karacabey, Tur.	C11	28
Karačaevo-Čerkesija, state, Russia	F6	32
Karacasu, Tur.	F11	28
Karačev, Russia	G17	10
Karachay see Karačaevo-Čerkesija, state, Russia	F6	32
Karachay-Cherkessia see Karačaevo-Čerkesija, state, Russia	F6	32
Karāchi, Pak.	E10	56
Karād, India	C2	53
Karaftit, Russia	F11	34
Karaganda *see* Karagandy, Kaz.	E12	32
Karagandy (Karaganda), Kaz.	E12	32
Karagayly *see* Qarqaraly, Kaz.	E13	32
Karaginskij, ostrov, i., Russia	E21	34
Karaginskij zaliv, b., Russia	E21	34
Karagoš, gora, mtn., Russia	D15	32
Karahallı, Tur.	E12	28
Kāraikkudi, India	F4	53
Karaisalı, Tur.	A6	58
Karaj, Iran	B7	56
Kara-Kala, Turkmen.	B8	56
Karakaralong, Pulau, is., Indon.	E8	44
Karakax, stm., China	A7	54
Karakol, Kyrg.	F13	32
Karakoram Pass, p., Asia	A6	54
Karakoram Range, mts., Asia	A4	46
Karakul', Uzb.	G10	32
Kara-Kum Canal see Garagumskij kanal, can., Turkmen.	B9	56
Karama, stm., Indon.	E11	50
Karamai *see* Karamay, China	B1	36
Karaman, Tur.	A4	58
Karaman, state, Tur.	A4	58
Karamanlı, Tur.	F12	28
Karamay, China	B1	36
Karamea Bight, b., N.Z.	E4	80
Karamürsel, Tur.	C12	28
Karamyševo, Russia	C18	32
Karamzino, Russia	D17	10
Karangasem, Indon.	H9	50
Karangnunggal, Indon.	G6	50
Kāranja, India	H6	54
Karanjia, India	H10	54
Karapınar, Tur.	A4	58
Karaqoyyn köli, l., Kaz.	E11	32
Karas, state, Nmb.	E3	70
Karaşar, Tur.	C14	28
Karasburg, Nmb.	F4	70
Kara Sea see Karskoe more, s., Russia	B10	30
Karasjok, Nor.	B11	8
Karasu, Tur.	B13	28
Karasu, stm., Tur.	B4	56
Karasuk, Russia	D13	32
Karatal, Kaz.	E15	32
Karataş Burun, c., Tur.	B6	58
Karatau, hrebet see Qarataū zhotasy, mts., Kaz.	F11	32
Karatau Range see Qarataū zhotasy, mts., Kaz.	F11	32
Karatöbe, Kaz.	E8	32
Karatsu, Japan	F2	40
Karaul, Russia	B5	34
Karauli, India	E6	54
Karawa, D.R.C.	D4	66
Karawang, Indon.	G5	50
Karawang, Tanjung, c., Indon.	F5	50
Karawanken, mts., Eur.	D11	22
Karažal *see* Qarazhal, Kaz.	E12	32
Karbalā', Iraq	C5	56
Kårböle, Swe.	E6	8
Karcag, Hung.	B7	26
Kardámaina, Grc.	G9	28
Kardeljevo, Cro.	G14	22
Kárditsa, Grc.	D4	28
Kärdla, Est.	G10	8
Kărdžali, Blg.	H12	26
Karelia see Karelija, state, Russia	D15	8
Karelia, hist. reg., Eur.	E14	8
Karelija, state, Russia	D15	8
Karelija see Karelia, hist. reg., Eur.	E14	8
Karel'skij Gorodok, Russia	B19	10
Karema, Tan.	F6	66
Karen, India	F7	46
Karesuando, Swe.	B9	8
Kärevere, Est.	B9	10
Kargasok, Russia	C14	32
Kargat, Russia	C14	32
Kargil, India	A5	54
Kargopol', Russia	F18	8
Kariba, Zimb.	D4	68
Kariba, Lake, res., Afr.	D4	68
Karibib, Nmb.	B2	70
Kariega, stm., S. Afr.	H6	70
Karimata, Kepulauan, is., Indon.	D6	50
Karimata, Selat, strt., Indon.	E6	50
Karīmganj, India	F14	54
Karīmnagar, India	B4	53
Karimunjawa, Kepulauan, is., Indon.	F7	50
Karimunjawa, Pulau, i., Indon.	F7	50
Karisimbi, vol., Afr.	E5	66
Káristos, Grc.	E7	28
Kariya, Japan	D10	40
Kārkal, India	E2	53
Karkaralinsk *see* Qarqaraly, Kaz.	E13	32
Karkar Island, i., Pap. N. Gui.	a4	79a
Karkonoski Park Narodowy, p.o.i., Pol.	F11	16
Karkūk, Iraq	B5	56
Karleby *see* Kokkola, Fin.	E10	8
Karlino, Pol.	B11	16
Karl-Marx-Stadt *see* Chemnitz, Ger.	F8	16
Karlovac, Cro.	E12	22
Karlovo, Blg.	G11	26
Karlovy Vary, Czech Rep.	F8	16
Karlsborg, Swe.	D10	8
Karlsburg *see* Alba Iulia, Rom.	C10	26
Karlshamn, Swe.	H6	8
Karlskoga, Swe.	G6	8
Karlskrona, Swe.	H6	8
Karlsruhe, Ger.	G4	16
Karlstad, Swe.	G5	8
Karlstadt, Ger.	G5	16
Karluk, Ak., U.S.	E9	140
Karma, Bela.	H14	10
Karma, Niger	G5	64
Karmah an Nuzul, Sudan	D6	62
Karmāla, India	B2	53
Karmøy, i., Nor.	G1	8
Karnack, Tx., U.S.	E4	122
Karnak, Il., U.S.	G9	120
Karnāl, India	D6	54
Karṇāli, stm., Asia	D8	54
Karnāli, stm., Nepal	D8	54
Karnaphuli Reservoir, res., Bngl.	G14	54
Karnātaka, state, India	D2	53
Karnobat, Blg.	G13	26
Kärnten, state, Aus.	D10	22
Karoli, India	G7	54
Karonga, Mwi.	B5	68
Karoo National Park, p.o.i., S. Afr.	H6	70
Karoonda, Austl.	J2	76
Karor, Pak.	C3	54
Kárpathos, Grc.	H10	28
Kárpathos, i., Grc.	H10	28
Karpats'kyi Pryrodnyi Natsional'nyi Park, p.o.i., Ukr.	A11	26
Karpenísi, Grc.	E4	28
Karpogory, Russia	D21	8
Karpuzlu, Tur.	F10	28
Karratha, Austl.	D3	74
Karrats Fjord, b., Grnld.	C14	141
Kars, Tur.	A5	56
Karsantı, Tur.	A6	58
Karši, Uzb.	G11	32
Karsin, Pol.	C13	16
Karskoe more (Kara Sea), s., Russia	B10	30
Kartala, vol., Com.	C7	68
Kartaly, Russia	D10	32
Kartārpur, India	C5	54
Karthaus, Pa., U.S.	C7	114
Kartuzy, Pol.	B14	16
Karufa, Indon.	F9	44
Karumba, Austl.	A3	76
Karungi, Swe.	C10	8
Karunjie, Austl.	C5	74
Karūr, India	F4	53
Karviná, Czech Rep.	G14	16
Kārwār, India	D1	53
Karyés, Grc.	C7	28
Karymskoe, Russia	F11	34
Kasai (Cassai), stm., Afr.	E3	66
Kasaji, D.R.C.	G4	66
Kasama, Japan	C13	40
Kasama, Zam.	C5	68
Kasane, Bots.	D3	68
Kasanga, Tan.	F6	66
Kasangulu, D.R.C.	E3	66
Kasaoka, Japan	E6	40
Kāsaragod, India	E2	53
Kasba, India	F11	54
Kasba Lake, l., Can.	C10	106
Kascjukouka, Bela.	H13	10
Kascjukovičy, Bela.	G14	10
Kaseda, Japan	H3	40
Kasempa, Zam.	C4	68
Kasenga, D.R.C.	G5	66
Kasenye, D.R.C.	D6	66
Kasese, D.R.C.	E5	66
Kasese, Ug.	D6	66
Kaset Sombun, Thai.	D5	48
Kāsganj, India	E7	54
Kāshān, Iran	C7	56
Kashgar *see* Kashi, China	B12	56
Kashi, China	B12	56
Kashihara, Japan	E8	40
Kashima, Japan	F3	40
Kashima-nada, s., Japan	C13	40
Kashing *see* Jiaxing, China	F9	42
Kāshīpur, India	D7	54
Kashiwazaki, Japan	B11	40
Kāshmar, Iran	B8	56
Kashmir, hist. reg., Asia	A3	46
Kasia, India	E9	54
Kasimbar, Indon.	D12	50
Kasimov, Russia	I19	8
Kašin, Russia	C20	10
Kašira, Russia	F21	10
Kasiruta, Pulau, i., Indon.	F8	44
Kaskaskia, stm., Il., U.S.	E9	120
Kaskinen, Fin.	E9	8
Kaslo, B.C., Can.	G13	138
Kasnja, Russia	E17	10
Kasongo, D.R.C.	E5	66
Kasongo-Lunda, D.R.C.	F3	66
Kásos, i., Grc.	H9	28
Kasota, Mn., U.S.	G5	118
Kaspijsk, Russia	F7	32
Kaspijskij, Russia	E7	32
Kaspijskoje more see Caspian Sea, s.	F7	32
Kasplja, stm., Eur.	E13	10
Kasr, Ra's, c., Afr.	D7	62
Kassab, Syria	C6	58
Kassalā, Sudan	D7	62
Kassándra, pen., Grc.	C6	28
Kassandra, Gulf of see Kassándras, Kólpos, b., Grc.	C6	28
Kassándras, Kólpos, b., Grc.	C6	28
Kassel, Ger.	E5	16
Kasserine, Tun.	B6	64
Kastamonu, Tur.	A3	56
Kastamonu, state, Tur.	B16	28
Kastélli, Grc.	H6	28
Kastoría, Grc.	C4	28
Kastorías, Límni, l., Grc.	C4	28
Kastrakíou, Technití Límni, res., Grc.	E4	28
Kasugai, Japan	D9	40
Kasulu, Tan.	E6	66
Kasumi, Japan	D7	40
Kasumiga-ura, l., Japan	C13	40
Kasungan, Indon.	E8	50
Kasūr, Pak.	C5	54
Kaszuby, hist. reg., Pol.	B13	16
Kataba, Zam.	D4	68
Katahdin, Mount, mtn., Me., U.S.	E7	110
Katako-Kombe, D.R.C.	E4	66
Katanga, hist. reg., D.R.C.	F4	66
Katanga, stm., Russia	C18	32
Katangi, India	G7	54
Katangli, Russia	F17	34
Katanning, Austl.	F3	74
Katchall Island, i., India	G7	46
Katepwa Beach, Sk., Can.	D10	124
Kateríni, Grc.	C5	28
Kates Needle, mtn., N.A.	D4	106
Katete, Zam.	C5	68
Katha, Mya.	D8	46
Katherîna, Gebel, mtn., Egypt	J4	58
Katherine, Austl.	B6	74
Katherine, stm., Austl.	B6	74
Katherine Creek, stm., Austl.	D4	76
Kāthiāwār Peninsula, pen., India	H3	54
Kathla, India	C6	54
Kāṭhmāṇḍāū (Kathmandu), Nepal	E10	54
Kathmandu *see* Kāṭhmāṇḍāū, Nepal	E10	54
Kathor, India	H4	54
Kathua, India	B5	54
Kati, Mali	G3	64
Katibas, stm., Malay.	C8	50
Katihār, India	F11	54
Katimik Lake, l., Mb., Can.	B14	124
Katiola, C. Iv.	H4	64
Katipunan, Phil.	F4	52
Ka Tiriti o te Moana see Southern Alps, mts., N.Z.	F4	80
Katmai, Mount, vol., Ak., U.S.	E8	140
Káto Achaía, Grc.	E4	28
Kātol, India	H7	54
Katoomba, Austl.	I8	76
Katowice, Pol.	F14	16
Katowice, state, Pol.	F15	16
Katrineholm, Swe.	G7	8
Katsina, Nig.	G6	64
Katsina Ala, stm., Afr.	H6	64
Katsuta, Japan	C13	40
Katsuura, Japan	D13	40
Katsuyama, Japan	C9	40
Katsuyama, Japan	D6	40
Kattakurgan, Uzb.	G11	32
Kattegat, strt., Eur.	H4	8
Katul, Jabal, mtn., Sudan	E5	62
Katun', stm., Russia	D15	32
Katunino, Russia	G21	8
Kātwa, India	G11	54
Katwijk aan Zee, Neth.	B13	14
Katyn, Russia	F14	10
Katzenbuckel, mtn., Ger.	G5	16
Kaua'i, i., Hi., U.S.	b2	78a
Kauai Channel, strt., Hi., U.S.	b3	78a
Kaufbeuren, Ger.	I6	16
Kaufman, Tx., U.S.	E2	122
Kaukauna, Wi., U.S.	D1	112
Kaukau Veld, plat., Afr.	D3	68
Kaulakahi Channel, strt., Hi., U.S.	b2	78a
Kaumalapau, Hi., U.S.	c4	78a
Kaunas, Lith.	F6	10
Kaura-Namoda, Nig.	G6	64
Kauriālā (Ghāghara), stm., Asia	D8	54
Kautokeino, Nor.	B10	8
Kau-ye Kyun, i., Mya.	G4	48
Kavača, Russia	D23	34
Kavadarci, Mac.	B5	28
Kavaja *see* Kavajë, Alb.	C13	24
Kavajë, Alb.	C13	24
Kavaklıdere, Tur.	F11	28
Kaváala, Grc.	C7	28
Kavalerovo, Russia	B11	38
Kāvali, India	D4	53
Kavaratti, India	F3	46
Kavaratti Island, i., India	F3	46
Kāveri (Cauvery), stm., India	F4	53
Kāveri Falls, wtfl., India	E3	53
Kavieng, Pap. N. Gui.	a5	79a
Kavīr, Dasht-e, des., Iran	C8	56
Kaw, Ok., U.S.	E12	128
Kawa, Mya.	D3	48
Kawagama Lake, l., On., Can.	C10	112
Kawagoe, Japan	D12	40
Kawaguchi, Japan	D12	40
Kawaihoa, c., Hi., U.S.	b1	78a
Kawaikini, mtn., Hi., U.S.	a2	78a
Kawambwa, Zam.	B4	68
Kawanoe, Japan	E6	40
Kawardha, India	H8	54
Kawasaki, Japan	D12	40
Kawatana, Japan	F2	40
Kawdut, Mya.	E3	48
Kaweenakumik Lake, l., Mb., Can.	B14	124
Kawhia Harbour, b., N.Z.	D6	80
Kawich Peak, mtn., Nv., U.S.	F9	134
Kawkareik, Mya.	D4	48
Kaw Lake, res., Ok., U.S.	E12	128
Kawludo, Mya.	C3	48
Kawnipi Lake, l., On., Can.	C7	118
Kawthaung, Mya.	H4	48
Kaxgar, stm., China	B12	56
Kaya, Burkina	G4	64
Kayah, state, Mya.	C3	48
Kayak Island, i., Ak., U.S.	E11	140
Kāyalpattinam, India	G4	53
Kayan, Mya.	D3	48
Kayan, stm., Indon.	B10	50
Kāyankulam, India	G3	53
Kaycee, Wy., U.S.	D6	126
Kayenta, Az., U.S.	G6	132
Kayes, Mali	G2	64
Kayin, state, Mya.	D3	48
Kaymaz, Tur.	D14	28
Kayseri, Tur.	B4	56
Kaysville, Ut., U.S.	B4	132
Kayuadi, Pulau, i., Indon.	G12	50
Kayuagung, Indon.	E4	50
Kayumas, Indon.	G9	50
Kazače, Russia	B16	34
Kazačinskoe, Russia	E7	34
Kazačinskoe, Russia	C19	32
Kazahskij melkosopočnik see Qazaqtyng usaqshoqylyghy, hills, Kaz.	D12	32
Kazakh Hills see Qazaqtyng usaqshoqylyghy, hills, Kaz.	E12	32
Kazakhstan, ctry., Asia	E10	32
Kazaki, Russia	H21	10
Kazan', Russia	C7	32
Kazan, stm., Can.	C11	106
Kazanlăk, Blg.	G12	26
Kazanlı, Tur.	B5	58
Kazan-rettō, is., Japan	G18	30
Kazanskoe, Russia	C11	32
Kāzerūn, Iran	D7	56
Kazimierza Wielka, Pol.	F16	16
Kazincbarcika, Hung.	A7	26
Kaziranga National Park, p.o.i., India	E14	54
Kazlų Rūda, Lith.	F6	10
Kaztalovka, Kaz.	E7	32
Kazula, Moz.	D5	68
Kazym, Russia	B11	32
Kazym, stm., Russia	B11	32
Kazyr, stm., Russia	D16	32
Kbal Dâmrei, Camb.	E7	48
Kdyně, Czech Rep.	G9	16
Kéa, Grc.	F7	28
Kéa, i., Grc.	F7	28
Keahole Point, c., Hi., U.S.	d5	78a
Kealaikahiki Channel, strt., Hi., U.S.	c5	78a
Keams Canyon, Az., U.S.	H6	132
Keanapapa Point, c., Hi., U.S.	c4	78a
Kearney, Mo., U.S.	E3	120
Kearney, Ne., U.S.	G13	126
Kearns, Ut., U.S.	C4	132
Kearny, Az., U.S.	J6	132
Keban Barajı, res., Tur.	B4	56
Keban Reservoir see Keban Barajı, res., Tur.	B4	56
Kébèmer, Sen.	F1	64
Kebnekaise, mtn., Swe.	B8	8
K'ebrī Dehar, Eth.	F8	62
Kech, stm., Pak.	D9	56
Kechika, stm., B.C., Can.	D5	106
Keçiborlu, Tur.	F13	28
Kecskemét, Hung.	C6	26
Kedah, state, Malay.	J5	48
Kėdainiai, Lith.	E6	10
Kediri, Indon.	G8	50
Kedon, Russia	D20	34
Kédougou, Sen.	G2	64
Kędzierzyn-Koźle, Pol.	F14	16
Keefers, B.C., Can.	F9	138
Keele, stm., N.T., Can.	C5	106
Keele Peak, mtn., Yk., Can.	C4	106
Keeling Islands see Cocos Islands, dep., Oc.	K12	142
Keelung *see* Chilung, Tai.	I9	42
Keene, Ky., U.S.	G13	120
Keene, N.H., U.S.	B13	114
Keene, Tx., U.S.	B10	130
Keeney Knob, mtn., W.V., U.S.	G5	114
Keer-Weer, Cape, c., Austl.	B8	74
Keeseville, N.Y., U.S.	F3	110
Keetmanshoop, Nmb.	E3	70
Keewatin, On., Can.	B4	118
Keewatin, Mn., U.S.	D5	118
Kefalloniá, i., Grc.	E3	28
Kefamenanu, Indon.	G7	44
Kefar Naḥum (Capernaum), sci., Isr.	F6	58
Kefar Sava, Isr.	F5	58
Keffi, Nig.	H6	64
Keflavík, Ice.	k28	8a
Ke Ga, Mui, c., Viet.	F9	48
Kegalla, Sri L.	H5	53
Keg River, Ab., Can.	D7	106
Kegums, Lat.	D7	10
Ke-hsi Mānsām, Mya.	B3	48
Keighley, Eng., U.K.	H10	12
Keila, Est.	G11	8
Keimoes, S. Afr.	F5	70
Keith, Scot., U.K.	D9	12
Keith Arm, b., N.T., Can.	B6	106
Keithley Creek, B.C., Can.	D9	138
Keithsburg, Il., U.S.	J8	118
Keiyasi, Fiji	p18	79e
Keizer, Or., U.S.	F3	136
Kejimkujik National Park, p.o.i., N.S., Can.	F11	110
Kejvy, mts., Russia	C17	8
Kekaha, Hi., U.S.	b2	78a
Kékes, mtn., Hung.	B7	26
Kekri, India	E5	54
K'elafo, Eth.	F8	62
Kelai, stm., Indon.	C10	50
Kelani, stm., Sri L.	H5	53
Kelantan, state, Malay.	J6	48
Kelantan, stm., Malay.	J6	48
Kelapa, Indon.	D4	50
Kelbia, Sebkhet, l., Tun.	I4	24
Kelheim, Ger.	H7	16
Kelibia, Tun.	H5	24
Kéllé, Congo	E2	66
Kellerberrin, Austl.	F3	74
Keller Lake, l., N.T., Can.	C6	106
Kellett, Cape, c., N.T., Can.	B14	140
Kelleys Island, i., Oh., U.S.	C3	114
Kellogg, Ia., U.S.	C5	120
Kellogg, Id., U.S.	C10	136
Kellogg, Mn., U.S.	G6	118
Kelloselkä, Fin.	C13	8
Kells, Ire.	H6	12
Kelmė, Lith.	E5	10
Kélo, Chad	F3	62
Kelolokan, Indon.	C10	50
Kelowna, B.C., Can.	G11	138
Kelsey Bay, B.C., Can.	F5	138
Kelseyville, Ca., U.S.	D3	134
Kelso, Scot., U.K.	F10	12
Kelso, Wa., U.S.	D4	136
Keluang, Malay.	K6	48
Kelvington, Sk., Can.	B10	124
Kelvin Island, i., On., Can.	B10	118
Kem', Russia	D16	8
Kem', stm., Russia	D15	8
Kemano, B.C., Can.	C2	138
Kemena, stm., Malay.	B8	50
Kemer, Tur.	F13	28
Kemer Barajı, res., Tur.	F11	28
Kemerhisar, Tur.	A5	58
Kemerovo, Russia	C15	32
Kemi, Fin.	D11	8
Kemijärvi, Fin.	C12	8
Kemijärvi, l., Fin.	C12	8
Kemijoki, stm., Fin.	C12	8
Kemmerer, Wy., U.S.	B6	132
Kemmuna (Comino), i., Malta	H8	24
Kemnath, Ger.	G7	16
Kemp, Tx., U.S.	E2	122
Kemp, Lake, res., Tx., U.S.	H9	128
Kempner, Tx., U.S.	C9	130
Kempsey, Austl.	H9	76
Kempt, Lac, l., Qc., Can.	F16	106
Kempten, Ger.	I6	16
Kemptville, On., Can.	C14	112
Kemujan, Pulau, i., Indon.	F7	50
Kemul, Kong, mtn., Indon.	C9	50
Ken, stm., India	F8	54
Kenai, Ak., U.S.	D9	140
Kenai Mountains, mts., Ak., U.S.	E9	140
Kenai Peninsula, pen., Ak., U.S.	E9	140
Kenansville, Fl., U.S.	I5	116
Kenansville, N.C., U.S.	B7	116
Kenbridge, Va., U.S.	H7	114
Kendal, Sk., Can.	D10	124
Kendal, Indon.	G7	50
Kendal, Eng., U.K.	G10	12
Kendall, Austl.	H9	76
Kendall, Fl., U.S.	K5	116
Kendall, Wi., U.S.	H8	118
Kendall, Cape, c., Nu., Can.	C13	106
Kendari, Indon.	F7	44
Kendawangan, Indon.	E7	50
Kendrāparha, India	H11	54
Kendrew, S. Afr.	H7	70
Kendrick, Fl., U.S.	G3	116
Kendrick, Id., U.S.	D10	136
Kendujhargarh, India	H10	54
Kenedy, Tx., U.S.	F10	130
Kenema, S.L.	H2	64
Kenga, Russia	C14	32
Kenge, D.R.C.	E3	66
Keng Hkam, Mya.	B3	48
Kēng Tung, Mya.	B4	48
Kenhardt, S. Afr.	F5	70
Kenilworth, Ut., U.S.	D6	132
Kénitra, Mor.	C3	64
Kenly, N.C., U.S.	A7	116
Kenmare, Ire.	J3	12
Kenmare, N.D., U.S.	F11	124
Kennard, Tx., U.S.	F3	122
Kennebec, stm., Me., U.S.	F7	110
Kennebecasis Bay, b., N.B., Can.	E11	110
Kennebunk, Me., U.S.	G6	110
Kennedy, Al., U.S.	D11	122
Kennedy, Cape see Canaveral, Cape, c., Fl., U.S.	H5	116
Kennedy, Mount, mtn., B.C., Can.	F5	138
Kennedy, Mount, mtn., Yk., Can.	C3	106
Kennedy Lake, l., B.C., Can.	G5	138
Kenner, La., U.S.	G8	122
Kennetcook, N.S., Can.	E13	110
Kennett, Mo., U.S.	H7	120
Kennewick, Wa., U.S.	D7	136
Kenney Dam, dam, B.C., Can.	C6	138
Kenogami, stm., On., Can.	E13	106
Kénogami, Lac, res., Qc., Can.	B5	110
Keno Hill, Yk., Can.	C3	106
Kenora, On., Can.	B4	118
Kenosha, Wi., U.S.	F2	112
Kenozero, ozero, l., Russia	E18	8
Kensal, N.D., U.S.	G15	124
Kensett, Ar., U.S.	B7	122
Kensington, Ks., U.S.	B9	128
Kensington Park, Fl., U.S.	I3	116
Kent, Oh., U.S.	C4	114
Kent, Wa., U.S.	C4	136
Kentaū, Kaz.	F11	32
Kent Group, is., Austl.	L6	76
Kentland, In., U.S.	H2	112
Kenton, Mi., U.S.	E10	118
Kenton, Tn., U.S.	H8	120
Kent Peninsula, pen., Nu., Can.	B9	106
Kentrikí Makedonía, state, Grc.	C6	28
Kentucky, state, U.S.	G12	120
Kentucky, stm., Ky., U.S.	F13	120
Kentucky, Middle Fork, stm., Ky., U.S.	G2	114
Kentucky, North Fork, stm., Ky., U.S.	G2	114
Kentucky Lake, res., U.S.	H9	120
Kentville, N.S., Can.	E12	110
Kentwood, La., U.S.	G8	122
Kenya, ctry., Afr.	D7	66
Kenya, Mount see Kirinyaga, mtn., Kenya	E7	66
Kenyon, Mn., U.S.	G6	118
Keokuk, Ia., U.S.	D6	120
Keoladeo National Park, p.o.i., India	E6	54
Keo Nua, Deo, p., Asia	C7	48
Keosauqua, Ia., U.S.	D5	120
Keota, Ia., U.S.	C6	120
Keota, Ok., U.S.	B4	122
Keowee, Lake, res., S.C., U.S.	B2	116
Kepi, Indon.	G10	44
Kepina, Russia	D19	8
Kępno, Pol.	E13	16
Keppel Bay, b., Austl.	D8	76
Kepsut, Tur.	D11	28
Kerala, state, India	F3	53
Keramadoo, mtn., Palau	f8	78b
Keramian, Pulau, i., Indon.	F9	50
Kerang, Austl.	J4	76
Keratéa, Grc.	F6	28
Keravat, Pap. N. Gui.	a5	79a
Kerch, Ukr.	E5	32
Kerec, mys, c., Russia	D18	8
Kerema, Pap. N. Gui.	b4	79a
Keremeos, B.C., Can.	G11	138
Keren, Erit.	D7	62
Kerens, Tx., U.S.	E2	122
Keret', Russia	C15	8
Keret', ozero, l., Russia	D15	8
Kerewan, Gam.	G1	64
Kerguélen, Îles, is., Afr.	J17	4
Kerguelen Plateau, unds.	O10	142
Kerí, Grc.	F3	28
Kericho, Kenya	E7	66
Kerinci, Gunung, vol., Indon.	D2	50
Kerkenna, Îles, is., Tun.	C7	64
Kerkhoven, Mn., U.S.	F3	118
Kerkiči, Turkmen.	B10	56
Kerkrade, Neth.	F2	16
Kérkyra (Corfu), Grc.	D2	28
Kérkyra (Corfu), i., Grc.	D2	28
Kermadec Islands, is., N.Z.	F9	72
Kermadec Ridge, unds.	M20	142
Kermadec Trench, unds.	M21	142
Kermān, Iran	C8	56
Kermānshāh (Bākhtarān), Iran	C6	56
Kerme, Gulf of see Gökova Körfezi, b., Tur.	G10	28
Kermit, Tx., U.S.	C4	130
Kern, stm., Ca., U.S.	H7	134

Name — Map Ref. — Page

Kern, South Fork, stm., Ca., U.S. H7 134
Kernersville, N.C., U.S. H5 114
Kernville, Ca., U.S. H7 134
Kérouané, Gui. H3 64
Kerrobert, Sk., Can. C4 124
Kerrville, Tx., U.S. D8 130
Kerry, state, Ire. I2 12
Kerry Head, c., Ire. I2 12
Kershaw, S.C., U.S. B5 116
Kersley, B.C., Can. D8 138
Kertamulia, Indon. D6 50
Kerulen, stm., Asia B7 36
Kesagami Lake, l., On., Can. E14 106
Keşan, Tur. C9 28
Kesennuma, Japan E14 38
Keshan, China B10 36
Keshod, India H3 54
Kes'ma, Russia B20 10
Kesova Gora, Russia C20 10
Kestell, S. Afr. F9 70
Keswick, Eng., U.K. G9 12
Keszthely, Hung. C4 26
Ket', stm., Russia C14 32
Keta, Ghana H5 64
Keta, ozero, l., Russia C6 34
Ketapang, Indon. D6 50
Ketapang, Indon. F4 50
Ketchikan, Ak., U.S. E13 140
Ketchum, Id., U.S. G12 136
Kete-Krachi, Ghana H4 64
Ketoj, ostrov, i., Russia G19 34
Kętrzyn, Pol. B17 16
Kettering, Eng., U.K. I12 12
Kettering, Oh., U.S. E1 114
Kettle, stm., N.A. H12 138
Kettle Falls, Wa., U.S. B8 136
Kęty, Pol. G15 16
Keudeteunom, Indon. J2 48
Keuka Lake, l., N.Y., U.S. B8 114
Keukenhof, misc. cult., Neth. B13 14
Keul', Russia C18 32
Kevelaer, Ger. E2 16
Kevin, Mt., U.S. B14 136
Kew, T/C. Is. A12 102
Kewanee, Il., U.S. C7 120
Kewaunee, Wi., U.S. D2 112
Keweenaw Bay, b., Mi., U.S. E10 118
Keweenaw Peninsula, pen., Mi., U.S. D11 118
Keweenaw Point, c., Mi., U.S. D11 118
Key, Lough, l., Ire. G4 12
Keya Paha, stm., U.S. E13 126
Keyes, Ok., U.S. E6 128
Keyhole Reservoir, res., Wy., U.S. C8 126
Key Largo, Fl., U.S. K5 116
Key Largo, i., Fl., U.S. K5 116
Keyser, W.V., U.S. E7 114
Keystone, S.D., U.S. D9 126
Keystone, W.V., U.S. G4 114
Keystone Lake, res., Ok., U.S. A2 122
Keystone Peak, mtn., Az., U.S. L5 132
Keysville, Va., U.S. G7 114
Keytesville, Mo., U.S. E5 120
Key West, Fl., U.S. L4 116
Kezi, Zimb. B9 70
Kežma, Russia C18 32
Kežmarok, Slov. G16 16
Kgalagadi, state, Bots. D5 70
Kgatleng, state, Bots. D8 70
Khadki, India B1 53
Khadzhybeis'kyi lyman, l., Ukr. C17 26
Khagaria, India F11 54
Khairāgarh, India H8 54
Khairpur, Pak. E2 54
Khairpur, Pak. D4 54
Khajrāho, India F8 54
Khakassia see Hakasija, state, Russia D16 32
Kha Khaeng, stm., Thai. E4 48
Khakhea, Bots. D6 70
Khalatse, India A6 54
Khālidī, Khirbat al-, sci., Jord. I6 58
Khalîya, Gebel, mtn., Egypt I3 58
Khalūf, Oman E8 56
Khambhāliya, India G2 54
Khambhāt, India G4 54
Khambhāt, Gulf of, b., India H3 54
Khāmgaon, India H6 54
Khāmis, Ash-Shallāl al- (Fifth Cataract), wtfl., Sudan D6 62
Khamīs Mushayţ, Sau. Ar. F5 56
Khammam, India C5 53
Khan, stm., Laos C6 48
Khan, stm., Nmb. C2 70
Khānābād, Afg. B10 56
Khān Abū Shāmāt, Syria E7 58
Khancoban, Austl. K7 76
Khandela, India E5 54
Khandwa, India H6 54
Khānewāl, Pak. C3 54
Khāngarh, Pak. D3 54
Khangchendzonga National Park, p.o.i., India E12 54
Khangkhai, Laos C6 48
Khania, Gulf of see Chanión, Kólpos, b., Grc. H6 28
Khanka, Lake, l., Asia B10 38
Khanna, India C6 54
Khānpur, Pak. D3 54
Khansiir, Raas, c., Som. B9 66
Khantaū, Kaz. F12 32
Khān Yūnus, Gaza G5 58
Khao Laem Reservoir, res., Thai. E4 48
Khao Sok National Park, p.o.i., Thai. H4 48
Khao Yoi, Thai. F4 48
Kharagpur, India G11 54
Khārān, Pak. D10 56
Kharāyij, Sabkhat al-, l., Syria C8 58
Kharg Island see Khārk, Jazīreh-ye, i., Iran D7 56
Khargon, India H5 54
Khāriān Cantonment, Pak. B4 54
Khārk, Jazīreh-ye, i., Iran D7 56
Kharkiv, Ukr. D5 32
Kharmanli see Harmanli, Blg. H12 26
Khartoum see Al-Kharṭūm, Sudan D6 62
Khartoum North see Al-Kharṭām Baḥrī, Sudan D6 62
Khasebake, Bots. B7 70
Khāsh, Afg. C9 56
Khāsh, Iran D9 56
Khashm al-Qirbah, Sudan D7 62
Khaskovo see Haskovo, Blg. H12 26
Khatanga see Hatanga, Russia B9 34
Khatanga see Hatanga, stm., Russia B9 34
Khatauli, India D6 54
Khatt, Oued al, stm., W. Sah. D2 64
Khavast see Havast, Uzb. F11 32
Khawsa, Mya. E3 48
Khayung, stm., Thai. E7 48
Khed, India C1 53
Kheil, Katîb el-, sand, Egypt H3 58
Khemis el Khechna, Alg. H14 20
Khemis Melyana, Alg. H13 20
Khemmarat, Thai. D7 48
Khenchla, Alg. B6 64
Khenifra, Mor. C3 64
Kherson, Ukr. F15 6
Kheta see Heta, stm., Russia B8 34
Khetia, India H5 54
Khimki see Himki, Russia E20 10
Khipro, Pak. F2 54
Khisfīn, Golan F6 58
Khiva see Hiva, Uzb. F10 32
Khlong Thom, Thai. I4 48
Khlung, Thai. F6 48
Khok Kloi, Thai. H4 48
Khok Samrong, Thai. E5 48
Kholm, Afg. B10 56
Khomas, state, Nmb. C3 70
Khomeynīshahr, Iran C7 56
Khondmāl Hills, hills, India H10 54
Khong see Mekong, stm., Asia E10 46
Khon Kaen, Thai. D6 48
Khordha, India H10 54
Khorixas, Nmb. B2 70
Khorog see Horog, Taj. B11 56
Khorramābād, Iran C6 56
Khorramshahr, Iran C6 56
Khotyn, Ukr. A13 26
Khouribga, Mor. C3 64
Khowai, India F13 54
Khowst, Afg. C10 56
Khrisokhoús, Kólpos, b., Cyp. C3 58
Khuis, Bots. E5 70
Khuīyāla, India E3 54
Khulna, Bngl. G12 54
Khulna, state, Bngl. G12 54
Khun Tan, Doi, mtn., Thai. C4 48
Khunti, India G10 54
Khurai, India F7 54
Khurja, India D6 54
Khushāb, Pak. B4 54
Khust, Ukr. A10 26
Khuzdār, Pak. D10 56
Khvoy, Iran B6 56
Khwae Noi, stm., Thai. E4 48
Khyber Pass, p., Asia A3 54
Khyriv, Ukr. G18 16
Kiama, Austl. J8 76
Kiama, D.R.C. F3 66
Kiamba, Phil. H5 52
Kiambi, D.R.C. F5 66
Kiamichi, stm., Ok., U.S. C3 122
Kiamusze see Jiamusi, China B11 36
Kian see Ji'an, China H6 42
Kiangarow, Mount, mtn., Austl. F8 76
Kiang-si see Jiangxi, state, China H6 42
Kiangsi see Jiangxi, state, China H6 42
Kiang-sou see Jiangsu, state, China E8 42
Kiangsu see Jiangsu, state, China E8 42
Kiaohsien see Jiaoxian, China C8 42
Kibangou, Congo E2 66
Kibombo, D.R.C. E5 66
Kibondo, Tan. E6 66
Kibre Mengist, Eth. F7 62
Kıbrıs see Cyprus, ctry., Asia C4 58
Kıbrısçık, Tur. C14 28
Kibuye, Rw. E5 66
Kičevo, Mac. B3 28
Kickapoo, stm., Wi., U.S. H8 118
Kicking Horse Pass, p., Can. E14 138
Kidal, Mali F5 64
Kidapawan, Phil. G5 52
Kidatu, Tan. F7 66
Kidderminster, Eng., U.K. I10 12
Kidira, Sen. G2 64
Kidnappers, Cape, c., N.Z. D7 80
Kidston, Austl. B5 76
Kiefersfelden, Ger. I8 16
Kiel, Ger. B6 16
Kiel, Wi., U.S. H10 118
Kiel Bay see Kieler Bucht, b., Ger. B6 16
Kiel Canal see Nord-Ostsee-Kanal, can., Ger. B5 16
Kielce, Pol. F16 16
Kielce, state, Pol. F16 16
Kieler Bucht, b., Ger. B6 16
Kiester, Mn., U.S. H5 118
Kiev see Kyïv, Ukr. D4 32
Kīevka, Kaz. D12 32
Kiev Reservoir see Kyïvs'ke vodoskhovyshche, res., Ukr. D4 32
Kiffa, Maur. F2 64
Kifisiá, Grc. E6 28
Kigali, Rw. E6 66
Kigoma, Tan. E5 66
Kihčik, Russia F20 34
Kīhei, Hi., U.S. c5 78a
Kihniö, Fin. E10 8
Kihnu, i., Est. G10 8
Kii-hantō, pen., Japan F8 40
Kiik, Kaz. E12 32
Kii-suidō, strt., Japan F7 40
Kikerino, Russia A12 10
Kikinda, Serb. D7 26
Kikládes (Cyclades), is., Grc. F7 28
Kikori, Pap. N. Gui. b3 79a
Kikori, stm., Pap. N. Gui. b3 79a
Kikuchi, Japan G3 40
Kikwit, D.R.C. F3 66
Kīlakkarai, India G4 53
Kilauea, Hi., U.S. a2 78a
Kīlauea Crater, crat., Hi., U.S. d6 78a
Kılbasan, Tur. A4 58
Kilbuck Mountains, mts., Ak., U.S. D8 140
Kilchu-ŭp, Kor., N. D8 38
Kilcoy, Austl. F9 76
Kildare, state, Ire. H6 12
Kildare, Cape, c., P.E., Can. D13 110
Kildurk, Austl. C5 74
Kilembe, D.R.C. F3 66
Kilgore, Tx., U.S. E4 122
Kilian Island, i., Nu., Can. B18 140
Kılıç, Tur. C12 28
Kiliia, Ukr. D16 26
Kilikollūr, India G3 53
Kilimanjaro, mtn., Tan. E7 66
Kilimli, Tur. B14 28
Kilindoni, Tan. F7 66
Kilis, Tur. B8 58
Kilkee, Ire. I3 12
Kilkenny, Ire. I5 12
Kilkenny, state, Ire. I5 12
Kilkís, Grc. C5 28
Killaloe, Ire. I4 12
Killaloe Station, On., Can. C12 112
Killam, Ab., Can. D19 138
Killarney, Austl. G9 76
Killarney, Mb., Can. E14 124
Killarney, On., Can. C8 112
Killarney, Ire. I3 12
Killdeer, N.D., U.S. G11 124
Killeen, Tx., U.S. C10 130
Killen, Al., U.S. C11 122
Killington Peak, mtn., Vt., U.S. G4 110
Killiniq Island, i., Can. E13 141
Killybegs, Ire. G4 12
Kilmarnock, Scot., U.K. F8 12
Kilmarnock, Va., U.S. G9 114
Kilmore, Austl. K5 76
Kilo, Indon. H11 50
Kilombero, stm., Tan. F7 66
Kilomines, D.R.C. D5 66
Kilosa, Tan. F7 66
Kilrush, Ire. I3 12
Kilttān Island, i., India F3 46
Kilwa, D.R.C. F5 66
Kilwa Kivinje, Tan. F7 66
Kim, Co., U.S. D5 128
Kimba, Austl. F7 74
Kimball, Ne., U.S. F9 126
Kimball, S.D., U.S. D13 126
Kimbe Bay, b., Pap. N. Gui. b5 79a
Kimberley, B.C., Can. G15 138
Kimberley, S. Afr. F7 70
Kimberley Downs, Austl. C4 74
Kimberley Plateau, plat., Austl. C5 74
Kimberling City, Mo., U.S. H4 120
Kimberly, Id., U.S. H12 136
Kimberly, Wi., U.S. G10 118
Kimch'aek, Kor., N. D8 38
Kimch'ŏn, Kor., S. F8 38
Kimhae, Kor., S. D1 40
Kimito, Fin. F10 8
Kim-me-ni-oli Wash, stm., N.M., U.S. H8 132
Kimmirut, Nu., Can. C17 106
Kímolos, i., Grc. G7 28
Kimovsk, Russia F21 10
Kimpō-zan, mtn., Japan D11 40
Kimry, Russia D20 10
Kinabalu, Gunong (Kinabalu, Mount), mtn., Malay. G1 52
Kinabalu National Park, p.o.i., Malay. H1 52
Kinabatangan, stm., Malay. H2 52
Kinbasket Lake, res., B.C., Can. D12 138
Kincaid, Sk., Can. E6 124
Kincardine, On., Can. D8 112
Kinchafoonee Creek, stm., Ga., U.S. F14 122
Kinchega National Park, p.o.i., Austl. I4 76
Kinda, D.R.C. F4 66
Kinde, Mi., U.S. E7 112
Kinder, La., U.S. G6 122
Kindersley, Sk., Can. C4 124
Kindia, Gui. G2 64
Kindu, D.R.C. E5 66
Kinešma, Russia H19 8
King, N.C., U.S. H5 114
King and Queen Court House, Va., U.S. G9 114
Kingaok (Bathurst Inlet), Nu., Can. B9 106
Kingaroy, Austl. F8 76
King City, On., Can. E10 112
King City, Ca., U.S. G4 134
Kingfield, Me., U.S. F6 110
Kingfisher, Ok., U.S. F10 128
King George, Va., U.S. F8 114
King George, Mount, mtn., B.C., Can. F15 138
King George Islands, is., Nu., Can. D14 106
King George Sound, strt., Austl. G3 74
King Hill, Id., U.S. G11 136
Kingisepp, Russia A11 10
King Island, i., Austl. m12 77a
King Island, i., B.C., Can. D3 138
King Leopold Ranges, mts., Austl. C4 74
Kingman, Az., U.S. H2 132
Kingman, Ks., U.S. D10 128
Kingman Reef, rf., Oc. C10 72
King Mountain, mtn., Or., U.S. H3 136
Kingombe, D.R.C. E5 66
Kingoonya, Austl. F7 74
King Peak, mtn., Ca., U.S. C1 134
Kings, stm., Ca., U.S. G6 134
Kings Beach, Ca., U.S. D5 134
Kingsbridge, Eng., U.K. K9 12
Kingsburg, Ca., U.S. G6 134
Kings Canyon National Park, p.o.i., Ca., U.S. G7 134
Kingsford, Mi., U.S. C1 112
Kingshill, V.I.U.S. h10 104c
Kingsland, Ar., U.S. D6 122
Kingsland, Ga., U.S. F4 116
Kingsley, S. Afr. E10 70
Kingsley, Ia., U.S. B2 120
Kingsley, Mi., U.S. D4 112
Kingsley Dam, dam, Ne., U.S. F11 126
King's Lynn, Eng., U.K. I13 12
Kings Mountain, N.C., U.S. A4 116
King Solomon's Mines see Mikhrot Timna', hist., Isr. I5 58
King Sound, strt., Austl. C4 74
Kings Peak, mtn., Ut., U.S. C6 132
Kingsport, Tn., U.S. H3 114
Kingston, N.S., Can. E11 110
Kingston, On., Can. D13 112
Kingston, Jam. i14 104d
Kingston, Norf. I. y25 78i
Kingston, N.Z. G3 80
Kingston, Ga., U.S. C14 122
Kingston, Mo., U.S. E3 120
Kingston, N.Y., U.S. C11 114
Kingston, Ok., U.S. C2 122
Kingston, Pa., U.S. C9 114
Kingston, Tn., U.S. I13 120
Kingston Southeast, Austl. K2 76
Kingston upon Hull, Eng., U.K. H12 12
Kingston upon Thames, Eng., U.K. J12 12
Kingstown, St. Vin. o11 105e
Kingstree, S.C., U.S. C6 116
Kingsville, On., Can. G7 112
Kingsville, Tx., U.S. G10 130
Kingtechen see Jingdezhen, China G7 42
King William Island, i., Nu., Can. B11 106
King William's Town, S. Afr. H8 70
Kinhwa see Jinhua, China G8 42
Kınık, Tur. D10 28
Kinira, stm., S. Afr. G9 70
Kinistino, Sk., Can. B9 124
Kinkala, Congo E2 66
Kinlochleven, Scot., U.K. E8 12
Kinnaird Head, c., Scot., U.K. D10 12
Kinneret, Yam (Galilee, Sea of), l., Isr. F6 58
Kinngait (Cape Dorset), Nu., Can. C15 106
Kinosaki, Japan D7 40
Kinpoku-san, mtn., Japan A11 40
Kinross, Scot., U.K. E9 12
Kinsale, Monts. D3 105a
Kinsale, Old Head of, c., Ire. J4 12
Kinsarvik, Nor. F2 8
Kinshasa (Léopoldville), D.R.C. E3 66
Kinsley, Ks., U.S. D9 128
Kinsman, Oh., U.S. C5 114
Kinston, N.C., U.S. A8 116
Kintampo, Ghana H4 64
Kintyre, pen., Scot., U.K. F7 12
Kintyre, Mull of, c., Scot., U.K. F7 12
Kinuseo Falls, wtfl., B.C., Can. B9 138
Kinuso, Ab., Can. A15 138
Kinyangiri, Tan. E6 66
Kinyeti, mtn., Sudan G6 62
Kinzia, D.R.C. E3 66
Kinzua, Or., U.S. E7 136
Kinzua Dam, dam, Pa., U.S. C6 114
Kiowa, Co., U.S. B4 128
Kiowa, Ok., U.S. C3 122
Kiowa Creek, stm., Co., U.S. A4 128
Kipawa, stm., Qc., Can. B11 112
Kipawa, Lac, res., Qc., Can. A10 112
Kipembawe, Tan. F6 66
Kipengere Range, mts., Tan. F6 66
Kipili, Tan. F6 66
Kipini, Kenya E8 66
Kipling, Sk., Can. D11 124
Kipnuk, Ak., U.S. E7 140
Kipushi, D.R.C. G5 66
Kirakira, Sol. Is. f9 79b
Kirandul, India B5 53
Kiraṷsk, Bela. G12 10
Kirazlı, Tur. C9 28
Kirbla, Est. B6 10
Kirchberg, Ger. G5 16
Kirchmöser, Ger. D8 16
Kireevsk, Russia G20 10
Kirejkovo, Russia G18 10
Kirenga, stm., Russia C19 32
Kirensk, Russia C19 32
Kirghizia see Kyrgyzstan, ctry., Asia F12 32
Kirgiz Range, mts., Asia F12 32
Kirgiz Soviet Socialist Republic see Kyrgyzstan, ctry., Asia F12 32
Kiri, D.R.C. E3 66
Kiribati, ctry., Oc. D9 72
Kırıkhan, Tur. B7 58
Kırıkkale, Tur. B3 56
Kirillovo, Russia H21 8
Kirin see Jilin, China C7 38
Kirin see Jilin, state, China C10 36
Kirinyaga (Kenya, Mount), mtn., Kenya E7 66
Kirishima-Yaku-kokuritsu-kōen, p.o.i., Japan H3 40
Kirishima-yama, vol., Japan H3 40
Kiriši, Russia A15 10
Kiritimati (Christmas Island), at., Kir. C11 72
Kiriwina Islands (Trobriand Islands), is., Pap. N. Gui. b5 79a
Kırka, Tur. D13 28
Kırkağaç, Tur. D10 28
Kirkcaldy, Scot., U.K. E9 12
Kirkcudbright, Scot., U.K. G8 12
Kirkenes, Nor. B14 8
Kirkland, Il., U.S. B9 120
Kirkland, Tx., U.S. G8 128
Kirkland, Wa., U.S. C4 136
Kirkland Lake, On., Can. F14 106
Kırklareli, Tur. B10 28
Kırklareli, state, Tur. B10 28
Kirklin, In., U.S. H3 112
Kirkpatrick, Mount, mtn., Ant. D21 81
Kirksville, Mo., U.S. D5 120
Kirkwall, Scot., U.K. B9 12
Kirkwood, S. Afr. H7 70
Kirkwood, Mo., U.S. F7 120
Kirmir, stm., Tur. C15 28
Kirn, Ger. G3 16
Kirov, Russia F17 10
Kirov, Russia C7 32
Kirovakan see Vanadzor, Arm. A5 56
Kirovohrad, Ukr. E4 32
Kirovohrad, co., Ukr. A17 26
Kirovsk, Russia C15 8
Kirovsk, Turkmen. B9 56
Kirovskaja oblast', co., Russia F22 8
Kirovskij, Russia F20 34
Kirovskij, Russia B10 38
Kīrovskīy, Kaz. F13 32
Kirriemuir, Scot., U.K. E9 12
Kirs, Russia C8 32
Kirsanov, Russia D6 32
Kırşehir, Tur. B3 56
Kīrthar Range, mts., Pak. D10 56
Kirtland, N.M., U.S. G8 132
Kiruna, Swe. C8 8
Kirundu, D.R.C. E5 66
Kirwin, Ks., U.S. B9 128
Kiryū, Japan C12 40
Kiržač, Russia D21 10
Kisa, Swe. G6 8
Kisangani (Stanleyville), D.R.C. D5 66
Kisar, Pulau, i., Indon. G8 44
Kisaran, Indon. B1 50
Kisarazu, Japan D12 40
Kisbey, Sk., Can. E11 124
Kiselëvsk, Russia D15 32
Kīsh, Jazīreh-ye, i., Iran D7 56
Kishanganj, India E11 54
Kishangarh, India E3 54
Kishangarh Bās, India E5 54
Kishi, Nig. H5 64
Kishinev see Chişinău, Mol. B15 26
Kishiwada, Japan E8 40
Kishorganj, Bngl. F13 54
Kisii, Kenya E6 66
Kisiju, Tan. F7 66
Kisiwada see Kishiwada, Japan E8 40
Kiska Island, i., Ak., U.S. g22 140a
Kiskatinaw, stm., B.C., Can. A10 138
Kiska Volcano, vol., Ak., U.S. g22 140a
Kiskörei-viztároló, res., Hung. B7 26
Kiskőrös, Hung. C6 26
Kiskunfélegyháza, Hung. C6 26
Kiskunhalas, Hung. C6 26
Kiskunmajsa, Hung. C6 26
Kiskunsági Nemzeti Park, p.o.i., Hung. C6 26
Kislovodsk, Russia F6 32
Kismaayo, Som. E8 66
Kiso, stm., Japan D9 40
Kiso-sammyaku, mts., Japan D10 40
Kissidougou, Gui. H2 64
Kissimmee, Fl., U.S. H4 116
Kissimmee, stm., Fl., U.S. I4 116
Kissimmee, Lake, l., Fl., U.S. I4 116
Kississing Lake, l., Mb., Can. D10 106
Kisújszállás, Hung. B7 26
Kisuki, Japan D5 40
Kisumu, Kenya E6 66
Kisvárda, Hung. A9 26
Kita, Mali G3 64
Kitaa see Vestgrønland, state, Grnld. D16 141
Kitaibaraki, Japan C13 40
Kitakami, stm., Japan E14 38
Kitakata, Japan B12 40
Kitakyūshū, Japan F3 40
Kitale, Kenya D7 66
Kitami, Japan C15 38
Kitangiri, Lake, l., Tan. E6 66
Kitchener, On., Can. E9 112
Kithārah, Khirbat, sci., Jord. I6 58
Kitimat, B.C., Can. B2 138
Kitimat Ranges, mts., B.C., Can. C2 138
Kitinen, stm., Fin. C12 8
Kitíou, Akrotírion, c., Cyp. D4 58
Kitridge Point, c., Barb. n9 105d
Kitsuki, Japan F4 40
Kittanning, Pa., U.S. D6 114
Kittitas, Wa., U.S. D6 136
Kitt Peak National Observatory, sci., Az., U.S. K5 132
Kitui, Kenya E7 66
Kitunda, Tan. F6 66
Kitwanga, B.C., Can. A2 138
Kitwe, Zam. C4 68
Kityang see Jieyang, China J7 42
Kitzbühel, Aus. C9 22
Kitzingen, Ger. G6 16
Kiukiang see Jiujiang, China G6 42
Kiunga, Pap. N. Gui. b3 79a
Kiuruvesi, Fin. E12 8
Kivalina, Ak., U.S. C7 140
Kivijärvi, l., Fin. E11 8
Kiviõli, Est. G12 8
Kivu, Lake, l., Afr. E5 66
Kıyıköy, Tur. B11 28
Kiyiu Lake, l., Sk., Can. C5 124
Kızıl Adalar, is., Tur. C11 28
Kızılcabölük, Tur. F11 28
Kızılcahamam, Tur. C15 28
Kızıldağ Milli Parkı, p.o.i., Tur. F14 28
Kızılırmak, stm., Tur. A4 56
Kızılören, Tur. F15 28
Kizimkazi, Tan. F7 66
Kızkalesi, sci., Tur. B4 58
Kizljar, Russia F7 32
Kizyl-Atrek, Turkmen. B7 56
Kizyl-Su, Turkmen. B7 56
Kjahta, Russia F10 34
Kjungej-Ala-Too, hrebet, mts., Asia F13 32
Kjusjur, Russia B14 34
Kjustendil, Blg. G9 26
Klabat, Gunung, vol., Indon. E8 44
Kladno, Czech Rep. F10 16
Kladovo, Serb. E9 26
Klagan, Malay. G1 52
Klagenfurt, Aus. D11 22
Klaipėda (Memel), Lith. E3 10
Klakah, Indon. G8 50
Klamath, stm., U.S. B2 134
Klamath Falls, Or., U.S. A3 134
Klamath Marsh, sw., Or., U.S. H5 136
Klamath Mountains, mts., U.S. B2 134
Klamono, Indon. F9 44
Klang, Malay. K5 48
Klangenan, Indon. G6 50
Klangenang, Indon. G6 50
Klangpi, Mya. G14 54
Klatovy, Czech Rep. G9 16
Klawer, S. Afr. G4 70
Kleck, Bela. G9 10
Kleczew, Pol. D14 16
Kleena Kleene, B.C., Can. E5 138
Klein Curaçao, i., Neth. Ant. q22 104g
Klein Karroo see Little Karroo, plat., S. Afr. H5 70
Klein Namaland see Little Namaqualand, hist. reg., S. Afr. F3 70
Klekovača, mtn., Bos. E3 26
Klemme, Ia., U.S. A4 120
Klemtu, B.C., Can. D2 138
Klerksdorp, S. Afr. E8 70
Kletnja, Russia G16 10
Kleve, Ger. E2 16
Klickitat, stm., Wa., U.S. E5 136
Klimavičy, Bela. G14 10
Klimino, Russia C17 32
Klimovo, Russia H15 10
Klimovsk, Russia E20 10
Klimpfjäll, Swe. D6 8
Klin, Russia D19 10
Klinaklini, stm., B.C., Can. E5 138
Klincy, Russia H15 10
Klingenthal, Ger. F8 16
Klínovec, mtn., Czech Rep. F8 16
Klintehamn, Swe. H8 8
Klip, stm., S. Afr. E9 70
Klipdale, S. Afr. I4 70
Klipplaat, S. Afr. H7 70
Klisura, Blg. G11 26
Kljazma, stm., Russia E21 10
Ključ, Bos. E3 26
Ključevskaja Sopka, vulkan, vol., Russia E21 34
Ključi, Russia E21 34
Kljukvenka, Russia C15 32
Kłobuck, Pol. F14 16
Kłodawa, Pol. D14 16
Kłodzko, Pol. F12 16
Klondike, hist. reg., Yk., Can. C3 106
Klooga, Est. A7 10
Klosterneuburg, Aus. B13 22
Kloten, Switz. C5 22
Klotz, Lac, l., Qc., Can. C16 106
Klötze, Ger. D7 16
Kluane Lake, l., Yk., Can. C3 106
Kluczbork, Pol. F14 16
Klungkung, Indon. H9 50
Knaddah, Syria C7 58
Knapp, Wi., U.S. G6 118
Kneehills Creek, stm., Ab., Can. E17 138
Knee Lake, l., Mb., Can. D12 106
Kneža, Blg. F11 26
Knić, Serb. F7 26
Knickerbocker, Tx., U.S. C7 130
Knife, stm., N.D., U.S. G12 124
Knight Inlet, b., B.C., Can. F4 138
Knights Landing, Ca., U.S. E4 134
Knin, Cro. F13 22
Knippa, Tx., U.S. E8 130
Knittelfeld, Aus. C11 22
Knjaževac, Serb. F9 26
Knob Noster, Mo., U.S. F4 120
Knokke-Heist, Bel. C12 14
Knosós, sci., Grc. H8 28
Knox, Pa., U.S. C6 114
Knox, Cape, c., B.C., Can. E4 106
Knox City, Tx., U.S. H9 128
Knox Coast, cst., Ant. B15 81
Knoxville, Ga., U.S. D2 116
Knoxville, Il., U.S. D7 120
Knoxville, Tn., U.S. I2 114
Knuckles, mtn., Sri L. H5 53
Knud Rasmussen Land, reg., Grnld. A14 141
Knysna, S. Afr. I6 70
Knyszyn, Pol. C18 16
Kob', Russia C18 32
Kobar Sink, depr., Eth. E8 62
Kobayashi, Japan H3 40
Kōbe, Japan E8 40
København (Copenhagen), Den. I4 8
København, state, Den. I5 8
Kobjaj, Russia D14 34
Koblenz, Ger. F3 16
K'obo, Eth. E7 62
Koboža, Russia B18 10
Koboža, stm., Russia A18 10
Kobroor, Pulau, i., Indon. G10 44
Kobryn, Bela. H7 10
Kobuk, Ak., U.S. C8 140
Kobuk, stm., Ak., U.S. C8 140
Kobuleti, Geor. F6 32
Kobylin, Pol. E13 16
Kocaali, Tur. B13 28
Kocaavşar, stm., Tur. D10 28
Kocaeli, state, Tur. C12 28
Kočani, Mac. B5 28
Koçarlı, Tur. F10 28
Kočečum, stm., Russia C8 34
Kočevje, Slvn. E11 22
Kočevo, Russia C8 32
Kŏch'ang, Kor., S. G7 38
Koch Bihār, India E12 54
Kocher, stm., Ger. G5 16
Kochi (Cochin), India G3 53
Kōchi, Japan F6 40
Kōchi, state, Japan F6 40
Koch Island, i., Nu., Can. B15 106
Kochiu see Gejiu, China G5 36
Kochnay Darvīshān, Afg. C9 56
Kodaikānal, India F3 53
Kodar, hrebet, mts., Russia E12 34
Kodāri, Nepal E10 54
Kodarma, India F10 54
Kodiak, Ak., U.S. E9 140
Kodiak Island, i., Ak., U.S. E9 140
Kodinār, India H3 54
Kodok, Sudan F6 62
Kodyma, Ukr. A16 26
Kodyma, stm., Ukr. B17 26
Koës, Nmb. D4 70
Köflach, Aus. C11 22
Koforidua, Ghana H4 64
Kōfu, Japan D11 40
Koga, Japan C12 40
Kogaluc, stm., Qc., Can. D15 106
Kogaluc, Baie, b., Qc., Can. D15 106
Kogan, Austl. F8 76
Køge, Den. I5 8
Kogon, stm., Gui. G2 64
Koẖanava, Bela. F12 10
Kohāt, Pak. B3 54
Kohīma, India C7 46
Kohler, Wi., U.S. E2 112
Kohtla-Järve, Est. G12 8
Kohyl'nyk (Cogâlnic), stm., Eur. C15 26
Koide, Japan B11 40
Koigi, Est. B8 10
Koindu, S.L. H2 64
Koiva (Gauja), stm., Eur. C7 10
Kojda, Russia C20 8
Kŏje-do, i., Kor., S. E1 40
Kojgorodok, Russia B8 32
Kojonup, Austl. F3 74
Kok (Hkok), stm., Asia B4 48
Kokand, Uzb. F12 32
Kokas, Indon. F9 44
Kokemäki, Fin. F9 8
Kokenau, Indon. F10 44
Kokhav HaYarden, sci., Isr. F6 58
Kokiu see Gejiu, China G5 36
Kokkilai Lagoon, b., Sri L. G5 53
Kokkola, Fin. E10 8
Kokoda, Pap. N. Gui. b4 79a
Kokomo, In., U.S. H3 112
Kokomo, Ms., U.S. F8 122
Kokong, Bots. D6 70
Kokopo, Pap. N. Gui. a5 79a
Kokorevka, Russia H17 10
Koksan-ŭp, Kor., N. E7 38
Kökshetaū, Kaz. D12 32
Kökshetaū see Kokčetav, Kaz. D12 32
Koksoak, stm., Qc., Can. D17 106
Kokstad, S. Afr. G9 70
Kokubu, Japan H3 40
Kola, Russia B15 8
Kolachel, India G3 53
Kolaka, Indon. F7 44
Kolangār, Afg. A2 54
Kola Peninsula see Kol'skij poluostrov, pen., Russia C17 8
Kolār, India E3 53
Kolāras, India F6 54
Kolār Gold Fields, India E4 53
Kolárovo, Slov. I13 16
Kolašin, Mont. G6 26
Kolbio, Kenya E8 66
Kolbuszowa, Pol. F17 16
Kol'čugino, Russia D22 10
Kolda, Sen. G2 64
Kolding, Den. I3 8
Kole, D.R.C. E4 66
Kolea, Alg. H13 20
Kolguev, ostrov, i., Russia B18 6
Kolhāpur, India C4 53
Kolhāpur, India C1 53
Koli, Russia A17 10
Kolín, Czech Rep. F11 16
Koljubakino, Russia E19 10
Kolkata (Calcutta), India G12 54
Kollam see Quilon, India G3 53
Kollegāl, India E3 53
Kolleru Lake, l., India C5 53
Kolmogorovo, Russia C16 32
Köln (Cologne), Ger. E2 16
Kolno, Pol. C17 16
Koło, Pol. D14 16
Koloa, Hi., U.S. b2 78a
Kołobrzeg, Pol. B11 16
Kolodnja, Russia F15 10
Kolokani, Mali G3 64
Kolombangara Island, i., Sol. Is. d7 79b
Kolomna, Russia E21 10
Kolomyia, Ukr. A12 26
Kolonga, Tonga n14 78e
Kolonia, Micron. m11 78d
Kolonodale, Indon. F7 44
Kolosib, India F14 54
Kolosovka, Russia C12 32
Kolovai, Tonga n13 78e
Kolozsvár see Cluj-Napoca, Rom. C10 26
Kolp', stm., Russia A19 10
Kolpaševo, Russia C14 32
Kolpino, Russia A13 10
Kolpny, Russia H19 10
Kol'skij poluostrov (Kola Peninsula), pen., Russia C17 8
Kolwezi, D.R.C. G5 66
Kolyma, stm., Russia C20 34
Kolyma Plain see Kolymskaja nizmennost', pl., Russia C19 34
Kolymskaja, Russia C20 34
Kolymskaja nizmennost' (Kolyma Plain), pl., Russia C19 34
Kom, mtn., Blg. F10 26
Koma, Mya. E4 48
Komadugu Gana, stm., Nig. G7 64
Komagane, Japan D10 40
Komandorskie ostrova, is., Russia D20 30
Komandorski Islands see Komandorskie ostrova, is., Russia D20 30
Komárno, Slov. I13 16
Komarnyky, Ukr. G19 16
Komárom, Hung. B5 26
Komárom-Esztergom, state, Hung. B5 26
Komati (Incomati), stm., Afr. E10 70
Komatipoort, S. Afr. D10 70
Komatsu, Japan C9 40
Komatsushima, Japan E7 40
Kome Island, i., Ug. E6 66
Komering, stm., Indon. E4 50
Komfane, Indon. G9 44
Komi, state, Russia B8 32
Komissarovo, Russia B9 38
Komló, Hung. C5 26
Kommunizma, pik see Ismail Samani, pik, mtn., Taj. B11 56
Komodo, Pulau, i., Indon. H11 50
Komodo National Park, p.o.i., Indon. H11 50
Komoé, stm., Afr. H4 64
Kom Ombo, Egypt C6 62
Komoran, Pulau, i., Indon. G10 44
Komoro, Japan C11 40
Komotiní, Grc. B8 28
Kompasberg, mtn., S. Afr. G7 70
Komsomolets, Kaz. D10 32
Komsomolets shyghanaghy, b., Kaz. E8 32
Komsomol'sk, Russia H18 8
Komsomol'sk, Russia C15 32

Name	Map Ref.	Page
Komsomol'sk-na-Amure, Russia	F16	34
Komsomol'skoj Pravdy, ostrova, is., Russia	A10	34
Konakovo, Russia	D19	10
Konakpınar, Tur.	D10	28
Konar, stm., Asia	A3	54
Konārak, India	I11	54
Konawa, Ok., U.S.	C2	122
Konch, India	F7	54
Konda, stm., Russia	B10	32
Kondagaon, India	B5	53
Kondega, Russia	F15	8
Kondinin, Austl.	F3	74
Kondoa, Tan.	E7	66
Kondopoga, Russia	E16	8
Kondoz, Afg.	B10	56
Kondrovo, Russia	F18	10
Kondukūr, India	D4	53
Koné, N. Cal.	m15	79d
Kong, stm., Asia	F8	48
Kŏng, Kaôh, i., Camb.	G6	48
Kongcheng, China	F7	42
Kong Christian IX Land, reg., Grnld.	D18	141
Kong Christian X Land, reg., Grnld.	C19	141
Kong Frederik VIII Land, reg., Grnld.	B19	141
Kong Frederik VI Kyst, cst., Grnld.	E17	141
Kongjiawopeng, China	B5	38
Kongju, Kor., S.	F7	38
Kongmoon see Jiangmen, China	J5	42
Kongolo, D.R.C.	F5	66
Kongor, Sudan	F6	62
Kong Oscar Fjord, strt., Grnld.	C21	141
Kongsvinger, Nor.	F5	8
Kongur Shan, mtn., China	G13	32
Kong Wilhelms Land, reg., Grnld.	B21	141
Konice, Czech Rep.	G12	16
Königsberg see Kaliningrad, Russia	F3	10
Königswinter, Ger.	F3	16
Konin, Pol.	D14	16
Konin, state, Pol.	D14	16
Konispol, Alb.	E14	24
Kónitsa, Grc.	C3	28
Konjic, Bos.	F4	26
Konkiep, stm., Nmb.	E3	70
Konkouré, stm., Gui.	G2	64
Konna, Mali	G4	64
Konnevesi, l., Fin.	E12	8
Konnur, India	C2	53
Konoša, Russia	F18	8
Kōnosu, Japan	C12	40
Konotop, Ukr.	E15	6
Końskie, Pol.	E16	16
Konstantinovskij, Russia	C22	10
Konstanz, Ger.	I4	16
Kontagora, Nig.	G5	64
Kontcha, Cam.	C2	66
Kontha, Mya.	C3	48
Kontseba, Ukr.	A16	26
Kon Tum, Viet.	E8	48
Konya, Tur.	F15	28
Konya, state, Tur.	E15	28
Konz, Ger.	G2	16
Konza, Kenya	E7	66
Konžakovskij Kamen', gora, mtn., Russia	C9	32
Koocanusa, Lake, res., N.A.	B11	136
Kookynie, Austl.	E4	74
Koolatah, Austl.	C8	74
Kooloonong, Austl.	J4	76
Koontz Lake, In., U.S.	G3	112
Koorawatha, Austl.	J7	76
Koosa, Est.	B9	10
Kooskia, Id., U.S.	D11	136
Kootenai (Kootenay), stm., N.A.	G13	138
Kootenay (Kootenai), stm., N.A.	G13	138
Kootenay Lake, l., B.C., Can.	G14	138
Kootenay National Park, p.o.i., B.C., Can.	F14	138
Kopāganj, India	E9	54
Kopargaon, India	B2	53
Kópavogur, Ice.	k29	8a
Kopejsk, Russia	C10	32
Koper, Slvn.	E10	22
Kopervik, Nor.	G1	8
Kopet Mountains, mts., Asia	B8	56
Köping, Swe.	G6	8
Koplik, Alb.	B13	24
Koppal, India	D3	53
Koppang, Nor.	F4	8
Koppies, S. Afr.	E8	70
Koprivnica, Cro.	D13	22
Köprü, stm., Tur.	F14	28
Köprülü Kanyon Milli Parkı, p.o.i., Tur.	F14	28
Kopylovo, Russia	F21	8
Korab (Korabit, Maja e), mtn., Eur.	C14	24
Korabit, Maja e (Korab), mtn., Eur.	C14	24
Korāput, India	B6	53
Korarou, Lac, l., Mali	F4	64
Koratla, India	B4	53
Korba, India	G9	54
Korba, Tun.	H4	24
Korbach, Ger.	E4	16
Korça see Korçë, Alb.	D14	24
Korçë, Alb.	D14	24
Korčula, Cro.	H14	22
Korčula, Otok, i., Cro.	H13	22
Korea, North, ctry., Asia	D7	38
Korea, South, ctry., Asia	G8	38
Korea Bay, b., Asia	E5	38
Korea Strait, strt., Asia	E2	40
Korelakša, Russia	D15	8
Korenovsk, Russia	E5	32
Korf, Russia	D22	34
Korhogo, C. Iv.	H3	64
Korientzé, Mali	F4	64
Korim, Indon.	F10	44
Korinthiakós Kólpos (Corinth, Gulf of), b., Grc.	E5	28
Kórinthos, Grc.	F5	28
Kōriyama, Japan	B13	40
Korjakskaja Sopka, vulkan, vol., Russia	F20	34
Korjakskoe nagor'e, mts., Russia	D22	34
Korjažma, Russia	F22	8
Korkino, Russia	D10	32
Korkuteli, Tur.	F13	28
Korla, China	C2	36
Korliki, Russia	B14	32
Körmend, Hung.	C3	26
Kornat, Otok, i., Cro.	G12	22
Kornati, Nacionalni Park, p.o.i., Cro.	G12	22
Korner, Mt., U.S.	A14	136
Korneuburg, Aus.	B13	22
Koro, i., Fiji	p19	79e
Köroğlu Tepesi, mtn., Tur.	C14	28
Korogwe, Tan.	F7	66
Koroleve, Ukr.	H19	16
Koromere see East Cape, c., N.Z.	C8	80
Koronadal, Phil.	G5	52
Koróni, Grc.	G4	28
Korónia, Límni, l., Grc.	C6	28
Korópi, Grc.	F6	28
Koror, Palau	g8	78b
Körös, stm., Hung.	C7	26
Koro Sea, s., Fiji	p20	79e
Korosten', Ukr.	E14	6
Koro Toro, Chad	D3	62
Korotyš, Russia	H20	10
Korovin Volcano, vol., Ak., U.S.	g24	140a
Korovou, Fiji	p19	79e
Koroyanitu, mtn., Fiji	p18	79e
Korsakov, Russia	G17	34
Korsakovo, Russia	G20	10
Korsør, Den.	I4	8
Koršunovo, Russia	C20	32
Kortrijk, Bel.	D12	14
Korucam, Cape see Koruçam Burnu, c., N. Cyp.	C3	58
Koruçam Burnu, c., N. Cyp.	C3	58
Korucu, Tur.	D10	28
Korumburra, Austl.	L5	76
Koryak Mountains see Korjakskoe nagor'e, mts., Russia	D22	34
Koryŏng, Kor., S.	D1	40
Kos (Cos), i., Grc.	G10	28
Kosa, Russia	C8	32
Kosa, Russia	F10	34
Kosai, Japan	E10	40
Kosaja Gora, Russia	F20	10
Kościan, Pol.	D12	16
Kościerzyna, Pol.	B14	16
Kosciusko, Ms., U.S.	D9	122
Kosciuszko, Mount, mtn., Austl.	K6	76
Kosciuszko National Park, p.o.i., Austl.	K6	76
Kose, Est.	A8	10
Koshikijima-rettō, is., Japan	H2	40
Koshkonong, Lake, l., Wi., U.S.	B9	120
Kōshoku, Japan	C11	40
Košice, Slov.	H17	16
Kosi Kalan, India	E6	54
Kosimeer, l., S. Afr.	E11	70
Kosiv, Ukr.	A12	26
Köşk, Tur.	F11	28
Koslan, Russia	E23	8
Kosŏng, Kor., S.	E1	40
Kosŏng-ŭp, Kor., N.	E8	38
Kosovo-Metohija, state, Serb.	G7	26
Kosovska Mitrovica, Serb.	G7	26
Kosrae, i., Micron.	C7	72
Kösreli, Tur.	A6	58
Kosse, Tx., U.S.	F2	122
Kossou, Lac de, res., C. Iv.	H3	64
Kostenec, Blg.	G10	26
Koster, S. Afr.	D8	70
Kostomukša, Russia	D14	8
Kostonjärvi, l., Fin.	D12	8
Kostroma, Russia	H19	8
Kostroma, stm., Russia	G19	8
Kostromskaja oblast', co., Russia	G20	8
Kostrzyn, Pol.	D10	16
Kosum Phisai, Thai.	D6	48
Koszalin, Pol.	B12	16
Koszalin, state, Pol.	C12	16
Kőszeg, Hung.	B3	26
Kota, India	G9	54
Kota, India	F5	54
Kotaagung, Indon.	F4	50
Kotabangun, Indon.	D10	50
Kotabaru, Indon.	E10	50
Kota Belud, Malay.	G1	52
Kota Bharu, Malay.	I6	48
Kotabumi, Indon.	F4	50
Kotadabok, Indon.	D4	50
Kot Addu, Pak.	C3	54
Kota Kinabalu, Malay.	G1	52
Kotamobagu, Indon.	E7	44
Kotapinang, Indon.	C1	50
Kota Tinggi, Malay.	L6	48
Kotawaringin, Indon.	E7	50
Kotcho Lake, l., B.C., Can.	D6	106
Kot Chutta, Pak.	D3	54
Kotel'nič, Russia	C7	32
Kotel'nikovo, Russia	E6	32
Kotel'nyj, ostrov, i., Russia	A16	34
Kotelnyj, ostrov, i., Russia	B3	34
Köthen, Ger.	E7	16
Kotikovo, Russia	G17	34
Kotka, Fin.	F12	8
Kot Kapūra, India	C5	54
Kotlas, Russia	F22	8
Kotli, Pak.	B4	54
Kotlik, Ak., U.S.	D7	140
Kôtomo, Île, i., N. Cal.	n16	79d
Kotor, Mont.	G5	26
Kotoriba, Cro.	D13	22
Kotovs'k, Ukr.	B16	26
Kot Pūtli, India	E6	54
Kotri, Pak.	F2	54
Kottagūdem, India	C5	53
Kottayam, India	G3	53
Kotto, stm., C.A.R.	C4	66
Kottūru, India	D3	53
Kotuj, stm., Russia	B9	34
Kotzebue, Ak., U.S.	C7	140
Kotzebue Sound, strt., Ak., U.S.	C7	140
Kötzting, Ger.	G8	16
Kouang-si see Guangxi, state, China	G6	36
Kouang-tong see Guangdong, state, China	J6	42
Kouaoua, N. Cal.	m15	79d
Kouchibouguac National Park, p.o.i., N.B., Can.	D11	110
Koudougou, Burkina	G4	64
Kouei-tcheou see Guizhou, state, China	H2	42
Kouga, stm., S. Afr.	H7	70
Kougaberge, mts., S. Afr.	H6	70
Koukdjuak, stm., Nu., Can.	B16	106
Kouki, C.A.R.	C3	66
Koúklia, Cyp.	D3	58
Koulamoutou, Gabon	E2	66
Koulikoro, Mali	G3	64
Koumala, Austl.	C7	76
Koumbia, Gui.	G2	64
Koumpentoum, Sen.	G2	64
Koumra, Chad	F3	62
Koundâra, Gui.	G2	64
Kourou, Fr. Gu.	B7	84
Kouroussa, Gui.	G3	64
Kousséri, Cam.	B2	66
Koussi, Emi, mtn., Chad	D3	62
Koutiala, Mali	G3	64
Kouts, In., U.S.	G2	112
Kouvola, Fin.	F12	8
Kova, Russia	C18	32
Kovada Milli Parkı, p.o.i., Tur.	F13	28
Kovarskas, Lith.	E7	10
Kovdor, Russia	C14	8
Kovdozero, ozero, res., Russia	C14	8
Kovilpatti, India	G3	53
Kovrov, Russia	H19	8
Kovūr, India	D5	53
Kovža, Russia	F18	8
Kowalewo Pomorskie, Pol.	C14	16
Kowloon see Jiulong, China	J5	42
Kowŏn-ŭp, Kor., N.	E7	38
Kowt-e 'Ashrow, Afg.	C10	56
Koxtag, China	A4	46
Köyceğiz Gölü, l., Tur.	G11	28
Koyna Reservoir, res., India	C1	53
Koyuk, Ak., U.S.	D7	140
Koyukuk, Ak., U.S.	D8	140
Koyukuk, stm., Ak., U.S.	C8	140
Kō-zaki, c., Japan	E2	40
Kozan, Tur.	A6	58
Kozáni, Grc.	C4	28
Kožany, Russia	H14	10
Kozel'sk, Russia	F18	10
Koževnikovo, Russia	C14	32
Kozhikode (Calicut), India	F2	53
Kozienice, Pol.	E17	16
Kozlov Bereg, Russia	B10	10
Kozlovo, Russia	D19	10
Kozlu, Tur.	B14	28
Koz'mino, Russia	F22	8
Kožposëlok, Russia	E17	8
Kōzu-shima, i., Japan	E12	40
Kpalimé, Togo	H5	64
Kra, Isthmus of, isth., Asia	H4	48
Kraai, stm., S. Afr.	G8	70
Krabi, Thai.	H4	48
Krâchéh, Camb.	F8	48
Kraeva, Russia	B9	38
Kragan, Indon.	G7	50
Kragujevac, Serb.	F7	26
Krajenka, Pol.	C13	16
Krakatoa see Rakata, Pulau, i., Indon.	G4	50
Krakovets', Ukr.	G19	16
Kraków, Pol.	F15	16
Kraków, state, Pol.	G15	16
Kralendijk, Neth. Ant.	p23	104g
Kraljevo, Serb.	F7	26
Kralovice, Czech Rep.	G9	16
Kralupy nad Vltavou, Czech Rep.	F10	16
Kramators'k, Ukr.	E5	32
Kramfors, Swe.	E7	8
Kranídi, Grc.	F6	28
Kranj (Krainburg), Slvn.	D11	22
Kranskop, S. Afr.	F10	70
Krapivna, Russia	G18	10
Krasavino, Russia	F22	8
Krasieo, stm., Thai.	E4	48
Krasivaja Meča, stm., Russia	G20	10
Krāslava, Lat.	E10	10
Krasnae, Bela.	F10	10
Krasnaja Gorbatka, Russia	I19	8
Krasnaja Slabada, Bela.	H9	10
Krasnaluki, Bela.	F11	10
Krasneno, Russia	D23	34
Kraśnik, Pol.	F18	16
Kraśnik Fabryczny, Pol.	F18	16
Krasni Okny, Ukr.	B16	26
Krasnoarmejsk, Russia	D21	10
Krasnoarmejskij, Russia	C23	34
Krasnobród, Pol.	F19	16
Krasnodar, Russia	E5	32
Krasnoe, ozero, l., Russia	D23	34
Krasnoe Selo, Russia	A12	10
Krasnoe Znamja, Russia	C18	10
Krasnogorodskoe, Russia	D11	10
Krasnogorsk, Russia	E20	10
Krasnogorsk, Russia	G17	34
Krasnojarovo, Russia	F14	34
Krasnojarsk, Russia	C16	32
Krasnojarskoe vodohranilišče, res., Russia	D16	32
Krasnokamsk, Russia	C8	32
Krasnomajskij, Russia	C17	10
Krasnoščele, Russia	C17	8
Krasnosel'kup, Russia	A14	32
Krasnoturjinsk, Russia	C10	32
Krasnoufimsk, Russia	C9	32
Krasnoural'sk, Russia	C10	32
Krasnovišersk, Russia	B9	32
Krasnovodskij poluostrov, pen., Turkmen.	A7	56
Krasnozavodsk, Russia	D20	10
Krasnozërskoe, Russia	D14	32
Krasnoznamensk, Russia	F5	10
Krasnoznamenskoe, Kaz.	D11	32
Krasnye Gory, Russia	B12	10
Krasnyj Čikoj, Russia	F10	34
Krasnyj Gorodok, Russia	C16	10
Krasnyj Jar, Russia	C12	32
Krasnyj Luč, Russia	C13	10
Krasnyj Oktjabr', Russia	D21	10
Krasnyj Tkač, Russia	E22	10
Krasnystaw, Pol.	E19	16
Kratovo, Mac.	A5	28
Krâvanh, Chuŏr Phnum, mts., Camb.	F6	48
Krbava, reg., Cro.	F12	22
Krečetovo, Russia	F18	8
Krefeld, Ger.	E2	16
Kremastón, Technití Límni, res., Grc.	E4	28
Kremenchug Reservoir see Kremenchuts'ke vodoskhovyshche, res., Ukr.	E4	32
Kremenchuk, Ukr.	E4	32
Kremenchuts'ke vodoskhovyshche, res., Ukr.	E4	32
Kremenskoe, Russia	E18	10
Kremmling, Co., U.S.	C10	132
Krems an der Donau, Aus.	B12	22
Kress, Tx., U.S.	G7	128
Kresta, zaliv, b., Russia	C25	34
Krestcy, Russia	B15	10
Krestcy, Russia	B22	10
Krest-Maër, Russia	C17	34
Kretinga, Lith.	E4	10
Kribi, Cam.	D1	66
Křimice, Czech Rep.	G9	16
Krishna, stm., India	C5	53
Krishna, Mouths of the, mth., India	D5	53
Krishnagiri, India	E4	53
Krishnanagar, India	G12	54
Krishnarāja Sāgara, res., India	E3	53
Krishnarājpet, India	E3	53
Kristiansand, Nor.	G3	8
Kristianstad, Swe.	I6	8
Kristiansund, Nor.	E2	8
Kristiinankaupunki (Kristinestad), Fin.	E9	8
Kristinehamn, Swe.	G6	8
Kristinestad see Kristiinankaupunki, Fin.	E9	8
Kríti, state, Grc.	H7	28
Kríti (Crete), i., Grc.	H7	28
Kritikón Pélagos (Crete, Sea of), s., Grc.	H8	28
Kriva Palanka, Mac.	A5	28
Krivodol, Blg.	F10	26
Križevci, Cro.	D13	22
Krjukovo, Russia	E20	10
Krjukovo, Russia	C20	34
Krk, Otok, i., Cro.	E11	22
Krnov, Czech Rep.	F13	16
Krobia, Pol.	E12	16
Krøderen, l., Nor.	F3	8
Krokodil, stm., S. Afr.	D8	70
Krom, stm., S. Afr.	G4	70
Kroměříž, Czech Rep.	G13	16
Kromy, Russia	H18	10
Kronach, Ger.	F7	16
Krŏng Kaôh Kŏng, Camb.	G6	48
Krŏng Kêb, Camb.	G7	48
Kronoberg, state, Swe.	H6	8
Kronockaja Sopka, vulkan, vol., Russia	F21	34
Kronockij zaliv, b., Russia	F21	34
Kronoki, Russia	F21	34
Kronprins Christian Land, reg., Grnld.	A22	141
Kronštadt, Russia	A12	10
Kroonstad, S. Afr.	E8	70
Kropotkin, Russia	E12	34
Kropotkin, Russia	E6	32
Krośniewice, Pol.	D14	16
Krosno, Pol.	G17	16
Krosno, state, Pol.	G17	16
Krotoszyn, Pol.	E13	16
Krotz Springs, La., U.S.	G7	122
Kroya, Indon.	G6	50
Krško, Slvn.	E12	22
Kruger National Park, p.o.i., S. Afr.	C10	70
Krugersdorp, S. Afr.	E8	70
Kruhlae, Bela.	F12	10
Krui, Indon.	F3	50
Kruisfontein, S. Afr.	H7	70
Kruja see Krujë, Alb.	C13	24
Krujë, Alb.	C13	24
Krumbach, Ger.	H6	16
Krumovgrad, Blg.	H12	26
Krung Thep (Bangkok), Thai.	F5	48
Kruså, Den.	B5	16
Kruševac, Serb.	F8	26
Krušinovka, Bela.	G12	10
Krutcy, Russia	C12	10
Krutoe, Russia	H20	10
Kruzenšterna, proliv, strt., Russia	G19	34
Kruzof Island, i., Ak., U.S.	E12	140
Kryčau, Bela.	G14	10
Kryms'kyi pivostriv (Crimean Peninsula), pen., Ukr.	E4	32
Krynica, Pol.	G16	16
Krynychne, Ukr.	D15	26
Kryve Ozero, Ukr.	B17	26
Kryvošyn, Bela.	H8	10
Kryvyj Rih, Ukr.	E4	32
Kryzhopil', Ukr.	A15	26
Krzeszowice, Pol.	F15	16
Krzyż, Pol.	D11	16
Ksenevka, Russia	F12	34
Kstovo, Russia	H20	8
Kuah, Malay.	I4	48
Kuai, stm., China	E7	42
Kualacenako, Indon.	D3	50
Kuala Kangsar, Malay.	J5	48
Kualakapuas, Indon.	E9	50
Kuala Krai, Malay.	J6	48
Kuala Kubu Baharu, Malay.	K5	48
Kualakurun, Indon.	D8	50
Kualalangsa, Indon.	J4	48
Kuala Lipis, Malay.	J5	48
Kuala Lumpur, Malay.	K5	48
Kuala Nerang, Malay.	I5	48
Kualapesaguan, Indon.	E6	50
Kuala Pilah, Malay.	K6	48
Kuala Rompin, Malay.	K6	48
Kuala Sepetang, Malay.	J5	48
Kualasimpang, Indon.	J3	48
Kuala Terengganu, Malay.	J6	48
Kualu, stm., Indon.	B1	50
Kuamut, stm., Malay.	A10	50
Kuancheng, China	A8	42
Kuandian, China	D6	38
Kuan Shan, mtn., Tai.	J9	42
Kuantan, Malay.	K6	48
Kuanyün see Guanyun, China	D8	42
Kuban', stm., Russia	E6	32
Kubenskoe, ozero, l., Russia	G18	8
Kubokawa, Japan	F6	40
Kubrat, Blg.	F13	26
Kučema, Russia	D20	8
Kuchaiburi, India	G11	54
Kuchāman, India	E5	54
Kuching, Malay.	C7	50
Kuchurhan, stm., Eur.	B16	26
Kuçova see Kuçovë, Alb.	D13	24
Kuçovë, Alb.	D13	24
Kūd, India	B5	54
Kudamatsu, Japan	F4	40
Kudat, Malay.	G1	52
Kudever', Russia	D12	10
Kudirkos Naumiestis, Lith.	F5	10
Kudus, Indon.	G7	50
Kudymkar, Russia	C8	32
Kū'ē'ē Ruins, sci., Hi., U.S.	d6	78a
Kueisui see Hohhot, China	A4	42
Kueiyang see Guiyang, China	H2	42
K'uerhlo see Korla, China	C2	36
Kufstein, Aus.	C9	22
Kugluktuk (Coppermine), Nu., Can.	B8	106
Kugmallit Bay, b., N.T., Can.	C13	140
Kuhësi see Kukës, Alb.	B14	24
Kuhmoinen, Fin.	F11	8
Kuhn Ø, i., Grnld.	C22	141
Kuial'nyts'kyi lyman, l., Ukr.	C17	26
Kuiseb, stm., S. Afr.	C2	70
Kuitan, China	J7	42
Kuito, Ang.	C2	68
Kuiu Island, i., Ak., U.S.	E13	140
Kuivastu, Est.	G10	8
Kuja, Russia	D18	8
Kujang-ŭp, Kor., N.	E7	38
Kujawy, reg., Pol.	D14	16
Kujbyšev, Russia	C13	32
Kujbyševskoe vodohranilišče, res., Russia	D7	32
Kujū-san, vol., Japan	F4	40
Kukalaya, stm., Nic.	F6	102
Kukawa, Nig.	G7	64
Kukës, Alb.	B14	24
Kukoboj, Russia	B22	10
Kükong see Shaoguan, China	I5	42
Kukshi, India	G5	54
Kukuj, Russia	A15	10
Kukukus Lake, l., On., Can.	B7	118
Kukurtli, Turkmen.	B8	56
Kula, Blg.	F9	26
Kula, Tur.	E11	28
Kula, Serb.	D6	26
Kulagi, Russia	H15	10
Kula Gulf, strt., Sol. Is.	e7	79b
Kulai, Malay.	L6	48
Kula Kangri, mtn., Bhu.	E13	54
Kular, Russia	B15	34
Kulaura, Bngl.	F13	54
Kuldīga, Lat.	D5	10
Kuldja see Yining, China	F14	32
Kule, Bots.	C5	70
Kulebaki, Russia	I20	8
Kulen Vakuf, Bos.	E3	26
Kulim, Malay.	J5	48
Kuljab, Taj.	B10	56
Kulkyne Creek, stm., Austl.	H5	76
Kullu, India	B6	54
Kulm, N.D., U.S.	A13	126
Kulmbach, Ger.	F7	16
Kuloj, Russia	F20	8
Kuloj, Russia	D20	8
Kuloj, stm., Russia	D20	8
Kulsary, Kaz.	E8	32
Kulti, India	G11	54
Kultuk, Russia	D18	32
Kulu, Tur.	D16	28
Kulunda, Russia	D13	32
Kulundinskaja ravnina, pl., Asia	D13	32
Kulundinskoe, ozero, l., Russia	D13	32
Kulwin, Austl.	J4	76
Kumagaya, Japan	C12	40
Kumai, Indon.	E8	50
Kumai, Teluk, b., Indon.	E7	50
Kumajri see Gjumri, Arm.	A5	56
Kumamoto, Japan	G3	40
Kumamoto, state, Japan	G3	40
Kumano, Japan	F9	40
Kumano-nada, s., Japan	F9	40
Kumanovo, Mac.	A4	28
Kumara, Russia	F14	34
Kumārghāt, India	F14	54
Kumasi, Ghana	H4	64
Kumba, Cam.	D1	66
Kumbakonam, India	F4	53
Kumbarilla, Austl.	F8	76
Kumdanlı, Tur.	E13	28
Kume-jima, i., Japan	I18	39a
Kŭm-gang, stm., Kor., S.	F7	38
Kumla, Swe.	G6	8
Kumluca, Tur.	G13	28
Kumluca, Tur.	B15	28
Kumo, Nig.	H7	64
Kumon Range, mts., Mya.	C8	46
Kumora, Russia	E11	34
Kumta, India	D2	53
Kumu, D.R.C.	D5	66
Kumukahi, Cape, c., Hi., U.S.	o16	135a
Kümüx, China	C2	36
Kŭmya-ŭp, Kor., N.	E7	38
Kuna, Id., U.S.	G10	136
Kunašir, ostrov (Kunashiri-tō), i., Russia	C16	38
Kunda, Est.	G12	8
Kunda Hills, hills, India	F3	53
Kundāpura, India	E2	53
Kundar, stm., Asia	C2	54
Kunderu, stm., India	D4	53
Kundiān, Pak.	B3	54
Kundiawa, Pap. N. Gui.	b3	79a
Kundla, India	H3	54
Kundur, Pulau, i., Indon.	C3	50
Kunene, state, Nmb.	B2	70
Kunene (Cunene), stm., Afr.	D1	68
Kunes, Nor.	A12	8
Kungchuling see Gongzhuling, China	C6	38
Kunggyü Yumco, l., China	C9	54
Kunghit Island, i., B.C., Can.	E4	106
Kungrad, Uzb.	F9	32
Kungsbacka, Swe.	H4	8
Kungur, Russia	C9	32
Kunhegyes, Hung.	B7	26
Kuningan, Indon.	G6	50
Kunisaki, Japan	F4	40
Kunisaki-hantō, pen., Japan	F4	40
Kunja, Russia	D13	10
Kunja, stm., Russia	D13	10
Kunlong, Mya.	D8	46
Kunlun Mountains see Kunlun Shan, mts., China	A5	46
Kunlun Shan, mts., China	A5	46
Kunming, China	F5	36
Kunnamkulam, India	F2	53
Kunsan, Kor., S.	F7	38
Kunshan, China	F9	42
Kunting, China	G9	42
Kununurra, Austl.	C5	74
Kunwi, Kor., S.	C1	40
Kunya, Nig.	G6	64
Künzelsau, Ger.	G5	16
Kuopio, Fin.	E12	8
Kupa, stm., Eur.	E12	22
Kupang, Indon.	H7	44
Kupanskoe, Russia	D21	10
Kup'ians'k, Ukr.	E5	32
Kupino, Russia	D13	32
Kupiškis, Lith.	E7	10
Kupreanof Island, i., Ak., U.S.	E13	140
Kuqa, China	F14	32
Kuqa, China	F14	32
Kuragino, Russia	D16	32
Kuranec, Bela.	F9	10
Kurashiki, Japan	E6	40
Kurasiki see Kurashiki, Japan	E6	40
Kurauli, India	E7	54
Kuraymah, Sudan	D6	62
Kurayoshi, Japan	D6	40
Kurčatov, Russia	D5	32
Kürchatov, Kaz.	D13	32
Kurdistan, hist. reg., Asia	B5	56
Kurdistān see Kurdistan, hist. reg., Asia	B5	56
Kurdufān, state, Sudan	E6	62
Kurduvādi, India	B2	53
Kure, Japan	E5	40
Kurejka, stm., Russia	C7	34
Kuresaare, Est.	G10	8
Kurgan, Russia	C11	32
Kurgan-Tjube, Taj.	B10	56
Kuria, i., Kir.	C8	72
Kuria Muria Islands see Ḥallānīyah, Juzur al-, is., Oman	F8	56
Kuridala, Austl.	C3	76
Kurīgrām, Bngl.	F12	54
Kurikka, Fin.	E10	8
Kuril Islands see Kuril'skie ostrova, is., Russia	E19	30
Kuril'sk, Russia	B14	36
Kuril'skie ostrova (Kuril Islands), is., Russia	E19	30
Kuril Strait see Pervyj Kuril'skij proliv, strt., Russia	F20	34
Kuril Trench, unds.	E18	142
Kurinjippadi, India	F4	53
Kurinwás, stm., Nic.	F5	102
Kurjanovskaja, Russia	F19	8
Kurkliai, Lith.	E8	10
Kurmuk, Sudan	E6	62
Kurnool, India	D3	53
Kurobe, Japan	C10	40
Kurort Schmalkalden, Ger.	F6	16
Kurovskoe, Russia	E21	10
Kurow, N.Z.	G4	80
Kuršėnai, Lith.	D6	10
Kurseong, India	E12	54
Kürshim, Kaz.	E14	32
Kuršiu nerija (Kurššskaja kosa), spit, Eur.	E3	10
Kursk, Russia	D5	32
Kurskaja oblast', co., Russia	H19	10
Kurššskaja kosa (Kuršiu nerija), spit, Eur.	E3	10
Kuršumlija, Serb.	F8	26
Kurşunlu, Tur.	C16	28
Kūrtī, Sudan	D6	62
Kurtistown, Hi., U.S.	d6	78a
Kurtoğlu Burnu, c., Tur.	G11	28
Kuruktag, mts., China	C2	36
Kuruman, S. Afr.	E6	70
Kuruman, stm., S. Afr.	E5	70
Kurumanheuwels, mts., S. Afr.	E6	70
Kurume, Japan	F3	40
Kurumkan, Russia	F11	34
Kurunegala, Sri L.	H5	53
Kuruqi, China	B9	36
Kuryongp'o, Kor., S.	C2	40
Kuşadası, Tur.	F10	28
Kuşadası Körfezi, b., Tur.	F9	28
Kusan-ni, Kor., S.	B1	40
Kusawa Lake, l., Yk., Can.	D12	140
Kuş Gölü, l., Tur.	C10	28
Kuş Gölü Milli Parkı, p.o.i., Tur.	C10	28
Kushālgarh, India	G5	54
Kusheriki, Nig.	G6	64
Kushikino, Japan	H3	40
Kushima, Japan	H4	40
Kushiro, Japan	C16	38
Kushnytsia, Ukr.	A10	26
Kushtia, Bngl.	G12	54
Kushui, China	C3	36
Kusiro see Kushiro, Japan	C16	38
Kusiyāra, stm., Bngl.	F13	54
Kuskokwim, stm., Ak., U.S.	D7	140
Kuskokwim Bay, b., Ak., U.S.	E7	140
Kuskokwim Mountains, mts., Ak., U.S.	D8	140
Kuśmā, Nepal	D9	54
Kusmuryn, Kaz.	D10	32
Kusmuryn köli, l., Kaz.	D10	32
Kustanaj see Qostanay, Kaz.	D10	32
Kūstī, Sudan	E6	62
Kusu, Japan	F4	40
Kut, Ko, i., Thai.	G6	48
Kutabaru, Indon.	D3	50
Kutacane, Indon.	K3	48
Kütahya, Tur.	D13	28
Kütahya, state, Tur.	D12	28
Kutaisi, Geor.	F6	32
Kutch, Rann of (Kachchh, Rann of), reg., Asia	D2	46
Kutima, Russia	C19	32
Kutina, Cro.	E13	22
Kutiyāna, India	H3	54
Kutná Hora, Czech Rep.	G11	16
Kutno, Pol.	D15	16
Kutse Game Reserve, Bots.	C7	70
Kutu, D.R.C.	E3	66
Kutubdia Island, i., Bngl.	H13	54
Kutum, Sudan	E4	62
Kúty, Slov.	H13	16
Kuujjuaq, Qc., Can.	D17	106
Kuuli-Majak, Turkmen.	A7	56
Kuusamo, Fin.	D13	8
Kuusankoski, Fin.	F12	8
Kuvango, Ang.	C2	68
Kuvšinovo, Russia	C16	10
Kuwait see Al-Kuwayt, Kuw.	D6	56
Kuwait, ctry., Asia	D6	56
Kuwana, Japan	D9	40
Kuybyshev Reservoir see Kujbyševskoe vodohranilišče, res., Russia	D7	32
Kuye, stm., China	B4	42
Kuytun, Mount, mtn., Asia	E15	32
Kuženkino, Russia	C16	10
Kuz'miniči, Russia	F16	10
Kuz'movka, Russia	B16	32
Kuzneck, Russia	D7	32
Kuzneckij Alatau, mts., Russia	D15	32
Kuznecovka, Russia	D11	10
Kuznetsk see Kuzneck, Russia	D7	32
Kuzomen', Russia	C17	8
Kvænangen, b., Nor.	A9	8
Kvaløya, i., Nor.	B8	8
Kvaløya, i., Nor.	A10	8
Kvam, Nor.	F3	8
Kvarnbergsvattnet, l., Swe.	D5	8
Kvarner, b., Cro.	F11	22
Kvarnerić, b., Cro.	F11	22
Kverkfjöll, vol., Ice.	k31	8a
Kvichak Bay, b., Ak., U.S.	E8	140
Kwa, stm., D.R.C.	E3	66
Kwai see Khwae Noi, stm., Thai.	E4	48
Kwajalein, at., Marsh. Is.	C7	72
Kwakoegron, Sur.	B6	84
Kwamisa, mtn., Ghana	H4	64
Kwamouth, D.R.C.	E3	66
Kwando (Cuando), stm., Afr.	D3	68
Kwangchow see Guangzhou, China	J5	42
Kwangju, Kor., S.	G7	38
Kwango (Cuango), stm., Afr.	E3	66
Kwangsi Chuang see Guangxi, state, China	G6	36
Kwangtung see Guangdong, state, China	J6	42
KwaZulu-Natal, state, S. Afr.	F10	70
Kweichow see Guizhou, state, China	F6	36
Kweihwa see Hohhot, China	A4	42
Kweilin see Guilin, China	I4	42
Kweisui see Hohhot, China	A4	42
Kweiyang see Guiyang, China	H2	42
Kwekwe, Zimb.	D4	68
Kweneng, state, Bots.	C7	70
Kwenge (Caengo), stm., Afr.	B2	68
Kwethluk, Ak., U.S.	D7	140
Kwidzyn, Pol.	C14	16
Kwigillingok, Ak., U.S.	E7	140
Kwilu (Cuilo), stm., Afr.	F3	66
Kyabra, Austl.	F4	76
Kyabra Creek, stm., Austl.	E4	76
Kyabram, Austl.	K5	76
Kyaikkami, Mya.	D3	48
Kyaiklat, Mya.	D2	48
Kyaikto, Mya.	D3	48
Kya-in, Mya.	D4	48
Kyalite, Austl.	J4	76
Kyancutta, Austl.	F7	74
Ky Anh, Viet.	C8	48
Kyaukhnyat, Mya.	C3	48
Kyaukme, Mya.	A3	48
Kyaukpa, Mya.	F4	48
Kyaukpyu, Mya.	C1	48
Kyaukse, Mya.	B2	48
Kyauktaw, Mya.	D7	46
Kyaunggon, Mya.	D2	48
Kybartai, Lith.	F5	10
Kyebang-san, mtn., Kor., S.	B1	40
Kyeikdon, Mya.	E4	48
Kyidaunggan, Mya.	C3	48
Kyïv (Kiev), Ukr.	D4	32
Kyïvs'ke vodoskhovyshche, res., Ukr.	D4	32
Kyjov, Czech Rep.	G13	16
Kykotsmovi Village, Az., U.S.	H6	132
Kyle, Sk., Can.	D5	124
Kyle, S.D., U.S.	D10	126
Kyle, Lake, res., Zimb.	B10	70
Kyllíni, Grc.	F4	28
Kyneton, Austl.	K5	76
Kynšperk nad Ohří, Czech Rep.	F8	16
Kyoga, Lake, l., Ug.	D6	66
Kyogle, Austl.	G9	76
Kyŏngju, Kor., S.	D2	40
Kyŏngsan, Kor., S.	D1	40
Kyŏngsang-bukto, state, Kor., S.	C1	40
Kyŏngsang-namdo, state, Kor., S.	D1	40
Kyŏngsŏng-ŭp, Kor., N.	D8	38
Kyônkadun, Mya.	D2	48
Kyonpyaw, Mya.	D2	48
Kyōto, Japan	D8	40
Kyōto, state, Japan	D8	40
Kyparissía, Grc.	F4	28
Kyparissiakós Kólpos, b., Grc.	F4	28
Kyra, Russia	G11	34
Kyren, Russia	D18	32
Kyrgyzstan, ctry., Asia	F12	32
Kyritz, Ger.	D8	16
Kyrönjoki, stm., Fin.	E10	8
Kyrösjärvi, l., Fin.	F10	8
Kyštym, Russia	C10	32
Kýthira, Grc.	G5	28
Kýthira, i., Grc.	G5	28
Kýthnos, i., Grc.	F7	28
Kyundon, Mya.	B2	48
Kyungyi, i., Mya.	E3	48
Kyuquot, B.C., Can.	F3	138
Kyūshū, i., Japan	G2	40
Kyushu-Palau Ridge, unds.	H16	142
Kyūshū-sanchi, mts., Japan	G4	40
Kywong, Austl.	J6	76
Kyyjärvi, Fin.	E11	8
Kyyvesi, l., Fin.	E12	8
Kyzyl, Russia	D16	32
Kyzylbair, Turkmen.	B8	56
Kyzyl-Kija, Kyrg.	F12	32
Kyzylkum, des., Asia	F10	32
Kzyl-Orda see Qyzylorda, Kaz.	F11	32

L

Name	Map Ref.	Page
La Aguja, Cabo de, c., Col.	B4	86
La Albuera, Spain	F4	20
La Alcarria, reg., Spain	D8	20
La Algaba, Spain	G4	20

Name | Map Ref. | Page

La Almunia de Doña Godina, Spain C9 20
La Antigua, Salina, pl., Arg. D4 92
La Araucanía, state, Chile I1 92
Laascaanood, Som. C9 66
La Ascención, hill, Mex. C8 100
La Asunción, Ven. B10 86
Laau Point, c., Hi., U.S. b4 78a
Laayoune see El Aaiún, W. Sah. D2 64
La Azufrosa, Mex. F7 130
La Babia, Mex. A7 100
Labadieville, La., U.S. H8 122
La Baie, Qc., Can. B6 110
La Banda, Arg. C5 92
La Bandera, Cerro, mtn., Mex. C6 100
La Bañeza, Spain B4 20
La Barca, Mex. E7 100
La Barge, Wy., U.S. H16 136
Labasa, Fiji p19 79e
La Baule-Escoublac, Fr. G6 14
Labé, Gui. G2 64
Labe (Elbe), stm., Eur. C5 16
Labelle, Qc., Can. D2 110
La Belle, Mo., U.S. D5 120
Laberge, Lake, l., Yk., Can. C4 106
Labi, Bru. A9 50
Labian, Tanjong, c., Malay. A11 50
La Biche, stm., Ab., Can. B18 138
Labis, Malay. K6 48
La Bisbal d'Empordà, Spain C13 20
Łabiszyn, Pol. D13 16
La Blanca Grande, Laguna, l., Arg. I5 92
Labná, sci., Mex. B3 102
Laboe, Ger. B6 16
Laborde, Arg. F6 92
Laborie, St. Luc. m7 105c
La Bostonnais, Qc., Can. C4 110
Laboulaye, Arg. G6 92
Labrador, reg., Nf., Can. E18 106
Labrador Basin, unds. C9 144
Labrador City, Nf., Can. E17 106
Labrador Sea, s., N.A. D17 94
Lábrea, Braz. E5 84
La Brea, Trin. s12 105f
Labuan, Malay. A9 50
Labuan, state, Malay. A9 50
Labuan, Pulau, i., Malay. A9 50
Labuchongshan, mts., China C10 54
La Bufadora, Mex. L9 134
Labuhan, Indon. G4 50
Labuhanbajo, Indon. H11 50
Labuhanbilik, Indon. B2 50
Labuhanpandan, Indon. H10 50
Labuhanruku, Indon. B1 50
Labuk, stm., Malay. H1 52
Labuk, Telukan, b., Malay. G1 52
Labu Kananga, Indon. H10 50
Labutta, Mya. D2 48
Labytnangi, Russia A11 32
Laç, Alb. C13 24
Lača, ozero, l., Russia F18 8
Lac-à-Beauce, Qc., Can. C4 110
La Cadena, Mex. I3 130
La Calera, Chile F2 92
La Campana, Spain G5 20
La Canada Flintridge, Ca., U.S. I7 134
La Candelaria, Arg. C5 92
La Candelaria, Mex. C1 130
Lacantum, stm., Mex. D2 102
La Capelle-en-Thiérache, Fr. D12 14
La Carlota, Arg. F6 92
La Carlota, Phil. E4 52
La Carolina, Spain F7 20
Lacaune, Fr. F8 18
Laccadive Islands see Lakshadweep, is., India F3 46
Lac-Édouard, Qc., Can. C4 110
La Ceiba, Hond. E4 102
Lacepede Bay, b., Austl. K2 76
Lac-Etchemin, Qc., Can. D6 110
Lacey, Wa., U.S. C4 136
Lac-Frontière, Qc., Can. D6 110
La Chapelle-d'Angillon, Fr. G11 14
La Châtaigneraie, Fr. C5 18
La Chaux-de-Fonds, Switz. C3 22
Lachhmangarh Sīkar, India E5 54
Lachine, ngh., Qc., Can. E3 110
Lachlan, stm., Austl. J5 76
La Chorrera, Col. H5 86
La Chorrera, Pan. H8 102
Lachute, Qc., Can. E2 110
Laçi see Laç, Alb. C13 24
La Ciénaga, Arg. C4 92
La Ciotat, Fr. F11 18
La Citadelle, hist., Haiti C11 102
La Ciudad, Mex. D6 100
Lackawanna, N.Y., U.S. B6 114
Lac La Biche, Ab., Can. B18 138
Lac la Hache, B.C., Can. E9 138
Laclede, Id., U.S. B10 136
Laclede, Mo., U.S. E4 120
La Clotilde, Arg. C7 92
Lac-Mégantic, Qc., Can. E6 110
La Colorada, Mex. A3 100
La Coma, Mex. C9 100
Lacombe, Ab., Can. D17 138
Lacombe, La., U.S. G9 122
Lacona, Ia., U.S. C4 120
La Concepción, Pan. H6 102
La Concepción, Ven. B5 86
Laconi, Italy E2 24
Laconia, N.H., U.S. G5 110
Laconia, Gulf of see Lakonikós Kólpos, b., Grc. G5 28
La Consulta, Arg. F3 92
Lacoochee, Fl., U.S. H3 116
La Coruña see A Coruña, Spain A2 20
La Coruña see A Coruña, co., Spain A2 20
La Coste, Tx., U.S. E9 130
La Courtine, Fr. D8 18
La Crescent, Mn., U.S. H7 118
La Crosse, Ks., U.S. C9 128
La Crosse, Va., U.S. H7 114
Lacrosse, Wa., U.S. D9 136
La Crosse, Wi., U.S. H7 118
La Cruz, Arg. D9 92
La Cruz, Col. G3 86
La Cruz, Mex. G2 130
La Cruz de Río Grande, Nic. F5 102
Lac Seul, On., Can. A6 118
La Cuesta, P.R. B2 104a
La Cumbre, Arg. E5 92
La Cygne, Ks., U.S. F3 120
Ladākh, hist. reg., Pak. A6 54
Ladākh Range, mts., Asia A6 54
Ladder Creek, stm., Ks., U.S. C7 128
Laddonia, Mo., U.S. E6 120
La Désirade, i., Guad. h6 105c
La Digue, i., Sey. j13 69b
Ladismith, S. Afr. H5 70
Ladispoli, Italy I8 22
Lādīz, Iran D9 56
Ladner, B.C., Can. G7 138
Lādnūn, India E5 54
Ladoga, In., U.S. I3 112
Ladoga, Lake see Ladožskoe ozero, l., Russia F14 8
La Dorada, Col. E4 86
La Dormida, Arg. F4 92
Ladožskoe ozero (Ladoga, Lake), l., Russia F14 8
Laduškin, Russia F3 10
Ladva-Vetka, Russia F15 8
Lady Ann Strait, strt., Nu., Can. B10 141
Lady Barron, Austl. n14 77a
Ladybrand, S. Afr. F8 70
Lady Elliot Island, i., Austl. E9 76
Ladysmith, B.C., Can. H7 138
Ladysmith, S. Afr. F9 70
Ladysmith, Wi., U.S. F7 118
Lae, Pap. N. Gui. b4 79a
La Encantada, Mex. C8 100
La Escondida, Mex. H8 130
La Esmeralda, Mex. B7 100
Læsø, i., Den. H4 8
La Esperanza, Cuba A5 102
La Esperanza, Hond. E3 102
La Esperanza, Mex. H4 130
La Esperanza, P.R. B3 104a
La Estrada see A Estrada, Spain B2 20
Lafa, China C7 38
La Falda, Arg. E5 92
La Farge, Wi., U.S. H8 118
Lafayette, Al., U.S. E13 122
Lafayette, Ca., U.S. F3 134
Lafayette, Co., U.S. A3 128
Lafayette, Ga., U.S. C13 122
Lafayette, In., U.S. H3 112
Lafayette, La., U.S. G6 122
Lafayette, Tn., U.S. H11 120
Lafayette, Mount, mtn., N.H., U.S. F5 110
La Feria, Tx., U.S. H10 130
La Ferté-Bernard, Fr. F9 14
La Ferté-Saint-Aubin, Fr. G10 14
Lafia, Nig. H6 64
Lafiagi, Nig. H6 64
Lafleche, Sk., Can. E7 124
La Flèche, Fr. G8 14
La Florida, Guat. D2 102
La Foa, N. Cal. m15 79d
La Follette, Tn., U.S. H1 114
Lafourche, Bayou, stm., La., U.S. H8 122
La Fragua, Arg. C5 92
La Fría, Ven. C5 86
La Fuente de San Esteban, Spain D4 20
La Galite, i., Tun. G2 24
La Gallareta, Arg. D7 92
Lagan, stm., Swe. E3 8
Lagarto, Braz. F7 88
Lagawe, Phil. B3 52
Lage, China D10 54
Lågen, stm., Nor. F4 8
Lages, Braz. C12 92
Laghmān, state, Afg. A3 54
Laghouat, Alg. C5 64
Lagkadás, Grc. C5 28
Lagoa da Prata, Braz. K3 88
Lagoa Vermelha, Braz. D12 92
Lago da Pedra, Braz. C3 88
Lago Kolonie, Aruba p20 104g
Lagolândia, Braz. H1 88
Lagonegro, Italy D9 24
Lagonoy Gulf, b., Phil. D4 52
Lago Posadas, Arg. I2 90
Lagos, Nig. H5 64
Lagos, Port. G2 20
Lagos de Moreno, Mex. E8 100
La Gouèra, W. Sah. E1 64
La Goulette, Tun. H4 24
Lago Viedma, Arg. I2 90
La Granadella, Spain C11 20
La Grande, Or., U.S. E8 136
La Grande Deux, Réservoir, res., Qc., Can. E15 106
La Grande Quatre, Réservoir, res., Qc., Can. E16 106
LaGrange, Austl. C4 74
La Grange, Ga., U.S. D13 122
La Grange, Ky., U.S. F12 120
La Grange, Mo., U.S. D6 120
La Grange, Tx., U.S. E11 130
Lagrange, Wy., U.S. F8 126
Lagrange Bay, b., Austl. C4 74
La Gran Sabana, pl., Ven. E10 86
La Guadeloupe, Qc., Can. E6 110
La Guajira, state, Col. G11 102
La Guajira, Península de, pen., S.A. A6 86
La Guardia, Arg. D5 92
La Guardia, Bol. C4 90
La Guardia see A Guardia, Spain C1 20
La Guerche-sur-l'Aubois, Fr. G11 14
Laguiole, Fr. E8 18
Laguna, Braz. D13 92
Laguna, N.M., U.S. H9 132
Laguna, Ilha da, i., Braz. D7 84
Laguna Beach, Ca., U.S. J8 134
Laguna Dam, dam, U.S. K2 132
Laguna de Jaco, Mex. G4 130
Laguna Larga, Arg. E6 92
Laguna Paiva, Arg. E7 92
Lagunas, Peru E2 84
Lagunas de Chacagua, Parque Nacional, p.o.i., Mex. H9 100
Lagunillas, Bol. C4 90
Laha, China B9 36
La Habana (Havana), Cuba A6 102
Lahad Datu, Malay. A11 50
Lahad Datu, Telukan, b., Malay. A11 50
La Harpe, Il., U.S. K7 118
La Harpe, Ks., U.S. G2 120
Lahat, Indon. E3 50
Lahdenpohja, Russia F14 8
Lahemaa rahrus, p.o.i., Est. G11 8
Lahewa, Indon. L3 48
Lahfân, Bîr, well, Egypt G4 58
Laḥij, Yemen G5 56
Lāhījān, Iran B7 56
Lahnstein, Ger. F3 16
Laholm, Swe. H5 8
Lahontan Reservoir, res., Nv., U.S. D6 134
Lahore, Pak. C5 54
La Horqueta, Col. F5 86
Lahr, Ger. H3 16
Lahti, Fin. F11 8
La Huerta, N.M., U.S. B3 130
Laḫva, Bela. H10 10
Laï, Chad F3 62
Laiagam, Pap. N. Gui. b3 79a
Laibin, China J3 42
Lai Chau, Viet. A6 48
Laichow Bay see Laizhou Wan, b., China C8 42
Laifeng, China G3 42
L'Aigle, Fr. F9 14
Laihia, Fin. E9 8
Laïmbélé, Mont, mtn., Vanuatu k16 79d
Laingsburg, S. Afr. H5 70
Laingsburg, Mi., U.S. B1 114
Lainioälven, stm., Swe. C10 8
Lainsitz see Lužnice, stm., Eur. G10 16
Laird Hill, Tx., U.S. E3 122
Lais, Indon. E3 50
Lais, Indon. C12 50
Lais, Phil. G5 52
Laitila, Fin. F9 8
Laiwu, China C7 42
Laixi, China C9 42
Laiyang, China C9 42
Laizhou Bay see Laizhou Wan, b., China C8 42
Laizhou Wan (Laizhou Bay), b., China C8 42
Laja, stm., Chile H2 92
Laja, Laguna de la, l., Chile H2 92
Laja, Salto del, wtfl., Chile H2 92
La Jara, Co., U.S. D2 128
La Jara, reg., Spain E5 20
La Jara Canyon, p., N.M., U.S. G9 132
La Jarita, Mex. F4 130
Lajas, P.R. B1 104a
Laje, Braz. G6 88
Lajeado, Braz. D11 92
Lajedo, Braz. E7 88
Lajes, Braz. C7 88
Lajinha, Braz. K5 88
Laji Shan, mts., China D5 36
Lajosmizse, Hung. B6 26
Lajta (Leitha), stm., Eur. H12 16
La Junta, Co., U.S. D5 128
Lakar Kūh, mtn., Iran C8 56
Lakatoro, Vanuatu k16 79d
Lake, Ms., U.S. E9 122
Lake Alfred, Fl., U.S. H4 116
Lake Andes, S.D., U.S. D14 126
Lake Arthur, La., U.S. G6 122
Lakeba, i., Fiji q20 79e
Lakeba Passage, strt., Fiji q20 79e
Lake Benton, Mn., U.S. G2 118
Lake Brownwood, Tx., U.S. C8 130
Lake Cargelligo, Austl. I6 76
Lake Charles, La., U.S. G5 122
Lake Chelan National Recreation Area, p.o.i., Wa., U.S. B6 136
Lake City, Ar., U.S. B8 122
Lake City, Co., U.S. E9 132
Lake City, Fl., U.S. F3 116
Lake City, Mi., U.S. D4 112
Lake City, Pa., U.S. B5 114
Lake City, S.C., U.S. C6 116
Lake City, Tn., U.S. H1 114
Lake Cowichan, B.C., Can. H6 138
Lake Crystal, Mn., U.S. G4 118
Lake Dallas, Tx., U.S. A10 130
Lake Delton, Wi., U.S. H9 118
Lake District National Park, p.o.i., Eng., U.K. G9 12
Lake Elsinore, Ca., U.S. J8 134
Lakefield, On., Can. D11 112
Lakefield, Mn., U.S. H3 118
Lake Forest, Il., U.S. F2 112
Lake Fork Reservoir, res., Tx., U.S. E3 122
Lake Geneva, Wi., U.S. B9 120
Lake George, N.Y., U.S. G3 110
Lake Harbor, Fl., U.S. J5 116
Lake Havasu City, Az., U.S. I2 132
Lake Helen, Fl., U.S. H4 116
Lakehurst, N.J., U.S. D11 114
Lake Jackson, Tx., U.S. E12 130
Lake King, Austl. F3 74
Lakeland, Fl., U.S. H3 116
Lakeland, Ga., U.S. E2 116
Lake Linden, Mi., U.S. D10 118
Lake Louise, Ab., Can. E14 138
Lake Mead National Recreation Area, p.o.i., U.S. G2 132
Lake Mills, Wi., U.S. A8 120
Lake Minchumina, Ak., U.S. D9 140
Lake Mohawk see Sparta, N.J., U.S. C11 114
Lake Nash, Austl. D7 74
Lake Norden, S.D., U.S. C15 126
Lake Oswego, Or., U.S. E4 136
Lake Ozark, Mo., U.S. F5 120
Lake Park, Fl., U.S. J5 116
Lake Park, Ia., U.S. H3 118
Lake Placid, Fl., U.S. I4 116
Lake Placid, N.Y., U.S. F3 110
Lake Pleasant, N.Y., U.S. G2 110
Lakeport, Ca., U.S. D3 134
Lakeport, Mi., U.S. E7 112
Lake Preston, S.D., U.S. C15 126
Lakes Entrance, Austl. K7 76
Lakeshore, Ms., U.S. G9 122
Lakeside, Ca., U.S. K8 134
Lakeside, Mt., U.S. B12 136
Lake Stevens, Wa., U.S. B4 136
Laketown, Ut., U.S. B5 132
Lake View, Ar., U.S. C8 122
Lake View, Ia., U.S. B2 120
Lakeview, Mi., U.S. E4 112
Lakeview, Mi., U.S. F4 112
Lakeview, Oh., U.S. D2 114
Lakeview, Or., U.S. A5 134
Lake Village, Ar., U.S. D7 122
Lakeville, Mn., U.S. G5 118
Lake Wales, Fl., U.S. I4 116
Lake Wilson, Mn., U.S. G2 118
Lakewood, Co., U.S. B3 128
Lakewood, N.J., U.S. D11 114
Lakewood, Oh., U.S. C4 114
Lakewood, Wa., U.S. C4 136
Lakewood, Wi., U.S. C1 112
Lakewood Park, N.D., U.S. F15 124
Lake Worth, Fl., U.S. J5 116
Lakhdaria, Alg. H14 20
Lākheri, India F5 54
Lakhīmpur, India D8 54
Lakhipur, India F14 54
Lakhnādon, India G7 54
Lakinsk, Russia H18 8
Lakonikós Kólpos (Laconia, Gulf of), b., Grc. G5 28
Lakota, N.D., U.S. F15 124
Laksefjorden, b., Nor. A12 8
Lakshadweep, state, India F3 46
Lakshadweep, is., India F3 46
Lakshadweep Sea, s., Asia G3 46
Lākshām, Bngl. G13 54
Lakshmeshwar, India D2 53
La Laja, Chile H1 92
Lāla Mūsa, Pak. B4 54
Lâlapaşa, Tur. B9 28
L'Albufera, l., Spain E10 20
Laleham, Austl. D7 76
La Leona, Mex. I6 130
La Leonesa, Arg. C8 92
Lālganj, India F10 54
Lalībela, Eth. E7 62
La Libertad, Guat. D2 102
La Ligua, Chile F2 92
La Lima, Hond. E3 102
Lalin, stm., China B7 38
Lalindi, Indon. I12 50
La Línea de la Concepción, Spain H5 20
Lalitpur, India F7 54
Lalitpur, Nepal E10 54
Lalla Khedidja, Tamgout de, mtn., Alg. H14 20
Lālmanir Hāt, Bngl. F12 54
La Loche, Sk., Can. D9 106
La Lora, plat., Spain B7 20
La Louvière, Bel. D13 14
L'Alpe-d'Huez, Fr. D12 18
Lālpur, India G2 54
Lālsot, India E6 54
La Luz, Mex. C10 100
La Luz, Mex. I10 130
Lama, ozero, l., Russia C7 34
La Macarena, Parque Nacional, p.o.i., Col. F5 86
La Macarena, Serranía de, mts., Col. F5 86
La Maddalena, Italy C3 24
La Madrid, Arg. C5 92
Lamadrid, Mex. G6 130
La Magdalena, Mex. H1 130
Lama-Kara, Togo H5 64
La Malbaie, Qc., Can. C6 110
La Mancha, reg., Spain E8 20
Lamandau, stm., Indon. E7 50
Lamap, Vanuatu k16 79d
Lamar, Co., U.S. C6 128
Lamar, Mo., U.S. G3 120
Lamarche, Fr. F14 14
La Marmora, Punta, mtn., Italy D3 24
La Maroma, Mex. F7 130
La Marque, Tx., U.S. H4 122
La Marsa, Tun. H4 24
La Martre, Qc., Can. A10 110
Lamas, Peru E2 84
Lamballe, Fr. F6 14
Lambaréné, Gabon E1 66
Lambari, stm., Braz. J3 88
Lambayeque, Peru E2 84
Lambay Island, i., Ire. H7 12
Lambert, Ms., U.S. C8 122
Lambert, Mt., U.S. G9 124
Lambert, Cape, c., Pap. N. Gui. a5 79a
Lambert Glacier, ice, Ant. C11 81
Lambert Land, reg., Grnld. B21 141
Lamberton, Mn., U.S. G3 118
Lambertsbaai see Lambert's Bay, S. Afr. H3 70
Lambert's Bay, S. Afr. H3 70
Lambton, Cape, c., N.T., Can. A6 106
Lame Deer, Mt., U.S. B6 126
La Media Luna, Arrecifes de, rf., Hond. E6 102
Lamentin, Guad. h5 105c
Lamèque, N.B., Can. C12 110
Lamèque, Île, i., N.B., Can. C12 110
La Merced, Arg. B5 92
La Merced, Arg. D5 92
Lameroo, Austl. J3 76
La Mesa, Ca., U.S. K8 134
Lamesa, Tx., U.S. B6 130
Lamía, Grc. E5 28
Lamine, stm., Mo., U.S. F5 120
Lamington National Park, p.o.i., Austl. G9 76
La Misión, Mex. K9 134
Lamitan, Phil. G4 52
Lamlam, Mount, hill, Guam j9 78c
Lammeulo, Indon. J2 48
La Moille, Il., U.S. C8 120
Lamoille, Nv., U.S. C1 132
Lamoille, stm., Vt., U.S. F4 110
Lamon Bay, b., Phil. C4 52
Lamone, stm., Italy F9 22
Lamongan, Indon. G8 50
Lamoni, Ia., U.S. D3 120
Lamont, Ca., U.S. H6 134
Lamont, Ia., U.S. I7 118
Lamont, Ok., U.S. E11 128
La Monte, Mo., U.S. F4 120
La Mothe, Lac, l., Qc., Can. B5 110
La Mothe-Achard, Fr. H7 14
Lamotrek, at., Micron. C5 72
Lamotte-Beuvron, Fr. G10 14
Lampang, Thai. C4 48
Lampasas, Tx., U.S. C9 130
Lampasas, stm., Tx., U.S. C9 130
Lampazos de Naranjo, Mex. B8 100
Lampedusa, Isola di, i., Italy I6 24
Lampertheim, Ger. G4 16
Lamphun, Thai. C4 48
Lampman, Sk., Can. E11 124
Lampung, state, Indon. F4 50
Lamskoe, Russia H21 10
Lamu, Kenya E8 66
La Mure, Fr. E11 18
Lan', stm., Bela. H10 10
Lana, Italy D8 22
Lāna'i, i., Hi., U.S. c4 78a
Lanai City, Hi., U.S. c4 78a
Lanaihale, mtn., Hi., U.S. c5 78a
Lanalhue, Lago, l., Chile I1 92
Lanark, On., Can. C13 112
Lanark, Scot., U.K. F9 12
Lanbi Kyun, i., Mya. G4 48
Lancang, China A4 48
Lancang see Mekong, stm., Asia D9 46
Lancaster, Eng., U.K. G10 12
Lancaster, Ca., U.S. I7 134
Lancaster, Mn., U.S. C2 118
Lancaster, Mo., U.S. D5 120
Lancaster, N.H., U.S. F5 110
Lancaster, Oh., U.S. E3 114
Lancaster, Pa., U.S. D9 114
Lancaster, S.C., U.S. B5 116
Lancaster, Tx., U.S. E2 122
Lancaster, Va., U.S. G9 114
Lancaster, Wi., U.S. B7 120
Lancaster Sound, strt., Nu., Can. C8 141
Lance Creek, Wy., U.S. D8 126
Lancelin, Austl. F2 74
Lanchou see Lanzhou, China D5 36
Lanchow see Lanzhou, China D5 36
Lanciano, Italy H11 22
Lancun, China C9 42
Łańcut, Pol. F18 16
Lândana, Ang. B1 68
Landau an der Isar, Ger. H8 16
Landau in der Pfalz, Ger. G4 16
Landeck, Aus. C7 22
Lander, Wy., U.S. E4 126
Landerneau, Fr. F4 14
Landes, state, Fr. F5 18
Landes, reg., Fr. E5 18
Landete, Spain E9 20
Landis, Sk., Can. B5 124
Lando, S.C., U.S. B4 116
Land O'Lakes, Wi., U.S. E9 118
Landösjön, l., Swe. E5 8
Landri Sales, Braz. D3 88
Landrum, S.C., U.S. A3 116
Landsborough Creek, stm., Austl. D5 76
Land's End, c., Eng., U.K. K7 12
Landshut, Ger. H7 16
Landskrona, Swe. I5 8
Lane, mth., Fr. G9 14
Lanesboro, Mn., U.S. H6 118
Lanett, Al., U.S. E13 122
Lanezi Lake, l., B.C., Can. C10 138
La'nga Co, l., China C8 54
Langa-Langa, D.R.C. E3 66
Langbank, Sk., Can. D11 124
Lang Bay, B.C., Can. G6 138
Langdale, Al., U.S. E13 122
Langdon, N.D., U.S. F15 124
Langeac, Fr. D9 18
Langeberg, mts., S. Afr. H5 70
Langeland, i., Den. I4 8
Langenhagen, Ger. D5 16
Langenthal, Switz. C4 22
Langfang, China B7 42
Langford, S.D., U.S. B15 126
Langgam, Indon. C2 50
Langham, Sk., Can. B6 124
Langhe, hist. reg., Italy F5 22
Langholm, Scot., U.K. F9 12
Langjökull, ice, Ice. k29 8a
Langkawi, Pulau, i., Malay. I4 48
Langley, B.C., Can. G8 138
Langley, Ok., U.S. A3 122
Langlo, stm., Austl. E5 76
Langnau im Emmental, Switz. C4 22
Langogne, Fr. E9 18
Langøya, i., Nor. B6 8
Langping, China F4 42
Langreo, Spain A5 20
Langres, Fr. G14 14
Langruth, Mb., Can. D15 124
Langsa, Indon. J3 48
Langsa, Teluk, b., Indon. J4 48
Langshan, China A2 42
Lang Son, Viet. B8 48
Lang Suan, Thai. H4 48
Languedoc, hist. reg., Fr. F8 18
L'Anguille, stm., Ar., U.S. C8 122
Langxi, China F8 42
Langzhong, China F1 42
Lanigan, Sk., Can. C8 124
Lanigan Creek, stm., Sk., Can. C9 124
Lanín, Volcán, vol., S.A. G2 90
Länkäran, Azer. B6 56
Länkipohja, Fin. F11 8
Lannemezan, Fr. F6 18
Lannion, Fr. F5 14
Lanping, China F4 36
Lansdowne, India D7 54
Lansdowne House, On., Can. E13 106
L'Anse, Mi., U.S. B1 112
Lansing, Ia., U.S. H7 118
Lansing, Mi., U.S. B1 114
Länsi-Suomi, state, Fin. E10 8
Lantana, Fl., U.S. J5 116
Lantau Island, i., China J6 42
Lanta Yai, Ko, i., Thai. I4 48
Lantian, China D3 42
La Nurra, reg., Italy D2 24
Lanusei, Italy E3 24
Lanxi, China G8 42
Lan Yü, i., Tai. J9 42
Lanzhou, China D5 36
Lanzo Torinese, Italy E4 22
Lao, stm., Thai. C4 48
Laoag, Phil. A3 52
Laoang, Phil. D5 52
Lao Cai, Viet. A6 48
Laodao, stm., China G5 42
Laofu, China C3 38
Laoha, stm., China C4 38
Laohekou, China E4 42
Laohokow see Laohekou, China E4 42
Laois, state, Ire. I5 12
Lao Ling, mtn., China C9 38
Laon, Fr. E12 14
Laona, Wi., U.S. F10 118
La Orchila, Isla, i., Ven. B8 86
La Oroya, Peru F2 84
Laos, ctry., Asia C6 48
Laoshan Wan, b., China C9 42
Lapa, Braz. B13 92
Lapai, Nig. H6 64
Lapalisse, Fr. C9 18
La Palma, Col. E4 86
La Palma, Pan. H8 102
La Palma, Pan. I7 102
La Palma del Condado, Spain G4 20
La Paloma, Ur. G10 92
La Pampa, state, Arg. G3 90
La Paragua, Ven. D10 86
La Pasión, stm., Guat. D2 102
La Paya, Parque Nacional, p.o.i., Col. G4 86
La Paz, Arg. E8 92
La Paz, Arg. F4 92
La Paz, Bol. C3 90
La Paz, Col. B5 86
La Paz, Hond. E4 102
La Paz, Mex. C3 100
La Paz, Mex. D8 100
La Paz, Ur. G9 92
La Paz, Bahía de, b., Mex. C3 100
La Perla, Mex. A6 100
La Perouse, Bahía, b., Chile e30 78l
La Perouse Strait, strt., Asia B13 36
La Pesca, Mex. D10 100
La Piedad de Cabadas, Mex. E7 100
La Pine, Or., U.S. G5 136
La Place, La., U.S. G8 122
Lap Lae, Thai. D4 48
Lapland, hist. reg., Eur. C11 8
La Plata, Arg. G8 92
La Plata, Col. F4 86
La Plata, Md., U.S. F9 114
La Plata, Mo., U.S. D5 120
La Plata Peak, mtn., Co., U.S. D10 132
La Pobla de Segur, Spain B11 20
La Pocatière, Qc., Can. C6 110
Lapominka, Russia D19 8
Laporte, Co., U.S. G7 126
La Porte, In., U.S. G3 112
Laporte, Pa., U.S. C9 114
La Porte City, Ia., U.S. B5 120
La Potherie, Lac, l., Qc., Can. D16 106
La Poza Grande, Mex. C2 100
Lappajärvi, l., Fin. E10 8
Lappeenranta, Fin. F12 8
Lappi, state, Fin. C12 8
Laprida, Arg. D5 92
Laprida, Arg. H7 92
La Pryor, Tx., U.S. F8 130
Lapta, N. Cyp. C4 58
Laptev Sea see Laptevyh, more, s., Russia B4 32
Laptevyh, more, s., Russia B4 32
La Puebla de Montalbán, Spain E6 20
La Puerta, Arg. D5 92
La Puerta de Cabrera, Mex. H2 130
Lapu-Lapu, Phil. E4 52
La Purísima, Mex. B2 100
Lăpuş, Rom. B11 26
Lapwai, Id., U.S. D10 136
La Quiaca, Arg. D3 90
L'Áquila, Italy H10 22
Lār, Iran D7 56
Lara, state, Ven. B7 86
Laracha, Spain A2 20
Larache, Mor. B3 64
Laramie, Wy., U.S. F7 126
Laramie, stm., U.S. E8 126
Laramie Mountains, mts., Wy., U.S. F7 126
Laramie Peak, mtn., Wy., U.S. E7 126
Laranjal, Braz. K4 88
Laranjeiras, Braz. F7 88
Laranjeiras do Sul, Braz. B11 92
Larantuka, Indon. G7 44
Larap, Phil. C4 52
Larat, Indon. G9 44
Larat, Pulau, i., Indon. G9 44
Larche Pass, p., Eur. E12 18
Larchwood, Ia., U.S. H2 118
Larde, Moz. D6 68
L'Ardoise, N.S., Can. E16 110
Laredo, Spain A7 20
Laredo, Tx., U.S. G8 130
La Reforma, Mex. C4 100
Lares, P.R. B2 104a
Larga, Mol. A13 26
Larga, Laguna, l., Tx., U.S. G10 130
Largo, Fl., U.S. I3 116
Largo, Cañon, p., N.M., U.S. G9 132
Largo, Cayo, i., Cuba B7 102
Largs, Scot., U.K. F8 12
Lariang, stm., Indon. D11 50
Larimore, N.D., U.S. G16 124
Larino, Italy I11 22
Lario see Como, Lago di, l., Italy D6 22
La Rioja, Arg. D4 92
La Rioja, state, Arg. D4 92
La Rioja, state, Spain B8 20
Lárisa, Grc. D5 28
Larjak, Russia B14 32
Lārkāna, Pak. D10 56
Lárnakos, Kólpos, b., Cyp. D4 58
Larne, N. Ire., U.K. G7 12
Larned, Ks., U.S. C9 128
La Robla, Spain B5 20
La Rochefoucauld, Fr. D6 18
La Rochelle, Fr. C4 18
La Roche-sur-Yon, Fr. H7 14
La Roda, Spain E8 20
La Romaine, Qc., Can. i21 107a
La Romana, Dom. Rep. C13 102
La Ronge, Sk., Can. D10 106
Laroquebrou, Fr. D8 18
Larose, Pointe, c., Mart. k7 105c
Larroque, Arg. F8 92
Larrys River, N.S., Can. E15 110
Larsen Ice Shelf, ice, Ant. B34 81
La Rubia, Arg. E7 92
La Rue, Oh., U.S. D2 114
Larvik, Nor. G3 8
Larzac, Causse du, plat., Fr. F9 18
La Sabanilla, Mex. C8 100
La Sal, Ut., U.S. E7 132
La Salle, Co., U.S. G8 126
La Salle, Il., U.S. C8 120
La Salle, stm., Mb., Can. E16 124
Lasan, Indon. C9 50
Las Animas, Co., U.S. C5 128
Las Arenas, P.R. B1 104a
La Sarre, Qc., Can. F15 106
Las Arrias, Arg. E6 92
Las Ballenas, Canal de, strt., Mex. G6 98
Las Breñas, Arg. C7 92
Las Cabezas de San Juan, Spain G5 20
Las Cabras, Chile G2 92
Lascano, Ur. F10 92
Las Casitas, mtn., Mex. D4 100
Las Catitas, Arg. F3 92
Las Choapas, Mex. G11 100
Las Chorreras, Mex. A6 100
Las Cruces, N.M., U.S. K10 132
Las Cuatas, Mex. D1 130
Las Cuevas, Mex. A8 100
Las Cumaraguas, Ven. p20 104g
La Selle, Morne, mtn., Haiti C11 102
La Serena, Chile D2 92
La Serena, reg., Spain F5 20
La Seu d'Urgell, Spain B12 20
La Seyne, Fr. F11 18
La Seyne, Fr. F11 18
Las Flores, Arg. G8 92
Las Flores, P.R. B3 104a
Las Flores, Arroyo, stm., Arg. H7 92
Las Garcitas, Arg. C7 92
Las Guayabas, Mex. C10 100
Lashburn, Sk., Can. A4 124
Las Heras, Arg. F3 92
Las Heras, Arg. I3 90
Lashio, Mya. A3 48
Lashkar Gāh, Afg. C9 56
Las Hormigas, Mex. C9 100
Lasia, Pulau, i., Indon. K3 48
Łasin, Pol. C15 16
La Sirena, Ven. p20 104g
Łaskarzew, Pol. E17 16
Las Lajas, Arg. I2 92
Las Lajas, Pan. H7 102
Las Lomitas, Arg. B7 92
Las Malvinas, Arg. G3 92
Las Mareas, P.R. C3 104a
Las Margaritas, Mex. G13 100
Las Marianas, Arg. G8 92
Las Marías, P.R. B1 104a
Las Minas, Cerro, mtn., Hond. E3 102
Las Nopaleras, Cerro, mtn., Mex. C7 100
La Solana, Spain F7 20
Las Ovejas, Arg. H2 92
Las Palmas, Arg. C8 92
Las Palmas, P.R. C3 104a
Las Palomas, Mex. F9 98
La Spezia, Italy F6 22
Las Piedras, P.R. B4 104a
Las Piedras, Ur. G9 92
Las Piedras, stm., Peru F3 84
Las Plumas, Arg. H3 90
Lasqueti Island, i., B.C., Can. G6 138
Las Rosas, Arg. F7 92
Las Rosas, Mex. G12 100
Lassance, Braz. I3 88
Lassen Peak, vol., Ca., U.S. C4 134
Lassen Volcanic National Park, p.o.i., Ca., U.S. C4 134
L'Assomption, stm., Qc., Can. D3 110
Las Tablas, Pan. I7 102
Las Tinajas, Arg. C6 92
Last Mountain Lake, l., Sk., Can. C8 124
Las Tórtolas, Cerro (Tórtolas, Cerro de las), mtn., S.A. D2 92
Lastoursville, Gabon E2 66
Las Tunas, Cuba B9 102
Las Tunas Grandes, Laguna, l., Arg. H6 92
Las Varas, Mex. E6 100
Las Varas, Mex. G8 98
Las Varillas, Arg. E6 92
Las Vegas, P.R. B1 104a
Las Vegas, N.M., U.S. F3 128
Las Vegas, Nv., U.S. G1 132
Las Vegas, Ven. C7 86
Latacunga, Ec. H2 86
La Tagua, Col. H4 86
Latakia see Al-Lādhiqīyah, Syria C6 58
Lata Mountain, vol., Am. Sam. h13 79c
Latehar, India G10 54
La Teste-de-Buch, Fr. E4 18
Lāthi, India H3 54
Lathrop, Mo., U.S. E3 120
Latimer, Ia., U.S. I5 118
Latina, Italy C6 24
Latisana, Italy E10 22
Latium see Lazio, state, Italy B6 24
Latjuga, Russia D23 8
La Torrecilla, mtn., P.R. B3 104a
La Tortuga, Isla, i., Ven. B9 86
Latouche Treville, Cape, c., Austl. C4 74
La Tour-d'Auvergne, Fr. D8 18
La Trimouille, Fr. C7 18
La Trinidad, Nic. F4 102
La Trinidad, Phil. B3 52
La Trinidad de Orichuna, Ven. D7 86
La Trinité, Mart. k6 105c
Latrobe, Pa., U.S. D6 114
Latta, S.C., U.S. B6 116
La Tuque, Qc., Can. C4 110
Lātūr, India B3 53
Latvia, ctry., Eur. D7 10
Lau, Nig. H7 64
Lauchhammer, Ger. E9 16
Lauenburg, Ger. C6 16
Lauf an der Pegnitz, Ger. G7 16
Lauge Koch Kyst, cst., Grnld. B13 141
Laughlin, Nv., U.S. H2 132
Laughlin Peak, mtn., N.M., U.S. E4 128
Lau Group, is., Fiji p20 79e
Lauis see Lugano, Switz. D5 22
Laukaa, Fin. E11 8
Laun, Thai. G4 48
Launceston, Austl. n13 77a
Launceston, Eng., U.K. K8 12
La Unión, Chile H2 90
La Unión, El Sal. F4 102
La Unión, Mex. G8 100
La Unión, Spain G10 20
La Union, N.M., U.S. L10 132
La Unión, Ven. C8 86
Laupheim, Ger. H5 16
Laura, Austl. C8 74
La Urbana, Ven. D8 86
Laurel, Fl., U.S. I3 116
Laurel, In., U.S. E12 120
Laurel, Md., U.S. E9 114
Laurel, Ms., U.S. F9 122
Laurel, Mt., U.S. B4 126
Laurel, Ne., U.S. E15 126
Laurel Bay, S.C., U.S. D5 116

Name	Map Ref.	Page
Laureldale, Pa., U.S.	D10	114
Laureles, Ur.	E9	92
Laurel River Lake, res., Ky., U.S.	G1	114
Laurelville, Oh., U.S.	E15	120
Laurencekirk, Scot., U.K.	E10	12
Laurens, S.C., U.S.	B3	116
Laurentides, Les, plat., Qc., Can.	F16	106
Lau Ridge, unds.	L21	142
Laurier, Mb., Can.	D14	124
Laurier-Station, Qc., Can.	D5	110
Laurinburg, N.C., U.S.	B6	116
Laurium, Mi., U.S.	D10	118
Lausanne, Switz.	D3	22
Lausitzer Neisse (Nysa Łużycka), stm., Eur.	F10	16
Laut, Pulau, i., Indon.	A5	50
Laut, Pulau, i., Indon.	E10	50
Laut, Selat, strt., Indon.	E9	50
Lauta, Ger.	E9	16
Lautaro, Chile	I1	92
Lauterbach, Ger.	F5	16
Lauter Sachsen, Ger.	F8	16
Laut Kecil, Kepulauan, is., Indon.	F9	50
Lautoka, Fiji	p18	79e
Lauzerte, Fr.	E7	18
Lava (Łyna), stm., Eur.	B16	16
Lava Beds National Monument, p.o.i., Ca., U.S.	B4	134
Lavaca, stm., Tx., U.S.	E11	130
Laval, Qc., Can.	E3	110
Laval, Fr.	F8	14
La Vall d'Uixó, Spain	E10	20
Lavalle, Arg.	D5	92
Lavalle, Arg.	D8	92
Lavapié, Punta, c., Chile	H1	92
Lavassaare, Est.	G11	8
La Vega, Dom. Rep.	C12	102
La Vela de Coro, Ven.	B7	86
Lavelanet, Fr.	G7	18
Lavello, Italy	C9	24
La Venada, Mex.	I10	130
La Venta, sci., Mex.	F11	100
La Ventura, Mex.	C8	100
La Vera, reg., Spain	D5	20
La Vergne, Tn., U.S.	H11	120
Laverne, Ok., U.S.	E9	128
Laverton, Austl.	E4	74
La Veta, Co., U.S.	D4	128
Lavieille, Lake, l., On., Can.	C11	112
La Vila Joiosa, Spain	F10	20
Lavillette, N.B., Can.	C11	110
La Viña, Arg.	B5	92
Lavina, Mt., U.S.	A4	126
La Vista, Ne., U.S.	C1	120
La Voulte-sur-Rhône, Fr.	E10	18
Lavras, Braz.	K3	88
Lávrio, Grc.	F7	28
Lavumisa, Swaz.	E10	70
Lawang, Indon.	G8	50
Lawas, Malay.	A9	50
Lawdar, Yemen	G6	56
Lawers, Ben, mtn., Scot., U.K.	E8	12
Lawgi, Austl.	E8	76
Lawksawk, Mya.	B3	48
Lawler, Ia., U.S.	A5	120
Lawn, Tx., U.S.	B8	130
Lawndale, N.C., U.S.	A4	116
Lawn Hill, Austl.	C7	74
Lawn Hill Creek, stm., Austl.	C7	74
Lawrence, In., U.S.	I3	112
Lawrence, Ks., U.S.	F2	120
Lawrence, Ma., U.S.	B14	114
Lawrenceburg, In., U.S.	E12	120
Lawrenceburg, Ky., U.S.	F12	120
Lawrenceburg, Tn., U.S.	B11	122
Lawrenceville, Il., U.S.	F10	120
Lawrenceville, N.J., U.S.	D11	114
Lawson, Mo., U.S.	E3	120
Lawtey, Fl., U.S.	F3	116
Lawton, N.D., U.S.	F15	124
Lawton, Ok., U.S.	G10	128
Lawu, Gunung, vol., Indon.	G7	50
Lawz, Jabal al-, mtn., Sau. Ar.	J6	58
Laxå, Swe.	G6	8
Laxe, Spain	A1	20
Lay Lake, res., Al., U.S.	D12	122
Layou, St. Vin.	o11	105e
Layton, Ut., U.S.	B4	132
Laytonville, Ca., U.S.	D2	134
La Zarca, Mex.	C6	100
Lazarev, Russia	F17	34
Lázaro Cárdenas, Mex.	G7	100
Lázaro Cárdenas, Presa, res., Mex.	C6	100
Lazdijai, Lith.	F6	10
Lazio, state, Italy	B6	24
Léach, Camb.	F6	48
Leachville, Ar., U.S.	I7	120
Lead, S.D., U.S.	C9	126
Leadbetter Point, c., Wa., U.S.	D2	136
Leader, Sk., Can.	D4	124
Lead Hill, hill, Mo., U.S.	H4	120
Leadore, Id., U.S.	F13	136
Leadville, Co., U.S.	D10	132
Leaf, stm., Ms., U.S.	F10	122
Leaf Lake, l., Sk., Can.	A11	124
Leaghur, Lake, l., Austl.	I4	76
League City, Tx., U.S.	H3	122
Leakey, Tx., U.S.	E8	130
Leaksville, N.C., U.S.	H5	114
Lealman, Fl., U.S.	I3	116
Leamington, On., Can.	F7	112
Le'an, China	H6	42
Leandro, Braz.	C3	88
Leandro N. Alem, Arg.	C10	92
Leary, Ga., U.S.	F14	122
Leatherman Peak, mtn., Id., U.S.	F13	136
Leavenworth, Ks., U.S.	E2	120
Leavenworth, Wa., U.S.	C6	136
Leawood, Ks., U.S.	F3	120
Lebak, Phil.	G5	52
Lebam, Wa., U.S.	D3	136
Lebanon, In., U.S.	H3	112
Lebanon, Ks., U.S.	B10	128
Lebanon, Ky., U.S.	G12	120
Lebanon, N.H., U.S.	G4	110
Lebanon, Oh., U.S.	E1	114
Lebanon, Or., U.S.	F3	136
Lebanon, Pa., U.S.	D9	114
Lebanon, S.D., U.S.	B13	126
Lebanon, Tn., U.S.	H11	120
Lebanon, Va., U.S.	H3	114
Lebanon, ctry., Asia	E6	58
Lebec, Ca., U.S.	I7	134
Lebesby, Nor.	A12	8
Le Bic, Qc., Can.	B8	110
Le Blanc, Fr.	H10	14
Lebo, D.R.C.	D4	66
Lebo, Ks., U.S.	F2	120
Lębork, Pol.	B13	16
Lebrija, Spain	H4	20
Lebrija, stm., Col.	D5	86
Łebsko, Jezioro, l., Pol.	B13	16
Lebu, Chile	H1	92
Lebyazh'e, Kaz.	D13	32
Le Carbet, Mart.	k6	105c
Lecce, Italy	D12	24
Lecco, Italy	E6	22
Le Center, Mn., U.S.	G5	118
Lech, stm., Eur.	H6	16
Lechainá, Grc.	F4	28
Lechang, China	I5	42
Le Chesne, Fr.	E13	14
Lechiguanas, Islas de las, is., Arg.	F8	92
Lechuguilla, Cerro, mtn., Mex.	D6	100
Lecompte, La., U.S.	F6	122
Le Creusot, Fr.	H13	14
Le Croisic, Fr.	G6	14
Łęczyca, Pol.	D15	16
Ledesma, Spain	C4	20
Le Diamant, Mart.	l6	105c
Ledjanaja, gora, mtn., Russia	D23	34
Ledo, India	C8	46
Ledo, Indon.	C6	50
Ledong, China	L3	42
Le Dorat, Fr.	C7	18
Ledu, China	D5	36
Leduc, Ab., Can.	C17	138
Leechburg, Pa., U.S.	D6	114
Leech Lake, l., Mn., U.S.	D4	118
Leedey, Ok., U.S.	F9	128
Leeds, Eng., U.K.	H11	12
Leeds, Al., U.S.	D12	122
Leek, Eng., U.K.	H10	12
Leelanau, Lake, l., Mi., U.S.	D4	112
Leelanau Peninsula, pen., Mi., U.S.	C4	112
Leer, Ger.	C3	16
Leesburg, Fl., U.S.	H4	116
Leesburg, Ga., U.S.	E1	116
Leesburg, Va., U.S.	E8	114
Lees Summit, Mo., U.S.	F3	120
Leesville, La., U.S.	F5	122
Leesville, Tx., U.S.	E10	130
Leeton, Austl.	J6	76
Leeu-Gamka, S. Afr.	H6	70
Leeuwarden, Neth.	A14	14
Leeuwin, Cape, c., Austl.	F2	74
Lee Vining, Ca., U.S.	F6	134
Leeward Islands, is., N.A.	h15	96a
Lefkáda, Grc.	E3	28
Lefkáda, i., Grc.	E3	28
Lefke, N. Cyp.	C3	58
Lefkosía see Nicosia, Cyp.	C4	58
Lefors, Tx., U.S.	F8	128
Le François, Mart.	k7	105c
Lefroy, Lake, l., Austl.	F4	74
Legal, Ab., Can.	C17	138
Leganés, Spain	D7	20
Legaspi, Phil.	D4	52
Leggett, Ca., U.S.	D2	134
Leghorn see Livorno, Italy	G7	22
Legion, Zimb.	B9	70
Legionowo, Pol.	D16	16
Legnago, Italy	E8	22
Legnano, Italy	E5	22
Legnica, Pol.	E12	16
Legnica, state, Pol.	E12	16
Le Gosier, Guad.	h6	105c
Le Grand, Ca., U.S.	F5	134
Le Guelta, Alg.	H11	20
Legume, Austl.	G9	76
Leh, India	A6	54
Le Havre, Fr.	E8	14
Lehčevo, Blg.	F10	26
Lehigh, Ia., U.S.	B3	120
Lehigh, Ok., U.S.	C2	122
Lehigh Acres, Fl., U.S.	J4	116
Lehighton, Pa., U.S.	D10	114
Lehrte, Ger.	D5	16
Lehtse, Est.	A8	10
Lehua, i., Hi., U.S.	a1	78a
Lehututu, Bots.	C5	70
Lei, stm., China	I5	42
Leiah, Pak.	C3	54
Leibnitz, Aus.	D12	22
Leicester, Eng., U.K.	I11	12
Leichhardt, stm., Austl.	A2	76
Leichhardt Falls, wtfl., Austl.	B2	76
Leiden (Leyden), Neth.	B13	14
Leigh Creek South, Austl.	H2	76
Leighton, Al., U.S.	C11	122
Leighton Buzzard, Eng., U.K.	J12	12
Leinan, Sk., Can.	D6	124
Leine, stm., Ger.	D5	16
Leinster, hist. reg., Ire.	I6	12
Leinster, Mount, mtn., Ire.	I6	12
Leipalingis, Lith.	F6	10
Leipsic, Oh., U.S.	C1	114
Leipsoi, i., Grc.	F9	28
Leipzig, Ger.	E8	16
Leiria, Port.	E2	20
Leiria, state, Port.	E2	20
Leisler, Mount, mtn., Austl.	D6	74
Leitariegos, Puerto de, p., Spain	A4	20
Leitha (Lajta), stm., Eur.	H12	16
Leitrim, Ire.	H4	12
Leitrim, state, Ire.	H5	12
Leivádia, Grc.	E5	28
Leiyang, China	H5	42
Leizhou Bandao, pen., China	K3	42
Lejasciems, Lat.	C9	10
Lekeitio, Spain	A8	20
Leksozero, ozero, l., Russia	E14	8
Le Lamentin, Mart.	k6	105c
Leland, Il., U.S.	C9	120
Leland, Mi., U.S.	C4	112
Leland, Ms., U.S.	D8	122
Leleiwi Point, c., Hi., U.S.	d7	78a
Leleque, Arg.	H2	90
Leles, Indon.	G5	50
Leli Shan, mtn., China	B8	54
Le Locle, Switz.	C3	22
Lelystad, Neth.	B14	14
Le Maire, Estrecho de, strt., Arg.	J4	90
Le Mans, Fr.	G9	14
Le Marin, Mart.	l7	105c
Le Mars, Ia., U.S.	B1	120
Lema Shilindi, Eth.	G8	62
Lemay, Mo., U.S.	F7	120
Lembak, Indon.	C10	50
Lemdiyya, Alg.	H13	20
Leme, Braz.	L2	88
Lemesós (Limassol), Cyp.	D4	58
Lemhi, stm., Id., U.S.	F13	136
Lemhi Pass, p., U.S.	F13	136
Lemhi Range, mts., Id., U.S.	F13	136
Lemieux Islands, is., Nu., Can.	E13	141
Leming, Tx., U.S.	E9	130
Lemitar, N.M., U.S.	I10	132
Lemmatsi, Est.	B9	10
Lemmenjoen kansallispuisto, p.o.i., Fin.	B11	8
Lemmon, S.D., U.S.	B10	126
Lemmon, Mount, mtn., Az., U.S.	K6	132
Lemnos see Límnos, i., Grc.	D8	28
Lemoncove, Ca., U.S.	G7	134
Le Mont-Dore, N. Cal.	n16	79d
Lemoore, Ca., U.S.	G6	134
Le Moule, Guad.	h6	105c
Lempa, stm., N.A.	F3	102
Lempe, Indon.	D12	50
Lemro, stm., Mya.	B1	48
Le Murge, hills, Italy	D10	24
Le Muy, Fr.	F12	18
Lemyethna, Mya.	D2	48
Lena, Il., U.S.	B8	120
Lena, Wi., U.S.	D1	112
Lena, stm., Russia	B14	34
Lenart, Slvn.	D12	22
Lençóis, Braz.	G5	88
Lençóis Maranhenses, Parque Nacional dos, p.o.i., Braz.	B4	88
Lendery, Russia	E14	8
Lendinara, Italy	E8	22
Lenger, Kaz.	F12	32
Lenggor, stm., Malay.	K6	48
Lenghu, China	D3	36
Lengshuitan, China	H4	42
Lenhovda, Swe.	H6	8
Leningrad see Sankt-Peterburg, Russia	A13	10
Leningradskaja oblast', co., Russia	G15	8
Leninogor see Leninogorsk, Kaz.	D14	32
Leninogorsk, Kaz.	D14	32
Lenin Peak, mtn., Asia	B11	56
Leninsk, Kaz.	E10	32
Leninsk, Uzb.	F12	32
Leninskij, Russia	F20	10
Leninsk-Kuzneckij, Russia	D15	32
Leninskoe, Russia	G15	34
Lennonville, Austl.	E3	74
Lennox, S.D., U.S.	H2	118
Lennox, Isla, i., Chile	K3	90
Lennoxville, Qc., Can.	E5	110
Lenoir, N.C., U.S.	I4	114
Lenora, Czech Rep.	H9	16
Lenore Lake, l., Sk., Can.	B9	124
Lenox, Ga., U.S.	E2	116
Lenox, Ia., U.S.	D3	120
Lenox, Tn., U.S.	H8	120
Lens, Fr.	D11	14
Lensk, Russia	B20	32
Lenti, Hung.	C3	26
Lentini, Italy	G9	24
Lentua, l., Fin.	D13	8
Lentvaris, Lith.	F8	10
Lenya, stm., Mya.	G4	48
Léo, Burkina	G4	64
Leoben, Aus.	C12	22
Léogâne, Haiti	C11	102
Leola, Ar., U.S.	C6	122
Leola, S.D., U.S.	B14	126
Leominster, Eng., U.K.	I10	12
Leominster, Ma., U.S.	B14	114
Léon, Fr.	F4	18
León, Mex.	E8	100
León, Nic.	F4	102
León, Spain	B5	20
Leon, Ks., U.S.	D12	128
León, co., Spain	B5	20
Leon, stm., Tx., U.S.	C10	130
León, Montes de, mts., Spain	B4	20
Leona, stm., Tx., U.S.	F8	130
Leonard, Tx., U.S.	D2	122
Leonardtown, Md., U.S.	F9	114
Leonardville, Ks., U.S.	B11	128
Leonberg, Ger.	H4	16
Leones, Arg.	F6	92
Leonforte, Italy	G8	24
Leongatha, Austl.	L5	76
Leoniha, Russia	G18	8
Leonora, Austl.	E4	74
Leopold and Astrid Coast, cst., Ant.	B13	81
Leopoldina, Braz.	K4	88
Leopoldo de Bulhões, Braz.	I1	88
Léopoldville see Kinshasa, D.R.C.	E3	66
Leoti, Ks., U.S.	C7	128
Leova, Mol.	C15	26
Lepanto see Náfpaktos, Grc.	E4	28
Lepanto, Ar., U.S.	B8	122
Lepar, Pulau, i., Indon.	E5	50
Lepe, Spain	G3	20
Lepel', Bela.	F11	10
Leping, China	G7	42
L'Épiphanie, Qc., Can.	E3	110
Lepontine Alps, mts., Eur.	C14	18
Lepreau, Point, c., N.B., Can.	E10	110
Le Prêcheur, Mart.	k6	105c
Lepsi, Kaz.	E13	32
Lepsy see Lepsi, Kaz.	E13	32
Le Puy, Fr.	D9	18
Lequeitio see Lekeitio, Spain	A8	20
Lercara Friddi, Italy	G7	24
Lerdo, Mex.	C7	100
Lerici, Italy	F6	22
Lérida, Col.	G6	86
Lérida see Lleida, Spain	C11	20
Lerma, stm., Mex.	E8	100
Le Roy, Il., U.S.	D9	120
Le Roy, Ks., U.S.	F2	120
Le Roy, N.Y., U.S.	B7	114
Lerum, Swe.	H5	8
Lerwick, Scot., U.K.	n18	12a
Les Abymes, Guad.	h5	105c
Le Saint-Esprit, Mart.	k7	105c
Les Andelys, Fr.	E10	14
Les Anses-d'Arlets, Mart.	l6	105c
Les Borges Blanques, Spain	C11	20
Lesbos see Lésvos, i., Grc.	D9	28
Les Cayes, Haiti	C11	102
Leshan, China	F5	36
Les Herbiers, Fr.	H7	14
Lesina, Lago di, b., Italy	I12	22
Lesko, Pol.	G18	16
Leskovac, Serb.	F8	26
Leskov Island, i., S. Geor.	K12	82
Les Laurentides see Laurentides, Les, plat., Qc., Can.	F16	106
Leslie, Ar., U.S.	I5	120
Leslie, Mi., U.S.	B1	114
Leslie, W.V., U.S.	F5	114
Lesneven, Fr.	F4	14
Lesnoe, Russia	B18	10
Lesogorsk, Russia	G17	34
Lesosibirsk, Russia	E7	34
Lesotho, ctry., Afr.	F9	70
Lesozavodsk, Russia	B10	38
Lesozavodskij, Russia	C15	8
Les Sables-d'Olonne, Fr.	H7	14
Les Saintes, is., Guad.	i5	105c
Lesser Antilles, is.	D8	82
Lesser Khingan Range see Xiao Hinggan Ling, mts., China	B10	36
Lesser Slave, stm., Ab., Can.	A16	138
Lesser Slave Lake, l., Ab., Can.	D8	106
Lesser Sunda Islands see Tenggara, Nusa, is., Indon.	G6	44
L'Esterre, Gren.	q10	105e
Lestock, Sk., Can.	C9	124
Le Sueur, Mn., U.S.	G4	118
Le Sueur, stm., Mn., U.S.	G5	118
Lešukonskoe, Russia	D21	8
Lésvos (Lesbos), i., Grc.	D9	28
Leszno, Pol.	E12	16
Leszno, state, Pol.	E12	16
Letaba, stm., S. Afr.	C10	70
Letcher, S.D., U.S.	D14	126
Letea, Ostrovul, i., Rom.	D16	26
Letenye, Hung.	C3	26
Lethbridge, Ab., Can.	G18	138
Lethem, Guy.	F12	86
Le Thillot, Fr.	B12	18
Leti, Kepulauan, is., Indon.	G8	44
Leticia, Col.	D4	84
Letlhakane, Bots.	B7	70
Letlhakeng, Bots.	D7	70
Letnjaja Zolotica, Russia	D17	8
Letpadan, Mya.	D2	48
Le Tréport, Fr.	D10	14
Letsôk-aw Kyun, i., Mya.	G3	48
Letung, Indon.	B4	50
Leucas see Lefkáda, i., Grc.	E3	28
Leucate, Étang de, l., Fr.	G9	18
Leuk, Switz.	D4	22
Leuser, Gunung, mtn., Indon.	K3	48
Leutkirch, Ger.	I6	16
Leuven, Bel.	D13	14
Levack, On., Can.	B8	112
Levan, Ut., U.S.	D5	132
Levanger, Nor.	E4	8
Levante, Riviera di, cst., Italy	F6	22
Levanzo, Isola di, i., Italy	F6	24
Le Vauclin, Mart.	k7	105c
Levelland, Tx., U.S.	H6	128
Leveque, Cape, c., Austl.	C4	74
Leverkusen, Ger.	E3	16
Levice, Slov.	H14	16
Levin, N.Z.	E6	80
Lévis, Qc., Can.	D5	110
Levisa Fork, stm., U.S.	G3	114
Levittown, P.R.	b3	104a
Levittown, N.Y., U.S.	D12	114
Levittown, Pa., U.S.	D11	114
Levkosía see Nicosia, Cyp.	C4	58
Levoča, Slov.	H16	16
Levski, Blg.	F12	26
Levuka, Fiji	p19	79e
Lévuo, stm., Lith.	E7	10
Lewe, Mya.	C2	48
Lewellen, Ne., U.S.	F10	126
Lewer, stm., Nmb.	D3	70
Lewes, De., U.S.	F10	114
Lewin Brzeski, Pol.	F13	16
Lewis, Ia., U.S.	J3	118
Lewis, Butt of, c., Scot., U.K.	C6	12
Lewis, Isle of, i., Scot., U.K.	C6	12
Lewis, Mount, mtn., Nv., U.S.	C8	134
Lewis and Clark Lake, res., U.S.	E15	126
Lewis and Clark Range, mts., Mt., U.S.	C13	136
Lewisburg, Ky., U.S.	H10	120
Lewisburg, Pa., U.S.	D8	114
Lewisburg, Tn., U.S.	B12	122
Lewis Range, mts., N.A.	B13	136
Lewis Run, Pa., U.S.	C7	114
Lewis Smith Lake, res., Al., U.S.	C11	122
Lewiston, Ca., U.S.	C3	134
Lewiston, Id., U.S.	D10	136
Lewiston, Me., U.S.	F6	110
Lewiston, Mi., U.S.	D5	112
Lewiston, Mn., U.S.	H7	118
Lewiston, Ut., U.S.	B5	132
Lewiston Orchards, Id., U.S.	D10	136
Lewistown, Il., U.S.	D7	120
Lewistown, Mt., U.S.	C17	136
Lewistown, Pa., U.S.	D8	114
Lewisville, N.B., Can.	D12	110
Lewisville, Ar., U.S.	D5	122
Lewisville, Tx., U.S.	A10	130
Lewisville Lake, res., Tx., U.S.	H12	128
Lewvan, Sk., Can.	D9	124
Lexa, Ar., U.S.	C8	122
Lexington, Ga., U.S.	C2	116
Lexington, Il., U.S.	D9	120
Lexington, Ky., U.S.	F1	114
Lexington, Ma., U.S.	B14	114
Lexington, Mi., U.S.	E7	112
Lexington, Ms., U.S.	D8	122
Lexington, N.C., U.S.	I5	114
Lexington, Ok., U.S.	F11	128
Lexington, Or., U.S.	E7	136
Lexington, S.C., U.S.	C4	116
Lexington, Tx., U.S.	D10	130
Lexington, Va., U.S.	G6	114
Lexington Park, Md., U.S.	F9	114
Leyden see Leiden, Neth.	B13	14
Leye, China	I2	42
Leyte, i., Phil.	E5	52
Leyte Gulf, b., Phil.	E5	52
Lezhë, Alb.	C13	24
Lezhi, China	F1	42
Lëzna, Bela.	E13	10
L'gov, Russia	D5	32
Lhasa, China	D13	54
Lhasa, stm., China	C13	54
Lhazê, China	D11	54
Lhoknga, Indon.	J2	48
Lhokseumawe, Indon.	J3	48
Lhoksukon, Indon.	J3	48
Lhorong, China	E4	36
L'Hospitalet de Llobregat, Spain	C13	20
Lhuntsi Dzong, Bhu.	E13	54
Li, Thai.	D4	48
Li, stm., China	G4	42
Li, stm., Thai.	D4	48
Liamuiga, Mount, vol., St. K./N.	c2	105a
Lian, stm., China	I5	42
Liancheng, China	I7	42
Lianga, Phil.	F6	52
Liangbao, China	D4	42
Liangbuaya, Indon.	C10	50
Liangdang, China	E1	42
Lianghekou, China	G3	42
Liangmentou, China	G9	42
Liangping, China	F2	42
Liangyuan, China	E7	42
Liangzi Hu, l., China	F6	42
Lianhuapao, China	B8	38
Lianhua Shan, mts., China	J6	42
Lianjiang, China	K4	42
Liannan, China	I5	42
Lianshui, China	E8	42
Lianxian, China	I5	42
Lianyuan, China	H4	42
Lianyungang, China	D8	42
Liao, stm., China	D5	38
Liaocheng, China	C7	42
Liaodong Bandao (Liaotung Peninsula), pen., China	D5	38
Liaodong Wan (Liaotung, Gulf of), b., China	A9	42
Liaoning, state, China	D5	38
Liaotung, Gulf of see Liaodong Wan, b., China	A9	42
Liaotung Peninsula see Liaodong Bandao, pen., China	E5	38
Liaoyang, China	D5	38
Liaoyuan, China	C6	38
Liaozhong, China	D5	38
Liard, stm., Can.	C6	106
Liat, Pulau, i., Indon.	E5	50
Libagon, Phil.	E5	52
Líbano, Col.	E4	86
Libby, Mt., U.S.	B11	136
Libby Dam, dam, Mt., U.S.	B11	136
Libenge, D.R.C.	D3	66
Liberal, Ks., U.S.	D7	128
Liberal, Mo., U.S.	G3	120
Liberec, Czech Rep.	F11	16
Liberia, C.R.	G5	102
Liberia, ctry., Afr.	H3	64
Liberta, Antig.	f4	105b
Libertad, Ven.	C7	86
Libertad, Ven.	C7	86
Libertador General Bernardo O'Higgins, state, Chile	G2	92
Liberty, Mo., U.S.	E3	120
Liberty, Ms., U.S.	F8	122
Liberty, N.C., U.S.	I6	114
Liberty, N.Y., U.S.	C11	114
Liberty, S.C., U.S.	B3	116
Liberty, Tx., U.S.	G4	122
Liberty Center, Oh., U.S.	G5	112
Libertyville, Il., U.S.	B9	120
Libo, China	I2	42
Libobo, Tanjung, c., Indon.	F8	44
Libode, S. Afr.	G9	70
Libourne, Fr.	E5	18
Librazhd, Alb.	C14	24
Libres, Mex.	F10	100
Libreville, Gabon	D1	66
Liburung, Indon.	F12	50
Libya, ctry., Afr.	B3	62
Libyan Desert, des., Afr.	C5	62
Libyan Plateau, plat., Afr.	A4	62
Licancábur, Volcán, vol., S.A.	D3	90
Licantén, Chile	G1	92
Licata, Italy	G7	24
Lich, Ger.	F4	16
Licheng, China	C5	42
Licheng see Liyang, China	F8	42
Lichfield, Eng., U.K.	I11	12
Lichinga, Moz.	C6	68
Lichtenau, Ger.	E5	16
Lichtenburg, S. Afr.	E7	70
Lichtenfels, Ger.	F7	16
Lichuan, China	H7	42
Lichuan, China	F3	42
Licking, Mo., U.S.	G6	120
Licking, stm., Ky., U.S.	F1	114
Ličko Polje, val., Cro.	F12	22
Lida, Bela.	G8	10
Liddon Gulf, b., N.T., Can.	B17	140
Liden, Swe.	E7	8
Lidgerwood, N.D., U.S.	E1	118
Lidköping, Swe.	G5	8
Lido di Ostia, Italy	I9	22
Lidzbark, Pol.	C15	16
Lidzbark Warmiński, Pol.	B16	16
Liebenbergsvlei, stm., S. Afr.	E9	70
Liebig, Mount, mtn., Austl.	D6	74
Liechtenstein, ctry., Eur.	C6	22
Liège (Luik), Bel.	D14	14
Lielais Liepu kalns, hill, Lat.	D10	10
Lielvārde, Lat.	D7	10
Lienchou see Hepu, China	K3	42
Lienz, Aus.	D9	22
Liepāja, Lat.	D3	10
Liepājas ezers, l., Lat.	D4	10
Lier, Bel.	C13	14
Lierre see Lier, Bel.	C13	14
Liestal, Switz.	C4	22
Liești, Rom.	D14	26
Liévin, Fr.	D11	14
Lièvre, stm., Qc., Can.	C14	112
Liezen, Aus.	C11	22
Liffey, stm., Ire.	H6	12
Lifford, Ire.	G5	12
Lifou, i., N. Cal.	m16	79d
Līgatne, Lat.	C7	10
Lighthouse Point, Fl., U.S.	J5	116
Lighthouse Point, c., Fl., U.S.	H14	122
Lighthouse Point, c., Mi., U.S.	C4	112
Lightning Creek, stm., Wy., U.S.	D7	126
Lightning Ridge, Austl.	G6	76
Lignite, N.D., U.S.	F11	124
Ligny-en-Barrois, Fr.	F14	14
Ligonha, stm., Moz.	D6	68
Ligonier, In., U.S.	G4	112
Ligonier, Pa., U.S.	H10	112
Liguria, state, Italy	F5	22
Ligurian Sea, s., Eur.	G5	22
Lihir Island, i., Pap. N. Gui.	a5	79a
Lihoslavl', Russia	C18	10
Lihou Reefs and Cays, rf., Austl.	A8	76
Lihue, Hi., U.S.	b2	78a
Lihuel Calel, Parque Nacional, p.o.i., Arg.	H5	92
Lihula, Est.	B6	10
Lijiang, China	F5	36
Lik, stm., Laos	C6	48
Likasi (Jadotville), D.R.C.	G5	66
Likati, D.R.C.	D4	66
Likely, B.C., Can.	D9	138
Liki, Indon.	D2	50
Likino-Dulevo, Russia	E21	10
Lilbourn, Mo., U.S.	H8	120
Lilibeo, Capo see Boeo, Capo, c., Italy	G6	24
Lilienfeld, Aus.	B12	22
Liling, China	H5	42
Lille, Fr.	D12	14
Lillebælt, strt., Den.	I3	8
Lillebonne, Fr.	E9	14
Lillehammer, Nor.	F3	8
Lillers, Fr.	D11	14
Lillestrøm, Nor.	F4	8
Lillhärdal, Swe.	F6	8
Lillington, N.C., U.S.	A7	116
Lillooet, B.C., Can.	F9	138
Lillooet, stm., B.C., Can.	G8	138
Lillooet Lake, l., B.C., Can.	F8	138
Lilongwe, Mwi.	C5	68
Liloy, Phil.	F4	52
Lilydale, Austl.	n13	77a
Lim, stm., Eur.	G16	22
Lima, Para.	A9	92
Lima, Peru	F2	84
Lima, Mt., U.S.	F14	136
Lima, N.Y., U.S.	B8	114
Lima, Oh., U.S.	D1	114
Lima (Limia), stm., Eur.	C2	20
Limarí, stm., Chile	E2	92
Limas, Indon.	C4	50
Limassol see Lemesós, Cyp.	D4	58
Limavady, N. Ire., U.K.	F6	12
Limay, stm., Arg.	G3	90
Limay Mahuida, Arg.	H4	92
Limbang, Malay.	A9	50
Limbang, stm., Malay.	A9	50
Līmbdi, India	G3	54
Limbe, Cam.	D1	66
Limbé, Haiti	C11	102
Limbujan see Pio V. Corpuz, Phil.	E5	52
Limburg an der Lahn, Ger.	F4	16
Limeira, Braz.	L2	88
Limerick, Sk., Can.	E7	124
Limerick (Luimneach), Ire.	I4	12
Limerick, state, Ire.	I4	12
Limestone, Me., U.S.	D9	110
Limestone, Lake, res., Tx., U.S.	F2	122
Limfjorden, l., Den.	H3	8
Limia (Lima), stm., Eur.	C2	20
Limingen, l., Nor.	D5	8
Limmared, Swe.	H5	8
Limmen Bight, b., Austl.	B7	74
Límnos, i., Grc.	D8	28
Limoeiro, Braz.	D8	88
Limoeiro do Norte, Braz.	C6	88
Limoges, Fr.	D7	18
Limón, Hond.	E5	102
Limone Piemonte, Italy	F4	22
Limoux, Fr.	F8	18
Limpopo, stm., Afr.	D8	70
Limpopo, Parque Nacional do, p.o.i., Moz.	C10	70
Linahamari, Russia	B14	8
Lin'an, China	F8	42
Linapacan Island, i., Phil.	E2	52
Linares, Chile	G2	92
Linares, Mex.	C9	100
Linares, Spain	F7	20
Linch, Wy., U.S.	D6	126
Lincheng, China	C6	42
Linch'ing see Linqing, China	C6	42
Lincoln, Arg.	G7	92
Lincoln, Eng., U.K.	H12	12
Lincoln, Ar., U.S.	I3	120
Lincoln, Ca., U.S.	E4	134
Lincoln, Il., U.S.	D8	120
Lincoln, Ks., U.S.	B10	128
Lincoln, Mi., U.S.	D6	112
Lincoln, Mo., U.S.	F4	120
Lincoln, Mt., U.S.	D14	136
Lincoln, Ne., U.S.	K2	118
Lincoln, N.H., U.S.	F5	110
Lincoln, Mount, mtn., Co., U.S.	B2	128
Lincoln City, Or., U.S.	F2	136
Lincoln Creek, stm., Ne., U.S.	F15	126
Lincoln Park, Co., U.S.	C3	128
Lincoln Park, Mi., U.S.	B2	114
Lincoln Sea, s., N.A.	A13	141
Lincolnton, Ga., U.S.	C3	116
Lincolnton, N.C., U.S.	A4	116
Lincoln Village, Ca., U.S.	F4	134
Lindale, Ga., U.S.	C13	122
Lindale, Tx., U.S.	E3	122
Lindau, Ger.	I5	16
Linde, stm., Russia	C13	34
Linden, Guy.	B6	84
Linden, Al., U.S.	E11	122
Linden, In., U.S.	H3	112
Linden, Mi., U.S.	B2	114
Linden, Tn., U.S.	B11	122
Lindesnes, c., Nor.	H2	8
Lindi, Tan.	F7	66
Lindi, stm., D.R.C.	D5	66
Líndos, sci., Grc.	G10	28
Lind Point, c., V.I.U.S.	e7	104b
Lindsay, On., Can.	D11	112
Lindsay, Ca., U.S.	G6	134
Lindsay, Ne., U.S.	F15	126
Lindsay, Ok., U.S.	G11	128
Line Islands, is., Oc.	D11	72
Linesville, Pa., U.S.	C5	114
Lineville, Al., U.S.	D13	122
Lineville, Ia., U.S.	D4	120
Linfen, China	C4	42
Linganamakki Reservoir, res., India	D2	53
Lingao, China	L3	42
Lingayen, Phil.	B3	52
Lingayen Gulf, b., Phil.	B3	52
Lingbi, China	E7	42
Lingbo, Swe.	F7	8
Lingchuan, China	D5	42
Lingen, Ger.	D3	16
Lingfengwei, China	I6	42
Lingga, Kepulauan, is., Indon.	C4	50
Lingga, Pulau, i., Indon.	D4	50
Lingomo II, D.R.C.	D4	66
Lingqiu, China	B6	42
Lingshan, China	J3	42
Lingshi, China	C4	42
Lingshui, China	L4	42
Linguère, Sen.	F2	64
Lingwu, China	B2	42
Lingxian, China	H5	42
Lingyuan, China	A8	42
Linh, Ngoc, mtn., Viet.	E9	48
Linhai, China	G9	42
Linhares, Braz.	J5	88
Linhe, China	A2	42
Linhsia see Linxia, China	D5	36
Lini see Linyi, China	D8	42
Linjiang, China	D7	38
Linköping, Swe.	G6	8
Linkou, China	B9	38
Linksmakalnis, Lith.	F6	10
Linkuva, Lith.	D6	10
Linn, Ks., U.S.	B11	128
Linn, Mo., U.S.	F6	120
Linnansaaren kansallispuisto, p.o.i., Fin.	E13	8
Linnhe, Loch, b., Scot., U.K.	E7	12
Linqi, China	D5	42
Linqing, China	C6	42
Linqu, China	C8	42
Linquan, China	E6	42
Linru, China	D5	42
Lins, Braz.	K1	88
Linstead, Jam.	i13	104d
Lintan, China	E5	36
Linton, In., U.S.	E10	120
Linton, N.D., U.S.	A12	126
Lintong, China	D3	42
Linwu, China	I5	42
Linxi, China	C8	36
Linxi, China	C3	38
Linxia, China	D5	36
Linxian, China	C4	42
Linxian, China	C5	42
Linyi, China	D8	42
Linyi, China	C7	42
Linyü see Shanhaiguan, China	A8	42
Linz, Aus.	B11	22
Lio Matoh, Malay.	B9	50
Lion, Golfe du, b., Fr.	G10	18
Lion, Gulf of see Lion, Golfe du, b., Fr.	G10	18
Lionel Town, Jam.	j13	104d
Liouesso, Congo	D3	66
Lipa, Phil.	D3	52
Lipan, Tx., U.S.	B9	130
Lipari, Italy	F8	24
Lipari, Isola, i., Italy	F9	24
Lipari, Isole see Eolie, Isole, is., Italy	F8	24
Lipcani, Mol.	A13	26
Lipeck, Russia	D6	32
Lípez, Cerro, mtn., Bol.	D3	90
Lipicy, Russia	G20	10
Liping, China	H3	42
Lipki, Russia	G20	10
Lipník nad Bečvou, Czech Rep.	G13	16
Lipno, Pol.	D15	16
Lipno, údolní nádrž, res., Czech Rep.	H10	16
Lipova, Rom.	C8	26
Lipovcy, Russia	B9	38
Lippe, stm., Ger.	E2	16
Lippstadt, Ger.	E4	16
Lipscomb, Tx., U.S.	E8	128
Liptovská Teplička, Slov.	G15	16
Liptovský Mikuláš, Slov.	G15	16
Liptrap, Cape, c., Austl.	L5	76
Lipu, China	I4	42
Lira, Ug.	D6	66
Liri, stm., Italy	C7	24
Liria see Llíria, Spain	E10	20
Liro, Vanuatu	k17	79d
Lisala, D.R.C.	D4	66
Lisboa (Lisbon), Port.	F1	20
Lisboa, state, Port.	E1	20
Lisbon see Lisboa, Port.	F1	20
Lisbon, N.D., U.S.	A15	126
Lisbon, N.H., U.S.	F5	110
Lisbon, Oh., U.S.	D5	114
Lisburn, N. Ire., U.K.	G6	12
Lisburne, Cape, c., Ak., U.S.	C6	140
Lishi, China	C4	42
Lishu, China	C6	38
Lishui, China	G8	42
Lishuzhen, China	B9	38
Lisicy, Russia	D19	10
Lisieux, Sk., Can.	E7	124
Lisieux, Fr.	E9	14
Liski, Russia	D5	32
L'Isle-Jourdain, Fr.	C6	18
Lisman, Al., U.S.	E10	122
Lismore, Austl.	G9	76
Lismore, N.S., Can.	E14	110
Lišov, Czech Rep.	G10	16
Listowel, On., Can.	E9	112
Listowel, Ire.	I3	12
Litang, China	E5	36
Litang, China	J3	42
Litchfield, Il., U.S.	E8	120
Litchfield, Mn., U.S.	F4	118
Litchfield, Ne., U.S.	F13	126
Litchville, N.D., U.S.	A14	126
Lithgow, Austl.	I8	76
Líthino, Ákra, c., Grc.	I7	28
Lithonia, Ga., U.S.	D14	122
Lithuania, ctry., Eur.	E7	10
Litija, Slvn.	D11	22
Lititz, Pa., U.S.	D9	114
Litoměřice, Czech Rep.	F10	16
Litomyšl, Czech Rep.	G12	16
Litovko, Russia	G16	34
Little, stm., Ga., U.S.	C3	116
Little, stm., N.C., U.S.	A7	116
Little, stm., Ok., U.S.	F11	128
Little, stm., Tx., U.S.	D11	130
Little, stm., U.S.	B8	122

Name Map Ref. Page

Little, stm., U.S. D5 122
Little, Mountain Fork, stm., U.S. C4 122
Little Abaco, i., Bah. B9 96
Little Andaman, i., India F7 46
Little Arkansas, stm., Ks., U.S. C11 128
Little Beaver Creek, stm., U.S. B7 128
Little Beaver Creek, stm., U.S. A8 126
Little Belt see Lillebælt, strt., Den. I3 8
Little Belt Mountains, mts., Mt., U.S. D16 136
Little Bighorn, stm., U.S. B5 126
Little Bighorn Battlefield National Monument, p.o.i., Mt., U.S. B5 126
Little Blue, stm., U.S. G15 126
Little Buffalo, stm., Can. C8 106
Little Carpathians see Malé Karpaty, mts., Slov. H13 16
Little Cayman, i., Cay. Is. C7 102
Little Chute, Wi., U.S. D1 112
Little Colorado, stm., Az., U.S. H5 132
Little Current, On., Can. C8 112
Little Current, stm., On., Can. A12 118
Little Deep Creek, stm., N.D., U.S. F12 124
Little Deschutes, stm., Or., U.S. G5 136
Little Desert, des., Austl. K3 76
Little Desert National Park, p.o.i., Austl. K3 76
Little Dry Creek, stm., Mt., U.S. G7 124
Little Falls, Mn., U.S. E4 118
Little Falls, N.Y., U.S. E15 112
Littlefork, Mn., U.S. C5 118
Little Fork, stm., Mn., U.S. C5 118
Little Hurricane Creek, stm., Ga., U.S. E3 116
Little Inagua, i., Bah. B11 102
Little Kanawha, stm., W.V., U.S. E4 114
Little Karroo (Klein Karroo), plat., S. Afr. H5 70
Little Lake, l., La., U.S. H8 122
Little London, Jam. i12 104d
Little Lost, stm., Id., U.S. F13 136
Little Mexico, Tx., U.S. D4 130
Little Missouri, stm., Ar., U.S. D5 122
Little Missouri, stm., U.S. B7 108
Little Namaqualand (Klein Namaland), hist. reg., S. Afr. F3 70
Little Nicobar, i., India G7 46
Little Osage, stm., U.S. G3 120
Little Pee Dee, stm., S.C., U.S. B6 116
Little Pic, stm., On., Can. C12 118
Little Powder, stm., U.S. B7 126
Little Quill Lake, l., Sk., Can. C10 124
Little Rann of Kachchh, reg., India G3 54
Little Red, stm., Ar., U.S. B7 122
Little Red, Middle Fork, stm., Ar., U.S. B6 122
Little Red Deer, stm., Ab., Can. E16 138
Little River, Ks., U.S. C10 128
Little Rock, Ar., U.S. C6 122
Little Rock, stm., U.S. H2 118
Little Sable Point, c., Mi., U.S. E3 112
Little Saint Bernard Pass, p., Eur. D12 18
Little Sandy Creek, stm., Wy., U.S. E3 126
Little Sioux, stm., U.S. J3 118
Little Sioux, West Fork, stm., Ia., U.S. B2 120
Little Smoky, stm., Ab., Can. A14 138
Little Snake, stm., U.S. C8 132
Littlestown, Pa., U.S. E8 114
Little Tallapoosa, stm., U.S. D13 122
Little Tennessee, stm., U.S. A1 116
Little Tobago, i., Trin. r13 105f
Littleton, Co., U.S. B3 128
Littleton, N.H., U.S. F5 110
Littleton, W.V., U.S. E5 114
Little Valley, N.Y., U.S. B7 114
Little Wabash, stm., Il., U.S. F9 120
Little White, stm., S.D., U.S. D12 126
Little Wood, stm., Id., U.S. G12 136
Litvínov, Czech Rep. F9 16
Liu, stm., China C6 38
Liu, stm., China C5 38
Liu, stm., China I3 42
Liuaniua see Ontong Java, at., Sol. Is. D7 72
Liuba, China E2 42
Liuboml', Ukr. E20 16
Liuchen, China J4 42
Liucheng, China I3 42
Liuchow see Liuzhou, China I3 42
Liucura, Chile I2 92
Liufang, China H7 42
Liuhe, China C6 38
Liuheng Dao, i., China G10 42
Liujiazi, China A9 42
Liupan Shan, mts., China D2 42
Liushuquan, China F16 32
Liuxi, stm., China J5 42
Liuyang, China G5 42
Liuyang, stm., China G5 42
Liuzhou, China I3 42
Livada, Rom. B10 26
Livadija, Russia C10 38
Līvāni, Lat. D9 10
Livanjsko Polje, val., Bos. F3 26
Lively, On., Can. B8 112
Lively Island, i., Falk. Is. J5 90
Live Oak, Ca., U.S. D4 134
Live Oak, Fl., U.S. F2 116
Liveringa, Austl. C4 74
Livermore, Ca., U.S. F4 134
Livermore, Ia., U.S. B3 120
Livermore, Ky., U.S. G10 120
Livermore, Mount, mtn., Tx., U.S. D3 130
Livermore Falls, Me., U.S. F6 110
Liverpool, N.S., Can. F12 110
Liverpool, Eng., U.K. H10 12
Liverpool, Cape, c., Nu., Can. C10 141
Liverpool Bay, b., N.T., Can. A5 106
Liverpool Bay, b., Eng., U.K. H9 12
Lívingston, Guat. E3 102
Livingston, Al., U.S. E10 122
Livingston, Il., U.S. F8 120
Livingston, La., U.S. G8 122
Livingston, Mt., U.S. E16 136
Livingston, Tn., U.S. H12 120
Livingston, Tx., U.S. G4 122
Livingston, Wi., U.S. B7 120
Livingston, Lake, res., Tx., U.S. G3 122
Livingstone, Zam. D4 68
Livingstone Falls, wtfl., Afr. A1 68
Livingstonia, Mwi. C5 68
Livingston Manor, N.Y., U.S. C11 114
Livno, Bos. F4 26
Livny, Russia H20 10
Livonia, La., U.S. G7 122
Livonia, Mi., U.S. B2 114
Livonia, N.Y., U.S. B8 114
Livorno (Leghorn), Italy G7 22
Livramento do Brumado, Braz. G5 88
Liwale, Tan. F7 66
Lixi, China G6 42
Lixian, China G4 42
Lixian, China D1 42
Lixian see Black, stm., Asia D9 56
Lixin, China E7 42
Lixoúri, Grc. E3 28
Liyang, China F8 42
Lizarda, Braz. E2 88
Lizard Point, c., Eng., U.K. L7 12
Lizarra see Estella, Spain B8 20
Ljady, Bela. F14 10
Ljahavičy, Bela. G9 10
Ljahovskie ostrova, is., Russia B17 34
Ljamca, Russia D17 8
Ljaskavičy, Bela. H11 10
Ljasnaja, Bela. G8 10
Ljuban', Bela. H10 10
Ljuban', Russia A14 10
Ljubercy, Russia E20 10
Ljubimec, Blg. H12 26
Ljubljana, Slvn. D11 22
Ljubnica, Russia C15 10
Ljubohna, Russia G17 10
Ljubuški, Bos. F4 26
Ljudinovo, Russia G17 10
Ljudkovo, Russia F17 10
Ljungan, stm., Swe. E5 8
Ljungby, Swe. H5 8
Ljusdal, Swe. F7 8
Ljusina, Bela. H9 10
Ljusnan, stm., Swe. F6 8
Llancanelo, Laguna, l., Arg. G3 92
Llandeilo, Wales, U.K. J8 12
Llandrindod Wells, Wales, U.K. I9 12
Llandudno, Wales, U.K. H9 12
Llanelli, Wales, U.K. J8 12
Llangefni, Wales, U.K. H8 12
Llanidloes, Wales, U.K. I9 12
Llano, stm., Tx., U.S. D8 130
Llano Colorado, Mex. L9 134
Llanos, pl., S.A. E7 86
Llanquihue, Lago, l., Chile H2 90
Lleida, Spain C11 20
Lleida, co., Spain B12 20
Llera de Canales, Mex. D9 100
Llerena, Spain F4 20
Lleulleu, Lago, l., Chile I1 92
Llico, Chile G1 92
Llíria, Spain E10 20
Llivia, Spain B12 20
Llobregat, stm., Spain C12 20
Lloydminster, Sk., Can. E9 106
Llucena, Spain D10 20
Lluchmayor see Llucmajor, Spain E13 20
Llucmajor, Spain E13 20
Llullaillaco, Volcán, vol., S.A. B3 92
Lo (Panlong), stm., Asia A7 48
Loa, Ut., U.S. E5 132
Loa, stm., Chile D3 90
Loanda, Braz. D6 90
Loange (Luangue), stm., Afr. F3 66
Lobamba, Swaz. E10 70
Lobanovo, Russia G21 10
Lobatse, Bots. D7 70
Löbau, Ger. E10 16
Lobaye, stm., C.A.R. D3 66
Lobelville, Tn., U.S. B11 122
Lobería, Arg. I8 92
Lobnja, Russia D20 10
Lobos, Arg. G8 92
Lobos, Cay, i., Bah. A9 102
Lobos, Isla, i., Mex. B3 100
Lobskoe, Russia E16 8
Łobżenica, Pol. C13 16
Locarno, Switz. D5 22
Loches, Fr. G10 14
Loch Garman see Wexford, Ire. I6 12
Lochinver, Scot., U.K. C7 12
Lochsa, stm., Id., U.S. D12 136
Lock, Austl. F7 74
Lockeport, N.S., Can. G11 110
Lockerbie, Scot., U.K. F9 12
Lockesburg, Ar., U.S. D4 122
Lockhart, Austl. J6 76
Lock Haven, Pa., U.S. C8 114
Lockney, Tx., U.S. G7 128
Lockport, Il., U.S. C9 120
Lockport, La., U.S. H8 122
Lockport, N.Y., U.S. E11 112
Lockwood, Mo., U.S. G4 120
Locminé, Fr. G6 14
Loc Ninh, Viet. G8 48
Locust Creek, stm., U.S. D4 120
Locust Fork, stm., Al., U.S. D11 122
Locust Grove, Ok., U.S. H2 120
Lod (Lydda), Isr. G5 58
Lodalskåpa, mtn., Nor. F2 8
Loddon, stm., Austl. K4 76
Lodejnoe Pole, Russia F15 8
Lodève, Fr. F9 18
Lodge Creek, stm., N.A. F4 124
Lodge Grass, Mt., U.S. B5 126
Lodgepole, Ab., Can. C15 138
Lodgepole, Ne., U.S. F10 126
Lodgepole Creek, stm., U.S. F10 126
Lodhrān, Pak. D3 54
Lodi, Italy E6 22
Lodi, Ca., U.S. E4 134
Lodi, Wi., U.S. H9 118
Lodja, D.R.C. E4 66
Lodwar, Kenya D7 66
Łódź, Pol. E15 16
Łódź, state, Pol. E15 16
Loei, Thai. D5 48
Loei, stm., Thai. D5 48
Loeriesfontein, S. Afr. G4 70
Lofer, Aus. C9 22
Lofoten, is., Nor. B5 8
Lofoten Basin, unds. A14 144
Loga, Niger G5 64
Logan, Ia., U.S. C2 120
Logan, Ks., U.S. B9 128
Logan, Oh., U.S. E3 114
Logan, Ut., U.S. B5 132
Logan, W.V., U.S. G4 114
Logan, Mount, mtn., Yk., Can. C2 106
Logan Creek, stm., Ne., U.S. E15 126
Logan Island, i., On., Can. A10 118
Logan Martin Lake, res., Al., U.S. D12 122
Logan Mountains, mts., Yk., Can. C5 106
Logan Pass, p., Mt., U.S. B13 136
Logansport, In., U.S. H3 112
Logansport, La., U.S. F5 122
Loganville, Ga., U.S. C2 116
Logone, stm., Afr. F3 62
Logroño, Spain B8 20
Løgstør, Den. H3 8
Logudoro, reg., Italy D2 24
Lohārdaga, India G10 54
Lohiniva, Fin. C11 8
Lohne, Ger. D4 16
Loho see Luohe, China E6 42
Lohrville, Ia., U.S. B3 120
Loi (Nanlei), stm., Asia B4 48
Loi, Phou, mtn., Laos B6 48
Loi-kaw, Mya. C3 48
Loi Mwe, Mya. B4 48
Loing, stm., Fr. F11 14
Loing, Canal du, can., Fr. F11 14
Loir, stm., Fr. G8 14
Loire, state, Fr. D10 18
Loire, stm., Fr. B4 18
Loire, Canal latéral à la, can., Fr. C9 18
Loire-Atlantique, state, Fr. G7 14
Loiret, state, Fr. F11 14
Loir-et-Cher, state, Fr. G10 14
Loja, Ec. D2 84
Loja, Spain G6 20
Lokandu, D.R.C. E5 66
Lokan Reservoir see Lokan tekojärvi, res., Fin. C12 8
Lokan tekojärvi, res., Fin. C12 8
Lokeren, Bel. C13 14
Loket, Czech Rep. F8 16
Lokichar, Kenya D7 66
Lokichokio, Kenya D6 66
Loknja, Russia D13 10
Lokoja, Nig. H6 64
Lokolama, D.R.C. E3 66
Lokot', Russia H17 10
Loksa, Est. A8 10
Loks Land, i., Nu., Can. E13 141
Lola, Gui. H3 64
Loleta, Ca., U.S. C1 134
Loliondo, Tan. E7 66
Lolita, Tx., U.S. F11 130
Lolland, i., Den. I4 8
Lolo, Mt., U.S. D12 136
Lolodorf, Cam. D2 66
Lolo Pass, p., U.S. D12 136
Lolowai, Vanuatu j16 79d
Loltong, Vanuatu j16 79d
Lolvavana, Passage, strt., Vanuatu j16 79d
Lom, Blg. F10 26
Lom, Nor. F3 8
Lom, stm., Afr. F2 62
Lomami, stm., D.R.C. D4 66
Lomas de Zamora, Arg. G8 92
Lomax, Il., U.S. D6 120
Łomazy, Pol. E19 16
Lombardia, state, Italy E6 22
Lombardy see Lombardia, state, Italy E6 22
Lomblen, Pulau, i., Indon. G7 44
Lombok, Indon. H10 50
Lombok, i., Indon. H10 50
Lombok, Selat, strt., Indon. H9 50
Lomé, Togo H5 64
Lomela, D.R.C. E4 66
Lomela, stm., D.R.C. E4 66
Lometa, Tx., U.S. C9 130
Lomié, Cam. D2 66
Lomira, Wi., U.S. H10 118
Lommel, Bel. C14 14
Lomond, Loch, l., Scot., U.K. E8 12
Lomonosov, Russia A12 10
Lomonosovka, Kaz. D11 32
Lomovoe, Russia D19 8
Lompobatang, Gunung, mtn., Indon. F11 50
Lompoc, Ca., U.S. I5 134
Lom Sak, Thai. D5 48
Łomża, Pol. C18 16
Łomża, state, Pol. C18 16
Lonaconing, Md., U.S. E7 114
Lonāvale, India B1 53
Loncoche, Chile G2 90
Loncopué, Arg. I2 92
London, On., Can. F8 112
London, Eng., U.K. J12 12
London, Ar., U.S. B5 122
London, Ky., U.S. G1 114
London, Tx., U.S. D8 130
Londonderry, N.S., Can. E13 110
Londonderry (Derry), N. Ire., U.K. F6 12
Londonderry, Cape, c., Austl. B5 74
Londonderry, Isla, i., Chile K2 90
Londrina, Braz. D6 90
Lone Grove, Ok., U.S. G11 128
Lone Oak, Ky., U.S. G9 120
Lone Pine, Ca., U.S. G7 134
Lone Rock, Wi., U.S. A7 120
Lone Tree, Ia., U.S. C6 120
Lone Wolf, Ok., U.S. G9 128
Long, stm., China I3 42
Longa, Ang. C2 68
Longá, stm., Braz. B5 88
Longa, proliv, strt., Russia B24 34
Long Akah, Malay. B9 50
Longana, Vanuatu j17 79d
Longarone, Italy D9 22
Longaví, Chile G2 92
Longbangun, Indon. C9 50
Long Bay, b., U.S. C7 116
Long Beach, Ca., U.S. J7 134
Long Beach, Ms., U.S. G9 122
Long Beach, N.Y., U.S. D12 114
Long Beach, Wa., U.S. D2 136
Long Beach, cst., N.J., U.S. E11 114
Longboat Key, Fl., U.S. I3 116
Long Branch, N.J., U.S. D12 114
Long Cay, i., Bah. m18 104f
Longchang, China G1 42
Longchuan, China I6 42
Long Creek, stm., N.A. E10 124
Longde, China D2 42
Long Eaton, Eng., U.K. I11 12
Longford, Austl. L6 76
Longford, Ire. H5 12
Longford, state, Ire. H5 12
Long Hu, l., China F6 42
Longhua, China A7 42
Longhui, China H4 42
Longiram, Indon. C9 50
Long Island, i., Antig. f4 105b
Long Island, i., Austl. D7 76
Long Island, i., Bah. A10 102
Long Island, i., N.S., Can. F10 110
Long Island, i., Nu., Can. E14 106
Long Island, i., N.Y., U.S. D12 114
Long Island Sound, strt., U.S. D12 114
Longitudinal, Valle, val., Chile H1 92
Longjiang, China B9 36
Longkou, China C9 42
Long Lake, N.Y., U.S. G2 110
Long Lake, l., On., Can. B11 118
Longleaf, La., U.S. F6 122
Long Leaf Park, N.C., U.S. B8 116
Longli, China H2 42
Longlin, China G6 36
Longling, China G4 36
Longmeadow, Ma., U.S. B13 114
Long Moc, Viet. C7 48
Longmont, Co., U.S. A3 128
Long Mountain, mtn., Mo., U.S. H5 120
Longnan, China I6 42
Longnawan, Indon. C9 50
Long Pine, Ne., U.S. E13 126
Long Point, c., Bah. n18 104f
Long Point, c., N.S., Can. D16 110
Long Point, pen., Mb., Can. A15 124
Long Point, pen., On., Can. F9 112
Long Point Bay, b., On., Can. F9 112
Longquan, China G8 42
Long Range Mountains, mts., Nf., Can. j22 107a
Longreach, Austl. D5 76
Long-Sault, On., Can. E2 110
Longsegah, Indon. B10 50
Longshan, China G3 42
Longsheng, China I3 42
Longs Peak, mtn., Co., U.S. A3 128
Long Swamp, Br. Vir. Is. e8 104b
Long Thanh, Viet. G8 48
Longton, Ks., U.S. G1 120
Longtown, Eng., U.K. F10 12
Longueuil, Qc., Can. E3 110
Longuyon, Fr. E14 14
Longview, Ab., Can. F16 138
Long View, N.C., U.S. I4 114
Longview, Tx., U.S. E4 122
Longview, Wa., U.S. D4 136
Longwai, Indon. C10 50
Longwy, Fr. E14 14
Longxi, China E5 36
Longxian, China D2 42
Long Xuyen, Viet. G7 48
Longyan, China I7 42
Longyou, China G8 42
Longzhen, China B10 36
Longzhou, China J2 42
Lonigo, Italy E8 22
Löningen, Ger. D3 16
Lonja, stm., Cro. E13 22
Lonoke, Ar., U.S. C7 122
Lonquimay, Volcán, vol., Chile I2 92
Lonsdale, Mn., U.S. G5 118
Lons-le-Saunier, Fr. H14 14
Lontra, stm., Braz. D1 88
Loogootee, In., U.S. F11 120
Lookout, Cape, c., N.C., U.S. B9 116
Lookout Mountain, mts., U.S. C13 122
Lookout Pass, p., U.S. C11 136
Lookout Ridge, mts., Ak., U.S. C8 140
Loolmalassin, vol., Tan. E7 66
Loomis, Ne., U.S. G13 126
Loomis, Wa., U.S. B7 136
Loop, Tx., U.S. B5 130
Loop Head, c., Ire. I2 12
Lop, China A5 46
Lop, stm., Viet. F8 48
Lopatina, gora, mtn., Russia F17 34
Lopatka, mys, c., Russia F20 34
Lopatovo, Russia D12 10
Lop Buri, Thai. E5 48
Lopévi, i., Vanuatu k17 79d
Lopez, Cap, c., Gabon E1 66
Lop Nur, l., China C3 36
Loptjuga, Russia E22 8
Lora, Hāmūn-i-, l., Asia D9 56
Lora del Río, Spain G5 20
Lorain, Oh., U.S. C3 114
Loraine, Tx., U.S. B7 130
Loralai, Pak. C2 54
Lorca, Spain G9 20
Lord Howe Island, i., Austl. G6 72
Lord Howe Rise, unds. L19 142
Lord Mayor Bay, b., Nu., Can. B12 106
Lordsburg, N.M., U.S. K8 132
Loreauville, La., U.S. G7 122
Loreley, misc. cult., Ger. F3 16
Lorena, Braz. L3 88
Lorengau, Pap. N. Gui. a4 79a
Lorenzo, Tx., U.S. H7 128
Lorenzo Geyres, Ur. F9 92
Loreto, Arg. C9 92
Loreto, Mex. D8 100
Loreto, Mex. B3 100
Loreto, state, Peru H4 86
Loretto, Ky., U.S. G12 120
Loretto, Tn., U.S. B11 122
Lorica, Col. C4 86
Lorient, Fr. G5 14
Lorimor, Ia., U.S. C3 120
Loriol-sur-Drôme, Fr. E10 18
Loris, S.C., U.S. B7 116
Lorman, Ms., U.S. F7 122
Lorn, Firth of, b., Scot., U.K. E7 12
Lorne, Austl. L5 76
Lorne, N.B., Can. C10 110
Lörrach, Ger. I3 16
Lorraine, hist. reg., Fr. F14 14
Los, Îles de, is., Gui. H2 64
Losada, stm., Col. F4 86
Los Alamos, N.M., U.S. F2 128
Los Aldamas, Mex. B9 100
Los Andes, Chile F2 92
Los Angeles, Chile H1 92
Los Angeles, Ca., U.S. I7 134
Los Angeles Aqueduct, aq., Ca., U.S. H7 134
Los Antiguos, Arg. I2 90
Los Banos, Ca., U.S. F5 134
Los Blancos, Arg. D4 90
Los Bolones, Cerro, mtn., Mex. G12 100
Los Cerrillos, Arg. E5 92
Los Conquistadores, Arg. E8 92
Los Fresnos, Tx., U.S. H10 130
Los Garza, Mex. H8 130
Los Gatos, Ca., U.S. F4 134
Loshan see Leshan, China F5 36
Los Hermanos, Islas, is., Ven. B9 86
Łosice, Pol. D18 16
Los Idolos, Parque Arquelógico de, hist., Col. G3 86
Lošinj, Otok, i., Cro. F11 22
Losinoborskaja, Russia C15 32
Los Juríes, Arg. D6 92
Los Lagos, Chile G2 90
Los Llanos, P.R. B3 104a
Los López, Mex. H8 130
Los Lunas, N.M., U.S. I10 132
Los Mochis, Mex. C4 100
Los Nogales, Mex. H8 130
Losolava, Vanuatu j16 79d
Los Padillas, N.M., U.S. I10 132
Los Palacios, Arg. D3 92
Los Palacios, Cuba A6 102
Los Palacios y Villafranca, Spain G4 20
Los Picachos, Parque Nacional, p.o.i., Col. F4 86
Los Rábanos, P.R. B2 104a
Los Ríos, state, Ec. H2 86
Los Roques, Islas, is., Ven. B8 86
Los Sauces, Chile H1 92
Lossiemouth, Scot., U.K. D9 12
Lost, stm., U.S. A4 134
Los Taques, Ven. B6 86
Los Teques, Ven. B8 86
Los Testigos, Islas, is., Ven. B10 86
Lost Hills, Ca., U.S. H6 134
Lost Nation, Ia., U.S. C7 120
Lost River Range, mts., Id., U.S. F13 136
Lost Trail Pass, p., U.S. E13 136
Losuia, Pap. N. Gui. b5 79a
Los Vidrios, Mex. F6 98
Los Vilos, Chile E2 92
Los Yébenes, Spain E6 20
Lot, state, Fr. E7 18
Lot, stm., Fr. E7 18
Lota, Chile H1 92
Lot-et-Garonne, state, Fr. E6 18
Lothair, S. Afr. E10 70
Lotošino, Russia D18 10
Lotsane, stm., Bots. C8 70
Lotta, stm., Eur. B13 8
Lotuke, Jabal, mtn., Sudan G6 62
Lotung, Tai. I9 42
Louang Namtha, Laos B5 48
Louangphrabang, Laos C6 48
Loubomo, Congo E2 66
Loudon, Tn., U.S. A1 116
Loudonville, Oh., U.S. D3 114
Loudun, Fr. G9 14
Loue, stm., Fr. H14 14
Louga, Sen. F1 64
Louge, Arg. H7 92
Loughborough, Eng., U.K. I11 12
Loughrea, Ire. H4 12
Louhi, Russia C15 8
Louin, Ms., U.S. E9 122
Louisa, Ky., U.S. F3 114
Louisbourg, N.S., Can. E16 110
Louisburg, Ks., U.S. F3 120
Louisburg, N.C., U.S. H7 114
Louise, Ms., U.S. D8 122
Louise, Tx., U.S. H2 122
Louiseville, Qc., Can. D3 110
Louisiade Archipelago, is., Pap. N. Gui. B10 74
Louisiana, Mo., U.S. E6 120
Louisiana, state, U.S. F6 122
Louis Trichardt, S. Afr. C9 70
Louisville, Al., U.S. F13 122
Louisville, Ga., U.S. C3 116
Louisville, Ky., U.S. F12 120
Louisville, Ne., U.S. D1 120
Louisville, Oh., U.S. D4 114
Louisville Ridge, unds. M22 142
Louis-XIV, Pointe, c., Qc., Can. E14 106
Loulé, Port. G2 20
Loum, Cam. D1 66
Lount Lake, l., On., Can. A4 118
Louny, Czech Rep. F9 16
Loup, stm., Ne., U.S. F14 126
Loup City, Ne., U.S. F14 126
Loups Marins, Lacs des, l., Qc., Can. D16 106
Lourdes, Fr. F5 18
Lourenço Marques see Maputo, Moz. D11 70
Lourinhã, Port. E1 20
Lousã, Port. D2 20
Louth, Austl. H5 76
Louth, Ire. H6 12
Louth, Eng., U.K. H13 12
Louth, state, Ire. H6 12
Loutrá Aidipsoú, Grc. E6 28
Louvain see Leuven, Bel. D13 14
Louviers, Fr. E10 14
Louviers, Co., U.S. B4 128
Lovat', stm., Russia B14 10
Loveč, Blg. F11 26
Loveč, state, Blg. F11 26
Loveland, Co., U.S. G7 126
Lovell, Wy., U.S. C4 126
Lovell Village, St. Vin. p11 105e
Lovelock, Nv., U.S. C7 134
Lovely, Ky., U.S. G3 114
Lovere, Italy E6 22
Loves Park, Il., U.S. B8 120
Loving, N.M., U.S. B3 130
Loving, Tx., U.S. H10 128
Lovingston, Va., U.S. G7 114
Lovington, N.M., U.S. B4 130
Lovosice, Czech Rep. F9 16
Lovozero, Russia D13 8
Lovozero, ozero, l., Russia C16 8
Lóvua, Ang. B3 68
Low, Qc., Can. C14 112
Low, Cape, c., Nu., Can. C13 106
Lowa, D.R.C. E5 66
Lowa, stm., D.R.C. E5 66
Lowden, Ia., U.S. C7 120
Lowell, Ar., U.S. H3 120
Lowell, In., U.S. G2 112
Lowell, Ma., U.S. B14 114
Lowell, Or., U.S. G4 136
Lowell, Lake, res., Id., U.S. G10 136
Löwen, stm., Nmb. E3 70
Löwenberg, Ger. D8 16
Lower Arrow Lake, res., B.C., Can. G12 138
Lower Austria see Niederösterreich, state, Aus. B12 22
Lower California see Baja California, pen., Mex. B2 96
Lower Egypt see Misr el-Bahrî, hist. reg., Egypt G2 58
Lower Glenelg National Park, p.o.i., Austl. L3 76
Lower Hutt, N.Z. E6 80
Lower Lake, l., U.S. B5 134
Lower Manitou Lake, l., On., Can. B6 118
Lower Post, B.C., Can. D5 106
Lower Red Lake, l., Mn., U.S. D3 118
Lower Saxony see Niedersachsen, state, Ger. D4 16
Lower Trajan's Wall, misc. cult., Eur. D15 26
Lower West End Point, c., Anguilla A1 105a
Lower Woods Harbour, N.S., Can. G10 110
Lowestoft, Eng., U.K. I14 12
Lowgar, state, Afg. A2 54
Łowicz, Pol. D15 16
Lowmoor, Va., U.S. G6 114
Low Rocky Point, c., Austl. o12 77a
Lowry City, Mo., U.S. F4 120
Lowville, N.Y., U.S. E14 112
Loxton, Austl. J3 76
Loyal, Wi., U.S. G8 118
Loyalton, Ca., U.S. D5 134
Loyalty Islands see Loyauté, Îles, is., N. Cal. m16 79d
Loyang see Luoyang, China D5 42
Loyauté, Îles (Loyalty Islands), is., N. Cal. m16 79d
Loyoro, Ug. D6 66
Lozère, state, Fr. E9 18
Loznica, Serb. E6 26
Lualaba, stm., Afr. E5 66
Luama, stm., D.R.C. E5 66
Lu'an, China F7 42
Luan, stm., China E3 38
Luancheng, China J3 42
Luanda, Ang. B1 68
Luando, stm., Ang. C2 68
Luang, Khao (Maw Taung), mtn., Asia G4 48
Luang, Thale, l., Thai. I5 48
Luang Chiang Dao, Doi, mtn., Thai. C4 48
Luanginga, stm., Afr. G4 66
Luang Prabang see Louangphrabang, Laos C6 48
Luangue (Loange), stm., Afr. F3 66
Luangwa, stm., Afr. C5 68
Luanping, China A7 42
Luanshya, Zam. C4 68
Luan Toro, Arg. H5 92
Luanxian, China B8 42
Luapula, stm., Afr. C4 68
Luar, Danau, l., Indon. C8 50
Luarca, Spain A4 20
Luba, Eq. Gui. I6 64
Lubaantun, sci., Belize D3 102
Lubań, Pol. E11 16
Lubāna, Lat. D9 10
Lubang Islands, is., Phil. D2 52
Lubango, Ang. C1 68
Lubāns, l., Lat. D9 10
Lubartów, Pol. E18 16
Lübben, Ger. E9 16
Lübbenau, Ger. E9 16
Lubbock, Tx., U.S. H7 128
Lübeck, Ger. C6 16
Lubefu, D.R.C. E4 66
Lubefu, stm., D.R.C. E4 66
Lubień Kujawski, Pol. D15 16
Lubilash, stm., D.R.C. F4 66
Lubin, Pol. E12 16
Lublin, Pol. E18 16
Lublin, state, Pol. E18 16
Lubliniec, Pol. F14 16
Lubny, Ukr. E4 32
Luboń, Pol. D12 16
Lubsko, Pol. E10 16
Lübtheen, Ger. C7 16
Lubuagan, Phil. B3 52
Lubudi, D.R.C. G5 66
Lubukbatang, Indon. F3 50
Lubuklinggau, Indon. E3 50
Lubukpakam, Indon. B1 50
Lubuksikaping, Indon. C1 50
Lubumbashi (Élisabethville), D.R.C. G5 66
Lubutu, D.R.C. E5 66
Lübz, Ger. C7 16
Lucan, On., Can. E8 112
Lucanas, Peru F3 84
Lucania, hist. reg., Italy D10 24
Lucania, Mount, mtn., Yk., Can. C3 106
Lucapa, Ang. B3 68
Lucas, Ia., U.S. C4 120
Lucas, Ks., U.S. B10 128
Lucban, Phil. C3 52
Lucca, Italy G7 22
Lucea, Jam. i12 104d
Luce Bay, b., Scot., U.K. G8 12
Lucedale, Ms., U.S. G10 122
Lucena, Phil. D3 52
Lucena, Spain G6 20
Lucena del Cid see Llucena, Spain D10 20
Lučenec, Slov. H15 16
Lucera, Italy C9 24
Lucerne see Luzern, Switz. C5 22
Lucerne, Ca., U.S. D3 134
Lucerne, Lake of see Vierwaldstätter See, l., Switz. D5 22
Luchou see Luzhou, China G1 42
Luchow see Luzhou, China G1 42
Lüchow, Ger. C7 16
Luchuan, China J4 42
Lucinda, Austl. B6 76
Lucira, Ang. C1 68
Luckau, Ger. E9 16
Luckenwalde, Ger. D9 16
Luckhoff, S. Afr. F7 70
Luck Lake, l., Sk., Can. C6 124
Lucknow, On., Can. E8 112
Lucknow, India E8 54
Lucky Lake, Sk., Can. D6 124
Luçon, Fr. C4 18
Lucusse, Ang. C3 68
Luda Kamčija, stm., Blg. G14 26
Ludao, China C8 38
Lüdenscheid, Ger. E3 16
Lüderitz, Nmb. E2 70
Ludhiāna, India C5 54
Ludian, China F5 36
Ludington, Mi., U.S. E3 112
Ludlow, Eng., U.K. I10 12
Ludlow, Ma., U.S. B13 114
Ludogorie, reg., Blg. F13 26
Ludowici, Ga., U.S. E4 116
Luduș, Rom. C11 26
Ludvika, Swe. F6 8
Ludwigsburg, Ger. H4 16
Ludwigsfelde, Ger. D9 16
Ludwigshafen am Rhein, Ger. G4 16
Ludwigslust, Ger. C7 16
Ludza, Lat. D10 10
Luebo, D.R.C. F4 66
Lueders, Tx., U.S. B8 130
Luena, Ang. C3 68
Luena, D.R.C. F5 66
Luena, stm., Ang. C3 68
Luepa, Ven. E11 86
Lueyang, China E2 42
Lufeng, China J6 42
Lufico, Ang. B1 68
Lufira, stm., D.R.C. F5 66
Lufkin, Tx., U.S. F4 122
Luga, Russia B12 10
Luga, stm., Russia A11 10
Lugano, Switz. D5 22
Lugano, Lago di, l., Eur. D14 18
Luganville, Vanuatu j16 79d
Lugards Falls, wtfl., Kenya E7 66
Lugenda, stm., Moz. C6 68
Luggarus see Locarno, Switz. D5 22
Lugnaquillia Mountain, mtn., Ire. I6 12
Lugo, Italy F8 22
Lugo, Spain A3 20
Lugo, co., Spain B3 20
Lugoj, Rom. D8 26
Lūgovoy, Kaz. F12 32
Lugovskij, Russia E11 34
Luhans'k, Ukr. E5 32
Luhe, China E8 42
Luhovicy, Russia F21 10
Luhsien see Luzhou, China G1 42
Luiana, Ang. D3 68
Luido, Moz. B12 70
Luik see Liège, Bel. D14 14
Luimneach see Limerick, Ire. I4 12
Luino, Italy D5 22
Luishia, D.R.C. G5 66
Luis L. León, Presa, res., Mex. F2 130
Luis Muñoz Marin, Aeropuerto Internacional, P.R. B3 104a
Luitpold Coast, cst., Ant. C1 81
Luiza, D.R.C. F4 66
Luján, Arg. F4 92
Luján de Cuyo, Arg. F3 92
Lujiang, China F7 42
Lukang, Tai. I9 42
Lukenie, stm., D.R.C. E3 66
Lukeville, Az., U.S. L4 132
Lukojanov, Russia I21 8
Lukolela, D.R.C. E3 66
Lukolela, D.R.C. F4 66
Lukovit, Blg. F11 26
Łuków, Pol. E18 16
Lukuga, stm., D.R.C. F5 66
Lukula, D.R.C. F2 66
Lukulu, Zam. C3 68
Lulaka, stm., D.R.C. E4 66
Luleå, Swe. D10 8
Luleälven, stm., Swe. C9 8
Lüleburgaz, Tur. B10 28
Lules, Arg. C5 92
Luliang, China G5 36
Lüliang Shan, mts., China C4 42
Luling, Tx., U.S. E10 130
Lulonga, stm., D.R.C. D3 66
Lulua, stm., D.R.C. F4 66
Luluabourg see Kananga, D.R.C. F4 66
Lumajang, Indon. H8 50
Lumajangdong Co, l., China B8 54
Lumaku, Gunong, mtn., Malay. A9 50
Lumana, D.R.C. E5 66
Lumbala Kaquengue, Ang. C3 68
Lumbala N'guimbo, Ang. C3 68
Lumber, stm., U.S. B6 116
Lumber City, Ga., U.S. E3 116
Lumberport, W.V., U.S. E5 114
Lumberton, N.C., U.S. B7 116
Lumberton, Tx., U.S. G4 122
Lumbis, Indon. A10 50
Lumbrales, Spain D4 20
Lumby, B.C., Can. F12 138
Lumding, India F14 54
Lumpkin, Ga., U.S. E14 122
Lumu, Indon. E11 50
Lumut, Malay. J5 48
Lumut, Tanjung, c., Indon. E4 50
Luna Pier, Mi., U.S. C2 114
Lūnāvāda, India G4 54
Lund, B.C., Can. G6 138
Lund, Swe. I5 8
Lund, Nv., U.S. E2 132
Lundazi, Zam. C5 68
Lundy, i., Eng., U.K. J8 12
Lüneburg, Ger. C6 16
Lüneburger Heide, reg., Ger. D6 16
Lunel, Fr. F10 18
Lünen, Ger. E3 16
Lunenburg, N.S., Can. F12 110
Lunenburg, Va., U.S. H7 114
Lunéville, Fr. F15 14
Lungch'i see Zhangzhou, China I7 42
Lunge'nake, China C10 54
Lunglei, India G14 54
Lungtsin see Longzhou, China J2 42
Lungué-Bungo (Lungwebungu), stm., Afr. C3 68

Name	Map Ref.	Page
Lungwebungu (Lungué-Bungo), stm., Afr.	C3	68
Lūni, India	E4	54
Lūni, stm., India	F4	54
Luninec, Bela.	H9	10
Luninets see Luninec, Bela.	H9	10
Lūnkaransar, India	D4	54
Luntai, China	F14	32
Luo, stm., China	D4	42
Luo, stm., China	D4	42
Luobei, China	B11	36
Luobu, China	I3	42
Luocheng, China	I3	42
Luoding, China	J4	42
Luofu, D.R.C.	E5	66
Luohe, China	E6	42
Luoji, China	E7	42
Luonan, China	D4	42
Luoning, China	D4	42
Luoqi, China	G2	42
Luotian, China	F6	42
Luowenba, China	F2	42
Luoxiao Shan, mts., China	H6	42
Luoyang, China	D5	42
Luoyuan, China	H8	42
Luozi, D.R.C.	F2	66
Lupanshui, China	F5	36
Lupar, stm., Malay.	C7	50
Łupawa, Pol.	B13	16
Lupeni, Rom.	D10	26
Lupin see Manzhouli, China	B8	36
Luputa, D.R.C.	F4	66
Luqiao, China	E7	42
Luqiao, China	G9	42
Luqu, China	E5	36
Luque, Spain	G6	20
Luquillo, P.R.	B4	104a
Lure, Fr.	G15	14
Luremo, Ang.	B2	68
Lurgan, N. Ire., U.K.	G6	12
Luribay, Bol.	C3	90
Lurín, Peru	F2	84
Lúrio, Moz.	C7	68
Lúrio, stm., Moz.	C6	68
Lusaka, Zam.	D4	68
Lusambo, D.R.C.	E4	66
Lusanga, D.R.C.	E3	66
Lusangi, D.R.C.	E5	66
Luscar, Ab., Can.	C13	138
Luseland, Sk., Can.	B4	124
Lushan, China	E5	42
Lu Shan, mtn., China	G6	42
Lushnja see Lushnjë, Alb.	D13	24
Lushnjë, Alb.	D13	24
Lushoto, Tan.	E7	66
Lüshun (Port Arthur), China	E4	38
Lusk, Wy., U.S.	E8	126
Lussac-les-Châteaux, Fr.	C6	18
Lūt, Dasht-e, des., Iran	C8	56
Lü-ta see Dalian, China	B9	42
Lü Tao, i., Tai.	J9	42
Lutembo, Ang.	C3	68
Lutesville, Mo., U.S.	G7	120
Luther, Mi., U.S.	D4	112
Luther, Ok., U.S.	F11	128
Lutherstadt Eisleben, Ger.	E7	16
Lutherstadt Wittenberg, Ger.	E8	16
Luti, Sol. Is.	d7	79b
Luton, Eng., U.K.	J12	12
Lutong, Malay.	A8	50
Łutselk'e, N.T., Can.	C8	106
Lutz, Fl., U.S.	H3	116
Lützow, Ger.	C7	16
Lutzow-Holm Bay, b., Ant.	B8	81
Luuq, Som.	D8	66
Luverne, Al., U.S.	F12	122
Lu Verne, Ia., U.S.	I4	118
Luverne, Mn., U.S.	H2	118
Luvua, stm., D.R.C.	F5	66
Luvuvhu, stm., S. Afr.	C10	70
Luwegu, stm., Tan.	F7	66
Luwingu, Zam.	C4	68
Luwuk, Indon.	F7	44
Luxapallila Creek, stm., U.S.	D11	122
Luxembourg, Lux.	E14	14
Luxembourg, ctry., Eur.	E15	14
Luxemburg, Wi., U.S.	D2	112
Luxeuil-les-Bains, Fr.	G15	14
Luxi, China	G4	36
Luxor see El-Uqsor, Egypt	B6	62
Luz, Braz.	J3	88
Luza, Russia	F22	8
Luža, Russia	A14	10
Luzern (Lucerne), Switz.	C5	22
Luzhai, China	I3	42
Luzhou, China	G1	42
Luziânia, Braz.	I2	88
Luzilândia, Braz.	B4	88
Lužki, Bela.	E10	10
Lužnice, stm., Eur.	G10	16
Luzon, i., Phil.	B3	52
Luzon Strait, strt., Asia	G16	30
L'viv, Ukr.	F13	6
L'viv, co., Ukr.	G19	16
L'vovskij, Russia	E20	10
Lwówek, Pol.	D12	16
Lyallpur see Faisalabad, Pak.	C4	54
Lyčkovo, Russia	C15	10
Lycksele, Swe.	D8	8
Lydenburg, S. Afr.	D10	70
Lydia Mills, S.C., U.S.	B3	116
Lyell, Mount, mtn., Can.	E13	138
Lyerly, Ga., U.S.	C13	122
Lyford, Tx., U.S.	H10	130
Lykošino, Russia	B16	10
Lyle, Mn., U.S.	H6	118
Lyman, Ne., U.S.	F8	126
Lyman, S.C., U.S.	B3	116
Lymans'ke, Ukr.	C17	26
Lyme Bay, b., Eng., U.K.	K9	12
Łyna (Lava), stm., Eur.	B16	16
Lynch, Ne., U.S.	E14	126
Lynchburg, Oh., U.S.	E2	114
Lynchburg, S.C., U.S.	B5	116
Lynchburg, Tn., U.S.	B12	122
Lynchburg, Va., U.S.	G6	114
Lynd, stm., Austl.	A4	76
Lynden, Wa., U.S.	B4	136
Lyndhurst, Austl.	B5	76
Lyndon, Ks., U.S.	F2	120
Lyndon, Ky., U.S.	F12	120
Lyndon, stm., Austl.	D2	74
Lyndon B. Johnson, Lake, res., Tx., U.S.	D9	130
Lyndon B. Johnson Space Center, sci., Tx., U.S.	H3	122
Lyngen, b., Nor.	B9	8
Lyngseidet, Nor.	B8	8
Lynn, Al., U.S.	C11	122
Lynn, Ma., U.S.	B14	114
Lynndyl, Ut., U.S.	D4	132
Lynn Haven, Fl., U.S.	G13	122
Lynn Lake, Mb., Can.	D10	106
Lyntupy, Bela.	E9	10
Lynx Lake, l., N.T., Can.	C9	106
Lyon, Fr.	D10	18
Lyon Inlet, b., Nu., Can.	B14	106
Lyon Mountain, N.Y., U.S.	F2	110
Lyonnais, hist. reg., Fr.	D10	18
Lyons, In., U.S.	F10	120
Lyons, Ks., U.S.	C10	128
Lyons, Mi., U.S.	F5	112
Lyons, Ne., U.S.	C1	120
Lyons, N.Y., U.S.	E13	112
Lyons, stm., Austl.	D3	74
Lysa Hora, Ukr.	A18	26
Łysica, mtn., Pol.	F16	16
Lyskovo, Russia	H21	8
Lys'va, Russia	C9	32
Lysychans'k, Ukr.	E5	32
Lytham Saint Anne's, Eng., U.K.	H9	12
Lytle, Tx., U.S.	E9	130
M		
Ma, stm., Asia	C7	48
Ma'ān, Jord.	H6	58
Ma'ān, state, Jord.	H7	58
Ma'anshan, China	F8	42
Maardu, Est.	G11	8
Maarianhamina see Mariehamn, Fin.	F9	8
Ma'arrat an-Nu'mān, Syria	C7	58
Maas (Meuse), stm., Eur.	D14	14
Maasin, Phil.	E5	52
Maastricht, Neth.	D14	14
Mabalane, Moz.	C11	70
Mabank, Tx., U.S.	E2	122
Mabaruma, Guy.	C12	86
Mabeleapodi, Bots.	B6	70
Mabel Lake, l., B.C., Can.	F12	138
Maben, Ms., U.S.	D9	122
Mablethorpe, Eng., U.K.	H13	12
Mableton, Ga., U.S.	D14	122
Mabton, Wa., U.S.	D6	136
Mabuasehube Game Reserve, Bots.	D6	70
Mača, Russia	E12	34
Maca, Cerro, vol., Chile	H2	90
Macachín, Arg.	H6	92
Macaé, Braz.	L5	88
Macaíba, Braz.	C8	88
Macajuba, Braz.	G5	88
Macalister, B.C., Can.	D8	138
Macalister, stm., Austl.	K6	76
Macalister, Mount, mtn., Austl.	J7	76
MacAlpine Lake, l., Nu., Can.	B10	106
Macan, Kepulauan, is., Indon.	G12	50
Macapá, Braz.	C7	84
Macará, Ec.	D2	84
Macareo, Caño, stm., Ven.	C11	86
MacArthur, Phil.	E5	52
Macas, Ec.	I2	86
Macau, Braz.	C7	88
Macau see Aomen, China	J5	42
Macaúbas, Braz.	G4	88
MacClenny, Fl., U.S.	F3	116
Macclesfield, Eng., U.K.	H10	12
Macdhui, Ben, mtn., Afr.	G9	70
Macdonald, Lake, l., Austl.	D5	74
MacDonald Pass, p., Mt., U.S.	D14	136
MacDonnell Ranges, mts., Austl.	D6	74
Macdui, Ben, mtn., Scot., U.K.	D9	12
Macedonia, ctry., Eur.	B4	28
Macedonia, hist. reg., Eur.	H10	26
Maceió, Braz.	E8	88
Macenta, Gui.	H3	64
Maceo, Col.	D4	86
Macerata, Italy	G10	22
MacFarlane, stm., Sk., Can.	D9	106
Macgillycuddy's Reeks, mts., Ire.	J3	12
MacGregor, Mb., Can.	D15	124
Machado, Braz.	K3	88
Machado, stm., Braz.	F5	84
Machagai, Arg.	C7	92
Machaíla, Moz.	C11	70
Machakos, Kenya	E7	66
Machala, Ec.	D2	84
Machalí, Chile	G2	92
Machalilla, Parque Nacional, p.o.i., Ec.	H1	86
Machanga, Moz.	B12	70
Machaquilá, stm., Guat.	D3	102
Machattie, Lake, l., Austl.	E2	76
Machaze, Moz.	B11	70
Macheng, China	F6	42
Mācherla, India	C4	53
Machias, Me., U.S.	F9	110
Machilīpatnam (Bandar), India	C5	53
Machiques, Ven.	B5	86
Machkund, res., India	B6	53
Macho, Arroyo del, stm., N.M., U.S.	H4	128
Machu Picchu see Machupicchu, sci., Peru	F3	84
Machupicchu, sci., Peru	F3	84
Maciá, Arg.	F8	92
Macia, Moz.	D11	70
Măcin, Rom.	D15	26
Macintyre, stm., Austl.	G7	76
Mackay, Austl.	C7	76
Mackay, Id., U.S.	G13	136
Mackay, Lake, l., Austl.	D5	74
MacKay Lake, l., N.T., Can.	C8	106
Mackenzie, stm., Austl.	D7	76
Mackenzie, stm., N.T., Can.	B4	106
Mackenzie Bay, b., Can.	C12	140
Mackenzie King Island, i., Can.	B3	141
Mackenzie Mountains, mts., Can.	C4	106
Mackinac, Straits of, strt., Mi., U.S.	C4	112
Mackinac Bridge, Mi., U.S.	C5	112
Mackinac Island, Mi., U.S.	C5	112
Mackinaw, stm., Il., U.S.	D9	120
Mackinaw City, Mi., U.S.	C5	112
Mackinnon Road, Kenya	E7	66
Macklin, Sk., Can.	B4	124
Macksville, Austl.	H9	76
Macksville, Ks., U.S.	C9	128
Maclean, Austl.	G9	76
Maclear, S. Afr.	G9	70
Macleay, stm., Austl.	H9	76
Macleod, Lake, l., Austl.	D2	74
Macmillan, stm., Yk., Can.	C4	106
Macomb, Il., U.S.	D7	120
Macomer, Italy	D2	24
Mâcon, Fr.	C10	18
Macon, Ga., U.S.	D2	116
Macon, Il., U.S.	E9	120
Macon, Mo., U.S.	E5	120
Macon, Ms., U.S.	D10	122
Macon, Bayou, stm., U.S.	E7	122
Macondo, Ang.	C3	68
Macorís, Cabo, c., Dom. Rep.	C12	102
Macoupin Creek, stm., Il., U.S.	E8	120
Macovane, Moz.	B12	70
Macquarie, stm., Austl.	H6	76
Macquarie, stm., Austl.	n13	77a
Macquarie, Lake, l., Austl.	I8	76
Macquarie Harbour, b., Austl.	o12	77a
Macquarie Island, i., Austl.	A20	81
Macquarie Marshes, sw., Austl.	H6	76
Macquarie Ridge, unds.	O18	142
Mac. Robertson Land, reg., Ant.	B10	81
Macucuau, stm., Braz.	H11	86
Macugnaga, Italy	E4	22
Macumba, stm., Austl.	E7	74
Macuro, Ven.	B10	86
Macusani, Peru	F3	84
Macuspana, Mex.	G12	100
Mad, stm., Ca., U.S.	C2	134
Mādabā, Jord.	G6	58
Madagascar, ctry., Afr.	D8	68
Madagascar Basin, unds.	L8	142
Madagascar Plateau, unds.	M7	142
Madan, Blg.	H11	26
Madanapalle, India	E4	53
Madang, Pap. N. Gui.	b4	79a
Madaoua, Niger	G6	64
Mādārīpur, Bngl.	G13	54
Madawaska, Me., U.S.	C8	110
Madawaska, stm., On., Can.	C13	112
Madawaska Highlands, plat., On., Can.	C12	112
Madaya, Mya.	A3	48
Maddalena, Isola, i., Italy	C3	24
Maddaloni, Italy	C8	24
Maddock, N.D., U.S.	G14	124
Madeira, i., Port.	C1	64
Madeira, stm., S.A.	E5	84
Madeira, Arquipélago da (Madeira Islands), is., Port.	C1	64
Madeira Islands see Madeira, Arquipélago da, is., Port.	C1	64
Mädelegabel, mtn., Eur.	I6	16
Madeleine, Îles de la, is., Qc., Can.	C15	110
Madeleine-Centre, Qc., Can.	A11	110
Madeline Island, i., Wi., U.S.	E8	118
Madera, Mex.	A4	100
Madera, Ca., U.S.	G5	134
Madera see Madeira, stm., S.A.	E5	84
Madgaon, India	D1	53
Madhepura, India	F11	54
Madhubani, India	E10	54
Madhugiri, India	E3	53
Madhupur, India	F11	54
Madhya Pradesh, state, India	D4	46
Madibogo, S. Afr.	E7	70
Madida, China	C9	38
Madidi, stm., Bol.	B3	90
Madill, Ok., U.S.	C2	122
Madimba, D.R.C.	E3	66
Madīnat ash-Sha'b, Yemen	G5	56
Madingo-Kayes, Congo	E2	66
Madingou, Congo	E2	66
Madirovalo, Madag.	D8	68
Madison, Al., U.S.	C12	122
Madison, Fl., U.S.	F2	116
Madison, Ga., U.S.	C2	116
Madison, In., U.S.	F12	120
Madison, Me., U.S.	F6	110
Madison, Mn., U.S.	F2	118
Madison, Mo., U.S.	E5	120
Madison, N.C., U.S.	H5	114
Madison, Ne., U.S.	F15	126
Madison, S.D., U.S.	C15	126
Madison, Wi., U.S.	A8	120
Madison, W.V., U.S.	F4	114
Madison, stm., U.S.	E15	136
Madison Heights, Va., U.S.	G6	114
Madison Range, mts., Mt., U.S.	E15	136
Madisonville, Ky., U.S.	G10	120
Madisonville, La., U.S.	G8	122
Madisonville, Tn., U.S.	A1	116
Madisonville, Tx., U.S.	G2	122
Madiun, Indon.	G7	50
Madiyi, China	G4	42
Mado Gashi, Kenya	D7	66
Madoi, China	E4	36
Madona, Lat.	D9	10
Madora, Bela.	G13	10
Madrakah, Ra's al-, c., Oman	F8	56
Madras see Chennai, India	E5	53
Madras, Or., U.S.	F5	136
Madre, Laguna, b., Mex.	C10	100
Madre, Laguna, b., Tx., U.S.	H10	130
Madre, Sierra, mts., Phil.	B3	52
Madre de Chiapas, Sierra, mts., N.A.	G12	100
Madre de Dios, stm., S.A.	F4	84
Madre de Dios, Isla, i., Chile	J1	90
Madre del Sur, Sierra, mts., Mex.	G9	100
Madre Occidental, Sierra, mts., Mex.	B3	96
Madre Oriental, Sierra, mts., Mex.	C8	100
Madrid, Spain	D7	20
Madrid, Al., U.S.	F13	122
Madrid, Ne., U.S.	G11	126
Madrid, state, Spain	D7	20
Madridejos, Spain	E7	20
Madura, i., Indon.	G8	50
Madura, Selat, strt., Indon.	G8	50
Madurai, India	G4	53
Madurāntakam, India	E4	53
Maduru, stm., Sri L.	H5	53
Maebashi, Japan	C11	40
Mae Hong Son, Thai.	C3	48
Mae Klong, stm., Thai.	E4	48
Mae Ping Mae Hat Mae Kor National Park, p.o.i., Thai.	D4	48
Mae Ramat, Thai.	D4	48
Mae Sariang, Thai.	C3	48
Maeser, Ut., U.S.	C7	132
Mae Sot, Thai.	D4	48
Maestra, Sierra, mts., Cuba	B9	102
Maestu, Spain	B8	20
Mae Tha, Thai.	C4	48
Maevatanana, Madag.	D8	68
Maéwo, i., Vanuatu	j17	79d
Mafeking, Mb., Can.	B12	124
Mafeking see Mafikeng, S. Afr.	D7	70
Mafeteng, Leso.	F8	70
Maffra, Austl.	K6	76
Mafia Island, i., Tan.	F8	66
Mafikeng, S. Afr.	D7	70
Mafra, Braz.	C13	92
Magadan, Russia	E19	34
Magadi, Kenya	E7	66
Magaguadavic Lake, l., N.B., Can.	E9	110
Magalhães de Almeida, Braz.	B4	88
Magallanes, Phil.	D4	52
Magangué, Col.	C4	86
Magaria, Niger	G6	64
Magazine Mountain, mtn., Ar., U.S.	B5	122
Magdagači, Russia	F14	34
Magdalena, Arg.	G9	92
Magdalena, Bol.	B4	90
Magdalena, Mex.	E7	100
Magdalena, N.M., U.S.	I9	132
Magdalena, state, Col.	B4	86
Magdalena, stm., Col.	B4	86
Magdalena, stm., Mex.	F7	98
Magdalena, Bahía, b., Mex.	C2	100
Magdalena, Isla, i., Chile	H2	90
Magdalena, Punta, c., Col.	F3	86
Magdalena de Kino, Mex.	F7	98
Magdeburg, Ger.	D7	16
Magelang, Indon.	G7	50
Magellen, Strait of, strt., S.A.	J2	90
Magenta, Italy	E5	22
Magetan, Indon.	G7	50
Maggiore, Lago, l., Eur.	C14	18
Maghâgha, Egypt	J1	58
Maghama, Maur.	F2	64
Mágina, mtn., Spain	G7	20
Maglaj, Bos.	E5	26
Maglić, mtn., Bos.	F5	26
Maglie, Italy	D12	24
Magnet, Mb., Can.	C14	124
Magnetawan, stm., On., Can.	C10	112
Magnetic Island, i., Austl.	B6	76
Magnitogorsk, Russia	D9	32
Magnolia, Ar., U.S.	D5	122
Magnolia, Ms., U.S.	F8	122
Mago, i., Fiji	p20	79e
Magog, Qc., Can.	E4	110
Magozal, Mex.	E10	100
Magrath, Ab., Can.	G18	138
Maguan, China	A7	48
Maguari, Cabo, c., Braz.	D8	84
Magumeri, Nig.	G7	64
Māgura, Bngl.	G12	54
Maguse Lake, l., Nu., Can.	C12	106
Magway, Mya.	B2	48
Magway, state, Mya.	B2	48
Mahābād, Iran	B6	56
Mahābaleshwar, India	C1	53
Mahabe, Madag.	D8	68
Mahābhārat Lek, mts., Nepal	E11	54
Mahabharat Range see Mahābhārat Lek, mts., Nepal	E11	54
Mahabo, Madag.	E7	68
Mahačkala, Russia	F7	32
Mahād, India	B1	53
Mahādeo Range, mts., India	C2	53
Mahagi, D.R.C.	D6	66
Mahajamba, stm., Madag.	D8	68
Mahājan, India	D4	54
Mahajanga, Madag.	D8	68
Mahākālī (Sārda), stm., Asia	D8	54
Mahakam, stm., Indon.	D9	50
Mahalapye, Bots.	E4	68
Maham, India	D6	54
Mahānadi, stm., India	H10	54
Mahanoro, Madag.	D8	68
Mahanoy City, Pa., U.S.	D9	114
Maharagama, Sri L.	H4	53
Mahārājganj, India	E10	54
Mahārājpur, India	F7	54
Mahārāshtra, state, India	E4	46
Mahāsamund, India	H9	54
Maha Sarakham, Thai.	D6	48
Mahaut, Dom.	j6	105c
Mahaweli, stm., Sri L.	H5	53
Mahaxai, Laos	D7	48
Mahbūbābād, India	C4	53
Mahbūbnagar, India	C4	53
Mahd adh-Dhahab, Sau. Ar.	E5	56
Mahdia, Guy.	E12	86
Mahe, India	F2	53
Mahé, i., Sey.	j13	69b
Mahébourg, Mrts.	i10	69a
Mahendra Giri, mtn., India	B7	53
Mahendranagar, Nepal	D7	54
Mahenge, Tan.	F7	66
Mahesāna, India	G4	54
Maheshwar, India	G5	54
Mahi, stm., India	G4	54
Mahia Peninsula, pen., N.Z.	D7	80
Mahilëu, Bela.	G13	10
Mahilëu, state, Bela.	G13	10
Mahina, Fr. Poly.	u21	78h
Mahlabatini, S. Afr.	F10	70
Mahmūdābād, India	E8	54
Mahmudiye, Tur.	D14	28
Mahoba, India	F7	54
Mahogany Mountain, mtn., Or., U.S.	G9	136
Mahogany Tree, Anguilla	A1	105a
Mahomet, Il., U.S.	D9	120
Mahón see Maó, Spain	E15	20
Mahone Bay, N.S., Can.	F12	110
Mahone Bay, b., N.S., Can.	F12	110
Mahood Lake, l., B.C., Can.	E10	138
Mahora, Spain	E9	20
Mahrāt, Jabal, plat., Yemen	F7	56
Mahrauni, India	F7	54
Mahuva, India	H3	54
Maiaky, Ukr.	C17	26
Maicao, Col.	B5	86
Maichen, China	K3	42
Maicuru, stm., Braz.	D7	84
Maiden, N.C., U.S.	A4	116
Maidenhead, Eng., U.K.	J12	12
Maidstone, Sk., Can.	A4	124
Maidstone, Eng., U.K.	J13	12
Maiduguri, Nig.	G7	64
Maihar, India	F8	54
Maijoma, Mex.	F3	130
Maikala Range, mts., India	G8	54
Maikoor, Pulau, i., Indon.	G9	44
Mailāni, India	D8	54
Main, stm., Ger.	F4	16
Maināguri, India	E12	54
Mainburg, Ger.	H7	16
Main Channel, strt., On., Can.	C8	112
Mai-Ndombe, Lac, l., D.R.C.	E3	66
Main-Donau-Kanal, can., Ger.	G7	16
Maine, state, U.S.	E7	110
Maine, hist. reg., Fr.	F8	14
Maine, Gulf of, b., N.A.	G8	110
Maine-et-Loire, state, Fr.	G8	14
Maïné-Soroa, Niger	G7	64
Mainhardt, Ger.	G5	16
Mainland, i., Scot., U.K.	n18	12a
Mainland, i., Scot., U.K.	B9	12
Mainpuri, India	E7	54
Maintirano, Madag.	D7	68
Mainz, Ger.	G4	16
Maio, i., C.V.	k10	65a
Maipo, stm., Chile	F2	92
Maipo, Volcán, vol., S.A.	G3	92
Maipú, Arg.	F3	92
Maipú, Arg.	H8	92
Maipú, ngh., Chile	F2	92
Maiqihamiao, China	C4	38
Maiquetía, Ven.	B8	86
Maišiagala, Lith.	F8	10
Maiskhāl Island, i., Bngl.	H13	54
Maitembge, Bots.	E4	68
Maitland, Austl.	I8	76
Maitland, Austl.	F7	74
Maitland, stm., On., Can.	E8	112
Maitri, sci., Ant.	C6	81
Maíz, Islas del, is., Nic.	F6	102
Maizuru, Japan	D8	40
Maja, stm., Russia	E15	34
Majari, stm., Braz.	F11	86
Majene, Indon.	E11	50
Majī, Eth.	F7	62
Majia, stm., China	C7	42
Majiang, China	J4	42
Majiangzong, China	C12	54
Majja, Russia	D15	34
Majkain see Mayqayyng, Kaz.	D13	32
Majkop, Russia	F6	32
Major, Puig, mtn., Spain	E13	20
Majorca see Mallorca, i., Spain	E13	20
Majskij, Russia	F14	34
Majuro, at., Marsh. Is.	C8	72
Maka, Sen.	G2	64
Makabana, Congo	E2	66
Makale, Indon.	E11	50
Makallé, Arg.	C8	92
Makālu, mtn., Asia	E11	54
Makapu'u Head, c., Hi., U.S.	b4	78a
Makarakomburu, Mount, mtn., Sol. Is.	e8	79b
Makarev, Russia	H20	8
Makarov, Russia	G17	34
Makasar, Selat (Makassar Strait), strt., Indon.	D11	50
Makassar Strait see Makasar, Selat, strt., Indon.	D11	50
Makawao, Hi., U.S.	c5	78a
Makeni, S.L.	H2	64
Makgadikgadi, pl., Bots.	E4	68
Makgadikgadi Pans Game Reserve, Bots.	B7	70
Makhaleng, stm., Afr.	G8	70
Makham, Thai.	F5	48
Maki, Indon.	F9	44
Makiivka, Ukr.	E5	32
Makindu, Kenya	E7	66
Makinsk, Kaz.	D11	32
Makira, state, Sol. Is.	f10	79b
Makira Harbour, b., Sol. Is.	f9	79b
Makkah (Mekka), Sau. Ar.	E4	56
Makkovik, Nf., Can.	D19	106
Makó, Hung.	C7	26
Makokou, Gabon	D2	66
Makongolosi, Tan.	F6	66
Makoua, Congo	E3	66
Maków Mazowiecki, Pol.	D16	16
Makrai, India	G6	54
Makrāna, India	E5	54
Makrān Coast, cst., Asia	D9	56
Maksatiha, Russia	C18	10
Maksimkin Jar, Russia	C15	32
Maktar, Tun.	I3	24
Makumbi, D.R.C.	F4	66
Makung, Tai.	J8	42
Makurdi, Nig.	H6	64
Makushin Volcano, vol., Ak., U.S.	F6	140
Makušino, Russia	C11	32
Makwassie, S. Afr.	E8	70
Māl, India	E12	54
Mala see Mallow, Ire.	I4	12
Mala, Punta, c., Pan.	I8	102
Malabang, Phil.	G5	52
Malabar Coast, cst., India	F2	53
Malabo, Eq. Gui.	I6	64
Malacacheta, Braz.	I4	88
Malacca see Melaka, Malay.	K6	48
Malacca, Strait of, strt., Asia	B2	50
Malacky, Slov.	H13	16
Malad, stm., U.S.	H14	136
Malad City, Id., U.S.	A4	132
Maladzečna, Bela.	F9	10
Málaga, Col.	D5	86
Málaga, Spain	H6	20
Málaga, co., Spain	H6	20
Malagarasi, Tan.	F6	66
Malagash, N.S., Can.	E13	110
Malagasy Republic see Madagascar, ctry., Afr.	D8	68
Malagón, Spain	E7	20
Malaimbandy, Madag.	E8	68
Malaita, state, Sol. Is.	d9	79b
Malaita, i., Sol. Is.	e9	79b
Malaja Kuril'skaja Grjada (Habomai-shotō), is., Russia	C17	38
Malaja Višera, Russia	B15	10
Malaka, Sempitan, strt., Indon.	J2	48
Malakāl, Sudan	F6	62
Malākand, Pak.	A3	54
Malakoff, Tx., U.S.	E3	122
Malakula, state, Vanuatu	k16	79d
Malakula, i., Vanuatu	k16	79d
Malambo, Col.	B4	86
Malang, Indon.	H8	50
Malanggwā, Nepal	E10	54
Malanje, Ang.	B2	68
Malanville, Benin	G5	64
Malanzán, Arg.	E4	92
Mała Panew, stm., Pol.	F14	16
Mälaren, l., Swe.	G7	8
Malargüe, Arg.	G3	92
Malaspina, Arg.	H3	90
Malaspina Glacier, ice, Ak., U.S.	E11	140
Malatya, Tur.	B4	56
Malau, Vanuatu	j16	79d
Malaut, India	C5	54
Malavalli, India	E3	53
Malawali, Pulau, i., Malay.	G1	52
Malawi, ctry., Afr.	C5	68
Malaŵi, Lake see Nyasa, Lake, l., Afr.	C5	68
Malaya see Semenanjung Malaysia, hist. reg., Malay.	K6	48
Malayagiri, mtn., India	H10	54
Malaybalay, Phil.	F5	52
Malāyer, Iran	C6	56
Malay Peninsula, pen., Asia	J5	48
Malay Reef, rf., Austl.	B7	76
Malaysia, ctry., Asia	E3	44
Malbon, Austl.	C3	76
Malbork, Pol.	B15	16
Malbrán, Arg.	D6	92
Malchin, Ger.	C8	16
Malchow, Ger.	C8	16
Malcolm, Austl.	E4	74
Malcolm Island, i., B.C., Can.	F4	138
Malcom, Ia., U.S.	C5	120
Malczyce, Pol.	E12	16
Malden, i., Kir.	D11	72
Mal di Ventre, Isola di, i., Italy	E2	24
Maldives, ctry., Asia	I11	30
Maldonado, Ur.	G10	92
Male', Mald.	i12	46a
Male, Mya.	A2	48
Maléas, Ákra, c., Grc.	G6	28
Male' Atoll, at., Mald.	i12	46a
Mālegaon, India	H5	54
Malé Karpaty (Little Carpathians), mts., Slov.	H13	16
Malema, Moz.	C6	68
Malente, Ger.	B6	16
Māler Kotla, India	C5	54
Malesherbes, Fr.	F11	14
Malgomaj, l., Swe.	D6	8
Malhanskij hrebet, mts., Russia	F10	34
Malheur, stm., Or., U.S.	F9	136
Malheur, South Fork, stm., Or., U.S.	G8	136
Malheur Lake, l., Or., U.S.	G8	136
Mali, Gui.	G2	64
Mali, ctry., Afr.	F4	64
Mali, stm., Mya.	C8	46
Malīk, Sudan	F6	62
Malik, Wādī al-, val., Sudan	D5	62
Mali Kyun, i., Mya.	F4	48
Malili, Indon.	E12	50
Malin, Or., U.S.	A4	134
Malinaltepec, Mex.	G9	100
Malinau, Indon.	B10	50
Malindi, Kenya	E8	66
Malines see Mechelen, Bel.	C13	14
Malingping, Indon.	G4	50
Malin Head, c., Ire.	F5	12
Malino, Bukit, mtn., Indon.	C12	50
Malita, Phil.	G5	52
Malizhen, China	A7	48
Maljamar, N.M., U.S.	B4	130
Malka, Russia	F20	34
Malkāpur, India	H5	54
Malkara, Tur.	C9	28
Mallāḥ, Syria	F7	58
Mallan luonnonpuisto, p.o.i., Fin.	B9	8
Mallawi, Egypt.	K1	58
Mallersdorf-Pfaffenberg, Ger.	H8	16
Mallery Lake, l., Nu., Can.	C11	106
Mallet, Braz.	B12	92
Malligasta, Arg.	D4	92
Mallorca (Majorca), i., Spain	E13	20
Mallow, Ire.	I4	12
Malm, Nor.	D4	8
Malmberget, Swe.	C8	8
Malmesbury, S. Afr.	H4	70
Malmö, Swe.	I5	8
Malmok, c., Neth. Ant.	p23	104g
Malo, i., Vanuatu	j16	79d
Maloelap, at., Marsh. Is.	C8	72
Maloe Skuratovo, Russia	G19	10
Malojaroslavec, Russia	E19	10
Malolos, Phil.	C3	52
Malone, Fl., U.S.	G13	122
Malone, N.Y., U.S.	F2	110
Malonga, D.R.C.	G4	66
Małopolska, reg., Pol.	F17	16
Malošujka, Russia	E17	8
Malott, Wa., U.S.	B7	136
Małowice, Pol.	E11	16
Måløy, Nor.	E1	8
Malozemel'skaja Tundra, reg., Russia	C24	8
Malpas, Austl.	J3	76
Malpe, India	E2	53
Malpeque Bay, b., P.E., Can.	D13	110
Malprabha, stm., India	D2	53
Mālpura, India	E5	54
Malta, Braz.	D7	88
Malta, Lat.	D10	10
Malta, Mt., U.S.	F6	124
Malta, ctry., Eur.	I8	24
Malta, i., Malta	I8	24
Malta Channel, strt., Eur.	H8	24
Maltahöhe, Nmb.	D3	70
Maluku (Moluccas), is., Indon.	F8	44
Maluku, Laut (Molucca Sea), s., Indon.	F8	44
Ma'lūlā, Syria	E7	58
Malu Mare, Rom.	E10	26
Malunda, Indon.	E11	50
Mālvan, India	C1	53
Malvern, Ar., U.S.	C6	122
Malvern, Ia., U.S.	K3	118
Malvern, Oh., U.S.	D4	114
Malvérnia, Moz.	C10	70
Malvinas Sur, Arg.	D8	92
Malý Dunaj, stm., Slov.	H13	16
Malyja Haradzjačy, Bela.	H11	10
Malyj Anjuj, stm., Russia	C21	34
Malyj Enisej, stm., Russia	F8	34
Malyj Tajmyr, ostrov, i., Russia	A10	34
Mama, Russia	E11	34
Mamaia, Rom.	E15	26
Mamanguape, Braz.	D8	88
Mamasa, Indon.	E11	50
Mamasa, stm., Indon.	E11	50
Mambajao, Phil.	F5	52
Mambasa, D.R.C.	D5	66
Mamberamo, stm., Indon.	F10	44
Mamburao, Phil.	D3	52
Mamehaktebo, Indon.	C9	50
Mameigwess Lake, l., On., Can.	B6	118
Ma-Me-O Beach, Ab., Can.	C17	138
Mamfe, Cam.	C1	66
Mamlyutka, Kaz.	D11	32
Mammoth, Az., U.S.	K6	132
Mammoth Cave National Park, p.o.i., Ky., U.S.	G11	120
Mammoth Lakes, Ca., U.S.	F7	134
Mammoth Spring, Ar., U.S.	H6	120
Mamonovo, Russia	F2	10
Mamoré, stm., S.A.	F4	84
Mamou, Gui.	G2	64
Mampikony, Madag.	D8	68
Mamry, Jezioro, l., Pol.	B17	16
Mamuju, Indon.	E11	50
Mamuno, Bots.	C5	70
Man, C. Iv.	H3	64
Man, W.V., U.S.	G4	114
Man, Isle of see Isle of Man, dep., Eur.	G8	12
Mana, Hi., U.S.	a2	78a
Manabí, state, Ec.	H2	86
Manacacías, stm., Col.	F5	86
Manacapuru, Braz.	I11	86
Manacapuru, stm., Braz.	I11	86
Manacor, Spain	E14	20
Manado (Menado), Indon.	E7	44
Manaenki, Russia	G19	10
Managua, Nic.	F4	102
Managua, Lago de, l., Nic.	F4	102
Manakara, Madag.	E8	68
Manakau, mtn., N.Z.	F5	80
Manāli, India	B6	54
Manama see Al-Manāmah, Bahr.	D7	56
Manam Island, i., Pap. N. Gui.	a4	79a
Mánamo, Caño, stm., Ven.	C10	86
Mananara Avaratra, Madag.	D8	68
Mananjary, Madag.	E8	68
Manantenina, Madag.	E8	68
Manapire, stm., Ven.	D8	86
Manappārai, India	F4	53
Manār, stm., India	B3	53
Manas, China	C2	36
Manās, stm., Asia	E13	54
Manasarowar Lake see Mapam Yumco, l., China	C8	54
Manas Hu, l., China	B2	36
Manāslu, mtn., Nepal	D10	54
Manasquan, N.J., U.S.	D11	114
Manassas, Va., U.S.	F8	114
Mânăstirea, Rom.	E13	26
Manatí, Col.	B4	86
Manatí, P.R.	B3	104a
Manatuto, E. Timor	G8	44
Manaung, Mya.	C1	48
Manaus, Braz.	D5	84
Manavgat, Tur.	G14	28
Manawa, Wi., U.S.	G10	118
Manāwar, India	G5	54
Manawoka, Pulau, i., Indon.	F9	44
Manban, China	A6	48
Manbij, Syria	B8	58
Mancelona, Mi., U.S.	D4	112
Mancha Real, Spain	G7	20
Manche, state, Fr.	E7	14
Mancheng, China	B6	42
Mancherāl, India	B4	53
Manchester, Eng., U.K.	H10	12
Manchester, Ct., U.S.	C13	114
Manchester, Ga., U.S.	E14	122
Manchester, Ia., U.S.	B6	120
Manchester, Ky., U.S.	G2	114
Manchester, N.H., U.S.	H5	110
Manchester, Oh., U.S.	F2	114
Manchester, Vt., U.S.	G3	110
Manchioneal, Jam.	i14	104d
Manchouli see Manzhouli, China	B8	36
Manchuria see Dong San Shen, hist. reg., China	B5	38
Manciano, Italy	H8	22
Mancos, Co., U.S.	F8	132
Mancos, stm., U.S.	F8	132
Mānd, stm., India	G9	54
Mand, stm., Iran	D7	56
Manda, Tan.	G6	66
Manda, Jabal, mtn., Sudan	F4	62
Mandabe, Madag.	E7	68
Mandaguari, Braz.	A12	92
Manda Island, i., Kenya	E8	66
Mandal, Mong.	B6	36
Mandala, Puncak, mtn., Indon.	F10	44
Mandalay, Mya.	A2	48
Mandalay, state, Mya.	B2	48
Mandan, N.D., U.S.	A11	126
Mandar, Teluk, b., Indon.	E11	50
Mandara, Monts (Mandara Mountains), mts., Afr.	G7	64
Mandara Mountains (Mandara, Monts), mts., Afr.	G7	64
Mandas, Italy	E3	24
Mandaue, Phil.	E4	52
Mandeb, Bab el, strt.	E8	62
Mandera, Kenya	D8	66
Manderson, Wy., U.S.	C5	126
Mandeville, Jam.	i13	104d
Mandi, India	C6	54
Mandi Bahāuddīn, Pak.	B4	54
Mandi Būrewāla, Pak.	C4	54
Mandi Dabwāli, India	D5	54
Mandimba, Moz.	C6	68
Mandioli, Pulau, i., Indon.	F8	44
Mandioré, Lagoa, l., S.A.	G6	84

Name | Map Ref. | Page

Mandioré, Laguna see Mandioré, Lagoa, l., S.A. G6 84
Mandla, India G8 54
Mandlakazi, Moz. D11 70
Mandora, Austl. C4 74
Mandra, Pak. B4 54
Mandritsara, Madag. D8 68
Mandsaur, India F5 54
Mandun, China A4 48
Manduria, Italy D11 24
Māndvi, India H4 54
Māndvi, India G2 54
Mandya, India E3 53
Manendragarh, India G9 54
Manfalût, Egypt K1 58
Manfredonia, Italy I12 22
Manfredonia, Golfo di, b., Italy C10 24
Manga, Braz. H3 88
Manga, reg., Niger F7 64
Mangabeiras, Chapada das, hills, Braz. E2 88
Mangagoy, Phil. F6 52
Mangai, D.R.C. E3 66
Mangalagiri, India C5 53
Mangaldai, India E14 54
Mangalia, Rom. F15 26
Mangalore, India E2 53
Mangalvedha, India C2 53
Mangchang, China I2 42
Mange, China B9 54
Mangela, Mount see Nanggala Hill, mtn., Sol. Is. e7 79b
Manggar, Indon. E6 50
Mangham, La., U.S. E7 122
Mangin Range, mts., Mya. C8 46
Mangkalihat, Tanjung, c., Indon. C11 50
Manglares, Cabo, c., Col. G2 86
Mangla Reservoir, res., Pak. B4 54
Mangnai, China G16 32
Mangochi, Mwi. C6 68
Mangoky, stm., Madag. E7 68
Mangole, Pulau, i., Indon. F8 44
Mangrol, India H2 54
Mangrūl Pīr, India H6 54
Mangsang, Indon. E4 50
Mangshi see Luxi, China G4 36
Mangueira, Lagoa, b., Braz. F11 92
Mangueirinha, Braz. B11 92
Mangum, Ok., U.S. G9 128
Mangya, China D3 36
Manhattan, Ks., U.S. B12 128
Manhattan, Mt., U.S. E15 136
Manhiça, Moz. D11 70
Mān Hpāng, Mya. A4 48
Manhuaçu, Braz. K4 88
Manhuaçu, stm., Braz. J5 88
Manhumirim, Braz. K4 88
Maniago, Italy D9 22
Manica, Moz. D5 68
Manica, state, Moz. B11 70
Manicaland, state, Zimb. B11 70
Manic Deux, Réservoir, res., Qc., Can. A8 110
Manicoré, Braz. E5 84
Manicouagan, stm., Qc., Can. E17 106
Manicouagan, Réservoir, res., Qc., Can. E17 106
Maniganggo, China E4 36
Manigotagan, Mb., Can. C17 124
Manigotagan, stm., Can. C17 124
Manihiki, at., Cook Is. E10 72
Maniitsoq see Sukkertoppen, Grnld. D15 141
Mānikganj, Bngl. G13 54
Mānikpur, India F8 54
Manila, Phil. C3 52
Manila, Ar., U.S. I7 120
Manila, Ut., U.S. C7 132
Manila Bay, b., Phil. C3 52
Manilla, Austl. H8 76
Manily, Russia D22 34
Maningrida, Austl. B6 74
Maninjau, Danau, l., Indon. D1 50
Manipa, Selat, strt., Indon. F8 44
Manipur, state, India C7 46
Manipur, stm., Asia A1 48
Manisa, Tur. E10 28
Manisa, state, Tur. E11 28
Manistee, Mi., U.S. D3 112
Manistee, stm., Mi., U.S. D3 112
Manistique, Mi., U.S. C3 112
Manistique Lake, l., Mi., U.S. B4 112
Manito, Il., U.S. K9 118
Manitoba, state, Can. D11 106
Manitoba, Lake, l., Mb., Can. D15 124
Manitou, stm., On., Can. B5 118
Manitou, Lake, l., On., Can. C7 112
Manitou Beach, Sk., Can. C8 124
Manitou Lake, l., Sk., Can. B4 124
Manitoulin Island, i., On., Can. C7 112
Manitou Springs, Co., U.S. C3 128
Manitowaning, On., Can. C8 112
Manitowoc, Wi., U.S. D2 112
Maniwaki, Qc., Can. B13 112
Manizales, Col. E4 86
Manja, Madag. E7 68
Manjakandriana, Madag. D8 68
Manjeri, India F3 53
Mānjra, stm., India B3 53
Mankanza, D.R.C. D3 66
Mankato, Ks., U.S. B10 128
Mankato, Mn., U.S. G4 118
Mankera, Pak. C3 54
Mankota, Sk., Can. E6 124
Manley Hot Springs, Ak., U.S. D9 140
Manlleu, Spain B13 20
Manmād, India H5 54
Manna, Indon. F3 50
Mannahill, Austl. I3 76
Mannar, Sri L. G4 53
Mannar, Gulf of, b., Asia G4 53
Mannārgudi, India F4 53
Mannford, Ok., U.S. A2 122
Mannheim, Ger. G4 16
Manning, N.D., U.S. G11 124
Manning, S.C., U.S. C5 116
Manning Strait, strt., Sol. Is. d7 79b
Mannum, Austl. J2 76
Mannville, Ab., Can. C19 138
Manoharpur, India G10 54
Manokwari, Indon. F9 44
Manombo Atsimo, Madag. E7 68
Manono, D.R.C. F5 66
Manor, Sk., Can. E11 124
Manor, Tx., U.S. D10 130
Manosque, Fr. F11 18
Manouane, Lac, l., Qc., Can. C2 110
Manouane, Lac, res., Qc., Can. E16 106
Manp'o, Kor., N. D7 38
Mānpur, India H8 54
Manra, at., Kir. D9 72
Manresa, Spain C12 20
Mānsa, India C5 54
Mansa, Zam. C4 68
Mansafīs, Egypt J1 58
Mānsehra, Pak. A4 54
Mansel Island, i., Nu., Can. C14 106
Mansfield, Eng., U.K. H11 12
Mansfield, Ga., U.S. C2 116
Mansfield, Il., U.S. D9 120
Mansfield, La., U.S. E5 122
Mansfield, Mo., U.S. G5 120
Mansfield, Oh., U.S. D3 114
Mansfield, Pa., U.S. C8 114
Mansfield, Tx., U.S. B10 130
Mansfield, Mount, mtn., Vt., U.S. F4 110
Mansion, St. K./N. C2 105a
Mansôa, Gui.-B. G1 64
Manson, Ia., U.S. B3 120
Mansucum, Pan. H9 102
Mansura, La., U.S. F6 122
Manta, Ec. H1 86
Manta, Bahía de, b., Ec. H1 86
Mantagao, stm., Mb., Can. C16 124
Mantalingajan, Mount, mtn., Phil. F1 52
Mantanani Besar, Pulau, i., Malay. G1 52
Manteca, Ca., U.S. F4 134
Mantecal, Ven. D7 86
Mantena, Braz. J5 88
Manteo, N.C., U.S. I10 114
Mantes-la-Jolie, Fr. F10 14
Manti, Ut., U.S. D5 132
Mantiqueira, Serra da, mts., Braz. L3 88
Manton, Mi., U.S. D4 112
Mántova, Italy E7 22
Mantua, Cuba A5 102
Mantua see Mántova, Italy E7 22
Mantua, Oh., U.S. C4 114
Manturovo, Russia G21 8
Mäntyharju, Fin. F12 8
Manu, Peru F3 84
Manuae, at., Cook Is. E11 72
Manuae, at., Fr. Poly. E11 72
Manua Islands, is., Am. Sam. h13 79c
Manuel, Mex. D9 100
Manuel Alves, stm., Braz. F2 88
Manuel Alves Grande, stm., Braz. D2 88
Manuel Benavides, Mex. A6 100
Manuel F. Mantilla see Pedro R. Fernández, Arg. D8 92
Manuguru, India B5 53
Manui, Pulau, i., Indon. F7 44
Manukau, N.Z. C6 80
Manukau Harbour, b., N.Z. C6 80
Manus Island, i., Pap. N. Gui. a4 79a
Mānwat, India B3 53
Many, La., U.S. F5 122
Manyara, Lake, l., Tan. E7 66
Manyberries, Ab., Can. E3 124
Many Island Lake, l., Can. D3 124
Manyoni, Tan. F6 66
Many Peaks, Austl. E8 76
Manza, D.R.C. F5 66
Manzala, Bahra el-, l., Egypt G3 58
Manzanares, Spain E7 20
Manzanilla Point, c., Trin. s13 105f
Manzanillo, Cuba B9 102
Manzanillo, Mex. F6 100
Manzanillo Bay, b., N.A. C11 102
Manzano, N.M., U.S. G2 128
Manzano Peak, mtn., N.M., U.S. G2 128
Manzhouli, China B8 36
Manzini, Swaz. E10 70
Mao, Chad E3 62
Mao, Dom. Rep. C12 102
Maó, Spain E15 20
Maoba, China F3 42
Maoke, Pegunungan, mts., Indon. a2 79a
Maolin, China C5 38
Maoming, China K4 42
Mapaga, Indon. D11 50
Mapam Yumco, l., China C8 54
Mapane, Indon. D12 50
Mapari, stm., Braz. I8 86
Mapastepec, Mex. H12 100
Mapi, Indon. G10 44
Mapimí, Mex. C6 100
Mapimí, Bolsón de, des., Mex. B6 100
Mapire, Ven. D9 86
Mapiri, Bol. C3 90
Mapixari, Ilha, i., Braz. I9 86
Maple, stm., Ia., U.S. B2 120
Maple, stm., Mi., U.S. E5 112
Maple, stm., N.D., U.S. H16 124
Maple Creek, Sk., Can. E4 124
Maple Lake, Mn., U.S. F4 118
Maple Mount, Ky., U.S. G10 120
Maple Ridge, B.C., Can. G8 138
Mapleton, Ia., U.S. B2 120
Mapleton, Or., U.S. F3 136
Mapleton, Ut., U.S. C5 132
Mapuera, stm., Braz. C6 84
Maputo, Moz. D11 70
Maputo, state, Moz. D11 70
Maputo, stm., Afr. E11 70
Maqanshy, Kaz. E14 32
Maqat, Kaz. E8 32
Maqên Gangri, mtn., China E4 36
Maqna, Sau. Ar. J5 58
Maquan, stm., China D10 54
Maquela do Zombo, Ang. B2 68
Maquereau, Pointe au, c., Qc., Can. B12 110
Maquinchao, Arg. H3 90
Maquoketa, Ia., U.S. B7 120
Maquoketa, stm., Ia., U.S. B7 120
Maquoketa, North Fork, stm., Ia., U.S. B7 120
Mar, Serra do, mts., Braz. B13 92
Mara, stm., Afr. E7 66
Maraã, Braz. H9 86
Maraa, Fr. Poly. v21 78h
Marabá, Braz. C1 88
Marabahan, Indon. E9 50
Maraboon, Lake, res., Austl. D6 76
Maracá, Ilha de, i., Braz. F11 86
Maracá, Ilha de, i., Braz. C7 84
Maracaçumé, stm., Braz. A3 88
Maracaibo, Ven. B5 86
Maracaibo, Lago de, l., Ven. C6 86
Maracaju, Braz. D5 90
Maracanaú, Braz. B6 88
Maracás, Braz. G5 88
Maracay, Ven. B8 86
Marādah, Libya B3 62
Maradi, Niger G6 64
Marāghah, Sabkhat al-, l., Syria C8 58
Marāgheh, Iran B6 56
Maragogipe, Braz. G6 88
Maragoji, Braz. E8 88
Marahuaca, Cerro, mtn., Ven. F9 86
Maraial, Braz. E8 88
Marais des Cygnes, stm., U.S. F3 120
Marajó, Baía de, b., Braz. D8 84
Marajó, Ilha de, i., Braz. D8 84
Maralal, Kenya D7 66
Marali, C.A.R. C3 66
Maralinga, Austl. F6 74
Marambio, sci., Ant. B35 81
Marampa, S.L. H2 64
Maramsilli Reservoir, res., India H8 54
Maramureș, state, Rom. B10 26
Maran, Malay. K6 48
Marana, Az., U.S. K5 132
Marand, Iran B6 56
Marang, Malay. J6 48
Marangas, Phil. F1 52
Maranguape, Braz. B6 88
Maranhão, state, Braz. C3 88
Maranhão, stm., Braz. D9 84
Marano, Laguna di, b., Italy E10 22
Maranoa, stm., Austl. F7 76
Marañón, stm., Peru D2 84
Marasende, Pulau, i., Indon. F10 50
Mărășești, Rom. D14 26
Maratasã, stm., Braz. C4 88
Marathon, Austl. C4 76
Marathon, On., Can. C12 118
Marathon, Tx., U.S. D4 130
Marathon, Wi., U.S. G9 118
Marathónas, Grc. E6 28
Maratua, Pulau, i., Indon. B11 50
Marau, Braz. D11 92
Maraú, Braz. H6 88
Marauiá, stm., Braz. H9 86
Maravilha, Braz. C11 92
Maravillas, Mex. B6 100
Maravillas Creek, stm., Tx., U.S. E4 130
Marav Lake, l., Pak. D2 54
Maravovo, Sol. Is. e8 79b
Marawi, Phil. F5 52
Marawwah, i., U.A.E. E7 56
Marayes, Arg. E4 92
Marbella, Spain H6 20
Marble, N.C., U.S. A2 116
Marble Bar, Austl. D3 74
Marble Canyon, p., Az., U.S. G5 132
Marble Falls, Tx., U.S. D9 130
Marble Hall, S. Afr. D9 70
Marble Hill, Mo., U.S. G8 120
Marblemount, Wa., U.S. B5 136
Marble Rock, Ia., U.S. I6 118
Marburg, Ger. F4 16
Marburg, S. Afr. G10 70
Marca, Ponta da, c., Ang. D1 68
Marcal, stm., Hung. B4 26
Marcelin, Sk., Can. B7 124
Marceline, Mo., U.S. E5 120
March, Eng., U.K. I12 12
March (Morava), stm., Eur. H12 16
Marche, state, Italy G10 22
Marche, hist. reg., Fr. C8 18
Marche-en-Famenne, Bel. D14 14
Marchena, Spain G5 20
Marches see Marche, state, Italy G10 22
Mar Chiquita, Laguna, b., Arg. H9 92
Mar Chiquita, Laguna, l., Arg. E6 92
Marcigny, Fr. C10 18
Marco, Braz. B5 88
Marcos Juárez, Arg. F6 92
Marcus, Ia., U.S. B2 120
Marcus Baker, Mount, mtn., Ak., U.S. D10 140
Marcus Island see Minami-Tori-shima, i., Japan G19 30
Marcy, Mount, mtn., N.Y., U.S. F2 110
Mardān, Pak. A4 54
Mardarivka, Ukr. B16 26
Mar del Plata, Arg. H9 92
Mardin, Tur. B5 56
Maré, i., N. Cal. m17 79d
Mare a Brăilei, Insula, i., Rom. D14 26
Marea de Portillo, Cuba C9 102
Marechal Cândido Rondon, Braz. B10 92
Marechal Deodoro, Braz. E8 88
Maree, Loch, l., Scot., U.K. D7 12
Mareeba, Austl. A5 76
Maremma, reg., Italy H8 22
Marengo, Ia., U.S. C5 120
Marengo, Il., U.S. B9 120
Marenisco, Mi., U.S. E9 118
Marennes, Fr. D4 18
Marettimo, Isola, i., Italy G5 24
Marfa, Tx., U.S. D3 130
Margai Caka, l., China A6 46
Margaree Harbour, N.S., Can. D15 110
Margaret, stm., Austl. C5 74
Margaret Bay, B.C., Can. E3 138
Margaret River, Austl. F2 74
Margaretville, N.Y., U.S. B11 114
Margarita, Isla de, i., Ven. B9 86
Margate, S. Afr. G10 70
Margate, Eng., U.K. J14 12
Margate, Fl., U.S. J5 116
Margecany, Slov. H16 16
Margelan see Margilan, Uzb. F12 32
Margherita di Savoia, Italy C10 24
Margherita Peak, mtn., Afr. D5 66
Margilan, Uzb. F12 32
Margonin, Pol. D13 16
Margosatubig, Phil. G4 52
Mārgow, Dasht-e, des., Afg. C9 56
Marha, Russia D13 34
Marha, stm., Russia C12 34
Maria, Îles, is., Fr. Poly. F11 72
María Cleofas, Isla, i., Mex. E5 100
María Elena, Chile D3 90
María Grande, Arg. E8 92
María Ignacia, Arg. H8 92
Maria Island, i., Austl. B7 74
Maria Island National Park, p.o.i., Austl. o14 77a
Mariakani, Kenya E7 66
María Madre, Isla, i., Mex. E5 100
María Magdalena, Isla, i., Mex. E5 100
Mariana, Braz. K4 88
Mariana Islands, is., Oc. B5 72
Mariana Ridge, unds. H17 142
Mariana Trench, unds. H17 142
Marian Lake, l., N.T., Can. C7 106
Marianna, Ar., U.S. C8 122
Marianna, Fl., U.S. G13 122
Mariano I. Loza, Arg. D8 92
Mariánské Lázně, Czech Rep. G8 16
Marias, stm., Mt., U.S. B16 136
Marias Pass, p., Mt., U.S. B13 136
María Teresa, Arg. G6 92
Mariato, Punta, c., Pan. I7 102
Maribo, Den. B7 16
Maribor, Slvn. D12 22
Maricao, P.R. B2 104a
Marico, stm., Afr. D8 70
Maricopa, Az., U.S. J4 132
Maricunga, Salar de, pl., Chile C3 92
Marié, stm., Braz. H8 86
Marie Byrd Land, reg., Ant. C29 81
Marie-Galante, i., Guad. i6 105c
Mariehamn, Fin. F9 8
Mariental, Nmb. D4 70
Marienville, Pa., U.S. C6 114
Mariestad, Swe. G5 8
Marieta, stm., Ven. E8 86
Marietta, Ga., U.S. D14 122
Marietta, Mn., U.S. G2 118
Marietta, Oh., U.S. E4 114
Marieville, Qc., Can. E3 110
Marignane, Fr. F11 18
Marigot, Dom. i6 105c
Marigot, Guad. A1 105a
Mariinsk, Russia C15 32
Mariinskoe, Russia F17 34
Marijampolė, Lith. F6 10
Marij El, state, Russia C7 32
Marília, Braz. D7 90
Marimba, Ang. B2 68
Marín, Mex. I7 130
Marín, Spain B2 20
Marina di Ravenna, Italy F9 22
Marina Fall, wtfl., Guy. E12 86
Mar''ina Horka, Bela. G11 10
Marinduque, i., Phil. D3 52
Marine City, Mi., U.S. B3 114
Marinette, Wi., U.S. C2 112
Maringá, Braz. D6 90
Marino, Vanuatu j16 79d
Marintu, Indon. C6 50
Marion, Al., U.S. E11 122
Marion, Ar., U.S. B8 122
Marion, Ia., U.S. B6 120
Marion, Il., U.S. G9 120
Marion, In., U.S. H4 112
Marion, Ks., U.S. C12 128
Marion, Ky., U.S. G9 120
Marion, La., U.S. E6 122
Marion, Ms., U.S. E10 122
Marion, N.C., U.S. I4 114
Marion, N.D., U.S. A14 126
Marion, Oh., U.S. D2 114
Marion, S.C., U.S. B6 116
Marion, Va., U.S. H4 114
Marion, Lake, res., S.C., U.S. C5 116
Marion Bay, b., Austl. o13 77a
Marion County Lake, res., Ks., U.S. C11 128
Marion Downs, Austl. D2 76
Marion Junction, Al., U.S. E11 122
Marion Reef, rf., Austl. B9 76
Marionville, Mo., U.S. G4 120
Maripa, Ven. D9 86
Mariposa, Ca., U.S. F5 134
Mariquita, Col. E4 86
Mariscal Estigarribia, Para. D4 90
Maritime Alps, mts., Eur. E12 18
Maritsa (Évros) (Marica) (Meriç), stm., Eur. C9 28
Mariupol', Ukr. E5 32
Mariusa, Caño, stm., Ven. C11 86
Mariveles, Phil. C3 52
Mariyampole see Marijampolė, Lith. F6 10
Marjanovka, Russia D12 32
Marka, Som. D8 66
Mārkāpur, India D4 53
Markaryd, Swe. H5 8
Markdale, On., Can. D9 112
Marked Tree, Ar., U.S. B8 122
Markesan, Wi., U.S. H10 118
Market Harborough, Eng., U.K. I12 12
Markham, On., Can. E10 112
Markham, Tx., U.S. F11 130
Markham Bay, b., Nu., Can. C16 106
Markit, China B12 56
Markle, In., U.S. H4 112
Markleeville, Ca., U.S. E6 134
Markovo, Russia D23 34
Marks, Russia D7 32
Marks, Ms., U.S. C8 122
Marktheidenfeld, Ger. G5 16
Marktoberdorf, Ger. I6 16
Marktredwitz, Ger. G8 16
Mark Twain Lake, res., Mo., U.S. E6 120
Marlboro, Ab., Can. C14 138
Marlboro, N.Y., U.S. C11 114
Marlborough, Austl. D7 76
Marlborough, Guy. B6 84
Marlborough, Ma., U.S. B14 114
Marlette, Mi., U.S. E6 112
Marlinton, W.V., U.S. F5 114
Marlow, Ok., U.S. G11 128
Marmaduke, Ar., U.S. H7 120
Marmande, Fr. E6 18
Marmara, Sea of see Marmara Denizi, s., Tur. C11 28
Marmara Adası, i., Tur. C10 28
Marmara Denizi (Marmara, Sea of), s., Tur. C11 28
Marmara Ereğlisi, Tur. C10 28
Marmara Gölü, l., Tur. E10 28
Marmaris, Tur. G11 28
Marmaton, stm., U.S. G3 120
Marmelos, stm., Braz. E5 84
Marmet, W.V., U.S. F4 114
Marmion Lake, l., On., Can. C7 118
Marmolada, mtn., Italy D8 22
Marmora, On., Can. D12 112
Marnay, Fr. G14 14
Marne, Ger. C4 16
Marne, Mi., U.S. E4 112
Marne, state, Fr. E13 14
Marne, stm., Fr. E11 14
Marne à la Saône, Canal de la, can., Fr. F14 14
Maroa, Ven. F8 86
Maroantsetra, Madag. D8 68
Maromandia, Madag. C8 68
Maromme, Fr. E10 14
Maromokotro, mtn., Madag. C8 68
Marondera, Zimb. D5 68
Maroni (Marowijne), stm., S.A. C7 84
Maros, Indon. F11 50
Maros (Mureș), stm., Eur. C7 26
Maroua, Cam. B2 66
Marovoay, Madag. D8 68
Marowijne (Maroni), stm., S.A. C7 84
Marqakól köli, l., Kaz. E15 32
Marquand, Mo., U.S. G7 120
Marquard, S. Afr. F8 70
Marquesas Islands see Marquises, Îles, is., Fr. Poly. D12 72
Marquesas Keys, is., Fl., U.S. L3 116
Marquette, Ks., U.S. C11 128
Marquette, Mi., U.S. B2 112
Marquis, Gren. q10 105e
Marquises, Îles, is., Fr. Poly. D12 72
Marradi, Italy F8 22
Marrah, Jabal, hill, Sudan E4 62
Marrakech, Mor. C3 64
Marrakesh see Marrakech, Mor. C3 64
Marrawah, Austl. n12 77a
Marree, Austl. E7 74
Marrero, La., U.S. H8 122
Marromeu, Moz. D6 68
Marrupa, Moz. C6 68
Marsá al-Burayqah, Libya A3 62
Marsabit, Kenya D7 66
Marsala, Italy G6 24
Marsciano, Italy H9 22
Marseille, Fr. F11 18
Marseilles, Il., U.S. C9 120
Marsfjället, mtn., Swe. D6 8
Marshall, Lib. H2 64
Marshall, Ak., U.S. D7 140
Marshall, Ar., U.S. I5 120
Marshall, Mi., U.S. B1 114
Marshall, Mn., U.S. G3 118
Marshall, Mo., U.S. E4 120
Marshall, N.C., U.S. I3 114
Marshall, Tx., U.S. E4 122
Marshall, Va., U.S. F8 114
Marshall, stm., Austl. D7 74
Marshallberg, N.C., U.S. B9 116
Marshall Islands, ctry., Oc. H19 142
Marshall Islands, is., Marsh. Is. B7 72
Marshalltown, Ia., U.S. B5 120
Marshfield, Mo., U.S. G4 120
Marshfield, Wi., U.S. G8 118
Mars Hill, Me., U.S. D9 110
Mars Hill, N.C., U.S. I3 114
Marsh Island, i., La., U.S. H7 122
Marshville, N.C., U.S. A5 116
Marsing, Id., U.S. G10 136
Märsta, Swe. G7 8
Marstal, Den. B6 16
Martaban, Gulf of, b., Mya. D3 48
Martapura, Indon. E9 50
Martapura, Indon. F4 50
Marte R. Gómez, Presa, res., Mex. H9 130
Marthaguy Creek, stm., Austl. H6 76
Martha's Vineyard, i., Ma., U.S. C15 114
Martí, Cuba B9 102
Martigny, Switz. D4 22
Martigues, Fr. F11 18
Martin, Slov. G14 16
Martin, Ky., U.S. G3 114
Martin, Mi., U.S. F4 112
Martin, N.D., U.S. G13 124
Martin, Tn., U.S. H9 120
Martín, stm., Spain C10 20
Martina Franca, Italy D11 24
Martindale, Tx., U.S. E10 130
Mărtinești, Rom. D14 26
Martinez, Ca., U.S. E3 134
Martinez, Ga., U.S. C3 116
Martínez de la Torre, Mex. E10 100
Martinho Campos, Braz. J3 88
Martinique, dep., N.A. i15 96a
Martinique Passage, strt., N.A. k6 105c
Martin Lake, res., Al., U.S. E12 122
Martinópole, Braz. B5 88
Martinsberg, Aus. B12 22
Martinsburg, W.V., U.S. E7 114
Martins Ferry, Oh., U.S. D5 114
Martinsville, Il., U.S. E10 120
Martinsville, In., U.S. E11 120
Martinsville, Va., U.S. H5 114
Martin Vaz, Ilhas, is., Braz. H12 82
Martos, Spain G7 20
Martre, Lac la, l., N.T., Can. C7 106
Martti, Fin. C13 8
Marudi, Malay. A9 50
Marudu, Telukan, b., Malay. G1 52
Marugame, Japan E6 40
Maruim, Braz. F7 88
Maruoka, Japan C9 40
Marutea, at., Fr. Poly. E12 72
Marv Dasht, Iran D7 56
Marvine, Mount, mtn., Ut., U.S. E5 132
Mārwār, India F4 54
Mary, Turkmen. B9 56
Mary, stm., Austl. E9 76
Maryborough, Austl. E9 76
Maryborough, Austl. K4 76
Marydale, S. Afr. F5 70
Maryfield, Sk., Can. E12 124
Mary Kathleen, Austl. C2 76
Maryland, state, U.S. E8 114
Maryneal, Tx., U.S. B7 130
Maryport, Eng., U.K. G9 12
Marysvale, Ut., U.S. E4 132
Marysville, N.B., Can. D10 110
Marysville, Ca., U.S. D4 134
Marysville, Ks., U.S. L2 118
Marysville, Mi., U.S. B3 114
Marysville, Oh., U.S. D2 114
Marysville, Wa., U.S. B4 136
Maryville, Mo., U.S. D3 120
Maryville, Tn., U.S. I2 114
Marzagão, Braz. I1 88
Marzo, Punta, c., Col. D3 86
Masada see Mezada, Horvot, sci., Isr. G6 58
Masai Mara Game Reserve, Kenya E7 66
Masai Steppe, plat., Tan. E7 66
Masaka, Ug. E6 66
Masalembu Besar, Pulau, i., Indon. F9 50
Masamba, Indon. E12 50
Masan, Kor., S. D1 40
Masasi, Tan. G7 66
Masatepe, Nic. G4 102
Masaya, Nic. G4 102
Masbate, Phil. D4 52
Masbate, i., Phil. E4 52
Mascarene Basin, unds. K8 142
Mascarene Islands, is., Afr. i10 69a
Mascarene Plateau, unds. J8 142
Mascot, Tn., U.S. H2 114
Mascota, Mex. E6 100
Mascoutah, Il., U.S. F8 120
Maseru, Leso. F8 70
Mashan, China J3 42
Mashava, Zimb. D5 68
Mashhad, Iran B8 56
Mashi, China G6 42
Mashiko, Japan C13 40
Mashra'ar Raqq, Sudan F5 62
Masi-Manimba, D.R.C. E3 66
Masindi, Ug. D6 66
Masira, Gulf of see Maṣīrah, Khalīj, b., Oman F8 56
Maṣīrah, i., Oman E8 56
Maṣīrah, Khalīj, b., Oman F8 56
Masisea, Peru E3 84
Masjed-e Soleymān, Iran C6 56
Mask, Lough, l., Ire. H3 12
Maskanah, Syria B8 58
Masljanino, Russia D14 32
Mason, Mi., U.S. F5 112
Mason, Oh., U.S. E1 114
Mason, Tx., U.S. D8 130
Mason, W.V., U.S. E3 114
Mason City, Ia., U.S. A4 120
Mason City, Il., U.S. D8 120
Mason City, Ne., U.S. F13 126
Masqaṭ (Muscat), Oman E8 56
Massa, Italy F7 22
Massachusetts, state, U.S. B14 114
Massachusetts Bay, b., Ma., U.S. B15 114
Massafra, Italy D11 24
Massaguet, Chad E3 62
Massa Marittima, Italy G7 22
Massangena, Moz. B11 70
Massawa (Mitsiwa), Erit. D7 62
Massena, Ia., U.S. C3 120
Massena, N.Y., U.S. F2 110
Massenya, Chad E3 62
Massey, On., Can. B7 112
Massey Sound, strt., Nu., Can. B7 141
Massiac, Fr. D9 18
Massillon, Oh., U.S. D4 114
Massina, reg., Mali G4 64
Massinga, Moz. C12 70
Massingir, Moz. C11 70
Massive, Mount, mtn., Co., U.S. D10 132
Masson Island, i., Ant. B14 81
Mastābah, Sau. Ar. E4 56
Masterson, Tx., U.S. F6 128
Masterton, N.Z. E6 80
Mastic Point, Bah. K8 116
Mastung, Pak. D10 56
Masty, Bela. G7 10
Masuda, Japan E4 40
Masurai, Gunung, mtn., Indon. E2 50
Masuria see Mazury, reg., Pol. C16 16
Masvingo, Zimb. E5 68
Masvingo, state, Zimb. B10 70
Maṣyāf, Syria C7 58
Mata Amarilla, Arg. I2 90
Matabeleland North, state, Zimb. A9 70
Matabeleland South, state, Zimb. B9 70
Matabuena, Spain C7 20
Matacuni, stm., Ven. F9 86
Mata de São João, Braz. G6 88
Matadi, D.R.C. F2 66
Matagalpa, Nic. F5 102
Matagami, Qc., Can. F15 106
Matagorda, Tx., U.S. F12 130
Matagorda Island, i., Tx., U.S. F11 130
Matagorda Peninsula, pen., Tx., U.S. F11 130
Matahiae, Pointe, c., Fr. Poly. w22 78h
Matâi, Egypt J1 58
Mataiea, Fr. Poly. w22 78h
Mataiva, at., Fr. Poly. E12 72
Matak, Pulau, i., Indon. B5 50
Matakana, Austl. I5 76
Matale, Sri L. H5 53
Matam, Sen. F2 64
Matamoros, Mex. C10 100
Matamoros, Mex. C7 100
Matan, Indon. D7 50
Matandu, stm., Tan. F7 66
Matane, Qc., Can. B9 110
Matanni, Pak. B3 54
Matanzas, Cuba A7 102
Matanzas, Mex. E8 100
Matapan, Cape see Taínaro, Ákra, c., Grc. G5 28
Matape, stm., Mex. A3 100
Matapédia, Qc., Can. C9 110
Matapédia, Lac, l., Qc., Can. B9 110
Mataquito, stm., Chile G2 92
Matara, Sri L. I5 53
Mataram, Indon. H9 50
Mataranka, Austl. B6 74
Mataró, Spain C13 20
Matasiri, Pulau, i., Indon. F9 50
Matatiele, S. Afr. G9 70
Matatula, Cape, c., Am. Sam. h12 79c
Matâ'utu, Wal./F. E9 72
Matavera, Cook Is. a27 78j
Mataveri, Chile e29 78l
Mataveri, Aeropuerto, Chile f29 78l
Mataveri Airstrip see Mataveri, Aeropuerto, Chile f29 78l
Matehuala, Mex. D8 100
Mateke Hills, hills, Zimb. B10 70
Matera, Italy D10 24
Mateur, Tun. G3 24
Matha, Fr. D5 18
Mather, Mb., Can. E14 124
Mather, Pa., U.S. E5 114
Matheson, On., Can. F14 106
Mathews, Va., U.S. G9 114
Mathis, Tx., U.S. F10 130
Mathura (Muttra), India E6 54
Matias Barbosa, Braz. K4 88
Matías Romero, Mex. G11 100
Matícora, stm., Ven. B6 86
Matinha, Braz. B3 88
Matipó, Braz. K4 88
Matiyure, stm., Ven. D7 86
Mātli, Pak. F2 54
Mato, Cerro, mtn., Ven. D9 86
Mato Grosso, state, Braz. F6 84
Mato Grosso, Planalto do, plat., Braz. B5 90
Mato Grosso, Plateau of see Mato Grosso, Planalto do, plat., Braz. B5 90
Mato Grosso do Sul, state, Braz. C6 90
Matola Rio, Moz. D11 70
Matopos, Zimb. B9 70
Matosinhos, Port. C2 20
Matouying, China B8 42
Matozinhos, Braz. J3 88
Maṭraḥ, Oman E8 56
Matsudo, Japan D12 40
Matsue, Japan D6 40
Matsumoto, Japan C10 40
Matsusaka, Japan E9 40
Matsu Tao, i., Tai. H8 42
Matsutō, Japan C9 40
Matsuura, Japan F2 40
Matsuyama, Japan F5 40
Mattagami, stm., On., Can. F14 106
Mattamuskeet, Lake, l., N.C., U.S. A9 116
Mattaponi, stm., Va., U.S. G8 114
Mattawa, On., Can. B11 112
Mattawa, Wa., U.S. D7 136
Mattawamkeag, stm., Me., U.S. E8 110
Matterhorn, mtn., Eur. D13 18
Matterhorn, mtn., Nv., U.S. B1 132
Matthews Mountain, hill, Mo., U.S. G7 120
Matthew Town, Bah. C10 96
Mattighofen, Aus. B10 22
Mattoon, Il., U.S. E9 120
Mattoon, Wi., U.S. F9 118
Mattydale, N.Y., U.S. E13 112
Matua, Indon. E7 50
Matudo see Matsudo, Japan D12 40
Matue see Matsue, Japan D6 40
Matuku, i., Fiji q19 79e
Matumoto see Matsumoto, Japan C10 40
Maturín, Ven. C10 86
Matutina, Braz. J2 88
Matuzaka see Matsusaka, Japan E9 40
Maú (Ireng), stm., S.A. F12 86
Maúa, Moz. C6 68
Mau Aimma, India F8 54
Maubeuge, Fr. D12 14
Maud, Tx., U.S. D4 122
Maudaha, India F7 54
Maude, Austl. J5 76
Maués, Braz. D6 84
Maués, stm., Braz. D6 84
Mauganj, India F8 54
Maui, i., Hi., U.S. c5 78a
Mauk, Indon. F5 50
Mauldin, S.C., U.S. B3 116
Maule, state, Chile G2 92
Maule, stm., Chile G1 92
Maule, Laguna del, l., Chile G2 92
Mauléon-Licharre, Fr. F5 18
Maumee, Oh., U.S. G6 112
Maumee, stm., U.S. G6 112
Maumelle, Lake, res., Ar., U.S. C6 122
Maumere, Indon. G7 44
Maun, Bots. D3 68
Maunabo, P.R. B4 104a
Mauna Kea, vol., Hi., U.S. d6 78a
Maunaloa, Hi., U.S. b4 78a
Mauna Loa, vol., Hi., U.S. d6 78a
Maunath Bhanjan, India F9 54
Maungdaw, Mya. H14 54
Maungmagan, Mya. E3 48
Maunoir, Lac, l., N.T., Can. B6 106
Maupihaa, at., Fr. Poly. E11 72
Mau Rānīpur, India F7 54
Maurepas, Lake, l., La., U.S. G8 122
Maurice, Lake, l., Austl. E6 74
Mauricie, Parc national de la, p.o.i., Qc., Can. D3 110
Mauritania, ctry., Afr. F2 64
Mauritanie see Mauritania, ctry., Afr. F2 64
Mauritius, ctry., Afr. h10 69a
Mauron, Fr. F6 14
Mauston, Wi., U.S. H8 118
Mautau, c., Fr. Poly. r19 78g
Mauterndorf, Aus. C10 22
Mauthen, Aus. D9 22
Mauvais Coulee, stm., N.D., U.S. F14 124
Mava, Pap. N. Gui. b3 79a
Maverick, Az., U.S. J7 132
Mavinga, Ang. D3 68
Mavrovo Nacionalni Park, p.o.i., Mac. B3 28
Mavuradonha Mountains, mts., Zimb. D5 68
Mawchi, Mya. C3 48
Mawlaik, Mya. D7 46
Mawlamyine (Moulmein), Mya. D3 48
Mawson, sci., Ant. B11 81

Name	Map Ref.	Page

Maw Taung (Luang, Khao), mtn., Asia — G4 48
Max, N.D., U.S. — G12 124
Maxaranguape, Braz. — C8 88
Maxcanú, Mex. — B3 102
Maxixe, Moz. — C12 70
Maxville, On., Can. — E2 110
Maxwell, Ca., U.S. — D3 134
Maxwell, Ne., U.S. — F12 126
Maxwell, N.M., U.S. — E4 128
May, Tx., U.S. — B9 130
May, Cape, pen., N.J., U.S. — F11 114
May, Mount, mtn., Ab., Can. — B11 138
Maya, Pulau, i., Indon. — D6 50
Mayaguana, i., Bah. — A11 102
Mayaguana Passage, strt., Bah. — A11 102
Mayagüez, P.R. — B1 104a
Mayang, China — H3 42
Mayari, Cuba — B10 102
Maybole, Scot., U.K. — F8 12
Maydena, Austl. — o13 77a
Mayd, Som. — B9 66
Mayen, Ger. — F3 16
Mayenne, Fr. — F8 14
Mayenne, state, Fr. — F8 14
Mayenne, stm., Fr. — F8 14
Mayer, Az., U.S. — I4 132
Mayerthorpe, Ab., Can. — C15 138
Mayfield, Ky., U.S. — H9 120
Mayfield, Ut., U.S. — D5 132
Mayflower, Ar., U.S. — C6 122
Mayir, Syria — B8 58
Maykain see Mayqayyng, Kaz. — D13 32
Maymyo, Mya. — A3 48
Maynard, La., U.S. — B6 120
Maynardville, Tn., U.S. — H2 114
Mayne, stm., Austl. — D3 76
Mayo, Yk., Can. — C3 106
Mayo, Fl., U.S. — F2 116
Mayo, state, Ire. — H3 12
Mayo, stm., Arg. — I3 90
Mayo, stm., Mex. — B4 100
Mayon Volcano, vol., Phil. — D4 52
Mayor Buratovich, Arg. — G4 90
Mayotte, dep., Afr. — C8 68
Mayoyouque, Col. — G4 86
May Pen, Jam. — j13 104d
Mayqayyng, Kaz. — D13 32
Mayreau, i., St. Vin. — p11 105e
Mayskoe, Kaz. — D13 32
Mays Landing, N.J., U.S. — E11 114
Maysville, Ky., U.S. — F2 114
Maysville, Mo., U.S. — E3 120
Maysville, N.C., U.S. — B8 116
Maysville, Ok., U.S. — G11 128
Mayumba, Gabon — E2 66
Mayūram, India — F4 53
Mayville, Mi., U.S. — E6 112
Mayville, N.D., U.S. — G16 124
Mayville, N.Y., U.S. — B6 114
Maywood, Ne., U.S. — G12 126
Maza, Arg. — H6 92
Mazabuka, Zam. — D4 68
Mazagão, Braz. — D7 84
Mazamet, Fr. — F8 18
Mazán, stm., Peru — I4 86
Mazara, Val di, reg., Italy — G7 24
Mazara del Vallo, Italy — G6 24
Mazār-e Sharīf, Afg. — B10 56
Mazarrón, Golfo de, b., Spain — G9 20
Mazaruni, stm., Guy. — D11 86
Mazatenango, Guat. — E2 102
Mazatlán, Mex. — D5 100
Mažeikiai, Lith. — D5 10
Mazenod, Sk., Can. — E7 124
Mazinga, mtn., Neth. Ant. — C2 105a
Mazirbe, Lat. — C5 10
Mazon, Il., U.S. — C9 120
Mazowe, stm., Afr. — D5 68
Mazury (Masuria), reg., Pol. — C16 16
Mazyr, Bela. — D3 32
Mbabane, Swaz. — E10 70
M'bahiakro, C. Iv. — H4 64
Mbaïki, C.A.R. — D3 66
Mbaké, Sen. — G1 64
Mbala, Zam. — B5 68
Mbalabala, Zimb. — B9 70
Mbale, Ug. — D6 66
Mbalmayo, Cam. — D2 66
Mbamba Bay, Tan. — G7 66
Mbandaka (Coquilhatville), D.R.C. — D3 66
Mbanga, Cam. — D1 66
Mbanika Island, i., Sol. Is. — e8 79b
M'banza Congo, Ang. — B1 68
Mbanza-Ngungu, D.R.C. — F3 66
Mbarara, Ug. — E6 66
Mbashe, stm., S. Afr. — H9 70
Mbava Island, i., Sol. Is. — d7 79b
Mbé, Cam. — C2 66
Mberengwa, Zimb. — B9 70
Mbeya, Tan. — F6 66
Mbigou, Gabon — E2 66
Mbinda, Congo — E2 66
Mbini, Eq. Gui. — I6 64
Mbini, stm., Afr. — I6 64
Mboi, C.A.R. — F4 66
Mboki, C.A.R. — C5 66
Mbola, Sol. Is. — e9 79b
Mborokua, i., Sol. Is. — e8 79b
Mbouda, Cam. — H12 50
Mbour, Sen. — G1 64
Mbout, Maur. — F2 64
Mbuji-Mayi (Bakwanga), D.R.C. — F4 66
Mbuluzi, stm., Swaz. — E10 70
Mbwemwu, stm., Tan. — F7 66
McAdam, N.B., Can. — E9 110
McAdoo, Pa., U.S. — D9 114
McAlester, Ok., U.S. — C3 122
McAllen, Tx., U.S. — H9 130
McArthur, Oh., U.S. — E3 114
McArthur, stm., Austl. — C7 74
McArthur River, Austl. — C7 74
McBain, Mi., U.S. — D4 112
McBee, S.C., U.S. — B5 116
McBeth Fjord, b., Nu., Can. — B17 106
McBride, B.C., Can. — C10 138
McCall Creek, Ms., U.S. — F8 122
McCamey, Tx., U.S. — C5 130
McCammon, Id., U.S. — H14 136
McCauley Island, i., B.C., Can. — E4 106
McCleary, Wa., U.S. — C3 136
McClellan Creek, stm., Tx., U.S. — F8 128
McClellanville, S.C., U.S. — C6 116
McClintock, Mount, mtn., Ant. — D21 81
McCloud, Ca., U.S. — B3 134
McCloud, stm., Ca., U.S. — B3 134
McClure, Il., U.S. — G8 120
McClusky, N.D., U.S. — G13 124
McColl, S.C., U.S. — B6 116
McComb, Ms., U.S. — F8 122
McConaughy, Lake, res., Ne., U.S. — F11 126
McConnellsburg, Pa., U.S. — E7 114
McConnelsville, Oh., U.S. — E4 114
McCook, Ne., U.S. — A8 128
McCormick, S.C., U.S. — C3 116
McCreary, Mb., Can. — D14 124
McCullough Mountain, mtn., Nv., U.S. — H1 132
McCune, Ks., U.S. — G2 120
McCurtain, Ok., U.S. — B4 122
McDade, Tx., U.S. — D10 130
McDermitt, Nv., U.S. — B8 134
McDermott, Oh., U.S. — F2 114

McDonald, Ks., U.S. — B7 128
McDonald, Lake, l., Mt., U.S. — B12 136
McDowell Peak, mtn., Az., U.S. — J4 132
Mcensk, Russia — G19 10
McEwen, Tn., U.S. — H10 120
McFadden, Wy., U.S. — B10 132
McFarland, Ca., U.S. — H6 134
McGehee, Ar., U.S. — D7 122
McGill, Nv., U.S. — D2 132
McGrath, Ak., U.S. — D8 140
McGraw, N.Y., U.S. — B9 114
McGregor, Tx., U.S. — C10 130
McGregor, stm., B.C., Can. — B9 138
McGregor Lake, l., Ab., Can. — F18 138
McHenry, Il., U.S. — B9 120
McHenry, Ms., U.S. — G9 122
Mchinji, Mwi. — C5 68
McIntosh, Mn., U.S. — D3 118
McIntyre Bay, b., On., Can. — C17 106
McKeand, stm., Nu., Can. — C17 106
McKee, Ky., U.S. — G2 114
McKeesport, Pa., U.S. — D6 114
McKenzie, Tn., U.S. — H9 120
McKenzie, stm., Or., U.S. — F4 136
McKenzie Bridge, Or., U.S. — F4 136
McKenzie Island, On., Can. — E12 106
McKinlay, Austl. — C3 76
McKinlay, stm., Austl. — C3 76
McKinley, Mount, mtn., Ak., U.S. — D9 140
McKinleyville, Ca., U.S. — C1 134
McKinney, Tx., U.S. — D2 122
McKittrick Summit, mtn., Ca., U.S. — H6 134
McLain, Ms., U.S. — F10 122
McLaurin, Ms., U.S. — F9 122
McLean, Il., U.S. — D8 120
McLeansboro, Il., U.S. — F9 120
McLennan, Ab., Can. — D7 106
McLeod, stm., Ab., Can. — C15 138
McLeod Bay, b., N.T., Can. — C8 106
McLeod Lake, B.C., Can. — B7 138
M'Clintock Channel, strt., Nu., Can. — A10 106
McLoughlin, Mount, mtn., Or., U.S. — A3 134
McLouth, Ks., U.S. — E2 120
M'Clure Strait, strt., N.T., Can. — B16 140
McMahon, Sk., Can. — D6 124
McMinnville, Or., U.S. — E3 136
McMinnville, Tn., U.S. — B13 122
McMurdo, sci., Ant. — C22 81
McMurdo Sound, strt., Ant. — C22 81
McNary, Az., U.S. — I7 132
McNeil, Ar., U.S. — D5 122
McPherson, Ks., U.S. — C11 128
McQueeney, Tx., U.S. — E9 130
McRae, Ar., U.S. — B7 122
McRae, Ga., U.S. — D3 116
McVeigh, Ky., U.S. — G3 114
McVille, N.D., U.S. — G15 124
McWilliams, Al., U.S. — F11 122
Mdantsane, S. Afr. — H8 70
M'drak, Viet. — F9 48
Mead, Ne., U.S. — C1 120
Mead, Lake, res., U.S. — G2 132
Meade, Ks., U.S. — D8 128
Meaden Peak, mtn., Co., U.S. — C9 132
Meadow, Ut., U.S. — E4 132
Meadow Lake, Sk., Can. — E9 106
Meadow Valley Wash, stm., Nv., U.S. — F2 132
Meadowview, Va., U.S. — H3 114
Meadville, Mo., U.S. — E4 120
Meadville, Ms., U.S. — F7 122
Meadville, Pa., U.S. — C5 114
Meaford, On., Can. — D9 112
Mealhada, Port. — D2 20
Meandarra, Austl. — F7 76
Meander River, Ab., Can. — D7 106
Mearim, stm., Braz. — B3 88
Meath, state, Ire. — H6 12
Meath, hist. reg., Ire. — H6 12
Meaux, Fr. — F11 14
Mecaya, stm., Col. — G4 86
Mecca see Makkah, Sau. Ar. — E4 56
Mechanicsville, Ia., U.S. — C6 120
Mechanicsville, Va., U.S. — G8 114
Mechanicville, N.Y., U.S. — B12 114
Mechelen (Malines), Bel. — C13 14
Mecklenburg, hist. reg., Ger. — C7 16
Mecklenburger Bucht, b., Ger. — B7 16
Mecklenburg-Vorpommern, state, Ger. — C8 16
Mecubúri, Moz. — C6 68
Mecula, Moz. — C6 68
Meda, Port. — D3 20
Medak, India — B4 53
Medan, Indon. — B1 50
Medanosa, Punta, c., Arg. — I3 90
Mede, Italy — E5 22
Medeiros Neto, Braz. — I5 88
Medellín, Col. — D4 86
Médenine, Tun. — C6 64
Mederdra, Maur. — F1 64
Medford, Or., U.S. — A2 134
Medford, Wi., U.S. — F8 118
Medgidia, Rom. — E15 26
Mediapolis, Ia., U.S. — C6 120
Mediaș, Rom. — C11 26
Medicine Bow, Wy., U.S. — B10 132
Medicine Bow, stm., Wy., U.S. — A10 132
Medicine Bow Mountains, mts., U.S. — F6 126
Medicine Creek, stm., Mo., U.S. — E4 120
Medicine Hat, Ab., Can. — D3 124
Medicine Lake, Mt., U.S. — F9 124
Medicine Lodge, Ks., U.S. — D10 128
Medicine Lodge, stm., U.S. — D10 128
Medina, Braz. — I5 88
Medina see Al-Madīnah, Sau. Ar. — E4 56
Medina, N.Y., U.S. — E11 112
Medina, Oh., U.S. — C4 114
Medina, Tn., U.S. — B10 120
Medina, Tx., U.S. — E9 130
Medinaceli, Spain — C8 20
Medina del Campo, Spain — C6 20
Medina-Sidonia, Spain — H5 20
Medinipur, India — G11 54
Medio, Punta, c., Chile — C2 92
Medio Creek, stm., Tx., U.S. — F10 130
Mediterranean Sea, s. — A4 62
Medje, D.R.C. — D5 66
Medjez el Bab, Tun. — H3 24
Medkovec, Blg. — F10 26
Medora, N.D., U.S. — H10 124
Mêdog, reg., Fr. — D4 18
Médouneu, Gabon — D2 66
Meductic, N.B., Can. — E9 110
Medvedica, stm., Russia — C19 10
Medvedica, stm., Russia — D6 32
Medvegalis, hill, Lith. — E5 10
Medvež'jegorsk, Russia — E15 8
Medvež'i ostrova, is., Russia — B21 34
Medyn', Russia — F18 10
Meekatharra, Austl. — E3 74
Meeker, Co., U.S. — C8 132
Meeks Bay, Ca., U.S. — D5 134
Meeladeen, Som. — B9 66

Meerane, Ger. — F8 16
Meersburg, Ger. — I5 16
Meerut, India — D6 54
Mēga, Eth. — G7 62
Mega, Pulau, i., Indon. — E2 50
Megalópoli, Grc. — F4 28
Megántic, Lac, l., Qc., Can. — E5 110
Mégara, Grc. — E6 28
Megargel, Tx., U.S. — H9 128
Meghâlaya, state, India — F13 54
Meghna, stm., Bngl. — G13 54
Megisti, i., Grc. — G12 28
Megra, Russia — C19 8
Meharry, Mount, mtn., Austl. — D3 74
Mehedinți, state, Rom. — E10 26
Mehekar, India — H6 54
Meherrin, stm., U.S. — H7 114
Mehidpur, India — G5 54
Mehikoorma, Est. — B10 10
Mehrdäwal, India — E9 54
Mehren'ga, Russia — F19 8
Mehrenga, stm., Russia — E19 8
Mehtar Läm, Afg. — C11 56
Mehun-sur-Yèvre, Fr. — G11 14
Mei, stm., China — H7 42
Mei, stm., China — I7 42
Meia Meia, Tan. — F7 66
Meia Ponte, stm., Braz. — I1 88
Meiganga, Cam. — C2 66
Meighen Island, i., Nu., Can. — A5 141
Meigs, Ga., U.S. — E1 116
Meihekou, China — C6 38
Meihsien see Meizhou, China — I7 42
Meikeng, China — J6 42
Meiktila, Mya. — B2 48
Meiners Oaks, Ca., U.S. — I6 134
Meiningen, Ger. — F6 16
Meishan, China — E5 36
Meissen, Ger. — E9 16
Meitan, China — H2 42
Meizhou, China — I7 42
Mejillones, Chile — D2 90
Mejillones, Península, pen., Chile — A2 92
Mejinrjyl'gyno, Russia — D24 34
Mékambo, Gabon — D2 66
Mek'elē, Eth. — E7 62
Mékhé, Sen. — F1 64
Mekhtar, Pak. — C3 54
Mekka see Makkah, Sau. Ar. — E4 56
Meknès, Mor. — C3 64
Mekong (Mékôngk) (Khong) (Lancang), stm., Asia — F9 46
Mekongga, Gunung, mtn., Indon. — F7 44
Mékôngk see Mekong, stm., Asia — F10 46
Melado, stm., Chile — H2 92
Melaka, Malay. — K6 48
Melaka, state, Malay. — K6 48
Melanesia, is., Oc. — D7 72
Melawi, stm., Indon. — D8 50
Melbourne, Austl. — K5 76
Melbourne, Ar., U.S. — H6 120
Melbourne, Fl., U.S. — H5 116
Melbourne, Ia., U.S. — J5 118
Melbourne Island, i., Nu., Can. — B10 106
Melchor, Isla, i., Chile — I2 90
Melchor Múzquiz, Mex. — B8 100
Meldorf, Ger. — B4 16
Meldrum Bay, On., Can. — C6 112
Melfi, Chad — E3 62
Melfi, Italy — C9 24
Melfort, Sk., Can. — B9 124
Meliane, Oued, stm., Tun. — H4 24
Meliau, Indon. — D7 50
Meligalás, Grc. — F4 28
Melilla, Sp. N. Afr. — B4 64
Melimoyu, Cerro, vol., Chile — H2 92
Melincué, Arg. — F7 92
Melita, Mb., Can. — E12 124
Melitopol', Ukr. — E5 32
Melivoia, Grc. — D5 28
Mellansel, Swe. — E7 8
Mellen, Wi., U.S. — E8 118
Mellerud, Swe. — G5 8
Mellish Reef, at., Austl. — C11 74
Mellit, Sudan — E5 62
Mělník, Czech Rep. — F10 16
Melo, Ur. — F10 92
Melolo, Indon. — H12 50
Melos see Milos, i., Grc. — G7 28
Melrhir, Chott, l., Alg. — C6 64
Melrose, Austl. — I4 76
Melrose, Mn., U.S. — F4 118
Melrose, N.M., U.S. — G5 128
Melrose, Wi., U.S. — G8 118
Melsungen, Ger. — E5 16
Meltaus, Fin. — C11 8
Melton Mowbray, Eng., U.K. — I12 12
Melūr, India — F4 53
Melvern, Ks., U.S. — F2 120
Melvern Lake, res., Ks., U.S. — F2 120
Melville, Sk., Can. — D11 124
Melville, La., U.S. — G7 122
Melville, Cape, c., Austl. — B9 74
Melville Bugt, b., Grnld. — B12 141
Melville Hall Airport, Dom. — i6 105c
Melville Hills, hills, Can. — B7 106
Melville Island, i., Austl. — B6 74
Melville Island, i., Can. — A17 140
Melville Peninsula, pen., Nu., Can. — B14 106
Melvin, Ky., U.S. — G3 114
Melvin, Tx., U.S. — C8 130
Melyana, Alg. — H13 20
Mélykút, Hung. — C6 26
Mémar Co, l., China — A9 54
Memba, Moz. — C7 68
Membalong, Indon. — E5 50
Memboro, Indon. — H11 50
Memel see Klaipėda, Lith. — E3 10
Memel, S. Afr. — E9 70
Mêmêle (Nemunélis), stm., Eur. — D7 10
Mempawah, Indon. — C6 50
Memphis, Fl., U.S. — I3 116
Memphis, Mi., U.S. — B3 114
Memphis, Tn., U.S. — B8 122
Memphis, Tx., U.S. — G8 128
Memphremagog, Lac (Memphremagog, Lake), l., N.A. — E4 110
Memphrémagog, Lake (Memphrémagog, Lac), l., N.A. — E4 110
Memramcook, N.B., Can. — D12 110
Mena, Ar., U.S. — C4 122
Menado see Manado, Indon. — E7 44
Ménaka, Mali — F5 64
Menan, Id., U.S. — G15 136
Menard, Tx., U.S. — D8 130
Menasha, Wi., U.S. — G10 118
Menate, Indon. — D8 50
Mendawai, Indon. — E8 50
Mendawai, stm., Indon. — E8 50
Mende, Fr. — E9 18
Mendebo, mts., Eth. — F7 62
Mendenhall, Ms., U.S. — F9 122

Mendī, Eth. — F7 62
Mendi, Pap. N. Gui. — b3 79a
Mendocino, Ca., U.S. — D2 134
Mendocino, Cape, c., U.S. — C1 134
Mendocino Fracture Zone, unds. — E24 142
Mendon, Il., U.S. — D6 120
Mendota, Ca., U.S. — G5 134
Mendoza, Arg. — F3 92
Mendoza, state, Arg. — G3 92
Mendoza, stm., Arg. — F3 92
Mene de Mauroa, Ven. — B6 86
Mene Grande, Ven. — C6 86
Menemen, Tur. — E9 28
Menen, Bel. — D12 14
Menfi, Italy — G6 24
Mengban, China — A5 48
Mengcheng, China — E7 42
Mengellang, Palau — f8 78b
Menggala, Indon. — F4 50
Menggudai, China — B5 48
Menghai, China — B5 48
Mengjiawan, China — B3 42
Menglian, China — A4 48
Mengxian, China — D5 42
Mengyin, China — D7 42
Mengzi, China — A6 48
Menihek Lakes, l., Nf., Can. — E17 106
Menin see Menen, Bel. — D12 14
Menindee, Austl. — I4 76
Meningie, Austl. — J2 76
Menlo Park, Ca., U.S. — F3 134
Menno, S.D., U.S. — D15 126
Meno, Ok., U.S. — E10 128
Menominee, Mi., U.S. — C2 112
Menominee, stm., U.S. — C2 112
Menomonee Falls, Wi., U.S. — A9 120
Menomonie, Wi., U.S. — G7 118
Menongue, Ang. — C2 68
Menor, Mar, b., Spain — G10 20
Menorca (Minorca), i., Spain — D15 20
Mentasta Lake, Ak., U.S. — D11 140
Mentawai, Kepulauan, is., Indon. — E1 50
Mentawai, Selat, strt., Indon. — D2 50
Menton, Fr. — F13 18
Mentor, Oh., U.S. — C4 114
Menyapa, Gunung, mtn., Indon. — C9 50
Menzel Bourguiba, Tun. — G3 24
Menzel Bou Zelfa, Tun. — H4 24
Menzelinsk, Russia — C8 32
Menzel Temime, Tun. — H5 24
Menzies, Austl. — E4 74
Menzies, Mount, mtn., Ant. — C10 81
Meobbaai, b., Nmb. — D2 70
Meoqui, Mex. — A6 100
Meota, Sk., Can. — A5 124
Meppel, Neth. — B15 14
Meppen, Ger. — D3 16
Megerghane, Sebkha, pl., Alg. — D5 64
Mequinenza, Embalse de, res., Spain — C10 20
Mequon, Wi., U.S. — E2 112
Merah, Indon. — C10 50
Meramec, stm., Mo., U.S. — F7 120
Meran see Merano, Italy — D8 22
Merano (Meran), Italy — D8 22
Meratus, Pegunungan, mts., Indon. — E9 50
Merauke, Indon. — G11 44
Merbau, Indon. — C3 50
Merbein, Austl. — J4 76
Mercaderes, Col. — G3 86
Mercara, India — E2 53
Merced, Ca., U.S. — F5 134
Merced, stm., Ca., U.S. — F5 134
Mercedario, Cerro, mtn., Arg. — E2 92
Mercedes, Arg. — D8 92
Mercedes, Arg. — F8 92
Mercedes, Ur. — F8 92
Mercedes, Tx., U.S. — H10 130
Mercer, Mo., U.S. — D4 120
Mercer, Pa., U.S. — C5 114
Mercersburg, Pa., U.S. — E7 114
Merchants Bay, b., Nu., Can. — D13 141
Mercoal, Ab., Can. — C13 138
Mercury, Nv., U.S. — G10 134
Mercury Islands, is., N.Z. — C6 80
Mercy, Cape, c., Nu., Can. — E13 141
Mercy Bay, b., N.T., Can. — B16 140
Meredith, Lake, res., Tx., U.S. — F7 128
Meredosia, Il., U.S. — E7 120
Mereeg, Som. — D9 66
Méré Lava, i., Vanuatu — j17 79d
Merevari, stm., Ven. — E9 86
Mereža, Russia — A19 10
Mergui, Mya. — F4 48
Mergui Archipelago, is., Mya. — G3 48
Meribah, Austl. — J3 76
Mérida, Mex. — B3 102
Mérida, Spain — F4 20
Mérida, Ven. — C6 86
Mérida, state, Ven. — C6 86
Mérida, Cordillera de, mts., Ven. — C6 86
Meridian, Ga., U.S. — E4 116
Meridian, Ms., U.S. — E10 122
Meridian, Tx., U.S. — C10 130
Meridianville, Al., U.S. — C12 122
Mérignac, Fr. — E5 18
Merigold, Ms., U.S. — D8 122
Merikarvia, Fin. — F9 8
Merimbula, Austl. — K7 76
Merin, Laguna (Mirim, Lagoa), b., S.A. — F11 92
Merinda, Austl. — B6 76
Merino, Co., U.S. — G9 126
Merino, Ur. — F9 92
Merizo, Guam — j9 78c
Merkinė, Lith. — F7 10
Merlin, On., Can. — F7 112
Merlin, Or., U.S. — H3 136
Merna, Ne., U.S. — F13 126
Meron, Har (Meron, Mount), mtn., Isr. — E6 58
Meron, Mount see Meron, Har, mtn., Isr. — E6 58
Merouane, Chott, l., Alg. — C6 64
Merredin, Austl. — F3 74
Merrick, mtn., Scot., U.K. — F8 12
Merrill, Ia., U.S. — B1 120
Merrill, Mi., U.S. — E5 112
Merrill, Or., U.S. — A4 134
Merrill, Wi., U.S. — G8 118
Merrillan, Wi., U.S. — G8 118
Merrillville, In., U.S. — G2 112
Merriman, Ne., U.S. — E11 126
Merritt, B.C., Can. — F10 138
Merritt Island, Fl., U.S. — H5 116
Merriwa, Austl. — I8 76
Merrygoen, Austl. — H7 76
Merryville, La., U.S. — G4 122
Mersa Matruh, Egypt — A5 62
Mersea Island, i., Eng., U.K. — J13 12
Mersey, stm., Austl. — n13 77a
Mersey, stm., Eng., U.K. — H10 12
Mersin, Tur. — B4 58
Mersing, Malay. — K6 48
Mērsrags, Lat. — C6 10
Merta, India — E5 54
Merthyr Tydfil, Wales, U.K. — J9 12
Mértola, Port. — G3 20

Mertz Glacier Tongue, ice, Ant. — B19 81
Méru, Fr. — E11 14
Meru, Kenya — D7 66
Meruoca, Braz. — B5 88
Merweville, S. Afr. — H5 70
Merzifon, Tur. — A4 56
Merzig, Ger. — G2 16
Mesa, Az., U.S. — J5 132
Mesabi Range, hills, Mn., U.S. — D6 118
Mesagne, Italy — D11 24
Mesa Verde National Park, p.o.i., Co., U.S. — F8 132
Mescalero, N.M., U.S. — H3 128
Meščerino, Russia — G20 10
Meschede, Ger. — E4 16
Meščura, Russia — E24 8
Mesewa see Massawa, Erit. — D7 62
Mesgouez, Lac, l., Qc., Can. — E16 106
Mesick, Mi., U.S. — D4 112
Mesilla, N.M., U.S. — K10 132
Meškuičiai, Lith. — D6 10
Mesolóngi, Grc. — E4 28
Mesopotamia, hist. reg., Asia — C5 56
Mesquite, Tx., U.S. — E2 122
Messalo, stm., Moz. — C6 68
Messina, S. Afr. — C9 70
Messina, Gulf of see Messiniakós Kólpos, b., Grc. — G5 28
Messina, Stretto di, strt., Italy — F9 24
Messini, Grc. — F4 28
Messíni, sci., Grc. — F4 28
Messiniakós Kólpos, b., Grc. — G5 28
Messkirch, Ger. — H5 16
Messojaha, stm., Russia — C4 34
Mesta (Néstos), stm., Eur. — B6 28
Mestghanem, Alg. — B4 64
Mestre, ngh., Italy — E9 22
Mesuji, stm., Indon. — F4 50
Meta, stm., S.A. — D7 86
Metabetchouan, Qc., Can. — B5 110
Métabetchouane, stm., Qc., Can. — B4 110
Meta Incognita Peninsula, pen., Nu., Can. — C17 106
Metairie, La., U.S. — H8 122
Metaline Falls, Wa., U.S. — B9 136
Metamora, Il., U.S. — D8 120
Metán, Arg. — B5 92
Metangula, Moz. — C5 68
Metapán, El Sal. — E3 102
Metaponto, sci., Italy — D10 24
Metapontum see Metaponto, sci., Italy — D10 24
Meteor Crater, crat., Az., U.S. — I6 132
Methow, stm., Wa., U.S. — B7 136
Methven, N.Z. — F4 80
Metica, stm., Col. — E5 86
Metiskow, Ab., Can. — B3 124
Metlakatla, Ak., U.S. — E13 140
Metlika, Slvn. — E12 22
Metropolis, Il., U.S. — G9 120
Metropolitan, Mi., U.S. — C2 112
Metter, Ga., U.S. — D3 116
Mettuppâlaiyam, India — F3 53
Mettur, India — F3 53
Metz, Fr. — E15 14
Metzingen, Ger. — H5 16
Meu, stm., Fr. — F7 14
Meulaboh, Indon. — J2 48
Meureudu, Indon. — J3 48
Meurthe, stm., Fr. — F15 14
Meurthe-et-Moselle, state, Fr. — F15 14
Meuse, state, Fr. — E14 14
Meuse (Maas), stm., Eur. — D14 14
Meuselwitz, Ger. — F8 16
Mexia, Tx., U.S. — D2 122
Mexiana, Ilha, i., Braz. — C8 84
Mexicali, Mex. — K10 134
Mexican Hat, Ut., U.S. — F7 132
México see Ciudad de México, Mex. — F9 100
Mexico, Mo., U.S. — F6 120
Mexico, N.Y., U.S. — E13 112
Mexico, state, Mex. — F9 100
Mexico, Gulf of, b., N.A. — B6 96
Mexico Basin, unds. — F5 144
Mexico Beach, Fl., U.S. — H13 122
Mexico City see Ciudad de México, Mex. — F9 100
Meycauayan, Phil. — C3 52
Meydan Khvolah, Afg. — B2 54
Meyersdale, Pa., U.S. — E6 114
Meymaneh, Afg. — C9 56
Meymeh, Iran — C7 56
Meyronne, Sk., Can. — E7 124
Meyungs, Palau — g7 78b
Mèza (M'oža), stm., Eur. — E14 10
Mezada, Horvot (Masada), sci., Isr. — G6 58
Mezcala, Mex. — F9 100
Mezcalapa, stm., Mex. — G12 100
Mezdra, Blg. — F10 26
Mèze, Fr. — F9 18
Mezen', Russia — D21 8
Mezen', stm., Russia — D21 8
Mezenskaja guba, b., Russia — C20 8
Mezhdurečensk, Russia — D15 32
Mezhgor'e, Russia — C9 32
Mezőberény, Hung. — B7 26
Mezőkövesd, Hung. — B7 26
Mezőtúr, Hung. — B7 26
Mezquital, stm., Mex. — D6 100
Mezquitic, Mex. — E6 100
Mfangano Island, i., Kenya — E6 66
Mgači, Russia — F17 34
M'Goun, Irhil, mtn., Mor. — C3 64
M'Hai, B'nom, mtn., Viet. — G8 48
Mhasvad, India — C2 53
Mhow, India — G5 54
Mi, stm., China — H5 42
Mi, stm., China — H5 42
Mia, stm., China, Alg. — C13 28
Miahuatlán de Porfirio Díaz, Mex. — G10 100
Miajadas, Spain — E5 20
Miami, Az., U.S. — J6 132
Miami, Fl., U.S. — K5 116
Miami, Mb., Can. — E15 124
Miami, Tx., U.S. — F8 128
Miami, stm., Oh., U.S. — H3 120
Miami Beach, Fl., U.S. — K5 116
Miami Canal, can., Fl., U.S. — J5 116
Miamisburg, Oh., U.S. — E1 114
Miami Springs, Fl., U.S. — K5 116
Mianchi, China — D4 42
Mian Channún, Pak. — C4 54
Miandrivazo, Madag. — D8 68
Miāndurab, Iran — B6 56
Mâneh, Iran — B8 56
Miānganj, India — E8 54
Miangas, Pulau, i., Indon. — E9 44
Mianning, China — F5 36
Mianwâli, Pak. — B3 54
Mianxian, China — E2 42
Mianyang, China — F1 42
Mianzhu, China — E5 36
Miaodao Qundao, is., China — B9 42
Miaoli, Tai. — I9 42
Miao Ling, mts., China — H2 42

Miass, Russia — C10 32
Miass, stm., Russia — C10 32
Miastko, Pol. — B12 16
Micang Shan, mts., China — E2 42
Michalovce, Slov. — H17 16
Michaud, Point, c., N.S., Can. — E16 110
Micheal Peak, mtn., B.C., Can. — C4 138
Michel, B.C., Can. — G16 138
Miches, Dom. Rep. — C13 102
Michigan, N.D., U.S. — F15 124
Michigan, state, U.S. — D4 112
Michigan, stm., Co., U.S. — G6 126
Michigan, Lake, l., U.S. — E2 112
Michigan City, In., U.S. — G3 112
Michipicoten Island, i., On., Can. — F13 106
Michoacán, state, Mex. — F8 100
Micoud, St. Luc. — m7 105c
Micronesia, is., Oc. — B6 72
Micronesia, Federated States of, ctry., Oc. — C6 72
Mičurinsk, Russia — D6 32
Midai, Pulau, i., Indon. — B5 50
Midale, Sk., Can. — E10 124
Mid-Atlantic Ridge, unds. — F9 144
Middelburg, Neth. — C12 14
Middelburg, S. Afr. — G7 70
Middelburg, S. Afr. — G7 70
Middle, stm., Ia., U.S. — C3 120
Middle, stm., Mn., U.S. — C2 118
Middle Alkali Lake, l., Ca., U.S. — B5 134
Middle America Trench, unds. — H29 142
Middle Andaman, i., India. — F7 46
Middleboro, Ma., U.S. — C15 114
Middlebourne, W.V., U.S. — E5 114
Middleburg, N.Y., U.S. — B11 114
Middleburg, Pa., U.S. — D8 114
Middlebury, Vt., U.S. — F3 110
Middle Caicos, i., T./C. Is. — B12 102
Middle Fabius, stm., Mo., U.S. — D5 120
Middlefield, Oh., U.S. — C4 114
Middlegate, Norf. I. — y25 78i
Middle Loup, stm., Ne., U.S. — F14 126
Middlemount, Austl. — D7 76
Middle Musquodoboit, N.S., Can. — E13 110
Middleport, Oh., U.S. — E3 114
Middle Raccoon, stm., Ia., U.S. — J4 118
Middlesboro, Ky., U.S. — H2 114
Middlesbrough, Eng., U.K. — G11 12
Middlesex, Belize — D3 102
Middle Stewiacke, N.S., Can. — E13 110
Middleton, N.S., Can. — F11 110
Middleton, Mi., U.S. — E5 112
Middleton, Id., U.S. — A8 120
Middleton Island, i., Ak., U.S. — E10 140
Middleton Reef, at., Austl. — E11 74
Middletown, Ca., U.S. — E3 134
Middletown, Ct., U.S. — C13 114
Middletown, Il., U.S. — K9 118
Middletown, In., U.S. — H4 112
Middletown, Ky., U.S. — F12 120
Middletown, Md., U.S. — E8 114
Middletown, N.Y., U.S. — C11 114
Middletown, Oh., U.S. — E1 114
Middletown, Pa., U.S. — D9 114
Middletown, R.I., U.S. — C14 114
Middleville, Mi., U.S. — F4 112
Midgic, N.B., Can. — E12 110
Midi, Canal du, can., Fr. — F9 18
Midi de Bigorre, Pic du, mtn., Fr. — G5 18
Mid-Indian Basin, unds. — J10 142
Mid-Indian Ridge, unds. — K10 142
Midland, On., Can. — D9 112
Midland, Ca., U.S. — J2 132
Midland, Mi., U.S. — E5 112
Midland, S.D., U.S. — C11 126
Midland, Tx., U.S. — C5 130
Midlands, state, Zimb. — B10 70
Midleton, Ire. — J4 12
Midlothian, Tx., U.S. — B10 130
Midnapore, Ab., Can. — F16 138
Midongy Atsimo, Madag. — E8 68
Mid-Pacific Mountains, unds. — G19 142
Midsayap, Phil. — G5 52
Midville, Ga., U.S. — D3 116
Midway, B.C., Can. — G12 138
Midway, Ky., U.S. — F13 120
Midway, Tx., U.S. — F3 122
Midway Islands, dep., Oc. — G22 30
Midway Park, N.C., U.S. — B8 116
Midwest City, Ok., U.S. — F11 128
Midyan, reg., Sau. Ar. — J6 58
Midžur (Midžor), mtn., Eur. — F9 26
Mie, state, Japan — E9 40
Miedzybórz, Pol. — E12 16
Miedzylesie, Pol. — F12 16
Miedzyrzec Podlaski, Pol. — D18 16
Miedzyrzecz, Pol. — D11 16
Mielan, Fr. — F6 18
Mielec, Pol. — F17 16
Mier, Mex. — B9 100
Mier y Noriega, Mex. — D8 100
Miesbach, Ger. — I7 16
Mi'eso, Eth. — F8 62
Mieszkowice, Pol. — D10 16
Mifflinburg, Pa., U.S. — H12 112
Miguel Alemán, Presa, res., Mex. — F10 100
Miguel Alves, Braz. — C4 88
Miguel Auza, Mex. — C7 100
Miguel Calmon, Braz. — F5 88
Miguel Hidalgo, Presa, res., Mex. — B4 100
Miguelópolis, Braz. — K1 88
Miguel Riglos, Arg. — H6 92
Mihăilești, Rom. — E12 26
Mihajlov, Russia — D6 32
Mihajlovka, Russia — C10 38
Mihajlovka, Russia — D14 32
Mihajlovskij, Russia — F20 8
Mihalıçcık, Tur. — C13 28
Mihara, Japan — E5 40
Mihara-yama, vol., Japan — E21 8
Miḥninskaja, Russia — F21 8
Mikame, Japan — F5 40
Mikasa, Japan — C14 38
Mikaševičy, Bela. — G10 10
Mikhrot Timna ('King Solomon's Mines'), hist., Isr. — I5 58
Mikindani, Tan. — G8 66
Mikkeli (Sankt Michel), Fin. — F12 8
Mikołajki, Pol. — C17 16
Mikołów, Pol. — F14 16
Mikrá Préspa, Limni, l., Eur. — C18 10
Mikšino, Russia — C18 10
Mikulino, Russia — F7 66
Mikumi, Tan. — F7 66
Mikun', Russia — E23 8
Mikuni, Japan — C9 40
Miladummadulu Atoll, at., Mald. — h12 46a
Milagro, Arg. — E5 92
Milagro, Ec. — I2 86
Milagros, Phil. — D4 52
Milan see Milano, Italy — E6 22
Milan, Ga., U.S. — D2 116
Milan, In., U.S. — E12 120

Name	Map Ref.	Page
Milan, Mi., U.S.	B2	114
Milan, Mn., U.S.	F3	118
Milan, Mo., U.S.	D4	120
Milan, N.M., U.S.	H8	132
Milang, Austl.	J2	76
Milange, Moz.	D6	68
Milano (Milan), Italy	E6	22
Milas, Tur.	F10	28
Milavidy, Bela.	H8	10
Milazzo, Italy	F9	24
Milazzo, Golfo di, b., Italy	F9	24
Milbank, Sk., Can.	F2	118
Milburn, Ok., U.S.	C2	122
Milden, Sk., Can.	C6	124
Mildmay, On., Can.	D8	112
Mildura, Austl.	J4	76
Mile, China	G5	36
Miles, Austl.	F8	76
Miles, Tx., U.S.	C7	130
Miles City, Mt., U.S.	A7	126
Milestone, Sk., Can.	E9	124
Milet, sci., Tur.	F10	28
Milford, De., U.S.	F10	114
Milford, Ia., U.S.	H3	118
Milford, Ma., U.S.	B14	114
Milford, Me., U.S.	F8	110
Milford, Mi., U.S.	B2	114
Milford, N.H., U.S.	B14	114
Milford, Pa., U.S.	C11	114
Milford, Ut., U.S.	E4	132
Milford Center, Oh., U.S.	D2	114
Milford Haven, Wales, U.K.	J7	12
Milford Lake, res., Ks., U.S.	B11	128
Milford Sound, strt, N.Z.	G2	80
Mili, at., Marsh. Is.	C8	72
Milian, stm., Malay.	A10	50
Milicz, Pol.	E13	16
Miljatino, Russia	F17	10
Milk, stm., N.A.	B6	108
Milk, North Fork (North Milk), stm., N.A.	B13	136
Mil'kovo, Russia	F20	34
Milk River, Ab., Can.	G18	138
Millard, Ne., U.S.	C1	120
Millau, Fr.	E9	18
Millboro, Va., U.S.	F6	114
Millbrook, N.Y., U.S.	C12	114
Mill City, Or., U.S.	F4	136
Millcreek, Pa., U.S.	B5	114
Millcreek, Ut., U.S.	C5	132
Mill Creek, W.V., U.S.	F5	114
Milledgeville, Ga., U.S.	C2	116
Milledgeville, Il., U.S.	C8	120
Mille Lacs, Lac des, l., On., Can.	C8	118
Mille Lacs Lake, l., Mn., U.S.	C8	118
Millen, Ga., U.S.	D4	116
Miller, Mo., U.S.	G4	120
Miller, S.D., U.S.	C14	126
Miller Mountain, mtn., Nv., U.S.	E7	134
Millerovo, Russia	E6	32
Millersburg, Ky., U.S.	F1	114
Millersburg, Mi., U.S.	C5	112
Millersburg, Oh., U.S.	D4	114
Millersport, Oh., U.S.	I7	112
Millerton, N.Y., U.S.	C12	114
Millet, Ab., Can.	C17	138
Millevaches, Plateau de, plat., Fr.	D7	18
Millicent, Austl.	K3	76
Milligan, Fl., U.S.	G12	122
Milligan, Ne., U.S.	G15	126
Millington, Mi., U.S.	E6	112
Millington, Tn., U.S.	B9	122
Millinocket, Me., U.S.	F8	110
Mill Island, i., Ant.	B15	81
Mill Island, i., Nu., Can.	C15	106
Millry, Al., U.S.	F10	122
Mills, Wy., U.S.	E6	126
Mills Creek, stm., Austl.	D4	76
Mills Lake, l., N.T., Can.	C7	106
Millstream, Austl.	D3	74
Milltown, Mt., U.S.	D13	136
Milltown, Wi., U.S.	F6	118
Milltown Malbay, Ire.	I3	12
Mill Valley, Ca., U.S.	F3	134
Millville, N.J., U.S.	E10	114
Millwood, Va., U.S.	E7	114
Millwood Lake, res., Ar., U.S.	D4	122
Milne Land, i., Grnld.	C20	141
Milnor, N.D., U.S.	A15	126
Milo, Ab., Can.	F18	138
Milos, i., Grc.	G7	28
Miłosław, Pol.	D13	16
Milparinka, Austl.	G3	76
Milroy, In., U.S.	E12	120
Milroy, Pa., U.S.	D8	114
Miltenberg, Ger.	G5	16
Milton, On., Can.	E10	112
Milton, N.Z.	H4	80
Milton, Fl., U.S.	G11	122
Milton, Ia., U.S.	D5	120
Milton, Pa., U.S.	G13	112
Milton, Wi., U.S.	B9	120
Milton-Freewater, Or., U.S.	E8	136
Milton Keynes, Eng., U.K.	I12	12
Miltonvale, Ks., U.S.	B11	128
Miltou, Chad	E3	62
Miluo, China	G5	42
Milwaukee, Wi., U.S.	E2	112
Milwaukee, stm., Wi., U.S.	H11	118
Milwaukie, Or., U.S.	E4	136
Mimbres, stm., N.M., U.S.	K9	132
Mimizan-les-Bains, Fr.	E4	18
Mimoň, Czech Rep.	F10	16
Mimoso do Sul, Braz.	K5	88
Mims, Fl., U.S.	H5	116
Min, stm., China	F5	36
Min, stm., China	I8	42
Mina, Mex.	H7	130
Mina, Nv., U.S.	E7	134
Mīnā' al-Ahmadī, Kuw.	D6	56
Mināb, Iran	D8	56
Minahasa, pen., Indon.	E7	44
Minakuchi, Japan	E9	40
Minamata, Japan	G3	40
Minami-Alps-kokuritsu-kōen, p.o.i., Japan	D11	40
Minami-Tori-shima, i., Japan	G19	30
Minas, Cuba	B9	102
Minas, Indon.	C2	50
Minas, Ur.	G10	92
Minas Basin, b., N.S., Can.	E12	110
Minas de Barroterán, Mex.	B8	100
Minas de Corrales, Ur.	E10	92
Minas de Matahambre, Cuba	A5	102
Minas Gerais, state, Braz.	C8	90
Minas Novas, Braz.	I4	88
Minatare, Ne., U.S.	F9	126
Minatitlán, Mex.	F11	100
Minbu, Mya.	B2	48
Minbya, Mya.	B1	48
Minbyin, Mya.	C1	48
Mincio, stm., Italy.	E7	22
Minco, Ok., U.S.	F11	128
Mindanao, i., Phil.	G5	52
Mindanao, stm., Phil.	G5	52
Mindelheim, Ger.	H6	16
Mindelo, C.V.	k10	65a
Mindemoya, On., Can.	C7	112
Minden, On., Can.	D11	112
Minden, Ger.	D4	16
Minden, La., U.S.	E5	122
Minden, Ne., U.S.	G14	126
Minden, Nv., U.S.	E6	134
Minden City, Mi., U.S.	E7	112
Mindoro, i., Phil.	D3	52
Mindoro Strait, strt., Phil.	D2	52
Mine, Japan.	E4	40
Mine Centre, On., Can.	C6	118
Minehead, Eng., U.K.	J9	12
Mineiros, Braz.	G7	84
Mineola, Tx., U.S.	E3	122
Mineral, Wa., U.S.	D4	136
Mineral Point, Wi., U.S.	B7	120
Mineral Springs, Ar., U.S.	D5	122
Mineral Wells, Tx., U.S.	B9	130
Minersville, Pa., U.S.	H13	112
Minerva, Oh., U.S.	D4	114
Minervino Murge, Italy	C9	24
Mineville, N.Y., U.S.	F3	110
Minfeng, China	A5	46
Minga, D.R.C.	G5	66
Mingäçevir, Azer.	A6	56
Mingäora, Pak.	C11	56
Mingary, Austl.	I3	76
Mingene, Austl.	E3	74
Mingin, Mya.	A2	48
Minglanilla, Spain	E9	20
Mingo Junction, Oh., U.S.	D5	114
Mingo Lake, l., Nu., Can.	C16	106
Mingshui, China	B10	36
Mingulay, i., Scot., U.K.	E5	12
Mingyuegou, China	C8	38
Minhang, China	H9	42
Minh Hai, Viet.	H7	48
Minhla, Mya.	B2	48
Minhla, Mya.	C2	48
Minho, hist. reg., Port.	C2	20
Minho (Miño), stm., Eur.	B2	20
Miníčevo, Serb.	F9	26
Minicoy Island, i., India	G3	46
Minigwal, Lake, l., Austl.	E4	74
Minija, stm., Lith.	E4	10
Minilya, Austl.	D2	74
Minilya, stm., Austl.	D2	74
Miniota, Mb., Can.	D12	124
Minitonas, Mb., Can.	B12	124
Minle, China	D5	36
Minna, Nig.	H6	64
Minneapolis, Ks., U.S.	B11	128
Minneapolis, Mn., U.S.	G5	118
Minnedosa, Mb., Can.	D13	124
Minneola, Ks., U.S.	D8	128
Minnesota, Mn., U.S.	G2	118
Minnesota, state, U.S.	E4	118
Minnesota, stm., Mn., U.S.	G5	118
Minnesota Lake, Mn., U.S.	H5	118
Minnewanka, Lake, res., Ab., Can.	E15	138
Minnitaki Lake, l., On., Can.	B6	118
Mino, Japan	D9	40
Miño (Minho), stm., Eur.	B2	20
Minocqua, Wi., U.S.	F9	118
Minong, Wi., U.S.	E7	118
Minonk, Il., U.S.	D8	120
Minorca see Menorca, i., Spain	D15	20
Minot, N.D., U.S.	F12	124
Minqing, China	H8	42
Minquan, China	D6	42
Minquiers, Plateau des, is., Jersey	E6	14
Min Shan, mts., China	E5	36
Minsk, Bela.	G10	10
Minsk, state, Bela.	G10	10
Minskaye uzvyša, plat., Bela.	G10	10
Mińsk Mazowiecki, Pol.	D17	16
Minta, Cam.	D2	66
Minto, Mb., Can.	E13	124
Minto, Yk., Can.	C3	106
Minto, N.T., Can.	C1	118
Minto, Lac, l., Qc., Can.	D16	106
Minto, Mount, mtn., Ant.	C22	81
Minto Inlet, b., N.T., Can.	A7	106
Minton, Sk., Can.	E9	124
Minturn, Co., U.S.	D10	132
Minūf, Egypt	H1	58
Minusinsk, Russia	D16	32
Minvoul, Gabon	D2	66
Minxian, China	A5	42
Minya see El-Minya, Egypt	J1	58
Minya el-Qamh, Egypt	H2	58
Mio, Mi., U.S.	D5	112
Miquan, China	F15	32
Mir, Bela.	G9	10
Mira, stm., Col.	G2	86
Mīrābād, Afg.	C9	56
Mirabella, Gulf of see Mirampéllou, Kólpos, b., Grc.	H8	28
Miracema do Tocantins, Braz.	E1	88
Mirador, Braz.	D3	88
Miradouro, Braz.	K4	88
Miraflores, Col.	G5	86
Miraflores, Col.	E5	86
Miraj, India	C2	53
Miramar, Arg.	I9	92
Miramar, Moz.	C12	70
Miramas, Fr.	F10	18
Miramichi Bay, b., N.B., Can.	C11	110
Mirampéllou, Kólpos, b., Grc.	H8	28
Mirānī, Pak.	C3	54
Miranda, Braz.	D5	90
Miranda, Col.	F3	86
Miranda, state, Ven.	B8	86
Miranda, stm., Braz.	D5	90
Miranda de Ebro, Spain	B7	20
Mirande, Fr.	F6	18
Mirando City, Tx., U.S.	G8	130
Mirandola, Italy	F8	22
Mira Taglio, Italy	E7	22
Miravalles, Volcán, vol., C.R.	G5	102
Miravete, Puerto de, p., Spain	E5	20
Mirbāt, Oman	F7	56
Mirecourt, Fr.	F14	14
Miri, Malay.	A9	50
Miria, Niger	G6	64
Miriam Vale, Austl.	D8	76
Mirim, Lagoa (Merin, Laguna), b., S.A.	F11	92
Miriñay, stm., Arg.	D9	92
Miritiparaná, stm., Col.	H6	86
Miriyama, Pap. N. Gui.	a3	79a
Mirnoe Ozero, Russia	C13	32
Mirny, sci., Ant.	B14	81
Mirnyj, Russia	D11	34
Mirnyy, sci., Ant.	B14	81
Miroslav, Czech Rep.	H12	16
Mirow, Ger.	C8	16
Mirpur, Bngl.	G13	54
Mirpur, Pak.	B4	54
Mirpur Batoro, Pak.	F2	54
Mirpur Khās, Pak.	F2	54
Mirror, Ab., Can.	D17	138
Miryang, Kor., S.	D1	40
Mirzāpur, India	F9	54
Misantla, Mex.	F10	100
Misawa, Japan	D14	38
Miscou Centre, N.B., Can.	C12	110
Miscou Island, i., N.B., Can.	C12	110
Miscou Point, c., N.B., Can.	C12	110
Mishan, China	B9	38
Mishawaka, In., U.S.	G3	112
Mishicot, Wi., U.S.	D2	112
Misima Island, i., Pap. N. Gui.	B10	74
Misiones, state, Arg.	C10	92
Misión Santa Rosa, Para.	D4	90
Misión San Vicente, Mex.	F4	98
Miskitos, Cayos, is., Nic.	E6	102
Miskolc, Hung.	A7	26
Mishevo, Russia	G19	10
Misool, Pulau, i., Indon.	F9	44
Mişrātah, Libya	A3	62
Misr el-Bahri (Lower Egypt), hist. reg., Egypt	H1	58
Misrikh, India.	E8	54
Missinaibi, stm., On., Can.	E14	106
Missinaibi Lake, l., On., Can.	F14	106
Mission, B.C., Can.	G8	138
Mission, S.D., U.S.	D12	126
Mission, Tx., U.S.	H9	130
Mission Mountain, hill, Ok., U.S.	H3	120
Mission Viejo, Ca., U.S.	J8	134
Mississagi, stm., On., Can.	B6	112
Mississauga, On., Can.	E10	112
Mississinewa, stm., U.S.	H4	112
Mississippi, state, U.S.	D9	122
Mississippi, stm., On., Can.	C13	112
Mississippi, stm., U.S.	E9	108
Mississippi Lake, l., On., Can.	C13	112
Mississippi River Delta, La., U.S.	H9	122
Mississippi Sound, strt., U.S.	G10	122
Mississippi State, Ms., U.S.	D10	122
Missoula, Mt., U.S.	D12	136
Missouri, state, U.S.	F5	120
Missouri, stm., U.S.	D9	108
Missouri City, Tx., U.S.	H3	122
Mistake Creek, stm., Austl.	D6	76
Mistassibi, stm., Qc., Can.	A4	110
Mistassini, Qc., Can.	E16	106
Mistassini, Qc., Can.	B4	110
Mistassini, stm., Qc., Can.	B4	110
Mistassini, Lac, l., Qc., Can.	E16	106
Mistatim, Sk., Can.	B10	124
Mistelbach an der Zaya, Aus.	B13	22
Misterbianco, Italy	G9	24
Misti, Volcán, vol., Peru	G3	84
Misumi, Japan	E4	40
Mita, Punta de, c., Mex.	E6	100
Mitchell, Austl.	F6	76
Mitchell, On., Can.	E8	112
Mitchell, In., U.S.	F11	120
Mitchell, Or., U.S.	F6	136
Mitchell, S.D., U.S.	D14	126
Mitchell, stm., Austl.	K6	76
Mitchell, stm., Austl.	C8	74
Mitchell, Mount, mtn., N.C., U.S.	I3	114
Mitchinamecus, stm., Qc., Can.	C2	110
Mitchinamecus, Réservoir, res., Qc., Can.	C1	110
Mit Ghamr, Egypt.	H2	58
Mithapur, India	G2	54
Mithi, Pak.	F2	54
Mitidja, Plaine de la, pl., Alg.	H14	20
Mitíškovo, Russia	F16	10
Mitla, sci., Mex.	G10	100
Mito, Japan	C13	40
Mitsio, Nosy, i., Madag.	C8	68
Mitsukaidō, Japan	C13	40
Mitsuke, Japan	B11	40
Mittellandkanal, can., Ger.	D5	16
Mittenwald, Ger.	I7	16
Mittersill, Aus.	C9	22
Mittimatalik (Pond Inlet), Nu., Can.	A15	106
Mittweida, Ger.	E9	16
Mitú, Col.	G6	86
Mitumba, Monts, mts., D.R.C.	F5	66
Mitwaba, D.R.C.	F5	66
Mitzic, Gabon	D2	66
Miura, Japan	D12	40
Miura-hantō, pen., Japan	D12	40
Mixian, China	D5	42
Miyagi, state, Japan	A13	40
Miyake-jima, i., Japan	E12	40
Miyako, Japan	E14	38
Miyako-jima, i., Japan	G10	36
Miyakonojō, Japan	H4	40
Miyama, Japan	E9	40
Miyanojō, Japan	H3	40
Miyazaki, Japan	H4	40
Miyazaki, state, Japan	G4	40
Miyazu, Japan	D8	40
Miyoshi, Japan	E5	40
Miyun, China	A7	42
Miyun Shuiku, res., China	A7	42
Mīzān Teferī, Eth.	F7	62
Mizdah, Libya	A2	62
Mize, Ms., U.S.	F9	122
Mizen Head, c., Ire.	J3	12
Mizen Head, c., Ire.	I6	12
Mizhhir'ia, Ukr.	A10	26
Mizhi, China	C4	42
Mizil, Rom.	E13	26
Mizoram, state, India	G14	54
Mizpah Creek, stm., Mt., U.S.	A7	126
Mizque, Bol.	C3	90
Mizukaidō see Mitsukaidō, Japan	C13	40
Mizusawa, Japan	E14	38
Mjadzel, Bela.	F9	10
Mjakit, Russia	D19	34
Mjaksa, Russia	B19	10
Mjölby, Swe.	G6	8
Mjøsa, l., Nor.	F4	8
Mkalama, Tan.	E6	66
Mkhondvo, stm., Afr.	E10	70
Mkokotoni, Tan.	F7	66
Mkomazi, stm., S. Afr.	G10	70
Mkulwe, Tan.	F6	66
Mkushi, Zam.	C4	68
Mkuze, stm., S. Afr.	E11	70
Mkuze Game Reserve, S. Afr.	E11	70
Mladá Boleslav, Czech Rep.	F11	16
Mladenovac, Serb.	E7	26
Mlava, state, Serb.	E8	26
Mława, Pol.	C16	16
Mljet, Otok, i., Cro.	H14	22
Mljet Nacionalni Park, p.o.i., Cro.	H14	22
Mmabatho, S. Afr.	D7	70
Mmadinare, Bots.	B8	70
Moa, stm., Afr.	H2	64
Moab, Ut., U.S.	E7	132
Moala, i., Fiji.	q18	79e
Moamba, Moz.	D11	70
Moanda, Gabon	E2	66
Moar Lake, l., Can.	C18	124
Moate, Ire.	H5	12
Moba, D.R.C.	F5	66
Mobara, Japan	D13	40
Mobaye, C.A.R.	D4	66
Mobeetie, Tx., U.S.	F8	128
Moberly, Mo., U.S.	E5	120
Mobile, Al., U.S.	G11	122
Mobile, stm., Al., U.S.	G11	122
Mobile Bay, b., Al., U.S.	G11	122
Mobridge, S.D., U.S.	B12	126
Moca, Dom. Rep.	C12	102
Mo Cay, Viet.	G8	48
Mocha see Al-Mukhā, Yemen	G5	56
Mochudi, Bots.	D8	70
Mocksville, N.C., U.S.	I5	114
Moclips, Wa., U.S.	C2	136
Mōco, Morro de, mtn., Ang.	C2	68
Mocoa, Col.	G3	86
Mococa, Braz.	K2	88
Mocodoene, Moz.	C12	70
Mocoreta, Arg.	C9	92
Moctezuma, Mex.	G8	98
Moctezuma, Mex.	H14	96a
Moctezuma, Mex.	E9	100
Moctezuma, stm., Mex.	D5	114
Mocuba, Moz.	D6	68
Modane, Fr.	D12	18
Modāsa, India	G4	54
Modder, stm., S. Afr.	F7	70
Módena, Italy	F7	22
Modeste, Mount, mtn., B.C., Can.	H6	138
Modesto, Ca., U.S.	F4	134
Modica, Italy	H8	24
Mödling, Aus.	B13	22
Modowi, Indon.	F9	44
Modra, Slov.	H13	16
Moe, Austl.	L6	76
Moeda, Braz.	K3	88
Moei (Thaungyin), stm., Asia	D3	48
Moema, Braz.	J3	88
Moengo, Sur.	B7	84
Moen-jo-Daro, sci., Pak.	D10	56
Moenkopi, Az., U.S.	G5	132
Moenkopi Wash, stm., Az., U.S.	G6	132
Moeris, Lake see Qārūn, Birket, l., Egypt.	I1	58
Moeskroen see Mouscron, Bel.	D12	14
Moffat, Scot., U.K.	F9	12
Moga, India	C5	54
Mogadiscio see Muqdisho, Som.	D9	66
Mogadishu see Muqdisho, Som.	D9	66
Mogalakwena, stm., S. Afr.	C9	70
Mogami, stm., Japan	A13	40
Mogaung, Mya.	C8	46
Mogdy, Russia	F15	34
Mogilno, Pol.	D13	16
Mogincual, Moz.	D7	68
Mogoča, Russia	F12	34
Mogočin, Russia	C14	32
Mogogh, Sudan	F6	62
Mogok, Mya.	A3	48
Mogollon Rim, clf., Az., U.S.	I6	132
Mogor, Afg.	B1	54
Mogotes, Col.	D5	86
Mogotón, mtn., N.A.	F4	102
Moguer, Spain	G4	20
Mogzon, Russia	F11	34
Mohács, Hung.	C5	26
Mohall, N.D., U.S.	F12	124
Mohammed, Râs, c., Egypt	K5	58
Mohammedia, Mor.	C3	64
Mohania, India	F9	54
Mohawk, Mi., U.S.	D10	118
Mohawk, stm., N.Y., U.S.	B11	114
Mohe, China	F13	34
Mohéli see Mwali, i., Com.	C7	68
Mohnyin, Mya.	D8	46
Mohokare (Caledon), stm., Afr.	F8	70
Mohyliv-Podil's'kyi, Ukr.	A14	26
Moi, Nor.	G2	8
Moineşti, Rom.	C13	26
Moira, stm., On., Can.	D12	112
Moiraba, Braz.	B1	88
Moirana, Nor.	C5	8
Moiseevka, Russia	C13	32
Moisés Ville, Arg.	E7	92
Moisie, Qc., Can.	E17	106
Moisie, stm., Qc., Can.	E17	106
Moitaco, Ven.	C9	86
Mojácar, Spain	G9	20
Mojave, Ca., U.S.	H7	134
Mojave, stm., Ca., U.S.	H9	134
Mojave Desert, des., Ca., U.S.	D4	98
Mojero, stm., Russia	C9	34
Mojiguaçu, stm., Braz.	K2	88
Mojikit Lake, res., On., Can.	A10	118
Moji-Mirim, Braz.	L2	88
Mojo, Eth.	F7	62
Moju, Braz.	A1	88
Moju, stm., Braz.	D8	84
Moka, Japan	C12	40
Mokala, India	F10	54
Mōkapu Peninsula, pen., Hi., U.S.	b4	78a
Mokau, stm., N.Z.	D6	80
Mokelumne, stm., Ca., U.S.	E5	134
Mokoreale, Italy	F7	24
Moknine, Tun.	B7	64
Mokochu, Khao, mtn., Thai.	E4	48
Mokokchūng, India	C7	46
Mokolo, Cam.	B2	66
Mokolo, stm., S. Afr.	C8	70
Mokp'o, Kor., S.	G7	38
Mokša, stm., Russia	D6	32
Mokwa, Nig.	H5	64
Mol, Bel.	C14	14
Mola di Bari, Italy	C11	24
Molat, Otok, i., Cro.	F11	22
Moldau see Vltava, stm., Czech Rep.	F10	16
Molde, Nor.	E2	8
Moldova, ctry., Eur.	B15	26
Moldova, stm., Rom.	C13	26
Moldoveanu, Vârful, mtn., Rom.	D11	26
Môle, Cap du, c., Haiti	C11	102
Mole Creek, Austl.	n13	77a
Molega Lake, l., N.S., Can.	F12	110
Molène, Île de, i., Fr.	F3	14
Molepolole, Bots.	D7	70
Molêtai, Lith.	E8	10
Molfetta, Italy	C10	24
Molina, Chile	G2	92
Molina de Aragón, Spain	D9	20
Molina de Segura, Spain	F9	20
Moline, Il., U.S.	C7	120
Moline, Ks., U.S.	D12	128
Molino, Fl., U.S.	G11	122
Molino de Valdo de Piedras, Mex.	E3	130
Molinos, Arg.	B4	92
Molise, state, Italy	C8	24
Mollendo, Peru	G3	84
Mölln, Ger.	C6	16
Mölndal, Swe.	H4	8
Molodečno see Maladzečna, Bela.	F9	10
Molodogvardeyskoe, Kaz.	D11	32
Molong, Austl.	I7	76
Molopo, stm., Afr.	E5	70
Moloundou, Cam.	D3	66
Molson Lake, l., Mb., Can.	E11	106
Molu, Pulau, i., Indon.	G9	44
Moluccas see Maluku, is., Indon.	F8	44
Molucca Sea see Maluku, Laut, s., Indon.	F8	44
Molvoticy, Russia	C15	10
Moma, Moz.	D6	68
Moma, stm., Russia	C18	34
Mombaça, Braz.	C6	88
Mombasa, Kenya	E7	66
Mombetsu, Japan	B15	38
Mombo, Tan.	E7	66
Momchilgrad, Bul.	H12	26
Mömi, Fiji	p18	79e
Momotombo, Volcán, vol., Nic.	F4	102
Mompono, D.R.C.	D4	66
Mompós, Col.	C5	86
Momskij hrebet, mts., Russia	C18	34
Møn, i., Den.	I5	8
Møn, state, Mya.	D3	48
Mona, Pan.	H8	102
Mona, Isla de, i., P.R.	H14	96a
Mona, Punta, c., C.R.	H6	102
Monach Islands, is., Scot., U.K.	D5	12
Monaco, Mon.	G4	22
Monaco, ctry., Eur.	F13	18
Monadnock Mountain, mtn., N.H., U.S.	B13	114
Monagas, state, Ven.	C10	86
Monaghan, Ire.	G6	12
Monaghan, state, Ire.	G6	12
Monahans, Tx., U.S.	C5	130
Monapo, Moz.	C7	68
Monarch, S.C., U.S.	B4	116
Monarch Mountain, mtn., B.C., Can.	E5	138
Monarch Pass, p., Co., U.S.	E10	132
Monashee Mountains, mts., B.C., Can.	F12	138
Monastir, Tun.	I4	24
Moncalieri, Italy	F4	22
Moncalvo, Italy	E5	22
Monção, Braz.	B3	88
Monchegorsk, Russia	B15	8
Mönchengladbach, Ger.	E2	16
Monchique, Port.	G2	20
Moncks Corner, S.C., U.S.	C5	116
Monclova, Mex.	B8	100
Moncton, N.B., Can.	D12	110
Monday, stm., Para.	B10	92
Mondego, stm., Port.	D3	20
Mondombe, D.R.C.	D4	66
Mondoubleau, Fr.	F9	14
Mondovi, Wi., U.S.	G7	118
Mondragone, Italy	C7	24
Monemvasía, Grc.	G6	28
Monessen, Pa., U.S.	D5	114
Monesterio, Spain	F4	20
Monett, Mo., U.S.	H4	120
Monette, Ar., U.S.	I7	120
Monfalcone, Italy	E10	22
Monferrato, hist. reg., Italy	F5	22
Monforte de Lemos, Spain	B3	20
Monga, D.R.C.	D4	66
Mongaguá, Braz.	B14	92
Mongalla, Sudan	F6	62
Mongers Lake, l., Austl.	E3	74
Monggon Qulu, China	B8	36
Mông Hai, Mya.	B4	48
Mông Hsat, Mya.	B4	48
Mongibello see Etna, Monte, vol., Italy	G8	24
Möng Küng, Mya.	B3	48
Mông Ma, Mya.	B3	48
Mông Nai, Mya.	B3	48
Mongo, Chad	E3	62
Mongol Altayn nuruu, mts., Asia	E16	32
Mongolia, ctry., Asia	E14	30
Mongonu, Nig.	G7	64
Mông Pai, Mya.	B3	48
Mông Pawn, Mya.	B3	48
Mông Yai, Mya.	A4	48
Monico, Wi., U.S.	F9	118
Monida Pass, p., U.S.	F14	136
Monino, Russia	E21	10
Moniquirá, Col.	E5	86
Mõniste, Est.	H12	8
Monitor Valley, val., Nv., U.S.	E9	134
Monivea, Pol.	C18	16
Monkira, Austl.	E3	76
Monmouth, Wales, U.K.	J10	12
Monmouth, Il., U.S.	D7	120
Monmouth, Or., U.S.	F3	136
Monmouth Mountain, mtn., B.C., Can.	E7	138
Mono, stm., Afr.	H5	64
Mono, Caño, stm., Col.	E7	86
Mono Island, i., Sol. Is.	d6	79b
Mono Lake, l., Ca., U.S.	E7	134
Monon, In., U.S.	H3	112
Monona, Ia., U.S.	H7	118
Monona, Wi., U.S.	A8	120
Monongahela, stm., U.S.	E6	114
Monopoli, Italy	D11	24
Monor, Hung.	B6	26
Monreal del Campo, Spain	D9	20
Monreale, Italy	F7	24
Monroe, La., U.S.	E6	122
Monroe, Mi., U.S.	C2	114
Monroe, N.C., U.S.	B5	116
Monroe, N.Y., U.S.	C11	114
Monroe, Ut., U.S.	E4	132
Monroe, Va., U.S.	G6	114
Monroe, Wa., U.S.	C5	136
Monroe, Wi., U.S.	B8	120
Monroe City, In., U.S.	F10	120
Monroe Lake, res., In., U.S.	E11	120
Monroeville, Al., U.S.	F11	122
Monroeville, In., U.S.	C1	114
Monroeville, Oh., U.S.	D6	114
Monroeville, Pa., U.S.	D6	114
Monrovia, Lib.	H2	64
Mons, Bel.	D12	14
Monselice, Italy	E8	22
Monsenhor Hipólito, Braz.	D5	88
Monsenhor Tabosa, Braz.	C5	88
Monserrato, Italy	E2	24
Montabaur, Ger.	F3	16
Montagne, Neth. Ant.	p23	104g
Montagu, S. Afr.	H5	70
Montague, P.E.I., Can.	D14	110
Montague, Mi., U.S.	E3	112
Montague, Tx., U.S.	H11	128
Montague, Isla, i., Mex.	F5	98
Montague Island, i., Ak., U.S.	E10	140
Montaigu, Fr.	H7	14
Montalbano Ionico, Italy	D10	24
Montalegre, Port.	C3	20
Montana, Blg.	F10	26
Montana, state, U.S.	C6	108
Montánchez, Spain	E4	20
Montana, Braz.	J5	88
Montargis, Fr.	G11	14
Montauban, Fr.	E7	18
Montauk Point, c., N.Y., U.S.	C14	114
Montbard, Fr.	G13	14
Montbéliard, Fr.	G15	14
Mont Belvieu, Tx., U.S.	H3	122
Montblanc, Spain	C11	20
Montblanc see Montblanc, Spain	C11	20
Montbrison, Fr.	D9	18
Montceau-les-Mines, Fr.	H13	14
Montclair, Ca., U.S.	I8	134
Mont-de-Marsan, Fr.	F5	18
Montdidier, Fr.	E11	14
Monte, Laguna del, l., Arg.	H6	92
Monteagudo, Bol.	C4	90
Montebello, Qc., Can.	E1	110
Monte Albán, sci., Mex.	G10	100
Monte Azul, Braz.	H4	88
Montebello, Qc., Can.	C14	112
Montecarlo, Arg.	C10	92
Monte Caseros, Arg.	E8	92
Montecatini Terme, Italy	G7	22
Montecito, Ca., U.S.	I6	134
Monte Comán, Arg.	G4	92
Monte Creek, B.C., Can.	F11	138
Monte Cristi, Dom. Rep.	C12	102
Monte Cristo, Bol.	B4	90
Montecristo, Isola di, i., Italy	H7	22
Monte do Carmo, Braz.	F1	88
Monte Escobedo, Mex.	D7	100
Montefalco, Italy	H9	22
Montefiascone, Italy	H8	22
Montego Bay, Jam.	i12	104d
Monteiro, Braz.	D7	88
Monteiçar, Spain	G7	20
Montejinni, Austl.	C6	74
Montelibano, Col.	C4	86
Montélimar, Fr.	E10	18
Monte Lindo, stm., Para.	A9	92
Montellano, Spain	H5	20
Montello, Nv., U.S.	B2	132
Montello, Wi., U.S.	H9	118
Monte Maíz, Arg.	F6	92
Montemayor, Meseta de, plat., Arg.	H3	90
Montemorelos, Mex.	C9	100
Montemor-o-Velho, Port.	D2	20
Montemuro, mtn., Port.	C2	20
Montenegro, Braz.	D12	92
Montenegro, ctry., Eur.	G6	26
Monte Pascoal, Parque Nacional de, p.o.i., Braz.	I5	88
Monte Patria, Chile	E2	92
Montepuez, Moz.	C6	68
Montepulciano, Italy	G8	22
Monte Quemado, Arg.	B6	92
Montereau-Faut-Yonne, Fr.	F11	14
Monterey, Ca., U.S.	G3	134
Monterey, Va., U.S.	F6	114
Monterey Bay, b., Ca., U.S.	G3	134
Montería, Col.	C3	86
Monteros, Arg.	C5	92
Monterotondo, Italy	H9	22
Monterrey, Mex.	C8	100
Montesano, Wa., U.S.	C3	136
Monte Sant'Angelo, Italy	I12	22
Monte Santu, Capo di, c., Italy	D3	24
Montes Claros, Braz.	I3	88
Montesilvano Marina, Italy	H11	22
Montevallo, Al., U.S.	D12	122
Montevarchi, Italy	G8	22
Montevideo, Ur.	G9	92
Montevideo, Mn., U.S.	G3	118
Monte Vista, Co., U.S.	D2	132
Montezuma, Ga., U.S.	D1	116
Montezuma, In., U.S.	I2	112
Montezuma, Ks., U.S.	D8	128
Montezuma Castle National Monument, p.o.i., Az., U.S.	I4	132
Montgenèvre, Col de, p., Fr.	E12	18
Montgomery, Al., U.S.	E12	122
Montgomery, Mn., U.S.	F6	122
Montgomery, Mn., U.S.	G5	118
Montgomery, Pa., U.S.	C8	114
Montgomery, Tx., U.S.	G3	122
Montgomery City, Mo., U.S.	E6	120
Montguyon, Fr.	D5	18
Monthey, Switz.	D3	22
Monticello, Ar., U.S.	D7	122
Monticello, Fl., U.S.	F2	116
Monticello, Il., U.S.	D9	120
Monticello, In., U.S.	H3	112
Monticello, Ky., U.S.	H13	120
Monticello, Mn., U.S.	F5	118
Monticello, Ms., U.S.	F8	122
Monticello, N.Y., U.S.	C11	114
Monticello, Ut., U.S.	F7	132
Monticello, hist., Va., U.S.	G7	114
Montigny-le-Roi, Fr.	G14	14
Montigny-lès-Metz, Fr.	E15	14
Montijo, Port.	F2	20
Montijo, Spain	F4	20
Montijo, Golfo de, b., Pan.	I7	102
Montilla, Spain	G6	20
Montivilliers, Fr.	E9	14
Mont-Joli, Qc., Can.	B14	112
Mont-Laurier, Qc., Can.	B14	112
Montluçon, Fr.	C8	18
Montmagny, Qc., Can.	D6	110
Montmédy, Fr.	E14	14
Montmorillon, Fr.	C7	18
Montmorris, Austl.	E8	76
Monto, Austl.	E8	76
Montoro, Spain	F6	20
Montour Falls, N.Y., U.S.	B9	114
Montpelier, Jam.	i13	104d
Montpelier, Id., U.S.	H15	136
Montpelier, In., U.S.	H4	112
Montpelier, Oh., U.S.	C1	114
Montpelier, Vt., U.S.	F4	110
Montpellier, Fr.	F9	18
Montréal, Qc., Can.	E3	110
Montreal, Wi., U.S.	E8	118
Montreal, stm., On., Can.	A10	112
Montreal Lake, l., Sk., Can.	E9	106
Montréal-Nord, Qc., Can.	E3	110
Montreuil-sur-Mer, Fr.	D10	14
Montrose, Scot., U.K.	E10	12
Montrose, Co., U.S.	E9	132
Montrose, Mi., U.S.	E6	112
Montrose, Pa., U.S.	C10	114
Montrose, S.D., U.S.	D15	126
Montross, Va., U.S.	F9	114
Monts, Pointe des, c., Qc., Can.	A9	110
Mont-Saint-Michel, Baie du, b., Fr.	F7	14
Mont-Saint-Michel, Le, rel., Fr.	F7	14
Mont-Tremblant, Parc de récréation du, p.o.i., Qc., Can.	D2	110
Montserrat, dep., N.A.	h15	96a
Montaña de Covadonga, Parque Nacional de la, p.o.i., Spain	A5	20
Monument, Or., U.S.	F7	136
Monument Draw, stm., U.S.	B5	130
Monument Peak, mtn., Co., U.S.	D9	132
Monument Valley, val., U.S.	F6	132
Monyo, Mya.	C2	48
Monywa, Mya.	A2	48
Monza, Italy	E6	22
Monze, Zam.	D4	68
Monzón, Spain	C11	20
Mooi, stm., S. Afr.	F10	70
Mooiawatana, Austl.	G2	76
Moonbi, Mountains of the see Ruwenzori, mts., Afr.	D6	66
Moonie, Austl.	F7	76
Moonie, stm., Austl.	G7	76
Moorcroft, Wy., U.S.	G13	136
Moore, Id., U.S.	G13	136
Moore, Ok., U.S.	F11	128
Moore, Tx., U.S.	E8	130
Moore, Lake, l., Austl.	E3	74
Moorea, i., Fr. Poly.	v20	78h
Moorefield, W.V., U.S.	E7	114
Moore Haven, Fl., U.S.	J4	116
Mooreland, Ok., U.S.	E9	128
Mooresville, N.C., U.S.	A5	116
Mooresville, In., U.S.	E2	120
Moorhead, Ms., U.S.	D8	122
Moorhead, Mn., U.S.	E2	118
Moornanyah Lake, l., Austl.	I4	76
Moorreesburg, S. Afr.	H4	70
Moose, stm., On., Can.	E14	106
Moosehead Lake, l., Me., U.S.	E7	110
Moose Island, i., Mb., Can.	C16	124
Moose Jaw, Sk., Can.	D8	124

Name	Map Ref.	Page
Moose Jaw, stm., Sk., Can.	D8	124
Moose Lake, Mn., U.S.	E6	118
Moose Lake, l., Ab., Can.	B19	138
Mooselookmeguntic Lake, l., Me., U.S.	F5	110
Moose Mountain, mtn., Sk., Can.	E11	124
Moose Mountain Creek, stm., Sk., Can.	E11	124
Moose Pass, Ak., U.S.	D10	140
Moosomin, Sk., Can.	D12	124
Moosonee, On., Can.	E14	106
Mootwingee National Park, p.o.i., Austl.	H4	76
Mopane, S. Afr.	C9	70
Mopipi, Bots.	B7	70
Moppo see Mokp'o, Kor., S.	G7	38
Mopti, Mali	G4	64
Moquegua, Peru	G3	84
Mór, Hung.	B5	26
Mòr, Glen, val., Scot., U.K.	D8	12
Mora, Cam.	B2	66
Mora, Port.	F2	20
Mora, Swe.	F6	8
Mora, Mn., U.S.	F5	118
Mora, stm., N.M., U.S.	F4	128
Morač, stm., Bela.	H10	10
Morādābād, India	D7	54
Morada Nova, Braz.	C6	88
Morada Nova de Minas, Braz.	J3	88
Morąg, Pol.	C15	16
Moral de Calatrava, Spain	F7	20
Moraleda, Canal, strt., Chile	H2	90
Morales, Laguna de, b., Mex.	D10	100
Moramanga, Madag.	D8	68
Moran, Ks., U.S.	G2	120
Moran, Mi., U.S.	B5	112
Moran, Tx., U.S.	B8	130
Morant Bay, Jam.	j14	104d
Morant Cays, is., Jam.	D10	102
Morant Point, c., Jam.	j14	104d
Morar, Loch, l., Scot., U.K.	E7	12
Moratalla, Spain	F9	20
Moratuwa, Sri L.	H4	53
Morava, hist. reg., Czech Rep.	G13	16
Morava (March), stm., Eur.	H12	16
Moravia, N.Y., U.S.	B9	114
Moravské Budějovice, Czech Rep.	G11	16
Morawa, Austl.	E3	74
Morawhanna, Guy.	C12	86
Moray Firth, b., Scot., U.K.	D9	12
Morbi, India	G3	54
Morbihan, state, Fr.	G6	14
Morcenx, Fr.	E5	18
Morden, Mb., Can.	E15	124
Mordovia see Mordovija, state, Russia	D6	32
Mordovija, state, Russia	D6	32
Mordves, Russia	F21	10
Mordvinia see Mordovija, state, Russia	D6	32
Mordy, Pol.	D18	16
More, Ben, mtn., Scot., U.K.	E7	12
Moreau, stm., S.D., U.S.	B12	126
Moreau, North Fork, stm., S.D., U.S.	B9	126
Moreau, South Fork, stm., S.D., U.S.	B9	126
Moreau Peak, mtn., S.D., U.S.	B9	126
Moreauville, La., U.S.	F7	122
Morecambe, Eng., U.K.	G9	12
Morecambe Bay, b., Eng., U.K.	H9	12
Moree, Austl.	G7	76
Morehead, Ky., U.S.	F2	114
Morehead City, N.C., U.S.	B9	116
Moreland, Ga., U.S.	D14	122
Moreland, Ky., U.S.	G13	120
Morelia, Mex.	F8	100
Morell, P.E., Can.	D14	110
Morella, Austl.	D4	76
Morelos, Mex.	I2	130
Morelos, Mex.	B5	100
Morelos, state, Mex.	F9	100
Morena, India	E6	54
Morena, Sierra, mts., Spain	F5	20
Morenci, Az., U.S.	J7	132
Moreni, Rom.	D12	26
Moreno, Bahía, b., Chile	A2	92
Møre og Romsdal, state, Nor.	E2	8
Moresby Island, i., B.C., Can.	E4	106
Moreton, Austl.	B8	74
Moreton Island, i., Austl.	F9	76
Moreuil, Fr.	E11	14
Morez, Fr.	H14	14
Morgan, Mn., U.S.	G3	118
Morgan, Mt., U.S.	F6	124
Morgan, Tx., U.S.	B10	130
Morgan, Ut., U.S.	B5	132
Morgan City, Al., U.S.	C12	122
Morgan City, La., U.S.	H7	122
Morganfield, Ky., U.S.	G10	120
Morgan Hill, Ca., U.S.	F4	134
Morganito, Ven.	E8	86
Morganton, N.C., U.S.	I4	114
Morgantown, In., U.S.	E11	120
Morgantown, Ms., U.S.	F8	122
Morgantown, Ms., U.S.	F7	122
Morgantown, W.V., U.S.	E6	114
Morgenzon, S. Afr.	E9	70
Morghāb (Murgab), stm., Asia	B9	56
Moriah, Mount, mtn., Nv., U.S.	D2	132
Moriarty, N.M., U.S.	G2	128
Morice, stm., B.C., Can.	B4	138
Morice Lake, l., B.C., Can.	B3	138
Morichal Largo, stm., Ven.	C10	86
Moricsala rezervāts, Lat.	C5	10
Moriki, Nig.	G6	64
Morino, Russia	C13	10
Morinville, Ab., Can.	C17	138
Morioka, Japan	E14	38
Morīri, Tso, l., India	B6	54
Morisset, Austl.	I8	76
Morjakovskij Zaton, Russia	C14	32
Morkoka, stm., Russia	D11	34
Morlaix, Fr.	F5	14
Morley, Mi., U.S.	E4	112
Mormal', Bela.	H12	10
Mormugao, India	D1	53
Morne-à-l'Eau, Guad.	h5	105c
Morne du Vitet, hill, Guad.	B2	105a
Morne Trois Pitons National Park, p.o.i., Dom.	j6	105c
Morney, Austl.	E3	76
Morning Sun, Ia., U.S.	C6	120
Mornington, Austl.	L5	76
Mornington, Isla, i., Chile	I1	90
Mornington Island, i., Austl.	C7	74
Morobe, Pap. N. Gui.	b4	79a
Morocco, In., U.S.	H2	112
Morocco, ctry., Afr.	C3	64
Moro Creek, stm., Ar., U.S.	D6	122
Morogoro, Tan.	F7	66
Moro Gulf, b., Phil.	G4	52
Moroleón, Mex.	E8	100
Morombe, Madag.	E7	68
Morón, Arg.	G8	92
Morón, Cuba	A8	102
Mörön, Mong.	B5	36
Morón, Ven.	B7	86
Morona, stm., S.A.	I3	86
Morona Santiago, state, Ec.	I3	86
Morondava, Madag.	E7	68
Morón de Almazán, Spain	C8	20
Morón de la Frontera, Spain	G5	20
Moroni, Com.	C7	68
Moroni, Ut., U.S.	D5	132
Moron Us, stm., China	E3	36
Morošečnoe, Russia	E20	34
Morotai, i., Indon.	E8	44
Moroto, Ug.	D6	66
Moroto, mtn., Ug.	D6	66
Morovis, P.R.	B3	104a
Morozovsk, Russia	E6	32
Morpeth, Eng., U.K.	F11	12
Morrilton, Ar., U.S.	B6	122
Morrin, Ab., Can.	E18	138
Morrinhos, Braz.	I1	88
Morrinhos, Braz.	B5	88
Morrinsville, N.Z.	C6	80
Morris, Mb., Can.	E16	124
Morris, Il., U.S.	C9	120
Morris, Mn., U.S.	F2	118
Morrisburg, On., Can.	D14	112
Morris Jesup, Kap, c., Grnld.	A19	141
Morrison, Arg.	F6	92
Morrison, Il., U.S.	C8	120
Morrisonville, Il., U.S.	E8	120
Morristown, Az., U.S.	J4	132
Morristown, In., U.S.	E12	120
Morristown, S.D., U.S.	B11	126
Morristown, Tn., U.S.	H2	114
Morrisville, Pa., U.S.	H15	112
Morro, Punta, c., Mex.	C2	102
Morro Bay, Ca., U.S.	H5	134
Morro do Chapéu, Braz.	F5	88
Morros, Braz.	B3	88
Morrosquillo, Golfo de, b., Col.	C3	86
Morrow, La., U.S.	G6	122
Morrumbala, Moz.	D6	68
Morrumbene, Moz.	C12	70
Morse, La., U.S.	G6	122
Morse, Tx., U.S.	E7	128
Morsi, India	H6	54
Mörskom see Myrskylä, Fin.	F11	8
Morson, On., Can.	B4	118
Mortagne-sur-Sèvre, Fr.	H8	14
Mortara, Italy	E5	22
Morteau, Fr.	G15	14
Morteros, Arg.	E6	92
Mortes, stm., Braz.	F7	84
Mortlach, Sk., Can.	D7	124
Mortlock Islands, is., Micron.	C6	72
Morton, Il., U.S.	D8	120
Morton, Mn., U.S.	G4	118
Morton, Tx., U.S.	H6	128
Morton, Wa., U.S.	D4	136
Morton National Park, p.o.i., Austl.	J7	76
Morua, Vanuatu	k17	79d
Moruya, Austl.	J7	76
Morvan, mts., Fr.	G13	14
Morvant, Trin.	s12	105f
Morven, Austl.	F6	76
Morven, Ga., U.S.	F2	116
Morven, N.C., U.S.	B5	116
Morwell, Austl.	L6	76
Moryń, Pol.	D10	16
Moržovec, ostrov, i., Russia	C20	8
Mosal'sk, Russia	F17	10
Mosbach, Ger.	G5	16
Moscos Islands, is., Mya.	E3	48
Moscow see Moskva, Russia	E20	10
Moscow, Id., U.S.	D10	136
Moscow see Moskva, stm., Russia	E21	10
Mosel (Moselle), stm., Eur.	G2	16
Moselebe, stm., Bots.	D7	70
Moselle, Ms., U.S.	F9	122
Moselle, state, Fr.	F15	14
Moselle (Mosel), stm., Eur.	G2	16
Moses Lake, Wa., U.S.	C7	136
Moses Point, Ak., U.S.	D7	140
Moshaweng, stm., S. Afr.	E6	70
Mosheim, Tn., U.S.	H3	114
Moshi, Tan.	E7	66
Mosinee, Wi., U.S.	G9	118
Mosjøen, Nor.	D5	8
Moskalvo, Russia	F17	34
Moskenesøya, i., Nor.	C5	8
Moskovskaja oblast', co., Russia	D19	10
Moskovskaja vozvyšennost', plat., Russia	E19	10
Moskva (Moscow), Russia	E20	10
Moskva, stm., Russia	E21	10
Moskvy, kanal imeni, can., Russia	D20	10
Mosomane, Bots.	C8	70
Mosonmagyaróvár, Hung.	B4	26
Mosopa, Bots.	D7	70
Mosqueiro, Braz.	D8	84
Mosquera, Col.	F2	86
Mosquito Coast see Mosquitos, Costa de, hist. reg., Nic.	F6	102
Mosquitos, Costa de, hist. reg., Nic.	F6	102
Mosquitos, Golfo de los, b., Pan.	H7	102
Moss, Nor.	G4	8
Mossaka, Congo	E3	66
Mossbank, Sk., Can.	E7	124
Mossburn, N.Z.	G2	80
Mosselbaai (Mossel Bay), S. Afr.	I6	70
Mossel Bay see Mosselbaai, S. Afr.	I6	70
Mossleigh, Ab., Can.	F17	138
Mossman, Austl.	C9	74
Moss Mountain, mtn., Ar., U.S.	C6	122
Mossoró, Braz.	C7	88
Moss Point, Ms., U.S.	G10	122
Moss Vale, Austl.	J8	76
Mossy, stm., Mb., Can.	C13	124
Most, Czech Rep.	F9	16
Mostar, Bos.	F4	26
Mostardas, Braz.	E12	92
Møsting, Kap, c., Grnld.	E17	141
Mostovaja, Russia	D16	10
Mostyn, Malay.	A11	50
Mosul see Al-Mawṣil, Iraq	B5	56
Møsvatnet, l., Nor.	G2	8
Mot'a, Eth.	E7	62
Mota del Cuervo, Spain	E8	20
Mota del Marqués, Spain	C5	20
Motagua, stm., N.A.	E3	102
Motal', Bela.	H8	10
Motala, Swe.	G6	8
Mota Lava, i., Vanuatu	i16	79d
Motaze, Moz.	D11	70
Moteve, Cap, c., Fr. Poly.	s18	78g
Motherwell, Scot., U.K.	F9	12
Motihāri, India	E10	54
Motloutse, stm., Bots.	B9	70
Motopu, Fr. Poly.	s18	78g
Motozintla de Mendoza, Mex.	H12	100
Motril, Spain	H7	20
Motru, Rom.	E10	26
Mott, N.D., U.S.	A10	126
Motu, stm., N.Z.	C7	80
Motueka, N.Z.	E5	80
Motul de Felipe Carrillo Puerto, Mex.	B3	102
Motutapu, i., Cook Is.	a27	78j
Motygino, Russia	C17	32
Motyklejka, Russia	E18	34
Mouaskar, Alg.	B5	64
Mouchoir Passage, strt., N.A.	B12	102
Moudjéria, Maur.	F2	64
Moúdros, Grc.	D8	28
Mouila, Gabon	E2	66
Mould Bay, N.T., Can.	A16	140
Moule à Chique, Cap, c., St. Luc.	m7	105c
Moulins, Fr.	H12	14
Moulmein see Mawlamyine, Mya.	D3	48
Moulmeingyun, Mya.	D2	48
Moulouya, Oued, stm., Mor.	C4	64
Moulton, Al., U.S.	C11	122
Moulton, Ia., U.S.	D5	120
Moulton, Tx., U.S.	E10	130
Moultrie, Ga., U.S.	E2	116
Moultrie, Lake, res., S.C., U.S.	C5	116
Mouly, N. Cal.	m16	79d
Mounana, Gabon	E2	66
Mound City, Ks., U.S.	F3	120
Mound City, Mo., U.S.	D2	120
Mound City, S.D., U.S.	B12	126
Moundou, Chad	F3	62
Moundridge, Ks., U.S.	C11	128
Mounds, Ok., U.S.	B2	122
Moundsville, W.V., U.S.	E5	114
Moundville, Al., U.S.	E11	122
Mounlapamôk, Laos	E7	48
Mountain, Wi., U.S.	C1	112
Mountain, stm., N.T., Can.	C5	106
Mountainair, N.M., U.S.	G2	128
Mountainaire, Az., U.S.	H5	132
Mountain Brook, Al., U.S.	D12	122
Mountain City, Ga., U.S.	B2	116
Mountain City, Nv., U.S.	B1	132
Mountain Creek, Al., U.S.	E12	122
Mountain Grove, Mo., U.S.	G5	120
Mountain Home, Ar., U.S.	H5	120
Mountain Home, Id., U.S.	G11	136
Mountain Iron, Mn., U.S.	D6	118
Mountain Lake, Mn., U.S.	H3	118
Mountain Nile, stm., Afr.	F6	62
Mountain Park, Ab., Can.	D13	138
Mountain Pine, Ar., U.S.	C5	122
Mountain View, Ar., U.S.	I5	120
Mountain View, Ca., U.S.	F3	134
Mountain View, Ok., U.S.	F10	128
Mountain View, Wy., U.S.	E6	126
Mountain Village, Ak., U.S.	D7	140
Mountain Zebra National Park, p.o.i., S. Afr.	H7	70
Mount Airy, N.C., U.S.	H5	114
Mount Alida, S. Afr.	F10	70
Mount Angel, Or., U.S.	E4	136
Mount Aspiring National Park, p.o.i., N.Z.	G3	80
Mount Athos see Ágio Óros, state, Grc.	C7	28
Mount Ayliff, S. Afr.	G9	70
Mount Ayr, Ia., U.S.	D3	120
Mount Barker, Austl.	F3	74
Mount Barker, Austl.	J2	76
Mount Berry, Ga., U.S.	C13	122
Mount Buffalo National Park, p.o.i., Austl.	K5	76
Mount Calm, Tx., U.S.	C11	130
Mount Carmel, Il., U.S.	F10	120
Mount Carmel, Pa., U.S.	D9	114
Mount Carroll, Il., U.S.	B7	120
Mount Clemens, Mi., U.S.	B3	114
Mount Cook National Park, p.o.i., N.Z.	F4	80
Mount Dora, Fl., U.S.	H4	116
Mount Enterprise, Tx., U.S.	F4	122
Mount Field National Park, p.o.i., Austl.	o13	77a
Mount Forest, On., Can.	D9	112
Mount Frere, S. Afr.	G9	70
Mount Gambier, Austl.	K3	76
Mount Garnet, Austl.	A5	76
Mount Gay, W.V., U.S.	G3	114
Mount Hagen, Pap. N. Gui.	b3	79a
Mount Holly, N.C., U.S.	A4	116
Mount Holly Springs, Pa., U.S.	H12	112
Mount Hope, Austl.	F7	74
Mount Hope, Ks., U.S.	D11	128
Mount Horeb, Wi., U.S.	B8	120
Mount Ida, Ar., U.S.	C5	122
Mount Isa, Austl.	C2	76
Mount Jackson, Va., U.S.	F7	114
Mount Juliet, Tn., U.S.	H11	120
Mount Kaputar National Park, p.o.i., Austl.	H8	76
Mount Lebanon, Pa., U.S.	D6	114
Mount Lofty Ranges, mts., Austl.	I2	76
Mount Magnet, Austl.	E3	74
Mount Manara, Austl.	I4	76
Mount Margaret, Austl.	F4	76
Mount Morgan, Austl.	D8	76
Mount Morris, Il., U.S.	I9	118
Mount Morris, Mi., U.S.	E6	112
Mount Olive, Il., U.S.	E8	120
Mount Olive, Ms., U.S.	F9	122
Mount Olive, N.C., U.S.	A7	116
Mount Orab, Oh., U.S.	E2	114
Mount Perry, Austl.	E8	76
Mount Pleasant, On., Can.	E9	112
Mount Pleasant, Ia., U.S.	D6	120
Mount Pleasant, Mi., U.S.	E5	112
Mount Pleasant, Pa., U.S.	D6	114
Mount Pleasant, S.C., U.S.	D6	116
Mount Pleasant, Tn., U.S.	B11	122
Mount Pleasant, Tx., U.S.	D4	122
Mount Pleasant, Ut., U.S.	D5	132
Mount Pulaski, Il., U.S.	D8	120
Mount Rainier National Park, p.o.i., Wa., U.S.	D5	136
Mount Revelstoke National Park, p.o.i., B.C., Can.	E12	138
Mount Riddock, Austl.	D6	74
Mount Saint Helens National Volcanic Monument, p.o.i., Wa., U.S.	D5	136
Mount Selinda, Zimb.	B11	70
Mount Somers, N.Z.	F4	80
Mount Sterling, Il., U.S.	E7	120
Mount Sterling, Ky., U.S.	F2	114
Mount Sterling, Oh., U.S.	E2	114
Mount Uniacke, N.S., Can.	F12	110
Mount Union, Pa., U.S.	D8	114
Mount Vernon, Austl.	D3	74
Mount Vernon, Al., U.S.	F10	122
Mount Vernon, Ga., U.S.	D3	116
Mount Vernon, Ia., U.S.	C6	120
Mount Vernon, Il., U.S.	F8	120
Mount Vernon, Ky., U.S.	G1	114
Mount Vernon, Mo., U.S.	G4	120
Mount Vernon, Oh., U.S.	D3	114
Mount Vernon, Or., U.S.	F7	136
Mount Vernon, S.D., U.S.	D14	126
Mount Vernon, Wa., U.S.	B4	136
Mount Vernon, hist., Va., U.S.	F8	114
Mount William National Park, p.o.i., Austl.	n13	77a
Mount Willoughby, Austl.	E6	74
Mount Wolf, Pa., U.S.	H13	112
Moura, Braz.	H11	86
Moura, Port.	F3	20
Mourdi, Dépression du, depr., Chad	D4	62
Mourdiah, Mali	G3	64
Mourne Mountains, mts., N. Ire., U.K.	G6	12
Mouscron, Bel.	D12	14
Moussa 'Ali, mtn., Afr.	B8	66
Moussoro, Chad	E3	62
Moutier, Switz.	C4	22
Moutong, Indon.	E7	44
Mouzáki, Grc.	D4	28
Movenda, D.R.C.	D4	66
Moweaqua, Il., U.S.	E8	120
Moxotó, stm., Braz.	E7	88
Moyahua, Mex.	E7	100
Moyale, Kenya	D7	66
Moyamba, S.L.	H2	64
Moyen Atlas, mts., Mor.	C4	64
Moyeuvre-Grande, Fr.	E14	14
Moyie, B.C., Can.	G15	138
Moyie, stm., N.A.	H14	138
Moyo, Pulau, i., Indon.	H10	50
Moyobamba, Peru	E2	84
Moyu, China	A4	46
M'oža (Měža), stm., Eur.	E14	10
Možajsk, Russia	E18	10
Mozambique, ctry., Afr.	D5	68
Mozambique Channel, strt., Afr.	D7	68
Mozambique Plateau, unds.	M6	142
Mozdok, Russia	F6	32
Mozolevo, Russia	A16	10
Mpala, D.R.C.	F5	66
Mpanda, Tan.	F6	66
Mphoengs, Zimb.	B8	70
Mpika, Zam.	C5	68
Mporokoso, Zam.	B5	68
Mpui, Tan.	F6	66
Mpumalanga, state, S. Afr.	E9	70
Mpwapwa, Tan.	F7	66
Mqanduli, S. Afr.	G9	70
Mrągowo, Pol.	C17	16
Mrkonjić Grad, Bos.	E3	26
M'Saken, Tun.	I4	24
Mscislau, Bela.	F14	10
Msciž, Bela.	F11	10
Msta, Russia	C17	10
Msta, stm., Russia	B15	10
Mszczonów, Pol.	E16	16
Mtama, Tan.	G7	66
Mtamvuna, stm., S. Afr.	G9	70
Mtwara, Tan.	G8	66
Mu, N. Cal.	m16	79d
Mu, stm., Mya.	A2	48
Mu, Cerro, mtn., S.A.	C5	86
Mu'a, Tonga	n14	78e
Mualang, Indon.	C7	50
Muanda, D.R.C.	F2	66
Muang Hay, Laos	B5	48
Muang Hôngsa, Laos	C5	48
Muang Hounxianghoung, Laos	B6	48
Muang Khammouan, Laos	D7	48
Muang Khao, Laos	C6	48
Muang Không, Laos	E7	48
Muang Khôngxédôn, Laos	E7	48
Muang La, Laos	B6	48
Muang Long, Laos	B5	48
Muang Ngoy, Laos	B6	48
Muang Nong, Laos	D8	48
Muang Ou Tai, Laos	A5	48
Muang Pak-Lay, Laos	C5	48
Muang Paktha, Laos	B5	48
Muang Pakxan, Laos	C6	48
Muang Phalan, Laos	D7	48
Muang Phônthong, Laos	E7	48
Muang Sam Sip, Thai.	E7	48
Muang Sing, Laos	B5	48
Muang Souvannakhili, Laos	E7	48
Muang Sung, Laos	B6	48
Muang Thatèng, Laos	E8	48
Muang Va, Laos	B6	48
Muang Vangviang, Laos	C6	48
Muang Xaignabouri, Laos	C5	48
Muang Xamtong, Laos	C6	48
Muang Xépôn, Laos	D7	48
Muang Yo, Laos	B5	48
Muar, Malay.	L6	48
Muar, stm., Malay.	K6	48
Muara, Bru.	A9	50
Muaraancalung, Indon.	C10	50
Muarabenangin, Indon.	D9	50
Muarabungo, Indon.	D2	50
Muaradua, Indon.	F4	50
Muaraenim, Indon.	E3	50
Muarajuloi, Indon.	D8	50
Muarakelingi, Indon.	E3	50
Muaralabuh, Indon.	D2	50
Muaralakitan, Indon.	E3	50
Muaralembu, Indon.	D2	50
Muarapangean, Indon.	B10	50
Muarapayang, Indon.	D9	50
Muarasabak, Indon.	D3	50
Muarasiberut, Indon.	D1	50
Muaratebo, Indon.	D3	50
Muarateladang, Indon.	E4	50
Muaratembesi, Indon.	D3	50
Muaratewe, Indon.	D9	50
Muaratunan, Indon.	D10	50
Mubārakpur, India	E9	54
Mubende, Ug.	D6	66
Mubi, Nig.	G7	64
Mubur, Pulau, i., Indon.	B4	50
Mucaitá, stm., Braz.	D4	88
Mucajaí, stm., Braz.	F11	86
Muchinga Escarpment, clf., Zam.	C4	68
Muchinga Mountains, mts., Zam.	C5	68
Muckadilla, Austl.	F7	76
Mučkas, Russia	D23	8
Mucojo, Moz.	C7	68
Muconda, Ang.	C3	68
Mucujê, Braz.	G5	88
Muçum, Braz.	D11	92
Mucuri, Braz.	J6	88
Mucuri, stm., Braz.	J6	88
Muda, stm., Malay.	J5	48
Mudan, stm., China	B10	36
Mudanjiang, China	B8	38
Mudanya, Tur.	C11	28
Mud Creek, stm., Ne., U.S.	F13	126
Mud Creek, stm., Tx., U.S.	E3	122
Muddus Nationalpark, p.o.i., Swe.	C9	8
Muddy, stm., Nv., U.S.	G2	132
Muddy Boggy Creek, stm., Ok., U.S.	C3	122
Muddy Creek, stm., Ut., U.S.	E6	132
Mudgee, Austl.	I7	76
Mudhol, India	C2	53
Mudjuga, Russia	E18	8
Mud Lake, l., Nv., U.S.	F8	134
Mudon, Mya.	D3	48
Mudurnu, Tur.	C14	28
Muelle de los Bueyes, Nic.	G5	102
Muenster, Tx., U.S.	H11	128
Muerto, Mar, l., Mex.	G11	100
Mufulira, Zam.	C4	68
Mufu Shan, mtn., China	G5	42
Mufu Shan, mts., China	G6	42
Mughal Sarāi, India	F9	54
Mugi, Japan	F7	40
Mu Gia, Deo, p., Asia	D7	48
Muğla, Tur.	F11	28
Muğla, state, Tur.	F11	28
Muḥammad Qawl, Sudan	C7	62
Muhanovo, Russia	D21	10
Muhavec, stm., Bela.	H7	10
Muhino, Russia	F14	34
Mühlacker, Ger.	H4	16
Mühldorf am Inn, Ger.	H8	16
Mühlhausen, Ger.	E6	16
Muhlig-Hofmann Mountains, mts., Ant.	C5	81
Mühlviertel, reg., Aus.	B11	22
Muḥradah, Syria	C7	58
Muhu, i., Est.	G10	8
Muié, Ang.	C3	68
Mui Hopohoponga Point, c., Tonga	n14	78e
Muineachán see Monaghan, Ire.	G6	12
Muine Bheag, Ire.	I6	12
Muite, Moz.	C6	68
Muja, Russia	E12	34
Mujnak, Uzb.	F9	32
Mukah, Malay.	B8	50
Mukalla see Al-Mukallā, Yemen	G6	56
Mukatsjeve, Ukr.	A9	26
Mukāwir, sci., Jord.	G6	58
Mukdahan, Thai.	D7	48
Mukden see Shenyang, China	D5	38
Mukeriān, India	C5	54
Mukharram al-Fawqānī, Syria	D7	58
Mukilteo, Wa., U.S.	C4	136
Mukinbudin, Austl.	F3	74
Mukomuko, Indon.	E2	50
Mukry, Turkmen.	B10	56
Muktsar, India	C5	54
Mūl, India	A4	53
Mula, China	F5	36
Mula, Spain	F9	20
Mula, stm., India	B1	53
Mula, stm., India	B2	53
Mulaku Atoll, at., Mald.	i12	46a
Mulan, China	B10	36
Mulas, Punta de, c., Cuba	B10	102
Mulatos, Mex.	A4	100
Mulbāgal, India	E4	53
Mulberry, Ar., U.S.	B4	122
Mulberry, Fl., U.S.	I4	116
Mulberry Fork, stm., Al., U.S.	D12	122
Mulberry Mountain, mtn., Ar., U.S.	I5	120
Mulchatna, stm., Ak., U.S.	D8	140
Mulchén, Chile	H1	92
Mulde, stm., Ger.	E8	16
Muldoon, Tx., U.S.	E10	130
Muldraugh, Ky., U.S.	G12	120
Muldrow, Ok., U.S.	B4	122
Muleshoe, Tx., U.S.	G6	128
Mulgowie, Austl.	F9	76
Mulgrave, N.S., Can.	E15	110
Mulhacén, mtn., Spain	G7	20
Mulhall, Ok., U.S.	E11	128
Mulhouse, Fr.	G16	14
Muling, China	B9	38
Muling, China	B9	38
Muling, stm., China	B9	38
Mulinu'u, Cape, c., Samoa	g11	79c
Mūlki, India	E2	53
Mull, Island of, i., Scot., U.K.	E6	12
Mullengudgery, Austl.	H6	76
Muller, Pegunungan, mts., Indon.	C8	50
Mullet Peninsula, pen., Ire.	G2	12
Mullet Pond Bay, Neth. Ant.	A1	105a
Mullett Lake, l., Mi., U.S.	C5	112
Mullewa, Austl.	E3	74
Müllheim, Ger.	I3	16
Mullin, Tx., U.S.	C9	130
Mullingar, Ire.	H5	12
Mullins, S.C., U.S.	B6	116
Mulobezi, Zam.	D4	68
Mulongo, D.R.C.	F5	66
Mulshi Lake, res., India	B1	53
Multai, India	H7	54
Multān, Pak.	C3	54
Multé, Mex.	D2	102
Mulumbe, Monts, mts., D.R.C.	F5	66
Mulvane, Ks., U.S.	D11	128
Mumbai (Bombay), India	B1	53
Mumbwa, Zam.	D4	68
Mumen, China	E2	42
Mumeng, Pap. N. Gui.	b4	79a
Mumford, Tx., U.S.	G2	122
Mun, stm., Thai.	E7	48
Muna, stm., Russia	C13	34
Muna, Pulau, i., Indon.	F7	44
Muncar, Indon.	H9	50
Münchberg, Ger.	F7	16
München (Munich), Ger.	H7	16
Munchique, Cerro, mtn., Col.	F3	86
Munchique, Parque Nacional, p.o.i., Col.	F3	86
Muncie, In., U.S.	H4	112
Muncy, Pa., U.S.	C9	114
Mundare, Ab., Can.	C18	138
Munday, Tx., U.S.	H9	128
Mundelein, Il., U.S.	B9	120
Münden, Ger.	E5	16
Mundra, India	G2	54
Mundrabilla, Austl.	F5	74
Mundubbera, Austl.	E8	76
Munfordville, Ky., U.S.	G12	120
Mungallala Creek, stm., Austl.	F6	76
Mungana, Austl.	C8	74
Mungar Junction, Austl.	E9	76
Mungbere, D.R.C.	D5	66
Mungeli, India	G8	54
Munger, India	F11	54
Mungindi, Austl.	G7	76
Mungo, Ang.	C2	68
Mungo National Park, p.o.i., Austl.	I4	76
Munhango, Ang.	C2	68
Munich see München, Ger.	H7	16
Muniesa, Spain	C10	20
Munim, stm., Braz.	B3	88
Munising, Mi., U.S.	B3	112
Muniz Freire, Braz.	K5	88
Munku-Sardyk, gora, mtn., Asia	D17	32
Münsingen, Ger.	H5	16
Munson, Ab., Can.	E18	138
Münster, Ger.	D3	16
Munster, Ger.	C6	16
Munster, hist. reg., Ire.	I3	12
Munte, Indon.	C11	50
Muntok, Indon.	E4	50
Munuscong Lake, l., N.A.	B5	112
Muong Hinh, Viet.	C7	48
Muong Saiapoun, Laos	C5	48
Muonio, Fin.	C10	8
Muping, China	C9	42
Muqdisho (Mogadiscio), Som.	D9	66
Muqui, Braz.	K5	88
Mur (Mura), stm., Eur.	D12	22
Mura (Mur), stm., Eur.	D12	22
Murajá, Braz.	D8	84
Murakami, Japan	A12	40
Murana, Indon.	F9	44
Muraši, Russia	C7	32
Murat, Fr.	D8	18
Murat, stm., Tur.	H17	6
Murat Dağı, mtn., Tur.	E12	28
Muratlı, Tur.	B10	28
Muravera, Italy	E3	24
Murayama, Japan	A13	40
Murça, Port.	C3	20
Murchison, Tx., U.S.	E3	122
Murchison, stm., Austl.	E2	74
Murchison, Mount, mtn., N.Z.	F4	80
Murcia, Spain	G9	20
Murcia, state, Spain	G9	20
Mur-de-Barrez, Fr.	E8	18
Murdo, S.D., U.S.	D12	126
Mürefte, Tur.	C10	28
Mureș, state, Rom.	C11	26
Mureș (Maros), stm., Eur.	C8	26
Muret, Fr.	F7	18
Murewa, Zimb.	D5	68
Murfreesboro, Ar., U.S.	C5	122
Murfreesboro, Tn., U.S.	I11	120
Murgab, Taj.	B11	56
Murgab (Morghāb), stm., Asia	B9	56
Murgha Kibzai, Pak.	C2	54
Murgon, Austl.	F8	76
Muri, Cook Is.	a27	78j
Muriaé, Braz.	K4	88
Muriaé, stm., Braz.	K5	88
Muribeca dos Guararapes, Braz.	E8	88
Murici, Braz.	E8	88
Muricizal, stm., Braz.	D1	88
Murīdke, Pak.	C5	54
Muriege, Ang.	C3	68
Müritz, l., Ger.	C8	16
Murmansk, Russia	B15	8
Murmanskaja oblast', co., Russia	C16	8
Murnau, Ger.	I7	16
Muro Lucano, Italy	D9	24
Murom, Russia	I19	8
Muromcevo, Russia	C13	32
Muroran, Japan	C14	38
Muroto, Japan	F7	40
Muroto-zaki, c., Japan	F7	40
Murowana Goślina, Pol.	D13	16
Murphy, Id., U.S.	G10	136
Murphy, N.C., U.S.	A1	116
Murphys, Ca., U.S.	E5	134
Murra Murra, Austl.	G6	76
Murrat el-Kubra, Buheirat (Great Bitter Lake), l., Egypt	H3	58
Murray, Ia., U.S.	C3	120
Murray, Ky., U.S.	H9	120
Murray, Ut., U.S.	C5	132
Murray, stm., Austl.	J2	76
Murray, stm., B.C., Can.	B9	138
Murray, Lake, l., Pap. N. Gui.	b3	79a
Murray, Lake, res., S.C., U.S.	B4	116
Murray Bridge, Austl.	J2	76
Murray Fracture Zone, unds.	F24	142
Murray Harbour, P.E., Can.	E14	110
Murray Maxwell Bay, b., Nu., Can.	A14	106
Murray River, P.E., Can.	D14	110
Murraysburg, S. Afr.	G6	70
Murree, Pak.	B4	54
Murrhardt, Ger.	H5	16
Murrumbidgee, stm., Austl.	J4	76
Murrumburrah, Austl.	J7	76
Murrupula, Moz.	D6	68
Mursala, Pulau, i., Indon.	L4	48
Murshidābād, India	F12	54
Murska Sobota, Slvn.	D13	22
Murtajāpur, India	H6	54
Murtee, Austl.	H4	76
Murter, Otok, i., Cro.	G12	22
Murtle Lake, l., B.C., Can.	D11	138
Murtoa, Austl.	K4	76
Murtosa, Port.	D2	20
Muru, Capu di, c., Fr.	H14	18
Murud, India	B1	53
Murud, Gunong, mtn., Malay.	B9	50
Murukta, Russia	C9	34
Murung, stm., Indon.	C9	50
Mururoa, at., Fr. Poly.	F13	72
Murwāra (Katni), India	G8	54
Murwillumbah, Austl.	G9	76
Murzuq, Libya	B2	62
Murzūq, Idhān, des., Libya	C2	62
Mürzzuschlag, Aus.	C12	22
Muş, Tur.	B5	56
Mūša (Mūsa), stm., Eur.	D6	10
Mūsa (Mūša), stm., Eur.	D6	10
Mûsa, Gebel (Sinai, Mount), mtn., Egypt	J5	58
Musadi, D.R.C.	E4	66
Musā'id, Libya	A4	62
Musala, mtn., Blg.	G10	26
Musan-ŭp, Kor., N.	C8	38
Muscat see Masqaṭ, Oman	E8	56
Muscat and Oman see Oman, ctry., Asia	F8	56
Muscatine, Ia., U.S.	C6	120
Muscle Shoals, Al., U.S.	C11	122
Musclow, Mount, mtn., B.C., Can.	C3	138
Muscoda, Wi., U.S.	A7	120
Musgrave, Austl.	B8	74
Mus-Haja, gora, mtn., Russia	D17	34
Mushie, D.R.C.	E3	66
Mushin, Nig.	H5	64
Mūsi, stm., India	C4	53
Musi, stm., Indon.	E4	50
Musicians Seamounts, unds.	F22	142
Muskegon, Mi., U.S.	E3	112
Muskegon, stm., Mi., U.S.	E4	112
Muskingum, stm., Oh., U.S.	E4	114
Muskogee, Ok., U.S.	I2	120
Muskoka, Lake, l., On., Can.	D10	112
Musoma, Tan.	E6	66
Musquodoboit Harbour, N.S., Can.	F13	110
Mussau Island, i., Pap. N. Gui.	a4	79a
Musselshell, stm., Mt., U.S.	G6	124
Mussende, Ang.	C2	68
Mussidan, Fr.	D6	18
Mussomeli, Italy	G7	24
Mussuma, Ang.	C3	68
Mustafakemalpaşa, Tur.	C11	28
Mustafa Kemal Paşa, stm., Tur.	D11	28
Mustahīl, Eth.	F8	62
Mustāng, Nepal	D9	54
Mustang Draw, stm., Tx., U.S.	B5	130
Mustang Island, i., Tx., U.S.	G10	130
Musters, Lago, l., Arg.	I3	90
Mustla, Est.	B8	10
Mustvee, Est.	B9	10
Muswellbrook, Austl.	I8	76
Mût, Egypt	B5	62
Mut, Tur.	B4	58
Mutá, Ponta do, c., Braz.	G6	88
Mutanchiang see Mudanjiang, China	B8	38
Mutankiang see Mudanjiang, China	B8	38
Mutare, Zimb.	D5	68
Mutlu (Rezovska), stm., Eur.	G14	26
Mutoko, Zimb.	D5	68
Mutoraj, Russia	B17	32
Mutsamudu, Com.	C7	68
Mutshatsha, D.R.C.	G4	66
Mutsu, Japan	D14	38
Mutsu-wan, b., Japan	D14	38
Mutton Bay, Qc., Can.	i22	107a
Mutuípe, Braz.	G6	88
Mutum, Braz.	J5	88
Mu Us Shamo (Ordos Desert), des., China	B3	42
Mūvattupula, India	F3	53
Muxima, Ang.	B1	68
Muyinga, Bdi.	E6	66
Muyumba, D.R.C.	F5	66
Muzaffarābād, Pak.	A4	54
Muzaffargarh, Pak.	C3	54
Muzaffarnagar, India	D6	54
Muzaffarpur, India	E10	54
Muzat, stm., China	C2	36
Muži, Russia	A10	32
Muzillac, Fr.	G6	14
Muztag, mtn., China	A5	46
Muztag, mtn., China	D2	36
Mvolo, Sudan	F6	62
Mvoti, stm., S. Afr.	F10	70
Mvuma, Zimb.	D5	68
Mwadui, Tan.	E6	66
Mwali, i., Com.	C7	68
Mwanza, Tan.	E6	66
Mweelrea, mtn., Ire.	H3	12
Mweka, D.R.C.	E4	66
Mwene-Ditu, D.R.C.	F4	66
Mwenezi, Zimb.	B10	70

Name	Map Ref.	Page
Mwenezi, stm., Afr.	B10	70
Mweru, Lake, l., Afr.	B4	68
Mweru Wantipa, Lake, l., Zam.	B4	68
Mwilitua Islands (Purdy Islands), is., Pap. N. Gui.	a4	79a
Mwinilunga, Zam.	C3	68
Myäjlär, India	E3	54
Myall Lakes National Park, p.o.i., Austl.	I9	76
Myanaung, Mya.	C2	48
Myanmar (Burma), ctry., Asia	D8	46
Myaungmya, Mya.	D2	48
Mycenae see Mykines, sci., Grc.	F5	28
Myebon, Mya.	B1	48
Myingyan, Mya.	B2	48
Myitkyinä, Mya.	C8	46
Myitnge, stm., Mya.	B3	48
Myitta, Mya.	E4	48
Myittha, Mya.	B2	48
Myittha, stm., Mya.	B2	48
Myjava, Slov.	H13	16
Mykines, i., Far. Is.	m34	8b
Mykines, sci., Grc.	F5	28
Mykolaïv, Ukr.	F5	6
Mykolaïv, co., Ukr.	B17	26
Mykolaïvka, Ukr.	C16	26
Mýkonos, i., Grc.	F8	28
Myla, India	D24	8
Mymensingh (Nasirābād), Bngl.	F13	54
Mynaral, Kaz.	E12	32
Mynfontein, S. Afr.	G6	70
Myohaung, Mya.	B1	48
Myohyang-san, mtn., Kor., N.	D7	38
Myökö-san, vol., Japan	C11	40
Myra, sci., Tur.	G12	28
Mýrdalsjökull, ice, Ice.	l30	8a
Myrskylä, Fin.	F11	8
Myrtle Beach, S.C., U.S.	C7	116
Myrtle Creek, Or., U.S.	G3	136
Myrtle Grove, Fl., U.S.	G11	122
Myrtle Point, Or., U.S.	G2	136
Myrtletowne, Ca., U.S.	C1	134
Myrtöön Pélagos, s., Grc.	G6	28
Myškino, Russia	C21	10
Myślenice, Pol.	G15	16
Myślibórz, Pol.	D10	16
Mysłowice, Pol.	F15	16
Mysore, India	E3	53
Mysore see Karnätaka, state, India	F4	46
Mystic, Ct., U.S.	C14	114
Mystrás, sci., Grc.	F5	28
Mys Vhodnoj, Russia	B6	34
Myszków, Pol.	F15	16
Myt, Russia	H20	8
My Tho, Viet.	G8	48
Mytilíni, Grc.	D9	28
Mytišči, Russia	E20	10
Myton, Ut., U.S.	C6	132
Mývatn, l., Ice.	k31	8a
Mzimba, Mwi.	C5	68
Mzimvubu, stm., S. Afr.	G9	70
Mzintlava, stm., S. Afr.	G9	70
Mzuzu, Mwi.	C5	68

N

Name	Map Ref.	Page
Na (Tengtiao), stm., Asia	A6	48
Naab, stm., Ger.	G7	16
Nä'älehu, Hi., U.S.	d6	78a
Naas, Ire.	H6	12
Nababeep, S. Afr.	F3	70
Nabari, Japan	E9	40
Nabberu, Lake, l., Austl.	E4	74
Nabburg, Ger.	G8	16
Naberežnye Čelny, Russia	C8	32
Nabeul, Tun.	H4	24
Näbha, India	C6	54
Nabire, Indon.	F10	44
Nabi Shu'ayb, Jabal an-, mtn., Yemen	F5	56
Nabouwalu, Fiji	p19	79e
Nabq, Egypt	J5	58
Nabula, China	C7	54
Näbulus, W.B.	F6	58
Nacala-a-Velha, Moz.	C7	68
Nachingwea, Tan.	G7	66
Nächna, India	E3	54
Náchod, Czech Rep.	F12	16
Nachvak Fiord, b., Nf., Can.	F13	141
Nacimiento, Chile	H1	92
Nacimiento, Lake, res., Ca., U.S.	H5	134
Naco, Mex.	F8	98
Naco, Az., U.S.	L6	132
Nacogdoches, Tx., U.S.	F4	122
Nácori Chico, Mex.	G8	98
Nacozari de García, Mex.	F8	98
Nacunday, Para.	B10	92
Nadarivatu, Fiji	p18	79e
Nadela, Spain	B3	20
Nadiäd, India	G4	54
Nadi Bay, b., Fiji	p18	79e
Nädlac, Rom.	C7	26
Naduri, Fiji	p19	79e
Nadvoicy, Russia	E16	8
Nadym, Russia	A12	32
Nadym, stm., Russia	A12	32
Naenwa, India	F5	54
Nærbø, Nor.	G1	8
Næstved, Den.	I4	8
Nafada, Nig.	G7	64
Nafi, Sau. Ar.	D5	56
Näfpaktos, Grc.	E4	28
Näfplio, Grc.	F5	28
Nafüsah, Jabal, hills, Libya	A2	62
Naga, Phil.	D4	52
Nagahama, Japan	D9	40
Nagahama, Japan	F5	40
Naga Hills, mts., Asia	F5	40
Nagai, Japan	A12	40
Nagai Island, i., Ak., U.S.	F7	140
Nägaland, state, India	C7	46
Nagano, Japan	C11	40
Nagano, state, Japan	C11	40
Nagaoka, Japan	B11	40
Nagaon, India	E14	54
Nägappattinam, India	F4	53
Nägara, stm., Japan	D9	40
Nagarhole Tiger Reserve, India	E2	53
Nägärjuna Ságar, res., India	C4	53
Nagarote, Nic.	F4	102
Nagasaki, Japan	G2	40
Nagasaki, state, Japan	G2	40
Nagaur, India	E4	54
Nagaur, India	E4	54
Nägävali, stm., India	B6	53
Nagda, India	G5	54
Nägercoil, India	G3	53
Nagina, India	D7	54
Nagłowice, Pol.	F15	16
Nago, Japan	I19	39a
Nagod, Ger.	H4	16
Nagornyj, Russia	E13	34
Nagoya, Japan	D9	40
Nägpur, India	H7	54
Nagqu, China	C14	54
Nagua, Dom. Rep.	C12	102
Naguabo, P.R.	B4	104a
Nagyatád, Hung.	C4	26
Nagybánya see Baia Mare, Rom.	B10	26
Nagyecsed, Hung.	B9	26
Nagykanizsa, Hung.	C4	26
Nagykáta, Hung.	B6	26
Nagykőrös, Hung.	B6	26
Naha, Japan	I18	39a
Nahabuan, Indon.	C9	50
Nähan, India	C6	54
Nahanni Butte, N.T., Can.	C6	106
Nahariyya, Isr.	E5	58
Nahävand, Iran	C6	56
Nahe, China	B9	36
Nahe, stm., Ger.	G3	16
Nahma, Mi., U.S.	C3	112
Nahodka, Russia	C10	38
Nahodka, Russia	A13	32
Nahoe, Fr. Poly.	r19	78g
Nahoi, Cap, c., Vanuatu	j16	79d
Nahuel Huapi, Lago, l., Arg.	H2	90
Nahuel Niyeu, Arg.	H3	90
Naica, Mex.	B6	100
Naicam, Sk., Can.	B9	124
Naila, Ger.	F7	16
Naiman Qi, China	C4	38
Nā'in, Iran	C7	56
Naini Tāl, India	D7	54
Nainpur, India	G8	54
Nairai, i., Fiji	p19	79e
Nairn, La., U.S.	H9	122
Nairobi, Kenya	E7	66
Naitauba, i., Fiji	p20	79e
Naivasha, Kenya	E7	66
Naizishan, China	C7	38
Najac, Fr.	E8	18
Najafäbäd, Iran	C7	56
Najasa, stm., Cuba	B9	102
Najd (Nejd), hist. reg., Sau. Ar.	D5	56
Najïbäbäd, India	D7	54
Najin, Kor., N.	C9	38
Naka, stm., Japan	C13	40
Nakajö, Japan	A12	40
Nakama, Japan	F3	40
Nakaminato, Japan	C13	40
Nakamura, Japan	G5	40
Nakano, Japan	C11	40
Nakano-shima, i., Japan	k19	39a
Nakasongola, Ug.	D6	66
Nakatsu, Japan	F4	40
Nakatsugawa, Japan	D10	40
Nakhl, Egypt	I4	58
Nakhon Nayok, Thai.	E5	48
Nakhon Pathom, Thai.	F5	48
Nakhon Phanom, Thai.	D7	48
Nakhon Ratchasima, Thai.	E6	48
Nakhon Sawan, Thai.	E5	48
Nakhon Si Thammarat, Thai.	H5	48
Nakhon Thai, Thai.	D5	48
Nakina, On., Can.	A12	118
Naklo nad Notecią, Pol.	C13	16
Nakodar, India	C5	54
Nakonde, Zam.	B5	68
Nakskov, Den.	I4	8
Naktong-gang, stm., Kor., S.	C1	40
Nakuru, Kenya	E7	66
Nakusp, B.C., Can.	F13	138
Nälanda, India	F10	54
Nalayh, Mong.	B6	36
Nalbäri, India	E13	54
Nal'čik, Russia	F6	32
Nalęczów, Pol.	E18	16
Nalgonda, India	C4	53
Nallamala Hills, mts., India	D4	53
Nallïhan, Tur.	C14	28
Nalón, stm., Spain	A5	20
Nalong, China	J2	42
Nälüt, Libya	A2	62
Nam (Nan'a), stm., Asia	B4	48
Namaacha, Moz.	D10	70
Namacurra, Moz.	D6	68
Namadgi National Park, p.o.i., Austl.	J7	76
Namak, Daryächeh-ye, l., Iran	C7	56
Namakan Lake, l., N.A.	C6	118
Nämakkal, India	F4	53
Namangan, Uzb.	F12	32
Namanyere, Tan.	F6	66
Namapa, Moz.	C6	68
Namarrói, Moz.	D6	68
Namatanai, Pap. N. Gui.	a5	79a
Nambour, Austl.	F9	76
Nam Co, l., China	C13	54
Nam Dinh, Viet.	B7	48
Nam Du, Quan Dao, is., Viet.	H6	48
Nameh, Indon.	B10	50
Namen see Namur, Bel.	D13	14
Namerikawa, Japan	C10	40
Nametil, Moz.	D6	68
Nam-gang, stm., Kor., N.	E7	38
Namhae-do, i., Kor., S.	G8	38
Namhan-gang, stm., Kor., S.	F7	38
Namhkam, Mya.	D8	46
Namib Desert, des., Nmb.	E1	68
Namibe, Ang.	D1	68
Namibia, ctry., Afr.	E2	68
Namib Naukluft Park, p.o.i., Nmb.	D2	70
Namie, Japan	B14	40
Namies, S. Afr.	F4	70
Namji-ri, Kor., S.	D1	40
Namlea, Indon.	F8	44
Namling, China	D12	54
Nam Nao National Park, p.o.i., Thai.	D5	48
Nam Ngum Reservoir, res., Laos	C6	48
Namnoi, Khao, mtn., Mya.	G4	48
Namoi, stm., Austl.	H7	76
Nampa, Id., U.S.	G10	136
Nampala, Mali.	F3	64
Nam Pat, Thai.	D5	48
Nampawng, Mya.	A3	48
Nam Phan (Cochin China), hist. reg., Viet.	G8	48
Nampo, Kor., N.	E6	38
Nampula, Moz.	D6	68
Namsang, Mya.	B3	48
Namsen, stm., Nor.	D5	8
Namsos, Nor.	D4	8
Nam Tok, Thai.	E4	48
Nam Tok Mae Surin National Park, p.o.i., Thai.	C4	48
Namtu, Mya.	A3	48
Namu, B.C., Can.	E3	138
Namuka-I-Lau, i., Fiji	q20	79e
Namúli, Serra, mts., Moz.	D6	68
Namur (Namen), Bel.	D13	14
Namwala, Zam.	D4	68
Namwon, Kor., S.	G7	38
Namysłów, Pol.	E13	16
Nan, Thai.	C5	48
Nan, stm., Thai.	D5	48
Nan'a (Nam), stm., Asia	B4	48
Nanam, Kor., N.	D8	38
Nanango, Austl.	F8	76
Nanao, Japan	B9	40
Nanatsu-jima, is., Japan	B9	40
Nanbu, China	F1	42
Nanchang, China	G6	42
Nancheng, China	H7	42
Nancheng see Hanzhong, China	E2	42
Nanching see Nanjing, China	E8	42
Nanchong, China	F2	42
Nanchuan, China	G2	42
Nanch'ung see Nanchong, China	F2	42
Nancowry Island, i., India	G7	46
Nancy, Fr.	F15	14
Nanda Devi, mtn., India	C7	54
Nandaime, Nic.	G4	102
Nandan, Japan	E7	40
Nänded, India	B3	53
Nändgaon, India	H5	54
Nandi Drug, mtn., India	E3	53
Nandikotkür, India	D4	53
Nandu, China	F8	42
Nandu, stm., China	L4	42
Nändüra, India	H6	54
Nandurbär, India	H4	54
Nandyäl, India	D4	53
Nanfen, China	D5	38
Nanfeng, China	H7	42
Nanga-Eboko, Cam.	D2	66
Nangakelawit, Indon.	C8	50
Nangamau, Indon.	D7	50
Nangaobat, Indon.	C8	50
Nanga Parbat, mtn., Pak.	B11	56
Nangapinoh, Indon.	D7	50
Nangarhär, state, Afg.	A3	54
Nangatayap, Indon.	D7	50
Nanggala Hill, mtn., Sol. Is.	e7	79b
Nangin, Mya.	G4	48
Nangnim-üp, Kor., N.	D7	38
Nangong, China	C6	42
Nang Rong, Thai.	E6	48
Nanguan, China	C5	42
Nanhua, China	F5	36
Nan Hulsan Hu, l., China	D4	36
Nanika Lake, l., B.C., Can.	C3	138
Nanjangüd, India	E3	53
Nanjiang, China	E2	42
Nanjing, China	I7	42
Nanjing (Nanking), China	E8	42
Nankang, China	I6	42
Nanking see Nanjing, China	E8	42
Nankoku, Japan	F6	40
Nankye, Mya.	F4	48
Nanle, China	C6	42
Nanlei (Loi), stm., Asia	A4	48
Nanling, China	H6	42
Nan Ling, mts., China	I5	42
Nanliu, stm., China	J3	42
Nanlou Shan, mtn., China	C7	38
Nannine, Austl.	E3	74
Nanning, China	J3	42
Na Noi, Thai.	C5	48
Nanortalik, Grnld.	E16	141
Nanpan, stm., China	G5	36
Nänpära, India	E8	54
Nanpiao, China	A9	42
Nanping, China	H8	42
Nanping, China	E5	36
Nansei, Japan.	E9	40
Nansei-shotö (Ryukyu Islands), is., Japan	k19	39a
Nan Shan see Qilian Shan, mts., China	D4	36
Nanshan Island, i., Asia	C6	44
Nantais, Lac, l., Qc., Can.	C16	106
Nantai-zan, vol., Japan	C12	40
Nanterre, Fr.	F11	14
Nantes, Fr.	G7	14
Nantes à Brest, Canal de, can., Fr.	F5	14
Nanticoke, Pa., U.S.	C9	114
Nanto, Japan	E9	40
Nanton, Ab., Can.	F17	138
Nantong, China	E9	42
Nant'ou, Tai.	J9	42
Nantucket, Ma., U.S.	C15	114
Nantucket Island, i., Ma., U.S.	C15	114
Nantucket Sound, strt., Ma., U.S.	C15	114
Nantulo, Moz.	C6	68
Nantung see Nantong, China.	E9	42
Nanty Glo, Pa., U.S.	H11	112
Nanu, Pap. N. Gui.	b3	79a
Nanuku Passage, strt., Fiji	p20	79e
Nanumea, at., Tuvalu	D8	72
Nanuque, Braz.	I5	88
Nanusa, Kepulauan, is., Indon.	E8	44
Nanxi, China	G1	42
Nanxian, China	G5	42
Nanxiang, China	F9	42
Nanxiong, China	I6	42
Nanyang, China.	J4	42
Nanyang Hu, l., China	D7	42
Nanyi Hu, l., China	F8	42
Nan-yö, Japan	A13	40
Nanyuki, Kenya	D7	66
Nanzamu, China	C6	38
Nanzhao, China	E5	42
Nao, Cabo de la see Nau, Cap de la, c., Spain	F11	20
Naococane, Lac, l., Qc., Can.	E16	106
Naogaon, Bngl.	F12	54
Naokot, Pak.	F2	54
Náousa, Grc.	C5	28
Napa, Ca., U.S.	E3	134
Napa, stm., Ca., U.S.	E3	134
Napaku, Indon.	B9	50
Napakovo, Russia	C3	34
Napanee, On., Can.	D12	112
Napassoq, Grnld.	D15	141
Naperville, Il., U.S.	C9	120
Napido, Indon.	F10	44
Napier, N.Z.	D7	80
Napier, Mount, hill, Austl.	C5	74
Napier Mountains, mts., Ant.	B10	81
Naples see Napoli, Italy	D8	24
Naples, Fl., U.S.	J4	116
Naples, N.Y., U.S.	B8	114
Naples, Tx., U.S.	D4	122
Napo, state, Ec.	H3	86
Napo, stm., S.A.	D3	84
Napoleon, N.D., U.S.	A13	126
Napoleonville, La., U.S.	H7	122
Napoli (Naples), Italy	D8	24
Napoli, Golfo di, b., Italy	D8	24
Nappamerrie, Austl.	F3	76
Nappanee, In., U.S.	G4	112
Napu, Indon.	H11	50
Nara, Japan	E8	40
Nara, Mali.	F3	64
Nara, state, Japan	E8	40
Nära, stm., Pak.	F2	54
Naracoorte, Austl.	K3	76
Naradhan, Austl.	I6	76
Naraini, India	F8	54
Naramata, B.C., Can.	G11	138
Naranjal, Ec.	I2	86
Naranjito, P.R.	B3	104a
Narasannapeta, India	B7	53
Narasapur, India	C5	53
Narasaraopet, India	C5	53
Narasun, Russia	A7	36
Narathiwat, Thai.	I5	48
Naraü (Narew), stm., Eur.	D17	16
Näräjanganj, Bngl.	G13	54
Näräjani (Gandaki), stm., Asia	E10	54
Näräjanpet, India	C3	53
Narbonne, Fr.	F8	18
Nardò, Italy	D11	24
Nares Strait, strt., N.A.	B11	141
Nares (Narau), stm., Eur.	D17	16
Nargund, India	D2	53
Nariño, state, Col.	G3	86
Narita, Japan	D13	40
Nariva Swamp, sw., Trin.	s12	105f
Nar'jan-Mar, Russia	C25	8
Narli, Tur.	A8	58
Narmada, stm., India	H4	54
Narnaul, India	D6	54
Narodnaja, gora, mtn., Russia	B10	32
Narodnaya, Mount see Narodnaja, gora, mtn., Russia	B10	32
Naro-Fominsk, Russia	E19	10
Narol, Pol.	F19	16
Narooma, Austl.	K8	76
Närowäl, Pak.	B5	54
Narrabri, Austl.	H7	76
Narran, stm., Austl.	G7	76
Narrandera, Austl.	J6	76
Narraway, stm., Can.	B11	138
Narrogin, Austl.	F3	74
Narromine, Austl.	I6	76
Narsaq see Narssaq, Grnld.	E16	141
Narsimhapur, India	G7	54
Narsinghgarh, India	G6	54
Narsïpatnam, India	C6	53
Narssaq, Grnld.	E16	141
Naruto, Japan	G1	40
Naruto, Japan	E7	40
Narva, Est.	G13	8
Narva, Russia	C16	32
Narva, stm., Eur.	A11	10
Narvik, Nor.	B7	8
Narvskoe vodohranilišče, l., Eur.	A10	10
Narwäna, India	D6	54
Narwietooma, Austl.	D6	74
Narym, Russia	C14	32
Naryn, Kyrg.	F13	32
Naryn, stm., Asia	F13	32
Narynkol, Kaz.	F13	32
Näsåker, Swe.	E7	8
Na San, Thai.	H4	48
Nasawa, Vanuatu	j17	79d
Nasbinals, Fr.	E9	18
Nasca, Peru	F2	84
Nase see Naze, Japan	k19	39a
Nash, Tx., U.S.	D4	122
Näshik, India	H4	54
Nashua, Ia., U.S.	B5	120
Nashua, N.H., U.S.	B14	114
Nashville, Ar., U.S.	D5	122
Nashville, Il., U.S.	F8	120
Nashville, In., U.S.	E11	120
Nashville, Mi., U.S.	F4	112
Nashville, N.C., U.S.	I8	114
Nashville, Tn., U.S.	H11	120
Nashwaak, stm., N.B., Can.	D10	110
Nashwauk, Mn., U.S.	D5	118
Nasielsk, Pol.	D16	16
Näsijärvi, l., Fin.	F10	8
Näsir, Sudan	F6	62
Näsir, Buheirat see Nasser, Lake, res., Afr.	C6	62
Näsïräbäd, India	E5	54
Nasr, Egypt	H1	58
Nass, stm., B.C., Can.	E5	106
Nassarawa, Nig.	H6	64
Nassau, Bah.	m18	104f
Nassau, N.Y., U.S.	B12	114
Nassau International Airport, Bah.	m18	104f
Nassau Island, i., Cook Is.	E10	72
Nassawadox, Va., U.S.	G10	114
Nasser, Lake (Näsir, Buheirat), res., Afr.	C6	62
Nässjö, Swe.	H6	8
Nastapoka Islands, is., Can.	D15	106
Nasugbu, Phil.	C3	52
Nasu-dake, vol., Japan	B12	40
Nasukoin Mountain, mtn., Mt., U.S.	B12	136
Nasva, Russia	D13	10
Nata, Bots.	E4	68
Nata, stm., Afr.	B8	70
Natal, Braz.	C8	88
Natal, B.C., Can.	G16	138
Natal, Indon.	C1	50
Natal see KwaZulu-Natal, state, S. Afr.	F10	70
Natalia, Tx., U.S.	E9	130
Natalkuz Lake, res., B.C., Can.	C5	138
Natanes Plateau, plat., Az., U.S.	J6	132
Natashquan, stm., Can.	i21	107a
Natchez, Ms., U.S.	F7	122
Natchez Trace Parkway, p.o.i., U.S.	E9	122
Natchitoches, La., U.S.	F5	122
Natewa Bay, b., Fiji	p19	79e
Näthdwära, India	F4	54
Natimuk, Austl.	K3	76
Nation, stm., B.C., Can.	A7	138
National City, Ca., U.S.	K8	134
Natitingou, Benin	G5	64
Native Bay, b., Nu., Can.	C14	106
Natividade, Braz.	F2	88
Natkyizin, Mya.	E3	48
Natoma, Ks., U.S.	B9	128
Nator, Bngl.	F12	54
Natori, Japan	A13	40
Natron, Lake, l., Afr.	E7	66
Natrün, Wadi el-, val., Egypt	H1	58
Nattaung, mtn., Mya.	C3	48
Natuna Besar, i., Indon.	A6	50
Natuna Besar, Kepulauan, is., Indon.	A5	50
Natuna Selatan, Kepulauan, is., Indon.	B6	50
Natural Bridge, misc. cult., Va., U.S.	G6	114
Natural Bridges National Monument, p.o.i., Ut., U.S.	F6	132
Naturaliste, Cape, c., Austl.	F2	74
Naturno, Italy	D7	22
Nau, Cap de la, c., Spain	F11	20
Naucelle, Fr.	E8	18
Naucratis, hist., Egypt	H1	58
Nauen, Ger.	D8	16
Naugatuck, Ct., U.S.	C12	114
Naughton, On., Can.	B8	112
Naujaat (Repulse Bay), Nu., Can.	B13	106
Naujamiestis, Lith.	E6	10
Naujan, Lake, l., Phil.	D3	52
Naujoji Akmenė, Lith.	D5	10
Naumburg, Ger.	E7	16
Naunglon, Mya.	D3	48
Nä'ür, Jord.	G6	58
Nauru, state, Oc.	p17	78f
Nauru International Airport, Nauru	q17	78f
Nauši, Russia	F10	34
Nausori, Fiji	p19	79e
Nauta, Peru	D3	84
Nautanwa, India	E9	54
Nautla, Mex.	E10	100
Navadwip, India	G12	54
Navahrudak, Bela.	G8	10
Navajo Mountain, mtn., Ut., U.S.	H7	132
Navajo National Monument, p.o.i., Az., U.S.	G6	132
Navajo Reservoir, res., U.S.	G9	132
Navalmoral de la Mata, Spain	E5	20
Navalvillar de Pela, Spain	E5	20
Navan, Ire.	H6	12
Navapolack, Bela.	E11	10
Navarin, Mys, c., Russia	D24	34
Navarino, Isla, i., Chile	K3	90
Navarra, state, Spain	B9	20
Navarro Mills Lake, res., Tx., U.S.	F2	122
Navasëlki, Bela.	H7	10
Navasota, Tx., U.S.	G2	122
Navasota, stm., Tx., U.S.	D11	130
Navassa, N.C., U.S.	B7	116
Navassa Island, i., N.A.	C10	102
Navesnoe, Russia	H20	10
Navia, Arg.	G4	92
Navia, stm., Spain	A4	20
Navidad, Chile	F1	92
Navidad, stm., Tx., U.S.	E11	130
Navio, Riacho do, stm., Braz.	E6	88
Naviti, i., Fiji	p18	79e
Navlja, Russia	H17	10
Navodari, Rom.	E15	26
Navoi, Uzb.	F11	32
Navojoa, Mex.	B4	100
Navolato, Mex.	C5	100
Nawa, see Naha, Japan	I18	39a
Nawäbganj, Bngl.	F12	54
Nawäbganj, India	F10	54
Nawäbshäh, Pak.	E2	54
Nawada, India	F10	54
Nawäh, Afg.	B1	54
Nawalgarh, India	E5	54
Nawäpära, India	H8	54
Naxçivan, Azer.	B6	56
Náxos, i., Grc.	F8	28
Nayägarh, India	H10	54
Nayarit, state, Mex.	E6	100
Näy Band, Küh-e, mtn., Iran	C8	56
Naylor, Mo., U.S.	H7	120
Nayoro, Japan	B15	38
Nazaré, Braz.	D2	88
Nazaré, Port.	E1	20
Nazaré da Mata, Braz.	D8	88
Nazaré do Piauí, Braz.	D4	88
Nazareth see Nazerat, Isr.	F6	58
Nazarovo, Russia	C16	32
Nazas, Mex.	C6	100
Nazas, stm., Mex.	C6	100
Nazca Ridge, unds.	K5	144
Naze, Japan	k19	39a
Naze, The see Lindesnes, c., Nor.	H2	8
Nazerat (Nazareth), Isr.	F6	58
Nazerat 'Illit, Isr.	F6	58
Nazija, Russia	A14	10
Nazilli, Tur.	F11	28
Nazina, Russia	B13	32
Nazko, stm., B.C., Can.	D8	138
Nazlet el-'Amüdein, Egypt	J1	58
Nazran', Russia	F7	32
Nazrët, Eth.	F7	62
Nazwá, Oman	E8	56
Nazyvaevsk, Russia	C12	32
Nčeckij avtonomnyj okrug, Russia	C23	8
Ndalatando, Ang.	B1	68
Ndali, Benin	H5	64
Ndélé, C.A.R.	C4	66
Ndendé, Gabon	E2	66
N'Djamena (Fort-Lamy), Chad	E3	62
Ndjolé, Gabon	E2	66
Ndogo, Lagune, l., Gabon	E2	66
Ndola, Zam.	C4	68
Ndumu Game Reserve, S. Afr.	E11	70
Neabul Creek, stm., Austl.	F6	76
Neagh, Lough, l., N. Ire., U.K.	G6	12
Neah Bay, Wa., U.S.	B2	136
Neale, Lake, l., Austl.	D6	74
Neamt, state, Rom.	B13	26
Néa Páfos (Paphos), Cyp.	C7	58
Neápoli, Grc.	G6	28
Near Islands, is., Ak., U.S.	g21	140a
Neath, Wales, U.K.	J9	12
Nebine Creek, stm., Austl.	G6	76
Nebitdag, Turkmen.	B7	56
Neblina, Cerro de la see Neblina, Pico da, mtn., S.A.	G9	86
Neblina, Pico da, mtn., S.A.	G9	86
Nebo, Il., U.S.	E7	120
Nebo, Mount, mtn., Ut., U.S.	D5	132
Nebolči, Russia	A16	10
Nebraska, state, U.S.	C7	108
Nebraska City, Ne., U.S.	D1	120
Necedah, Wi., U.S.	G8	118
Nechako, stm., B.C., Can.	C7	138
Nechako Reservoir, res., B.C., Can.	C5	138
Neches, Tx., U.S.	F3	122
Neches, stm., Tx., U.S.	G4	122
Nechi, Col.	C4	86
Nechí, stm., Col.	D4	86
Nechranice, vodni nádrž, res., Czech Rep.	F9	16
Neckarsulm, Ger.	G5	16
Necker Island, i., Br. Vir. Is.	d9	104b
Necochea, Arg.	I8	92
Nederland, Tx., U.S.	H4	122
Nédong, China	D13	54
Needham Point, c., Barb.	n8	105d
Needle Mountain, mtn., Wy., U.S.	F17	136
Needles, Ca., U.S.	I2	132
Needville, Tx., U.S.	H3	122
Neembucu, state, Para.	C8	92
Neenah, Wi., U.S.	G10	118
Neepawa, Mb., Can.	D14	124
Nefëdovo, Russia	C12	32
Nefta, Tun.	C6	64
Neftçala, Azer.	B6	56
Nefteçala, Russia	B12	32
Nefta, Tun.	H3	24
Negage, Ang.	B2	68
Negara, Indon.	H9	50
Negara, stm., Indon.	E9	50
Negara, stm., Indon.	D9	50
Negele, Eth.	F7	62
Negeri Sembilan, state, Malay.	K6	48
Negev Desert see HaNegev, reg., Isr.	H5	58
Negombo, Sri L.	H4	53
Negra, Laguna, l., Ur.	G11	92
Negreira, Spain	B2	20
Nègres, Pointe des, c., Mart.	k6	105c
Negresti-Oas, Rom.	B10	26
Negritos, Peru	D1	84
Negro, stm., Arg.	H4	90
Negro, stm., Braz.	C13	92
Negro, stm., Col.	B9	86
Negro, stm., Para.	B9	92
Negro, stm., S.A.	I3	86
Negro, stm., S.A.	F9	92
Negros, i., Phil.	E4	52
Nehalem, stm., Or., U.S.	E3	136
Nehbandän, Iran	C9	56
Nehe, China	B9	36
Néhoué, Baie de, b., N. Cal.	m14	79d
Neiba, Dom. Rep.	C12	102
Neijiang, China	F1	42
Neidpath, Sk., Can.	D6	124
Neikiang see Neijiang, China	F1	42
Neilburg, Sk., Can.	B4	124
Neillsville, Wi., U.S.	G8	118
Neiqiu, China	C6	42
Neira, Col.	E4	86
Neisse see Lausitzer Neisse, stm., Eur.	F10	16
Neisse see Nysa Łużycka, stm., Eur.	E10	16
Neiva, Col.	F4	86
Neixiang, China	E4	42
Neja, Russia	G20	8
Nejapa de Madero, Mex.	G11	100
Nejd see Najd, hist. reg., Sau. Ar.	D5	56
Nejdek, Czech Rep.	F8	16
Nek'emtë, Eth.	F7	62
Nelichu, mtn., Sudan	F6	62
Nelidovo, Russia	D15	10
Neligh, Ne., U.S.	E14	126
Nel'kan, Russia	D16	34
Nellikuppam, India	C5	53
Nellore, India	H4	53
Nel'ma, Russia	G16	34
Nelson, B.C., Can.	G13	138
Nelson, N.Z.	E5	80
Nelson, stm., Can.	A10	128
Nelson, stm., Mb., Can.	D12	106
Nelson, Cape, c., Austl.	L3	76
Nelson, Estrecho, strt., Chile	J2	90
Nelson Lakes National Park, p.o.i., N.Z.	E5	80
Nelsonville, Oh., U.S.	E3	114
Nelspoort, S. Afr.	H6	70
Nelspruit, S. Afr.	D10	70
Néma, Maur.	F3	64
Nemadji, stm., U.S.	E6	118
Neman, Russia	E4	10
Neman (Nemunas), stm., Eur.	E4	10
Nembe, Nig.	I6	64
Nemenčinė, Lith.	F8	10
Nemerči, Russia	G16	10
Nemours, Fr.	F11	14
Nemunas (Neman), stm., Eur.	E4	10
Nemuro, Japan	C16	38
Nemuro Strait, strt., Asia	C16	38
Nen, stm., China	B9	36
Nenagh, Ire.	I4	12
Nenana, Ak., U.S.	D10	140
Nenana, stm., Ak., U.S.	D10	140
Nendo, i., Sol. Is.	E7	72
Nenjiang, China	B10	36
Nenusa, Kepulauan, is., Indon.	E8	44
Neosho, Mo., U.S.	H3	120
Neosho, stm., U.S.	H2	120
Nepa, stm., Russia	C19	32
Nepal, ctry., Asia	E9	54
Nepälganj, Nepal	D8	54
Nepa Nagar, India	H6	54
Nepeña, Peru	E2	84
Nephi, Ut., U.S.	D5	132
Nephin, mtn., Ire.	G3	12
Nepisiguit, stm., N.B., Can.	C10	110
Nepisiguit Bay, b., N.B., Can.	C11	110
Neptune, N.J., U.S.	D11	114
Neptune Beach, Fl., U.S.	F4	116
Nérac, Fr.	E6	18
Nerča, stm., Russia	F12	34
Nerčinsk, Russia	F12	34
Nerčinskij Zavod, Russia	F12	34
Nerehta, Russia	H19	8
Neretva, stm., Eur.	G15	22
Neriquinha, Ang.	D3	68
Neris (Vilija), stm., Eur.	F6	10
Nerja, Spain	H7	20
Nerjungri, Russia	E13	34
Nerl', Russia	C20	10
Nerl', stm., Russia	D22	10
Neropolis, Braz.	I1	88
Nerussa, stm., Russia	H16	10
Nerva, Spain	G4	20
Nes, Neth.	C1	16
Nesbyen, Nor.	F3	8
Neščarda, vozero, l., Bela.	E12	10
Neskaupstadur, Ice.	k32	8a
Nesna, Nor.	C5	8
Nespelem, Wa., U.S.	B7	136
Ness, Loch, l., Scot., U.K.	D8	12
Ness City, Ks., U.S.	C8	128
Nesselrode, Mount, mtn., N.A.	D4	106
Nesterkovo, Russia	A13	10
Nestoita, Ukr.	B16	26
Netanya, Isr.	F5	58
Netherdale, Austl.	B14	14
Netherlands Antilles, dep., N.A.	i14	96a
Netherlands Guiana see Surinam, ctry., S.A.	C6	84
Netrakona, Bngl.	F13	54
Nettilling Fiord, b., Nu., Can.	B17	106
Nettilling Lake, l., Nu., Can.	B17	106
Nett Lake, l., Mn., U.S.	C5	118
Nettuno, Italy	C6	24
Neubrandenburg, Ger.	C9	16
Neuburg an der Donau, Ger.	H7	16
Neuchâtel, Switz.	D3	22
Neuchâtel, Lac de, l., Switz.	D3	22
Neudorf, Sk., Can.	D11	124
Neuenburg see Neuchâtel, Switz.	D3	22
Neuenhagen, Ger.	D9	16
Neuerburg, Ger.	F2	16
Neufchâteau, Fr.	F14	14
Neufchâtel-en-Bray, Fr.	E10	14
Neu-Isenburg, Ger.	F4	16
Neumarkt in der Oberpfalz, Ger.	G7	16
Neumünster, Ger.	B6	16
Neun, Nam, stm., Laos	C6	48
Neunkirchen, Aus.	C13	22
Neunkirchen, Ger.	G3	16
Neuquén, Arg.	G3	90
Neuquén, state, Arg.	G3	90
Neuquén, stm., Arg.	G3	90
Neuruppin, Ger.	D8	16
Neuse, stm., N.C., U.S.	A8	116
Neusiedl am See, Aus.	C13	22
Neuss, Ger.	E2	16
Neustadt an der Aisch, Ger.	G6	16
Neustadt an der Weinstrasse, Ger.	G4	16
Neustadt bei Coburg, Ger.	F6	16
Neustadt in Holstein, Ger.	B6	16
Neustrelitz, Ger.	C9	16
Neutral Hills, hills, Ab., Can.	B3	124
Neu-Ulm, Ger.	H6	16
Neuvic, Fr.	D8	18
Neuville, Fr.	F13	16
Neuwied, Ger.	F3	16
Nevada, Ia., U.S.	B4	120
Nevada, Mo., U.S.	G3	120
Nevada, state, U.S.	D4	108

Name	Map Ref.	Page
Nevada, Sierra, mts., Spain	G7	20
Nevada, Sierra, mts., Ca., U.S.	F6	134
Nevada City, Ca., U.S.	D4	134
Nevado, Cerro, mtn., Arg.	G3	92
Nevado, Cerro, mtn., Col.	E4	86
Nevado de Colima, Parque Nacional del, p.o.i., Mex.	F7	100
Nevado de Toluca, Parque Nacional, p.o.i., Mex.	F8	100
Neve, Serra da, mts., Ang.	C1	68
Nevel', Russia	D12	10
Nevel'sk, Russia	G17	34
Nevel'skogo, proliv, strt., Russia	F17	34
Never, Russia	F13	34
Nevers, Fr.	G12	14
Nevesinje, Bos.	F5	26
Nevinnomyssk, Russia	F6	32
Nevis, i., St. K./N.	C2	105a
Nevis, Ben, mtn., Scot., U.K.	E7	12
Nevis Peak, vol., St. K./N.	C2	105a
Nevjansk, Russia	C10	32
Nevşehir, Tur.	B3	56
New, stm., Belize	D3	102
New, stm., Guy.	C6	84
New, stm., S.C., U.S.	D4	116
New, stm., U.S.	F4	114
Newala, Tan.	G7	66
New Albany, In., U.S.	F12	120
New Albany, Ms., U.S.	C9	122
New Amsterdam, Guy.	B6	84
New Angledool, Austl.	G6	76
Newark, Ar., U.S.	B7	122
Newark, De., U.S.	E10	114
Newark, N.J., U.S.	D11	114
Newark, N.Y., U.S.	A8	114
Newark, Oh., U.S.	D3	114
Newark Lake, l., Nv., U.S.	D1	132
Newark Valley, N.Y., U.S.	B9	114
Newark-on-Trent, Eng., U.K.	H12	12
New Athens, Il., U.S.	F8	120
New Augusta, Ms., U.S.	F9	122
New Baden, Il., U.S.	F8	120
New Bedford, Ma., U.S.	C15	114
Newberg, Or., U.S.	E4	136
New Berlin, Il., U.S.	E7	120
New Berlin, N.Y., U.S.	B10	114
New Berlin, Wi., U.S.	F1	112
Newbern, Al., U.S.	E11	122
Newbern, N.C., U.S.	A8	116
Newbern, Tn., U.S.	H8	120
Newberry, Fl., U.S.	G3	116
Newberry, S.C., U.S.	B4	116
Newberry National Volcanic Monument, p.o.i., Or., U.S.	G5	136
New Bethlehem, Pa., U.S.	D6	114
New Bloomfield, Pa., U.S.	H12	112
New Boston, Oh., U.S.	F3	114
New Boston, Tx., U.S.	D4	122
New Braunfels, Tx., U.S.	E9	130
New Britain, Ct., U.S.	C13	114
New Britain, i., Pap. N. Gui.	b5	79a
New Brockton, Al., U.S.	F12	122
Newbrook, Ab., Can.	B17	138
New Brunswick, N.J., U.S.	D11	114
New Brunswick, state, Can.	D10	110
Newburg, Mo., U.S.	G6	120
Newburgh, In., U.S.	G10	120
Newburgh, N.Y., U.S.	C11	114
Newbury, Eng., U.K.	J11	12
Newburyport, Ma., U.S.	B15	114
New Caledonia Nouvelle-Calédonie, i., N. Cal.	m15	79d
New Caledonia Basin, unds.	L19	142
New Carlisle, Qc., Can.	B11	110
New Carlisle, Oh., U.S.	E2	114
New Castile see Castilla la Nueva, hist. reg., Spain	E7	20
Newcastle, Austl.	I8	76
Newcastle, N.B., Can.	C11	110
Newcastle, S. Afr.	E9	70
Newcastle, St. K./N.	C2	105a
Newcastle, N. Ire., U.K.	G7	12
New Castle, Co., U.S.	D9	132
New Castle, De., U.S.	E10	114
New Castle, In., U.S.	I4	112
Newcastle, Ne., U.S.	I2	118
Newcastle, Ok., U.S.	F11	128
New Castle, Pa., U.S.	D5	114
Newcastle, Tx., U.S.	A9	130
New Castle, Va., U.S.	G5	114
Newcastle, Wy., U.S.	D8	126
Newcastle Bay, b., Austl.	B8	74
Newcastle-under-Lyme, Eng., U.K.	I10	12
Newcastle upon Tyne, Eng., U.K.	G10	12
Newcastle Waters, Austl.	C6	74
Newcastle West, Ire.	I3	12
New City, N.Y., U.S.	C11	114
Newcomerstown, Oh., U.S.	D4	114
New Concord, Oh., U.S.	D4	114
New Cumberland, W.V., U.S.	D5	114
Newdegate, Austl.	F3	74
New Delhi, India	D6	54
New Denver, B.C., Can.	F13	138
New Edinburg, Ar., U.S.	D6	122
New Effington, S.D., U.S.	F1	118
Newell, Ia., U.S.	B2	120
Newell, W.V., U.S.	D5	114
Newell, Lake, l., Ab., Can.	F19	138
New Ellenton, S.C., U.S.	C4	116
Newellton, La., U.S.	E7	122
New England, N.D., U.S.	A10	126
New England National Park, p.o.i., Austl.	H9	76
Newfane, N.Y., U.S.	E11	112
Newfane, Vt., U.S.	A13	114
New Florence, Pa., U.S.	D6	114
New Hebrides see Vanuatu, ctry., Oc.	k16	79d
New Hebrides, is., Vanuatu	k16	79d
New Hebrides Trench, unds.	L20	142
Newhebron, Ms., U.S.	F9	122
New Holland, Oh., U.S.	E2	114
New Holland, Pa., U.S.	D9	114
New Holstein, Wi., U.S.	E1	112
New Hope, Al., U.S.	C12	122
New Iberia, La., U.S.	G7	122
New Ireland, i., Pap. N. Gui.	a5	79a
New Jersey, state, U.S.	D11	114
New Johnsonville, Tn., U.S.	H10	120
New Kensington, Pa., U.S.	D6	114
New Kent, Va., U.S.	G9	114
Newkirk, Ok., U.S.	E11	128
New Kowloon see Xinjiulong, China	J6	42
New Lexington, Oh., U.S.	E3	114
New Lisbon, Wi., U.S.	H8	118
New Liskeard, On., Can.	F14	106
New Llano, La., U.S.	F5	122
New London, Ct., U.S.	C13	114
New London, Mo., U.S.	E6	120
New London, N.H., U.S.	G5	110
New London, Oh., U.S.	C3	114
New London, Tx., U.S.	E4	122
New London, Wi., U.S.	G10	118
New Madrid, Mo., U.S.	H8	120
Newman, Austl.	D3	74
Newman, Ca., U.S.	F4	134
Newman Grove, Ne., U.S.	F15	126
Newmarket, On., Can.	D10	112
Newmarket, Eng., U.K.	I13	12
New Market, Al., U.S.	C12	122
New Market, Ia., U.S.	D3	120
Newmarket, N.H., U.S.	G5	110
New Market, Va., U.S.	F7	114
New Martinsville, W.V., U.S.	E4	114
New Mexico, state, U.S.	D9	98
New Milford, Ct., U.S.	C12	114
New Milford, Pa., U.S.	C10	114
Newnan, Ga., U.S.	D14	122
New Norfolk, Austl.	o13	77a
New Orleans, La., U.S.	G8	122
New Paris, Oh., U.S.	I5	112
New Philadelphia, Oh., U.S.	D4	114
New Pine Creek, Or., U.S.	A5	134
New Plymouth, N.Z.	D5	80
New Plymouth, Id., U.S.	G10	136
Newport, Eng., U.K.	K11	12
Newport, Wales, U.K.	J10	12
Newport, Ar., U.S.	B7	122
Newport, Ky., U.S.	E1	114
Newport, Me., U.S.	F7	110
Newport, N.C., U.S.	B8	116
Newport, N.H., U.S.	G4	110
Newport, Or., U.S.	F2	136
Newport, Pa., U.S.	D8	114
Newport, R.I., U.S.	C14	114
Newport, Tn., U.S.	I2	114
Newport, Vt., U.S.	F4	110
Newport Beach, Ca., U.S.	J7	134
Newport News, Va., U.S.	G9	114
New Port Richey, Fl., U.S.	H3	116
New Providence, i., Bah.	C9	96
Newquay, Eng., U.K.	K7	12
New Richland, Mn., U.S.	H5	118
New Richmond, Qc., Can.	B10	110
New Richmond, Wi., U.S.	F6	118
New River, St. K./N.	C2	105a
New Road, N.S., Can.	F13	110
New Roads, La., U.S.	G7	122
New Rochelle, N.Y., U.S.	D12	114
New Ross, N.S., Can.	F12	110
New Ross, Ire.	I6	12
Newry, N. Ire., U.K.	G6	12
Newry, S.C., U.S.	B3	116
New Salem, N.D., U.S.	A11	126
New Schwabenland, reg., Ant.	C5	81
New Sharon, Ia., U.S.	C5	120
New Siberian Islands see Novosibirskie ostrova, is., Russia	A18	34
New Smyrna Beach, Fl., U.S.	G5	116
New South Wales, state, Austl.	I6	76
New Tazewell, Tn., U.S.	H2	114
New Tecumseth, On., Can.	D9	112
Newton, Ga., U.S.	F14	122
Newton, Ia., U.S.	C4	120
Newton, Il., U.S.	F9	120
Newton, Ks., U.S.	C11	128
Newton, Ma., U.S.	B14	114
Newton, Ms., U.S.	E9	122
Newton, N.J., U.S.	C11	114
Newton, Tx., U.S.	G5	122
Newton Falls, N.Y., U.S.	F2	110
Newton Stewart, Scot., U.K.	G8	12
New Town, N.D., U.S.	F11	124
Newtownabbey, N. Ire., U.K.	G6	12
Newtownards, N. Ire., U.K.	G7	12
New Ulm, Mn., U.S.	G4	118
New Ulm, Tx., U.S.	H2	122
New Washington, Oh., U.S.	D3	114
New Waterford, N.S., Can.	D16	110
New Waverly, Tx., U.S.	G3	122
New Westminster, B.C., Can.	G8	138
New Whiteland, In., U.S.	E11	120
New York, N.Y., U.S.	D12	114
New York, state, U.S.	C12	108
New York Mills, Mn., U.S.	E3	118
New York State Barge Canal, can., N.Y., U.S.	E12	112
New Zealand, ctry., Oc.	D4	80
Neyrīz, Iran	D7	56
Neyshābūr, Iran	B8	56
Neyveli, India	F4	53
Neyyāttinkara, India	G3	53
Nezahualcóyotl, Presa, res., Mex.	G12	100
Nezperce, Id., U.S.	D10	136
Ngabang, Indon.	C6	50
Ngabé, Congo	E3	66
Ngambé, Cam.	D2	66
Ngami, Lake, l., Bots.	B6	70
Ngamiland, state, Bots.	B6	70
Ngan-chouei see Anhui, state, China	F7	42
Nganglaring Ringco, l., China	C9	54
Nganglong Kangri, mts., China	B9	54
Ngangzê Co, l., China	C11	54
Nganjuk, Indon.	G7	50
Ngao, Thai.	C5	48
Ngaoui, Mont, mtn., Afr.	F3	62
Ngaoundéré, Cam.	C2	66
Ngape, Mya.	B2	48
Ngaputaw, Mya.	D2	48
Ngara, Tan.	E6	66
Ngatangiia, Cook Is.	a27	78j
Ngatangiia Harbour, b., Cook Is.	a27	78j
Ngawi, Indon.	G7	50
Ngay Nua, Laos	B5	48
Ngcheangel, is., Palau	D9	44
Ngeaur, i., Palau	D9	44
Ngeregielmadel, Palau	g8	78b
Ngerkeai, Palau	f7	78b
Ngeruktabel, i., Palau	h7	78b
Ngetbong, Palau	f8	78b
Nggatokae Island, i., Sol. Is.	e9	79b
Nggela Pile, i., Sol. Is.	e9	79b
Nghia Hanh, Viet.	E9	48
Ngiap, stm., Laos	C6	48
Ngidinga, D.R.C.	F3	66
Ng'iro, mtn., Kenya	D7	66
Ngiva, Ewaso, stm., Kenya	D7	66
Ngo, Congo	E3	66
Ngoko, stm., Afr.	D3	66
Ngom, stm., China	B8	46
Ngomeni, Ras, c., Kenya	E8	66
Ngong, Kenya	E7	66
Ngoring Hu, l., China	E4	36
Ngounié, stm., Gabon.	E2	66
Ngouri, Chad	E3	62
Nguigmi, Niger.	G7	64
Ngulu, at., Micron.	C4	72
Ngum, stm., Laos	C6	48
Nguna, Île, i., Vanuatu	k17	79d
Nguru, Nig.	G7	64
Nhacoongo, Moz.	D12	70
Nhamundá, stm., Braz.	D6	84
Nha Trang, Viet.	F9	48
Nhill, Austl.	K3	76
Nhoma, stm., Afr.	D2	68
Niafounké, Mali	F4	64
Niagara, Wi., U.S.	C1	112
Niagara Falls, On., Can.	E10	112
Niagara Falls, N.Y., U.S.	A6	114
Niagara Falls, wtfl., N.A.	E10	112
Niagara-on-the-Lake, On., Can.	E10	112
Niagassola, Gui.	G3	64
Niah, Malay.	B8	50
Niamey, Niger	G5	64
Niangara, D.R.C.	D5	66
Niangay, Lac, l., Mali	F4	64
Niangoloko, Burkina	G4	64
Niangua, stm., Mo., U.S.	G5	120
Nia-Nia, D.R.C.	D5	66
Niantic, Il., U.S.	E8	120
Nianyushan, China	G7	42
Nianzishan, China	B9	36
Niari, stm., Congo	E2	66
Nias, Pulau, i., Indon.	L3	48
Nicaragua, ctry., N.A.	F5	102
Nicaragua, Lago de, l., Nic.	G5	102
Nicaragua, Lake see Nicaragua, Lago de, l., Nic.	G5	102
Nicastro, Italy	F10	24
Nice, Fr.	F13	18
Niceville, Fl., U.S.	G12	122
Nichinan, Japan	H4	40
Nicholas Channel (San Nicolás, Canal de), strt., N.A.	G11	108
Nicholasville, Ky., U.S.	G13	120
Nicholls, Ga., U.S.	E3	116
Nicholl's Town, Bah.	B9	96
Nicholson, Pa., U.S.	C10	114
Nickel Centre, On., Can.	B8	112
Nickerson, Ks., U.S.	C10	128
Nicobar Islands, is., India.	F7	46
Nicola, B.C., Can.	F10	138
Nicola, stm., B.C., Can.	F9	138
Nicolae Bălcescu, Rom.	B13	26
Nicolet, Qc., Can.	D4	110
Nicolet, Lake, l., Mi., U.S.	B5	112
Nicolet Sud-Ouest, stm., Qc., Can.	E5	110
Nicollet, Mn., U.S.	G4	118
Nicosia (Lefkosía), Cyp.	C4	58
Nicosia, Italy	G8	24
Nicoya, Golfo de, b., C.R.	H5	102
Nicoya, Península de, pen., C.R.	H5	102
Nida, Lith.	E3	10
Nida, stm., Pol.	F16	16
Nidadavole, India	C5	53
Nidzica, Pol.	C16	16
Niebüll, Ger.	B4	16
Niedere Tauern, mts., Aus.	C10	22
Niederösterreich, state, Aus.	B12	22
Niedersachsen, state, Ger.	D4	16
Niekerkshoop, S. Afr.	F6	70
Niemba, D.R.C.	F5	66
Niemodlin, Pol.	F13	16
Nienburg, Ger.	D5	16
Niers, stm., Eur.	C15	14
Niesky, Ger.	E10	16
Nieszawa, Pol.	D14	16
Nieu-Bethesda, S. Afr.	G7	70
Nieuport see Nieuwpoort, Bel.	C11	14
Nieuw Amsterdam, Sur.	B6	84
Nieuw Nickerie, Sur.	B6	84
Nieuwpoort, Bel.	C11	14
Nieuwpoort, Neth. Ant.	p22	104g
Nièvre, state, Fr.	G12	14
Nīfīsha, Egypt	H3	58
Niğde, Tur.	H15	6
Niğde, state, Tur.	A5	58
Nigel Island, i., B.C., Can.	F3	138
Nigel, S. Afr.	E9	70
Niger, ctry., Afr.	F6	64
Niger, stm., Afr.	H6	64
Niger Delta, Nig.	I6	64
Nigeria, ctry., Afr.	H6	64
Nightcaps, N.Z.	G3	80
Nighthawk, Wa., U.S.	B7	136
Nigríta, Grc.	C6	28
Nihefdāt el-Sūd, Gebel el-, mtn., Egypt	J3	58
Nihommatsu, Japan	B13	40
Nihuil, Embalse del, res., Arg.	G3	92
Niigata, Japan	B11	40
Niigata, state, Japan	B11	40
Niihama, Japan	F6	40
Ni'ihau, i., Hi., U.S.	b1	78a
Nii-jima, i., Japan	E12	40
Niitsu, Japan	B12	40
Nijar, Spain	H8	20
Nijmegen, Neth.	C14	14
Nijvel see Nivelles, Bel.	D13	14
Nikel', Russia	B14	8
Nikkō, Japan	C12	40
Nikkō-kokuritsu-kōen, p.o.i., Japan	B12	40
Nikolaevo, Russia	B12	10
Nikolaevsk-na-Amure, Russia	F17	34
Nikol'sk, Russia	C6	32
Nikol'sk, Russia	G21	8
Nikolski, Ak., U.S.	F6	140
Nikol'skij, Russia	F15	8
Nikol'skoe, Russia	E22	34
Nikol'skoe, Russia	H19	10
Nikopol', Ukr.	E4	32
Nikshahr, Iran	D9	56
Nikšić, Mont.	G5	26
Nikumaroro, at., Kir.	D9	72
Nikunau, i., Kir.	D8	72
Nil, Bahr el- see Nile, stm., Afr.	B6	62
Nil, Nahr an- see Nile, stm., Afr.	D6	62
Nila, Pulau, i., Indon.	G9	44
Nilakka, l., Fin.	E12	8
Nile, stm., Afr.	D6	62
Nile Delta, Egypt	H1	58
Niles, Il., U.S.	B10	120
Niles, Mi., U.S.	G3	112
Niles, Oh., U.S.	C5	114
Nilgiri, India	H11	54
Nilka, China	F14	32
Nilsiä, Fin.	E12	8
Nimach, India	F5	54
Nimba, Mount, mtn., Afr.	H3	64
Nîmes, Fr.	F10	18
Nimpkish Lake, l., B.C., Can.	F3	138
Nimule, Sudan	G6	62
Nindigully, Austl.	G7	76
Nine Degree Channel, strt., India	G3	46
Ninette, Mb., Can.	E14	124
Ninety Mile Beach, cst., Austl.	L6	76
Ninety Six, S.C., U.S.	B3	116
Ninfas, Punta, c., Arg.	H4	90
Ninga, Mb., Can.	E14	124
Ning'an, China	B8	38
Ningbo, China	G9	42
Ningcheng, China	C8	38
Ningde, China	H8	42
Ningdu, China	H6	42
Ningguo, China	F8	42
Ninghai, China	G9	42
Ning-hia see Ningxia, state, China	D6	36
Ninghua, China	H7	42
Ningi, Nig.	G6	64
Ningjing Shan, mts., China	F4	36
Ningming, China	J2	42
Ningnan, China	F5	36
Ningpo see Ningbo, China	G9	42
Ningqiang, China	E2	42
Ningshan, China	E3	42
Ningsia see Yinchuan, China	B2	42
Ningsia Hui see Ningxia, state, China	D6	36
Ningsia Hui Autonomous Region see Ningxia, state, China	D6	36
Ningwu, China	B4	42
Ningxia, state, China	D6	36
Ningxiang, China	G5	42
Ningyuan, China	I4	42
Ninh Binh, Viet.	B7	48
Ninh Hoa, Viet.	F9	48
Ninhue, Chile.	H1	92
Ninigo Group, is., Pap. N. Gui.	a3	79a
Ninnescah, North Fork, stm., Ks., U.S.	D10	128
Ninnescah, South Fork, stm., Ks., U.S.	D10	128
Ninohe, Japan	D14	38
Nioaque, Braz.	D5	90
Niobrara, stm., U.S.	E14	126
Nioghalvfjerdsfjorden, ice, Grnld.	B22	141
Nioki, D.R.C.	E3	66
Niono, Mali	G3	64
Nioro, Mali	F3	64
Niort, Fr.	C5	18
Niota, Tn., U.S.	B14	122
Nipāni, India	C2	53
Nipawin, Sk., Can.	E10	106
Nipe, Bahía de, b., Cuba	B10	102
Nipigon, On., Can.	B10	118
Nipigon, Lake, res., On., Can.	B10	118
Nipigon Bay, b., On., Can.	C10	118
Nipissing, Lake, l., On., Can.	B10	112
Nipomo, Ca., U.S.	H5	134
Niquelândia, Braz.	H1	88
Niquero, Cuba	B9	102
Niquivil, Arg.	E3	92
Nira, stm., India	B2	53
Nirasaki, Japan	D11	40
Nirmal, India	B4	53
Nirmali, India	E11	54
Niš, Serb.	F8	26
Nişab, Yemen	G6	56
Nišava, stm., Eur.	F9	26
Niscemi, Italy	G8	24
Nishio, Japan	E10	40
Nishiwaki, Japan	E7	40
Nisporeni, Mol.	B15	26
Nisqually, stm., Wa., U.S.	D4	136
Nisswa, Mn., U.S.	E4	118
Nitaure, Lat.	C8	10
Niterói, Braz.	L4	88
Nith, stm., On., Can.	E9	112
Nitinat Lake, l., B.C., Can.	H6	138
Nitra, Slov.	H14	16
Nitra, stm., Slov.	H14	16
Nitro, W.V., U.S.	F4	114
Niue, dep., Oc.	E10	72
Niulakita, i., Tuvalu.	E8	72
Niut, Gunung, mtn., Indon.	C6	50
Niutao, i., Tuvalu.	D8	72
Niutoushan, China	B7	38
Niutou Shan, i., China	G9	42
Niuzhuang, China	A10	42
Nive, stm., Austl.	E6	76
Nivelles, Bel.	D13	14
Nivernais, hist. reg., Fr.	G12	14
Niverville, Mb., Can.	E16	124
Nixa, Mo., U.S.	G4	120
Nixon, Nv., U.S.	D6	134
Niža, Russia	C20	8
Nizāmābād, India	B4	53
Nizām Sāgar, res., India	C3	53
Nižegorodskaja oblast', co., Russia	H21	8
Nizip, Tur.	A8	58
Nízke Tatry, Narodny Park, p.o.i., Slov.	H15	16
Nižneangarsk, Russia	E10	34
Nižneje Kujto, ozero, l., Russia	D14	8
Nižneilimsk, Russia	C18	32
Nižnekamsk, Russia	C8	32
Nižnekolymskoe, vodohraniliŝe, res., Russia	C8	32
Nižneudinsk, Russia	D17	32
Nižnevartovsk, Russia	B13	32
Nižnij Casučej, Russia	F12	34
Nižnij Kuranah, Russia	E14	34
Nižnij Novgorod (Gorki), Russia	H21	8
Nižnij Pjandž, Taj.	B10	56
Nižnij Tagil, Russia	C10	32
Nižnjaja Peša, Russia	C22	8
Nižnjaja Pojma, Russia	C17	32
Nižnjaja Tavda, Russia	C11	32
Nižnjaja Tunguska, stm., Russia	B16	32
Nizza Monferrato, Italy.	F5	22
Njandoma, Russia	F19	8
Njasviž, Bela.	G9	10
Njazidja, i., Com.	C7	68
Njombe, stm., Tan.	F7	66
Njombe, Tan.	F6	66
Njuhča, Russia	E22	8
Njuja, stm., Russia	D12	34
Njuja, stm., Russia	B20	32
Njuk, ozero, l., Russia	D14	8
Njuksenica, Russia	F21	8
Njurba, Russia	D12	34
Njuvčim, Russia	B8	32
Nkambe, Cam.	C2	66
Nkawkaw, Ghana	H4	64
Nkayi, Zimb.	D4	68
Nkhata Bay, Mwi.	C5	68
Nkhotakota, Mwi.	C5	68
Nkomi, Lagune, l., Gabon	E1	66
Nkongsamba, Cam.	D1	66
Nkululu, S. Afr.	F10	70
Nkwalendewok, Mwi.	C6	68
Nmai, stm., Mya.	C8	46
Noākhāli, Bngl.	G13	54
Noatak, Ak., U.S.	C8	140
Noatak, stm., Ak., U.S.	C8	140
Nobeoka, Japan	F4	40
Noble, Il., U.S.	F9	120
Noblesville, In., U.S.	H3	112
Noboribetsu, Japan	C14	38
Nobres, Braz.	F6	84
Nocatee, Fl., U.S.	I4	116
Nocera Inferiore, Italy	D8	24
Noce, stm., Italy.	D8	22
Nocona, Tx., U.S.	H11	128
Nocupétaro, Mex.	F8	100
Noetinger, Arg.	F6	92
Nogales, Mex.	F7	98
Nogales, Az., U.S.	L5	132
Nogara, Italy.	E8	22
Nogat, stm., Pol.	C15	16
Nogent-le-Rotrou, Fr.	F9	14
Nogent-sur-Seine, Fr.	F12	14
Noginsk, Russia	E21	10
Nogliki, Russia	F17	34
Nogoá, Arg.	F7	92
Nógrád, state, Hung.	B6	26
Noguera Pallaresa, stm., Spain	B12	20
Noguera Ribagorçana, stm., Spain.	B11	20
Nohar, India	D5	54
Noia, Spain.	B2	20
Noir, Causse, plat., Fr.	E9	18
Noir, Isla, i., Chile.	J2	90
Noire, stm., Qc., Can.	B13	112
Noirmoutier, Île de, i., Fr.	H6	14
Noirmoutier-en-l'Île, Fr.	H6	14
Nojima-zaki, c., Japan	E12	40
Nokha Mandi, India	E4	54
Nokia, Fin.	F10	8
Nokomis, Sk., Can.	C8	124
Nokomis, Il., U.S.	E8	120
Nokou, Chad	E2	62
Nokuku, Vanuatu	j16	79d
Nola, C.A.R.	D3	66
Nola, Italy.	D8	24
Nolichucky, stm., U.S.	H2	114
Nolin, stm., Ky., U.S.	G11	120
Nolin Lake, res., Ky., U.S.	G11	120
Nolinsk, Russia	C8	32
Nólsoy, i., Far. Is.	n34	8b
Nombre de Dios, Pan.	H8	102
Nome, Ak., U.S.	D6	140
Nomozaki, Japan	G2	40
Nomtsas, Nmb.	D3	70
Nonacho Lake, l., N.T., Can.	C8	106
Nonburg, Russia	D24	8
Nondalton, Ak., U.S.	D8	140
Nong'an, China	B6	38
Nong Han, Thai.	D6	48
Nong Khai, Thai.	D6	48
Nongoma, S. Afr.	E10	70
Nongpoh, India	F13	54
Nongstoin, India	F13	54
Nonoava, Mex.	B5	100
Nonogasta, Arg.	D4	92
Nonouti, at., Kir.	D8	72
Nonsuch Bay, b., Antig.	f4	105b
Nonthaburi, Thai.	F5	48
Nooksack, Wa., U.S.	B4	136
Noonkanbah, Austl.	C4	74
Noordoostpolder, reg., Neth.	B14	14
Noordpunt, c., Neth. Ant.	p21	104g
Noordwijk aan Zee, Neth.	B13	14
Noorvik, Ak., U.S.	C7	140
Nootka Island, i., B.C., Can.	G4	138
Nóqui, Ang.	B1	68
Nora, i., Erit.	D7	62
Nora Islands see Nora, is., Erit.	D7	62
Noralee, B.C., Can.	B4	138
Nora Springs, Ia., U.S.	A5	120
Norcatur, Ks., U.S.	B8	128
Norcia, Italy	H10	22
Norcross, Ga., U.S.	D14	122
Nord, state, Fr.	D12	14
Nord, Canal du, can., Fr.	D11	14
Nord, Canal du, can., Fr.	D12	14
Nordaustlandet, i., Nor.	B29	141
Nordborg, Den.	A5	16
Nordegg, Ab., Can.	D14	138
Nordegg, stm., Ab., Can.	D15	138
Norden, Ger.	C3	16
Nordenham, Ger.	C4	16
Nordenšel'da, arhipelag, is., Russia	A8	34
Norderstedt, Ger.	C6	16
Nordfjord, b., Nor.	F1	8
Nordfold, Nor.	C6	8
Nordgrønland (Avanersuaq), state, Grnld.	B15	141
Nordhausen, Ger.	E6	16
Nordhorn, Ger.	D2	16
Nordjylland, state, Den.	H4	8
Nordkapp (North Cape), c., Nor.	A11	8
Nordkinnhalvøya, pen., Nor.	A12	8
Nordland, state, Nor.	C6	8
Nördlingen, Ger.	H6	16
Nordmaling, Swe.	E8	8
Nordman, Id., U.S.	B10	136
Nordostrundingen, c., Grnld.	A23	141
Nord-Ostsee-Kanal (Kiel Canal), can., Ger.	B5	16
Nordrhein-Westfalen, state, Ger.	E4	16
Nordstrand, i., Ger.	B4	16
Nord-Trøndelag, state, Nor.	D5	8
Nordvik, Russia	B11	34
Norfolk, Ne., U.S.	E15	126
Norfolk, Va., U.S.	H9	114
Norfolk Island, dep., Oc.	x25	78i
Norfolk Island National Park, p.o.i., Norf. I.	y25	78i
Norfolk Ridge, unds.	L19	142
Norfork Lake, res., U.S.	H5	120
Norikura-dake, vol., Japan	C10	40
Noril'sk, Russia	C6	34
Norlina, N.C., U.S.	H7	114
Normal, Il., U.S.	D9	120
Norman, Ar., U.S.	C5	122
Norman, Ok., U.S.	F11	128
Norman, stm., Austl.	B3	76
Norman, Lake, res., N.C., U.S.	A4	116
Normanby Island, i., Pap. N. Gui.	c5	79a
Normandes, Îles see Channel Islands, is., Eur.	L10	12
Normandie, hist. reg., Fr.	F8	14
Normandie, Collines de, hills, Fr.	F8	14
Normandin, Qc., Can.	B4	110
Normandy see Normandie, hist. reg., Fr.	F8	14
Normandy, Hills of see Normandie, Collines de, hills, Fr.	F8	14
Normangee, Tx., U.S.	F2	122
Norman Park, Ga., U.S.	E2	116
Normanton, Austl.	B3	76
Norman Wells, N.T., Can.	B5	106
Norogachi, Mex.	B5	100
Norquay, Sk., Can.	C11	124
Norquincó, Arg.	H2	90
Norra Storfjället, mtn., Swe.	D6	8
Norrbotten, state, Swe.	C8	8
Norresundby, Den.	H3	8
Norridgewock, Me., U.S.	F6	110
Norris, Tn., U.S.	H1	114
Norris Lake, res., Tn., U.S.	H2	114
Norristown, Pa., U.S.	D10	114
Norrköping, Swe.	G7	8
Norrtälje, Swe.	G8	8
Norseman, Austl.	F4	74
Norsjö, Swe.	D8	8
Norsk, Russia	F16	34
Norske Øer, is., Grnld.	B22	141
Norsup, Vanuatu	k16	79d
Norte, Cabo, c., Braz.	C8	84
Norte, Serra do, plat., Braz.	F6	84
Norte de Santander, state, Col.	D5	86
Northampton, Austl.	E2	74
Northampton, Eng., U.K.	I12	12
Northampton, Ma., U.S.	B13	114
North Andaman, i., India	F7	46
North Atlanta, Ga., U.S.	C1	116
North Augusta, S.C., U.S.	C4	116
North Aulatsivik Island, i., Nf., Can.	F13	141
North Baltimore, Oh., U.S.	C2	114
North Battleford, Sk., Can.	B5	124
North Bay, Pa., Can.	B10	112
North Bay, B.C., Can.	G9	138
North Bend, Or., U.S.	G2	136
North Bend, Ne., U.S.	J2	118
North Bennington, Vt., U.S.	B12	114
North Berwick, Scot., U.K.	E10	12
North Berwick, Me., U.S.	G6	110
North Borneo see Sabah, state, Malay.	H1	52
North Bourke, Austl.	H5	76
North Branch, Mi., U.S.	E6	112
North Caicos, i., T./C. Is.	B11	102
North Canadian, stm., Ok., U.S.	F12	128
North Canton, Ga., U.S.	C14	122
North Canton, Oh., U.S.	D4	114
North Cape, c., P.E., Can.	C13	110
North Cape see Nordkapp, c., Nor.	A11	8
North Cape, c., N.Z.	B5	80
North Caribou Lake, l., On., Can.	E12	106
North Carolina, state, U.S.	D11	108
North Cascades National Park, p.o.i., Wa., U.S.	B5	136
North Channel, strt., On., Can.	B7	112
North Channel, strt., U.K.	F7	12
North Charleston, S.C., U.S.	D5	116
North Chicago, Il., U.S.	F2	112
North Chungcheong see Ch'ungch'ŏng-bukto, state, Kor., S.	B1	40
North College Hill, Oh., U.S.	F13	120
North Collins, N.Y., U.S.	F11	112
North Concho, stm., Tx., U.S.	C7	130
North Conway, N.H., U.S.	F5	110
North Crossett, Ar., U.S.	D6	122
North Cyprus see Cyprus, North, ctry., Asia.	C4	58
North Dakota, state, U.S.	G13	124
North Downs, hills, Eng., U.K.	J13	12
North Eagle Butte, S.D., U.S.	B11	126
North East, Md., U.S.	E9	114
North-East, state, Bots.	B8	70
Northeast Cape, Ak., U.S.	D6	140
Northeast Cape Fear, stm., N.C., U.S.	B8	116
North East Point, c., Bah.	A11	102
Northeast Providence Channel, strt., Bah.	B9	96
North English, Ia., U.S.	C5	120
Northern see HaZafon, state, Isr.	F6	58
Northern Cape, state, S. Afr.	F5	70
Northern Cook Islands, is., Cook Is.	E10	72
Northern Division, state, Fiji.	p20	79e
Northern Dvina see Severnaja Dvina, stm., Russia	E19	8
Northern Indian Lake, l., Mb., Can.	D11	106
Northern Ireland, state, U.K.	G6	12
Northern Mariana Islands, dep., Oc.	B6	72
Northern Province, state, S. Afr.	C9	70
Northern Sporades see Vóreioi Sporádes, is., Grc.	D6	28
Northern Territory, state, Austl.	D6	74
North Fabius, stm., U.S.	E5	120
Northfield, Mn., U.S.	G5	118
Northfield, Vt., U.S.	F4	110
North Fiji Basin, unds.	K20	142
North Flinders Range, mts., Austl.	H2	76
North Fond du Lac, Wi., U.S.	H10	118
North Foreland, c., Eng., U.K.	J14	12
North Fork, Ca., U.S.	F6	134
North Fork, S.C., U.S.	H5	120
North Fork Ft. Myers, Fl., U.S.	J4	116
North Frisian Islands, is., Eur.	B3	16
North Gulfport, Ms., U.S.	G9	122
North Gyeongsang see Kyŏngsang-bukto, state, Kor., S.	C1	40
North Henik Lake, l., Nu., Can.	C11	106
North Hero, Vt., U.S.	F3	110
North Highlands, Ca., U.S.	E4	134
North Horr, Kenya	D7	66
North Island, i., N.Z.	C5	80
North Judson, In., U.S.	G3	112
North Kent Island, i., Nu., Can.	B7	141
North Kingsville, Oh., U.S.	C5	114
North Knife Lake, l., Mb., Can.	D11	106
North Korea see Korea, North, ctry., Asia.	D7	38
North Lakhimpur, India	C7	46
North La Veta Pass, p., Co., U.S.	D3	128
North Little Rock, Ar., U.S.	C6	122
North Llano, stm., Tx., U.S.	D8	130
North Logan, Ut., U.S.	B5	132
North Loup, Ne., U.S.	F14	126
North Loup, stm., Ne., U.S.	F14	126
North Magnetic Pole, misc. cult.	A3	141
North Mamm Peak, mtn., Co., U.S.	D9	132
North Manchester, In., U.S.	H4	112
North Manitou Island, i., Mi., U.S.	C3	112
North Mankato, Mn., U.S.	G4	118
North Miami, Fl., U.S.	K5	116
North Miami Beach, Fl., U.S.	K5	116
North Milk (Milk, North Fork), stm., N.A.	B13	136
North Myrtle Beach, S.C., U.S.	C7	116
North New River Canal, can., Fl., U.S.	J5	116
North Newton, Ks., U.S.	C11	128
North Ossetia see Severnaja Osetija, state, Russia	F6	32
North Palisade, mtn., Ca., U.S.	F7	134
North Palm Beach, Fl., U.S.	J5	116
North Park, Il., U.S.	B8	120
North Plains, pl., N.M., U.S.	I8	132
North Platte, Ne., U.S.	F12	126
North Platte, stm., U.S.	F11	126
North Pole, misc. cult.	A4	94
Northport, Al., U.S.	D11	122

Name Map Ref. Page

Northport, Mi., U.S. C4 112
Northport, Wa., U.S. B9 136
North Portal, Sk., Can. E11 124
North Raccoon, stm., Ia., U.S. C3 120
North Rhine-Westphalia see Nordrhein-Westfalen, state, Ger. E4 16
North Richland Hills, Tx., U.S. B10 130
North Rim, Az., U.S. G4 132
North Ronaldsay, i., Scot., U.K. B10 12
North Rustico, P.E., Can. D13 110
North Salt Lake, Ut., U.S. C5 132
North Saskatchewan, stm., Can. E9 106
North Sea, s., Eur. D9 6
North Shoal Lake, l., Mb., Can. D16 124
North Shore City, N.Z. C6 80
North Shoshone Peak, mtn., Nv., U.S. D8 134
North Siberain Lowland see Severo-Sibirskaja nizmennost', pl., Russia B6 34
North Skunk, stm., Ia., U.S. C5 120
North Solitary Island, i., Austl. G9 76
North Solomons, state, Pap. N. Gui. d7 79b
North Spicer Island, i., Nu., Can. B15 106
North Stradbroke Island, i., Austl. F9 76
North Sumatra see Sumatera Utara, state, Indon. K4 48
North Sydney, N.S., Can. D16 110
North Taranaki Bight, b., N.Z. D5 80
North Terre Haute, In., U.S. E10 120
North Thompson, stm., B.C., Can. F10 138
North Troy, Vt., U.S. F4 110
North Tunica, Ms., U.S. C8 122
North Uist, i., Scot., U.K. D5 12
Northumberland Isles, is., Austl. C7 76
Northumberland National Park, p.o.i., Eng., U.K. F10 12
Northumberland Strait, strt., Can. D12 110
North Umpqua, stm., Or., U.S. G4 136
North Vancouver, B.C., Can. G7 138
North Vietnam see Vietnam, ctry., Asia E9 48
Northville, N.Y., U.S. G2 110
North-West, state, S. Afr. E7 70
North West Bluff, c., Monts. D3 105a
North West Cape, c., Austl. D2 74
North-West Frontier, state, Pak. A4 54
Northwest Miramichi, stm., N.B., Can. C10 110
Northwest Pacific Basin, unds. F18 142
Northwest Providence Channel, strt., Bah. m17 104f
Northwest Territories, state, Can. C6 106
North Wichita, stm., Tx., U.S. H9 128
North Wilkesboro, N.C., U.S. H4 114
North Windham, Me., U.S. G6 110
Northwood, Ia., U.S. H5 118
Northwood, N.D., U.S. G16 124
North York, ngh., On., Can. E10 112
North York Moors National Park, p.o.i., Eng., U.K. G12 12
North Zulch, Tx., U.S. G2 122
Norton, Ks., U.S. B9 128
Norton, Va., U.S. H3 114
Norton Shores, Mi., U.S. E3 112
Norton Sound, strt., Ak., U.S. D6 140
Nortonville, Ks., U.S. E2 120
Norvegia, Cape, c., Ant. C3 81
Norwalk, Ct., U.S. C12 114
Norwalk, Ia., U.S. C4 120
Norwalk, Oh., U.S. C3 114
Norway, Ia., U.S. C6 120
Norway, Me., U.S. F6 110
Norway, ctry., Eur. E3 8
Norway Bay, b., Nu., Can. A10 106
Norway House, Mb., Can. E11 106
Norwegian Basin, unds. B13 144
Norwegian Sea, s., Eur. C3 30
Norwich, On., Can. E9 112
Norwich, Eng., U.K. I14 12
Norwich, Ct., U.S. C13 114
Norwich, N.Y., U.S. B10 114
Norwood, On., Can. D11 112
Norwood, Co., U.S. E8 132
Norwood, Ma., U.S. B14 114
Norwood, Mn., U.S. G5 118
Norwood, N.C., U.S. A5 116
Norwood, Oh., U.S. E1 114
Noshiro, Japan D13 38
Nosop (Nossob), stm., Afr. D5 70
Nosovaja, Russia B26 8
Nosovščina, Russia E17 8
Nossa Senhora das Dores, Braz. F7 88
Nossob (Nosop), stm., Afr. D5 70
Nosy-Varika, Madag. E8 68
Notasulga, Al., U.S. E13 122
Notch Hill, B.C., Can. F11 138
Noteć, stm., Pol. D11 16
Nótio Aigaío, state, Grc. G9 28
Noto, Italy H9 24
Noto, Japan B10 40
Noto, Golfo di, b., Italy H9 24
Noto-hantō, pen., Japan B10 40
Notozero, ozero, l., Russia C14 8
Notre-Dame, N.B., Can. D12 110
Notre-Dame, Monts, mts., Qc., Can. B9 110
Notre Dame Bay, b., Nf., Can. j22 107a
Notre-Dame-du-Laus, Qc., Can. B14 112
Notrees, Tx., U.S. C5 130
Nottawasaga, stm., On., Can. D10 112
Nottawasaga Bay, b., On., Can. D9 112
Nottaway, stm., Qc., Can. E15 106
Nottingham, Eng., U.K. I11 12
Nottingham Island, i., Nu., Can. C15 106
Nottoway, stm., Va., U.S. H8 114
Notukeu Creek, stm., Sk., Can. E6 124
Notwane, stm., Afr. D8 70
Nouâdhibou, Maur. E1 64
Nouâdhibou, Râs, c., Afr. E1 64
Nouakchott, Maur. F1 64
Nouâmghâr, Maur. F1 64
Nouméa, N. Cal. n16 79d
Noupoort, S. Afr. G7 70
Nouveau-Québec, Cratère du, crat., Qc., Can. C16 106
Nouvelle, Qc., Can. B10 110
Nouvelle-Calédonie (New Caledonia), i., N. Cal. m15 79d
Nouvelle-Écosse see Nova Scotia, state, Can. G18 106
Nouvelle-France, Cap de, c., Qc., Can. C16 106
Nova Andradina, Braz. D6 90
Nová Baňa, Slov. H14 16
Nova Caipemba, Ang. B1 68
Nova Era, Braz. J4 88
Nova Friburgo, Braz. L4 88
Nova Gorica, Slvn. D10 22
Nova Gradiška, Cro. E14 22
Nova Granada, Braz. K1 88
Nova Iguaçu, Braz. L4 88
Novaja Ladoga, Russia F14 8
Novaja Maluksa, Russia A14 10
Novaja Sibir', ostrov, i., Russia B19 34
Novaja Zemlja, is., Russia B8 30
Nova Kakhovka, Ukr. E4 32
Nova Lamego, Gui.-B. G2 64
Nova Lima, Braz. K4 88
Novalukoml', Bela. F11 10
Nova Mambone, Moz. B12 70
Nova Olinda, Braz. D6 88
Nová Paka, Czech Rep. F11 16
Nova Ponte, Braz. J2 88
Nova Prata, Braz. D12 92
Novara, Italy E5 22
Nova Roma, Braz. G2 88
Nova Russas, Braz. C5 88
Nova Scotia, state, Can. G18 106
Nova Soure, Braz. F6 88
Novato, Ca., U.S. E3 134
Nova Venécia, Braz. J5 88
Nova Vida, Braz. F5 84
Novaya Kazanka, Kaz. E7 32
Novaya Zemlya see Novaja Zemlja, is., Russia B8 30
Nova Zagora, Blg. G13 26
Nové Hrady, Czech Rep. H10 16
Novelda, Spain F10 20
Nové Město nad Váhom, Slov. H13 16
Nové Město na Moravě, Czech Rep. G12 16
Nové Zámky, Slov. I14 16
Novgorod, Russia B14 10
Novgorodskaja oblast', co., Russia B15 10
Novi Bečej, Serb. D7 26
Novi Beograd, Serb. E7 26
Novice, Tx., U.S. C8 130
Novigrad, Cro. E10 22
Novikovo, Russia G17 34
Novi Ligure, Italy F5 22
Novinger, Mo., U.S. D5 120
Novi Pazar, Blg. F14 26
Novi Pazar, Serb. F7 26
Novi Sad, Serb. D6 26
Novo, Lago, l., Braz. C7 84
Novo Airão, Braz. H11 86
Novoaltajsk, Russia D14 32
Novo Aripuanã, Braz. E5 84
Novočerkassk, Russia E6 32
Novodvinsk, Russia D19 8
Novoe, Russia C11 32
Novoenisejsk, Russia C16 32
Novo Hamburgo, Braz. D12 92
Novo Horizonte, Braz. K1 88
Novoizborsk, Russia C10 10
Novokačalinsk, Russia B10 38
Novokaširsk, Russia F21 10
Novokazalinsk see Zhangaqazaly, Kaz. E10 32
Novokujbyševsk, Russia D7 32
Novokuzneck, Russia D15 32
Novolazarevskaja, sci., Ant. C6 81
Novo Mesto, Slvn. E12 22
Novomoskovsk (Stalinogorsk), Russia F21 10
Novo Oriente, Braz. C5 88
Novopetrovskoe, Russia E19 10
Novorossijsk, Russia F5 32
Novorybnoe, Russia B10 34
Novoržev, Russia C12 10
Novošahtinsk, Russia E6 32
Novosëlovo, Russia E7 34
Novoselytsia, Ukr. A13 26
Novosergievka, Russia D8 32
Novosibirsk, Russia C14 32
Novosibirskie ostrova, is., Russia A18 34
Novosibirskoe vodohranilišče, res., Russia D14 32
Novosil's'ke, Ukr. D15 26
Novosokol'niki, Russia D12 10
Novotroick, Russia D9 32
Novouzensk, Russia D7 32
Novovjatsk, Russia C7 32
Novozavidovskij, Russia D19 10
Novozybkov, Russia H14 10
Novska, Cro. E13 22
Nový Bohumín, Czech Rep. G14 16
Nový Bor, Czech Rep. F10 16
Novyja Valosavičy, Bela. F11 10
Nový Jičín, Czech Rep. G13 16
Novyj Nekouz, Russia C20 10
Novyj Port, Russia A12 32
Novyj Uzen' see Zhangaözen, Kaz. F8 32
Novyj Vasjugan, Russia C13 32
Novy Pahost, Bela. E10 10
Nowa Ruda, Pol. F12 16
Nowa Sól, Pol. E11 16
Nowe, Pol. C14 16
Nowe Miasto nad Pilicą, Pol. E16 16
Nowendoc, Austl. H8 76
Nowgong, India F7 54
Nowitna, stm., Ak., U.S. D9 140
Nowogard, Pol. C11 16
Nowogrodziec, Pol. E11 16
Nowood, stm., Wy., U.S. C5 126
Nowra, Austl. J8 76
Nowrangapur, India B6 53
Nowshāk, mtn., Asia B11 56
Nowshera, Pak. C11 56
Nowshera, Pak. B4 54
Nowy Dwór Mazowiecki, Pol. D16 16
Nowy Sącz, Pol. G16 16
Nowy Sącz, state, Pol. G16 16
Nowy Staw, Pol. B15 16
Nowy Targ, Pol. G15 16
Noxapater, Ms., U.S. E9 122
Noxen, Pa., U.S. C9 114
Noxon, Mt., U.S. B11 136
Noxubee, stm., U.S. D10 122
Noy, stm., Laos D7 48
Noya see Noia, Spain B2 20
Noyant, Fr. G9 14
Noyon, Fr. E11 14
Nsanje, Mwi. D6 68
Nsawam, Ghana H4 64
Nsok, Eq. Gui. I7 64
Nsukka, Nig. H6 64
Nsuta, Ghana H4 64
Ntwetwe Pan, pl., Bots. B7 70
Nu see Salween, stm., Asia C8 46
Nūbah, Jibāl an-, mts., Sudan E6 62
Nubian Desert, des., Sudan C6 62
Ñuble, stm., Chile H2 92
Nucet, Rom. C9 26
Nudol'-Šarino, Russia D19 10
Nueces, stm., Tx., U.S. G10 130
Nueces Plains, pl., Tx., U.S. F8 130
Nueltin Lake, l., Can. C11 106
Nuestra Señora de Talavera, Arg. B6 92
Nueva, Isla, i., Chile K3 90
Nueva Antioquia, Col. D7 86
Nueva Ciudad Guerrero, Mex. B9 100
Nueva Esparta, state, Ven. B9 86
Nueva Galia, Arg. G5 92
Nueva Germania, Para. A9 92
Nueva Gerona, Cuba B6 102
Nueva Imperial, Chile G2 90
Nueva Italia de Ruiz, Mex. F7 100
Nueva Loja, Ec. G3 86
Nueva Palmira, Ur. F8 92
Nueva Rosita, Mex. A8 100
Nueva San Salvador, El Sal. F3 102
Nueva Toltén, Chile G2 90
Nueve, Canal Numero, can., Arg. H8 92
Nueve de Julio, Arg. G7 92
Nuevitas, Cuba B9 102
Nuevo, Bajo, unds., Col. E8 102
Nuevo, Cayo, i., Mex. E12 100
Nuevo, Golfo, b., Arg. H4 90
Nuevo Camarón, Mex. G8 130
Nuevo Casas Grandes, Mex. F9 98
Nuevo Delicias, Mex. B7 100
Nuevo Laredo, Mex. B9 100
Nuevo León, state, Mex. B8 100
Nuevo Primero de Mayo, Mex. H9 130
Nuevo Progreso, Mex. F12 100
Nuevo Rocafuerte, Ec. H4 86
Nuevo San Lucas, Mex. F2 130
Nûgssuaq, pen., Grnld. C15 141
Nugu, res., India F3 53
Nui, at., Tuvalu D8 72
Nuku'alofa, Tonga n14 78e
Nukuhu, Pap. N. Gui. b4 79a
Nukus, Uzb. F9 32
Nul, Vanuatu k17 79d
Nulato, Ak., U.S. D8 140
Nullagine, Austl. D4 74
Nullarbor, Austl. F6 74
Nullarbor Plain, pl., Austl. F5 74
Numan, Nig. H7 64
Numancia (Numantia), sci., Spain C8 20
Numantia see Numancia, sci., Spain C8 20
Numata, Japan C12 40
Numazu, Japan D11 40
Numfoor, Pulau, i., Indon. F10 44
Numto, Russia B12 32
Nunavut, state, Can. B12 106
Nunda, N.Y., U.S. B7 114
Nuneaton, Eng., U.K. I11 12
Nuñez, Cape, c., S. Geor. J9 90
Nunivak Island, i., Ak., U.S. D6 140
Nunjiang, China B10 36
Nunkun, mtn., India A6 54
Nunnelly, Tn., U.S. I10 120
Nuomin, stm., China B10 36
Nuoro, Italy D3 24
Nuquí, Col. E3 86
Nura, Kaz. E12 32
Nura, stm., Kaz. E12 32
Nur Dağları, mts., Tur. B7 58
Nuremberg see Nürnberg, Ger. G6 16
Nuremburg see Nürnberg, Ger. G6 16
Nuriootpa, Austl. J2 76
Nürnberg (Nuremberg), Ger. G6 16
Nūrpur, India B5 54
Nürtingen, Ger. H5 16
Nusa Tenggara Barat, state, Indon. G10 50
Nusa Tenggara Timur, state, Indon. H12 50
Nuṣayrīyah, Jabal an-, mts., Syria C7 58
Nu Shan, mts., China F4 36
Nüshan Hu, l., China E8 42
Nushki, Pak. D10 56
Nutrioso, Az., U.S. J7 132
Nutter Fort, W.V., U.S. E5 114
Nuuk see Godthåb, Grnld. E15 141
Nuwerus, S. Afr. G4 70
Nuweveldberge, mts., S. Afr. H5 70
Nūzvīd, India C5 53
Nyabéssan, Cam. D2 66
Nyabing, Austl. F3 74
Nyack, N.Y., U.S. C12 114
Nyahanga, Tan. E6 66
Nyainqêntanglha Feng, mtn., China C13 54
Nyainqêntanglha Shan, mts., China C6 46
Nyainrong, China B14 54
Nyakanazi, Tan. E6 66
Nyala, Sudan E5 62
Nyalam, China D10 54
Nyamlell, Sudan F5 62
Nyamtumbo, Tan. G7 66
Nyang, stm., China D14 54
Nyanga, stm., Afr. J7 64
Nyasa, Lake, l., Afr. C5 68
Nyaunglebin, Mya. C3 48
Nyboe Land, reg., Grnld. A14 141
Nyborg, Den. I4 8
Nybro, Swe. H6 8
Nyda, Russia A12 32
Nyêmo, China C7 46
Nyeri, Kenya E7 66
Nyerol, Sudan F6 62
Nyimba, Zam. C5 68
Nyingchi, China F3 36
Nyírbátor, Hung. B9 26
Nyíregyháza, Hung. B8 26
Nykøbing, Den. I4 8
Nyköping, Swe. G7 8
Nylstroom, S. Afr. D9 70
Nymboida, stm., Austl. G9 76
Nymburk, Czech Rep. F11 16
Nynäshamn, Swe. G7 8
Nyngan, Austl. H6 76
Nyon, Switz. D3 22
Nyons, Fr. E11 18
Nýrsko, Czech Rep. G9 16
Nyš, Russia F17 34
Nysa, Pol. F13 16
Nysa Kłodzka, stm., Pol. F12 16
Nysa Łużycka (Lausitzer Neisse), stm., Eur. E10 16
Nyslott see Savonlinna, Fin. F13 8
Nysted, Den. B7 16
Nyunzu, D.R.C. F5 66
Nyūzen, Japan C10 40
Nyvrovo, Russia F17 34
Nzébéla, Gui. H3 64
Nzérékoré, Gui. H3 64
N'zeto, Ang. B1 68
Nzwani, i., Com. C7 68

O

Oahe, Lake, res., U.S. A12 126
Oahe Dam, dam, S.D., U.S. C12 126
O'ahu, i., Hi., U.S. b4 78a
Oakbank, Austl. I3 76
Oak Bay, B.C., Can. H7 138
Oak Bluffs, Ma., U.S. C15 114
Oakburn, Mb., Can. D13 124
Oak City, N.C., U.S. I8 114
Oak City, Ut., U.S. D4 132
Oakdale, Ca., U.S. F5 134
Oakdale, La., U.S. G6 122
Oakdale, Ne., U.S. E14 126
Oakes, N.D., U.S. A14 126
Oakesdale, Wa., U.S. C9 136
Oakey, Austl. F8 76
Oakfield, Me., U.S. D8 110
Oakfield, Wi., U.S. H10 118
Oak Grove, La., U.S. E7 122
Oak Harbor, Wa., U.S. B4 136
Oak Hill, Fl., U.S. H5 116
Oak Hill, Oh., U.S. F3 114
Oak Hill, W.V., U.S. G4 114
Oakhurst, Ca., U.S. F6 134
Oak Knolls, Ca., U.S. I5 134
Oak Lake, Mb., Can. E13 124
Oak Lake, l., Mb., Can. E13 124
Oak Lake, l., On., Can. A5 118
Oakland, Ca., U.S. F3 134
Oakland, Ia., U.S. C2 120
Oakland, Md., U.S. E6 114
Oakland, Me., U.S. F7 110
Oakland, Ms., U.S. C9 122
Oakland, Ne., U.S. C1 120
Oakland, Or., U.S. G3 136
Oakland City, In., U.S. F10 120
Oakland Park, Fl., U.S. J5 116
Oak Lawn, Il., U.S. G2 112
Oakley, Id., U.S. H13 136
Oakley, Ks., U.S. B8 128
Oakman, Al., U.S. D11 122
Oakohay Creek, stm., Ms., U.S. F9 122
Oakover, stm., Austl. D4 74
Oak Park, Il., U.S. G2 112
Oak Ridge, Tn., U.S. H1 114
Oak Ridge National Laboratory, sci., Tn., U.S. H1 114
Oaktown, In., U.S. F10 120
Oak View, Ca., U.S. I6 134
Oakville, Mb., Can. E15 124
Oakville, On., Can. E10 112
Oakwood, Oh., U.S. C1 114
Oamaru, N.Z. G4 80
Oancea, Rom. D14 26
Ōarai, Japan C13 40
Oatman, Az., U.S. H2 132
Oaxaca, state, Mex. G10 100
Oaxaca de Juárez, Mex. G10 100
Ob', stm., Russia A11 32
Obabika Lake, l., On., Can. A9 112
Obaghan, stm., Kaz. D10 32
Obal', stm., Bela. E12 10
Obala, Cam. D2 66
Obama, Japan D8 40
Obama, Japan G3 40
Oban, Austl. C2 76
Oban, Scot., U.K. E7 12
Obanazawa, Japan A13 40
O Barco de Valdeorras, Spain B3 20
Ob Bay see Obskaja guba, b., Russia A12 32
Obed, Ab., Can. C13 138
Obeliai, Lith. E8 10
Oberá, Arg. C10 92
Oberhausen, Ger. E2 16
Oberlin, La., U.S. G6 122
Oberlin, Oh., U.S. C3 114
Oberösterreich, state, Aus. B10 22
Oberpullendorf, Aus. C13 22
Oberursel, Ger. F4 16
Oberviechtach, Ger. G8 16
Ob Gulf see Obskaja guba, b., Russia A12 32
Obi, Kepulauan, is., Indon. F8 44
Obi, Pulau, i., Indon. F8 44
Obi, Selat, strt., Indon. F8 44
Óbidos, Braz. D6 84
Obihiro, Japan C15 38
Obi Islands see Obi, Kepulauan, is., Indon. F8 44
Obion, Tn., U.S. H8 120
Obion, stm., Tn., U.S. H8 120
Obion, Middle Fork, stm., Tn., U.S. H9 120
Oblačnaja, gora, mtn., Russia C11 38
Oblong, Il., U.S. F9 120
Obluče, Russia G15 34
Obninsk, Russia E19 10
Obnova, Blg. F12 26
Obo, C.A.R. C5 66
Obock, Dji. E8 62
Obokote, D.R.C. E5 66
Obozërskij, Russia E19 8
O'Brien, Or., U.S. A2 134
Obrovac, Cro. F12 22
Obša, stm., Russia E16 10
Obščij syrt, mts., Eur. D8 32
Obskaja guba, b., Russia A12 32
Obuasi, Ghana H4 64
Obudu, Nig. H6 64
Ocala, Fl., U.S. G3 116
Ocamo, stm., Ven. F9 86
Ocampo, Mex. A4 100
Ocaña, Col. C5 86
Ocaña, Spain E7 20
Occhito, Lago di, res., Italy C8 24
Occidental, Cordillera, mts., Col. E3 86
Oceana, W.V., U.S. G4 114
Ocean Cape, c., Ak., U.S. E12 140
Ocean City, Md., U.S. F10 114
Ocean City, N.J., U.S. E11 114
Ocean Falls, B.C., Can. D3 138
Ocean Island see Banaba, i., Kir. D7 72
Ocean Park, Wa., U.S. D2 136
Oceanside, Ca., U.S. J8 134
Ocean Springs, Ms., U.S. G10 122
Ocheyedan, Ia., U.S. H3 118
Ōchi, Japan E7 40
Ochlocknee, Ga., U.S. F1 116
Ochlockonee, stm., U.S. G14 122
Ocho Rios, Jam. i13 104d
Ochsenfurt, Ger. G5 16
Ocilla, Ga., U.S. E2 116
Ockelbo, Swe. F7 8
Ocmulgee National Monument, p.o.i., Ga., U.S. D2 116
Ocnița, Mol. A14 26
Ocoa, Bahía de, b., Dom. Rep. C12 102
Ocoee, Fl., U.S. H4 116
Ocoña, stm., Peru G3 84
Oconee, stm., Ga., U.S. D3 116
Oconee, Lake, res., Ga., U.S. C2 116
Oconomowoc, Wi., U.S. A9 120
Oconto, Wi., U.S. D2 112
Oconto Falls, Wi., U.S. D1 112
Ocosingo, Mex. G12 100
Ocotal, Nic. F4 102
Ocotes, Cerro, mtn., Mex. B5 100
Ocotlán, Mex. E7 100
Ocotlán de Morelos, Mex. G10 100
Ocozocuautla, Mex. G12 100
Ocracoke Island, i., N.C., U.S. A10 116
Ocumare del Tuy, Ven. B8 86
Oda, Ghana H4 64
Ōda, Japan D5 40
Oda, Jabal, mtn., Sudan C7 62
Odaka, Japan B14 40
Ōdate, Japan D14 38
Odawara, Japan D12 40
Odebolt, Ia., U.S. B2 120
Odell, Il., U.S. D9 120
Odell, Tx., U.S. G9 128
Odem, Tx., U.S. G10 130
Odemira, Port. G2 20
Ödemiș, Tur. E10 28
Odendaalsrus, S. Afr. E8 70
Odense, Den. I3 8
Odenwald, mts., Ger. G4 16
Oder (Odra), stm., Eur. D10 16
Oderzo, Italy E9 22
Odesa, Ukr. C17 26
Odesa, co., Ukr. C16 26
Odessa see Odesa, Ukr. C17 26
Odessa, Mo., U.S. F3 120
Odessa, Tx., U.S. C5 130
Odessa, Wa., U.S. C8 136
Odesskoe, Russia D12 32
Odiel, stm., Spain G4 20
Odienné, C. Iv. H3 64
Odin, Mount, mtn., B.C., Can. F12 138
Odincovo, Russia E20 10
Odobești, Rom. D13 26
Odolanów, Pol. E13 16
Odon, In., U.S. F11 120
O'Donnell, Tx., U.S. B6 130
Odorheiu Secuiesc, Rom. C12 26
Odra (Oder), stm., Eur. D10 16
Odrzywół, Pol. E16 16
Odum, Ga., U.S. E3 116
Odžaci, Serb. D6 26
Oebisfelde, Ger. D6 16
Oeiras, Braz. D4 88
Oelsnitz, Ger. F8 16
Oelwein, Ia., U.S. B6 120
Oenpelli, Austl. B6 74
Oetz, Aus. C7 22
O'Fallon, Mo., U.S. F7 120
Ofanto, stm., Italy D9 24
Ofaqim, Isr. G5 58
Offa, Nig. H5 64
Offaly, state, Ire. H5 12
Offenbach am Main, Ger. F4 16
Offenburg, Ger. H3 16
Oficina Alemania, Chile B3 92
Ofu, i., Am. Sam. h13 79c
Ogaden, reg., Afr. F8 62
Ōgaki, Japan D9 40
Ogallala, Ne., U.S. F11 126
Ogan, stm., Indon. E4 50
Ogasawara-guntō, is., Japan G18 30
Ogatsu, Japan A14 40
Ogawa, Japan G3 40
Ogbomosho, Nig. H5 64
Ogden, Ks., U.S. B12 128
Ogden, Ut., U.S. B5 132
Ogdensburg, N.Y., U.S. D14 112
Ogeechee, stm., Ga., U.S. D4 116
Ogema, Sk., Can. E8 124
Ogidaki Mountain, hill, On., Can. A6 112
Ogilvie, Mn., U.S. F5 118
Ogilvie Mountains, mts., Yk., Can. C3 106
Oglesby, Il., U.S. C8 120
Oglethorpe, Ga., U.S. D1 116
Ogliastra, reg., Italy E3 24
Oglio, stm., Italy E6 22
Ogmore, Austl. D7 76
Ognon, stm., Fr. G15 14
Ogoja, Nig. H6 64
Ogoki, stm., On., Can. E13 106
Ogooué, stm., Afr. I7 64
Ogōri, Japan E4 40
Ogosta, stm., Blg. F10 26
Ogre, Lat. D7 10
Ogre, stm., Lat. D8 10
O Grove, Spain B2 20
Ogulin, Cro. E12 22
Ogunquit, Me., U.S. G6 110
Ogurdžaly, ostrov, i., Turkmen. B7 56
Oğuzeli, Tur. B8 58
Oha, Russia F17 34
Ohanet, Alg. D6 64
Ōhara, Japan D13 40
O'Higgins, Cabo, c., Chile e30 78l
O'Higgins, Lago (San Martín, Lago), l., S.A. I2 90
Ohio, state, U.S. D3 114
Ohio, stm., U.S. G9 120
Ohio Peak, mtn., Co., U.S. E9 132
'Ohonua, Tonga o15 78e
Ohoopee, stm., Ga., U.S. D3 116
Ohota, stm., Russia E17 34
Ohotsk, Russia E17 34
Ohře, stm., Eur. F9 16
Ohrid, Mac. B3 28
Ohrid, Lake, l., Eur. D14 24
Ohrigstad, S. Afr. D10 70
Öhringen, Ger. G5 16
Ohuira, Bahía de, l., Mex. C4 100
Ōi, stm., Japan E11 40
Oiapoque, Braz. C7 84
Oiapoque (Oyapok), stm., S.A. C7 84
Oies, Île aux, i., Qc., Can. C6 110
Oil Center, N.M., U.S. B4 130
Oil City, La., U.S. E4 122
Oil City, Pa., U.S. C6 114
Oildale, Ca., U.S. H7 134
Oilton, Ok., U.S. A2 122
Oilton, Tx., U.S. G9 130
Oil Trough, Ar., U.S. B7 122
Oise, state, Fr. E11 14
Oise, stm., Eur. E11 14
Oistins, Barb. n8 105d
Ōita, Japan F4 40
Ōita, state, Japan F4 40
Oituz, Pasul, p., Rom. C13 26
Ojat', stm., Russia F16 8
Öje, Swe. F5 8
Ojinaga, Mex. A6 100
Ojiya, Japan B11 40
Ojmjakon, Russia D17 34
Ojocaliente, Mex. D7 100
Ojo de la Casa, Mex. C1 130
Ojo del Carrizo, Mex. E2 130
Ojo de Liebre, Laguna, b., Mex. B1 100
Ojos del Salado, Nevado, mtn., S.A. C3 92
Ojos Negros, Mex. L9 134
Oka, stm., Russia D6 32
Oka, stm., Russia D18 32
Okaba, Indon. G10 44
Okahandja, Nmb. B3 70
Okaihau, N.Z. B5 80
Okak Islands, is., Nf., Can. F13 141
Okanagan (Okanogan), stm., N.A. G11 138
Okanagan Falls, B.C., Can. G11 138
Okanagan Lake, l., B.C., Can. G10 138
Okanagan Landing, B.C., Can. F11 138
Okanogan, Wa., U.S. B7 136
Okanogan (Okanagan), stm., N.A. G11 138
Okanogan Range, mts., Can. A6 136
Okāra, Pak. C4 54
Okaukuejo, Nmb. D2 68
Okavango (Cubango), stm., Afr. D2 68
Okavango Delta, Bots. D3 68
Ōkawa, Japan F3 40
Okawville, Il., U.S. F8 120
Okaya, Japan C11 40
Okayama, Japan E6 40
Okayama, state, Japan E6 40
Okazaki, Japan E10 40
Okeechobee, Fl., U.S. I5 116
Okeechobee, Lake, l., Fl., U.S. J5 116
Okeene, Ok., U.S. E10 128
Okefenokee Swamp, sw., U.S. F3 116
Okemos, Mi., U.S. B1 114
Okene, Nig. H6 64
Okhaldhunggā, Nepal E11 54
Okhotsk, Sea of, s., Asia D18 30
Okhotsk Basin, unds. D17 142
Okhtyrka, Ukr. D4 32
Okiep, S. Afr. F3 70
Okinawa, Japan I18 39a
Okinawa Island see Okinawa-jima, i., Japan I19 39a
Okinawa-jima, i., Japan I19 39a
Okinawa-shotō, is., Japan I18 39a
Okino-Erabu-shima, i., Japan I19 39a
Oki-shotō, is., Japan C6 40
Okitipupa, Nig. H5 64
Oklahoma, state, U.S. F11 128
Oklahoma City, Ok., U.S. F11 128
Oklawaha, Fl., U.S. G4 116
Oklee, Mn., U.S. D3 118
Okmulgee, Ok., U.S. B3 122
Okollo, Ug. D6 66
Okolona, Ar., U.S. D5 122
Okolona, Ky., U.S. F12 120
Okondja, Gabon E2 66
Okonek, Pol. C12 16
Okotoks, Ab., Can. F16 138
Okoyo, Congo E2 66
Oktjabr', Russia C20 10
Oktjabr'skij, Russia D8 32
Oktjabr'skij, Russia F14 34
Oktjabr'skij, Russia G21 8
Oktjabr'skij, Russia F20 8
Oktjabr'skoe, Russia B10 32
Oktyabr'sk, Kaz. E9 32
Oktyabr'skoe, Kaz. D11 32
Ōkuchi, Japan G3 40
Okulovka, Russia B16 10
Okunëv Nos, Russia C25 8
Okushiri-tō, i., Japan C13 38
Okuta, Nig. H5 64
Okwa, stm., Afr. C6 70
Ola, Russia E19 34
Ola, Ar., U.S. B5 122
Ólafsfjörður, Ice. j30 8a
Olancha, Ca., U.S. G8 134
Olancha Peak, mtn., Ca., U.S. G7 134
Olanchito, Hond. E4 102
Öland, i., Swe. H7 8
Olanta, S.C., U.S. C6 116
Olary, Austl. I3 76
Olathe, Co., U.S. E8 132
Olathe, Ks., U.S. F3 120
Olavarría, Arg. H7 92
Oława (Ohlau), Pol. F13 16
Olbia, Italy D3 24
Olcott, N.Y., U.S. E11 112
Old Castille see Castilla la Vieja, hist. reg., Spain C7 20
Old Cork, Austl. D3 76
Old Crow, Yk., Can. C12 140
Old Crow, stm., N.A. C11 140
Olden, Tx., U.S. B9 130
Oldenburg, Ger. C3 16
Oldenburg, hist. reg., Ger. C4 16
Oldenburg in Holstein, Ger. B6 16
Oldenzaal, Neth. B15 14
Old Faithful Geyser, gysr., Wy., U.S. F16 136
Old Forge, Pa., U.S. C10 114
Old Fort Bay see Vieux-Fort, Qc., Can. i22 107a
Oldham, Eng., U.K. H10 12
Oldham, S.D., U.S. C15 126
Old Harbor, Ak., U.S. E9 140
Old Harbour, Jam. j13 104d
Old Hickory Lake, res., Tn., U.S. H11 120
Oldman, stm., Ab., Can. G19 138
Old Mkushi, Zam. C4 68
Old Norwood, Monts. D3 105a
Old Road, Antig. f4 105b
Old Road Bluff, c., Antig. f4 105b
Old Road Town, St. K./N. C2 105a
Olds, Ab., Can. E16 138
Old Saybrook, Ct., U.S. C13 114
Old Speck Mountain, mtn., Me., U.S. F5 110
Old Tate, Bots. B8 70
Old Town, Me., U.S. F8 110
Olduvai Gorge, val., Tan. E7 66
Old Wives Lake, l., Sk., Can. D8 124
Olean, N.Y., U.S. B7 114
O'Leary, P.E., Can. D12 110
Olecko, Pol. B18 16
Olëkma, stm., Russia E13 34
Olekminsk, Russia D13 34
Olëkminskij Stanovik, mts., Russia F12 34
Ølen, Nor. G1 8
Olenegorsk, Russia B15 8
Olenëk, Russia C11 34
Olenëk, stm., Russia C12 34
Olenëkskij zaliv, b., Russia B13 34
Olenij, ostrov, i., Russia B4 34
Olenino, Russia D16 10
Oléron, Île d', i., Fr. D4 18
Oleśnica, Pol. E13 16
Olesno, Pol. F14 16
Ol'ga, Russia C11 38
Olga, Mount, mtn., Austl. D6 74
Olgastretet, strt., Nor. B30 141
Ölgiy, Mong. E16 32
Olhão, Port. G3 20
Olho d'Água das Flores, Braz. E7 88
Ol'hon, ostrov, i., Russia F10 34
Olib, Otok, i., Cro. F11 22
Olifants (Elefantes), stm., Afr. D10 70
Olifants, stm., S. Afr. H6 70
Olifants, stm., S. Afr. H4 70
Olifantshoek, S. Afr. E6 70
Ólimbos (Olympus), mtn., Cyp. C3 58
Olímpia, Braz. K1 88
Olin, Ia., U.S. B6 120
Olinda, Braz. D8 88
Olio, Austl. C4 76
Olite, Spain B9 20
Oliva, Arg. F6 92
Oliva, Spain F10 20
Oliva de la Frontera, Spain F3 20
Olivares, Cerro de, mtn., S.A. E2 92
Olive Branch, Ms., U.S. C9 122
Olivees Mountain, mtn., St. K./N. C2 105a
Olive Hill, Ky., U.S. F2 114
Olivehurst, Ca., U.S. D4 134
Oliveira, Braz. K3 88
Oliveira dos Brejinhos, Braz. G4 88
Olivenza, Spain F3 20
Oliver Springs, Tn., U.S. H13 120
Olivet, Mi., U.S. B1 114
Olivet, S.D., U.S. D15 126
Olji Moron, stm., China B4 38
Oljutorskij, mys, c., Russia E23 34
Oljutorskij zaliv, b., Russia D22 34
Olla, La., U.S. F6 122
Ollagüe, Chile D3 90
Ollagüe, Volcán, vol., S.A. D3 90
Ollei, Palau f8 78b
Olmedo, Spain C6 20
Olmos, Peru E2 84
Olney, Mt., U.S. B12 136
Olney, Tx., U.S. H10 128
Olomouc, Czech Rep. G13 16
Olonec, Russia F15 8
Olongapo, Phil. C2 52
Oloron-Sainte-Marie, Fr. F5 18
Olot, Spain B13 20
Olovjannaja, Russia F12 34
Olpe, Ger. E3 16
Olpe, Ks., U.S. F1 120
Olsufevo, Russia G16 10
Olsztyn, Pol. C16 16
Olsztyn, state, Pol. C16 16
Olt, state, Rom. E11 26
Olt, stm., Rom. D11 26
Olta, Arg. E4 92
Olten, Switz. C4 22
Olteni, Rom. E12 26
Oltenița, Rom. E13 26
Olteț, stm., Rom. E10 26
Olton, Tx., U.S. G6 128
Oluan Pi, c., Tai. K9 42
Olustee, Fl., U.S. F3 116
Olutanga Island, i., Phil. G4 52
Olvera, Spain H5 20
Olympia, Wa., U.S. C3 136
Olympiá, sci., Grc. F4 28
Olympia see Olympiá, sci., Grc. F4 28
Olympic Mountains, mts., Wa., U.S. C3 136

Name	Map Ref.	Page
Olympic National Park, p.o.i., Wa., U.S.	C3	136
Ólympos (Olympus, Mount), mtn., Grc.	C5	28
Olympus see Ólimbos, mtn., Cyp.	C3	58
Olympus, Mount see Ólympos, mtn., Grc.	C5	28
Olympus, Mount, mtn., Wa., U.S.	C3	136
Om', stm., Russia	D13	32
Ōmachi, Japan	C10	40
Omae-zaki, c., Japan	E11	40
Ōmagari, Japan	E14	38
Omagh, N. Ire., U.K.	G5	12
Omaha, Ne., U.S.	C2	120
Omaha, Tx., U.S.	D4	122
Omaheke, state, Nmb.	C4	70
Omak, Wa., U.S.	B7	136
Oman, ctry., Asia	F8	56
Oman, Gulf of, b., Asia	E8	56
Omaruru, Nmb.	B3	70
Omaruru, stm., Nmb.	B2	70
Omatako, mtn., Nmb.	B3	70
Omatako, stm., Nmb.	B3	70
Omate, Peru	G3	84
Omboué, Gabon	E1	66
Ombrone, stm., Italy	H8	22
Omčak, Russia	D18	34
Omdurman see Umm Durmān, Sudan	D6	62
Ōme, Japan	D12	40
Omega, Ga., U.S.	E2	116
Omegna, Italy	E5	22
Omemee, On., Can.	D11	112
Omeo, Austl.	K6	76
Ömerköy, Tur.	D10	28
Ömerli Barajı, res., Tur.	C12	28
Ometepe, Isla de, i., Nic.	G5	102
Ometepec, Mex.	G9	100
Ōmi-hachiman, Japan	D8	40
Omineca, stm., B.C., Can.	D6	106
Omineca Mountains, mts., B.C., Can.	D5	106
Ōmiya, Japan	D12	40
Ommaney, Cape, c., Ak., U.S.	E13	140
Ommanney Bay, b., Nu., Can.	A10	106
Omo, stm., Afr.	F7	62
Omoloj, stm., Russia	B15	34
Omolon, stm., Russia	C20	34
Omsk, Russia	C12	32
Omsukčan, Russia	D20	34
Omul, Vârful, mtn., Rom.	D12	26
Ōmura, Japan	G2	40
Omurtag, Blg.	F13	26
Ōmuta, Japan	F3	40
Omutinskij, Russia	C11	32
Omutninsk, Russia	C8	32
Onabas, Mex.	A4	100
Onaga, Ks., U.S.	E1	120
Onaman Lake, l., On., Can.	A11	118
Onamia, Mn., U.S.	E5	118
Onangué, Lac, l., Gabon	E1	66
Onaping Lake, l., On., Can.	A8	112
Onarga, Il., U.S.	D10	120
Onatchiway, Lac, res., Qc., Can.	A5	110
Onawa, Ia., U.S.	B1	120
Onaway, Mi., U.S.	C5	112
Oncativo, Arg.	E6	92
Once, Canal Numero, can., Arg.	H8	92
Oncócua, Ang.	D1	68
Onda, Spain	E10	20
Ondangwa, Nmb.	D2	68
Ondas, stm., Braz.	G3	88
Ondava, stm., Slov.	H17	16
Ondjiva, Ang.	D2	68
Ondo, Japan	E5	40
Ondo, Nig.	H5	64
Öndörhaan, Mong.	B7	36
Ondozero, ozero, l., Russia	E15	8
Oneco, Fl., U.S.	I3	116
Onega, Russia	E17	8
Onega, stm., Russia	E18	8
Onega, Lake see Onežskoe ozero, l., Russia	F16	8
Onega Bay see Onežskaja guba, b., Russia	D17	8
One Hundred and Two, stm., Mo., U.S.	D3	120
One Hundred Fifty Mile House, B.C., Can.	D9	138
One Hundred Mile House, B.C., Can.	E9	138
Oneida, Il., U.S.	C7	120
Oneida, N.Y., U.S.	E14	112
Oneida, Tn., U.S.	H13	120
Oneida Lake, l., N.Y., U.S.	E14	112
O'Neill, Ne., U.S.	E14	126
Onekama, Mi., U.S.	D3	112
Onekotan, ostrov, i., Russia	G20	34
Oneonta, Al., U.S.	D12	122
Oneonta, N.Y., U.S.	B10	114
Onești, Rom.	C13	26
Onevai, i., Tonga	n14	78e
Onežskaja guba (Onega Bay), b., Russia	D17	8
Onežskij poluostrov, pen., Russia	D17	8
Onežskoe ozero (Onega, Lake), l., Russia	F16	8
Ongjin-ŭp, Kor., N.	F6	38
Ongniud Qi, China	C3	38
Ongole, India	D5	53
Onilahy, stm., Madag.	F7	68
Onion Creek, stm., Tx., U.S.	D10	130
Onitsha, Nig.	H6	64
Ōno, Japan	D9	40
Onoda, Japan	F4	40
Onomichi, Japan	E6	40
Onon, Mong.	B7	36
Onon Gol, stm., Asia	G11	34
Onoto, Ven.	C9	86
Onotoa, at., Kir.	D8	72
Onoway, Ab., Can.	C16	138
Ons, Illa de, i., Spain	B1	20
Onset, Ma., U.S.	C15	114
Onslow, Austl.	D3	74
Onslow Bay, b., N.C., U.S.	B8	116
On-take, vol., Japan	H3	40
Ontake-san, vol., Japan	D10	40
Ontario, Ca., U.S.	I8	134
Ontario, Or., U.S.	F10	136
Ontario, state, Can.	E13	106
Ontario, Lake, l., N.A.	E11	112
Ontinyent, Spain	F10	20
Ontojärvi, l., Fin.	D13	8
Ontonagon, Mi., U.S.	E9	118
Ontong Java, at., Sol. Is.	D7	72
Onverwacht, Sur.	B6	84
Oodnadatta, Austl.	E7	74
Ooldea, Austl.	F6	74
Oologah, Ok., U.S.	H2	120
Oologah Lake, res., Ok., U.S.	H2	120
Oorlogskloof, stm., S. Afr.	G4	70
Oos-Londen see East London, S. Afr.	H8	70
Oostburg, Wi., U.S.	E2	112
Oostelijk Flevoland, reg., Neth.	B14	14
Oostende, Bel.	C11	14
Oosterhout, Neth.	C13	14
Oosterschelde, est., Neth.	C12	14
Ootsa Lake, B.C., Can.	C4	138
Ootsa Lake, res., B.C., Can.	C4	138
Opaka, Blg.	F13	26
Opala, D.R.C.	E4	66
Oparino, Russia	G22	8
Opatija, Cro.	E11	22
Opava, Czech Rep.	G13	16
Opawica, stm., Qc., Can.	A2	110
Opečenskij Posad, Russia	B17	10
Opelika, Al., U.S.	E13	122
Opelousas, La., U.S.	G6	122
Opeongo, stm., On., Can.	C12	112
Opeongo Lake, l., On., Can.	C11	112
Ophir, Ak., U.S.	D8	140
Ophir, Or., U.S.	H2	136
Opihikao, Hi., U.S.	d7	78a
Opinaca, stm., Qc., Can.	E15	106
Opiscotéo, Lac, l., Qc., Can.	E17	106
Opobo, Nig.	I6	64
Opočka, Russia	D11	10
Opoczno, Pol.	E16	16
Opole, Pol.	F13	16
Opole, state, Pol.	F13	16
Opotiki, N.Z.	D7	80
Oppdal, Nor.	E3	8
Oppland, state, Nor.	F3	8
Opportunity, Mt., U.S.	D14	136
Opportunity, Wa., U.S.	C9	136
Optima Lake, res., Ok., U.S.	E7	128
Opua, N.Z.	B6	80
Opunake, N.Z.	D5	80
Opuwo, Nmb.	D1	68
Oqsuqtooq (Gjoa Haven), Nu., Can.	B11	106
Oquawka, Il., U.S.	K7	118
Or, Côte d', mts., Fr.	G13	14
Oracle, Az., U.S.	K6	132
Oradea, Rom.	B8	26
Öræfajökull, ice, Ice.	k31	8a
Orahovica, Cro.	E14	22
Orai, India	F7	54
Oraibi Wash, stm., Az., U.S.	H6	132
Oral, Kaz.	D8	32
Oran see Wahran, Alg.	B4	64
Orange, Austl.	I7	76
Orange, Fr.	E10	18
Orange, Ma., U.S.	B13	114
Orange, Tx., U.S.	G5	122
Orange, Va., U.S.	F7	114
Orange (Oranje) (Senqu), stm., Afr.	F3	70
Orange, Cabo, c., Braz.	C7	84
Orangeburg, S.C., U.S.	C4	116
Orange City, Ia., U.S.	A1	120
Orange Cove, Ca., U.S.	G6	134
Orange Free State see Free State, state, S. Afr.	F8	70
Orange Grove, Tx., U.S.	G9	130
Orange Lake, Fl., U.S.	G3	116
Orange Lake, l., Fl., U.S.	G3	116
Orangeville, On., Can.	E9	112
Orangeville, Ut., U.S.	D5	132
Orange Walk, Belize	C3	102
Orango, Ilha de, i., Gui.-B.	G1	64
Orani, Phil.	C3	52
Oranienburg, Ger.	D8	16
Oranje see Orange, stm., Afr.	F3	70
Oranje Gebergte, mts., Sur.	C6	84
Oranjemund, Nmb.	F3	70
Oranjestad, Aruba	o19	104g
Oranjestad, Neth. Ant.	C1	105a
Oranje Vrijstaat see Free State, state, S. Afr.	F8	70
Orăștie, Rom.	D10	26
Orba Co, l., China	A8	54
Orbetello, Italy	H8	22
Órbigo, stm., Spain	B5	20
Orbisonia, Pa., U.S.	D8	114
Orbost, Austl.	K7	76
Örbyhus, Swe.	F7	8
Orcadas, sci., Ant.	B36	81
Orchard City, Co., U.S.	E8	132
Orchard Homes, Mt., U.S.	D12	136
Orchard Mesa, Co., U.S.	E8	132
Orchard Park, N.Y., U.S.	B7	114
Ord, Ne., U.S.	F14	126
Ord, stm., Austl.	C5	74
Ord, Mount, mtn., Austl.	C5	74
Ordenes see Ordes, Spain	A2	20
Orderville, Ut., U.S.	F4	132
Ordes, Spain	A2	20
Ordesa y Monte Perdido, Parque Nacional de, p.o.i., Spain	B10	20
Ord Mountain, mtn., Ca., U.S.	I9	134
Ordos Desert see Mu Us Shamo, des., China	B3	42
Ord River, Austl.	C5	74
Ordu, Tur.	A4	56
Ordway, Co., U.S.	C5	128
Ordžonikidzeabad, Taj.	B10	56
Örebro, Swe.	G6	8
Örebro, state, Swe.	G6	8
Oredež, Russia	B13	10
Oredež, stm., Russia	B13	10
Oregon, Il., U.S.	B8	120
Oregon, Mo., U.S.	D2	120
Oregon, Oh., U.S.	C2	114
Oregon, state, U.S.	G6	136
Oregon Caves National Monument, p.o.i., Or., U.S.	A2	134
Oregon City, Or., U.S.	E4	136
Oregon Dunes National Recreation Area, p.o.i., Or., U.S.	G2	136
Orehovo-Zuevo, Russia	E21	10
Orel, Russia	G18	10
Orel', ozero, l., Russia	F16	34
Orellana, Peru	E2	84
Orellana, state, Ec.	H3	86
Orellana, Embalse de, res., Spain	E5	20
Orem, Ut., U.S.	C5	132
Ore Mountains, mts., Eur.	F8	16
Orenburg, Russia	D8	32
Örencik, Tur.	D12	28
Orense, Arg.	I8	92
Orense see Ourense, Spain	B3	20
Orense see Ourense, co., Spain	B3	20
Oreor, i., Palau	g8	78b
Orestes Pereyra, Mex.	B6	100
Orestiáda, Grc.	B9	28
Orford Ness, c., Eng., U.K.	I14	12
Organ Pipe Cactus National Monument, p.o.i., Az., U.S.	K4	132
Orgelet, Fr.	H14	14
Orgosolo, Italy	D3	24
Orgun, Afg.	C10	56
Orhangazi, Tur.	C12	28
Orhei, Mol.	B15	26
Orhon, stm., Mong.	B5	36
Orichuna, stm., Ven.	D7	86
Orick, Ca., U.S.	B1	134
Orient, Ia., U.S.	C3	120
Orient, Wa., U.S.	B8	136
Oriental, Cordillera, mts., Col.	E5	86
Oriental, Cordillera, mts., Peru	F3	84
Orientos, Austl.	G3	76
Orihuela see Oriola, Spain	F10	20
Orillia, On., Can.	D10	112
Orimattila, Fin.	F11	8
Orinduik, Guy.	E11	86
Orinoco, stm., S.A.	C10	86
Orinoco, Delta del, Ven.	C11	86
Oriola, Spain	F10	20
Orion, Il., U.S.	C7	120
Oriskany, N.Y., U.S.	E14	112
Orissa, state, India	D5	46
Orissaare, Est.	B5	10
Oristano, Italy	E2	24
Oristano, Golfo di, b., Italy	E2	24
Orituco, stm., Ven.	C8	86
Orivesi, l., Fin.	E13	8
Oriximiná, Braz.	D6	84
Orizaba, Mex.	F10	100
Orjahovo, Blg.	F10	26
Orjen, mtn., Mont.	G5	26
Orkney, Sk., Can.	E5	124
Orkney, S. Afr.	E8	70
Orkney Islands, is., Scot., U.K.	C10	12
Orlândia, Braz.	K1	88
Orlando, Fl., U.S.	H4	116
Orléanais, hist. reg., Fr.	F11	14
Orleans, On., Can.	C14	112
Orléans, Fr.	G10	14
Orleans, Ca., U.S.	B2	134
Orleans, Ma., U.S.	C15	114
Orleans, Ne., U.S.	A9	128
Orleans, Vt., U.S.	F4	110
Orléans, Canal d', can., Fr.	G11	14
Orléans, Île d', i., Qc., Can.	D6	110
Orlik, Russia	D18	32
Orlovskaja oblast', co., Russia	H19	10
Orly, Fr.	F11	14
Ormāra, Pak.	D9	56
Ormiston, Sk., Can.	E8	124
Ormoc, Phil.	E5	52
Ormond Beach, Fl., U.S.	G4	116
Ornain, stm., Fr.	F14	14
Ornans, Fr.	G15	14
Orne, state, Fr.	F8	14
Orne, stm., Fr.	F8	14
Orne, stm., Fr.	E14	14
Ornö, i., Swe.	G8	8
Örnsköldsvik, Swe.	E8	8
Oročen, Russia	E14	34
Orocovis, P.R.	B3	104a
Orocué, Col.	E6	86
Orofino, Id., U.S.	D10	136
Orog nuur, l., Mong.	B5	36
Orohena, Mont, mtn., Fr. Poly.	v22	78h
Oroluk, at., Micron.	C6	72
Oromocto, N.B., Can.	E10	110
Oromocto Lake, l., N.B., Can.	E10	110
Oron, Nig.	I6	64
Orona, at., Kir.	D9	72
Orono, On., Can.	D11	112
Orono, Me., U.S.	F8	110
Orontes (Asi), stm., Asia	B7	58
Oroquieta, Phil.	F4	52
Orós, Braz.	D6	88
Orós, Açude, res., Braz.	D6	88
Orosei, Italy	D3	24
Orosei, Golfo di, b., Italy	D3	24
Orosháza, Hung.	C7	26
Oroszlány, Hung.	B5	26
Orote Peninsula, pen., Guam	j9	78c
Oroville, Ca., U.S.	D4	134
Oroville, Lake, res., Ca., U.S.	D4	134
Orpheus Island, i., Austl.	B6	76
Orrick, Mo., U.S.	E3	120
Orrin, N.D., U.S.	F13	124
Orroroo, Austl.	I2	76
Orrs Island, Me., U.S.	G7	110
Orša, Bela.	F13	10
Orsk, Russia	D9	32
Orșova, Rom.	E9	26
Ortaca, Tur.	G11	28
Ortakent, Tur.	F10	28
Ortaklar, Tur.	F10	28
Orta Nova, Italy	C9	24
Ortega, Col.	F4	86
Ortegal, Cabo, c., Spain	A2	20
Orteguaza, stm., Col.	G4	86
Orthon, stm., Bol.	B3	90
Ortigueira, Spain	A3	20
Orting, Wa., U.S.	C4	136
Ortiz, Mex.	A3	100
Ortiz, Ven.	C8	86
Ortona, Italy	H11	22
Ortonville, Mn., U.S.	F2	118
Orūmīyeh, Iran	B6	56
Orūmīyeh, Daryācheh-ye (Urmia, Lake), l., Iran	B6	56
Orust, i., Swe.	G4	8
Orvieto, Italy	H9	22
Orwell, Oh., U.S.	C5	114
Orxon, stm., China	B8	36
Orzinuovi, Italy	E6	22
Orzyc, stm., Pol.	D17	16
Oš, Kyrg.	F12	32
Os, Nor.	E4	8
Osa, Península de, pen., C.R.	H6	102
Osage, Ia., U.S.	H6	118
Osage, Wy., U.S.	D8	126
Osage, stm., Mo., U.S.	F5	120
Osage Beach, Mo., U.S.	F5	120
Osage City, Ks., U.S.	F2	120
Ōsaka, Japan	E8	40
Ōsaka, state, Japan	E8	40
Osakarovka, Kaz.	D12	32
Ōsaka-wan, b., Japan	E8	40
Osăm, stm., Blg.	F11	26
Osawatomie, Ks., U.S.	F3	120
Osborne, Ks., U.S.	B10	128
Osburn, Id., U.S.	C11	136
Osceola, Ar., U.S.	B8	122
Osceola, Ia., U.S.	C4	120
Osceola, Mo., U.S.	F4	120
Osceola, Wi., U.S.	F6	118
Osceola Mills, Pa., U.S.	D7	114
Oschatz, Ger.	E8	16
Oschersleben, Ger.	D7	16
Osečina, Serb.	E6	26
Osëtr, stm., Russia	F21	10
Osetrovo, Russia	E10	34
Osgood, In., U.S.	E12	120
Oshawa, On., Can.	E11	112
Oshika, Japan	A14	40
Oshika-hantō, pen., Japan	A14	40
Ō-shima, i., Japan	E12	40
Oshima-hantō, pen., Japan	C14	38
Oshkosh, Ne., U.S.	F10	126
Oshkosh, Wi., U.S.	G10	118
Oshogbo, Nig.	H5	64
Oshwe, D.R.C.	E3	66
Osica de Jos, Rom.	E11	26
Osijek, Cro.	E15	22
Osilo, Italy	D2	24
Osimo, Italy	G10	22
Osinniki, Russia	D15	32
Osipovo Selo, Russia	D13	10
Osire Süd, Nmb.	B3	70
Oskaloosa, Ia., U.S.	C5	120
Oskaloosa, Ks., U.S.	E2	120
Oskarshamn, Swe.	H7	8
Öskemen, Kaz.	E14	32
Oskolkovo, Russia	B26	8
Oslo, Nor.	G4	8
Oslo, state, Nor.	F4	8
Oslofjorden, b., Nor.	G4	8
Osmānābād, India	B3	53
Osmaneli, Tur.	C12	28
Osmaniye, Tur.	A7	58
Os'mino, Russia	A11	10
Osmussaar, i., Est.	A6	10
Osnabrück, Ger.	D4	16
Osorno, Chile	H2	90
Osorno, Spain	B6	20
Osoyoos, B.C., Can.	G11	138
Oss, Neth.	C14	14
Ossa, Mount, mtn., Austl.	n13	77a
Ossabaw Island, i., Ga., U.S.	E4	116
Osseo, Wi., U.S.	G7	118
Ossian, Ia., U.S.	A6	120
Ossining, N.Y., U.S.	C12	114
Ossipee, N.H., U.S.	G5	110
Ossjøen, l., Nor.	F4	8
Ossora, Russia	E21	34
Ostaškov, Russia	C16	10
Ostašovo, Russia	E18	10
Ostende see Oostende, Bel.	C11	14
Ostër (Ascör), stm., Eur.	G15	10
Osterburg, Ger.	D7	16
Östergötland, state, Swe.	G7	8
Osterholz-Scharmbeck, Ger.	C4	16
Osterode am Harz, Ger.	E6	16
Osterøyni, i., Nor.	F1	8
Östersund, Swe.	E6	8
Osterwieck, Ger.	E6	16
Østfold, state, Nor.	G4	8
Ostfriesische Inseln (East Frisian Islands), is., Ger.	C3	16
Ostfriesland, hist. reg., Ger.	C3	16
Østgrønland (Tunu), state, Grnld.	C18	141
Östhammar, Swe.	F8	8
Ostpreussen, hist. reg., Eur.	F4	10
Ostrava, Czech Rep.	G14	16
Ostróda, Pol.	C15	16
Ostrogožsk, Russia	D5	32
Ostrołęka, Pol.	C17	16
Ostrołęka, state, Pol.	D17	16
Ostroróg, Pol.	D12	16
Ostrov, Czech Rep.	F8	16
Ostrov, Russia	C11	10
Ostrov, i., Slov.	I13	16
Ostrov-Zalit, Russia	B11	10
Ostrowiec Świętokrzyski, Pol.	F17	16
Ostrów Mazowiecka, Pol.	D17	16
Ostrów Wielkopolski, Pol.	E13	16
Ostrzeszów, Pol.	E13	16
Ostuni, Italy	D11	24
O'Sullivan Lake, l., On., Can.	A11	118
Osum, stm., Alb.	D14	24
Ōsumi-hantō, pen., Japan	H3	40
Osumi Islands see Ōsumi-shotō, is., Japan	I9	38
Ōsumi-kaikyō, strt., Japan	I9	38
Ōsumi-shotō, is., Japan	I9	38
Osuna, Spain	G5	20
Oswego, Il., U.S.	C9	120
Oswego, Ks., U.S.	G2	120
Oswego, N.Y., U.S.	E13	112
Oswestry, Eng., U.K.	I9	12
Oświęcim (Auschwitz), Pol.	F15	16
Osyka, Ms., U.S.	F8	122
Ōta, Japan	C12	40
Otaci, Mol.	A14	26
Ōtake, Japan	E5	40
Otaki, N.Z.	E6	80
Otaru, Japan	C14	38
Otautau, N.Z.	H2	80
Otava, Fin.	F12	8
Otava, stm., Czech Rep.	G9	16
Otavalo, Ec.	G2	86
Otavi, Nmb.	D2	68
Ōtawara, Japan	C12	40
Otego Creek, stm., N.Y., U.S.	G3	110
Oteotea, Sol. Is.	e9	79b
Oteros, stm., Mex.	B4	100
Otinapa, Mex.	C6	100
Otis, Co., U.S.	A6	128
Otis, Ks., U.S.	C9	128
Otish, Monts, mts., Qc., Can.	E16	106
Otjimbingwe, Nmb.	C2	70
Otjinene, Nmb.	B4	70
Otjiwarongo, Nmb.	B3	70
Otjozondjou, stm., Nmb.	B5	70
Otjozondjupa, state, Nmb.	B3	70
Otočac, Cro.	F12	22
Otoskwin, stm., On., Can.	E13	106
Otra, stm., Nor.	G2	8
Otradnyj, Russia	D8	32
Ótranto, Italy	D12	24
Otranto, Strait of, strt., Eur.	D12	24
Otrokovice, Czech Rep.	G13	16
Otrøya, i., Nor.	E2	8
Ötscher, mtn., Aus.	C12	22
Ōtsu, Japan	D8	40
Otta, Nor.	F3	8
Ottawa, On., Can.	C14	112
Ottawa, Il., U.S.	C9	120
Ottawa, Ks., U.S.	F2	120
Ottawa, Oh., U.S.	C1	114
Ottawa (Outaouais), stm., Can.	C15	112
Ottawa Islands, is., Nu., Can.	D14	106
Otterburne, Mb., Can.	E16	124
Otter Creek, Fl., U.S.	G3	116
Otter Creek, stm., Vt., U.S.	F3	110
Otter Lake, Mi., U.S.	E6	112
Otterøya see Otrøya, i., Nor.	E2	8
Otter Tail, stm., Mn., U.S.	E2	118
Otter Tail Lake, l., Mn., U.S.	E2	118
Otterville, Mo., U.S.	F5	120
Ottosdal, S. Afr.	E7	70
Ottoshoop, S. Afr.	D8	70
Ottoville, Oh., U.S.	D1	114
Ottumwa, Ia., U.S.	C5	120
Ottweiler, Ger.	G3	16
Otway, Cape, c., Austl.	L4	76
Otwock, Pol.	D17	16
Ötztaler Alpen (Venoste, Alpi), mts., Eur.	D7	22
Ou, stm., China	I5	42
Ou, stm., China	G9	42
Ou, stm., Laos	B6	48
Ouacha, Niger	G6	64
Ouachita, stm., U.S.	F7	122
Ouachita, Lake, res., Ar., U.S.	C5	122
Ouachita Mountains, mts., U.S.	C4	122
Ouaco, N. Cal.	m15	79d
Ouadda, C.A.R.	C4	66
Ouagadougou, Burkina	G4	64
Ouahigouya, Burkina	G4	64
Ouahran see Wahran, Alg.	B4	64
Ouaka, stm., C.A.R.	C4	66
Oualâta, Maur.	F3	64
Ouallene, Alg.	E5	64
Ouanary, Fr. Gu.	C7	84
Ouanda Djallé, C.A.R.	C4	66
Ouango, C.A.R.	D4	66
Ouangolodougou, C. Iv.	H3	64
Ouarâne, reg., Maur.	E2	64
Ouarkziz, Jbel, mts., Afr.	D3	64
Ouarzazate, Mor.	C3	64
Ouasiemsca, stm., Qc., Can.	A4	110
Oubangui (Ubangi), stm., Afr.	E3	66
Oudenaarde, Bel.	D12	14
Oudtshoorn, S. Afr.	H6	70
Oued Fodda, Alg.	H12	20
Oued-Zem, Mor.	C3	64
Ouémé, stm., Benin	H5	64
Ouen, Île, i., N. Cal.	n16	79d
Ouessant, Île d' (Ushant), i., Fr.	F3	14
Ouesso, Congo	D3	66
Ouezzane, Mor.	C3	64
Ouham, stm., Afr.	F3	62
Ouidah, Benin	H5	64
Ouimet Canyon, misc. cult., On., Can.	C10	118
Ouistreham, Fr.	E8	14
Oujda, Mor.	C4	64
Oulangan kansallispuisto, p.o.i., Fin.	C13	8
Oulu (Uleåborg), Fin.	D11	8
Oulu, state, Fin.	D12	8
Oulujärvi, l., Fin.	D12	8
Oum-Chalouba, Chad	D4	62
Oumé, C. Iv.	H3	64
Oum-Hadjer, Chad	E3	62
Oumiao, China	F5	42
Ounasjoki, stm., Fin.	C11	8
Ounianga Kébir, Chad	D3	62
Ourém, Braz.	A2	88
Ourense, Spain	B3	20
Ourense, co., Spain	B3	20
Ouricuri, Braz.	D5	88
Ourinhos, Braz.	D7	90
Ouro Branco, Braz.	D7	88
Ouro Fino, Braz.	L2	88
Ouro Preto, Braz.	K4	88
Ours, Grande chute à l', wtfl., Qc., Can.	B4	110
Ourthe, stm., Bel.	D14	14
Ōu-sammyaku, mts., Japan	E14	38
Oust, can., Fr.	F6	14
Outaouais (Ottawa), stm., Can.	C15	112
Outardes, stm., Qc., Can.	E17	106
Outer Hebrides, is., Scot., U.K.	D5	12
Outer Island, i., Wi., U.S.	D8	118
Outer Santa Barbara Passage, strt., Ca., U.S.	J7	134
Outjo, Nmb.	B3	70
Outlook, Sk., Can.	C6	124
Outlook, Mt., U.S.	F9	124
Out Skerries, is., Scot., U.K.	n19	12a
Ouvéa, i., N. Cal.	m16	79d
Ouyen, Austl.	J4	76
Ovacık, Tur.	B15	28
Ovada, Italy	F5	22
Ovalle, Chile	E2	92
Ovana, Cerro, mtn., Ven.	E8	86
Ovar, Port.	D2	20
Ovejas, Col.	C4	86
Overbrook, Ks., U.S.	F2	120
Overflowing, stm., Can.	A12	124
Overland Park, Ks., U.S.	F3	120
Overton, Ne., U.S.	G13	126
Overton, Tx., U.S.	E4	122
Overton Arm, b., Nv., U.S.	G2	132
Övertorneå, Swe.	C10	8
Ovett, Ms., U.S.	F9	122
Ovid, N.Y., U.S.	B9	114
Ovidiopol', Ukr.	C17	26
Oviedo, Spain	A5	20
Ovinišče, Russia	B20	10
Ovīši, Lat.	C4	10
Ovoot, Mong.	B7	36
Øvre Anárjohka Nasjonalpark, p.o.i., Nor.	B13	8
Øvre Dividal Nasjonalpark, p.o.i., Nor.	B8	8
Ovstug, Russia	G16	10
Owando, Congo	E3	66
Owase, Japan	E9	40
Owasso, Ok., U.S.	H2	120
Owatonna, Mn., U.S.	G5	118
Owbī, Afg.	C9	56
Owego, N.Y., U.S.	B9	114
Owen, Wi., U.S.	G8	118
Owendo, Gabon	D1	66
Owens, stm., Ca., U.S.	F7	134
Owensboro, Ky., U.S.	G10	120
Owens Lake, l., Ca., U.S.	G8	134
Owen Sound, On., Can.	D8	112
Owen Sound, b., On., Can.	D9	112
Owen Stanley Range, mts., Pap. N. Gui.	b4	79a
Owensville, In., U.S.	F10	120
Owensville, Mo., U.S.	F6	120
Owerri, Nig.	H6	64
Owikeno Lake, l., B.C., Can.	E3	138
Owingsville, Ky., U.S.	F2	114
Owl, stm., Ab., Can.	A19	138
Owl, stm., Mb., Can.	D12	106
Owo, Nig.	H6	64
Owosso, Mi., U.S.	E5	112
Owyhee, Nv., U.S.	B9	134
Owyhee, stm., U.S.	G9	136
Owyhee, Lake, res., Or., U.S.	G9	136
Owyhee, South Fork, stm., U.S.	H10	136
Öxarfjörður, b., Ice.	j31	8a
Oxbow, Sk., Can.	E11	124
Oxelösund, Swe.	G7	8
Oxford, N.S., Can.	E13	110
Oxford, N.Z.	F5	80
Oxford, Eng., U.K.	J11	12
Oxford, Al., U.S.	D13	122
Oxford, In., U.S.	H2	112
Oxford, Ks., U.S.	D11	128
Oxford, Md., U.S.	F9	114
Oxford, Me., U.S.	F6	110
Oxford, Ms., U.S.	C9	122
Oxford, N.C., U.S.	H7	114
Oxford, N.Y., U.S.	B10	114
Oxford, Oh., U.S.	E13	120
Oxford, Pa., U.S.	I14	112
Oxford, Wi., U.S.	H9	118
Oxford Junction, Ia., U.S.	J8	118
Oxford Lake, l., Mb., Can.	E11	106
Oxford Peak, mtn., Id., U.S.	H14	136
Oxkutzcab, Mex.	B3	102
Oxley Downs, Austl.	J4	76
Oxley Wild Rivers National Park, p.o.i., Austl.	H8	76
Oxnard, Ca., U.S.	I6	134
Oxus see Amu Darya, stm., Asia	F10	32
Oya, stm., Malay.	B8	50
Oyabe, Japan	C9	40
Oyama, Japan	C12	40
Ōyano, Japan	G3	40
Oyapok (Oiapoque), stm., S.A.	C7	84
Oyem, Gabon	D2	66
Oyen, Ab., Can.	C3	124
Oyo, Nig.	H5	64
Oyonnax, Fr.	C11	18
Oyster Creek, mth., Tx., U.S.	E12	130
Oyyl, Kaz.	E8	32
Ozamis, Phil.	F4	52
Ozark, Al., U.S.	F13	122
Ozark, Ar., U.S.	B5	122
Ozark, Mo., U.S.	G4	120
Ozark Plateau, plat., U.S.	H4	120
Ozarks, Lake of the, res., Mo., U.S.	F5	120
Ózd, Hung.	A7	26
Oželele, Russia	F21	10
Ozernovskij, Russia	F20	34
Ozërnyj, Russia	D10	32
Ozery, Russia	F21	10
Ozette Lake, l., Wa., U.S.	B2	136
Ozieri, Italy	D2	24
Ozimek, Pol.	F14	16
Ozinki, Russia	D7	32
Ozorków, Pol.	E15	16
Ōzu, Japan	F5	40
Ozuluama, Mex.	E9	100
Ozurgeti, Geor.	F6	32

P

Name	Map Ref.	Page
Paagoumène, N. Cal.	m14	79d
Paama, state, Vanuatu	k17	79d
Paama, i., Vanuatu	k17	79d
Paamiut see Frederikshåb, Grnld.	E15	141
Paarl, S. Afr.	H4	70
Pa'auilo, Hi., U.S.	c6	78a
Pabbay, i., Scot., U.K.	D5	12
Pabbiring, Kepulauan, is., Indon.	F11	50
Pabean, Indon.	G9	50
Pabellón, Ensenada del, b., Mex.	C4	100
Pabianice, Pol.	E15	16
Pablo, Mt., U.S.	C12	136
Pābna, Bngl.	G12	54
Pabradė, Lith.	F8	10
Pacaás Novos, Serra dos, mts., Braz.	F5	84
Pacajus, Braz.	C6	88
Pacasmayo, Peru	E2	84
Pacatuba, Braz.	C6	88
Pachino, Italy	H9	24
Pachitea, stm., Peru	E3	84
Pachmarhi, India	G7	54
Pāchora, India	H5	54
Pachuca de Soto, Mex.	E9	100
Pacific, B.C., Can.	B2	138
Pacific, Mo., U.S.	F7	120
Pacifica, Ca., U.S.	F3	134
Pacific-Antarctic Ridge, unds.	P22	142
Pacific Grove, Ca., U.S.	G3	134
Pacific Ocean	F20	142
Pacific Ranges, mts., B.C., Can.	E5	138
Pacific Rim National Park, p.o.i., B.C., Can.	H5	138
Paciran, Indon.	G8	50
Pacitan, Indon.	H7	50
Pacora, Pan.	C2	86
Pacov, Czech Rep.	G11	16
Pacuí, stm., Braz.	I3	88
Padada, Phil.	G5	52
Padamo, stm., Ven.	F9	86
Padampur, India	H9	54
Padang, Indon.	D2	50
Padang, Indon.	G12	50
Padang, Indon.	D6	50
Padang, Pulau, i., Indon.	C3	50
Padang Endau, Malay.	K6	48
Padangpanjang, Indon.	D2	50
Padangsidempuan, Indon.	C1	50
Padany, Russia	E15	8
Padas, stm., Malay.	A9	50
Padauari, stm., Braz.	G9	86
Paddle, stm., Ab., Can.	B16	138
Paddle Prairie, Ab., Can.	D7	106
Paderborn, Ger.	E4	16
Padjelanta Nationalpark, p.o.i., Swe.	C7	8
Padloping Island, i., Nu., Can.	D13	141
Padma see Ganges, stm., Asia	G13	54
Pádova (Padua), Italy	E8	22
Pādra, India	G4	54
Padrauna, India	E9	54
Padre Bernardo, Braz.	H1	88
Padre Island, i., Tx., U.S.	G10	130
Padre Island National Seashore, p.o.i., Tx., U.S.	G10	130
Padre Paraíso, Braz.	I5	88
Padstow, Eng., U.K.	K8	12
Padua see Pádova, Italy	E8	22
Paducah, Ky., U.S.	G9	120
Paducah, Tx., U.S.	G8	128
Paea, Fr. Poly.	v21	78h
Paedun, Kor., S.	D1	40
Paektu-san, mtn., Asia	C10	36
Paestum, sci., Italy	D8	24
Páez, stm., Col.	F4	86
Pafúri, Moz.	C10	70
Pag, Otok, i., Cro.	F11	22
Pagadenbaru, Indon.	G5	50
Pagadian, Phil.	G4	52
Pagai Selatan, Pulau, i., Indon.	E2	50
Pagai Utara, Pulau, i., Indon.	E2	50
Pagan, Mya.	B2	48
Pagan, i., N. Mar. Is.	B5	72
Pagaralam, Indon.	E3	50
Pagasitikós Kólpos, b., Grc.	D5	28
Page, Az., U.S.	G5	132
Page, N.D., U.S.	G16	124
Pagėgiai, Lith.	E4	10
Pagerdewa, Indon.	E4	50
Paget, Mount, mtn., S. Geor.	J9	90
Pagoda Peak, mtn., Co., U.S.	C9	132
Pagoda Point, c., Mya.	E2	48
Pagon, Bukit, mtn., Asia	A9	50
Pago Pago, Am. Sam.	h12	79c
Pagosa Springs, Co., U.S.	F9	132
Paguate, N.M., U.S.	H9	132
Pagudpud, Phil.	A3	52
Pahača, Russia	D22	34
Pāhala, Hi., U.S.	d6	78a
Pahang, state, Malay.	K6	48
Pahang, stm., Malay.	K6	48
Pahokee, Fl., U.S.	J5	116
Pahost, Bela.	G12	10
Pahrump, Nv., U.S.	G10	134
Pai, Thai.	C4	48
Pai, stm., Asia	C3	48
Paico, Peru	F3	84
Paide, Est.	B8	10
Paige, Tx., U.S.	D10	130
Paignton, Eng., U.K.	K9	12
Paiguano, Chile	E2	92
Päijänne, l., Fin.	F11	8
Paikü Co, l., China	D10	54
Pailolo Channel, strt., Hi., U.S.	b5	78a
Paimpol, Fr.	F5	14
Painan, Indon.	D2	50
Painesdale, Mi., U.S.	D10	118
Painesville, Oh., U.S.	C4	114
Paint, stm., Mi., U.S.	E10	118
Paint Creek, stm., Oh., U.S.	E14	120
Painted Desert, des., Az., U.S.	H5	132
Painted Rock Reservoir, res., Az., U.S.	K3	132
Paintsville, Ky., U.S.	G3	114
Paisley, Scot., U.K.	F8	12
Paisley, Or., U.S.	H6	136
Païta, N. Cal.	n16	79d
Paita, Peru	E1	84
Paitan, Telukan, b., Malay.	G1	52
Paiton, Indon.	G8	50
Pajala, Swe.	C10	8
Paján, Ec.	H1	86
Pajares, Puerto de, p., Spain	B5	20
Pajaros Point, c., Br. Vir. Is.	d9	104b
Pajęczno, Pol.	E14	16
Pajer, gora, mtn., Russia	C1	34
Pajeú, stm., Braz.	E6	88
Paj-Hoj, hills, Russia	A10	32
Paka, Malay.	J6	48
Pākāla, India	E4	53
Pakaraima Mountains, mts., S.A.	E11	86
Pakashkan Lake, l., On., Can.	B8	118
Pākaur, India	F11	54
Pak Chong, Thai.	E5	48
Pākhāl, l., India	C5	53
Pákhna, Cyp.	D3	58
Pakhoi see Beihai, China	K3	42
Pakistan, ctry., Asia	C2	46
Paklenica Nacionalni Park, p.o.i., Cro.	F12	22
Pakokku, Mya.	B2	48
Pakowki Lake, l., Ab., Can.	E2	124
Pākpattan, Pak.	C4	54
Pak Phanang, Thai.	H5	48
Pak Phayun, Thai.	I5	48
Pak Phraek, Thai.	H5	48
Pakrac, Cro.	E14	22
Pakruojis, Lith.	E6	10
Paks, Hung.	C5	26
Paktīā, state, Afg.	B2	54
Paktīkā, state, Afg.	B2	54
Pakwash Lake, l., On., Can.	A5	118
Pakxé, Laos	E7	48
Pala, Chad	F2	62
Pala, Mya.	F4	48
Palacios, Tx., U.S.	F11	130
Palagruža, Otoci, is., Cro.	H13	22
Palai, India	G3	53
Palaiochóra, Grc.	H6	28
Pālakodu, India	C5	53
Palamós, Spain	C14	20

Name	Map Ref.	Page
Pālampur, India	B6	54
Palamu National Park, p.o.i., India	G10	54
Palamut, Tur.	D10	28
Palana, Russia	E20	34
Palanan Bay, b., Phil.	B4	52
Palanga, Lith.	E3	10
Palangkaraya, Indon.	E8	50
Palani, India	F3	53
Pālanpur, India	F4	54
Palaoa Point, c., Hi., U.S.	c4	78a
Palapye, Bots.	C8	70
Pālār, stm., India	E4	53
Palas de Rei, Spain	B3	20
Palatka, Russia	D19	34
Palatka, Fl., U.S.	G4	116
Palau, Italy	C3	24
Palau, ctry., Oc.	g8	78b
Palau Islands, is., Palau	D10	44
Palauk, Mya.	F4	48
Palaw, Mya.	F4	48
Palawan, i., Phil.	F2	52
Palawan Passage, strt., Phil.	F1	52
Palayan, Phil.	C3	52
Pālayankottai, India	G3	53
Palembang, Indon.	E4	50
Palena, Italy	I11	22
Palena, stm., S.A.	H2	90
Palencia, Spain	B6	20
Palencia, co., Spain	B6	20
Palen Lake, l., Ca., U.S.	J1	132
Palenque, Mex.	G13	100
Palenque, sci., Mex.	G12	100
Palermo, Col.	F4	86
Palermo, Italy	F7	24
Palermo, Ur.	F10	92
Palestina, Mex.	E6	130
Palestine, Ar., U.S.	B7	122
Palestine, Il., U.S.	E10	120
Palestine, Tx., U.S.	F3	122
Palestine, hist. reg., Asia	G6	58
Palestine, Lake, res., Tx., U.S.	E3	122
Palestrina, Italy	I9	22
Paletwa, Mya.	D7	46
Pālghāt, India	F3	53
Palgrave Point, c., Nmb.	E1	68
Palhano, stm., Braz.	C6	88
Pāli, India	F4	54
Palikir, Micron.	m11	78d
Palima, Indon.	F12	50
Palinuro, Capo, c., Italy	D9	24
Palisade, Ne., U.S.	A7	128
Palisades, Id., U.S.	G15	136
Palisades Reservoir, res., U.S.	G15	136
Pālitāna, India	H3	54
Palivere, Est.	A6	10
Palizada, Mex.	F12	100
Palk Bay, b., Asia	G4	53
Palkino, Russia	G20	8
Pālkonda, India	B6	53
Pālkonda Range, mts., India	D4	53
Palk Strait, strt., Asia	G4	53
Pallastunturi, mtn., Fin.	B11	8
Palliser, Cape, c., N.Z.	E6	80
Palma, Braz.	K4	88
Palma, Moz.	C7	68
Palma, stm., Braz.	G2	88
Palma, Badia de, b., Spain	E13	20
Palmácia, Braz.	C6	88
Palma del Río, Spain	G5	20
Palma de Mallorca, Spain	E13	20
Palma di Montechiaro, Italy	G7	24
Palmar, stm., Ven.	B6	86
Palmar, Lago Artificial del, res., Ur.	F9	92
Palmar Camp, Belize	D3	102
Palmarejo, P.R.	B1	104a
Palmares, Braz.	E8	88
Palmarito, Ven.	D6	86
Palmarola, Isola, i., Italy	D6	24
Palmas, Braz.	F1	88
Palmas, Braz.	C12	92
Palmas Bellas, Pan.	H7	102
Palmas de Monte Alto, Braz.	H4	88
Palma Soriano, Cuba	B9	102
Palm Bay, Fl., U.S.	H5	116
Palm Beach, Fl., U.S.	J5	116
Palmdale, Ca., U.S.	I7	134
Palm Desert, Ca., U.S.	J9	134
Palmeira, Braz.	B13	92
Palmeira das Missões, Braz.	C11	92
Palmeira dos Índios, Braz.	E7	88
Palmeiras, stm., Braz.	F2	88
Palmeirinhas, Ponta das, c., Ang.	B1	68
Palmelo, Braz.	I1	88
Palmer, P.R.	B4	104a
Palmer, Ak., U.S.	D10	140
Palmer, Ma., U.S.	B13	114
Palmer, Ne., U.S.	F14	126
Palmer, Tn., U.S.	B13	122
Palmer, sci., Ant.	B34	81
Palmer Lake, Co., U.S.	B3	128
Palmer Land, reg., Ant.	C34	81
Palmerston, N.Z.	G4	80
Palmerston, at., Cook Is.	E10	72
Palmerston, Cape, c., Austl.	C7	76
Palmerston North, N.Z.	E6	80
Palmerton, Pa., U.S.	D10	114
Palmetto, Ga., U.S.	D14	122
Palmetto, La., U.S.	G6	122
Palmetto Point, c., Antig.	e4	105b
Palmi, Italy	F9	24
Palmira, Col.	F3	86
Palmira, Cuba	A7	102
Palmira, Ec.	I2	86
Palmitas, Ur.	F9	92
Palm Springs, Ca., U.S.	J9	134
Palmyra *see* Tudmur, Syria	D9	58
Palmyra, Il., U.S.	E7	120
Palmyra, Mo., U.S.	E6	120
Palmyra, N.Y., U.S.	A8	114
Palmyra, Va., U.S.	G7	114
Palmyra, sci., Syria	D9	58
Palmyra Atoll, at., Oc.	C10	72
Palo Alto, Mex.	H8	130
Palo Alto, Ca., U.S.	F3	134
Palo Blanco, P.R.	B2	104a
Palo Flechado Pass, p., N.M., U.S.	E3	128
Paloh, Malay.	B7	50
Paloich, Sudan	E6	62
Palojoensuu, Fin.	B10	8
Palomar Mountain, mtn., Ca., U.S.	J9	134
Palomas, Mex.	F4	130
Palo Pinto, Tx., U.S.	B9	130
Palopo, Indon.	E12	50
Palos, Cabo de, c., Spain	G10	20
Palo Santo, Arg.	B8	92
Palos Verdes Point, c., Ca., U.S.	J7	134
Palouse, stm., U.S.	D8	136
Palo Verde, Ca., U.S.	J2	132
Palpa, Peru	F2	84
Palpalá, Arg.	B5	92
Palu, Indon.	D11	50
Palu, Teluk, b., Indon.	D11	50
Paluga, Russia	D21	8
Palwal, India	D6	54
Pama, Burkina	G5	64
Pamanukan, Indon.	G5	50
Pāmban Channel, strt., India	G4	53
Pāmban Island, i., India	G4	53
Pamekasan, Indon.	G8	50
Pamenang, Indon.	E3	50
Pameungpeuk, Indon.	G5	50
Pamiers, Fr.	F7	18
Pamir, mts., Asia	B11	56
Pamlico Sound, strt., N.C., U.S.	A10	116
Pampa, Tx., U.S.	F8	128
Pampã, stm., Braz.	I5	88
Pampa (Pampas), reg., Arg.	G4	90
Pampa Almirón, Arg.	C8	92
Pampa del Chañar, Arg.	E3	92
Pampa del Indio, Arg.	B7	92
Pampanga, stm., Phil.	C3	52
Pampanua, Indon.	F12	50
Pampas, Peru	F3	84
Pampas, stm., Peru	F3	84
Pampas see Pampa, reg., Arg.	F4	90
Pamplico, S.C., U.S.	B6	116
Pamplona, Col.	D5	86
Pamplona, Spain	B9	20
Pamukkale (Hierapolis), sci., Tur.	F12	28
Pamukova, Tur.	C13	28
Pana, Il., U.S.	E8	120
Panabá, Mex.	B3	102
Panabo, Phil.	G5	52
Panacea, Fl., U.S.	G14	122
Panadura, Sri L.	H4	53
Panagjurište, Blg.	G11	26
Panaitan, Pulau, i., Indon.	G4	50
Panaji, India	D1	53
Panamá, Pan.	H8	102
Panama, Ok., U.S.	B4	122
Panama, ctry., N.A.	F9	96
Panamá, Bahía de, b., Pan.	H8	102
Panamá, Canal de (Panama Canal), can., Pan.	H8	102
Panamá, Golfo de, b., Pan.	D2	86
Panama, Gulf of see Panamá, Golfo de, b., Pan.	D2	86
Panama, Isthmus of see Panamá, Istmo de, isth., Pan.	H8	102
Panamá, Istmo de (Panama, Isthmus of), isth., Pan.	H8	102
Panama Basin, unds.	H5	144
Panama Canal see Panamá, Canal de, can., Pan.	H8	102
Panama City, Fl., U.S.	G13	122
Panambi, Braz.	D11	92
Panamint Range, mts., Ca., U.S.	G8	134
Panamint Valley, val., Ca., U.S.	G8	134
Panao, Peru	E2	84
Panarea, Isola, i., Italy	F9	24
Panaro, stm., Italy	F8	22
Panay, i., Phil.	E4	52
Panay Gulf, b., Phil.	E4	52
Pančevo, Serb.	E7	26
Panciu, Rom.	D14	26
Panda, Moz.	D12	70
Pandaria, India	G8	54
Pan de Azúcar, Ur.	G10	92
Pandėlys, Lith.	D8	10
Pāndharkawada, India	A4	53
Pandharpur, India	C2	53
Pāndhurna, India	H7	54
Pando, Ur.	G10	92
Panevėžys, Lith.	E7	10
Pāng, stm., Mya.	B4	48
Panga, D.R.C.	D5	66
Pangala, Congo	E2	66
Pangandaran, Indon.	G6	50
Pangani, Tan.	F7	66
Pangani, stm., Tan.	E7	66
Pangburn, Ar., U.S.	B7	122
Pangfou *see* Bengbu, China	E7	42
Panghkam, Mya.	D8	46
Pangi, D.R.C.	E5	66
Pangkajene, Indon.	F11	50
Pangkalanbrandan, Indon.	J4	48
Pangkalanbuun, Indon.	E7	50
Pangkalpinang, Indon.	E5	50
Pango Aluquem, Ang.	B1	68
Pangŏjin, Kor., S.	D2	40
Pangong Tso, l., Asia	B7	54
Panguiranan, Phil.	D4	52
Panguitch, Ut., U.S.	F4	132
Pangutaran, Phil.	G3	52
Pangutaran Group, is., Phil.	G3	52
Panhandle, Tx., U.S.	F7	128
Pānī'au, mtn., Hi., U.S.	b1	78a
Panié, Mont, mtn., N. Cal.	m15	79d
Panīpāt, India	D6	54
Panitan, Phil.	E4	52
Panj (Pjandž), stm., Asia	B11	56
Panjang, Indon.	F4	50
Panjang, Selat, strt., Indon.	C3	50
Pankshin, Nig.	H6	64
Panlong (Lo), stm., Asia	A7	48
P'anmunjŏm-ni, Kor., N.	E7	38
Panna, India	F8	54
Panna National Park, p.o.i., India	F7	54
Pannawonica, Austl.	D3	74
Pannirtuuq, Nu., Can.	B17	106
Panola, U.S.	E10	122
Páno Lévkara, Cyp.	D4	58
Panopah, Indon.	D7	50
Panorama, Braz.	D6	90
Panovo, Russia	C18	32
Panruti, India	F4	53
Panshan, China	D4	38
Pantanal, reg., S.A.	C5	90
Pantanaw, Mya.	D2	48
Pantar, Pulau, i., Indon.	G7	44
Pantelleria, Isola di, i., Italy	H6	24
Pantonlabu, Indon.	J3	48
Pánuco, Mex.	E10	100
Pánuco, stm., Mex.	E9	100
Panxian, China	F5	36
Panyam, Nig.	H6	64
Panzós, Guat.	E3	102
Pao, stm., Thai.	D6	48
Pao, stm., Ven.	C9	86
Pao, stm., Ven.	C8	86
Paochi *see* Baoji, China	D2	42
Paoki *see* Baoji, China	D2	42
Paola, Italy	E9	24
Paola, Ks., U.S.	F3	120
Paoli, In., U.S.	F11	120
Paopao, Fr. Poly.	v20	78h
Paoting *see* Baoding, China	B6	42
Paotou *see* Baotou, China	A4	42
Paotow *see* Baotou, China	A4	42
Pápa, Hung.	B4	26
Papagaio, stm., Braz.	I10	86
Papagaios, Braz.	D3	88
Papagayo, Golfo de, b., C.R.	G4	102
Pāpa'ikou, Hi., U.S.	d6	78a
Papantla de Olarte, Mex.	E10	100
Papara, Fr. Poly.	v22	78h
Papa Stour, i., Scot., U.K.	n18	12a
Papeari, Fr. Poly.	w22	78h
Papeete, Fr. Poly.	v21	78h
Papenburg, Ger.	C3	16
Papetoai, Fr. Poly.	v20	78h
Paphos *see* Néa Páfos, Cyp.	D3	58
Papigochic, stm., Mex.	G8	98
Papillion, Ne., U.S.	C1	120
Paposo, Chile	B2	92
Papua, Gulf of, b., Pap. N. Gui.	D5	72
Papua New Guinea, ctry., Oc.	D5	72
Papulovo, Russia	F23	8
Papun, Mya.	C3	48
Papunáua, stm., Col.	G6	86
Papurí (Papuri), stm., S.A.	G6	86
Papuri (Papurí), stm., S.A.	G6	86
Pará, state, Braz.	D7	84
Pará, stm., Braz.	A1	88
Pará, stm., Braz.	J3	88
Parabel', Russia	C14	32
Paraburdoo, Austl.	D3	74
Paracatu, Braz.	I2	88
Paracatu, stm., Braz.	I3	88
Paracel Islands see Xisha Qundao, is., China	B5	50
Pārachinār, Pak.	B3	54
Paracho de Verduzco, Mex.	F7	100
Parachute, Co., U.S.	D8	132
Paraćin, Serb.	F8	26
Paracuru, Braz.	B6	88
Parada, Punta, c., Peru	G2	84
Paradise, Ca., U.S.	D4	134
Paradise, Mt., U.S.	C12	136
Paradise, Nv., U.S.	G1	132
Paradise Island, i., Bah.	m18	104f
Paradise Valley, Az., U.S.	J5	132
Paradise Valley, Nv., U.S.	B8	134
Pāradwīp, India	H11	54
Paragonah, Ut., U.S.	F4	132
Paragould, Ar., U.S.	H7	120
Paraguá, stm., Bol.	B4	90
Paragua, stm., Ven.	D10	86
Paraguaçu, stm., Braz.	G6	88
Paraguai (Paraguay), stm., S.A.	D5	90
Paraguaipoa, Ven.	B6	86
Paraguaná, Península de, pen., Ven.	A6	86
Paraguarí, Para.	B9	92
Paraguarí, state, Para.	C9	92
Paraguay, ctry., S.A.	D5	90
Paraguay (Paraguai), stm., S.A.	E5	90
Paraíba, state, Braz.	D7	88
Paraíba do Sul, stm., Braz.	K5	88
Paraibano, Braz.	D3	88
Parainen, Fin.	F9	8
Paraíso, Mex.	F12	100
Paraiso, Pan.	H8	102
Parakou, Benin	H5	64
Paramakkudi, India	G4	53
Paramaribo, Sur.	B6	84
Parambu, Braz.	D5	88
Paramillo, Parque Nacional, p.o.i., Col.	D3	86
Paramirim, Braz.	G4	88
Paramirim, stm., Braz.	F4	88
Páramo de Masa, Puerto de, p., Spain	B7	20
Paramušir, ostrov, i., Russia	F20	34
Paramythiá, Grc.	D3	28
Paran, Naḥal (Girafi, Wadi), stm.	I5	58
Paraná, Arg.	E7	92
Paranã, Braz.	G1	88
Paraná, state, Braz.	D6	90
Paranã, stm., Braz.	G1	88
Paraná, stm., S.A.	F5	90
Paranaguá, Braz.	B13	92
Paranaguá, Baía de, b., Braz.	B13	92
Paranaíba, Braz.	C6	90
Paranaíba, stm., Braz.	C6	90
Paranaidji, Braz.	D2	88
Paranapanema, stm., Braz.	D6	90
Paranapiacaba, Serra do, mts., Braz.	B13	92
Paranavaí, Braz.	D6	90
Parang, Phil.	G5	52
Parang, Pulau, i., Indon.	F7	50
Parângu Mare, Vârful, mtn., Rom.	D10	26
Paranhos, Braz.	A10	92
Paranoá, Lago do, res., Braz.	H2	88
Paraopeba, Braz.	J3	88
Parapetí, stm., Bol.	C4	90
Parara, Indon.	E12	50
Paratinga, Braz.	G4	88
Paratoo, Austl.	I2	76
Paray-le-Monial, Fr.	C9	18
Pārbati, stm., India	F6	54
Pārbatipur, Bngl.	F12	54
Parbhani, India	B3	53
Parchim, Ger.	C7	16
Pardeeville, Wi., U.S.	H9	118
Pārdi, India	H4	54
Parding, China	B12	54
Pardo, stm., Braz.	D6	90
Pardo, stm., Braz.	H6	88
Pardo, stm., Braz.	L1	88
Pardo, stm., Braz.	D11	92
Pardo, stm., Braz.	K1	88
Pardubice, Czech Rep.	F11	16
Paredón, Mex.	C8	100
Parelhas, Braz.	D7	88
Paren', Russia	D21	34
Paren', stm., Russia	D21	34
Parent, Qc., Can.	C2	110
Parentis-en-Born, Fr.	E4	18
Parepare, Indon.	E11	50
Parera, Arg.	G5	92
Parfenevo, Russia	F20	8
Párga, Grc.	D3	28
Parham, Antig.	f4	105b
Paria, Gulf of, b.	B10	86
Paria, Península de, pen., Ven.	B10	86
Pariaguán, Ven.	C9	86
Pariaman, Indon.	D1	50
Paricutín, vol., Mex.	F7	100
Parigi, Indon.	D12	50
Parika, Guy.	B6	84
Parikkala, Fin.	F13	8
Parima, stm., Braz.	F10	86
Parima, Serra (Parima, Sierra), mts., S.A.	F9	86
Parima, Sierra (Parima, Serra), mts., S.A.	F9	86
Parima Tapirapecó, Parque Nacional, p.o.i., Ven.	F9	86
Parintins, Braz.	D6	84
Paris, On., Can.	E9	112
Paris, Fr.	F11	14
Paris, Ar., U.S.	B5	122
Paris, Il., U.S.	I2	112
Paris, Ky., U.S.	F1	114
Paris, Mo., U.S.	E5	120
Paris, Tn., U.S.	H9	120
Paris, Tx., U.S.	D3	122
Parisienne, Ile, i., On., Can.	B5	112
Parita, Bahía de, b., Pan.	H7	102
Parit Buntar, Malay.	J5	48
Parkano, Fin.	E10	8
Park City, Mt., U.S.	B3	126
Park City, Ut., U.S.	C5	132
Parkdale, Or., U.S.	E5	136
Parker, Az., U.S.	I2	132
Parker, Co., U.S.	B4	128
Parker, Fl., U.S.	G13	122
Parker, Cape, c., Nu., Can.	B10	141
Parker City, In., U.S.	H4	112
Parker Dam, Ca., U.S.	I2	132
Parker Dam, dam, U.S.	I2	132
Parkersburg, Ia., U.S.	B5	120
Parkersburg, Il., U.S.	F9	120
Parkersburg, W.V., U.S.	E4	114
Parkes, Austl.	I7	76
Park Falls, Wi., U.S.	F8	118
Park Forest, Il., U.S.	G2	112
Parkhill, On., Can.	E8	112
Parkland, Wa., U.S.	C4	136
Park Range, mts., Co., U.S.	C10	132
Park Rapids, Mn., U.S.	E3	118
Parkrose, Or., U.S.	E4	136
Park Rynie, S. Afr.	G10	70
Parksley, Va., U.S.	G10	114
Parkston, S.D., U.S.	D14	126
Parksville, B.C., Can.	G6	138
Parkville, Md., U.S.	E9	114
Parkville, Mo., U.S.	E3	120
Parla, Spain	D7	20
Parlākimidi, India	B7	53
Parli, India	B3	53
Parma, Italy	F7	22
Parma, Mo., U.S.	H8	120
Parma, Oh., U.S.	C4	114
Parnaguá, Braz.	F3	88
Parnaíba, Braz.	B5	88
Parnaíba, stm., Braz.	B5	88
Parnaibinha, stm., Braz.	E2	88
Parnamirim, Braz.	E6	88
Parnassós, mtn., Grc.	E5	28
Párnitha, mtn., Grc.	E6	28
Pärnu, Est.	G11	8
Pärnu laht, b., Est.	G11	8
Paro, Bhu.	E12	54
Pārola, India	H5	54
Paromaj, Russia	F17	34
Paroo, stm., Austl.	G5	76
Páros, i., Grc.	F8	28
Parowan, Ut., U.S.	F4	132
Parque Nacional da Chapada da Diamantina, p.o.i., Braz.	G4	88
Parral, Chile	H2	92
Parral, stm., Mex.	B6	100
Parramatta, Austl.	I8	76
Parras de la Fuente, Mex.	C7	100
Parrish, Fl., U.S.	I3	116
Parrsboro, N.S., Can.	E12	110
Parry, Cape, c., N.T., Can.	A6	106
Parry Bay, b., Nu., Can.	B14	106
Parry Island, i., On., Can.	C9	112
Parry Peninsula, pen., N.T., Can.	B6	106
Parry Sound, On., Can.	C9	112
Parsberg, Ger.	G7	16
Parsęta, stm., Pol.	B11	16
Parshall, N.D., U.S.	G11	124
Paršino, Russia	C20	32
Parsnip, stm., B.C., Can.	A8	138
Parsons, Ks., U.S.	G2	120
Parsons, Tn., U.S.	B10	122
Pärsti, Est.	B8	10
Partanna, Italy	G6	24
Parthenay, Fr.	H8	14
Partinico, Italy	F7	24
Partizansk, Russia	C10	38
Partizánske, Slov.	H14	16
Paru, stm., Braz.	D7	84
Parú, stm., Ven.	E9	86
Paru de Oeste, stm., Braz.	C6	84
Parūr, India	F3	53
Pārvatīpuram, India	B6	53
Paryang, China	C9	54
Parys, S. Afr.	E8	70
Pasadena, Ca., U.S.	I7	134
Pasadena, Tx., U.S.	H3	122
Pasaje, Ec.	D2	84
Pa Sak, stm., Thai.	E5	48
Paşaköy, N. Cyp.	C4	58
Pasarbantal, Indon.	E2	50
Pasawng, Mya.	C3	48
Pascagoula, Ms., U.S.	G10	122
Pascagoula, stm., Ms., U.S.	G10	122
Paşcani, Rom.	B13	26
Pasco, Wa., U.S.	D7	136
Pascoag, R.I., U.S.	C14	114
Pascua, Isla de (Easter Island) (Rapa Nui), i., Chile	f30	78l
Pas-de-Calais, state, Fr.	D11	14
Pasewalk, Ger.	C10	16
Pasir Mas, Malay.	J6	48
Pasirpengarayan, Indon.	C2	50
Pasir Puteh, Malay.	J6	48
Paškovo, Russia	G15	34
Pasłęka, stm., Pol.	C16	16
Pasley Bay, b., Nu., Can.	A11	106
Pašman, Otok, i., Cro.	G12	22
Pasmore, stm., Austl.	H2	76
Pasni, Pak.	D9	56
Paso de Indios, Arg.	H3	90
Paso del Cerro, Ur.	E9	92
Paso de los Libres, Arg.	D9	92
Paso de los Toros, Ur.	F9	92
Paso de Patria, Para.	C8	92
Paso de San Antonio, Mex.	E3	130
Paso Hondo, Mex.	H13	100
Paso Robles, Ca., U.S.	H5	134
Pašozero, Russia	F16	8
Pasquia Hills, hills, Sk., Can.	A11	124
Pasrūr, Pak.	B5	54
Passadumkeag, Me., U.S.	E8	110
Passadumkeag Mountain, hill, Me., U.S.	E8	110
Passage Point, c., N.T., Can.	B16	140
Passaic, N.J., U.S.	H15	112
Passamaquoddy Bay, b., N.A.	E10	110
Passau, Ger.	H9	16
Passero, Capo, c., Italy	H9	24
Passo Fundo, Braz.	D11	92
Passo Real, Represa do, res., Braz.	D11	92
Passos, Braz.	K2	88
Pastavy, Bela.	E9	10
Pastaza, state, Ec.	H3	86
Pastaza, stm., S.A.	D2	84
Pastillo, P.R.	B3	104a
Pasto, Col.	G3	86
Pastos Bons, Braz.	D3	88
Pasuruan, Indon.	G8	50
Pasvalys, Lith.	D7	10
Pásztó, Hung.	B6	26
Patacamaya, Bol.	C3	90
Patadkal, sci., India	C3	53
Patagonia, Az., U.S.	L6	132
Patagonia, reg., Arg.	I2	90
Pātan, India	G3	54
Patchogue, N.Y., U.S.	D13	114
Patea, N.Z.	D6	80
Pategi, Nig.	H6	64
Pate Island, i., Kenya	E8	66
Patensie, S. Afr.	H7	70
Paterna, Spain	E10	20
Paternion, Aus.	D10	22
Paternò, Italy	G8	24
Paterson, N.J., U.S.	D11	114
Pathānkot, India	B5	54
Pathein, Mya.	D2	48
Pathfinder Reservoir, res., Wy., U.S.	E5	126
Pathiu, Thai.	G4	48
Pathum Thani, Thai.	E5	48
Pati, Indon.	G7	50
Patía, Col.	F3	86
Patía, stm., Col.	F2	86
Patiāla, India	C6	54
Patillas, P.R.	B3	104a
Pati Point, c., Guam	i10	78c
Pativilca, Peru	F2	84
Pātkai Range, mts., Asia	F4	36
Pat Mayse Lake, res., Tx., U.S.	D3	122
Pátmos, i., Grc.	F9	28
Patna, India	F10	54
Patna, India	H11	54
Patnāgarh, India	H9	54
Patnanongan Island, i., Phil.	C4	52
Pato Branco, Braz.	C11	92
Patoka, Il., U.S.	F8	120
Patoka, stm., In., U.S.	F10	120
Patoka Lake, res., In., U.S.	F11	120
Patomskoe nagor'e, plat., Russia	E12	34
Patonga, Ug.	D6	66
Patos, Braz.	D7	88
Patos, stm., Arg.	E3	92
Patos, Lagoa dos, b., Braz.	E12	92
Patos de Minas, Braz.	J2	88
Patquía, Arg.	D4	92
Pátra, Grc.	E4	28
Patrai, Gulf of see Patraïkós Kólpos, b., Grc.	E4	28
Patraïkós Kólpos, b., Grc.	E4	28
Patricio Lynch, Isla, i., Chile	I1	90
Patrocínio, Braz.	J2	88
Pattani, Thai.	I5	48
Pattaya, Thai.	F5	48
Patten, Me., U.S.	D8	110
Patterson, Ca., U.S.	F4	134
Patterson, Ga., U.S.	E3	116
Patterson, Mount, mtn., Yk., Can.	C4	106
Patti, Golfo di, b., Italy	F9	24
Pattison, Ms., U.S.	F8	122
Pattoki, Pak.	C4	54
Pattonsburg, Mo., U.S.	D3	120
Pattukkottai, India	F4	53
Pattullo, Mount, mtn., B.C., Can.	D5	106
Patuākhāli, Bngl.	G13	54
Patuca, stm., Hond.	E5	102
Pātūr, India	H6	54
Patusi, Pap. N. Gui.	a4	79a
Patuxent, stm., Md., U.S.	F9	114
Pátzcuaro, Mex.	F8	100
Pau, Fr.	F5	18
Pau, Gave de, stm., Fr.	F5	18
Pau Brasil, Braz.	H6	88
Pau dos Ferros, Braz.	D6	88
Pauh, Indon.	E3	50
Pauini, stm., Braz.	E4	84
Pauini, stm., Braz.	H10	86
Pauk, Mya.	B2	48
Pauksa Taung, mtn., Mya.	C2	48
Paul, Id., U.S.	H13	136
Paulding, Ms., U.S.	E9	122
Paulicéia, Braz.	D6	90
Paulina Peak, mtn., Or., U.S.	G5	136
Pauline, Mount, mtn., Can.	C11	138
Paulino Neves, Braz.	B4	88
Paulistana, Braz.	E5	88
Paulistas, Braz.	J4	88
Paullina, Ia., U.S.	B2	120
Paulo Afonso, Braz.	E6	88
Paulo Afonso, Cachoeira de, wtfl., Braz.	E6	88
Paulpietersburg, S. Afr.	E10	70
Pauls Valley, Ok., U.S.	G11	128
Paung, Mya.	D3	48
Paungde, Mya.	C2	48
Pauri, India	C7	54
Paute, Ec.	I2	86
Paute, stm., Ec.	I2	86
Pauto, stm., Col.	E6	86
Pavia, Italy	E6	22
Pavilion, B.C., Can.	F9	138
Pāvilosta, Lat.	D4	10
Pavlikeni, Blg.	F12	26
Pavlodar, Kaz.	D13	32
Pavlof Volcano, vol., Ak., U.S.	E7	140
Pavlovo, Russia	I20	8
Pavlovsk, Russia	A13	10
Pavlovsk, Russia	D14	32
Pavlovskij Posad, Russia	E21	10
Pavo, Ga., U.S.	F2	116
Pavullo nel Frignano, Italy	F7	22
Pavuvu Island, i., Sol. Is.	e8	79b
Pawan, stm., Indon.	D7	50
Pawhuska, Ok., U.S.	E12	128
Pawn, stm., Mya.	C3	48
Pawnee, Il., U.S.	E8	120
Pawnee, Ok., U.S.	A2	122
Pawnee, stm., Ks., U.S.	C9	128
Pawnee Rock, Ks., U.S.	C9	128
Pawni, India	H7	54
Pawota, Mya.	D3	48
Paw Paw, Il., U.S.	C8	120
Paw Paw, Mi., U.S.	F4	112
Pawtucket, R.I., U.S.	C14	114
Paxoí, i., Grc.	D3	28
Paxson, Ak., U.S.	D10	140
Paxton, Ne., U.S.	F11	126
Paya, Hond.	E5	102
Payakumbuh, Indon.	D2	50
Payamlı, Tur.	A9	58
Payerne, Switz.	D3	22
Payeti, Indon.	H12	50
Payette, Id., U.S.	F10	136
Payette, stm., Id., U.S.	G10	136
Payette, North Fork, stm., Id., U.S.	F11	136
Payette, South Fork, stm., Id., U.S.	F11	136
Payne, Oh., U.S.	C1	114
Payne, Lac, l., Can.	D16	106
Paynes Find, Austl.	E3	74
Paynton, Sk., Can.	A5	124
Paysandú, Ur.	F8	92
Payson, Az., U.S.	I5	132
Payson, Il., U.S.	E6	120
Payson, Ut., U.S.	C5	132
Payún, Cerro, mtn., Arg.	H3	92
Pazarbaşı Burnu, c., Tur.	B13	28
Pazarcık, Tur.	A8	58
Pazardžik, Blg.	G11	26
Pazaryeri, Tur.	D12	28
Paz de Ariporo, Col.	E6	86
Pčevža, Russia	A15	10
Pe, Mya.	F4	48
Pea, stm., U.S.	F12	122
Peabody, Ks., U.S.	C11	128
Peabody, Ma., U.S.	B14	114
Peace, stm., Can.	D8	106
Peace, stm., Fl., U.S.	I4	116
Peace River, Ab., Can.	D7	106
Peachland, B.C., Can.	G11	138
Peach Orchard, Ga., U.S.	C3	116
Peach Springs, Az., U.S.	H3	132
Peak District National Park, p.o.i., Eng., U.K.	H11	12
Peak Downs, Austl.	D7	76
Peak Hill, Austl.	E3	74
Peak Hill, Austl.	I7	76
Peäldoajvi, mtn., Fin.	B12	8
Peale, Mount, mtn., Ut., U.S.	E7	132
Pearisburg, Va., U.S.	G5	114
Pearl, Il., U.S.	E7	120
Pearl, Ms., U.S.	E8	122
Pearl, stm., U.S.	G9	122
Pearland, Tx., U.S.	H3	122
Pearl Harbor, b., Hi., U.S.	b3	78a
Pearl Peak, mtn., Nv., U.S.	C1	132
Pearl River, La., U.S.	G9	122
Pearson, Ga., U.S.	E3	116
Peary Land, reg., Grnld.	A18	141
Pease, stm., Tx., U.S.	G9	128
Pebane, Moz.	D6	68
Pebas, Peru	D3	84
Pebble Island, i., Falk. Is.	J5	90
Peć, Serb.	G7	26
Pecan Gap, Tx., U.S.	D3	122
Peçanha, Braz.	J4	88
Peças, Ilha das, i., Braz.	B13	92
Pecatonica, Il., U.S.	B8	120
Pecatonica, stm., U.S.	B8	120
Pečenga, Russia	B14	8
Pechenizhyn, Ukr.	A11	26
Pechora see Pečora, stm., Russia	C25	8
Pechora Bay see Pečorskaja guba, b., Russia	A8	32
Pečora, Russia	A9	32
Pečora (Pechora), stm., Russia	A8	32
Pecoraro, Monte, mtn., Italy	F10	24
Pečorskaja guba, b., Russia	A8	32
Pečorskoe more, s., Russia	A8	32
Pečory, Russia	C10	10
Pecos, N.M., U.S.	F3	128
Pecos, Tx., U.S.	C4	130
Pecos, stm., U.S.	F12	98
Pecos National Monument, p.o.i., N.M., U.S.	F3	128
Pécs, Hung.	C5	26
Pedana, India	C5	53
Pedasí, Pan.	I7	102
Pedder, Lake, res., Austl.	o12	77a
Peddie, S. Afr.	H8	70
Pededze, stm., Eur.	C10	10
Pedernales, Dom. Rep.	C12	102
Pedernales, Ven.	C10	86
Pedernales, stm., Tx., U.S.	D9	130
Pedernales, Salar de, pl., Chile	C3	92
Pedra Azul, Braz.	I5	88
Pedra Branca, Braz.	C6	88
Pedra Lume, C.V.	k10	65a
Pedras de Fogo, Braz.	D8	88
Pedras Salgadas, Port.	C3	20
Pedraza, Col.	B4	86
Pedregal, Ven.	B6	86
Pedreiras, Braz.	C3	88
Pedriceña, Mex.	C6	100
Pedro, Point, c., Sri L.	G5	53
Pedro Afonso, Braz.	E1	88
Pedro Avelino, Braz.	C7	88
Pedro Cays, is., Jam.	D9	102
Pedro Gomes, Braz.	G7	84
Pedro II, Braz.	C5	88
Pedro II, Ilha, i., S.A.	G8	86
Pedro Juan Caballero, Para.	D5	90
Pedro Leopoldo, Braz.	J3	88
Pedro Osório, Braz.	E11	92
Pedro R. Fernández, Arg.	D8	92
Pedro Velho, Braz.	D8	88
Peebles, Scot., U.K.	F9	12
Peebles, Oh., U.S.	F2	114
Pee Dee, stm., U.S.	A6	116
Peekskill, N.Y., U.S.	C12	114
Peel, I. of Man	G8	12
Peel, stm., Can.	B4	106
Peel Point, c., N.T., Can.	B17	140
Peel Sound, strt., Nu., Can.	A11	106
Peene, stm., Ger.	C9	16
Peerless, Mt., U.S.	F8	124
Peesane, Sk., Can.	B10	124
Peetz, Co., U.S.	G9	126
Pegasus Bay, b., N.Z.	F5	80
Pegnitz, Ger.	G7	16
Pegu, stm., Mya.	D3	48
Pegu Yoma, mts., Mya.	C2	48
Pegyš, Russia	E24	8
Pehlivanköy, Tur.	B9	28
Pehuajó, Arg.	G7	92
Peian *see* Bei'an, China	B10	36
Peiching *see* Beijing, China	B7	42
Peihai *see* Beihai, China	K3	42
Peikang, Tai.	J9	42
Peine, Ger.	D6	16
Peine, Pointe à, c., Dom.	j6	105c
Peinnechaung, i., Mya.	I14	54
Peip'ing *see* Beijing, China	B7	42
Peipus, Lake, l., Eur.	B10	10
Peiraiás (Piraeus), Grc.	F6	28
Peissenberg, Ger.	I7	16
Peixe, Braz.	G1	88
Peixe, stm., Braz.	D6	90
Peixian, China	D7	42
Peixoto, Represa de, res., Braz.	K2	88
Pekalongan, Indon.	G6	50
Pekan, Malay.	K6	48
Pekanbaru, Indon.	C2	50
Pekin, Il., U.S.	D8	120
Pekin, In., U.S.	F11	120
Peking *see* Beijing, China	B7	42
Peklino, Russia	G16	10
Pekul'nej, hrebet, mts., Russia	C24	34
Pelabohan Klang, Malay.	K5	48
Pelabuhanratu, Indon.	G5	50
Pelagie, Isole, is., Italy	I6	24
Pelaihari, Indon.	E9	50
Pelat, Mont, mtn., Fr.	E12	18
Pełczyce, Pol.	C11	16
Peleduj, Russia	C20	32
Pelée, Montagne, vol., Mart.	k6	105c
Pelee, Point, c., On., Can.	G7	112
Pelee Island, i., On., Can.	G7	112
Pelega, Vârful, mtn., Rom.	D9	26
Peleliu see Beliliou, i., Palau	D9	44
Peleng, Pulau, i., Indon.	F7	44
Pelham, Al., U.S.	D12	122
Pelham, Ga., U.S.	E1	116
Pelhřimov, Czech Rep.	G11	16
Pelican, Ak., U.S.	E12	140
Pelican Bay, b., Mb., Can.	B13	124
Pelican Lake, Wi., U.S.	F9	118
Pelican Lake, l., Mb., Can.	B13	124
Pelican Lake, l., Mb., Can.	E14	124
Pelican Lake, l., Mn., U.S.	C5	118
Pelican Rapids, Mb., Can.	B13	124
Pelican Rapids, Mn., U.S.	E2	118
Pelister Nacionalni Park, p.o.i., Mac.	B4	28
Peljekaise Nationalpark see Pieljekaise Nationalpark, p.o.i., Swe.	C6	8
Pelješac, Poluotok, pen., Cro.	H14	22
Peljušnja, Russia	B15	10
Pella, Ia., U.S.	C5	120
Pélla, sci., Grc.	C5	28
Pell City, Al., U.S.	D12	122
Pellegrini, Arg.	H6	92
Pellegrini, Lago, l., Arg.	I4	92
Pello, Fin.	C11	8
Pellworm, i., Ger.	B4	16
Pelly, Sk., Can.	C12	124
Pelly, stm., Yk., Can.	C4	106
Pelly Bay, b., Nu., Can.	B12	106
Pelly Crossing, Yk., Can.	C3	106
Pelly Lake, l., Nu., Can.	B10	106
Pelly Mountains, mts., Yk., Can.	C4	106
Pelón de Ñado, mtn., Mex.	E9	100
Peloponnesus see Pelopónnisos, pen., Grc.	F5	28
Pelopónnisos, state, Grc.	F5	28
Pelopónnisos (Peloponnesus), pen., Grc.	F5	28
Pelotas, Braz.	E11	92
Pelotas, stm., Braz.	C12	92
Pelusium Bay see Tīna, Khalīg el-, b., Egypt	G3	58
Pemadumcook Lake, l., Me., U.S.	E7	110
Pemalang, Indon.	G6	50
Pemangkat, Indon.	C6	50
Pematangsiantar, Indon.	B1	50
Pemba, Moz.	C7	68
Pemba, Zam.	D4	68
Pemba, i., Tan.	F7	66
Pemberton, Austl.	F3	74
Pemberton, B.C., Can.	F8	138
Pembina, N.D., U.S.	C1	118
Pembina, stm., Ab., Can.	B16	138
Pembina, stm., N.A.	F16	124
Pembina Hills, hills, N.A.	E15	124
Pembroke, On., Can.	C12	112
Pembroke, Wales, U.K.	J7	12
Pembroke, Ga., U.S.	D4	116
Pembroke, Ky., U.S.	H10	120
Pembroke, Me., U.S.	F9	110
Pembroke, N.C., U.S.	B6	116
Pembroke, Cape, c., Nu., Can.	C14	106
Pembroke Pines, Fl., U.S.	K5	116
Pembrokeshire Coast National Park, p.o.i., Wales, U.K.	J7	12
Pembuang, Indon.	E7	50
Pembuang, stm., Indon.	D8	50

Name | Map Ref. | Page

Pemigewasset, stm., N.H., U.S. G5 110
Pemuco, Chile H1 92
Penafiel, Port. C2 20
Peñalara, Pico de, mtn., Spain D6 20
Penalva, Braz. B3 88
Penang see George Town, Malay. J4 48
Peñaranda de Bracamonte, Spain D5 20
Pen Argyl, Pa., U.S. D10 114
Peñarroya-Pueblonuevo, Spain F5 20
Peñas, Cabo de, c., Spain A5 20
Penas, Golfo de, b., Chile I2 90
Penasco, N.M., U.S. E3 128
Pench National Park, p.o.i., India H7 54
Pendembu, S.L. H2 64
Pendembu, S.L. H2 64
Pendências, Braz. C7 88
Pendleton, In., U.S. H4 112
Pendleton, Or., U.S. E8 136
Pendleton, S.C., U.S. B3 116
Pendolo, Indon. E12 50
Pend Oreille, stm., N.A. B9 136
Pend Oreille, Lake, l., Id., U.S. B10 136
Pendžikent, Taj. B10 56
Penebel, Indon. H9 50
Penedo, Braz. F7 88
Penetanguishene, On., Can. D9 112
Peneus see Pineiós, stm., Grc. D5 28
Penfield, Pa., U.S. C7 114
Penganga, stm., India H6 54
Penghu, China I8 42
P'enghu Ch'üntao (Pescadores), is., Tai. J8 42
P'enghu Shuitao, strt., Tai. J8 42
Pengkou, China I7 42
Penglai, China C9 42
Pengpu see Bengbu, China E7 42
Pengshui, China G2 42
Pengwaluote Shan, mtn., China B11 54
Pengxi, China F1 42
Pengxian, China E5 36
Pengze, China G7 42
Penha, Braz. C13 92
Penhsi see Benxi, China D5 38
Penibética, Cordillera, mts., Spain G8 20
Peniche, Port. E1 20
Penicuik, Scot., U.K. F9 12
Penida, Nusa, i., Indon. H9 50
Peninsular Malaysia see Semenanjung Malaysia, hist. reg., Malay. K6 48
Peníscola, Spain D11 20
Penki see Benxi, China D5 38
Pennant Station, Sk., Can. D5 124
Penne, Italy H10 22
Penneru, stm., India D4 53
Penn Hills, Pa., U.S. H10 112
Pennine Alps, mts., Eur. C13 18
Pennines, mts., Eng., U.K. G10 12
Pennington Gap, Va., U.S. H2 114
Pennsboro, W.V., U.S. E4 114
Pennsylvania, state, U.S. C8 114
Penn Yan, N.Y., U.S. B8 114
Penny Ice Cap, ice, Nu., Can. B17 106
Penny Strait, strt., Nu., Can. B6 141
Peno, Russia D15 10
Penobscot, stm., Me., U.S. F8 110
Penobscot, East Branch, stm., Me., U.S. D8 110
Penobscot, West Branch, stm., Me., U.S. D7 110
Penobscot Bay, b., Me., U.S. F7 110
Penola, Austl. K3 76
Peñón de Ifac see Penyal d'Ifac, misc. cult., Spain F11 20
Penong, Austl. F6 74
Penonomé, Pan. H7 102
Penrhyn, at., Cook Is. D11 72
Penrith, Austl. I8 76
Penrith, Eng., U.K. G10 12
Pensacola, Fl., U.S. G11 122
Pensacola Bay, b., Fl., U.S. G11 122
Pensacola Mountains, mts., Ant. D36 81
Pense, Sk., Can. D9 124
Pensilvania, Col. E4 86
Pentagon Mountain, mtn., Mt., U.S. C13 136
Pentecostes, Braz. B6 88
Pentecost Island see Pentecôte, i., Vanuatu j17 79d
Pentecôte, state, Vanuatu j17 79d
Pentecôte (Pentecost Island), i., Vanuatu j17 79d
Penticton, B.C., Can. G11 138
Pentland, Austl. C5 76
Pentland Firth, strt., Scot., U.K. C9 12
Pentwater, Mi., U.S. E3 112
Penuba, Indon. D4 50
Peñuelas, P.R. B2 104a
Penuguan, Indon. E4 50
Penukonda, India D3 53
Penyal d'Ifac, misc. cult., Spain F11 20
Penza, Russia D7 32
Penzance, Eng., U.K. K7 12
Penzberg, Ger. I7 16
Penžina, stm., Russia D22 34
Penžinskaja guba, b., Russia D21 34
Penžinskij hrebet, mts., Russia D22 34
Peoples Creek, stm., Mt., U.S. F5 124
People's Democratic Republic of Korea see Korea, North, ctry., Asia D7 38
Peoria, Az., U.S. J4 132
Peoria, Il., U.S. D8 120
Peoria Heights, Il., U.S. K9 118
Peotone, Il., U.S. G2 112
Pepel, S.L. H2 64
Pepin, Wi., U.S. G6 118
Pepin, Lake, l., U.S. G7 118
Peqin, Alb. C13 24
Perabumulih, Indon. E4 50
Perak, state, Malay. J5 48
Perak, stm., Malay. J5 48
Perak, Kuala, b., Malay. J5 48
Perales de Alfambra, Spain D9 20
Peralillo, Chile G2 92
Peralta, N.M., U.S. I10 132
Perambalur, India F4 53
Percé, Qc., Can. B12 110
Perchas, P.R. B2 104a
Perche, Collines du, hills, Fr. F9 14
Percival Lakes, l., Austl. D4 74
Percy Isles, is., Austl. C8 76
Perdida, stm., Braz. E2 88
Perdido, stm., U.S. G11 122
Perdido, Monte, mtn., Spain B10 20
Perdizes, Braz. J2 88
Perdue, Sk., Can. B6 124
Perechyn, Ukr. H18 16
Pereež'na, Russia G22 8
Pereira, Col. E4 86
Perelazy, Russia G14 10
Peremyšl', Russia F18 10
Pereslavl'-Zalesskij, Russia D21 10
Pérez, Arg. F7 92
Pergamino, Arg. F7 92
Pergamum, sci., Tur. D10 28
Pergine Valsugana, Italy D8 22
Perham, Mn., U.S. E3 118
Péribonka, Qc., Can. B4 110
Péribonka, stm., Qc., Can. B5 110
Péribonka, Lac, l., Qc., Can. E16 106
Perico, Arg. B5 92
Pericumã, stm., Braz. B3 88
Peridot, Az., U.S. J6 132
Perigiraja, Indon. D3 50
Périgord, hist. reg., Fr. D6 18
Périgueux, Fr. D6 18
Perijá, Serranía de, mts., S.A. C5 86
Perim see Barīm, i., Yemen G5 56
Peri-Mirim, Braz. B3 88
Perito Moreno, Arg. I2 90
Peritoró, Braz. C3 88
Periyār, stm., India F3 53
Periyar Tiger Reserve, India G3 53
Perkasie, Pa., U.S. D10 114
Perkins, Ok., U.S. A2 122
Perlas, Archipiélago de las, is., Pan. H8 102
Perlas, Laguna de, b., Nic. F6 102
Perleberg, Ger. C7 16
Perlez, Serb. D7 26
Perlis, state, Malay. I5 48
Perm', Russia C9 32
Përmet, Alb. D14 24
Pernambuco, state, Braz. E6 88
Pernik, Blg. G10 26
Péronne, Fr. E11 14
Perote, Mex. F10 100
Perow, B.C., Can. B4 138
Perpignan, Fr. G8 18
Perrault Falls, On., Can. A5 118
Perrin, Tx., U.S. A9 130
Perrine, Fl., U.S. K5 116
Perris, Ca., U.S. J8 134
Perro, Laguna del, l., N.M., U.S. G3 128
Perro, Punta del, c., Spain H4 20
Perros, Bahía de, strt., Cuba A8 102
Perros-Guirec, Fr. F5 14
Perry, Fl., U.S. F2 116
Perry, Ia., U.S. C3 120
Perry, Ks., U.S. E2 120
Perry, Mi., U.S. B1 114
Perry, Mo., U.S. E6 120
Perry, N.Y., U.S. B7 114
Perry, Kap, c., Grnld. B11 141
Perry Lake, res., Ks., U.S. E2 120
Perrysburg, Oh., U.S. C2 114
Perry's Victory and International Peace Memorial, hist., Oh., U.S. C2 114
Perrysville, Oh., U.S. D3 114
Perryton, Tx., U.S. E8 128
Perryville, Ak., U.S. E8 140
Perryville, Ar., U.S. B6 122
Perryville, Ky., U.S. G12 120
Perseverancia, Bol. B4 90
Persia, Ia., U.S. C2 120
Persia see Iran, ctry., Asia C7 56
Persian Gulf, b., Asia D7 56
Perth, Austl. F3 74
Perth, On., Can. D13 112
Perth, Scot., U.K. E9 12
Perth Amboy, N.J., U.S. D11 114
Perth Basin, unds. L13 142
Pertominsk, Russia D18 8
Peru, Il., U.S. C8 120
Peru, In., U.S. H3 112
Peru, Ne., U.S. D2 120
Peru, N.Y., U.S. F3 110
Peru, ctry., S.A. E2 84
Peru Basin, unds. J5 144
Perućac, Jezero, res., Eur. G16 22
Peru-Chile Trench, unds. K6 144
Perugia, Italy G9 22
Perugorría, Arg. D8 92
Peruíbe, Braz. B14 92
Perušić, Cro. F12 22
Pervomais'k, Ukr. A17 26
Pervomajsk, Russia I20 8
Pervomajskij, Russia F15 10
Pervoural'sk, Russia C9 32
Pervyj Kuril'skij proliv, strt., Russia F20 34
Pes', Russia B17 10
Pesaro, Italy G9 22
Pescadores see P'enghu Ch'üntao, is., Tai. J8 42
Pescadores Channel see P'enghu Shuitao, strt., Tai. J8 42
Pescara, Italy H11 22
Pescara, stm., Italy H11 22
Pescasseroli, Italy C7 24
Pescia, Italy G7 22
Pesé, Pan. D1 86
Peshāwar, Pak. B3 54
Peshkopi, Alb. C14 24
Peshkopija see Peshkopi, Alb. C14 24
Peshtigo, Wi., U.S. C2 112
Peshtigo, stm., Wi., U.S. F10 118
Peski, Bela. G7 10
Pesočnoe, Russia B22 10
Peso da Régua, Port. C3 20
Pesquería, stm., Mex. I8 130
Pessac, Fr. E5 18
Pest, state, Hung. B6 26
Peštera, Blg. G11 26
Pestovo, Russia B18 10
Pëstraja Dresva, Russia D20 34
Petacalco, Bahía, b., Mex. G7 100
Petah Tiqwa, Isr. F5 58
Petal, Ms., U.S. F9 122
Petalcingo, Mex. G12 100
Petalión, Kólpos, b., Grc. F7 28
Petaluma, Ca., U.S. E3 134
Petare, Ven. B8 86
Petatlán, Mex. G8 100
Petawawa, On., Can. C12 112
Petén Itzá, Lago, l., Guat. D2 102
Petenwell Lake, res., Wi., U.S. G8 118
Peterborough, Austl. I2 76
Peterborough, On., Can. D11 112
Peterborough, Eng., U.K. I12 12
Peterhead, Scot., U.K. D11 12
Peter Island, i., Br. Vir. Is. e8 104b
Peter Isøy, i., Ant. B31 81
Peter Lake, l., Nu., Can. C12 106
Peterlee, Eng., U.K. G11 12
Peterman, Al., U.S. F11 122
Peter Pond Lake, l., Sk., Can. D9 106
Petersburg, Ak., U.S. E13 140
Petersburg, Il., U.S. K9 118
Petersburg, In., U.S. F10 120
Petersburg, Tn., U.S. B12 122
Petersburg, Tx., U.S. H7 128
Petersburg, Va., U.S. G8 114
Petersburg, W.V., U.S. F6 114
Petersfield, Eng., U.K. J12 12
Peterson, Ia., U.S. B2 120
Peter the Great Bay see Petra Velikogo, zaliv, b., Russia C9 38
Petilia Policastro, Italy E10 24
Pétion-Ville, Haiti C11 102
Petit-Bourg, Guad. h5 105c
Petitcodiac, N.B., Can. E11 110
Petite Rivière Noire, Piton de la, mtn., Mrts. i10 69a
Petites-Anses, Guad. i5 105c
Petit-Goâve, Haiti C11 102
Petit Jean, stm., Ar., U.S. B5 122
Petitot, stm., Can. D6 106
Petit Piton, vol., St. Luc. m6 105c
Petitsikapau Lake, l., Nf., Can. E17 106
Petlād, India G4 54
Peto, Mex. B3 102
Petoskey, Mi., U.S. C5 112
Petra see Al-Batrā', sci., Jord. H6 58
Petra Velikogo, zaliv (Peter the Great Bay), b., Russia C9 38
Petre, Point, c., On., Can. E12 112
Petrič, Blg. H10 26
Petrified Forest National Park, p.o.i., Az., U.S. I7 132
Petrila, Rom. D10 26
Petrinja, Cro. E13 22
Petriščevo, Russia E19 10
Petrodvorec, Russia A12 10
Petrolândia, Braz. E6 88
Petrólea, Col. C5 86
Petrolia, Tx., U.S. G10 128
Petrolina, Braz. E5 88
Petrolina de Goiás, Braz. I1 88
Petrona, Punta, c., P.R. C3 104a
Petropavl see Petropavlovsk, Kaz. D11 32
Petropavlovka, Russia F10 34
Petropavlovsk, Kaz. D11 32
Petropavlovsk-Kamčatskij, Russia F20 34
Petrópolis, Braz. L4 88
Petros, Tn., U.S. H13 120
Petroşani, Rom. D10 26
Petrovac, Serb. E8 26
Petrovsk, Russia D6 32
Petrovskij, Russia H18 8
Petrovsk-Zabajkal'skij, Russia F10 34
Petrozavodsk, Russia F15 8
Petrusburg, S. Afr. F7 70
Petrusville, S. Afr. G7 70
Petrykau, Bela. H11 10
Pettus, Tx., U.S. F10 130
Petuhovo, Russia C11 32
Peuetsagoe, Gunung, vol., Indon. J3 48
Peureulak, Indon. J3 48
Peusangan, stm., Indon. J3 48
Pevek, Russia C23 34
Peza, stm., Russia D23 8
Pezawa Taung, mtn., Mya. C2 48
Pézenas, Fr. F9 18
Pezinok, Slov. H13 16
Pfarrkirchen, Ger. H8 16
Pforzheim, Ger. H4 16
Pfronten, Ger. I6 16
Pfunds, Aus. D7 22
Pfungstadt, Ger. G4 16
Pha-an, Mya. D3 48
Phagwāra, India C5 54
Phalaborwa, S. Afr. C10 70
Phalodi, India E4 54
Phaltan, India C2 53
Phan, Thai. C4 48
Phanat Nikhom, Thai. F5 48
Phangan, Ko, i., Thai. H5 48
Phangnga, Thai. H4 48
Phaniang, stm., Thai. D6 48
Phanom Dongrak Range (Dângrêk, Chuŏr Phnum), mts., Asia C3 44
Phan Rang, Viet. G9 48
Phan Thiet, Viet. G9 48
Phan Thong, Thai. F5 48
Pharenda, India E9 54
Pharr, Tx., U.S. H9 130
Phat Diem, Viet. B8 48
Phatthalung, Thai. I5 48
Phayao, Thai. C4 48
Phelps, N.Y., U.S. B8 114
Phelps, Wi., U.S. E9 118
Phelps Lake, l., N.C., U.S. I9 114
Phenix City, Al., U.S. E13 122
Phepane, stm., S. Afr. E6 70
Phet Buri, stm., Thai. F4 48
Phetchabun, Thai. D5 48
Phetchabun, Thiu Khao, mts., Thai. D5 48
Phetchaburi, Thai. F4 48
Phibun Mangsahan, Thai. E7 48
Phichai, Thai. D5 48
Phichit, Thai. D5 48
Philadelphia, Ms., U.S. E9 122
Philadelphia, N.Y., U.S. D14 112
Philadelphia, Pa., U.S. E10 114
Phil Campbell, Al., U.S. C11 122
Philip, S.D., U.S. C11 126
Philippeville see Skikda, Alg. B6 64
Philippeville, Bel. D13 14
Philippi, W.V., U.S. E5 114
Philippi see Fílippoi, sci., Grc. B7 28
Philippi, Lake, l., Austl. E2 76
Philippine Basin, unds. H15 142
Philippines, ctry., Asia C4 52
Philippine Sea, s. H15 142
Philippine Trench, unds. I15 142
Philippolis, S. Afr. G7 70
Philipsburg, Mt., U.S. D13 136
Philipsburg, Pa., U.S. D7 114
Philip Smith Mountains, mts., Ak., U.S. C10 140
Philipstown, S. Afr. G7 70
Phillaur, India C5 54
Phillip Island, i., Austl. L5 76
Phillips, Me., U.S. F6 110
Phillips, Tx., U.S. F7 128
Phillips, Wi., U.S. F8 118
Phillipsburg, Ga., U.S. E2 116
Phillipsburg, N.J., U.S. D10 114
Philo, Il., U.S. E9 120
Philo, Oh., U.S. E4 114
Philpots Island, i., Nu., Can. C10 141
Phimai, Thai. E6 48
Phitsanulok, Thai. D5 48
Phnom Penh see Phnum Pénh, Camb. G7 48
Phnum Pénh (Phnom Penh), Camb. G7 48
Phoenix, Az., U.S. J4 132
Phoenix, N.Y., U.S. E13 112
Phoenix, Or., U.S. A3 134
Phoenix Islands, is., Kir. D9 72
Phoenixville, Pa., U.S. D10 114
Phofung (Sources, Mont-aux-), mtn., Afr. F9 70
Phon, Thai. E6 48
Phong, stm., Thai. D6 48
Phôngsali, Laos B6 48
Phon Phisai, Thai. D6 48
Phra Chedi Sam Ong, p., Asia E4 48
Phrae, Thai. C5 48
Phra Nakhon Si Ayutthaya, Thai. E5 48
Phran Kratai, Thai. D4 48
Phrom Phiram, Thai. D5 48
Phu Cat, Viet. E9 48
Phuket, Thai. I4 48
Phuket, Ko, i., Thai. I4 48
Phu Ly, Viet. B7 48
Phum Duang, stm., Thai. H4 48
Phumĭ Bâ Khăm, Camb. F8 48
Phumĭ Béng, Camb. F7 48
Phumĭ Châmbák, Camb. G7 48
Phumĭ Chhuk, Camb. G7 48
Phumĭ Chruŏy Slêng, Camb. F8 48
Phumĭ Kâmpóng Srâlau, Camb. E7 48
Phumĭ Kâmpóng Trâbâk, Camb. F7 48
Phumĭ Kaôh Kért, Camb. F7 48
Phumĭ Khpôb, Camb. G7 48
Phumĭ Lvéa Kraôm, Camb. F6 48
Phumĭ Narŭng, Camb. F7 48
Phumĭ Prêk Kák, Camb. F7 48
Phumĭ Puŏk Chăs, Camb. F6 48
Phumĭ Sâmraông, Camb. E6 48
Phumĭ Srê Kôkir, Camb. F8 48
Phumĭ Tbêng, Camb. F7 48
Phumĭ Thmâ Pôk, Camb. F6 48
Phumĭ Tœk Choŭ, Camb. F6 48
Phu My, Viet. E9 48
Phuoc Long, Viet. G8 48
Phuoc Long, Viet. H7 48
Phu Pan National Park, p.o.i., Thai. D6 48
Phu Quoc, Dao, i., Viet. G6 48
Phu Tho, Viet. B7 48
Phu Vang, Viet. D8 48
Pi, stm., China F7 42
Piaçabuçu, Braz. F7 88
Piacenza, Italy E6 22
Pialba, Austl. E9 76
Piancó, Braz. D7 88
Pianosa, Isola, i., Italy H6 22
Pianosa, Isola, i., Italy H12 22
Piapot, Sk., Can. E4 124
Piaseczno, Pol. D16 16
Piaski, Pol. E18 16
Piatã, Braz. G5 88
Piatra-Neamţ, Rom. B13 26
Piauí, state, Braz. D4 88
Piauí, stm., Braz. D4 88
Piauí, Morro do, mtn., Braz. H2 88
Piave, stm., Italy E9 22
Piaxtla, stm., Mex. D5 100
Piazza Armerina, Italy G8 24
Pibor Post, Sudan F6 62
Pic, stm., On., Can. B12 118
Picacho, Az., U.S. K5 132
Picardie, hist. reg., Fr. E11 14
Picardy see Picardie, hist. reg., Fr. E11 14
Picayune, Ms., U.S. G9 122
Pichanal, Arg. D4 90
Picher, Ok., U.S. H3 120
Pichilemu, Chile G1 92
Pichimá, Col. E3 86
Pichi Mahuida, Arg. I5 92
Pichincha, state, Ec. H2 86
Pichucalco, Mex. G12 100
Pickardville, Ab., Can. B16 138
Pickens, Ms., U.S. E9 122
Pickens, S.C., U.S. B3 116
Pickensville, Al., U.S. D10 122
Pickerel Lake, l., Mb., Can. B14 124
Pickering, Eng., U.K. G12 12
Pickle Lake, On., Can. E12 106
Pickstown, S.D., U.S. D14 126
Pickton, Tx., U.S. D3 122
Pickwick Lake, res., U.S. B10 122
Pico, mtn., C.V. I10 65a
Pico, i., Port. C3 60
Pico da Neblina, Parque Nacional, p.o.i., Braz. G9 86
Pico de Orizaba, Parque Nacional, p.o.i., Mex. F10 100
Pico de Orizaba, Volcán (Citlaltépetl, Volcán), vol., Mex. F10 100
Picos, Braz. D5 88
Picquigny, Fr. E11 14
Picton, On., Can. D12 112
Picton, N.Z. E6 80
Picton, Isla, i., Chile K3 90
Pictou, N.S., Can. E14 110
Pictou Island, i., N.S., Can. E14 110
Picture Butte, Ab., Can. G18 138
Pictured Rocks National Lakeshore, p.o.i., Mi., U.S. B3 112
Picuí, Braz. D7 88
Picún Leufú, Arg. G3 90
Pidálion, Akrotírion, c., Cyp. D5 58
Pidhorodna, Ukr. A17 26
Pidurutalagala, mtn., Sri L. H5 53
Piedecuesta, Col. D5 86
Piedimonte Matese, Italy C8 24
Piedmont, Al., U.S. D13 122
Piedmont, Mo., U.S. G7 120
Piedmont see Piemonte, state, Italy F5 22
Piedra, stm., Co., U.S. F9 132
Piedra, Cerro, mtn., Chile H1 92
Piedra del Águila, Arg. H3 90
Piedrafita, Puerto de, p., Spain B3 20
Piedrahita, Spain D5 20
Piedras, Punta, c., Arg. G9 92
Piedras, Punta, c., Ven. B11 86
Piedras Blancas, Arg. E8 92
Piedras Negras, Guat. D2 102
Piedras Negras, Mex. A8 100
Pieksämäki, Fin. E12 8
Pielinen, l., Fin. E13 8
Pieljekaise Nationalpark, p.o.i., Swe. C6 8
Piemonte, state, Italy F5 22
Pienaarsrivier, S. Afr. D8 70
Pieniężno, Pol. B16 16
Pieniński Park Narodowy, p.o.i., Pol. G16 16
Pienza, Italy G8 22
Pierce, Co., U.S. G8 126
Pierce, Id., U.S. D11 136
Pierce City, Mo., U.S. E14 128
Pierpont, S.D., U.S. B15 126
Pierre, S.D., U.S. C12 126
Pierre, Bayou, stm., La., U.S. F5 122
Pierre, Bayou, stm., Ms., U.S. E8 122
Pierre Part, La., U.S. G7 122
Pierreville, Trin. s13 105f
Pierz, Mn., U.S. F4 118
Piešt'any, Slov. H13 16
Pietarsaari, Fin. E10 8
Pietermaritzburg, S. Afr. F10 70
Pietersburg, S. Afr. C9 70
Pietrasanta, Italy F7 22
Piet Retief, S. Afr. E10 70
Pietrosu, Vârful, mtn., Rom. B12 26
Pigeon, Mi., U.S. E6 112
Pigeon, stm., Mb., Can. B17 124
Pigeon Forge, Tn., U.S. I2 114
Pigeon Lake, l., Ab., Can. C16 138
Pigeon Lake, l., On., Can. D11 112
Piggs Peak, Swaz. E10 70
Pigs, Bay of see Cochinos, Bahía de, b., Cuba B7 102
Pigüé, Arg. H6 92
Pihāri, India E8 54
Pihlajavesi, l., Fin. F13 8
Pihtipudas, Fin. E11 8
Pijijiapan, Mex. H12 100
Pikalëvo, Russia A17 10
Pikangikum, On., Can. E12 106
Pikes Peak, mtn., Co., U.S. C3 128
Pikes Rocks, hill, Pa., U.S. C6 114
Pikesville, Md., U.S. E9 114
Piketberg, S. Afr. H4 70
Piketon, Oh., U.S. E2 114
Pikeville, Tn., U.S. B13 122
Pikou, China B10 42
Pikounda, Congo D3 66
Piła, Pol. C12 16
Piła, state, Pol. C12 16
Pilanesberg Game Reserve, p.o.i., S. Afr. D8 70
Pilão Arcado, Braz. E4 88
Pilar, Arg. E5 92
Pilar, Braz. E8 88
Pilar, Para. C8 92
Pilar de Goiás, Braz. H1 88
Pilar do Sul, Braz. A14 92
Pilares, Mex. D3 130
Pilas Group, is., Phil. G3 52
Pilawa, Pol. D17 16
Pilcomayo, stm., S.A. D4 90
Pilcomayo, Brazo Norte, stm., Para. B8 92
Pilcomayo, Brazo Sur del, stm., S.A. B8 92
Pilcomayo, Parque Nacional, p.o.i., Arg. B8 92
Pilger, Ne., U.S. E15 126
Pilgrim's Rest, S. Afr. D10 70
Pili, Phil. D4 52
Pīlībhīt, India D7 54
Pilica, stm., Pol. E16 16
Pilliga, Austl. H7 76
Pilot, The, mtn., Austl. K7 76
Pilot Butte, Sk., Can. D9 124
Pilot Knob, Mo., U.S. G7 120
Pilot Knob, mtn., Id., U.S. E11 136
Pilot Mound, Mb., Can. E15 124
Pilot Mountain, N.C., U.S. H5 114
Pilot Peak, mtn., Nv., U.S. E8 134
Pilot Peak, mtn., Wy., U.S. F16 136
Pilot Rock, Or., U.S. E8 136
Pilottown, La., U.S. H9 122
Pilsen see Plzeň, Czech Rep. G9 16
Pilu, stm., Mya. B3 48
Pilzno, Pol. G17 16
Pima, Az., U.S. K7 132
Pimba, Austl. F7 74
Pimenteira, Vereda, stm., Braz. F4 88
Pimentel, Braz. B3 88
Pinang, Pulau, i., Malay. J4 48
Pınarbaşı, Tur. B16 28
Pinar del Río, Cuba A5 102
Pinarello, Fr. H15 18
Pınarhisar, Tur. B10 28
Pinas, Arg. E5 92
Pinatubo, Mount, vol., Phil. C3 52
Pincher Creek, Ab., Can. G17 138
Pinchi Lake, l., B.C., Can. B6 138
Pinckneyville, Il., U.S. F8 120
Pinconning, Mi., U.S. E5 112
Pindale, Mya. B2 48
Pindamonhangaba, Braz. L3 88
Pindaré, stm., Braz. B3 88
Pindaré-Mirim, Braz. B3 88
Pindi Gheb, Pak. B4 54
Pindobaçu, Braz. F5 88
Píndos Óros (Pindus Mountains), mts., Grc. D4 28
Pindus Mountains see Píndos Óros, mts., Grc. D4 28
Pindwāra, India F4 54
Pine, stm., Mi., U.S. E5 112
Pine Apple, Al., U.S. F11 122
Pine Barrens, reg., N.J., U.S. E11 114
Pine Bluff, Ar., U.S. C7 122
Pine Bush, N.Y., U.S. C11 114
Pine Castle, Fl., U.S. H4 116
Pine City, Mn., U.S. F6 118
Pine Creek, Austl. B6 74
Pine Creek, stm., Nv., U.S. C9 134
Pine Creek, stm., Pa., U.S. C8 114
Pine Falls, Mb., Can. D17 124
Pinega, Russia D20 8
Pinega, stm., Russia D20 8
Pine Grove, W.V., U.S. E5 114
Pine Hill, Austl. D6 76
Pine Hill, Al., U.S. F11 122
Pine Hills, Fl., U.S. H4 116
Pinehouse Lake, l., Sk., Can. D9 106
Pinehurst, Ga., U.S. D2 116
Pinehurst, Id., U.S. E10 136
Pinehurst, N.C., U.S. A6 116
Pinehurst Lake, l., Ab., Can. B19 138
Pineiós (Peneus), stm., Grc. D5 28
Pine Island, Mn., U.S. G6 118
Pine Island, i., Fl., U.S. J3 116
Pine Island Bay, b., Ant. C30 81
Pinellas Park, Fl., U.S. I3 116
Pine Mountain, mtn., Ca., U.S. H4 134
Pine Pass, p., B.C., Can. A8 138
Pine Point, N.T., Can. C8 106
Pine Ridge, S.D., U.S. D10 126
Pine River, Mb., Can. C13 124
Pine River, Mn., U.S. E4 118
Pinerolo, Italy F4 22
Piñeros, Isla, i., P.R. B4 104a
Pines, Isle of see Juventud, Isla de la, i., Cuba B6 102
Pines, Lake O' The, res., Tx., U.S. E4 122
Pine Swamp Knob, mtn., W.V., U.S. E6 114
Pinetop-Lakeside, Az., U.S. I6 132
Pinetops, N.C., U.S. I8 114
Pinetown, S. Afr. F10 70
Pine Valley, val., Ut., U.S. E3 132
Pineville, Ky., U.S. H2 114
Pineville, La., U.S. F6 122
Pineville, Mo., U.S. H3 120
Pineville, W.V., U.S. G4 114
Pinewood, S.C., U.S. C5 116
Ping, stm., Thai. E5 48
Ping'an, China B5 38
Pingba, China H2 42
Pingchang, China F2 42
Pingding, China C5 42
Pingdingshan, China E5 42
Pingdu, China C8 42
Pingelly, Austl. F3 74
Pinghe, China A6 48
Pinghu, China F9 42
Pingjiang, China G5 42
Pingle, China I4 42
Pingli, China E3 42
Pingliang, China D2 42
Pingluo, China B2 42
Pingnan, China H8 42
Pingnan, China J4 42
Pingquan, China A8 42
Pingshi, China I5 42
Pingtan, China I8 42
Pingtan Dao, i., China I8 42
P'ingtung, Tai. J9 42
Pingwu, China E5 36
Pingxiang, China H5 42
Pingxiang, China J2 42
Pingyang, China H9 42
Pingyao, China C5 42
Pingyi, China D7 42
Pingyin, China C7 42
Pingyuan, China I6 42
Pinhão, Braz. F7 88
Pinheiro, Braz. B3 88
Pinheiros, Braz. J5 88
Pinhel, Port. D3 20
Pini, Pulau, i., Indon. E2 44
Pinillos, Col. C4 86
Pinjarra, Austl. F3 74
Pinjug, Russia F22 8
Pinkiang see Harbin, China B7 38
Pink Mountain, B.C., Can. D6 106
Pinnacle, mtn., Va., U.S. E7 114
Pinnacle Buttes, mtn., Wy., U.S. G17 136
Pinnacles National Monument, p.o.i., Ca., U.S. G4 134
Pinnaroo, Austl. J3 76
Pinneberg, Ger. C5 16
Pinos, Mex. D8 100
Pinos, Isla de see Juventud, Isla de la, i., Cuba B6 102
Pinos, Mount, mtn., Ca., U.S. I6 134
Pinos Puente, Spain G7 20
Pinrang, Indon. E11 50
Pins, Île des, i., N. Cal. n16 79d
Pins, Pointe aux, c., On., Can. F8 112
Pinsk, Bela. H9 10
Pinsk Marshes see Pripet Marshes, reg., Eur. H12 10
Pinson, Al., U.S. D12 122
Pinta, Isla, i., Ec. h11 84a
Pintada Arroyo, stm., N.M., U.S. G3 128
Pintados, Chile D3 90
Pintasan, Malay. A10 50
Pinto Butte, mtn., Sk., Can. E6 124
Pintoyacu, stm., Ec. H3 86
Pin Valley National Park, p.o.i., India C6 54
Pioche, Nv., U.S. F2 132
Piombino, Italy H7 22
Pioneer Mine, B.C., Can. F8 138
Pionerskij, Russia F3 10
Pionki, Pol. E17 16
Piorini, stm., Braz. D5 84
Piorini, Lago, l., Braz. D5 84
Piotrków, state, Pol. E15 16
Piotrków Trybunalski, Pol. E15 16
Pio V. Corpuz, Phil. E5 52
Piove di Sacco, Italy E8 22
Pio XII, Braz. B3 88
Pipanaco, Salar de, pl., Arg. D4 92
Pīpār, India E4 54
Piparia, India G7 54
Pīpar Road, India E4 54
Pipe Spring National Monument, p.o.i., Az., U.S. G4 132
Pipestem Creek, stm., N.D., U.S. G14 124
Pipestone, Mn., U.S. H2 118
Pipestone, stm., On., Can. E12 106
Pipestone Creek, stm., Can. E12 124
Pipestone National Monument, p.o.i., Mn., U.S. G2 118
Pipinas, Arg. G9 92
Piplān, Pak. B3 54
Pipmuacan, Réservoir, res., Qc., Can. A6 110
Piqua, Oh., U.S. D1 114
Piquet Carneiro, Braz. C6 88
Piquiri, stm., Braz. B11 92
Piracanjuba, Braz. I1 88
Piracanjuba, stm., Braz. I1 88
Piracicaba, Braz. L2 88
Piracicaba, stm., Braz. L1 88
Piracuruca, Braz. B5 88
Pirae, Fr. Poly. v21 78h
Piraeus see Peiraiás, Grc. F6 28
Piraí do Sul, Braz. B12 92
Piraju, Braz. L1 88
Pirajuí, Braz. L1 88
Piram Island, i., India H4 54
Piran, Slvn. E10 22
Pirané, Arg. B8 92
Piranga, Braz. K4 88
Piranhas, Braz. G7 84
Piranhas, stm., Braz. E1 88
Piranhas, stm., Braz. C7 88
Piranji, stm., Braz. C6 88
Pirapemas, Braz. B3 88
Pirapora, Braz. I3 88
Piraquara, Braz. B13 92
Pirassununga, Braz. K2 88
Pirata, Monte, hill, P.R. B4 104a
Piratinga, stm., Braz. H2 88
Piratini, Braz. E11 92
Piratini, stm., Braz. D10 92
Piratuba, Braz. C11 92
Pires do Rio, Braz. I1 88
Piriápolis, Ur. G10 92
Pirin, Parki Narodowe, p.o.i., Blg. H10 26
Piripiri, Braz. C5 88
Píritu, Ven. C7 86
Pirmasens, Ger. G3 16
Pirna, Ger. F9 16
Pirojpur, Bngl. G12 54
Pirot, Serb. F9 26
Pirovano, Arg. H7 92
Pirovskoe, Russia C16 32
Pīr Panjāl Range, mts., Asia B5 54
Pirtleville, Az., U.S. L7 132
Pirttikylä, Fin. E9 8
Piru, Indon. F8 44
Pisa, Italy G7 22
Pisagua, Chile C2 90
Pisco, Peru F2 84
Pişcolt, Rom. B9 26
Písek, Czech Rep. G10 16
Pishan, China A4 46
Pishchanka, Ukr. A15 26
Pisinemo, Az., U.S. K4 132
Pismo Beach, Ca., U.S. H5 134
Pisticci, Italy D10 24
Pistoia, Italy G7 22
Pisuerga, stm., Spain C6 20
Pit, stm., Ca., U.S. B4 134
Pit, North Fork, stm., Ca., U.S. B5 134
Pita, Gui. G2 64
Pitalito, Col. G4 86
Pitanga, Braz. B12 92
Pitangui, Braz. J3 88
Pitcairn, dep., Pit. c28 78k
Piteå, Swe. D9 8
Piteälven, stm., Swe. D8 8
Piteşti, Rom. E11 26
Pithapuram, India C6 53
Pithiviers, Fr. F11 14
Pithom, hist., Egypt H2 58
Pithorāgarh, India D8 54
Pitinga, stm., Braz. H12 86
Pitiquito, Mex. F6 98
Pitkjaranta, Russia F14 8
Pitljar, Russia C2 34
Pitomača, Cro. D14 22
Pitrufquén, Chile G2 90
Pitt Island, i., B.C., Can. E5 106
Pitt Lake, l., B.C., Can. G8 138
Pittsboro, N.C., U.S. I6 114
Pittsburg, Ks., U.S. G3 120
Pittsburg, Tx., U.S. E4 122
Pittsburgh, Pa., U.S. D6 114
Pittsfield, Il., U.S. E7 120
Pittsfield, Ma., U.S. B12 114
Pittsfield, Me., U.S. F7 110
Pittsford, Mi., U.S. C1 114
Pittston, Pa., U.S. C10 114
Pittsview, Al., U.S. E13 122
Pittsworth, Austl. F8 76
Pituil, Arg. D4 92
Pium, Braz. F1 88
Piura, Peru E1 84
Piute Peak, mtn., Ca., U.S. H7 134
Pivan', Russia F16 34
Pivdennyy Buh, stm., Ukr. A17 26
Pizarro, Col. E3 86
Pizzo, Italy F10 24
Pjakupur, stm., Russia B13 32
Pjalka, Russia C19 8
Pjandž (Panj), stm., Asia B11 56
Pjaozero, ozero, l., Russia C14 8
Pjasina, stm., Russia B6 34
Pjasino, ozero, l., Russia B6 34
Pjasinskij zaliv, b., Russia B5 34
Pjatigorsk, Russia F6 32
Pjatovskij, Russia F19 10
Pjažieva Sel'ga, Russia F16 8
Placentia Bay, b., Nf., Can. j23 107a
Placerville, Ca., U.S. E5 134
Placetas, Cuba A8 102
Plácido Rosas, Ur. F11 92
Plai Mat, stm., Thai. E6 48
Plain City, Ut., U.S. B4 132
Plain Dealing, La., U.S. E5 122
Plainfield, Ct., U.S. C13 114
Plainfield, In., U.S. I3 112
Plainfield, N.J., U.S. D11 114

Name | Map Ref. | Page

Plains, Ga., U.S. E14 122
Plains, Ks., U.S. D8 128
Plains, Mt., U.S. C12 136
Plainview, Mn., U.S. G6 118
Plainview, Ne., U.S. E15 126
Plainview, Tx., U.S. G7 128
Plainville, In., U.S. F10 120
Plainwell, Mi., U.S. F4 112
Plakhtiïvka, Ukr. C16 26
Plamondon, Ab., Can. B18 138
Plampang, Indon. H10 50
Planá, Czech Rep. G8 16
Plana, L'Illa, i., Spain F10 20
Planada, Ca., U.S. F5 134
Planalto, Braz. C11 92
Planchón, Cerro del (El Planchón, Volcán), vol., S.A. G2 92
Planeta Rica, Col. C4 86
Plano, Il., U.S. C9 120
Plano, Tx., U.S. D2 122
Plantagenet, On., Can. E2 110
Plantation, Fl., U.S. J5 116
Plant City, Fl., U.S. I3 116
Plantersville, Ms., U.S. C10 122
Plantsite, Az., U.S. J7 132
Plaquemine, La., U.S. G7 122
Plasencia, Spain D4 20
Plaster Rock, N.B., Can. D9 110
Plasy, Czech Rep. G9 16
Plata, Isla de la, i., Ec. H1 86
Plata, Río de la, est., S.A. G9 92
Plato, Col. C4 86
Platte, stm., Ne., U.S. C7 108
Platte, stm., U.S. E3 120
Platte, Île, i., Sey. k13 69b
Platte Center, Ne., U.S. F15 126
Platte City, Mo., U.S. E3 120
Platteville, Co., U.S. A4 128
Platteville, Wi., U.S. B7 120
Plattsburgh, N.Y., U.S. F3 110
Plattsmouth, Ne., U.S. D2 120
Plau, Ger. C8 16
Plauen, Ger. F8 16
Plav, Mont. G6 26
Plavsk, Russia G20 10
Playa Azul, Mex. G7 100
Playa de Fajardo, P.R. B4 104a
Playa de Guayanilla, P.R. B2 104a
Playa de Naguabo, P.R. B4 104a
Playa de Ponce, P.R. C2 104a
Playa Noriega, Laguna, l., Mex. A3 100
Playa Vicente, Mex. G11 100
Playgreen Lake, l., Mb., Can. E11 106
Play Ku, Viet. F8 48
Plaza, N.D., U.S. F12 124
Pleasant, Mount, hill, N.B., Can. E9 110
Pleasant Bay, N.S., Can. D16 110
Pleasantdale, Sk., Can. B9 124
Pleasant Grove, Ut., U.S. C5 132
Pleasant Hill, Il., U.S. E7 120
Pleasant Hill, La., U.S. F5 122
Pleasant Hill, Mo., U.S. F3 120
Pleasanton, Ks., U.S. F3 120
Pleasanton, Tx., U.S. F9 130
Pleasantville, N.J., U.S. E11 114
Pleasantville, Pa., U.S. C6 114
Pleaux, Fr. D8 18
Plehanovo, Russia F20 10
Plenty, Sk., Can. C5 124
Plenty, Bay of, b., N.Z. C7 80
Plentywood, Mt., U.S. F9 124
Pleščeevo, ozero, l., Russia D21 10
Pleseck, Russia. E19 8
Plessisville, Qc., Can. D5 110
Pleszew, Pol. E13 16
Plétipi, Lac, l., Qc., Can. E16 106
Plettenbergbaai, S. Afr. I6 70
Pleven, Blg. F11 26
Plevna, Mt., U.S. A8 126
Plitvička Jezera Nacionalni Park, p.o.i., Cro. F12 22
Pljevlja, Mont. F6 26
Pljuskovo, Russia H16 10
Pljussa, stm., Russia A11 10
Płock, Pol. D15 16
Płock, state, Pol. D15 16
Ploërmel, Fr. G6 14
Ploiești, Rom. E12 26
Plomb du Cantal, mtn., Fr. D8 18
Plomer, Point, c., Austl. H9 76
Plön, Ger. B6 16
Płońsk, Pol. D16 16
Ploskoe, Russia H21 10
Plotnica, Bela. H9 10
Ploudalmézeau, Fr. F4 14
Plovdiv, Blg. G11 26
Plovdiv, state, Blg. G11 26
Plumerville, Ar., U.S. B6 122
Plummer, Id., U.S. C9 136
Plumridge Lakes, l., Austl. E5 74
Plumtree, Zimb. B8 70
Plungė, Lith. E4 10
Plutarco Elías Calles, Presa, res., Mex. G8 98
Plymouth, Monts. D3 105a
Plymouth, Eng., U.K. K8 12
Plymouth, Ca., U.S. E5 134
Plymouth, Il., U.S. D6 120
Plymouth, Ma., U.S. C15 114
Plymouth, N.C., U.S. I9 114
Plymouth, Ne., U.S. A11 128
Plymouth, N.H., U.S. G5 110
Plymouth, Oh., U.S. C3 114
Plymouth, Pa., U.S. C10 114
Plzeň, Czech Rep. G9 16
Pô, Burkina G4 64
Po, stm., Italy F8 22
Po, Foci del, mth., Italy F9 22
Po, Mouths of the see Po, Foci del, mth., Italy F9 22
Poarta Orientală, Pasul, p., Rom. D9 26
Pobè, Benin H5 64
Pobeda, gora, mtn., Russia C18 34
Pobedino, Russia G17 34
Pobedy, pik, mtn., Asia F14 32
Poblado Cerro Gordo, P.R. A3 104a
Poblado Jacaguas, P.R. B2 104a
Poblado Mediania Alta, P.R. B4 104a
Poblado Santana, P.R. B2 104a
Pobra de Trives, Spain B3 20
Pocahontas, Ar., U.S. H6 120
Pocahontas, Ia., U.S. B3 120
Poção, Braz. E7 88
Pocatello, Id., U.S. H14 136
Počep, Russia H16 10
Počinok, Russia D4 32
Pocitos, Salar, pl., Arg. B4 92
Poço da Cruz, Açude, res., Braz. E7 88
Poções, Braz. H5 88
Pocola, Ok., U.S. B4 122
Pocomoke City, Md., U.S. F10 114
Poconé, Braz. G6 84
Pocono Mountains, hills, Pa., U.S. C10 114
Pocono Summit, Pa., U.S. C10 114
Poço Redondo, Braz. E7 88
Poços de Caldas, Braz. K2 88
Pocrane, Braz. J5 88
Podbereze, Russia D13 10
Podborove, Russia A18 10
Poddębice, Pol. E14 16
Poddore, Russia C13 10
Poděbrady, Czech Rep. F11 16
Podgorica, Mont. G6 26
Podjuga, Russia F19 8
Podkamennaja Tunguska, Russia B16 32
Podkamennaja Tunguska, stm., Russia B16 32
Podlasie, reg., Pol. D19 16
Podol'sk, Russia E20 10
Podor, Sen. F2 64
Podporože, Russia F16 8
Podravina, reg., Cro. E15 22
Podtësovo, Russia C16 32
Podujevo, Serb. G8 26
Poel, i., Ger. B7 16
Poelela, Lagoa, l., Moz. D12 70
Pofadder, S. Afr. F4 70
Pogar, Russia H16 10
Poggibonsi, Italy G8 22
Pogoanele, Rom. E13 26
Pogoreloe Gorodišče, Russia D17 10
Pogradec, Alb. D14 24
Pogradeci see Pogradec, Alb. D14 24
Pograničnyj, Russia B9 38
P'ohang, Kor., S. C2 40
Pohjanmaa, reg., Fin. D11 8
Pohnpei, i., Micron. I11 78d
Pohri, India F6 54
Pohvistnevo, Russia D8 32
Pöide, Est. B6 10
Poinsett, Cape, c., Ant. B16 81
Poinsett, Lake, l., S.D., U.S. C15 126
Point, Tx., U.S. E3 122
Point Arena, Ca., U.S. E2 134
Point Au Fer Island, i., La., U.S. H7 122
Point Baker, Ak., U.S. E13 140
Pointe-à-la-Garde, Qc., Can. B10 110
Pointe à la Hache, La., U.S. H9 122
Pointe-à-Pitre, Guad. h5 105c
Pointe-à-Pitre-le Raizet, Aéroport de, Guad. h5 105c
Pointe du Canonnier, c., Guad. A1 105a
Pointe Edward, On., Can. E7 112
Pointe-Noire, Congo E2 66
Pointe-Noire, Guad. h5 105c
Point Fortin, Trin. s12 105f
Point Hope, Ak., U.S. C6 140
Point Jupiter, c., St. Vin. p11 105e
Point Lake, l., N.T., Can. B8 106
Point Marion, Pa., U.S. E5 114
Point Pelee National Park, p.o.i., On., Can. G7 112
Point Pleasant, N.J., U.S. D11 114
Point Reyes National Seashore, p.o.i., Ca., U.S. E2 134
Point Roberts, Wa., U.S. B3 136
Point Salines International Airport, Gren. q10 105e
Point Sapin, N.B., Can. D12 110
Poisson Blanc, Lac du, res., Qc., Can. B14 112
Poissy, Fr. F10 14
Poitiers, Fr. H9 14
Poitou, hist. reg., Fr. C5 18
Poivre Atoll, i., Sey. k12 69b
Pojarkovo, Russia G14 34
Pojoaque Valley, N.M., U.S. F2 128
Pojuca, Braz. G6 88
Pojuca, stm., Braz. G6 88
Pokaran, India E3 54
Pokataroo, Austl. G7 76
Pokharā, Nepal D10 54
Poko, D.R.C. D5 66
Pokrovsk, Russia D14 34
Pokrovskoe, Russia H19 10
Pola, stm., Russia C14 10
Polacca Wash, stm., Az., U.S. H6 132
Polack, Bela. E11 10
Pola de Lena, Spain A5 20
Pola de Siero, Spain A5 20
Poland, ctry., Eur. D15 16
Polanów, Pol. B12 16
Polatlı, Tur. D15 28
Polcura, Chile. H2 92
Poldnevica, Russia G22 8
Polebridge, Mt., U.S. B12 136
Pol-e Khomrī, Afg. B10 56
Polesie see Pripet Marshes, reg., Eur. H12 10
Polesine, reg., Italy E8 22
Polewali, Indon. E11 50
Polgár, Hung. B8 26
Poli, Cam. C2 66
Poli, China D8 42
Policastro, Golfo di, b., Italy E9 24
Police (Pölitz), Pol. C10 16
Polička, Czech Rep. G12 16
Polillo Island, i., Phil. C3 52
Polillo Islands, is., Phil. C4 52
Polis, Cyp. C3 58
Polist', stm., Russia C14 10
Polistena, Italy F10 24
Poljarnyj, Russia C24 34
Poljarnyj, Russia B15 8
Poljarnyj Ural, mts., Russia A10 32
Polk, Ne., U.S. F15 126
Polk, Pa., U.S. C6 114
Pol'kino, Russia B8 34
Pollāchi, India F3 53
Pöllau, Aus. C12 22
Pollino, Monte, mtn., Italy E10 24
Pollock, La., U.S. F6 122
Pollock, S.D., U.S. B12 126
Polnovo-Seliger, Russia C15 10
Polo, Il., U.S. B8 120
Polomet', stm., Russia C15 10
Polonnaruwa, Sri L. H5 53
Polonnaruwa, sci., Sri L. H5 53
Polotnjanyj, Russia F18 10
Polski Trămbeš, Blg. F12 26
Polson, Mt., U.S. C12 136
Poltava, Ukr. E4 32
Poltimore, Qc., Can. C14 112
Põltsamaa, Est. G12 8
Poluj, stm., Russia A11 32
Polunočnoe, Russia B10 32
Polur, India E4 53
Polvijärvi, Fin. E13 8
Polyaigos, i., Grc. G8 28
Polynesia, is., Oc. J22 142
Polysajevo, Russia F6 34
Pomarkku, Fin. F9 8
Pombal, Braz. D7 88
Pomerania, hist. reg., Eur. C11 16
Pomeranian Bay, b., Eur. B10 16
Pomerode, Braz. C13 92
Pomeroy, Ia., U.S. B3 120
Pomeroy, Oh., U.S. E4 114
Pomeroy, Wa., U.S. D9 136
Pomfret, S. Afr. D6 70
Pomi, Rom. B10 26
Pomme de Terre, stm., Mn., U.S. F3 118
Pomme de Terre, stm., Mo., U.S. G4 120
Pomme de Terre Lake, res., Mo., U.S. G4 120
Pomona, Ca., U.S. I8 134
Pomona, Ks., U.S. F2 120
Pomona Lake, res., Ks., U.S. F2 120
Pomorskij proliv, strt., Russia B24 8
Pompano Beach, Fl., U.S. J5 116
Pompei, sci., Italy D8 24
Pompejevka, Russia G15 34
Pompéu, Braz. J3 88
Pomquet, N.S., Can. E15 110
Ponass Lakes, l., Sk., Can. B9 124
Ponazyrevo, Russia G22 8
Ponca, Ne., U.S. B1 120
Ponca City, Ok., U.S. E11 128
Ponca Creek, stm., U.S. E14 126
Ponce, P.R. B2 104a
Ponce, Aeropuerto, P.R. B2 104a
Ponce de Leon, Fl., U.S. G12 122
Poncha Pass, p., Co., U.S. C2 128
Pond Creek, Ok., U.S. E11 128
Ponderay, Id., U.S. B10 136
Pondicherry (Puduchcheri), India F4 53
Pondicherry, state, India E5 53
Pond Inlet see Mittimatalik, Nu., Can. A15 106
Pond Inlet, b., Nu., Can. A15 106
Pondosa, Ca., U.S. B4 134
Ponente, Riviera di, cst., Italy F5 22
Ponérihouen, N. Cal. m15 79d
Ponferrada, Spain B4 20
Pongolo, stm., S. Afr. E10 70
Poniatowa, Pol. E17 16
Ponizove, Russia E14 10
Ponnaiyār, stm., India E4 53
Ponnāni, India F2 53
Ponnūru Nidubrolu, India C5 53
Ponoj, Russia C19 8
Ponoj, stm., Russia C18 8
Ponoka, Ab., Can. D17 138
Ponorogo, Indon. G7 50
Pons, Fr. D5 18
Ponta Delgada, Port. C3 60
Ponta Grossa, Braz. B12 92
Pontalina, Braz. I1 88
Ponta Porã, Braz. D5 90
Pontarlier, Fr. H15 14
Pontas de Pedra, Braz. D8 88
Pontassieve, Italy G8 22
Pontchartrain, Lake, l., La., U.S. G8 122
Pontchâteau, Fr. G6 14
Pont-de-Vaux, Fr. C10 18
Ponte Alta do Bom Jesus, Braz. G2 88
Ponte-Caldelas, Spain B2 20
Ponte de Lima, Port. C2 20
Pontedera, Italy G7 22
Pontedeume, Spain A2 20
Ponte do Púngoè, Moz. A12 70
Ponteix, Sk., Can. E6 124
Ponte Nova, Braz. K4 88
Ponte Serrada, Braz. C12 92
Pontevedra, Spain B2 20
Pontevedra, co., Spain B2 20
Pontiac, Il., U.S. D9 120
Pontiac, Mi., U.S. B2 114
Pontianak, Indon. C6 50
Pontine Islands see Ponziane, Isole, is., Italy D6 24
Pontivy, Fr. F5 14
Pontoise, Fr. E11 14
Pontotoc, Ms., U.S. C9 122
Pontotoc, Tx., U.S. D9 130
Pontremoli, Italy F6 22
Pontresina, Switz. D6 22
Pont-Rouge, Qc., Can. D5 110
Ponts, Spain C12 20
Pont-sur-Yonne, Fr. F12 14
Pontus Mountains see Doğu Karadeniz Dağları, mts., Tur. A5 56
Pontypridd, Wales, U.K. J9 12
Ponyri, Russia H19 10
Ponziane, Isole (Pontine Islands), is., Italy D6 24
Poole, Eng., U.K. K11 12
Pooley Island, i., B.C., Can. D2 138
Poolville, Tx., U.S. B10 130
Pooncarie, Austl. I4 76
Poopó, Bol. C3 90
Poopó, Lago, l., Bol. C3 90
Popayán, Col. F3 86
Pope, Ms., U.S. C8 122
Popești-Leordeni, Rom. E13 26
Popham Bay, b., Nu., Can. C17 106
Popigaj, Russia B11 34
Popigaj, stm., Russia B10 34
Popiltah Lake, l., Austl. I3 76
Poplar, Mt., U.S. F8 124
Poplar, stm., Can. B16 124
Poplar, stm., N.A. F8 124
Poplar, West Fork (West Poplar), stm., N.A. F8 124
Poplar Bluff, Mo., U.S. H7 120
Poplar Hill, On., Can. E12 106
Poplar Point, Mb., Can. D16 124
Poplarville, Ms., U.S. G9 122
Popocatépetl, Volcán, vol., Mex. F9 100
Popoh, Indon. H7 50
Popokabaka, D.R.C. F3 66
Popoli, Italy H10 22
Popondetta, Pap. N. Gui. b4 79a
Popovo, Blg. F13 26
Poprad, Slov. G16 16
Poprad, stm., Eur. G16 16
Popricani, Rom. B14 26
Pŏptong-ŭp, Kor., N. E7 38
Poquoson, Va., U.S. G9 114
Porangatu, Braz. G1 88
Porbandar, India H2 54
Porce, stm., Col. D4 86
Porcher Island, i., B.C., Can. E4 106
Porco, Bol. C3 90
Porcos, stm., Braz. G3 88
Porcuna, Spain G6 20
Porcupine, stm., N.A. C3 106
Pordenone, Italy D9 22
Pordim, Blg. F11 26
Poreče, Russia E18 10
Poreče-Rybnoe, Russia C22 10
Porhov, Russia C12 10
Pori (Björneborg), Fin. F9 8
Porjaguba, Russia C15 8
Porlamar, Ven. B10 86
Porog, Russia E18 8
Poronajsk, Russia G17 34
Poroshkove, Ukr. H18 16
Porpoise Bay, b., Ant. B17 81
Porrentruy, Switz. C3 22
Porretta Terme, Italy F7 22
Porsangen, b., Nor. A11 8
Porsangerhalvøya, pen., Nor. A11 8
Porsgrunn, Nor. G3 8
Porsuk, stm., Tur. D13 28
Portachuelo, Bol. C4 90
Port Adelaide, Austl. J2 76
Portadown, N. Ire., U.K. G6 12
Portage, Mi., U.S. F4 112
Portage, Ut., U.S. B4 132
Portage Bay, b., Mb., Can. C15 124
Portage Lake, l., Mi., U.S. D10 118
Portage la Prairie, Mb., Can. E15 124
Portageville, Mo., U.S. H8 120
Portal, Ga., U.S. D4 116
Portal, N.D., U.S. F11 124
Port Alberni, B.C., Can. G6 138
Portalegre, Port. E3 20
Portalegre, state, Port. E3 20
Portales, N.M., U.S. G5 128
Port Alfred, S. Afr. H8 70
Port Alice, B.C., Can. F3 138
Port Allen, La., U.S. G7 122
Port Alma, Austl. D8 76
Port Angeles, Wa., U.S. B3 136
Port Antonio, Jam. i14 104d
Port Aransas, Tx., U.S. G10 130
Portarlington, Ire. H5 12
Port Arthur, Austl. o13 77a
Port Arthur see Lüshun, China E4 38
Port Arthur, Tx., U.S. H4 122
Port Askaig, Scot., U.K. F6 12
Port Augusta, Austl. I2 76
Port au Port Peninsula, pen., Nf., Can. B17 110
Port-au-Prince, Haiti C11 102
Port-au-Prince, Baie de, b., Haiti C11 102
Port Austin, Mi., U.S. D6 112
Port Blair, India F7 46
Port Borden, P.E., Can. D13 110
Port Byron, Il., U.S. J8 118
Port Canning, India G12 54
Port-Cartier, Qc., Can. E17 106
Port Chalmers, N.Z. G4 80
Port Charlotte, Fl., U.S. J3 116
Port Clinton, Oh., U.S. C3 114
Port Clyde, Me., U.S. G7 110
Port Colborne, On., Can. F10 112
Port Coquitlam, B.C., Can. G8 138
Port-de-Paix, Haiti C11 102
Port Dickson, Malay. K5 48
Porte Crayon, Mount, mtn., W.V., U.S. F6 114
Port Edward see Weihai, China C10 42
Port Edward, S. Afr. G10 70
Port Edwards, Wi., U.S. G9 118
Porteirinha, Braz. H4 88
Portel, Braz. D7 84
Portel, Port. F3 20
Port Elgin, N.B., Can. D12 110
Port Elgin, On., Can. D8 112
Port Elizabeth, S. Afr. H7 70
Port-en-Bessin, Fr. E8 14
Porter, Tx., U.S. G3 122
Port Erin, I. of Man G8 12
Porter Point, c., St. Vin. o11 105e
Porterville, S. Afr. H4 70
Porterville, Ca., U.S. G7 134
Porterville, Ms., U.S. E10 122
Portete, Bahía, b., Col. A6 86
Port Fairy, Austl. L4 76
Port Gamble, Wa., U.S. C4 136
Port-Gentil, Gabon E1 66
Port Gibson, Ms., U.S. F8 122
Port Graham, Ak., U.S. E9 140
Port Harcourt, Nig. I6 64
Port Hardy, B.C., Can. F3 138
Port Hawkesbury, N.S., Can. E15 110
Port Hedland, Austl. D3 74
Port Heiden, Ak., U.S. E8 140
Port Hill, P.E., Can. D13 110
Porthmadog, Wales, U.K. I8 12
Port Hood, N.S., Can. D15 110
Port Hope, On., Can. E11 112
Port Hope, Mi., U.S. E7 112
Port Huron, Mi., U.S. B3 114
Portimão, Port. G2 20
Port Isabel, Tx., U.S. H10 130
Port Jervis, N.Y., U.S. C11 114
Port Kembla, Austl. J8 76
Port Laige see Waterford, Ire. I5 12
Portland, Austl. L3 76
Portland, Austl. I7 76
Portland, Ar., U.S. D7 122
Portland, In., U.S. H5 112
Portland, Me., U.S. G6 110
Portland, N.D., U.S. G16 124
Portland, Or., U.S. E4 136
Portland, Tn., U.S. H11 120
Portland, Tx., U.S. G10 130
Portland, Bill of, c., Eng., U.K. K10 12
Portland, Cape, c., Austl. n13 77a
Portland, Isle of, i., Eng., U.K. K10 12
Portland Bay, b., Austl. L3 76
Portland Bight, b., Jam. j13 104d
Portland Point, c., Jam. j13 104d
Portlaoise, Ire. H5 12
Port Lavaca, Tx., U.S. F11 130
Port Leyden, N.Y., U.S. E14 112
Port Lincoln, Austl. F7 74
Port Loko, S.L. H2 64
Port-Louis, Guad. h5 105c
Port Louis, Mrts. h10 69a
Port-Lyautey see Kénitra, Mor. C3 64
Port MacDonnell, Austl. L3 76
Port Macquarie, Austl. H9 76
Port Maria, Jam. i14 104d
Port McNeill, B.C., Can. F3 138
Port McNicoll, On., Can. D10 112
Port Moller, Ak., U.S. E7 140
Port Morant, Jam. j14 104d
Portmore, Jam. j13 104d
Port Moresby, Pap. N. Gui. b4 79a
Port Morien, N.S., Can. D17 110
Port Neches, Tx., U.S. H4 122
Port Nelson, Mb., Can. D12 106
Portneuf, stm., Qc., Can. B7 110
Portneuf, stm., Id., U.S. H14 136
Port Neville, B.C., Can. F4 138
Port Nolloth, S. Afr. F3 70
Port Norris, N.J., U.S. E10 114
Porto, Port. C2 20
Porto, state, Port. C2 20
Porto Acre, Braz. E4 84
Porto Alegre, Braz. E12 92
Porto Alegre, S. Tom./P. J6 64
Porto Amboim, Ang. C1 68
Portobelo, Pan. H8 102
Porto Calvo, Braz. E8 88
Porto de Moz, Braz. D7 84
Porto de Pedras, Braz. E8 88
Porto dos Gaúchos, Braz. F6 84
Porto Empedocle, Italy G7 24
Porto Esperança, Braz. C5 90
Porto Esperidião, Braz. G6 84
Porto Feliz, Braz. L2 88
Portoferraio, Italy H7 22
Porto Ferreira, Braz. K2 88
Port of Ness, Scot., U.K. C6 12
Porto Franco, Braz. D2 88
Port of Spain, Trin. s12 105f
Portogruaro, Italy E9 22
Portola, Ca., U.S. D5 134
Portomaggiore, Italy F8 22
Porto Mendes, Braz. B10 92
Porto Murtinho, Braz. D5 90
Porto Nacional, Braz. F1 88
Porto-Novo, Benin H5 64
Porto Novo, India F4 53
Port Orange, Fl., U.S. G5 116
Port Orchard, Wa., U.S. C4 136
Port Orford, Or., U.S. H2 136
Porto San Giorgio, Italy G10 22
Porto Santana, Braz. D7 84
Porto Santo, i., Port. C1 64
Porto Santo Stefano, ngh., Italy H7 22
Porto Seguro, Braz. I6 88
Porto Tolle, Italy F9 22
Porto Torres, Italy D2 24
Porto União, Braz. C12 92
Porto Válter, Braz. E3 84
Porto-Vecchio, Fr. H15 18
Porto Velho, Braz. E5 84
Portoviejo, Ec. H1 86
Port Patrick, Vanuatu m17 79d
Port Perry, On., Can. D11 112
Port Phillip Bay, b., Austl. L5 76
Port Pirie, Austl. F7 74
Portree, Scot., U.K. D6 12
Port Renfrew, B.C., Can. H6 138
Port Rowan, On., Can. F9 112
Port Royal, Jam. j14 104d
Port Royal, Pa., U.S. D8 114
Port Royal, S.C., U.S. D5 116
Port Said see Būr Sa'īd, Egypt G3 58
Port Saint Joe, Fl., U.S. H13 122
Port Saint Johns, S. Afr. G9 70
Port Saint Lucie, Fl., U.S. I5 116
Port Sanilac, Mi., U.S. E8 112
Port Saunders, Nf., Can. i22 107a
Portsea, Austl. L5 76
Portsmouth, Dom. i6 105c
Portsmouth, Eng., U.K. K11 12
Portsmouth, N.H., U.S. G6 110
Portsmouth, Oh., U.S. F2 114
Portsmouth, Va., U.S. H9 114
Portsoy, Scot., U.K. D10 12
Port Stanley, On., Can. F8 112
Port Sudan see Būr Sūdān, Sudan D7 62
Port Sulphur, La., U.S. H9 122
Port Talbot, Wales, U.K. J9 12
Porttipahdan tekojärvi, l., Fin. B12 8
Port Townsend, Wa., U.S. B4 136
Portugal, ctry., Eur. D3 20
Portugalete, Spain A7 20
Portuguesa, state, Ven. C7 86
Portuguesa, stm., Ven. C8 86
Portuguese Guinea see Guinea-Bissau, ctry., Afr. G1 64
Port Vila, Vanuatu k17 79d
Portville, N.Y., U.S. B7 114
Port-Vladimir, Russia B15 8
Port Wentworth, Ga., U.S. D4 116
Port Wing, Wi., U.S. E7 118
Porus, Jam. i13 104d
Porvenir, Chile J2 90
Porvoo, Fin. F11 8
Porzuna, Spain E6 20
Posadas, Arg. C9 92
Posadas, Spain G5 20
Posavina, val., Eur. E14 22
Pošehon'e, Russia B22 10
Poseidonos, Naós toy, sci., Grc. F6 28
Posen, Mi., U.S. C6 112
Poshan see Boshan, China C7 42
Posio, Fin. C12 8
Poso, Indon. D12 50
Poso, Danau, l., Indon. D12 50
Poso, Teluk, b., Indon. D12 50
Pospeliha, Russia D14 32
Posse, Braz. H2 88
Possession Island, i., Nmb. E2 70
Pössneck, Ger. F7 16
Possum Kingdom Lake, res., Tx., U.S. B9 130
Post, Tx., U.S. A6 130
Posta de Jihuites, Mex. I2 130
Postelle, Tn., U.S. A1 116
Postmasburg, S. Afr. F6 70
Postojna, Slvn. E11 22
Postrervalle, Bol. C4 90
Postville, Ia., U.S. A6 120
Potaro, stm., Guy. E12 86
Potaro-Siparuni, state, Guy. E12 86
Potchefstroom, S. Afr. E8 70
Poté, Braz. I5 88
Poteau, Ok., U.S. B4 122
Poteet, Tx., U.S. E9 130
Potenza, Italy D9 24
Potgietersrus, S. Afr. D9 70
Poth, Tx., U.S. E9 130
Potholes Reservoir, res., Wa., U.S. D7 136
Poti, Geor. F6 32
Poti, stm., Braz. C4 88
Potiraguá, Braz. H6 88
Potiskum, Nig. G7 64
Potomac, Il., U.S. H2 112
Potomac, stm., U.S. F9 114
Potomac, North Fork South Branch, stm., U.S. F6 114
Potomac, South Branch, stm., U.S. E7 114
Potomac Heights, Md., U.S. F8 114
Potosí, Bol. C3 90
Potosi, Mo., U.S. G7 120
Potrerillos, Chile. C3 92
Potro, Cerro del (El Potro, Cerro), mtn., S.A. D3 92
Potsdam, Ger. D9 16
Potsdam, N.Y., U.S. F2 110
Pott, Île, i., N. Cal. I14 79d
Potter, Ne., U.S. F9 126
Potterville, Mi., U.S. B1 114
Potts Camp, Ms., U.S. C9 122
Pottstown, Pa., U.S. D10 114
Pottsville, Pa., U.S. D9 114
Pouancé, Fr. G7 14
Poughkeepsie, N.Y., U.S. C11 114
Poulan, Ga., U.S. E2 116
Poulsbo, Wa., U.S. C4 136
Poultney, Vt., U.S. G3 110
Poum, N. Cal. m14 79d
Pouso Alegre, Braz. L3 88
Poŭthĭsăt, Camb. F6 48
Poŭthĭsăt, stm., Camb. F6 48
Poutini see Westland National Park, p.o.i., N.Z. F3 80
Poutrincourt, Lac, l., Qc., Can. A2 110
Považská Bystrica, Slov. G14 16
Povenec, Russia E16 8
Póvoa de Varzim, Port. C2 20
Povorino, Russia D6 32
Povorotnyj, mys, c., Russia C10 38
Povungnituk, Qc., Can. C15 106
Povungnituk, stm., Qc., Can. C15 106
Powassan, On., Can. B10 112
Poway, Ca., U.S. K9 134
Powder, stm., Or., U.S. F9 136
Powder, stm., U.S. A7 126
Powder, South Fork, stm., Wy., U.S. D6 126
Powder River Pass, p., Wy., U.S. C5 126
Powderly, Tx., U.S. D3 122
Powell, Wy., U.S. C4 126
Powell, stm., U.S. H2 114
Powell, Lake, res., U.S. F5 132
Powell Creek, stm., Austl. E5 76
Powellhurst, Or., U.S. E4 136
Powell Lake, l., B.C., Can. F6 138
Powell River, B.C., Can. G6 138
Powers, Mi., U.S. C2 112
Powers, Or., U.S. H2 136
Powers Lake, N.D., U.S. F11 124
Powhatan, Va., U.S. G7 114
Powhatan Point, Oh., U.S. E4 114
Poxoréu, Braz. G7 84
Poya, N. Cal. m15 79d
Poyang Hu, l., China G7 42
Poyen, Ar., U.S. C6 122
Poygan, Lake, l., Wi., U.S. G9 118
Požarevac, Serb. E7 26
Poza Rica de Hidalgo, Mex. E10 100
Požega, Cro. E14 22
Požega, Serb. F7 26
Poznań, Pol. D12 16
Poznań, state, Pol. D12 16
Pozoblanco, Spain F6 20
Pozo-Cañada, Spain F9 20
Pozo del Molle, Arg. F6 92
Pozo del Tigre, Arg. B7 92
Pozuelos, Ven. B9 86
Pozzallo, Italy H8 24
Pozzuoli, Italy D8 24
Prachatice, Czech Rep. G10 16
Prachin Buri, Thai. E5 48
Prachuap Khiri Khan, Thai. G4 48
Pradera, Col. F3 86
Prado, Braz. I6 88
Pradópolis, Braz. K3 88
Præstø, Den. A8 16
Prague see Praha, Czech Rep. F10 16
Prague, Ne., U.S. F16 126
Prague, Ok., U.S. B2 122
Praha (Prague), Czech Rep. F10 16
Praha, state, Czech Rep. F10 16
Praha, mtn., Czech Rep. G9 16
Prahova, state, Rom. D13 26
Prahova, stm., Rom. E13 26
Praia, C.V. l10 65a
Praia Grande, Braz. D13 92
Prainha Nova, Braz. E5 84
Prairie, Austl. C5 76
Prairie, stm., Mi., U.S. G4 112
Prairie City, Ia., U.S. C4 120
Prairie City, Il., U.S. D7 120
Prairie Creek, stm., Ne., U.S. F15 126
Prairie Dog Creek, stm., Ks., U.S. B8 128
Prairie du Chien, Wi., U.S. A6 120
Prairie du Sac, Wi., U.S. H9 118
Prairie River, Sk., Can. B11 124
Prairies, Coteau des, hills, U.S. C16 126
Prairies, Lake of the, res., Can. C12 124
Prairie View, Tx., U.S. G3 122
Prairie Village, Ks., U.S. B14 128
Pran Buri, Thai. F4 48
Pran Buri, stm., Thai. F4 48
Prānhita, stm., India B5 53
Praslin, i., Sey. j13 69b
Prasonísi, Ákra, c., Grc. H10 28
Praszka, Pol. E14 16
Prata, Braz. J1 88
Prata, stm., Braz. J1 88
Prata, stm., Braz. I2 88
Pratāpgarh, India F5 54
Pratápolis, Braz. K2 88
Pratas Island see Tungsha Tao, i., Tai. K7 42
Prat de Llobregat see El Prat de Llobregat, Spain C12 20
Prato, Italy G8 22
Pratt, Ks., U.S. D10 128
Prattville, Al., U.S. E12 122
Pratudão, stm., Braz. H3 88
Pravdinskij, Russia D20 10
Pravia, Spain A4 20
Praya, Indon. H10 50
Preajba, Rom. E12 26
Prečistoe, Russia G19 8
Predeal, Rom. D12 26
Preeceville, Sk., Can. C11 124
Preetz, Ger. B6 16
Pregolja, stm., Russia F3 10
Pregonero, Ven. D6 86
Preguiças, stm., Braz. B4 88
Preila, Lith. E4 10
Prêk Poŭthĭ, Camb. G7 48
Prelate, Sk., Can. D4 124
Premnitz, Ger. D8 16
Premont, Tx., U.S. G9 130
Premuda, Otok, i., Cro. F11 22
Prenjasi see Prrenjas, Alb. C14 24
Prentiss, Ms., U.S. F9 122
Prenzlau, Ger. C9 16
Preobraženie, Russia C10 38
Preparis Island, i., Mya. F7 46
Preparis North Channel, strt., Mya. E7 46
Preparis South Channel, strt., Mya. F7 46
Přerov, Czech Rep. G13 16
Prescott, On., Can. D14 112
Prescott, Ar., U.S. D5 122
Prescott, Az., U.S. I4 132
Prescott, Wi., U.S. G6 118
Prescott Island, i., Nu., Can. A11 106
Presidencia de la Plaza, Arg. C7 92
Presidencia Roca, Arg. C8 92
Presidencia Roque Sáenz Peña, Arg. C7 92
Presidente Dutra, Braz. C3 88
Presidente Epitácio, Braz. D6 90
Presidente Hayes, state, Para. B8 92
Presidente Prudente, Braz. D6 90
Presidio, Tx., U.S. E3 130
Presidio, stm., Mex. D6 100
Presnogor'kovka, Kaz. D11 32
Prešov, Slov. H17 16
Prespa, Lake, l., Eur. D14 24
Presque Isle, Me., U.S. D8 110
Presque Isle, pen., Pa., U.S. B5 114
Prestea, Ghana H4 64
Preston, Eng., U.K. H10 12
Preston, Ia., U.S. B7 120
Preston, Id., U.S. A5 132
Preston, Ks., U.S. D10 128
Preston, Mn., U.S. H6 118
Prestonsburg, Ky., U.S. G3 114
Prestwick, Scot., U.K. F8 12
Preto, stm., Braz. I2 88
Preto, stm., Braz. G1 88
Preto, stm., Braz. B4 88
Preto, stm., Braz. K1 88
Preto, stm., Braz. I9 86
Preto, stm., Braz. F3 88
Preto do Igapó-açu, stm., Braz. E5 84
Pretoria (Tshwane), S. Afr. D9 70
Pretty Prairie, Ks., U.S. D10 128
Préveza, Grc. E3 28
Prey Lvéa, Camb. G7 48
Prey Vêng, Camb. G7 48
Pribilof Islands, is., Ak., U.S. E5 140
Priboj, Serb. F6 26
Příbram, Czech Rep. G10 16
Price, Ut., U.S. D6 132
Price, stm., Ut., U.S. D6 132
Price Island, i., B.C., Can. D2 138
Prichard, Al., U.S. G10 122
Prickly Pear Cays, is., Anguilla A1 105a
Priddy, Tx., U.S. C9 130
Priego de Córdoba, Spain G6 20
Priekule, Lat. D4 10
Priekulė, Lith. E4 10
Prieska, S. Afr. F6 70
Priest, stm., Id., U.S. B10 136
Priest Lake, res., Id., U.S. B9 136
Priest River, Id., U.S. B9 136
Prieta, Peña, mtn., Spain A6 20
Prieto Diaz, Phil. D5 52
Prievidza, Slov. H14 16
Prijedor, Bos. E3 26
Prilep, Mac. B4 28
Priluki, Russia A22 10
Primeira Cruz, Braz. B4 88
Primera, Tx., U.S. H10 130
Primero, stm., Arg. E6 92
Primghar, Ia., U.S. A2 120
Primorsk, Russia F13 8
Primorskij, Russia C9 38
Primorskij hrebet, mts., Russia F10 34
Primo Tapia, Mex. K8 134
Primrose Lake, l., Can. E9 106
Prince Albert, Sk., Can. A8 124
Prince Albert, S. Afr. H6 70
Prince Albert Sound, strt., N.T., Can. A7 106
Prince Alfred, Cape, c., N.T., Can. B15 140
Prince Charles Island, i., Nu., Can. B15 106
Prince Charles Mountains, mts., Ant. C11 81
Prince Edward Island, state, Can. D13 110
Prince Edward Island, i., P.E., Can. F18 106
Prince Edward Island National Park, p.o.i., P.E., Can. D13 110
Prince Frederick, Md., U.S. F9 114
Prince George, B.C., Can. C8 138
Prince George, Va., U.S. G8 114
Prince Gustaf Adolf Sea, s., Can. B4 141
Prince of Wales Island, i., Austl. B8 74
Prince of Wales Island, i., Nu., Can. A11 106

Name | Map Ref. | Page

Prince of Wales Island, i., Ak., U.S. E13 140
Prince of Wales Strait, strt., N.T., Can. B15 140
Prince Olav Coast, cst., Ant. B9 81
Prince Patrick Island, i., N.T., Can. A16 140
Prince Regent Inlet, b., Nu., Can. A12 106
Prince Rupert, B.C., Can. E4 106
Prince Rupert Bluff Point, c., Dom. i5 105c
Princes Islands see Kızıl Adalar, is., Tur. C11 28
Princess Anne, Md., U.S. F10 114
Princess Astrid Coast, cst., Ant. C6 81
Princess Charlotte Bay, b., Austl. B8 74
Princess Martha Coast, cst., Ant. C4 81
Princess Ragnhild Coast, cst., Ant. C7 81
Princess Royal Island, i., B.C., Can. C1 138
Princes Town, Trin. s12 105f
Princeton, B.C., Can. G10 138
Princeton, Ca., U.S. D3 134
Princeton, In., U.S. F10 120
Princeton, Ky., U.S. G9 120
Princeton, Me., U.S. E9 110
Princeton, Mi., U.S. B2 112
Princeton, N.C., U.S. A7 116
Princeton, N.J., U.S. D11 114
Princeton, Wi., U.S. H9 118
Princeton, W.V., U.S. G4 114
Princeville, Qc., Can. D4 110
Princeville, Il., U.S. D8 120
Prince William Sound, strt., Ak., U.S. D10 140
Príncipe, i., S. Tom./P. I6 64
Príncipe da Beira, Braz. F5 84
Prineville, Or., U.S. F6 136
Pringsewu, Indon. F4 50
Prinses Margrietkanaal, can., Neth. A14 14
Prins Karls Forland, i., Nor. B27 141
Prinzapolka, stm., Nic. F5 102
Priozersk, Russia F14 8
Pripet (Prypjac'), stm., Eur. H10 10
Pripet Marshes, reg., Eur. H12 10
Pripoljarnyj Ural, mts., Russia A9 32
Priština, Serb. G8 26
Pritchett, Co., U.S. D6 128
Pritzwalk, Ger. C8 16
Privas, Fr. E10 18
Priverno, Italy C7 24
Privodino, Russia F22 8
Prizren, Serb. G7 26
Prjaža, Russia F15 8
Probolinggo, Indon. G8 50
Probstzella, Ger. F7 16
Procida, Isola di, i., Italy D7 24
Procter, B.C., Can. G13 138
Proctor, Mn., U.S. E6 118
Proctor Lake, res., Tx., U.S. C9 130
Proddatūr, India D4 53
Proença-a-Nova, Port. E2 20
Progreso, Mex. B3 102
Progreso, Mex. B8 100
Progreso, Mex. K10 134
Progreso, Ur. G9 92
Prohladnyj, Russia F6 32
Project City, Ca., U.S. C3 134
Prokopevsk, Russia D15 32
Prokuplje, Serb. F8 26
Prokuševo, Russia G16 8
Proletarskij, Russia E20 10
Prome (Pyè), Mya. C2 48
Pronja, stm., Bela. G14 10
Pronja, stm., Russia F21 10
Prony, Baie de, b., N. Cal. n16 79d
Prophet, stm., B.C., Can. D6 106
Prophetstown, Il., U.S. C8 120
Propriá, Braz. F7 88
Propriano, Fr. H14 18
Proserpine, Austl. C7 76
Prosna, stm., Pol. E14 16
Prospect, Oh., U.S. D2 114
Prosperidad, Phil. F5 52
Prosser, Wa., U.S. D7 136
Prostějov, Czech Rep. G12 16
Prostki, Pol. C18 16
Proston, Austl. F8 76
Proszowice, Pol. F16 16
Protection, Ks., U.S. D9 128
Protem, S. Afr. I5 70
Protva, stm., Russia F20 10
Provadija, Blg. F14 26
Prøven (Kangersuatsiaq), Grnld. C14 141
Provence, hist. reg., Fr. F12 18
Providence, Ky., U.S. G10 120
Providence, R.I., U.S. C14 114
Providence, Ut., U.S. B5 132
Providence, Atoll de, i., Sey. k12 69b
Providence, Cape, c., N.Z. H2 80
Providencia, Mex. G4 130
Providencia, Isla de, i., Col. F7 102
Providenciales, i., T./C. Is. B11 102
Providenija, Russia D26 34
Provincetown, Ma., U.S. B15 114
Provins, Fr. F12 14
Provo, Ut., U.S. C5 132
Provo, stm., Ut., U.S. C5 132
Provost, Ab., Can. B3 124
Prrenjas, Alb. C14 24
Prudentópolis, Braz. B12 92
Prudhoe Bay, Ak., U.S. B10 140
Prudhoe Island, i., Austl. C7 76
Prudnik, Pol. F13 16
Pruszków, Pol. D16 16
Prut, stm., Eur. D15 26
Pružany, Bela. H7 10
Prydz Bay, b., Ant. B12 81
Pryluky, Ukr. D4 32
Pryor, Ok., U.S. H2 120
Przasnysz, Pol. D16 16
Przedbórz, Pol. E15 16
Przemyśl, Pol. G18 16
Przemyśl, state, Pol. F18 16
Przeworsk, Pol. F18 16
Psachná, Grc. E6 28
Pskov, Russia C11 10
Pskov, Lake, l., Eur. B11 10
Pskovskaja oblast', co., Russia C11 10
Pszczyna, Pol. G14 16
Ptarmigan, Cape, c., N.T., Can. A7 106
Ptolemaís, Grc. C4 28
Ptuj, Slvn. D12 22
Puakatike, Volcán, vol., Chile e30 78l
Puán, Arg. H6 92
Pucallpa, Peru. E3 84
Pucará, Bol. C4 90
Pučeveem, stm., Russia C23 34
Pučež, Russia H20 8
Pucheng, China H8 42
Pucheng, China D3 42
Púchov, Slov. G14 16
Pučišća, Cro. G13 22
Pudasjärvi, Fin. D12 8
Pudož, Russia F17 8
Puduari, stm., Braz. I11 86
Puduchcheri *see* Pondicherry, India F4 53
Pudukkottai, India F4 53
Puebla, state, Mex. F10 100
Puebla de Don Fadrique, Spain G8 20
Puebla de Sanabria, Spain B4 20
Puebla de Zaragoza, Mex. F9 100
Pueblito, Mex. E2 130
Pueblito de Ponce, P.R. B1 104a
Pueblo, Co., U.S. C4 128
Pueblonuevo, Col. C4 86
Pueblo Nuevo, P.R. B2 104a
Pueblo Nuevo, Ven. B7 86
Pueblo Viejo, Laguna, l., Mex. D10 100
Pueblo Yaqui, Mex. B4 100
Puente-Caldelas *see* Ponte-Caldelas, Spain B2 20
Puente del Arzobispo, Spain E5 20
Puentedeume *see* Pontedeume, Spain A2 20
Puente Genil, Spain G6 20
Puerca, Punta, c., P.R. B4 104a
Puerco, stm., N.M., U.S. I10 132
Puerco, stm., U.S. I7 132
Puerto Acosta, Bol. C3 90
Puerto Adela, Para. B10 92
Puerto Aisén, Chile I2 90
Puerto Alegre, Bol. B4 90
Puerto Ángel, Mex. H10 100
Puerto Arista, Mex. H11 100
Puerto Armuelles, Pan. H6 102
Puerto Asís, Col. G3 86
Puerto Ayacucho, Ven. E8 86
Puerto Baquerizo Moreno, Ec. i12 84a
Puerto Barrios, Guat. E3 102
Puerto Bermúdez, Peru F3 84
Puerto Berrío, Col. D4 86
Puerto Bolívar, Col. A5 86
Puerto Boyacá, Col. E4 86
Puerto Cabello, Ven. B7 86
Puerto Cabezas, Nic. F6 102
Puerto Carreño, Col. D8 86
Puerto Chicama, Peru E2 84
Puerto Colombia, Col. B4 86
Puerto Cortés, Hond. E3 102
Puerto Cumarebo, Ven. B7 86
Puerto Deseado, Arg. I3 90
Puerto Escondido, Mex. H10 100
Puerto Escondido, c., Ven. p20 104g
Puerto Esperanza, Arg. B10 92
Puerto Fonciere, Para. D5 90
Puerto Francisco de Orellana, Ec. H3 86
Puerto Heath, Bol. B3 90
Puerto Iguazú, Arg. B10 92
Puerto Ingeniero Ibáñez, Chile I2 90
Puerto Inírida, Col. F7 86
Puerto Juárez, Mex. B4 102
Puerto la Cruz, Ven. B9 86
Puerto Leguízamo, Col. H4 86
Puerto Libertad, Mex. G6 98
Puerto Limón, Col. F5 86
Puerto Limón, C.R. G6 102
Puertollano, Spain F6 20
Puerto Lobos, Arg. H4 90
Puerto López, Col. E5 86
Puerto Madero, Mex. H12 100
Puerto Madryn, Arg. H3 90
Puerto Maldonado, Peru F4 84
Puerto Montt, Chile H2 90
Puerto Morelos, Mex. B4 102
Puerto Natales, Chile J2 90
Puerto Padre, Cuba B9 102
Puerto Páez, Ven. D8 86
Puerto Palmer, Pico, mtn., Mex. G6 130
Puerto Peñasco, Mex. F6 98
Puerto Pinasco, Para. D5 90
Puerto Pirámides, Arg. H4 90
Puerto Piray, Arg. C10 92
Puerto Píritu, Ven. B9 86
Puerto Plata, Dom. Rep. C12 102
Puerto Princesa, Phil. F2 52
Puerto Real, P.R. B1 104a
Puerto Real, Spain H4 20
Puerto Rico, Arg. C10 92
Puerto Rico, Bol. B3 90
Puerto Rico, Col. G4 86
Puerto Rico, dep., N.A. b3 104a
Puerto Rico Trench, unds. G7 144
Puerto Rondón, Col. D6 86
Puerto San José, Guat. F2 102
Puerto San Julián, Arg. I3 90
Puerto Santa Cruz, Arg. J3 90
Puerto Sastre, Para. D5 90
Puerto Suárez, Bol. C5 90
Puerto Tejada, Col. F3 86
Puerto Tolosa, Col. H4 86
Puerto Umbría, Col. G3 86
Puerto Vallarta, Mex. E6 100
Puerto Varas, Chile H2 90
Puerto Victoria, Arg. C10 92
Puerto Viejo, C.R. G5 102
Puerto Villamil, Ec. i11 84a
Puerto Villamizar, Col. C5 86
Puerto Wilches, Col. D5 86
Puerto Ybapobó, Para. D5 90
Pueyrredón, Lago (Cochrane, Lago), l., S.A. I2 90
Pugačov, Russia D7 32
Puget Sound, strt., Wa., U.S. C4 136
Puglia, state, Italy C10 24
Pugŏ-ri, Kor., N. D9 38
Puhi-waero see South West Cape, c., N.Z. H2 80
Puhja, Est. B9 10
Puiești, Rom. C14 26
Puigcerdà, Spain B12 20
Puigmal d' Err (Puigmal), mtn., Eur. G8 18
Pujiang, China G8 42
Pujilí, Ec. H2 86
Puka *see* Pukë, Alb. B13 24
Pukaki, Lake, l., N.Z. F3 80
Pukch'ŏng-ŭp, Kor., N. D8 38
Pukë, Alb. B13 24
Pukekohe, N.Z. C6 80
Pukhrāyān, India E7 54
Pukou, China H8 42
Puksoozero, Russia E19 8
Pula, Cro. F10 22
Pula, Italy F3 24
Pulacayo, Bol. D3 90
Pulantien *see* Xinjin, China B9 42
Pulap, at., Micron. C5 72
Púlar, Cerro, vol., Chile B3 92
Pulaski, N.Y., U.S. E13 112
Pulaski, Tn., U.S. B11 122
Pulaski, Va., U.S. G5 114
Pulau, stm., Indon. G10 44
Pulaukida, Indon. E3 50
Pulau Pinang, state, Malay. J5 48
Puławy, Pol. E18 16
Pulgaon, India H7 54
Puli, Tai. J9 42
Pulicat, India E5 53
Pulicat Lake, l., India E4 53
Puliyangudi, India G3 53
Pullman, Wa., U.S. D9 136
Pulog, Mount, mtn., Phil. B3 52
Pulon'ga, Russia C18 8
Pułtusk, Pol. D16 16
Puma Yumco, l., China D13 54
Pumei, China A7 48
Pumpkin Buttes, mtn., Wy., U.S. D7 126
Pumpkin Creek, stm., Mt., U.S. B7 126
Pumpkin Creek, stm., Ne., U.S. F10 126
Puná, Isla, i., Ec. I1 86
Punaauia, Fr. Poly. v21 78h
Punakha, Bhu. E12 54
Punan, Indon. B10 50
Punata, Bol. C3 90
Pūnch, India B5 54
Punchaw, B.C., Can. C7 138
Pune (Poona), India B1 53
Punganūru, India E4 53
P'ungsan-ŭp, Kor., N. D7 38
Pungué, stm., Afr. A12 70
Punia, D.R.C. E5 66
Punilla, Sierra de la, mts., Arg. D3 92
Punitaqui, Chile E2 92
Punjab, state, India C5 54
Punjab, state, Pak. C4 54
Punnichy, Sk., Can. C9 124
Puno, Peru G3 84
Punta, Cerro de, mtn., P.R. B2 104a
Punta Alta, Arg. I6 92
Punta Arenas, Chile J2 90
Punta Banda, Cabo, c., Mex. L9 134
Punta Cardón, Ven. B6 86
Punta Colnett, Mex. F4 98
Punta de Agua Creek (Tramperos Creek), stm., U.S. E5 128
Punta de Díaz, Chile C2 92
Punta del Cobre, Chile C2 92
Punta del Este, Ur. G10 92
Punta Delgada, Arg. H4 90
Punta de los Llanos, Arg. E4 92
Punta de Piedras, Ven. B9 86
Punta Gorda, Nic. G6 102
Punta Gorda, Fl., U.S. J3 116
Punta Gorda, Bahía de, b., Nic. G6 102
Punta Negra, Salar de, pl., Chile B3 92
Punta Prieta, Mex. A1 100
Puntarenas, C.R. G5 102
Punta Santiago, P.R. B4 104a
Punto Fijo, Ven. B6 86
Punung, Indon. H7 50
Puper, Indon. F9 44
Puppy's Point, c., Norf. I. y24 78i
Puqi, China G5 42
Puqian, China L4 42
Puquio, Peru F3 84
Pur, stm., Russia A13 32
Puracé, Volcán, vol., Col. F3 86
Pūranpur, India D7 54
Purcell, Ok., U.S. F11 128
Purcell Mountains, mts., N.A. F14 138
Purcellville, Va., U.S. E8 114
Purdy, Mo., U.S. H3 120
Puré (Puruí), stm., S.A. I6 86
Purgatoire, stm., Co., U.S. D5 128
Puri, India I10 54
Purificación, Col. F4 86
Purificación, stm., Mex. C9 100
Purísima, Mex. E7 130
Purmerend, Neth. B13 14
Pūrna, stm., India H5 54
Pūrna, stm., India H6 54
Pūrnia, India F11 54
Puronga, Russia F19 8
Puruí (Puré), stm., S.A. I6 86
Puruliya, India G11 54
Puruni, stm., Guy. D12 86
Purús, stm., S.A. E4 84
Puruvesi, l., Fin. F13 8
Purvis, Ms., U.S. F9 122
Purwakarta, Indon. G5 50
Purwodadi, Indon. G6 50
Purwodadi, Indon. G7 50
Purwokerto, Indon. G6 50
Purworejo, Indon. G6 50
Pusa, Malay. C7 50
Pusad, India B3 53
Pusan (Fusan), Kor., S. D2 40
Pusan-jikhalsi, state, Kor., S. D2 40
Pusat Gayo, Pegunungan, mts., Indon. J3 48
Pushkar, India E5 54
Puškin, Russia A13 10
Puškino, Russia D20 10
Püspökladány, Hung. B8 26
Püssi, Est. A10 10
Pustozersk, Russia C25 8
Putaendo, Chile F2 92
Putao, Mya. C8 46
Putian, China I8 42
Putian, China G6 42
Putignano, Italy D10 24
Puting, Tanjung, c., Indon. E7 50
Putnam, Ct., U.S. C14 114
Putney, Ga., U.S. E1 116
Putney, Vt., U.S. B13 114
Putorana, plato, plat., Russia C7 34
Puttalam, Sri L. G4 53
Puttalam Lagoon, b., Sri L. G4 53
Puttūr, India E4 53
Putú, Chile G1 92
Putumayo, state, Col. G4 86
Putumayo (Içá), stm., S.A. D3 84
Putuo, China F10 42
Putussibau, Indon. C8 50
Putyla, Ukr. B12 26
Puula, l., Fin. F12 8
Puurmani, Est. B9 10
Puyallup, Wa., U.S. C4 136
Puyang, China D6 42
Puy-de-Dôme, state, Fr. D9 18
Puymorens, Col de, p., Fr. G7 18
Puyo, Ec. H3 86
Pweto, D.R.C. F5 66
Pwinbyu, Mya. B2 48
Pyalo, Mya. C2 48
Pyapon, Mya. D2 48
Pyawbwe, Mya. B3 48
Pyhäjärvi, l., Fin. E11 8
Pyhäjärvi, l., Fin. F9 8
Pyhäjoki, Fin. D10 8
Pyhäjoki, stm., Fin. D11 8
Pyhäselkä, l., Fin. E13 8
Pyhätunturi, mtn., Fin. C12 8
Pyinbongyi, Mya. D3 48
Pyinmana, Mya. C3 48
Pyin Oo Lwin *see* Maymyo, Mya. A3 48
Pýlos, Grc. G4 28
Pymatuning Reservoir, res., U.S. C5 114
Pyŏktong-ŭp, Kor., N. D6 38
P'yŏngch'ang, Kor., S. B1 40
P'yonghae, Kor., S. C2 40
P'yŏngt'aek, Kor., S. F7 38
P'yŏngyang, Kor., N. E6 38
Pyote, Tx., U.S. C4 130
Pyramid Lake, l., Nv., U.S. D6 134
Pyramid Peak, mtn., Wy., U.S. G16 136
Pyrenees, mts., Eur. G6 18
Pyrénées-Atlantiques, state, Fr. F5 18
Pyrénées Occident, Parc National des, p.o.i., Fr. G5 18
Pyrénées-Orientales, state, Fr. G8 18
Pýrgos, Grc. F4 28
Pytalovo, Russia C10 10
Pyu, Mya. C3 48
Pyūṭhān, Nepal D9 54

Q

Qaanaaq *see* Thule, Grnld. B12 141
Qabbāsīn, Syria B8 58
Qacentina (Constantine), Alg. B6 64
Qā'en, Iran C8 56
Qagan Moron, stm., China C3 38
Qagan Nur, l., China C7 36
Qahar Youyi Zhongqi, China A5 42
Qaidam, stm., China D4 36
Qaidam Pendi, bas., China D3 36
Qalāt, Afg. C10 56
Qal'at ash-Shaqīf (Beaufort Castle), sci., Leb. E6 58
Qal'at Bīshah, Sau. Ar. E5 56
Qal'at Ṣāliḥ, Iraq C6 56
Qal'eh-ye Now, Afg. C9 56
Qallābāt, Sudan E7 62
Qalyûb, Egypt H2 58
Qamani'tuaq (Baker Lake), Nu., Can. C11 106
Qamar, Ghubbat al-, b., Yemen F7 56
Qamdo, China E4 36
Qamea, i., Fiji p20 79e
Qamīnis, Libya A3 62
Qānā, Leb. E6 58
Qandahār *see* Kandahār, Afg. C10 56
Qandala, Som. B9 66
Qapshaghay, Kaz. F13 32
Qaqortoq *see* Julianehåb, Grnld. E16 141
Qarabutaq, Kaz. D10 32
Qārah, Syria D7 58
Qaratal, stm., Kaz. E13 32
Qarataū, Kaz. F11 32
Qarataū zhotasy, mts., Kaz. F11 32
Qaraton, Kaz. E8 32
Qaraūyl, Kaz. E13 32
Qarazhal, Kaz. E12 32
Qardho, Som. C9 66
Qarqan, stm., China G15 32
Qarqaraly, Kaz. E13 32
Qarsaqbay, Kaz. E11 32
Qârûn, Birket (Moeris, Lake), l., Egypt I1 58
Qarwāw, Ra's, c., Oman F8 56
Qasigiannguit *see* Christanshåb, Grnld. D15 141
Qaṣr al-Azraq, sci., Jord. G7 58
Qaṣr al-Kharānah, sci., Jord. G7 58
Qaṣr al-Mushattá, sci., Jord. G7 58
Qaṣr aṭ-Ṭūbah, sci., Jord. G7 58
Qaṣr Ḍab'ah, sci., Jord. G7 58
Qaṣr-e Shīrīn, Iran C6 56
Qasr Farâfra, Egypt B5 62
Qaṭanā, Syria E6 58
Qatar, ctry., Asia D7 56
Qatrani, Gebel, hill, Egypt I1 58
Qattâra, Munkhafad el- (Qattara Depression), depr., Egypt B5 62
Qattara Depression see Qattâra, Munkhafad el-, depr., Egypt B5 62
Qaṭṭīnah, Buḥayrat, res., Syria D7 58
Qausuittuq (Resolute), Nu., Can. C7 141
Qayghy, Kaz. D10 32
Qazaly, Kaz. E10 32
Qazaqtyng usaqshoqylyghy (Kazakh Hills), hills, Kaz. D12 32
Qāzigund, India B5 54
Qazımämmäd, Azer. B6 56
Qazvīn, Iran B6 56
Qena, Egypt B6 62
Qena, Wadi (Qinā, Wādī), stm., Egypt K3 58
Qeqertarsuaq *see* Godhavn, Grnld. D15 141
Qesari, Horbat (Caesarea), sci., Isr. F5 58
Qeshm, Jazīreh-ye, i., Iran D8 56
Qetura, Isr. I5 58
Qezel Owzan, stm., Iran B6 56
Qian, stm., China J3 42
Qian'an, China B6 38
Qian Gorlos, China B6 38
Qianning, China E5 36
Qianshan, China F7 42
Qianwei, China F5 36
Qianxi, China H1 42
Qianyang, China H3 42
Qiaolima, China A8 54
Qiaowan, China C4 36
Qidong, China H5 42
Qiemo, China G15 32
Qigong, China F5 36
Qijiang, China G2 42
Qila Saifullāh, Pak. C2 54
Qilian Shan, mtn., China D4 36
Qilian Shan, mts., China D4 36
Qimen, China G7 42
Qin, stm., China D5 42
Qing, stm., China F4 42
Qingcheng, China C7 42
Qingchengzi, China D5 38
Qingdao (Tsingtao), China C9 42
Qingfeng, China D6 42
Qinggang, China B10 36
Qinghai, state, China D4 36
Qinghai Hu, l., China D5 36
Qingjiang, China G6 42
Qingjiang, China E8 42
Qinglong, China F6 36
Qinglonggang, China F9 42
Qingshen, China F5 36
Qingshui, China D2 42
Qingshui, China D4 36
Qingshui, stm., China C2 42
Qingshui, stm., China H3 42
Qingtang, China I5 42
Qingyang, China F7 42
Qingyang, China B8 38
Qingyang, China C2 42
Qingyuan, China J5 42
Qingyuan, China H8 42
Qingyuan, China I3 42
Qingyuan, China C6 38
Qing Zang Gaoyuan (Tibet, Plateau of), plat., China B6 46
Qingzhen, China H2 42
Qinhuangdao, China B8 42
Qin Ling, mts., China E3 42
Qinshihuang Mausoleum (Terra Cotta Army), sci., China D3 42
Qinshui, China D5 42
Qinxian, China C5 42
Qinyang, China D5 42
Qinyuan, China C5 42
Qinzhou, China J3 42
Qionghai, China L4 42
Qionglai, China E5 36
Qionglaishan, mts., China E5 36
Qiongzhong, China L3 42
Qiongzhou Haixia, strt., China K4 42
Qiqian, China F13 34
Qiqihar, China B9 36
Qira, China A5 46
Qiryat Ata, Isr. F6 58
Qiryat Gat, Isr. G5 58
Qiryat Shemona, Isr. E6 58
Qishn, Yemen F7 56
Qitai, China C2 36
Qitaihe, China B11 36
Qitamu, China B7 38
Qixia, China C9 42
Qixian, China D6 42
Qiyang, China H4 42
Qizhou, China F6 42
Qizil Jilga, China A7 54
Qom, Iran C7 56
Qomsheh, Iran C7 56
Qonggyai, China D13 54
Qongyrat, Kaz. E12 32
Qorghalzhyn, Kaz. D12 32
Qôrnoq, Grnld. E15 141
Qosshaghyl, Kaz. E8 32
Qostanay, Kaz. D10 32
Qowowuyag (Chopu), mtn., Asia D11 54
Qu, stm., China F2 42
Qu, stm., China G8 42
Quabbin Reservoir, res., Ma., U.S. B13 114
Quadra Island, i., B.C., Can. F5 138
Quadros, Lagoa dos, l., Braz. D12 92
Quakenbrück, Ger. D3 16
Qualicum Beach, B.C., Can. G6 138
Quambatook, Austl. J4 76
Quang Ngai, Viet. E9 48
Quang Trach, Viet. D8 48
Quantico, Va., U.S. F8 114
Quanyang, China C7 38
Quanzhou, China I8 42
Qu'Appelle, Sk., Can. D10 124
Qu'Appelle, stm., Can. D12 124
Qu'Appelle Dam, dam, Sk., Can. D7 124
Quaraí, Braz. E9 92
Quaraí (Cuareim), stm., S.A. E9 92
Quarles, Pegunungan, mts., Indon. E11 50
Quarryville, Pa., U.S. E9 114
Quartier d'Orléans, Guad. A1 105a
Quartu Sant'Elena, Italy E3 24
Quartz Lake, l., Nu., Can. A14 106
Quartz Mountain, mtn., Or., U.S. G4 136
Quartzsite, Az., U.S. J2 132
Quba, Azer. A6 56
Qūchān, Iran B8 56
Quchijie, China G4 42
Queanbeyan, Austl. J7 76
Québec, Qc., Can. D5 110
Québec, state, Can. E16 106
Quebeck, Tn., U.S. I12 120
Quebra-Anzol, stm., Braz. J2 88
Quebracho, Ur. E9 92
Quebrada Seca, P.R. B4 104a
Quedal, Cabo, c., Chile H2 90
Quedlinburg, Ger. E7 16
Queen Charlotte Islands, is., B.C., Can. E4 106
Queen Charlotte Sound, strt., B.C., Can. E2 138
Queen Charlotte Strait, strt., B.C., Can. F3 138
Queen City, Mo., U.S. D5 120
Queen City, Tx., U.S. D4 122
Queen Elizabeth Islands, is., Can. B13 94
Queen Mary Coast, cst., Ant. B14 81
Queen Maud Gulf, b., Nu., Can. B10 106
Queen Maud Land, reg., Ant. C4 81
Queen Maud Mountains, mts., Ant. D23 81
Queenscliff, Austl. L5 76
Queensland, state, Austl. D8 74
Queensport, N.S., Can. E15 110
Queenstown, Austl. o12 77a
Queenstown, N.Z. G3 80
Queenstown, S. Afr. G8 70
Queguay Grande, stm., Ur. F9 92
Queimada Nova, Braz. E5 88
Queimadas, Braz. F6 88
Queimados, Braz. L4 88
Quela, Ang. B2 68
Quelelevu, i., Fiji p20 79e
Quelimane, Moz. D6 68
Quelpart Island see Cheju-do, i., Kor., S. H7 38
Quemado, Tx., U.S. F7 130
Quemado, Punta de, c., Cuba B10 102
Quemoy see Chinmen Tao, i., Tai. I8 42
Quemú Quemú, Arg. H6 92
Quequén, Arg. I8 92
Querary, stm., Col. G6 86
Quercy, hist. reg., Fr. E7 18
Querétaro, Mex. E8 100
Querétaro, state, Mex. E8 100
Querobabi, Mex. F7 98
Quesada, Spain G7 20
Queshan, China E5 42
Quesnel, B.C., Can. C8 138
Quesnel, stm., B.C., Can. D8 138
Quesnel Lake, l., B.C., Can. D9 138
Que Son, Viet. E9 48
Questa, N.M., U.S. E3 128
Quetico Lake, l., On., Can. C7 118
Quetta, Pak. C10 56
Quetzaltenango, Guat. E2 102
Quevedo, Ec. H2 86
Quezon City, Phil. C3 52
Qufu, China D7 42
Quibala, Ang. C2 68
Quibdó, Col. E3 86
Quiberon, Fr. G5 14
Quíbor, Ven. C7 86
Quiculungo, Ang. B2 68
Quila, Mex. C5 100
Quilengues, Ang. C1 68
Quilimarí, Chile F2 92
Quillabamba, Peru F3 84
Quillacollo, Bol. C3 90
Quill Lake, Sk., Can. B9 124
Quillota, Chile F2 92
Quilon, India G3 53
Quilpie, Austl. F5 76
Quilpué, Chile F2 92
Quimarí, Alto de, mtn., Col. C3 86
Quimaria, Ang. B1 68
Quimby, Ia., U.S. B2 120
Quimilí, Arg. C6 92
Quimper (Kemper), Fr. F5 14
Quimperlé, Fr. G5 14
Quinault, stm., Wa., U.S. C3 136
Quince Mil, Peru F3 84
Quincy, Ca., U.S. D4 134
Quincy, Fl., U.S. G14 122
Quincy, Il., U.S. E6 120
Quincy, Ma., U.S. B14 114
Quincy, Wa., U.S. C7 136
Quindío, state, Col. E4 86
Quines, Arg. F5 92
Quinhagak, Ak., U.S. E7 140
Quinlan, Tx., U.S. E2 122
Quinn, stm., Nv., U.S. B7 134
Quintanar de la Orden, Spain E7 20
Quintana Roo, state, Mex. C3 102
Quinte, Bay of, b., On., Can. D12 112
Quinto, Spain C10 20
Quinto, stm., Arg. G5 92
Quinton, Ok., U.S. B3 122
Quipapá, Braz. E7 88
Quirauk Mountain, mtn., Md., U.S. E8 114
Quiriguá, sci., Guat. E3 102
Quirihue, Chile H1 92
Quirindi, Austl. H8 76
Quirinópolis, Braz. C6 90
Quiriquire, Ven. C10 86
Quiroga, Mex. F8 100
Quiros, Cap, c., Vanuatu j16 79d
Quissanga, Moz. C7 68
Quissico, Moz. D12 70
Quitaque, Tx., U.S. G7 128
Quitasueño, unds., Col. E7 102
Quitasueño, Banco see Quitasueño, unds., Col. E7 102
Quita Sueno Bank see Quitasueño, unds., Col. E7 102
Quiterajo, Moz. C7 68
Quitilipi, Arg. C7 92
Quitman, Ga., U.S. F2 116
Quitman, Tx., U.S. E3 122
Quito, Ec. H2 86
Quixadá, Braz. C6 88
Quixeramobim, Braz. C6 88
Qujiadian, China C5 38
Qujing, China F5 36
Qujiu, China J2 42
Qulin, Mo., U.S. H7 120
Qumarlêb, China E4 36
Qumrān, Khirbat, hist., W.B. G6 58
Quoich, stm., Nu., Can. C12 106
Quorn, Austl. F7 74
Quoxo, stm., Bots. C7 70
Qurdūd, Sudan E5 62
Qus, Egypt B6 62
Quseir, Egypt B6 62
Qutdligssat, Grnld. C15 141
Quthing, Leso. G8 70
Quweisna, Egypt H2 58
Quxian, China F2 42
Qüxü, China D13 54
Quyang, China B6 42
Quyghan, Kaz. E12 32
Quy Nhon, Viet. F9 48
Quyon, Qc., Can. C13 112
Quyquyó, Para. C9 92
Quzhou, China G8 42
Quzhou, China C6 42
Qyzylorda, Kaz. F11 32
Qyzyltū, Kaz. D12 32

R

Raab (Rába), stm., Eur. D12 22
Raalte, Neth. B15 14
Ra'ananna, Isr. F5 58
Raas, Pulau, i., Indon. G9 50
Raasay, i., Scot., U.K. D6 12
Raasiku, Est. A8 10
Rab, Otok, i., Cro. F11 22
Raba, Indon. H11 50
Rába (Raab), stm., Eur. D12 22
Rábade, Spain A3 20
Rabak, Sudan E6 62
Rabat, Malta I8 24
Rabat, Malta H8 24
Rabat, Mor. C3 64
Rabaul, Pap. N. Gui. a5 79a
Rabbit Creek, stm., S.D., U.S. B10 126
Rabbit Ears Pass, p., Co., U.S. C10 132
Rabi, i., Fiji p20 79e
Rābi', Ash-Shallāl ar- (Fourth Cataract), wtfl., Sudan D6 62
Rābigh, Sau. Ar. E4 56
Rabka, Pol. G15 16
Rabkavi Banhatti, India C2 53
Râbnița, Mol. B16 26
Rabočeostrovsk, Russia D16 8
Rabwāh, Pak. C4 54
Rabyānah, Ramlat, des., Libya C4 62
Raccoon, stm., Ia., U.S. C4 120
Raccoon Creek, stm., Oh., U.S. E15 120
Race, Cape, c., Nf., Can. j23 107a
Race Point, c., Ma., U.S. B15 114
Rach Gia, Viet. G7 48
Rach Gia, Vinh, b., Viet. H7 48
Raciąż, Pol. D16 16
Racibórz, Pol. F14 16
Racine, Wi., U.S. F2 112
Radaškovičy, Bela. F10 10
Rădăuți, Rom. B12 26
Radcliff, Ky., U.S. G12 120
Radeberg, Ger. E9 16
Radebeul, Ger. E9 16
Radford, Va., U.S. G5 114
Rādhanpur, India G3 54
Rădinești, Rom. E10 26
Radisson, Sk., Can. B6 124
Radium Hot Springs, B.C., Can. F14 138
Radnice, Czech Rep. G9 16
Radofinnikovo, Russia A13 10
Radom, Pol. E17 16
Radom, state, Pol. E16 16
Radomsko, Pol. E15 16
Radomyśl Wielki, Pol. F17 16
Radoviš, Mac. B5 28
Radstadt, Aus. C10 22
Radutino, Russia H17 10
Radviliškis, Lith. E6 10
Radville, Sk., Can. E9 124
Radymno, Pol. G18 16
Radzyń Chełmiński, Pol. C14 16
Rae, N.T., Can. C7 106
Rae, stm., Nu., Can. B7 106
Rāe Bareli, India E8 54
Raeford, N.C., U.S. B6 116
Rae Isthmus, isth., Nu., Can. B13 106
Rae Strait, strt., Nu., Can. B12 106
Rafaela, Arg. E7 92
Rafael Freyre, Cuba B10 102
Rafaḥ, Gaza G5 58
Rafḥā', Sau. Ar. D5 56
Rafsanjān, Iran C8 56
Raft, stm., U.S. H13 136
Raga, Sudan F5 62
Ragay Gulf, b., Phil. D4 52
Ragged Island, i., Bah. A10 102
Ragged Island Range, is., Bah. A10 102
Ragged Top Mountain, mtn., Wy., U.S. F7 126
Ragland, Al., U.S. D12 122
Raguva, Lith. E7 10
Rahačoŭ, Bela. G12 10
Rahad al-Bardī, Sudan E4 62
Rāhatgarh, India G7 54
Rahimatpur, India C1 53
Rahīm Ki Bāzār, Pak. F2 54
Rahīmyār Khān, Pak. D3 54
Rāichūr, India C3 53
Raiganj, India F12 54
Raigarh, India H9 54
Rāikot, India C5 54
Railroad Valley, val., Nv., U.S. E10 134
Railton, Austl. n13 77a
Rainbow Bridge National Monument, p.o.i., Ut., U.S. F6 132
Rainbow Falls, wtfl., B.C., Can. D11 138
Rainelle, W.V., U.S. G5 114
Rainier, Mount, vol., Wa., U.S. D5 136
Rainy, stm., N.A. C4 118
Rainy Lake, l., N.A. C5 118
Rainy River, On., Can. C4 118
Raipur, India H8 54
Raipur Uplands, plat., India H9 54
Raisen, India G6 54
Raisin, stm., Mi., U.S. G6 112
Raivavae, i., Fr. Poly. F12 72
Rajabasa, Indon. F4 50
Rājahmundry, India C5 53
Rājaldesar, India E5 54
Rājampet, India D4 53
Rajang, stm., Malay. B7 50
Rājapālaiyam, India G3 53
Rājāpur, India C1 53
Rājasthān, state, India E4 54
Rājbāri, Bngl. G12 54

Name	Map Ref.	Page
Rajčihinsk, Russia	G14	34
Rāj Gangpur, India	G10	54
Rājgarh, India	E6	54
Rājgarh, India	G6	54
Rājgarh, India	D5	54
Rajik, Indon.	E4	50
Rājkot, India	G3	54
Rāj Nāndgaon, India	H8	54
Rājpipla, India	H4	54
Rājpur, India	G5	54
Rājpura, India	C6	54
Rājshāhi, Bngl.	F12	54
Rājshāhi, state, Bngl.	F12	54
Rājula, India	H3	54
Raka, stm., China	D11	54
Rakamaz, Hung.	A8	26
Rakaposhi, mtn., Pak.	B11	56
Rakata, Pulau (Krakatoa), i., Indon.	G4	50
Rakhine, state, Mya.	C1	48
Rakhiv, Ukr.	A11	26
Rakitnoe, Russia	B11	36
Rakiura see Stewart Island, i., N.Z.	H3	80
Rakoniewice, Pol.	D12	16
Rakops, Bots.	B7	70
Rakovník, Czech Rep.	F9	16
Råkvåg see Råkvågen, Nor.	E4	8
Råkvågen, Nor.	E4	8
Rakvere, Est.	G12	8
Raleigh, Ms., U.S.	E9	122
Raleigh, N.C., U.S.	I7	114
Ralik Chain, is., Marsh. Is.	C7	72
Ralls, Tx., U.S.	H7	128
Ralston, Pa., U.S.	C9	114
Ramah, N.M., U.S.	H8	132
Rām Allāh, W.B.	G6	58
Rāmanagaram, India	E3	53
Rāmanāthapuram, India	G4	53
Rāmānuj Ganj, India	G9	54
Ramat Gan, Isr.	F5	58
Ramat HaSharon, Isr.	F5	58
Ramatlabama, Bots.	D7	70
Rambervillers, Fr.	F15	14
Rambouillet, Fr.	F10	14
Rambutyo Island, i., Pap. N. Gui.	a4	79a
Rām Dās, India	B5	54
Rāmdurg, India	C2	53
Ramea, Nf., Can.	j22	107a
Ramene, Russia	F20	8
Ramenskoe, Russia	E21	10
Rāmeswaram, India	G4	53
Rāmgarh, Bngl.	G13	54
Rāmgarh, India	E5	54
Rāmgarh, India	G10	54
Ram Head, c., V.I.U.S.	e8	104b
Rāmhormoz, Iran	C6	56
Ramírez, Mex.	I10	130
Ramírez, Mex.	G7	130
Ramla, Isr.	G5	58
Ramlu, mtn., Afr.	E8	62
Ramm, Jabal, mtn., Jord.	I6	58
Rāmnagar, India	F9	54
Rāmnagar, India	D7	54
Râmnicu Sărat, Rom.	D14	26
Râmnicu Vâlcea, Rom.	D11	26
Ramona, Ca., U.S.	J9	134
Ramona, S.D., U.S.	C15	126
Ramos, Mex.	D8	100
Ramos, stm., Mex.	C6	100
Ramotswa, Bots.	D7	70
Rampart, Ak., U.S.	C9	140
Ramparts, stm., N.T., Can.	B4	106
Rāmpur, India	D7	54
Rāmpur, India	C6	54
Rāmpura, India	F5	54
Rāmpur Hāt, India	F11	54
Ramree Island, i., Mya.	C1	48
Ramseur, N.C., U.S.	I6	114
Ramsey, I. of Man	G8	12
Ramsey Lake, l., On., Can.	A7	112
Ramsgate, Eng., U.K.	J14	12
Ramshorn Peak, mtn., Mt., U.S.	E15	136
Rāmtek, India	H7	54
Rāmu, Bngl.	H14	54
Ramu, stm., Pap. N. Gui.	a3	79a
Ramville, Îlet, i., Mart.	k7	105c
Ramygala, Lith.	E7	10
Rānāghāt, India	G12	54
Rana Kao, Volcán, vol., Chile	f29	78l
Rāna Pratāp Sāgar, res., India	F5	54
Ranau, Malay.	H1	52
Ranau, Danau, l., Indon.	F3	50
Ranburne, Al., U.S.	D13	122
Rancagua, Chile	G2	92
Rancah, Indon.	G6	50
Rancevo, Russia	D16	10
Rancharia, Braz.	D6	90
Ranchería, stm., Col.	B5	86
Ranchester, Wy., U.S.	C5	126
Rānchi, India	G10	54
Ranchillos, Arg.	C5	92
Ranch Lake, l., Sk., Can.	B9	124
Rancho Cordova, Ca., U.S.	E4	134
Rancho Nuevo, Mex.	H7	130
Ranchos, Arg.	G8	92
Ranco, Lago, l., Chile	H2	90
Rancul, Arg.	G5	92
Randazzo, Italy	G8	24
Randers, Den.	H4	8
Randleman, N.C., U.S.	I6	114
Randlett, Ok., U.S.	G10	128
Randolph, Az., U.S.	K5	132
Randolph, Me., U.S.	F7	110
Randolph, Ne., U.S.	E15	126
Randolph, N.Y., U.S.	B7	114
Randolph, Ut., U.S.	B5	132
Random Lake, Wi., U.S.	E2	112
Randsfjorden, l., Nor.	F3	8
Ranfurly, N.Z.	G4	80
Rāngāmāti, Bngl.	G13	54
Rangantemiang, Indon.	D8	50
Rangas, Tanjung, c., Indon.	E11	50
Rangasa, Tanjung, c., Indon.	E11	50
Rangaunu Bay, b., N.Z.	B5	80
Rangeley, Me., U.S.	E6	110
Ranger, Tx., U.S.	B9	130
Rangia, India	E13	54
Rangitaiki, stm., N.Z.	D7	80
Rangitata, stm., N.Z.	F4	80
Rangitikei, stm., N.Z.	D7	80
Rangkasbitung, Indon.	G4	50
Rangoon see Yangon, Mya.	D2	48
Rangoon, stm., Mya.	D3	48
Rangpur, Bngl.	F12	54
Rangpur, Pak.	C3	54
Rangsang, Pulau, i., Indon.	C3	50
Rānībennur, India	D2	53
Rānīganj, India	G11	54
Rānikhet, India	D7	54
Rankamhaeng National Park, p.o.i., Thai.	D4	48
Ranken, stm., Austl.	D7	74
Ranken Store, Austl.	C7	74
Rankin, Il., U.S.	H2	112
Rankin, Tx., U.S.	C6	130
Rankin Inlet see Kangiqsliniq, Nu., Can.	C12	106
Rankins Springs, Austl.	I6	76
Rann of Kutch see Kutch, Rann of, reg., Asia	D2	46
Ranong, Thai.	H4	48
Ranongga Island, i., Sol. Is.	e7	79b
Ranot, Thai.	I5	48
Ransiki, Indon.	F9	44
Ransom, Ks., U.S.	C8	128
Ranson, W.V., U.S.	E8	114
Rantabe, Madag.	D8	68
Rantaukampar, Indon.	C2	50
Rantaupanjang, Indon.	D2	50
Rantauprapat, Indon.	B1	50
Rantekombola, Bulu, mtn., Indon.	E12	50
Rantepao, Indon.	E11	50
Rantoul, Il., U.S.	D9	120
Raohe, China	B11	36
Raoping, China	J7	42
Raoul, Ga., U.S.	B2	116
Raoul-Blanchard, Mont, mtn., Qc., Can.	C6	110
Raoul Island, i., N.Z.	F9	72
Rapa, i., Fr. Poly.	F12	72
Rapallo, Italy	F6	22
Rapang, Indon.	E11	50
Rapa Nui see Pascua, Isla de, i., Chile	f30	78l
Rāpar, India	G3	54
Rapel, stm., Chile	F2	92
Rapel, Embalse, res., Chile	G2	92
Rapelli, Arg.	C5	92
Raper, Cape, c., Nu., Can.	B17	106
Rapidan, stm., Va., U.S.	F7	114
Rapid City, Mb., Can.	D13	124
Rapid City, S.D., U.S.	C9	126
Rapid Creek, stm., S.D., U.S.	D9	126
Rapide-Blanc, Qc., Can.	C4	110
Rapid River, Mi., U.S.	C2	112
Räpina, Est.	G12	8
Rappahannock, stm., Va., U.S.	G9	114
Rāpti, stm., Asia	E9	54
Rapu Rapu Island, i., Phil.	D5	52
Raraka, at., Fr. Poly.	E12	72
Rarotonga, i., Cook Is.	a26	78j
Rarotonga International Airport, Cook Is.	a26	78j
Rasa, Punta, c., Arg.	H9	92
Ra's al-Khaymah, U.A.E.	D8	56
Ra's Ba'labakk, Leb.	D7	58
Râșcani, Mol.	B14	26
Rașcov, Mol.	B15	26
Ras Dashen Terara, mtn., Eth.	E7	62
Ras Dejen see Ras Dashen Terara, mtn., Eth.	E7	62
Ras Djebel, Tun.	G4	24
Raseiniai, Lith.	E5	10
Râs el-Barr, Egypt	G2	58
Rashād, Sudan	E6	62
Rashid (Rosetta), Egypt	G1	58
Rashid, Masabb (Rosetta Mouth), mth., Egypt	G1	58
Rasht, Iran	B6	56
Raška, Serb.	F7	26
Rās Koh, mtn., Pak.	D10	56
Rasm al-Arwām, Sabkhat, l., Syria	C8	58
Râșnov, Rom.	D12	26
Rasra, India	F9	54
Rasšua, ostrov, i., Russia	G19	34
Rast, Rom.	F10	26
Rastatt, Ger.	H4	16
Rastede, Ger.	C4	16
Rastenburg see Kętrzyn, Pol.	B17	16
Rásttigáisá, mtn., Nor.	A12	8
Ratak Chain, is., Marsh. Is.	C8	72
Ratamka, Bela.	G10	10
Ratangarh, India	D5	54
Rat Buri, Thai.	F4	48
Rāth, India	F7	54
Rathbun Lake, res., Ia., U.S.	D4	120
Rathdrum, Id., U.S.	C9	136
Rathenow, Ger.	D8	16
Rathkeale, Ire.	I3	12
Ráth Luirc, Ire.	I4	12
Rathwell, Mb., Can.	E15	124
Rat Island, i., Ak., U.S.	g22	140a
Rat Islands, is., Ak., U.S.	g22	140a
Ratlām, India	G5	54
Ratmanova, ostrov, i., Russia	C27	34
Ratnāgiri, India	C1	53
Ratnapura, Sri L.	H5	53
Raton, N.M., U.S.	E4	128
Raton Pass, p., N.M., U.S.	E4	128
Rats, stm., Qc., Can.	A4	110
Rattanaburi, Thai.	E6	48
Rattaphum, Thai.	I5	48
Rattlesnake, Mt., U.S.	D13	136
Rattlesnake Creek, stm., Ks., U.S.	D10	128
Ratz, Mount, mtn., B.C., Can.	D4	106
Ratzeburg, Ger.	C6	16
Rau, Indon.	C2	50
Raub, Malay.	K5	48
Rauch, Arg.	H8	92
Raul Soares, Braz.	K4	88
Rauma, Fin.	F9	8
Rauma, stm., Nor.	E2	8
Rauna, Lat.	C8	10
Raung, Gunung, vol., Indon.	H9	50
Raurkela, India	G10	54
Răut, stm., Mol.	B14	26
Ravalgaon, India	H5	54
Ravanusa, Italy	G7	24
Ravena, N.Y., U.S.	B12	114
Ravenna, Italy	F9	22
Ravenna, Ky., U.S.	G2	114
Ravenna, Ne., U.S.	F13	126
Ravenna, Oh., U.S.	G8	112
Ravensburg, Ger.	I5	16
Ravenscrag, Sk., Can.	E4	124
Ravenshoe, Austl.	A5	76
Ravensthorpe, Austl.	F4	74
Ravenswood, W.V., U.S.	F4	114
Rāvi, stm., Asia	C4	54
Ravnina, Turkmen.	B9	56
Rāwah, Iraq	C5	56
Rawaki, at., Kir.	D9	72
Rāwalpindi, Pak.	B4	54
Rawas, stm., Indon.	E3	50
Rawdon, Qc., Can.	D3	110
Rawicz, Pol.	E12	16
Rawlinna, Austl.	F4	74
Rawlins, Wy., U.S.	B9	132
Rawson, Arg.	H4	90
Rawson, Arg.	G7	92
Raxāul, India	E10	54
Ray, Cape, c., Nf., Can.	C17	110
Raya, Indon.	C11	50
Raya, Bukit, mtn., Indon.	D8	50
Rāyachoti, India	D4	53
Rāyadurg, India	D3	53
Rāyagarha, India	B6	53
Ray Hubbard, Lake, res., Tx., U.S.	E2	122
Raymond, Ab., Can.	G18	138
Raymond, Il., U.S.	E8	120
Raymond, Mn., U.S.	F3	118
Raymond, Wa., U.S.	D3	136
Raymond Terrace, Austl.	I8	76
Raymondville, Tx., U.S.	H10	130
Raymore, Sk., Can.	C9	124
Rayne, La., U.S.	G6	122
Rayones, Mex.	C8	100
Rayong, Thai.	F5	48
Rayside-Balfour, On., Can.	B8	112
Raytown, Mo., U.S.	E3	120
Rayville, La., U.S.	E7	122
Raz, Pointe du, c., Fr.	F4	14
Războieni, Rom.	B13	26
Razdolinsk, Russia	C16	32
Răzeni, Mol.	C15	26
Razgrad, Blg.	F13	26
Razim, Lacul, l., Rom.	E15	26
Rāznas ezers, l., Lat.	D10	10
Razorback Mountain, mtn., B.C., Can.	E6	138
Răzvani, Rom.	E13	26
Ré, Île de, i., Fr.	C4	18
Reading, Eng., U.K.	J11	12
Reading, Mi., U.S.	C1	114
Reading, Oh., U.S.	E1	114
Reading, Pa., U.S.	D9	114
Readlyn, Ia., U.S.	B5	120
Readstown, Wi., U.S.	H8	118
Real, stm., Braz.	F6	88
Real, Cordillera, mts., S.A.	G4	84
Real del Castillo, Mex.	L9	134
Real del Padre, Arg.	G4	92
Realicó, Arg.	G5	92
Reardan, Wa., U.S.	C8	136
Reata, Mex.	B8	100
Reay, Scot., U.K.	C9	12
Rebecca, Lake, l., Austl.	F4	74
Rebiana Sand Sea see Rabyānah, Ramlat, des., Libya	C4	62
Reboly, Russia	E14	8
Rebouças, Braz.	B12	92
Rebun-tō, i., Japan	B14	38
Recanati, Italy	G10	22
Recherche, Archipelago of the, is., Austl.	F4	74
Recife, Braz.	E8	88
Recinto, Chile	H2	92
Recklinghausen, Ger.	E2	16
Reconquista, Arg.	D8	92
Recreio, Braz.	K4	88
Recreo, Arg.	D5	92
Rector, Ar., U.S.	H7	120
Rèčyča, Bela.	H13	10
Recz, Pol.	C11	16
Red (Hong, Song) (Yuan), stm., Asia	D9	46
Red, stm., N.A.	A2	118
Red, stm., U.S.	H10	120
Red, stm., U.S.	E9	108
Red, Elm Fork, stm., U.S.	F8	128
Red, North Fork, stm., U.S.	G9	128
Red, Prairie Dog Town Fork, stm., U.S.	H7	122
Red, Salt Fork, stm., U.S.	G9	128
Redang, Pulau, i., Malay.	J6	48
Red Bank, N.J., U.S.	D11	114
Red Bank, Tn., U.S.	B13	122
Red Bay, Nf., Can.	i22	107a
Red Bay, Al., U.S.	C10	122
Redbay, Fl., U.S.	G12	122
Redberry Lake, l., Sk., Can.	B6	124
Red Bluff, Ca., U.S.	C3	134
Red Bluff Reservoir, res., U.S.	C4	130
Red Boiling Springs, Tn., U.S.	H12	120
Red Canyon, p., S.D., U.S.	D9	126
Redcar, Eng., U.K.	G11	12
Red Cedar, stm., Mi., U.S.	F5	112
Red Cedar Lake, l., On., Can.	B9	112
Redcliff, Ab., Can.	D3	124
Red Cliff, Co., U.S.	D10	132
Redcliff see Red Cliff, Co., U.S.	D10	132
Redcliffe, Austl.	F9	76
Redcliffe, Mount, mtn., Austl.	E4	74
Red Cliffs, Austl.	J3	76
Red Cloud, Ne., U.S.	A10	128
Red Creek, stm., Ms., U.S.	G10	122
Red Deer, Ab., Can.	D17	138
Red Deer, stm., Can.	F19	138
Red Deer, stm., Can.	B12	124
Red Deer Lake, l., Mb., Can.	B12	124
Reddersburg, S. Afr.	F8	70
Red Devil, Ak., U.S.	D8	140
Redding, Ca., U.S.	C3	134
Redditch, Eng., U.K.	I10	12
Redenção, Braz.	C6	88
Redfield, S.D., U.S.	C14	126
Redford, Tx., U.S.	E3	130
Redhead, Trin.	s13	105f
Redja, stm., Russia	C14	10
Redkey, In., U.S.	H4	112
Redkino, Russia	D19	10
Red Lake, On., Can.	E12	106
Red Lake, l., On., Can.	E12	106
Red Lake, l., Az., U.S.	H2	132
Red Lake, stm., Mn., U.S.	D2	118
Red Lake Falls, Mn., U.S.	D2	118
Red Lake Road, On., Can.	B5	118
Redlands, Ca., U.S.	I8	134
Redlands, Co., U.S.	D8	132
Red Level, Al., U.S.	F12	122
Red Lion, Pa., U.S.	E9	114
Red Lodge, Mt., U.S.	B3	126
Redmond, Or., U.S.	F5	136
Redmond, Ut., U.S.	D5	132
Redmond, Wa., U.S.	C4	136
Red Mountain, mtn., Mt., U.S.	C14	136
Red Mountain Pass, p., Co., U.S.	F9	132
Red Oak, Ia., U.S.	D2	120
Redon, Fr.	G6	14
Redonda, Isla, i., Ven.	t12	105f
Redonda Islands, is., B.C., Can.	F6	138
Redondela, Spain	B2	20
Redondo, Port.	F3	20
Redondo Beach, Ca., U.S.	J7	134
Redoubt Volcano, vol., Ak., U.S.	D9	140
Red Pass, B.C., Can.	D11	138
Red Rock, B.C., Can.	C8	138
Red Rock, On., Can.	C10	118
Red Rock, stm., Mt., U.S.	F14	136
Red Rock, Lake, res., Ia., U.S.	C4	120
Redruth, Eng., U.K.	K7	12
Red Sea, s.	C7	62
Redvers, Sk., Can.	E12	124
Redwater, Ab., Can.	C17	138
Redwater, stm., Mt., U.S.	G8	124
Redwillow, stm., Can.	A11	138
Red Willow Creek, stm., Ne., U.S.	G12	126
Red Wing, Mn., U.S.	G6	118
Redwood, stm., Mn., U.S.	G3	118
Redwood Falls, Mn., U.S.	G3	118
Redwood National Park, p.o.i., Ca., U.S.	B1	134
Ree, Lough, l., Ire.	H5	12
Reed City, Mi., U.S.	E4	112
Reeder, N.D., U.S.	A10	126
Reed Lake, l., Sk., Can.	D6	124
Reedley, Ca., U.S.	G6	134
Reedsburg, Wi., U.S.	H8	118
Reedsville, Wi., U.S.	D2	112
Reefton, N.Z.	F4	80
Reelfoot Lake, l., Tn., U.S.	H8	120
Rees, Ger.	E2	16
Reese, Mi., U.S.	E6	112
Reese, stm., Nv., U.S.	C9	134
Reeseville, Wi., U.S.	H10	118
Refuge Cove, B.C., Can.	F6	138
Refugio, Tx., U.S.	F10	130
Rega, stm., Pol.	C11	16
Regência, Braz.	J6	88
Regeneração, Braz.	D4	88
Regensburg, Ger.	H8	16
Regent, N.D., U.S.	A10	126
Reggâne, Alg.	D5	64
Reggio di Calabria, Italy	F9	24
Reggio nell'Emilia, Italy	F7	22
Reghin, Rom.	C11	26
Regina, Sk., Can.	D9	124
Región Metropolitana, state, Chile	F2	92
Registan see Rīgestān, reg., Afg.	C9	56
Registro, Braz.	B14	92
Regozero, Russia	D14	8
Rehau, Ger.	F7	16
Rehoboth, Nmb.	C3	70
Rehoboth Beach, De., U.S.	F10	114
Reẖovot, Isr.	G5	58
Reichenbach, Ger.	F8	16
Reidsville, Ga., U.S.	D3	116
Reidsville, N.C., U.S.	H6	114
Reigate, Eng., U.K.	J12	12
Reihoku, Japan	G2	40
Reims (Rheims), Fr.	E12	14
Rein Anteriur (Vorderrhein), stm., Switz.	D6	22
Reinbeck, Ia., U.S.	B5	120
Reindeer Lake, l., Can.	D10	106
Reinga, Cape, c., N.Z.	B5	80
Reinosa, Spain	A6	20
Reisa Nasjonalpark, p.o.i., Nor.	B10	8
Reisterstown, Md., U.S.	E9	114
Reitz, S. Afr.	E9	70
Reliance, N.T., Can.	C9	106
Remada, Tun.	C7	64
Remagen, Ger.	F3	16
Remanso, Braz.	E4	88
Rembang, Indon.	G7	50
Remedios, Col.	D4	86
Remedios, Pan.	H7	102
Remedios, Punta, c., El Sal.	F2	102
Remer, Mn., U.S.	D5	118
Remington, Va., U.S.	F8	114
Rémire, Fr. Gu.	C7	84
Remiremont, Fr.	G15	14
Remoulins, Fr.	F10	18
Rempang, Pulau, i., Indon.	C3	50
Remscheid, Ger.	E3	16
Remsen, Ia., U.S.	B1	120
Remus, Mi., U.S.	E4	112
Renaix see Ronse, Bel.	D12	14
Renata, B.C., Can.	G12	138
Rencēni, Lat.	C8	10
Rende, Italy	E10	24
Rend Lake, res., Il., U.S.	F8	120
Rendova Island, i., Sol. Is.	e7	79b
Rendsburg, Ger.	B5	16
Renfrew, On., Can.	C13	112
Rengat, Indon.	D3	50
Rengel, Indon.	G8	50
Rengo, Chile	G2	92
Reng Tlāng, mtn., Asia	H14	54
Renheji, China	F6	42
Renhuai, China	H2	42
Reni, Ukr.	D15	26
Renland, reg., Grnld.	C20	141
Renmark, Austl.	J3	76
Rennell, i., Sol. Is.	E7	72
Rennell, Islas, is., Chile	J2	90
Rennell and Bellona, state, Sol. Is.	f9	79b
Rennes, Fr.	F7	14
Rennie, Mb., Can.	E18	124
Reno, Nv., U.S.	D6	134
Reno, stm., Italy	F8	22
Reno Hill, mtn., Wy., U.S.	E6	126
Renoster, stm., S. Afr.	G5	70
Renous, N.B., Can.	D11	110
Renovo, Pa., U.S.	C8	114
Rensjön, Swe.	B8	8
Rensselaer, In., U.S.	H2	112
Rensselaer, N.Y., U.S.	B12	114
Rentería, Spain	A9	20
Renton, Wa., U.S.	C4	136
Renville, Mn., U.S.	G3	118
Renwick, Ia., U.S.	B4	120
Reo, Indon.	H12	50
Repetek, Turkmen.	B9	56
Repton, Al., U.S.	F11	122
Republic, Mi., U.S.	B1	112
Republic, Mo., U.S.	G4	120
Republic, Wa., U.S.	B8	136
Republican, stm., U.S.	B11	128
Republican, North Fork, stm., U.S.	A6	128
Republican, South Fork, stm., U.S.	B7	128
Republic of Korea see Korea, South, ctry., Asia	G8	38
Repulse Bay see Naujaat, Nu., Can.	B13	106
Repulse Bay, b., Austl.	C7	76
Repvåg, Nor.	A11	8
Requena, Spain	E9	20
Reriutaba, Braz.	C5	88
Reşadiye Yarımadası, pen., Tur.	G10	28
Reschenpass (Resia, Passo di), p., Eur.	C16	18
Reschenscheideck see Reschenpass, p., Eur.	C16	18
Reschenscheideck see Resia, Passo di, p., Eur.	C16	18
Resen, Mac.	B4	28
Reserva, Braz.	B12	92
Reserve, La., U.S.	G8	122
Reserve, N.M., U.S.	J8	132
Resia, Passo di (Reschenpass), p., Eur.	C16	18
Resistencia, Arg.	C8	92
Reşiţa, Rom.	D8	26
Resko, Pol.	C11	16
Resolute see Qausuittuq, Nu., Can.	C7	141
Resolution Island, i., Nu., Can.	E12	141
Resolution Island, i., N.Z.	G2	80
Resplendor, Braz.	J5	88
Restigouche, stm., Can.	C9	110
Restinga Seca, Braz.	D11	92
Reston, Mb., Can.	E12	124
Retalhuleu, Guat.	E2	102
Retamosa, Ur.	F10	92
Retezat, Parcul Național, p.o.i., Rom.	D9	26
Rethel, Fr.	E13	14
Réthymno, Grc.	H7	28
Rettihovka, Russia	B10	38
Reunion, dep., Afr.	I11	60
Reus, Spain	C12	20
Reuss, stm., Switz.	C5	22
Reuterstadt Stavenhagen, Ger.	C8	16
Reutlingen, Ger.	H5	16
Revda, Russia	C16	8
Revelstoke, B.C., Can.	F12	138
Revelstoke, Lake, res., B.C., Can.	E12	138
Reventazón, Peru	E1	84
Revilla del Campo, Spain	B7	20
Revillagigedo, Islas, is., Mex.	F2	100
Revillagigedo Island, i., Ak., U.S.	E13	140
Revillagigedo Islands see Revillagigedo, Islas, is., Mex.	F2	100
Revin, Fr.	E13	14
Revolución, Mex.	H2	130
Rewa, India	F8	54
Rewāri, India	D6	54
Rexburg, Id., U.S.	G15	136
Rexford, Ks., U.S.	B8	128
Rexford, Mt., U.S.	B11	136
Rey, Isla del, i., Pan.	H8	102
Rey, Laguna del, l., Mex.	B7	100
Reyes, Bol.	B3	90
Reyes, Point, c., Ca., U.S.	F2	134
Reyhanlı, Tur.	B7	58
Reykjanes Ridge, unds.	C10	144
Reykjavík, Ice.	k28	8a
Reyno, Ar., U.S.	H7	120
Reynolds, Ga., U.S.	D1	116
Reynolds, N.D., U.S.	G16	124
Reynosa, Mex.	B9	100
Rezé, Fr.	G7	14
Rēzekne, Lat.	D10	10
Rezina, Mol.	B15	26
Rezovo, Blg.	G15	26
Rezovska (Mutlu), stm., Eur.	G14	26
Rhaetian Alps, mts., Eur.	C15	18
Rhame, N.D., U.S.	A9	126
Rheda-Wiedenbrück, Ger.	E4	16
Rheims see Reims, Fr.	E12	14
Rhein, Sk., Can.	C11	124
Rhein see Rhine, stm., Eur.	C15	14
Rheine, Ger.	D3	16
Rheinland-Pfalz, state, Ger.	G3	16
Rhine, Ga., U.S.	E2	116
Rhine (Rhein) (Rhin), stm., Eur.	C15	14
Rhinelander, Wi., U.S.	F9	118
Rhineland-Palatinate see Rheinland-Pfalz, state, Ger.	G3	16
Rhinns Point, c., Scot., U.K.	F6	12
Rhir, Cap, c., Mor.	C2	64
Rho, Italy	E5	22
Rhode Island, state, U.S.	C14	114
Rhode Island Sound, strt., U.S.	C14	114
Rhodes see Ródos, Grc.	G11	28
Rhodes see Ródos, i., Grc.	G10	28
Rhodesia see Zimbabwe, ctry., Afr.	D4	68
Rhodes Matopos National Park, p.o.i., Zimb.	B8	70
Rhodes' Tomb, hist., Zimb.	B9	70
Rhodope Mountains, mts., Eur.	H11	26
Rhön, mts., Ger.	F5	16
Rhondda, Wales, U.K.	J9	12
Rhône, state, Fr.	D10	18
Rhône, stm., Eur.	F10	18
Rhyl, Wales, U.K.	H9	12
Riachão, Braz.	D2	88
Riachão do Jacuípe, Braz.	F6	88
Riacho de Santana, Braz.	G4	88
Riachos, Islas de los, is., Arg.	H4	90
Riamkanan, Waduk, res., Indon.	E9	50
Riaño, Spain	A6	20
Riau, state, Indon.	D2	50
Riau, Kepulauan, is., Indon.	C4	50
Riaza, Spain	C7	20
Ribadeo, Spain	A3	20
Ribas do Rio Pardo, Braz.	D6	90
Ribáuè, Moz.	C6	68
Ribe, Den.	I3	8
Ribe, state, Den.	I3	8
Ribeira, Braz.	B13	92
Ribeira do Pombal, Braz.	F6	88
Ribeirão, Braz.	E8	88
Ribeirão Preto, Braz.	K2	88
Ribeirão Vermelho, Braz.	K3	88
Ribeiro Gonçalves, Braz.	D3	88
Ribera, Italy	G7	24
Riberalta, Bol.	B3	90
Rib Lake, Wi., U.S.	F8	118
Ribnica, Slvn.	E11	22
Ribnitz-Damgarten, Ger.	B8	16
Ribstone Creek, stm., Ab., Can.	D19	138
Ricardo Flores Magón, Mex.	F9	98
Riccione, Italy	F9	22
Rice, Tx., U.S.	E2	122
Rice Lake, l., On., Can.	D11	112
Riceville, Ia., U.S.	H6	118
Riceville, Tn., U.S.	B14	122
Richan, On., Can.	B6	118
Richard B. Russell Lake, res., U.S.	B3	116
Richard Collinson Inlet, b., N.T., Can.	B17	140
Richards, Tx., U.S.	G3	122
Richards Bay, S. Afr.	F11	70
Richards Bay, b., S. Afr.	F11	70
Richards Island, i., N.T., Can.	C13	140
Richardson, Tx., U.S.	E2	122
Richardson, Wa., U.S.	B4	136
Richardson Mountains, mts., Can.	B3	106
Richard Toll, Sen.	F1	64
Riche, Pointe, c., Nf., Can.	i22	107a
Richelieu, Fr.	G9	14
Richelieu, stm., Qc., Can.	E3	110
Richer, Mb., Can.	E17	124
Richey, Mt., U.S.	G8	124
Richfield, Mn., U.S.	G5	118
Richfield, Pa., U.S.	D8	114
Richfield, Ut., U.S.	E4	132
Richfield Springs, N.Y., U.S.	B11	114
Richford, Vt., U.S.	F4	110
Rich Hill, Mo., U.S.	F3	120
Richibucto, N.B., Can.	D12	110
Richland, Ga., U.S.	E14	122
Richland, Mi., U.S.	F4	112
Richland, Mt., U.S.	F7	124
Richland, Wa., U.S.	D7	136
Richland Center, Wi., U.S.	H8	118
Richland Creek, stm., Tx., U.S.	C11	130
Richlands, Va., U.S.	G4	114
Richland Springs, Tx., U.S.	C9	130
Richmond, Austl.	C4	76
Richmond, Austl.	I8	76
Richmond, B.C., Can.	G7	138
Richmond, On., Can.	C14	112
Richmond, Qc., Can.	E4	110
Richmond, N.Z.	E5	80
Richmond, S. Afr.	G6	70
Richmond, S. Afr.	F10	70
Richmond, Eng., U.K.	G11	12
Richmond, Ca., U.S.	F3	134
Richmond, In., U.S.	I5	112
Richmond, Ky., U.S.	G1	114
Richmond, Me., U.S.	F7	110
Richmond, Mi., U.S.	B3	114
Richmond, Mn., U.S.	F4	118
Richmond, Mo., U.S.	E4	120
Richmond, Tx., U.S.	H3	122
Richmond, Ut., U.S.	B5	132
Richmond, Va., U.S.	G8	114
Richmond Heights, Fl., U.S.	K5	116
Richmond Highlands, Wa., U.S.	C4	136
Richmond Hill, On., Can.	E10	112
Richmond Hill, Ga., U.S.	E4	116
Richmond Peak, mtn., St. Vin.	o11	105e
Richton, Ms., U.S.	F9	122
Richwood, Oh., U.S.	D2	114
Richwood, W.V., U.S.	F5	114
Ricobayo, Embalse de, res., Spain	C4	20
Riddle, Or., U.S.	H3	136
Rideau, stm., On., Can.	C14	112
Ridgecrest, Ca., U.S.	H8	134
Ridgedale, Sk., Can.	A9	124
Ridgeland, Ms., U.S.	E8	122
Ridgeland, S.C., U.S.	D4	116
Ridgetown, On., Can.	F8	112
Ridgeville, Mb., Can.	E16	124
Ridgeville, S.C., U.S.	C5	116
Ridgeway, Mo., U.S.	D4	120
Ridgway, Co., U.S.	E9	132
Ridgway, Il., U.S.	G9	120
Ridgway, Pa., U.S.	C7	114
Riding Mountain National Park, p.o.i., Mb., Can.	D13	124
Riegelwood, N.C., U.S.	B7	116
Riesa, Ger.	E9	16
Riesco, Isla, i., Chile	J2	90
Riesi, Italy	G8	24
Riet, stm., S. Afr.	F7	70
Riet, stm., S. Afr.	H5	70
Rietavas, Lith.	E4	10
Rietfontein (Buitsivango), stm., Afr.	B4	70
Rieti, Italy	H9	22
Rif, mts., Mor.	C4	64
Riffe Lake, res., Wa., U.S.	D4	136
Rifle, Co., U.S.	D9	132
Rifstangi, c., Ice.	j31	8a
Rift Valley, val., Afr.	F7	62
Rīga, Lat.	D7	10
Riga, Gulf of, b., Eur.	C6	10
Rigaih, Indon.	J2	48
Rigby, Id., U.S.	G14	136
Rīgestān, reg., Afg.	C9	56
Riggins, Id., U.S.	E10	136
Rigi, mtn., Switz.	C5	22
Rigo, Pap. N. Gui.	b4	79a
Rig-Rig, Chad	E2	62
Riihimäki, Fin.	F11	8
Riiser-Larsen Peninsula, pen., Ant.	B8	81
Riječki Zaljev, b., Cro.	E11	22
Rijeka (Fiume), Cro.	E11	22
Rijssen, Neth.	D2	16
Rillito, Az., U.S.	K5	132
Rimatara, i., Fr. Poly.	F11	72
Rimavská Sobota, Slov.	H15	16
Rimbey, Ab., Can.	D16	138
Rimersburg, Pa., U.S.	C6	114
Rimini, Italy	F9	22
Rimouski, Qc., Can.	B8	110
Rimouski, stm., Qc., Can.	B8	110
Rinbung, China	C7	46
Rinca, Pulau, i., Indon.	H11	50
Rincon, Ga., U.S.	D4	116
Rincon, N.M., U.S.	K9	132
Rinconada, Arg.	D3	90
Rincón del Bonete, Lago Artificial de, res., Ur.	F9	92
Rincón de Romos, Mex.	D7	100
Rīngas, India	E5	54
Ringdove, Vanuatu	k16	79d
Ringebu, Nor.	F4	8
Ringgold, Ga., U.S.	C13	122
Ringim, Nig.	G6	64
Ringkøbing, Den.	H2	8
Ringkøbing, state, Den.	H3	8
Ringkøbing Fjord, b., Den.	H2	8
Ringling, Ok., U.S.	G11	128
Ringsted, Ia., U.S.	H4	118
Ringvassøya, i., Nor.	A8	8
Rinjani, Gunung, vol., Indon.	H10	50
Rinteln, Ger.	D5	16
Rio, Wi., U.S.	H9	118
Riobamba, Ec.	H2	86
Río Blanco, Chile	F2	92
Rio Branco, Braz.	E4	84
Río Branco, Ur.	F11	92
Río Bravo, Mex.	C9	100
Río Bravo, Parque Internacional del, p.o.i., Mex.	F5	130
Rio Brilhante, Braz.	D6	90
Río Bueno, Chile	H2	90
Rio Casca, Braz.	K4	88
Río Ceballos, Arg.	E5	92
Río Chico, Ven.	B9	86
Rio Claro, Braz.	L2	88
Rio Claro, Trin.	s12	105f
Río Colorado, Arg.	I5	92
Río Cuarto, Arg.	F5	92
Rio das Pedras, Moz.	C12	70
Rio de Janeiro, Braz.	L4	88
Rio de Janeiro, state, Braz.	L4	88
Rio Dell, Ca., U.S.	C1	134
Río de Oro, Col.	C5	86
Rio do Sul, Braz.	C13	92
Rio Espera, Braz.	K4	88
Rio Felix, stm., N.M., U.S.	H3	128
Río Gallegos, Arg.	J3	90
Río Grande, Arg.	J3	90
Rio Grande, Braz.	F11	92
Río Grande, Mex.	D7	100
Río Grande, Nic.	F4	102
Río Grande, P.R.	B4	104a
Rio Grande (Bravo), stm., N.A.	H13	98
Rio Grande do Norte, state, Braz.	C7	88
Rio Grande do Sul, state, Braz.	D11	92
Ríohacha, Col.	B5	86
Río Hato, Pan.	H7	102
Rio Hondo, Tx., U.S.	H10	130
Rio Hondo, stm., N.M., U.S.	H3	128
Rio Hondo, Embalse, res., Arg.	C5	92
Río Jueyes, P.R.	B3	104a
Riolândia, Braz.	D6	90
Rio Largo, Braz.	E8	88
Riom, Fr.	D9	18
Río Mayo, Arg.	I2	90
Río Mulatos, Bol.	C3	90
Riondel, B.C., Can.	G14	138
Rio Negro, Braz.	C13	92
Ríonegro, Col.	D5	86
Río Negro, state, Arg.	G3	90
Rio Negro, Pantanal do, sw., Braz.	C5	90
Rionero in Vulture, Italy	D9	24
Riópar, Spain	F8	20
Rio Pardo, Braz.	E11	92
Rio Pardo de Minas, Braz.	H4	88
Río Piedras, P.R.	B3	104a
Rio Piracicaba, Braz.	J4	88
Rio Pomba, Braz.	K4	88
Rio Preto, Braz.	L3	88
Rio Rancho, N.M., U.S.	H10	132
Rio Real, Braz.	F6	88
Río Segundo, Arg.	E5	92
Ríosucio, Col.	E4	86
Río Tercero, Arg.	F5	92
Rio Tinto, Braz.	D8	88
Rio Verde, Braz.	G7	84
Ríoverde, Mex.	E8	100
Rio Verde de Mato Grosso, Braz.	C6	90
Rio Vista, Ca., U.S.	E4	134
Riozinho, stm., Braz.	E3	88
Riozinho, stm., Braz.	D4	84
Ripley, N.Y., U.S.	B6	114
Ripley, Oh., U.S.	F2	114
Ripley, Tn., U.S.	B9	122
Ripoll, Spain	B13	20
Ripon, Qc., Can.	E1	110
Ripon, Eng., U.K.	G11	12
Ripon, Ca., U.S.	F4	134
Ripon, Wi., U.S.	H10	118
Riposto, Italy	G9	24
Risaralda, state, Col.	E3	86
Risbäck, Swe.	D6	8
Rishīkesh, India	C7	54
Rishiri-suidō, strt., Japan	B14	38
Rishiri-tō, i., Japan	B14	38
Rishon LeẔiyyon, Isr.	G5	58
Rising Star, Tx., U.S.	B9	130
Rising Sun, In., U.S.	F12	120
Rising Sun, Md., U.S.	E9	114
Risle, stm., Fr.	E9	14
Risnjak, mtn., Cro.	E11	22
Risti, Est.	A7	10
Ristna, Est.	G9	8
Rita Blanca Creek, stm., Tx., U.S.	F6	128
Ritchie, S. Afr.	F7	70
Ritidian Point, c., Guam	i10	78c
Ritter, Mount, mtn., Ca., U.S.	F6	134
Rittman, Oh., U.S.	D4	114
Ritzville, Wa., U.S.	C8	136
Rivadavia, Arg.	E3	92
Rivadavia, Arg.	G6	92
Rivadavia, Chile	D2	92
Riva del Garda, Italy	E7	22
Rivas, Nic.	G5	102
Rive-de-Gier, Fr.	D10	18
Rivera, Arg.	H6	92
Rivera, Ur.	E10	92
River Cess, Lib.	H3	64

Name	Map Ref.	Page
Riverdale, Ca., U.S.	G6	134
Riverdale, N.D., U.S.	G12	124
River Falls, Al., U.S.	F12	122
River Falls, Wi., U.S.	G6	118
Riverhead, N.Y., U.S.	D13	114
Riverhurst, Sk., Can.	D7	124
Riverina, reg., Austl.	J5	76
River John, N.S., Can.	E13	110
River Jordan, B.C., Can.	H6	138
River Road, Or., U.S.	F3	136
Rivers, Mb., Can.	D13	124
Riversdale, S. Afr.	I5	70
Riverside, Ca., U.S.	J8	134
Riverside, Ia., U.S.	C6	120
Riverside, Tx., U.S.	G3	122
Riverside, Wa., U.S.	B7	136
Rivers Inlet, B.C., Can.	E3	138
Riversleigh, Austl.	C7	74
Riverton, N.Z.	H2	80
Riverton, Il., U.S.	E8	120
Riverton, Ne., U.S.	A10	128
Riverton, Ut., U.S.	C4	132
Riverton, Va., U.S.	F7	114
Riverton, Wy., U.S.	D4	126
Riverton Heights, Wa., U.S.	C4	136
River View, Al., U.S.	E13	122
Rives, Tn., U.S.	H8	120
Rivesville, W.V., U.S.	E5	114
Riviera, Tx., U.S.	G10	130
Riviera Beach, Fl., U.S.	J5	116
Rivière-à-Pierre, Qc., Can.	C5	110
Rivière-Bleue, Qc., Can.	C7	110
Rivière-de-la-Chaloupe, Qc., Can.	A14	110
Rivière-du-Loup, Qc., Can.	C7	110
Rivière-Matawin, Qc., Can.	D3	110
Rivière-Pilote, Mart.	l7	105c
Rivière-Salée, Mart.	k7	105c
Rivne, Ukr.	E14	6
Rivoli, Italy	E4	22
Rivoli Bay, b., Austl.	K2	76
Riyadh see Ar-Riyāḍ, Sau. Ar.	E6	56
Rīyāq, Leb.	E7	58
Rize, Tur.	A5	56
Rizzuto, Capo, c., Italy	F11	24
Rjad, Russia	C18	10
Rjazan', Russia	D5	32
Rjazancevo, Russia	D22	10
Rjazanskaja oblast', co., Russia	I19	8
Rjažsk, Russia	D6	32
Rjukan, Nor.	G3	8
Ro, N. Cal.	m16	79d
Roachdale, In., U.S.	I3	112
Road Town, Br. Vir. Is.	e8	104b
Roan Mountain, Tn., U.S.	H3	114
Roanne, Fr.	C9	18
Roanoke, Al., U.S.	D13	122
Roanoke, Il., U.S.	D8	120
Roanoke, Va., U.S.	G6	114
Roanoke, stm., U.S.	H8	114
Roanoke Island, i., N.C., U.S.	I10	114
Roanoke Rapids, N.C., U.S.	H8	114
Roanoke Rapids Lake Dam, dam, N.C., U.S.	H8	114
Roan Plateau, plat., U.S.	D7	132
Roaring Spring, Pa., U.S.	D7	114
Roaring Springs, Tx., U.S.	H7	128
Roatán, Isla de, i., Hond.	D4	102
Robbins, N.C., U.S.	A6	116
Robbins, Tn., U.S.	H13	120
Robbins Island, i., Austl.	n12	77a
Robbinsville, N.C., U.S.	A2	116
Robe, Austl.	K2	76
Robe, Mount, hill, Austl.	H3	76
Röbel, Ger.	C8	16
Robersonville, N.C., U.S.	I8	114
Roberta, Ga., U.S.	D1	116
Robert Lee, Tx., U.S.	C7	130
Robert Louis Stevenson's Tomb, hist., Samoa	g12	79c
Roberts, Id., U.S.	G14	136
Roberts, Mt., U.S.	B3	126
Robertsdale, Al., U.S.	G11	122
Robertsfors, Swe.	D9	8
Robert S. Kerr Lake, res., Ok., U.S.	B3	122
Robertson, S. Afr.	H4	70
Roberts Peak, mtn., B.C., Can.	D10	138
Roberts Port, Lib.	H2	64
Roberval, Qc., Can.	B4	110
Robinson, Il., U.S.	E10	120
Robinson, Tx., U.S.	C10	130
Róbinson Crusoe, Isla, i., Chile	I7	82
Robinvale, Austl.	J4	76
Robledo, Spain	F8	20
Roblin, Mb., Can.	C12	124
Roboré, Bol.	C5	90
Rob Roy Island, i., Sol. Is.	d7	79b
Robson, Mount, mtn., B.C., Can.	C11	138
Robstown, Tx., U.S.	G10	130
Roby, Tx., U.S.	B7	130
Roca, Cabo da, c., Port.	F1	20
Roçado, Braz.	D3	88
Rocafuerte, Ec.	H1	86
Roca Partida, Isla, i., Mex.	F2	100
Rocas, Atol das, at., Braz.	F11	82
Rocciamelone, mtn., Italy	E4	22
Rocha, Ur.	G10	92
Rochdale, Eng., U.K.	H10	12
Rochechouart, Fr.	D6	18
Rochefort, Fr.	D5	18
Rochelle, Ga., U.S.	E2	116
Rochelle, Il., U.S.	C8	120
Roche-Percée, Sk., Can.	E10	124
Rochester, In., U.S.	G3	112
Rochester, Mi., U.S.	B2	114
Rochester, Mn., U.S.	G6	118
Rochester, N.H., U.S.	G5	110
Rochester, N.Y., U.S.	E12	112
Rochester, Tx., U.S.	H9	128
Rochlitz, Ger.	E8	16
Rock, stm., U.S.	J8	118
Rock, stm., U.S.	H2	118
Rockall, i., Scot., U.K.	D6	6
Rockall Rise, unds.	C12	144
Rock Bay, B.C., Can.	F5	138
Rock Creek, B.C., Can.	G11	138
Rock Creek, stm., N.A.	F7	124
Rock Creek, stm., Mt., U.S.	D13	136
Rock Creek, stm., Nv., U.S.	C9	134
Rock Creek Butte, mtn., Or., U.S.	F8	136
Rockdale, Il., U.S.	C9	120
Rockdale, Tx., U.S.	D11	130
Rockefeller Plateau, plat., Ant.	D27	81
Rockenhausen, Ger.	G3	16
Rock Falls, Il., U.S.	C8	120
Rockford, Ia., U.S.	A5	120
Rockford, Il., U.S.	B8	120
Rockford, Oh., U.S.	D1	114
Rockford, Tn., U.S.	B15	122
Rockglen, Sk., Can.	E8	124
Rockhampton, Austl.	D8	76
Rockhampton Downs, Austl.	C7	74
Rock Hill, S.C., U.S.	B4	116
Rockingham, N.C., U.S.	B6	116
Rockingham Bay, b., Austl.	B6	76
Rock Island, Il., U.S.	C7	120
Rocklake, N.D., U.S.	F14	124
Rockland, On., Can.	C14	112
Rockland, Id., U.S.	H14	136
Rockland, Ma., U.S.	B15	114
Rockland, Me., U.S.	F7	110
Rocklands Reservoir, l., Austl.	K3	76
Rockledge, Fl., U.S.	H5	116
Rocklin, Ca., U.S.	E4	134
Rockmart, Ga., U.S.	D13	122
Rockport, In., U.S.	G10	120
Rockport, Ky., U.S.	G11	120
Rockport, Ma., U.S.	B15	114
Rockport, Me., U.S.	F7	110
Rock Port, Mo., U.S.	D2	120
Rock Rapids, Ia., U.S.	H2	118
Rock River, Wy., U.S.	F6	126
Rocksprings, Tx., U.S.	E7	130
Rock Springs, Wy., U.S.	B7	132
Rockstone, Guy.	B6	84
Rock Tombs see *Speos, hist., Egypt*	K1	58
Rock Valley, Ia., U.S.	H2	118
Rockville, In., U.S.	I2	112
Rockville, Md., U.S.	E8	114
Rockwall, Tx., U.S.	E2	122
Rockwell, Ia., U.S.	B4	120
Rockwell, N.C., U.S.	A5	116
Rockwood, Me., U.S.	E7	110
Rockwood, Pa., U.S.	I10	112
Rockwood, Tn., U.S.	I13	120
Rocky Cape National Park, p.o.i., Austl.	n12	77a
Rockyford, Ab., Can.	E17	138
Rocky Ford, Co., U.S.	C5	128
Rocky Mount, N.C., U.S.	I8	114
Rocky Mount, Va., U.S.	H5	114
Rocky Mountain, mtn., Mt., U.S.	C14	136
Rocky Mountain House, Ab., Can.	D16	138
Rocky Mountain National Park, p.o.i., Co., U.S.	G7	126
Rocky Mountains, mts., N.A.	D6	106
Rocky Mountain Trench, val., N.A.	G15	138
Rocky Point, c., Bah.	K8	116
Rodalben, Ger.	G3	16
Rodbār, Afg.	C9	56
Rødbyhavn, Den.	I4	8
Rodeo, Arg.	E3	92
Rodeo, Mex.	C6	100
Rodeo, N.M., U.S.	L7	132
Roderick Island, i., B.C., Can.	D2	138
Rodewisch, Ger.	F8	16
Rodez, Fr.	E8	18
Roding, Ger.	G8	16
Rodino, Russia	G21	8
Rodney, On., Can.	F8	112
Rodney, Cape, c., Ak., U.S.	D6	140
Rodniki, Russia	H19	8
Ródos (Rhodes), Grc.	G11	28
Ródos (Rhodes), i., Grc.	G10	28
Rodrigues, i., Mrts.	K9	142
Roebourne, Austl.	D3	74
Roebuck Bay, b., Austl.	C4	74
Roeland Park, Ks., U.S.	E3	120
Roermond, Neth.	C14	14
Roeselare, Bel.	D11	14
Roes Welcome Sound, strt., Nu., Can.	C13	106
Roff, Ok., U.S.	C2	122
Rogačevo, Russia	D20	10
Rogagua, Laguna, l., Bol.	B3	90
Rogaguado, Laguna, l., Bol.	B3	90
Rogaland, state, Nor.	G2	8
Rogaška Slatina, Slvn.	D12	22
Rogers, Ar., U.S.	H3	120
Rogers, Tx., U.S.	D10	130
Rogers, Mount, mtn., Va., U.S.	H4	114
Rogers Lake, l., Ca., U.S.	I8	134
Rogers Pass, p., B.C., Can.	E13	138
Rogersville, N.B., Can.	D11	110
Rogersville, Al., U.S.	C11	122
Rogersville, Tn., U.S.	H3	114
Roggewein, Cabo, c., Chile	e30	78l
Rogliano, Fr.	G15	18
Rognedino, Russia	G16	10
Rogue, stm., Or., U.S.	H2	136
Rohri, Pak.	E2	54
Rohtak, India	D6	54
Roi Et, Thai.	E6	48
Roi Georges, Îles du, is., Fr. Poly.	E12	72
Roilianka, Ukr.	C16	26
Rojas, Arg.	G7	92
Rojo, Cabo, c., Mex.	E10	100
Rojo, Cabo, c., P.R.	C1	104a
Rokan, Indon.	C2	50
Rokan, stm., Indon.	C2	50
Rokel, stm., S.L.	H2	64
Rokiškis, Lith.	E8	10
Rokycany, Czech Rep.	G9	16
Roland, Mb., Can.	E16	124
Roland, Ar., U.S.	C6	122
Roland, Ia., U.S.	B4	120
Rolândia, Braz.	D6	90
Roldanillo, Col.	E3	86
Rolfe, Ia., U.S.	B3	120
Roll, Az., U.S.	K2	132
Rolla, Mo., U.S.	G6	120
Rolla, N.D., U.S.	F14	124
Rolling Fork, Ms., U.S.	E8	122
Rolling Fork, stm., Ky., U.S.	G12	120
Rollingstone, Austl.	B6	76
Rollins, Mt., U.S.	C12	136
Rolvsøya, i., Nor.	A10	8
Roma, Austl.	F7	76
Roma (Rome), Italy	I9	22
Roma, Leso.	F8	70
Roma, Tx., U.S.	H8	130
Romagna, hist. reg., Italy	F9	22
Roman, Rom.	C13	26
Romanche Gap, unds.	I12	144
Romang, Pulau, i., Indon.	G8	44
Romania, ctry., Eur.	D11	26
Roman Nose Mountain, mtn., Or., U.S.	G3	136
Romano, Cape, c., Fl., U.S.	K4	116
Romano, Cayo, i., Cuba	A9	102
Romans-sur-Isère, Fr.	D10	18
Romanzof Mountains, mts., Ak., U.S.	C11	140
Romblon, Phil.	D4	52
Rome see Roma, Italy	I9	22
Rome, Ga., U.S.	C13	122
Rome, N.Y., U.S.	E14	112
Romeo, Mi., U.S.	B2	114
Romilly-sur-Seine, Fr.	F12	14
Romney, W.V., U.S.	E7	114
Romny, Ukr.	D4	32
Romont, Switz.	D3	22
Romorantin-Lanthenay, Fr.	G10	14
Rompin, stm., Malay.	K6	48
Romsey, Eng., U.K.	J11	12
Ron, Mui, c., Viet.	C8	48
Rona, i., Scot., U.K.	D7	12
Rona, i., Scot., U.K.	B7	12
Ronan, Mt., U.S.	C12	136
Roncador, Banco see *Roncador, Cayos de, unds., Col.*	F7	102
Roncador, Cayos de, unds., Col.	F7	102
Roncador, Serra do, plat., Braz.	F7	84
Roncador Bank see *Roncador, Cayos de, unds., Col.*	F7	102
Ronda, Spain	H5	20
Ronda, Serranía de, mts., Spain	H5	20
Rondane Nasjonalpark, p.o.i., Nor.	F3	8
Ronde, Pointe, c., Dom.	i5	105c
Rondônia, state, Braz.	F5	84
Rondonópolis, Braz.	G7	84
Rong, stm., China	I3	42
Rong'an, China	I3	42
Rongcheng, China	C10	42
Ronge, Lac la, l., Sk., Can.	D10	106
Rongelap, at., Marsh. Is.	B7	72
Rongjiang, China	I3	42
Rongkop, Indon.	H7	50
Rongshui, China	I3	42
Rongxian, China	J4	42
Rønne, Den.	I6	8
Ronneby, Swe.	H6	8
Ronne Ice Shelf, ice, Ant.	C34	81
Ronse, Bel.	D12	14
Ronuro, stm., Braz.	F7	84
Roodhouse, Il., U.S.	E7	120
Roof Butte, mtn., Az., U.S.	G7	132
Rooiboklaagte, stm., Nmb.	B5	70
Roorkee, India	D6	54
Roosendaal, Neth.	C13	14
Roosevelt, Mn., U.S.	C3	118
Roosevelt, Ok., U.S.	G9	128
Roosevelt, Ut., U.S.	C6	132
Roosevelt, stm., Braz.	E5	84
Roosevelt Campobello International Park, p.o.i., N.B., Can.	F10	110
Roosevelt Island, i., Ant.	C24	81
Root, stm., Mn., U.S.	H7	118
Ropaži, Lat.	C7	10
Roper, N.C., U.S.	I9	114
Roper, stm., Austl.	B6	74
Roper Valley, Austl.	B6	74
Ropesville, Tx., U.S.	H6	128
Roque, Braz.	B3	88
Roquefort, Fr.	E5	18
Roraima, state, Braz.	C5	84
Roraima, Mount, mtn., S.A.	E11	86
Røros, Nor.	E4	8
Rosa, Lake, l., Bah.	B11	102
Rosales, Mex.	A6	100
Rosalia, Wa., U.S.	C9	136
Rosamond, Ca., U.S.	I7	134
Rosamond Lake, l., Ca., U.S.	I7	134
Rosario, Arg.	F7	92
Rosário, Braz.	B3	88
Rosario, Mex.	D5	100
Rosario, Mex.	B4	100
Rosario, Para.	B9	92
Rosario, Ur.	G9	92
Rosario, stm., Arg.	B5	92
Rosario, Bahía del, b., Mex.	G4	98
Rosario, Islas del, is., Col.	B4	86
Rosario de Arriba, Mex.	F4	98
Rosario de la Frontera, Arg.	B5	92
Rosario de Lerma, Arg.	B5	92
Rosario del Tala, Arg.	F8	92
Rosário do Sul, Braz.	E10	92
Rosário Oeste, Braz.	F6	84
Rosarito, Mex.	K8	134
Rosarito, Mex.	A2	100
Rosarno, Italy	F9	24
Rosas, Mex.	H4	130
Roscoe, S.D., U.S.	B13	126
Roscoe, Tx., U.S.	B7	130
Roscommon, Ire.	H4	12
Roscommon, state, Ire.	H4	12
Roscrea, Ire.	I5	12
Rose, Mount, mtn., Nv., U.S.	D5	134
Roseau, Dom.	j6	105c
Roseau, Mn., U.S.	C3	118
Roseau, stm., N.A.	C2	118
Roseberth, Austl.	E2	76
Rosebery, Austl.	n12	77a
Roseboro, N.C., U.S.	B7	116
Rosebud, Mt., U.S.	A6	126
Rosebud, S.D., U.S.	D12	126
Rosebud, Tx., U.S.	C11	130
Rosebud, stm., Ab., Can.	E17	138
Rosebud Creek, stm., Mt., U.S.	A6	126
Roseburg, Or., U.S.	G3	136
Rosebush, Mi., U.S.	E5	112
Rose City, Mi., U.S.	D5	112
Rosedale, Austl.	E8	76
Rosedale, Ab., Can.	E18	138
Rosedale, La., U.S.	G7	122
Rosedale, Ms., U.S.	D7	122
Rose Hill, N.C., U.S.	B7	116
Rose Hill, Va., U.S.	H2	114
Rose Island, i., Bah.	K8	116
Rosemary, Ab., Can.	F18	138
Rosenberg, Tx., U.S.	H3	122
Rosenheim, Ger.	I8	16
Rosepine, La., U.S.	G5	122
Roses, Golf de, b., Spain	B14	20
Roses, Golfo de see *Roses, Golf de, b., Spain*	B14	20
Roseto degli Abruzzi, Italy	H11	22
Rosetown, Sk., Can.	C6	124
Rosetta see Rashid, Egypt	G1	58
Rosetta Mouth see *Rashid, Masabb, mth., Egypt*	G1	58
Rose Valley, Sk., Can.	B10	124
Roseville, Il., U.S.	D7	120
Roseville, Mi., U.S.	F7	112
Roseville, Mn., U.S.	F5	118
Rosholt, S.D., U.S.	F2	118
Rosholt, Wi., U.S.	G9	118
Rosica, stm., Blg.	F12	26
Rosiclare, Il., U.S.	G9	120
Rosignol, Guy.	B6	84
Roşiori de Vede, Rom.	E12	26
Roskilde, Den.	I4	8
Roskilde, state, Den.	I5	8
Roslavl', Russia	G15	10
Rosman, N.C., U.S.	A3	116
Rosmead, S. Afr.	G7	70
Ros Mhic Thriúin see New Ross, Ire.	I6	12
Ross, Austl.	o13	77a
Ross, stm., Yk., Can.	C4	106
Rossano, Italy	E10	24
Rossasna, Bela.	F13	10
Rossburn, Mb., Can.	D13	124
Rosseau, Lake, l., On., Can.	C10	112
Rossel, Cap, c., N. Cal.	m16	79d
Rossell y Rius, Ur.	F10	92
Rossford, Oh., U.S.	C2	114
Ross Ice Shelf, ice, Ant.	D23	81
Rossignol, Lake, l., N.S., Can.	F11	110
Ross Island, i., Ant.	C22	81
Ross Lake, res., N.A.	B5	136
Rossland, B.C., Can.	G13	138
Rosslau, Ger.	E8	16
Rosso, Maur.	F1	64
Ross-on-Wye, Eng., U.K.	J10	12
Rossoš', Russia	D5	32
Ross R. Barnett Reservoir, res., Ms., U.S.	E9	122
Ross River, Yk., Can.	C4	106
Ross Sea, s., Ant.	C23	81
Røssvatnet, l., Nor.	D5	8
Rossville, Ga., U.S.	C13	122
Rossville, Il., U.S.	H2	112
Rossville, Ks., U.S.	E2	120
Røst, is., Nor.	C4	8
Rosthern, Sk., Can.	B7	124
Roštkala, Taj.	B11	56
Rostock, Ger.	B7	16
Rostov, Russia	C22	10
Rostov-na-Donu, Russia	E6	32
Rosvinskoe, Russia	C24	8
Roswell, Ga., U.S.	B1	116
Roswell, N.M., U.S.	H4	128
Rota, i., N. Mar. Is.	B5	72
Rotan, Tx., U.S.	B7	130
Rotenburg, Ger.	C5	16
Roth, Ger.	G7	16
Rothenburg ob der Tauber, Ger.	G6	16
Rothera, sci., Ant.	B34	81
Rotherham, Eng., U.K.	H11	12
Rothesay, N.B., Can.	E11	110
Rothesay, Scot., U.K.	F7	12
Rothsay, Mn., U.S.	E2	118
Rothwell, N.B., Can.	D10	110
Roti, Pulau, i., Indon.	H7	44
Roto, Austl.	I5	76
Rotondella, Italy	D10	24
Rotorua, N.Z.	D7	80
Rottenburg am Neckar, Ger.	H4	16
Rottenburg an der Laaber, Ger.	H8	16
Rotterdam, Neth.	C13	14
Rotterdam, N.Y., U.S.	B11	114
Rottweil, Ger.	H4	16
Rotuma, i., Fiji	E8	72
Roubaix, Fr.	D12	14
Roudnice nad Labem, Czech Rep.	F9	16
Rouen, Fr.	E10	14
Rouge, stm., Qc., Can.	E2	110
Rough, stm., Ky., U.S.	G11	120
Rough River Lake, res., Ky., U.S.	G11	120
Rouleau, Sk., Can.	D9	124
Roulers see Roeselare, Bel.	D11	14
Roulette, Pa., U.S.	C7	114
Round Hill Head, c., Austl.	E8	76
Round Lake, Mn., U.S.	H3	118
Round Lake, l., On., Can.	C12	112
Round Mound, hill, Ks., U.S.	C9	128
Round Mountain, Nv., U.S.	E8	134
Round Mountain, mtn., Austl.	H9	76
Round Rock, Tx., U.S.	D10	130
Roundup, Mt., U.S.	A4	126
Rousay, i., Scot., U.K.	B9	12
Rouses Point, N.Y., U.S.	E3	110
Roussillon, hist. reg., Fr.	G8	18
Routhierville, Qc., Can.	B9	110
Rouyn-Noranda, Qc., Can.	F15	106
Rovaniemi, Fin.	C11	8
Rovenskaja Slabada, Bela.	H13	10
Rovereto, Italy	E8	22
Roversi, Arg.	C6	92
Rovigo, Italy	E8	22
Rovuma (Ruvuma), stm., Afr.	C6	68
Rowan Lake, l., On., Can.	B5	118
Rowena, Austl.	G7	76
Rowland, N.C., U.S.	B6	116
Rowley, stm., Nu., Can.	A15	106
Rowley Island, i., Nu., Can.	B14	106
Roxas, Phil.	E4	52
Roxboro, N.C., U.S.	H7	114
Roxborough, Trin.	r13	105f
Roxburgh, N.Z.	G3	80
Roxton, Tx., U.S.	D3	122
Roy, N.M., U.S.	F4	128
Roy, Ut., U.S.	B4	132
Roy, Wa., U.S.	C4	136
Royal Bardiyā Wild Life Reserve, India	D8	54
Royal Canal, can., Ire.	H6	12
Royal Center, In., U.S.	H3	112
Royal Chitwan National Park, p.o.i., Nepal	E10	54
Royal City, Wa., U.S.	D7	136
Royale, Isle, i., Mi., U.S.	D10	118
Royal Gorge, p., Co., U.S.	C3	128
Royal Leamington Spa, Eng., U.K.	I11	12
Royal Natal National Park, p.o.i., S. Afr.	F9	70
Royal Oak, Mi., U.S.	B2	114
Royalton, Mn., U.S.	F4	118
Royal Tunbridge Wells, Eng., U.K.	J13	12
Royan, Fr.	D5	18
Roye, Fr.	E11	14
Royston, Eng., U.K.	I12	12
Royston, Ga., U.S.	B2	116
Różan, Pol.	D17	16
Roždestveno, Russia	C20	10
Rozdil'na, Ukr.	C17	26
Rozewie, Przylądek, c., Pol.	B14	16
Rožňava, Slov.	H16	16
Roznov, Rom.	C13	26
Rożnów, Pol.	G16	16
Roztocze, hills, Eur.	F19	16
Roztoky, Czech Rep.	F10	16
Rrogozhina see Rrogozhinë, Alb.	C13	24
Rrogozhinë, Alb.	C13	24
Rtiščevo, Russia	D6	32
Ru, stm., China	E6	42
Ruacana Falls, wtfl., Afr.	D1	68
Ruahine Range, mts., N.Z.	D7	80
Ruapehu, Mount, vol., N.Z.	D6	80
Ruapuke Island, i., N.Z.	H3	80
Rubbestadneset, Nor.	G1	8
Rubcovsk, Russia	D14	32
Rubi, stm., D.R.C.	D5	66
Rubio, Ven.	D5	86
Rubondo Island, i., Tan.	E6	66
Ruby, Ak., U.S.	D8	140
Ruby, stm., Mt., U.S.	E14	136
Ruby Dome, mtn., Nv., U.S.	C1	132
Ruby Lake, sw., Nv., U.S.	C1	132
Ruby Mountains, mts., Nv., U.S.	C1	132
Ruby Valley, val., Nv., U.S.	C1	132
Rucheng, China	I5	42
Ruciane-Nida, Pol.	C17	16
Ruda Śląska, Pol.	F14	16
Rudauli, India	E8	54
Rüdersdorf, Ger.	D9	16
Rudkøbing, Den.	B6	16
Rudnaja Pristan', Russia	B11	38
Rudnja, Russia	F14	10
Rudnyj see Rūdnyy, Kaz.	D10	32
Rudnyj, Russia	B11	38
Rūdnyy, Kaz.	D10	32
Rudo, Bos.	F6	26
Rudolf, Lake (Turkana, Lake), l., Afr.	D7	66
Rudolf Häyk' see *Rudolf, Lake, l., Afr.*	D7	66
Rudolstadt, Ger.	F7	16
Rudong, China	E9	42
Rudozem, Blg.	H11	26
Rudyard, Mi., U.S.	B5	112
Rue, Fr.	D10	14
Rufā'ah, Sudan	E6	62
Ruffin, S.C., U.S.	C5	116
Rufiji, stm., Tan.	F7	66
Rufino, Arg.	G6	92
Rufisque, Sen.	G1	64
Rufunsa, Zam.	D4	68
Rufus, Or., U.S.	E6	136
Rugāji, Lat.	D10	10
Rugao, China	E9	42
Rugby, Eng., U.K.	I11	12
Rugby, N.D., U.S.	F14	124
Rügen, i., Ger.	B9	16
Rugged Mountain, mtn., B.C., Can.	F4	138
Ruhan', Russia	G15	10
Ruhengeri, Rw.	E5	66
Ruhpolding, Ger.	I8	16
Ruhr, stm., Ger.	E3	16
Ruhunu National Park, p.o.i., Sri L.	H5	53
Rui'an, China	H9	42
Ruidoso, N.M., U.S.	H3	128
Ruidoso, stm., N.M., U.S.	H3	128
Ruihong, China	G7	42
Ruijin, China	I6	42
Ruiz, Mex.	D6	100
Ruiz, Nevado del, vol., Col.	E4	86
Ruiz de Montoya, Arg.	C10	92
Ruki, stm., D.R.C.	E3	66
Rukwa, Lake, l., Tan.	F6	66
Rule, Tx., U.S.	A8	130
Ruleville, Ms., U.S.	D8	122
Rulo, Ne., U.S.	D2	120
Rúm, i., Scot., U.K.	D6	12
Rum, stm., Mn., U.S.	F5	118
Ruma, Serb.	D6	26
Rumbek, Sudan	F5	62
Rum Cay, i., Bah.	C10	96
Rumia, Pol.	B14	16
Rumigny, Fr.	E13	14
Rum Jungle, Austl.	B6	74
Rumoi, Japan	B14	38
Runan, China	E6	42
Runanga, N.Z.	F4	80
Runde, stm., Zimb.	B10	70
Rundēni, Lat.	D10	10
Rundu, Nmb.	D2	68
Rŭng, Kaôh, i., Camb.	G6	48
Runge, Tx., U.S.	F10	130
Rungwa, Tan.	F6	66
Rungwa, stm., Tan.	F6	66
Running Water Draw, stm., U.S.	G6	128
Ruo, stm., China	C4	36
Ruoqiang, China	D2	36
Ruoxi, China	G6	42
Rupat, Pulau, i., Indon.	C2	50
Rupert, Id., U.S.	H13	136
Rupert, W.V., U.S.	G5	114
Rupert, stm., Qc., Can.	E15	106
Rupert Creek, stm., Austl.	C4	76
Rupununi, stm., Guy.	F12	86
Rur, stm., Eur.	D15	14
Rural Retreat, Va., U.S.	H4	114
Rurrenabaque, Bol.	B3	90
Rurutu, i., Fr. Poly.	F11	72
Rusape, Zimb.	D5	68
Ruṣayriṣ, Khazzān ar-, res., Afr.	E6	62
Ruse, Blg.	F12	26
Ruse, state, Blg.	F13	26
Rusera, India	F11	54
Rushan, China	C9	42
Rush Center, Ks., U.S.	C9	128
Rush City, Mn., U.S.	F5	118
Rush Creek, stm., Co., U.S.	C5	128
Rushford, Mn., U.S.	H7	118
Rushmore, Mn., U.S.	H3	118
Rushville, Il., U.S.	D7	120
Rushville, In., U.S.	E12	120
Rusinga Island, i., Kenya	E6	66
Rusizi, stm., Afr.	E5	66
Rusk, Tx., U.S.	F3	122
Ruskin, Fl., U.S.	I3	116
Rusnė, Lith.	E4	10
Russas, Braz.	C6	88
Russell, Mb., Can.	D12	124
Russell, Ia., U.S.	D4	120
Russell, Ks., U.S.	C10	128
Russell, Ky., U.S.	F3	114
Russell, Cape, c., N.T., Can.	A16	140
Russell Cave National Monument, p.o.i., Al., U.S.	C13	122
Russell Islands, is., Sol. Is.	e8	79b
Russellkonda, India	I10	54
Russells Point, Oh., U.S.	D2	114
Russell Springs, Ky., U.S.	G12	120
Russellville, Al., U.S.	C11	122
Russellville, Ar., U.S.	B5	122
Russellville, Ky., U.S.	H11	120
Rüsselsheim, Ger.	G4	16
Russia, ctry., Eur.	B18	2
Russian, stm., Ca., U.S.	E2	134
Russiaville, In., U.S.	H3	112
Russkij, Russia	C9	38
Rust, Aus.	C13	22
Rustavi, Geor.	F7	32
Rustburg, Va., U.S.	G6	114
Rustenburg, S. Afr.	D8	70
Ruston, La., U.S.	E6	122
Rutana, Bdi.	E6	66
Rute, Spain	G6	20
Ruteng, Indon.	H12	50
Ruth, Nv., U.S.	D1	132
Rutherford, Tn., U.S.	H8	120
Rutherfordton, N.C., U.S.	A3	116
Ruthin, Wales, U.K.	H9	12
Ruthven, Ia., U.S.	H4	118
Rutland, B.C., Can.	G11	138
Rutland, N.D., U.S.	A15	126
Rutland, Vt., U.S.	G4	110
Rutledge, Ga., U.S.	C2	116
Rutog, China	B7	54
Rutshuru, D.R.C.	E5	66
Rutter, On., Can.	B9	112
Ruvuma (Rovuma), stm., Afr.	C6	68
Ruwenzori, mts., Afr.	D6	66
Ruwenzori Range see *Ruwenzori, mts., Afr.*	D6	66
Ruy Barbosa, Braz.	G5	88
Ruza, Russia	E19	10
Ruza, stm., Russia	E18	10
Ruzaevka, Russia	D7	32
Ružany, Bela.	H7	10
Ružomberok, Slov.	G15	16
Rwanda, ctry., Afr.	E6	66
Ryan, Ok., U.S.	G11	128
Ryan Peak, mtn., Id., U.S.	G12	136
Rybach'e, Kaz.	E14	32
Rybačij, poluostrov, pen., Russia	B15	8
Rybinsk, Russia	B21	10
Rybinskoe vodohranilišče (Rybinsk Reservoir), res., Russia	B21	10
Rybinsk Reservoir see *Rybinskoe vodohranilišče, res., Russia*	B21	10
Rybnik, Pol.	F14	16
Rybnoje, Russia	E7	34
Ryde, Eng., U.K.	K11	12
Ryderwood, Wa., U.S.	D3	136
Rydzyna, Pol.	E12	16
Ryegate, Mt., U.S.	A3	126
Rye Patch Reservoir, res., Nv., U.S.	C7	134
Ryfoss, Nor.	F3	8
Ryley, Ab., Can.	C18	138
Rylovići, Russia	H15	10
Ryl'sk, Russia	D4	32
Rýmařov, Czech Rep.	G13	16
Ryōhaku-sanchi, mts., Japan	C9	40
Ryōtsu, Japan	A11	40
Rysy, mtn., Eur.	G15	16
Ryūgasaki, Japan	D13	40
Ryukyu Islands see *Nansei-shotō, is., Japan*	k19	39a
Ryukyu Trench, unds.	G15	142
Ržanica, Russia	G16	10
Rzeszów, Pol.	F18	16
Rzeszów, state, Pol.	F17	16
Ržev, Russia	D17	10

S

Name	Map Ref.	Page
Sa, Thai.	C5	48
Saale, stm., Ger.	E7	16
Saalfeld, Ger.	F7	16
Saar see *Saarland, state, Ger.*	G2	16
Saarbrücken, Ger.	G2	16
Saarburg, Ger.	G2	16
Saaremaa, i., Est.	G9	8
Saarijärvi, Fin.	E11	8
Saaristomeren kansallispuisto, p.o.i., Fin.	G9	8
Saarland, state, Ger.	G2	16
Saarlouis, Ger.	G2	16
Saavedra, Arg.	H6	92
Saba, i., Neth. Ant.	B1	105a
Šabac, Serb.	E6	26
Sabadell, Spain	C13	20
Sabae, Japan	D9	40
Sabah, state, Malay.	H1	52
Sabah, hist. reg., Malay.	D6	44
Sabak, Malay.	K5	48
Sabalana, Kepulauan, is., Indon.	G11	50
Sabana, Archipiélago de, is., Cuba	A7	102
Sabana de la Mar, Dom. Rep.	C13	102
Sabana de Mendoza, Ven.	C6	86
Sabanagrande, Hond.	F4	102
Sabana Grande, P.R.	B2	104a
Sabanalarga, Col.	B4	86
Sabana Llana, P.R.	B3	104a
Sabang, Indon.	J2	48
Sabang, Indon.	C11	50
Sabarei, Kenya	D7	66
Sābari, stm., India	C5	53
Sābarmati, stm., India	G4	54
Sab'atayn, Ramlat as-, sand, Yemen	F6	56
Sabbioneta, Italy	E7	22
Şāberī, Hāmūn-e, l., Asia	C9	56
Sabetha, Ks., U.S.	E2	120
Sabhā, Libya	B2	62
Sabidana, Jabal, mtn., Sudan	D7	62
Sabie, S. Afr.	D10	70
Sabiè, stm., Afr.	D10	70
Sabile, Lat.	C5	10
Sabina, Oh., U.S.	E2	114
Sabina, hist. reg., Italy	H9	22
Sabinal, Tx., U.S.	E8	130
Sabinal, stm., Tx., U.S.	E8	130
Sabinal, Cayo, i., Cuba	B9	102
Sabiñánigo, Spain	B10	20
Sabinas, Mex.	B8	100
Sabinas, stm., Mex.	B9	100
Sabinas, stm., Mex.	B8	100
Sabinas Hidalgo, Mex.	B8	100
Sabine, stm., U.S.	G5	122
Sabine Bay, b., Can.	A17	140
Sabine Lake, l., U.S.	H5	122
Sabine Pass, strt., U.S.	H5	122
Sabinópolis, Braz.	J4	88
Sabiote, Spain	F7	20
Šabla, Blg.	F15	26
Sable, Cape, c., N.S., Can.	G11	110
Sable, Cape, pen., Fl., U.S.	K4	116
Sable Island, i., N.S., Can.	G16	110
Sablūkah, Shallāl as- (Sixth Cataract), wtfl., Sudan	D6	62
Šablykino, Russia	H18	10
Sabor, stm., Port.	C4	20
Sabou, Burkina	G4	64
Sabrina Coast, cst., Ant.	B16	81
Şabyā, Sau. Ar.	F5	56
Sabyin, Mya.	C2	48
Sabzevār, Iran	B8	56
Sac, stm., Mo., U.S.	G4	120
Sacaton, Az., U.S.	J5	132
Sac City, Ia., U.S.	B3	120
Săcele, Rom.	D12	26
Sachayoj, Arg.	C6	92
Sachsen, state, Ger.	F9	16
Sachsen (Saxony), hist. reg., Ger.	D5	16
Sachsen-Anhalt, state, Ger.	D7	16
Sachs Harbour, N.T., Can.	B14	140
Šack, Bela.	G10	10
Sackets Harbor, N.Y., U.S.	E13	112
Sackville, N.B., Can.	E12	110
Saco, Me., U.S.	G6	110
Saco, stm., U.S.	F5	110
Sacramento, Braz.	J2	88
Sacramento, Ca., U.S.	E4	134
Sacramento, stm., Ca., U.S.	E4	134
Sacramento Mountains, mts., N.M., U.S.	E10	98
Sacramento Valley, val., Ca., U.S.	D3	134
Sacramento Wash, stm., Az., U.S.	H2	132
Sacred Heart, Mn., U.S.	G3	118
Sádaba, Spain	B9	20
Şa'dah, Yemen	F5	56
Sadaik Taung, mtn., Mya.	E4	48
Sada-misaki, c., Japan	F4	40
Sada-misaki-hantō, pen., Japan	F5	40
Sadang, stm., Indon.	E11	50
Sa Dao, Thai.	I5	48
Sadda, Pak.	B3	54
Saddle Mountain, mtn., Co., U.S.	C3	128
Saddle Mountain, mtn., Or., U.S.	E3	136
Saddle Peak, mtn., India	F7	46
Sa Dec, Viet.	G7	48
Sādiqābād, Pak.	D3	54
Sadiya, India	C8	46
Sadlers, St. K./N.	C2	105a
Sado, i., Japan	A11	40
Sado, stm., Port.	F2	20
Sado-kaikyō, strt., Japan	B11	40
Sadowara, Japan	G4	40
Sādri, India	F4	54
Šadrinsk, Russia	C10	32
Sädvaluspen, Swe.	C7	8
Saegertown, Pa., U.S.	C5	114
Saerluojia Hu, l., China	B11	54
Šafárikovo, Slov.	H16	16
Säffle, Swe.	G5	8
Saffron Walden, Eng., U.K.	I13	12
Safi, Mor.	C3	64
Safīd Koh, Selseleh-ye, mts., Afg.	C9	56
Safonovo, Russia	E16	10
Safonovo, Russia	D22	8
Safranbolu, Tur.	B15	28
Saga, China	D10	54
Saga, Japan	F3	40
Saga, state, Japan	F3	40
Sagae, Japan	A13	40
Sagaing, Mya.	B2	48
Sagaing, state, Mya.	A2	48
Sagamihara, Japan	D12	40
Sagami-nada, b., Japan	D12	40
Saganaga Lake, l., N.A.	C7	118
Saganoseki, Japan	F4	40
Saganthit Kyun, i., Mya.	F4	48
Sāgar, India	G7	54
Sāgar, India	D2	53
Sagara, Japan	E11	40
Sagaranten, Indon.	G5	50
Sagavanirktok, stm., Ak., U.S.	C10	140
Sagay, Phil.	E4	52
Sage, Mount, mtn., Br. Vir. Is.	e8	104b
Sage Creek, stm., Mt., U.S.	B16	136
Sagerton, Tx., U.S.	A8	130
Saginaw, Mi., U.S.	E6	112
Saginaw, stm., Mi., U.S.	E5	112
Saginaw Bay, b., Mi., U.S.	E6	112
Sağkaya, Tur.	A6	58
Sagleipie, Lib.	H3	64
Saglek Bay, b., Nf., Can.	F13	141
Šagonar, Russia	D16	32
Şagu, Rom.	C8	26
Saguache, Co., U.S.	C2	128
Saguache Creek, stm., Co., U.S.	C2	128
Sagua de Tánamo, Cuba	B10	102
Sagua la Grande, Cuba	A7	102
Saguaro National Park, p.o.i., Az., U.S.	K5	132
Saguenay, stm., Qc., Can.	B7	110
Sagunt, Spain	E10	20
Sagunto see Sagunt, Spain	E10	20
Sāgwāra, India	G4	54
Sa'gya, China	D12	54

Name	Map Ref.	Page
Sahagún, Col.	C4	86
Sahagún, Spain	B5	20
Sahalin, ostrov, i., Russia	F17	34
Sahalinskij zaliv, b., Russia	F17	34
Sahara, des., Afr.	E5	64
Sahāranpur, India	C6	54
Saharsa, India	F11	54
Sahel see Sudan, reg., Afr.	E4	62
Sāhibganj, India	F11	54
Sāhīwāl, Pak.	C4	54
Sāhīwāl, Pak.	C4	54
Šahovskaja, Russia	D18	10
Šahrisabz, Uzb.	G11	32
Šahtjorsk, Russia	G17	34
Šahty, Russia	E6	32
Sahuaripa, Mex.	A4	100
Sahuarita, Az., U.S.	L5	132
Sahuayo de José María Morelos, Mex.	E7	100
Šahunja, Russia	H22	8
Šahy, Slov.	H14	16
Sai Buri, Thai.	I5	48
Sai Buri, stm., Thai.	I5	48
Saidor, Pap. N. Gui.	b4	79a
Saidpur, Bngl.	F12	54
Saidu, Pak.	C11	56
Saigō, Japan	C6	40
Saigon *see* Thanh Pho Ho Chi Minh, Viet.	G8	48
Saijō, Japan	F6	40
Saiki, Japan	G4	40
Šaim, Russia	B10	32
Saimaa, l., Fin.	F13	8
Sainte Agathe, Mb., Can.	E16	124
Sainte-Agathe-des-Monts, Qc., Can.	D2	110
Saint-Agrève, Fr.	D10	18
Saint Alban's, Nf., Can.	j22	107a
Saint Albans, Eng., U.K.	J12	12
Saint Albans, Vt., U.S.	F3	110
Saint Albans, W.V., U.S.	F4	114
Saint Albert, Ab., Can.	C17	138
Saint Aldhelm's Head, c., Eng., U.K.	K10	12
Saint-Alexis-des-Monts, Qc., Can.	D3	110
Saint-Amand-Mont-Rond, Fr.	H11	14
Saint-André-Avellin, Qc., Can.	E1	110
Saint Andrew, Barb.	n8	105d
Saint Andrew, Mount, mtn., St. Vin.	o11	105e
Saint Andrews, N.B., Can.	E9	110
Saint Andrews, Scot., U.K.	E10	12
Saint Andrews, S.C., U.S.	D5	116
Sainte-Anne, Guad.	h6	105c
Sainte-Anne, Mart.	I7	105c
Sainte Anne, Lac, l., Ab., Can.	C16	138
Sainte-Anne-de-Beaupré, Qc., Can.	C5	110
Sainte-Anne-de-Madawaska, N.B., Can.	C8	110
Sainte-Anne-des-Monts, Qc., Can.	A10	110
Sainte-Anne-du-Lac, Qc., Can.	D1	110
Saint Ann's Bay, Jam.	i13	104d
Saint-Anselme, Qc., Can.	D6	110
Saint Ansgar, Ia., U.S.	H5	118
Saint Anthony, Nf., Can.	i22	107a
Saint Anthony, Id., U.S.	G15	136
Saint Arnaud, Austl.	K4	76
Saint Augustin, Qc., Can.	i22	107a
Saint Augustine, Fl., U.S.	G4	116
Saint Austell, Eng., U.K.	K8	12
Saint-Avold, Fr.	E15	14
Saint-Barthélemy, i., Guad.	B2	105a
Saint-Basile, N.B., Can.	C8	110
Saint Bathans, Mount, mtn., N.Z.	G3	80
Saint Bees Head, c., Eng., U.K.	G9	12
Saint-Boniface-de-Shawinigan, Qc., Can.	D3	110
Saint-Bonnet, Fr.	E11	18
Saint Brides Bay, b., Wales, U.K.	J7	12
Saint-Brieuc, Fr.	F6	14
Saint-Brieuc, Baie de, b., Fr.	F6	14
Saint Catharines, On., Can.	E10	112
Saint Catherine, Mount, vol., Gren.	q10	105e
Saint Catherines Island, i., Ga., U.S.	E4	116
Saint Catherine's Point, c., Eng., U.K.	K11	12
Saint-Céré, Fr.	E7	18
Saint-Chamond, Fr.	D10	18
Saint Charles, Id., U.S.	A5	132
Saint Charles, Il., U.S.	C9	120
Saint Charles, Mi., U.S.	E5	112
Saint Charles, Mn., U.S.	H6	118
Saint Charles, Mo., U.S.	F7	120
Saint Charles Mesa, Co., U.S.	C4	128
Saint Christopher (Saint Kitts), i., St. K./N.	C2	105a
Saint Christopher and Nevis see Saint Kitts and Nevis, ctry., N.A.	C2	105a
Saint Clair, Mi., U.S.	B3	114
Saint Clair, Mo., U.S.	F6	120
Saint Clair, stm., N.A.	B3	114
Saint Clair, Lake, l., N.A.	B3	114
Saint Clair Shores, Mi., U.S.	B3	114
Saint-Claud, Fr.	D6	18
Saint Claude, Mb., Can.	E15	124
Saint-Claude, Fr.	C11	18
Saint-Claude, Guad.	h5	105c
Saint Cloud, Fl., U.S.	H4	116
Saint Cloud, Mn., U.S.	F4	118
Sainte-Croix, Qc., Can.	D5	110
Saint Croix, i., V.I.U.S.	g10	104c
Saint Croix, stm., N.A.	E9	110
Saint Croix, stm., U.S.	G6	118
Saint Croix Falls, Wi., U.S.	F6	118
Saint Croix Island National Monument, p.o.i., Me., U.S.	E10	110
Saint-Cyr, stm., Qc., Can.	A1	110
Saint David, Az., U.S.	L6	132
Saint David's, Wales, U.K.	J7	12
Saint David's Head, c., Wales, U.K.	J7	12
Saint David's Island, i., Ber.	k16	104e
Saint-Denis, Fr.	E11	14
Saint-Denis, Reu.	i10	69a
Saint-Dié, Fr.	F15	14
Saint-Dizier, Fr.	F13	14
Saint-Donat-de-Montcalm, Qc., Can.	D2	110
Saint Edward, Ne., U.S.	F15	126
Saint Elias, Cape, c., Ak., U.S.	E11	140
Saint Elias, Mount, mtn., N.A.	C2	106
Saint Elias Mountains, mts., N.A.	D12	140
Saint-Élie, Fr. Gu.	C7	84
Saint Elmo, Il., U.S.	E9	120
Saint-Étienne, Fr.	D10	18
Saint-Étienne-du-Rouvray, Fr.	E10	14
Saint-Eugène, Qc., Can.	B4	110
Saint-Eustache, Qc., Can.	E2	110
Saint-Fabien, Qc., Can.	B8	110
Saint-Félicien, Qc., Can.	B4	110
Saint-Félix-de-Valois, Qc., Can.	D3	110
Saint-Florent-sur-Cher, Fr.	G11	14
Saint-Flour, Fr.	D9	18
Sainte-Foy, ngh., Qc., Can.	D5	110
Sainte-Foy-la-Grande, Fr.	E6	18
Saint Francis, Ks., U.S.	B7	128
Saint Francis, Wi., U.S.	I11	118
Saint Francis, stm., N.A.	C7	110
Saint Francis, stm., U.S.	C8	122
Saint Francis, Cape, c., S. Afr.	I7	70
Saint Francis Bay, b., S. Afr.	I7	70
Saint Francisville, Il., U.S.	F10	120
Saint Francisville, La., U.S.	G7	122
Saint-François, Guad.	h6	105c
Saint-François, stm., Qc., Can.	D4	110
Saint-François, Lac, l., Can.	E2	110
Saint-François, Lac, res., Qc., Can.	E5	110
Saint-Gabriel, Can.	B8	110
Saint-Gabriel-de-Gaspé, Qc., Can.	B12	110
Saint-Gall *see* Sankt Gallen, Switz.	C6	22
Saint-Gaudens, Fr.	F6	18
Sainte Genevieve, Mo., U.S.	G7	120
Saint George, Austl.	G7	76
Saint George, Ber.	k16	104e
Saint George, N.B., Can.	E10	110
Saint George, On., Can.	E9	112
Saint George, Ut., U.S.	F3	132
Saint George, Cape, c., Fl., U.S.	H13	122
Saint George, Point, c., Ca., U.S.	B1	134
Saint George Island, i., Fl., U.S.	H14	122
Saint-Georges, Qc., Can.	D6	110
Saint-Georges, Qc., Can.	D4	110
Saint-Georges, Fr. Gu.	C7	84
Saint George's, Gren.	q10	105e
Saint George's Bay, b., Nf., Can.	j22	107a
Saint Georges Bay, b., N.S., Can.	E15	110
Saint George's Channel, strt., Eur.	J7	12
Saint George's Channel, strt., Pap. N. Gui.	a5	79a
Saint-Gilles-Croix-de-Vie, Fr.	H6	14
Saint Gotthard Pass see San Gottardo, Passo del, p., Switz.	D5	22
Saint Helena, Ca., U.S.	E3	134
Saint Helena, dep., Afr.	H5	60
Saint Helena Bay see Sint Helenabaai, b., S. Afr.	H3	70
Saint Helens, Eng., U.K.	H10	12
Saint Helens, Or., U.S.	E4	136
Saint Helens, Mount, vol., Wa., U.S.	D4	136
Saint Helier, Jersey	E6	14
Saint-Hilaire-du-Harcouët, Fr.	F7	14
Saint-Hyacinthe, Qc., Can.	E4	110
Saint Ignace Island, i., On., Can.	C11	118
Saint Ignatius, Guy.	F12	86
Saint Ignatius, Mt., U.S.	C12	136
Saint-Isidore, N.B., Can.	C11	110
Saint Ives, Eng., U.K.	K7	12
Saint James, Mi., U.S.	C4	112
Saint James, Mn., U.S.	G4	118
Saint James, Mo., U.S.	G6	120
Saint James, Cape, c., B.C., Can.	E4	106
Saint James Islands, is., V.I.U.S.	e7	104b
Saint-Jean, Guad.	B2	105a
Saint-Jean, Lac, res., Qc., Can.	B4	110
Saint Jean Baptiste, Mb., Can.	E16	124
Saint-Jean-d'Angély, Fr.	C5	18
Saint-Jean-de-Luz, Fr.	F4	18
Saint-Jean-de-Maurienne, Fr.	D12	18
Saint-Jean-du-Gard, Fr.	E9	18
Saint-Jean-Port-Joli, Qc., Can.	C6	110
Saint-Jean-sur-Richelieu, Qc., Can.	E3	110
Saint-Jérôme, Qc., Can.	E3	110
Saint Jo, Tx., U.S.	H11	128
Saint Joe, stm., Id., U.S.	C11	136
Saint John, N.B., Can.	E10	110
Saint John, N.D., U.S.	F14	124
Saint John, Wa., U.S.	C9	136
Saint John, i., V.I.U.S.	e8	104b
Saint John, stm., N.A.	E10	110
Saint John, Cape, c., Nf., Can.	E19	106
Saint John's, Antig.	f4	105b
Saint John's, Nf., Can.	j23	107a
Saint Johns, Az., U.S.	I7	132
Saint Johns, Mi., U.S.	E5	112
Saint Johns, stm., Fl., U.S.	G4	116
Saint Johnsbury, Vt., U.S.	F4	110
Saint Joseph, Dom.	j6	105c
Saint Joseph, Il., U.S.	D9	120
Saint Joseph, Mi., U.S.	F3	112
Saint Joseph, Mn., U.S.	F4	118
Saint Joseph, Mo., U.S.	E3	120
Saint Joseph, stm., U.S.	G5	112
Saint Joseph, stm., U.S.	G3	112
Saint Joseph, Lake, l., On., Can.	E12	106
Saint-Joseph-de-Beauce, Qc., Can.	D6	110
Saint Joseph Island, i., On., Can.	B6	112
Saint-Jovite, Qc., Can.	D2	110
Saint-Julien-en-Born, Fr.	E4	18
Sainte-Julienne, Qc., Can.	E3	110
Saint-Junien, Fr.	D6	18
Saint Just, P.R.	B4	104a
Saint Kilda, i., Scot., U.K.	D4	12
Saint Kitts see Saint Christopher, i., St. K./N.	C2	105a
Saint Kitts and Nevis, ctry., N.A.	C2	105a
Saint-Lambert, ngh., Qc., Can.	E3	110
Saint Landry, La., U.S.	G6	122
Saint Laurent, Mb., Can.	D16	124
Saint-Laurent (Saint Lawrence), stm., N.A.	B8	110
Saint-Laurent du Maroni, Fr. Gu.	B7	84
Saint Lawrence, Austl.	D7	76
Saint Lawrence (Saint-Laurent), stm., N.A.	B8	110
Saint Lawrence, Gulf of, b., Can.	F18	106
Saint Lawrence Island, i., Ak., U.S.	D5	140
Saint-Léandre, Qc., Can.	B9	110
Saint-Léonard, N.B., Can.	C9	110
Saint-Lô, Fr.	E7	14
Saint Louis, Sk., Can.	B8	124
Saint-Louis, Guad.	i6	105c
Saint-Louis, Sen.	F1	64
Saint Louis, Mi., U.S.	E5	112
Saint Louis, Mo., U.S.	F7	120
Saint Louis, stm., U.S.	E6	118
Saint-Louis, Lac, l., Qc., Can.	E3	110
Saint-Louis de Kent, N.B., Can.	D12	110
Saint Louis Park, Mn., U.S.	G5	118
Saint-Loup-sur-Semouse, Fr.	G14	14
Sainte-Luce, Mart.	I7	105c
Saint Lucia, ctry., N.A.	m6	105c
Saint Lucia, Cape, c., S. Afr.	F11	70
Saint Lucia, Lake, l., S. Afr.	E11	70
Saint Lucia Channel, strt., N.A.	I6	105c
Saint Lucia Game Reserve, S. Afr.	F11	70
Saint Lucie Canal, can., Fl., U.S.	J5	116
Saint Magnus Bay, b., Scot., U.K.	n18	12a
Saint-Malo, Fr.	F7	14
Saint-Malo, Golfe de, b., Fr.	F6	14
Saint-Marc, Haiti	C11	102
Saint-Marc, Canal de, strt., Haiti	C11	102
Saint-Marc-des-Carrières, Qc., Can.	D4	110
Sainte-Marie, Mart.	k7	105c
Sainte Marie, Nosy, i., Madag.	D9	68
Saint Maries, Id., U.S.	C10	136
Saint Marks, stm., Fl., U.S.	F1	116
Saint-Martin (Sint Maarten), i., N.A.	A1	105a
Saint-Martin, Cap, c., Mart.	k6	105c
Saint Martin, Lake, l., Mb., Can.	C15	124
Saint Martins, N.B., Can.	E11	110
Saint Martinville, La., U.S.	G7	122
Saint Mary, Mo., U.S.	G8	120
Saint Mary, stm., N.A.	G18	138
Saint Mary Peak, mtn., Austl.	H2	76
Saint Mary Reservoir, res., Ab., Can.	G17	138
Saint Marys, Austl.	n14	77a
Saint Marys, Ak., U.S.	D7	140
Saint Marys, Ga., U.S.	F4	116
Saint Marys, Ks., U.S.	E1	120
Saint Marys, Pa., U.S.	C7	114
Saint Marys, W.V., U.S.	E4	114
Saint Mary's, i., Eng., U.K.	L6	12
Saint Marys, stm., U.S.	H5	112
Saint Marys, stm., U.S.	F4	116
Saint Mary's Bay, b., Nf., Can.	j23	107a
Saint Marys Bay, b., N.S., Can.	F10	110
Saint Marys City, Md., U.S.	F9	114
Saint-Mathieu, Fr.	D6	18
Saint Matthew Island, i., Ak., U.S.	D5	140
Saint Matthews, Ky., U.S.	F12	120
Saint-Maurice, stm., Qc., Can.	D4	110
Sainte-Maxime, Fr.	F12	18
Saint Meinrad, In., U.S.	F11	120
Saint Michael, Ak., U.S.	D7	140
Saint Michaels, Md., U.S.	F9	114
Saint-Michel-des-Saints, Qc., Can.	D2	110
Saint-Mihiel, Fr.	F14	14
Saint Moritz *see* Sankt Moritz, Switz.	D6	22
Saint-Nazaire, Fr.	G6	14
Saint-Nicolas *see* Sint-Niklaas, Bel.	C12	14
Saint-Omer, Fr.	D11	14
Saintonge, hist. reg., Fr.	D5	18
Saint-Pacôme, Qc., Can.	C7	110
Saint-Pamphile, Qc., Can.	D7	110
Saint Paris, Oh., U.S.	D2	114
Saint-Patrice, Lac, l., Qc., Can.	B12	112
Saint Paul, Ab., Can.	B19	138
Saint-Paul, Reu.	i10	69a
Saint Paul, In., U.S.	E12	120
Saint Paul, Ks., U.S.	G2	120
Saint Paul, Mn., U.S.	G5	118
Saint Paul, Va., U.S.	H3	114
Saint Paul, stm., Lib.	H2	64
Saint-Paul, Île, i., Afr.	M10	142
Saint Paul Island, i., Ak., U.S.	E6	140
Saint Paul's, St. K./N.	C2	105a
Saint Pauls, N.C., U.S.	B7	116
Saint Paul's Point, c., Pit.	c28	78k
Saint Peter, Mn., U.S.	G4	118
Saint Peter Port, Guern.	E6	14
Saint Peters, N.S., Can.	E16	110
Saint Peters Bay, P.E., Can.	D14	110
Saint Petersburg *see* Sankt-Peterburg, Russia	A13	10
Saint Petersburg, Fl., U.S.	I3	116
Saint-Pierre, Mart.	k6	105c
Saint-Pierre, Reu.	i10	69a
Saint-Pierre, St. P./M.	j22	107a
Saint Pierre, i., Sey.	k12	69b
Saint-Pierre, Lac, l., Qc., Can.	D3	110
Saint Pierre and Miquelon, dep., N.A.	j22	107a
Saint Pierre-Jolys, Mb., Can.	E16	124
Saint-Pierre-sur-Dives, Fr.	E8	14
Saint-Pol-sur-Ternoise, Fr.	D11	14
Saint-Pons-de-Thomères, Fr.	F8	18
Saint-Prime, Qc., Can.	B4	110
Saint-Prosper-de-Dorchester, Qc., Can.	D6	110
Saint-Quentin, N.B., Can.	C9	110
Saint-Quentin, Fr.	E12	14
Saint-Raphaël, Fr.	F12	18
Saint-Raymond, Qc., Can.	D5	110
Saint Regis Falls, N.Y., U.S.	F2	110
Saint-Rémy-de-Provence, Fr.	F10	18
Saint Robert, Mo., U.S.	G5	120
Saint-Roch-de-Mékinac, Qc., Can.	D3	110
Saint-Romuald, Qc., Can.	D5	110
Sainte-Rose-du-dégelis *see* Dégelis, Can.	C8	110
Sainte Rose du Lac, Mb., Can.	C14	124
Saintes, Fr.	D5	18
Saint-Savin, Fr.	H9	14
Saint-Siméon, Qc., Can.	C6	110
Saint Simons Island, Ga., U.S.	E4	116
Saint Simons Island, i., Ga., U.S.	E4	116
Saintes-Maries-de-la-Mer, Fr.	F10	18
Saint Stephen, S.C., U.S.	C6	116
Sainte-Thérèse-de-Blainville, Qc., Can.	E3	110
Saint Thomas, On., Can.	F8	112
Saint Thomas, N.D., U.S.	F16	124
Saint Thomas, i., V.I.U.S.	e7	104b
Saint-Tite, Qc., Can.	D4	110
Saint-Trond *see* Sint-Truiden, Bel.	D14	14
Saint-Tropez, Fr.	F12	18
Saint-Ubalde, Qc., Can.	D4	110
Saint-Urbain-de-Charlevoix, Qc., Can.	C6	110
Saint-Valéry-en-Caux, Fr.	E9	14
Saint-Vallier, Fr.	D10	18
Sainte-Véronique, Qc., Can.	D2	110
Saint Vincent, Mn., U.S.	C1	118
Saint Vincent, i., St. Vin.	o11	105e
Saint-Vincent, Baie de, b., N. Cal.	n15	79d
Saint Vincent, Gulf, b., Austl.	J2	76
Saint Vincent and the Grenadines, ctry., N.A.	p10	105e
Saint Vincent Passage, strt., N.A.	m7	105c
Saint-Vith, Bel.	D14	14
Saint Walburg, Sk., Can.	E9	106
Saint-Yrieix-la-Perche, Fr.	D7	18
Saint-Yvon, Qc., Can.	A12	110
Saipan, i., N. Mar. Is.	B5	72
Saiqi, China	H8	42
Saitama, state, Japan	C12	40
Saito, Japan	G4	40
Sai Yok National Park, p.o.i., Thai.	E4	48
Sajama, Nevado, mtn., Bol.	C3	90
Sajanogorsk, Russia	D16	32
Sajat, Turkmen.	B9	56
Šajman, Taj.	B11	56
Sajószentpéter, Hung.	A7	26
Sak, stm., S. Afr.	G5	70
Sa Kaeo, Thai.	F6	48
Sakai, Japan	E8	40
Sakaide, Japan	E6	40
Sakaiminato, Japan	D6	40
Sakakawea, Lake, res., N.D., U.S.	G12	124
Sakala, Pulau, i., Indon.	G10	50
Sakami, stm., Qc., Can.	E15	106
Sakami, Lac, l., Qc., Can.	E15	106
Sakania, D.R.C.	G5	66
Sakaraha, Madag.	E7	68
Sakarya, Tur.	C13	28
Sakarya, state, Tur.	C13	28
Sakarya (Sangarius), stm., Tur.	B13	28
Sakata, Japan	A12	40
Sakawa, Japan	F6	40
Sakchu-ŭp, Kor., N.	D6	38
Sakété, Benin	H5	64
Sakhalin see Sahalin, ostrov, i., Russia	F17	34
Sakhnin, Isr.	F6	58
Sakht Sar, Iran	B7	56
Šakiai, Lith.	E6	10
Sakiet Sidi Youssef, Tun.	H2	24
Sakishima-shotō, is., Japan	G9	36
Sakon Nakhon, Thai.	D6	48
Sakrand, Pak.	E2	54
Saks, Al., U.S.	D13	122
Sakti, India	H9	54
Saku, Japan	C11	40
Sakuma, Japan	D10	40
Sakurai, Japan	E8	40
Sal, i., C.V.	k10	65a
Šal'a, Slov.	H13	16
Sala, Swe.	F7	8
Salaberry-de-Valleyfield, Qc., Can.	E2	110
Salacgrīva, Lat.	C7	10
Sala Consilina, Italy	D9	24
Salada, Laguna, l., Mex.	F5	98
Saladas, Arg.	D8	92
Saladillo, Arg.	G8	92
Saladillo, stm., Arg.	D6	92
Saladillo Dulce, Arroyo, stm., Arg.	E7	92
Salado, stm., Arg.	D4	92
Salado, stm., Arg.	G9	92
Salado, stm., Arg.	E7	92
Salado, stm., Arg.	I5	92
Salado, stm., Cuba	B9	102
Salado, stm., Mex.	B9	100
Salado, stm., N.M., U.S.	I9	132
Salaga, Ghana	H4	64
Salairskij krjaž, mts., Russia	D14	32
Sălaj, state, Rom.	B10	26
Šalakuša, Russia	E19	8
Salal, Chad	E3	62
Şalālah, Oman	F7	56
Salālah, Sudan	C7	62
Salamanca, Chile	E2	92
Salamanca, Mex.	E8	100
Salamanca, Spain	D5	20
Salamanca, N.Y., U.S.	F11	112
Salamanca, co., Spain	D4	20
Salamanga, Moz.	E11	70
Salamat, Bahr, stm., Chad	F3	62
Salamina, Col.	E4	86
Salamína, Grc.	F6	28
Salamína, i., Grc.	F6	28
Salamis, sci., N. Cyp.	C4	58
Salamīyah, Syria	C8	58
Salamonie, stm., In., U.S.	H4	112
Salantai, Lith.	D4	10
Salaquí, Col.	D3	86
Salaquí, stm., Col.	D3	86
Salas, Peru	E2	84
Salas de los Infantes, Spain	B7	20
Salatiga, Indon.	G7	50
Salavat, Russia	D9	32
Salaverry, Peru	E2	84
Salawati, i., Indon.	F9	44
Salāya, India	G2	54
Sala y Gómez, Isla, i., Chile	L28	142
Sala y Gomez Ridge, unds.	L29	142
Şalbani, India	G11	54
Šalčininkai, Lith.	F8	10
Salcombe, Eng., U.K.	K9	12
Saldaña, Spain	B6	20
Saldaña, stm., Col.	F4	86
Saldanha, S. Afr.	H3	70
Saldungaray, Arg.	I7	92
Saldus, Lat.	D5	10
Sale, Austl.	L6	76
Salé, Mor.	C3	64
Sale Creek, Tn., U.S.	B13	122
Saleh, Teluk, b., Indon.	H10	50
Salehard, Russia	A11	32
Salem, India	F4	53
Salem, Monts.	D3	105a
Salem, Ar., U.S.	H6	120
Salem, Ia., U.S.	D6	120
Salem, Il., U.S.	F9	120
Salem, Ma., U.S.	B15	114
Salem, Mo., U.S.	G6	120
Salem, N.H., U.S.	B14	114
Salem, N.J., U.S.	E10	114
Salem, N.Y., U.S.	G3	110
Salem, Oh., U.S.	D5	114
Salem, Or., U.S.	F3	136
Salem, S.D., U.S.	D15	126
Salem, Va., U.S.	G5	114
Salem, W.V., U.S.	E5	114
Salemi, Italy	G6	24
Salem Upland, plat., Mo., U.S.	G6	120
Salentina, Penisola, pen., Italy	D12	24
Salerno, Italy	D8	24
Salerno, Golfo di, b., Italy	D8	24
Salers, Fr.	D8	18
Salgar, Col.	D4	86
Salgótarján, Hung.	A6	26
Salgueiro, Braz.	E6	88
Salher, mtn., India	H4	54
Sali, Cro.	G12	22
Salida, Co., U.S.	C3	128
Salihli, Tur.	E11	28
Salihorsk, Bela.	H10	10
Salima, Mwi.	C5	68
Salimbatu, Indon.	B10	50
Salin, Mya.	B2	48
Salina, Ks., U.S.	C11	128
Salina, Ut., U.S.	E5	132
Salina Cruz, Mex.	G11	100
Salina Point, c., Bah.	A10	102
Salinas, Braz.	I4	88
Salinas, Ec.	I1	86
Salinas, Mex.	G5	130
Salinas, P.R.	C3	104a
Salinas, Ca., U.S.	G4	134
Salinas, stm., Braz.	I4	88
Salinas, stm., N.A.	D2	102
Salinas, stm., Ca., U.S.	G4	134
Salinas, Pampa de las, pl., Arg.	E4	92
Salinas de Hidalgo, Mex.	D8	100
Salinas Pueblo Missions National Monument, p.o.i., N.M., U.S.	G2	128
Salinas Victoria, Mex.	I7	130
Saline, Mi., U.S.	B2	114
Saline, stm., Ar., U.S.	D6	122
Saline, stm., Ar., U.S.	C4	122
Saline, stm., Ks., U.S.	C11	128
Saline Bayou, stm., La., U.S.	E6	122
Saline Lake, l., La., U.S.	F6	122
Salines, Cap de ses, c., Spain	E14	20
Salines, Point, c., Gren.	r10	105e
Salines, Pointe des, c., Mart.	I7	105c
Salinópolis, Braz.	D8	84
Salipolo, Indon.	E11	50
Salisbury, Austl.	J2	76
Salisbury, Eng., U.K.	J11	12
Salisbury, Md., U.S.	F10	114
Salisbury, Mo., U.S.	E5	120
Salisbury, N.C., U.S.	I5	114
Salisbury, Pa., U.S.	E6	114
Salisbury *see* Harare, Zimb.	D5	68
Salisbury Island, i., Nu., Can.	C15	106
Salisbury Plain, pl., Eng., U.K.	J11	12
Salish Mountains, mts., Mt., U.S.	B12	136
Salitpa, Al., U.S.	F10	122
Salitre, stm., Braz.	E5	88
Şalkhad, Syria	F7	58
Salles-Curan, Fr.	E8	18
Salliq (Coral Harbour), Nu., Can.	C14	106
Sallisaw, Ok., U.S.	B4	122
Salluit, Qc., Can.	C15	106
Salmi, Russia	F14	8
Salmo, B.C., Can.	G13	138
Salmon, stm., B.C., Can.	B8	138
Salmon, stm., N.B., Can.	D11	110
Salmon, stm., Id., U.S.	E10	136
Salmon, Middle Fork, stm., Id., U.S.	E12	136
Salmon, South Fork, stm., Id., U.S.	E11	136
Salmon Arm, B.C., Can.	F11	138
Salmon Falls Creek, stm., U.S.	H12	136
Salmon Gums, Austl.	F4	74
Salmon Peak, mtn., Tx., U.S.	E7	130
Salmon River Mountains, mts., Id., U.S.	F12	136
Salmon Valley, B.C., Can.	B8	138
Salo, Fin.	F10	8
Salò, Italy	E7	22
Salome, Az., U.S.	J3	132
Salomon, Cap, c., Mart.	I6	105c
Salon-de-Provence, Fr.	F11	18
Salonga, Parc National de la, p.o.i., D.R.C.	E4	66
Salonika *see* Thessaloníki, Grc.	C6	28
Salonika, Gulf of see Thermaïkós Kólpos, b., Grc.	C6	28
Salonta, Rom.	C8	26
Salor, stm., Spain	E4	20
Salpausselʹkja, mts., Eur.	B3	32
Sal Rei, C.V.	k10	65a
Salsacate, Arg.	E5	92
Salsipuedes, Canal, strt., Mex.	A2	100
Sal'sk, Russia	E6	32
Salsomaggiore Terme, Italy	F6	22
Salt, stm., Az., U.S.	J4	132
Salt, stm., Mo., U.S.	E6	120
Salt, Middle Fork, stm., Mo., U.S.	E5	120
Salt, North Fork, stm., Mo., U.S.	E5	120
Salta, Arg.	B5	92
Salta, state, Arg.	D4	90
Saltanovka, Russia	H17	10
Saltash, Eng., U.K.	K8	12
Salt Basin, l., Tx., U.S.	C2	130
Salt Cay, i., Bah.	m18	104f
Saltcoats, Sk., Can.	C11	124
Salt Creek, stm., Il., U.S.	D8	120
Saltee Islands, is., Ire.	I6	12
Saltfjellet Svartisen Nasjonalpark, p.o.i., Nor.	C6	8
Saltillo, Mex.	C8	100
Saltillo, Tn., U.S.	B10	122
Salt Lake City, Ut., U.S.	C4	132
Salto, Arg.	G7	92
Salto, Ur.	E9	92
Salto del Guairá, Para.	A10	92
Salto Grande, Embalse, res., S.A.	E8	92
Salton City, Ca., U.S.	J9	134
Salton Sea, l., Ca., U.S.	J10	134
Salto Santiago, Represa de, res., Braz.	B11	92
Saltspring Island, i., B.C., Can.	H7	138
Saltville, Va., U.S.	H4	114
Saluda, Va., U.S.	G9	114
Saluda, stm., S.C., U.S.	B4	116
Salûm, Egypt	A5	62
Sālūmbar, India	F5	54
Sālūr, India	B6	53
Saluzzo, Italy	F4	22
Salvador, Braz.	G6	88
Salvador, El see El Salvador, ctry., N.A.	F3	102
Salvador, Lake, l., La., U.S.	H8	122
Salvatierra, Mex.	E8	100
Salviac, Fr.	E7	18
Salween (Nu) (Khong) (Thanlwin), stm., Asia	E8	46
Salyan, Azer.	B6	56
Salyān, Nepal	D9	54
Salyer, Ca., U.S.	C2	134
Salyersville, Ky., U.S.	G2	114
Salzach, stm., Eur.	B9	22
Salzburg, Aus.	C10	22
Salzburg, state, Aus.	C10	22
Salzgitter, Ger.	D6	16
Salzkammergut, reg., Aus.	C10	22
Salzwedel, Ger.	D7	16
Samacá, Col.	E5	86
Samacèvičy, Bela.	G14	10
Samagaltaj, Russia	D16	32
Samah, Libya	B3	62
Samales Group, is., Phil.	G3	52
Samalga Pass, strt., Ak., U.S.	g25	140a
Samal Island, i., Phil.	G5	52
Sāmalkot, India	C6	53
Samâlût, Egypt	J1	58
Samaná, Dom. Rep.	C13	102
Samāna, India	C5	54
Samaná, Bahía de, b., Dom. Rep.	C13	102
Samaná, Cabo, c., Dom. Rep.	C13	102
Samana Cay, i., Bah.	A11	102
Samandağı, Tur.	B6	58
Samaniego, Col.	G3	86
Samaqua, stm., Qc., Can.	A4	110
Samar, i., Phil.	E5	52
Samara, Russia	D8	32
Samara, stm., Russia	D8	32
Samarai, Pap. N. Gui.	c5	79a
Samaria, Id., U.S.	A4	132
Samaria Gorge see Samariás, Farángi, p., Grc.	H6	28
Samariapo, Ven.	E8	86
Samariás, Farángi (Samaria Gorge), p., Grc.	H6	28
Samarinda, Indon.	D10	50
Samarka, Russia	B10	38
Samarkand, Uzb.	G11	32
Sāmarrā', Iraq	C5	56
Samastīpur, India	F10	54
Samaúna, Braz.	E5	84
Samba Caju, Ang.	B2	68
Sambaíba, Braz.	D3	88
Sambalpur, India	H9	54
Sambar, Tanjung, c., Indon.	E7	50
Sambas, Indon.	C6	50
Sambava, Madag.	C9	68
Şambayat, Tur.	A9	58
Sambhal, India	D7	54
Sāmbhar, India	E5	54
Sāmbhar Lake, l., India	E5	54
Sambir, Ukr.	G19	16
Sambit, Pulau, i., Indon.	C11	50
Sambito, stm., Braz.	D5	88
Samboja, Indon.	D10	50
Sâmbor, Camb.	F7	48
Samborombón, stm., Arg.	G9	92
Samborombón, Bahía, b., Arg.	G9	92
Sambre, stm., Eur.	D12	14
Sambre à l'Oise, Canal de la, can., Fr.	E12	14
Sambriāl, Pak.	B5	54
Samch'ŏk, Kor., S.	B2	40
Sam Chom, Khao, mtn., Thai.	H4	48
Same, Tan.	E7	66
Sam Ford Fiord, b., Nu., Can.	A16	106
Samfya, Zam.	C4	68
Samka, Mya.	B3	48
Samnangjin, Kor., S.	D1	40
Sam Ngao, Thai.	D4	48
Samoa, ctry., Oc.	g12	79c
Samoa Islands, is., Oc.	h12	79c
Samo Alto, Chile	E2	92
Samobor, Cro.	E12	22
Samoded, Russia	E19	8
Samokov, Blg.	G10	26
Sámos, i., Grc.	F9	28
Samoset, Fl., U.S.	I3	116
Samosir, Pulau, i., Indon.	B1	50
Samothrace see Samothráki, i., Grc.	C8	28
Samothráki, Grc.	C8	28
Samothráki (Samothrace), i., Grc.	C8	28
Sampacho, Arg.	F5	92
Sampanahan, Indon.	E10	50
Sampang, Indon.	G8	50
Sampit, Indon.	E8	50
Sampit, stm., Indon.	E8	50
Sampit, Teluk, b., Indon.	E8	50
Sampwe, D.R.C.	F5	66
Sam Rayburn Reservoir, res., Tx., U.S.	F4	122
Samro, ozero, l., Russia	B11	10
Sam Son, Viet.	C7	48
Samsun, Tur.	A4	56
Samsu-ŭp, Kor., N.	D7	38
Samtown, La., U.S.	F6	122
Samuhú, Arg.	C7	92
Samui, Ko, i., Thai.	H5	48
Samundri, Pak.	C4	54
Samut Prakan, Thai.	F5	48
Samut Sakhon, Thai.	F5	48
Samut Songkhram, Thai.	F5	48
San, Mali	G3	64
San (Xan), stm., Asia	F8	48
San, stm., China	E8	42
San (Syan), stm., Eur.	F18	16
Saña, Peru	E2	84
Şan'ā', Yemen	F5	56
Sana, stm., Bos.	E3	26
Sanaa *see* Şan'ā', Yemen	F5	56
Sanabu, Egypt	K1	58
Sanaga, stm., Cam.	D2	66
San Agustín, Arg.	E5	92
San Agustín, Arg.	I8	92
San Agustín, Mex.	C1	130
San Agustin, Cape, c., Phil.	G6	52
Sanak Islands, is., Ak., U.S.	F7	140
San Alberto, Mex.	G6	130
San Ambrosio, Isla, i., Chile	H7	82
Sanana, Pulau, i., Indon.	F8	44
Sānand, India	G4	54
Sanandaj, Iran	B6	56
San Andreas, Ca., U.S.	E5	134
San Andrés, Col.	F7	102
San Andrés, Isla de, i., Col.	F7	102
San Andres Mountains, mts., N.M., U.S.	H2	128
San Andrés Sajcabajá, Guat.	E2	102
San Andrés Tuxtla, Mex.	F11	100
San Andrés y Providencia, state, Col.	F7	102
Sananduva, Braz.	C12	92
San Angelo, Tx., U.S.	C7	130
San Antero, Col.	C4	86
San Antonio, Arg.	D5	92
San Antonio, Chile	F2	92
San Antonio, Col.	F4	86
San Antonio, Ur.	E9	92
San Antonio, N.M., U.S.	J9	132
San Antonio, N.M., U.S.	F2	128
San Antonio, Tx., U.S.	E9	130
San Antonio, stm., Tx., U.S.	F10	130
San Antonio, Cabo, pen., Arg.	H9	92
San Antonio, Cabo de, c., Cuba	B5	102
San Antonio, Lake, res., Ca., U.S.	H4	134
San Antonio, Mount, mtn., Ca., U.S.	I8	134
San Antonio, Punta, c., Mex.	B3	100
San Antonio Abad *see* Sant Antoni de Portmany, Spain	F12	20
San Antonio Bay, b., Tx., U.S.	F11	130
San Antonio de Bravo, Mex.	D3	130
San Antonio de La Paz *see* San Antonio, Arg.	D5	92
San Antonio de los Baños, Cuba	A6	102
San Antonio de los Cobres, Arg.	B4	92
San Antonio del Táchira, Ven.	D5	86
San Antonio de Tamanaco, Ven.	C8	86
San Antonio el Grande, Mex.	F2	130
San Antonio Mountain, mtn., N.M., U.S.	E2	128
San Antonio Oeste, Arg.	H4	90
Sanatorium, Ms., U.S.	F9	122
San Augustine, Tx., U.S.	F4	122
San Augustin Pass, p., N.M., U.S.	K10	132
Sanāw, Yemen	F7	56
Sanāwad, India	G6	54
San Bartolomeo in Galdo, Italy	C9	24
San Benedetto del Tronto, Italy	H10	22
San Benedetto Po, Italy	E7	22
San Benedicto, Isla, i., Mex.	F3	100
San Benito, Tx., U.S.	H10	130
San Benito, stm., Ca., U.S.	G4	134
San Benito Mountain, mtn., Ca., U.S.	G5	134
San Bernard, stm., Tx., U.S.	E12	130
San Bernardino, Ca., U.S.	I8	134
San Bernardino Mountains, mts., Ca., U.S.	I9	134
San Bernardino Strait, strt., Phil.	D5	52
San Bernardo, Chile	F2	92
San Bernardo, Islas de, is., Col.	C3	86
San Bernardo del Viento, Col.	C3	86
Sanbe-yama, vol., Japan	D5	40
San Blas, Mex.	E6	100
San Blas, Mex.	B4	100
San Blas, Cape, c., Fl., U.S.	H13	122
San Blas, Golfo de, b., Pan.	H8	102
San Blas, Serranía de, mts., Pan.	H8	102
San Borja, Bol.	B3	90
Sanborn, Ia., U.S.	H3	118
Sanborn, N.D., U.S.	H15	124
San Bruno, Ca., U.S.	F3	134
San Buenaventura, Bol.	B3	90
San Buenaventura, Mex.	B8	100

Name | Map Ref. | Page

San Buenaventura see Ventura, Ca., U.S. I6 134
San Carlos, Chile H2 92
San Carlos, Mex. C9 100
San Carlos, Mex. A8 100
San Carlos, Nic. G5 102
San Carlos, Phil. E4 52
San Carlos, Phil. C3 52
San Carlos, Ur. G10 92
San Carlos, Az., U.S. J6 132
San Carlos, Ca., U.S. F3 134
San Carlos, Ven. C7 86
San Carlos, stm., C.R. G5 102
San Carlos, stm., Ven. C7 86
San Carlos Centro, Arg. E7 92
San Carlos de Bariloche, Arg. H2 90
San Carlos de Bolívar, Arg. H7 92
San Carlos de Guaroa, Col. F5 86
San Carlos del Zulia, Ven. C5 86
San Carlos de Río Negro, Ven. G8 86
San Carlos Reservoir, res., Az., U.S. J6 132
San Cataldo, Italy G7 24
San Cayetano, Arg. I8 92
Sancha, stm., China H1 42
Sanchahe, China B7 38
Sanchenglong, China B4 38
San Ciro de Acosta, Mex. E9 100
San Clemente, Spain E8 20
San Clemente, Ca., U.S. J8 134
San Clemente Island, i., Ca., U.S. K7 134
San Cristóbal, Arg. E7 92
San Cristóbal, Dom. Rep. C12 102
San Cristóbal, Ven. D5 86
San Cristobal, i., Sol. Is. f9 79b
San Cristóbal, Bahía, b., Mex. B1 100
San Cristóbal, Isla, i., Ec. i12 84a
San Cristóbal, Volcán, vol., Nic. F4 102
San Cristóbal de las Casas, Mex. G12 100
Sancti Spíritus, Cuba A8 102
Sancy, Puy de, mtn., Fr. D8 18
Sand, Nor. G2 8
Sand, stm., Ab., Can. B19 138
Sand, stm., S. Afr. F8 70
Sand, stm., S. Afr. C9 70
Sandai, Indon. D7 50
Sandakan, Malay. H2 52
Sândăn, Camb. F8 48
Sandaré, Mali G2 64
Sand Arroyo, stm., U.S. D7 128
Sanday, i., Scot., U.K. B10 12
Sandefjord, Nor. G4 8
Sanderson, Tx., U.S. D5 130
Sandersville, Ga., U.S. D3 116
Sandersville, Ms., U.S. F9 122
Sand Fork, W.V., U.S. F5 114
Sand Hill, stm., Mn., U.S. D2 118
Sand Hills, hills, Ne., U.S. F11 126
Sāndi, India E8 54
Sandia, Peru F4 84
San Diego, Ca., U.S. K8 134
San Diego, Tx., U.S. G9 130
San Diego, Cabo, c., Arg. J3 90
San Diego Aqueduct, aq., Ca., U.S. J8 134
Sandıklı, Tur. E13 28
Sandīla, India E8 54
Sandilands Village, Bah. m18 104f
Sand Key, i., Fl., U.S. I3 116
Sand Lake, l., On., Can. A4 118
Sandnes, Nor. G1 8
Sandoa, D.R.C. F4 66
Sandomierz, Pol. F17 16
Sandoná, Col. G3 86
San Donà di Piave, Italy E9 22
Sandovo, Russia B19 10
Sandoway, Mya. C2 48
Sandown, Eng., U.K. K11 12
Sand Point, Ak., U.S. E7 140
Sandpoint, Id., U.S. B10 136
Sandringham, Austl. E2 76
Sandspit, B.C., Can. E4 106
Sand Springs, Ok., U.S. A2 122
Sand Springs, Tx., U.S. B6 130
Sandstone, Austl. E3 74
Sandstone, Mn., U.S. E5 118
Sandu Ao, b., China H8 42
Sandusky, Mi., U.S. E7 112
Sandusky, Oh., U.S. C3 114
Sandvika, Nor. G4 8
Sandviken, Swe. F7 8
Sandwich, Eng., U.K. J14 12
Sandwich Bay, b., Nmb. C2 70
Sandwick, B.C., Can. G5 138
Sandwīp Island, i., Bngl. G13 54
Sandy, Or., U.S. E4 136
Sandy, Ut., U.S. C5 132
Sandy Bay Mountain, mtn., Me., U.S. E6 110
Sandy Cape, c., Austl. E9 76
Sandy Cape, c., Austl. n12 77a
Sandy Creek, stm., Austl. I5 76
Sandy Hook, Ky., U.S. F2 114
Sandy Hook, spit, N.J., U.S. D12 114
Sandykači, Turkmen. B9 56
Sandy Lake, l., On., Can. E12 106
Sandy Point, c., Trin. r13 105f
Sandy Point Town, St. K./N. C2 105a
Sandy Springs, Ga., U.S. C1 116
Sandžak, reg., Eur. F6 26
San Elizario, Tx., U.S. C1 130
San Enrique, Arg. G7 92
San Estanislao, Para. B9 92
San Esteban, Isla, i., Mex. A2 100
San Esteban de Gormaz, Spain C7 20
San Felipe, Chile F2 92
San Felipe, Col. G8 86
San Felipe, Mex. E8 100
San Felipe, Mex. F5 98
San Felipe, Ven. B7 86
San Felipe, Cayos de, is., Cuba B6 102
San Felipe Nuevo Mercurio, Mex. C7 100
San Felipe Pueblo, N.M., U.S. F2 128
San Felíu de Guixols see Sant Feliu de Guíxols, Spain C14 20
San Félix, Isla, i., Chile H6 82
San Fernando, Chile G2 92
San Fernando, Mex. C9 100
San Fernando, Mex. F6 130
San Fernando, Phil. B2 52
San Fernando, Phil. C3 52
San Fernando, Spain H4 20
San Fernando, Trin. s12 105f
San Fernando, Ca., U.S. I7 134
San Fernando de Apure, Ven. D8 86
San Fernando de Atabapo, Ven. E8 86
San Fernando del Valle de Catamarca, Arg. D4 92
Sånfjällets Nationalpark, p.o.i., Swe. E5 8
Sanford, Co., U.S. D2 128
Sanford, Fl., U.S. H4 116
Sanford, Me., U.S. G6 110
Sanford, N.C., U.S. A6 116
Sanford, Tx., U.S. F7 128
Sanford, stm., Austl. E3 74
Sanford, Mount, vol., Ak., U.S. D11 140
San Francisco, Arg. E6 92
San Francisco, El Sal. F3 102
San Francisco, Ca., U.S. F3 134
San Francisco, stm., Arg. B5 92
San Francisco, stm., U.S. J8 132
San Francisco, Paso de, p., S.A. C3 92
San Francisco Bay, b., Ca., U.S. F3 134
San Francisco Creek, stm., Tx., U.S. E5 130
San Francisco de Borja, Mex. B5 100
San Francisco de Horizonte, Mex. I4 130
San Francisco del Chañar, Arg. D5 92
San Francisco del Oro, Mex. B5 100
San Francisco del Rincón, Mex. E7 100
San Francisco de Macorís, Dom. Rep. C12 102
San Francisco de Mostazal, Chile F2 92
San Gabriel, Ec. G3 86
San Gabriel Chilac, Mex. F10 100
San Gabriel Mountains, mts., Ca., U.S. I8 134
Sangamankanda Point, c., Sri L. H5 53
Sangamner, India B1 53
Sangamon, stm., Il., U.S. D7 120
Sangar, Russia D14 34
Sangasanga-dalam, Indon. D10 50
San Gavino Monreale, Italy E2 24
Sangay, vol., Ec. I2 86
Sangay, Parque Nacional, p.o.i., Ec. H3 86
Sange, D.R.C. F5 66
Sangeang, Pulau, i., Indon. H11 50
Sanger, Ca., U.S. G6 134
Sanger, Tx., U.S. H11 128
Sângera, Mol. B15 26
Sangerhausen, Ger. E7 16
San Germán, P.R. B1 104a
Sangerville, Me., U.S. E7 110
Sanggan, stm., China A6 42
Sanggau, Indon. C7 50
Sangha, stm., Afr. E3 66
Sanghar, Pak. E2 54
Sangihe, Kepulauan, is., Indon. E7 44
Sangihe, Pulau, i., Indon. E8 44
San Gil, Col. D5 86
Sangilen, hrebet, mts., Russia D17 32
San Gimignano, Italy G7 22
San Giovanni in Fiore, Italy E10 24
San Giovanni in Persiceto, Italy F8 22
San Giovanni Rotondo, Italy C9 24
San Giovanni Valdarno, Italy G8 22
Sangiyn Dalay nuur, l., Mong. B4 36
Sangju, Kor., S. F8 38
Sangkapura, Indon. F8 50
Sângkê, stm., Camb. F6 48
Sangkulirang, Indon. C10 50
Sāngli, India C2 53
Sangmélima, Cam. D2 66
Sāngole, India C2 53
Sangolquí, Ec. H2 86
San Gorgonio Mountain, mtn., Ca., U.S. I9 134
San Gottardo, Passo del, p., Switz. D5 22
Sangre de Cristo Mountains, mts., U.S. E3 128
San Gregorio, Arg. G6 92
Sangre Grande, Trin. s12 105f
Sangro, stm., Italy H11 22
Sangrūr, India C5 54
Sangsang, China D11 54
Sangue, stm., Braz. F6 84
Sangutane, stm., Moz. C11 70
Sangya, China C13 54
San Hipólito, Punta, c., Mex. B1 100
Sanhu, China H6 42
Sânhûr, Egypt I1 58
Sanibel Island, i., Fl., U.S. J3 116
San Ignacio, Arg. C10 92
San Ignacio, Mex. B2 100
San Ignacio, Mex. D8 100
San Ignacio, Para. C9 92
San Ignacio, Isla, i., Mex. C4 100
San Ignacio, Laguna, b., Mex. B2 100
San Ignacio de Moxo, Bol. B3 90
San Ignacio de Velasco, Bol. C4 90
San Isidro, Arg. D5 92
San Isidro, Arg. G8 92
San Isidro del General, C.R. H5 102
San Jacinto, Col. C4 86
San Jacinto, Ca., U.S. J9 134
San Jacinto Peak, mtn., Ca., U.S. J9 134
San Jaime, Arg. E8 92
San Javier, Arg. E8 92
San Javier, Arg. C10 92
San Javier, Bol. C4 90
San Javier, Chile G2 92
San Javier, Mex. H8 130
San Javier, Ur. F8 92
San Javier, stm., Arg. E8 92
Sanjay National Park, p.o.i., India G8 54
San Jerónimo, Guat. E2 102
Sanjiang, China I3 42
Sanjō, Japan B11 40
San Joaquín, Bol. B4 90
San Joaquín, stm., Bol. B4 90
San Joaquin, stm., Ca., U.S. E4 134
San Joaquín de Omaguas, Peru D3 84
San Joaquin Valley, val., Ca., U.S. G5 134
San Jorge, Arg. E6 92
San Jorge, stm., Col. C4 86
San Jorge, Bahía de, b., Mex. F6 98
San Jorge, Golfo, b., Arg. I3 90
San Jorge Island, i., Sol. Is. e8 79b
San José, C.R. H5 102
San José, Mex. F7 130
San Jose, Phil. E3 52
San Jose, Ca., U.S. F4 134
San Jose, Il., U.S. D8 120
San Jose, N.M., U.S. F3 128
San José, Ven. q19 104g
San Jose, stm., N.M., U.S. I9 132
San José, Cerro, mtn., Mex. H2 130
San José, Isla, i., Mex. C3 100
San José, Isla, i., Pan. H8 102
San José, Laguna, b., P.R. B3 104a
San José de Bácum, Mex. B3 100
San José de Batuc, Mex. A3 100
San José de Chiquitos, Bol. C4 90
San José de Feliciano, Arg. E8 92
San José de Guanipa, Ven. C9 86
San José de Jáchal, Arg. E3 92
San José de la Popa, Mex. H7 130
San José de las Lajas, Cuba A6 102
San José del Cabo, Mex. D4 100
San José del Guaviare, Col. F5 86
San José de Mayo, Ur. G9 92
San José de Ocuné, Col. E6 86
San José de Tiznados, Ven. C8 86
San Jose Island, i., Tx., U.S. G11 130
San Juan, Arg. E3 92
San Juan, Mex. E3 130
San Juan, P.R. B3 104a
San Juan, state, Arg. E3 92
San Juan, stm., Arg. F4 92
San Juan, stm., Col. E3 86
San Juan, stm., Mex. H8 130
San Juan, stm., N.A. G5 102
San Juan, stm., U.S. F6 132
San Juan, stm., Ven. B10 86
San Juan, Cabezas de, c., P.R. B4 104a
San Juan, Cabo, c., Arg. J4 90
San Juan Basin, bas., N.M., U.S. G8 132
San Juan Bautista, Mex. H6 130
San Juan Bautista, Para. C9 92
San Juan Bautista see Sant Joan de Labritja, Spain E12 20
San Juan Bautista, Ca., U.S. G4 134
San Juan Creek, stm., Ca., U.S. H5 134
San Juan de Colón, Ven. C5 86
San Juan de Guadalupe, Mex. C7 100
San Juan de la Maguana, Dom. Rep. C12 102
San Juan del Norte, Nic. G6 102
San Juan de los Cayos, Ven. B7 86
San Juan de los Morros, Ven. C8 86
San Juan del Río, Mex. E8 100
San Juan del Río, Mex. C6 100
San Juan del Sur, Nic. G4 102
San Juan de Micay, stm., Col. F3 86
San Juan de Payara, Ven. D8 86
San Juan de Sabinas, Mex. G6 130
San Juanico, Mex. B2 100
San Juan Islands, is., Wa., U.S. B3 136
San Juanito, Isla, i., Mex. E5 100
San Juan Mountains, mts., Co., U.S. C9 98
San Juan Nepomuceno, Col. C4 86
San Juan Nepomuceno, Para. C9 92
San Justo, Arg. E7 92
Sankarani, stm., Afr. G3 64
Sankeshwar, India C2 53
Sankh, stm., India G10 54
Sankheda, India G4 54
Sankosh, stm., Asia E13 54
Sankt Anton am Arlberg, Aus. C7 22
Sankt Gallen, Switz. C6 22
Sankt Goarshausen, Ger. F3 16
Sankt Ingbert, Ger. G3 16
Sankt Michel see Mikkeli, Fin. F12 8
Sankt Moritz, Switz. D6 22
Sankt-Peterburg (Saint Petersburg), Russia A13 10
Sankt Peter-Ording, Ger. B4 16
Sankt Pölten, Aus. B12 22
Sankt Veit an der Glan, Aus. D11 22
Sankt-Vith see Saint-Vith, Bel. D14 14
Sankt Wendel, Ger. G3 16
Sankuru, stm., D.R.C. E4 66
San Lázaro, Cabo, c., Mex. C2 100
San Leandro, Ca., U.S. F3 134
San Leonardo, Mex. G3 130
Şanlıurfa (Urfa), Tur. A9 58
Şanlıurfa, state, Tur. A9 58
San Lorenzo, Arg. F7 92
San Lorenzo, Arg. D8 92
San Lorenzo, Bol. D4 90
San Lorenzo, Ec. G2 86
San Lorenzo, Mex. C7 100
San Lorenzo, P.R. B4 104a
San Lorenzo, stm., Mex. C5 100
San Lorenzo, Cabo, c., Ec. H1 86
San Lorenzo, Isla, i., Mex. A2 100
San Lorenzo, Monte (Cochrane, Cerro), mtn., S.A. I2 90
San Lorenzo de la Parrilla, Spain E8 20
Sanlúcar de Barrameda, Spain H4 20
San Lucas, Bol. D3 90
San Lucas, Mex. D3 100
San Lucas, Cabo, c., Mex. D4 100
San Luis, Arg. F4 92
San Luis, Cuba B10 102
San Luis, Guat. D3 102
San Luis, Co., U.S. D3 128
San Luis, Ven. B7 86
San Luis, state, Arg. F5 92
San Luís, Laguna, l., Bol. B4 90
San Luis, Sierra de, mts., Arg. F5 92
San Luis Creek, stm., Co., U.S. C3 128
San Luis de la Paz, Mex. E8 100
San Luis Gonzaga, Mex. C3 100
San Luis Gonzaga, Bahía, b., Mex. G5 98
San Luis Jilotepeque, Guat. E3 102
San Luis Obispo, Ca., U.S. H5 134
San Luis Potosí, Mex. D8 100
San Luis Potosí, state, Mex. D8 100
San Luis Reservoir, res., Ca., U.S. F4 134
San Luis Río Colorado, Mex. E5 98
San Luis Valley, val., Co., U.S. D3 128
San Manuel, Arg. H8 92
San Manuel, Az., U.S. K6 132
San Marcial, stm., Mex. A3 100
San Marcos, Col. C4 86
San Marcos, Mex. G9 100
San Marcos, Tx., U.S. E9 130
San Marcos, Isla, i., Mex. B2 100
San Marino, S. Mar. G9 22
San Marino, ctry., Eur. G9 22
San Martín, Arg. F3 92
San Martín, Arg. D5 92
San Martín, Col. F5 86
San Martín, stm., Bol. B4 90
San Martín, sci., Ant. B34 81
San Martín, Lago (O'Higgins, Lago), l., S.A. I2 90
San Martín de los Andes, Arg. H2 90
San Martino di Castrozza, ngh., Italy D8 22
San Mateo, Mex. G1 130
San Mateo see Sant Mateu del Maestrat, Spain D10 20
San Mateo, Ca., U.S. F3 134
San Mateo, Fl., U.S. G4 116
San Mateo, N.M., U.S. H9 132
San Matías, Bol. C5 90
San Matías, Golfo, b., Arg. H4 90
Sanmen, China G9 42
Sanmenhsia see Sanmenxia, China D4 42
Sanmenxia, China D4 42
San Miguel, Ec. H2 86
San Miguel, El Sal. F3 102
San Miguel, Mex. A8 100
San Miguel, Pan. H8 102
San Miguel, stm., Bol. B4 90
San Miguel, stm., S.A. G3 86
San Miguel, stm., Co., U.S. E8 132
San Miguel, Golfo de, b., Pan. H8 102
San Miguel de Allende, Mex. E8 100
San Miguel de Cruces, Mex. C6 100
San Miguel del Monte, Arg. G8 92
San Miguel de Salcedo, Ec. H2 86
San Miguel de Tucumán, Arg. C4 92
San Miguel Island, i., Ca., U.S. I5 134
Sanming, China H7 42
San Miniato, Italy G7 22
Sannār, Sudan E6 62
Sannicandro Garganico, Italy I12 22
San Nicolás, Peru G2 84
San Nicolas, Phil. A3 52
San Nicolás de los Arroyos, Arg. F7 92
San Nicolás de los Garza, Mex. C8 100
San Nicolas Island, i., Ca., U.S. J6 134
Sânnicolau Mare, Rom. C7 26
Sannieshof, S. Afr. E7 70
Sannikova, proliv, strt., Russia B16 34
Sano, Japan C12 40
Sanok, Pol. G18 16
Sânon, stm., Fr. F15 14
San Pablo, Phil. C3 52
San Pablo Bay, b., Ca., U.S. E3 134
San Pasqual, Punta, c., Mex. C3 100
San Pedro, Arg. B5 92
San Pedro, Arg. F8 92
San Pedro, Arg. C5 92
San Pedro, Chile F2 92
San-Pédro, C. Iv. I3 64
San Pedro, Col. C4 86
San Pedro, Neth. Ant. A1 105a
San Pedro, state, Para. B9 92
San Pedro, stm., Mex. F8 98
San Pedro, stm., Mex. G2 130
San Pedro, stm., N.A. K6 132
San Pedro, stm., N.A. D2 102
San Pedro, Punta, c., Chile B2 92
San Pedro, Volcán, vol., Chile D3 90
San Pedro Carchá, Guat. E2 102
San Pedro de Jujuy see San Pedro, Arg. B5 92
San Pedro de las Colonias, Mex. C7 100
San Pedro del Gallo, Mex. C6 100
San Pedro del Paraná, Para. C9 92
San Pedro de Macorís, Dom. Rep. C13 102
San Pedro de Ycuamandiyú, Para. B9 92
San Pedro Peaks, mtn., N.M., U.S. G10 132
San Pedro Sula, Hond. E3 102
San Pedro Tabasco, Mex. D2 102
San Pellegrino Terme, Italy E6 22
San Pietro, Isola di, i., Italy E2 24
San Pitch, stm., Ut., U.S. D5 132
Sanquhar, Scot., U.K. F9 12
Sanquianga, Parque Nacional, p.o.i., Col. F2 86
San Quintín, Cabo, c., Mex. F4 98
San Rafael, Arg. G3 92
San Rafael, Chile G2 92
San Rafael, Mex. C8 100
San Rafael, Ca., U.S. E3 134
San Rafael, N.M., U.S. H8 132
San Rafael, Ven. B6 86
San Rafael, stm., Mex. F5 98
San Rafael, stm., Ut., U.S. E6 132
San Rafael del Norte, Nic. F4 102
San Rafael Swell, plat., Ut., U.S. E6 132
San Ramón, Arg. C5 92
San Ramón, Bol. B4 90
San Ramón de la Nueva Orán, Arg. D4 90
San Remo, Italy G4 22
San Rodrigo, stm., Mex. F6 130
San Roque, Arg. D8 92
San Roque, Punta, c., Mex. B1 100
San Saba, Tx., U.S. C9 130
San Saba, stm., Tx., U.S. C9 130
San Salvador, Arg. E8 92
San Salvador, El Sal. F3 102
San Salvador, i., Bah. C10 96
San Salvador de Jujuy, Arg. A5 92
Sansanné-Mango, Togo G5 64
San Sebastián, P.R. B1 104a
San Sebastián see Donostia-San Sebastián, Spain A9 20
San Sebastián, Bahía, b., Arg. J3 90
Sansepolcro, Italy G9 22
San Severo, Italy I12 22
Sansha, China H9 42
San Simon, Az., U.S. K7 132
San Simon, stm., Az., U.S. K7 132
San Simon Wash, stm., Az., U.S. K4 132
Sanski Most, Bos. E3 26
San Solano, Arg. E4 92
Sans-Souci, sci., Haiti C11 102
Santa, stm., Peru E2 84
Santa Adélia, Braz. K1 88
Santa Amalia, Spain E4 20
Santa Ana, Bol. B3 90
Santa Ana, Ec. H1 86
Santa Ana, El Sal. E3 102
Santa Ana, Mex. F7 98
Santa Ana, Mex. C8 100
Santa Ana, Ca., U.S. J8 134
Santa Ana, Ven. C9 86
Santa Ana del Alto Beni, Bol. C3 90
Santa Anna, Tx., U.S. C8 130
Santa Bárbara, Chile H2 92
Santa Barbara, Col. E4 86
Santa Bárbara, Hond. E3 102
Santa Bárbara, Mex. B6 100
Santa Barbara, Ca., U.S. I6 134
Santa Bárbara, Ven. D6 86
Santa Barbara Channel, strt., Ca., U.S. I6 134
Santa Barbara Island, i., Ca., U.S. J7 134
Santa Catalina, Gulf of, b., Ca., U.S. J7 134
Santa Catalina, Isla, i., Mex. C3 100
Santa Catalina Island, i., Ca., U.S. J7 134
Santa Catarina, Mex. C8 100
Santa Catarina, Mex. L10 134
Santa Catarina, state, Braz. C12 92
Santa Catarina, Ilha de, i., Braz. C13 92
Santa Cecília, Braz. C12 92
Santa Clara, Col. I7 86
Santa Clara, Cuba A7 102
Santa Clara, Ca., U.S. F3 134
Santa Clara, Ut., U.S. F3 132
Santa Clara, stm., Ca., U.S. I7 134
Santa Clarita, Ca., U.S. I7 134
Santa Clotilde, Peru D3 84
Santa Coloma de Farners, Spain C13 20
Santa Coloma de Farnés see Santa Coloma de Farners, Spain C13 20
Santa Comba, Spain A2 20
Santa Cruz, Braz. D8 88
Santa Cruz, Braz. J5 88
Santa Cruz, C.R. G5 102
Santa Cruz, Phil. D4 52
Santa Cruz, Phil. C3 52
Santa Cruz, Phil. C2 52
Santa Cruz, Ca., U.S. G3 134
Santa Cruz, state, Arg. I2 90
Santa Cruz, stm., Arg. J3 90
Santa Cruz, stm., N.A. J4 132
Santa Cruz, Isla, i., Ec. i11 84a
Santa Cruz Cabrália, Braz. I6 88
Santa Cruz de la Sierra, Bol. C4 90
Santa Cruz del Quiché, Guat. E2 102
Santa Cruz del Sur, Cuba B9 102
Santa Cruz de Mudela, Spain F7 20
Santa Cruz do Capibaribe, Braz. D7 88
Santa Cruz do Piauí, Braz. D5 88
Santa Cruz do Rio Pardo, Braz. L1 88
Santa Cruz do Sul, Braz. D11 92
Santa Cruz Island, i., Ca., U.S. J6 134
Santa Cruz Islands, is., Sol. Is. E7 72
Santa Elena, Arg. E8 92
Santa Elena, Ec. I1 86
Santa Elena, Mex. B7 100
Santa Elena, Bahía de, b., Ec. H1 86
Santa Elena, Cabo, c., C.R. G4 102
Santa Eufemia, Spain F6 20
Santa Eulalia, Spain D9 20
Santa Eulalia del Río see Santa Eulària del Riu, Spain E12 20
Santa Eulària del Riu, Spain E12 20
Santa Fe, Arg. E7 92
Santa Fe, Spain G7 20
Santa Fe, N.M., U.S. F3 128
Santa Fe, state, Arg. D7 92
Santa Fe, stm., Fl., U.S. G3 116
Santa Fe Baldy, mtn., N.M., U.S. F3 128
Santa Fe de Bogotá see Bogotá, Col. E4 86
Santa Fe de Minas, Braz. I3 88
Santa Fé do Sul, Braz. D6 90
Santa Filomena, Braz. E3 88
Sant'Agata di Militello, Italy F8 24
Santa Gertrudis, Mex. G2 130
Santa Helena, Braz. B3 88
Santa Helena de Goiás, Braz. G7 84
Santai, China F1 42
Santa Inês, Braz. G5 88
Santa Inés, Bahía, b., Mex. B3 100
Santa Inés, Isla, i., Chile J2 90
Santa Isabel, Arg. H4 92
Santa Isabel, P.R. C3 104a
Santa Isabel, i., Sol. Is. e8 79b
Santa Isabel, stm., Mex. F1 130
Santa Isabel, Pico de, mtn., Eq. Gui. I6 64
Santa Isabel Creek, stm., Tx., U.S. G8 130
Santa Juliana, Braz. J2 88
Santal, Baie du, b., N. Cal. m16 79d
Santa Lucía, Arg. D8 92
Santa Lucía, Ur. G9 92
Santa Lucia Range, mts., Ca., U.S. G4 134
Santaluz, Braz. F6 88
Santa Luzia, Braz. D7 88
Santa Magdalena, Arg. G6 92
Santa Magdalena, Isla, i., Mex. C2 100
Santa Margarita, Ca., U.S. H5 134
Santa Margarita, Isla, i., Mex. C2 100
Santa Margherita Ligure, Italy F6 22
Santa María, Arg. C4 92
Santa Maria, Braz. D10 92
Santa María, Mex. F6 130
Santa Maria, Ca., U.S. I5 134
Santa Maria, i., Vanuatu j16 79d
Santa Maria, stm., Braz. E10 92
Santa María, stm., Mex. F9 98
Santa María, stm., Mex. E8 100
Santa Maria, stm., Az., U.S. I3 132
Santa María, Bahía, b., Mex. C4 100
Santa María, Cabo, c., Ur. G10 92
Santa Maria, Cabo de, c., Ang. C1 68
Santa Maria, Cabo de, c., Port. H3 20
Santa María, Isla, i., Chile H1 92
Santa María, Isla, i., Ec. i11 84a
Santa María, Laguna de, l., Mex. F9 98
Santa María Asunción Tlaxiaco, Mex. G10 100
Santa Maria Capua Vetere, Italy C7 24
Santa María Colotepec, Mex. H10 100
Santa Maria da Boa Vista, Braz. E5 88
Santa Maria da Vitória, Braz. G3 88
Santa Maria de Itabira, Braz. J4 88
Santa María del Oro, Mex. C6 100
Santa María del Río, Mex. E8 100
Santa Maria di Leuca, Capo, c., Italy E12 24
Santa Maria do Suaçuí, Braz. J4 88
Santa María la Real de Nieva, Spain C6 20
Santa Marinella, Italy H8 22
Santa Marta, Col. B4 86
Santa Marta, Cabo de, c., Ang. C1 68
Santa Marta, Ciénaga Grande, b., Col. B4 86
Santa Mónica, Mex. F7 130
Santa Monica, Ca., U.S. I7 134
Santa Monica Bay, b., Ca., U.S. J7 134
Santan, Indon. D10 50
Santana, Braz. G3 88
Santana, Coxilha de (Santa Ana, Cuchilla de), hills, S.A. E10 92
Santana, Ilha de, i., Braz. B4 88
Santana da Boa Vista, Braz. E11 92
Santana do Ipanema, Braz. E7 88
Santana do Livramento, Braz. E9 92
Santander, Col. F3 86
Santander, Phil. F4 52
Santander, Spain A7 20
Santander, state, Col. D5 86
Santander Jiménez, Mex. C9 100
Sant'Andrea, Isola, i., Italy D11 24
Santanghu, China C3 36
Santanilla, Islas, is., Hond. D6 102
Sant'Antine, Nuraghe, hist., Italy D2 24
Sant'Antioco, Italy E2 24
Sant'Antioco, Isola di, i., Italy E2 24
Sant Antoni de Portmany, Spain F12 20
Santanyí, Spain E14 20
Santa Paula, Ca., U.S. I6 134
Santaquin, Ut., U.S. D5 132
Santa Quitéria, Braz. C5 88
Santa Quitéria do Maranhão, Braz. B4 88
Santarcangelo di Romagna, Italy F9 22
Santarém, Braz. D7 84
Santarém, Port. E2 20
Santarém, state, Port. E2 20
Santaren Channel, strt., Bah. C9 96
Santa Rita, Braz. D8 88
Santa Rita, Col. G5 86
Santa Rita, Hond. E3 102
Santa Rita, Mex. G7 130
Santa Rita, Mt., U.S. B14 136
Santa Rita, Ven. B6 86
Santa Rosa, Arg. H5 92
Santa Rosa, Braz. C10 92
Santa Rosa, Braz. H2 88
Santa Rosa, Col. F7 86
Santa Rosa, Ec. D2 84
Santa Rosa, Ca., U.S. E3 134
Santa Rosa, Tx., U.S. H10 130
Santa Rosa, Ven. C7 86
Santa Rosa, Ven. D7 86
Santa Rosa, Mount, hill, Guam i10 78c
Santa Rosa Beach, Fl., U.S. G12 122
Santa Rosa de Copán, Hond. E3 102
Santa Rosa del Conlara, Arg. F5 92
Santa Rosa de Leales, Arg. C5 92
Santa Rosa de Osos, Col. D4 86
Santa Rosa de Sucumbíos, Ec. G3 86
Santa Rosa de Viterbo, Col. E5 86
Santa Rosa Island, i., Ca., U.S. J5 134
Santa Rosalía, Mex. B2 100
Santa Rosalía, Mex. H9 130
Santa Rosalía, Ven. C7 86
Santa Rosa Wash, stm., Az., U.S. K5 132
Šantarskie ostrova, is., Russia E16 34
Santa Sylvina, Arg. C7 92
Santa Teresa, Braz. J5 88
Santa Teresa, Mex. C9 100
Santa Teresa, stm., Braz. G1 88
Santa Teresa, Embalse de, res., Spain D5 20
Santa Teresa, Fortaleza de, hist., Ur. F11 92
Santa Uxía, Spain B1 20
Santa Vitória do Palmar, Braz. F11 92
Santee, Ca., U.S. K8 134
Santee, stm., S.C., U.S. C6 116
Santee Dam, dam, S.C., U.S. C5 116
Sant'Eufemia, Golfo di, b., Italy F9 24
Sant Feliu de Guíxols, Spain C14 20
Santhià, Italy E5 22
Santiago, Braz. D10 92
Santiago, Chile F2 92
Santiago, Mex. D4 100
Santiago, Pan. H7 102
Santiago, Para. C9 92
Santiago, i., C.V. I10 65a
Santiago, stm., Mex. C6 100
Santiago, stm., S.A. D2 84
Santiago, Isla, i., Ec. i11 84a
Santiago de Compostela, Spain B2 20
Santiago de Cuba, Cuba C9 102
Santiago del Estero, Arg. C5 92
Santiago del Estero, state, Arg. C5 92
Santiago de los Caballeros, Dom. Rep. C12 102
Santiago Island, i., Phil. B2 52
Santiago Ixcuintla, Mex. E6 100
Santiago Jamiltepec, Mex. G10 100
Santiago Larre, Arg. G8 92
Santiago Papasquiaro, Mex. C6 100
Santiago Peak, mtn., Ca., U.S. J8 134
Santiago Peak, mtn., Tx., U.S. E4 130
Santiaguillo, Laguna, l., Mex. C6 100
Santiam Pass, p., Or., U.S. F5 136
Säntis, mtn., Switz. C6 22
Santisteban del Puerto, Spain F7 20
Sant Joan de Labritja, Spain E12 20
Sant Jordi, Golf de, b., Spain D11 20
Sant Mateu del Maestrat, Spain D10 20
Santo Amaro, Braz. G6 88
Santo Amaro, Braz. B4 88
Santo André, Braz. L2 88
Santo Ângelo, Braz. D10 92
Santo Antão, i., C.V. k10 65a
Santo Antônio, Braz. D8 88
Santo António, S. Tom./P. I6 64
Santo Antônio, stm., Braz. I3 88
Santo Antônio, stm., Braz. F1 88
Santo Antônio da Patrulha, Braz. D12 92
Santo Antônio de Jesus, Braz. G6 88
Santo Antônio de Pádua, Braz. K4 88
Santo Antônio do Amparo, Braz. K3 88
Santo Antônio do Içá, Braz. D4 84
Santo Augusto, Braz. C11 92
Santo Domingo, Dom. Rep. C13 102
Santo Domingo, Mex. I3 130
Santo Domingo, Mex. D8 100
Santo Domingo, Mex. C2 100
Santo Domingo, Ven. D5 86
Santo Domingo de la Calzada, Spain B7 20
Santo Domingo de los Colorados, Ec. H1 86
Santo Domingo Pueblo, N.M., U.S. F2 128
Santo Domingo Tehuantepec, Mex. G11 100
Santo Domingo Zanatepec, Mex. G11 100
Santo Estêvão, Braz. G6 88
Santo / Malo, state, Vanuatu j16 79d
San Tomé, Ven. C9 86
Santo Onofre, stm., Braz. G4 88
Santorini see Thíra, i., Grc. G8 28
Santos, Braz. L2 88
Santos Dumont, Braz. K4 88
Santo Tirso, Port. C2 20
Santo Tomás, Mex. L9 134
Santo Tomás, Punta, c., Mex. L9 134
Santo Tomé, Arg. E7 92
Santo Tomé, Arg. D9 92
San Vicente de Alcántara, Spain E3 20
San Vicente de Baracaldo see Barakaldo, Spain A8 20
San Vicente del Caguán, Col. F4 86
San Vincente, Arg. D5 92
San Vincenzo, Italy G7 22
San Vito, Capo, c., Italy F6 24
Sanya, China L3 42
Sanyati, stm., Zimb. D4 68
Sanyō, Japan E4 40
Sanyuan, China D3 42
Sanzao Dao, i., China K5 42
Sanza Pombo, Ang. B2 68
São Benedito, Braz. C5 88
São Benedito do Rio Preto, Braz. B3 88
São Bento, Braz. B3 88
São Bento do Norte, Braz. C7 88
São Bento do Sul, Braz. C13 92
São Bento do Una, Braz. E7 88
São Borja, Braz. D10 92
São Caetano do Sul, Braz. L2 88
São Carlos, Braz. L2 88
São Cristóvão, Braz. F7 88
São Domingos, Braz. G2 88
São Domingos, Braz. C11 92
São Domingos, Gui.-B. G1 64

Name	Map Ref.	Page
São Domingos do Maranhão, Braz.	C3	88
São Felipe, Braz.	H5	88
São Félix de Balsas, Braz.	D3	88
São Francisco, Braz.	H3	88
São Francisco, stm., Braz.	H5	88
São Francisco, stm., Braz.	E6	88
São Francisco, Baía de, b., Braz.	C13	92
São Francisco, Ilha de, i., Braz.	C13	92
São Francisco de Assis, Braz.	D10	92
São Francisco de Goiás, Braz.	H1	88
São Francisco de Paula, Braz.	D12	92
São Francisco do Maranhão, Braz.	D4	88
São Francisco do Sul, Braz.	C13	92
São Gabriel, Braz.	E10	92
São Gabriel, Braz.	F5	88
São Gabriel da Palha, Braz.	J5	88
São Gabriel de Goiás, Braz.	H2	88
São Gonçalo do Sapucaí, Braz.	K3	88
São Gonçalo dos Campos, Braz.	G6	88
São Hill, Tan.	F7	66
São Jerônimo, Braz.	E12	92
São Jerônimo da Serra, Braz.	A12	92
São João da Aliança, Braz.	H2	88
São João da Barra, Braz.	K5	88
São João da Boa Vista, Braz.	L2	88
São João de Cortês, Braz.	B3	88
São João Del Rei, Braz.	K3	88
São João do Araguaia, Braz.	C1	88
São João do Jaguaribe, Braz.	C6	88
São João do Piauí, Braz.	E4	88
São João dos Patos, Braz.	D4	88
São Joaquim, Braz.	D12	92
São Joaquim, Parque Nacional de, p.o.i., Braz.	D13	92
São Joaquim da Barra, Braz.	K1	88
São José, Braz.	C13	92
São José, stm., Braz.	J5	88
São José da Laje, Braz.	E7	88
São José das Piranhas, Braz.	D6	88
São José de Anauá, Braz.	G11	86
São José do Cedro, Braz.	C11	92
São José do Egito, Braz.	D7	88
São José do Gurupi, Braz.	A2	88
São José do Mipibu, Braz.	D8	88
São José do Peixe, Braz.	D4	88
São José do Rio Preto, Braz.	K1	88
São José dos Campos, Braz.	L3	88
São José dos Pinhais, Braz.	B13	92
São Leopoldo, Braz.	D12	92
São Lourenço, Braz.	L3	88
São Lourenço, Pantanal de, sw., Braz.	C5	90
São Lourenço do Sul, Braz.	E12	92
São Luís, Braz.	B3	88
São Luís do Curu, Braz.	B6	88
São Luís do Quitunde, Braz.	E8	88
São Luís Gonzaga, Braz.	D10	92
São Manuel, Braz.	L1	88
São Manuel, stm., Braz.	E6	84
São Marcos, stm., Braz.	I2	88
São Marcos, Baía de, b., Braz.	B3	88
São Mateus, Braz.	J6	88
São Mateus, Braço Norte, stm., Braz.	J5	88
São Mateus do Sul, Braz.	B12	92
São Miguel, Braz.	D6	88
São Miguel, i., Port.	C3	60
São Miguel do Araguaia, Braz.	F7	84
São Miguel d'Oeste, Braz.	C11	92
São Miguel do Guamá, Braz.	A2	88
São Miguel dos Campos, Braz.	E7	88
São Miguel do Tapuio, Braz.	C5	88
Saona, Isla, i., Dom. Rep.	C13	102
Saône, stm., Fr.	C10	18
Saône-et-Loire, state, Fr.	C10	18
Saoner, India	H7	54
São Nicolau, i., C.V.	k10	65a
São Nicolau, stm., Braz.	C5	88
São Paulo, Braz.	L2	88
São Paulo, state, Braz.	D7	90
São Paulo de Olivença, Braz.	D4	84
São Paulo do Potengi, Braz.	C7	88
São Pedro do Piauí, Braz.	C4	88
São Pedro do Sul, Port.	D2	20
São Raimundo das Mangabeiras, Braz.	D3	88
São Raimundo Nonato, Braz.	E4	88
São Romão, Braz.	I3	88
São Roque, Braz.	L2	88
São Roque, Cabo de, c., Braz.	C8	88
São Sebastião, Braz.	L3	88
São Sebastião, Ilha de, i., Braz.	L3	88
São Sebastião, Ponta, c., Moz.	C12	70
São Sebastião do Paraíso, Braz.	K2	88
São Sepé, Braz.	E11	92
São Simão, Braz.	K2	88
São Simão, Represa de, res., Braz.	C7	90
São Timóteo, Braz.	G4	88
São Tomé, Braz.	C7	88
São Tomé, S. Tom./P.	I6	64
São Tomé, i., S. Tom./P.	I6	64
São Tomé, Cabo de, c., Braz.	L5	88
São Tomé, Pico de, mtn., S. Tom./P.	I6	64
Sao Tome and Principe, ctry., Afr.	I6	64
Saoura, Oued, stm., Alg.	D4	64
São Valério, stm., Braz.	F1	88
São Vicente, Braz.	M2	88
São Vicente, i., C.V.	k9	65a
São Vicente, Cabo de, c., Port.	H1	20
Sapanca, Tur.	C13	28
Sape, Selat, strt., Indon.	H11	50
Sapele, Nig.	H6	64
Sapelo Island, i., Ga., U.S.	E4	116
Sápes, Port.	B8	28
Sapitwa, mtn., Mwi.	D6	68
Sapkina, stm., Russia	A14	10
Sapkina, stm., Russia	C26	8
Sapockin, Bela.	G6	10
Sappa Creek, stm., U.S.	A9	128
Sappa Creek, South Fork, stm., Ks., U.S.	B8	128
Sappho, Wa., U.S.	B2	136
Sapporo, Japan	C14	38
Sap Songkhla, Thale, l., Thai	I5	48
Saptakośī, stm., Nepal	E11	54
Sapudi, Pulau, i., Indon.	G9	50
Sapulpa, Ok., U.S.	A2	122
Sapwe, D.R.C.	G5	66
Saqqâra, Egypt	I2	58
Saqqâra, Pyramides de (Step Pyramid), hist., Egypt	I1	58
Saqqez, Iran	B6	56
Sarana, Baie, b., Qc., Can.	B11	110
Sarāb, Iran	B6	56
Saraburi, Thai	E5	48
Saracura, stm., Braz.	C4	130
Saragosa see Zaragoza, Spain	C10	20
Saraji, Austl.	D7	76
Sarakhs, Iran	B9	56
Saraktaš, Russia	D9	32
Saraland, Al., U.S.	G10	122
Saran', Kaz.	E12	32
Saran, Gunung, mtn., Indon.	D7	50
Saranac, Mi., U.S.	F4	112
Saranac, stm., N.Y., U.S.	F3	110
Saranda see Sarandë, Alb.	E13	24
Sarandë, Alb.	E13	24
Sarandi, Braz.	C11	92
Sarandi del Yi, Ur.	F10	92
Sarandí Grande, Ur.	F9	92
Sarangani Bay, b., Phil.	H5	52
Sarangani Islands, is., Phil.	H5	52
Sarangani Strait, strt., Phil.	H5	52
Sārangarh, India	H9	54
Saransk, Russia	D6	32
Saraphi, Thai	C4	48
Sarapul, Russia	C8	32
Sarāqib, Syria	C7	58
Sarare, stm., Ven.	D6	86
Sarasota, Fl., U.S.	I3	116
Sarata, Ukr.	C16	26
Saratoga, Ca., U.S.	F3	134
Saratoga, Tx., U.S.	G4	122
Saratoga, Wy., U.S.	B10	132
Saratoga Springs, N.Y., U.S.	G2	110
Saratov, Russia	D7	32
Saratov Reservoir see Saratovskoe vodohranilišče, res., Russia	D7	32
Saratovskoe vodohranilišče, res., Russia	D7	32
Sarāvān, Iran	D9	56
Saravan, Laos	E8	48
Saravena, Col.	D5	86
Sarawak, state, Malay.	B8	50
Sarawak, hist. reg., Malay.	C5	50
Saray, Tur.	B10	28
Saraya, Gui.	G2	64
Sarayevo see Sarajevo, Bos.	F5	26
Sarayköy, Tur.	F11	28
Sarayönü, Tur.	E15	28
Sarbāz, Iran	D9	56
Sarcelle, Passe de la, strt., N. Cal.	n16	79d
Sarcidano, reg., Italy	E3	24
Sarcoxie, Mo., U.S.	G3	120
Sárda (Mahākālī), stm., Asia	D8	54
Sardarpur, India	G5	54
Sardārshahr, India	D5	54
Sardegna, state, Italy	D4	24
Sardegna (Sardinia), i., Italy	D3	24
Sardinata, Col.	H11	102
Sardinia see Sardegna, state, Italy	D4	24
Sardinia see Sardegna, i., Italy	D3	24
Sardis, Al., U.S.	E12	122
Sardis, Ga., U.S.	D4	116
Sardis, Tn., U.S.	B10	122
Sardis, sci., Tur.	E10	28
Sardis Lake, res., Ms., U.S.	C9	122
Sardis Lake, res., Ok., U.S.	C3	122
Sardonem', Russia	E21	8
Sarek, mtn., Swe.	C7	8
Sareks Nationalpark, p.o.i., Swe.	C7	8
Sar-e Pol, Afg.	B10	56
Sarepta, La., U.S.	E5	122
Sargent, Ga., U.S.	D14	122
Sargent, Ne., U.S.	F13	126
Sargodha, Pak.	B4	54
Sarh, Chad	F3	62
Sārī, Iran	B7	56
Saría, i., Grc.	H10	28
Sarıgöl, Tur.	E11	28
Sarıkaya, Tur.	E15	28
Sariki, Malay.	B7	50
Sarina, Austl.	C7	76
Sariñena, Spain	C10	20
Sariska Tiger Reserve, India	E6	54
Sarita, Tx., U.S.	G10	130
Sariwŏn, Kor., N.	E6	38
Sariyar Baraji, res., Tur.	D14	28
Sark, i., Guern.	E6	14
Šarkauščyna, Bela.	E10	10
Şarkikaraağaç, Tur.	E14	28
Şarköy, Tur.	C10	28
Sarles, N.D., U.S.	F15	124
Sărmaşu, stm., Russia	D9	32
Sarmi, Indon.	F10	44
Sarmiento, Arg.	I3	90
Särna, Swe.	F5	8
Sarnia, On., Can.	F7	112
Sarny, Ukr.	D8	24
Sarolangun, Indon.	E3	50
Saronic Gulf see Saronikós Kólpos, b., Grc.	F6	28
Saronikós Kólpos, b., Grc.	F6	28
Saronno, Italy	E6	22
Saros Körfezi, b., Tur.	C9	28
Sárospatak, Hung.	A8	26
Sarowbi, Afg.	C10	56
Sarpsborg, Nor.	G4	8
Sarqan, Kaz.	E13	32
Sarralbe, Fr.	E15	14
Sarre (Saar), stm., Eur.	E15	14
Sarrebourg, Fr.	F16	14
Sarreguemines, Fr.	E15	14
Šarščin, Bela.	H14	10
Sartell, Mn., U.S.	F4	118
Sartène, Fr.	H14	18
Sarthe, state, Fr.	G9	14
Sarthe, stm., Fr.	G8	14
Sárvár, Hung.	B3	26
Sárviz, can., Hung.	C5	26
Saryg-Sep, Russia	D17	32
Sarykamysskoe ozero, l., Asia	A8	56
Saryözek, Kaz.	F13	32
Saryqopa köli, l., Kaz.	C10	32
Saryqopa köli, l., Kaz.	E10	32
Sarysū, stm., Kaz.	E10	32
Sary-Taš, Kyrg.	G12	32
Sarzana, Italy	F7	22
Sasabeneh, Eth.	F8	62
Sasaginnigak Lake, l., Mb., Can.	C17	124
Sasakwa, Ok., U.S.	C2	122
Sasamungga, Sol. Is.	d7	79b
Sāsarām, India	F10	54
Sásd, Hung.	C5	26
Sasebo, Japan	G2	40
Saskatchewan, state, Can.	E9	106
Saskatchewan, stm., Can.	E10	106
Saskatoon, Sk., Can.	B7	124
Saskylah, Russia	B11	34
Sasolburg, S. Afr.	E8	70
Sasovo, Russia	D6	32
Sassafras Mountain, mtn., U.S.	A3	116
Sassandra, C. Iv.	I3	64
Sassandra, stm., C. Iv.	I3	64
Sassari, Italy	D2	24
Sasso Marconi, Italy	F8	22
Sassuolo, Italy	F7	22
Sasyqköl, l., Ukr.	D16	26
Sasyqqöl köli, l., Kaz.	E14	32
Satadougou, Mali	G2	64
Satah Mountain, vol., B.C., Can.	D6	138
Sata-misaki, c., Japan	H3	40
Satāna, India	H5	54
Satão, Port.	D3	20
Sātāra, India	C1	53
Satara Ruskamp, S. Afr.	D10	70
Satélite, Mex.	C1	130
Satellite Beach, Fl., U.S.	H5	116
Satengar, Pulau, i., Indon.	G10	50
Satevó, Mex.	G1	130
Satevó, stm., Mex.	G1	130
Satilla, stm., Ga., U.S.	E4	116
Satiro Dias, Braz.	F6	88
Satīt (Tekezē), stm., Afr.	E7	62
Šatki, Russia	I20	8
Satluj see Sutlej, stm., Asia	C5	54
Satna, India	F8	54
Sátoraljaújhely, Hung.	A8	26
Sātpura Range, mts., India	H6	54
Satsuma-hantō, pen., Japan	H3	40
Satsunan-shotō, is., Japan	k19	39a
Sattahip, Thai	F5	48
Satuj, Indon.	F9	50
Satu Mare, Rom.	B9	26
Satu Mare, state, Rom.	B10	26
Satun, Thai	I4	48
Šatura, Russia	I18	8
Saturnino M. Laspiur, Arg.	E6	92
Satyamangalam, India	F3	53
Sauce, Arg.	E8	92
Sauce Corto, Arroyo, stm., Arg.	H7	92
Saucier, Ms., U.S.	G9	122
Saucillo, Mex.	A6	100
Sauðárkrókur, Ice.	k30	8a
Saudi Arabia, ctry., Asia	E5	56
Sauerland, reg., Ger.	E4	16
Saueruiná, stm., Braz.	F6	84
Saugatuck, Mi., U.S.	F3	112
Saugeen, stm., On., Can.	D8	112
Saugerties, N.Y., U.S.	B12	114
Saugstad, Mount, mtn., B.C., Can.	D4	138
Saujil, Arg.	D3	90
Sauk, stm., Mn., U.S.	F4	118
Sauk Centre, Mn., U.S.	F4	118
Sauk City, Wi., U.S.	H9	118
Sauk Rapids, Mn., U.S.	F4	118
Saukville, Wi., U.S.	E1	112
Saül, Fr. Gu.	C7	84
Sauldre, Canal de la, can., Fr.	B8	18
Saulgau, Ger.	I5	16
Saulieu, Fr.	G13	14
Sault aux Cochons, stm., Qc., Can.	A7	110
Sault-de-Vaucluse, Fr.	E11	18
Saulteaux, stm., Ab., Can.	B16	138
Sault Sainte Marie, On., Can.	B5	112
Sault Sainte Marie, Mi., U.S.	B5	112
Saumarez Reef, rf., Austl.	C9	76
Saumlaki, Indon.	G9	44
Saumur, Fr.	G8	14
Saunders Island, i., Falk. Is.	J4	90
Saunders Island, i., S. Geor.	K12	82
Sauquoit, N.Y., U.S.	B10	114
Saurimo, Ang.	B3	68
Sausar, India	H7	54
Sausu, Indon.	D12	50
Sautar, Ang.	C2	68
Sauteurs, Gren.	q10	105e
Sauveterre-de-Guyenne, Fr.	E5	18
Sauwald, for., Aus.	B10	22
Sauzal, Mex.	C1	130
Sava, stm., Eur.	F16	22
Savai'i, i., Samoa	g11	79c
Savalou, Benin	H5	64
Savanna, Il., U.S.	B7	120
Savanna, Ok., U.S.	C3	122
Savannah, Ga., U.S.	D4	116
Savannah, Tn., U.S.	B10	122
Savannah, stm., U.S.	D4	116
Savannah River Plant, sci., S.C., U.S.	C4	116
Savannah Sound, Bah.	K9	116
Savannakhét, Laos	D7	48
Savanna-la-Mar, Jam.	i12	104d
Savant Lake, On., Can.	A8	118
Savant Lake, l., On., Can.	A8	118
Sāvantvādi, India	D1	53
Savanūr, India	D2	53
Savaştepe, Tur.	D10	28
Savè, Benin	H5	64
Save (Sabi), stm., Afr.	B10	70
Sāveh, Iran	B7	56
Savelugu, Ghana	H4	64
Savenay, Fr.	G7	14
Saverdun, Fr.	F7	18
Savigliano, Italy	F4	22
Savino-Borisovskaja, Russia	E21	8
Savinskij, Russia	E19	8
Savissik, Grnld.	B13	141
Šavnik, Mont.	G6	26
Savoie, state, Fr.	D12	18
Savoie, hist. reg., Fr.	D12	18
Savo Island, i., Sol. Is.	e8	79b
Savona, B.C., Can.	F10	138
Savona, Italy	F5	22
Savonlinna, Fin.	F13	8
Savoy, Tx., U.S.	D2	122
Savoy see Savoie, hist. reg., Fr.	D12	18
Savran', Ukr.	A17	26
Savusavu Bay, b., Fiji	p19	79e
Savu Sea see Sawu, Laut, s., Indon.	G7	44
Sawah, Indon.	B9	50
Sawahlunto, Indon.	D2	50
Sawāi Mādhopur, India	E6	54
Sawākin, Sudan	D7	62
Sawankhalok, Thai	D4	48
Sawara, Japan	D13	40
Sawara, Japan	A11	40
Sawatch Range, mts., Co., U.S.	B2	128
Sawda', Jabal, mtn., Sau. Ar.	F5	56
Sawda', Jabal as-, hills, Libya	A4	62
Sawda', Qurnat as-, mtn., Leb.	D7	58
Sawdirī, Sudan	E5	62
Sawqirah, Oman	F8	56
Sawqirah, Dawhat, b., Oman	F8	56
Sawtooth National Recreation Area, p.o.i., Id., U.S.	F12	136
Sawu, Laut (Savu Sea), s., Indon.	G7	44
Sawu, Pulau, i., Indon.	H7	44
Sawyer, Mi., U.S.	G3	112
Sawyer, N.D., U.S.	F12	124
Saxby, stm., Austl.	B3	76
Saxon, Wi., U.S.	E8	118
Saxony see Sachsen, state, Ger.	F9	16
Saxony see Sachsen, hist. reg., Ger.	D5	16
Saxony-Anhalt see Sachsen-Anhalt, state, Ger.	D7	16
Saxton, Pa., U.S.	D7	114
Say, Niger	G5	64
Sayan Mountains, mts., Asia	D17	32
Sayaxché, Guat.	D2	102
Saydā (Sidon), Leb.	E6	58
Şaydā, state, Leb.	E6	58
Sāyḥūt, Yemen	F7	56
Saȳil, sci., Mex.	B3	102
Saylac, Som.	B8	66
Saylūn, Khirbat (Shiloh), hist., W.B.	F6	58
Sayram Hu, l., China	F14	32
Sayre, Ok., U.S.	F9	128
Sayre, Pa., U.S.	C9	114
Sayreville, N.J., U.S.	D11	114
Sayward, B.C., Can.	F5	138
Saywūn, Yemen	F6	56
Saza, Japan	F2	40
Sazan, i., Alb.	D13	24
Sba, Alg.	D4	64
Ščadryn, Bela.	H12	10
Scafell Pike, mtn., Eng., U.K.	G9	12
Scalea, Italy	E9	24
Scammon Bay, Ak., U.S.	D6	140
Scandia, Ks., U.S.	B11	128
Scanlon, Mn., U.S.	E6	118
Scapa Flow, b., Scot., U.K.	C9	12
Scapegoat Mountain, mtn., Mt., U.S.	C14	136
Scappoose, Or., U.S.	E3	136
Ščara, stm., Bela.	G8	10
Scarborough, St. K./N.	C2	105a
Scarborough, Trin.	r13	105f
Scarborough, Eng., U.K.	G12	12
Scarborough, ngh., Can., Can.	E10	112
Scărișoara, Rom.	F11	26
Ščelkovo, Russia	E20	10
Ščekino, Russia	F20	10
Scarja, Scot., U.K.	C5	12
Scawfell Island, i., Austl.	C7	76
Ščedro, Otok, i., Cro.	G13	22
Ščekino, Russia	F20	10
Ščelkovo, Russia	E20	10
Sceptre, Sk., Can.	D4	124
Ščerbakovo, Russia	C21	34
Ščerbinka, Russia	E20	10
Schaffhausen, Switz.	C5	22
Schaffhouse see Schaffhausen, Switz.	C5	22
Schärding, Aus.	B10	22
Schefferville, Qc., Can.	E17	106
Scheinfeld, Ger.	G6	16
Schelde, stm., Eur.	C13	14
Schell Creek Range, mtn., Nv., U.S.	D2	132
Schenectady, N.Y., U.S.	B11	114
Schenevus Creek, stm., N.Y., U.S.	B11	114
Schertz, Tx., U.S.	E9	130
Schiedam, Neth.	C13	14
Schiermonnikoog, i., Neth.	C2	16
Schiltigheim, Fr.	F16	14
Schio, Italy	E8	22
Schkeuditz, Ger.	E8	16
Schladming, Aus.	C10	22
Schlater, Ms., U.S.	D8	122
Schleiden, Ger.	F2	16
Schleswig, Ger.	B5	16
Schleswig, Ia., U.S.	B2	120
Schleswig-Holstein, state, Ger.	B6	16
Schlitz, Ger.	F5	16
Schlüchtern, Ger.	F5	16
Schmölln, Ger.	F8	16
Schneeberg, Ger.	F8	16
Schneeberg, mtn., Ger.	F7	16
Schneverdingen, Ger.	C5	16
Schœlcher, Mart.	k6	105c
Schofield, Wi., U.S.	G9	118
Schoharie, N.Y., U.S.	B11	114
Schoharie Creek, stm., N.Y., U.S.	B11	114
Schönebeck, Ger.	D7	16
Schongau, Ger.	I6	16
Schopfheim, Ger.	I3	16
Schorndorf, Ger.	H5	16
Schouten, Kepulauan, is., Indon.	F10	44
Schouten Island, i., Austl.	o14	77a
Schouten Islands, is., Pap. N. Gui.	a3	79a
Schramberg, Ger.	H4	16
Schreiber, On., Can.	C11	118
Schriever, La., U.S.	H8	122
Schroon Lake, N.Y., U.S.	F3	110
Schulenburg, Tx., U.S.	E11	130
Schultz Lake, l., Nu., Can.	C11	106
Schuyler, Va., U.S.	G7	114
Schuylkill, stm., Pa., U.S.	D10	114
Schuylkill Haven, Pa., U.S.	D9	114
Schwabach, Ger.	G7	16
Schwaben, hist. reg., Ger.	H5	16
Schwäbische Alb, mts., Ger.	H5	16
Schwäbisch Gmünd, Ger.	H5	16
Schwäbisch Hall, Ger.	G5	16
Schwabmünchen, Ger.	H6	16
Schwandorf in Bayern, Ger.	G7	16
Schwaner, Pegunungan, mts., Indon.	D8	50
Schwarzach im Pongau, Aus.	C10	22
Schwarzwald (Black Forest), mts., Ger.	H4	16
Schwatka Mountains, mts., Ak., U.S.	C8	140
Schwaz, Aus.	C8	22
Schwechat, Aus.	B13	22
Schwedt, Ger.	C10	16
Schweinfurt, Ger.	F5	16
Schweizer Nationalpark, p.o.i., Switz.	D7	22
Schweizer-Reineke, S. Afr.	E7	70
Schwerin, Ger.	C7	16
Schweriner See, l., Ger.	C7	16
Schwyz, Switz.	C5	22
Sciacca, Italy	G7	24
Scicli, Italy	H8	24
Scilly, Isles of, is., Eng., U.K.	L6	12
Scio, Oh., U.S.	D4	114
Scioto, stm., Oh., U.S.	F3	114
Ščit, mtn., Bos.	E13	26
Scobey, Mt., U.S.	F8	124
Scone, Austl.	I8	76
Scooba, Ms., U.S.	E10	122
Scoresby Land, reg., Grnld.	C21	141
Scoresbysund (Ittoqqortoormiit), Grnld.	C21	141
Scoresby Sund, strt., Grnld.	C21	141
Scotia Ridge, unds.	N8	144
Scotia Sea, s.	K10	82
Scotland, Ont., Can.	E9	112
Scotland, S.D., U.S.	D15	126
Scotland, Tx., U.S.	H10	128
Scotland, state, U.K.	E8	12
Scotlandville, La., U.S.	G7	122
Scotsburn, N.S., Can.	E14	110
Scott, Sk., Can.	B5	124
Scott, Ms., U.S.	D7	122
Scott, Cape, c., B.C., Can.	F2	138
Scott, Mount, mtn., Or., U.S.	H4	136
Scott City, Ks., U.S.	C7	128
Scott City, Mo., U.S.	G8	120
Scott Coast, cst., Ant.	C20	81
Scott Base, sci., Ant.	C22	81
Scott Island, i., Ant.	B23	81
Scott Islands, is., B.C., Can.	F1	138
Scott Peak, mtn., Id., U.S.	F14	136
Scott Reef, rf., Austl.	B4	74
Scotts Bluff National Monument, p.o.i., Ne., U.S.	F9	126
Scottsboro, Al., U.S.	C12	122
Scottsburg, In., U.S.	F12	120
Scottsdale, Austl.	n13	77a
Scottsdale, Az., U.S.	J5	132
Scotts Head, c., Dom.	j6	105c
Scotts Hill, Tn., U.S.	B10	122
Scottsville, Ky., U.S.	H11	120
Scottville, Mi., U.S.	E3	112
Scourie, Scot., U.K.	C7	12
Scout Lake, Sk., Can.	E8	124
Scranton, N.D., U.S.	A9	126
Scranton, Pa., U.S.	C10	114
Screven, Ga., U.S.	E3	116
Scribner, Ne., U.S.	J2	118
Scrub Island, i., Anguilla	A2	105a
Ščuče, Russia	C10	32
Ščučinsk see Shchūchinsk, Kaz.	D12	32
Ščučyn, Bela.	G7	10
Scugog, Lake, l., On., Can.	D11	112
Scunthorpe, Eng., U.K.	H12	12
Scutari, Lake, l., Eur.	H16	22
Ščytkavičy, Bela.	G10	10
Seabrook, Lake, l., Austl.	F3	74
Seaford, De., U.S.	F10	114
Seaforth, On., Can.	E8	112
Seahorse Point, c., Nu., Can.	C15	106
Sea Islands, is., U.S.	E5	116
Sea Isle City, N.J., U.S.	E11	114
Seal, stm., Mb., Can.	D11	106
Seal, Cape, c., S. Afr.	I6	70
Seal Lake, Austl.	J4	76
Sealark Channel, strt., Sol. Is.	e9	79b
Seal Cays, is., T./C. Is.	B12	102
Sealevel, N.C., U.S.	B9	116
Seal Island, i., N.S., Can.	G10	110
Sealy, Tx., U.S.	H2	122
Seara, Braz.	C11	92
Searcy, Ar., U.S.	B7	122
Searles Lake, l., Ca., U.S.	H8	134
Searsport, Me., U.S.	F7	110
Seaside, Ca., U.S.	G4	134
Seaside, Or., U.S.	D2	136
Seaside Park, N.J., U.S.	E11	114
Seattle, Wa., U.S.	C4	136
Sebago Lake, l., Me., U.S.	G6	110
Sebakung, Indon.	D10	50
Sebangan, Teluk, b., Indon.	E8	50
Sebangka, Pulau, i., Indon.	C4	50
Sebastian, Tx., U.S.	H10	130
Sebastian, Cape, c., Or., U.S.	A1	134
Sebastián Vizcaíno, Bahía, b., Mex.	A1	100
Sebastopol, Ca., U.S.	E3	134
Sebastopol, Ms., U.S.	E9	122
Sebdou, Alg.	C4	64
Sebeş Körös (Crișul Repede), stm., Eur.	B8	26
Sebewaing, Mi., U.S.	E6	112
Sebež, Russia	D11	10
Sebuku, Indon.	A10	50
Sebuku, Teluk, b., Indon.	A11	50
Sebuyau, Malay.	C7	50
Sechelt, B.C., Can.	G7	138
Sechura, Peru	E1	84
Sechura, Desierto de, des., Peru	E1	84
Seda, China	E5	36
Seda, Lith.	D5	10
Sedalia, Ab., Can.	B4	124
Sedalia, Mo., U.S.	F4	120
Sedan, Fr.	E13	14
Sedano, Russia	C18	32
Sedayu, Indon.	G8	50
Seddon, Kap, c., Grnld.	B14	141
Sedel'nikovo, Russia	C13	32
Séderon, Fr.	E11	18
Sedgewick, Ab., Can.	D19	138
Sedgwick, Co., U.S.	G10	126
Sedgwick, Ks., U.S.	D11	128
Sédhiou, Sen.	G1	64
Sedley, Sk., Can.	D10	124
Sedom (Sodom), hist., Isr.	G6	58
Sedova, Lith.	E7	10
Seduva, Lith.	E6	10
Seehausen, Ger.	D7	16
Seeheim, Nmb.	E3	70
Seeis, Nmb.	C3	70
Seekoei, stm., S. Afr.	G7	70
Seeley Lake, Mt., U.S.	C13	136
Seeleys Bay, On., Can.	C13	112
Sées, Fr.	F9	14
Seesen, Ger.	E6	16
Sefadu, S.L.	H2	64
Seferihisar, Tur.	E9	28
Segama, stm., Malay.	A11	50
Segamat, Malay.	K6	48
Segezha, Russia	E16	8
Seget, Indon.	F9	44
Segni, Italy	C7	24
Segorbe, Spain	E10	20
Ségou, Mali	G3	64
Segovary, Russia	E20	8
Segovia, Spain	D6	20
Segovia, co., Spain	C6	20
Segozero, ozero, l., Russia	E15	8
Segre, stm., Spain	C11	20
Seguam Island, i., Ak., U.S.	g24	140a
Séguédine, Niger	E7	64
Séguéla, C. Iv.	H3	64
Seguin, Tx., U.S.	E10	130
Segundo, stm., Arg.	E6	92
Segura, stm., Spain	F10	20
Segura, Sierra de, mts., Spain	G8	20
Séhithwa, Bots.	B6	70
Sehore, India	G6	54
Sehwān, Pak.	D10	56
Seibert, Co., U.S.	B6	128
Seikpyu, Myan.	B2	48
Seiland, i., Nor.	A10	8
Seiling, Ok., U.S.	E10	128
Seim, stm., Eur.	D4	32
Seinäjoki, Fin.	E10	8
Seine, stm., Mb., Can.	E17	124
Seine, stm., Fr.	F11	14
Seine, Baie de la, b., Fr.	E7	14
Seine-et-Marne, state, Fr.	F12	14
Seine-Maritime, state, Fr.	E9	14
Seixal, Port.	F1	20
Seixas, Ponta do, c., Braz.	D8	88
Sejmčan, Russia	D19	34
Sejny, Pol.	B19	16
Seka, Eth.	F7	62
Sekayu, Indon.	E3	50
Seki, Japan	D9	40
Sekiu, Wa., U.S.	B2	136
Sekoma, Bots.	D6	70
Sekondi, Ghana	I4	64
Sékota, Eth.	E7	62
Selatan, Tanjung, c., Indon.	F9	50
Selatpanjang, Indon.	C3	50
Selawik, Ak., U.S.	C8	140
Selawik Lake, l., Ak., U.S.	C7	140
Selayar, Pulau, i., Indon.	G12	50
Selayar, Selat, strt., Indon.	F12	50
Selb, Ger.	F8	16
Selbusjøen, l., Nor.	E4	8
Selby, Eng., U.K.	H11	12
Selby, S.D., U.S.	B12	126
Selbyville, De., U.S.	F10	114
Sel'co, Russia	G17	10
Sel'co, Russia	E19	8
Selçuk, Tur.	F10	28
Seldovia, Ak., U.S.	D9	140
Selebi-Phikwe, Bots.	C9	70
Selečnja, Russia	H17	10
Selehov, Russia	D18	32
Selemdža, stm., Russia	F14	34
Selemdžinsk, Russia	F15	34
Selenduma, Russia	F10	34
Selenge, D.R.C.	E3	66
Selenge, stm., Asia	G9	34
Selenicë, Alb.	D13	24
Selennjah, stm., Russia	C16	34
Sélestat, Fr.	F16	14
Seleznëvo, Russia	F13	8
Selfoss, Ice.	l29	8a
Selfridge, N.D., U.S.	A11	126
Seliger, ozero, l., Russia	C15	10
Seligman, Az., U.S.	H4	132
Selihova, zaliv, b., Russia	D20	34
Selimbau, Indon.	C8	50
Selinsgrove, Pa., U.S.	D8	114
Selinunte, sci., Italy	G6	24
Selišče, Russia	D16	10
Selišče, Russia	D16	10
Selizarovo, Russia	D17	124
Selkirk, Mb., Can.	D17	124
Selkirk, Scot., U.K.	F10	12
Selkirk Mountains, mts., N.A.	F13	138
Sellers, S.C., U.S.	B6	116
Sellersburg, In., U.S.	F12	120
Selles-sur-Cher, Fr.	G10	14
Selm, Ger.	E3	16
Selma, Al., U.S.	E11	122
Selma, Ca., U.S.	G6	134
Selma, N.C., U.S.	A7	116
Selmer, Tn., U.S.	B10	122
Selmont, Al., U.S.	E11	122
Selon', stm., Russia	B13	10
Selong, Indon.	H10	50
Selva, Arg.	D6	92
Selvagens, Ilhas, is., Port.	C1	64
Selvas, for., Braz.	F8	82
Selway, stm., Id., U.S.	D11	136
Selwyn, Austl.	C3	76
Selwyn, Passage, strt., Vanuatu	k16	79d
Selwyn Lake, l., Can.	D10	106
Selwyn Mountains, mts., Can.	C4	106
Selwyn Range, mts., Austl.	C3	76
Seman, stm., Alb.	D13	24
Semangka, Teluk, b., Indon.	F4	50
Semara, W. Sah.	D2	64
Semarang, Indon.	G7	50
Semayang, Kenohan, l., Indon.	D10	50
Sembakung, stm., Indon.	B10	50
Semcy, Russia	H16	10
Semenanjung Malaysia, hist. reg., Malay.	K6	48
Semeru, Gunung, vol., Indon.	H8	50
Semey (Semipalatinsk), Kaz.	D13	32
Semežava, Bela.	H10	10
Semichi Islands, is., Ak., U.S.	g21	140a
Semiluki, Russia	D5	32
Semily, Czech Rep.	F11	16
Seminary, Ms., U.S.	F9	122
Seminoe Reservoir, res., Wy., U.S.	A9	132
Seminole, Ok., U.S.	B2	122
Seminole, Tx., U.S.	B5	130
Seminole, Lake, res., U.S.	G14	122
Seminole Draw, stm., U.S.	B5	130
Semiozernoe, Kaz.	D10	32
Semipalatinsk see Semey, Kaz.	D13	32
Semitau, Indon.	C7	50
Semizbughy, Kaz.	D13	32
Semliki, stm., Afr.	D6	66
Semnān, Iran	B7	56
Semois, stm., Eur.	E13	14
Semporna, Malay.	A11	50
Semuda, Indon.	E8	50
Sena, Bol.	B3	90
Sên, stm., Camb.	F7	48
Senador Canedo, Braz.	I1	88
Senador Pompeu, Braz.	C6	88
Senaki, Geor.	F6	32
Sena Madureira, Braz.	E4	84
Senanayake Samudra, res., Sri L.	H5	53
Senanga, Zam.	D3	68
Senath, Mo., U.S.	H7	120
Senatobia, Ms., U.S.	C9	122
Sendai, Japan	H3	40
Sendai, Japan	A13	40
Sendelingsdrif, Nmb.	F3	70
Sendhwa, India	H5	54
Sendurjana, India	H7	54
Senduruhan, Indon.	D7	50
Senebui, Tanjung, c., Indon.	C3	50
Seneca, Il., U.S.	C9	120
Seneca, Ks., U.S.	E1	120
Seneca, Mo., U.S.	H3	120
Seneca, Or., U.S.	F8	136
Seneca, S.C., U.S.	B3	116
Seneca Falls, N.Y., U.S.	B9	114
Seneca Lake, l., N.Y., U.S.	B8	114
Senegal, ctry., Afr.	G2	64
Sénégal, stm., Afr.	F2	64
Sénékal, S. Afr.	F8	70
Senetosa, Capo di, c., Fr.	H14	18
Senetosa, Capo di (Senetosa, Punta di), c., Fr.	H14	18
Senftenberg, Ger.	E10	16
Sengés, Braz.	B13	92
Sênggê, stm., China	B8	54
Senhor do Bonfim, Braz.	F5	88
Senica, Slov.	H13	16
Senigallia, Italy	G10	22
Senj, Cro.	F11	22
Senja, i., Nor.	B7	8
Senkaku-shotō, is., Japan	F9	36
Senköy, Tur.	B7	58
Senlis, Fr.	E11	14
Senmonorom, Camb.	F8	48
Senneterre, Qc., Can.	F15	106
Senneville, Qc., Can.	E18	112
Senoia, Ga., U.S.	D14	122
Sens, Fr.	G12	14
Senta, Serb.	D7	26
Sentarum, Danau, l., Indon.	C7	50
Sentinel Butte, mtn., N.D., U.S.	A8	126
Seonāth, stm., India	H8	54

Name	Map Ref.	Page
Seoni, India	G7	54
Seoni Mālwa, India	G6	54
Seoul see Sŏul, Kor., S.	F7	38
Sepanjang, Pulau, i., Indon.	G9	50
Sepasu, Indon.	C10	50
Sepetiba, Baía de, b., Braz.	L4	88
Sepi, Sol. Is.	e8	79b
Sepik, strm., Pap. N. Gui.	a3	79a
Sepopol, Pol.	B17	16
Sept-Îles, Qc., Can.	E17	106
Sepúlveda, Spain	C7	20
Seputih, strm., Indon.	F4	50
Sequatchie, stm., Tn., U.S.	B13	122
Sequillo, stm., Spain	C5	20
Sequim, Wa., U.S.	B3	136
Sequoia National Park, p.o.i., Ca., U.S.	G7	134
Šerabad, Uzb.	B10	56
Serafimovič, Russia	E6	32
Seraing, Bel.	D14	14
Seram (Ceram), i., Indon.	F8	44
Seram, Laut (Ceram Sea), s., Indon.	F8	44
Serang, Indon.	G5	50
Serasan, Pulau, i., Indon.	B6	50
Serasan, Selat, strt., Indon.	B6	50
Serayevo see Sarajevo, Bos.	F5	26
Serbeulangit, Pegunungan, mts., Indon.	K3	48
Serbia, ctry., Eur.	F7	26
Serdo, Eth.	E8	62
Serdobsk, Russia	D6	32
Séré'ama, Mont, mtn., Vanuatu	i16	79d
Serebrjanye Prudy, Russia	F21	10
Serebrjansk, Russia	E14	32
Sered', Slov.	H13	16
Seredejskij, Russia	F18	10
Serëdka, Russia	B11	10
Seremban, Malay.	K5	48
Serengeti National Park, p.o.i., Tan.	E6	66
Serengeti Plain, pl., Tan.	E6	66
Serengka, Indon.	D7	50
Serenje, Zam.	C5	68
Seret (Siret), stm., Eur.	A12	26
Sergač, Russia	I21	8
Sergeevka, Kaz.	D11	32
Sergeevka, Russia	C10	38
Sergeja Kirova, ostrova, is., Russia	A6	34
Sergen, Tur.	B10	28
Sergiev Posad, Russia	D21	10
Serginskij, Russia	B10	32
Sergipe, state, Braz.	F7	88
Sergozero, ozero, l., Russia	C17	8
Seria, Bru.	A9	50
Serian, Malay.	C7	50
Seribudolok, Indon.	B1	50
Seridó, stm., Braz.	D7	88
Sérifos, i., Grc.	F7	28
Serik, Tur.	G14	28
Serinyol, Tur.	B7	58
Serio, strm., Italy	E6	22
Serkovo, Russia	A15	32
Šerlovaja Gora, Russia	F12	34
Serov, Russia	C10	32
Serowe, Bots.	C8	70
Serpejsk, Russia	F17	10
Serpentine Lakes, l., Austl.	E5	74
Serpents Mouth, strt.	C11	86
Serpuhov, Russia	F20	10
Serra, Braz.	K5	88
Serra Branca, Braz.	D7	88
Serra da Canastra, Parque Nacional da, p.o.i., Braz.	K2	88
Serra da Capivara, Parque Nacional da, p.o.i., Braz.	E4	88
Serra de Outes, Spain	B1	20
Serra do Navio, Braz.	C7	84
Serra do Salitre, Braz.	J2	88
Serra dos Órgãos, Parque Nacional da, p.o.i., Braz.	L4	88
Serrana, Braz.	K2	88
Serrana, Cayo de, unds., Col.	E7	102
Serrana Bank see Serrana, Cayo de, unds., Col.	E7	102
Serrania, Braz.	K2	88
Serranía de la Neblina, Parque Nacional, p.o.i., Ven.	G8	86
Serranilla, Banco see Serranilla, Cayo de, unds., Col.	E8	102
Serranilla, Cayo de, unds., Col.	E8	102
Serranilla Bank see Serranilla, Cayo de, unds., Col.	E8	102
Serrano, Banco see Serrana, Cayo de, unds., Col.	E7	102
Serra Talhada, Braz.	E8	88
Serres, Fr.	E11	18
Sérres, Grc.	B6	28
Serrezuela, Arg.	E5	92
Serrinha, Braz.	F6	88
Serrita, Braz.	D6	88
Sertânia, Braz.	E7	88
Sertãozinho, Braz.	K1	88
Serui, Indon.	F10	44
Serule, Bots.	B8	70
Serutu, Pulau, i., Indon.	D6	50
Seruwai, Indon.	J4	48
Sērxü, China	E4	36
Serýševo, Russia	F14	34
Sesayap, strm., Indon.	B10	50
Sesayap Lama, Indon.	B10	50
Seseganaga Lake, l., On., Can.	A8	118
Sese Islands, is., Ug.	E6	66
Sesfontein, Nmb.	D1	68
Sesheke, Zam.	D3	68
Sesia, stm., Italy	E5	22
Sesibu, Indon.	A10	50
Sessa Aurunca, Italy	C7	24
Sestao, Spain	A7	20
Sestri Levante, Italy	F6	22
Sestroreck, Russia	F14	8
Šešupė, stm., Eur.	F5	10
Šeta, Lith.	E7	10
Sète, Fr.	F9	18
Sete Barras, Braz.	B13	92
Sete Cidades, Parque Nacional da, p.o.i., Braz.	C5	88
Sete Lagoas, Braz.	J3	88
Sete Quedas, Parque Nacional da, p.o.i., Braz.	A11	92
Sete Quedas, Salto das (Guairá, Salto del), wtfl., S.A.	B10	92
Seth Ward, Tx., U.S.	G7	128
Seto, Japan	D10	40
Seto-naikai (Inland Sea), s., Japan	E5	40
Seton Portage, B.C., Can.	F8	138
Settat, Mor.	C3	64
Sette Cama, Gabon	E1	66
Sette-Daban, hrebet, mts., Russia	D16	34
Settlers, S. Afr.	D9	70
Setúbal, Port.	F1	20
Setúbal, Baía de b., Port.	F2	20
Seul, Lac, l., On., Can.	A6	118
Seul Choix Point, c., Mi., U.S.	C4	112
Seulimeum, Indon.	J2	48
Sevan, Lake see Sevana Lich, l., Arm.	A6	56
Sevana Lich, l., Arm.	A6	56
Sevastopol', Ukr.	G15	6
Ševelevskaja, Russia	F20	8
Seven Persons, Ab., Can.	E3	124
Seven Sisters Peaks, mtn., B.C., Can.	B2	138
Seventy Mile House, B.C., Can.	E9	138
Severn, stm., On., Can.	E12	106
Severn, stm., U.K.	J10	12
Severnaja Dvina (Northern Dvina), stm., Russia	E19	8
Severnaja Osetija, state, Russia	F6	32
Severnaja Sos'va, stm., Russia	B10	32
Severnaja Zemlja, is., Russia	B12	30
Severna Park, Md., U.S.	E9	114
Severnoe, Russia	C13	32
Severnye uvaly, hills, Russia	C7	32
Severnyj Ural, mts., Russia	B9	32
Severočeskij, state, Czech Rep.	F10	16
Severodvinsk (Molotovsk), Russia	D18	8
Severo-Enisejskij, Russia	B16	32
Severo-Kuril'sk, Russia	F20	34
Severomorsk, Russia	B15	8
Severo-Sibirskaja nizmennost' (North Siberian Lowland), pl., Russia	B6	34
Severoural'sk (Severouralsk), Russia	B9	32
Severo-Zadonsk, Russia	F21	10
Severy, Ks., U.S.	D12	128
Sevettijärvi, Fin.	B13	8
Sevier, stm., Ut., U.S.	D4	132
Sevier, East Fork, stm., Ut., U.S.	F5	132
Sevier Desert, des., Ut., U.S.	D4	132
Sevier Lake, l., Ut., U.S.	B6	98
Sevierville, Tn., U.S.	I2	114
Sevilla, Col.	E4	86
Sevilla, Spain	G5	20
Sevilla, co., Spain	G5	20
Seville see Sevilla, Spain	G5	20
Seville, Fl., U.S.	G4	116
Sevlievo, Blg.	F12	26
Sevnica, Slvn.	D5	54
Seward, Ak., U.S.	D10	140
Seward, Ne., U.S.	G15	126
Seward, Pa., U.S.	D7	114
Seward Peninsula, pen., Ak., U.S.	C7	140
Sexsmith, Ab., Can.	A12	138
Sextín, stm., Mex.	C6	100
Seybaplaya, Mex.	C2	102
Seychelles, ctry., Afr.	k12	69b
Seychelles, is., Sey.	k13	69b
Seydişehir, Tur.	F14	28
Seydisfjördur, Ice.	k32	8a
Seyhan (Sarus), stm., Tur.	B6	58
Seyhan Baraji, res., Tur.	A6	58
Seymour, Austl.	K6	76
Seymour, S. Afr.	H8	70
Seymour, Ct., U.S.	C12	114
Seymour, In., U.S.	F12	120
Seymour, Mo., U.S.	G5	120
Seymour, Tx., U.S.	H9	128
Seymour, Wi., U.S.	D1	112
Sežana, Slvn.	E10	22
Sézanne, Fr.	F12	14
Sfákia, Grc.	H7	28
Sfântu Gheorghe, Rom.	D12	26
Sfântu Gheorghe, Bratul, stm., Rom.	E16	26
Sfântu Gheorghe, Ostrovul, i., Rom.	D16	26
Sfax, Tun.	C7	64
's-Gravenhage (The Hague), Neth.	B13	14
Sha, stm., China	H7	42
Sha, stm., China	E6	42
Shaanxi, state, China	E3	42
Shabeelle (Shebelē Wenz, Wabē), stm., Afr.	D8	66
Shabunda, D.R.C.	E5	66
Shabwah, Yemen	F6	56
Shache (Yarkant), China	B12	56
Shackleton Ice Shelf, ice, Ant.	B14	81
Shackleton Range, mts., Ant.	D2	81
Shady Cove, Or., U.S.	A3	134
Shady Grove, Fl., U.S.	F2	116
Shadyside, Oh., U.S.	E5	114
Shageluk, Ak., U.S.	D8	140
Shag Rocks, r., S. Geor.	J8	90
Shāhābād, India	C3	53
Shāhābād, India	C6	54
Shāhābād, India	E7	54
Shāhābād, India	H5	54
Shah Alam, Malay.	K5	48
Shāhdādpur, Pak.	F2	54
Shahdol, India	G8	54
Shahe, China	J3	42
Shahezhen, China	A7	42
Shāhjahānpur, India	E7	54
Shāh Kot, Pak.	C4	54
Shāhpur, India	C3	53
Shāhpur, Pak.	D2	54
Shāhpura, India	E5	54
Shāhpura, India	G8	54
Shāhpura, India	F5	54
Shahr-e Kord, Iran	C7	56
Shaighālu, Pak.	C2	54
Shājāpur, India	G6	54
Shakawe, Bots.	D3	68
Shaker Heights, Oh., U.S.	G8	112
Shakespeare Island, i., On., Can.	B10	118
Shakhtinsk, Kaz.	E12	32
Shaki, Nig.	H5	64
Shakopee, Mn., U.S.	G5	118
Shakotan-hantō, pen., Japan	C14	38
Shaktoolik, Ak., U.S.	D7	140
Shala, Lake see Shala Hāyk', l., Eth.	F7	62
Shala Hāyk', l., Eth.	F7	62
Shalalth, B.C., Can.	F8	138
Shaler Mountains, mts., Can.	A8	106
Shallowater, Tx., U.S.	H6	128
Shalqar, Kaz.	E9	32
Shaluli Shan, mts., China	E4	36
Shām, Jabal ash-, mtn., Oman	E8	56
Shamattawa, Mb., Can.	D12	106
Shambe, Sudan	F6	62
Shambu, Eth.	F7	62
Shāmli, India	D6	54
Shamokin, Pa., U.S.	D9	114
Shamrock, Fl., U.S.	G2	116
Shamrock, Tx., U.S.	F8	128
Shamva, Zimb.	D5	68
Shan, state, Mya.	B4	48
Shancheng, China	D5	36
Shandan, China	D5	36
Shāndī, Sudan	D6	62
Shandong, state, China	C7	42
Shandong Bandao (Shantung Peninsula), pen., China	C9	42
Shandur Pass, p., Pak.	B11	56
Shangani, Zimb.	A9	70
Shangani, stm., Zimb.	D4	68
Shangbahe, China	F6	42
Shangcheng, China	F6	42
Shangch'iu see Shangqiu, China	D6	42
Shangchuan Dao, i., China	K5	42
Shangdu, China	C7	36
Shanghai, China	F9	42
Shanghai, state, China	F9	42
Shanghai Shih see Shanghai, state, China	F9	42
Shanghang, China	I7	42
Shanghe, China	C7	42
Shangrao see Shangrao, China	G7	42
Shangjin, China	E4	42
Shanglin, China	J3	42
Shangqing, China	I8	42
Shangqiu, China	D6	42
Shangrao, China	G7	42
Shangshui, China	E6	42
Shangsi, China	J2	42
Shangxian, China	E3	42
Shangyi, China	A6	42
Shangying, China	B7	38
Shangyou Shuiku, res., China	I6	42
Shangyu, China	F9	42
Shangzhi, China	B8	38
Shanhaiguan, China	A8	42
Shanhaikuan see Shanhaiguan, China	A8	42
Shanhetun, China	B7	38
Shankou, China	K3	42
Shannon, Il., U.S.	B8	120
Shannon, Ms., U.S.	C10	122
Shannon, stm., Ire.	I3	12
Shannon Ø, i., Grnld.	B22	141
Shannontown, S.C., U.S.	C5	116
Shanshan, China	C3	36
Shansi see Shanxi, state, China	B5	42
Shantar Islands see Šantarskie ostrova, is., Russia	E16	34
Shāntipur, India	G12	54
Shantou, China	J7	42
Shantung see Shandong, state, China	C7	42
Shantung Peninsula see Shandong Bandao, pen., China	C9	42
Shanwei, China	J6	42
Shanxi, state, China	B5	42
Shanxian, China	D7	42
Shanyang, China	E3	42
Shanyin, China	B5	42
Shaoguan, China	I5	42
Shaohing see Shaoxing, China	G9	42
Shaokuan see Shaoguan, China	G9	42
Shaoling, stm., China	C3	38
Shaowu, China	H7	42
Shaoxing, China	G9	42
Shaoyang, China	H4	42
Shaqqā, Syria	F7	58
Shaqrā', Sau. Ar.	D6	56
Shaqrā', Yemen	G6	56
Shar, Kaz.	E14	32
Shara, gora, mtn., Asia	A5	56
Sharbaqty, Kaz.	D13	32
Shardara, Kaz.	F11	32
Shardara bögeni, res., Asia	A10	56
Shari-dake, mtn., Japan	C16	38
Sharin Gol, Mong.	B6	36
Sharjah see Ash-Shāriqah, U.A.E.	D8	56
Shark Bay, b., Austl.	E2	74
Sharktooth Mountain, mtn., B.C., Can.	D5	106
Sharm el-Sheikh, Egypt	K5	58
Sharon, Pa., U.S.	C5	114
Sharon, Tn., U.S.	H9	120
Sharon, Wi., U.S.	B9	120
Sharpe, Lake, res., S.D., U.S.	C12	126
Sharpsville, In., U.S.	H3	112
Shashe, stm., Afr.	B9	70
Shashemenē, Eth.	F7	62
Shashi, China	F5	42
Shasi see Shashi, China	F5	42
Shasta, Mount, vol., Ca., U.S.	B3	134
Shasta Lake, res., Ca., U.S.	C3	134
Shāti', Wādī ash-, stm., Libya	B2	62
Shats'k, Ukr.	E19	16
Shats'kyi Pryrodnyi Natsional'nyi Park, p.o.i., Ukr.	E19	16
Shattuck, Ok., U.S.	E9	128
Shaunavon, Sk., Can.	E5	124
Shaw, Ms., U.S.	D8	122
Shawan, China	C2	36
Shawinigan, Qc., Can.	D4	110
Shawinigan-Sud, Qc., Can.	D4	110
Shawnee, Ks., U.S.	E3	120
Shawnee, Oh., U.S.	E3	114
Shawnee, Ok., U.S.	B2	122
Shawneetown, Il., U.S.	G9	120
Shawville, Qc., Can.	C13	112
Shaxian, China	H7	42
Shayang, China	F5	42
Shay Gap, Austl.	D4	74
Shaykh Miskin, Syria	F7	58
Shaykh 'Uthmān, Yemen	G6	56
Shchūchīnsk, Kaz.	D12	32
She, stm., China	F6	42
Shebele Wenz, Wabē (Shabeelle), stm., Afr.	C8	66
Sheberghān, Afg.	B10	56
Sheboygan, Wi., U.S.	E2	112
Sheboygan, stm., Wi., U.S.	E1	112
Sheboygan Falls, Wi., U.S.	E1	112
Shechem, sci., W.B.	F6	58
Shediac, N.B., Can.	D12	110
Sheenjek, stm., Ak., U.S.	C11	140
Sheep Mountain, mtn., Wy., U.S.	K2	132
Sheerness, Eng., U.K.	J13	12
Sheet Harbour, N.S., Can.	F14	110
Sheffield, Eng., U.K.	H11	12
Sheffield, Al., U.S.	C11	122
Sheffield, Ia., U.S.	B4	120
Sheffield, Il., U.S.	J9	118
Sheffield, Pa., U.S.	C7	114
Shegaon, India	H6	54
Shēha, Sk., Can.	C10	124
Shehong, China	F1	42
Sheikhpura, India	F10	54
Shekhūpura, Pak.	C5	54
Shekki see Zhongshan, China	J5	42
Shelbyville, Mo., U.S.	E5	120
Shelbyville, Tn., U.S.	B12	122
Shelbyville, Lake, res., Il., U.S.	E8	120
Sheldon, Ia., U.S.	H3	118
Sheldon, Mo., U.S.	G3	120
Shelek, Kaz.	F13	32
Shelekhov, Gulf of see Šelihova, zaliv, b., Russia	D20	34
Shelikof Strait, strt., Ak., U.S.	E9	140
Shell, stm., Mb., Can.	C12	124
Shellbrook, Sk., Can.	A7	124
Shell Creek, stm., Ne., U.S.	F15	126
Shelley, B.C., Can.	C8	138
Shellharbour, Austl.	J8	76
Shell Lake, Wi., U.S.	F7	118
Shellman, Ga., U.S.	F14	122
Shellmouth Dam, dam, Mb., Can.	D12	124
Shelton, Ct., U.S.	C12	114
Shelton, Ne., U.S.	G14	126
Shemogue, N.B., Can.	D12	110
Shemonaïkha, Kaz.	D14	32
Shemonaïkha see Šemonaihaa, Kaz.	D14	32
Shenandoah, Ia., U.S.	D2	120
Shenandoah, Va., U.S.	F7	114
Shenandoah, stm., U.S.	E8	114
Shenandoah, North Fork, stm., Va., U.S.	F7	114
Shenandoah, South Fork, stm., Va., U.S.	F7	114
Shenandoah National Park, p.o.i., Va., U.S.	F7	114
Shenber, Kaz.	E11	32
Shenchi, China	B4	42
Shencottah, India	G3	53
Shendam, Nig.	H6	64
Shenge, S.L.	H2	64
Shengsi Liedao, is., China	I5	38
Shengxian, China	G9	42
Shengze, China	F9	42
Shenjing, China	J5	42
Shenmu, China	B4	42
Shenqiu, China	E6	42
Shensi see Shaanxi, state, China	E3	42
Shenton, Mount, mtn., Austl.	E4	74
Shenyang (Mukden), China	D5	38
Shenzhen, China	J6	42
Sheoganj, India	F4	54
Sheopur, India	F6	54
Shepard, Ab., Can.	E17	138
Shepherd, Mi., U.S.	E5	112
Shepherd, state, Vanuatu	k17	79d
Shepherd, Îles, is., Vanuatu	k17	79d
Shepherdstown, W.V., U.S.	E7	114
Shepherdsville, Ky., U.S.	F12	120
Shepparton, Austl.	K5	76
Sheppey, Isle of, i., Eng., U.K.	J13	12
Sheqi, China	E5	42
Sherard, Cape, c., Nu., Can.	C10	141
Sherard Osborn Fjord, b., Grnld.	A14	141
Sherborne, Eng., U.K.	K10	12
Sherbro Island, i., S.L.	H2	64
Sherbrooke, N.S., Can.	E14	110
Sherbrooke, Qc., Can.	E5	110
Sherburn, Mn., U.S.	H4	118
Sherburne, N.Y., U.S.	B10	114
Sheridan, Ar., U.S.	C6	122
Sheridan, In., U.S.	H3	112
Sheridan, Or., U.S.	E3	136
Sheridan, Tx., U.S.	E11	130
Sheridan, Wy., U.S.	C6	126
Sherman, N.Y., U.S.	B6	114
Sherman, Tx., U.S.	D2	122
Sherman Mills, Me., U.S.	D8	110
Sherman Mountain, mtn., Ar., U.S.	I4	120
Sherman Station, Me., U.S.	E8	110
Sherpur, Bngl.	F12	54
Sherpur, Bngl.	F13	54
Sherridon, Mb., Can.	E10	106
Sherrill, N.Y., U.S.	E14	112
Shertallai, India	G3	53
's-Hertogenbosch, Neth.	C14	14
Sherwood, Ar., U.S.	C6	122
Sherwood, Oh., U.S.	C1	114
Sherwood, Tn., U.S.	B12	122
Sherwood Park, Ab., Can.	C17	138
Sherwood Shores, Tx., U.S.	D9	130
Shesh Gāv, Afg.	B2	54
Shetland Islands, is., Scot., U.K.	n17	12a
Shetrunji, stm., India	H3	54
Shexian, China	G8	42
Sheyang, China	E9	42
Sheyenne, N.D., U.S.	G14	124
Sheyenne, stm., N.D., U.S.	H16	124
Sheykhābād, Afg.	A2	54
Shiant Islands, is., Scot., U.K.	D6	12
Shibām, Yemen	F6	56
Shibata, Japan	B12	40
Shibīn el-Kôm, Egypt	H1	58
Shibing, China	H2	42
Shibukawa, Japan	C12	40
Shicheng, China	H7	42
Shickley, Ne., U.S.	G15	126
Shidai, China	F7	42
Shidao, China	C10	42
Shidler, Ok., U.S.	E12	128
Shieli, Kaz.	F11	32
Shiga, state, Japan	D9	40
Shigatse see Xigazê, China	D12	54
Shigouyi, China	C2	42
Shiguaigou, China	A4	42
Shihchiachuang see Shijiazhuang, China	C6	42
Shih-lu see Zhongshan, China	J5	42
Shihtsuishan see Shizuishan, China	B2	42
Shihung, S. Kor.	F7	38
Shijaku, Alb.	C13	24
Shijiazhuang, China	C6	42
Shijiu Hu, l., China	F8	42
Shikārpur, India	D5	53
Shikārpur, Pak.	E2	54
Shikohābād, India	E7	54
Shikoku, i., Japan	F5	40
Shikoku-sanchi, mts., Japan	F6	40
Shikotsu-ko, l., Japan	C14	38
Shiliguri, India	E12	54
Shilka, Russia	F12	34
Shilka, stm., Russia	F13	34
Shillong, India	F13	54
Shiloh see Saylūn, Khirbat, hist., W.B.	F6	58
Shilong, China	J5	42
Shimabara, Japan	G2	40
Shimada, Japan	E11	40
Shimane, state, Japan	D5	40
Shimbiris, mtn., Som.	B9	66
Shimian, China	F5	36
Shimizu, Japan	D11	40
Shimla, India	C6	54
Shimminato, Japan	C10	40
Shimoda, Japan	E12	40
Shimoga, India	E2	53
Shimoni, Kenya	E7	66
Shimonoseki, Japan	F3	40
Shimono-shima, i., Japan	E2	40
Shin, Loch, l., Scot., U.K.	C8	12
Shinano, stm., Japan	B11	40
Shindand, Afg.	C9	56
Shingbwiyang, Mya.	C8	46
Shingū, Japan	F9	40
Shingū, Japan	E7	40
Shingwidzi, S. Afr.	C10	70
Shingwidzi (Singuédeze), stm., Afr.	C10	70
Shinji-ko, l., Japan	D5	40
Shinjō, Japan	A13	40
Shinnston, W.V., U.S.	E6	114
Shinshiro, Japan	D10	40
Shinyanga, Tan.	E6	66
Shiocton, Wi., U.S.	G10	118
Shiogama, Japan	A14	40
Shiojiri, Japan	C10	40
Shiono-misaki, c., Japan	F8	40
Shioya-zaki, c., Japan	C13	40
Shiping, China	G5	36
Shiping, China	G2	42
Shipka Pass see Šipčenski Prohod, p., Blg.	G12	26
Shipman, Va., U.S.	G7	114
Shippegan, N.B., Can.	C12	110
Shippensburg, Pa., U.S.	D8	114
Shiprock, N.M., U.S.	G8	132
Ship Rock, mtn., N.M., U.S.	G8	132
Shipshaw, stm., Qc., Can.	B6	110
Shipu, China	G9	42
Shiquan, China	E2	42
Shirahama, Japan	F8	40
Shirakawa, Japan	B13	40
Shīrāz, Iran	D7	56
Shirbīn, Egypt	G2	58
Shiretoko-misaki, c., Japan	B16	38
Shīr Kūh, mtn., Iran	C7	56
Shirley, In., U.S.	I3	112
Shiroishi, Japan	A13	40
Shirone, Japan	B11	40
Shirpur, India	H5	54
Shirvān, Iran	B8	56
Shisanzhan, China	F14	34
Shishaldin Volcano, vol., Ak., U.S.	F7	140
Shishi, China	I8	42
Shishmaref, Ak., U.S.	C6	140
Shishou, China	G5	42
Shitang, China	I4	42
Shiv, India	E3	54
Shively, Ky., U.S.	F12	120
Shivpuri, India	F6	54
Shivta, Horvot (Subeita), sci., Isr.	H5	58
Shivwits Plateau, plat., Az., U.S.	G3	132
Shiwu, China	C6	38
Shixing, China	E4	42
Shizhu, China	G8	42
Shizugawa, Japan	A14	40
Shizui, China	C6	38
Shizunai, Japan	C15	38
Shizuoka, Japan	E11	40
Shizuoka, state, Japan	E10	40
Shkodër, Alb.	B13	24
Shkodra see Shkodër, Alb.	B13	24
Shkumbin, stm., Alb.	C14	24
Shō, stm., Japan	C10	40
Shoal, stm., Fl., U.S.	G12	122
Shoal Creek, stm., Mo., U.S.	E4	120
Shoal Creek, stm., U.S.	H3	120
Shoalhaven, stm., Austl.	J8	76
Shoal Lake, l., Can.	D3	118
Shoals, In., U.S.	F11	120
Shoalwater Bay, b., Austl.	D8	76
Shōbara, Japan	E6	40
Shōdo-shima, i., Japan	E7	40
Sholaqqorghan, Kaz.	F11	32
Sholingnur, India	E4	53
Shonzhy, Kaz.	F13	32
Shoqpar, Kaz.	F12	32
Shorāpur, India	C3	53
Shoreacres, B.C., Can.	G13	138
Shorewood, Wi., U.S.	E2	112
Shorkot, Pak.	C4	54
Shortandy, Kaz.	D12	32
Shortland Island, i., Sol. Is.	d6	79b
Shortland Islands, is., Sol. Is.	d6	79b
Shoshone, Id., U.S.	H12	136
Shoshone, stm., Wy., U.S.	C4	126
Shoshone, South Fork, stm., Wy., U.S.	G17	136
Shoshone Lake, l., Wy., U.S.	F15	136
Shoshone Mountains, mts., Nv., U.S.	E8	134
Shoshone Peak, mtn., Nv., U.S.	G9	134
Shoshone Range, mts., Nv., U.S.	C9	134
Shoshong, Bots.	C8	70
Shostka, Ukr.	D4	32
Shouchang, China	G8	42
Shouguang, China	C8	42
Shouning, China	H8	42
Shouxian, China	E7	42
Shouyang, China	C5	42
Show Low, Az., U.S.	I6	132
Shqipëria see Albania, ctry., Eur.	C14	24
Shreve, Oh., U.S.	D4	114
Shreveport, La., U.S.	E5	122
Shrewsbury, Eng., U.K.	I10	12
Shri Düngargarh, India	D5	54
Shri Mohangarh, India	E3	54
Shū, Kaz.	F12	32
Shū, stm., China	D8	42
Shuajingsi, China	E5	36
Shuangcheng, China	B7	38
Shuangfeng, China	H5	42
Shuanggou, China	D7	42
Shuangji, stm., China	D5	42
Shuangjiang, China	G4	36
Shuangliao, China	C5	38
Shuangshan, China	A4	42
Shuangshipu see Fengxian, China	E2	42
Shuangyashan, China	B11	36
Shubarqudyq, Kaz.	E9	32
Shubrā al-Kheima, Egypt	H1	58
Shubuta, Ms., U.S.	F10	122
Shucheng, China	F7	42
Shuibatang, China	H2	42
Shuicheng, China	F5	36
Shuiji, China	H7	42
Shuijingtang, China	H5	42
Shuikoushan, China	H4	42
Shuitou, China	I8	42
Shuiye, China	C6	42
Shujāābād, Pak.	D3	54
Shujālpur, India	G6	54
Shuksan, Mount, mtn., Wa., U.S.	B5	136
Shulan, China	B6	38
Shulaps Peak, mtn., B.C., Can.	F8	138
Shule, China	B12	56
Shule, stm., China	D4	36
Shumagin Islands, is., Ak., U.S.	F7	140
Shunchang, China	H7	42
Shunde, China	J5	42
Shungnak, Ak., U.S.	C8	140
Shunyi, China	B7	42
Shuqualak, Ms., U.S.	E10	122
Shūr, stm., Iran	C8	56
Shurugwi, Zimb.	D5	68
Shūshtar, Iran	C6	56
Shuswap, stm., B.C., Can.	F12	138
Shuswap Lake, l., B.C., Can.	F11	138
Shuwak, Sudan	E7	62
Shuyak Island, i., Ak., U.S.	E9	140
Shuyang, China	D8	42
Shwangliao see Liaoyuan, China	C6	38
Shwebo, Mya.	A2	48
Shwegun, Mya.	D3	48
Shwegyin, Mya.	D3	48
Shyghys-Qongyrat, Kaz.	E13	32
Shymkent, Kaz.	F11	32
Shyok, India	A7	54
Shyok, stm., Asia	B4	46
Si, stm., China	D7	42
Sia, Indon.	G9	44
Siahan Range, mts., Pak.	D9	56
Siak, strm., Indon.	C2	50
Siak Sri Indrapura, Indon.	C3	50
Siālkot, Pak.	B5	54
Siam see Thailand, ctry., Asia	E5	48
Siam, Gulf of see Thailand, Gulf of, b., Asia	G5	48
Sian see Xi'an, China	D3	42
Siangtan see Xiangtan, China	H5	42
Sianów, Pol.	B12	16
Siantan, Pulau, i., Indon.	B4	50
Siapa, stm., Ven.	G9	86
Siargao Island, i., Phil.	F6	52
Siasconset, Ma., U.S.	C15	114
Siasi, Phil.	H3	52
Siasi Island, i., Phil.	H3	52
Siasköten, ostrov, i., Russia	G19	34
Siau, Pulau, i., Indon.	E7	44
Šiauliai, Lith.	E6	10
Sibaj, Russia	D9	32
Sibayi, Lake, l., S. Afr.	E11	70
Šibenik, Cro.	G12	22
Siberia see Sibir', reg., Russia	C12	34
Siberut, Pulau, i., Indon.	D1	50
Sibi, Pak.	D10	56
Sibigo, Indon.	K2	48
Sibir', reg., Russia	C12	34
Sibircevo, Russia	B10	38
Sibirjakova, ostrov, i., Russia	B4	34
Sibiti, Congo	E2	66
Sibiu, Rom.	D11	26
Sibiu, state, Rom.	D11	26
Sibley, Ia., U.S.	H3	118
Sibley, La., U.S.	E5	122
Sibley, Ms., U.S.	F7	122
Sibley Peninsula, pen., On., Can.	C10	118
Sibolga, Indon.	C1	50
Sibsagar, India	C7	46
Sibu, Malay.	B7	50
Sibuguey Bay, b., Phil.	G4	52
Sibut, C.A.R.	C3	66
Sibutu Island, i., Phil.	H2	52
Sibutu Passage, strt., Asia	H2	52
Sibuyan Island, i., Phil.	D4	52
Sibuyan Sea, s., Phil.	D4	52
Sicapoo, Mount, mtn., Phil.	B3	52
Siccus, stm., Austl.	H2	76
Sichang see Xichang, China	F5	36
Si Chon, Thai.	H4	48
Sichuan, state, China	E5	36
Sichuan Pendi, bas., China	F1	42
Sichuanzhai, China	A5	48
Sicié, stm., Italy	F8	24
Sicilia (Sicily), i., Italy	G7	24
Sicily see Sicilia, state, Italy	F8	24
Sicily see Sicilia, i., Italy	G7	24
Sicily, Strait of, strt.	G5	24
Sicily Island, La., U.S.	F7	122
Sicuani, Peru	F3	84
Sidareja, Indon.	G6	50
Sidas, Indon.	C7	50
Siddhapur, India	G4	54
Siddipet, India	B4	53
Sidéradougou, Burkina	G4	64
Siderno, Italy	F10	24
Siderópolis, Braz.	D13	92
Sideros, Akra, c., Grc.	H9	28
Sidhi, India	F8	54
Sīdī Barrānī, Egypt	A5	62
Sidi Bel Abbès, Alg.	B4	64
Sidi-Ifni, Mor.	D2	64
Siding Spring Mountain, mtn., Austl.	H7	76
Sidirókastro, Grc.	B6	28
Sīdī Sālim, Egypt	G1	58
Sidlaghatta, India	E3	53
Sidley, Mount, mtn., Ant.	C28	81
Sidmouth, Eng., U.K.	K9	12
Sidnaw, Mi., U.S.	E10	118
Sidney, B.C., Can.	H7	138
Sidney, Ia., U.S.	D2	120
Sidney, Il., U.S.	D9	120
Sidney, N.Y., U.S.	B10	114
Sidney, Ne., U.S.	F10	126
Sidney, Oh., U.S.	D1	114
Sidney Lanier, Lake, res., Ga., U.S.	B2	116
Sidon see Şaydā, Leb.	E6	58
Sidorovsk, Russia	A14	32
Sidra see Surt, Khalīj, b., Libya	A3	62
Sidrolândia, Braz.	D6	90
Siedlce, Pol.	D18	16
Siedlce, state, Pol.	D17	16
Siegburg, Ger.	F3	16
Siegen, Ger.	E4	16
Siem Reap, Camb.	F6	48
Siemianowice Śląskie, Pol.	F15	16
Siemiatycze, Pol.	D18	16
Siena, Italy	G8	22
Sieradz, Pol.	E14	16
Sieradz, state, Pol.	E14	16
Sieraków, Pol.	D12	16
Sierpc, Pol.	D15	16
Sierra Blanca, Tx., U.S.	C2	130
Sierra Blanca Peak, mtn., N.M., U.S.	H3	128
Sierra Chica, Arg.	H7	92
Sierra Colorada, Arg.	H3	90
Sierra Gorda, Chile	D3	90
Sierra Grande, Arg.	H4	90
Sierra Leone, ctry., Afr.	H2	64
Sierra Mojada, Mex.	G4	130
Sierra Nevada, Parque Nacional, p.o.i., Ven.	C6	86
Sierra Vista, Az., U.S.	L6	132
Sierre, Switz.	D4	22
Siesta Key, Fl., U.S.	I3	116
Sífnos, i., Grc.	F7	28
Sifton, Mb., Can.	C13	124
Sigatoka, Fiji	q19	79e
Sigep, Indon.	D1	50
Sighetu Marmaţiei, Rom.	B10	26
Sighişoara, Rom.	C11	26
Siglan, Russia	E18	34
Sigli, Indon.	J2	48
Siglufjördur, Ice.	j30	8a
Signal Mountain, Tn., U.S.	B13	122
Signal Mountain, mtn., Vt., U.S.	F4	110
Signy, sci., Ant.	B36	81
Sigourney, Ia., U.S.	C5	120
Sigsig, Ec.	D2	84
Siguatepeque, Hond.	E4	102
Sigüenza, Spain	C8	20
Siguiri, Gui.	G3	64
Sigulda, Lat.	C7	10

Name	Map Ref.	Page
Sigurd, Ut., U.S.	E5	132
Siguri Falls, wtfl., Tan.	F7	66
Sihabuhabu, Dolok, mtn., Indon.	B1	50
Sihanoukville see Kâmpóng Saôm, Camb.	G6	48
Sihor, India.	H3	54
Sihorã, India	G8	54
Sihote-Alin', mts., Russia	E17	30
Sihtovo, Russia	E15	10
Sihui, China	J5	42
Siirt, Tur.	B5	56
Sija, Russia	E19	8
Sijunjung, Indon.	D2	50
Sikandarābād, India	D6	54
Sikanni Chief, stm., B.C., Can.	D6	106
Sikao, Thai.	I4	48
Sikar, India	E5	54
Sikasso, Mali	G3	64
Sikeston, Mo., U.S.	H8	120
Sihote-Alin Mountains see Sihote-Alin', mts., Russia	E17	30
Sikiang see Xi, stm., China	J5	42
Siking see Xi'an, China	D3	42
Sikinos, i., Grc.	G8	28
Sikkim, state, India.	E12	54
Sikonge, Tan.	F6	66
Sikotan, ostrov (Shikotan-tō), i., Russia	C17	38
Siktjah, Russia	B13	34
Sikuati, Malay.	G1	52
Sikyón, sci., Grc.	F5	28
Şil, stm., Spain	B3	20
Šila, Russia	E7	34
Šilalė Lith.	E5	10
Silao, Mex.	E8	100
Silas, Al., U.S.	F10	122
Silaut, Indon.	E2	50
Silay, Phil.	E4	52
Silchar, India	F14	54
Şile, Tur.	B12	28
Şiler City, N.C., U.S.	I6	114
Sileru, stm., India	C5	53
Silesia, hist. reg., Eur.	F13	16
Silettengiz koli, l., Kaz.	D12	32
Siletz, Or., U.S.	F3	136
Siletz, stm., Or., U.S.	F3	136
Silgadhī, Nepal	D8	54
Silghāt, India.	E14	54
Silhouette, i., Sey.	j13	69b
Siliana, Tun.	H3	24
Siliana, Oued, stm., Tun.	I3	24
Silifke, Tur.	B4	58
Silifng Co, l., China	E14	26
Silistra, Blg.	E14	26
Šilivri, Tur.	B11	28
Siljan, l., Swe.	F6	8
Šilka, Russia	F12	34
Šilka, stm., Russia	F12	34
Silkeborg, Den.	H3	8
Sillamäe, Est.	A10	10
Sillem Island, i., Nu., Can.	A16	106
Sillian, Aus.	D9	22
Sillon de Talbert, pen., Fr.	F5	14
Šiloviči, Russia	E15	10
Silsbee, Tx., U.S.	G4	122
Silton, Sk., Can.	D9	124
Siluas, Indon.	C6	50
Šilutė Lith.	E4	10
Silvassa, Braz.	H4	54
Silver, Tx., U.S.	B7	130
Silver Bank Passage, strt., N.A.	B12	102
Silver Bell, Az., U.S.	K5	132
Silver City, N.C., U.S.	B6	116
Silver City, N.M., U.S.	K8	132
Silver Creek, Ms., U.S.	F9	122
Silver Creek, Ne., U.S.	F15	126
Silver Creek, stm., Az., U.S.	I6	132
Silver Creek, stm., Or., U.S.	G7	136
Silverdale, Wa., U.S.	C4	136
Silver Lake, Ks., U.S.	E2	120
Silver Lake, Mn., U.S.	G4	118
Silver Lake, Wi., U.S.	F1	112
Silver Lake, l., Or., U.S.	G7	136
Silver Lake, l., Or., U.S.	G5	136
Silver Spring, Md., U.S.	E8	114
Silver Star Mountain, mtn., Wa., U.S.	B6	136
Silverthrone Mountain, vol., B.C., Can.	E4	138
Silverton, Austl.	H3	76
Silverton, B.C., Can.	G13	138
Silverton, Or., U.S.	F9	132
Silverton, Tx., U.S.	G7	128
Silvi, Italy	H11	22
Silvia, Col.	F3	86
Silvies, stm., Or., U.S.	G7	136
Šimanovsk, Russia	F14	34
Simao, China	A5	48
Simão Dias, Braz.	F6	88
Simav, Tur.	D11	28
Simav, stm., Tur.	C11	28
Simbach, Ger.	H8	16
Simbo Island, i., Sol. Is.	e7	79b
Simcoe, On., Can.	F9	112
Simcoe, Lake, l., On., Can.	D10	112
Simdega, India	G10	54
Simeria, Rom.	D10	26
Simeulue, Pulau, i., Indon.	K2	48
Simferopol', Ukr.	G15	6
Simikot, Nepal	C8	54
Similkameen, stm., N.A.	G10	138
Simití, Col.	D4	86
Simi Valley, Ca., U.S.	I7	134
Simizu see Shimizu, Japan	D11	40
Simla, Co., U.S.	B4	128
Simmern, Ger.	G3	16
Simmie, Sk., Can.	E5	124
Simms, Mt., U.S.	C15	136
Simnas, Lith.	F6	10
Simoca, Arg.	C5	92
Simões, Braz.	D5	88
Simojärvi, l., Fin.	C12	8
Simojovel, Mex.	G12	100
Simon, Lac, l., Qc., Can.	E1	110
Simonette, stm., Ab., Can.	A12	138
Simonoseki see Shimonoseki, Japan	F3	40
Simonstad see Simon's Town, S. Afr.	I4	70
Simon's Town, S. Afr.	I4	70
Simoom Sound, B.C., Can.	F4	138
Simpang, Indon.	D3	50
Simpang-kiri, stm., Indon.	K3	48
Simpson Desert, des., Austl.	D7	74
Simpson Island, i., On., Can.	C11	118
Simpson Peninsula, pen., Nu., Can.	B11	106
Simpson Strait, strt., Nu., Can.	B11	106
Simpsonville, S.C., U.S.	B3	116
Simrishamn, Swe.	I6	8
Simsonbaai, Neth. Ant.	A1	105a
Simunjan, Malay.	C7	50
Simušir, ostrov, i., Russia	G19	34
Sina, stm., India	B2	53
Sinabang, Indon.	K3	48
Sinai (Sīnā Peninsula), pen., Egypt.	J4	58
Sinai, Mount, vol., Gren.	q10	105e
Sinai, Mount, vol., Egypt.	J5	58
Sinaia, Rom.	D12	26
Sinai Peninsula see Sinai, pen., Egypt	J4	58
Sinaloa, state, Mex.	C5	100
Sinaloa, stm., Mex.	C5	100
Sinamaica, Ven.	B6	86
Sinan, China.	H3	42
Sinanpaşa, Tur.	E13	28
Sinawin, Libya	A2	62
Sincan, Tur.	D15	28
Since, Col.	B2	84
Sincelejo, Col.	C4	86
Sinch'ang-ŭp, Kor., N.	D8	38
Sin-ch'on, Kor., N.	E6	38
Sinclair, Wy., U.S.	B9	132
Sinclair, Lake, res., Ga., U.S.	C2	116
Sinclair Mills, B.C., Can.	B9	138
Sind, state, Pak.	F2	54
Sind, stm., India	F7	54
Sindañgan, Phil.	F4	52
Sindangbarang, Indon.	G5	50
Sindara, Gabon	E2	66
Sindari, India	F3	54
Sindelfingen, Ger.	H4	16
Sindhnūr, India	D3	53
Sindhuli Mārdi, Nepal	E10	54
Sindingale, Mya.	C2	48
Sindri, India	B10	54
Sines, Port.	G2	20
Sinfra, C. Iv.	H3	64
Singalamwe, Nmb.	D3	68
Singapore, Sing.	C3	50
Singapore, ctry., Asia	L6	48
Singapore, Strait of, strt., Asia.	C4	50
Singaraja, Indon.	H9	50
Sing Buri, Thai.	E5	48
Singen, Ger.	I4	16
Singida, Tan.	E6	66
Singitic Gulf see Agíou Órous, Kólpos, b., Grc.	C6	28
Singkaling Hkámti, Mya.	C8	46
Singkang, Indon.	F11	50
Singkawang, Indon.	D4	50
Singkep, Pulau, i., Indon.	D4	50
Singkil, Indon.	K3	48
Singkuang, Indon.	C1	50
Singleton, Austl.	I8	76
Singleton, Mount, mtn., Austl.	E3	74
Singuédeze (Shingwidzi), stm., Afr.	C10	70
Sining see Xining, China.	D5	36
Sinjai, Indon.	F12	50
Sinjai, stm., Eur.	D11	10
Sinjaja, stm., Russia	D14	34
Sinjuga, Russia	E12	34
Sinkāt, Sudan	D7	62
Sinkiang see Xinjiang, state, China	A5	46
Sinnamahoning, Pa., U.S.	C7	114
Sinnamary, Fr. Gu.	B7	84
Sinnar, India	B2	53
Sinnūris, Egypt	I1	58
Sinnyŏng, Kor., S.	C1	40
Sinoie, Lacul, l., Rom.	E15	26
Sinop, Tur.	A4	56
Sinsheim, Ger.	G4	16
Sinsiang see Xinxiang, China	D5	42
Sinskoe, Russia	D14	34
Sintang, Indon.	C7	50
Sint Christoffelberg, hill, Neth. Ant.	p21	104g
Sint Eustatius, i., Neth. Ant.	B1	105a
Sint Helenabaai, b., S. Afr.	H3	70
Sint Kruis, Neth. Ant.	p21	104g
Sint Maarten (Saint-Martin), i., N.A.	A1	105a
Sint Nicolaas, Aruba.	p20	104g
Sint-Niklaas, Bel.	C12	14
Sintra, Port.	F1	20
Sint-Truiden, Bel.	D14	14
Sinú, stm., Col.	C4	86
Sinŭiju, Kor., N.	D6	38
Sió, stm., Hung.	C5	26
Siocon, Phil.	F4	52
Siófok, Hung.	C5	26
Sion, Switz.	D4	22
Sioraoaluk, Grnld.	B12	141
Sioux Center, Ia., U.S.	H2	118
Sioux City, Ia., U.S.	B1	120
Sioux Falls, S.D., U.S.	H2	118
Sioux Lookout, On., Can.	A6	118
Sioux Narrows, On., Can.	B4	118
Sioux Rapids, Ia., U.S.	B2	120
Sipalay, Phil.	F4	52
Sipan, Otok, i., Cro.	H14	22
Sipapo, stm., Ven.	E8	86
Siparia, Trin.	s12	105f
Šipčenski Prohod (Shipka Pass), p., Blg.	G12	26
Sipicyno, Russia	F22	8
Siping, China.	C6	38
Sipiwesk Lake, l., Mb., Can.	D11	106
Siple, Mount, mtn., Ant.	C28	81
Siple Island, i., Ant.	C28	81
Si Prachan, Thai.	E4	48
Sipsey, stm., Al., U.S.	D10	122
Sipunskij, mys, c., Russia	F21	34
Sipura, Pulau, i., Indon.	E1	50
Siqueira Campos, Braz.	A12	92
Siquia, stm., Nic.	F5	102
Siquijor, Phil.	F4	52
Siquijor Island, i., Phil.	F4	52
Siquirres, C.R.	G6	102
Šira, India	E3	53
Šira, Russia	D16	32
Sira, stm., Nor.	G2	8
Si Racha, Thai.	F5	48
Siracusa, Italy	G9	24
Sirāhã, Nepal	E11	54
Sirājganj, Bngl.	F12	54
Sirdar, B.C., Can.	G14	138
Sir Douglas, Mount, mtn., Can.	F15	138
Siret, Rom.	B12	26
Siret (Seret), stm., Eur.	A12	26
Sīrhān, Wādī as-, val., Sau. Ar.	H8	58
Sirik, Tanjong, c., Malay.	B7	50
Sirikit Reservoir, res., Thai.	D5	48
Sirino, Monte, mtn., Italy	D9	24
Sir James MacBrien, Mount, mtn., N.T., Can.	C4	106
Sīrjān, Iran	C8	56
Sirkeli, Tur.	C15	28
Sirocina, India	F4	54
Sirohi, India	F4	54
Širokovo, Russia	C17	32
Sironj, India	F6	54
Sırpsındığı, Tur.	B9	28
Sirri, Jazīreh-ye, i., Iran	D7	56
Sirsa, India	D5	54
Sirsi, India.	E3	54
Sirsi, India.	D2	53
Sirsilla, India.	B4	53
Sirte, Gulf of see Surt, Khalīj, b., Libya	A3	62
Sir Timothy's Hill, hill, St. K./N.	C2	105a
Sirupa, stm., Mex.	F7	98
Sirvintos, Lith.	E7	10
Sisaba, mtn., Tan.	F6	66
Sisak, Cro.	E13	22
Si Sa Ket, Thai.	E7	48
Sishui, China	G7	42
Sisili, China	G7	42
Sisib Lake, l., Mb., Can.	B14	124
Sisimiut see Holsteinsborg, Grnld.	D15	141
Siskiyou Pass, p., Or., U.S.	A3	134
Sisseton, S.D., U.S.	F1	118
Sīstān, reg., Asia	C9	56
Sister Bay, Wi., U.S.	C2	112
Sisteron, Fr.	E11	18
Sisters, Or., U.S.	F5	136
Sistersville, W.V., U.S.	E5	114
Sit', stm., Russia	B20	10
Sitāmarhi, India.	E10	54
Sitāpur, India	E8	54
Siteia, Grc.	H9	28
Siteki, Swaz.	E10	70
Sitia see Siteia, Grc.	H9	28
Sithonía, pen., Grc.	C6	28
Sitidgi Lake, l., N.T., Can.	B4	106
Sítio d'Abadia, Braz.	H2	88
Sitka, Ak., U.S.	E12	140
Sitkalidak Island, i., Ak., U.S.	E9	140
Sittard, Neth.	C14	14
Sitten see Sion, Switz.	D4	22
Sittoung, stm., Mya.	C3	48
Sittwe, Mya.	D7	46
Siuri, India	G11	54
Siuslaw, stm., Or., U.S.	G3	136
Sivaganga, India	G4	53
Sivakāsi, India	G3	53
Sivaki, Russia	F14	34
Sīvas, Tur.	B4	56
Šiveluč, vulkan, vol., Russia	E21	34
Siverek, Tur.	B4	56
Siverskij, Russia	A12	10
Sivrihisar, Tur.	D14	28
Siwa, Egypt.	B5	62
Siwalik Range, mts., India	C6	54
Siwān, India	E10	54
Sixian, China	E7	42
Sixth Cataract see Sablūkah, Shallāl as-, wtfl., Sudan	D6	62
Siyang, China	E8	42
Sizuoka see Shizuoka, Japan	E11	40
Sjælland, i., Den.	I4	8
Sjalec, Bela.	G13	10
Sjamža, Russia	F19	8
Sjarheevičy, Bela.	G10	10
Sjas', stm., Russia	A15	10
Sjas'stroj, Russia	F15	8
Sjenica, Serb.	F7	26
Sjuzikozero, Russia	F17	8
Skærfjorden, b., Grnld.	B22	141
Skaftafell Nasjonalpark, p.o.i., Ice.	k31	8a
Skagafjördur, b., Ice.	j31	8a
Skagen, Den.	H4	8
Skagerrak, strt., Eur.	H3	8
Skagit, stm., N.A.	H8	138
Skagway, Ak., U.S.	E12	140
Skaistkalne, Lat.	D7	10
Skalbmierz, Pol.	F16	16
Skalino, Russia	G18	8
Skalistyj Golec, gora, mtn., Russia	E12	34
Skalka, l., Swe.	C8	8
Skåne, state, Swe.	H5	8
Skärdu, Pak.	B12	56
Skarszewy, Pol.	B14	16
Skarżysko-Kamienna, Pol.	E16	16
Skawina, Pol.	F15	16
Skeena, stm., B.C., Can.	B1	138
Skeena Crossing, B.C., Can.	A3	138
Skeena Mountains, mts., B.C., Can.	D5	106
Skegness, Eng., U.K.	H13	12
Skei, Nor.	F2	8
Skeleton Coast, cst., Nmb.	B1	70
Skellefteå, Swe.	D9	8
Skellefteälven, stm., Swe.	D8	8
Skellytown, Tx., U.S.	F7	128
Skerpyvore, Scot., U.K.	E5	12
Ski, Nor.	G4	8
Skiatook, Ok., U.S.	H1	120
Skibbereen, Ire.	J3	12
Skidal', Bela.	G7	10
Skiddaw, mtn., Eng., U.K.	G9	12
Skidmore, Tx., U.S.	F10	130
Skien, Nor.	G3	8
Skierniewice, Pol.	E16	16
Skierniewice, state, Pol.	D16	16
Skikda, Alg.	B6	64
Skilak Lake, l., Ak., U.S.	D9	140
Skillet Fork, stm., Il., U.S.	F9	120
Skinnastaðir, Ice.	j31	8a
Skipton, Austl.	K4	76
Skipton, Eng., U.K.	H10	12
Skive, Den.	H3	8
Skjálfandafljót, stm., Ice.	k31	8a
Sklad, Russia	B13	34
Šklou, Bela.	F13	10
Škofja Loka, Slvn.	D11	22
Skoganvarre, Nor.	B11	8
Skoganvarri see Skoganvarre, Nor.	B11	8
Skokie, Il., U.S.	F2	112
Skón, Camb.	F7	48
Skópelos, i., Grc.	D6	28
Skopin, Russia	D5	32
Skopje, Mac.	A4	28
Skopje see Skopje, Mac.	A4	28
Skórcz, Pol.	C14	16
Skövde, Swe.	G5	8
Skowhegan, Me., U.S.	F7	110
Skownan, Mb., Can.	C14	124
Skriplivka, Russia	C13	10
Skrudaliena, Lat.	E9	10
Skudeneshavn, Nor.	G1	8
Skukuza, S. Afr.	D10	70
Skull Valley, Az., U.S.	I4	132
Skuna, can., Ms., U.S.	D9	122
Skunk, stm., Ia., U.S.	C6	120
Skuodas, Lith.	D4	10
Skuratovskij, Russia	F20	10
Skwierzyna, Pol.	D11	16
Skye, Island of, i., Scot., U.K.	D6	12
Skyland, N.C., U.S.	A3	116
Skyring, Peninsula, pen., Chile.	I1	90
Skyring, Seno, strt., Chile.	J2	90
Skyros, i., Grc.	D8	28
Slabada, Bela.	G11	10
Slagelse, Den.	I4	8
Slagnäs, Swe.	D8	8
Slamet, Gunung, vol., Indon.	G6	50
Slancy, Russia	A11	10
Slānic, Rom.	D12	26
Slano, Cro.	H14	22
Slaný, Czech Rep.	F10	16
Slater, Ia., U.S.	C4	120
Slater, Mo., U.S.	E4	120
Slatina, Rom.	E12	26
Slaughter, La., U.S.	G7	122
Slaughter, Ia., U.S.	C4	116
Slave, stm., Can.	C12	106
Slave Coast, cst., Afr.	H5	64
Slave Lake, Ab., Can.	A16	138
Slavgorod, Russia	D13	32
Slavkov, Russia.	C9	38
Slavjanka, Russia	C10	38
Slavjansk-na-Kubani, Russia	E5	32
Slavkoviči, Russia	C12	10
Slavonia see Slavonija, hist. reg., Cro.	E14	22
Slavonija, hist. reg., Cro.	E14	22
Slavonski Brod, Cro.	E15	22
Slavuta, Ukr.	E16	6
Slawno, Pol.	B12	16
Slayton, Mn., U.S.	G3	118
Sleaford, Eng., U.K.	H12	12
Sledge, Ms., U.S.	C8	122
Sledzjuki, Bela.	G13	10
Sleeper Islands, is., Nu., Can.	D14	106
Sleeping Bear Dunes National Lakeshore, p.o.i., Mi., U.S.	D3	112
Sleepy Eye, Mn., U.S.	G4	118
Slesin, Pol.	D14	16
Slidell, La., U.S.	G9	122
Slide Mountain, mtn., N.Y., U.S.	B11	114
Sliema, Malta	I8	24
Slievekilmalta, mtn., Ire.	I4	12
Sligeach see Sligo, Ire.	G4	12
Sligo, Ire.	G4	12
Sligo, Pa., U.S.	C6	114
Sligo, state, Ire.	G4	12
Sligo Bay, b., Ire.	G4	12
Slinger, Wi., U.S.	H10	118
Slíno, ozero, l., Russia	C16	10
Slippery Rock, Pa., U.S.	C5	114
Slissel'burg, Russia	A13	10
Slitere Rezervāts, Lat.	C5	10
Sliven, Blg.	G13	26
Sljudjanka, Russia	D18	32
Sloan, Nv., U.S.	H1	132
Slobidka, Ukr.	B16	26
Slobodka, Russia.	F14	26
Slobozia, Mol.	C16	26
Slobozia, Rom.	E14	26
Slobozia, Rom.	F12	26
Slocan, B.C., Can.	G13	138
Slocan Lake, l., B.C., Can.	G13	138
Slocomb, Al., U.S.	F13	122
Slomniki, Pol.	F15	16
Slonim, Bela.	G8	10
Slough, Eng., U.K.	J12	12
Slovakia, ctry., Eur.	H14	16
Slovenia, ctry., Eur.	E11	22
Slovenija see Slovenia, ctry., Eur.	E11	22
Slovenské rudohorie, mts., Slov.	H15	16
Słowiński Park Narodowy, p.o.i., Pol.	B13	16
Słubice, Pol.	D10	16
Sluč, stm., Bela.	H10	10
Sluck, Bela.	G10	10
Šluknov, Czech Rep.	E10	16
Slupca, Pol.	D13	16
Slupia, stm., Pol.	B13	16
Slupsk (Stolp), Pol.	B13	16
Slupsk, state, Pol.	B13	16
Slutsk see Sluck, Bela.	G10	10
Småland, state, Swe.	H6	8
Smålandsfarvandet, b., Den.	I4	8
Smalininkai, Lith.	E5	10
Smaljavičy, Bela.	F10	10
Smallwood Reservoir, res., Nf., Can.	E18	106
Smalouka, Bela.	E13	10
Smarhon', Bela.	F9	10
Smederevo, Serb.	E7	26
Smeralda, Costa, cst., Italy	C3	24
Smethport, Pa., U.S.	C7	114
Šmidovič, Russia	G15	34
Šmidta, poluostrov, pen., Russia	F16	10
Smigiel, Pol.	D12	16
Smila, Ukr.	E16	6
Smiley, Sk., Can.	C4	124
Smiltene, Lat.	C8	10
Smith, Ab., Can.	A16	138
Smith, stm., Ca., U.S.	B2	134
Smith, stm., Mt., U.S.	C15	136
Smith, stm., Or., U.S.	G3	136
Smith, stm., U.S.	H5	114
Smith Arm, b., N.T., Can.	B6	106
Smith Bay, b., Nu., Can.	B10	141
Smith Bay, b., Ak., U.S.	B8	140
Smith Canyon, p., Co., U.S.	D5	128
Smithers, B.C., Can.	B3	138
Smithfield, S. Afr.	G8	70
Smithfield, Ut., U.S.	A7	116
Smithfield, N.C., U.S.	A7	116
Smith Island see Sumisu-jima, i., Japan	E13	36
Smith Island, i., N.C., U.S.	C8	116
Smithland, Ky., U.S.	G9	120
Smith Mountain Lake, res., Va., U.S.	G6	114
Smith Point, N.J., U.S.	E13	110
Smith River, B.C., Can.	B1	134
Smith River, Ca., U.S.	B1	134
Smiths, Al., U.S.	E13	122
Smiths Falls, On., Can.	D13	112
Smiths Grove, Ky., U.S.	G11	120
Smithville, Ga., U.S.	E1	116
Smithville, Ms., U.S.	C10	122
Smithville, Tn., U.S.	I12	120
Smithville, Tx., U.S.	D10	130
Smjadovo, Blg.	F13	26
Smoke Creek Desert, des., Nv., U.S.	C6	134
Smokey, Cape, c., N.S., Can.	D16	110
Smoky, stm., Ab., Can.	A12	138
Smoky Cape, c., Austl.	H9	76
Smoky Dome, mtn., Id., U.S.	G12	136
Smoky Hill, stm., U.S.	B7	128
Smoky Hill, North Fork, stm., U.S.	B18	128
Smoky Lake, Ab., Can.	E2	8
Smoke Mountains see Great Smoky Mountains, mts., U.S.	F15	10
Smolensk, Russia	E10	32
Smolensk, co., Russia	B14	34
Smolensk, oblast', co., Russia	F16	10
Smolenskaja-Moskovskaja vozvyšennost', plat., Eur.	F16	10
Smolenskaja oblast', co., Russia	F15	10
Smoljan, Blg.	H11	26
Smolskoje, Russia	B8	38
Smoothrock Lake, l., On., Can.	A9	118
Smorodovka, Russia	C12	10
Smyrna see İzmir, Tur.	E10	28
Smyrna, Ga., U.S.	D14	122
Smyrna, Tn., U.S.	I11	120
Smythe, Mount, mtn., B.C., Can.	D6	106
Snaefell, mtn., Isle of Man	G8	12
Snæfellsnes, pen., Ice.	k28	8a
Snag, Yk., Can.	C3	106
Snake, stm., Mn., U.S.	E5	118
Snake, stm., Ne., U.S.	E11	126
Snake, stm., U.S.	D7	108
Snake, stm., Yk., Can.	B4	126
Snake River Plain, pl., Id., U.S.	D3	132
Snake Valley, val., U.S.	G4	134
Snåsavatnet, l., Nor.	D4	8
Sneads, Fl., U.S.	G14	122
Sneedville, Tn., U.S.	A14	14
Sneek, Neth.	F11	16
Śniardwy, Jezioro, l., Pol.	C17	16
Sniatyn, Ukr.	H15	18
Snipe Lake, l., Ab., Can.	A14	138
Snjadin, Bela.	H11	10
Snøhetta, mtn., Nor.	E3	8
Snohomish, Wa., U.S.	C4	136
Snoqualmie Pass, p., Wa., U.S.	C5	136
Snøtinden, mtn., Nor.	C5	8
Snov, stm., Eur.	H15	10
Snover, Mi., U.S.	E7	112
Snowbird Lake, l., N.T., Can.	C10	106
Snowdon, mtn., Wales, U.K.	H8	12
Snowdonia National Park, p.o.i., Wales, U.K.	I8	12
Snowflake, Az., U.S.	I6	132
Snow Hill, Md., U.S.	F10	114
Snow Hill, N.C., U.S.	A8	116
Snow Lake, Mb., Can.	E10	106
Snowmass Mountain, mtn., Co., U.S.	D9	132
Snow Mountain, mtn., Ca., U.S.	D3	134
Snowtown, Austl.	I2	76
Snowy, stm., Austl.	K7	76
Snowy Mountain, mtn., N.Y., U.S.	G2	110
Snowy Mountains, mts., Austl.	K7	76
Snowy River National Park, p.o.i., Austl.	K6	76
Snudl, Camb.	F8	48
Snyder, Tx., U.S.	B7	130
Soacha, Col.	E4	86
Soalala, Madag.	D8	68
Soap Lake, Wa., U.S.	C7	136
Soavinandriana, Madag.	D8	68
Sobaek-sanmaek, mts., Kor., S.	C1	40
Sobeslav, Czech Rep.	G10	16
Sobinka, Russia	I19	8
Sobradinho, Braz.	D11	92
Sobradinho, Represa de, res., Braz.	E5	88
Sobral, Braz.	B5	88
Sobrance, Slov.	H18	16
Sobrarbe, hist. reg., Spain	B10	20
Sochaczew, Pol.	D16	16
Soch'e see Shache, China.	B12	56
Soči, Russia	F5	32
Société, Archipel de la (Society Islands), is., Fr. Poly.	E11	72
Society Hill, S.C., U.S.	B6	116
Society Islands see Société, Archipel de la, is., Fr. Poly.	E11	72
Soco, stm., Dom. Rep.	C13	102
Socompa, Paso (Socompa, Portezuelo de), p., S.A.	B3	92
Socompa, Portezuelo de (Socompa, Paso), p., S.A.	B3	92
Socorro, Col.	D5	86
Socorro, N.M., U.S.	I10	132
Socorro, Tx., U.S.	C1	130
Socorro, Isla, i., Mex.	F3	100
Socotra see Suquţrā, i., Yemen	G8	56
Soc Trang, Viet.	H8	48
Socuéllamos, Spain	E8	20
Soda Creek, B.C., Can.	D8	138
Soda Springs, Id., U.S.	H15	136
Söderhamn, Swe.	F7	8
Södermanland, state, Swe.	G7	8
Södertälje, Swe.	G7	8
Sodo, Eth.	F7	62
Sodom see Sedom, hist., Isr.	G6	58
Sodus, N.Y., U.S.	E12	112
Soekmekaar, S. Afr.	C9	70
Soest, Ger.	E4	16
Soest, Neth.	B14	14
Sofala, Moz.	B12	70
Sofala, state, Moz.	B12	70
Sofia see Sofija, Blg.	G10	26
Sofiivka, Ukr.	E4	32
Sofija (Sofia), Blg.	G10	26
Sofija, state, Blg.	G10	26
Sofijsk, Russia	F16	34
Sofjanga, Russia	D14	8
Sofrino, Russia	D9	32
Sofronovo, Col.	E5	86
Sogamoso, stm., Col.	D5	86
Soğanlı, stm., Tur.	C15	28
Sogcho see Sokch'o, Kor., S.	A1	40
Sogda, Russia	F15	34
Sognefjorden, b., Nor.	F1	8
Sogn og Fjordane, state, Nor.	F2	8
Sogod, Phil.	E5	52
Sogo Nur, l., China	C5	36
Sogoža, stm., Russia	B22	10
Sogruma Milli Parkı, p.o.i., Tur.	F12	28
Söğüt Gölü, l., Tur.	F12	28
Söğütlü, Tur.	C13	28
Sog Xian, China	E3	36
Sohāgpur, India	G6	54
Sohar see Şuḥār, Oman.	E8	56
Sohna, India	D6	54
Sŏho, stm., China	D9	36
Soignies, Bel.	D12	14
Sointula, B.C., Can.	F4	138
Soira, mtn., Erit.	E7	62
Soissons, Fr.	E12	14
Sojana, Russia	D20	8
Sojat, India	F4	54
Sojoši-man, b., Kor., N.	E6	38
Sokch'o, Kor., S.	A1	40
Söke, Tur.	F10	28
Sokele, D.R.C.	F4	66
Sokodé, Togo	H5	64
Sokol, Russia	G19	8
Sokol, Russia	B14	34
Sokolka, Pol.	C19	16
Sokolov, Czech Rep.	F8	16
Sokol'niki, Russia	G16	10
Sokoł-nyki, Russia.	G16	10
Sokołów Małopolski, Pol.	F18	16
Sokone, Sen.	G1	64
Sokoto, Nig.	G5	64
Sokoto, state, Nig.	G5	64
Sokyriany, Ukr.	A13	26
Sol, Costa del, cst., Spain	H7	20
Sola, Vanuatu	i16	79d
Solacolu, Kenya.	D7	66
Solai, Kenya.	D7	66
Solana, Phil.	B3	52
Solāpur, India	C2	53
Solca, Rom.	B12	26
Sol'cy, Russia	B14	10
Soldanı Gölü, l., Tur.	C12	28
Soldiers Grove, Wi., U.S.	H8	118
Soldotna, Ak., U.S.	D9	140
Soledad, Ca., U.S.	G4	134
Soledad, Col.	B5	86
Soledad, Picacho, mtn., Mex.	B5	100
Soledade, Braz.	D11	92
Soledad Díez Gutiérrez, Mex.	D8	100
Soledade, Braz.	E2	88
Solen, N.D., U.S.	A12	126
Soleure see Solothurn, Switz.	C4	22
Solginskij, Russia	E19	8
Soligorsk see Salihorsk, Bela.	H10	10
Solihull, Eng., U.K.	I11	12
Solikamsk, Russia	C9	32
Sol'-Ileck, Russia	D8	32
Soliman, Tun.	H4	24
Solingen, Ger.	E3	16
Solis, Russia	B14	10
Sollefteå, Swe.	E7	8
Sollentuna, Swe.	G7	8
Sóller, Spain	E13	20
Solnečnogorsk, Russia	D19	10
Sologne, reg., Fr.	G10	14
Solok, Indon.	D2	50
Solomennoe, Russia	F16	8
Solomon, Az., U.S.	K7	132
Solomon, stm., Ks., U.S.	B11	128
Solomon, North Fork, stm., Ks., U.S.	B10	128
Solomon, South Fork, stm., Ks., U.S.	B10	128
Solomon Basin, unds.	D7	72
Solomon Islands, i., Oc.	I18	142
Solomon Islands, is., Oc.	d7	79b
Solomon Sea, s., Oc.	D6	72
Solomon's Pools see Sulaymān, Birak, sci., W.B.	G5	58
Solon, China	B9	36
Solon, Ia., U.S.	C6	120
Solon Springs, Wi., U.S.	F7	110
Solothurn, Switz.	C4	22
Solovecskie ostrova, is., Russia	D16	8
Solov'evsk, Russia	F12	34
Solov'evsk, Russia	F13	34
Solsona, Spain	C12	20
Šolta, Otok, i., Cro.	G13	22
Soltānābād, Iran	B8	56
Soltau, Ger.	C6	16
Solvang, Ca., U.S.	I5	134
Solvay, N.Y., U.S.	A9	114
Solvychegodsk, Russia	F22	8
Solway Firth, b., U.K.	G9	12
Solwezi, Zam.	C4	68
Solza, Russia	D18	8
Sóma, Tur.	D10	28
Somabhula, Zimb.	D4	68
Somalia, ctry., Afr.	D9	66
Somali Basin, unds.	I8	142
Somaliland see Somalia, Afr.	D9	66
Somali Republic see Somalia, ctry., Afr.	D9	66
Sombo, Ang.	B3	68
Sombor, Serb.	D6	26
Sombrerete, Mex.	D7	100
Sombreretillo, Mex.	H7	130
Sombrero Channel, strt., India	G7	46
Sombrio, Braz.	D13	92
Sombrio, Lagoa do, l., Braz.	D13	92
Somdari, India	F4	54
Somerset, Austl.	n12	77a
Somerset, Co., U.S.	E9	132
Somerset, Ky., U.S.	G13	120
Somerset, Oh., U.S.	E3	114
Somerset, Pa., U.S.	D6	114
Somerset, Tx., U.S.	E9	130
Somerset East, S. Afr.	H7	70
Somerset Island, i., Nu., Can.	A12	106
Somerset West, S. Afr.	I4	70
Somers Point, N.J., U.S.	E11	114
Somersworth, N.H., U.S.	G5	110
Somerton, Az., U.S.	K2	132
Somerville, N.J., U.S.	D11	114
Somerville, Tn., U.S.	B9	122
Somerville, Tx., U.S.	G2	122
Somerville Lake, res., Tx., U.S.	D11	130
Someş (Szamos), stm., Eur.	B9	26
Somino, Russia	A17	10
Somme, state, Fr.	D11	14
Somme, stm., Fr.	E11	14
Somme, Baie de la, b., Fr.	D10	14
Sommen, l., Swe.	H6	8
Sömmerda, Ger.	E7	16
Somogy, state, Hung.	C4	26
Somosierra, Puerto de, p., Spain	C7	20
Somosomo, Fiji	p20	79e
Somosomo Strait, strt., Fiji	p19	79e
Somoto, Nic.	F4	102
Somovo, Russia	H17	10
Somport, Col du (Somport, Puerto de), p., Eur.	G5	18
Somport, Puerto de (Somport, Col du), p., Eur.	F13	14
Sompuis, Fr.	F13	14
Son, stm., India	F10	54
Sonāmukhi, India	A5	54
Sonāmukhi, India	G11	54
Sonari, India.	G11	54
Sŏnch'ŏn-ŭp, Kor., N.	E6	38
Sönderborg, Den.	I3	8
Sondershausen, Ger.	E6	16
Søndre Strømfjord, Grnld.	D15	141
Sondrio, Italy.	D6	22
Sonepur, India	H9	54
Song, Nig.	H7	64
Song Bay Hap, Cua, b., Viet.	H7	48
Song Cau, Viet.	F9	48
Song Da see Black, stm., Asia	D9	46
Songe, Nor.	G3	8
Songea, Tan.	G7	66
Song Hong see Red, stm., Asia	D9	46
Songhua, stm., China	B11	36
Songhua Hu, res., China	C7	38
Songjiang, China	F9	42
Songjŏng, Kor., S.	D1	40
Songkhla, Thai.	I5	48
Songkhram, stm., Thai.	D6	48
Songlinba, China.	C8	48
Songnam, Kor., S.	F7	38
Songpan, China	E5	36
Songnim, Kor., N.	E6	38
Songpan, China	E5	36
Song Phi Nong, Thai.	E4	48
Songxi, China	H8	42
Songxian, China	D4	42
Song Youqi, China	C7	36
Sonid Zuoqi, China	C7	36
Sonīpat, India.	D6	54
Son La, Viet.	D6	48
Sonmiāni, Pak.	D10	56
Sonmiāni Bay, b., Pak.	D10	56
Sonning, Eng., U.K.	I11	12
Sonningdale, Sk., Can.	B6	124
Sono, stm., Braz.	E1	88
Sono, stm., Braz.	E1	88
Sonora, Ca., U.S.	F5	134
Sonora, Tx., U.S.	D7	130
Sonora, state, Mex.	G7	98
Sonora, stm., Mex.	G7	98
Sonora, Desierto de, des., N.A.	F6	98
Sonoyta, Mex.	F6	98
Sonqor, Kor., S.	C1	40
Sonsón, Col.	E4	86
Sonsonate, El Sal.	F3	102
Sonsorol Islands, is., Palau	D9	44
Sonstraal, S. Afr.	E6	70
Son Tay, Viet.	B7	48
Soochow see Suzhou, China	F9	42
Soonchon see Suncheon, China	I6	42
Sooner Lake, res., Ok., U.S.	A1	122
Sopchoppy, Fl., U.S.	G14	122
Soperton, Ga., U.S.	D3	116
Sopki, Russia	C13	10
Sopot, Bela.	H11	10
Sopot, Pol.	B14	16

Name | Map Ref. | Page

Sop Pong, Laos — A6 48
Sopron, Hung. — B3 26
Sopur, India — A5 54
Sora, Italy — I10 22
Sorada, India — I10 54
Sorata, Bol. — C3 90
Sorbhog, India — E13 54
Sorel, Qc., Can. — D3 110
Sorell, Cape, c., Austl. — o12 77a
Sorfold, Nor. — C6 8
Sorgues, Fr. — E10 18
Soria, Spain — C8 20
Soria, co., Spain — C8 20
Soriano, Ur. — F8 92
Sørli, Nor. — D5 8
Soro, Den. — I4 8
Soro, India — H11 54
Soro, Monte, mtn., Italy — G8 24
Soroca, Mol. — A15 26
Sorocaba, Braz. — L2 88
Soročinsk, Russia — D8 32
Soroco, P.R. — B4 104a
Sorol, at., Micron. — C5 72
Soron, India — E7 54
Sorong, Indon. — F9 44
Sorónb, stm., Braz. — C1 88
Sorot', stm., Russia — C12 10
Soroti, Ug. — D6 66
Sørøya, i., Nor. — A10 8
Sorrento, Italy — D8 24
Sorrento, La., U.S. — G8 122
Sorris-Sorris, Nmb. — B2 70
Sor Rondane Mountains, mts., Ant. — C7 81
Sorsk, Russia — D16 32
Sorso, Italy — D2 24
Sorsogon, Phil. — D4 52
Sort, Spain — B12 20
Sortavala, Russia — F14 8
Sør-Trøndelag, state, Nor. — E4 8
Sørve neem, c., Est. — C4 10
Sösa, stm., Russia — D18 10
Sos del Rey Católico, Spain — B9 20
Soskovo, Russia — H18 10
Sosna, stm., Russia — H21 10
Sosneado, Cerro, mtn., Arg. — G3 92
Sosnogorsk, Russia — B8 32
Sosnovec, Russia — D15 8
Sosnovka, Kaz. — D13 32
Sosnovka, Russia — C19 8
Sosnovo-Ozerskoe, Russia — F11 34
Sosnovskoe, Russia — I20 8
Sosnovyj Bor, Russia — A11 10
Sosnowiec, Pol. — F15 16
Soso, Ms., U.S. — F9 122
Sos'va, Russia — B10 32
Sotkamo, Fin. — D13 8
Soto, Mex. — F1 130
Soto la Marina, Mex. — D9 100
Soto la Marina, Barra, i., Mex. — C10 100
Sotra see Store Sotra, i., Nor. — F1 8
Sotteville-lès-Rouen, Fr. — E9 14
Souanké, Congo — D2 66
Soubré, C. Iv. — A3 64
Soudan, Austl. — D7 74
Souderton, Pa., U.S. — D10 114
Soufrière, St. Luc. — m6 105c
Soufrière, vol., Guad. — h5 105c
Soufrière, vol., St. Vin. — o11 105e
Soufrière Hills, vol., Monts. — d3 105a
Souillac, Fr. — E7 18
Sôul (Seoul), Kor., S. — F7 38
Soulac-sur-Mer, Fr. — D4 18
Sound, The, strt., Eur. — I5 8
Sounding Creek, stm., Ab., Can. — E19 138
Sounding Lake, l., Ab., Can. — B3 124
Sources, Mont-aux- (Phofung), mtn., Afr. — F9 70
Soure, Braz. — D8 84
Sour el Ghozlane, Alg. — H14 20
Souris, Mb., Can. — E13 124
Souris, stm., N.A. — E13 124
Sourlake, Tx., U.S. — G4 122
Sourland Mountain, hill, N.J., U.S. — D11 114
Sousa, Braz. — D6 88
Sousel, Port. — F3 20
Souse, Tun. — I4 24
Sout, stm., S. Afr. — H6 70
South, stm., N.C., U.S. — B7 116
South Africa, ctry., Afr. — F7 70
South America, cont. — G9 4
Southampton, On., Can. — D8 112
Southampton, Eng., U.K. — K11 12
Southampton, N.Y., U.S. — D13 114
Southampton, Cape, c., Nu., Can. — C13 106
Southampton Island, i., Nu., Can. — C14 106
South Andaman, i., India — F7 46
South Anna, stm., Va., U.S. — G8 114
South Antler Creek see Antler, stm., N.A. — E12 124
South Australia, state, Austl. — E6 74
South Australian Basin, unds. — M15 142
Southaven, Ms., U.S. — B8 122
South Baldy, mtn., N.M., U.S. — J9 132
Southbank, B.C., Can. — C5 138
South Bay, Fl., U.S. — J5 116
South Bay, b., Nu., Can. — C14 106
South Bay, b., On., Can. — C8 112
South Baymouth, On., Can. — C7 112
South Bend, In., U.S. — G3 112
South Bend, Wa., U.S. — D3 136
South Bohemia see Jihočeský kraj, state, Czech Rep. — G10 16
South Borneo see Kalimantan Selatan, state, Indon. — E9 50
South Boston, Va., U.S. — H6 114
Southbridge, N.Z. — F5 80
Southbridge, Ma., U.S. — B13 114
South Brookfield, N.S., Can. — F11 110
South Bruny Island, i., Austl. — o13 77a
South Burlington, Vt., U.S. — F3 110
South Carolina, state, U.S. — C5 116
South Celebes see Sulawesi Selatan, state, Indon. — E11 50
South Charleston, W.V., U.S. — F4 114
South China Basin, unds. — H14 142
South China Sea, s., Asia — H15 30
South Dakota, state, U.S. — C12 126
South Downs, hills, Eng., U.K. — K12 12
South East, state, Bots. — D7 70
South East Cape, c., Austl. — o13 77a
Southeast Indian Ridge, unds. — N12 142
Southeast Pacific Basin, unds. — P25 142
South East Point, c., Austl. — L6 76
Southern, state, Bots. — D7 70
Southern see HaDarom, state, Isr. — H5 58
Southern Alps, mts., N.Z. — F4 80
Southern Bug see Pivdennyj Buh, stm., Ukr. — A17 26
Southern Cook Islands, is., Cook Is. — E10 72
Southern Cross, Austl. — F3 74

Southern Ghāts, mts., India — G3 53
Southern Indian Lake, l., Mb., Can. — D10 106
Southern Ocean — P7 142
Southern Pines, N.C., U.S. — A6 116
South Esk, stm., Austl. — n13 77a
South Fabius, stm., Mo., U.S. — E6 120
South Fallsburg, N.Y., U.S. — C11 114
Southfield, Mi., U.S. — B2 114
South Fiji Basin, unds. — L20 142
South Foreland, c., Eng., U.K. — J14 12
South Fork, Co., U.S. — F10 132
South Fulton, Tn., U.S. — H8 120
Southgate, Mi., U.S. — B2 114
South Georgia, i., S. Geor. — J9 90
South Georgia and the South Sandwich Islands, dep., S.A. — K11 82
South Grand, stm., Mo., U.S. — F3 120
South Hātia Island, i., Bngl. — G13 54
South Haven, Mi., U.S. — F3 112
South Henderson, N.C., U.S. — H7 114
South Henik Lake, l., Nu., Can. — C11 106
South Hero, Vt., U.S. — F3 110
South Hill Village, Anguilla — A1 105a
South Holston Lake, res., U.S. — H3 114
South Honshu Ridge, unds. — G16 142
South Houston, Tx., U.S. — H3 122
South Indian Basin, unds. — O12 142
South Indian Lake, Mb., Can. — D11 106
South International Falls, Mn., U.S. — C5 118
South Island, i., N.Z. — G5 80
South Konkan Hills, hills, India — C1 53
South Korea see Korea, South, ctry., Asia — G8 38
South Lake Tahoe, Ca., U.S. — E5 134
Southland, N.Z. — H2 128
Southlawn, Il., U.S. — E8 120
South Llano, stm., Tx., U.S. — D8 130
South Loup, stm., Ne., U.S. — F13 126
South Lyon, Mi., U.S. — F6 112
South Magnetic Pole, misc. cult. — B18 81
South Manitou Island, i., Mi., U.S. — C3 112
South Miami, Fl., U.S. — K5 116
South Milwaukee, Wi., U.S. — F2 112
South Moravia see Jihomoravský kraj, state, Czech Rep. — G12 16
South Nahanni, stm., N.T., Can. — C5 106
South Nation, stm., On., Can. — C14 112
South Negril Point, c., Jam. — i12 104d
South Ogden, Ut., U.S. — B5 132
South Orkney Islands, is., Ant. — B36 81
South Paris, Me., U.S. — F6 110
South Pass, p., Wy., U.S. — E4 126
South Pekin, Il., U.S. — D8 120
South Pittsburg, Tn., U.S. — B13 122
South Platte, stm., U.S. — F11 126
South Point, c., Barb. — n8 105d
South Pole, misc. cult., Ant. — D1 81
Southport (Gold Coast), Austl. — F9 76
Southport, Austl. — o13 77a
Southport, Eng., U.K. — H9 12
Southport, In., U.S. — E11 120
Southport, N.C., U.S. — C7 116
South Portland, Me., U.S. — G6 110
South Range, Mi., U.S. — D10 118
South River, On., Can. — C10 112
South Ronaldsay, i., Scot., U.K. — C10 12
South Sandwich Islands, is., S. Geor. — K11 82
South Sandwich Trench, unds. — N11 144
South Saskatchewan, stm., Can. — A8 124
South Shetland Islands, is., Ant. — B35 81
South Sioux City, Ne., U.S. — I2 118
South Skunk, stm., Ia., U.S. — C5 120
South Slocan, B.C., Can. — G13 138
South Sound, b., Br. Vir. Is. — e9 104b
South Spicer Island, i., Nu., Can. — B15 106
South Sulphur, stm., Tx., U.S. — D3 122
South Sumatra see Sumatera Selatan, state, Indon. — E4 50
South Taranaki Bight, b., N.Z. — D5 80
South Tasman Rise, unds. — N17 142
South Thompson, stm., B.C., Can. — F11 138
South Torrington, Wy., U.S. — E8 126
South Uist, i., Scot., U.K. — D5 12
South Umpqua, stm., Or., U.S. — G3 136
South Ventana Cone, mtn., Ca., U.S. — G4 134
South Vietnam see Vietnam, ctry., Asia — E9 48
South West Africa see Namibia, ctry., Afr. — E2 68
South West Cape, c., Austl. — o12 77a
South West Cape, c., N.Z. — H2 80
South West City, Mo., U.S. — H3 120
Southwest Harbor, Me., U.S. — F8 110
Southwest Indian Ridge, unds. — M8 142
Southwest Miramichi, stm., N.B., Can. — D10 110
Southwest National Park, p.o.i., Austl. — o12 77a
Southwest Pacific Basin, unds. — M23 142
Southwest Point, c., Bah. — K8 116
South Whitley, In., U.S. — G4 112
South Wichita, stm., Tx., U.S. — H9 128
South Windham, Me., U.S. — G6 110
Southwold, Eng., U.K. — I14 12
Soutpansberg, mts., S. Afr. — C9 70
Sovetsk, Russia — G20 10
Sovetsk, Russia — E4 10
Sovetsk, Russia — C7 32
Sovetskaja Gavan', Russia — G17 34
Sovetskij, Russia — F13 8
Sovpole, Russia — D20 8
Sowa Pan, pl., Bots. — B7 70
Soweto, S. Afr. — E8 70
Soya-misaki, c., Japan — B14 38
Soyang-chösuji, res., Kor., S. — F7 38
Soyo, Ang. — B1 68
Sož, stm., Eur. — H13 10
Sozaq, Kaz. — F11 32
Sozimskij, Russia — C8 32
Sozopol, Blg. — G14 26
Spa, Bel. — D14 14
Spain, ctry., Eur. — E7 20
Spalding, Sk., Can. — B9 124
Spalding, Eng., U.K. — I12 12
Spanish, On., Can. — B7 112

Spanish, stm., On., Can. — B8 112
Spanish Fork, Ut., U.S. — C5 132
Spanish Point, c., Ber. — k15 104e
Spanish Sahara see Western Sahara, dep., Afr. — E2 64
Spanish Town, Br. Vir. Is. — e9 104b
Spanish Town, Jam. — H13 104d
Spanta, Ákra, c., Grc. — H6 28
Sparkman, Ar., U.S. — D6 122
Sparks, Nv., U.S. — D6 134
Sparland, Il., U.S. — C8 120
Sparlingville, Mi., U.S. — F7 112
Sparrows Point, Md., U.S. — E9 114
Sparta, Ga., U.S. — C3 116
Sparta, Il., U.S. — F8 120
Sparta, Ky., U.S. — F13 120
Sparta, N.C., U.S. — H4 114
Sparta, N.J., U.S. — C11 114
Sparta, Tn., U.S. — I12 120
Sparta, Wi., U.S. — H8 118
Spartanburg, S.C., U.S. — B4 116
Spárti, Grc. — F5 28
Spartivento, Capo, c., Italy — G10 24
Spartivento, Capo, c., Italy — F2 24
Spas-Klepiki, Russia — I19 8
Spassk-Dal'nij, Russia — B10 38
Spearfish, S.D., U.S. — C8 126
Spearville, Ks., U.S. — D9 128
Spednic Lake, l., N.A. — E9 110
Speedway, In., U.S. — I3 112
Speightstown, Barb. — n8 105d
Speikkogel, mtn., Aus. — C12 22
Speke Gulf, b., Tan. — E6 66
Spencer, Ia., U.S. — H3 118
Spencer, In., U.S. — E11 120
Spencer, Ne., U.S. — E14 126
Spencer, Wi., U.S. — G8 118
Spencer, W.V., U.S. — F4 114
Spencer, Cape, c., Austl. — E11 110
Spencer Gulf, b., Austl. — F7 74
Spencerville, Oh., U.S. — D1 114
Spences Bridge, B.C., Can. — F9 138
Speos (Rock Tombs), hist., Egypt — K1 58
Sperryville, Va., U.S. — F7 114
Spétses, i., Grc. — F6 28
Spey, stm., Scot., U.K. — D9 12
Spezia see La Spezia, Italy — F6 22
Spezzano Albanese, Italy — E10 24
Sphinx see Abū el-Hul, hist., Egypt — I1 58
Spickard, Mo., U.S. — D4 120
Spilimbergo, Italy — D9 22
Spillville, Ia., U.S. — H6 118
Spinazzola, Italy — D10 24
Spindale, N.C., U.S. — A4 116
Spires see Speyer, Ger. — G4 16
Spirit Lake, Ia., U.S. — H3 118
Spirit River, Ab., Can. — D7 106
Spiro, Ok., U.S. — B4 122
Spišská Nová Ves, Slov. — H16 16
Spitsbergen, i., Nor. — B4 30
Spitsbergen Bank, unds. — B5 30
Spittal an der Drau, Aus. — D10 22
Split, Cro. — G13 22
Split Lake, res., Mb., Can. — D11 106
Spogi, Lat. — D9 10
Spokane, Wa., U.S. — C9 136
Spokane, stm., U.S. — C8 136
Spoleto, Italy — H9 22
Spoon, stm., Il., U.S. — D7 120
Spooner, Wi., U.S. — F7 118
Sporava, Bela. — H8 10
Spornoe, Russia — D19 34
Spotsylvania, Va., U.S. — F8 114
Sprague, Wa., U.S. — C9 136
Spratly Islands, is., Asia — D5 44
Spray, Or., U.S. — F7 136
Spree, stm., Ger. — E10 16
Spremberg, Ger. — E10 16
Spring, stm., U.S. — H6 120
Spring, stm., U.S. — H3 120
Spring, South Fork, stm., U.S. — H6 120
Spring City, Tn., U.S. — B14 122
Spring City, Ut., U.S. — D5 132
Spring Creek, Austl. — D3 76
Spring Creek, stm., N.D., U.S. — G11 124
Spring Creek, stm., S.D., U.S. — C8 134
Springdale, Nf., Can. — j22 107a
Springdale, Ar., U.S. — H3 120
Springdale, N.D., U.S. — G12 124
Springdale, Wa., U.S. — B9 136
Springe, Ger. — D5 16
Springerville, Az., U.S. — I7 132
Springfield, N.S., Can. — F12 110
Springfield, Co., U.S. — D6 128
Springfield, Fl., U.S. — G13 122
Springfield, Il., U.S. — E8 120
Springfield, Ky., U.S. — G12 120
Springfield, Ma., U.S. — B13 114
Springfield, Mn., U.S. — G4 118
Springfield, Mo., U.S. — G4 120
Springfield, Oh., U.S. — E2 114
Springfield, Or., U.S. — F3 136
Springfield, S.C., U.S. — C4 116
Springfield, S.D., U.S. — E14 126
Springfield, Tn., U.S. — H10 120
Springfontein, S. Afr. — G7 70
Spring Glen, Ut., U.S. — D5 132
Spring Green, Wi., U.S. — A7 118
Spring Grove, Mn., U.S. — H7 118
Springhill, La., U.S. — D5 122
Spring Hope, N.C., U.S. — I7 114
Springhouse, B.C., Can. — E8 138
Spring Lake, N.C., U.S. — A7 116
Springs, S. Afr. — E9 70
Springside, Austl. — D3 76
Springvale, Austl. — I7 76
Springvale, Me., U.S. — G6 110
Spring Valley, Ca., U.S. — K9 134
Spring Valley, Il., U.S. — J9 118
Spring Valley, N.Y., U.S. — C11 114
Spring Valley, Wi., U.S. — G6 118
Spring Valley, val., Nv., U.S. — D2 132
Springview, Ne., U.S. — E13 126
Springville, Al., U.S. — D12 122
Springville, Ca., U.S. — G7 134
Springville, Ut., U.S. — C5 132
Sproat Lake, l., B.C., Can. — G5 138
Spruce Grove, Ab., Can. — C17 138
Spruce Knob, mtn., W.V., U.S. — F6 114
Spruce Mountain, mtn., Az., U.S. — I4 132
Spruce Pine, N.C., U.S. — I3 114
Spulico, Capo, c., Italy — E10 24
Spurfield, Ab., Can. — A16 138
Spurger, Tx., U.S. — G4 122
Spuzzum, B.C., Can. — G9 138
Squamish, B.C., Can. — G7 138
Squamish, stm., B.C., Can. — F5 138
Square Lake, l., N.H., U.S. — G5 110
Square Lake, l., Me., U.S. — D8 110
Squatec, Qc., Can. — C8 110
Squaw Cap Mountain, mtn., N.B., Can. — C10 110
Squaw Peak, mtn., Ut., U.S. — C12 136
Squilax, B.C., Can. — F11 138
Squillace, Golfo di, b., Italy — F10 24
Squinzano, Italy — D12 24
Sragen, Indon. — G7 50
Srbobran, Serb. — D6 26
Srě Âmběl, Camb. — G6 48

Sredninyj hrebet, mts., Russia — E20 34
Sredna Gora, mts., Blg. — G11 26
Srednee Kujto, ozero, Russia — D14 8
Srednekolymsk, Russia — C19 34
Srednerusskaja vozvyšennost', plat., Russia — D5 32
Srednesibirskoe ploskogor'e (Central Siberian Uplands), plat., Russia — C10 34
Srednij Ural, mts., Russia — C9 32
Srednij Vasjugan, Russia — C13 32
Srednij Olëkma, Russia — E13 34
Šrem, Pol. — D13 16
Srě Moăt, Camb. — F8 48
Sremska Mitrovica, Serb. — E6 26
Sremski Karlovci, Serb. — D6 26
Srěng, stm., Camb. — F6 48
Srěpôk, stm., Camb. — F8 48
Sretensk, Russia — F12 34
Sri Aman, Malay. — C7 50
Sri Jayewardenepura Kotte, Sri L. — H4 53
Srikākulam, India — B6 53
Sri Kālahasti, India — E4 53
Sri Lanka, ctry., Asia — G5 53
Srīnagar, India — A5 54
Srirampur, India — B2 53
Srivardhan, India — B1 53
Śrīvilliputtūr, India — B3 53
Środa Śląska, Pol. — E12 16
Środa Wielkopolska, Pol. — D13 16
Sseu-tch'ouan see Sichuan, state, China — E5 36
Ssup'ing see Siping, China — C6 38
Staaten, stm., Austl. — C8 74
Stacyville, Ia., U.S. — H6 118
Stade, Ger. — C5 16
Stadlandet, pen., Nor. — E1 8
Stadl-Paura, Aus. — B10 22
Stadskanaal, Neth. — A16 14
Stadtallendorf, Ger. — F5 16
Stadtoldendorf, Ger. — E5 16
Stafford, Eng., U.K. — I10 12
Stafford, Ks., U.S. — D10 128
Stafford Springs, Ct., U.S. — C13 114
Staffordsville, Ky., U.S. — G14 120
Stagen, Indon. — E10 50
Staines, Eng., U.K. — J12 12
Staked Plain see Estacado, Llano, pl., U.S. — H6 128
Stakhanov, Ukr. — E5 32
Stalać, Serb. — F8 26
Stalowa Wola, Pol. — F18 16
Stamford, Austl. — C4 76
Stamford, Eng., U.K. — I12 12
Stamford, Ct., U.S. — C12 114
Stamford, N.Y., U.S. — B11 114
Stamford, Tx., U.S. — B8 130
Stamford Lake, res., Tx., U.S. — A8 130
Stamps, Ar., U.S. — D5 122
Stanaford, W.V., U.S. — G4 114
Stanardsville, Va., U.S. — F7 114
Stanberry, Mo., U.S. — D3 120
Stancionno-Ojašinskij, Russia — C14 32
Standard, Ab., Can. — E18 138
Standerton, S. Afr. — E9 70
Standish, Mi., U.S. — E6 112
Stanfield, Or., U.S. — E7 136
Stanford, B.C., Can. — D4 106
Stanford, Ky., U.S. — C3 106
Stanford, Mt., U.S. — C16 136
Stanger, S. Afr. — F10 70
Stanislaus, stm., Ca., U.S. — F5 134
Stanley, Austl. — n12 77a
Stanley, N.B., Can. — D10 110
Stanley, Falk. Is. — J5 90
Stanley, N.D., U.S. — A4 116
Stanley, Wi., U.S. — G7 118
Stanley Falls, wtfl., D.R.C. — D4 66
Stanley Reservoir, res., India — F3 53
Stanleyville see Kisangani, D.R.C. — D5 66
Stanovoe nagor'e, mts., Russia — E11 34
Stanovoj hrebet, mts., Russia — E14 34
Stanovoy Mountains see Stanovoe nagor'e, mts., Russia — E11 34
Stanthorpe, Austl. — G8 76
Stanton, Ky., U.S. — G2 114
Stanton, Ne., U.S. — E8 112
Stanton, N.D., U.S. — G12 124
Stanton, Ne., U.S. — F15 126
Stanton, Tn., U.S. — B9 122
Stantonsburg, N.C., U.S. — A8 116
Stanwood, Wa., U.S. — B4 136
Staples, Mn., U.S. — E4 118
Stapleton, Al., U.S. — G11 122
Stāporków, Pol. — E16 16
Star, Ms., U.S. — E8 122
Star, N.C., U.S. — A6 116
Starachowice, Pol. — E17 16
Staraja Rudnja, Bela. — H13 10
Staraja Russa, Russia — B14 10
Stara Zagora, Blg. — G12 26
Starbuck, Mb., Can. — E16 124
Starbuck, Wa., U.S. — D8 136
Starbuck, i., Kir. — D11 72
Star City, Sk., Can. — B9 124
Star City, Ar., U.S. — D7 122
Stargard Szczeciński, Pol. — C11 16
Stargo, Az., U.S. — J7 132
Stari Harbour, B., Sol. Is. — f10 79b
Stari Grad, Cro. — G13 22
Starij Rjad, Russia — B17 10
Stari Vlah, reg., Serb. — F7 26
Starke, Fl., U.S. — G3 116
Starkville, Ms., U.S. — D10 122
Star Lake, l., Wi., U.S. — I7 118
Starnberg, Ger. — H7 16
Starnberger See, l., Ger. — I7 16
Staroe Rahino, Russia — B15 10
Starogard Gdański, Pol. — C14 16
Starokostjantyniv, Ukr. — C16 26
Star Peak, mtn., Nv., U.S. — C7 134
Starý Medvěd', Russia — B13 10
Staryj Oskol, Russia — D5 32
Stary Sącz, Pol. — G16 16
Stassfurt, Ger. — E7 16
State College, Pa., U.S. — D7 114
State Line, Ms., U.S. — F10 122
Stateline, Nv., U.S. — E5 134
Staten Island see Estados, Isla de los, i., Arg. — J4 90
State Road, N.C., U.S. — H4 114
Statesboro, Ga., U.S. — D4 116
Statesville, N.C., U.S. — I4 114
Staubun, Bela. — H14 10
Staunton, Il., U.S. — E8 120
Staunton, Va., U.S. — F6 114
Staunton see Roanoke, stm., U.S. — H8 114
Stavanger, Nor. — G1 8
Stavely, Ab., Can. — F17 138
Stavne, Ukr. — G18 16
Stavropol', Russia — E6 32
Stavropol', Austl. — K4 76
Stawell, stm., Austl. — C4 76
Stawiszyn, Pol. — E14 16
Stayner, On., Can. — D9 112
Steamboat Springs, Co., U.S. — A4 132
Stearns, Ky., U.S. — H13 120
Stebark, Pol. — C16 16
Steele, Mo., U.S. — H8 120

Steele, N.D., U.S. — H14 124
Steele, Mount, mtn., Wy., U.S. — B9 132
Steels Point, c., Norf. I. — y25 78i
Steelville, Mo., U.S. — G6 120
Steensby Inlet, b., Nu., Can. — A15 106
Steenwijk, Neth. — B15 14
Steep Rock, Mb., Can. — C15 124
Stefanie, Lake, l., Afr. — G7 62
Stefansson Island, i., Nu., Can. — A9 106
Štefan Vodă, Rom. — E14 26
Stege, Den. — B8 16
Stehekin, Wa., U.S. — B6 136
Steiermark, state, Aus. — C11 22
Steinach, Aus. — C8 22
Steinbach, Mb., Can. — E17 124
Steinfurt, Ger. — D3 16
Steinhausen, Nmb. — B4 70
Steinkjer, Nor. — D4 8
Stekljanka, Russia — G19 8
Stella, S. Afr. — E7 70
Stellarton, N.S., Can. — E14 110
Stellenbosch, S. Afr. — H4 70
Stelvio, Parco Nazionale dello, p.o.i., Italy — D7 22
Stelvio, Passo dello, p., Italy — D7 22
Stendal, Ger. — D7 16
Stende, Lat. — C5 10
Stephen, Mn., U.S. — C2 118
Stephens, Ar., U.S. — D5 122
Stephens, Port, b., Austl. — I9 76
Stephens City, Va., U.S. — E7 114
Stephens Creek, Austl. — H3 76
Stephens Lake, res., Mb., Can. — D11 106
Stephenville, Nf., Can. — j22 107a
Stephenville, Tx., U.S. — B9 130
Stepnjak, Kaz. — D12 32
Step Pyramid see Saqqāra, Pyramides de, hist., Egypt — I1 58
Steptoe Valley, val., Nv., U.S. — D2 132
Sterkstroom, S. Afr. — G8 70
Sterling, Co., U.S. — G9 126
Sterling, Il., U.S. — C8 120
Sterling, Ks., U.S. — C10 128
Sterling, Mi., U.S. — D5 112
Sterling, Ne., U.S. — D1 120
Sterling City, Tx., U.S. — C7 130
Sterling, La., U.S. — E6 122
Sterlitamak, Russia — D9 32
Šternberk, Czech Rep. — G13 16
Sterzing see Vipiteno, Italy — D8 22
Stettin see Szczecin, Pol. — C10 16
Stettler, Ab., Can. — D18 138
Steubenville, Oh., U.S. — D5 114
Stevenage, Eng., U.K. — J12 12
Stevenson, Al., U.S. — C13 122
Stevenson Entrance, strt., Ak., U.S. — E9 140
Stevens Pass, p., Wa., U.S. — C5 136
Stevens Peak, mtn., Id., U.S. — C11 136
Stevens Point, Wi., U.S. — G9 118
Stevensville, Mi., U.S. — F3 112
Stevensville, Mt., U.S. — D12 136
Stewardson, Il., U.S. — E9 120
Stewart, B.C., Can. — D4 106
Stewart, stm., Yk., Can. — C3 106
Stewart, Isla, i., Chile — J2 90
Stewart Island, i., N.Z. — H3 80
Stewartstown, Pa., U.S. — E9 114
Stewart Valley, Sk., Can. — D6 124
Stewartville, Mn., U.S. — H6 118
Steyerville, S. Afr. — H7 70
Steyr, Aus. — B11 22
Steytlerville, S. Afr. — H7 70
Stickney, S.D., U.S. — D14 126
Stiene, Lat. — C7 10
Stif, Alg. — B6 64
Stigler, Ok., U.S. — B3 122
Stih, hora, mtn., Ukr. — A10 26
Stikine, stm., N.A. — D4 106
Stikine Ranges, mts., B.C., Can. — D4 106
Stilbaai, S. Afr. — I5 70
Stilfontein, S. Afr. — E8 70
Stillhouse Hollow Lake, res., Tx., U.S. — D10 130
Stillwater, B.C., Can. — G6 138
Stillwater, Mn., U.S. — F6 118
Stillwater, Ok., U.S. — A1 122
Stilwell, Ok., U.S. — B3 122
Stînca-Costeşti, Lacul, res., Eur. — B14 26
Stine Mountain, mtn., Mt., U.S. — E13 136
Stinking Water Creek, stm., Ne., U.S. — G11 126
Stinnett, Tx., U.S. — F7 128
Štip, Mac. — B5 28
Stirling, Austl. — F3 74
Stirling, On., Can. — D12 112
Stirling, Scot., U.K. — E8 12
Stirling City, Ca., U.S. — D4 134
Stirrat, W.V., U.S. — G15 120
Stjno, i., Nor. — A9 8
Štúrovo, Czech Rep. — G10 16
Stobi, sci., Mac. — B4 28
Stockach, Ger. — I5 16
Stockbridge, Ga., U.S. — C1 116
Stockbridge, Mi., U.S. — B1 114
Stockdale, Tn., U.S. — E9 130
Stockerau, Aus. — B13 22
Stockholm, Swe. — G8 8
Stockholm, state, Swe. — G8 8
Stockport, Eng., U.K. — H10 12
Stockton, Austl. — I9 76
Stockton, Al., U.S. — G11 122
Stockton, Ca., U.S. — F4 134
Stockton, Il., U.S. — B8 120
Stockton, Ks., U.S. — B9 128
Stockton, Mo., U.S. — G4 120
Stockton Plateau, plat., Tx., U.S. — D5 130
Stockton Reservoir, res., Mo., U.S. — G4 120
Stockton Springs, Me., U.S. — F8 110
Stoczek Łukowski, Pol. — D18 16
Støeng Trěng, Camb. — F8 48
Stobja, S. Afr. — F7 70
Stoke-on-Trent, Eng., U.K. — H11 12
Stokes Point, c., Austl. — n11 77a
Stolberg, Ger. — F2 16
Stolbovo, Russia — H17 10
Stolbovoj, ostrov, i., Russia — B16 34
Stoneboro, Pa., U.S. — C5 114
Stone Harbor, N.J., U.S. — E11 114
Stonehaven, Scot., U.K. — E10 12
Stonehenge, hist., Eng., U.K. — J11 12
Stoner, B.C., Can. — C8 138
Stone Mountain, mtn., Vt., U.S. — F5 110
Stoneville, N.C., U.S. — H5 114
Stonewall, Mb., Can. — D16 124
Stonewall, Ms., U.S. — E10 122
Stonington, Me., U.S. — F8 110
Stonington, Il., U.S. — E8 120
Stony Lake, l., Mb., Can. — D11 106
Stony Lake, l., On., Can. — D11 112
Stony Plain, Ab., Can. — C16 138
Stony Point, N.C., U.S. — I4 114

Stony Rapids, Sk., Can. — D9 106
Stony River, Ak., U.S. — D8 140
Stopnica, Pol. — F16 16
Stora Lulevatten, l., Swe. — C8 8
Storavan, l., Swe. — D8 8
Stord, i., Nor. — G1 8
Storebælt, strt., Den. — I4 8
Store Koldewey, i., Grnld. — B22 141
Støren, Nor. — E4 8
Store Sotra, i., Nor. — F1 8
Storkerson Bay, b., N.T., Can. — B14 140
Storkerson Peninsula, pen., Nu., Can. — A9 106
Storlien, Swe. — E5 8
Storm Bay, b., Austl. — o13 77a
Storm Lake, Ia., U.S. — B2 120
Stornoway, Scot., U.K. — C6 12
Storozhynets', Ukr. — A12 26
Storrs, Ct., U.S. — C13 114
Storsjøen, l., Nor. — F4 8
Storsjön, l., Swe. — E5 8
Storstrøm, state, Den. — I5 8
Storthoaks, Sk., Can. — E12 124
Storuman, Swe. — D7 8
Storuman, l., Swe. — D6 8
Storvindeln, l., Swe. — D7 8
Storvreta, Swe. — F7 8
Story City, Ia., U.S. — B4 120
Stošch, Isla, i., Chile — I1 90
Stoṳbcy, Bela. — H10 10
Stoughton, Sk., Can. — E10 124
Stoughton, Ma., U.S. — B14 114
Stoughton, Wi., U.S. — B8 120
Stoụng, stm., Camb. — F7 48
Stow, Oh., U.S. — C4 114
Stowe, Vt., U.S. — F4 110
Stowell, Tx., U.S. — H4 122
Stoyomarket, strg., U.K. — I14 12
Stoyomarket Mountain, mtn., B.C., Can. — G9 138
Stradella, Italy — E6 22
Stradzečy, Bela. — I6 10
Strahan, Austl. — o12 77a
Strakonice, Czech Rep. — G9 16
Stralsund, Ger. — B9 16
Strand, S. Afr. — I4 70
Stranraer, Scot., U.K. — G8 12
Strasbourg, Sk., Can. — C9 124
Strasbourg, Fr. — F16 14
Strasburg, Ger. — C9 16
Strasburg, N.D., U.S. — A12 126
Strasburg, Oh., U.S. — D4 114
Strasburg, Pa., U.S. — E9 114
Strasburg, Va., U.S. — B15 26
Stratford, N.Z. — D6 80
Stratford, On., Can. — G6 134
Stratford, Ct., U.S. — C12 114
Stratford, Pol. — B4 120
Stratford, Ok., U.S. — C2 122
Stratford, Tx., U.S. — G8 118
Stratford-upon-Avon, Eng., U.K. — I11 12
Strathalbyn, Austl. — J2 76
Strathclair, Mb., Can. — D13 124
Strathgordon, Austl. — o12 77a
Strathmore, N.S., Can. — D15 110
Strathmore, Ab., Can. — E9 12
Strathroy, On., Can. — F8 112
Strathy Point, c., Scot., U.K. — C8 12
Stratton, Co., U.S. — B6 128
Stratton, Me., U.S. — F5 110
Stratton, Ne., U.S. — A7 128
Straubing, Ger. — H8 16
Strausberg, Ger. — D9 16
Strawberry, stm., Ar., U.S. — H6 120
Strawberry, stm., Ut., U.S. — C6 132
Strawberry Mountain, mtn., Or., U.S. — F8 136
Strawberry Reservoir, res., Ut., U.S. — C5 132
Strawn, Tx., U.S. — B9 130
Strážnice, Czech Rep. — H13 16
Streaky Bay, b., Austl. — F6 74
Streatham, B.C., Can. — C9 138
Streator, Il., U.S. — C9 120
Středočeský kraj, state, Czech Rep. — G10 16
Streeter, N.D., U.S. — A13 126
Streetsboro, Oh., U.S. — C4 114
Streetsville, On., Can. — E10 112
Strehaia, Rom. — F11 26
Strelka-Čunja, Russia — B18 32
Strel'na, stm., Russia — C18 8
Strel'skaja, Russia — G22 8
Strenči, Lat. — C8 10
Strěšyn, Bela. — H13 10
Strickland, stm., Pap. N. Gui. — b3 79a
Strymonikós Kólpos (Strimon, Gulf of), b., Grc. — C6 28
Strjama, stm., Blg. — G11 26
Stroeder, Arg. — H4 90
Strofádes, is., Grc. — F3 24
Stromboli, Isola, i., Italy — F9 24
Strome, Ab., Can. — D18 138
Stromeferry, Scot., U.K. — D7 12
Stromsburg, Ne., U.S. — F15 126
Strömstad, Swe. — G4 8
Strömsund, Swe. — E6 8
Strong City, Ks., U.S. — C12 128
Stronghurst, Il., U.S. — D6 120
Stronsay, i., Scot., U.K. — B10 12
Stropkov, Slov. — G17 16
Stroud, Austl. — I8 76
Stroud, Eng., U.K. — J10 12
Stroud, Ok., U.S. — B2 122
Stroudsburg, Pa., U.S. — D10 114
Struga, Mac. — B3 28
Struma, stm., Eur. — H10 26
Strumble Head, c., Wales, U.K. — I7 12
Struthers, Oh., U.S. — C5 114
Strunino, Russia — D21 10
Stryi, stm., Ukr. — A11 26
Stryker, Mt., U.S. — B12 136
Stryker, Oh., U.S. — C1 114
Stryn, Nor. — F2 8
Stryków, Pol. — E15 16
Strzegom, Pol. — F12 16
Strzelce Krajeńskie, Pol. — D11 16
Strzelce Opolskie, Pol. — F14 16
Strzelecki Creek, stm., Austl. — G3 76
Strzelecki Desert, des., Austl. — E4 76
Strzelecki National Park, p.o.i., Austl. — n13 77a
Strzelin, Pol. — F13 16
Strzelno, Pol. — D14 16
Stuart, Fl., U.S. — I5 116
Stuart, Ne., U.S. — E13 126
Stuart, Va., U.S. — H5 114
Stuart, stm., B.C., Can. — B7 138
Stuart Island, i., Ak., U.S. — D7 140
Stuarts Draft, Va., U.S. — F6 114
Stuart Lake, l., B.C., Can. — B5 138
Stuck Kladenec, jazovir, res., Blg. — H12 26
Stuie, B.C., Can. — D4 138
Stupino, Russia — F20 10
Stura di Demonte, stm., Italy — F4 22
Sturge Island, i., Ant. — B21 81
Sturgeon, stm., On., Can. — B9 112
Sturgeon, stm., On., Can. — E10 118
Sturgeon Bay, b., Mb., Can. — D2 112
Sturgeon Bay, Wi., U.S. — B15 124

Name	Map Ref.	Page
Sturgeon Falls, On., Can.	B10	112
Sturgeon Lake, I., Ab., Can.	A13	138
Sturgeon Lake, I., On., Can.	A7	118
Sturgeon Lake, I., On., Can.	D11	112
Sturgis, Sk., Can.	C11	124
Sturgis, Ky., U.S.	G10	120
Sturgis, Mi., U.S.	G4	112
Sturgis, S.D., U.S.	C9	126
Šturovo, Slovak.	I14	16
Sturt, Mount, mtn., Austl.	G3	76
Sturtevant, Wi., U.S.	F2	112
Sturt National Park, p.o.i., Austl.	G3	76
Sturt Stony Desert, des., Austl.	G3	76
Stutterheim, S. Afr.	H8	70
Stuttgart, Ger.	H5	16
Stuttgart, Ar., U.S.	C7	122
Stylis, Grc.	E5	28
Styr, stm., Eur.	H9	10
Styria see Steiermark, state, Aus.	C11	22
Šu see Shū, Kaz.	F12	32
Suaqui Grande, stm., Braz.	J4	88
Suai, Malay.	B8	50
Suaita, Col.	D5	86
Suapure, stm., Ven.	D8	86
Suaqui Grande, Mex.	A4	100
Subah, Indon.	G6	50
Subang, Indon.	G5	50
Subansiri, stm., Asia.	D14	54
Subarnarekha, stm., India	G11	54
Subät, stm., Sudan	F6	62
Subate, Lat.	D8	10
Subei, China	D3	36
Subeita see Shivta, Horvot, sci., Isr.	H5	58
Subiaco, Italy	I10	22
Sublette, Ks., U.S.	D8	128
Sublett Range, mts., Id., U.S.	H14	136
Subotica, Serb.	C6	26
Sucarnoochee, stm., U.S.	E10	122
Succotah, hist., Egypt	H3	58
Suceava, Rom.	B13	26
Suceava, state, Rom.	B12	26
Suchań, Pol.	C11	16
Suchou see Suzhou, China	F9	42
Süchow see Xuzhou, China	D7	42
Sucio, stm., Col.	D3	86
Sucre, Bol.	C3	90
Sucre, Col.	C4	86
Sucre, state, Col.	C4	86
Sucre, state, Ven.	B10	86
Sucuaro, Col.	E7	86
Sucumbíos, state, Ec.	H3	86
Sucuriju, Braz.	C8	84
Sucuriú, stm., Braz.	C6	90
Sud, state, N. Cal.	m16	79d
Sud, Canal du, strt., Haiti	C11	102
Suda, Russia	A20	10
Suda, stm., Russia	A20	10
Sudan, Tx., U.S.	G6	128
Sudan, cty., Afr.	E5	62
Sudan, reg., Afr.	E4	62
Sudbišči, Russia	H20	10
Sudbury, On., Can.	B8	112
Sudbury, Eng., U.K.	I13	12
Sudd see As-Sudd, reg., Sudan	F6	62
Sudetes, mts., Eur.	F11	16
Sudogda, Russia	H19	8
Sudomskaja vozvyšennost', plat., Russia	C12	10
Sudost', stm., Eur.	H16	10
Südtirol see Trentino-Alto Adige, state, Italy	D8	22
Suduroy, i., Far. Is.	n34	8b
Sue, stm., Sudan	F5	62
Sueca, Spain	E10	20
Suez see El-Suweis, Egypt.	I3	58
Suez, Gulf of see Suweis, Khalîg el-, b., Egypt	J4	58
Suez Canal see Suweis, Qanâ el-, can., Egypt	H3	58
Suffield, Ab., Can.	D2	124
Suffolk, Va., U.S.	H9	114
Sufu see Kashi, China	B12	56
Sugar City, Id., U.S.	G15	136
Sugar Hill, Ga., U.S.	B1	116
Sugar Island, i., Mi., U.S.	B5	112
Sugar Land, Tx., U.S.	H3	122
Sugarloaf, Hill, Oh., U.S.	C4	114
Sugarloaf Mountain, mtn., Me., U.S.	E6	110
Sugarloaf Point, c., Austl.	I9	76
Suğla Gölü, l., Tur.	F14	28
Sugoj, stm., Russia	D20	34
Suğun, stm., Malay.	G1	52
Suhag, Egypt	B6	62
Suhai Hu, l., China	G16	32
Suhana, Russia	C12	34
Şuhār, Oman.	E8	56
Sühbaatar, Mong.	A6	36
Suhindol, Blg.	F12	26
Suhiniči, Russia	F18	10
Suhl, Ger.	F6	16
Suhodol'skij, Russia	G21	10
Suhona, stm., Russia	F22	8
Suhoverkovo, Russia	D18	10
Suhumi, Geor.	F6	32
Şuhut, Tur.	E13	28
Suiá-Miçu, stm., Braz.	F7	84
Suichuan, China	H6	42
Suide, China	C4	42
Suifu see Yibin, China	F5	36
Suihua, China	B10	36
Suijiang, China	F5	36
Suileng, China	B10	36
Suining, China	E7	42
Suining, China	F1	42
Suipacha, Arg.	G8	92
Suiping, China	E5	42
Suippes, Fr.	E13	14
Suir, stm., Ire.	I5	12
Suixi, China	E7	42
Suiyang, China	H2	42
Suiyang, China	B9	38
Suiyangdian, China	E5	42
Suizhong, China	A9	42
Suizhou, China	F5	42
Šuja, Russia	H19	8
Šuja, stm., Russia	E15	8
Sujângarh, India	E5	54
Sujāwal, Pak.	F2	54
Sukabumi, Indon.	G5	50
Sukadana, Indon.	D6	50
Sukadana, Indon.	F4	50
Sukadana, Teluk, b., Indon.	D6	50
Sukagawa, Japan	B13	40
Sukamara, Indon.	E7	50
Sukaraja, Indon.	E7	50
Sukau, Malay.	A11	50
Sukhothai, Thai.	D4	48
Sukhumi see Suhumi, Geor.	F6	32
Sukkertoppen (Maniitsoq), Grnld.	D15	141
Sukkozero, Russia	E14	8
Sukkur, Pak.	E2	54
Sukoharjo, Indon.	G7	50
Sukromlja, Russia	D17	10
Sukses, Nmb.	B3	70
Sukumo, Japan	G5	40
Sukunka, stm., B.C., Can.	A9	138
Sul, Baía do, b., Braz.	C13	92
Sula, i., Nor.	E1	8
Sula, stm., Russia	C23	8
Sula, Kepulauan (Sula Islands), is., Indon.	F8	44
Sulaimān Range, mts., Pak.	C3	54
Sula Islands see Sula, Kepulauan, is., Indon.	F8	44
Sulawesi (Celebes), i., Indon.	F7	44

Name	Map Ref.	Page
Sulawesi Selatan, state, Indon.	E11	50
Sulawesi Tengah, state, Indon.	D12	50
Sulawesi Tenggara, state, Indon.	E12	50
Sulaymān, Birak (Solomon's Pools), sci., W.B.	G5	58
Sulcis, reg., Italy	E2	24
Sulechów, Pol.	D11	16
Sulęcin, Pol.	D11	16
Sulejówek, Pol.	D17	16
Sulen, Mount, mtn., Pap. N. Gui.	a3	79a
Sulina, Rom.	D16	26
Sulina, Brațul, stm., Rom.	D16	26
Sulingen, Ger.	D4	16
Sulitelma, mtn., Eur.	C7	8
Sullana, Peru	D1	84
Sulligent, Al., U.S.	D10	122
Sullivan, Il., U.S.	E9	120
Sullivan, In., U.S.	E10	120
Sullivan Lake, l., Ab., Can.	E18	138
Sullivan, Italy	H10	22
Sulphur, La., U.S.	G5	122
Sulphur, Ok., U.S.	C2	122
Sulphur, stm., U.S.	D5	122
Sulphur Springs, Tx., U.S.	D3	122
Sulphur Springs Draw, stm., U.S.	H6	128
Sulphur Springs Valley, val., Az., U.S.	L7	132
Sultan, Wa., U.S.	C5	136
Sultan Alonto, Lake, l., Phil.	G5	52
Sultandağı, Tur.	E14	28
Sultanhisar, Tur.	F11	28
Sultan Kudarat, Phil.	G4	52
Sultānpur, India	E8	54
Sulu Archipelago, is., Phil.	H3	52
Sulu Chi, l., China	C11	54
Sulug, Libya	A4	62
Sulu Sea, s., Asia	F2	52
Sulzbach-Rosenberg, Ger.	G7	16
Šum, Russia	A14	10
Šumadija, reg., Serb.	E7	26
Sumangat, Tanjong, c., Malay.	G1	52
Sumatera (Sumatra), i., Indon.	E3	44
Sumatera Barat, state, Indon.	D2	50
Sumatera Selatan, state, Indon.	E4	50
Sumatera Utara, state, Indon.	K4	48
Sumatra see Sumatera, i., Indon.	E3	44
Sumba, Far. Is.	n34	8b
Sumba, i., Indon.	H11	50
Sumba, Selat, strt., Indon.	H11	50
Sumbawa, i., Indon.	H10	50
Sumbawa Besar, Indon.	H10	50
Sumbawanga, Tan.	F6	66
Sumbe, Ang.	C1	68
Sumburgh Head, c., Scot., U.K.	o18	12a
Sumé, Braz.	D7	88
Sumedang, Indon.	G5	50
Sümeg, Hung.	B4	26
Šumen, Blg.	F13	26
Sumenep, Indon.	G8	50
Šumerlja, Russia	C7	32
Sumisu-jima (Smith Island), i., Japan	E13	36
Sumjači, Russia	G15	10
Summerfield, Fl., U.S.	G3	116
Summerfield, N.C., U.S.	H6	114
Summer Lake, l., Or., U.S.	H6	136
Summerland, B.C., Can.	G11	138
Summerside, P.E., Can.	D13	110
Summersville, Mo., U.S.	G6	120
Summerton, S.C., U.S.	C5	116
Summerville, Ga., U.S.	C13	122
Summerville, S.C., U.S.	C5	116
Summit, S.D., U.S.	F1	118
Summit Lake, B.C., Can.	B8	138
Summit Mountain, mtn., Nv., U.S.	D9	134
Sumner, Ia., U.S.	B5	120
Sumner, Ne., U.S.	D8	122
Sumner, Wa., U.S.	C4	136
Sumoto, Japan	E7	40
Sumpangbinangae, Indon.	F11	50
Šumperk, Czech Rep.	G13	16
Sumpiuh, Indon.	G6	50
Sumqayıt, Azer.	A6	56
Sumsu, ostrov, i., Russia.	D20	34
Sumter, S.C., U.S.	C5	116
Sumuşta el-Waqf, Egypt	J1	58
Sumy, Ukr.	D4	32
Sumzom, China	F4	36
Sun, stm., Mt., U.S.	C14	136
Sunämganj, Bngl.	F13	54
Sunbright, Tn., U.S.	H13	120
Sunburst, Mt., U.S.	B14	136
Sunbury, Austl.	K5	76
Sunbury, Oh., U.S.	D3	114
Sunbury, Pa., U.S.	D9	114
Sunchales, Arg.	E7	92
Suncho Corral, Arg.	C6	92
Sunch'ŏn, Kor., S.	G7	38
Sunch'ŏn-ŭp, Kor., N.	E6	38
Sun City, Az., U.S.	J4	132
Suncook, N.H., U.S.	G5	110
Sunda, Selat (Sunda Strait), strt., Indon.	G4	50
Sundance, Wy., U.S.	C8	126
Sundarbans, reg., Asia	H12	54
Sundargarh, India.	G9	54
Sunda Shelf, unds.	I13	142
Sunda Strait see Sunda, Selat, strt., Indon.	G4	50
Sundays, stm., S. Afr.	H7	70
Sunde, Nor.	G1	8
Sunderland, Eng., U.K.	G11	12
Sundown, Tx., U.S.	H6	128
Sundridge, On., Can.	C10	112
Sundsvall, Swe.	E7	8
Sunflower, Ms., U.S.	D8	122
Sunflower, Mount, mtn., Ks., U.S.	B7	128
Sungaianyar, Indon.	E10	50
Sungaibuntu, Indon.	F5	50
Sungaidareh, Indon.	D2	50
Sungaiguntung, Indon.	C3	50
Sungai Kolok, Thai.	I5	48
Sungailangsat, Indon.	D2	50
Sungailimau, Indon.	D1	50
Sungaipenuh, Indon.	E2	50
Sungai Petani, Malay.	J5	48
Sungaipinang, Indon.	D8	50
Sungairotan, Indon.	E4	50
Sungaiselan, Indon.	E5	50
Sungari see Songhua, stm., China	B11	36
Sungari Reservoir see Songhua Hu, res., China	C7	38
Sungchiang see Songjiang, China	F9	42
Sungguminasa, Indon.	F11	50
Sungsang, Indon.	E4	50
Sunland Park, N.M., U.S.	L10	132
Sunne, Swe.	G5	8
Sunnyside, Ut., U.S.	E19	138
Sunnyside, Wa., U.S.	D7	136
Sunnyslope, Ab., Can.	E17	138
Sunnyvale, Ca., U.S.	F3	134
Sun Prairie, Wi., U.S.	A8	120
Sunrise, Fl., U.S.	J5	116
Sunrise, Wy., U.S.	E8	126
Sunrise Manor, Nv., U.S.	G1	132
Sunset, La., U.S.	G6	122
Sunset, Tx., U.S.	H11	128

Name	Map Ref.	Page
Sunset Country, reg., Austl.	J3	76
Sunset Crater National Monument, p.o.i., Az., U.S.	H5	132
Sunshine, Austl.	K5	76
Suntar, Russia	D12	34
Suntar-Hajata, hrebet, mts., Russia	D17	34
Sun Valley, Id., U.S.	G12	136
Sunwu, China	B10	36
Sunwui see Jiangmen, China	J5	42
Sunyani, Ghana	H4	64
Suojarvi, Russia	E15	8
Suomussalmi, Fin.	D13	8
Suõ-nada, s., Japan	F4	40
Suordah, Russia	C15	34
Supamo, stm., Ven.	D10	86
Supaul, India	E11	54
Supai see La Merced, Arg...	D5	92
Superior, Az., U.S.	J5	132
Superior, Mt., U.S.	C12	136
Superior, Wi., U.S.	E6	118
Superior, Wy., U.S.	B7	132
Superior, Laguna, b., Mex.	G11	100
Superior, Lake, l., N.A.	B10	108
Supetar, Cro.	G13	22
Suphan Buri, Thai.	E4	48
Suphan Buri, stm., Thai.	E5	48
Suponevo, Russia	G17	10
Supung Reservoir, res., Asia.	D6	38
Suqian, China	E8	42
Sūq Suwayq, Sau. Ar.	E4	56
Suqutrā (Socotra), i., Yemen	G7	56
Şūr (Tyre), Leb.	E6	58
Şūr, Oman	E8	56
Sur, Point, c., Ca., U.S.	G4	134
Sura, stm., Russia	C7	32
Surabaya, Indon.	G8	50
Surakarta, Indon.	G7	50
Şūrān, Syria	C7	58
Surany, Slov.	H14	16
Surat, Austl.	F7	76
Sūrat, India	H4	54
Sūratgarh, India	D4	54
Surat Thani, Thai.	H4	48
Suraž, Bela.	E13	10
Suraž, Russia	G15	10
Surendranagar, India	G3	54
Surf City, N.J., U.S.	E11	114
Surfers Paradise, Austl.	G9	76
Surgères, Fr.	C5	18
Surgoinsville, Tn., U.S.	H3	114
Surgut, Russia	B12	32
Suriāpet, India	C4	53
Surigao, Phil.	F5	52
Surin, Thai.	E6	48
Surinam, ctry., S.A.	C6	84
Suriname, stm., Sur.	C6	84
Surprise Valley, val., U.S.	B5	134
Surrency, Ga., U.S.	E3	116
Surrey, N.D., U.S.	F12	124
Surry, Va., U.S.	G9	114
Sursee, Switz.	C5	22
Sursk, Russia	D7	32
Surt, Khalīj (Sidra, Gulf of), b., Libya	A3	62
Surtanāhu, Pak.	E2	54
Surtsey, i., Ice.	I29	8a
Suru, Pap. N. Gui.	b3	79a
Sürüç, Tur.	A9	58
Suruga-wan, b., Japan	E11	40
Surulangun, Indon.	E3	50
Şurumu, stm., Braz.	F11	86
Suruyskary, Russia	A10	32
Susa, Italy	E4	22
Sušac, Otok, i., Cro.	H13	22
Süsah, Libya	A4	62
Susaki, Japan	F6	40
Susanino, Russia	F17	34
Susanville, Ca., U.S.	C5	134
Šušenskoe, Russia	D16	32
Susitna, stm., Ak., U.S.	D9	140
Susleni, Mol.	B15	26
Susoh, Indon.	K3	48
Susong, China	F7	42
Suspiro del Moro, Puerto, p., Spain	G7	20
Susquehanna, Pa., U.S.	C10	114
Susquehanna, stm., U.S.	E9	114
Susquehanna, West Branch, stm., Pa., U.S.	C8	114
Susques, Arg.	D3	90
Sussex, N.B., Can.	E11	110
Sussex, N.J., U.S.	C11	114
Sussex, Va., U.S.	H8	114
Susuman, Russia	D18	34
Susurluk, Tur.	D11	28
Susuzmüselim, Tur.	B9	28
Sušvė, stm., Lith.	E6	10
Sutak, India	A7	54
Sutherland, S. Afr.	H5	70
Sutherland, Ia., U.S.	A2	120
Sutherlin, Or., U.S.	G3	136
Sutjeska Nacionalni Park, p.o.i., Bos.	F5	26
Sutlej (Langqên) (Satluj), stm., Asia	D4	54
Sutter, Ca., U.S.	D4	134
Sutter Buttes, mtn., Ca., U.S.	D4	134
Sutter Creek, Ca., U.S.	E5	134
Sutton, Ak., U.S.	D10	140
Sutton, W.V., U.S.	F5	114
Sutton, Monts see Green Mountains, mts., N.A.	G4	110
Sutton in Ashfield, Eng., U.K.	H11	12
Sutton West, On., Can.	D10	112
Suttor, stm., Austl.	C6	76
Sutwik Island, i., Ak., U.S.	E8	140
Suure-Jaani, Est.	B8	10
Suur Munamägi, hill, Est.	C9	10
Suur Pakri, i., Est.	A6	10
Suva, Fiji	q19	79e
Suvadiva Atoll, at., Mald.	i12	46a
Suvarli, Tur.	A8	58
Suvasvesi, l., Fin.	E12	8
Suvorov, Russia	F19	10
Suwa, Japan	C11	40
Suwałki, Pol.	B18	16
Suwałki, state, Pol.	C18	16
Suwannaphum, Thai.	E6	48
Suwannee, stm., U.S.	G2	116
Suwanose-jima, i., Japan	k19	39a
Suwarrow, at., Cook Is.	E10	72
Suweis, Khalîg el- (Suez, Gulf of), b., Egypt	J4	58
Suweis, Qanâ el- (Suez Canal), can., Egypt	H3	58
Suwŏn, Kor., S.	F7	38
Suzaka, Japan	C11	40
Suzdal', Russia	H19	8
Suzhou, China	F9	42
Suzhou, China	E7	42
Suzigou, China	A10	42
Suzuka, Japan	E9	40
Suzuka-sammyaku, mts., Japan	D9	40
Suzu-misaki, c., Japan	B10	40
Suzun, Russia	D14	32
Suzzara, Italy	F7	22
Svalbard, dep., Eur.	B6	30
Svaliava, Ukr.	A10	26
Svapa, stm., Russia	H18	10
Svappavaara, Swe.	C9	8
Svarstad, Nor.	G3	8
Svartenhut, pen., Grnld.	C15	141
Svartisen, vit, Nor.	C6	8
Svataj, Russia	C19	34
Svay Riĕng, Camb.	G7	48
Svĕdasai, Lith.	E8	10
Švec šna, Lith.	E4	10
Švegssjön, l., Swe.	E6	8
Švek'šna, Lith.	E4	10
Svelvik, Nor.	G4	8

Name	Map Ref.	Page
Švenčionėliai, Lith.	E8	10
Švenčionys, Lith.	E9	10
Svendborg, Den.	A6	16
Šventoji, Russia	D16	10
Šventoji, stm., Lith.	E7	10
Sverdlovsk see Ekaterinburg, Russia	C10	32
Sverdrup, ostrov, i., Russia	B4	34
Sverdrup Channel, strt., Nu., Can.	A6	141
Sverdrup Islands, is., Nu., Can.	B5	141
Sveti Nikole, Mac.	B4	28
Svetlahorsk, Bela.	H12	10
Svetlaja, Russia	B12	36
Svetlogorsk, Russia	F2	10
Svetlograd, Russia	E6	32
Svetlyj, Russia	D10	32
Svetlyj, Russia	F3	10
Svetlyj, Russia	E12	34
Svetogorsk, Russia	F13	8
Svetozarevo, Serb.	F8	26
Svidník, Slov.	G17	16
Svilengrad, Blg.	H13	26
Svinoy, i., Far. Is.	m34	8b
Svir, Bela.	F9	10
Svir', stm., Russia	F16	8
Svirica, Russia	F15	8
Svirsk, Russia	D18	32
Svislač, stm., Bela.	G11	10
Svištov, Blg.	F12	26
Svit, Slov.	G16	16
Svitavy, Czech Rep.	G12	16
Svjacilavičy, Bela.	H14	10
Svjatoj Nos, mys, c., Russia	B18	8
Svjatoj Nos, mys, c., Russia	B17	34
Svobodnyj, Russia	F14	34
Svolvær, Nor.	B6	8
Svratka, stm., Czech Rep.	G12	16
Swabia see Schwaben, hist. reg., Ger.	H5	16
Swain Reefs, rf., Austl.	C9	76
Swainsboro, Ga., U.S.	D3	116
Swains Island, at., Am. Sam.	E9	72
Swakop, stm., Nmb.	C2	70
Swakopmund, Nmb.	C2	70
Swale, stm., Eng., U.K.	G11	12
Swan, stm., Ab., Can.	A13	138
Swan, stm., Can.	B13	124
Swan, stm., Can.	C13	136
Swan Peak, mtn., Mt., U.S.	C13	136
Swanquarter, N.C., U.S.	A9	116
Swan Range, mts., Mt., U.S.	C13	136
Swan Reach, Austl.	J2	76
Swan River, Mb., Can.	B12	124
Swansboro, N.C., U.S.	B8	116
Swansea, Austl.	o13	77a
Swansea, Wales, U.K.	J8	12
Swanton, Vt., U.S.	F3	110
Swanville, Mn., U.S.	F4	118
Swart-Mfolozi, stm., S. Afr.	F10	70
Swartz Creek, Mi., U.S.	F6	112
Swarzędz, Pol.	D13	16
Swät, stm., Pak.	A4	54
Swatow see Shantou, China	J7	42
Swaziland, ctry., Afr.	E10	70
Sweden, ctry., Eur.	E6	8
Swedish Knoll, mtn., Ut., U.S.	D5	132
Swedru, Ghana	H4	64
Sweeny, Tx., U.S.	E12	130
Sweet Briar, Va., U.S.	G6	114
Sweetgrass, Mt., U.S.	A15	136
Sweet Grass Hills, hills, Mt., U.S.	B15	136
Sweet Home, Tx., U.S.	E10	130
Sweet Springs, Mo., U.S.	F4	120
Sweetwater, Tn., U.S.	A1	116
Sweetwater, Tx., U.S.	B7	130
Sweetwater, stm., Wy., U.S.	E5	126
Swellendam, S. Afr.	H5	70
Świdnica, Pol.	F12	16
Świdnik, Pol.	E18	16
Świdwin, Pol.	C11	16
Świebodzice, Pol.	F12	16
Świebodzin, Pol.	D11	16
Świecie, Pol.	C14	16
Świerzawa, Pol.	E11	16
Świętokrzyski Park Narodowy, p.o.i., Pol.	F16	16
Swift Current, Sk., Can.	D6	124
Swift Current Creek, stm., Sk., Can.	D6	124
Swinburne, Cape, c., Nu., Can.	A11	106
Swindle Island, i., B.C., Can.	D2	138
Swindon, Eng., U.K.	J11	12
Swinford, Ire.	H4	12
Swinoujście (Swinemünde), Pol.	C9	16
Switzerland, ctry., Eur.	C14	18
Swords, Ire.	H6	12
Syalah, Russia	C13	34
Syan (San), stm., Eur.	F18	16
Sycamore, Ga., U.S.	E2	116
Sycamore, Oh., U.S.	C2	114
Syčovka, Russia	E17	10
Sydenham, stm., On., Can.	F7	112
Sydney, Austl.	I8	76
Sydney, N.S., Can.	D16	110
Sydney Bay, b., Norf. I.	y25	78i
Sydney Mines, N.S., Can.	D16	110
Syčyk, Bela.	H12	10
Syke, Ger.	D4	16
Sykesville, Pa., U.S.	C7	114
Syktyvkar, Russia	B8	32
Sylacauga, Al., U.S.	D12	122
Sylhet, Bngl.	F13	54
Syloga, Russia	E20	8
Sylt, i., Ger.	B4	16
Sylva, N.C., U.S.	A2	116
Sylvan Grove, Ks., U.S.	C10	128
Sylvania, Ga., U.S.	D4	116
Sylvan Lake, l., Ab., Can.	D16	138
Sylvan Pass, p., Wy., U.S.	F16	136
Sylvester, Tx., U.S.	B7	130
Sym, Russia	B15	32
Sym, stm., Russia	C15	32
Sými, i., Grc.	G10	28
Šymkent see Shymkent, Kaz.	F11	32
Synevyr, Ukr.	A11	26
Syowa, sci., Ant.	C9	81
Syracuse, In., U.S.	G3	112
Syracuse, Ks., U.S.	C7	128
Syracuse, Ut., U.S.	B4	132
Syracuse, N.Y., U.S.	A9	114
Syrdarja see Syr Darya, stm., Asia	F11	32
Syrdar'ja, Uzb.	A10	56
Syr Darya (Syrdariya), stm., Asia	F11	32
Syria, ctry., Asia	D3	56
Syriam, Mya.	D3	48
Syrian Desert (Shām, Bādiyat ash-), des., Asia	C4	56
Sýrna, i., Grc.	G9	28

Name	Map Ref.	Page
Sýros, i., Grc.	F7	28
Sysmä, Fin.	F11	8
Syston, Eng., U.K.		
Sysola, stm., Russia	B8	32
Syt'kovo, Russia	D16	10
Syväri, l., Fin.	E13	8
Syzran', Russia	D7	32
Szabolcs-Szatmár-Bereg, state, Hung.	A9	26
Szamos (Somes), stm., Eur.	B9	26
Szamotuły, Pol.	D12	16
Szarvas, Hung.	C7	26
Szczawnica, Pol.	G16	16
Szczecin (Stettin), Pol.	C10	16
Szczecin, state, Pol.	C11	16
Szczecinek, Pol.	C12	16
Szczuczyn, Pol.	C18	16
Szczytno, Pol.	C17	16
Szechwan see Sichuan, China	E5	36
Szechwan Basin see Sichuan Pendi, bas., China	F1	42
Szeged, Hung.	C7	26
Szeghalom, Hung.	B8	26
Székesfehérvár, Hung.	B5	26
Szekszárd, Hung.	C5	26
Szentendre, Hung.	B5	26
Szentes, Hung.	C7	26
Szeping see Siping, China	C6	38
Szerencs, Hung.	A8	26
Szob, Hung.	B5	26
Szolnok, Hung.	B7	26
Szombathely, Hung.	B3	26
Szprotawa, Pol.	E11	16
Szubin, Pol.	C13	16
Szypliszki, Pol.	B19	16

T

Name	Map Ref.	Page
Taal, Lake, l., Phil.	D3	52
Tábara, Spain	C5	20
Tabar Islands, is., Pap. N. Gui.	a5	79a
Tabarka, Tun.	H2	24
Tabasco, state, Mex.	D6	96
Tabelbala, Alg.	D4	64
Taber, Ab., Can.	G18	138
Tabernes de Valldigna see Tavernes de la Valldigna, Spain	E10	20
Tabira, Braz.	D7	88
Tablas de Daimiel, Parque Nacional de las, p.o.i., Spain	E7	20
Tablas Island, i., Phil.	D4	52
Tablas Strait, strt., Phil.	D3	52
Tablat, Alg.	H14	20
Table Mountain, mtn., Az., U.S.	K6	132
Table Rock, Ne., U.S.	D1	120
Table Rock Lake, res., U.S.	H4	120
Table Top, mtn., Az., U.S.	K4	132
Tablones, P.R.	B4	104a
Taboi, Mount, hill, St. Vin.	p11	105e
Tábor, Czech Rep.	G10	16
Tabor, Ia., U.S.	D2	120
Tabora, Tan.	E6	66
Tabor City, N.C., U.S.	B7	116
Tabou, C. Iv.	I3	64
Tabriz, Iran	B6	56
Tabuaeran, at., Kir.	C11	72
Tabu-dong, Kor., S.	C1	40
Tabuk, Phil.	B3	52
Tabūk, Sau. Ar.	J7	58
Tabuleiro do Norte, Braz.	C6	88
Tabwémasana, Mont, mtn., Vanuatu	j16	79d
Tacámbaro de Codallos, Mex.	F8	100
Tacaná, Volcán, vol., N.A.	H12	100
Tacañitas, Arg.	D6	92
Taché, Lac, l., N.T., Can.	C7	106
Tacheng, China	B1	36
Tachichitte, Isla de, i., Mex.	C4	100
Tachie, stm., B.C., Can.	B6	138
Táchira, state, Ven.	D6	86
Tachoshui, Tai.	I9	42
Tacima, Braz.	D8	88
Tacloban, Phil.	E5	52
Tacobo, Phil.	G4	52
Tacna, Peru	G3	84
Tacna, Az., U.S.	K3	132
Tacoma, Wa., U.S.	C4	136
Taconic Range, mts., U.S.	B12	114
Taco Pozo, Arg.	B6	92
Tacuarembó, Ur.	E10	92
Tacuarembó, stm., Ur.	E10	92
Tacuba, Sed.	I3	60
Tacuru (Takutu), stm., S.A.	F11	86
Tademaït, Plateau du, plat., Alg.	D5	64
Tadepallegŭdem, India	C5	53
Tadjemout, Alg.	C6	64
Tadjerouine, Tun.	C9	40
Tadjoura, Dji.	E8	62
Tadoule Lake, l., Mb., Can.	D11	106
Tadoussac, Qc., Can.	B7	110
Tādpatri, India	D4	53
Tādpatri, India	A7	60
T'aean, Kor., S.	F7	38
T'aebaek-sanmaek, mts., Asia	F8	38
Taech'ŏn, Kor., S.	A8	54
Taegangjŏng, stm., Kor., N.	D1	40
Taegu, Kor., S.	D1	40
Taejŏn, Kor., N.	D8	38
Taejŏn, Kor., S.	C7	38
Taejŏn, Kor., S.	C1	40
Taekwang-ni, Kor., N.	G8	38
Taël, Cro.	C1	40
Takhli, Thai.	E4	48
Tafahi, i., Tonga	E9	72
Tafalla, Spain	B9	20
Taféa, state, Vanuatu	l17	79d
Tafelberg, hill, Neth. Ant.	p22	104g
Tafi Viejo, Arg.	C5	92
Tafira, Ghana	H5	64
Taft, Ca., U.S.	H7	134
Taft, Tx., U.S.	F10	130
Taftān, Küh-e, vol., Iran	D9	56
Taga, Samoa	g11	79c
Tagajō, Japan	A14	40
Taganrog, Russia	E5	32
Tagant, reg., Maur.	F2	64
Tagaytay, Phil.	C3	52
Tage, Pap. N. Gui.	b3	79a
Tagish Lake, l., Can.	C3	106
Tagliamento, stm., Italy	D9	22
Táglio di Po, Italy	E9	22
Tagula, Pap. N. Gui.	c10	79a
Tagula Island, i., Pap. N. Gui.	c10	79a
Tagum, Phil., Alg.	F6	52
Tagus (Tajo) (Tejo), stm., Eur.	E2	20
Tahakopa, N.Z.	H3	80
Tahan, Gunong, mtn., Malay.	J6	48
Tahat, mtn., Alg.	F6	64
Tahching Shan see Daqing Shan, mts., China	A4	42
Tahe, China	A10	36
Tahifet, Alg.	F6	64
Tāhirpur, India	J6	48
Tahiti, i., Fr. Poly.	v23	78h
Tahiti-Faaa, Aéroport International de, Fr. Poly.	v21	78h
Tahlequah, Ok., U.S.	I3	120

Name	Map Ref.	Page
Tahoe, Lake, l., U.S.	E5	134
Tahoe City, Ca., U.S.	D5	134
Taho Lake, l., Nu., Can.	A8	106
Tahoka, Tx., U.S.	A6	130
Tahoua, Niger	F5	64
Tahquamenon, stm., Mi., U.S.	B4	112
Tahta, Egypt	L2	58
Tahta, Russia	E6	32
Tahta-Bazar, Turkmen.	B9	56
Tahtaköprü, Tur.	D12	28
Tahtamygda, Russia	F13	34
Tahtsa Lake, res., B.C., Can.	C3	138
Tahtsa Peak, mtn., B.C., Can.	C3	138
Tahuata, i., Fr. Poly.	s18	78g
Tahulandang, Pulau, i., Indon.	E7	44
Tahuna, Indon.	E8	44
Tahune, stm., China	C7	42
Taiarapu, Presqu'île de, pen., Fr. Poly.	w22	78h
Taibai Shan, mtn., China	E2	42
Taibilla, Sierra de, mts., Spain	F8	20
Taibus Qi, China	C8	36
Taicang, China	F9	42
T'aichou see Taizhou, China	E8	42
T'aichung, Tai.	I9	42
Taieri, stm., N.Z.	G4	80
Taigu, China	C5	42
Taihang Shan, mts., China	C5	42
Taihape, N.Z.	D6	80
Taihe, China	H6	42
Taihe, China	B5	42
Taihe, China	B5	38
T'aihsien see Taizhou, China	F7	42
Taihu, China	F7	42
Tai Hu, l., China	F9	42
Taikang, China	D6	42
Taikou, China	F4	42
Tailai, China	B9	36
Tai Lake see Tai Hu, l., China	F9	42
Tailem Bend, Austl.	J2	76
Taimba, Russia	B17	32
Taining, China	H7	42
Taiobeiras, Braz.	H4	88
T'aipei, Tai.	I9	42
T'aipeihsien, Tai.	I9	42
Taiping, China	J2	42
Taiping, Malay.	J5	48
Taipingdian, China	E5	42
Taipu, Braz.	C8	88
Tais, Indon.	F3	50
Taisha, Japan	D5	40
Taishan, China	J5	42
Tai Shan see Yuhuang Ding, mtn., China	C9	42
Taishun, China	H8	42
Taitao, Península de, pen., Chile	I2	90
T'aitung, Tai.	J9	42
Taiwan, ctry., Asia	J9	42
Taiwan Strait, strt., Asia	I8	42
Taixian, China	E9	42
Taixing, China	E9	42
Taiyiba, Isr.	F6	58
Taiyuan, China	C5	42
Taizhao, China	D14	54
Taizhou, China	J5	42
Tajbola, Russia	B15	8
Taga, Russia	C15	32
Tajgonos, mys, c., Russia	D21	34
Tajgonos, poluostrov, pen., Russia	D21	34
Tajikistan, ctry., Asia	B11	56
Tajimi, Japan	B12	40
Tajimi, Japan	D10	40
Tajitos, Mex.	G2	128
Tāj Mahal, hist., India	E7	54
Tajmura, stm., Russia	B18	32
Tajmyr, ozero, l., Russia	B9	34
Tajmyr, poluostrov, pen., Russia	B7	34
Tajo see Tagus, stm., Eur.	C17	32
Tajumulco, Volcán, vol., Guat.	E2	102
Tajuña, stm., Spain	D7	20
Tak, Thai.	D4	48
Takachu, Bots.	C5	70
Takahagi, Japan	C13	40
Takaishi, Japan	H7	40
Takahe, Mount, mtn., Ant.	C29	81
Takaka, N.Z.	E5	80
Takakkaw Falls, wtfl., B.C., Can.	E14	138
Takalar, Indon.	F11	50
Takamatsu, Japan	E7	40
Takanabe, Japan	G4	40
Takaoka, Japan	C9	40
Takapau, N.Z.	E7	80
Takasago, Japan	E7	40
Takasaki, Japan	C11	40
Takatsuki, Japan	E8	40
Ta-kaw, Mya.	B4	48
Takayama, Japan	C10	40
Takefu, Japan	D9	40
Takenake, Japan	A8	54
Takengon, Indon.	J3	48
Takeo, Japan	F3	40
Takeo-shima, is., Japan	B4	40
Takhatpur, India	G8	54
Takhli, Thai.	E4	48
Takhta-Bazar see Tahta-Bazar, Turkmen.	B9	56
Takijuq Lake, l., Nu., Can.	B8	106
Takikawa, Japan	C14	38
Takla Lake, l., B.C., Can.	A5	138
Takla Landing, B.C., Can.	D5	106
Takla Makan Desert see Taklimakan Shamo, des., China	G14	32
Taklimakan Shamo (Takla Makan Desert), des., China	G14	32
Tako, Ghana	H5	64
Takokelewa, Pegunungan, mts., Indon.	E11	50
Taksimo, Russia	E10	34
Taku, stm., N.A.	D3	106
Takua Pa, Thai.	H4	48
Takum, Nig.	H6	64
Takutu, stm., Cook Is.	E11	72
Takutu (Tacutu), stm., S.A.	F11	86
Tala, Ur.	E10	92
Talachyn, Bela.	F12	10
Talagante, Chile	F2	92
Talaimannar, Sri L.	G4	53
Tālāja, India	H4	54
Talal, i., Niger	H6	64
Talang, Gunung, vol., Indon.	D2	50
Talangbetutu, Indon.	E4	50
Talangpadang, Indon.	F4	50
Talara, Peru	D1	84
Talas, Kyrg.	F12	32
Talasea, Pap. N. Gui.	b5	79a
Talata Mafara, Nig.	G6	64
Talaud, Kepulauan (Talaud Islands), is., Indon.	E8	44
Talaud Islands see Talaud, Kepulauan, is., Indon.	E8	44

Name	Map Ref.	Page

Talavera de la Reina, Spain .. D5 20
Talawanta, Austl. B3 76
Talawdĭ, Sudan E6 62
Talayan, Phil. G5 52
Talbotton, Ga., U.S. E14 122
Talbragar, stm., Austl. I7 76
Talca, Chile G2 92
Talcahuano, Chile H1 92
Tālcher, India H10 54
Talco, Tx., U.S. D3 122
Taldom, Russia D20 10
Taldykorgan see
  Taldyqorghan, Kaz. F13 32
Taldyqorghan, Kaz. F13 32
Talence, Fr. E5 18
Talent, Or., U.S. A3 134
Talgar see Talghar, Kaz. F13 32
Talghar, Kaz. F13 32
Talhăr, Pak. F2 54
Taliabu, Pulau, i., Indon. F7 44
Talibon, Phil. E5 52
Taliparamba, India E2 53
Talisay, Phil. E4 52
Taliwang, Indon. H10 50
Talkeetna, Ak., U.S. D9 140
Talkeetna Mountains,
  mts., Ak., U.S. D10 140
Talla, Egypt J1 58
Talladega, Al., U.S. D12 122
Tallahala Creek, stm.,
  Ms., U.S. F9 122
Tallahassee, Fl., U.S. F1 116
Tallahatchie, stm., Ms., U.S. .. D8 122
Tallangatta, Austl. K6 76
Tallapoosa, Ga., U.S. D13 122
Tallapoosa, stm., U.S. E12 122
Tallard, Fr. E11 18
Tallassee, Al., U.S. E12 122
Tall as-Sulṭān, sci., Gaza G6 58
Tall Bīsah, Syria D7 58
Tallinn, Est. G11 8
Tallmadge, Oh., U.S. C4 114
Tall Rifʿat, Syria B8 58
Tallulah, La., U.S. E7 122
Talmage, Ca., U.S. D2 134
Talmage, Ne., U.S. K2 118
Talʾmenka, Russia D14 32
Talnakh, Russia C6 34
Taloda, India H5 54
Taloga, Ok., U.S. E10 128
Talok, Indon. C11 50
Talogan, Afg. B10 56
Talovka, Russia F7 32
Talquin, Lake, res., Fl., U.S. .. G14 122
Talsi, Lat. C5 10
Taltal, Chile B2 92
Taltson, stm., N.T., Can. C8 106
Talu, Indon. C1 50
Taluk, Indon. D2 50
Talumphuk, Laem, c., Thai. ... H5 48
Taluriquak, Nu., Can. B12 106
Talvikjulja, Russia B13 8
Talwood, Austl. G7 76
Tama, Arg. E4 92
Tama, Ia., U.S. C5 120
Tamalameque, Col. C5 86
Tamale, Ghana H4 64
Tamalea, Indon. E11 50
Tamalpais, Mount, mtn.,
  Ca., U.S. F3 134
Tamana, Japan G3 40
Tamana, Mount, hill, Trin. s12 105f
Tamanaco, stm., Ven. C9 86
Tamaniquá, Braz. I9 86
Taman Negara, p.o.i.,
  Malay. J6 48
Tamano, Japan E6 40
Tamanquaré, Ilha,
  i., Braz. H9 86
Tamapatz, Mex. E9 100
Tamar, stm., Austl. n13 77a
Tamarac, stm., Mn., U.S. C2 118
Tamaroa, Il., U.S. F8 120
Tamási, Hung. C5 26
Tamaulipas, state, Mex. C9 100
Tamazulapan del
  Progreso, Mex. G9 100
Tamazunchale, Mex. E9 100
Tambacounda, Sen. G2 64
Tambakboyo, Indon. G7 50
Tamba-kōchi, plat., Japan D8 40
Tambangsawah, Indon. E3 50
Tambara, Moz. D5 68
Tambaram, India E5 53
Tambej, Russia B3 34
Tambelan, Kepulauan,
  is., Indon. C5 50
Tamberías, Arg. E3 92
Tambo, stm., Austl. K6 76
Tambohorano, Madag. D7 68
Tamboliongang, Pulau, i.,
  Indon. G12 50
Tambora, Gunung, vol.,
  Indon. H10 50
Tamboril, Braz. C5 88
Tamboryacu, stm., Peru H4 86
Tambov, Russia D6 32
Tambre, stm., Spain A2 20
Tambu, Teluk, b., Indon. C11 50
Tamburan, Malay. H1 52
Tambura, Sudan F5 62
Tămchekket, Maur. F2 64
Tame, Col. D6 86
Tameapa, Mex. C5 100
Tamega, stm., Port. C3 20
Tamel Aike, Arg. I2 90
Tamenghest, Alg. E6 64
Tamenghest, Oued, stm.,
  Alg. E5 64
Tamga, Russia B10 38
Tamgak, Adrar, mtn., Niger . . F6 64
Tamiahua, Mex. E10 100
Tamiahua, Laguna de, l.,
  Mex. E10 100
Tamiami Canal, can.,
  Fl., U.S. K4 116
Tamil Nādu, state, India F4 53
Tamiš (Timiş), stm., Eur. D7 26
Tămîya, Egypt I1 58
Tamkūhi, India E10 54
Tam Ky, Viet. E9 48
Tammerfors see Tampere,
  Fin. F10 8
Tammisaari, Fin. G10 8
Tamms, Il., U.S. G8 120
Tampa, Fl., U.S. I3 116
Tampa Bay, b., Fl., U.S. I3 116
Tampang, Indon. F4 50
Tampaon, stm., Mex. E9 100
Tampere (Tammerfors), Fin. .. F10 8
Tampico, Mex. D10 100
Tampico, II., U.S. C8 120
Tampin, Malay. K6 48
Tamsagbulag, Mong. B8 36
Tamshiyacu, Peru D3 84
Tamsweg, Aus. C10 22
Tamu, Mya. D7 46
Tamuning, Guam j10 78c
Tamworth, Austl. H8 76
Tamworth, Eng., U.K. I11 12
Tana (Teno), stm., Eur. B12 8
Tana, stm., Kenya D8 66
Tana, Lake see
  Tʾana Hāyk', l., Eth. E7 62
Tanabe, Japan F8 40
Tanabi, Braz. K1 88
Tana bru, Nor. A12 8
Tanacross, Ak., U.S. D11 140
Tanafjorden, b., Nor. A13 8
Tanaga Island, i., Ak., U.S. ... g23 140a

Tʾana Hāyk', l., Eth. E7 62
Tanahbala, Pulau, i.,
  Indon. F2 44
Tanahgrogot, Indon. D10 50
Tanahjampea, Pulau, i.,
  Indon. G12 50
Tanahmasa, Pulau, i.,
  Indon. F2 44
Tanahmerah, Indon. G10 44
Tanah Merah, Malay. J6 48
Tanahputih, Indon. C2 50
Tanakeke, Pulau, i.,
  Indon. F11 50
Tanakpur, India D7 54
Tanami Desert, des., Austl. ... C5 74
Tan An, Viet. G8 48
Tanana, Ak., U.S. C9 140
Tanana, stm., Ak., U.S. D10 140
Tananarive see
  Antananarivo, Madag. D8 68
Tanbar, Austl. E3 76
Tanch'ŏn-ŭp, Kor., N. D8 38
Tancítaro, Pico de,
  mtn., Mex. F7 100
Tanda, Egypt K1 58
Tānda, India E9 54
Tānda, India C5 54
Tandag, Phil. E6 52
Tandāltī, Sudan E6 62
Tăndărei, Rom. E14 26
Tandil, Arg. H8 92
Tando Ādam, Pak. F2 54
Tando Allāhyār, Pak. F2 54
Tandou Lake, l., Austl. I3 76
Tandula Tank, res., India H8 54
Tandun, Indon. C2 50
Tăndŭr, India C3 53
Tanega-shima, i., Japan I9 38
Tanezrouft, des., Afr. E4 64
Tang, stm., China E7 42
Tang, stm., China E5 42
Tang, stm., China B6 42
Tanga, Russia F11 34
Tanga, Tan. F7 66
Tangail, Bngl. F12 54
Tanga Islands, is., Pap.
  N. Gui. a5 79a
Tanga Langua, c., Gren. q10 105e
Tanganyika see Tanzania,
  ctry., Afr. F6 66
Tanganyika, Lake, l., Afr. F6 66
Tangarana, stm., Peru I4 86
Tangarare, Sol. Is. e8 79b
Tanger (Tangier), Mor. B3 64
Tangerang, Indon. G5 50
Tangerhütte, Ger. D7 16
Tangermünde, Ger. D7 16
Tanggu, China B7 42
Tanggulashan, China A14 54
Tanggula Shan, mts., China .. E3 36
Tanggula Shankou, p.,
  China B13 54
Tangi, Indon. E5 42
Tangi, Pak. A3 54
Tangier, N.S., Can. F14 110
Tangier see Tanger, Mor. B3 64
Tangier, Va., U.S. G10 114
Tangipahoa, stm., U.S. G8 122
Tangjiagou, China F7 42
Tangkou, China F8 42
Tangmai, China E4 36
Tango-hantō, pen., Japan D8 40
Tangra Yumco, l., China C11 54
Tangshan, China B8 42
Tangtou, China D8 42
Tangyan, Mya. A4 48
Tangyin, China D6 42
Tangyuan, China B10 36
Tanhoj, Russia F10 34
Taniantaweng Shan, mts.,
  China F4 36
Tanigawa-dake, mtn., Japan . C11 40
Tanimbar, Kepulauan,
  is., Indon. G9 44
Tanintharyi, state, Mya. H2 58
Tanis, hist., Egypt H2 58
Tanjay, Phil. F4 52
Tanjung, Indon. H10 50
Tanjung, Indon. E9 50
Tanjungbalai, Indon. B1 50
Tanjungbatu, Indon. C3 50
Tanjungbatu, Indon. B11 50
Tanjungkarang-Telukbetung
  see Bandar Lampung,
  Indon. F4 50
Tanjunglabu, Indon. E5 50
Tanjungpandan, Indon. E5 50
Tanjungpinang, Indon. C4 50
Tanjungpura, Indon. K4 48
Tanjungraja, Indon. E4 50
Tanjungredep, Indon. B10 50
Tanjungselor, Indon. B10 50
Tanjunguban, Indon. C4 50
Tank, Pak. B3 54
Tankwa, stm., S. Afr. H5 70
Tanna, i., Vanuatu l17 79d
Tannenberg see
  Stębark, Pol. C16 16
Tanner, Mount, mtn.,
  B.C., Can. G12 138
Tannu-Ola, hrebet, mts.,
  Asia D16 32
Tannūrah, Ra's, c., Sau. Ar. .. D7 56
Tanon Strait, strt., Phil. E4 52
Tanout, Niger F6 64
Tanquinho, Braz. G6 88
Tanshui, Tai. I9 42
Tanta, Egypt H2 58
Tan-Tan, Mor. D2 64
Tantoyuca, Mex. E9 100
Tanuku, India C5 53
Tanvald, Czech Rep. F11 16
Tanyang, Kor., S. C1 40
Tanzania, ctry., Afr. F6 66
Tao'er, stm., China B5 38
Taohuazhen, China A6 42
Taole, China B2 42
Taonan, China B5 38
Taongi, at., Marsh. Is. B7 72
Taormina, Italy G9 24
Taos, Mo., U.S. F5 120
Taos, N.M., U.S. E3 128
Taos Pueblo, N.M., U.S. E4 64
Taoudenni, Mali E4 64
Taounate, Mor. C4 64
Taourirt, Mor. C4 64
Taoyuan, China G4 42
Taoyüan, Tai. I9 42
Tapa, Est. G11 8
Tapachula, Mex. H12 100
Tapaga, Cape, c., Samoa h12 79c
Tapah, Malay. J5 48
Tapajós, stm., Braz. D7 84
Tapaktuan, Indon. K3 48
Tapalqué, Arg. H7 92
Tapauá, stm., Braz. E4 84
Tapejara, Braz. D12 92
Taperoá, Braz. D7 88
Tapes, Braz. E12 92
Tapeta, Lib. H3 64
Taphan Hin, Thai. D5 48
Taphoen, stm., Thai. E4 48
Tapi, stm., India H4 54
Ta Pi, stm., Thai. H4 48
Tapiche, stm., Peru E3 84
Tapini, Pap. N. Gui. b4 79a
Taplan National Park,
  p.o.i., Thai. E6 48
Táplejunga, Nepal. E11 54
Tapp, N.D., U.S. H14 124
Tapuae-o-Uenuku, mtn.,
  N.Z. E5 80
Tapuio, Braz. C3 88

Tapul Group, is., Phil. H3 52
Tapun, Mya. C2 48
Tapuruquara, Braz. H9 86
Taqătu' Hayyā, Sudan D7 62
Taquara, Braz. D12 92
Taquaras, Ponta das, c.,
  Braz. C13 92
Taquari, stm., Braz. D12 92
Taquari Novo, stm., Braz. C5 90
Taquari, stm., Braz. K1 88
Tar, stm., N.C., U.S. I8 114
Tara, Austl. F8 76
Tara, Russia C12 32
Tara, stm., Eur. G16 22
Tara, stm., Russia C13 32
Taraba, stm., Nig. H7 64
Tarabuco, Bol. C3 90
Ṭarābulus (Tripoli), Leb. D6 58
Ṭarābulus (Tripoli), Libya A2 62
Ṭarābulus (Tripolitania),
  hist. reg., Libya A2 62
Taraclia, Mol. D15 26
Tarago, Austl. J7 76
Taraira (Traíra), stm., S.A. ... H7 86
Taraju, Indon. G6 50
Tarakan, Indon. B10 50
Tarakan, Pulau, i., Indon. B10 50
Taralga, Austl. J7 76
Tara Nacionalni Park,
  p.o.i., Serb. F6 26
Tárānagar, India D5 54
Taranaki, Mount (Egmont,
  Mount), vol., N.Z. D6 80
Tarancón, Spain D8 20
Taranto, Italy D11 24
Taranto, Golfo di, b., Italy ... E10 24
Tarapoto, Peru E2 84
Taraquá, Braz. G7 86
Tarare, Fr. D10 18
Tarariras, Ur. G9 92
Tārāsa Dwīp, i., India G7 46
Tarascon, Fr. F10 18
Tarascon-sur-Ariège, Fr. G7 18
Tarasovo, Russia C13 32
Tarat, Alg. D6 64
Tarata, Bol. C3 90
Taratakbuluh, Indon. C2 50
Tarauacá, stm., Braz. E3 84
Taravao, Isthme de,
  isth., Fr. Poly. v22 78h
Tarawa, at., Kir. C8 72
Tarawera, N.Z. D7 80
Taraz (Žambyl), Kaz. F12 32
Tarazona, Spain C9 20
Tarbagatai, hrebet see
  Tarbagatay, khrebet,
  mts., Asia E14 32
Tarbagatay, khrebet,
  mts., Asia E14 32
Tarbagatay Shan see
  Tarbagatay, khrebet,
  mts., Asia E14 32
Tarbela Reservoir, res., Pak. .. A4 54
Tarbert, Scot., U.K. D6 12
Tarbes, Fr. F6 18
Tarboro, N.C., U.S. I8 114
Tarbū, Libya B3 62
Tarcoola, Austl. F6 74
Tardoki-Jani, gora, mtn.,
  Russia G16 34
Tarée, Austl. H9 76
Tareja, Russia B7 34
Tārendö, Swe. C10 8
Tarentum, Pa., U.S. D6 114
Tarfa, Wadi el-, stm., Egypt .. J2 58
Tarfaya, Mor. D2 64
Targhee Pass, p., U.S. F15 136
Tărgovište, Blg. F13 26
Târgu Bujor, Rom. D14 26
Târgu Frumos, Rom. B14 26
Târgu Jiu, Rom. D10 26
Târgu Mureş, Rom. C11 26
Târgu-Neamţ, Rom. B13 26
Târgu Ocna, Rom. C13 26
Târgu Secuiesc, Rom. C13 26
Tarifa, Spain H5 20
Tarifa, Punta de, c., Spain ... H5 20
Tarija, Bol. D4 90
Tarikere, India E2 53
Tarim, stm., China F14 32
Tarim Pendi, bas., China F12 30
Taritatu, stm., Indon. F10 44
Tarkastad, S. Afr. G8 70
Tarkio, Mo., U.S. D2 120
Tarkio, stm., U.S. D2 120
Tarko-Sale, Russia B13 32
Tarkwa, Ghana H4 64
Tarlac, Phil. C3 52
Tarm, Den. I3 8
Tarma, Peru F2 84
Tarn, state, Fr. F7 18
Tarn, stm., Fr. F7 18
Tårnaby, Swe. D6 8
Tarnak, stm., Afg. B1 54
Târnava Mare, stm., Rom. ... C11 26
Târnăveni, Rom. C11 26
Tarn-et-Garonne, state, Fr. ... F7 18
Tarnobrzeg, Pol. F17 16
Tarnobrzeg, state, Pol. F18 16
Tarnogród, Pol. F18 16
Tarnów, Pol. A14 26
Tarnów, state, Pol. G16 16
Tarnowskie Góry, Pol. F14 16
Taro, Sol. Is. d7 79b
Taro, stm., Italy F7 22
Taron, Pap. N. Gui. a5 79a
Tarong, Austl. F7 76
Taroom, Austl. E7 76
Taroudannt, Mor. C3 64
Ta Roun, co, mtn., Viet. D8 48
Tarpon Springs, Fl., U.S. H3 116
Tarquinia, Italy H8 22
Tarra, stm., S.A. C5 86
Tarrafal, C.V. k10 65a
Tarragona, Spain C12 20
Tarragona, co., Spain D11 20
Tarraleah, Austl. o13 77a
Tarrasa see Terrassa, Spain .. C13 20
Tàrrega, Spain C12 20
Tàrrega see Tàrrega, Spain .. C12 20
Tarsus, Tur. B5 58
Tartagal, Arg. D4 90
Tartas, Fr. F5 18
Ţarţūs, Syria D6 58
Ţarţūs, state, Syria D7 58
Tarum, stm., Indon. G5 50
Tarumirim, Braz. J5 88
Tarumizu, Japan I4 40
Tarutao, Ko, i., Thai. I4 48
Tarutao National Park,
  p.o.i., Thai. I4 48
Tarutino, Russia E19 10
Tarutung, Indon. B1 50
Tarvisio, Italy D10 22
Tarzan, Tx., U.S. B6 130
Taşağıl, Tur. B2 58
Tasāwah, Libya H11 8
Tasböget, Kaz. F11 32
Taseeva, stm., Russia C16 32
Taseevo, Russia C17 32
Taseko Lakes, l., B.C., Can. .. E7 138
Taseko Mountain, mtn.,
  B.C., Can. E7 138
Tāsgaon, India D12 92
Tashi Gang Dzong, Bhu. E13 54
Tashk, Daryācheh-ye,
  l., Iran D7 56
Tashkent see
  Toshkent, Uzb. F11 32
Taškino, Russia C21 32
Taš-Kumyr, Kyrg. F12 32

Tasman Basin, unds. N18 142
Tasman Bay, b., N.Z. E5 80
Tasmania, state, Austl. n13 77a
Tasmania, i., Austl. o13 77a
Tasman Peninsula, pen.,
  Austl. o13 77a
Tasman Sea, s., Oc. G7 72
Taşnad, Rom. B9 26
Tassialouc, Lac, l., Qc., Can. .. D16 106
Taštagol, Russia D15 32
Tastiota, Mex. A3 100
Tata, Hung. B5 26
Tata, Mor. D3 64
Tatabánya, Hung. B5 26
Tatarbunary, Ukr. D16 26
Tatarija, state, Russia C8 32
Tatarinka, Russia E16 10
Tatarsk, Russia C13 32
Tatarskij proliv, strt.,
  Russia G17 34
Tatarstan see Tatarija,
  state, Russia C8 32
Tatar Strait see Tatarskij
  proliv, strt., Russia G17 34
Tate, Ga., U.S. B1 116
Tate, stm., Austl. A4 76
Tate (Harirud), stm., Asia B9 56
Teec Nos Pos, Az., U.S. F7 132
Tate-yama, vol., Japan C10 40
Tees, stm., Eng., U.K. G11 12
Tăranagar, India D5 54
Tatlína Lake, l., N.T., Can. ... C7 106
Tatlayoko Lake, B.C., Can. ... E6 138
Tatlayoko Lake, l.,
  B.C., Can. E6 138
Tatlow, Mount, mtn.,
  B.C., Can. E7 138
Tatnam, Cape, c., Mb., Can. .. D12 106
Tatranský Národny
  Park, p.o.i., Slov. G15 16
Tatrzański Park
  Narodowy, p.o.i., Pol. .... * G15 16
Tatsuno, Japan E7 40
Tatsuno, Japan D10 40
Tatui, Braz. L1 88
Tatum, N.M., U.S. H5 128
Tatum, Tx., U.S. E4 122
Tat'ung see Datong, China ... A5 42
Tatvan, Tur. B5 56
Tau, Am. Sam. h13 79c
Tau, Nor. G1 8
Tau, i., Am. Sam. h13 79c
Tauá, Braz. D5 88
Taubaté, Braz. L3 88
Tauberbischofsheim, Ger. ... G5 16
Taujskaja guba, b., Russia ... E18 34
Taumarunui, N.Z. D6 80
Taumaturgo, Braz. E3 84
Taum Sauk Mountain,
  mtn., Mo., U.S. G7 120
Taungbon, Mya. E3 48
Taungdwingyi, Mya. B3 48
Taunggyi, Mya. B3 48
Taungnyo Range, mts., Mya. . E4 48
Taungup, Mya. C2 48
Taungup Pass, p., Mya. C2 48
Taunsa, Pak. C3 54
Taunton, Eng., U.K. J9 12
Taunton, Ma., U.S. C14 114
Taupo, N.Z. D6 80
Taupo, Lake, l., N.Z. D7 80
Tauragé Lith. E5 10
Tauranga, N.Z. C7 80
Taurianova, Italy F9 24
Taurisano, Italy E12 24
Tauroa Point, c., N.Z. B5 80
Taurus Mountains see
  Toros Dağları, mts., Tur. ... A3 58
Taūshyq, Kaz. F8 32
Tautira, Fr. Poly. v23 78h
Tavares, Braz. D7 88
Tavas, Tur. F12 28
Tavastehus see
  Hämeenlinna, Fin. F10 8
Tavda, Russia C11 32
Tavda, stm., Russia C11 32
Taveuni, i., Fiji p20 79e
Taviano, Italy E11 24
Tavira, Port. G3 20
Tavistock, On., Can. E9 112
Tavistock, Eng., U.K. K8 12
Tavolara, Isola, i., Italy D3 24
Tavoy, Har, mtn., Isr. J3 8
Tavoy Point, c., Mya. F3 48
Tavşanlı, Tur. D12 28
Tavua, Fiji p18 79e
Tawaeli, Indon. D11 50
Tawakoni, Lake, res.,
  Tx., U.S. E2 122
Tawas City, Mi., U.S. D6 112
Tawau, Malay. A10 50
Tawila, Gezira, is., Egypt K4 58
Tawitawi Group, is., Phil. H3 52
Tawitawi Island, i., Phil. H2 52
Tawkar, Sudan D7 62
Taxco de Alarcón, Mex. F8 100
Taxkorgan Tajik
  Zizhixian, China B12 56
Tay, stm., Scot., U.K. E9 12
Tay, Firth of, b.,
  Scot., U.K. E9 12
Tay, Loch, l., Scot., U.K. E8 12
Tayabamba, Peru E2 84
Tayabas Bay, b., Phil. D3 52
Tayan, Indon. D7 50
Taylor, Az., U.S. I6 132
Taylor, B.C., Can. D7 138
Taylor, Tx., U.S. D10 130
Taylor, Mount, mtn.,
  N.M., U.S. H9 132
Taylors, S.C., U.S. B3 116
Taylorsville, Ky., U.S. F12 120
Taylorsville, Ms., U.S. F9 122
Taylorville, N.C., U.S. I4 114
Taylorville, Il., U.S. E8 120
Tayma', Sau. Ar. K9 58
Taymouth, N.B., Can. D10 110
Taymyr, poluostrov see
  Tajmyr, poluostrov,
  pen., Russia B7 34
Tay Ninh, Viet. G8 48
Tayoltita, Mex. C6 100
Tayport, Scot., U.K. E10 12
Tayshet, Russia C17 32
Tayu, Indon. G7 50
Taz, stm., Russia A14 32
Tazewell, Tn., U.S. H2 114
Tazewell, Va., U.S. G5 114
Tazin, stm., Russia C8 106
Tazin Lake, l., Sk., Can. D10 106
Tazovskaja guba, b., Russia .. A13 32
Tazovskij, Russia A13 32
Tazovskij poluostrov,
  pen., Russia C4 34
Tbessa, Alg. B6 64
Tbilisi, Geor. F6 32
Tchaourou, Benin H5 64
Tchentlo Lake, l., B.C., Can. .. A5 138
Tchesinkut Lake, l.,
  B.C., Can. B5 138
Tchibanga, Gabon E2 66
Tcho-kiang see Zhejiang,
  state, China G8 42
Tchollire, Cam. C2 66
Tchula, Ms., U.S. D8 122
Tczew, Pol. B14 16
Té, stm., Camb. F8 48
Teaca, Rom. C11 26
Teacapán, Mex. D5 100
Teague, Tx., U.S. F2 122

Te Anau, Lake, l., N.Z. G2 80
Teapa, Mex. G12 100
Te Awamutu, N.Z. C6 80
Teba, Spain H6 20
Tebakang, Malay. C7 50
Tebicuary, stm., Para. C9 92
Tebicuary-mí, stm., Para. C9 92
Tebingtinggi, Indon. B1 50
Tebingtinggi, Indon. E3 50
Tebingtinggi, Pulau, i.,
  Indon. H3 24
Tebourba, Tun. H3 24
Tébossouk, Tun. H3 24
Tecalitlán, Mex. F7 100
Tecate, Mex. K9 134
Techirghiol, Rom. E15 26
Techlé, W. Sah. E2 64
Techou see Dezhou, China ... C7 42
Tecka, Arg. H2 90
Tecka, stm., Arg. H2 90
Tecomán, Mex. F7 100
Tecopa, Ca., U.S. H9 134
Tecpan de Galeana, Mex. ... G8 100
Tecuala, Mex. D6 100
Tecuci, Rom. D14 26
Tecumseh, Ok., U.S. B2 122
Tedžen, Turkmen. B9 56
Tedžen (Harīrud), stm., Asia .. B9 56
Teeli, Russia D16 32
Teeswater, On., Can. D8 112
Tefé, Braz. D5 84
Tefé, stm., Braz. D4 84
Tefenni, Tur. F12 28
Tegal, Indon. G6 50
Tégama, reg., Niger F6 64
Tégéa, sci., Grc. F5 28
Tegineneng, Indon. F4 50
Tegucigalpa, Hond. E4 102
Teguldet, Russia C15 32
Tehachapi, Ca., U.S. H7 134
Tehachapi Pass, p., Ca., U.S. . H7 134
Tehek Lake, l., Nu., Can. C12 106
Tehran (Teheran), Iran B7 56
Tehrathum, Nepal. E11 54
Tehuacán, Mex. F10 100
Tehuantepec, Golfo de,
  b., Mex. H11 100
Tehuantepec, Gulf of see
  Tehuantepec, Golfo de,
  b., Mex. H11 100
Tehuantepec, Isthmus of
  see Tehuantepec,
  Istmo de, isth., Mex. G11 100
Tehuantepec, Istmo de,
  isth., Mex. G11 100
Teignmouth, Eng., U.K. K9 12
Teixeira, Braz. D7 88
Teixeira Pinto, Gui.-B. G1 64
Tejakula, Indon. H9 50
Tejo see Tagus, stm., Eur. ... C2 20
Tejon Pass, p., Ca., U.S. I7 134
Tejupilco de Hidalgo, Mex. .. F8 100
Tekamah, Ne., U.S. C1 120
Tekapo, Lake, l., N.Z. F4 80
Tekax, Mex. B3 102
Teke, Tur. B12 28
Teke Burnu, c., Tur. E9 28
Tekeli, Kaz. F13 32
Tekezē (Satīt), stm., Afr. E7 62
Tekirdağ, Tur. C10 28
Tekirdağ, state, Tur. B10 28
Tekkali, India B7 53
Tekoa, Wa., U.S. C9 136
Tekonsha, Mi., U.S. B1 114
Te Kuiti, N.Z. D6 80
Tela, Hond. E4 102
Telaopengsha Shan, mtn.,
  China C11 54
Telavi, Geor. F7 32
Tel Aviv-Jaffa see Tel
  Aviv-Yafo, Isr. F5 58
Tel Aviv-Yafo, Isr. F5 58
Telč, Czech Rep. G11 16
Telèckoe, ozero, l., Russia ... D15 32
Telefomin, Pap. N. Gui. b3 79a
Telegraph Creek, B.C., Can. .. D4 106
Telèmaco Borba, Braz. B12 92
Telemark, state, Nor. G3 8
Terdal, India C2 53
Terek, stm., Russia G18 6
Terengganu, state, Malay. ... J6 48
Terenos, Braz. C4 90
Teresina, Braz. C4 88
Teresópolis, Braz. L4 88
Terespol, Pol. D19 16
Tereváka, Cerro, mtn.,
  Chile e29 78l
Tergüün Bogd
  uul, mtn., Mong. C5 36
Teriang, stm., Malay. K6 48
Teriberka, Russia B16 8
Terihi, i., Fr. Poly. t19 78g
Terlingua, Tx., U.S. E4 130
Terlingua Creek, stm.,
  Tx., U.S. E4 130
Termas del Arapey, Ur. E9 92
Termez, Uzb. B10 56
Termini Imerese, Italy G7 24
Termini Imerese, Golfo
  di, b., Italy F7 24
Terminillo, Monte, mtn.,
  Italy H9 22
Términos, Laguna
  de, b., Mex. C2 102
Termoli, Italy H11 22
Termonde see
  Dendermonde, Bel. C12 14
Ternej, Russia B12 38
Terneuzen, Neth. C12 14
Terni, Italy H9 22
Ternitz, Aus. C12 22
Ternopil', Ukr. F14 6
Terpenija, mys, c., Russia ... G17 34
Terpenija, zaliv, b.,
  Russia G17 34
Terra Alta, W.V., U.S. E6 114
Terra Bella, Ca., U.S. H6 134
Terrace, B.C., Can. B2 138
Terrace Bay, On., Can. C7 24
Terra Santa, Braz. D6 84
Terrabonne Bay, b., La., U.S. . H5 122
Terrak, Nor. D5 8
Terre Haute, In., U.S. E2 122
Terrell, Tx., U.S. E2 122
Terre-Neuve see
  Newfoundland and
  Labrador, state, Can. i23 107a
Territoire du Yukon see
  Yukon, state, Can. B3 106
Territoires du Nord-Ouest
  see Northwest Territories,
  state, Can. C6 106
Terry, Ms., U.S. E8 122
Terry, Mt., U.S. A7 126
Terschelling, i., Neth. A14 14
Terskej-Alatau, hrebet,
  mts., Kyrg. F13 32
Tertenia, Italy E3 24
Teruel, Spain D10 20
Teruel, co., Spain D10 20
Tervola, Fin. C11 8

Name	Map Ref.	Page
Terzaghi Dam, dam, B.C., Can.	F8	138
Tes, stm., Asia	D16	32
Tescott, Ks., U.S.	B11	128
Teseney, Erit.	D7	62
Teshekpuk Lake, l., Ak., U.S.	B9	140
Teshio, Japan.	B14	38
Teshio, stm., Japan.	B15	38
Teslin, Yk., Can.	C4	106
Teslin, stm., Can.	C4	106
Teslin Lake, l., Can.	C4	106
Tёsovo, Russia.	E17	10
Tёsovo-Netyl'skij, Russia.	B13	10
Tёsovskij, Russia.	B13	10
Tessalit, Mali	E5	64
Tessaoua, Niger	G6	64
Testa, Capo, c., Italy	C3	24
Testour, Tun.	H3	24
Tetachuck Lake, res., B.C., Can.	C4	138
Tete, Moz.	D5	68
Tête Jaune Cache, B.C., Can.	D11	138
Tetepare Island, i., Sol. Is.	e7	79b
Teterow, Ger.	C8	16
Tetica, mtn., Spain	G8	20
Teton, Id., U.S.	G15	136
Teton, stm., Id., U.S.	G15	136
Teton, stm., Mt., U.S.	C15	136
Tetonia, Id., U.S.	G15	136
Teton Range, mts., Wy., U.S.	G16	136
Tetouan, Mor.	B4	64
Tetovo, Mac.	A4	28
Tetufera, Mont, mtn., Fr. Poly.	v22	78h
Teuco, stm., Arg.	D4	90
Teulada, Italy.	F2	24
Teulada, Capo, c., Italy	F2	24
Teulon, Mb., Can.	D16	124
Teutoburger Wald, hills, Ger.	D4	16
Teuva, Fin.	E9	8
Tevere (Tiber), stm., Italy	H9	22
Teverya, Isr.	F6	58
Te Waewae Bay, b., N.Z.	H2	80
Tewah, Indon.	D8	50
Tewantin-Noosa, Austl.	F9	76
Tewkesbury, Eng., U.K.	I11	12
Texada Island, i., B.C., Can.	G6	138
Texana, Lake, res., Tx., U.S.	F11	130
Texarkana, Ar., U.S.	D4	122
Texarkana, Tx., U.S.	D4	122
Texas, Austl.	G8	76
Texas, state, U.S.	E8	108
Texas City, Tx., U.S.	H4	122
Texel, i., Neth.	A13	14
Texhoma, Ok., U.S.	E7	128
Texico, N.M., U.S.	G5	128
Texoma, Lake, res., U.S.	D3	122
Teyateyaneng, Leso.	F8	70
Teyvareh, Afg.	C9	56
Teziutlán, Mex.	F10	100
Tezpur, India	E14	54
Tezzeron Lake, l., B.C., Can.	B6	138
Tha, stm., Laos	B5	48
Tha-anne, stm., Nu., Can.	C11	106
Thabana-Ntlenyana, mtn., Leso.	F9	70
Thabaung, Mya.	D2	48
Thabazimbi, S. Afr.	D8	70
Thabyu, Mya.	E4	48
Thagyettaw, Mya.	F3	48
Thai Binh, Viet.	B8	48
Thailand, ctry., Asia	E5	48
Thailand, Gulf of, b., Asia.	F5	48
Tha Nguyen, Viet.	B7	48
Thak, Pak.	C3	54
Thal, Pak.	B3	54
Thala, Tun.	I2	24
Thal Desert, des., Pak.	C3	54
Thalfang, Ger.	G2	16
Tha Li, Thai.	D5	48
Thalia, Tx., U.S.	H9	128
Thālith, Ash-Shallāl ath- (Third Cataract), wtfl., Sudan	D6	62
Thalwil, Switz.	C5	22
Thames, N.Z.	C6	80
Thames, stm., On., Can.	F8	112
Thames, stm., Eng., U.K.	J13	12
Thames, Firth of, b., N.Z.	C6	80
Thamesford, On., Can.	E8	112
Thamesville, On., Can.	F7	112
Thāna, India	B1	53
Thandaung, Mya.	C3	48
Thangoo, Austl.	C4	74
Thangool, Austl.	E8	76
Thanh Hoa, Viet.	C7	48
Thanh Pho Ho Chi Minh (Saigon), Viet.	G8	48
Thanjāvūr, India	F4	53
Thann, Fr.	B12	18
Thap Than, stm., Thai.	E6	48
Tharabwin West, Mya.	F4	48
Tharād, India.	F3	54
Thar Desert (Great Indian Desert), des., Asia.	D3	54
Thargomindah, Austl.	F5	76
Tharrawaddy, Mya.	D2	48
Tha Sala, Thai.	H4	48
Thásos, Grc.	C7	28
Thásos, i., Grc.	C7	28
Thásos, sci., Grc.	C7	28
Thaton, Mya.	D3	48
Tha Tum, Thai.	E6	48
Thau, Bassin de, l., Fr.	F9	18
Thaungyin (Moei), stm., Asia	D3	48
Thaya (Dyje), stm., Eur.	H12	16
Thayawthadangyi Kyun, i., Mya.	F3	48
Thayer, Ks., U.S.	G2	120
Thayer, Mo., U.S.	H6	120
Thayetchaung, Mya.	F4	48
Thayetmyo, Mya.	C2	48
Thazi, Mya.	B3	48
Thebes see Thíva, Grc.	E6	28
The Bottom, Neth. Ant.	B1	105a
The Cheviot, mtn., Eng., U.K.	F10	12
The Dalles, Or., U.S.	E5	136
Thedford, Ne., U.S.	E12	126
The Father see Ulawun, Mount, vol., Pap. N. Gui.	b5	79a
The Fens, reg., Eng., U.K.	I12	12
The Fishing Lakes, l., Sk., Can.	D10	124
The Granites, hill, Austl.	D6	74
The Hague see 's-Gravenhage, Neth.	B12	14
The Heads, c., Or., U.S.	H2	136
Theinkun, Mya.	G4	48
The Lakes National Park, p.o.i., Austl.	L6	76
The Little Minch, strt., Scot., U.K.	D6	12
Thelon, stm., Can.	C11	106
The Lynd, Austl.	B5	76
The Minch, strt., Scot., U.K.	D6	12
Thenia, Alg.	H14	20
Theodore, Austl.	E8	76
Theodore, Sk., Can.	C10	124
Theodore, Al., U.S.	G10	122
Theodore Roosevelt National Park North Unit, p.o.i., N.D., U.S.	G10	124
Theodore Roosevelt National Park South Unit, p.o.i., N.D., U.S.	G10	124
The Pas, Mb., Can.	E10	106
Thepha, Thai.	I5	48
The Pinnacle, hill, Mo., U.S.	E6	120
The Rand see Witwatersrand, mts., S. Afr.	D8	70
Theresa Creek, stm., Austl.	D6	76
The Rhins, pen., Scot., U.K.	G7	12
Thermaïkós Kólpos (Salonika, Gulf of), b., Grc.	C6	28
Thermopolis, Wy., U.S.	D4	126
Thermopylae see Thermopyles, hist., Grc.	E5	28
Thermopyles (Thermopylae), hist., Grc.	E5	28
The Rock, Austl.	J6	76
The Rockies, mtn., Wa., U.S.	D4	136
The Rope, clf., Pit.	c28	78k
Thesiger Bay, b., N.T., Can.	B15	140
The Slot see New Georgia Sound, strt., Sol. Is.	e8	79b
Thessalia, state, Grc.	D5	28
Thessalia, hist. reg., Grc.	D5	28
Thessalon, On., Can.	B6	112
Thessaloniki (Salonika), Grc.	C6	28
Thessaly see Thessalia, hist. reg., Grc.	D5	28
Thessalý, C. Iv.	H4	64
Ti'avea, Samoa	g12	79c
Tibaji, stm., Braz.	A12	92
Tibal-og, Phil.	G5	52
Tibasti, Sarir, des., Libya	C3	62
Tibati, Cam.	C2	66
Tibbie, Al., U.S.	F10	122
Tiber see Tevere, stm., Italy.	H9	22
Tiberias, Lake see Kinneret, Yam, l., Isr.	F6	58
Tibesti, mts., Afr.	C3	62
Tibet see Xizang, state, China	B5	46
Tibet, Plateau of see Qing Zang Gaoyuan, plat., China	B6	46
Tiblawan, Phil.	G6	52
Tibnīn, Leb.	E6	58
Tibooburra, Austl.	G4	76
Tiburón, Cabo, c.	C3	86
Tiburón, Isla, i., Mex.	G6	98
Tiča, Jazovir, res., Blg.	F13	26
Ticao Island, i., Phil.	D4	52
Tichît, Maur.	F3	64
Ticino, stm., Eur.	D14	18
Tickfaw, stm., U.S.	G8	122
Ticonderoga, N.Y., U.S.	G3	110
Ticul, Mex.	B3	102
Tidioute, Pa., U.S.	C6	114
Tidikin, Jbel, mtn., Mor.	C4	64
Tidjikja, Maur.	F2	64
Tiébissou, C. Iv.	H3	64
T'iehling see Tieling, China	C5	38
Tiel, Neth.	C14	14
Tieli, China	B10	36
Tieling, China	C5	38
Tielt, Bel.	C12	14
Tiémé, C. Iv.	H3	64
T'ienching see Tianjin, China	B7	42
Tien Yen, Viet.	B8	48
Tie Plant, Ms., U.S.	D9	122
Tierp, Swe.	F7	8
Tierra Amarilla, Chile	C2	92
Tierra Blanca, Mex.	F10	100
Tierra Blanca, stm., U.S.	G3	130
Tierra Blanca Creek, stm., U.S.	G6	128
Tierra de Campos, reg., Spain	C5	20
Tierra del Fuego, state, Arg.	J3	90
Tierra del Fuego, i., S.A.	J3	90
Tiétar, stm., Spain	E5	20
Tietê, Braz.	L2	88
Tietê, stm., Braz.	D6	90
Tiêti, N. Cal.	m15	79d
Tiffany Mountain, mtn., Wa., U.S.	B7	136
Tiffin, Oh., U.S.	C2	114
Tiffon, Ga., U.S.	E2	116
Tiga, Île, i., N. Cal.	m16	79d
Tigalda Island, i., Ak., U.S.	F7	140
Tigapuluh, Pegunungan, mts., Indon.	D3	50
Tighina, Mol.	C16	26
Tígil', Russia	E20	34
Tignall, Ga., U.S.	C3	116
Tignish, P.E., Can.	D12	110
Tigoda, stm., Russia	A14	10
Tigre, Col.	F7	86
Tigre, stm., Peru	D2	84
Tigre, stm., Ven.	C10	86
Tigris (Dicle) (Dijlah), stm., Asia	C5	56
Tiguentourine, Alg.	D6	64
Tihany, hist., Hung.	C4	26
Tihert, Alg.	B5	64
Tihon, Russia	G22	8
Tihookeanskij, Russia	C10	38
Tihoreck, Russia	E6	32
Tihua see Ürümqi, China	C2	36
Tihvin, Russia	A16	10
Tijuana, Mex.	K8	134
Tijuana, stm., N.A.	K9	134
Tijucas, Braz.	C13	92
Tijucas do Sul, Braz.	B13	92
Tijuco, stm., Braz.	J1	88
Tikal, sci., Guat.	D3	102
Tikal, Parque Nacional, p.o.i., Guat.	D3	102
Tikrīt, Iraq	C5	56
Tikša, Russia	D15	8
Tikšeozero, ozero, l., Russia	C14	8
Tiksi, Russia	B16	34
Tiladummati Atoll, at., Mald.	h12	46a
Tilburg, Neth.	C14	14
Tilbury, On., Can.	F7	112
Tilcha, Austl.	G3	76
Tilden, Il., U.S.	F8	120
Tilden, Ne., U.S.	E15	126
Tilden, Tx., U.S.	F9	130
Tilhar, India.	D7	54
Tilimsen, Alg.	B4	64
Tillabéri, Niger	G5	64
Tilley, Ab., Can.	F19	138
Tillia, Niger	F5	64
Tillmans Corner, Al., U.S.	G10	122
Tillson, N.Y., U.S.	C11	114
Tillsonburg, On., Can.	F8	112
Tilos, i., Grc.	G10	28
Tilpa, Austl.	H5	76
Tilton, Il., U.S.	H10	120
Tilton, N.H., U.S.	G5	110
Tiltonsville, Oh., U.S.	D5	114
Tima, Egypt	L2	58
Timanskij krjaž, hills, Russia	B8	32
Tīmaru, N.Z.	G4	80
Timbalier Bay, b., La., U.S.	H8	122
Timbaúba, Braz.	D8	88
Timbedgha, Maur.	F3	64
Timber Lake, S.D., U.S.	B11	126
Timbiras, Braz.	C4	88
Timbó, Braz.	C13	92
Timbo, Lib.	H3	64
Timbavati Game Reserve, S. Afr.	D10	70
Timbedgha see Timbedgha, Maur.	F3	64
Timber Lake see Timber Lake, S.D., U.S.	B11	126
Timétrine, Mali	F4	64
Timétrine, mts., Mali	F4	64
Timimoun, Alg.	D5	64
Timîrist, Râs, c., Maur.	F1	64
Timirjazevo, Russia	E4	10
Timiş, state, Rom.	D8	26
Timiş (Tamiš), stm., Eur.	D7	26
Timiškaming, Lake (Témiscamingue, Lac), res., Can.	B10	112
Timmendorfer Strand, Ger.	B7	16
Timmins, On., Can.	F14	106
Timmonsville, S.C., U.S.	B6	116
Timms Hill, mtn., Wi., U.S.	F8	118
Timna' see Mikhrot Timna', hist., Isr.	I5	58
Timók, stm., Eur.	E9	26
Timon, Braz.	H2	86
Timor, i., Asia	G8	44
Timor Sea, s.	K15	142
Timóšino, Russia	H21	8
Timotes, Ven.	C6	86
Timpanogos Cave National Monument, p.o.i., Ut., U.S.	C5	132
Timpton, stm., Russia	E14	34
Timşēr, Russia	B9	32
Tims Ford Lake, res., Tn., U.S.	B12	122
Tina, stm., S. Afr.	G9	70
Tina Tek Singh, Pak.	C4	54
Tinaca Point, c., Phil.	H5	52
Tinambung, Indon.	E11	50
Tinapagee, Austl.	G5	76
Tinaquillo, Ven.	C7	86
Tindivanam, India	E4	53
Tindouf, Alg.	D3	64
Tineba, Pegunungan, mts., Indon.	D12	50
Tineg, stm., Phil.	B3	52
Ting, stm., China	I7	42
Ting, Tinggi, Pulau, i., Malay.	K7	48
Tingha, Austl.	G8	76
Tinghert, Hamâdat (Tinghert, Plateau du), plat., Afr.	D7	64
Tinghert, Plateau du (Tinghert, Hamâdat), plat., Afr.	D6	64
Tinghsien see Dingxian, China	B6	42
Tinglev, Den.	B5	16
Tingo María, Peru	E2	84
Tingri, China	D11	54
Tingri see Dinggyê, China	D11	54
Tinguiririca, Volcán, vol., Chile	G2	92
Tinharé, Ilha de, i., Braz.	G6	88
Tinh Bien, Viet.	G7	48
Tinian, i., N. Mar. Is.	B5	72
Tinjar, stm., Malay.	B9	50
Tinos, Grc.	F8	28
Tinos, i., Grc.	F8	28
Tinsley, Ms., U.S.	E8	122
Tinsukia, India	C8	46
Tintagel, B.C., Can.	B5	138
Tintina, Arg.	C6	92
Tintinara, Austl.	J3	76
Tio, Erit.	E8	62
Tiobrad Árann see Tipperary, Ire.	I4	12
Tioga, N.D., U.S.	F11	124
Tiojala, Fin.	F10	8
Tioman, Pulau, i., Malay.	K7	48
Tionesta, Pa., U.S.	C6	114
Tipasa, Alg.	H13	20
Tipitapa, Nic.	F4	102
Tippecanoe, stm., In., U.S.	H3	112
Tipperary, Ire.	I4	12
Tipperary, state, Ire.	I5	12
Tipton, Ca., U.S.	G6	134
Tipton, In., U.S.	C6	120
Tipton, Mo., U.S.	F5	120
Tipton, Ok., U.S.	G9	128
Tipton, Mount, mtn., Az., U.S.	H2	132
Tiptonville, Tn., U.S.	H8	120
Tip Top Mountain, mtn., On., Can.	F13	106
Tiptūr, India	E3	53
Tiputini, stm., Ec.	H4	86
Tira, Isr.	F5	58
Tīrān, i., Sau. Ar.	K5	58
Tiran, Strait of, strt.	K5	58
Tirana see Tiranë, Alb.	C13	24
Tiranë, Alb.	C13	24
Tirano, Italy.	D7	22
Tiraspol, Mol.	C16	26
Tire, Tur.	E10	28
Tiree, i., Scot., U.K.	E6	12
Tirich Mīr, mtn., Pak.	B11	56
Tirna, stm., India	B3	53
Tirodi, India	H7	54
Tirol, state, Aus.	C8	22
Tiros, Braz.	J3	88
Tirso, stm., Italy	E2	24
Tirthahalli, India	E2	53
Tiruchchirāppalli, India	F3	53
Tiruchengodu, India	F3	53
Tirukkalukkunram, India	F4	53
Tirukkovilūr, India	F4	53
Tiruliai, Lith.	E6	10
Tirunelveli, India	G3	53
Tirupati, India	E4	53
Tiruppattūr, India	F4	53
Tiruppur, India	F3	53
Tirūr, India	F3	53
Tirutturaippūndi, India	F4	53
Tiruvalla, India	G3	53
Tiruvannāmalai, India	E4	53
Tiruvottiyūr, India	E5	53
Tiruvur, India	C5	53
Tisa (Tisza) (Tysa), stm., Eur.	D7	26
Tisaiyanvilai, India	G3	53
Tisdale, Sk., Can.	B9	124
Tishomingo, Ok., U.S.	C2	122
Tisīyah, Syria.	F7	58
Tiskilwa, Il., U.S.	C8	120
Tisovec, Slov.	H15	16
Tista, stm., Asia	F12	54
Tisza (Tisa) (Tysa), stm., Eur.	C7	26
Tiszaföldvár, Hung.	B7	26
Tiszaújváros, Hung.	A8	26
Titaf, Alg.	D4	64
Tit-Ary, Russia	B14	34
Titicaca, Lake, l., S.A.	G4	84
Titāgarh, India	H9	54
Titonka, Ia., U.S.	H4	118
Titov Veles, Mac.	B4	28
Titran, Nor.	E2	8
Tittabawassee, stm., Mi., U.S.	E5	112
Tittmoning, Ger.	H8	16
Titule, D.R.C.	D5	66
Toli, China	B1	36
Tiumpan Head, c., Scot., U.K.	C6	12
Titusville, Fl., U.S.	H5	116
Titusville, Pa., U.S.	C6	114
Tiuni, India	C6	54
Tivaouane, Sen.	F1	64
Tiverton, Eng., U.K.	K9	12
Tivoli, Italy.	I9	22
Tivoli, Tx., U.S.	F11	130
Tizimín, Mex.	B3	102
Tiznados, stm., Ven.	C8	86
Tizi-Ouzou, Alg.	B5	64
Tiznit, Mor.	D3	64
Tjačiv, Ukr.	A10	26
Tjörn, i., Swe.	G4	8
Tjukalinsk, Russia	C12	32
Tjul'gan, Russia	D9	32
Tjumen', Russia	C11	32
Tjung, stm., Russia	D13	34
Tjuva-Guba, Russia	B15	8
Tlacotalpan, Mex.	F11	100
Tlacotepec, Mex.	G9	100
Tlahualilo de Zaragoza, Mex.	B7	100
Tlalnepantla, Mex.	F9	100
Tlaltenango de Sánchez Román, Mex.	E7	100
Tlapaneco, stm., Mex.	G9	100
Tlaquepaque, Mex.	E7	100
Tlaxcala, state, Mex.	F9	100
Tlaxcala de Xicohténcatl, Mex.	F9	100
Tlaxiaco, Mex.	G9	100
Tłuszcz, Pol.	D17	16
Tmassah, Libya	B3	62
Tnáot, stm., Camb.	G7	48
Toa Alta, P.R.	B3	104a
Toa Baja, P.R.	B3	104a
Toachi, stm., Ec.	H2	86
Toahayana, Mex.	B5	100
Toamasina, Madag.	D8	68
Toba, Japan.	E9	40
Toba, Danau, l., Indon.	K4	48
Tobago, i., Trin.	r13	105f
Toba Inlet, b., B.C., Can.	F6	138
Toba Kākar Range, mts., Pak.	C10	56
Tobarra, Spain	F9	20
Tobas, Arg.	D6	92
Toba Tek Singh, Pak.	C4	54
Tobejuba, Isla, i., Ven.	C11	86
Tobermorey, Austl.	D7	74
Tobermory, On., Can.	C8	112
Tobermory, Scot., U.K.	E6	12
Tobias, Ne., U.S.	G15	126
Tobias Barreto, Braz.	F6	88
Tobin, Mount, mtn., Nv., U.S.	C8	134
Tobique, stm., N.B., Can.	C9	110
Toboali, Indon.	E5	50
Tobol (Tobyl), stm., Asia	C11	32
Toboli, Indon.	D12	50
Tobol'sk, Russia	C11	32
Tobruk see Tubruq, Libya	A4	62
Tobseda, Russia	B25	8
Tobyhanna, Pa., U.S.	C10	114
Tobyl, Kaz.	D10	32
Tobyl (Tobol), stm., Asia	D10	32
Tobylžan, Kaz.	D13	32
Tobyš, stm., Russia	C24	8
Tocantínia, Braz.	E1	88
Tocantinópolis, Braz.	D2	88
Tocantins, state, Braz.	E8	84
Tocantins, stm., Braz.	D8	84
Tocantins, stm., Braz.	F1	88
Tocantinzinho, stm., Braz.	H1	88
Tochcha Lake, l., B.C., Can.	B5	138
Tochigi, Japan	C12	40
Tochigi, state, Japan	C12	40
Tochio, Japan	C12	40
Toco, Trin.	s13	105f
Tocoa, Hond.	E5	102
Toconao, Chile	D3	90
Tocopilla, Chile	D2	90
Tocumwal, Austl.	J5	76
Tocuyo de la Costa, Ven.	B7	86
Toda Rāisingh, India	E5	54
Todi, Italy.	H9	22
Todos os Santos, Baía de, b., Braz.	G6	88
Todos Santos, Bol.	C3	90
Todos Santos, Mex.	D3	100
Todos Santos, Bahía de, b., Mex.	L8	134
Tofino, B.C., Can.	G5	138
Toga, i., Vanuatu	i16	79d
Togi, Japan	B9	40
Togiak, Ak., U.S.	E7	140
Togian, Kepulauan, is., Indon.	F7	44
Togo, ctry., Afr.	H5	64
Togtoh, China	A4	42
Toguçin, Russia	C14	32
Togur, Russia	C14	32
Togwotee Pass, p., Wy., U.S.	G15	136
Tōhaku, Japan	D6	40
Tohiea, Mont, mtn., Fr. Poly.	v20	78h
Tohopekaliga, Lake, l., Fl., U.S.	H4	116
Tohtamyš, Taj.	B11	56
Toi-misaki, c., Japan.	H4	40
Toiyabe Range, mts., Nv., U.S.	D8	134
Tōjō, Japan	E6	40
Tojtepa, Uzb.	F11	32
Tok, Ak., U.S.	D11	140
Tokachi, stm., Japan	C15	38
Tokachi-dake, vol., Japan.	C15	38
Tokaj, Hung.	A8	26
Tōkamachi, Japan	B11	40
Tokara-kaikyō, strt., Japan.	j19	39a
Tokara-rettō, is., Japan.	k19	39a
Tokat, Tur.	A4	56
Tōkchŏk-kundo, is., Kor., S.	F6	38
Tokelau, dep., Oc.	E9	72
Tokko, Russia	E12	34
Tokma, Russia	C19	32
Tokmak, Kyrg.	F12	32
Tokoro, stm., Japan	C15	38
Tokoroa, N.Z.	C6	80
Tok-to, is., Asia	B4	40
Toktogul, Kyrg.	F12	32
Tokuno-shima, i., Japan.	I19	39a
Tokur, Russia	F15	34
Tokushima, Japan	E6	40
Tokushima, state, Japan	E6	40
Tokuyama, Japan	E4	40
Tokwe, stm., Zimb.	B10	70
Tōkyō, Japan	D12	40
Tōkyō, state, Japan	D12	40
Tokyo Bay see Tōkyō-wan, b., Japan	D12	40
Tōkyō-daigaku-uchūkūkan-kenkyūsho, sci., Japan	H4	40
Tōkyō-wan, b., Japan	D12	40
Tōlañaro, Madag.	E8	68
Tolbo, Mong.	B3	36
Tôle bî, Kaz.	F12	32
Toledo, Braz.	B11	92
Toledo, Col.	D5	86
Toledo, Phil.	E4	52
Toledo, Spain	E6	20
Toledo, Il., U.S.	E9	120
Toledo, Oh., U.S.	C2	114
Toledo, Or., U.S.	F3	136
Toledo, co., Spain	E6	20
Toledo, Montes de, mts., Spain	E6	20
Toledo Bend Reservoir, res., U.S.	F4	122
Tolentino, Italy	G10	22
Toli, China	B1	36
Toliara, state, Madag.	E7	68
Tolima, state, Col.	E4	86
Tolima, Nevado del, vol., Col.	E4	86
Tolitoli, Indon.	C12	50
Toljatti, Russia	D7	32
Tol'ka, Russia	B14	32
Tolleson, Az., U.S.	J5	132
Tolloche, Arg.	C6	92
Tolmači, Russia	D18	10
Tolmezzo, Italy	D10	22
Tolmin, Slvn.	D10	22
Tolna, state, Hung.	C5	26
Tolo, Teluk, b., Indon.	F7	44
Tolosa, Spain	A8	20
Tolstoj, mys, c., Russia	E20	34
Tolú, Col.	C4	86
Toluca, Il., U.S.	C8	120
Toluca, Nevado de, vol., Mex.	F9	100
Toluca de Lerdo, Mex.	F9	100
Tom', stm., Russia	C14	32
Torna, Russia	B20	8
Tomah, Wi., U.S.	H8	118
Tomahawk, Wi., U.S.	F9	118
Tomakomai, Japan.	C14	38
Tomanivi, mtn., Fiji	p19	79e
Tomar, Port.	E2	20
Tomari, Russia	G17	34
Tomás Gomensoro, Ur.	E9	92
Tomasine, stm., Can.	B13	112
Tomaszów Lubelski, Pol.	F19	16
Tomaszów Mazowiecki, Pol.	E15	16
Tombador, Serra do, plat., Braz.	F6	84
Tomball, Tx., U.S.	G3	122
Tombigbee, stm., U.S.	F10	122
Tombos, Braz.	K5	88
Tombouctou (Timbuktu), Mali	F4	64
Tombstone, Az., U.S.	L6	132
Tombstone Mountain, mtn., Yk., Can.	C3	106
Tombua, Ang.	D1	68
Tom Burke, S. Afr.	C9	70
Tomé, Chile	H1	92
Tomé-Açu, Braz.	B1	88
Tomelilla, Swe.	I5	8
Tomelloso, Spain	E8	20
Tomichi Creek, stm., Co., U.S.	C2	128
Tomini, Indon.	C12	50
Tomini, Teluk, b., Indon.	F7	44
Tomioka, Japan	C11	40
Tommot, Russia	E14	34
Tomo, stm., Col.	E7	86
Tompkins, Sk., Can.	D5	124
Tompkinsville, Ky., U.S.	H12	120
Tompo, Indon.	C12	50
Tom Price, Austl.	D3	74
Tomptokan, Russia	E15	34
Tomsk, Russia	C15	32
Toms River, N.J., U.S.	E11	114
Tonalá, Mex.	G12	100
Tonami, Japan	C10	40
Tonantins, Braz.	I7	86
Tonantins, stm., Braz.	I7	86
Tonasket, Wa., U.S.	B7	136
Tonawanda, N.Y., U.S.	B6	114
Tonbo, Mya.	C2	48
Tonbridge, Eng., U.K.	J13	12
Tondano, Indon.	E8	44
Tonder, Den.	B4	16
Tondi, India	G4	53
Tone, stm., Japan	D13	40
Tonekābon, Iran	B7	56
Tonga, ctry., Oc.	E9	72
Tongaat, S. Afr.	F10	70
Tong'an, China	I7	42
Tonganoxie, Ks., U.S.	E2	120
Tonga Ridge, unds.	K21	142
Tongariro National Park, p.o.i., N.Z.	D6	80
Tongatapu, state, Tonga	o14	78e
Tongatapu, i., Tonga	n13	78e
Tonga Trench, unds.	L21	142
Tongbai, China	E5	42
Tongbai Shan, mts., China	E5	42
Tongbei, China	B10	36
Tongcheng, China	F7	42
Tongchuan, China	D3	42
Tongde, China	D5	36
Tongeren, Bel.	D14	14
Tongguan, China	G5	42
Tongguan, China	D3	42
Tonghai, China	G5	36
Tonghe, China	B10	36
Tonghua, China	D6	38
Tongjiang, China	B11	36
Tongjiang, China	F2	42
Tongjosŏn-man, b., Kor., N.	E7	38
Tongliao, China	C4	38
Tongling, China	F7	42
Tongling, China	J3	42
Tonglu, China	G8	42
Tongnae, Kor., S.	D2	40
Tongnan, China	F1	42
Tongo, Austl.	H4	76
Tongoa, i., Vanuatu	k17	79d
Tongoy, Chile	E2	92
Tongren, China	H3	42
Tongren, China	D5	36
Tongres see Tongeren, Bel.	D14	14
Tongsa Dzong, Bhu.	E13	54
Tongtian, stm., China	E4	36
Tongue, Scot., U.K.	C8	12
Tongue, stm., U.S.	A7	126
Tongue of the Ocean, unds.	C9	96
Tongwei, China	D1	42
Tongxian, China	B7	42
Tongxin, China	C1	42
Tongyang, China	D6	42
Tongyu, China	B5	38
Tongzi, China	G2	42
Tonj, Sudan	F5	62
Tonk, India	E5	54
Tonkawa, Ok., U.S.	E11	128
Tonkin see Bac Phan, hist. reg., Viet.	A7	48
Tonkin, Gulf of, b., Asia	C8	48
Tônlé Sab, Boeng, l., Camb.	F6	48
Tonle Sap see Tônlé Sab, Boeng, l., Camb.	F6	48
Tonneins, Fr.	E6	18
Tonopah, Nv., U.S.	E8	134
Tonoshō, Japan	E7	40
Tonosí, Pan.	D1	86
Tonotha, Bots.		
Tons, stm., India	C9	54
Tønsberg, Nor.	G4	8
Tonstad, Nor.	G2	8
Tonto National Monument, p.o.i., Az., U.S.	J5	132
Toodyay, Austl.	F3	74
Tooele, Ut., U.S.	C4	132
Toogoolawah, Austl.	F9	76
Toomsboro, Ga., U.S.	D2	116
Toora-Hem, Russia	D17	32
Toowoomba, Austl.	F8	76
Top Hill, hill, Gren.	q11	105e
Topia, Mex.	C5	100
Topki, Russia	C15	32
Topľa, gora, mtn., Russia	C2	114
Topley, B.C., Can.	B4	138
Topliţa, Rom.	C12	26
Topocalma, Punta, c., Chile	G1	92
Topol'čany, Slov.	H14	16
Topolobampo, Mex.	C4	100
Topolovăţu Mare, Rom.	D8	26
Toporok, Russia	B16	10
Topozero, ozero, l., Russia	D14	8
Toppenish, Wa., U.S.	D6	136
Top Springs, Austl.	C6	74
Tor, Eth.	F7	62
Torbalı, Tur.	E10	28
Torbat-e Heydarīyeh, Iran	B8	56
Torbat-e Jām, Iran	B9	56
Torbrook, N.S., Can.	F12	110
Torch Lake, l., Mi., U.S.	C4	112
Tordesillas, Spain	C5	20
Töre, Swe.	C10	8
Torgau, Ger.	E8	16
Torghay, Kaz.	E10	32
Torghay, stm., Kaz.	E10	32
Torghay üstirti, plat., Asia	D10	32
Torghay zhylgh, reg., Kaz.	D10	32
Torhout, Bel.	C12	14
Torhulu, Indon.		
Torino (Turin), Italy	E4	22
Torit, Sudan	G6	62
Tormes, stm., Spain	C5	20
Torna, Russia	B20	8
Torna, mtn., India.	B1	53

Name	Map Ref.	Page
Torneälven (Tornionjoki), stm., Eur.	C10	8
Torneträsk, l., Swe.	B8	8
Torngat Mountains, mts., Can.	F13	141
Tornillo, Tx., U.S.	C1	130
Tornionjoki (Torneälven), stm., Eur.	C10	8
Tornquist, Arg.	I6	92
Toro, Spain	C5	20
Toro, mtn., Mex.	F6	100
Toro, Lago del, l., Chile	J2	90
Toro, Punta, c., Chile	F1	92
Törökszentmiklós, Hung.	B7	26
Torom, Russia	F16	34
Toronto, On., Can.	E10	112
Toronto, Ks., U.S.	G1	120
Toronto, S.D., U.S.	G2	118
Toropec, Russia	D14	10
Tororo, Ug.	D6	66
Toros Dağları (Taurus Mountains), mts., Tur.	A3	58
Torosozero, Russia	E18	8
Toroume, hill, Cook Is.	b26	78j
Torquay, Sk., Can.	E10	124
Torquay (Torbay), Eng., U.K.	K9	12
Torrance, Ca., U.S.	J7	134
Torrão, Port.	F2	20
Torreblanca, Spain	D11	20
Torre del Greco, Italy	D8	24
Torredonjimeno, Spain	G6	20
Torrejoncillo, Spain	E4	20
Torrejón de Ardoz, Spain	D7	20
Torrejón-Tiétar, Embalse de, res., Spain	E5	20
Torrelavega, Spain	A6	20
Torremolinos, Spain	H6	20
Torrens, Lake, l., Austl.	F7	74
Torrens Creek, Austl.	C5	76
Torrens Creek, stm., Austl.	D5	76
Torrent, Arg.	D9	92
Torrent, Spain	E10	20
Torrente see Torrent, Spain	E10	20
Torrenueva, Spain	F7	20
Torreón, Mex.	C7	100
Torre Pellice, Italy	F4	22
Torreperojil, Spain	F7	20
Torres, Braz.	D13	92
Torres, Îles, is., Vanuatu	i16	79d
Torres Islands see Torres, Îles, is., Vanuatu	i16	79d
Torres Strait, strt., Oc.	b3	79a
Torres Vedras, Port.	E1	20
Torrevella, Spain	G10	20
Torrevieja see Torrevella, Spain	G10	20
Torridon, Scot., U.K.	D7	12
Torrijos, Spain	D6	20
Torrington, Ct., U.S.	C12	114
Torrington, Wy., U.S.	E8	126
Torröjen, l., Swe.	E5	8
Torsa (Amo), stm., Asia	E12	54
Torsby, Swe.	F5	8
Tórshavn (Thorshavn), Far. Is.	n34	8b
Tortola, i., Br. Vir. Is.	e8	104b
Tórtolas, Cerro de las (Las Tórtolas, Cerro), mtn., S.A.	D2	92
Tortona, Italy	F5	22
Tortorici, Italy	F8	24
Tortosa, Spain	D11	20
Tortosa, Cap de, c., Spain	D11	20
Tortue, Île de la, i., Haiti	B11	102
Tortuga Island see Tortue, Île de la, i., Haiti	B11	102
Tortuguero, Laguna, b., P.R.	B2	104a
Toruń, Pol.	C14	16
Toruń, state, Pol.	C15	16
Torup, Swe.	H5	8
Toržok, Russia	C17	10
Torzym, Pol.	D11	16
Tosa, Japan	F6	40
Tosa-shimizu, Japan	G5	40
Tosa-wan, b., Japan	F6	40
Tosca, S. Afr.	D6	70
Toscana, state, Italy	G8	22
Toses, Collada de, p., Spain	B12	20
Tosno, Russia	A13	10
Toson Hu, l., China	D4	36
Tosontsengel, Mong.	B4	36
Tostado, Arg.	D7	92
Tõstamaa, Est.	G10	8
Tosu, Japan	F3	40
Totana, Spain	G9	20
Toteng, Bots.	B6	70
Totiyas, Som.	D8	66
Tot'ma, Russia	F20	8
Totness, Sur.	B6	84
Totoya, i., Fiji	q20	79e
Tottenham, Austl.	I6	76
Tottenham, On., Can.	D10	112
Tottori, Japan	D7	40
Tottori, state, Japan	D6	40
Touba, C. Iv.	H3	64
Toubkal, Jebel, mtn., Mor.	C3	64
Touchet, stm., Wa., U.S.	D8	136
Touchwood Lake, l., Ab., Can.	B19	138
Toudao, stm., China	C7	38
Touggourt, Alg.	C6	64
Touho, N. Cal.	m15	79d
Toul, Fr.	F14	14
Touliu, Tai.	J9	42
Toulon, Fr.	F11	18
Toulon-sur-Arroux, Fr.	H13	14
Toulouse, Fr.	F7	18
Toumodi, C. Iv.	H3	64
Tounassine, Hamada, des., Alg.	D3	64
Toungo, Nig.	H7	64
Toungoo, Mya.	C3	48
Touraine, hist. reg., Fr.	G9	14
Tourcoing, Fr.	D11	14
Touriñan, Cabo, c., Spain	A1	20
Tournai, Bel.	D12	14
Tournon, Fr.	D10	18
Tournus, Fr.	H13	14
Touros, Braz.	C8	88
Tours, Fr.	G9	14
Toussidé, Pic, vol., Chad	C3	62
Touws, stm., S. Afr.	H5	70
Toužim, Czech Rep.	F9	16
Tovar, Ven.	C6	86
Tovarkovskij, Russia	G21	10
Tovuz, Azer.	A6	56
Tow, Tx., U.S.	D9	130
Towada, Japan	D14	38
Towanda, Ks., U.S.	D12	128
Towanda, Pa., U.S.	C9	114
Tower, Mn., U.S.	D6	118
Tower City, Pa., U.S.	D9	114
Tower Hill, Austl.	D5	76
Tower Hill, Il., U.S.	E9	120
Towerhill Creek, stm., Austl.	C5	76
Towla, Mount, mtn., Zimb.	B9	70
Town and Country, Wa., U.S.	C9	136
Town Hill, hill, Ber.	k16	104e
Townsend, Mt., U.S.	D15	136
Townshend Island, i., Austl.	D8	76
Townsville, Austl.	B6	76
Towson, Md., U.S.	E9	114
Towuti, Danau, l., Indon.	F7	44
Toyah, Tx., U.S.	C4	130
Toyah Creek, stm., Tx., U.S.	D4	130
Toyama, Japan	C10	40
Toyama, state, Japan	C10	40
Toyama-wan, b., Japan	C10	40
Tōyo, Japan	F6	40
Tōyō, Japan	F7	40
Toyohashi, Japan	E10	40
Toyokawa, Japan	E10	40
Toyonaka, Japan	E8	40
Toyooka, Japan	D7	40
Toyosaka, Japan	B12	40
Toyota, Japan	D10	40
Toyoura, Japan	E3	40
Tozeur, Tun.	C6	64
Trabzon, Tur.	A4	56
Tracadie, N.B., Can.	C12	110
Tracy, Qc., Can.	E3	110
Tracy, Ca., U.S.	F4	134
Tracy City, Tn., U.S.	B13	122
Tradewater, stm., Ky., U.S.	G10	120
Traer, Ia., U.S.	B5	120
Trafalgar, Cabo, c., Spain	H4	20
Traíd, Spain	D9	20
Tráighlí see Tralee, Ire.	I3	12
Traiguén, Chile	I1	92
Trail, B.C., Can.	G13	138
Traill Ø, i., Grnld.	C21	141
Traipu, Braz.	E7	88
Traíra (Taraira), stm., S.A.	H7	86
Trairi, Braz.	B6	88
Trakai, Lith.	F7	10
Tralee, Ire.	I3	12
Trá Lí see Tralee, Ire.	I3	12
Trammel, Va., U.S.	G3	114
Tramperos Creek (Punta de Agua Creek), stm., U.S.	E5	128
Tramping Lake, l., Sk., Can.	B5	124
Tra My, Viet.	E9	48
Trăn, Blg.	G9	26
Tranås, Swe.	G6	8
Trancas, Arg.	C5	92
Tranco de Beas, Embalse de, res., Spain	F8	20
Trang, Thai.	I4	48
Trangan, Pulau, i., Indon.	G9	44
Trang Dinh, Viet.	A8	48
Trani, Italy	C10	24
Tran Ninh see Xiangkhoang, Plateau de, plat., Laos	C6	48
Tranqueras, Ur.	E9	92
Transantarctic Mountains, mts., Ant.	D30	81
Transkei, hist. reg., S. Afr.	G8	70
Transylvania, hist. reg., Rom.	C10	26
Transylvanian Alps see Carpații Meridionali, mts., Rom.	D11	26
Trapani, Italy	F6	24
Trapper Peak, mtn., Mt., U.S.	E12	136
Traralgon, Austl.	L6	76
Trârza, reg., Maur.	F1	64
Trasimeno, Lago, l., Italy	G9	22
Trás-os-Montes, hist. reg., Port.	C3	20
Trat, Thai.	F6	48
Traun, Aus.	B11	22
Traun, stm., Aus.	B11	22
Traunstein, Ger.	I8	16
Travellers Lake, l., Austl.	I4	76
Traverse, Lake, res., U.S.	F2	118
Traverse City, Mi., U.S.	D4	112
Tra Vinh, Viet.	H8	48
Travis, Lake, l., Tx., U.S.	D10	130
Travnik, Bos.	E4	26
Trayning, Austl.	F3	74
Trbovlje, Slvn.	D12	22
Třebíč, Czech Rep.	G11	16
Trebinje, Bos.	G5	26
Trebišov, Slov.	H17	16
Treblinka, Pol.	D18	16
Trece Martires, Phil.	C3	52
Tregosse Islets, is., Austl.	A8	76
Tregubovo, Russia	B14	10
Treinta y Tres, Ur.	F10	92
Trélazé, Fr.	G8	14
Trelew, Arg.	H3	90
Trelleborg, Swe.	I5	8
Tremadog Bay, b., Wales, U.K.	I8	12
Tremblant, Mont, mtn., Qc., Can.	D2	110
Trembleur Lake, l., B.C., Can.	B5	138
Tremiti, Isole, is., Italy	H12	22
Tremont, Il., U.S.	K9	118
Tremonton, Ut., U.S.	B4	132
Tremp, Spain	B11	20
Trempealeau, Wi., U.S.	G7	118
Trenche, stm., Qc., Can.	B4	110
Trenčín, Slov.	H14	16
Trenel, Arg.	G5	92
Trêng, Camb.	F6	48
Trenggalek, Indon.	H7	50
Trenque Lauquen, Arg.	G6	92
Trent, stm., On., Can.	D12	112
Trent, stm., Eng., U.K.	H12	12
Trente et Un Milles, Lac des, l., Qc., Can.	B13	112
Trentino-Alto Adige, state, Italy	D8	22
Trento (Trent), Italy	D7	22
Trenton, N.S., Can.	E14	110
Trenton, On., Can.	D12	112
Trenton, Fl., U.S.	G3	116
Trenton, Ga., U.S.	C13	122
Trenton, Mo., U.S.	D4	120
Trenton, N.C., U.S.	A8	116
Trenton, Ne., U.S.	A8	128
Trenton, N.J., U.S.	D11	114
Trentwood, Wa., U.S.	C9	136
Trepassey, Nf., Can.	j23	107a
Tres Algarrobos, Arg.	G6	92
Tres Arroyos, Arg.	I7	92
Três Corações, Braz.	K3	88
Três Coroas, Braz.	D12	92
Três de Maio, Braz.	C10	92
Tres Esquinas, Col.	G4	86
Três Lagoas, Braz.	D6	90
Tres Lagos, Arg.	I2	90
Tres Lomas, Arg.	H6	92
Três Marias, Braz.	J3	88
Tres Marías, Islas, is., Mex.	E5	100
Três Marias, Represa de, res., Braz.	J3	88
Tres Montes, Península, pen., Chile	I1	90
Tres Montosas, mtn., N.M., U.S.	I9	132
Tres Palos, Laguna, l., Mex.	G9	100
Três Passos, Braz.	C11	92
Tres Picos, Cerro, mtn., Arg.	I6	92
Três Pontas, Braz.	K3	88
Tres Puntas, Cabo, c., Arg.	I3	90
Três Rios, Braz.	L4	88
Tres Vírgenes, Volcán de las, vol., Mex.	B2	100
Tres Zapotes, sci., Mex.	F11	100
Tretten, Nor.	F4	8
Treuchtlingen, Ger.	H6	16
Treuenbrietzen, Ger.	D8	16
Treviglio, Italy	E6	22
Treviso, Italy	E9	22
Trevorton, Pa., U.S.	D9	114
Trgovište, Serb.	G9	26
Triabunna, Austl.	o13	77a
Triberg, Ger.	H4	16
Tribugá, Ensenada de, b., Col.	E3	86
Tribune, Sk., Can.	E10	124
Tribune, Ks., U.S.	C7	128
Tricarico, Italy	D10	24
Tricase, Italy	E12	24
Trichonída, Límni, l., Grc.	E4	28
Trichūr, India	F3	53
Tri County Supply Canal, can., Ne., U.S.	G12	126
Trida, Austl.	I5	76
Trident Peak, mtn., Nv., U.S.	B7	134
Trier, Ger.	G2	16
Trieste (Trst), Italy	E10	22
Trieste, Gulf of, b., Eur.	E10	22
Triglav, mtn., Slvn.	D10	22
Triglavski narodni park, p.o.i., Slvn.	D10	22
Trigueros, Spain	G4	20
Tríkala, Grc.	D4	28
Trikora, Puncak, mtn., Indon.	F10	44
Trilby, Fl., U.S.	H3	116
Triman, Pak.	D2	54
Trincheras, Mex.	F7	98
Trincomalee, Sri L.	G5	53
Trindade, Braz.	I1	88
Trindade, i., Braz.	H12	82
Třinec, Czech Rep.	G14	16
Trinidad, Bol.	B3	90
Trinidad, Col.	E6	86
Trinidad, Cuba	B8	102
Trinidad, Ur.	F9	92
Trinidad, Co., U.S.	D4	128
Trinidad, Tx., U.S.	E2	122
Trinidad, i., Trin.	s13	105f
Trinidad, Isla, i., Arg.	I7	92
Trinidad and Tobago, ctry., N.A.	s13	105f
Trinity, Tx., U.S.	G3	122
Trinity, stm., Ca., U.S.	C2	134
Trinity, stm., Tx., U.S.	D13	130
Trinity, Elm Fork, stm., Tx., U.S.	H11	128
Trinity, South Fork, stm., Ca., U.S.	C2	134
Trinity, West Fork, stm., Tx., U.S.	H11	128
Trinity Bay, b., Nf., Can.	j23	107a
Trinity Bay, b., Tx., U.S.	H4	122
Trinity Islands, is., Ak., U.S.	E9	140
Trinity Peak, mtn., Nv., U.S.	C7	134
Trinity Site, hist., N.M., U.S.	H2	128
Trino, Italy	E5	22
Tripa, stm., Indon.	J3	48
Trípoli, Grc.	F5	28
Tripoli see Ṭarābulus, Leb.	D6	58
Tripoli see Ṭarābulus, Libya	A2	62
Tripoli, Ia., U.S.	I6	118
Tripolis, sci., Tur.	F12	28
Tripolitania see Ṭarābulus, hist. reg., Libya	A2	62
Tripp, S.D., U.S.	D15	126
Tripura, state, India	G13	54
Tristan da Cunha Group, is., St. Hel.	J4	60
Tristao, Îles, is., Gui.	G2	64
Triste, Spain	B10	20
Triste, Golfo, b., Ven.	B7	86
Tri Ton, Viet.	G7	48
Triumph, La., U.S.	H9	122
Trivandrum see Thiruvananthapuram , India	G3	53
Trnava, Slov.	H13	16
Trobriand Islands, is., Pap. N. Gui.	b5	79a
Trogir, Cro.	G13	22
Troia, Italy	C9	24
Troick, Russia	D10	32
Troickoe, Russia	D15	32
Troickoe, Russia	G16	34
Troicko-Pečorsk, Russia	B9	32
Troina, Italy	G8	24
Troisdorf, Ger.	F2	16
Trois-Pistoles, Qc., Can.	B7	110
Trois Pitons, Morne, vol., Dom.	j6	105c
Trois-Rivières, Qc., Can.	D4	110
Trois-Rivières, Guad.	i5	105c
Trojan, Blg.	G11	26
Trojanova Tabla, hist., Serb.	E9	26
Trollhättan, Swe.	G5	8
Trombetas, stm., Braz.	C6	84
Troms, state, Nor.	B8	8
Tromsø, Nor.	B8	8
Trona, Ca., U.S.	H8	134
Tronador, Cerro, mtn., S.A.	H2	90
Trondheim, Nor.	E4	8
Trondheimsfjorden, b., Nor.	E4	8
Troödos, Cyp.	D3	58
Troodos Mountains, mts., Cyp.	D3	58
Troon, Scot., U.K.	F8	12
Trophy Mountain, vol., B.C., Can.	E11	138
Tropic, Ut., U.S.	F4	132
Tropojë, Alb.	B14	24
Troškūnai, Lith.	E7	10
Trosna, Russia	H18	10
Trotuș, stm., Rom.	C13	26
Troup, Tx., U.S.	E3	122
Trout, La., U.S.	F6	122
Trout, stm., N.T., Can.	C6	106
Trout Creek, Mi., U.S.	E9	118
Trout Creek Pass, p., Co., U.S.	C3	128
Trout Lake, l., N.T., Can.	C6	106
Trout Lake, l., On., Can.	E12	106
Troutville, Va., U.S.	G6	114
Trouville-sur-Mer, Fr.	E9	14
Trowbridge, Eng., U.K.	J10	12
Troy, Al., U.S.	F13	122
Troy, Id., U.S.	D10	136
Troy, Mo., U.S.	F7	120
Troy, N.C., U.S.	A6	116
Troy, N.H., U.S.	B13	114
Troy, N.Y., U.S.	B12	114
Troy, Oh., U.S.	D1	114
Troy, Pa., U.S.	C9	114
Troy, Tn., U.S.	H8	120
Troy, Tx., U.S.	C10	130
Troy see Truva, sci., Tur.	D9	28
Troyes, Fr.	F13	14
Troy Peak, mtn., Nv., U.S.	E1	132
Trst see Trieste, Italy	E10	22
Trstená, Slov.	G15	16
Truax, Sk., Can.	E8	124
Trubč'evsk, Russia	H16	10
Truchas, N.M., U.S.	E3	128
Truchas Peak, mtn., N.M., U.S.	E3	128
Trucial States see United Arab Emirates, ctry., Asia	E7	56
Truckee, Ca., U.S.	D5	134
Truckee, stm., U.S.	D6	134
Trud, Russia	C16	10
Trujillo, Col.	E3	86
Trujillo, Hond.	E4	102
Trujillo, Peru	E2	84
Trujillo, Spain	E5	20
Trujillo, Ven.	C6	86
Trujillo, state, Ven.	C6	86
Trujillo Alto, P.R.	B4	104a
Truk Islands see Chuuk, is., Micron.	C6	72
Truman, Mn., U.S.	H4	118
Trumann, Ar., U.S.	B8	122
Trumansburg, N.Y., U.S.	B9	114
Trumbull, Ct., U.S.	C12	114
Trumbull, Mount, mtn., Az., U.S.	G3	132
Trundle, Austl.	I6	76
Trung Phan (Annam), hist. reg., Viet.	D8	48
Truro, N.S., Can.	E13	110
Truro, Eng., U.K.	K7	12
Trusan, stm., Malay.	A9	50
Truscott, Tx., U.S.	H9	128
Trușeni, Mol.	B15	26
Truth or Consequences, N.M., U.S.	J9	132
Trutnov, Czech Rep.	F11	16
Truva (Troy), sci., Tur.	D9	28
Truxton Wash, stm., Az., U.S.	H3	132
Truyère, stm., Fr.	E8	18
Tryon, N.C., U.S.	A3	116
Tryon, Ne., U.S.	F12	126
Trzcianka, Pol.	C12	16
Trzciel, Pol.	D11	16
Trzebiatów, Pol.	B11	16
Trzebinia, Pol.	F15	16
Trzebnica, Pol.	E13	16
Tsagaannuur, Mong.	E15	32
Tsaidam Basin see Qaidam Pendi, bas., China	D3	36
Tsala Apopka Lake, l., Fl., U.S.	H3	116
Tsamkong see Zhanjiang, China	K4	42
Ts'anghsien see Cangzhou, China	B7	42
T'sangwu see Wuzhou, China	J4	42
Tsaratanana, Madag.	D8	68
Tsaratanana, mts., Madag.	C8	68
Tsau, Bots.	E3	68
Tsavo, Kenya	E7	66
Tsaydaychuz Peak, mtn., B.C., Can.	C4	138
Tsebrykove, Ukr.	B17	26
Tses, Nmb.	D4	70
Tsetserleg, Mong.	B5	36
Tsévié, Togo	H5	64
Tshabong, Bots.	D6	70
Tshane, Bots.	D5	70
Tshela, D.R.C.	E2	66
Tshidilamolomo, S. Afr.	D7	70
Tshikapa, D.R.C.	F4	66
Tshofa, D.R.C.	F5	66
Tshuapa, stm., D.R.C.	E4	66
Tshumbe (Chiumbe), stm., Afr.	B3	68
Tshwane see Pretoria, S. Afr.	D9	70
Tsiafajavona, vol., Madag.	D8	68
Tsiigehtchic, N.T., Can.	B4	106
Tsimlyansk Reservoir see Cimljanskoe vodohranilišče, res., Russia	E6	32
Tsinan see Jinan, China	C7	42
Tsineng, S. Afr.	E6	70
Tsinghai see Qinghai, state, China	D4	36
Tsingkiang see Qingjiang, China	E8	42
Tsingtao see Qingdao, China	C9	42
Tsingyuan see Baoding, China	B6	42
Ts'in-hai see Qinghai, state, China	D4	36
Tsining see Jining, China	D7	42
Tsinling Shan see Qin Ling, mts., China	E3	42
Tsintsabis, Nmb.	D2	68
Tsiombe, Madag.	F8	68
Tsipa see Cipa, stm., Russia	F11	34
Tsiribihina, stm., Madag.	D7	68
Tsiroanomandidy, Madag.	D8	68
Tsitsihar see Qiqihar, China	B9	36
Tsna see Cna, stm., Russia	D6	32
Tsomo, stm., S. Afr.	H8	70
Tsomog, Mong.	B6	36
Tsu, Japan	E9	40
Tsubame, Japan	B11	40
Tsuchiura, Japan	C13	40
Tsugaru-kaikyō, strt., Japan	D14	38
Tsukumi, Japan	F4	40
Tsukushi-sanchi, mts., Japan	F3	40
Tsumeb, Nmb.	D2	68
Tsumkwe, Nmb.	D3	68
Tsuni see Zunyi, China	H2	42
Tsuruga, Japan	D9	40
Tsurugi-san, mtn., Japan	F7	40
Tsuruoka, Japan	A12	40
Tsushima, is., Japan	E2	40
Tsushima-kaikyō (Eastern Channel), strt., Japan	F2	40
Tsuyama, Japan	D7	40
Tswaane, Bots.	C6	70
Ttruchchendūr, India	G4	53
Tua, D.R.C.	E3	66
Tua, stm., Port.	C3	20
Tua, Tanjung, c., Indon.	F4	50
Tua Chua, Viet.	B6	48
Tual, Indon.	G9	44
Tuam, Ire.	H4	12
Tuamotu, Îles, is., Fr. Poly.	E12	72
Tuamotu Archipelago see Tuamotu, Îles, is., Fr. Poly.	E12	72
Tuamotu Ridge, unds.	K24	142
Tuanan, Indon.	E9	50
Tuangku, Pulau, i., Indon.	K3	48
Tuapse, Russia	F5	32
Tuasivi, Cape, c., Samoa	g11	79c
Tuba, Russia	C18	32
Tuba, stm., Russia	D16	32
Tubac, Az., U.S.	L5	132
Tuban, Indon.	G8	50
Tubarão, Braz.	D13	92
Ṭūbās, W.B.	F6	58
Tübingen, Ger.	H4	16
Ṭubruq, Libya	A4	62
Tubuai, i., Fr. Poly.	F12	72
Tucacas, Ven.	B7	86
Tucano, Braz.	F6	88
Tucheng, China	G2	42
Tuchów, Pol.	G17	16
Tuckerman, Ar., U.S.	B7	122
Tuckerton, N.J., U.S.	E11	114
Tučkovo, Russia	E19	10
Tucson, Az., U.S.	K5	132
Tucumán, state, Arg.	C5	92
Tucumcari, N.M., U.S.	F5	128
Tucunuco, Arg.	E3	92
Tucupido, Ven.	C9	86
Tucupita, Ven.	C11	86
Tucuruí, Braz.	D8	84
Tucuruí, Represa de, res., Braz.	D8	84
Tudela, Phil.	F4	52
Tudela, Spain	B9	20
Tudmur (Palmyra), Syria	D9	58
Tufānganj, India	E12	54
Tufi, Pap. N. Gui.	b4	79a
Tugela, stm., S. Afr.	F10	70
Tug Fork, stm., U.S.	G3	114
Tuggerah Lake, b., Austl.	I8	76
Tüghyl, Kaz.	E14	32
Tuguegarao City, Phil.	B3	52
Tugur, Russia	F16	34
Tuhai, stm., China	C7	42
Tuhuangba, China	F3	42
Tui, Spain	B2	20
Tuibo, China	C7	38
Tuira, stm., Pan.	D3	86
Tujmazy, Russia	D8	32
Tukangbesi, Kepulauan, is., Indon.	G7	44
Tukituki, stm., N.Z.	D7	80
Tukosméra, Mont, mtn., Vanuatu	I17	79d
Tūkrah, Libya	A4	62
Tuktoyaktuk, N.T., Can.	B4	106
Tukums, Lat.	D6	10
Tukuringra, hrebet, mts., Russia	F14	34
Tukuyu, Tan.	F6	66
Tula, Mex.	D9	100
Tula, Russia	F20	10
Tulach Mhór see Tullamore, Ire.	H5	12
Tulaghi, Sol. Is.	e8	79b
Tulancingo, Mex.	E9	100
Tulangbawang, stm., Indon.	F4	50
Tulare, Ca., U.S.	G6	134
Tulare, S.D., U.S.	C14	126
Tulare Lake Bed, reg., Ca., U.S.	G6	134
Tulare Lake Canal, can., Ca., U.S.	G6	134
Tularosa, N.M., U.S.	H2	128
Tularosa Valley, bas., N.M., U.S.	E9	98
Tulbagh, S. Afr.	H4	70
Tulcán, Ec.	G3	86
Tulcea, Rom.	D15	26
Tulcea, state, Rom.	D15	26
Tulelake, Ca., U.S.	B4	134
Tule Lake, l., Ca., U.S.	B4	134
Tulemalu Lake, l., Nu., Can.	C11	106
Tule Valley, val., Ut., U.S.	D3	132
Tuli, Zimb.	B9	70
Tuliszków, Pol.	D14	16
Tulita, N.T., Can.	C5	106
Ṭūlkarm, W.B.	F6	58
Tullahoma, Tn., U.S.	B12	122
Tullamore, Ire.	H5	12
Tulle, Fr.	D7	18
Tullibigeal, Austl.	I6	76
Tulln, Aus.	B13	22
Tullos, La., U.S.	F6	122
Tullus, Sudan	E4	62
Tully, Austl.	A5	76
Tulsa, Ok., U.S.	H2	120
Tulsequah, B.C., Can.	D4	106
Tul'skaja oblast', co., Russia	G20	10
Tuluá, Col.	E3	86
Tulum, Mex.	B4	102
Tulum, sci., Mex.	B4	102
Tulun, Russia	D18	32
Tulungagung, Indon.	H7	50
Tulungselapan, Indon.	E4	50
Tuma, stm., Nic.	F5	102
Tumacacori National Historical Park, p.o.i., Az., U.S.	L5	132
Tumaco, Col.	G2	86
Tumaco, Rada de, b., Col.	G2	86
Tuman-gang (Tumen), stm., Asia	C8	38
Tumanskij, Russia	D24	34
Tumany, Russia	D20	34
Tumbarumba, Austl.	J6	76
Tumbes, Peru	D1	84
Tumbes, Punta, c., Chile	H1	92
Tumbler Ridge, B.C., Can.	A10	138
Tumen, China	C8	38
Tumen (Tuman-gang), stm., Asia	C8	38
Tumeremo, Ven.	D11	86
Tumiritinga, Braz.	J5	88
Tumkūr, India	E3	53
Tumoteqi, China	A4	42
Tumpat, Malay.	I6	48
Tumsar, India	H7	54
Tumtum, Wa., U.S.	C9	136
Tumu, Ghana	G4	64
Tumuc-Humac Mountains, mts., S.A.	C6	84
Tumut, Austl.	J7	76
Tun, stm., Thai.	D4	48
Tunapuna, Trin.	s12	105f
Tunari, Cerro, mtn., Bol.	C3	90
Tunas de Zaza, Cuba	B8	102
Tunchang, China	L3	42
T'unch'i see Huangshan, China	G8	42
Tunduru, Tan.	G7	66
Tundža, stm., Eur.	G13	26
Tungabhadra, stm., India	D3	53
Tungabhadra Reservoir, res., India	D2	53
Tungaru, Sudan	E6	62
T'ungchou see Tongxian, China	B7	42
T'ungch'uan see Tongchuan, China	D3	42
Tung Hai see East China Sea, s., Asia	F9	36
T'unghsien see Tongxian, China	B7	42
T'unghua see Tonghua, China	D6	38
Tunghwa see Tonghua, China	D6	38
Tungkal, stm., Indon.	D3	50
Tungku, Malay.	A11	50
Tungla, Nic.	F5	102
T'ungliao see Tongliao, China	C4	38
Tungsha Tao (Pratas Island), i., Tai.	K7	42
Tungshih, Tai.	I9	42
Tungsten, N.T., Can.	C5	106
Tungurahua, state, Ec.	H2	86
Tungurahua, vol., Ec.	H2	86
Tuni, India	C6	53
Tunia, stm., Col.	G5	86
Tunis, Tun.	H4	24
Tunis, Golfe de, b., Tun.	G4	24
Tunis, Gulf of see Tunis, Golfe de, b., Tun.	G4	24
Tunisia, ctry., Afr.	C6	64
Tunisie see Tunisia, ctry., Afr.	C6	64
Tunja, Col.	E5	86
Tunkhannock, Pa., U.S.	C9	114
Tunliu, China	C5	42
Tunnel Hill, Ga., U.S.	C13	122
Tunnelton, W.V., U.S.	E6	114
Tunnsjøen, l., Nor.	D5	8
Tuntum, Braz.	C3	88
Tunu see Østgrønland, state, Grnld.	C18	141
Tununak, Ak., U.S.	D6	140
Tununirusiq (Arctic Bay), Nu., Can.	A14	106
Tunuyán, Arg.	F3	92
Tunuyán, stm., Arg.	F4	92
Tunxi, China	G8	42
Tuo, stm., China	E7	42
Tuo, stm., China	G1	42
Tuobalage, China	C12	54
Tuobuja, Russia	D13	34
Tuoj-Haja, Russia	B20	32
Tuokusidawan Ling, mtn., China	A6	46
Tuolumne, can., Ca., U.S.	F5	134
Tuong Duong, Viet.	C7	48
Tuotuo, stm., China	A13	54
Tupã, Braz.	D6	90
Tupaciguara, Braz.	J1	88
Tupanciretã, Braz.	D10	92
Tuparro, stm., Col.	E7	86
Tupelo, Ms., U.S.	C10	122
Tupelo, Ok., U.S.	C2	122
Tupik, Russia	F13	34
Tupinambarana, Ilha, i., Braz.	D6	84
Tupiraçaba, Braz.	H1	88
Tupiza, Bol.	D3	90
Tupper Lake, N.Y., U.S.	F2	110
Tupungato, Cerro, mtn., S.A.	F2	92
Tuquan, China	B9	36
Túquerres, Col.	G3	86
Tura, India	F13	54
Tura, Russia	B18	32
Tura, stm., Russia	C11	32
Turabah, Sau. Ar.	E5	56
Turaiyūr, India	F4	53
Turan, Russia	D16	32
Ṭurāq al-'Ilab, hills, Syria	E9	58
Turau, Bela.	H10	10
Turbaco, Col.	B4	86
Turbat, Pak.	D9	56
Turbo, Col.	C3	86
Turčasovo, Russia	E18	8
Turda, Rom.	C10	26
Turek, Pol.	D14	16
Turfan see Turpan, China	C2	36
Turfan Depression see Turpan Pendi, depr., China	C2	36
Turgaj see Torghay, stm., Kaz.	E10	32
Turgajskaja ložbina see Torghay zhylgh, reg., Kaz.	D10	32
Turgajskoe plato see Torghay üstirti, plat., Kaz.	D10	32
Turgay see Torghay, stm., Kaz.	E10	32
Turginovo, Russia	D18	10
Turgoš, Russia	A18	10
Turgutlu, Tur.	E10	28
Türi, Est.	B8	10
Turia (Túria), stm., Spain	D9	20
Túria (Turia), stm., Spain	D9	20
Turiaçu, Braz.	A3	88
Turiaçu, stm., Braz.	B3	88
Turimiquire, Cerro, mtn., Ven.	B10	86
Turin, Ab., Can.	F18	138
Turin see Torino, Italy	E4	22
Turinsk, Russia	C10	32
Turka, Ukr.	G19	16
Turkana, Lake see Rudolf, Lake, l., Afr.	D7	66
Turkestanskij hrebet, mts., Asia	B10	56
Túrkeve, Hung.	B7	26
Turkey, ctry., Asia	B3	56
Turkey, stm., Ia., U.S.	I7	118
Turkey Creek, stm., Ne., U.S.	K2	118
Turkish Republic of Northern Cyprus see Cyprus, North, ctry., Asia	C4	58
Türkistan, Kaz.	F11	32
Turkmenbaši, Turkmen.	B7	56
Turkmenia see Turkmenistan, ctry., Asia	B8	56
Turkmenistan, ctry., Asia	B8	56
Türkoğlu, Tur.	A7	58
Turks and Caicos Islands, dep., N.A.	A12	102
Turks Island Passage, strt., T./C. Is.	B12	102
Turks Islands, is., T./C. Is.	B12	102
Turku (Åbo), Fin.	F9	8
Turkwel, stm., Kenya	D7	66
Turley, Ok., U.S.	H2	120
Turlock, Ca., U.S.	F5	134
Turmalina, Braz.	I4	88
Turmantas, Lith.	E9	10
Turnagain, stm., B.C., Can.	D5	106
Turneffe Islands, is., Belize	D4	102
Turner, Mt., U.S.	F5	124
Turner, Or., U.S.	F4	136
Turners Falls, Ma., U.S.	B13	114
Turnhout, Bel.	C13	14
Turnov, Czech Rep.	F11	16
Turnu Măgurele, Rom.	F11	26
Turnu Roșu, Pasul, p., Rom.	D11	26
Turočak, Russia	D15	32
Turon, Ks., U.S.	D10	128
Turpan, China	C2	36
Turpan Pendi (Turfan Depression), depr., China	C2	36
Turquino, Pico, mtn., Cuba	C9	102
Turrell, Ar., U.S.	B8	122
Turret Peak, mtn., Az., U.S.	I5	132
Turtle, stm., Mb., Can.	D14	124
Turtle-Flambeau Flowage, res., Wi., U.S.	E8	118
Turtle Islands, is., S.L.	H2	64
Turtle Lake, N.D., U.S.	G13	124
Turtle Lake, Wi., U.S.	F6	118
Turu, stm., Russia	B18	32
Turuhan, stm., Russia	A14	32
Turuhansk, Russia	C6	34
Turvo, Braz.	D13	92
Turvo, stm., Braz.	K1	88
Turwi, stm., Zimb.	B10	70
Turzovka, Slov.	G14	16
Tuscaloosa, Al., U.S.	D11	122
Tuscaloosa, Lake, res., Al., U.S.	D11	122
Tuscany see Toscana, state, Italy	G8	22
Tuscarora Mountain, mts., Pa., U.S.	D8	114
Tuscola, Tx., U.S.	B8	130
Tuscumbia, Al., U.S.	C11	122
Tuscumbia, Mo., U.S.	F5	120
Tuskegee, Al., U.S.	E13	122
Tustumena Lake, l., Ak., U.S.	D9	140
Tutaev, Russia	C22	10
Tuticorin, India	G4	53
Tutin, Serb.	F7	26
Tutóia, Braz.	B4	88
Tutoko, Mount, mtn., N.Z.	G3	80
Tutrakan, Blg.	E13	26
Tuttle, N.D., U.S.	G14	124
Tuttle Creek Lake, res., Ks., U.S.	B12	128
Tutuala, E. Timor	G8	44
Tutuila, i., Am. Sam.	h12	79c
Tutupaca, Volcán, vol., Peru	G3	84
Tutwiler, Ms., U.S.	C8	122
Tutzing, Ger.	I7	16
Tuul, stm., Mong.	B6	36
Tuva, state, Russia	D16	32
Tuvalu, ctry., Oc.	D8	72
Tuvuca, i., Fiji	p20	79e
Ṭuwayq, Jabal, mts., Sau. Ar.	E6	56
Tuxford, Sk., Can.	D8	124
Tuxpan, Mex.	E6	100
Tuxpan de Rodríguez Cano, Mex.	E10	100
Tuxtepec, Mex.	F10	100
Tuxtla Gutiérrez, Mex.	G12	100
Túy see Tui, Spain	B2	20
Tuy, stm., Ven.	B8	86
Tuyen Hoa, Viet.	D8	48
Tuyen Quang, Viet.	B7	48
Tuy Hoa, Viet.	F9	48
Tuyün see Duyun, China	H2	42
Ṭuyūr, Burj aṭ-, hill, Sudan	C5	62
Tuz, Iraq	C5	56
Tuz Gölü, l., Tur.	B3	56
Tuzigoot National Monument, p.o.i., Az., U.S.	I4	132
Tuzla, Bos.	E5	26
Tuzly, Ukr.	D17	26
Tvardița, Mol.	C15	26
Tver' (Kalinin), Russia	D18	10
Tverca, stm., Russia	D18	10
Tverskaja oblast', co., Russia	D16	10
Tweed, On., Can.	D12	112
Tweed, stm., U.K.	F10	12
Tweed Heads, Austl.	G9	76
Twee Rivieren, S. Afr.	E5	70
Twelve Mile Lake, l., Sk., Can.	E7	124
Twenthekanaal, can., Neth.	B15	14
Twentynine Palms, Ca., U.S.	I9	134
Twin Buttes, mtn., Or., U.S.	F4	136
Twin Buttes Reservoir, res., Tx., U.S.	C7	130
Twin City, Ga., U.S.	D3	116
Twin Falls, Id., U.S.	H12	136
Twin Lakes, Ga., U.S.	F2	116
Twin Lakes, Wi., U.S.	B9	120
Twinsburg, Oh., U.S.	C4	114
Twisp, Wa., U.S.	B6	136
Twitchell Reservoir, res., Ca., U.S.	H5	134
Twitya, stm., N.T., Can.	C5	106
Two Butte Creek, stm., Co., U.S.	D6	128
Twofold Bay, b., Austl.	K7	76
Two Harbors, Mn., U.S.	D7	118

Name	Map Ref.	Page
Two Medicine, stm., Mt., U.S.	B14	136
Two Rivers, Wi., U.S.	D2	112
Tybee Island, Ga., U.S.	D5	116
Tychy, Pol.	F14	16
Tyczyn, Pol.	G18	16
Tye, Tx., U.S.	B8	130
Tygda, Russia	F14	34
Tyler, Mn., U.S.	G2	118
Tyler, Tx., U.S.	E3	122
Tylertown, Ms., U.S.	F8	122
Tylihul, stm., Ukr.	B17	26
Tylihul's'kyi lyman, l., Ukr.	B17	26
Tym, stm., Russia	C14	32
Tymovskoe, Russia	F17	34
Tynda, Russia	E13	34
Tyndall, S.D., U.S.	D15	126
Tyndaris, sci., Italy	F8	24
Tynemouth, Eng., U.K.	F11	12
Tynset, Nor.	E4	8
Tyre *see* Şūr, Leb.	E6	58
Tyrifjorden, l., Nor.	F3	8
Tyrma, Russia	F15	34
Tyrma, stm., Russia	F15	34
Tyrnavos, Grc.	D5	28
Tyrone, Ok., U.S.	E7	128
Tyrrell, Lake, l., Austl.	J4	76
Tyrrhenian Sea, s., Eur.	G11	6
Tysa (Tisa) (Tisza), stm., Eur.	A10	26
Tysnesøya, i., Nor.	F1	8
Tysse, Nor.	F1	8
Tytuvėnai, Lith.	E6	10
Ty Ty, Ga., U.S.	E2	116
Tyva see Tuva, state, Russia	D16	32
Tzaneen, S. Afr.	C9	70
Tzekung *see* Zigong, China	F5	36
Tzeliutsing *see* Zigong, China	F5	36
Tzucacab, Mex.	B3	102
Tzukung *see* Zigong, China	F5	36
Tzupo *see* Boshan, China	C7	42
Tzupo *see* Zibo, China	C8	42

U

Name	Map Ref.	Page
Uatumã, stm., Braz.	D6	84
Uauá, Braz.	E6	88
Uaupés, Braz.	H8	86
Uaupés (Vaupés), stm., S.A.	G7	86
Uaxactún, sci., Guat.	D3	102
Ubá, Braz.	K4	88
Ubaidullaganj, India	G6	54
Ubaitaba, Braz.	H6	88
Ubajara, Parque Nacional de, p.o.i., Braz.	B5	88
Ubangi (Oubangui), stm., Afr.	E3	66
Ubatã, Braz.	H6	88
Ubaté, Col.	E5	86
Ubatuba, Braz.	L3	88
Ube, Japan	F4	40
Úbeda, Spain	F7	20
Uberaba, Braz.	J2	88
Uberlândia, Braz.	J1	88
Überlingen, Ger.	I5	16
Ubiña, Peña, mtn., Spain	B4	20
Ubl'a, Slov.	H18	16
Ubly, Mi., U.S.	E7	112
Ubombo, S. Afr.	E11	70
Ubon Ratchathani, Thai.	E7	48
Ubrique, Spain	H5	20
Ubundu, D.R.C.	E5	66
Učaly, Russia	D9	32
Učami, Russia	B17	32
Ucayali, stm., Peru	D3	84
Uchinoura, Japan	H4	40
Uchiura-wan, b., Japan	C14	38
Uchiza, Peru	E2	84
Uchoa, Braz.	K1	88
Uckermark, reg., Ger.	C9	16
Ucon, Id., U.S.	G15	136
Učur, stm., Russia	E15	34
Uda, stm., Russia	F15	34
Uda, stm., Russia	C17	32
Udagamandalam, India	F3	53
Udaipur, India	F4	54
Udalguri, India	E13	54
Udall, Ks., U.S.	D11	128
Udamalpet, India	F3	53
Udankudi, India	G4	53
Udaquiola, Arg.	H8	92
Udaypur, Nepal	E11	54
Uddevalla, Swe.	G4	8
Uddjaur, l., Swe.	D8	8
Udgīr, India	B3	53
Udhampur, India	B5	54
Udimskij, Russia	F21	8
Udine, Italy	D10	22
Udmurtia see Udmurtija, state, Russia	C8	32
Udmurtija, state, Russia	C8	32
Udokan, hrebet, mts., Russia	E12	34
Udomlja, Russia	C17	10
Udon Thani, Thai.	D6	48
Udskaja guba, b., Russia	F16	34
Udskoe, Russia	F15	34
Udupi, India	E2	53
Udža, Russia	B12	34
Ueckermünde, Ger.	C10	16
Ueda, Japan	C11	40
Uele, stm., D.R.C.	D4	66
Uelen, Russia	C26	34
Uel'kal', Russia	C25	34
Uelzen, Ger.	C6	16
Ueno, Japan	E9	40
Uere, stm., D.R.C.	D5	66
Uetersen, Ger.	C5	16
Ufa, Russia	D9	32
Ufa, stm., Russia	C9	32
Uffenheim, Ger.	G6	16
Ugab, stm., Nmb.	E2	68
Uganda, ctry., Afr.	D6	66
Ugărčin, Blg.	F11	26
Ugarit, sci., Syria	C6	58
Ugashik, Ak., U.S.	E8	140
Uglegorsk, Russia	G17	34
Uglekamensk, Russia	C10	38
Uglič, Russia	C21	10
Ugljan, Otok, i., Cro.	F12	22
Ugodiči, Russia	C22	10
Ugodskij Zavod, Russia	E19	10
Ugra, stm., Russia	F18	10
Uherské Hradiště, Czech Rep.	G13	16
Uherský Brod, Czech Rep.	H13	16
Uhlenhorst, Nmb.	C3	70
Uhra, stm., Russia	B22	10
Uhta, Russia	B8	32
Uhta, Russia	F18	8
Uíge, Ang.	B1	68
Uinebona, stm., Ven.	E10	86
Uinta Mountains, mts., Ut., U.S.	C6	132
Uiraúna, Braz.	D6	88
Ŭisŏng, Kor., S.	C1	40
Uitenhage, S. Afr.	H7	70
Uithuizermeeden, Neth.	A15	14
Uj, stm., Asia	D10	32
Ujandina, stm., Russia	C17	34
Ujar, Russia	C16	32
Ujelang, at., Marsh. Is.	C7	72
Újfehértó, Hung.	B8	26
Ujhāni, India	D7	54
Uji, Japan	E8	40
Uji-guntō, is., Japan	H2	40
Ujiji, Tan.	E5	66
Ujjain, India	G5	54
Ujung, Indon.	G12	50
Ujunggenteng, Indon.	G5	50
Ujungkulon National Park, p.o.i., Indon.	G4	50
Ujungpandang (Makasar), Indon.	F11	50
Uk, Russia	C17	32
Uka, Russia	E21	34
Ukara Island, i., Tan.	E6	66
Ukerewe Island, i., Tan.	E6	66
Ukiah, Ca., U.S.	D2	134
Uki Ni Masi Island, i., Sol. Is.	f9	79b
Ukmergė, Lith.	E7	10
Ukraine, ctry., Eur.	F15	6
Ukui, Indon.	D3	50
Ukyr, Russia	G10	34
Ula, Bela.	E12	10
Ulaanbaatar, Mong.	B6	36
Ulaangom, Mong.	G7	34
Ulan, Austl.	I7	76
Ulan Bator *see* Ulaanbaatar, Mong.	B6	36
Ulan Buh Shamo, des., China	A2	42
Ulan-Burgasy, hrebet, mts., Russia	F10	34
Ulanhot, China	B9	36
Ulanów, Pol.	F18	16
Ulansuhai Nur, l., China	A3	42
Ulan-Ude, Russia	F10	34
Ulawa Island, i., Sol. Is.	e9	79b
Ulawun, Mount (The Father), vol., Pap. N. Gui.	b5	79a
Ulchin, Kor., S.	B2	40
Ulcinj, Mont.	H6	26
Ulco, S. Afr.	F7	70
Uldz, stm., Asia	B8	36
Uleåborg *see* Oulu, Fin.	D11	8
Ulen, Mn., U.S.	D2	118
Ulety, Russia	F11	34
Ulëz, Alb.	C13	24
Ulhāsnagar, India	B1	53
Ul'ianovka, Ukr.	A17	26
Uliastay, Mong.	B4	36
Ulindi, stm., D.R.C.	E5	66
Ulja, Russia	E17	34
Uljanovo, Russia	G18	10
Uljanovsk, Russia	D7	32
Ul'kan, Russia	C19	32
Ulla, stm., Spain	B2	20
Ulladulla, Austl.	J8	76
Ullin, Il., U.S.	G8	120
Ullŭng-do, i., Kor., S.	B3	40
Ulm, Ger.	H5	16
Ulm, Mt., U.S.	C15	136
Ulmarra, Austl.	G9	76
Ulmeni, Rom.	D13	26
Ulóngue, Moz.	C5	68
Ulsan, Kor., S.	D2	40
Ulster, hist. reg., Eur.	G5	12
Ulster Canal, can., Eur.	G5	12
Ulu, Indon.	E8	44
Ulu, Russia	D14	34
Ulúa, stm., Hond.	E3	102
Ulubat Gölü, l., Tur.	C11	28
Uluborlu, Tur.	E13	28
Uluçınar, Tur.	B6	58
Uludağ, mtn., Tur.	C12	28
Uludağ Yarımdası Milli Parkı, p.o.i., Tur.	C12	28
Ulukışla, Tur.	A5	58
Ulul, i., Micron.	C5	72
Ulungur, stm., China	B2	36
Ulungur Hu, l., China	B2	36
Ulunhan, Russia	F11	34
Uluru (Ayers Rock), mtn., Austl.	E6	74
Ulverston, Eng., U.K.	G9	12
Ulverstone, Austl.	n12	77a
Ulysses, Ks., U.S.	D7	128
Ulytaū zhotasy, mts., Kaz.	E11	32
Uma, China	F13	34
Umán, Mex.	B3	102
Umanak, Grnld.	C15	141
Umanak Fjord, b., Grnld.	C15	141
Umargāon, India	H4	54
Umaria, India	G8	54
Umarizal, Braz.	D7	88
Umarkot, Pak.	F2	54
Umatac, Guam	j9	78c
Umatilla, Fl., U.S.	H4	116
Umatilla, Or., U.S.	E7	136
Umatilla, stm., Or., U.S.	E7	136
Umatilla, Lake, res., U.S.	E4	136
Umba, Russia	C16	8
Umbertide, Italy	G9	22
Umboi Island, i., Pap. N. Gui.	b4	79a
Umbria, state, Italy	G9	22
Umbukul, Pap. N. Gui.	a4	79a
Umbuzero, ozero, l., Russia	C16	8
Umeå, Swe.	E9	8
Umeälven, stm., Swe.	D8	8
Umfolozi Game Reserve, S. Afr.	F10	70
Umfors, Swe.	C6	8
Umfreville Lake, res., On., Can.	A3	118
Umkomaas, S. Afr.	G10	70
Umm al-Arānib, Libya	B2	62
Umm al-Jimāl, Khirbat, sci., Jord.	F7	58
Umm al-Qaywayn, U.A.E.	D8	56
Umm as-Sa'd, sci., Syria	E7	58
Umm Bel, Sudan	E5	62
Umm Durmān (Omdurman), Sudan	D6	62
Umm el Faḥm, Isr.	F6	58
Umm Lajj, Sau. Ar.	D4	56
Umm Mitmam, sand, Egypt	H3	58
Umm Omeiyid, Râs, mtn., Egypt	K3	58
Umm Ruwābah, Sudan	E6	62
Umm Sayyālah, Sudan	E6	62
Umnak Island, i., Ak., U.S.	g25	140a
Umpqua, stm., Or., U.S.	G3	136
Umpulo, Ang.	C2	68
'Umrān, Yemen	F5	56
Umraniye, Tur.	D14	28
Umred, India	H7	54
Umreth, India	G4	54
Umtata, S. Afr.	G9	70
Umuarama, Braz.	A11	92
Umzingwani, stm., Zimb.	B9	70
Umzinto, S. Afr.	G10	70
Una, Braz.	H6	88
Una, India	H3	54
Una, stm., Eur.	E13	22
Unac, stm., Bos.	E3	26
Unadilla, Ga., U.S.	D2	116
Unadilla, N.Y., U.S.	B10	114
Unaí, Braz.	I2	88
Unalakleet, Ak., U.S.	D7	140
Unalaska, Ak., U.S.	F6	140
Unalaska Island, i., Ak., U.S.	F6	140
Unare, stm., Ven.	C9	86
'Unayzah, Sau. Ar.	D5	56
Uncia, Bol.	C3	90
Uncompahgre Peak, mtn., Co., U.S.	E9	132
Uncompahgre Plateau, plat., Co., U.S.	E8	132
Unden, l., Swe.	G5	8
Underberg, S. Afr.	F9	70
Undva nina, c., Est.	B4	10
Uneča, Russia	H15	10
Uneiuxi, stm., Braz.	H9	86
Unga Island, i., Ak., U.S.	E7	140
Ungava, Péninsule d', pen., Qc., Can.	D16	106
Ungava Bay, b., Can.	D17	106
Ungava Peninsula see Ungava, Péninsule d', pen., Qc., Can.	D16	106
Ungch'ŏn, Kor., S.	D1	40
Unggi-ŭp, Kor., N.	C9	38
Ungheni, Mol.	B14	26
União, Braz.	C4	88
União dos Palmares, Braz.	E7	88
Unicoi, Tn., U.S.	H3	114
Uniejów, Pol.	D14	16
Unimak Island, i., Ak., U.S.	F7	140
Unimak Pass, strt., Ak., U.S.	F6	140
Unini, stm., Braz.	H11	86
Unión, Arg.	G5	92
Unión, Para.	B9	92
Union, Ia., U.S.	B4	120
Union, La., U.S.	G8	122
Union, N.J., U.S.	D11	114
Union, Or., U.S.	E9	136
Union, S.C., U.S.	B4	116
Union, Wa., U.S.	C3	136
Union, W.V., U.S.	G5	114
Union Bay, B.C., Can.	G6	138
Union City, Ga., U.S.	D14	122
Union City, Mi., U.S.	F4	112
Union City, Oh., U.S.	D1	114
Union City, Pa., U.S.	C6	114
Union City, Tn., U.S.	H8	120
Unión de Reyes, Cuba	A7	102
Unión de Tula, Mex.	E7	100
Union Flat Creek, stm., U.S.	D9	136
Union Grove, Wi., U.S.	F1	112
Union Island, i., St. Vin.	p10	105e
Union Point, Ga., U.S.	C2	116
Union Springs, Al., U.S.	E13	122
Uniontown, Al., U.S.	E11	122
Uniontown, Ky., U.S.	G10	120
Uniontown, Pa., U.S.	E6	114
Unionville, Mi., U.S.	E6	112
United, Pa., U.S.	D6	114
United Arab Emirates, ctry., Asia	E7	56
United Arab Republic see Egypt, ctry., Afr.	B5	62
United Kingdom, ctry., Eur.	D8	6
United States, ctry., N.A.	C10	102
Unity, Sk., Can.	B4	124
Universal City, Tx., U.S.	E9	130
University, Ms., U.S.	C9	122
University City, Mo., U.S.	F7	120
University Park, N.M., U.S.	K10	132
University Park, Tx., U.S.	E2	122
Unjha, India	G4	54
Unnão, India	E8	54
Uno, Canal Numero, can., Arg.	H9	92
Unquillo, Arg.	E5	92
Unst, i., Scot., U.K.	n19	12a
Unstrut, stm., Ger.	E7	16
Unža, stm., Russia	G21	8
Unzen-dake, vol., Japan	G3	40
Uong Bi, Viet.	B8	48
Uozu, Japan	C10	40
Upa, stm., Russia	G20	10
Upanema, Braz.	C7	88
Upata, Ven.	C10	86
Upemba, Lac, l., D.R.C.	F5	66
Upernavik, Grnld.	C14	141
Upía, stm., Col.	E5	86
Upington, S. Afr.	F5	70
Upland, Ne., U.S.	A10	128
Upleta, India	H3	54
Upolu, i., Samoa	h11	79c
Upolu Point, c., Hi., U.S.	c6	78a
Upper Arlington, Oh., U.S.	D2	114
Upper Arrow Lake, l., B.C., Can.	F13	138
Upper Austria see Oberösterreich, state, Aus.	B10	22
Upper Blackville, N.B., Can.	D10	110
Upper Darby, Pa., U.S.	E10	114
Upper Egypt see El-Sa'īd, hist. reg., Egypt	J2	58
Upper Fraser, B.C., Can.	B8	138
Upper Ganga Canal (Upper Ganges Canal), can., India	D6	54
Upper Iowa, stm., U.S.	H7	118
Upper Kapuas Mountains, mts., Asia	C8	50
Upper Klamath Lake, l., Or., U.S.	H5	136
Upper Lake, Ca., U.S.	D3	134
Upper Lake, l., Ca., U.S.	B5	134
Upper Manitou Lake, l., On., Can.	B5	118
Upper Musquodoboit, N.S., Can.	E14	110
Upper Red Lake, l., Mn., U.S.	C4	118
Upper Sandusky, Oh., U.S.	D2	114
Upper Takutu-Upper Essequibo, state, Guy.	F12	86
Upper Trajan's Wall, misc. cult., Mol.	C15	26
Upper Volta see Burkina Faso, ctry., Afr.	G4	64
Uppsala, Swe.	G7	8
Uppsala, state, Swe.	F7	8
Upshi, India	B6	54
Upton, Ky., U.S.	G12	120
Urabá, Golfo de, b., Col.	C3	86
Uracoa, Ven.	C10	86
Uraj, Russia	B10	32
Urakawa, Japan	C15	38
Ural, stm.	E8	32
Ural Mountains see Ural'skie gory, mts., Russia	C9	32
Ural'sk *see* Oral, Kaz.	D8	32
Ural'skie gory (Ural Mountains), mts., Russia	C9	32
Urana, Austl.	J6	76
Urandangi, Austl.	D7	74
Urangan, Austl.	E9	76
Urania, La., U.S.	F6	122
Uranium City, Sk., Can.	D9	106
Uraricaá, stm., Braz.	F10	86
Uraricoera, Braz.	F11	86
Uraricoera, stm., Braz.	F11	86
Ura-Tjube, Taj.	B10	56
Uravakonda, India	D3	53
Uravan, Co., U.S.	E8	132
Urawa, Japan	D12	40
Urbana, Ar., U.S.	D6	122
Urbana, Il., U.S.	D9	120
Urbana, Oh., U.S.	D2	114
Urbandale, Ia., U.S.	C4	120
Urbania, Italy	G9	22
Urbino, Italy	G9	22
Urcos, Peru	F3	84
Urdinarrain, Arg.	F8	92
Ure, stm., Eng., U.K.	G11	12
Urèčča, Bela.	H10	10
Uren', Russia	H21	8
Ureña, Ven.	D5	86
Ures, Mex.	G7	98
Ureshino, Japan	F2	40
Urewera National Park, p.o.i., N.Z.	D7	80
Urgenč, Uzb.	F10	32
Urho Kekkosen kansallispuisto, p.o.i., Fin.	B12	8
Uriah, Al., U.S.	F11	122
Uriah, Mount, mtn., N.Z.	E4	80
Uribante, stm., Ven.	D6	86
Uribe, Col.	F4	86
Uribia, Col.	B5	86
Urich, Mo., U.S.	F4	120
Urique, stm., Mex.	B5	100
Ūritskīy, Kaz.	D11	32
Urjung-Haja, Russia	B11	34
Urjupinsk, Russia	D6	32
Urla, Tur.	E9	28
Urlaţi, Rom.	D13	26
Urlings, Antig.	f4	105b
Urmia *see* Orūmīyeh, Iran	B6	56
Urmia, Lake see Orūmīyeh, Daryācheh-ye, l., Iran	B6	56
Uromi, Nig.	H6	64
Uroševac, Serb.	G8	26
Urrao, Col.	D3	86
Ursa, Il., U.S.	D6	120
Uruaçu, Braz.	H1	88
Uruapan, Mex.	L9	134
Uruapan del Progreso, Mex.	F7	100
Urubamba, Peru	F3	84
Urubamba, stm., Peru	F3	84
Urubaxi, stm., Braz.	H9	86
Urubu, stm., Braz.	D6	84
Urubu, stm., Braz.	F1	88
Uruburetama, Braz.	B6	88
Urucará, Braz.	D6	84
Urucu, stm., Braz.	D5	84
Uruçuca, Braz.	H6	88
Uruçuí, Serra da, hills, Braz.	E3	88
Urucuia, stm., Braz.	I3	88
Uruçui-preto, stm., Braz.	E3	88
Uruguai (Uruguay), stm., S.A.	F8	92
Uruguaiana, Braz.	D9	92
Uruguay, ctry., S.A.	F10	92
Uruguay (Uruguai), stm., S.A.	F8	92
Urumchi *see* Ürümqi, China	C2	36
Ürümqi, China	C2	36
Urup, ostrov, i., Russia	G19	34
Urupês, Braz.	K1	88
Urutaí, Braz.	I1	88
Uruwira, Tan.	F6	66
Ürzhar, Kaz.	E14	32
Urziceni, Rom.	E13	26
Uržum, Russia	C7	32
Usa, Japan	F4	40
Usa, stm., Russia	A9	32
Uşak, Tur.	E12	28
Uşak, state, Tur.	E12	28
Ušaki, Russia	A13	10
Usakos, Nmb.	B2	70
Usborne, Mount, mtn., Falk. Is.	J5	90
Uščerpe, Russia	H14	10
U.S. Department of Energy Hanford Site, sci., Wa., U.S.	D7	136
Usedom, i., Eur.	B10	16
Ushant see Ouessant, Île d', i., Fr.	F3	14
Üsharal, Kaz.	E14	32
Ushashi, Tan.	E6	66
Üshtöbe, Kaz.	E13	32
Ushuaia, Arg.	J3	90
Usingen, Ger.	F4	16
Usinsk, Russia	A9	32
Usk, Wa., U.S.	B9	136
Usk, stm., Wales, U.K.	J9	12
Uslar, Ger.	E5	16
Usmas ezers, l., Lat.	C4	10
Usole, Russia	C9	32
Usole-Sibirskoe, Russia	D18	32
Uspallata, Arg.	F3	92
Uspanapa, stm., Mex.	G11	100
Ussuri (Wusuli), stm., Asia	C11	36
Ussurijsk, Russia	C10	38
Ust'-Barguzin, Russia	F10	34
Ust'-Belaja, Russia	C23	34
Ust'-Bolšereck, Russia	F20	34
Ust'-Čaun, Russia	C23	34
Ust'-Chorna, Ukr.	A10	26
Ust'-Cil'ma, Russia	D25	8
Uste, Russia	G18	8
Uster, Switz.	C5	22
Ustica, Isola di, i., Italy	F7	24
Ust'-Ilimsk, Russia	C18	32
Ust'-Ilimskoe vodohranilišče, res., Russia	C18	32
Ústí nad Labem, Czech Rep.	F10	16
Ústí nad Orlicí, Czech Rep.	G12	16
Ust'-Išim, Russia	C12	32
Ustja, stm., Russia	F21	8
Ust'-Javron'ga, Russia	E21	8
Ustjuckoe, Russia	B18	10
Ustjužna, Russia	B19	10
Ustka, Pol.	B12	16
Ust'-Kamčatsk, Russia	E21	34
Ust'-Kamenogorsk *see* Öskemen, Kaz.	E14	32
Ust'-Koksa, Russia	D15	32
Ust'-Kujda, Russia	B16	34
Ust'-Kulom, Russia	B8	32
Ust'-Kut, Russia	C19	32
Ust'-Lyža, Russia	A9	32
Ust'-Maja, Russia	D15	34
Ust'-Man'ja, Russia	B10	32
Ust'-Nera, Russia	D17	34
Ust'-Njukža, Russia	E13	34
Uštobe *see* Üshtöbe, Kaz.	E13	32
Ust'-Omčug, Russia	D18	34
Ust'-Ordynskij, Russia	D18	32
Ust'-Ozërnoe, Russia	C15	32
Ust'-Pinega, Russia	D19	8
Ust'-Reki, Russia	E22	8
Ustroń, Pol.	G14	16
Ust'-Sumy, Russia	D14	32
Ust'-Ulagan, Russia	D15	32
Ust'-Urgal, Russia	F15	34
Ust-Urt Plateau, plat., Asia	F9	32
Ust-Vyjskaja, Russia	E22	8
Usu, China	C1	36
Usuki, Japan	F4	40
Usulután, El Sal.	F3	102
Usumacinta, stm., N.A.	D2	102
Usumbura *see* Bujumbura, Bdi.	E5	66
Ušumun, Russia	F14	34
Usvjaty, Russia	E13	10
Utah, state, U.S.	D5	132
Utah Lake, l., Ut., U.S.	C5	132
Utata, Russia	D18	32
Ute, Ia., U.S.	B2	120
Ute Creek, stm., N.M., U.S.	F5	128
Utegi, Tan.	E6	66
Utena, Lith.	E8	10
Utete, Tan.	F7	66
Uthai Thani, Thai.	E4	48
Uthal, Pak.	D10	56
U Thong, Thai.	E4	48
Utiariti, Braz.	F6	84
Utica, Ks., U.S.	C8	128
Utica, Mi., U.S.	F6	112
Utica, Ms., U.S.	E8	122
Utica, N.Y., U.S.	E14	112
Utica, Oh., U.S.	D3	114
Utica see Utique, sci., Tun.	G3	24
Utiel, Spain	E9	20
Utila, Isla de, i., Hond.	D4	102
Utinga, stm., Braz.	G5	88
Utique (Utica), sci., Tun.	G3	24
Uto, Japan	G3	40
Utopia, Tx., U.S.	E8	130
Utorgoš, Russia	B13	10
Utraula, India	E9	54
Utrecht, Neth.	B14	14
Utrecht, S. Afr.	E10	70
Utrera, Spain	G5	20
Utrik, at., Marsh. Is.	B7	72
Utroja, stm., Eur.	D10	10
Utsunomiya, Japan	C12	40
Uttamapālaiyam, India	G3	53
Uttaradit, Thai.	D4	48
Uttaranchal, state, India	C7	54
Uttarkāshi, India	C7	54
Uttar Pradesh, state, India	E7	54
Utuado, P.R.	B2	104a
Utukok, stm., Ak., U.S.	C7	140
Utupua, i., Sol. Is.	E7	72
Uulu, Est.	B7	10
Uvá, stm., Col.	F7	86
Uvalda, Ga., U.S.	D3	116
Uvalde, Tx., U.S.	E8	130
Uvaravičy, Bela.	H13	10
Uvarovo, Russia	D6	32
Uvdal, Nor.	F3	8
Uvinza, Tan.	F6	66
Uvira, D.R.C.	E5	66
Uvs Lake see Uvsu-Nur, ozero, l., Asia	F7	34
Uvsu-Nur, ozero, l., Asia	F7	34
Uvworé, c., Vanuatu	I17	79d
Uwa, Japan	F5	40
Uwajima, Japan	F5	40
Uwayl, Sudan	F5	62
Uxbridge, On., Can.	D10	112
Uxmal, sci., Mex.	B3	102
Uyo, Nig.	H6	64
Uyuni, Bol.	D3	90
Uyuni, Salar de, pl., Bol.	D3	90
Uzbekistan, ctry., Asia	E10	30
Uzda, Bela.	G10	10
Uzerche, Fr.	D7	18
Uzgen, Kyrg.	F12	32
Uzhhorod, Ukr.	A9	26
Užice, Serb.	F6	26
Uzlovaja, Russia	F20	10
Üzümlü, Tur.	G12	28
Uzun Ada, i., Tur.	E9	28
Uzunköprü, Tur.	B9	28
Uzunkuduk, Uzb.	F11	32
Užur, Russia	C16	32
Užventis, Lith.	E5	10

V

Name	Map Ref.	Page
Vaal, stm., S. Afr.	F7	70
Vaaldam, res., S. Afr.	E8	70
Vaalwater, S. Afr.	D8	70
Vaasa (Vasa), Fin.	E9	8
Vabalninkas, Lith.	D7	10
Vác, Hung.	B6	26
Vacacaí, stm., Braz.	E11	92
Vacaria, Braz.	D12	92
Vacaria, stm., Braz.	I4	88
Vacaville, Ca., U.S.	E4	134
Vaccarès, Étang de, l., Fr.	F10	18
Vache, Île à, i., Haiti	C11	102
Vad, Russia	I21	8
Vadakara *see* Badagara, India	F2	53
Vădeni, Rom.	D14	26
Vadnagar, India	G4	54
Vado, N.M., U.S.	K10	132
Vadodara (Baroda), India	G4	54
Vado Ligure, Italy	F5	22
Vadsø, Nor.	A13	8
Vaduz, Liech.	C6	22
Vaga, stm., Russia	F20	8
Vågåmo, Nor.	F3	8
Vágar, i., Far. Is.	m34	8b
Vaghena Island, i., Sol. Is.	d7	79b
Vah, stm., Russia	B13	32
Váh, stm., Slov.	H13	16
Vahsel, Cape, c., S. Geor.	J9	90
Vaiden, Ms., U.S.	D9	122
Vaigai, stm., India	G4	53
Vaigat, strt., Grnld.	C15	141
Vaijāpur, India	B2	53
Vaikam, India	G3	53
Väike-Maarja, Est.	A9	10
Vail, Co., U.S.	D10	132
Vail, Ia., U.S.	B2	120
Vaimali, Vanuatu	k17	79d
Vaippār, stm., India	G4	53
Vaison-la-Romaine, Fr.	E11	18
Vaitahu, Fr. Poly.	s18	78g
Vākhān, hist. reg., Afg.	B11	56
Valaam, Russia	F14	8
Valadeces, Mex.	H9	130
Valandovo, Mac.	B5	28
Valašské Meziříčí, Czech Rep.	G13	16
Valatie, N.Y., U.S.	B12	114
Vâlcea, state, Rom.	E11	26
Vălčedrăm, Blg.	F10	26
Valcheta, Arg.	H3	90
Valdagno, Italy	E8	22
Valdai Hills see Valdajskaja vozvyšennost', hills, Russia	C15	10
Valdaj, Russia	B16	10
Valdaj, Russia	E16	8
Valdajskaja vozvyšennost' (Valdai Hills), hills, Russia	C15	10
Valdarno, val., Italy	G8	22
Val-de-Cães, Braz.	A1	88
Valdecañas, Embalse de, res., Spain	E5	20
Valdemarsvik, Swe.	G7	8
Valdepeñas, Spain	F7	20
Valderaduey, stm., Spain	C5	20
Valdés, Península, pen., Arg.	H4	90
Val-des-Bois, Qc., Can.	C14	112
Valdez, Ak., U.S.	D10	140
Valdivia, Chile	G2	90
Valdivia, Col.	D4	86
Valdobbiadene, Italy	E8	22
Val-d'Oise, state, Fr.	E10	14
Val-d'Or, Qc., Can.	F15	106
Valdosta, Ga., U.S.	F2	116
Valdoviño *see* Aviño, Spain	A2	20
Vale, Or., U.S.	G9	136
Valemount, B.C., Can.	D11	138
Valença, Braz.	L4	88
Valença, Braz.	G6	88
Valença, Port.	B2	20
Valença do Piauí, Braz.	D4	88
Valence, Fr.	E10	18
Valencia, Phil.	F5	52
València, Spain	E10	20
Valencia, Ven.	B7	86
València, state, Spain	E10	20
València, co., Spain	E10	20
València, Golf de, b., Spain	E10	20
Valencia, Golfo de see València, Golf de, b., Spain	E10	20
Valencia, Gulf of see València, Golf de, b., Spain	E10	20
Valencia, Lago de, l., Ven.	B8	86
Valencia de Alcántara, Spain	E3	20
Valencia de Don Juan, Spain	B5	20
Valencia Island, i., Ire.	J2	12
Valenciennes, Fr.	D12	14
Valente, Braz.	F6	88
Valentin, Russia	C11	38
Valentine, Ne., U.S.	E12	126
Valentine, Tx., U.S.	D3	130
Valenza, Italy	F5	22
Valera, Ven.	C6	86
Valga, Est.	H12	8
Valiente, Península, pen., Pan.	H7	102
Valili, mtn., Fiji	p19	79e
Valjevo, Serb.	E6	26
Valkeakoski, Fin.	F11	8
Valkenswaard, Neth.	C14	14
Valkininkas, Lith.	F7	10
Valladares, Mex.	H7	130
Valladolid, Mex.	B3	102
Valladolid, Spain	C6	20
Valladolid, co., Spain	C6	20
Vall de Uxó *see* La Vall d'Uixó, Spain	E10	20
Valle, Lat.	D7	10
Vallecillo, Mex.	H7	130
Valle d'Aosta, state, Italy	E4	22
Valle de Allende, Mex.	H2	130
Valle de la Pascua, Ven.	C8	86
Valle del Cauca, state, Col.	F3	86
Valle del Rosario, Mex.	G1	130
Valle de Olivos, Mex.	B5	100
Valle de Santiago, Mex.	E8	100
Valledupar, Col.	B5	86
Vallée d'Aoste see Valle d'Aosta, state, Italy	E4	22
Valle Edén, Ur.	E9	92
Vallegrande, Bol.	C4	90
Valle Hermoso, Mex.	C10	100
Vallejo, Ca., U.S.	E3	134
Vallenar, Chile	D2	92
Valle Redondo, Mex.	K9	134
Valletta, Malta	I8	24
Valley, Al., U.S.	E13	122
Valley, Ne., U.S.	C1	120
Valley, Wa., U.S.	B9	136
Valley, stm., Mb., Can.	C13	124
Valley Bend, W.V., U.S.	F6	114
Valley City, N.D., U.S.	H16	124
Valley East, On., Can.	B8	112
Valley Falls, Ks., U.S.	E2	120
Valley Farms, Az., U.S.	K5	132
Valley Head, Al., U.S.	C13	122
Valley Mills, Tx., U.S.	C10	130
Valley of the Kings, sci., Egypt	B6	62
Valley Springs, S.D., U.S.	H2	118
Valley Station, Ky., U.S.	F12	120
Valleyview, Ab., Can.	A13	138
Valley View, Tx., U.S.	H11	128
Vallimanca, Arroyo, stm., Arg.	H7	92
Vallorbe, Switz.	D3	22
Valls, Spain	C12	20
Valmeyer, Il., U.S.	F7	120
Valmiera, Lat.	C8	10
Valoria la Buena, Spain	C6	20
Valožyn, Bela.	F9	10
Vālpārai, India	F3	53
Valparaíso, Chile	F2	92
Valparaíso, Mex.	D7	100
Valparaiso, Fl., U.S.	G12	122
Valparaiso, In., U.S.	G2	112
Valparaiso, Ne., U.S.	F16	126
Valparaíso, state, Chile	F2	92
Valréas, Fr.	E10	18
Vals, stm., S. Afr.	E8	70
Vals, Tanjung, c., Indon.	G10	44
Valsbaai see False Bay, b., S. Afr.	I4	70
Valtimo, Fin.	E13	8
Valujki, Russia	D5	32
Valverde del Camino, Spain	G4	20
Valyncy, Bela.	E11	10
Vamori Wash, stm., Az., U.S.	L5	132
Van, Tur.	B5	56
Van, Lake see Van Gölü, l., Tur.	B5	56
Vanadzor, Arm.	A5	56
Vanajavesi, l., Fin.	F10	8
Van Alstyne, Tx., U.S.	D2	122
Vananda, B.C., Can.	G6	138
Vanavara, Russia	B18	32
Van Bruyssel, Qc., Can.	C4	110
Van Buren, Ar., U.S.	B4	122
Van Buren, Me., U.S.	C8	110
Vanceboro, Me., U.S.	E9	110
Vanceburg, Ky., U.S.	F2	114
Vancouver, B.C., Can.	G7	138
Vancouver, Wa., U.S.	E4	136
Vancouver Island, i., B.C., Can.	G4	138
Vancouver Island Ranges, mts., B.C., Can.	G5	138
Vandalia, Il., U.S.	F8	120
Vandalia, Mo., U.S.	E6	120
Vandalia, Oh., U.S.	E1	114
Vandavāsi, India	E4	53
Vanderbijlpark, S. Afr.	E8	70
Vanderbilt, Tx., U.S.	F11	130
Vanderhoof, B.C., Can.	B6	138
Vanderkloof Dam, res., S. Afr.	F7	70
Vanderlin Island, i., Austl.	C7	74
Vandervoort, Ar., U.S.	C4	122
Van Diemen Gulf, b., Austl.	B6	74
Vandry, Qc., Can.	C3	110
Vandžiogala, Lith.	E6	10
Vanegas, Mex.	D8	100
Vänern, l., Swe.	G5	8
Vänersborg, Swe.	G5	8
Vangaindrano, Madag.	E8	68
Van Gölü, l., Tur.	B5	56
Vangunu Island, i., Sol. Is.	e8	79b
Van Horn, Tx., U.S.	C3	130
Van Horne, Ia., U.S.	B5	120
Vanier, ngh., On., Can.	C14	112
Vanikolo, i., Sol. Is.	E7	72
Vanimo, Pap. N. Gui.	a3	79a
Vanino, Russia	G17	34
Vānīvilāsa Sāgara, res., India	E3	53
Vāniyambādi, India	E4	53
Vankarem, Russia	C25	34
Vankleek Hill, On., Can.	E2	110
Van Lear, Ky., U.S.	G3	114
Vanna, i., Nor.	A8	8
Vännäs, Swe.	E8	8
Vanndale, Ar., U.S.	B8	122
Vannes, Fr.	G6	14
Van Ninh, Viet.	F9	48
Van Phong, Vung, b., Viet.	F9	48
Van Phong Bay see Van Phong, Vung, b., Viet.	F9	48
Van Reenen, S. Afr.	F9	70
Van Rees, Pegunungan, mts., Indon.	F10	44
Vanrhynsdorp, S. Afr.	G4	70
Vansant, Va., U.S.	G3	114
Vansittart Island, i., Nu., Can.	B14	106
Vanskoe, Russia	B19	10
Vanthali, India	H3	54
Vanua Balavu, i., Fiji	p20	79e
Vanua Lava, i., Vanuatu	i16	79d
Vanua Levu, i., Fiji	p19	79e
Vanuatu (New Hebrides), ctry., Oc.	k16	79d
Van Wert, Oh., U.S.	D1	114
Van Wyksdorp, S. Afr.	H5	70
Van Zylsrus, S. Afr.	E6	70
Vao, N. Cal.	n16	79d
Var, state, Fr.	F12	18
Var, stm., Fr.	F13	18
Varada, stm., India	D2	53
Varallo, Italy	E5	22
Vārānasi (Benares), India	F9	54
Varandej, Russia	A9	32
Varangerfjorden, b., Nor.	A14	8
Varangerhalvøya, pen., Nor.	A13	8
Varano, Lago di, l., Italy	I12	22
Varaždin, Cro.	D13	22
Varazze, Italy	F5	22
Varberg, Swe.	H5	8
Vardak, state, Afg.	A2	54
Vardar (Axiós), stm., Eur.	B5	28
Varde, Den.	I3	8
Vardø, Nor.	A14	8
Varel, Ger.	C4	16
Varela, Arg.	G4	92
Varėna, Lith.	F7	10
Varennes-sur-Allier, Fr.	C9	18
Varese, Italy	E5	22
Vârfurile, Rom.	C9	26
Vargem, Riacho da, stm., Braz.	E6	88
Vargem Grande, Braz.	B3	88
Varginha, Braz.	K3	88
Varkallai, India	G3	53
Varkaus, Fin.	E12	8
Värmeln, l., Swe.	G5	8
Värmland, state, Swe.	G5	8
Varna, Blg.	F14	26
Varna, Russia	D10	32
Varna, state, Blg.	F14	26
Värnamo, Swe.	H6	8
Varniai, Lith.	E5	10
Varnjany, Bela.	F9	10
Varnsdorf, Czech Rep.	F10	16
Varnville, S.C., U.S.	D4	116
Várpalota, Hung.	B5	26
Värska, Est.	C10	10
Varvarin, Serb.	F8	26
Várzea, stm., Braz.	C11	92
Várzea Alegre, Braz.	D6	88
Várzea da Palma, Braz.	I3	88

Name	Map Ref.	Page
Várzea Grande, Braz.	G6	84
Varzino, Russia	B17	8
Vas, state, Hung.	B3	26
Vasa see Vaasa, Fin.	E9	8
Vasai, India	E3	46
Vasalemma, Est.	A7	10
Vasco, País see Euskal Herriko, state, Spain	A8	20
Vashkivtsi, Ukr.	A14	26
Vashkivtsi, Ukr.	A12	26
Vashon Island, i., Wa., U.S.	C4	136
Vasilevičy, Bela.	H12	10
Vasilevskij Moh, Russia	C18	10
Vasiliká, Grc.	C6	28
Vasjugan, stm., Russia	C13	32
Vaška, stm., Russia	D21	8
Vaskelovo, Russia	F14	8
Vaslui, Rom.	C14	26
Vaslui, state, Rom.	C14	26
Vassar, N.C., U.S.	A6	116
Vassar, Mi., U.S.	E6	112
Västerås, Swe.	G7	8
Västerbotten, state, Swe.	D8	8
Västernorrland, state, Swe.	E7	8
Västervik, Swe.	H7	8
Västmanland, state, Swe.	G7	8
Vasto, Italy	H11	22
Västra Götaland, state, Swe.	G4	8
Vásvár, Hung.	B3	26
Vatan, Fr.	G10	14
Vatican see Vatican City, ctry., Eur.	I9	22
Vatican City, ctry., Eur.	I9	22
Vaticano, Capo, c., Italy	F9	24
Vatnajökull, ice, Ice.	k31	8a
Vatomandry, Madag.	D8	68
Vatra Dornei, Rom.	B12	26
Vättern, l., Swe.	G6	8
Vatu-i-ra Channel, strt., Fiji	p19	79e
Vatukoula, Fiji	p18	79e
Vauclin, Montagne du, mtn., Mart.	k7	105c
Vaucluse, state, Fr.	F11	18
Vaucouleurs, Fr.	F14	14
Vaughan, On., Can.	E10	112
Vaughn, N.M., U.S.	G3	128
Vaukavysk, Bela.	G7	10
Vaupés, state, Col.	G6	86
Vaupés (Uaupés), stm., S.A.	G7	86
Vava'u, i., Tonga	E9	72
Vavoua, C. Iv.	H3	64
Vavuniya, Sri L.	G5	53
Växjö, Swe.	H6	8
Vaza-barris, stm., Braz.	E6	88
Vazante, Braz.	J2	88
Vazuza, stm., Russia	E17	10
Vazuzskoe vodohranilišče, res., Russia	E16	10
Veazie, Me., U.S.	F8	110
Veblen, S.D., U.S.	B15	126
Vecht (Vechte), stm., Eur.	B15	14
Vechta, Ger.	D4	16
Vechte (Vecht), stm., Eur.	B15	14
Vecpiebalga, Lat.	C8	10
Vecsés, Hung.	B6	26
Veddige, Swe.	H4	8
Vedea, stm., Rom.	F12	26
Vedia, Arg.	G7	92
Vednoe, Russia	C19	10
Veedersburg, In., U.S.	H2	112
Veendam, Neth.	A15	14
Veenendaal, Neth.	C14	14
Vega, i., Nor.	D4	8
Vega Alta, P.R.	B3	104a
Vega Baja, P.R.	B3	104a
Vegreville, Ab., Can.	C18	138
Veguita, N.M., U.S.	I10	132
Veinticinco de Mayo, Arg.	G7	92
Veiros, Braz.	D7	84
Veisiejai, Lith.	F6	10
Vejle, Den.	I3	8
Vejle, state, Den.	I3	8
Vela Luka, Cro.	H13	22
Velas, Cabo, c., C.R.	G4	102
Velázquez, Ur.	G10	92
Velden, Ger.	H8	16
Veleka, stm.	G14	26
Veleušćina, Bela.	F11	10
Vélez, Col.	D5	86
Vélez-Málaga, Spain	H6	20
Vel'gija, Russia	B17	10
Velhas, stm., Braz.	I3	88
Velikaja, stm., Russia	C11	10
Velikaja, stm., Russia	D23	34
Velikaja Kema, Russia	B12	38
Velika Morava, stm., Serb.	E8	26
Velikie Luki, Russia	D13	10
Velikij Ustjug, Russia	F21	8
Veliki Vítorog, mtn., Bos.	E4	26
Velikoe, Russia	G17	8
Velikoe, ozero, l., Russia	C19	10
Velikonda Hills, hills, India	D4	53
Veliko Tárnovo, Blg.	F12	26
Velikovisočnoe, Russia	C25	8
Veli Lošinj, Cro.	F11	22
Vélingara, Sen.	G2	64
Veliž, Russia	E14	10
Vel'ké Kapušany, Slov.	H18	16
Vel'ké Meziříčí, Czech Rep.	G12	16
Veila Gulf, strt., Sol. Is.	d7	79b
Veila Lavella, i., Sol. Is.	d7	79b
Vellār, stm., India	F4	53
Velletri, Italy	I9	22
Vellore, India	E4	53
Velma, Ok., U.S.	G11	128
Vel'sk, Russia	F20	8
Velten, Ger.	D9	16
Velva, N.D., U.S.	F13	124
Velyka Mykhailivka, Ukr.	B16	26
Velykodolyns'ke, Ukr.	C17	26
Velykoplos'ke, Ukr.	C17	26
Velykyj Bychkiv, Ukr.	B11	26
Velykyj Kuialnyk, stm., Ukr.	B17	26
Venadillo, Col.	E4	86
Venado Tuerto, Arg.	F6	92
Venafro, Italy	C8	24
Venâncio Aires, Braz.	D11	92
Vence, Fr.	F13	18
Venda, hist. reg., S. Afr.	C10	70
Vendas Novas, Port.	F2	20
Vendée, state, Fr.	C4	18
Vendéen, Bocage, reg., Fr.	C4	18
Vendôme, Fr.	G10	14
Vendrell see El Vendrell, Spain	C12	20
Veneta, Laguna, b., Italy	E9	22
Venetie, Ak., U.S.	C10	140
Veneto, state, Italy	E8	22
Venev, Russia	F21	10
Venézia (Venice), Italy	E9	22
Venezuela, ctry., S.A.	B8	86
Venezuela, Golfo de, b., S.A.	A3	84
Venezuela, Golfo de, b., S.A.	A3	84
Venezuelan Basin, unds.	G7	144
Vengerovo, Russia	C14	32
Venganga, India	D1	53
Veniaminof, Mount, vol., Ak., U.S.	E8	140
Venice see Venézia, Italy	E9	22
Venice, Fl., U.S.	I3	116
Venice, La., U.S.	H9	122
Venkatagiri, India	E4	53
Venlo, Neth.	C15	14
Venosa, Italy	C9	24
Venoste, Alpi (Ötztaler Alpen), mts., Eur.	D7	22
Venray, Neth.	C15	14
Venta, stm., Eur.	C4	10
Ventanas, Ec.	H2	86
Ventersdorp, S. Afr.	E8	70
Venterstad, S. Afr.	G7	70
Ventimiglia, Italy	G4	22
Ventotene, Isola, i., Italy	D7	24
Ventspils, Lat.	C4	10
Ventuari, stm., Ven.	E8	86
Ventura, Ca., U.S.	I6	134
Venturia, N.D., U.S.	B13	126
Venustiano Carranza, Mex.	G12	100
Venustiano Carranza, Presa, res., Mex.	B8	100
Vera, Arg.	D7	92
Vera, Spain	G9	20
Vera, Cape, c., Nu., Can.	B8	141
Veracruz, Mex.	F10	100
Veracruz, state, Mex.	F10	100
Veranópolis, Braz.	D12	92
Verával, India	H3	54
Verbania, Italy	E5	22
Verbano see Maggiore, Lago, l., Eur.	C14	18
Verbeek, Pegunungan, mts., Indon.	E12	50
Verbilki, Russia	D20	10
Vercelli, Italy	E5	22
Vercors, reg., Fr.	E11	18
Verde, stm., Braz.	D4	90
Verde, stm., Braz.	F4	88
Verde, stm., Braz.	H1	88
Verde, stm., Braz.	J1	88
Verde, stm., Braz.	F6	84
Verde, stm., Mex.	E7	100
Verde, stm., Az., U.S.	J5	132
Verde, Cape, c., Bah.	A10	102
Verde Grande, stm., Braz.	H4	88
Verden, Ger.	D5	16
Verden, Ok., U.S.	F10	128
Verde Pequeno, stm., Braz.	H4	88
Verdi, Nv., U.S.	D5	134
Verdigre, Ne., U.S.	E14	126
Verdigris, stm., U.S.	E13	128
Verdon, stm., Fr.	F12	18
Verdun, ngh., Qc., Can.	E3	110
Verdun-sur-Garonne, Fr.	F7	18
Verdun-sur-Meuse, Fr.	E14	14
Vereeniging, S. Afr.	E9	70
Veregin, Sk., Can.	C11	124
Veregin, stm., Russia	E19	10
Verešćagino, Russia	B15	32
Vergemont Creek, stm., Austl.	D4	76
Vergennes, Vt., U.S.	F3	110
Verhnedneprovskij, Russia	E16	10
Verhneimbatsk, Russia	B15	32
Verhnemulomskoe vodohranilišče, res., Russia	B14	8
Verhneural'sk, Russia	D9	32
Verhneviljujsk, Russia	D13	34
Verhnij Baskunčak, Russia	E7	32
Verhnij Most, Russia	C11	10
Verhnij Ufalej, Russia	C10	32
Verhnjaja Amga, Russia	E14	34
Verhnjaja Angara, stm., Russia	E11	34
Verhnjaja Inta, Russia	A10	32
Verhnjaja Salda, Russia	C10	32
Verhnjaja Tajmyra, stm., Russia	B8	34
Verhnjaja Tojma, Russia	E21	8
Verhojansk, Russia	C15	34
Verhojanskij hrebet (Verkhoyansk Mountains), mts., Russia	C14	34
Verhopuja, Russia	F19	8
Verhove, Russia	H20	10
Verigin see Veregin, Sk., Can.	C11	124
Verín, Spain	C3	20
Veríssimo, Braz.	J1	88
Verkhnovyna, Ukr.	A11	26
Verkhoyansk Mountains see Verhojanskij hrebet, mts., Russia	C14	34
Vermelho, stm., Braz.	E2	88
Vermilion, Oh., U.S.	C3	114
Vermilion, stm., Ab., Can.	C19	138
Vermilion, stm., On., Can.	B8	112
Vermilion, stm., U.S.	C6	118
Vermilion Bay, b., La., U.S.	H6	122
Vermilion Lake, l., On., Can.	A6	118
Vermilion Lake, l., Mn., U.S.	D8	118
Vermillion, S.D., U.S.	E16	126
Vermillion, stm., S.D., U.S.	E15	126
Vermillion, East Fork, stm., S.D., U.S.	D15	126
Vermillon, stm., Qc., Can.	C3	110
Vermont, Il., U.S.	D7	120
Vermont, state, U.S.	F4	110
Vernal, Ut., U.S.	C7	132
Verndale, Mn., U.S.	E3	118
Verneuil, Fr.	F9	14
Vernon, B.C., Can.	F11	138
Vernon, Fr.	E10	14
Vernon, Al., U.S.	D10	122
Vernon, Ct., U.S.	C13	114
Vernon, In., U.S.	F12	120
Vernon, Tx., U.S.	G9	128
Vernon, Ut., U.S.	C4	132
Vernonia, Or., U.S.	E3	136
Vernon Lake, res., La., U.S.	F5	122
Vernon River, P.E., Can.	D13	110
Vero Beach, Fl., U.S.	I5	116
Véroia, Grc.	C5	28
Verona, On., Can.	D13	112
Verona, Italy	E8	22
Verona, Ms., U.S.	C10	122
Verónica, Arg.	G9	92
Versailles, Fr.	F11	14
Versailles, Il., U.S.	E7	120
Versailles, In., U.S.	F13	120
Versailles, Ky., U.S.	F13	120
Versailles, Mo., U.S.	G5	120
Versailles, Oh., U.S.	D1	114
Veršino-Darasunskij, Russia	F12	34
Veršino-Šahtaminskij, Russia	F12	34
Vertedero, P.R.	B3	104a
Vertientes, Cuba	B8	102
Verulam, S. Afr.	E12	8
Verviers, Bel.	D14	14
Verwoerd Reservoir see Gariep Dam, res., S. Afr.	G7	70
Vescovato, Fr.	G15	18
Veseli nad Lužnicí, Czech Rep.	G10	16
Veselýj jar, Russia	C11	38
Vesolo, Monte, mtn., Italy	D9	24
Vesoul, Fr.	G14	14
Vespasiano, Braz.	J4	88
Vesta, C.R.	H6	102
Vest-Agder, state, Nor.	G2	8
Vestavia Hills, Al., U.S.	D12	122
Vesterålen, is., Nor.	B6	8
Vestfjorden, b., Nor.	C5	8
Vestfold, state, Nor.	G4	8
Vestgrønland (Kitaa), state, Grnld.	D16	141
Vestmannaeyjar, Ice.	I29	8a
Vestsjælland, state, Den.	I4	8
Vestvågøya, i., Nor.	B5	8
Vesuvio (Vesuvius), vol., Italy	D8	24
Vesuvius see Vesuvio, vol., Italy	D8	24
Veszprém, Hung.	B4	26
Veszprém, state, Hung.	B4	26
Vésztő, Hung.	C8	26
Vetapalem, India	D5	53
Vetluga, Russia	E24	8
Vetlanda, Swe.	H6	8
Vetluga, Russia	H21	8
Vetluga, stm., Russia	C7	32
Vetlužskij, Russia	G21	8
Vetlužskij, Russia	H21	8
Vetrișoaia, Rom.	C15	26
Vetschau, Ger.	E9	16
Veurne, Bel.	C11	14
Vevey, Switz.	D3	22
Vevay, state, S. Afr.	E11	18
Vézère, stm., Fr.	D7	18
Viacha, Bol.	C3	90
Viadana, Italy	F7	22
Viale, Arg.	E8	92
Viamão, Braz.	E12	92
Viamonte, Arg.	F6	92
Vian, Ok., U.S.	B4	122
Viana, Braz.	B3	88
Viana do Bolo, Spain	B3	20
Viana do Castelo, Port.	C1	20
Viana do Castelo, state, Port.	C2	20
Viangchan (Vientiane), Laos	D6	48
Viareggio, Italy	G7	22
Vibank, Sk., Can.	D10	124
Viborg, Den.	H3	8
Viborg, S.D., U.S.	D15	126
Viborg, state, Den.	H3	8
Vibo Valentia, Italy	F10	24
Vic, Spain	C13	20
Vicam, Mex.	B3	100
Vicebsk, Bela.	E13	10
Vicebsk, state, Bela.	E11	10
Vicente Guerrero, Mex.	D6	100
Vicente Guerrero, Presa, res., Mex.	D9	100
Vicenza, Italy	E8	22
Viceroy, Sk., Can.	E8	124
Vich see Vic, Spain	C13	20
Vichada, state, Col.	E7	86
Vichada, stm., Col.	E7	86
Vichadero, Ur.	E10	92
Vichra, stm., Eur.	F14	10
Vichuquén, Chile	G1	92
Vichy, Fr.	C9	18
Vici, Ok., U.S.	E9	128
Vicksburg, Ms., U.S.	E8	122
Vicksburg, Mi., U.S.	F4	112
Vic-sur-Cère, Fr.	E8	18
Viçosa do Ceará, Braz.	B5	88
Victor, Ia., U.S.	C5	120
Victor, Id., U.S.	G15	136
Victor, Mt., U.S.	D12	136
Victor Harbor, Austl.	J2	76
Victoria, Arg.	F7	92
Victoria, B.C., Can.	H7	138
Victoria, P.E., Can.	D13	110
Victoria, Chile	I1	92
Victoria see Labuan, Malay.	A9	50
Victoria see Rabat, Malta	H8	24
Victoria, Sey.	j13	69b
Victoria, Ks., U.S.	C9	128
Victoria, Tx., U.S.	F11	130
Victoria, Va., U.S.	G7	114
Victoria, state, Austl.	K4	76
Victoria, stm., Austl.	C6	74
Victoria, Chutes see Victoria Falls, wtfl., Afr.	D4	68
Victoria, Lake, l., Afr.	E6	66
Victoria, Lake, l., Austl.	I3	76
Victoria, Mount, mtn., Mya.	B8	48
Victoria, Mount, mtn., Pap. N. Gui.	b4	79a
Victoria Falls, wtfl., Afr.	D4	68
Victoria Fjord, b., Grnld.	A16	141
Victoria Harbour, On., Can.	D10	112
Victoria Island, i., Can.	A8	106
Victoria Land, reg., Ant.	C20	81
Victoria Nile, stm., Afr.	D6	66
Victoria Peak, mtn., Belize	D3	102
Victoria Peak, mtn., B.C., Can.	F4	138
Victoria River Downs, Austl.	C6	74
Victorias, Phil.	E4	52
Victoria Strait, strt., Nu., Can.	B10	106
Victoriaville, Qc., Can.	D4	110
Victoria West, S. Afr.	G6	70
Victorica, Arg.	H5	92
Victorino, Ven.	G8	86
Victorville, Ca., U.S.	I8	134
Vicuña, Chile	E2	92
Vicuña Mackenna, Arg.	F5	92
Vidalia, Ga., U.S.	D3	116
Vidalia, La., U.S.	F7	122
Vidal Ramos, Braz.	C13	92
Videira, Braz.	C12	92
Vidigueira, Port.	F3	20
Vidin, Blg.	F9	26
Vidisha, India	G6	54
Vidor, Tx., U.S.	G4	122
Vidra, Rom.	D13	26
Vidsel, Swe.	D9	8
Vidzeme, hist. reg., Lat.	C8	10
Viechtach, Ger.	H8	16
Viedma, Arg.	H4	90
Viedma, Lago, l., Arg.	I2	90
Viejo, Cerro, mtn., Peru	D2	84
Viella, Spain	B11	20
Vienna see Wien, Aus.	B13	22
Vienna, Ga., U.S.	D2	116
Vienna, Il., U.S.	G9	120
Vienna, Mo., U.S.	F5	120
Vienna, W.V., U.S.	E4	114
Vienna see Wien, state, Aus.	B13	22
Vienna Woods see Wienerwald, mts., Aus.	B13	22
Vienne, Fr.	D10	18
Vienne, state, Fr.	C6	18
Vienne, stm., Fr.	C6	18
Vientiane see Viangchan, Laos	D6	48
Vieques, P.R.	B5	104a
Vieques, Aeropuerto, P.R.	B5	104a
Vieques, Isla de, i., P.R.	B5	104a
Vieremä, Fin.	E12	8
Vierwaldstätter See (Lucerne, Lake of), l., Switz.	D5	22
Vierzon, Fr.	G11	14
Viesca, Mex.	C7	100
Vieste, Italy	I13	22
Vietnam, ctry., Asia	E9	48
Viet Tri, Viet.	D8	48
Vieux-Fort, Qc., Can.	i22	107a
Vieux-Fort, St. Luc.	m7	105c
Vieux-Fort, Pointe du, c., Guad.	i5	105c
Vieux-Habitants, Guad.	h5	105c
Vievis, Lith.	F7	10
Vigala, Est.	B7	10
Vigan, Phil.	B3	52
Vigevano, Italy	E5	22
Vigía, Braz.	D7	84
Vigía Airport, St. Luc.	I6	105c
Vigo, Spain	B2	20
Vigo, Ría de, est., Spain	B1	20
Vihari, Pak.	D4	54
Vihorevka, Russia	C18	32
Vihowa, stm., Pak.	C3	54
Vihren, mtn., Blg.	H10	26
Viiala, Fin.	F10	8
Viinijärvi, Fin.	E12	8
Viivikonna, Est.	A10	10
Vijaipur, India	E5	54
Vijayawāda, India	C5	53
Vijosë, stm., Alb.	D13	24
Vík, Ice.	l31	8a
Vikārābād, India	C4	53
Viking, Ab., Can.	C19	138
Vikna, Nor.	D4	8
Vikramasingapuram, India	G3	53
Vikulovo, Russia	C12	32
Vila da Ribeira Brava, C.V.	k10	65a
Vila do Bispo, Port.	G1	20
Vila do Conde, Port.	C2	20
Vila Fontes, Moz.	D6	68
Vilafranca del Panadés see Vilafranca del Penedès, Spain	C12	20
Vilafranca del Penedès, Spain	C12	20
Vila Franca de Xira, Port.	F2	20
Vila Gamito, Moz.	C5	68
Vilagarcía de Arousa, Spain	B1	20
Vilaine, stm., Fr.	G6	14
Vilaka, Lat.	C10	10
Vilalba, Spain	A3	20
Vilanandro, Tanjona, c., Madag.	D7	68
Vilāni, Lat.	D9	10
Vilankulo, Moz.	B12	70
Vila Nova de Famalicão, Port.	C2	20
Vila Nova de Gaia, Port.	C2	20
Vilanova i la Geltrú, Spain	C12	20
Vila Real, Port.	C3	20
Vila-Real, Spain	E10	20
Vila Real, state, Port.	C3	20
Vila Velha, Braz.	K5	88
Vila Verde, Port.	C2	20
Vilcabamba, Cordillera de, mts., Peru	F3	84
Vilejka, Bela.	F9	10
Vilelas, Arg.	C6	92
Vilhelmina, Swe.	D7	8
Vilhena, Braz.	F5	84
Vilija (Neris), stm., Eur.	F6	10
Viljandi, Est.	G11	8
Viljui, stm., Russia	D13	34
Viljujsk, Russia	D13	34
Viljujskoe vodohranilišče, res., Russia	B20	32
Vilkaviškis, Lith.	F6	10
Vil'kickogo, ostrov, i., Russia	A19	34
Vil'kickogo, proliv, strt., Russia	A9	34
Villa Abecia, Bol.	D3	90
Villa Ana, Arg.	D8	92
Villa Ángela, Arg.	C7	92
Villa Atamisqui, Arg.	D5	92
Villa Bella, Bol.	B3	90
Villa Berthet, Arg.	C7	92
Villablino, Spain	B4	20
Villa Bruzual, Ven.	C7	86
Villa Cañás, Arg.	G7	92
Villacañas, Spain	E7	20
Villa Carlos Paz, Arg.	F5	92
Villacarrillo, Spain	F7	20
Villacastín, Spain	D6	20
Villach, Aus.	D10	22
Villacidro, Italy	E2	24
Villa Clara, Arg.	E8	92
Villa Concepción del Tío, Arg.	E6	92
Villa Constitución, Arg.	F7	92
Villa de Arista, Mex.	D8	100
Villa de Cos, Mex.	D7	100
Villa de Cura, Ven.	B8	86
Villa del Carmen, Arg.	F5	92
Villa del Río, Spain	G6	20
Villa del Rosario, Arg.	E6	92
Villa del Rosario, Ven.	B5	86
Villa de Soto, Arg.	E5	92
Villadiego, Spain	B7	20
Villa Dolores, Arg.	F5	92
Villa Flores, Mex.	G12	100
Villa Florida, Para.	C9	92
Villafranca de los Barros, Spain	F4	20
Villafranca di Verona, Italy	E7	22
Villagarcía de Arosa see Vilagarcía de Arousa, Spain	B1	20
Village see The Village, Ok., U.S.	F11	128
Villa General Roca, Arg.	F4	92
Villa Gesell, Arg.	H9	92
Villa Grove, Il., U.S.	E9	120
Villaguay, Arg.	E8	92
Villa Guerrero, Mex.	F9	100
Villa Hayes, Para.	B9	92
Villahermosa, Mex.	G12	100
Villa Hidalgo, Mex.	H3	130
Villa Huidobro, Arg.	G5	92
Villa Insurgentes, Mex.	C3	100
Villa Iris, Arg.	I6	92
Villajoyosa see La Vila Joiosa, Spain	F10	20
Villa Juárez, Mex.	B3	100
Villa Krause, Arg.	E3	92
Villalba, P.R.	B3	104a
Villalba see Vilalba, Spain	A3	20
Villaldama, Mex.	B8	100
Villalonga, Arg.	G4	90
Villalpando, Spain	C5	20
Villa Mainero, Mex.	C9	100
Villa María, Arg.	F6	92
Villamartín, Spain	H5	20
Villa Mazán, Arg.	D4	92
Villa Media Agua, Arg.	E3	92
Villa Mercedes, Arg.	F5	92
Villa Montes, Bol.	D4	90
Villa Nueva, Arg.	E5	92
Villanueva, Col.	B5	86
Villanueva, Mex.	D7	100
Villanueva, N.M., U.S.	F3	128
Villanueva de Córdoba, Spain	F6	20
Villanueva de la Serena, Spain	F5	20
Villanueva de la Sierra, Spain	D4	20
Villanueva de los Infantes, Spain	F8	20
Villanueva del Río y Minas, Spain	G4	20
Villanueva y Geltrú see Vilanova i la Geltrú, Spain	C12	20
Villa Ocampo, Arg.	D8	92
Villa Ocampo, Mex.	C6	100
Villa Oliva, Para.	B9	92
Villa Pérez, P.R.	B2	104a
Villapinzón, Col.	E5	86
Villarcayo, Spain	B7	20
Villa Regina, Arg.	G3	90
Villa Reynolds, Arg.	F5	92
Villa Rica, Para.	B9	92
Villarreal see Vila-Real, Spain	E10	20
Villarrica, Para.	B9	92
Villarrobledo, Spain	E8	20
Villarrubia de los Ojos, Spain	E7	20
Villa San Giovanni, Italy	F9	24
Villa Santa Rita de Catuna, Arg.	E4	92
Villasayas, Spain	C8	20
Villa Serrano, Bol.	C4	90
Villasis, Phil.	B3	52
Villa Unión, Arg.	D6	92
Villa Unión, Arg.	D4	92
Villa Unión, Mex.	C5	100
Villa Unión, Mex.	D6	100
Villaviciosa de Córdoba, Spain	F5	20
Villazón, Bol.	D3	90
Villefranche-de-Rouergue, Fr.	E9	18
Villefranche-sur-Saône, Fr.	C10	18
Villena, Spain	F9	20
Villeneuve-sur-Lot, Fr.	E7	18
Villeneuve-sur-Yonne, Fr.	F12	14
Ville Platte, La., U.S.	G6	122
Villers-Cotterêts, Fr.	E12	14
Villerupt, Fr.	E14	14
Villeta, Col.	E4	86
Villeurbanne, Fr.	D10	18
Villiers, S. Afr.	E9	70
Villingen-Schwenningen, Ger.	H4	16
Villisca, Ia., U.S.	D3	120
Vilmanstrand see Lappeenranta, Fin.	F12	8
Vilnius, Lith.	F8	10
Vilsbiburg, Ger.	H8	16
Vil'shanka, Ukr.	A17	26
Vilshofen, Ger.	H9	16
Vilvoorde, Bel.	D13	14
Viluppuram, India	E4	53
Vilvorde see Vilvoorde, Bel.	D13	14
Vilyuy see Viljui, stm., Russia	D13	34
Vimmerby, Swe.	H6	8
Vimperk, Czech Rep.	G9	16
Vina, Ca., U.S.	D3	134
Vina, stm., Cam.	C2	66
Viña del Mar, Chile	F2	92
Vinalhaven, Me., U.S.	F8	110
Vinalhaven Island, i., Me., U.S.	F8	110
Vinaros see Vinaròs, Spain	D11	20
Vinaròs, Spain	D11	20
Vincennes, In., U.S.	F10	120
Vincennes Bay, b., Ant.	B15	81
Vincent, Al., U.S.	D12	122
Vinces, Ec.	H2	86
Vindelälven, stm., Swe.	D7	8
Vindhya Range, mts., India	G6	54
Vinegar Hill, mtn., Or., U.S.	F8	136
Vineland, N.J., U.S.	E10	114
Vinemont, Al., U.S.	C12	122
Vineyard Haven, Ma., U.S.	C15	114
Vineyard Sound, strt., Ma., U.S.	C15	114
Vinh, Viet.	C7	48
Vinh Long, Viet.	G8	48
Vinh Yen, Viet.	D8	48
Vinita, Ok., U.S.	H2	120
Vinkovci, Cro.	E15	22
Vinnytsia, Ukr.	F14	6
Vinnytsia, co., Ukr.	A16	26
Vinson Massif, mtn., Ant.	C32	81
Vintilă Vodă, Rom.	D13	26
Vinton, La., U.S.	G5	122
Vinton, Va., U.S.	G6	114
Viola, Il., U.S.	C7	120
Vioolsdrif, S. Afr.	F3	70
Vipiteno, Italy	D8	22
Vir, Otok, i., Cro.	F11	22
Virac, Phil.	D5	52
Viramgam, India	G4	54
Virarajendrapet, India	E2	53
Virbalis, Lith.	F5	10
Virden, Mb., Can.	E13	124
Virden, Il., U.S.	E8	120
Virden, N.M., U.S.	K8	132
Vire, Fr.	F7	14
Virei, Ang.	D1	68
Virgem da Lapa, Braz.	I4	88
Virgenes, Cabo, c., S.A.	J3	90
Virgil, Ks., U.S.	C13	128
Virgin, stm., U.S.	G2	132
Virgin Gorda, i., Br. Vir. Is.	e9	104b
Virginia, S. Afr.	F8	70
Virginia, Mn., U.S.	D6	118
Virginia, state, U.S.	G7	114
Virginia Beach, Va., U.S.	H10	114
Virginia City, Mt., U.S.	E14	136
Virginia City, Nv., U.S.	D6	134
Virginia Falls, wtfl., N.T., Can.	C5	106
Virginia Peak, mtn., Nv., U.S.	D6	134
Virgin Islands, dep., N.A.	h14	96a
Virgin Islands, is., N.A.	e7	104b
Virgin Islands National Park, p.o.i., V.I.U.S.	e7	104b
Virgin Passage, strt., N.A.	B5	104a
Virôhaure, l., Swe.	C7	8
Virje, Cro.	D13	22
Virojoki, Fin.	F12	8
Virovitica, Cro.	E14	22
Virrat, Fin.	E10	8
Virtaniemi, Fin.	B13	8
Virtsu, Est.	G10	8
Viru, Peru	E2	84
Virudunagar, India	G3	53
Virunga, Parc National de, p.o.i., D.R.C.	D5	66
Viru-Nigula, Est.	A9	10
Vis, Otok, i., Cro.	G13	22
Vis, i., Cro.	G13	22
Visale, Sol. Is.	e8	79b
Visalia, Ca., U.S.	G6	134
Visayan Sea, s., Phil.	E4	52
Visayas, is., Phil.	E4	52
Visby, Swe.	H8	8
Viscount Melville Sound, strt., Can.	A17	106
Viseu, Braz.	D7	84
Viseu, Port.	D3	20
Viseu, state, Port.	D3	20
Vishakhapatnam, India	C6	53
Visnagar, India	G4	54
Visoko, Bos.	F5	26
Visokoi Island, i., S. Geor.	K12	82
Visp, Switz.	D4	22
Visrivier, stm., Nmb.	C3	70
Vistina, Russia	A11	10
Vistula see Wisła, stm., Pol.	B14	16
Vita, Mb., Can.	E17	124
Vitarte, Peru	F2	84
Vite, India	C2	53
Viterbo, Italy	H9	22
Viti see Fiji, ctry., Oc.	E8	72
Vitichi, Bol.	D3	90
Vitigudino, Spain	D4	20
Viti Levu, i., Fiji	p19	79e
Vitim, stm., Russia	E11	34
Vitim, Russia	E12	34
Vitimskoe ploskogor'e, plat., Russia	F11	34
Vitína, Grc.	F5	28
Vitória, Braz.	K5	88
Vitória da Conquista, Braz.	H5	88
Vitória de Santo Antão, Braz.	D8	88
Vitória do Mearim, Braz.	B3	88
Vitorino Freire, Braz.	C3	88
Vitoria-Gasteiz, Spain	B8	20
Vitré, Fr.	F7	14
Vitry-le-François, Fr.	F13	14
Vitteaux, Fr.	G13	14
Vittoria, Italy	H8	24
Vittorio Veneto, Italy	E9	22
Viver, Spain	E10	20
Vivero see Viveiro, Spain	A3	20
Vivi, stm., Russia	C16	32
Vivian, La., U.S.	E5	122
Vizcaíno, Desierto de, des., Mex.	B2	100
Vizcaya see Bizkaiko, co., Spain	A8	20
Vize, Tur.	B10	28
Vizianagaram, India	B6	53
Vizille, Fr.	D11	18
Vizinga, Russia	B7	32
Vjalikaja Maščanica, Bela.	G12	10
Vjalikija Radaviči, Bela.	H7	10
Vjaseja, Russia	G10	10
Vjatka, stm., Russia	C8	32
Vjatskie Poljany, Russia	C8	32
Vjazemskij, Russia	G15	34
Vjaz'ma, Russia	E17	10
Vjazniki, Russia	H20	8
Vjazy', Bela.	F10	10
Vjosës (Aóos), stm., Eur.	D13	24
Vlaardingen, Neth.	C13	14
Vlădeasa, Vârful, mtn., Rom.	C9	26
Vladičin Han, Serb.	G8	26
Vladikavkaz, Russia	F6	32
Vladimir, Russia	H18	8
Vladimirskaja oblast', co., Russia	I19	8
Vladislavovka Tupik, Russia	E16	10
Vladivostok, Russia	C9	38
Vlasenica, Bos.	E5	26
Vlasotince, Serb.	G9	26
Vlasovo, Russia	B16	34
Vlieland, i., Neth.	A13	14
Vlissingen, Neth.	C12	14
Vlorë, Alb.	D13	24
Vltava (Moldau), stm., Czech Rep.	F10	16
Vnukovo, Russia	E20	10
Vöcklabruck, Aus.	C10	22
Vodila, stm., Russia	F17	8
Vodlozero, ozero, l., Russia	E16	8
Vodosalma, Russia	D14	8
Voël, stm., S. Afr.	H7	70
Voghera, Italy	F6	22
Voh, N. Cal.	m15	79d
Vohimena, Tanjona, c., Madag.	F8	68
Vohipeno, Madag.	E8	68
Vöhma, Est.	G11	8
Voi, Kenya	E7	66
Voineşti, Rom.	B14	26
Voinjama, Lib.	H3	64
Voiron, Fr.	D11	18
Voitsberg, Aus.	C12	22
Vojmsjön, l., Swe.	D6	8
Vojnica, Russia	D14	8
Vojvodina, state, Serb.	D7	26
Volcán, Pan.	H6	102
Volcano, Hi., U.S.	d6	78a
Volcano Islands see Kazan-rettō, is., Japan	G18	30
Volčiha, Russia	D14	32
Volda, Nor.	E2	8
Volga, S.D., U.S.	G2	118
Volga, stm., Russia	E7	32
Volga-Baltic Canal see Volgo-Baltijskij kanal, can., Russia	G17	8
Volgino, Russia	B16	10
Volgo-Baltijskij kanal, can., Russia	G17	8
Volgodonsk, Russia	E6	32
Volgograd, Russia	E6	32
Volgograd Reservoir see Volgogradskoe vodohranilišče, res., Russia	E7	32
Volgogradskoe vodohranilišče, res., Russia	D7	32
Volhov, Russia	A15	10
Volhov, stm., Russia	G14	8
Volissós, Grc.	E8	28
Völklingen, Ger.	G2	16
Volksrust, S. Afr.	E9	70
Voločanka, Russia	B7	34
Volodarskoe, Kaz.	D11	32
Volodarsk, Russia	H20	8
Vologda, Russia	F19	8
Vologda, stm., Russia	A22	10
Vologodskaja oblast', co., Russia	G19	8
Vologne, stm., Russia	D18	10
Volokolamsk, Russia	D18	10
Volonga, Russia	C22	8
Vólos, Grc.	D5	28
Volosovo, Russia	A12	10
Volot, Russia	C13	10
Volovo, Russia	G21	10
Vol'sk, Russia	D7	32
Volta, stm., Ghana	H5	64
Volta Blanche (White Volta), stm., Afr.	G4	64
Volta Lake, res., Ghana	H5	64
Volta Noire (Black Volta) (Mouhoun), stm., Afr.	G4	64
Volta Redonda, Braz.	L3	88
Volterra, Italy	G7	22
Volt'eva, Russia	D21	8
Vólturno, stm., Italy	C8	24
Volvi, Límni, l., Grc.	C6	28
Volyn', co., Ukr.	C7	32
Vónitsa, Grc.	E3	28
Vonavona Island, i., Sol. Is.	e7	79b
Vonda, Sk., Can.	B7	124
Vondrozo, Madag.	E8	68
Von Frank Mountain, mtn., Ak., U.S.	D8	140
Vopnafjörður, Ice.	k32	8a
Vopnafjörður, b., Ice.	k32	8a
Vorarlberg, state, Aus.	C6	22
Vorau, Aus.	C12	22
Vordemberg see Rein Anterior, stm., Switz.	D6	22
Vordingborg, Den.	I4	8
Vóreioi Sporádes, is., Grc.	D6	28
Vóreios Evvoïkós, b., Grc.	D5	28
Vorkuta, Russia	A10	32
Vormsi, i., Est.	G10	8
Vorob'evo, Russia	E14	10
Voronež, Russia	D5	32
Voronežskaja oblast', co., Russia	H21	10
Voronok, Russia	H15	10
Voropaevo, Bela.	E9	10
Vorpommern, hist. reg., Ger.	C9	16
Vørterkaka Nunatak, mtn., Ant.	C8	81
Võru, Est.	C10	10
Vosburg, S. Afr.	G6	70
Vosges, state, Fr.	F15	14
Vosges, mts., Fr.	F15	14
Voskresensk, Russia	F21	10
Voskresenskoe, Russia	B21	10
Voskresenskoe, Russia	E5	32
Vostočno-Sibirskoe more, s., Russia	B20	34
Vostočnyj Sajan, mts., Russia	D17	32
Vostok, i., Kir.	E11	72
Vostok, sci., Ant.	C15	81
Votice, Czech Rep.	G10	16
Votkinsk, Russia	C8	32
Votuporanga, Braz.	D7	90
Vouga, stm., Port.	D2	20
Vouziers, Fr.	E13	14
Voyageurs National Park, p.o.i., Mn., U.S.	C6	118

Name	Map Ref.	Page
Voyeykov Ice Shelf, ice, Ant.	B17	81
Vože, ozero, l., Russia	F18	8
Vožega, Russia	F19	8
Voznesene, Russia	F16	8
Vozroždenija, ostrov, i., Asia	E9	32
Vraca, Blg.	F10	26
Vradyïvka, Ukr.	B17	26
Vrancea, state, Rom.	D13	26
Vrangelja, ostrov (Wrangel Island), i., Russia	B24	34
Vranje, Serb.	G8	26
Vratsa *see* Vraca, Blg.	F10	26
Vrbas, Serb.	D6	26
Vrbas, stm., Bos.	E4	26
Vrbovec, Cro.	E13	22
Vrchlabí, Czech Rep.	F11	16
Vrede, S. Afr.	E9	70
Vredenburg, S. Afr.	H3	70
Vredenburgh, Al., U.S.	F11	122
Vredenburg-Saldanha *see* Vredenburg, S. Afr.	H3	70
Vredendal, S. Afr.	G4	70
Vriddhāchalam, India	F4	53
Vrindāvan, India	E6	54
Vršac, Serb.	D8	26
Vrútky, Slov.	G14	16
Vryburg, S. Afr.	E7	70
Vryheid, S. Afr.	E10	70
Vselug, ozero, l., Russia	C14	10
Vsetín, Czech Rep.	G13	16
Vsevidof, Mount, mtn., Ak., U.S.	F6	140
Vučitrn, Serb.	G7	26
Vukovar, Cro.	E16	22
Vulcan, Ab., Can.	F17	138
Vulcan, Rom.	D10	26
Vulcănești, Mol.	D15	26
Vulcano, Isola, i., Italy	F8	24
Vulsino see Bolsena, Lago di, l., Italy	H9	22
Vung Tau, Viet.	G8	48
Vunidawa, Fiji	p19	79e
Vunisea, Fiji	q18	79e
Vuohijärvi, l., Fin.	F11	8
Vuyyūru, India	C5	53
Vyāra, India	H4	54
Vyborg (Viipuri), Russia	F13	8
Vyčegda, stm., Russia	B7	32
Vyčegodskij, Russia	F22	8
Východočeský, state, Czech Rep.	F11	16
Východoslovenský Kraj, state, Slov.	H17	16
Vygoniči, Russia	G16	10
Vygozero, ozero, l., Russia	E16	8
Vyksa, Russia	I20	8
Vylkove, Ukr.	D16	26
Vynohradiv, Ukr.	A10	26
Vypolzovo, Russia	C16	10
Vyrica, Russia	A13	10
Vyšgorodok, Russia	C11	10
Vyskod', Russia	C13	10
Vyškov, Czech Rep.	G12	16
Vyšneol'šanoe, Russia	H20	10
Vyšnevolockoe vodohranilišče, res., Russia	C16	10
Vyšnij Voločok, Russia	C17	10
Vysoké Mýto, Czech Rep.	G12	16
Vysokiniči, Russia	F19	10
Vysokoe, Russia	D17	10
Vysokogornyj, Russia	G16	34
Vysokovsk, Russia	D19	10
Vytebet', stm., Russia	G18	10
Vytegra, Russia	F17	8
Vyzhnytsia, Ukr.	A12	26

W

Name	Map Ref.	Page
Wa, Ghana	G4	64
Waal, stm., Neth.	C14	14
Waalwijk, Neth.	C14	14
Wabag, Pap. N. Gui.	b3	79a
Wabakimi Lake, l., On., Can.	A8	118
Wabamun, Ab., Can.	C16	138
Wabamun Lake, l., Ab., Can.	C15	138
Wabana, Nf., Can.	j23	107a
Wabasca, stm., Ab., Can.	D7	106
Wabasca-Desmarais, Ab., Can.	D8	106
Wabash, In., U.S.	H4	112
Wabash, stm., U.S.	F9	120
Wabasha, Mn., U.S.	G6	118
Wabasso, Mn., U.S.	G3	118
Wabeno, Wi., U.S.	F10	118
Wabera, Eth.	F8	62
Wabowden, Mb., Can.	E11	106
Wąbrzeźno, Pol.	C14	16
Wabu Hu, l., China	E7	42
Waccamaw, stm., U.S.	C7	116
Waccamaw, Lake, l., N.C., U.S.	B7	116
Wachapreague, Va., U.S.	G10	114
Wachau, reg., Aus.	B12	22
Wacissa, Fl., U.S.	F2	116
Waco, Tx., U.S.	C10	130
Waco Lake, res., Tx., U.S.	C10	130
Waconda Lake, res., Ks., U.S.	B10	128
Wadayama, Japan	D7	40
Wad Bandah, Sudan	E5	62
Wadbilliga National Park, p.o.i., Austl.	K7	76
Waddenzee, strt., Neth.	A14	14
Waddington, N.Y., U.S.	D14	112
Waddington, Mount, mtn., B.C., Can.	E5	138
Wadena, Sk., Can.	C10	124
Wadena, Mn., U.S.	E3	118
Wadesboro, N.C., U.S.	B5	116
Wādī as-Sīr, Jord.	G6	58
Wādī Ḥalfā', Sudan	C6	62
Wadley, Al., U.S.	D13	122
Wadley, Ga., U.S.	D3	116
Wad Madanī, Sudan	E6	62
Wadowice, Pol.	G15	16
Wadsworth, Nv., U.S.	D6	134
Wadsworth, Oh., U.S.	C4	114
Wafangdian, China	B9	42
Wageningen, Neth.	C14	14
Wager Bay, b., Nu., Can.	B13	106
Wagga Wagga, Austl.	J6	76
Wagin, Austl.	F3	74
Waging am See, Ger.	I8	16
Wagner, S.D., U.S.	D14	126
Wagoner, Ok., U.S.	I2	120
Wagon Mound, N.M., U.S.	F4	128
Wagontire Mountain, mtn., Or., U.S.	G7	136
Wagrien, reg., Ger.	B6	16
Wągrowiec, Pol.	D13	16
Waha, Libya	B4	62
Wahai, Indon.	F8	44
Wāh Cantonment, Pak.	B4	54
Wahiawā, Hi., U.S.	b3	78a
Wahpeton, N.D., U.S.	E2	118
Wahran (Oran), Alg.	B4	64
Wai, India	B1	53
Waialua, Hi., U.S.	b3	78a
Wai'anae, Hi., U.S.	b3	78a
Waiau, N.Z.	F5	80
Waiau, stm., N.Z.	G2	80
Waiau, stm., N.Z.	F5	80
Waiblingen, Ger.	H5	16
Waidhofen an der Thaya, Aus.	B12	22
Waidhofen an der Ybbs, Aus.	C11	22
Waigeo, Pulau, i., Indon.	E9	44
Waihi, N.Z.	C6	80
Waikabubak, Indon.	H11	50
Waikato, stm., N.Z.	C6	80
Waikelo, Indon.	H11	50
Waikerie, Austl.	J2	76
Wailuku, Hi., U.S.	c5	78a
Waimate, N.Z.	G4	80
Waimea, Hi., U.S.	a2	78a
Wainganga, stm., India	H7	54
Waingapu, Indon.	H12	50
Waini, stm., Guy.	D12	86
Wainunu Bay, b., Fiji	p19	79e
Wainwright, Ab., Can.	B3	124
Wainwright, Ak., U.S.	B7	140
Waipukurau, N.Z.	E7	80
Wairarapa, Lake, l., N.Z.	E6	80
Wairau, stm., N.Z.	E5	80
Wairoa, N.Z.	D7	80
Wairoa, stm., N.Z.	B6	80
Waïsisi, Vanuatu	I17	79d
Waitaki, stm., N.Z.	G4	80
Waitara, N.Z.	D6	80
Waitemata, N.Z.	C6	80
Waite Park, Mn., U.S.	F4	118
Waitotara, N.Z.	D6	80
Waitsburg, Wa., U.S.	D8	136
Waiwo, Indon.	F9	44
Wajima, Japan	B9	40
Wajir, Kenya	D8	66
Waka, D.R.C.	D4	66
Waka, Eth.	F7	62
Wakarusa, In., U.S.	G3	112
Wakasa-wan, b., Japan	D8	40
Wakatipu, Lake, l., N.Z.	G3	80
Wakaw, Sk., Can.	B8	124
Wakayama, Japan	E8	40
Wakayama, state, Japan	F8	40
WaKeeney, Ks., U.S.	B9	128
Wakefield, Eng., U.K.	H11	12
Wakefield, Ks., U.S.	B11	128
Wakefield, Ne., U.S.	E15	126
Wakefield, Va., U.S.	H8	114
Wake Forest, N.C., U.S.	I7	114
Wake Island, dep., Oc.	B7	72
Wake Island, at., Wake I.	H19	142
Wakema, Mya.	D2	48
Waki, Japan	E7	40
Wakis, Pap. N. Gui.	b5	79a
Wakita, Ok., U.S.	E10	128
Wakkanai, Japan	B14	38
Wakomata Lake, l., On., Can.	B6	112
Wakonda, S.D., U.S.	E15	126
Waku Kungo, Ang.	C2	68
Walachia, hist. reg., Rom.	E11	26
Walanae, stm., Indon.	F12	50
Walawe, stm., Sri L.	H5	53
Wałbrzych, Pol.	F12	16
Wałbrzych, state, Pol.	F12	16
Walcha, Austl.	H8	76
Walcott, Ia., U.S.	C7	120
Walcott, N.D., U.S.	E1	118
Walcott, Lake, res., Id., U.S.	H13	136
Wałcz, Pol.	C12	16
Waldbröl, Ger.	F3	16
Walden, On., Can.	B8	112
Walden, Co., U.S.	C10	132
Waldheim, Sk., Can.	B7	124
Waldkirchen, Ger.	H9	16
Waldmünchen, Ger.	G8	16
Waldo, B.C., Can.	G15	138
Waldoboro, Me., U.S.	F7	110
Waldorf, Md., U.S.	F9	114
Waldport, Or., U.S.	F2	136
Waldron, Sk., Can.	D11	124
Waldron, Ar., U.S.	C4	122
Waldron, In., U.S.	E12	120
Waldshut-Tiengen, Ger.	I4	16
Waldviertel, reg., Aus.	B12	22
Wales, state, U.K.	I9	12
Wales Island, i., Nu., Can.	B13	106
Walewale, Ghana	G4	64
Walgett, Austl.	G6	76
Walgreen Coast, cst., Ant.	C30	81
Walhachin, B.C., Can.	F10	138
Walhalla, N.D., U.S.	F15	124
Walhalla, S.C., U.S.	B2	116
Walhalla, hist., Ger.	G8	16
Walker, Ia., U.S.	B6	120
Walker, stm., Nv., U.S.	D7	134
Walker Bay, b., S. Afr.	I4	70
Walker Lake, l., Nv., U.S.	E7	134
Walkerton, On., Can.	D8	112
Walkerton, In., U.S.	G3	112
Walkertown, N.C., U.S.	H5	114
Walkerville, Mt., U.S.	D14	136
Wall, S.D., U.S.	D10	126
Wallace, Id., U.S.	C11	136
Wallace, N.C., U.S.	B7	116
Wallace, Ne., U.S.	G11	126
Wallaceburg, On., Can.	F7	112
Wallal Downs, Austl.	C4	74
Wallam Creek, stm., Austl.	G6	76
Wallangarra, Austl.	G8	76
Wallaroo, Austl.	F7	74
Wallasey, Eng., U.K.	H9	12
Walla Walla, Wa., U.S.	D8	136
Wallingford, Ct., U.S.	C13	114
Wallingford, Vt., U.S.	G4	110
Wallis, Tx., U.S.	H2	122
Wallis, Îles, is., Wal./F.	E9	72
Wallis and Futuna, dep., Oc.	E9	72
Wallisville Lake, res., Tx., U.S.	H4	122
Wall Lake, Ia., U.S.	I3	118
Wallowa, Or., U.S.	E9	136
Wallowa, stm., Or., U.S.	E9	136
Walls of Jericho National Park, p.o.i., Austl.	n13	77a
Walnut, Ia., U.S.	C2	120
Walnut, Il., U.S.	C8	120
Walnut, Ms., U.S.	C10	122
Walnut, N.C., U.S.	I3	114
Walnut, stm., Ks., U.S.	D11	128
Walnut Canyon National Monument, p.o.i., Az., U.S.	H5	132
Walnut Cove, N.C., U.S.	H5	114
Walnut Creek, stm., Ks., U.S.	C9	128
Walnut Grove, Mn., U.S.	G3	118
Walnut Grove, Ms., U.S.	E9	122
Walnut Ridge, Ar., U.S.	H7	120
Walnut Springs, Tx., U.S.	B10	130
Walpole, Austl.	G3	74
Walpole, N.H., U.S.	G4	110
Walsall, Eng., U.K.	I11	12
Walsenburg, Co., U.S.	D4	128
Walsh, Austl.	C8	74
Walsh, Ab., Can.	E3	124
Walsh, stm., Austl.	A5	76
Walsrode, Ger.	D5	16
Walterboro, S.C., U.S.	D5	116
Walters, Ok., U.S.	G10	128
Waltershausen, Ger.	F6	16
Walthall, Ms., U.S.	D9	122
Walthill, Ne., U.S.	B1	120
Walton, N.S., Can.	E13	110
Walton, In., U.S.	H3	112
Walton, N.Y., U.S.	B10	114
Walvisbaai *see* Walvis Bay, Nmb.	C2	70
Walvis Bay (Walvisbaai), Nmb.	C2	70
Walvis Bay, b., Nmb.	C2	70
Walvis Ridge, unds.	K14	144
Walworth, Wi., U.S.	B9	120
Wamba, D.R.C.	D5	66
Wamba, Nig.	H6	64
Wamba (Uamba), stm., Afr.	F3	66
Wampsville, N.Y., U.S.	A10	114
Wampú, Hond.	E5	102
Wampú, stm., Hond.	E5	102
Wampum, Pa., U.S.	D5	114
Wamsutter, Wy., U.S.	B9	132
Wanaka, N.Z.	G3	80
Wanaka, Lake, l., N.Z.	G3	80
Wan'an, China	H6	42
Wanapa, Neth. Ant.	p23	104g
Wanapitei, stm., On., Can.	B9	112
Wanapitei Lake, l., On., Can.	B8	112
Wanbaoshan, China	B6	38
Wanbi, Austl.	J3	76
Wanblee, S.D., U.S.	D11	126
Wanchese, N.C., U.S.	I10	114
Wandel Hav, s., Grnld.	A22	141
Wandering, stm., Ab., Can.	A18	138
Wanfoxia, China	C4	36
Wang, stm., Thai.	D4	48
Wanganui, N.Z.	D6	80
Wanganui, stm., N.Z.	D6	80
Wangaratta, Austl.	K6	76
Wangcun, China	C7	42
Wangdu Phodrang, Bhu.	E12	54
Wangiwangi, Pulau, i., Indon.	G7	44
Wang Noi, Thai.	E5	48
Wangpan Yang, b., China	F9	42
Wangqing, China	C8	38
Wangtai, China	H7	42
Wangyehmiao *see* Ulanhot, China	B9	36
Wanhedian, China	E5	42
Wanhsien *see* Wanxian, China	F3	42
Wani, India	A4	53
Wanie-Rukula, D.R.C.	D5	66
Wanigela, Pap. N. Gui.	b4	79a
Wanipigow, stm., Can.	C18	124
Wānkāner, India	G3	54
Wanneroo, Austl.	F3	74
Wannian, China	G7	42
Wanning, China	L4	42
Wanparti, India	C4	53
Wantan, China	F4	42
Wanxian, China	F3	42
Wanyuan, China	E3	42
Wanzai, China	G6	42
Wanzleben, Ger.	D7	16
Wapakoneta, Oh., U.S.	D1	114
Wapanucka, Ok., U.S.	C2	122
Wapato, Wa., U.S.	D6	136
Wapello, Ia., U.S.	C6	120
Wāpi, India	H4	54
Wapiti, stm., Can.	A12	138
Wappingers Falls, N.Y., U.S.	C12	114
Wapsipinicon, stm., U.S.	J8	118
War, W.V., U.S.	G4	114
Warangal, India	B4	53
Wārāseoni, India	H7	54
Waratah, Austl.	n12	77a
Waratah Bay, b., Austl.	L5	76
Warburg, Ger.	E4	16
Warburton, Austl.	K5	76
Warburton Bay, b., N.T., Can.	C8	106
Ward, stm., Austl.	E6	76
Warden, S. Afr.	E9	70
Wardha, India	H7	54
Wardha, stm., India	H7	54
Ward Hill, hill, Scot., U.K.	C9	12
Wardlow, Ab., Can.	F19	138
Wardner, B.C., Can.	G15	138
Wardswell Draw, stm., U.S.	B5	130
Waremme, Bel.	D14	14
Waren, Ger.	C8	16
Waren, Indon.	F10	44
Warenai, stm., Indon.	F10	44
Warenda, Austl.	D3	76
Warendorf, Ger.	E3	16
Ware Shoals, S.C., U.S.	B3	116
Wargla, Alg.	C6	64
Warialda, Austl.	G8	76
Warin Chamrap, Thai.	E7	48
Warkworth, On., Can.	D11	112
Warman, Sk., Can.	B7	124
Warmandi, Indon.	F9	44
Warmbad, Nmb.	F4	70
Warmbad, S. Afr.	D9	70
Warm Baths *see* Warmbad, S. Afr.	D9	70
Warminster, Eng., U.K.	J10	12
Warminster, Pa., U.S.	D10	114
Warm Springs, Ga., U.S.	E14	122
Warm Springs, Mt., U.S.	D14	136
Warm Springs, Or., U.S.	F5	136
Warnemünde, ngh., Ger.	B7	16
Warner, Ab., Can.	G18	138
Warner, N.H., U.S.	G5	110
Warner Lakes, l., Or., U.S.	H6	136
Warner Mountains, mts., U.S.	B5	134
Warner Peak, mtn., Or., U.S.	A6	134
Warner Robins, Ga., U.S.	D2	116
Warnow, stm., Ger.	B8	16
Warra, Austl.	F8	76
Warracknabeal, Austl.	K4	76
Warragul, Austl.	L5	76
Warrawagine, Austl.	D4	74
Warrego, stm., Austl.	G5	76
Warren, Ar., U.S.	D6	122
Warren, In., U.S.	H4	112
Warren, Mi., U.S.	B2	114
Warren, Mn., U.S.	C2	118
Warren, Oh., U.S.	C5	114
Warren, Pa., U.S.	C6	114
Warrens, Wi., U.S.	G8	118
Warrensburg, Mo., U.S.	F4	120
Warrensburg, N.Y., U.S.	G3	110
Warrenton, S. Afr.	F7	70
Warrenton, Mo., U.S.	F6	120
Warrenton, N.C., U.S.	H7	114
Warrenton, Or., U.S.	D2	136
Warri, Nig.	H6	64
Warrington, Eng., U.K.	H10	12
Warrington, Fl., U.S.	G11	122
Warrior, Al., U.S.	D12	122
Warrnambool, Austl.	L4	76
Warroad, Mn., U.S.	C3	118
Warrumbungle National Park, p.o.i., Austl.	H7	76
Warsaw *see* Warszawa, Pol.	D16	16
Warsaw, Il., U.S.	D6	120
Warsaw, In., U.S.	G4	112
Warsaw, Ky., U.S.	F13	120
Warsaw, Mo., U.S.	F4	120
Warsaw, N.C., U.S.	A7	116
Warsaw, N.Y., U.S.	B7	114
Warspite, Ab., Can.	B18	138
Warszawa (Warsaw), Pol.	D16	16
Warszawa, state, Pol.	D16	16
Warta, Pol.	E14	16
Warta, stm., Pol.	D11	16
Wartburg, Tn., U.S.	H13	120
Wartrace, Tn., U.S.	B12	122
Warud, India	H7	54
Warwick, Austl.	G9	76
Warwick, Eng., U.K.	I11	12
Warwick, R.I., U.S.	C14	114
Warwick Channel, strt., Austl.	B7	74
Wasaga Beach, On., Can.	D10	112
Wasagu, Nig.	G6	64
Wasatch Range, mts., Ut., U.S.	C5	132
Wasbank, S. Afr.	F10	70
Wascana Creek, stm., Sk., Can.	D9	124
Wasco, Ca., U.S.	H6	134
Wasco, Or., U.S.	E6	136
Waseca, Mn., U.S.	G5	118
Wasgomuwa National Park, p.o.i., Sri L.	H5	53
Washademoak Lake, l., N.B., Can.	E11	110
Washburn, Il., U.S.	D8	120
Washburn, N.D., U.S.	G12	124
Washburn, Wi., U.S.	E7	118
Washburn, Mount, mtn., Wy., U.S.	F16	136
Washburn Lake, l., Nu., Can.	A9	106
Wāshīm, India	H6	54
Washington, D.C., U.S.	F8	114
Washington, Ga., U.S.	C3	116
Washington, Ia., U.S.	C6	120
Washington, Il., U.S.	D8	120
Washington, In., U.S.	F10	120
Washington, La., U.S.	G6	122
Washington, Mo., U.S.	F6	120
Washington, N.C., U.S.	A8	116
Washington, Pa., U.S.	D5	114
Washington, Tx., U.S.	G2	122
Washington, Ut., U.S.	F3	132
Washington, Va., U.S.	F7	114
Washington, state, U.S.	C6	136
Washington, Mount, mtn., N.H., U.S.	F5	110
Washington Court House, Oh., U.S.	E2	114
Washington Island, i., Wi., U.S.	C3	112
Washington Land, reg., Grnld.	A12	141
Washington Terrace, Ut., U.S.	B5	132
Washita, stm., U.S.	G12	128
Washow Bay, b., Mb., Can.	C17	124
Washpool National Park, p.o.i., Austl.	G9	76
Washtucna, Wa., U.S.	D8	136
Wasian, Indon.	F9	44
Wasilków, Pol.	C19	16
Wasior, Indon.	F9	44
Waskada, Mb., Can.	E13	124
Waskaganish, Qc., Can.	E15	106
Waskahigan, stm., Ab., Can.	B13	138
Waskom, Tx., U.S.	E4	122
Waspam, Nic.	E5	102
Wassenaar, Neth.	B13	14
Wasseralfingen, Ger.	H6	16
Wassy, Fr.	F13	14
Watampone, Indon.	F12	50
Watansopeng, Indon.	F11	50
Watatic, Mount, mtn., Ma., U.S.	B14	114
Waterberge, mts., S. Afr.	D8	70
Waterbury, Ct., U.S.	C12	114
Wateree Lake, res., S.C., U.S.	B5	116
Waterford (Port Lairge), Ire.	I5	12
Waterford, Ca., U.S.	F5	134
Waterford, Pa., U.S.	C6	114
Waterford, Wi., U.S.	B9	120
Waterford, state, Ire.	I5	12
Waterhen Lake, l., Mb., Can.	B14	124
Water Island, i., V.I.U.S.	e7	104b
Waterloo, Austl.	C5	74
Waterloo, Bel.	D13	14
Waterloo, On., Can.	E9	112
Waterloo, Qc., Can.	E4	110
Waterloo, Al., U.S.	C10	122
Waterloo, Ia., U.S.	B5	120
Waterloo, Il., U.S.	F7	120
Waterloo, N.Y., U.S.	B8	114
Waterloo, Wi., U.S.	A9	120
Waterman, Il., U.S.	C9	120
Waterproof, La., U.S.	F7	122
Watersmeet, Mi., U.S.	E9	118
Waterton-Glacier International Peace Park, p.o.i., N.A.	B13	136
Waterton Lakes National Park, p.o.i., Ab., Can.	G16	138
Watertown, N.Y., U.S.	E14	112
Watertown, S.D., U.S.	C15	126
Watertown, Wi., U.S.	A9	120
Waterval Boven, S. Afr.	D10	70
Water Valley, Ms., U.S.	C9	122
Waterville, N.S., Can.	E12	110
Waterville, Ks., U.S.	B12	128
Waterville, Me., U.S.	F7	110
Waterville, Oh., U.S.	C2	114
Waterville, Wa., U.S.	C6	136
Watervliet, N.Y., U.S.	B12	114
Watford, Eng., U.K.	J12	12
Watford City, N.D., U.S.	G10	124
Wathena, Ks., U.S.	E2	120
Watkins Glen, N.Y., U.S.	B9	114
Watkinsville, Ga., U.S.	C2	116
Watling Island see San Salvador, i., Bah.	C10	96
Watonga, Ok., U.S.	F10	128
Watrous, Sk., Can.	C8	124
Watsa, D.R.C.	D5	66
Watseka, Il., U.S.	H2	112
Watsikengo, D.R.C.	E4	66
Watson, Sk., Can.	B9	124
Watson Lake, Yk., Can.	C5	106
Watsonville, Ca., U.S.	G4	134
Watt Mountain, vol., Dom.	j6	105c
Watts Bar Lake, res., Tn., U.S.	B14	122
Watts Mills, S.C., U.S.	B4	116
Wattwil, Switz.	C5	22
Watubela, Kepulauan, is., Indon.	F9	44
Watzmann, mtn., Ger.	I8	16
Waubay Lake, l., S.D., U.S.	B15	126
Wauchope, Austl.	D6	74
Wauchula, Fl., U.S.	I4	116
Wauconda, Wa., U.S.	B7	136
Waugh, Mb., Can.	B3	118
Waukara, Bukit, mtn., Indon.	D11	50
Waukaringa, Austl.	I2	76
Waukarlycarly, Lake, l., Austl.	D4	74
Waukegan, Il., U.S.	F2	112
Waukesha, Wi., U.S.	A9	120
Waukon, Ia., U.S.	H7	118
Waunakee, Wi., U.S.	A8	120
Wauneta, Ne., U.S.	G11	126
Waupun, Wi., U.S.	H10	118
Waurika, Ok., U.S.	G11	128
Waurika Lake, res., Ok., U.S.	G10	128
Wausa, Ne., U.S.	E15	126
Wausau, Wi., U.S.	G9	118
Wauseon, Oh., U.S.	C1	114
Wautoma, Wi., U.S.	G9	118
Wauwatosa, Wi., U.S.	E1	112
Wauzeka, Wi., U.S.	A7	120
Wave Hill, Austl.	C6	74
Waverly, Ia., U.S.	B5	120
Waverly, Mo., U.S.	E4	120
Waverly, Ne., U.S.	D1	120
Waverly, N.Y., U.S.	B9	114
Waverly, Oh., U.S.	E2	114
Waverly, Tn., U.S.	H10	120
Waverly, Va., U.S.	G8	114
Waverly Hall, Ga., U.S.	E14	122
Wāw, Sudan	F5	62
Wawa, On., Can.	F14	106
Wawa, Nig.	H5	64
Wawa, stm., Nic.	E5	102
Wāw al-Kabīr, Libya	B3	62
Wawanesa, Mb., Can.	E14	124
Waxahachie, Tx., U.S.	B11	130
Waxhaw, N.C., U.S.	B5	116
Way, Lake, l., Austl.	E4	74
Waya, i., Fiji	p18	79e
Waycross, Ga., U.S.	E3	116
Wayland, Ia., U.S.	C6	120
Wayland, Ky., U.S.	G3	114
Wayland, Mi., U.S.	F4	112
Waylyn, S.C., U.S.	D6	116
Wayne, Ab., Can.	E18	138
Wayne, Mi., U.S.	B2	114
Wayne, Ne., U.S.	E15	126
Wayne, N.J., U.S.	D11	114
Wayne, W.V., U.S.	F3	114
Wayne City, Il., U.S.	F9	120
Waynesboro, Ms., U.S.	F10	122
Waynesboro, Tn., U.S.	B11	122
Waynesboro, Va., U.S.	F6	114
Waynesville, Il., U.S.	D8	120
Waynesville, N.C., U.S.	A3	116
Waynoka, Ok., U.S.	E10	128
Wāzah Khwāh, Afg.	B2	54
Wazīrābād, Pak.	B5	54
Wda, stm., Pol.	C14	16
Wé, N. Cal.	m16	79d
We, Pulau, i., Indon.	J2	48
Weatherford, Ok., U.S.	F10	128
Weatherford, Tx., U.S.	B10	130
Weatherly, Pa., U.S.	D10	114
Weaubleau, Mo., U.S.	G4	120
Weaver Lake, l., Mb., Can.	B17	124
Weaverville, Ca., U.S.	C3	134
Weaverville, N.C., U.S.	I3	114
Webb, Sk., Can.	D5	124
Webb, Ms., U.S.	D8	122
Webbwood, On., Can.	B7	112
Weber, stm., Ut., U.S.	B5	132
Weber City, Va., U.S.	H3	114
Webster, Ab., Can.	A12	138
Webster, Fl., U.S.	H3	116
Webster, Ma., U.S.	B14	114
Webster, Wi., U.S.	F6	118
Webster City, Ia., U.S.	B4	120
Weda, Indon.	E8	44
Weddell Island, i., Falk. Is.	J4	90
Weddell Sea, s., Ant.	B36	81
Wedderburn, Austl.	K4	76
Wedgeport, N.S., Can.	G11	110
Wedowee, Al., U.S.	D13	122
Weed, Ca., U.S.	B3	134
Weems, Va., U.S.	G9	114
Weenen, S. Afr.	F10	70
Weeping Water, Ne., U.S.	D1	120
Weert, Neth.	C14	14
Wee Waa, Austl.	H7	76
Węgorzewo, Pol.	B17	16
Węgrów, Pol.	D17	16
Wei, stm., China	C8	42
Wei, stm., China	C6	42
Wei, stm., China	D3	42
Weichang, China	C2	38
Weichuan, China	D6	42
Weida, Ger.	F8	16
Weiden in der Oberpfalz, Ger.	G7	16
Weifang, China	C8	42
Weihai, China	C10	42
Weihaiwei *see* Weihai, China	C10	42
Weihe, China	B8	38
Weilburg, Ger.	F4	16
Weilheim, Ger.	I7	16
Weilmoringle, Austl.	G6	76
Weimar, Ger.	E7	16
Weimar, Tx., U.S.	E11	130
Weinan, China	D3	42
Weinheim, Ger.	G4	16
Weipa, Austl.	B8	74
Weippe, Id., U.S.	D11	136
Weir, Ks., U.S.	D14	128
Weir, Ms., U.S.	D9	122
Weir, stm., Austl.	G8	76
Weirton, W.V., U.S.	D5	114
Weisburd, Arg.	C6	92
Weiser, Id., U.S.	F10	136
Weiser, stm., Id., U.S.	F10	136
Weishan Hu, l., China	D7	42
Weishi, China	D6	42
Weisner Mountain, mtn., Al., U.S.	C13	122
Weissenburg in Bayern, Ger.	G7	16
Weissenfels, Ger.	E7	16
Weiss Lake, res., U.S.	C13	122
Weisswasser, Ger.	E10	16
Weitra, Aus.	B11	22
Weixi, China	F4	36
Weixian, China	C6	42
Weiyuan, stm., China	A5	48
Weiz, Aus.	C12	22
Wejherowo, Pol.	B14	16
Wekoewa Punt, c., Neth. Ant.	p23	104g
Welaka, Fl., U.S.	G4	116
Welch, Ok., U.S.	H2	120
Welch, Tx., U.S.	B5	130
Welcome, Mn., U.S.	H4	118
Weldiya, Eth.	E7	62
Weldon, Sk., Can.	A8	124
Weldon, Il., U.S.	D9	120
Weldon, stm., U.S.	D4	120
Weleetka, Ok., U.S.	B2	122
Welk'īṭē, Eth.	F7	62
Welkom, S. Afr.	E8	70
Welland, On., Can.	F10	112
Welland, stm., Eng., U.K.	I12	12
Wellborn, Fl., U.S.	F3	116
Wellborn, Tx., U.S.	G2	122
Wellesley Islands, is., Austl.	C8	74
Wellingborough, Eng., U.K.	I12	12
Wellington, Austl.	I7	76
Wellington, On., Can.	E12	112
Wellington, N.Z.	E6	80
Wellington, S. Afr.	H4	70
Wellington, Eng., U.K.	K9	12
Wellington, Co., U.S.	G7	126
Wellington, Mo., U.S.	E4	120
Wellington, Oh., U.S.	C3	114
Wellington, Tx., U.S.	G8	128
Wellington, Ut., U.S.	D6	132
Wellington, Isla, i., Chile	I2	90
Wellington Bay, b., Nu., Can.	B9	106
Wellington Channel, strt., Nu., Can.	B7	141
Wellman, Ia., U.S.	C6	120
Wellman, Tx., U.S.	A5	130
Wells, Eng., U.K.	J10	12
Wells, Mi., U.S.	C2	112
Wells, Mn., U.S.	H5	118
Wells, N.Y., U.S.	G2	110
Wells, Tx., U.S.	F3	122
Wells, Lake, l., Austl.	E4	74
Wells, Mount, hill, Austl.	C5	74
Wellsboro, Pa., U.S.	C8	114
Wellsburg, Ia., U.S.	B4	120
Wellsburg, W.V., U.S.	D5	114
Wellsford, N.Z.	C6	80
Wells-next-the-Sea, Eng., U.K.	I13	12
Wellston, Oh., U.S.	E3	114
Wellsville, Ks., U.S.	C13	128
Wellsville, Mo., U.S.	E6	120
Wellsville, N.Y., U.S.	B8	114
Wellsville, Oh., U.S.	D5	114
Wellton, Az., U.S.	K2	132
Wels, Aus.	B10	22
Welsford, N.B., Can.	E10	110
Welshpool, Wales, U.K.	I9	12
Welwyn Garden City, Eng., U.K.	J12	12
Wembley, Ab., Can.	A11	138
Wena, D.R.C.	E4	66
Wenatchee, Wa., U.S.	C6	136
Wenatchee Mountains, mts., Wa., U.S.	C6	136
Wenceslau Braz, Braz.	L1	88
Wenchang, China	L4	42
Wencheng, China	H8	42
Wenchi, Ghana	H4	64
Wenchou *see* Wenzhou, China	F9	36
Wenchow *see* Wenzhou, China	F9	36
Wendell, Id., U.S.	H12	136
Wenden, Az., U.S.	J3	132
Wendeng, China	C10	42
Wendover, Ut., U.S.	C2	132
Weng, stm., China	I6	42
Weng'an, China	H2	42
Wenling, China	G9	42
Wenlock, stm., Austl.	B8	74
Wenquan, China	E14	32
Wenshan, China	A7	48
Wenshang, China	D7	42
Wenshui, China	C4	42
Wenshui, China	G2	42
Wensleydale, val., Eng., U.K.	G11	12
Wentworth, Austl.	J3	76
Wentworth, S.D., U.S.	G2	118
Wenxi, China	D4	42
Wenxian, China	D5	42
Wenzhou, China	F9	36
Wepener, S. Afr.	F8	70
Werda, Bots.	D6	70
Werdau, Ger.	F8	16
Werder, Ger.	D8	16
Wernadinga, Austl.	B2	76
Wernigerode, Ger.	E6	16
Werra, stm., Ger.	E5	16
Werribee, Austl.	K5	76
Werrikimbe National Park, p.o.i., Austl.	H9	76
Werris Creek, Austl.	H8	76
Wertheim, Ger.	G5	16
Wesel, Ger.	E2	16
Weser, stm., Ger.	C4	16
Weskan, Ks., U.S.	C7	128
Weslaco, Tx., U.S.	H10	130
Weslemkoon Lake, l., On., Can.	C12	112
Wesley, Dom.	i6	105c
Wesleyville, Pa., U.S.	B5	114
Wessel, Cape, c., Austl.	B7	74
Wessel Islands, is., Austl.	B7	74
Wessington, S.D., U.S.	C14	126
Wessington Springs, S.D., U.S.	C14	126
West, Ms., U.S.	D9	122
West, Tx., U.S.	C10	130
West Allis, Wi., U.S.	B9	120
West Antarctica, reg., Ant.	D30	81
Westbank, B.C., Can.	G11	138
West Bank, dep., Asia	F6	58
West Bay, N.S., Can.	E15	110
West Bay, b., Tx., U.S.	E12	130
West Bend, Ia., U.S.	B3	120
West Bend, Wi., U.S.	E1	112
West Bengal, state, India	G11	54
West Blocton, Al., U.S.	D11	122
West Bohemia see Západočeský kraj, state, Czech Rep.	G9	16
West Borneo see Kalimantan Barat, state, Indon.	D7	50
West Branch, Ia., U.S.	C6	120
Westbridge, B.C., Can.	G11	138
West Bromwich, Eng., U.K.	I11	12
Westbrook, Me., U.S.	G6	110
Westbrook, Mn., U.S.	G3	118
Westbrook, Tx., U.S.	B6	130
West Burlington, Ia., U.S.	D6	120
West Burra, i., Scot., U.K.	n18	12a
Westby, Austl.	J6	76
Westby, Wi., U.S.	H8	118
West Cache Creek, stm., Ok., U.S.	G10	128
West Caicos, i., T./C. Is.	B11	102
West Cape, c., N.Z.	G2	80
West Cape Howe, c., Austl.	G3	74
West Carlisle, Tx., U.S.	H6	128
West Caroline Basin, unds.	I16	142
West Chester, Pa., U.S.	E10	114
Westchester Station, N.S., Can.	E13	110
Westcliffe, Co., U.S.	C3	128
West Columbia, S.C., U.S.	B4	116
West Columbia, Tx., U.S.	H3	122
West Cote Blanche Bay, b., La., U.S.	H7	122
West Des Moines, Ia., U.S.	C4	120
West Dolores, stm., Co., U.S.	F8	132
West Elk Peak, mtn., Co., U.S.	E9	132
West End, Ar., U.S.	C6	122
West End, N.C., U.S.	A6	116
Westerland, Ger.	B4	16
Westerly, R.I., U.S.	C14	114
Western, state, Sol. Is.	e7	79b
Western, stm., Austl.	D4	76
Western Australia, state, Austl.	D4	74
Western Cape, state, S. Afr.	H5	70
Western Channel, strt., Asia	E2	40
Western Desert, des., Egypt	B5	62
Western Division, state, Fiji	p18	79e
Western Dvina (Daugava) (Zahodnjaja Dzvina) (Zapadnaja Dvina), stm., Eur.	D7	10
Western Ghāts, mts., India	E3	46
Westernport, Md., U.S.	E6	114
Western Sahara, dep., Afr.	E2	64
Western Samoa see Samoa, ctry., Oc.	g12	79c
Western Sayans see Zapadnyj Sajan, mts., Russia	D16	32
Western Shore, N.S., Can.	F12	110
Westerschelde, est., Neth.	C12	14
Westerstede, Ger.	C3	16
Westerville, Oh., U.S.	D3	114
Westerwald, mts., Ger.	F3	16
West European Basin, unds.	D12	144
West Falkland, i., Falk. Is.	J4	90
West Fargo, N.D., U.S.	E1	118
Westfield, Il., U.S.	E9	120
Westfield, In., U.S.	H3	112
Westfield, Ma., U.S.	H4	110
Westfield, N.J., U.S.	D11	114
Westfield, Pa., U.S.	C8	114
Westfield, Wi., U.S.	H9	118
West Fork, Ar., U.S.	I3	120
West Frankfort, Il., U.S.	G9	120
West Friese Eilanden, is., Neth.	A14	14
West Frisian Islands see West Friese Eilanden, is., Neth.	A14	14
Westgate, Austl.	F6	76
West Grand Lake, res., Me., U.S.	E8	110
West Hamlin, W.V., U.S.	F3	114
West Hartford, Ct., U.S.	C13	114
West Haven, Ct., U.S.	C13	114
West Helena, Ar., U.S.	C8	122
Westhoff, Tx., U.S.	E10	130
Westhope, N.D., U.S.	F12	124
West Ice Shelf, ice, Ant.	B13	81
West Indies, is.	C7	82
West Java see Jawa Barat, state, Indon.	G5	50
West Jefferson, N.C., U.S.	H4	114
West Jordan, Ut., U.S.	C4	132
West Kettle, stm., B.C., Can.	G11	138
West Kingston, R.I., U.S.	C14	114
West Lafayette, In., U.S.	H2	112
Westlake, La., U.S.	G5	122
Westland National Park, p.o.i., N.Z.	F3	80
West Laramie, Wy., U.S.	F7	126
West Lebanon, In., U.S.	H2	112
West Liberty, Ky., U.S.	G2	114
West Liberty, Oh., U.S.	D2	114
Westlock, Ab., Can.	B16	138
West Lorne, On., Can.	F8	112
Westmeath, state, Ire.	H5	12
West Memphis, Ar., U.S.	B8	122
Westminster, Co., U.S.	B3	128

Name	Map Ref.	Page
Westminster, Md., U.S.	E9	114
West Monroe, La., U.S.	E6	122
Westmoreland, Ks., U.S.	B12	128
Westmorland, Tn., U.S.	H11	120
Westmorland, Ca., U.S.	J10	134
West Nicholson, Zimb.	B9	70
West Nishnabotna, stm., Ia., U.S.	C2	120
West Nueces, stm., Tx., U.S.	E7	130
West Nusa Tenggara see Nusa Tenggara Barat, state, Indon.	G10	50
Weston, Id., U.S.	A4	132
Weston, Mo., U.S.	E3	120
Weston, Oh., U.S.	C2	114
Weston, Or., U.S.	E8	136
Weston, W.V., U.S.	E5	114
Weston-super-Mare, Eng., U.K.	J9	12
West Orange, Tx., U.S.	G5	122
Westover, Tn., U.S.	B10	122
West Palm Beach, Fl., U.S.	J5	116
West Palm Beach Canal, can., Fl., U.S.	J5	116
West Pensacola, Fl., U.S.	G11	122
Westphalia, Ks., U.S.	F2	120
West Plains, Mo., U.S.	H6	120
West Point, Ga., U.S.	E13	122
West Point, Ia., U.S.	D6	120
West Point, Ky., U.S.	F11	120
West Point, Ms., U.S.	D10	122
West Point, Ne., U.S.	J2	118
West Point, N.Y., U.S.	C11	114
West Point, Va., U.S.	G9	114
West Point Lake, res., U.S.	D13	122
West Poplar (Poplar, stm.), N.A.	F8	124
Westport, N.S., Can.	F10	110
Westport, On., Can.	D13	112
Westport, Ire.	H3	12
Westport, Ct., U.S.	C12	114
Westport, In., U.S.	E12	120
Westport, Or., U.S.	D3	136
Westpunt, c., Aruba	o19	104g
West Quoddy Head, c., Me., U.S.	F10	110
Westray, i., Scot., U.K.	B9	12
West Richland, Wa., U.S.	D7	136
West Road, stm., B.C., Can.	C7	138
West Rutland, Vt., U.S.	G3	110
West Salem, Il., U.S.	F9	120
West Salem, Oh., U.S.	D3	114
West Shoal Lake, l., Mb., Can.	D16	124
West Siberian Plain see Zapadno-Sibirskaja ravnina, pl., Russia	B12	32
West Slovakia see Západoslovenský Kraj, state, Slov.	H14	16
West Spanish Peak, mtn., Co., U.S.	D4	128
West Sumatra see Sumatera Barat, state, Indon.	D2	50
West Terre Haute, In., U.S.	E10	120
West Union, Ia., U.S.	B6	120
West Union, Oh., U.S.	F2	114
West Unity, Oh., U.S.	C1	114
West Valley City, Ut., U.S.	C4	132
West Vancouver, B.C., Can.	G7	138
Westville, N.S., Can.	E14	110
Westville, In., U.S.	G3	112
West Virginia, state, U.S.	F5	114
West Walker, stm., U.S.	E6	134
West Warwick, R.I., U.S.	C14	114
West Webster, N.Y., U.S.	E12	112
Westwold, B.C., Can.	F11	138
Westwood, Ca., U.S.	C5	134
Westwood Lakes, Fl., U.S.	K5	116
West Wyalong, Austl.	I6	76
West Yellowstone, Mt., U.S.	F15	136
Wetar, Pulau, i., Indon.	G8	44
Wetar, Selat, strt., Asia	G8	44
Wetaskiwin, Ab., Can.	C17	138
Wete, Tan.	E7	66
Wethersfield, Ct., U.S.	C13	114
Wetmore, Ks., U.S.	E2	120
Wetumka, Al., U.S.	E12	122
Wetzlar, Ger.	F4	16
Wewahitchka, Fl., U.S.	G13	122
Wewak, Pap. N. Gui.	a3	79a
Wewoka, Ok., U.S.	B2	122
Wexford, Ire.	I6	12
Wexford, state, Ire.	I6	12
Weyburn, Sk., Can.	E10	124
Weymontachie, Qc., Can.	C3	110
Weymouth, N.S., Can.	F10	110
Weymouth, Eng., U.K.	K10	12
Weymouth, Ma., U.S.	B15	114
Whakatane, N.Z.	C7	80
Whangarei, N.Z.	B6	80
Whapmagoostui, Qc., Can.	D15	106
Wharfe, stm., Eng., U.K.	H11	12
Wharton, W.V., U.S.	G4	114
Wharton Basin, unds.	K12	142
Wharton Lake, l., Nu., Can.	C10	106
Whataroa, N.Z.	F4	80
What Cheer, Ia., U.S.	C5	120
Whatley, Al., U.S.	F11	122
Wheatland, Ca., U.S.	D4	134
Wheatland, Ia., U.S.	C7	120
Wheatley, On., Can.	F7	112
Wheatley, Ar., U.S.	C7	122
Wheaton, Il., U.S.	C9	120
Wheaton, Md., U.S.	E8	114
Wheat Ridge, Co., U.S.	B3	128
Wheeler, Ms., U.S.	C10	122
Wheeler, Tx., U.S.	F8	128
Wheeler, stm., Qc., Can.	D17	106
Wheeler Lake, res., Al., U.S.	C11	122
Wheeler Peak, mtn., N.M., U.S.	E3	128
Wheeler Peak, mtn., Nv., U.S.	D2	132
Wheeling, W.V., U.S.	D5	114
Wheelwright, Arg.	F7	92
Wheelwright, Ky., U.S.	G3	114
Whidbey Island, i., Wa., U.S.	B4	136
Whiskey Peak, mtn., Wy., U.S.	E5	126
Whistler, B.C., Can.	F8	138
Whitakers, N.C., U.S.	H8	114
Whitby, On., Can.	E11	112
Whitby, Eng., U.K.	G12	12
Whitchurch, Eng., U.K.	H10	12
Whitchurch-Stouffville, On., Can.	D10	112
White, Ga., U.S.	C14	122
White, S.D., U.S.	C2	106
White, stm., N.A.	J6	132
White, stm., Az., U.S.	F10	120
White, stm., Tx., U.S.	F1	132
White, stm., Wa., U.S.	C5	136
White, stm., U.S.	D13	126
White, stm., U.S.	C7	122
White, East Fork, stm., In., U.S.	F10	120
White, Lake, l., Austl.	D5	74
White Bay, b., Nf., Can.	i22	107a
White Bear Lake, Mn., U.S.	F6	118
White Bluff, Tn., U.S.	H10	120
White Butte, mtn., N.D., U.S.	A9	126
White Castle, La., U.S.	G7	122
White City, Ks., U.S.	C12	128
White Cliffs, Austl.	H4	76
Whitecourt, Ab., Can.	B15	138
White Deer, Tx., U.S.	F7	128
Whiteface, stm., Mn., U.S.	D6	118
Whiteface Mountain, mtn., N.Y., U.S.	F3	110

Name	Map Ref.	Page
Whitefield, N.H., U.S.	F5	110
Whitefish, Mt., U.S.	B12	136
Whitefish Bay, Wi., U.S.	A10	120
Whitefish Bay, b., On., Can.	B4	118
Whitefish Bay, b., N.A.	B5	112
Whitefish Lake, l., Ab., Can.	B18	138
Whitefish Lake, l., N.T., Can.	C9	106
Whitefish Point, Mi., U.S.	B4	112
Whitefish Point, c., Mi., U.S.	B4	112
White Hall, Ar., U.S.	C6	122
White Hall, Il., U.S.	E7	120
Whitehall, Mi., U.S.	E3	112
Whitehall, N.Y., U.S.	G3	110
Whitehall, Wi., U.S.	G7	118
Whitehaven, Eng., U.K.	G9	12
Whitehorse, Yk., Can.	C4	106
White House, Tn., U.S.	H11	120
Whitehouse, Tx., U.S.	E3	122
White Island, i., Nu., Can.	B13	106
White Island, i., N.Z.	C7	80
White Lake, S.D., U.S.	D14	126
White Lake, Wi., U.S.	F10	118
White Lake, l., On., Can.	C13	112
White Lake, l., La., U.S.	H6	122
Whitemark, Austl.	n13	77a
White Mountain Peak, mtn., Ca., U.S.	F7	134
White Mountains, mts., N.H., U.S.	F5	110
Whitemouth, stm., Mb., Can.	E18	124
Whitemouth Lake, l., Mb., Can.	E18	124
Whitemud, stm., Mb., Can.	D15	124
White Nile (Abyad, Al-Bahr al-), stm., Afr.	E6	62
White Oak, Tx., U.S.	E4	122
White Oak Creek, stm., Tx., U.S.	D3	122
White Otter Lake, l., On., Can.	B6	118
White Pigeon, Mi., U.S.	G4	112
Whitepine, Mt., U.S.	C11	136
White Pine, Tn., U.S.	H2	114
White Plains, N.C., U.S.	H5	114
White Plains, N.Y., U.S.	C12	114
Whiteriver, Az., U.S.	J6	132
White River, S.D., U.S.	D12	126
White River Junction, Vt., U.S.	G4	110
White Rock, B.C., Can.	G8	138
White Russia see Belarus, ctry., Eur.	E14	6
Whitesail Lake, res., B.C., Can.	C3	138
Whitesand, stm., Sk., Can.	C11	124
White Sands National Monument, p.o.i., N.M., U.S.	B1	130
Whitesboro, Tx., U.S.	D2	122
White Sea see Beloe more, s., Russia	D18	8
White Settlement, Tx., U.S.	B10	130
White Springs, Fl., U.S.	F3	116
White Sulphur Springs, Mt., U.S.	D16	136
White Sulphur Springs, W.V., U.S.	G5	114
Whitesville, Ky., U.S.	G11	120
Whiteville, N.C., U.S.	B7	116
Whiteville, Tn., U.S.	B9	122
White Volta (Volta Blanche), stm., Afr.	G4	64
Whitewater, Mt., U.S.	B6	124
Whitewater, Wi., U.S.	B9	120
Whitewater, stm., U.S.	E13	120
Whitewater Baldy, mtn., N.M., U.S.	J8	132
Whitewater Creek, stm., N.A.	F6	124
Whitewater Lake, l., Mb., Can.	E13	124
White Woman Creek, stm., U.S.	C7	128
Whitewood, Austl.	C4	76
Whitewood, Sk., Can.	D11	124
Whitewood, S.D., U.S.	C9	126
Whithorn, Jam.	i12	104d
Whithorn, Scot., U.K.	G8	12
Whiting, In., U.S.	B2	120
Whiting, Ks., U.S.	E2	120
Whitley City, Ky., U.S.	H13	120
Whitman, Ma., U.S.	B15	114
Whitmire, S.C., U.S.	B4	116
Whitmore Mountains, mts., Ant.	D31	81
Whitney, On., Can.	C11	112
Whitney, Lake, res., Tx., U.S.	C10	130
Whitney, Mount, mtn., Ca., U.S.	G7	134
Whitney Point, N.Y., U.S.	B9	114
Whitsunday Island, i., Austl.	C7	76
Whittemore, Ia., U.S.	A3	120
Whittemore, Mi., U.S.	D6	112
Whittle, Cap, c., Qc., Can.	i22	107a
Whittlesea, Austl.	K5	76
Whittlesey, Mount, hill, Wi., U.S.	E8	118
Whitwell, Tn., U.S.	B13	122
Wholdaia Lake, l., N.T., Can.	C9	106
Whyalla, Austl.	F7	74
Whycocomagh, N.S., Can.	E15	110
Wiang Phan, Thai.	B4	48
Wiarton, On., Can.	D8	112
Wichian Buri, Thai.	E5	48
Wichita, Ks., U.S.	D11	128
Wichita, stm., Tx., U.S.	G10	128
Wichita Falls, Tx., U.S.	H10	128
Wick, Scot., U.K.	C9	12
Wickenburg, Az., U.S.	J4	132
Wickepin, Austl.	F3	74
Wickett, Tx., U.S.	C5	130
Wickham, Austl.	D3	74
Wickiup Reservoir, res., Or., U.S.	G5	136
Wickliffe, Ky., U.S.	H9	120
Wicklow, Ire.	H6	12
Wicklow, state, Ire.	H7	12
Wicklow Head, c., Ire.	I7	12
Wicklow Mountains, mts., Ire.	H6	12
Widgeegoara Creek, stm., Austl.	F6	76
Więcbork, Pol.	C13	16
Wieleń, Pol.	D12	16
Wieliczka, Pol.	F16	16
Wielkopolska, reg., Pol.	E13	16
Wielkopolski Park Narodowy, p.o.i., Pol.	D12	16
Wieluń, Pol.	E14	16
Wien (Vienna), Aus.	B13	22
Wien, state, Aus.	B13	22
Wiener Neustadt, Aus.	B13	22
Wieprz, stm., Pol.	E18	16
Wieprza, stm., Pol.	B12	16
Wieprz-Krzna, Kanał, can., Pol.	D2	16
Wierden, Neth.	D2	16
Wiergate, Tx., U.S.	F5	122
Wieruszów, Pol.	E14	16
Wiesbaden, Ger.	B14	16
Wiesloch, Ger.	G4	16
Wigan, Eng., U.K.	H10	12
Wiggins, Co., U.S.	A4	128
Wiggins, Ms., U.S.	G9	122
Wight, Isle of, i., Eng., U.K.	K11	12
Wigtown, Scot., U.K.	G8	12

Name	Map Ref.	Page
Wilbur, Wa., U.S.	C8	136
Wilburton, Ok., U.S.	C3	122
Wilcannia, Austl.	H4	76
Wilcox, Sk., Can.	D9	124
Wilcox, Ne., U.S.	A9	128
Wildcat Creek, stm., In., U.S.	H3	112
Wildcat Hill, mtn., Sk., Can.	A11	124
Wild Coast, cst., S. Afr.	H9	70
Wilder, Id., U.S.	G9	136
Wilder, Ga., U.S.	B2	116
Wilderness of Judaea (Midbar Yehuda), des., Asia	G6	58
Wildhay, stm., Ab., Can.	C13	138
Wildhorse Creek, stm., U.S.	G10	126
Wild Horse Lake, l., Mt., U.S.	B17	136
Wild Rice, stm., Mn., U.S.	D2	118
Wild Rice, stm., N.D., U.S.	H17	124
Wildrose, N.D., U.S.	F10	124
Wild Rose, Wi., U.S.	G9	118
Wildwood, Ab., Can.	C15	138
Wildwood, N.J., U.S.	F11	114
Wilge, stm., S. Afr.	E9	70
Wilhelm, Mount, mtn., Pap. N. Gui.	b3	79a
Wilhelmina Gebergte, mts., Sur.	C6	84
Wilhelmshaven, Ger.	C4	16
Wilhelmstal, Nmb.	B3	70
Wilkerson Pass, p., Co., U.S.	B3	128
Wilkes-Barre, Pa., U.S.	C10	114
Wilkesboro, N.C., U.S.	H4	114
Wilkes Land, reg., Ant.	C16	81
Wilkie, Sk., Can.	B5	124
Willacoochee, Ga., U.S.	E2	116
Willamette, stm., Or., U.S.	E4	136
Willamette, Middle Fork, stm., Or., U.S.	G4	136
Willamina, Or., U.S.	E3	136
Willandra Billabong Creek, stm., Austl.	I5	76
Willandra National Park, p.o.i., Austl.	I5	76
Willapa Bay, b., Wa., U.S.	D2	136
Willard, Mo., U.S.	G4	120
Willard, Oh., U.S.	C3	114
Willard, Ut., U.S.	B4	132
Willard, Punta, c., Mex.	A2	100
Willcox, Az., U.S.	K7	132
Willcox Playa, l., Az., U.S.	K7	132
Willemroo, Austl.	C6	74
Willemstad, Neth. Ant.	p22	104g
William "Bill" Dannelly Reservoir, res., Al., U.S.	E11	122
Williams, Ca., U.S.	D3	134
Williams, Ia., U.S.	I5	118
Williams, Mn., U.S.	C3	118
Williams, stm., Austl.	A3	76
Williamsburg, Ia., U.S.	C5	120
Williamsburg, Ky., U.S.	H1	114
Williamsburg, Va., U.S.	G9	114
Williams Lake, B.C., Can.	D8	138
Williamson, N.Y., U.S.	E12	112
Williamson, W.V., U.S.	G3	114
Williamson, stm., Or., U.S.	H5	136
Williamson, Mount, mtn., Ca., U.S.	G7	134
Williamsport, Pa., U.S.	C8	114
Williamston, Mi., U.S.	F5	112
Williamston, S.C., U.S.	B3	116
Williamstown, Ky., U.S.	F1	114
Williamstown, N.J., U.S.	E11	114
Williamsville, Il., U.S.	L9	118
Willikies, Antig.	f4	105b
Willimantic, Ct., U.S.	C13	114
Willingboro, N.J., U.S.	D10	114
Willis, Tx., U.S.	G3	122
Willis Group, is., Austl.	C10	74
Williston, Fl., U.S.	G3	116
Williston, N.D., U.S.	F10	124
Williston, S.C., U.S.	C4	116
Williston Lake, res., B.C., Can.	D6	106
Willits, Ca., U.S.	D2	134
Willmar, Mn., U.S.	F3	118
Willoughby, Oh., U.S.	C4	114
Willoughby Bay, b., Antig.	f4	105b
Willow, Ak., U.S.	D10	140
Willow, stm., B.C., Can.	C8	138
Willowbrook, Sk., Can.	C10	124
Willow Bunch, Sk., Can.	E8	124
Willow Bunch Lake, l., Sk., Can.	E8	124
Willow Creek, Ca., U.S.	C2	134
Willow Creek, Mt., U.S.	E15	136
Willow Creek, stm., Ab., Can.	F17	138
Willow Creek, stm., Or., U.S.	F9	136
Willow Creek, stm., Or., U.S.	E7	136
Willow Lake, S.D., U.S.	C15	126
Willow Lake, l., N.T., Can.	C7	106
Willowmore, S. Afr.	H6	70
Willowra, Austl.	D6	74
Willow Reservoir, res., Wi., U.S.	F9	118
Willows, Ca., U.S.	D3	134
Willow Springs, Mo., U.S.	H6	120
Willowvale, S. Afr.	H9	70
Wills Creek, stm., Austl.	D2	76
Wills Point, Tx., U.S.	D2	122
Wilmer, Al., U.S.	G10	122
Wilmer, Tx., U.S.	E2	122
Wilmette, Il., U.S.	F2	112
Wilmington, De., U.S.	E10	114
Wilmington, N.C., U.S.	B7	116
Wilmington, Oh., U.S.	E2	114
Wilmington, Vt., U.S.	H4	110
Wilmore, Ky., U.S.	G13	120
Wilmot, S.D., U.S.	F2	118
Wilpattu National Park, p.o.i., Sri L.	G4	53
Wilsall, Mt., U.S.	D16	136
Wilson, Austl.	H2	76
Wilson, Ks., U.S.	B8	122
Wilson, La., U.S.	G7	122
Wilson, N.C., U.S.	I7	114
Wilson, N.Y., U.S.	E11	112
Wilson, Ok., U.S.	G11	128
Wilson, Tx., U.S.	H7	128
Wilson, stm., Austl.	F4	76
Wilson, Cape, c., Nu., Can.	B14	106
Wilson, Mount, mtn., Az., U.S.	H2	132
Wilson, Mount, mtn., Co., U.S.	I7	134
Wilson Lake, res., Al., U.S.	C11	122
Wilson Lake, res., Ks., U.S.	C10	128
Wilsons Promontory, pen., Austl.	L6	76
Wilsons Promontory National Park, p.o.i., Austl.	L6	76
Wilson's Ranch, Nv., U.S.	A8	128
Wilton, Eng., U.K.	J11	12
Wilton, Me., U.S.	F6	110
Wilton, N.H., U.S.	B14	114
Wilton, Wi., U.S.	H8	118
Wiluna, Austl.	E4	74
Wimauma, Fl., U.S.	I3	116
Wimberley, Tx., U.S.	D9	130
Winamac, In., U.S.	G3	112
Winburg, S. Afr.	F8	70
Winchendon, Ma., U.S.	B13	114
Winchester, On., Can.	C14	112
Winchester, Eng., U.K.	J11	12

Name	Map Ref.	Page
Winchester, Il., U.S.	E7	120
Winchester, In., U.S.	H5	112
Winchester, Ky., U.S.	G1	114
Winchester, Tn., U.S.	B12	122
Winchester, Va., U.S.	E7	114
Wind, stm., Yk., Can.	B3	106
Wind, stm., Wy., U.S.	D4	126
Wind Cave National Park, p.o.i., S.D., U.S.	D9	126
Winder, Ga., U.S.	B2	116
Windermere, B.C., Can.	F15	138
Windermere, Eng., U.K.	G10	12
Windfall, Ab., Can.	B14	138
Windhoek, Nmb.	C3	70
Windigo, stm., Qc., Can.	C3	110
Windom, Mn., U.S.	H3	118
Windorah, Austl.	E4	76
Window Rock, Az., U.S.	H7	132
Wind River Peak, mtn., Wy., U.S.	E3	126
Wind River Range, mts., Wy., U.S.	D3	126
Windsor, Austl.	I8	76
Windsor, N.S., Can.	E12	110
Windsor, On., Can.	F6	112
Windsor, Qc., Can.	E5	110
Windsor, Eng., U.K.	J12	12
Windsor, Ca., U.S.	E3	134
Windsor, Ct., U.S.	C13	114
Windsor, Il., U.S.	E9	120
Windsor, Mo., U.S.	F4	120
Windsor, N.C., U.S.	I9	114
Windsor, Va., U.S.	H9	114
Windsor Forest, Ga., U.S.	E4	116
Windsor Locks, Ct., U.S.	C13	114
Windthorst, Tx., U.S.	H10	128
Windward, Gren.	p11	105e
Windward Islands, is., N.A.	k6	105c
Windward Passage, strt., N.A.	C11	102
Windy Peak, mtn., Co., U.S.	D11	122
Winfield, Al., U.S.	D11	122
Winfield, Ks., U.S.	D12	128
Winfield, Mo., U.S.	E7	120
Winfield, W.V., U.S.	F4	114
Wing, N.D., U.S.	G13	124
Wingate, N.C., U.S.	B5	116
Wingham, Austl.	H9	76
Wingham, On., Can.	E8	112
Winisk, stm., On., Can.	D13	106
Winisk, stm., On., Can.	E13	106
Winisk Lake, l., On., Can.	E13	106
Wink, Tx., U.S.	C4	130
Winkana, Mya.	E4	48
Winkelman, Az., U.S.	K6	132
Winkler, Mb., Can.	E16	124
Winlock, Wa., U.S.	D3	136
Winnebago, Mn., U.S.	H4	118
Winnebago, Ne., U.S.	B1	120
Winnebago, stm., Ia., U.S.	H5	118
Winnebago, Lake, l., Wi., U.S.	G10	118
Winneconne, Wi., U.S.	G10	118
Winnemucca, Nv., U.S.	B8	134
Winnemucca Lake, l., Nv., U.S.	C6	134
Winner, S.D., U.S.	D13	126
Winnetka, Il., U.S.	F2	112
Winnett, Mt., U.S.	H5	124
Winnibigoshish, Lake, res., Mn., U.S.	D4	118
Winnie, Tx., U.S.	H4	122
Winnipeg, Mb., Can.	D2	74
Winnipeg, Mb., Can.	E16	124
Winnipeg, stm., Can.	E11	106
Winnipeg, Lake, l., Mb., Can.	E11	106
Winnipeg Beach, Mb., Can.	D17	124
Winnipegosis, Mb., Can.	C13	124
Winnipegosis, Lake, l., Mb., Can.	B13	124
Winnipesaukee, Lake, l., N.H., U.S.	G5	110
Winnsboro, La., U.S.	E7	122
Winnsboro, S.C., U.S.	B4	116
Winnsboro, Tx., U.S.	C2	120
Winnsboro Mills, S.C., U.S.	I14	12
Winona, Ks., U.S.	B7	128
Winona, Mn., U.S.	G6	120
Winona, Mo., U.S.	G6	120
Winona, Ms., U.S.	D9	122
Winooski, stm., Vt., U.S.	F4	110
Winschoten, Neth.	A15	14
Winschoterdiep, can., Neth.	C6	16
Winsen, Ger.	C6	16
Winslow, Az., U.S.	H6	132
Winslow, In., U.S.	F10	120
Winslow, Me., U.S.	F7	110
Winsted, Mn., U.S.	G4	118
Winston, Fl., U.S.	H3	116
Winston, Or., U.S.	G3	136
Winston-Salem, N.C., U.S.	H5	114
Winter, Wi., U.S.	F8	118
Winter Garden, Fl., U.S.	H4	116
Winter Harbor, Me., U.S.	F8	110
Winter Harbour, B.C., Can.	F2	138
Winterhaven, Ca., U.S.	K2	132
Winter Haven, Fl., U.S.	I4	116
Winter Park, Fl., U.S.	H4	116
Winters, Ca., U.S.	E4	134
Winters, Tx., U.S.	C8	130
Winterset, Ia., U.S.	C3	120
Winterswijk, Neth.	B15	14
Winterthur, Switz.	C5	22
Winterville, Me., U.S.	D7	122
Winthrop, Me., U.S.	F7	110
Winthrop, Mn., U.S.	G4	118
Winthrop Harbor, Il., U.S.	F2	112
Wintinna, Austl.	E6	74
Winton, Austl.	D4	76
Winton, N.Z.	H3	80
Winton, N.C., U.S.	H8	114
Wirāṭnagar, Nepal	E11	54
Wirganj, India	E11	54
Wisbech, Eng., U.K.	I12	12
Wiscasset, Me., U.S.	G7	110
Wisconsin, state, U.S.	G9	118
Wisconsin, stm., Wi., U.S.	I8	118
Wisconsin Dells, Wi., U.S.	H9	118
Wisconsin Rapids, Wi., U.S.	G8	118
Wisdom, Mt., U.S.	E13	136
Wise, Va., U.S.	G3	114
Wishek, N.D., U.S.	A13	126
Wishram, Wa., U.S.	E5	136
Wisła, Pol.	G14	16
Wisła (Vistula), stm., Pol.	B14	16
Wiślany, Mierzeja, spit, Eur.	B15	16
Wisłok, stm., Pol.	F18	16
Wisłoka, stm., Pol.	F17	16
Wisner, La., U.S.	F7	122
Wisner, Ne., U.S.	C1	120
Wisznice, Pol.	E19	16
Witbank, S. Afr.	D9	70
Witham, stm., Eng., U.K.	H12	12
Withlacoochee, stm., U.S.	F2	116
Witkowo, Pol.	D13	16
Witney, Eng., U.K.	J11	12
Wit Nossob, stm., Nmb.	C4	70
Witt, Il., U.S.	E8	120
Wittenberg, Wi., U.S.	G9	118
Wittenberge, Ger.	C7	16
Wittenoom, Austl.	D3	74
Wittingen, Ger.	D6	16

Name	Map Ref.	Page
Wittlich, Ger.	G2	16
Wittmund, Ger.	C3	16
Wittstock, Ger.	C8	16
Witu Islands, is., Pap. N. Gui.	a5	79a
Witvlei, Nmb.	C4	70
Witwatersrand, mts., S. Afr.	D8	70
Witzenhausen, Ger.	E5	16
Wizajny, Pol.	B18	16
Wkra, stm., Pol.	C15	16
Wleń, Pol.	E11	16
Włocławek, Pol.	D15	16
Włocławek, state, Pol.	D14	16
Włoszczowa, Pol.	F15	16
Woburn, Ma., U.S.	B14	114
Wolcott, In., U.S.	K6	76
Wolcott, N.Y., U.S.	E13	112
Wolcottville, In., U.S.	G4	112
Woleai, at., Micron.	C5	72
Wolf, stm., Ms., U.S.	G9	122
Wolf, stm., Wi., U.S.	G10	118
Wolf, stm., U.S.	B9	122
Wolf, Volcán, vol., Ec.	h11	84a
Wolfach, Ger.	H4	16
Wolf Creek, Or., U.S.	H3	136
Wolf Creek, stm., Mt., U.S.	C17	136
Wolf Creek, stm., U.S.	E9	128
Wolf Creek Pass, p., Co., U.S.	F10	132
Wolf Creek Reservoir, res., Ks., U.S.	F2	120
Wolfeboro, N.H., U.S.	G5	110
Wolfe Island, i., On., Can.	D13	112
Wolfen, Ger.	E8	16
Wolfenbüttel, Ger.	D6	16
Wolfenden, Mount, mtn., B.C., Can.	F3	138
Wolfforth, Tx., U.S.	H6	128
Wolfhagen, Ger.	E4	16
Wolf Lake, l., Ab., Can.	B20	138
Wolf Point, Mt., U.S.	F8	124
Wolfratshausen, Ger.	I7	16
Wolf Rock, r., Eng., U.K.	L7	12
Wolfsberg, Aus.	D11	22
Wolfsburg, Ger.	D6	16
Wolfville, N.S., Can.	E12	110
Wolgast, Ger.	B9	16
Woliński Park Narodowy, p.o.i., Pol.	C10	16
Wollaston Lake, Sk., Can.	D10	106
Wollaston Peninsula, pen., Can.	B7	106
Wollemi National Park, p.o.i., Austl.	I7	76
Wollongong, Austl.	J8	76
Wołomin, Pol.	D17	16
Wołów, Pol.	E13	16
Wolseley, Sk., Can.	D10	124
Wolsey, S.D., U.S.	C14	126
Wolverhampton, Eng., U.K.	I10	12
Wolverton, Eng., U.K.	I11	12
Wonarah, Austl.	C7	74
Wondai, Austl.	F8	76
Wonderland, Ca., U.S.	C4	134
Wondinong, Austl.	E3	74
Wonewoc, Wi., U.S.	H8	118
Wŏnju, Kor., S.	F7	38
Wonogiri, Indon.	G7	50
Wonosari, Indon.	H7	50
Wonosobo, Indon.	G6	50
Wŏnsan, Kor., N.	E7	38
Wonthaggi, Austl.	L5	76
Wood, S.D., U.S.	D12	126
Wood, stm., Ne., U.S.	G13	126
Wood, Mount, mtn., Mt., U.S.	E17	136
Woodall Mountain, hill, Ms., U.S.	C10	122
Woodbine, Ga., U.S.	F4	116
Woodbine, Ia., U.S.	C2	120
Woodbridge, Eng., U.K.	I14	12
Woodbridge, Va., U.S.	F8	114
Woodburn, Or., U.S.	E4	136
Woodbury, Ga., U.S.	E14	122
Woodbury, N.J., U.S.	E10	114
Woodbury, Tn., U.S.	I11	120
Woodhull, Il., U.S.	C7	120
Woodlake, Ne., U.S.	G6	134
Woodland, Ca., U.S.	E4	134
Woodland, Me., U.S.	E9	110
Woodland, N.C., U.S.	H8	114
Woodland Park, Co., U.S.	E17	124
Woodridge, Mb., Can.	F2	132
Wood River, Il., U.S.	G14	126
Woodroffe, Mount, mtn., Austl.	E6	74
Woodruff, Fl., U.S.	I6	132
Woodruff, S.C., U.S.	B3	116
Woodruff, Wi., U.S.	F9	118
Woods, Lake, l., Austl.	C6	74
Woods, Lake of the, l., N.A.	B3	118
Woodsboro, Tx., U.S.	F10	130
Woodsfield, Oh., U.S.	E4	114
Woods Hole, Ma., U.S.	C15	114
Woodson, Tx., U.S.	A8	130
Woodstock, Austl.	D9	110
Woodstock, On., Can.	E9	112
Woodstock, Eng., U.K.	J11	12
Woodstock, N.B., Can.	D9	110
Woodstock, Ga., U.S.	B1	116
Woodstock, Il., U.S.	B9	120
Woodstock, N.Y., U.S.	B11	114
Woodstock, Vt., U.S.	G4	110
Woodsville, N.H., U.S.	F4	110
Woodville, N.Z.	E6	80
Woodville, On., Can.	C12	112
Woodville, Ms., U.S.	F7	122
Woodville, Oh., U.S.	C2	114
Woodville, Tx., U.S.	G4	122
Woodward, Ok., U.S.	E9	128
Woody, stm., Mb., Can.	B12	124
Woody Head, c., Austl.	G9	76
Woolmarket, Ms., U.S.	G9	122
Woomera, Austl.	F7	74
Woonsocket, R.I., U.S.	C14	114
Woonsocket, S.D., U.S.	C14	126
Woorabinda, Austl.	E7	76
Wooramel, Austl.	E2	74
Wooster, Oh., U.S.	D4	114
Worcester, S. Afr.	H4	70
Worcester, Eng., U.K.	I10	12
Worcester, Ma., U.S.	B14	114
Worden, Mt., U.S.	A4	126
Workington, Eng., U.K.	G9	12
Worksop, Eng., U.K.	H11	12
Worland, Wy., U.S.	C5	126
Worms, Ger.	G4	16
Worthing, Eng., U.K.	K12	12
Worthington, In., U.S.	E11	120
Worthington, Mn., U.S.	H3	118
Worthington, Oh., U.S.	D3	114
Worthington Peak, mtn., Nv., U.S.	E1	132
Wosi, Indon.	F8	44
Wota, at., Marsh. Is.	B7	72
Wotho, at., Marsh. Is.	B7	72
Wotu, Indon.	E12	50
Wouhta, Nic.	F6	102
Wounded Knee, S.D., U.S.	D10	126
Wounded Knee Creek, stm., S.D., U.S.	D10	126
Wowan, Austl.	D8	76
Wowoni, Pulau, i., Indon.	F7	44
Woy Woy, Austl.	I8	76

Name	Map Ref.	Page
Wrangel Island see Vrangelja, ostrov, i., Russia	B24	34
Wrangell, Ak., U.S.	E13	140
Wrangell, Cape, c., Ak., U.S.	g21	140a
Wrangell Mountains, mts., Ak., U.S.	D11	140
Wrath, Cape, c., Scot., U.K.	C8	12
Wrens, Ga., U.S.	C3	116
Wrentham, Ab., Can.	G18	138
Wrexham, Wales, U.K.	H10	12
Wright, Mount, mtn., Mt., U.S.	C13	136
Wright City, Mo., U.S.	F6	120
Wright Patman Lake, res., Tx., U.S.	D4	122
Wrightstown, Wi., U.S.	D1	112
Wrightsville, Ga., U.S.	D3	116
Wrightsville Beach, N.C., U.S.	B8	116
Wrigley, N.T., Can.	C6	106
Wrigley, Tn., U.S.	B13	116
Wrocław (Breslau), Pol.	E13	16
Wrocław, state, Pol.	E13	16
Wrong Lake, l., Mb., Can.	B17	124
Wrottesley, Cape, c., N.T., Can.	B15	140
Wroxton, Sk., Can.	C12	124
Września, Pol.	D13	16
Wschowa, Pol.	E12	16
Wu, stm., China	H3	42
Wu, stm., China	G7	42
Wu, stm., China	G2	42
Wu, stm., China	I5	42
Wu, stm., China	H4	42
Wubu, China	C4	42
Wuchang, China	B7	38
Wuchang Hu, l., China	F7	42
Wuchin see Changzhou, China	F8	42
Wuchou see Wuzhou, China	J4	42
Wuchow see Wuzhou, China	J4	42
Wuchuan, China	K4	42
Wuchuan, China	A4	42
Wuchung see Wuzhong, China	C2	42
Wuda, China	B2	42
Wudaoliang, China	D3	36
Wudi, China	C7	42
Wuding, China	F5	36
Wuding, stm., China	C4	42
Wudu, China	E5	36
Wufeng, China	F4	42
Wugang, China	H4	42
Wugong, China	D2	42
Wugong Shan, mts., China	H5	42
Wuhai, China	B2	42
Wuhan (Hankow), China	F6	42
Wuhsi see Wuxi, China	F9	42
Wuhsing see Huzhou, China	F8	42
Wuhu, China	J6	42
Wuhuanchi, China	C4	38
Wujiang, China	B7	54
Wujia, stm., China	H2	42
Wujiangdu, China	F8	42
Wukang, China	H6	64
Wukari, Nig.	H6	64
Wukeshu, China	B7	38
Wulatezhongqi, China	A3	42
Wuliang Shan, mts., China	G5	36
Wulong, China	G2	42
Wuluhan, Indon.	H8	50
Wulumuch'i see Ürümqi, China	C2	36
Wuluo, China	H3	42
Wuming, China	J3	42
Wundwin, Mya.	B2	48
Wunnummin Lake, l., On., Can.	E13	106
Wunstorf, Ger.	D5	16
Wupatki National Monument, p.o.i., Az., U.S.	H5	132
Wuppertal, Ger.	E3	16
Wuppertal, S. Afr.	H4	70
Wuqi, China	C3	42
Wuqia, China	B12	56
Wuqiang, China	B6	42
Wurno, Nig.	G6	64
Würzburg, Ger.	G5	16
Wurzen, Ger.	E8	16
Wusheng, China	F2	42
Wushenqi, China	B3	42
Wushi, China	J4	42
Wusih see Wuxi, China	F9	42
Wusuli (Ussuri), stm., Asia	B11	36
Wutai, China	B5	42
Wutai Shan, mtn., China	I3	42
Wutong, China	F5	36
Wutsin see Changzhou, China	F8	42
Wut'ungch'iao see Wutongqiao, China	F5	36
Wutungkiao see Wutongqiao, China	F5	36
Wuuvulu Island, i., Pap. N. Gui.	a3	79a
Wuwei, China	D5	36
Wuwei, China	F7	42
Wuxi, China	F9	42
Wuxi, China	F3	42
Wuxiang, China	H4	42
Wuyang, China	F9	42
Wuyi Shan, mts., China	H7	42
Wuyuan, China	A3	42
Wuyuan, China	G7	42
Wuzhai, China	B4	42
Wuzhi Shan (Wuzhi Peak), mtn., China	L3	42
Wuzhong, China	C2	42
Wuzhou, China	J4	42
Wyaconda, Mo., U.S.	D6	120
Wyandotte, Mi., U.S.	B2	114
Wyandra, Austl.	F5	76
Wyangala, Lake, res., Austl.	J7	76
Wyatt, Mo., U.S.	H8	120
Wycheproof, Austl.	K4	76
Wye, stm., U.K.	J10	12
Wyeville, Wi., U.S.	G8	118
Wylie, Lake, res., U.S.	A4	116
Wymark, Sk., Can.	D6	124
Wymondham, Eng., U.K.	I13	12
Wymore, Ne., U.S.	K2	118
Wyndham, Austl.	C5	74
Wyndmere, N.D., U.S.	E1	118
Wynne, Ar., U.S.	C6	122
Wynniatt Bay, b., Can.	A8	106
Wynona, Ok., U.S.	E12	128
Wynot, Ne., U.S.	E15	126
Wynyard, Austl.	n12	77a
Wynyard, Sk., Can.	C9	124
Wyodak, Wy., U.S.	C8	126
Wyoming, On., Can.	F7	112
Wyoming, Ia., U.S.	B6	120
Wyoming, Mn., U.S.	F5	118
Wyoming, state, U.S.	E5	126
Wyoming Peak, mtn., Wy., U.S.	H16	136
Wyong, Austl.	I8	76
Wyperfeld National Park, p.o.i., Austl.	J3	76
Wyśmierzyce, Pol.	E16	16
Wysokie Mazowieckie, Pol.	D18	16
Wyszków, Pol.	D17	16
Wytheville, Va., U.S.	H4	114

X

Name	Map Ref.	Page
Xaafuun, Raas, c., Som.	B10	66
Xàbia, Spain	F11	20
Xaidulla, China	A4	46
Xainza, China	C12	54
Xai-Xai, Moz.	D11	70
Xalapa (Jalapa), Mex.	F10	100
Xalin, Som.	C9	66
Xam (Chu), stm., Asia	B7	48
Xambioá, Braz.	D1	88
Xambrê, stm., Braz.	A11	92
Xam Nua, Laos	B7	48
Xá-Muteba, Ang.	B2	68
Xan (San), stm., Asia	E8	48
Xangongo, Ang.	D2	68
Xankändi, Azer.	B6	56
Xánthi, Grc.	B7	28
Xanxerê, Braz.	C11	92
Xapecó, stm., Braz.	C11	92
Xapuri, Braz.	F4	84
Xar Moron, stm., China	C3	38
Xàtiva, Spain	F10	20
Xau, Lake, pl., Bots.	B7	70
Xavantina, Braz.	D6	90
Xaxim, Braz.	C11	92
Xcalak, Mex.	C4	102
X-Can, Mex.	B4	102
Xelva, Spain	E9	20
Xenia, Oh., U.S.	E2	114
Xepenehe, N. Cal.	m16	79d
Xhumo, Bots.	B7	70
Xi, stm., China	J5	42
Xiachuan Dao, i., China	K5	42
Xiagaixin, China	A5	48
Xiamen (Amoy), China	I7	42
Xi'an (Sian), China	D3	42
Xianfeng, China	G3	42
Xiang, stm., China	G5	42
Xiangcheng, China	E5	42
Xiangfan, China	F4	42
Xianggang (Hong Kong), China	J6	42
Xiangkhoang, Laos	C6	48
Xiangkhoang, Plateau de (Tran Ninh), plat., Laos	C6	48
Xiangning, China	D4	42
Xiangride, China	D4	36
Xiangshan, China	G9	42
Xiangtan, China	H5	42
Xiangxiang, China	H5	42
Xiangyin, China	G5	42
Xiangyuan, China	C5	42
Xiangzhou, China	J3	42
Xianju, China	G9	42
Xianshui, stm., China	B9	46
Xiantao, China	F5	42
Xianyang, China	D3	42
Xianyang, China	G8	42
Xianyou, China	I8	42
Xiao, stm., China	G8	42
Xiaochengzi, China	C5	38
Xiaogan, China	F5	42
Xiaoguai, China	B1	36
Xiao Hinggan Ling (Lesser Khingan Range), mts., China	B10	36
Xiaojin, China	E5	36
Xiaojiu, China	B7	38
Xiaoluan, stm., China	D2	38
Xiaopingyang, China	J3	42
Xiaoshan, China	F9	42
Xiaoxian, China	D7	42
Xiaoyi, China	C4	42
Xiapu, China	H9	42
Xiawa, China	C4	38
Xiaxian, China	D4	42
Xibo, stm., China	D3	38
Xichang, China	F5	36
Xichong, China	F1	42
Xicoténcatl, Mex.	D9	100
Xié, stm., Braz.	G8	86
Xifei, stm., China	E7	42
Xifeng, China	H2	42
Xifeng, China	C6	38
Xigazê, China	D12	54
Xihan, stm., China	D1	42
Xihe, China	F5	42
Xiheying, China	B6	42
Xihua, China	E6	42
Xiji, China	D1	42
Xiliao, stm., China	C5	38
Xilin, China	D11	54
Xilinhot, China	C2	38
Ximakou, China	F5	42
Ximalin, China	A6	42
Ximiao, China	C5	36
Xin, stm., China	G7	42
Xin'an, China	C6	38
Xin'anjiang Shuiku, res., China	G8	42
Xinavane, Moz.	D11	70
Xin Barag Youqi, China	B8	36
Xin Barag Zuoqi, China	B8	36
Xinbin, China	D6	38
Xincai, China	E6	42
Xinchang, China	G9	42
Xincheng, China	B6	42
Xincheng, China	G6	36
Xindu, China	I4	42
Xinfeng, China	I6	42
Xinfeng Shuiku, res., China	J6	42
Xing'an, China	I4	42
Xingcheng, China	A9	42
Xingguo, China	H6	42
Xinghai, China	D4	36
Xinghe, China	A5	42
Xinghua, China	E8	42
Xinglong, China	D1	42
Xingren, China	F6	36
Xingrenbu, China	C1	42
Xingtai, China	C6	42
Xingtang, China	B6	42
Xingu, stm., Braz.	D7	84
Xingxian, China	B4	42
Xingyi, China	F5	36
Xinhe, China	C6	42
Xinhua, China	H4	42
Xinhui, China	J5	42
Xining, China	D5	36
Xinji, China	C6	42
Xinjiang, China	D4	42
Xinjiang, state, China	A5	46
Xinjin, China	E5	36
Xinjin, China	B9	42
Xinjiulong (New Kowloon), China	J6	42
Xinkai, stm., China	C5	38
Xinli, China	B7	38
Xinlitun, China	D5	38
Xinmin, China	C5	38
Xinning, China	H4	42
Xinshao, China	H4	42
Xintian, China	I5	42
Xinwen, China	D7	42
Xinxian, China	B5	42
Xinxian, China	F6	42
Xinxiang, China	D5	42
Xinxing, China	C8	38
Xinyang, China	E6	42
Xinye, China	E5	42
Xinyi, China	D8	42
Xinyu, China	H6	42
Xinzhou, China	L3	42
Xiongyuecheng, China	A9	42
Xiping, China	E6	42
Xiping, China	G8	42
Xiqing Shan, mts., China	E5	36
Xique-Xique, Braz.	F4	88
Xırdalan, Azer.	A6	56
Xishanqiao, China	F8	42
Xisha Qundao (Paracel Islands), is., China	B5	50
Xishui, China	F6	42
Xiti, China	B9	54
Xiu, stm., China	G6	42
Xi Ujimqin Qi, China	B2	38
Xiushui, China	G6	42
Xiuyan, China	A10	42
Xiva, Spain	E10	20
Xixabangma Feng, mtn., China	D10	54
Xixi, China	H8	42
Xixian, China	E6	42
Xixiang, China	E2	42
Xixona, Spain	F10	20
Xiyang, China	C5	42
Xizang (Tibet), state, China	B5	46
Xizi, China	D3	38
Xochicalco, sci., Mex.	F9	100
Xochistlahuaca, Mex.	G9	100
Xu, stm., China	H7	42
Xuancheng, China	F8	42
Xuan'en, China	F3	42
Xuang, stm., Laos	B6	48
Xuanhan, China	F2	42
Xuanhua, China	A6	42
Xuanwei, China	F5	36
Xuchang, China	D5	42
Xun, stm., China	J4	42
Xungru, China	D10	54
Xunwu, China	I6	42
Xupu, China	H4	42
Xúquer see Júcar, stm., Spain	E10	20
Xuwen, China	K4	42
Xuyi, China	E8	42
Xuyong, China	G1	42
Xuzhou, China	D7	42
Xylókastro, Grc.	E5	28

Y

Name	Map Ref.	Page
Yaak, Mt., U.S.	B11	136
Yaan, China	E5	36
Yaapeet, Austl.	J3	76
Yablonovy Range see Jablonovyj hrebet, mts., Russia	F11	34
Yabluniv, Ukr.	A12	26
Yabrīn, Sau. Ar.	E6	56
Yabucoa, P.R.	B4	104a
Yabuli, China	B8	38
Yacambu, Parque Nacional, p.o.i., Ven.	C7	86
Yacata, i., Fiji	p20	79e
Yacheng, China	L3	42
Yachi, stm., China	H2	42
Yaco see Iaco, stm., S.A.	F4	84
Yacuiba, Bol.	D4	90
Yacyretá, Isla, i., Para.	C9	92
Yādgīr, India	C3	53
Yadkin, stm., N.C., U.S.	H4	114
Yadkinville, N.C., U.S.	H5	114
Yadong, China	E12	54
Yafran, Libya	A2	62
Yagasa Cluster, i., Fiji	q20	79e
Yagoua, Cam.	B3	66
Yagradagzê Shan, mtn., China	D4	36
Yaguajay, Cuba	A8	102
Yaguarón (Jaguarão), stm., S.A.	F11	92
Yaguas, stm., S.A.	I6	86
Yahe, China	B9	38
Yahk, B.C., Can.	G14	138
Yahualica, Mex.	E7	100
Yai, Khao, mtn., Thai.	E4	48
Yainax Butte, mtn., Or., U.S.	A4	134
Yaita, Japan	C12	40
Yaitopya see Ethiopia, ctry., Afr.	F7	62
Yaizu, Japan	E11	40
Yajiang, China	E5	36
Yakacık, Tur.	B7	58
Yakeshi, China	B9	36
Yakima, Wa., U.S.	D6	136
Yakima, stm., Wa., U.S.	D7	136
Yakmach, Pak.	D9	56
Yako, Burkina	G4	64
Yakoma, D.R.C.	D4	66
Yakumo, Japan	C14	38
Yaku-shima, i., Japan	I9	38
Yakutat Bay, b., Ak., U.S.	E11	140
Yakutia see Jakutija, state, Russia	D14	34
Yala, Thai.	I5	48
Yalahau, Laguna de, b., Mex.	B4	102
Yale, B.C., Can.	G9	138
Yale, Mi., U.S.	E7	112
Yale, Ok., U.S.	A2	122
Yale, Mount, mtn., Co., U.S.	C2	128
Yalgoo, Austl.	E3	74
Yalinga, C.A.R.	C4	66
Yalobusha, stm., Ms., U.S.	D9	122
Yalong, stm., China	E5	36
Yalova, Tur.	C12	28
Yalpuh, ozero, l., Ukr.	D15	26
Yalu (Amnok-kang), stm., Asia	D7	38
Yalu, stm., China	D6	38
Yalvaç, Tur.	E14	28
Yamaga, Japan	F3	40
Yamagata, Japan	A13	40
Yamagata, state, Japan	A13	40
Yamaguchi, Japan	E4	40
Yamaguchi, state, Japan	E4	40
Yamal Peninsula see Jamal, poluostrov, pen., Russia	B2	34
Yamanaka, Japan	C9	40
Yamanashi, state, Japan	D11	40
Yamasaki, Japan	D7	40
Yamaska, stm., Qc., Can.	E4	110
Yamatengwumulu, China	D4	36
Yamba, Austl.	G9	76
Yambio, Sudan	G5	62
Yamdena, Pulau, i., Indon.	G9	44
Yame, Japan	F3	40
Ya Men, b., China	J5	42
Yamethin, Mya.	B3	48
Yamma Yamma, Lake, l., Austl.	F3	76
Yamoussoukro, C. Iv.	H4	64
Yampa, stm., Co., U.S.	C8	132
Yampil', Ukr.	A15	26
Yamsay Mountain, mtn., Or., U.S.	H5	136
Yamuna, stm., India	F8	54
Yamzho Yumco, l., China	D13	54
Yan, stm., China	C4	42
Yan, stm., Sri L.	G5	53
Yanac, Austl.	K3	76
Yanagawa, Japan	F3	40
Yanai, Japan	F5	40
Yanam, India	C6	53
Yan'an, China	C3	42
Yanbu' al-Baḥr, Sau. Ar.	E4	56
Yanceyville, N.C., U.S.	H6	114
Yanchang, China	C3	42
Yancheng, China	E9	42
Yanchi, China	C2	42
Yanco Creek, stm., Austl.	J5	76
Yanda Creek, stm., Austl.	H5	76
Yandama Creek, stm., Austl.	G3	76
Yandé, Île, i., N. Cal.	m14	79d
Yandina, Sol. Is.	e8	79b
Yandoon, Mya.	D2	48
Yanfolila, Mali	G3	64
Yang, stm., Thai.	D7	48
Yangambi, D.R.C.	D4	66
Yan'gang, China	I7	42
Yangbajain, China	C13	54
Yangcheng, China	D5	42
Yangchiang *see* Yangjiang, China	K4	42
Yangchou *see* Yangzhou, China	E8	42
Yangchow *see* Yangzhou, China	E8	42
Yangch'üan *see* Yangquan, China	C5	42
Yangchun, China	J4	42
Yangdachengzi, China	B6	38
Yanggao, China	A5	42
Yanghexi, China	G3	42
Yangjiang, China	K4	42
Yangkü *see* Taiyuan, China	C5	42
Yangliuqing, China	B7	42
Yangon (Rangoon), Mya.	D2	48
Yangon, state, Mya.	D3	48
Yangpingguan, China	E1	42
Yangquan, China	C5	42
Yangriwan, China	F4	42
Yangsan, Kor., S.	D2	40
Yangshan, China	I5	42
Yangshuo, China	I4	42
Yangtze see Chang, stm., China	F8	36
Yangtze see Jinsha, stm., China	F5	36
Yangxian, China	E2	42
Yangxin, China	G6	42
Yangyang, Kor., S.	A1	40
Yangyuan, China	A5	42
Yangzhou, China	E8	42
Yanhe, China	G3	42
Yanji, China	C8	38
Yanji, China	C8	38
Yanjiadian, China	B9	42
Yankeetown, Fl., U.S.	G3	116
Yankton, S.D., U.S.	E15	126
Yanqi, China	C2	36
Yanqing, China	A6	42
Yanshou, China	B8	38
Yantabulla, Austl.	G5	76
Yantai, China	C9	42
Yantan, China	G9	42
Yanting, China	F1	42
Yantongshan, China	C6	38
Yanyuan, China	F5	36
Yanzhou, China	D7	42
Yao, Chad	E3	62
Yaoundé, Cam.	D2	66
Yaoxian, China	D3	42
Yao Yai, Ko, i., Thai.	I4	48
Yap, i., Micron.	C4	72
Yapacana, Parque Nacional, p.o.i., Ven.	F8	86
Yapacaní, Bol.	C4	90
Yapen, Pulau, i., Indon.	F10	44
Yapen, Selat, strt., Indon.	F10	44
Yappar, stm., Austl.	B4	76
Yaque del Norte, stm., Dom. Rep.	C12	102
Yaqui, stm., Mex.	G8	98
Yaquina, stm., Or., U.S.	F3	136
Yaracuy, state, Ven.	B7	86
Yaraka, Austl.	E5	76
Yardımcı, Tur.	A10	58
Yardımcı Burnu, c., Tur.	G13	28
Yarí, stm., Col.	H5	86
Yariga-take, mtn., Japan	C10	40
Yarīm, Yemen	G5	56
Yaring, Thai.	I5	48
Yaritagua, Ven.	B7	86
Yarkand *see* Shache, China	B12	56
Yarkand see Yarkant, stm., China	G13	32
Yarkant *see* Shache, China	B12	56
Yarkant, stm., China	G13	32
Yarloop, Austl.	F3	74
Yarmouth, N.S., Can.	G10	110
Yarmouth, Me., U.S.	G6	110
Yarmu, Pap. N. Gui.	a3	79a
Yarram, Austl.	L6	76
Yarraman, Austl.	F9	76
Yarrawonga, Austl.	K5	76
Yarumal, Col.	D4	86
Yasawa Group, is., Fiji	p18	79e
Yashiro-jima, i., Japan	F5	40
Yasinia, Ukr.	A11	26
Yasothon, Thai.	E6	48
Yass, Austl.	J7	76
Yasugi, Japan	D6	40
Yasuní, stm., Ec.	H3	86
Yasuni, Parque Nacional, p.o.i., Ec.	H4	86
Yata, stm., Bol.	B3	90
Yatağan, Tur.	F11	28
Yaté, N. Cal.	n16	79d
Yates City, Il., U.S.	D7	120
Yathkyed Lake, l., Nu., Can.	C11	106
Yating, China	I2	42
Yatsuga-take, mtn., Japan	D11	40
Yatsuo, Japan	C10	40
Yatsushiro, Japan	G3	40
Yatsushiro-kai, b., Japan	G3	40
Yatuá, stm., Ven.	G8	86
Yauca, Peru	G3	84
Yauco, P.R.	B2	104a
Yautepec, Mex.	F9	100
Yavarí (Javari), stm., S.A.	D3	84
Yavaros, Mex.	B4	100
Yavatmāl, India	H7	54
Yaví, Cerro, mtn., Ven.	E9	86
Yavita, Ven.	F8	86
Yaviza, Pan.	H9	102
Yavoriv, Ukr.	G19	16
Yavuzeli, Tur.	A8	58
Yaw, stm., Mya.	B2	48
Yawatahama, Japan	F5	40
Yaxchilán, sci., Mex.	D2	102
Yayladağı, Tur.	C7	58
Yayuan, China	D7	38
Yazd, Iran	C7	56
Yazoo, stm., Ms., U.S.	E8	122
Yazoo City, Ms., U.S.	E8	122
Ybbs an der Donau, Aus.	B12	22
Yding Skovhøj, hill, Den.	I3	8
Ýdra (Hydra), i., Grc.	F6	28
Ye, Mya.	E3	48
Yebyu, Mya.	E4	48
Yecheng, China	B12	56
Yech'ŏn, Kor., S.	C1	40
Yecla, Spain	F9	20
Yedashe, Mya.	C3	48
Yedi Göller Milli Parkı, p.o.i., Tur.	B14	28
Yedseram, stm., Nig.	G7	64
Yeeda, Austl.	C4	74
Yeghegnador, Arm.	B6	56
Yei, Sudan	G6	62
Yeji, China	F6	42
Yela Island, i., Pap. N. Gui.	B10	74
Yelarbon, Austl.	G8	76
Yell, i., Scot., U.K.	n18	12a
Yellandu, India	C5	53
Yellow see Huang, stm., China	D8	36
Yellow, stm., Wi., U.S.	F7	118
Yellow, stm., Wi., U.S.	G8	118
Yellow Grass, Sk., Can.	E9	124
Yellowhead Pass, p., Can.	D12	138
Yellow House Draw, stm., Tx., U.S.	H3	122
Yellowknife, N.T., Can.	C8	106
Yellowknife, stm., N.T., Can.	C8	106
Yellow Sea, s., Asia	G5	38
Yellowstone, stm., U.S.	B7	108
Yellowstone, Clarks Fork, stm., U.S.	B3	126
Yellowstone Falls, wtfl., Wy., U.S.	F16	136
Yellowstone Lake, l., Wy., U.S.	F16	136
Yellowstone National Park, Wy., U.S.	F16	136
Yellowstone National Park, p.o.i., U.S.	F16	136
Yellowtail Dam, dam, Mt., U.S.	B4	126
Yellville, Ar., U.S.	H5	120
Yelverton Bay, b., Nu., Can.	A9	141
Yemen, ctry., Asia	F6	56
Yenagoa, Nig.	H6	64
Yenangyaung, Mya.	B2	48
Yenanma, Mya.	C2	48
Yen Bai, Viet.	B7	48
Yench'eng *see* Yancheng, China	E9	42
Yenchi *see* Yanji, China	C8	38
Yenda, Austl.	J6	76
Yendéré, Burkina	G4	64
Yendi, Ghana	H4	64
Ye-ngan, Mya.	B3	48
Yengisar, China	B12	56
Yengo National Park, p.o.i., Austl.	I8	76
Yenice, Tur.	A6	58
Yenice, stm., Tur.	B15	28
Yenicekale, Tur.	A7	58
Yenierenköy, N. Cyp.	C5	58
Yenimehmetli, Tur.	D15	28
Yenipazar, Tur.	C13	28
Yenişehir, Tur.	C12	28
Yenisey see Enisej, stm., Russia	C6	34
Yenshuichen, Tai.	J9	42
Yentai *see* Yantai, China	C9	42
Yeola, India	H5	54
Yeo Lake, l., Austl.	E4	74
Yeovil, Eng., U.K.	K10	12
Yepachic, Mex.	A4	100
Yeppoon, Austl.	D8	76
Yerevan (Erivan), Arm.	A5	56
Yerington, Nv., U.S.	E6	134
Yerköy, Tur.	B3	56
Yerlisu, Tur.	C9	28
Yermo, Ca., U.S.	I9	134
Yerupaja, Nevado, mtn., Peru	F2	84
Yerushalayim (Jerusalem), Isr.	G6	58
Yesa, Embalse de, res., Spain	B9	20
Yeşildere, Tur.	A4	58
Yeşilköy, Tur.	C11	28
Yeşiltepe, Tur.	A3	58
Yeso, N.M., U.S.	G4	128
Yetman, Austl.	G8	76
Yetti, reg., Afr.	D3	64
Ye-u, Mya.	A2	48
Yeu, Île d', i., Fr.	H6	14
Yevlax, Azer.	A6	56
Yexian, China	E5	42
Yexian, China	C8	42
Yeywa, Mya.	B3	48
Ygatimí, Para.	B10	92
Yguazú, stm., Para.	B10	92
Yhú, Para.	B10	92
Yi, stm., China	B6	42
Yi, stm., China	D5	42
Yi, stm., China	D8	42
Yi, stm., Ur.	F10	92
Yi'allaq, Gebel, mtn., Egypt	H4	58
Yi'an, China	B10	36
Yibin, China	F5	36
Yibug Caka, l., China	B11	54
Yichang, China	F4	42
Yicheng, China	F5	42
Yichuan, China	D5	42
Yichuan, China	C3	42
Yichuan *see* Yinchuan, China	B2	42
Yichun, China	B10	36
Yichun, China	H6	42
Yidie, China	C4	42
Yidu, China	C8	42
Yidu, China	F4	42
Yifeng, China	G6	42
Yığılca, Tur.	C14	28
Yilan, China	B10	36
Yilaxi, China	C7	38
Yiliang, China	F5	36
Yilong, China	F2	42
Yin, stm., Mya.	B2	48
Yinbaing, Mya.	D3	48
Yinchuan, China	B2	42
Ying, stm., China	E6	42
Yingcheng, China	F5	42
Yingcheng *see* Yingchengzi, China	B6	38
Yingchengzi, China	B6	38
Yingde, China	I5	42
Yingjin, stm., China	C3	38
Yingkou, China	A10	42
Yingkou, China	A9	42
Yingpan, China	I2	42
Yingshang, China	E6	42
Yingshouyingzi, China	A7	42
Yingtan, China	G7	42
Yining, China	F14	32
Yinjiang, China	G3	42
Yinkeng, China	H6	42
Yinmatu, stm., China	D2	38
Yinnyein, Mya.	D3	48
Yin Shan, mts., China	C6	36
Yi'ong, stm., China	E3	36
Yirga 'Alem, Eth.	F7	62
Yirol, Sudan	F6	62
Yishan, China	I3	42
Yishui, China	D8	42
Yisuhe, China	H5	42
Yitong, stm., China	C6	38
Yitulihe, China	A9	36
Yiwu, China	G8	42
Yiwu, China	A5	48
Yixian, China	D4	38
Yixing, China	F8	42
Yixun, stm., China	D2	38
Yiyang, China	G5	42
Yiyang, China	D4	42
Yiyang, China	G7	42
Yiyuan, China	C8	42
Yizhang, China	I5	42
Yli-Kitka, l., Fin.	C13	8
Ylivieska, Fin.	D11	8
Ymer Ø, i., Grnld.	C21	141
Ynykčanskij, Russia	D16	34
Yoakum, Tx., U.S.	E10	130
Yocona, stm., Ms., U.S.	C9	122
Yog Point, c., Phil.	C5	52
Yogyakarta, Indon.	G7	50
Yogyakarta, state, Indon.	H7	50
Yoho National Park, p.o.i., B.C., Can.	E14	138
Yōka, Japan	D7	40
Yokadouma, Cam.	D2	66
Yōkaichi, Japan	D9	40
Yokkaichi, Japan	D9	40
Yoko, Cam.	C2	66
Yokoate-jima, i., Japan	k19	39a
Yokohama, Japan	D12	40
Yokosuka, Japan	D12	40
Yokote, Japan	E14	38
Yola, Nig.	H7	64
Yolombo, D.R.C.	E4	66
Yom, stm., Thai.	D5	48
Yonago, Japan	D6	40
Yoncalla, Or., U.S.	G3	136
Yonezawa, Japan	B12	40
Yong'an, China	I7	42
Yongchang, China	D5	36
Yongcheng, China	D7	42
Yŏngch'ŏn, Kor., S.	D1	40
Yongchuan, China	G1	42
Yongding, China	I7	42
Yongding, stm., China	A6	42
Yŏngdŏk, Kor., S.	C2	40
Yŏngdong, Kor., S.	F7	38
Yongfeng, China	H6	42
Yonggi, Kor., S.	C1	40
Yongi, China	C7	38
Yŏngil-man, b., Kor., S.	C2	40
Yŏngju, Kor., S.	C1	40
Yongkang, China	G9	42
Yongle, stm., China	H5	42
Yongnian, China	C6	42
Yongning, China	J3	42
Yongning, China	B1	42
Yongping, China	F4	36
Yongren, China	F5	36
Yongshan, China	F5	36
Yongshou, China	D2	42
Yongtai, China	I8	42
Yŏngwŏl, Kor., S.	B1	40
Yongxing, China	H5	42
Yongxing, China	B4	42
Yongxiu, China	G6	42
Yŏngyang, Kor., S.	C2	40
Yongzhou, China	H4	42
Yonibana, S.L.	H2	64
Yonkers, N.Y., U.S.	D12	114
Yonne, state, Fr.	G12	14
Yonne, stm., Fr.	F12	14
Yopal, Col.	E5	86
Yopurga, China	B12	56
York, Austl.	F3	74
York, Eng., U.K.	H11	12
York, Al., U.S.	E10	122
York, N.D., U.S.	F14	124
York, Pa., U.S.	E9	114
York, S.C., U.S.	A4	116
York, Cape, c., Austl.	B8	74
York, Kap, c., Grnld.	B12	141
Yorke Peninsula, pen., Austl.	F7	74
Yorketown, Austl.	G7	74
York Factory, Mb., Can.	D12	106
Yorkshire Dales National Park, p.o.i., Eng., U.K.	G10	12
York Sound, strt., Austl.	B4	74
Yorkton, Sk., Can.	C11	124
Yorktown, Tx., U.S.	E10	130
Yorktown, Va., U.S.	G9	114
Yorkville, Il., U.S.	J10	118
Yorkville, N.Y., U.S.	E14	112
Yoro, Hond.	E4	102
Yoron-jima, i., Japan	I19	39a
Yosemite National Park, p.o.i., Ca., U.S.	F6	134
Yosemite Village, Ca., U.S.	F6	134
Yoshii, stm., Japan	E7	40
Yösöbulag *see* Altay, Mong.	B4	36
Yos Sudarso, Pulau, i., Indon.	G10	44
Yŏsu, Kor., S.	G7	38
You, stm., China	G6	36
You, stm., China	G4	42
Youanmi, Austl.	E3	74
Youghal, Ire.	J5	12
Young, Austl.	J7	76
Young, Sk., Can.	C8	124
Young, Ur.	F9	92
Young, Az., U.S.	I5	132
Younghusband Peninsula, pen., Austl.	K2	76
Young Island, i., Ant.	B21	81
Youngs Rock, r., Pit.	c28	78k
Youngstown, Ab., Can.	C2	124
Youngstown, N.Y., U.S.	E10	112
Youngstown, Oh., U.S.	C5	114
Youngsville, La., U.S.	G6	122
Youngsville, N.C., U.S.	H7	114
Yountville, Ca., U.S.	E3	134
Youssoufia, Mor.	C3	64
Youxian, China	H5	42
Youyang, China	G3	42
Yŏyang-ni, Kor., S.	B1	40
Yozgat, Tur.	B3	56
Ypres *see* Ieper, Bel.	D11	14
Ypsilanti, Mi., U.S.	B2	114
Yreka, Ca., U.S.	B3	134
Yrghyz, Kaz.	E10	32
Ysabel Channel, strt., Pap. N. Gui.	a4	79a
Ystad, Swe.	I5	8
Ystādeh-ye Moqor, Āb-e, l., Afg.	B2	54
Ytterhogdal, Swe.	E6	8
Yu, stm., China	J3	42
Yuam, stm., Thai.	C3	48
Yuan see Red, stm., Asia	D9	46
Yuan, stm., China	H6	42
Yuan, stm., China	G4	42
Yuanling, China	G4	42
Yuanmou, China	F5	36
Yuantan, China	J5	42
Yuanyang, China	D5	42
Yuasa, Japan	E8	40
Yuba City, Ca., U.S.	D4	134
Yūbari, Japan	C15	38
Yucaipa, Ca., U.S.	I8	134
Yucatán, state, Mex.	B3	102
Yucatán, Península de (Yucatan Peninsula), pen., N.A.	C3	102
Yucatan Channel, strt., N.A.	B4	102
Yucatan Peninsula see Yucatán, Península de, pen., N.A.	C3	102
Yucca, Az., U.S.	I2	132
Yucca Mountain, mtn., Nv., U.S.	G9	134
Yucca Valley, Ca., U.S.	I9	134
Yucheng, China	C7	42
Yuci, China	C5	42
Yudu, China	I6	42
Yuechi, China	F2	42
Yueqing, China	G9	42
Yuexi, China	F5	36
Yueyang, China	G5	42
Yufa, China	B7	42
Yugan, China	G7	42
Yuhebu, China	C3	42
Yuhuan Dao, i., China	G9	42
Yuhuang Ding, mtn., China	C9	42
Yukon, Ok., U.S.	F11	128
Yukon, state, Can.	B3	106
Yukon, stm., N.A.	D7	140
Yukon Flats, sw., Ak., U.S.	C11	140
Yukuhashi, Japan	F3	40
Yuli, China	F15	32
Yüli, Tai.	J9	42
Yulin, China	B3	42
Yulin, China	J3	42
Yulin, China	L3	42
Yuma, Az., U.S.	K2	132
Yuma, Co., U.S.	A6	128
Yuma, Bahía de, b., Dom. Rep.	C13	102
Yumare, Ven.	B7	86
Yumbel, Chile	H1	92
Yumbo, Col.	F3	86
Yumen, China	D4	36
Yumt uul, mtn., Mong.	C4	36
Yun, stm., China	F5	42
Yuna, stm., Dom. Rep.	C13	102
Yunak, Tur.	E14	28
Yunan, China	J4	42
Yuncheng, China	D4	42
Yuncheng, China	D6	42
Yungay, Chile	H2	92
Yungchi *see* Jilin, China	C7	38
Yungchia *see* Wenzhou, China	F9	36
Yungning *see* Nanning, China	J3	42
Yunkai Dashan, mts., China	J4	42
Yun Ling, mts., China	F4	36
Yunnan, state, China	G5	36
Yunnanfu *see* Kunming, China	F5	36
Yunta, Austl.	I2	76
Yunwu Shan, mtn., China	A7	42
Yunxi, China	E4	42
Yunxian, China	E4	42
Yunxiao, China	I7	42
Yunyang, China	F3	42
Yunyang *see* Yunxian, China	E4	42
Yunzalin, stm., Mya.	D3	48
Yuping, China	H3	42
Yuqing, China	H2	42
Yurimaguas, Peru	E2	84
Yuriria, Laguna de, l., Mex.	E8	100
Yuruá see Juruá, stm., S.A.	D4	84
Yuruarí, stm., Ven.	D11	86
Yurubi, Parque Nacional, p.o.i., Ven.	B7	86
Yurungkax, stm., China	A5	46
Yuscarán, Hond.	F4	102
Yûsef, Bahr (Yūsuf, Baḥr), can., Egypt	K1	58
Yushan, China	G8	42
Yü Shan, mtn., Tai.	J9	42
Yushanzhen, China	G3	42
Yushu, China	E4	36
Yushu, China	B7	38
Yutian, China	A5	46
Yutian, China	B7	42
Yuty, Para.	C9	92
Yütz'u *see* Yuci, China	C5	42
Yuxian, China	B6	42
Yuxian, China	B5	42
Yuxian, China	D5	42
Yuyao, China	F9	42
Yuzawa, Japan	E14	38
Yvelines, state, Fr.	F10	14
Yverdon-les-Bains, Switz.	D3	22
Ywathagyi, Mya.	A2	48

Z

Name	Map Ref.	Page
Zaandam *see* Zaanstad, Neth.	B13	14
Zaanstad, Neth.	B13	14
Zabalac', Bela.	G7	10
Zăbalț, Rom.	C8	26
Zabīd, Yemen	G5	56
Žabinka, Bela.	H6	10
Ząbkowice Śląskie, Pol.	F12	16
Žabljak, Mont.	F6	26
Żabno, Pol.	F16	16
Zābol, Iran	C9	56
Zābol, state, Afg.	C1	54
Zabolotiv, Ukr.	A12	26
Zabor"e, Bela.	E12	10
Zabore, Russia	F15	10
Zabory, Russia	E15	10
Zabrze, Pol.	F14	16
Zabyčanne, Bela.	G14	10
Zacapa, Guat.	E3	102
Zacapu, Mex.	F8	100
Zacatecas, Mex.	D7	100
Zacatecas, state, Mex.	D7	100
Zacatlán, Mex.	F10	100
Zacoalco de Torres, Mex.	E7	100
Zacualtipan, Mex.	E9	100
Zadar (Zara), Cro.	F12	22
Zadetkale Kyun, i., Mya.	G3	48
Zadetkyi Kyun, i., Mya.	H3	48
Zadoi, China	B8	46
Za'farâna, well, Egypt	I3	58
Zafer Burnu, c., N. Cyp.	C5	58
Zafirovo, Blg.	F13	26
Zafra, Spain	F4	20
Żagań, Pol.	E11	16
Žagare, Lith.	D6	10
Zagazig, Egypt	H2	58
Zaghouan, Tun.	H4	24
Zaghouan, Jebel, mtn., Tun.	H4	24
Zagora, Mor.	C3	64
Zagórz, Pol.	G18	16
Zagreb, Cro.	E12	22
Zāgros, Kūhhā-ye, mts., Iran	C7	56
Zagros Mountains see Zāgros, Kūhhā-ye, mts., Iran	C7	56
Za'gya, stm., China	B13	54
Zāhedān, Iran	D9	56
Zahīrābād, India	C3	53
Zaḥlah, Leb.	E6	58
Zahnitkiv, Ukr.	A15	26
Zahrebetnoe, Russia	B17	8
Zaire see Congo, Democratic Republic of the, ctry., Afr.	E4	66
Zaïre see Congo, stm., Afr.	F2	66
Zaječar, Serb.	F9	26
Zajsan *see* Zaysan, Kaz.	E14	32
Zajsan, ozero see Zhaysang köli, l., Kaz.	E14	32
Zaka, Zimb.	B10	70
Zakamensk, Russia	F9	34
Zakarpattia, co., Ukr.	A10	26
Zakhidnyy Buh (Bug) (Buh), stm., Eur.	D17	16
Zakho, Iraq	B5	56
Zakliczyn, Pol.	G16	16
Zakopane, Pol.	G16	16
Zakouma, Chad	E3	62
Zakroczym, Pol.	D16	16
Zákynthos, Grc.	F3	28
Zákynthos, i., Grc.	F3	28
Zala, state, Hung.	C3	26
Zala, stm., Hung.	C4	26
Zalaegerszeg, Hung.	C3	26
Zalamea de la Serena, Spain	F5	20
Zalantun, China	B9	36
Zalari, Russia	D18	32
Zalaszentgrót, Hung.	C4	26
Zalău, Rom.	B10	26
Zalese, Russia	F4	10
Zalim, Sau. Ar.	E5	56
Zalingei, Sudan	E4	62
Žaludok, Bela.	G7	10
Zama, Ms., U.S.	E9	122
Zamakh, Yemen	F6	56
Zamantı, stm., Tur.	A6	58
Zambeze, stm., Afr.	C3	68
Zambezi, Zam.	C3	68
Zambezi, stm., Afr.	D5	68
Zambezi Escarpment, clf., Zimb.	D4	68
Zambia, ctry., Afr.	C4	68
Zamboanga, Phil.	G3	52
Zamboanga Peninsula, pen., Phil.	G3	52
Zambrów, Pol.	C18	16
Žambyl *see* Taraz, Kaz.	F12	32
Zamežnaja, Russia	D24	8
Zami, stm., Mya.	D4	48
Zamora, Ec.	D2	84
Zamora, Spain	C5	20
Zamora, co., Spain	C5	20
Zamora de Hidalgo, Mex.	F7	100
Zamość, Pol.	F19	16
Zamość, state, Pol.	F19	16
Zanaga, Congo	E2	66
Záncara, stm., Spain	E8	20
Zanda, China	C7	54
Zanesville, Oh., U.S.	E3	114
Zanjān, Iran	B6	56
Zanjón, Arg.	C5	92
Žannetty, ostrov, i., Russia	A20	34
Zante see Zákynthos, i., Grc.	F3	28
Zanthus, Austl.	F4	74
Zanzibar, Tan.	F7	66
Zanzibar, i., Tan.	F7	66
Zanzibar Channel, strt., Tan.	F7	66
Zaostrove, Russia	F14	8
Zaō-zan, vol., Japan	A13	40
Zaozërnyj, Russia	C16	32
Zaozhuang, China	D7	42
Zap, N.D., U.S.	G12	124
Zapadnaja Dvina, Russia	D15	10

Name	Map Ref.	Page

Zapadna Morava, stm., Serb. — F8 — 26
Zapadno-Sibirskaja ravnina (West Siberian Plain), pl., Russia — B12 — 32
Zapadnyj hrebet, mts., Russia — F17 — 34
Zapadnyj Sajan, mts., Russia — D16 — 32
Západočeský kraj, state, Czech Rep. — G9 — 16
Západoslovenský kraj, state, Slov. — H14 — 16
Zapala, Arg. — G2 — 90
Zapata, Tx., U.S. — H8 — 130
Zapata, Península de, pen., Cuba — A7 — 102
Zapatoca, Col. — D5 — 86
Zapatosa, Ciénaga de, l., Col. — C5 — 86
Zapljuse, Russia — B12 — 10
Zapole, Russia — B12 — 10
Zapoljarnyj, Russia — B14 — 8
Zapopan, Mex. — E7 — 100
Zaporizhzhia, Ukr. — E5 — 32
Zapovednyj, Russia — C10 — 38
Zaprudnja, Russia — D20 — 10
Zaqatala, Azer. — A6 — 56
Zaragoza, Mex. — A8 — 100
Zaragoza, Mex. — C1 — 130
Zaragoza (Saragossa), Spain — C10 — 20
Zaragoza, co., Spain — C9 — 20
Zarajsk, Russia — F21 — 10
Zaranj, Afg. — C9 — 56
Zarasai, Lith. — E9 — 10
Zárate, Arg. — G8 — 92
Zarautz, Spain — A8 — 20
Zarauz see Zarautz, Spain — A8 — 20
Zaraza, Ven. — C9 — 86
Zareče, Russia — E21 — 8
Zarečensk, Russia — C14 — 8
Zarghon Shahr, Afg. — C10 — 56
Zaria, Nig. — G6 — 64
Żarma see Zharma, Kaz. — E14 — 32
Zărnești, Rom. — D12 — 26
Zarubino, Russia — C9 — 38
Zarumilla, Peru. — D1 — 84
Zary, Pol. — E11 — 16
Zarzaitine, Alg. — D6 — 64
Zarzal, Col. — E4 — 86
Zasa, Lat. — D8 — 10
Zāskār, stm., India — B6 — 54
Zāskār Mountains, mts., Asia — B7 — 54
Zaslaye, Bela. — F10 — 10
Zastava, Russia — G22 — 8
Zasule, Russia — D22 — 8
Žatec, Czech Rep. — F9 — 16
Zatyshshya, Ukr. — B16 — 26
Zavalla, Tx., U.S. — F4 — 122
Zave, Zimb. — D5 — 68
Zavet, Blg. — F13 — 26
Zavodoukovsk, Russia. — C11 — 32
Zavodovski Island, i., S. Geor. — K12 — 82
Zavolžsk, Russia — H20 — 8
Zawadzkie, Pol. — F14 — 16
Zawiercie, Pol. — F15 — 16
Zāwiyat al-Mukhaylá, Libya — A4 — 62
Zaysan, Kaz. — E14 — 32

Zaysan, Lake see Zhaysang köli, l., Kaz. — E14 — 32
Zayü, stm., China — C8 — 46
Zayzan see Zaysan, Kaz. — E14 — 32
Zaza, stm., Cuba — B8 — 102
Zaza, Presa, res., Cuba — B8 — 102
Zbąszynek, Pol. — D11 — 16
Zbraslav, Czech Rep. — G10 — 16
Žďár nad Sázavou, Czech Rep. — G11 — 16
Ždiar, Slov. — G16 — 16
Zduńska Wola, Pol. — E14 — 16
Zearing, Ia., U.S. — B4 — 120
Zeballos, B.C., Can. — G4 — 138
Zebulon, Ga., U.S. — C1 — 116
Zedang, China — C11 — 14
Zeebrugge, Bel. — C11 — 14
Zeehan, Austl. — n12 — 77a
Zeeland, Mi., U.S. — F4 — 112
Zeeland, N.D., U.S. — B13 — 126
Zeerust, S. Afr. — D7 — 70
Zefat, Isr. — F6 — 58
Zehdenick, Ger. — D9 — 16
Zehnder, mtn., Austl. — D6 — 74
Zeist, Neth. — B14 — 14
Zeitz, Ger. — E8 — 16
Zeja, Russia — F14 — 34
Zeja, stm., Russia — F14 — 34
Zejskoe vodohranilišče, res., Russia — F14 — 34
Zelee, Cape, c., Sol. Is. — e9 — 79b
Zelenoborskij, Russia — C14 — 8
Zelenogorsk, Russia — F13 — 8
Zelenograd, Russia — D20 — 10
Zelenogradsk, Russia — F3 — 10
Zelenokumsk, Russia — F6 — 32
Železnodorožnyj, Russia — B8 — 32
Železnodorožnyj, Russia — F4 — 10
Železnogorsk, Russia — H18 — 10
Železnogorsk-Ilimskij, Russia — C18 — 32
Zelienople, Pa., U.S. — D5 — 114
Zell am See, Aus. — F6 — 16
Zell am See, Aus. — C9 — 22
Zell am Ziller, Aus. — C8 — 22
Żel'va, Bela. — G7 — 10
Želva, Lith. — E8 — 10
Žemaitijos nacionalinis parkas, p.o.i., Lith. — D4 — 10
Zembin, Bela. — F11 — 10
Zembra, Île, i., Tun. — G4 — 24
Zémio, C.A.R. — C4 — 66
Zempoala, sci., Mex. — F10 — 100
Zemun, Serb. — E7 — 26
Zeng, stm., China — J5 — 42
Zenica, Bos. — E4 — 26
Zenon Park, Sk., Can. — A10 — 124
Zentsūji, Japan — E6 — 40
Zenza do Itombe, Ang. — B1 — 68
Zephyr, Tx., U.S. — C9 — 130
Zephyrhills, Fl., U.S. — H3 — 116
Zepu, China — B12 — 56
Zeravšan, stm., Asia — B10 — 56
Zeravšanskij hrebet, mts., Asia — B10 — 56
Zerbst, Ger. — D8 — 16
Żerków, Pol. — D13 — 16
Zerqan, Alb. — C14 — 24
Žešart, Russia — E23 — 8
Zeulenroda, Ger. — F7 — 16
Zeven, Ger. — C5 — 16

Zevenaar, Neth. — E2 — 16
Zeydābād, Afg. — A2 — 54
Zeytinbağı, Tur. — C11 — 28
Zêzere, stm., Port. — E2 — 20
Zgierz, Pol. — E15 — 16
Zgorzelec, Pol. — E11 — 16
Zhabuchaka Hu, l., China — C9 — 54
Zhakou, China — F5 — 42
Zhaltyr, Kaz. — D12 — 32
Zhambyl see Taraz, Kaz. — F12 — 32
Zhambyl, Kaz. — E12 — 32
Zhang, stm., China — I6 — 42
Zhang, stm., China — C5 — 42
Zhangaözen, Kaz. — F8 — 32
Zhanga Qalqotan, Kaz. — D11 — 32
Zhangaqazaly, Kaz. — E10 — 32
Zhangatas, Kaz. — F11 — 32
Zhangbei, China — A6 — 42
Zhangguangcai Ling, mts., China — B8 — 38
Zhanghuang, China — K3 — 42
Zhangjiakou, China — A6 — 42
Zhangping, China — I7 — 42
Zhangpu, China — I7 — 42
Zhangqiu, China — C7 — 42
Zhangshuping, China — F4 — 42
Zhangwu, China — C5 — 38
Zhangye, China — I7 — 42
Zhangzhou, China — I7 — 42
Zhānībek, Kaz. — E7 — 32
Zhanjiang, China — K4 — 42
Zhanyu, China — B5 — 38
Zhao'an, China — J7 — 42
Zhaodong, China — A7 — 38
Zhaojue, China — I4 — 42
Zhaoping, China — J5 — 42
Zhaoqing, China — J5 — 42
Zhaotong, China — F5 — 42
Zhaoxing, China — B11 — 36
Zhaoyuan, China — B10 — 36
Zharī Namco, l., China — C10 — 54
Zharkent, Kaz. — E14 — 32
Zharma, Kaz. — E14 — 32
Zharsuat, Kaz. — E12 — 32
Zhaxi Co, l., China — B10 — 54
Zhaxigang, China — B7 — 54
Zhaysang köli, l., Kaz. — E14 — 32
Zhayylma, Kaz. — D10 — 32
Zhayyq see Ural, stm. — E8 — 32
Zhecheng, China — D6 — 42
Zhegu, China — D13 — 54
Zhejiang, state, China — G8 — 42
Zhelezinka, Kaz. — D13 — 32
Zhelin, China — F9 — 42
Zhem see Embi, stm., Kaz. — E9 — 32
Zhenbeikou, China — B2 — 42
Zheng'an, China — G2 — 42
Zhengding, China — B6 — 42
Zhenglan Qi, China — H8 — 42
Zhenghe, China — C8 — 36
Zhengning, China — D3 — 42
Zhengyang, China — E4 — 42
Zhengzhou, China — D5 — 42
Zhenhai, China — G9 — 42
Zhenjiang, China — E8 — 42
Zhenlai, China — B9 — 36
Zhenning, China — H1 — 42
Zhenping, China — E5 — 42
Zhentou, stm., China — F5 — 42
Zhenxiong, China — F5 — 36
Zhenyu, China — H9 — 42
Zhenyuan, China — H3 — 42

Zhenyuan, China — D2 — 42
Zherong, China — H8 — 42
Zhetiqara, Kaz. — D10 — 32
Zhezdi, Kaz. — E11 — 32
Zhezqazghan, Kaz. — E11 — 32
Zhijiang, China — H3 — 42
Zhixia, China — G8 — 42
Zhob, Pak. — C2 — 54
Zhob, stm., Pak. — C10 — 56
Zholymbet, Kaz. — D12 — 32
Zhongba, China — C5 — 46
Zhongdian, China — F4 — 36
Zhongning, China — C1 — 42
Zhongpingchang, China — J5 — 42
Zhongshan, China — J5 — 42
Zhongshan, China — I4 — 42
Zhongshan, sci., Ant. — B12 — 81
Zhongtiao Shan, mts., China — D4 — 42
Zhongwei, China — C1 — 42
Zhongxian, China — F3 — 42
Zhongxiang, China — F5 — 42
Zhongyaozhan, China — F14 — 34
Zhosaly, Kaz. — E10 — 32
Zhoucun, China — C7 — 42
Zhouning, China — H8 — 42
Zhoushan Dao, i., China — F9 — 42
Zhoushan Qundao, is., China — F10 — 42
Zhouzhi, China — D3 — 42
Zhuanghe, China — B10 — 42
Zhuanglang, China — D1 — 42
Zhüantöbe, Kaz. — F11 — 32
Zhucang, China — H2 — 42
Zhucheng, China — D8 — 42
Zhuhe, China — G5 — 42
Zhuji, China — G9 — 42
Zhujia Jian, i., China — G10 — 42
Zhujiang Kou, est., China — J5 — 42
Zhumadian, China — E5 — 42
Zhuolu, China — A6 — 42
Zhuozhou, China — B6 — 42
Zhuozi, China — A5 — 42
Zhushan, China — E3 — 42
Zhuxi, China — E3 — 42
Zhuzhou, China — H5 — 42
Zhympity, Kaz. — D8 — 32
Zhytomyr, Ukr. — E14 — 6
Zi, stm., China — C8 — 42
Zi, stm., China — G4 — 42
Ziārat, Pak. — C10 — 56
Zibo, China — C8 — 42
Zichang, China — C3 — 42
Ziebice, Pol. — F13 — 16
Zielona Góra, Pol. — E11 — 16
Zielona Góra, state, Pol. — D11 — 16
Zierikzee, Neth. — C12 — 14
Ziesar, Ger. — D8 — 16
Zifta, Egypt — H2 — 58
Žigalovo, Russia — D19 — 32
Zigansk, Russia — C13 — 34
Zigong, China — F5 — 36
Zigui, China — F4 — 42
Ziguinchor, Sen. — G1 — 64
Zihuatanejo, Mex. — G8 — 100
Ziiyang, China — E3 — 42
Zijin, China — J6 — 42
Žilaja Tambica, Russia — E17 — 8
Žilina, Slov. — G14 — 16
Žilino, Russia — F4 — 10

Zillah, Libya — B3 — 62
Zillertaler Alpen (Aurine, Alpi), mts., Eur. — C8 — 22
Zilupe, Lat. — D11 — 10
Zilwaukee, Mi., U.S. — E6 — 112
Zima, Russia — D18 — 32
Zimapán, Mex. — E9 — 100
Zimbabwe, ctry., Afr. — D4 — 68
Zimbabwe Ruins, sci., Zimb. — B10 — 70
Zimi, S.L. — H2 — 64
Zimnicea, Rom. — F12 — 26
Zimonino, Russia — G14 — 10
Zinder, Niger — G6 — 64
Zinga Mulike, Tan. — F7 — 66
Zinnik see Soignies, Bel. — D12 — 14
Zion National Park, p.o.i., Ut., U.S. — F4 — 132
Zionsville, In., U.S. — I3 — 112
Zipaquirá, Col. — E5 — 86
Zirbitzkogel, mtn., Aus. — C11 — 22
Žirjatino, Russia — G16 — 10
Žirovnice, Czech Rep. — G11 — 16
Zitong, China — F1 — 42
Zittau, Ger. — F2 — 112
Ziway, Lake see Ziway Hāyk', l., Eth. — F7 — 62
Ziway Hāyk', l., Eth. — F7 — 62
Zixi, China — G7 — 42
Ziya, stm., China — B7 — 42
Ziyuan, China — I4 — 42
Žizdra, stm., Russia — F19 — 10
Zizhong, China — G1 — 42
Zizhou, China — C3 — 42
Žižica, Russia — D14 — 10
Žižickoe, ozero, l., Russia — D14 — 10
Zlaté Moravce, Slov. — H14 — 16
Zlatoust, Russia — C9 — 32
Zlatoustovsk, Russia — F15 — 34
Zlín, Czech Rep. — G13 — 16
Zlīṭan, Libya — A2 — 62
Żłobin, Bela. — H13 — 10
Złoczew, Pol. — E14 — 16
Złotoryja, Pol. — C8 — 42
Złotów, Pol. — C13 — 16
Zlynka, Russia — H14 — 10
Zmeinogorsk, Russia. — D14 — 32
Zmijiv, Ukr. — E12 — 16
Zmiinyi, ostriv, i., Ukr. — D17 — 26
Znamenka, Russia — F17 — 10
Znamensk, Russia — F4 — 10
Znamensk, Russia — C12 — 32
Žnin, Pol. — D13 — 16
Znojmo, Czech Rep. — H12 — 16
Zoar, S. Afr. — H5 — 70
Żodzina, Bela. — F11 — 10
Zoétélé, Cam. — D2 — 66
Zogang, China — F4 — 36
Zohreh, stm., Iran — C7 — 56
Zolotaja Gora, Russia — F14 — 34
Zomba, Mwi. — D6 — 68
Zonguldak, Tur. — B14 — 28
Zonguldak, state, Tur. — B15 — 28
Zonza, Fr. — H15 — 18
Zorita, Spain — E3 — 20
Zorra, Arroyo de la, stm., Mex. — E6 — 130
Zouar, Chad — C3 — 62
Zouérat, Maur. — E2 — 64
Zoug see Zug, Switz. — C5 — 22

Zouxian, China — D7 — 42
Zovka, Russia — B11 — 10
Zrenjanin, Serb. — D7 — 26
Zuata, stm., Ven. — C9 — 86
Zubaydīyah, Jabal az-, mtn., Syria — E8 — 58
Zubovo, Russia — F17 — 8
Zudáñez, Bol. — C4 — 90
Zuera, Spain — C10 — 20
Zufar (Dhofar), reg., Oman — F7 — 56
Zug, Switz. — C5 — 22
Zuger See, l., Switz. — C5 — 22
Zugdidi, Geor. — F6 — 32
Zugspitze, mtn., Eur. — I6 — 16
Zújar, stm., Spain — F5 — 20
Żukopa, Russia — D15 — 10
Žukovka, Russia — G16 — 10
Žukovskij, Russia — E21 — 10
Zuli, stm., China — D1 — 42
Zulia, state, Ven. — C5 — 86
Zulia, stm., S.A. — C5 — 86
Zululand, hist. reg., S. Afr. — F10 — 70
Zumbo, Moz. — D5 — 68
Zumbrota, Mn., U.S. — G6 — 118
Zungeru, Nig. — H6 — 64
Zunhua, China — A7 — 42
Zuni, stm., U.S. — I7 — 132
Zuni Pueblo, N.M., U.S. — H8 — 132
Zunyi, China — H2 — 42
Zuo, stm., China — J2 — 42
Zuodeng, China — J2 — 42
Zuomuchedong Hu, l., China — D12 — 54
Zuoyun, China — A5 — 42
Žuravičy, Bela. — G13 — 10
Zürich, On., Can. — E8 — 112
Zürich (Zurigo), Switz. — C5 — 22
Zurich, Lake see Zürichsee, l., Switz. — C5 — 22
Zürichsee, l., Switz. — C5 — 22
Zurigo see Zürich, Switz. — C5 — 22
Zurmi, Nig. — G6 — 64
Zuša, stm., Russia — G19 — 10
Zuṭ, Otok, i., Cro. — G12 — 22
Zuwārah, Libya — A2 — 62
Zuwayzā, Jord. — G6 — 58
Zvenigorod, Russia — E19 — 10
Zvezdec, Blg. — G14 — 26
Zvezdnyj, Russia — C19 — 32
Zvishavane, Zimb. — B9 — 70
Zvolen, Slov. — H15 — 16
Zwedru, Lib. — H3 — 64
Zweibrücken, Ger. — G3 — 16
Zweisimmen, Switz. — D4 — 22
Zwickau, Ger. — F8 — 16
Zwierzyniec, Pol. — F18 — 16
Zwolen, Pol. — E17 — 16
Zwolle, Neth. — B14 — 14
Zwolle, La., U.S. — F5 — 122
Żyrardów, Pol. — D16 — 16
Żyrjanka, Russia — C19 — 34
Zyryanovsk see Zyryanovsk, Kaz. — E14 — 32
Zyryanovsk, Russia — C15 — 32
Zyryan see Zyryanovsk, Kaz. — E14 — 32
Zyryanovsk, Kaz. — E14 — 32
Zyryanskoe, Russia — C15 — 32
Žytkavičy, Bela. — H10 — 10
Żywiec, Pol. — G15 — 16